IRISH COMPANY LAW REPORTS
(1963-1993)

AUSTRALIA
The Law Book Company
Brisbane • Sydney • Melbourne • Perth

CANADA
Carswell
Ottawa • Toronto • Calgary • Montreal • Vancouver

Agents
Steimatzky's Agency Ltd., Tel Aviv;
N.M. Tripathi (Private) Ltd., Bombay;
Easten Law House (Private) Ltd., Calcutta;
M.P.P. House, Bangalore;
Universal Book Traders, Delhi;
Aditya Books, Delhi;
MacmillanShuppan KK, Tokyo;
Pakistan Law House, Karachi, Lahore.

Irish Company Law Reports (1963-1993)

EDITOR

Bart D. Daly, Barrister-at-Law

EDITORIAL ADVISOR

Declan Murphy, Barrister-at-Law

REPORTERS

Agatha Clancy, Barrister-at-Law
Patricia McLaughlin, Barrister-at-Law
Alistair Rutherdale, Barrister-at-Law

ROUND HALL
Sweet & Maxwell

Published in 1996 by
Round Hall Sweet & Maxwell
Brehon House, 4 Upper Ormond Quay,
Dublin 7.

Typeset by
Gilbert Gough Typesetting, Dublin.

Printed by
Betaprint, Dublin.

ISBN 1-899738-07-X

A catalogue record for this book
is available from the British Library.

These reports may be cited as Irish Company Law Reports (1963-1993).

Round Hall Sweet & Maxwell
1996

PREFACE

In 1981, *Irish Law Reports Monthly* was commenced with the aim of providing a current law reporting service and the series came into being as a response to the growing number of reserved judgments being delivered each year. Since then the number has grown even more and while the ILRM and the *Irish Reports* have substantially increased their coverage, there are still many important cases left unreported.

In 1980 the ILRM commenced reporting volumes of selected previously unreported cases and produced volumes for 1976-77, 1978, 1979 and 1980. In April 1995 Brehon Publishing produced *Professional Negligence Law Reports* spanning the years 1968-1993 and deliberately chose a theme for the selection of cases. This volume also chooses a theme — company law. We have taken the Companies Act, 1963 as the starting point and organised the book by parts of that Act. We have also included a chapter of important cases under the Companies Act, 1990 and the Companies (Amendment) Act, 1990.

Many people have contributed to this volume. In particular we would like to thank the staff of the Central Office and Peggy McQuinn of the Office of the Supreme Court. We would also like to thank the many barristers and solicitors who consulted files for the names of colleagues for older cases where the court files were missing such information. Unfortunately, there still remained up to going to press many cases where we could not locate accurate information on the names of barristers and solicitors involved in some cases.

We would like to thank our diligent reporters Patricia McLaughlin BL, Agatha Clancy BL and Alistair Rutherdale BL and our editorial advisor, Declan Murphy, whose task it was to read all the headnotes and judgments and who made many suggestions which have enhanced the final work, and lastly but not least, to our in-house editor, Aidan Culhane who took over much of the checking in the final stages.

Bart D. Daly
Editor

November 1995

CONTENTS

CASES REPORTED

1963 ACT, PART II

Thomas Joseph Woods v. Paul Joseph Duggan: High Court 1970 No. 131P (Kenny J) 12 March 1971

Company Law – Agreement on formation of a new company – Plaintiff approached by defendant to join company – Terms upon which plaintiff agreed to become involved – Agreement never reduced to writing – Parties no longer able to work together – Action for specific performance of alleged agreement – Whether defendant agreed to transfer shares in a related company to the plaintiff – Plaintiff never requested transfer – Whether on the balance of probabilities such an agreement was ever concluded

Facts: The defendant was the majority shareholder in the Cork Shoe Company Ltd ("the shoe company") which had prospered since its incorporation in 1947. For some time prior to 1964, the defendant had considered the formation of a company ("the plastic company") which would manufacture a rubber compound, substantial amounts of which were required by the shoe company. The plaintiff was an accountant and marketing manager with Sunbeam Wolsey and had made a considerable amount of money through prudent investments. The defendant approached the plaintiff in relation to the formation of the new company and the plaintiff became convinced that such a project offered the potential of financial success. In 1964 the parties came to what they believed was an agreement as to the conditions upon which the plaintiff would become involved in the new company, which said agreement was never reduced to writing. In relation to the shoe company the plaintiff's salary, the duration of his appointment and the establishment of a non contributory pension scheme were agreed. The plaintiff also alleged that the defendant agreed that the plaintiff should receive two per cent commission on the profits of the shoe company and that the defendant would transfer 1,000 of his shares in that company to him. In relation to the plastic company, the plaintiff's salary, commission and non-contributory pension were agreed and this agreement was eventually put into writing in 1967. The plaintiff never demanded the transfer of the 1,000 shares to him and never received commission from the profits of the company. At some stage the defendant had decided to settle his shares in the shoe company on discretionary trusts and the plaintiff was present at these discussions but never mentioned that he had a claim on 1,000 of the shares. However, during the negotiations in relation to the formation of the plastic company the plaintiff did inform the bank manager who dealt with the accounts of the shoe company that the shares were to be transferred to him.

By 1969 unhappy differences had arisen between the parties to the extent that they found it impossible to work together. As a result the plaintiff resigned from both companies. The plaintiff brought an action for specific performance of the agreement to transfer the shares to him which, at the time of the hearing, were worth in or around £85,000: he made no claim in relation to the commission, which he had never been paid.

Held by Kenny J in dismissing the plaintiff's claim:
The probabilities favoured the defendant's case that he never agreed to transfer the shares to the plaintiff.

No cases referred to in judgment

Counsel's and solicitors' names not available

KENNY J **12 March 1971**

Cork Shoe company Ltd ("the shoe company") was incorporated in May 1974 with a nominal capital of £10,000 divided into 10,000 shares of £1 each. Since 1962 the defendant Paul Joseph Duggan has been owner of 7,101 of these while his mother had 100. The business of the shoe company has prospered since its incorporation so that in 1964 it was producing 12,000 pairs of slippers each week. It required a substantial amount of rubber compound which it did not manufacture and, for some time before 1964, the defendant had been considering the formation of a company which would manufacture this and sell it to the shoe company. The defendant has been successful in business but his character and methods of working are unusual. He makes decisions quickly, has little regard for the legal and financial problems which they created and leaves these to be sorted out by others. He is impulsive, does not like paper work and relies on personal contacts. The best illustration of his temperament is given by the facts in the case which was heard immediately after this one. He heard that the plaintiff's wife was not well, thought that her health would improve if the plaintiff and she moved into a good house, went immediately to the owner of what he thought was a suitable one, agreed a price and paid the total amount of it to the owner without any written contract or investigation of the title. There is also a vagueness in his mind in connection with legal and financial matters.

The defendant knew that a large amount of capital would be required to start a company to manufacture rubber and its compounds and that he would have to induce members of the public to subscribe for its shares. He knew that he would not be able to deal with the financial matters relating to the issue of shares and so he made diplomatic approaches to the plaintiff to leave the Sunbeam Wolsey group and to join the shoe company and the new company about to be formed.

The plaintiff is an accountant who in 1948 joined Sunbeam Wolsey and in 1957 was appointed marketing manager of that group. He has been remarkably successful, is very able and understands the complexities of modern company finance and taxation. He has made a considerable amount of money by prudent investment and is prepared to take part in any commercial transaction which offers the prospect of capital gain or profits which the Revenue Commissioners cannot assess to tax. When the defendant approached him, his salary from Sunbeam Wolsey was £3,000 and a bonus which was about £800. There was also a non-contributory pension scheme of which he was a member and he had the use of a company car. He is an entirely different type of man to the defendant: he is methodical, good at paper work, knows more about the law than most accountants and has a considerable appetite for money. He expresses himself with clarity while there is a vagueness and lack of precision in almost everything which the defendant says. Many discussions took place between these two men during which the prospects of the new company were exhaustively discussed. The plaintiff realised the size of the market available for its products and thought that it offered the chance of being as successful as the Sunbeam Wolsey group and Youghal Carpets Ltd. In both of these companies, those who had been associated with them from the beginning made very large sums of money when the shares in them were given a quotation on the stock exchange. I am convinced that the plaintiff thought that there was a good chance that the new company would be as successful as they were and that with his financial ability, the new company could make large profits. The two of them arrived at what they thought was an agreement which was never put into writing in the early part of 1964 and on 1 April the plaintiff resigned from Sunbeam Wolsey and took up his position as joint managing director of the shoe company on 1 June. The basis of the agreement between them was that a new company, Cork Rubber and Plastic Manufacturing Company Ltd ("the plastic company") would be formed in which there would be A ordinary shares with one vote for each share and ordinary shares with limited voting rights. The plastic company was incorporated on 4 June and the all the work in connection with this was done by the plaintiff. The plaintiff had also thought of having a bonus issue of shares in the plastic company under which those associated with that company, the defendant and he would get bonus shares for which they would not have to pay and which would not be taxable as profits from the office of director.

The terms agreed were that the plaintiff was to become joint managing director with the defendant in the two companies, that his salary in the shoe company was to be £2,500, that his contract was to be for 15 years and that there was to be a non-contributory pension scheme. The plaintiff says that it was also agreed between them that he was to get a commission of two per cent on the profits of the shoe company and that the defendant was to transfer 1,000 of his shares in it to him. The defendant denies vehemently that he agreed to pay a commission of two per cent on the profits to the plaintiff or that he would transfer any of his shares in the shoe company to him. It was also agreed between them that the plaintiff was to get a basic salary of £2,500 in the plastic company together with a commission of five per cent on the profits and that a non-contributory pension scheme was to be established in that company also. Throughout the negotiations the plaintiff consulted Mr Thompson, the manager of the bank where the shoe company had its account and kept him informed of the progress of the negotiations. The plaintiff told Mr Thompson that the defendant had agreed to transfer 1,000 shares in the shoe company to him but did not tell him anything about an agreement to pay him commission on the profits of that company. This evidence came from the defendant (Thompson did not give evidence) who admitted that in 1970 Mr Thompson said to the plaintiff in the presence of the defendant "You told me about the 1,000 shares but not about the commission".

At the beginning the plaintiff gave most of his time to the plastic company in which he had invested £3,000. There were many difficulties in connection with machinery, getting skilled labour and getting other people to put their capital into it. There was also the problem of the bonus shares in it on which the plaintiff took expert legal and accountancy advice and ultimately an immensely ingenious scheme was worked out. The shoe company entered into a contract with another company and the benefit of this was transferred to the plastic company for £20,000. The sum was not paid but was used to pay up in full 80,000 shares of five shillings each in the plastic company to which the shoe company then became entitled and it renounced its right to these shares in favour of the plaintiff, the defendant and the others. The shares were thus fully paid and there was no tax payable.

The plaintiff never demanded the transfer to him of the 1,000 shares in the shoe company although this was very successful. It made such profits that its assets are now worth about £600,000 so that the shares which the plaintiff claims are now worth about £85,000. The value of the assets of the shoe company when the plaintiff joined it as managing director was £100,000. At some date which the parties could not fix, the defendant decided to settle his shares in the shoe company on discretionary trusts so that large sums for the estate duty would not become payable on his death and the way in which this could be done was discussed with Mr O'Meara, a solicitor in Cork who specialises in this work. The plaintiff was at these discussions and never mentioned that he had a claim on 1,000 of these shares.

A written agreement between the plastic company and the plaintiff was made on the 21 September 1967 by which the plaintiff became joint managing director of that company for 15 years from the 1 October 1966, at a salary of £2,500 and an annual commission of five per cent of the net profits of that company. The agreement also provided that the plaintiff was to be given the use of a motor car and provision was made for a pension scheme. There was never a written agreement between the plaintiff and the shoe company.

In February 1969 the plaintiff went to Australia to build up an export market there for the products of the shoe company. He returned in April and the defendant and he found it impossible to work together and they quarrelled bitterly. The plaintiff had been dealing in building land near Leixlip and the defendant felt that he was giving too much time to these transactions. This however was not the only cause of the quarrel. Ultimately the plaintiff resigned from the shoe company. The plastic company had been taken over by the shoe company at an earlier date and the plaintiff also resigned from it. He has now brought this action claiming specific performance of the agreement to transfer the 1,000 shares to him: he was never paid the two per cent commission on the profits of the shoe company and does not now make any claim for this.

Both sides presented the case on the basis that the issue to be decided is whether I believe the evidence of the plaintiff or that of the defendant. I do not accept this approach because I am convinced that each of them now believes in the truth of the evidence which he has given. The contract was made in 1964, the parties have quarrelled bitterly, each feels that the other has treated him badly and so, when the case came to be heard in 1971, each had a strong conviction of the truth of the evidence which he was giving. The case must, I think, be decided by weighing the probabilities.

The strongest element in the plaintiff's case is that he told Mr Thompson, the bank manager, whom he consulted about the transaction in 1964, that he was getting 1,000 shares in the shoe company. The next matter which favours the plaintiff is that his main interest in joining the defendant's organisation was in capital appreciation. He wanted a good salary but as his main interest was in capital, he would have been interested in getting shares in the shoe company. I am convinced that the plaintiff thought that there would be very large profits made in the plastic company and that he thought he would be able to get a quotation for its shares on the stock exchange and so he gave most of his time to it. This was the company in which he had invested some of his capital. I am convinced that he never thought that the shoe company would become public because from the beginning the defendant had made it clear that he regarded it as his "powerhouse". The 1,000 shares claimed by the plaintiff would have given him a holding of 15 per cent of the equity and so the defendant would have retained a controlling interest.

The factors which support the defendant's case are that the plaintiff never made a demand for the transfer of the 1,000 shares to him between 1964 and 1970. The plaintiff says that he gave some hints about this but admits that he never demanded the transfer until the parties had quarrelled. The plaintiff did not say during his evidence where the agreement about the 1,000 shares was concluded. Very much in favour of the defendant is the uncontradicted evidence that at the discussion in connection with the establishment of the discretionary trust at which the plaintiff was present, Mr O'Meara was told that Mr Duggan had 7,101 shares in the shoe company. The plaintiff understood that the matter being discussed was the shares to be included in the discretionary trust and that Mr O'Meara was being told that the defendant owned 7,101 shares. If the plaintiff had a claim to 1,000 shares, it is astonishing that he did not mention it on this occasion. The agreement about the 1,000 shares was never put in writing and there was never a demand that it should be. For a man like the plaintiff who is money-conscious and who knew how prosperous the shoe company was, the omission to request that the agreement be put in writing is remarkable. The plaintiff's evidence about the defendant's agreement to pay him commission on the profits of the shoe company was contradicted. This commission must now be a large sum but is not being claimed by the plaintiff. When he was asked about his reason for not making the claim, he did not give a convincing reason why he had abandoned it. I have difficulty in understanding how the plaintiff expected to make a capital profit in the shoe company. He never believed that this company would get a quotation on the stock exchange and he could not have believed that the defendant would buy the shares from him for cash because the defendant finances himself with loans from the shoe company. Lastly, there is a factor that the claim for the 1,000 shares was made expressly only when a bitter quarrel between the parties had taken place.

In my view the probabilities strongly favour the defendant's case that he never agreed to transfer the 1,000 shares. I do not think his evidence that there was never a reference during the negotiations to a transfer of these shares to the plaintiff is correct. The plaintiff may have tried to get this as part of his contract but I am convinced that the defendant never agreed to transfer 1,000 shares.

Neither of the defendant's counsel mentioned the Statute of Frauds in their speeches so I think I am justified in assuming that it is not being relied on as an answer to the claim.

In my opinion the plaintiff has not established as a matter of probability that there was an agreement to transfer 1,000 shares in the shoe company to him or one to pay him commission on the profits of it. It follows that this action must be dismissed.

Patricia McLaughlin
Barrister

In the Matter of the Companies Act 1963: And in the Matter of Irish Visiting Motorists' Bureau Ltd: High Court (Kenny J) 27 January 1972

Company Law – Scheme established to provide insurance cover for motorists travelling to Britain and Northern Ireland – Bureau established in each country to operate scheme – Uniform agreement between bureaux – Agreement entered into between five Irish insurance companies and Irish bureau – Supplemental to agreement between bureau and Minister for Local Government – Companies became dissatisfied with burden of work imposed on them – Notice to terminate agreement given to minister

Petitioner applied for membership – Told new organisation to be formed – Petitioner applied for membership – Draft fundamental agreement provided that bureau would issue such international insurance cards as member required – Petitioner agreed to become a party to the fundamental agreement – Before agreement executed a resolution was passed providing that new members must provide security before cards issued – Only affected the petitioner – Whether the fundamental agreement could be relied upon to invalidate the resolution –

Whether petitioner could rely upon the earlier agreement to impugn the resolution – Whether resolution ultra vires *the company – Whether fundamental agreement imposed upon the bureau the obligation to issue any cards which a member might require – Whether requirement of security inconsistent with main purpose of agreement – Whether petitioner precluded from challenging the resolution when they had signed the fundamental agreement – Whether action of bureau oppressive to the petitioner as a member of the company – Whether resolution ceased to be effective when fundamental agreement executed – Companies Act 1963 (No. 33), section 205*

Facts: In order to achieve the position that third party insurance taken out in one country should be valid in others, a scheme was adopted by insurance companies in the Republic of Ireland, Northern Ireland and Britain whereby the insurance companies in each jurisdiction would establish a bureau which would issue international motor insurance cards, so-called green cards, to companies which were members of it or associated with it. This would indicate that the holder held a policy of insurance against third party liability in the State where he lived and that it had been extended to cover claims against him in other countries. If a holder of a card was involved in an accident in another country, the bureau which had been established there would handle the claim and would make any payments necessary to settle it. This bureau would then be paid the amount which the claim had cost them by the bureau which issued the card which would then recover this from the insurance company to which it had been given. This arrangement was expressed in a draft uniform agreement between bureau.

In 1953, five Irish insurance companies entered into an agreement with the Irish bureau, which then, as the duly authorised agent of such companies, entered into an agreement with the Minister for Local Government pursuant to article 4 of the uniform agreement. This latter agreement was stated to be determinable by the minister or the bureau on one year's notice. The 1953 agreement recited that the Irish bureau was to supply to each of the insurance companies such green cards as they might require and that each of them was to be entitled to issue these to any of their policy holders who might require them.

By 1967, the companies operating the scheme had become dissatisfied with the burden of work imposed upon them by it. Two factors contributed to this. In 1963 the Equitable Insurance Company had been wound up and a compensation fund had been set up which was financed by levies made on companies doing insurance business in Ireland. Further, with the increase in popularity of the motoring holiday, there was a significant increase in the number of claims in this country against motorists holding green cards issued by bureaux in other States. These had to be handled by the four Irish companies left operating the scheme and they became so dissatisfied with the burden of extra work which was imposed on them that they gave notice of termination of the agreement of 1953 to the minister.

The petitioner obtained a licence to provide motor insurance cover in 1967 and notified the Irish bureau of its wish to become members in order that it might provide insurance cover for its policy holders when visiting Northern Ireland. It was informed on that occasion that the bureau was about to be wound up and that a new organisation would be formed which would provide cards. The petitioner requested cards on a number of occasions, and negotiations were conducted as to the basis upon which it might be given cards, but ultimately the petitioner informed the bureau that it expected to become a member of the new organisation which was about to be formed.

In July 1969 the members of the Irish bureau and the British insurance companies and syndicates, transacting business in Ireland, agreed on the new form which the Irish bureau was to take and on the terms of the document which was to replace the agreement of 1953. On 27 August the Irish bureau passed a special resolution to insert a new article 3A in its articles of association which provided for the entering into of an agreement ("the fundamental agreement") with the members in the terms of the draft. A circular was sent to all insurers, including the petitioner, informing them that a new bureau would be constituted and that the necessary resolution to alter the articles had been passed, and that the wording of the new agreement had been agreed. Each new member was to apply for two shares to be sold at par. The petitioner acknowledged receipt of the circular and applied for two shares. It received its share certificate on 30 January 1970.

Before execution of the fundamental agreement, a resolution was passed at a meeting of the directors of the bureau on 9 March 1970. The directors were concerned that the petitioner could not operate profitably and that the issue of green cards could involve the bureau in heavy liabilities if any company to whom they were issued became insolvent as the other insurance companies would be ultimately responsible for these. The resolution, therefore, stipulated that members, other than the four founder members of the bureau, would be required to lodge a cash deposit or securities with an approved bank in order to obtain cards. All those at the meeting knew that the British insurance companies and syndicates did not intend to apply to the Irish bureau for cards and so the immediate effect of the resolution was that the petitioner would be the only company which would be required to give security for any cards for which it applied.

On 11 March, the chairman of the bureau wrote to the petitioner asking it to confirm that they would become a party to the fundamental agreement and also sent a circular as to the terms upon which cards would be issued to all members other than founder members. The petitioner confirmed that it would become a party to the fundamental agreement on 13 March. Clause III of the fundamental agreement, provided that the bureau should supply such international motor insurance cards as might be required and that each insurer should be entitled to issue these to any of its policy holders who might require one. It further provided that the Irish bureau might call upon its members to make a contribution to a fund to pay any liabilities which it might incur under the uniform agreement and to meet its expenses.

The petitioner submitted that the resolution of 9 March was invalid on the grounds that it attempted to regulate the issue of green cards in a manner which was contrary to the fundamental agreement. It also contended that the directors of the Irish bureau exercised their powers oppressively to it and in disregard of its interests as a member and that the resolution was not passed in good faith but was intended to impose a burden on it which was not placed on the Irish companies which were in competition with it.

Held by Kenny J in allowing the petition:

(1) As the fundamental agreement referred to in the special resolution passed on the 27 August 1969 had not been executed by the Irish bureau or by any of its members when the resolution of 9 March 1970 was passed it could not be relied upon to invalidate the resolution when passed and the petitioners could not successfully invoke the agreement of 1953 to impugn the resolution as they were not parties to it.

(2) The first object for which the company was incorporated was to enter into the agreement with the Minister for Local Government as mentioned in article 4 of its articles of association. The resolution of 9 March was therefore not *ultra vires* the company. Accordingly, the bureau was not under an obligation to issue green cards to its members on request, and the fundamental agreement did not get any extra force nor did its terms become an unalterable object of the company from the reference to it in article 3A.

(3) Clause III of the fundamental agreement provided that the bureau should supply to each insurer such international motor insurance cards as they might require and that each insurer should be entitled to issue the same to any of its policy holders who might require them. This imposed an obligation on the bureau to give to each party to the agreement any cards that they required without any condition as to security so long as they were members of the bureau.

(4) The requirement of security, although valid when passed by the directors, was so inconsistent with the main purpose of the fundamental agreement and with clause III that it must be regarded as having been rescinded by the bureau when it sealed the fundamental agreement.

(5) The petitioner did not accept the resolution of 9 March or preclude him from objecting to it by executing the fundamental agreement as the directors knew that the petitioner objected to the resolution but made no change to the wording of clause III which imposed an unconditional obligation on them to supply cards to members.

(6) The petitioners claim under section 205 of the Companies Act 1963 failed as the conduct or exercise complained of must affect the person making the complaint as a member and not as a creditor or a person having commercial dealings with the company. A member of the bureau did not acquire a right to be supplied with green cards because the articles of association did not confer this. The right derived from the fundamental agreement. As the issue of cards might have involved the Irish bureau in substantial liabilities, the interests of the members as shareholders were promoted by the bureau getting security from

each company which applied for cards and by imposing conditions which would make them difficult to obtain.

(7) The resolution passed by the directors on the 9 March 1970 ceased to be effective or valid on the 10 July 1970.

No cases referred to in judgment

Counsel's and solicitors' names not available

KENNY J **27 January 1972**

One of the features of tourism since 1950 has been the increase in the number of people who wish to take their cars with them when they visit other countries. Many States have imposed an obligation on motorists to insure themselves against claims arising out of the driving of vehicles but the policies issued did not cover liability in other countries and the insurance companies which issued them were often not authorised to carry on business in all the areas where the traveller wished to drive. The governments of some States in western Europe therefore tried to achieve the position that third party insurance taken out in one country should be valid in all others and that it should comply with the minimum compulsory insurance requirements of each State. The scheme adopted in Britain, Northern Ireland and the Republic of Ireland to do this was that the insurance companies in each country were to establish a bureau there which would issue an international motor insurance card to the companies which were members of it or associated with it. This would show that the holder of it held a policy of insurance against third party liability in the State where he lived and that it had been extended to cover claims against him in other countries. This card (called "a green card}) would show the countries to which the cover given by the policy had been extended and would be accepted by all governments as a compliance with the compulsory insurance requirements. If a holder of one was involved in an accident in another country, the bureau which had been established there would handle the claim and would make any payments necessary to settle it. This bureau would then be paid the amount which the claim had cost them by the bureau which issued the card and which would then recover this from the insurance company to which it had been given. This arrangement was expressed in a draft uniform agreement between bureaux which was intended to be made between the bureaux in two countries and it was hoped that there would be as many agreements as possible so that insurance cover in countries where this was compulsory would be available.

In Britain and Northern Ireland green cards were issued by the motor insurance bureau which was set up to make payments in cases where there was not a policy of insurance in force giving indemnity to the driver at the time of the accident but in 1952 the arrangements for the establishment of a similar institution in the Republic of Ireland had not been completed. The Minister for Local Government wished to have a bureau in this country which would issue and take liability for green cards and began negotiations with the five insurance companies incorporated in this State which carried on motor insurance business. The British insurance companies and syndicates which did insurance business here were not involved in the arrangement. These discussions led to the preparation of a draft agreement between the minister and the company which was to be established and to be called Irish Visiting Motorists' bureau Ltd ("the Irish bureau"). It was incorporated on 18 December 1952 and three of its objects were (a) to enter into and carry into effect with such modifications (if any) as might be agreed upon the agreement mentioned in article 4 of its articles of association (b) to act as the agents or representatives of companies or organisations carrying on motor insurance business either in this country or elsewhere and to deal with and settle claims by third parties against persons holding policies of insurance from such companies or organisations (c) to enter into agreements with the Minister for Industry and Commerce or any minister or department of State in relation to the payment of claims by third parties in respect of death or injury to person or property suffered in an accident arising out of or in consequence of the driving, management or control of a motor vehicle. Article 4 read:

> "The directors shall forthwith on behalf of the company take into consideration and if thought fit shall enter into (either with or without modification) the agreement which has already been prepared and is expressed to be made between the Minister for Local Government of the one part and the company of the other part in the terms of the draft which for the purposes of identification has been endorsed with the signatures of the subscribers hereto and shall carry the same into effect with full power nevertheless from time to time to agree to any modification of the terms of such agreement either before or after the execution thereof."

This draft was not proved in evidence but it was agreed that its terms were similar to those of an agreement of 7 January 1953 made between the Minister and the Irish bureau. This began with a recital that it was supplemental to an agreement of 2 January 1953 made between the Irish bureau of the one part and the Irish insurance companies of the other part. An agreement of 2 January was not proved but a copy of an agreement of 29 January 1953 between the Irish bureau and the five insurance companies incorporated in Ireland (the Hibernian Fire and General Insurance Company Ltd, the Insurance Corporation of Ireland Ltd, the Irish National Insurance Company Ltd, the Equitable Insurance Company Ltd and the Shield Insurance Company Ltd) was given in evidence and the case was conducted on the basis that the reference in the agreement of 7 January 1953 to the agreement of 2 January was to that of 29 January.

The agreement of 7 January, which must therefore be read as being supplemental to the agreement of 29 January 1953, provided that if a mechanically propelled vehicle of any person who was the holder of a card in respect of it issued by a bureau of the country between whom and the Irish bureau an international agreement was in force was involved in a motor accident in the

State and the accident occurred during the period while the card was in force, the Irish bureau undertook with the minister that they would take measures and do everything to ensure that all claims by third parties against the holder would be dealt with and the claim discharged as if they had been an insurance company carrying on motor insurance business and as if the holder had been insured by them for such vehicle in respect of a third party claim arising out of a motor accident. It also provided that the Irish bureau was making the agreement as the duly authorised agent of the five insurance companies which I have already mentioned and that it was to be determinable by the minister or by the Irish bureau on one year's notice.

The agreement of 29 January ("the 1953 agreement") made between the Irish bureau and the Irish insurance companies recited that they had entered into or were about to enter into arrangements with insurance organisations operating in the countries specified in the first schedule under which a motor accident insurance bureau would be established in the Republic of Ireland and in each of the countries specified in the schedule and that an owner of a mechanically propelled vehicle who wished to use it in some other country would be entitled to obtain a green card from the bureau in his own company. It also recited that if the holder or any other person specified in the card while in any of the countries named in it and while driving or being in control of the vehicle specified in it was involved in an accident, all claims by third parties in respect of death or personal injury were to be dealt with by the bureau of the country in which the accident occurred as if it were an insurance company which had issued a motor insurance policy to the owner of the vehicle and that the bureau handling the claim was to be indemnified against all claims by the bureau which had issued it. The parties then agreed that the Irish bureau was to supply to each of the Irish companies such green cards as they might require and that each of them was to be entitled to issue these to any of their policy holders who might require them. It also provided that the Irish bureau was to carry out the obligations of a bureau and of the Irish companies under the uniform agreement so that when a mechanically propelled vehicle of any person holding a green card issued by the bureau of another country in respect of that vehicle was involved in an accident in the Republic of Ireland and a claim was made by third parties, the Irish bureau was to deal with the claim and to make all payments in connection with it as if it had been an insurance company and had issued a policy of insurance to the owner. This agreement did not make any provision for the adherence to it of any company or syndicate carrying on motor insurance business in the Republic or of any company which was subsequently formed.

The British insurance companies and syndicates which carried on business in this country did not ask the Irish bureau for cards because they could get those which they required from the Motor Insurance bureau in London. Some of the Irish companies were authorised to do motor insurance business in Britain and Northern Ireland so that they could give cover to their policy holders when driving there and so did not require many cards. The Shield Insurance Company were not however authorised to carry on this business in Britain and Northern

Ireland and so whenever any of their policy holders wished to drive in Northern Ireland, they had to get a card from the Irish bureau and so they took the biggest proportion of them issued by the Irish bureau.

Shortly after the Irish bureau was established, an arrangement was made between the Irish companies that claims against motorists visiting the Republic of Ireland would be dealt with them in rotation. Claims against those who had got cards from the Irish bureau were sent to the company to which the card had been issued. The result was that the only function of the Irish bureau was the issue of cards to their five members. In 1963 the Equitable Insurance Company was ordered to be wound up by this court because it was insolvent and the Insurance Act 1964 set up a compensation fund to be financed by levies made on companies doing insurance business in Ireland and out of which the outstanding claims against the Equitable were to be met. I have been dealing with applications for payment out of this fund since it was established and the amount of the claims paid is now more that £100,000. This insolvency was referred to during this case and I think that the acceptance by the Government of the principle that the companies and syndicates should be liable to satisfy claims against insolvent insurance companies has had a considerable effect on those in this business. Since 1961 there have also been a number of failures of insurance companies in Britain which did motor work and many of the companies which are doing this type of insurance in the Republic had had heavy losses on this branch of their business during the last five years.

The introduction of car ferry services between this country and Britain and other European countries and the growing popularity of the caravan holiday led to a big increase in the number of claims in this country against motorists holding green cards issued by bureaux in other States. These had to be handled by the four Irish companies and they were so dissatisfied with the burden of extra work which was imposed on them that they gave notice of termination of the agreement of 7 January 1953 to the minister. Their purpose in doing this was, I think, to put pressure on the minister to compel the British companies to take part in the running of the Irish bureau and, in July 1967, agreement had been reached that the other insurance companies doing business in this country would take some of the work of the Irish bureau. The solicitors who acted for the Irish bureau were instructed to get advice as to whether it should be wound up and a new one established or whether its articles should be changed and the agreement of 1953 altered so that the other companies and syndicates would be parties to a new agreement. Mr Aubrey O'Callaghan, who had been the manager of the Irish National Insurance Company for many years, was the chairman of the Irish bureau and the other companies left the negotiation of the new terms with the British companies to him.

The P.M.P.A. Insurance Company Ltd ("the petitioners") were incorporated in April 1964. They were associated with a voluntary organisation called the Private Motorists' Protection Association whose spokesmen have consistently maintained that motor insurance at the premiums charged can be made profitable. Their views expressed in many public statements did not endear them to the insurance companies and they did not get a licence from the minister to enable them to carry on insurance business until 1967. They have never been authorised to carry on insurance business in Britain or Northern Ireland and so, when they got their licence in 1967, their policy holders could not get cover from them for any liabilities in Britain and Northern Ireland unless cards could be procured from the Irish bureau. On 7 July 1967 Mr Hughes, an official of the petitioners, called on Mr O'Callaghan to tell him that they wished to issue cards to their policy holders who wanted to go to Northern Ireland. Mr Hughes said that the petitioners had applied for membership of the Motor Insurance bureau of Ireland (an organisation financed by the insurance companies and established to pay claims when there is no policy of insurance in force), and that they wished to become members of the Irish bureau. Mr O'Callaghan told Mr Hughes that the Irish bureau was a company with limited liability which was going to be wound up and that they had given notice of termination of the agreement of 7 January 1953 to the minister. He also told Mr Hughes that a new organisation to provide cards was about to be formed and what he said gave Mr Hughes the impression that the petitioners could not get these unless they became members of the Irish bureau. On 25 July the petitioners wrote to the Irish bureau to apply for membership of it and on 11 August Mr O'Callaghan replied that this had been considered by the directors but that as it was in course of being would up, applications for membership could not be considered. The petitioners then made a complaint to the minister that the Irish bureau had refused to give them cards. An official of the department advised the petitioners to offer the Irish bureau a form of indemnity against any liabilities which might arise out of cards issued to them. A meeting took place on 28 August between Mr O'Callaghan and some of the petitioners' officers and a discussion took place as to the terms upon which cards could be issued to them. Mr O'Callaghan then gave Mr Dore a document which showed the conditions which had to be complied with by a new member of the Motor Insurance bureau in Britain before cards were given to it. These required that a new member should procure a guarantee granted by a British banker in favour of the Motor Insurance bureau for £10,000 for each 1,000 or part of 1,000 green cards issued and that the guarantee was to be operative for a period of five years in respect of liability which could be the responsibility of the British Motor Insurance bureau arising out of their issue or make a deposit with the bankers of the British Motor Insurance bureau in the joint names of the new member and he bureau of trustee investments the market value of which was to exceed £10,000 for each 1,000 cards issued by the bureau to the member within the preceding five years. The conditions also provided that no cards would be issued to a new member unless there were already sufficient investments deposited to cover any new ones as well as any which had been already provided.

At the meeting in August Mr O'Callaghan said that the Irish bureau would be prepared to issue cards to the petitioners if they complied with any of the conditions imposed by the British Motor Insurance bureau in respect of new members. On 29 August 1967 the petitioners wrote that they were prepared to give a guarantee and asked if one by the Munster and Leinster Bank would be sufficient. On 30 August Mr O'Callaghan confirmed that such a guarantee would be accepted and that he had written for a draft of it and he sent this on 5 September. The Munster and Leinster Bank were advised that they could not give a guarantee because of the provisions of the Insurance Act 1936. Correspondence then took place in relation to the deposit by the petitioners of securities. The petitioners were reluctant to lodge these in joint names but Mr O'Callaghan insisted on this being done. Another meeting took place on 28 September at which the deposit of securities was discussed and the petitioners then wrote to enquire whether they would be invited to take part in the reconstituted bureau on the same basis as the British companies. Mr O'Callaghan's answer was that he could not say what the position of the petitioners would be but that his personal view was that he saw no reason why an application from them for membership of the reconstructed bureau or of a new organisation would not be accepted. On 18 October Mr Dore telephoned Mr O'Callaghan to say that the petitioners were not proceeding with their request to be supplied with cards because they thought that the Irish bureau would be reconstructed or a new organisation would be set up early 1963 and that they expected to be accepted into it in the same way as other insurance companies had been. During the conversation Mr O'Callaghan told Mr Dore that his personal view was that the petitioners would be required to deposit securities for cards in the same way as this was required by the British Insurance bureau. The form of the new bureau or the alterations in the existing organisation had not been decided on when the petitioners wrote on 26 April 1968 for 100 green cards. This request was refused.

As the petitioners needed cards for their policy holders and as their inability to provide them was a serious handicap to them in their business, they purchased some from brokers associated with Belgian insurance companies. In 1969 the Insurance Corporation of Ireland, who were members of the Irish bureau, supplied cards to the petitioners and then decided to transfer some of the shares held by them in the Irish bureau to the petitioners so that they could become aware of it. The Irish bureau had a private company and its articles provided that shares might be transferred to any member of the company but that a share could not be transferred to a person who was not a member while any member or any person selected by the directors was willing to purchase it and that for the purpose of finding out whether a member was willing to purchase, a shareholder who wished to transfer his shares had to give notice to the Irish bureau of this. On 23 May 1969 the Insurance Corporation of Ireland wrote to Mr O'Callaghan that they had decided in principle to facilitate the petitioners to become members of the Irish bureau by transferring some of their shares in it to them and asked for "clearance" under article 18. This was treated by the board of directors as being an application to approve a transfer and at a meeting on 25 June they decided to refuse the request. On 9 July the petitioners made an application to Mr O'Callaghan for membership of the Irish bureau and informed him that the Insurance Corporation of Ireland had offered to transfer some of their shares in it to them and that approval to this had been refused. In answer to this Mr O'Callaghan wrote on 16 July that the Irish bureau was being reconstituted, that the final draft of the new articles of association were with counsel and that earlier correspondence and discussions had dealt fully with the application for membership and the conditions under which the Irish bureau were prepared to supply the petitioners with cards without the necessity of becoming a member of it.

In July 1969 the members of the Irish bureau and the British insurance companies and syndicates transacting motor insurance business in the Republic of Ireland agreed on the new form which the Irish bureau was to take and on the terms of the document which was to replace the agreement of 1953. The new arrangement was that all the companies incorporated in this country and all the British companies and syndicates doing motor insurance business here were to become members of the Irish bureau and that the articles of association were to be amended so that they would refer to the new agreement between the Irish bureau and all its members and would make provision for an increase in the number of directors and for a board which would represent all the companies and syndicates. A draft of the new agreement to which all the companies and syndicates were expressed to be parties was prepared and was sent to all the companies. This draft is not now available but it was conceded that the terms of it were similar to the agreement which was subsequently executed on 10 July 1970. This agreement however existed in draft form only when the resolution of 19 March 1970, the validity of which is the subject matter of this application, was passed.

On 27 August the Irish bureau passed a special resolution to insert a new article 3A in their articles of association. It read:

> "3A (1) The Company shall forthwith enter into an Agreement (herewith referred to as 'the fundamental agreement') with the members of the Company in the terms of the draft which for the purpose of identification has been signed by Ernest O. Knapp, a solicitor of the High Court of Justice and the directors shall carry the same into effect with full power nevertheless from time to time to agree to any modification thereof.
> (2) Thereafter no insurer shall be admitted as a member of the company unless such insurer shall have previously agreed in writing to become a party to the fundamental agreement and to be bound by its terms and on admission to execute such documents as it may be required to execute for the purpose of implementing clause 12 of the fundamental agreement.
> (3) The directors may at any time prior to an order or resolution to wind up the company and from time to time call upon the members for the payment between them rateably of such sums as the Company shall from time to time require in order to enable it to discharge its obligations or further its objects. In determining the amount of the contribution to be paid by a member the directors shall apply the provisions in that behalf contained in the fundamental agreement. Upon a call being made hereun-

der upon a member for his due contribution such member shall forthwith pay the amount thereof to the Company,
(4) In the event of a member (hereinafter called 'the defaulting member') not paying the amount of any such call as is provided for in sub-article (3) within sixty days after having received a written demand therefor from the Company then the defaulting member, at the request in writing of the directors made at any time after the expiration of the said period of sixty days, shall be bound to transfer its shares in the Company at part (this is an obvious error and should read 'at par') to such other member or members of the Company willing to purchase the same as shall be selected by the directors. If the defaulting member shall fail to comply with such request of the directors for the transfer of its shares as aforesaid, the Company may receive the purchase money from the member or members so selected by the directors, and the defaulting member shall be deemed to have appointed any one director or the Secretary of the Company as his agent to execute a transfer of the share of such member or members so selected as aforesaid, and upon the execution of such transfer the Company shall hold the purchase in trust for the defaulting member."

The Irish bureau then sent a circular letter to all insurers licensed to transact mechanically propelled vehicle insurance, to inform them that meetings had taken place between representatives of all licensed motor insurers (except the Insurance Corporation of Ireland) and officials of the Department of Local Government to arrange that all licensed motor insurers would be members of the Irish bureau and that the necessary resolutions to alter the articles had been passed and that the wording of the new agreement (a copy of which was sent) had been agreed. It confirmed that it had been agreed that new members would apply for two shares each which were to be made available for them by the existing shareholders and requested each company or syndicate to send Mr O'Callaghan a formal application for two shares to be sold at par. On 11 October the petitioners acknowledged receipt of the circular and applied for two shares in the Irish bureau and sent a cheque of £2 and on 21 October they wrote asking for 20 green cards. The reply to this on 23 October was that it would be some time before final arrangements were completed to operate the reconstituted bureau and that when the applications from all licensed insurers were received, the necessary transfers of shares would be made and the reconstituted bureau brought into operation. Mr O'Callaghan's letter continued:

> "In the meantime you will appreciate we are unable to supply the green cards as requested."

On 30 January 1970 the petitioners received their share certificate for the two shares and when they acknowledged it on 2 February, they asked for 20 cards. On 4 February Mr O'Callaghan answered by stating that the arrangements for the supply of cards would be dealt with immediately following the annual general meeting on 24 February.

A meeting of the directors of the Irish bureau was held on 24 February and when a discussion about the appointment of the secretary had taken place, the meeting was adjourned to 9 March. On that date Mr Fitzsimon who was chairman and eight other directors and Mr O'Callaghan who acted as secretary were present. Mr O'Callaghan told them that the petitioners had applied for green cards and a discussion as to the terms on which these should be issued took place. Everyone at the meeting knew the conditions which the British Motor Insurance bureau had laid down for the issue of cards to new members and that a number of British insurance companies which transacted motor insurance business had become insolvent and that some of these (Auto and Marine and the Vehicle and General) had lost large sums in motor insurance. All those at the meeting were convinced that this type of insurance could not be operated profitably and knew that the issue of green cards could involve the Irish bureau in heavy liabilities if the company to which they were issued became insolvent so that the other insurance companies would ultimately be responsible for these. Also they regarded the petitioners with considerable suspicion because their principal executives had little experience of motor insurance and were offering motor insurance on terms which were more favourable to the motorists than those which the other companies were making available. A resolution was drafted at the meeting to deal with the terms on which cards would be issued to the members but it was decided that these should not apply to the four companies incorporated in Ireland which had been members of the Irish bureau from its incorporation.

The resolution read:

> "That as and from this date, 9 March 1970, green cards will be issued to all members other than founder members on the basis of a cash deposit of £10,000 (ten thousand pounds) or the deposit of approved securities in the same sum lodged with a bank approved by the board in the names of the member, the bureau and the bank in respect of each one thousand or part thousand green cards. Each arrangement to be approved by the board. The charge for green cards shall be the cost of printing plus £2 per thousand cards."

This was intended to express the conditions which the British Motor Insurance bureau had attached to the issue of cards to new members but everyone overlooked that these conditions required that the cash deposit or lodgment of securities was to be in respect of liabilities arising from cards for a period of five years from the date of their issue. Mr O'Callaghan said in evidence that he omitted to draw the attention of those at the meeting to this and that it was his mistake. All those at the meeting knew that the British insurance companies and syndicates did not intend to apply to the Irish bureau for cards and so the immediate effects of the resolution was that the petitioners would be the only company which would have to give security for any cards for which they applied.

On 11 March Mr O'Callaghan wrote to the petitioners asking them to confirm that they would become a party to the fundamental agreement referred to in Article 3A and to inform them that all the other prospective members were prepared to do this. He also sent a circular letter setting out the terms upon which cards would be issued to all members other than founder members. On 13 March the petitioners confirmed that they would become a party to the fundamental agreement and added the remark that they had done this some months before.

The fundamental agreement was to be signed by the Irish companies in Dublin between 4 and 5 May (see the minute of 20 April 1970) and was then to be sent to the British insurance companies and syndicates for execution by them. It was ultimately dated 10 July which was probably the day which it was sent to the Irish bureau's solicitors for stamping. It contained recitals that the Irish bureau had been established to enter into agreements with bureaux in other countries in relation to the use of green cards, that the 1953 agreement had been made, that it had been agreed that it would be rescinded and that the parties would enter into a new one. Recital No. 6 read:

> "It is now the desire of all parties hereto that all the insurers should participate in the operation, benefits and obligations of the Uniform Agreement between bureaux and with the view to facilitating such participation and giving effect to the arrangements between them in that behalf the shares held by the four Irish companies (which were The Hibernian Insurance Company Ltd, The Insurance Corporation of Ireland Ltd, The Irish National Insurance Company Ltd and The Shield Insurance Company Ltd) have been divided up amongst all the insurers and certain alterations have been made in the articles of association of the Irish bureau."

The parties then agreed that the Irish bureau should be the duly authorised agent of each of the insurers for all the purposes of the uniform agreement, that it should supply to each of the insurers such international motor insurance cards as they might require and that each insurer should be entitled to issue these to any of its policy holders who might require one. It was also agreed that the Irish bureau might call upon its members to make a contribution to a fund to pay any liabilities which it might incur under the uniform agreement and to meet its expenses.

The petitioners have now brought this petition in which they seek to have the resolution of 9 March cancelled. They submit that it is invalid because it attempts to regulate the issue of green cards which is contrary to the fundamental agreement. They have also contended that the directors of the Irish bureau have exercised their powers oppressively to them and in disregard of their interests as members and that the resolution was not passed in good faith but was intended to impose a burden on them which was not placed on the Irish companies which were in competition with them.

As the fundamental agreement referred to in the special resolution passed on 27 August 1969 had not been executed by the Irish bureau or by any of its members when the resolution of 9 March 1970 was passed, it cannot be relied on to invalidate the resolution when passed and the petitioners cannot successfully invoke the agreement of 1953 to impugn the resolution because they were not parties to it. The first object for which the company was incorporated was to enter into the agreement mentioned in article 4 of the company's articles of association but this was the contract with the Minister for Local Government. The resolution of 9 March was not therefore *ultra vires* the company which was not made under an obligation to issue green cards to its members on request and the fundamental agreement does not get any extra force nor do its terms become an unalterable object of the company from the reference to it in article 3A.

But what was the effect on the resolution of 9 March of the subsequent execution of the fundamental agreement? In it "the insurers" are defined as "each of those insurance companies and members of the underwriting syndicates at Lloyds licensed to transact mechanically propelled vehicle insurance in the Republic of Ireland by or on whose behalf these presents are signed" and the petitioners are one of the companies which have executed it. I have already mentioned the terms of recital 6 which contemplates that all those who signed the fundamental agreement should take part in the operation of and have the benefit of the uniform agreement between bureaux. Clause III of it is of such importance that it must be quoted in the form in which it appears. It reads:

> "The Irish bureau shall supply to each of the insurers such international motor insurance cards as they may require and each insurer shall be entitled to issue the same to any of its policy holders who may require an international motor insurance card."

This in my view imposed on the Irish bureau an obligation to give to each of the parties to the agreement any green cards which they required without any condition as to security so long as they were members of the Irish bureau. The requirement that a member should be entitled to cards only when it had been given security of £10,000 for each 1,000 green cards, although valid when it was passed by the directors, is so inconsistent with the main purpose of the fundamental agreement and with clause III that it must be regarded as having been rescinded by the Irish bureau when it sealed the fundamental agreement. Counsel for the Irish bureau said that the question at issue was whether the directors were authorised by the memorandum and articles of association to pass the resolution of 9 March and that if they were, the petitioners could not successfully rely on the fundamental agreement to invalidate it because this was not an action for breach of contract. It seems to me however that clause III of the fundamental agreement prevents the directors of the Irish bureau from imposing any condition as to security when they are asked by a member to issue cards. They are entitled to require payment of a reasonable amount for their expenses in connection with the printing and other costs but subject to this, the obligation created by the fundamental agreement is to issue as many cards as a member may require. In my view the resolution of 9 March was rescinded by the subsequent agreement and is now ineffective. This does not have the result that the Irish bureau can be compelled to issue cards to an insolvent company because it will be unable to pay its contributions and its shares will then be compulsorily acquired and it will cease to be a member of the Irish bureau (see article 3A).

Counsel for the Irish bureau said that the petitioners signed the fundamental agreement when they knew that the resolution of 9 March had been passed and he submitted that the petitioners thereby accepted its validity and that they knew that the cards to be issued to them under the fundamental agreement would be subject to the terms imposed by the resolution when they became aware of it and had been advised that it was invalid when they signed the fundamental agreement. The directors of the Irish bureau knew that the petitioners objected to the resolution but made no changes in the wording of clause III which imposed an unconditional obligation on them to supply each of the insurance companies and syndicates which signed it with the cards which they required. In my opinion the petitioners did not accept the resolution of 9 March or preclude themselves from objecting to it by executing the fundamental agreement.

The next argument was that the resolution passed in March was an oppressive exercise by the directors of their powers and that the court should cancel it under section 205 of the Companies Act 1963 which reads:

> "205(1) Any member of a company who explains that the affairs of the company are being conducted or that the powers of the directors of the company are being exercised in a manner oppressive to him or any of the members (including himself), or in discharge of his or their interests as members, may apply to the court for an order under this section.
> (3) If, on any application under sub-section 1 . . . the court is of opinion that the company's affairs are being conducted or the directors' powers are being exercised as aforesaid, the court may, with a view to bringing to an end the matters complained of, make such order as it thinks fit, whether directing or prohibiting any act or cancelling or varying any transaction or for regulating the conduct of the company's affairs in future, or for the purchase of the shares of any members of the company by other members of the company or by the company and in the case of a purchase by the company, for the reduction accordingly of the company's capital, or otherwise."

This section, which had not been in any of the earlier Companies Acts, provides a remedy for a shareholder whose rights as a shareholder are affected by the way in which the affairs of the company are being conducted or in which the powers of the directors are being exercised. The shareholders' rights come from the Companies Act, equitable principles which have become part of company law and the memorandum and articles of association viewed as a contract created by membership of the company. See section 25 sub-section 1 of the Act of 1963 which reads:

> "25 (1) Subject to the provisions of this Act, the memorandum and articles shall, when registered, bind the company and the members thereof to the same extent as if they respectively had been signed and sealed by each member and contained covenants by each member to observe all the provisions of the memorandum and of the articles."

The conduct or exercise of the powers complained of under section 205 must affect the person making the complaint in his character as a member and not as a creditor or a person having commercial dealings with the company. A member of the Irish bureau does not by membership acquire a right to be supplied with green cards because the articles of association do not confer this. The right came from the fundamental agreement and, before it was executed, from the agreement of 1953. The Irish bureau does not make any charge for cards except for the cost of printing and administration and as their issue may involve the Irish bureau in substantial liabilities, the interests of the members as shareholders are promoted by the Irish bureau getting security from each company which applies for cards and by imposing conditions which will make them difficult to obtain. The fundamental agreement was entered into by the Irish bureau because of the obligation imposed on it by article 3A but this does not have the consequence that the right to cards is conferred on the parties to it by their membership of the Irish bureau. The claim then, insofar as it is based on section 205 fails but as the question whether the resolution was oppressive was discussed at length, I think I should express my views on it.

The affairs of a company may be conducted or the powers of the directors may be exercised in a manner oppressive to any of the members although those in charge of the company are acting honestly and in good faith. If one defines oppression as being conduct or depriving a person of rights to which he is entitled, the person whose conduct is in question may believe that he is exercising his rights in doing what he does. One of the most terrifying aspects of human history is that many of those whom we now regard as having been oppressors had a fanatical belief in the rightness of what they are doing. The question then when deciding whether the conduct of the affairs of a company or the passing of a resolution is oppressive is whether, judged by objective standards, it is.

Green cards which are issued for Britain and Northern Ireland are valid until the insurance policy in respect of which they are given has to be renewed so that the maximum period which they can cover is one year. The petitioners are not authorised to transact motor insurance business in Britain and Northern Ireland and as they have about 100,000 policy holders, it is reasonable to assume that they will require about 10,000 cards each year. The resolution passed in

March would require them therefore to deposit £100,000 each year and at the end of ten years, the Irish bureau would be holding securities worth one million pounds for the petitioners' contingent liabilities. At the meeting in March the directors intended to follow the precedent set by the British Motor Insurers bureau but overlooked the limitation that the deposit of £10,000 for each 1,000 cards was to relate to those issued within the preceding five years. The retention of the securities in respect of possible liabilities arising under cards issued ten years before is so unreasonable and involves such a large sum for security that I think it was oppressive. I accept the evidence that the omission of the reference to the five year period was a mistake and that the directors would probably have altered the resolution when this error was pointed out to them. The resolution, however, as passed was oppressive.

The petitioners also argued that the directors of the Irish bureau did not pass the resolution of March 1970 in the best interests of the company and charged that they acted in bad faith and with the intention of imposing a burden on one Irish company and not on the four others doing motor insurance business in the State. They relied on the failure of their attempts to get cards between July 1967 and March 1970 when, they said, Mr O'Callaghan and those in charge of the Irish bureau knew that the inability to provide them was a serious handicap in their business. At an early stage in the discussions Mr O'Callaghan had said that he was prepared to issue cards to the petitioners if they gave security. The petitioners thought that they would be entitled to them without giving security if they became shareholders in the Irish bureau and their principal grievance against Mr O'Callaghan is that he did not admit them as members and refused to approve of the transfer of shares by the Insurance Corporation of Ireland to them. Mr O'Callaghan was determined that the petitioners would not be admitted to membership until he had succeeded in getting the British insurance companies and syndicates to agree to become members of the Irish bureau. Notice to determine the agreement of 1953 had been given in 1966 because the burden on the Irish companies had become heavy and I think that Mr O'Callaghan thought that he could increase the official pressure on the British companies and syndicates to become members of the Irish bureau if he refused to allow the petitioners to join. This was, I think, his main motive. He was also suspicious of the ability of those in charge of the petitioners to conduct motor insurance at a profit. The failure of the Equitable Insurance Company and of some British companies and the acceptance by the Oireachtas of the view that all the insurance companies doing business in the State must accept responsibility for the liabilities of insolvent companies has made a profound impression on all those associated with insurance in Ireland. The conditions laid down by the British Motor Insurers bureau seemed to all those present at the meeting on 9 March to be a necessary precaution. Everybody at the meeting realised that cards when issued could impose substantial liabilities on the Irish bureau which had no reserves and which would therefore have to make levies on all its members if any of them failed in business. They were convinced that the terms being offered by the petitioners to motorists would involve them in the losses which the other companies had suffered. In my view the directors and Mr O'Callaghan did not act dishonestly nor were they actuated by unworthy motives when they passed the resolution in March. They acted in what they believed to be the best interests of the Irish bureau and of companies which they represented.

I shall declare that the resolution passed by the directors of the Irish bureau on March 1970 in relation to the issue of green cards ceased to be effective or valid on 10 July 1970.

Patricia McLaughlin
Barrister

In the Matter of Burke Clancy & Co. Ltd on the Application of John J. Fitzgerald, Receiver: High Court 1973 No. 1535p (Kenny J) 23 May 1974

Company Law – Objects of company – Power to borrow money limited to the amount of the issued share capital – Power to issue debentures – Power of company in general meeting to consent to borrowing sums greater than the issued share capital – Power of company to ratify ultra vires *acts of the directors – Whether or not the company in general meeting had given the directors power to borrow unlimited sums – Whether or not debenture secured only monies limited to the amount of the issued share capital of the company*

Facts: One of the stated objects of the company was to borrow money and to issue debentures. The authorised share capital of the company was £12,000 and its issued capital, at all relevant times, was £11,500. By Article 13 of the company's articles of association, the directors were given the power to borrow money, but this power was limited to borrowing a sum which, at any one time, did not exceed the amount of the issued share capital of the company, unless the company in general meeting consented to such increased borrowing. Article 13 enabled the directors to secure the repayment of any such sums by mortgage or charge upon the whole or any part of the property and assets of the company, present and future, including its uncalled capital. An ordinary general meeting of the company was held on 10 March 1954, the minutes of which stated that:

> "It was agreed by the directors that the company should have the right to borrow without limit and that the entry of this item in the minutes be accepted as the company's authority to do so."

The company organised an overdraft from the Provincial Bank of Ireland and the bank required the company to give a debenture charged on all its assets. This debenture was sealed on 8 February 1954 and was stated to be issued under clause 3(m) of the company's memorandum of association, under Article 13 of the company's Articles of Association and in pursuance of a resolution passed on 8 February 1954. The said resolution stated that:

> "The company do create a debenture for all such sums as are now or shall be from time to time hereafter become owing to the Provincial Bank of Ireland Ltd or shall for the time being remain unpaid by the company on the balance of its current account with the said bank. . . ."

The amount due by the company increased and by 12 January 1971 it was £60,260. On 15 September 1971 the bank appointed a receiver over all the assets of the company. He applied to the court for a determination of the questions as to whether the debenture was valid, whether it secured £11,500 only or whether it secured the total sum due under it which at the date of the proceedings was £98,000.

Held by Kenny J in dismissing the application:

(1) The resolution of 8 February 1954, forwarded to the bank, was a resolution of the directors and it was not authority to them under Article 13 to borrow an amount exceeding the issued share capital of the company.

(2) In the resolution of 10 March 1954, the words "directors" and "the company" were placed in the wrong position in the sentence. The resolution should read "It was agreed by the company that the directors should have the right to borrow without limits" and, as the meeting was an ordinary general meeting, constituted a consent of the company to such borrowing within Article 13.

(3) Therefore the company gave its consent to the directors borrowing more than the amount of the issued share capital of the company and the amount secured by the debenture was the whole amount now due.

(4) Even if the resolution of 10 March 1954 did not give the directors this authority, the minutes show that the balance sheets and accounts for a number of years after 1954 were accepted and signed at annual general meetings of the company. This would constitute ratification of the action of the directors in borrowing more than the issued share capital of the company and so would bind the company. It is established law that the members of a company may ratify acts which are outside the powers of the directors but are *intra vires* the company.

Cases referred to in judgment

Grant v. United Kingdom Switchback Railways Company (1889) 40 Ch D 135
Irvine v. The Union Bank of Australia (1877) 2 App Cas 366
Royal British Bank v. Turquand (1856) 6 E & B 327 (Exchequer)

Counsel's and solicitors' names not available

KENNY J **23 May 1974**

Burke Clancy & Co. Ltd ("the company") was incorporated on 12 February 1953. Its principal object was to acquire and take over as a going concern and carry on the business of public works contractors and builders carried on by John Burke and Michael Clancy and all or any of the assets and liabilities of the proprietors of that business in connection therewith. One of the objects in the memorandum was:

> "(m) To borrow or raise money in such manner as the company shall think fit, and in particular by the issue of debentures or debenture stock (perpetual or otherwise) and to secure the repayment of any money borrowed, raised, or owing, by mortgage, charge or lien upon the whole or any part of the company's property or assets (whether present or future) including its uncalled capital and also by a similar mortgage, charge or lien to secure and guarantee the performance by the company of any obligation or liability it may undertake."

The regulations contained in Table A in the First Schedule to the Companies (Consolidation) Act 1908 applied to the company, but regulation 73 was excluded. The share capital of the company was £12,000 and its issued capital, at all relevant times, was £11,500. Article 13 of its regulations of it read:

> "The directors may raise or borrow for the purposes of the company's business such sum or sums of money as they think fit, but so that the whole amount so raised or borrowed and outstanding at any one time shall not without the consent of the company in general meeting, exceed the amount of the share capital of the company for the time being issued or agreed to be issued. The directors may secure the repayment of or raise any such sum or sums as aforesaid by mortgage or charge upon the whole or any part of the property and assets of the company, present and future, including its uncalled capital or by the issue, at such price as they may think fit, of bonds, debentures or debenture stock, either upon the whole or any part of the property and assets of the company or not so charged, or in such other ways as the directors may think expedient."

An ordinary general meeting was held on 10 March 1954 and the minute of it read:

> "The first ordinary general meeting of the company was held at the company's office at Father Griffin Road at 4 p.m. Present were Mr John Burke, Mr Michael Clancy and Mr Gerald J. Fleming. The auditor's report was read and as no questions were raised, the accounts and balance sheet were accepted, signed and the auditor's appointment confirmed for the forthcoming year. It was agreed by the directors that the company should have the right to borrow without limit and that the entry of this item in the

minutes be accepted as the company's authority to do so. The meeting then adjourned."

The company entered into negotiations with the Provincial Bank of Ireland for an overdraft and the bank required the company to give a debenture charged on all its assets. The debenture was sealed on 8 February 1954 and was stated to be issued under clause 3(m) of the company's memorandum of association, under Article 13 of the company's Articles of Association and in pursuance of a resolution of the directors passed on 8 February 1954. By it the company charged all its premises and any property to which it might become entitled and its undertaking and all its other property and assets with repayment of the amounts advanced on the debenture. The conditions attached to the debenture provided that it was to rank as a first charge on the property and was, as regards the company's freehold and leasehold property, to be a fixed or specific charge and as regards all other property, present and future, a floating security. The resolution referred to as having been passed on 8 February 1954 does not appear in the company's minute book but a copy of it certified by a director and the secretary was sent to the bank. It read:

> "(1) That the company do create a debenture for all such sums as are now or shall from time to time hereafter become owing to the Provincial Bank of Ireland Ltd or shall for the time being remain unpaid by the company on the balance of its current account with the said bank whether in respect of monies advanced or paid to or for the use of the company or charges incurred on its account or in respect of negotiable instruments drawn accepted or endorsed by or on behalf of the company and discounted or paid or held by the said bank either at the company's request or in the course of business or otherwise or in respect of monies which the company shall become liable to pay to the said bank in any manner whatsoever and whether any such money shall be paid to or incurred on behalf of the company either alone or jointly with any other person or corporation together with interest until the day of payment at the rate or rates fixed by the said bank from time to time and calculated according to the custom of bankers and also the usual commission and other lawful bank charges and for all such sums for the payment of which the company is or may become liable to the said bank as surety or guarantor secured on all the undertaking and all the property and assets of the company legal and equitable present and future including its uncalled capital for the time being and goodwill.
>
> (2) That such debenture be in the form prepared by the solicitor for the said bank and approved of by the company's solicitor and now produced to the meeting and
>
> (3) that the said debenture be sealed with the common seal of the company."

The amount due by the company to the bank increased. On 12 January 1956, it was £14,571, on the same date in 1966 it was £13,081 and on the same date in 1971 it was £60,260. On 15 September 1971 the bank appointed Mr Fitzgerald, the applicant, to be receiver over all the assets of the company and he has applied to the court for a determination of the questions whether the debenture was valid, whether it secures £11,500 only or the total sum now due under it which is £98,000. One of the creditors has been appointed to represent the interests of the ordinary creditors.

The only resolution forwarded to the bank was that of 8 February 1954 but as this was a resolution of the directors, it was not an authority to them, under article 13, to borrow an amount exceeding the issued share capital of the company.

Counsel for the creditors has contended that the resolution passed on 10 March 1954 was not the consent of the company in general meeting to the directors borrowing more than the issued share capital. The meeting is stated to have been the first ordinary general meeting and was, therefore, not a directors' meeting. The minute reads that it was agreed by the directors that the company should have the right to borrow without limit but I think it obvious that the words "directors" and "company" have been placed in the wrong position in the sentence. If the minute had read: "It was agreed by the company that the directors should have the right to borrow without limit," it would have been a consent of the company to such borrowing within article 13 and as the meeting is stated to have been an ordinary general meeting, I think it is to be read as being a consent by the company to the directors borrowing without limit. The transposition of the words "directors" and "company" in the sentence has this effect and I have no doubt that this is what all those at the meeting intended to do. The company, in my opinion, gave its consent to the directors borrowing more than the issued share capital and the amount secured by the debenture is therefore not limited to £11,500 but is the whole amount now due.

The minutes show that the balance sheets and accounts for a number of years since 1954 were accepted and signed at annual general meetings of the company. These were prepared by auditors and though the accounts have not been put in evidence it is a reasonable assumption that the accounts showed the amounts which had been borrowed by the company. The approval of the company in general meeting of the accounts would, in my view, have been a ratification to the action of the directors in borrowing more than the issued share capital of the company even if the resolution of 10 March 1954 did not give them this authority. At the annual general meeting which was held on 4 December 1969, the chairman informed the meeting that the applicant, who was then acting as auditor for the company, had provided for the members a statement of accounts for the half-year ended 30 July 1969, and that these had been considered in detail. The borrowing by the directors of an amount exceeding the share capital was *intra vires* the company but *ultra vires* the directors if the resolution of 10 March 1954 did not give them this authority and the approval of these accounts by the company in general meeting would have been a ratification by the member of the unauthorised action of the directors and so, would have bound the company. It is established law that the members of a company may ratify acts which are outside the powers of the directors but are *intra vires* the company.

This is established by the advice of the Privy Council in *Irvine v. The Union Bank of Australia* (1877) 2 App Cas 366 and by the decision of the Court of Appeal in *Grant v. United Kingdom Switchback Railways Company* (1889) 40 Ch D 135. In the second of these cases Lindley LJ, a great authority on company law, said:

> "The appellant contends that the company could not ratify this contract except by special resolution. In my opinion that contention is unfounded. There is a broad distinction between altering the articles and merely saying this act was not authorised by the articles but we will ratify it. The shareholders can ratify any contract which comes within the powers of the company, and this contract clearly does, for the articles expressly authorise selling any part of the undertaking of the company."

In that case the articles of the company authorised the sale of part of its undertaking to any other company but contained a provision prohibiting any director from voting in respect of any contract in which he was interested. The directors entered on behalf of the company into a contract for a sale of part of its undertaking to another company of which all the directors of the first company except one were directors. The contract for sale was therefore *ultra vires* the directors because only one of them was qualified to vote but the approval of it by the company in general meeting made it binding on the company. Similarly, in this case, the approval of the accounts showing the amount borrowed was a ratification by the company of the action of the directors in borrowing an amount in excess of the issued share capital.

It was also argued for the bank that they were entitled to assume that a resolution under regulation 13 authorising the directors to borrow an amount in excess of the issued share capital had been passed because such a resolution would not have to be registered with the registrar of companies. This contention involves difficult questions as to the scope of the rule in the *Royal British Bank v. Turquand* (1856) 5 E and B 243: on appeal (1856) 6 E and B 327 but as no authorities were cited on this controversial branch of the law, I do not express any opinion on it. I reserve for future consideration the question whether when the Articles of Association limit the borrowing powers of the directors and prescribe that the directors may not borrow more than the authorised or issued share capital without the consent of the company in general meeting and an application is made to a lender for a loan which will exceed that limit, he may assume that the necessary resolution has been passed by the company giving the directors these powers. When articles contain such a provision, it would I think, be prudent for lenders to get proof that such a resolution has been passed by the company at a general meeting.

I shall accordingly rule that the debenture of 8 February 1954, given by the company in favour of the Provincial Bank of Ireland Ltd was and is a valid and effective debenture and that it created a valid charge against the assets of the company in respect of monies due by the company to the Provincial Bank of Ireland Ltd (now Allied Irish Banks Ltd) in excess of £11,500.

The creditors who appeared, Asbestos Cement Pipes Ltd, will be given their costs of these proceedings against the receiver, who will have them as part of his costs for acting as receiver. He will be declared entitled to his costs of these proceedings. The bank will be given their costs with their demand.

Patricia McLaughlin
Barrister

Azzouz Chaieb v. William Carter, Patrick Connery and Carter Connery & Co. Ltd: High Court 1982 No. 369P (McWilliam J) 11 January 1985

Separate legal entity – Contract – Agreement between plaintiff and individual defendants that the plaintiff would secure a contract for the sale of cattle to an Egyptian company – Plaintiff to be paid commission – Agreement concluded but subject to the condition that the Egyptian authorities approved the contract – Contract not approved – Defendants subsequently entered into fresh negotiations without the plaintiff – Company formed – Agreement concluded between new company and Egyptian company – Terms almost identical to prior agreement – Whether plaintiff was entitled to commission – Whether plaintiff was incidental in procuring second contract – Whether plaintiff had agreed to waive commission – "Without prejudice" – Separate legal personality – Whether defendants could avoid the consequences of the transactions which they were conducting by forming a company and continuing in the name of the company after it had been formed

Facts: The plaintiff agreed with the first and second defendants ("the exporters) to act as their representative in Egypt in order to secure a contract for the sale of cattle to an Egyptian company, for which it was agreed that the plaintiff would be paid commission. Different rates of commission were agreed in respect of beef cattle and feeding cattle. As a result of the efforts of the plaintiff, an agreement was concluded in June 1981 between the exporters and the Egyptian company for the sale of 30,000 heads of cattle. However, this agreement was stated to be conditional upon the approval of the Egyptian authorities which, in the event, was not forthcoming. Further negotiations then took place between the exporters and the Egyptian company, without the assistance of the plaintiff. As a result of these negotiations a contract was concluded in September 1981 between the Egyptian company and a company known as Carter, Connery &

Co. Ltd which had been incorporated on 31 August 1981 and which was controlled by the exporters. The terms of this agreement were almost identical to the June contract. When the plaintiff became aware of this, he arranged a meeting with the defendants in or around 22 September 1981. The exporters, although denying that they had any liability to the plaintiff, offered to pay him a substantially smaller rate on the feeding cattle sold as a result of the September contract. The plaintiff wrote to the exporters indicating that he would accept that figure but he stated that it was without prejudice to his rights under the June contract. The plaintiff claimed commission on the sale of 30,000 cattle and also claimed on the basis of fraud by the exporters in forming the defendant company for the purpose of having a new party to the contract and thereby depriving the plaintiff of his commission. At the hearing the plaintiff confined his claim to a claim for commission due on cattle supplied under the September contract at the rate agreed on his initial appointment in April 1981. The defendants submitted that the June contract became void and of no effect because the Egyptian authorities refused to approve it and they alleged that the September contract was a new contract with a different party. They also claimed that the plaintiff had agreed to accept the lower rate in full discharge of his commission.

Held by McWilliam J:

(1) The plaintiff was instrumental in securing the September contract. It was merely a variation of the June contract, there were no further tenders for it and it was based upon the tenders which had been submitted for the June contract.

(2) Although a company is a separate entity from its members, a group of people cannot form a company of which they are members to avoid the consequences of transactions which they were conducting when the company was formed and which they continued in the name of the company after it had been formed.

(3) The plaintiff's right to commission on the sale of beef cattle was not altered by his letter to the exporters of the 26 September 1981. The document referred only to the commission on feeding cattle and the defendants made no comment as to the 'without prejudice' provision.

(4) The plaintiff was entitled to commission on the sale of beef cattle at the rate originally agreed upon.

No cases referred to in judgment

Counsel's and solicitors' names not available

McWILLIAM J **11 January 1985**

The plaintiff's claim as pleaded is for commission alleged to be due to him by the defendants for negotiating a contract for the sale of 30,000 cattle by the defendants, William Carter and Patrick Connery (hereafter together called "the exporters"), to the Egyptian company for milk and meat production (hereinafter called "the Egyptian company").

The claim is based on an agreement dated 1 April 1981, signed by the exporters and containing the following provisions:— M/S W. Carter and P. Connery appoint Mr Azzouz Chaieb as their exclusive representative and porte-parole (spokesman) in Egypt for the supply of cattle to the entire Egyptian market. M/S Carter & Connery give full authority to Mr Azzouz Chaieb to negotiate and sign contracts on their behalf. Regarding the supply of 30,000 (thirty thousand) heads of cattle to the Egyptian company for meat and milk production/Cairo Mr Azzouz Chaieb's commission in respect of the above mentioned contract is fixed at USD110.00 (one hundred and ten US dollars) per metric ton of feeding cattle and USD60.00 (sixty US dollars) per metric ton of beef cattle.

This document contains an indorsement that it was sworn before T. Jackson, Commissioner for Oaths, at 30 Burlington Road, Dublin, on 29 June 1981. There is no indication of the nature of the oath which was administered and Mr Jackson was not called by either side to give evidence. The plaintiff and both the exporters gave evidence but their respective recollections of the date and circumstances of the execution of this document were not helpful. At first the plaintiff thought the document had been written out by him and signed on 1 April 1981, but this is not consistent with the other documentary evidence and I am satisfied that it was not prepared until later. The defendant, Patrick Connery, acknowledged his signature to the document of 1 April 1981, and agreed that it was sworn on 29 June but stated that he did not recollect signing it. The evidence of the defendant, William Carter, was somewhat similar but, on re-examination, stated that he signed before Mr Jackson in his presence. Although the actual date of the execution of the agreement by the exporters is not material to the issues in the case, the evidence of the three parties with regard to the matter suggests that their recollection of other facts may not be accurate.

Although the plaintiff is a citizen of Tunisia, he has had close associations with Ireland for a considerable time and is married to an Irish woman. At some stage he was involved in the export of furniture and prams from Ireland and, at another, he was involved with the exporters in a project for the manufacture of prayer mats in Mountrath. In 1973 he became involved with a brother, Tahar Chaieb, in the export of cattle to Tunis. Tahar Chaieb was also associated with the exporters in the cattle trade and, with them and another brother, formed a company, C.C.C. Meat and Livestock Exporters Ltd (hereinafter called "C.C.C.") in October 1973. The "C.C.C." apparently represents Carter, Connery and Chaieb and the company was owned by the exporters and the Chaiebs in equal shares with Tahar Chaieb one of the directors.

The exporters operated by themselves or with others under several different titles indicated by the documents before the court, that is to say:— Carter Connery, Timogue House, Stradbally; Carter & Connery (cattle exporters) of the same address; Carter Connery and Associates; Carter Connery & Associates Ltd; C.C.C. Meat Products and Livestock Exporters Ltd; and, finally and most recently, Carter Connery & Co. Ltd.

Although the agreement dated 1 April 1981, necessarily implied that the plaintiff would negotiate with the Egyptians on behalf of the exporters, his first negotiations were made in his own name as "Livestock Exporter", and the first tender to the Egyptian company, dated 28 April 1981, was made similarly. As the defendant, William Carter, stated in evidence that he got billheads printed in this form for the plaintiff to use, I do not accept the suggestion made on behalf of the defendants that the plaintiff was at this time acting on his own behalf.

The plaintiff put in a second tender dated 9 May 1981, this one expressed to be made on behalf of C.C.C. This was followed by a third tender dated 13 May 1981, at a lower price, expressed to be made by the plaintiff on behalf of the exporters.

It appears that, under Egyptian law, all such transactions must be conducted through an Egyptian national and the plaintiff was put in touch with a firm, Ali Labib & Co., known as Devco, and dealt with their representative, Gamal Kassim, who signed the tenders and other documents and presented them on behalf of Devco as exclusive agents for the supplier. Unfortunately the transactions between the plaintiff and the exporters became further complicated at a later stage by the conduct of this representative who seems to have acted somewhat irregularly on his behalf with regard to the commission which was payable to his employers.

As a result of the final tender, the Egyptian company entered into a contract with the exporters dated 15 June 1981, for the supply to it of 30,000 head of cattle of which 15,000, half bullocks and half heifers, were for slaughter and 15,000 in the same proportions of bullocks and heifers were for feeding, i.e., store cattle. This contract was made subject to certain conditions of which the first was that it should have the approval of the Egyptian authorities.

C.C.C. had at this time exported cattle for about two and a half years, but there seems to have been some falling out between Tahar Shaieb and the other directors or some of them and he brought proceedings of some sort against them. It is probable that the plaintiff and the exporters wished to keep Tahar Shaieb out of the Egyptian dealings, and that he was not informed of the final lower tender made within four days of the tender by C.C.C. and this may be the explanation of the two tenders within such a short period although there was no direct evidence to this effect. However this maybe, the two brothers were at loggerheads also and Tahar Chaieb felt that the contract should have been with C.C.C. and seems to have got himself into a position of being able to thwart the contract in some respect, and there is an illuminating telex of 6 June 1981, from the plaintiff to him in which the plaintiff suggested sharing his commission with his brother and referred to "no tricks".

One of the terms of the contract of 15 June 1981, was that the supplier should deposit a letter of guarantee amounting to 5 per cent of the total value of the contract and another was that the Egyptian company should open a letter of credit with the bank not later than 15 July 1981. Both parties delayed in complying with these terms, the exporters because they were having difficulty about arranging shipping and the Egyptian company probably as matter of policy.

At some stage before these important matters had been dealt with the Egyptian authorities indicated that they could not approve the contract because difficulties had arisen as a result of the import of diseased female cattle into Egypt. This led to further negotiations by the exporters with the Egyptian company but without the assistance or knowledge of a plaintiff. At a meeting between two representatives of the Egyptian company and the defendant, William Carter, and Gamal Kassim on 6 September 1981, terms were agreed for the supply of 22,500 male cattle by Carter Connery & Co. Ltd, which had been incorporated on 31 August 1981, and appears to have included amongst its members the persons who comprised the body previously known as Carter Connery & Associates.

This agreement was reached without any further tenders having been put in although the evidence has been to the effect that the Egyptian company could not enter into such a contract without at least two tenders having been received. A few days later a formal contract, dated 9 September 1981 was executed in terms almost identical with those contained in the June contract and containing an identical recital that "A committee from the company got offers from several exporting firms in Ireland, and reported the result to the Minister of Supply and Interior Trading".

The plaintiff states that he heard from his brother about the September contract, he thinks about 14 September and telephoned William Carter some days later and arranged to meet on 22 September with the exporters. It is not clear whether the plaintiff and the exporters met in Dublin or elsewhere but they appear to have met on or about 22 September, when the exporters offered to pay USD 20 per metric ton on the feeding cattle sold under the September contract but denied that they had any liability to the plaintiff for any commission. It is agreed that the plaintiff said he would have to think about it. Having thought about it, the plaintiff wrote to the exporters by letter dated 26 September 1981, stating as follows:

> "I Azzouz Chaieb, accept from M/S Carter, Connery and Company Ltd their undertaking to pay me the sum of U.S.D. 20 (twenty) per metric ton of feeding cattle on commission payable to me and without prejudice to the Egyptian contract awarded to M/S W. Carter and P. Connery on June 15 1981."

By his statement of claim, the plaintiff claimed commission on the sale of 30,000 cattle amounting to 1,027,500 United States dollars. He also claimed on the basis of fraud by the exporters by forming the defendant company for the purpose of having a new party to the contract and thereby depriving him of his commission.

By their defence, the defendants allege that the June contract became void and of no effect because the Egyptian authorities refused to approve it and, therefore, no commission became payable under this contract. They allege that the September contract was a new contract with a different party quite independent of the June contract and that, in any event, the plaintiff agreed to accept commission at the rate of 20 dollars per metric ton in respect of the feeding cattle in full discharge of all commission and that this was paid in full. The defendants, the exporters, also counterclaimed for the sum of £2,249,000 damages for loss sustained by them by reason of the failure of the June contract but made no allegation in the pleadings of fault on the part of the plaintiff in this respect.

At the hearing allegations were made by the parties that attempts were made by the opposing parties improperly to over-reach their opponents by obstructing the June contract.

At the hearing also the plaintiff's claim was reduced to a claim for commission due on the cattle supplied under the September contract at the rate agreed by the document of 1 April 1981, and the exporters did not pursue their counterclaim.

It is not necessary for me to discuss the motives or conduct of the various people involved in the transactions as I am satisfied that the plaintiff was instrumental in procuring the September contract for the defendants and, although a company is a separate entity from its members, I do not accept that a group of people, here the exporters and their associates, can, by forming a company of which they are all members, avoid the consequences of transactions which they were conducting when the company was formed and continued in the name of the company after it had been formed.

I am satisfied that the September contract was merely a variation of the June contract. There were no further tenders required for it and it was based on the tenders which had been submitted for the June contract. This being so, the plaintiff was equally instrumental in the procuring of this contract as in the procuring of the June contract.

In my opinion, the real issue in the case is as to the effect of the document of 26 September 1981. It is an unsatisfactory document but I do not see how the plaintiff can dispute his agreement to accept 20 dollars per metric ton for feeding cattle. The evidence with regard to the meeting which led to the execution of the document is inconclusive. The plaintiff says he was being pressed for money and felt he had to agree to it. The exporters stated that he was quite happy to sign it, that he had no right to any commission and that he was given this payment gratuitously because of the good relationship between them. This conclusion does not tally with the evidence of the defendant, Patrick Connery, that the plaintiff said he would have to think it over. In addition I cannot believe that there was, at this time, still a good relationship between the parties. Having thought it over and, possibly, seen his solicitor, the plaintiff prepared the document which reserved his rights under the June contract. In my opinion the parties were, at that stage, dealing at arms length and I must take the document as I find it, noting that the commission is stated only to refer to the feeding cattle and that the defendants did not make any comment with regard to the without prejudice provision, either by writing to say that the acceptance of the reduced commission on the feeding cattle covered all claims to commission or by refusing to pay this commission until the matter was cleared up.

I am of opinion that the plaintiff's rights to commission on the sale of beef cattle under the agreement of 1 April 1981, were not altered by this document. This means that the plaintiff is entitled to commission on the sale of the beef cattle at the rate of 60 American dollars per metric ton less whatever proportion of this commission was paid to G. Kassim or Devco.

The evidence before me is not sufficient to enable me to calculate the amount due to the plaintiff and the matter will either be re-entered before me or referred to the examiner if the parties cannot agree on the figures.

Patricia McLaughlin
Barrister

Edward Lynch v. Nicholas Bradley and Mary Josephine Kirby: High Court 1979 No. 2980p (Barrington J) 22 August 1984

Separate legal entity – Landlord and tenant – Real Property – House built for benefit of working classes – Grant by minister – Undertaking by Landlord Society against sale of premises without leave of minister – Society converted into limited company – Purported sale of premises – Whether company bound by covenant – Whether conversion into company mere device to evade undertaking – Industrial and Provident Societies Act 1893 (56 & 57 Vict c.39), section 54 – Housing (Financial and Miscellaneous Provisions) Act 1932 (No. 19) First Schedule – Housing (Amendment) Act 1948 (No. 1), sections 19, 20 – Housing (New Houses) Regulations 1948 (SI No. 90) Regs 22, 23, 27, 28, 30

Facts: The plaintiff occupied premises at 33 Somerton Park, Cork, which he claimed to hold as a weekly tenant and as successor in title to one Edward Lynch, to whom the premises were let on 17 July 1968 by Lee Utility Society Ltd ("the society"). The first defendant claimed to hold the landlord's interest in the tenancy, as successor in title to the society.

In October 1977, following the refusal of the plaintiff to pay an increased rent the first defendant purported to terminate the plaintiff's tenancy by notice to quit. He subsequently issued ejectment proceedings.

The premises were built and let by the society, pursuant to a scheme provided by section 20 of the Housing (Amendment) Act 1948 to benefit workers and agricultural labourers. The minister provided a grant of £250 towards the building costs, and in return the society gave an undertaking to the minister, pursuant to the Act, not to sell the house.

In 1975 the society, by special resolution, converted itself into a limited liability company called Lee Estates Company Ltd. In April 1976 the company passed a resolution that it be wound up voluntarily. The liquidator purported to transfer the landlord's interest in the premises to the first defendant. The approval of the minister was not sought.

Meanwhile the plaintiff had acquired the tenant's interest with the consent of Mr William Bradley, the principal person in the society, and an uncle of the first defendant. The plaintiff was told by Mr Bradley, and later by the first defendant, that if the house were ever for sale the plaintiff would have first option. Relying on this assurance the plaintiff carried out repairs, which the society could not afford to do, laid down concrete paths and painted the house. The plaintiff was, however, not given an opportunity to purchase the house.

The evidence was to the effect that the grant of £250 received from the minister was repaid in its entirety by the society prior to its conversion into a company.

The plaintiff issued proceedings claiming that the first defendant had no title to the premises.

Held by Barrington J in holding that the first defendant was still bound by the society's undertakings to the minister:

(1) There was no provision under the scheme set up by section 20 of the 1948 Act by which the sale of such houses could be approved and the undertaking required of the society appeared to be absolute.

(2) There was no evidence that the minister waived the undertaking of the society. Nor did it appear that the minister in any case had power to accept the return of the grant or to waive the undertaking.

(3) The conversion of the society into a limited liability company and the subsequent transfer of the property to the builder's nephew appeared to be a device to evade the society's undertaking to the minister.

(4) Under section 54(3) of the Industrial and Provident Society Act 1893 the new company was the same legal entity as the old society and was fixed with all the liabilities of the old society. *Moreland v. Woodward* [1940] 1 Ch 777 explained.

(5) The liquidator, once appointed, was obliged to realise the assets of the society. However, he did not have the power to convey the property, freed from the undertaking to the first defendant, who was not a *bona fide* purchaser for value without notice of the undertaking.

(6) Consequently the first defendant did not hold the property on terms any more favourable that those on which it was held by the society.

Cases referred to in judgment

McQuaid v. Lynam [1965] IR 564
Moreland v. Woodward [1940] 1 Ch 777; [1940] 3 All ER 665

Counsel's and solicitors' names not available

BARRINGTON J **22 August 1984**

The plaintiff is a mechanical fitter and is the occupier of premises known as 33 Somerton Park, Ballinlough in the City of Cork. The plaintiff claims to hold these premises as a weekly tenant and as successor in title to one Edward Lynch to whom the premises were let by memorandum of agreement dated 17 July 1968 and made between Lee Utility Society Ltd of the one part and the said Edward Lynch of the other part.

The first named defendant Nicholas Bradley claims to be entitled to the interest of the landlord in the said tenancy agreement as successor in title to the said Lee Utility Society Ltd. In pursuance of such claim the first named defendant by notice dated 21 October 1977, purported to raise the plaintiff's rent, and, when the plaintiff refused to pay the increased rent, by notice to quit dated 1 March 1978, purported to terminate the plaintiff's tenancy.

The first named defendant subsequently instituted ejectment proceedings in the Cork Circuit Court against the plaintiff in these proceedings and succeeded in recovering a decree for possession against him (see Southern Circuit, County of Cork, Record No. P41/1978 Nicholas Bradley, plaintiff and Edward Lynch, defendant). The plaintiff in these proceedings appealed to the High Court against the order for possession, and the appeal in the ejectment proceedings has been adjourned, on terms, pending determination of the matters at issue in these proceedings.

Background and pleadings

The plaintiff in these proceedings claims that the first named defendant in these proceedings has no title to the premises.

The premises at number 33, Somerton Park were constructed by the said Lee Utility Society Ltd, and let by that Society pursuant to and under the provisions of a scheme provided for by section 20 of the Housing (Amendment) Act 1948 and the regulations made thereunder including, in particular, Statutory Instrument No. 90 of 1948. The said society received a grant of £250 from the Minister for Local Government towards the cost of building the said house. In return for the said grant the said Society gave to the minister an undertaking pursuant to the Act and Regulations not to sell the said house. It is this undertaking which has given rise to the present proceedings.

The principal person in the Lee Utility Society Ltd was a builder called William Bradley, an uncle of the first named defendant. In or about the year 1975 the said Lee Utility Society Ltd, by special resolution, duly passed in accordance with the provisions of section 54 of the Industrial and Provident Societies' Act 1893, converted itself into a limited liability company called "Lee Estates Company Ltd".

On 2 April 1976 the members of Lee Estates Company Ltd, at an extraordinary general meeting, passed a special resolution that Lee Estates Company Ltd be wound up voluntarily and that Mr William Kirby F.C.A. be appointed liquidator. The second-named defendant is the widow and legal personal representative of the late Mr Kirby and no order is sought against her in these proceedings.

By transfer registered on 6 September 1976, the said William Kirby, in his capacity as liquidator of Lee Estates Company Ltd, purported to transfer the landlord's interest in number 33 Somerton Park to the first named defendant Nicholas Bradley. It does not appear that the approval of the minister was given or sought in respect of this transfer.

Meanwhile, the plaintiff Mr Lynch had, with the consent of Mr William Bradley, acquired the tenant's interest in the house. After he had acquired the tenant's interest the plaintiff approached Mr William Bradley and asked him if he could buy out the landlord's interest in the house. Mr William Bradley said he could not sell the house but that if the house was ever on the market he (the plaintiff) would be offered it first. At a later stage the plaintiff spoke to the first named defendant, Mr Nicholas Bradley, who was then secretary of the Utility Society, to get some landlord's repairs done. Mr Nicholas Bradley got some repairs done but said the society could not afford to do the remainder. At this stage he told the plaintiff that the plaintiff would be offered the house shortly. Relying on these assurances the plaintiff says that he himself carried out the repairs, laid down certain concrete paths, painted the house and generally kept it in good order. The plaintiff complains that, in spite of these assurances, he was never given an opportunity to buy the house.

The plaintiff's evidence on these points was not challenged. The plaintiff served on the first named defendant a notice to admit that Lee Utility Society Ltd had received a grant of £250 in respect of number 33 Somerton Park from the minister. The defendant, in his reply dated 15 June 1984, admitted that he had received such a grant and added the following words:

> "And it is further noted that the plaintiff admits that the grant of £250 was repaid in its entirely to Lee Utility Society prior to its conversion to the Lee Estates Company Ltd."

This is intended to record an alleged admission by the plaintiff's solicitor that the grant of £250 had been repaid by the Lee Utility Society to the minister. Mr Blayney, who appeared for the plaintiff in the hearing before me, agreed that his solicitor had made such an admission.

The case was opened to me on the basis that this grant of £250 had been paid by the minister to the society and repaid by the society to the minister. In the course of the hearing Mr O'Driscoll, who appeared for the first named defendant, expressed doubts as to whether the admission that the society had received a grant of £250 had been correctly made. It appeared that the society had received a loan from the Housing Authority as well as a grant from the minister. The loan had been paid off but a possibility existed of confusion between the loan and the grant. I allowed Mr O'Driscoll an opportunity to check on the true position. On this investigation it transpired that the society had, indeed, received a grant of £250. Mr Blayney then expressed doubts as to whether the admission made by his solicitor that the society had repaid a grant of £250 had been correctly made. Again I considered it fair to give Mr Blayney an opportunity to check on the position, notwithstanding the admission made by his solicitor. Mr Blayney's investigations, however, were inconclusive as apparently the Department of the Environment had no records from which it could establish whether the grant had been repaid or not.

Under these circumstances it appeared to me that the only safe course open to me was to consider the case on the basis of the formal admissions made by the parties. I therefore approach my decision on the basis that the minister did make a grant of £250 towards the cost of building the house and that this grant was repaid in its entirety by the Utility Society prior to its conversion into a limited liability company.

The law

The grant in the present case was made under section 20 of the Housing (Amendment) Act 1948, which provided that the Minister for Local Government could, in certain circumstances, make a grant to any public utility society erecting one or more than one house for occupation by a person of the working classes or an agricultural labourer.

Certain statutory conditions had to be fulfilled before a grant could be made. Erection of the house or houses had to be commenced on or after 1 November 1947, and to be completed on or before 1 April 1950. The house had to comply with rules set out in the first schedule of the Housing (Financial and Miscellaneous Provisions) Act 1932 (No. 19 of 1932). Finally, section 20 subsection (1), paragraph (c) of the 1948 Act provides as follows:

> "Such public utility society undertakes with the Minister that such a society will not sell such house or houses and will let such house or houses only at such rent and subject to such conditions as may be approved by the Minister".

Mr Blayney points out that the undertaking given by the Public Utility Society appears to be indefinite in point of time in that there is no statutory provision for the repayment of the grant or for the minister releasing the society from its undertaking. Mr Blayney further submits that the undertaking is given, not for the benefit of the minister only, but for the benefit of those persons, being members of working classes or agricultural labourers, housing of whom the Act seeks to assist.

Mr Blayney contrasts the wording of section 20 subsection (1) paragraph (c) with the wording of section 19 subsection (2) paragraph (c). Section 19 provides for grants being made by Housing Authorities. Under section 19 subsection (2) paragraph (c) the builder who accepts a grant must also give an undertaking but the wording of the relevant paragraph is significantly different. It reads as follows:

> "The person erecting the house undertakes with the housing authority that, *subject to such conditions as may be prescribed by regulations made under this section*, he will not sell the house and that he will let the house subject to such conditions as may be so prescribed". [emphasis added]

Regulations under sections 19 and 20 of the Housing (Amendment) Act 1948 are contained in Statutory Instrument No. 90 of 1948. Part IV of the Regulations applies to new houses in respect of which grants were given by a Housing Authority under section 19 of the 1948 Act.

Regulation 22, paragraph 8, provides as follows:

> "The title deed of a house to which this part of these Regulations applies shall have endorsed thereon a note to the effect that an undertaking has been given in pursuance of section 19 of the Act of 1948, that, subject to the provisions of these Regulations, the house will not be sold and that it will be let subject to the provisions of these Regulations."

Regulation 23 deals with the circumstances in which a house may be sold and is as follows:

> "A house to which this part of these Regulations applies may, with the consent of the housing authority, be sold if the following conditions are fulfilled;
> (a) the consent of the housing authority shall not be given before the first instalment of the grant has been paid by the housing authority;
> (b) the house shall not be sold while it is untenanted and shall be sold subject to the tenancy existing at the time of sale;
> (c) the house shall not be sold to the tenant thereof;
> (d) the vendor shall assign to the purchaser his interest in any instalments of the grant that have not been paid at the time of sale;
> (e) the purchaser shall give to the housing authority an undertaking that subject to the provisions of these Regulations, he will not sell the house and that he will let the house subject to the provisions of these Regulations and particulars of such undertaking shall be endorsed on the title deed of the house".

Part V of the Regulations deals with applications for grants under section 20 of the 1948 Act. Regulation 27 contemplates that a public utility society seeking a grant must submit a scheme to the minister. This scheme must be accompanied by detailed plans, specifications and detailed estimates of the cost of the work; a statement of the total all-in cost of the scheme; a statement showing the rent proposed to be charged for the house and the estimated annual income and expenditure under the scheme; and such evidence as the minister may require to satisfy himself that the public utility society is a utility society within the meaning of the Acts. Most important, however, for the purposes of the present case is that regulation 27(2)(d) contemplates that the scheme submitted to the minister shall be accompanied by:

> "An undertaking in writing signed by a responsible officer of the society that the house when completed will not be sold and will be let only on a

> monthly or lesser tenancy to a person of the working classes or an agricultural labourer as defined in the Labourers Acts 1883 to 1948, at a rent not exceeding such rent as may be approved by the Minister".

Under regulation 28 if the minister is satisfied that the public utility society is a public utility society within the meaning of the Acts, and that the scheme and the house to be erected thereunder comply with the requirements of the Acts and of the regulations, and as to the rent proposed to be charged for the house, he may approve of the scheme and of the rent.

Regulation 28, paragraph 2, provides as follows:

> "At any time before a house erected under the scheme is let the Minister may, on the application of the public utility society erecting the house, approve of an alteration of the rent to be charged under the scheme for that house".

Regulation 30 contemplates that when a scheme has been approved by the minister the public utility society is to keep separate accounts relating to the scheme and shall furnish accounts to the minister. It also provides that the public utility society shall, if required by the minister, permit any auditor nominated by him to have access to any books, deeds and accounts relating to the scheme.

It seems clear that the purpose of section 20 is to enable the minister to help, financially, in the provision of houses at a low rent for persons of the working classes and agricultural labourers. Section 20 appears to contemplate that such houses shall be let at a rent to be approved by the minister but, in marked contrast to section 19 of the Act, there is no provision whereby the sale of any such house can be approved and the undertaking required of the public utility society not to sell any such house appears to be absolute.

Needless to say the difficulties of this situation are made more acute by the great rise in the value of property which has taken place over the past 35 years and the fall in the value of money. Mr O'Driscoll, on behalf of the first named defendant, submits that it is absurd that a public utility society should be debarred forever from selling one of its houses even though the house was vacant or the society itself had become insolvent and was in the course of being wound up.

Mr Blayney, on the other hand, submits that it is wrong that a public utility society should be allowed, by turning itself into a limited liability company, to avoid its obligations to the minister and to treat as a normal commercial investment houses built with state aid to provide rented accommodation for members of the working classes.

The plaintiff in the present case is a mechanical fitter and would appear to fall within the category of persons for whom this house was provided. The defendant did not give evidence at the hearing before me and, apart from the admission by the plaintiff's solicitor that the grant of £250 was repaid to the minister, there is no evidence that the minister waived the undertaking of the society nor is it clear that the minister had power to accept the return of the grant or to waive the undertaking. In fact the defendants have formally admitted that the minister did not approve of the transfer of the landlord's interest in the house to the first named defendant. Indeed, the conversion of the society into a limited liability company and the subsequent transfer of the property to the builder's nephew have all the marks of a device designed to evade the society's undertaking to the minister.

Mr O'Driscoll submits that the society, once converted into a limited liability company, became a different legal entity and was no longer bound by the undertaking given to the minister. In support of this proposition he relies upon certain *dicta* of Farwell J, in *Moreland v. Woodward* [1940] 1 Ch 777. I cannot accept this proposition nor do I believe that the case cited supports it. In *Moreland v. Woodward* a society registered under the Industrial and Provident Societies Act 1893 had entered into trust deeds whereby certain sums were transferred to trustees for the establishment of a pension fund for the benefit of employees of the society, past and present. Subsequently, the society was converted into a limited company in pursuance of section 54 of the 1893 Act. Farwell J held that the society and the company were in substance the same thing and the trustees held the trust funds in their hands on exactly the same trusts as they had held them before the conversion.

This conclusion appears to be supported by the wording of section 54 itself. Subsection (1) provides that a registered society may, by special resolution, determine to convert itself into a company under the Companies Act. Subsection (2) provides that if the special resolution for converting the registered society contains the particulars required by the Companies Acts to be contained in the memorandum of association of a company and a copy thereof has been registered at the central office, a copy of such resolution under the seal or stamp of the central office shall have the same effect as a memorandum of association duly signed and attested under the Companies Acts. Subsection (3) however, goes on to provide as follows:

> "If a registered society is registered as, or amalgamates with, or transfers all its engagements to, a company, the registry of such society under this Act shall thereupon become void, and the same shall be cancelled by the chief registrar or by the assistant registrar for Scotland or Ireland under his direction; but the registration of a society as a company shall not affect any right or claim for the time being subsisting against such society, or any penalty for the time being incurred by such society; and, for the purpose of enforcing any such right, claim, or penalty, the society may be sued and proceeded against in the same manner as if it had not become registered as a company; and every such right or claim or the liability to such penalty, shall have priority, as against the property of such company, over all other rights or claims against or liabilities of such company".

It therefore appears to me that the new company may wear different corporate clothing and may have a different corporate structure but that it is the same legal entity as the old society and is fixed with all the liabilities of the old society.

The point which has caused me most difficulty in the present case is the point of whether the undertaking given by the society to the minister under section 20 of the 1948 Act was a matter of covenant only and affected only the rights of the society and the minister or whether it was a matter of title on which it is competent for the plaintiff to rely. Counsel have failed to find any case on section 20 of the 1948 Act relevant to this issue. However, in the case of *McQuaid v. Lynam* [1965] IR 564 Kenny J had to discuss the effect of an undertaking given to a Housing Authority under section 19 of the 1948 Act. In that case a builder had, in breach of his undertaking to the Housing Authority, agreed to sell a house to the plaintiff. The defendant later concluded that they could not sell the house because of their undertaking to the Housing Authority. The plaintiff then sued the defendants for damages in lieu of specific performance of the contract. The principal defence raised by the defendants was that there was not a sufficient note or memorandum of the alleged agreement for the purposes of the Statute of Frauds. But the defendants also raised the defence that the alleged agreement was illegal.

Kenny J held that the agreement was not illegal but clearly took the view that the defendants, being in breach of their undertaking to the Housing Authority under section 19, could not give a good title to the house.

The following passage appears at page 568 of the report:

> "At the time when the agreement between the plaintiff and the defendant was made, No. 1 Kinvara Road was untenanted and the defendants could not, therefore, give the purchaser a good title to the house. This conclusion is supported by sub-article 8 of Article 22 of the regulations which provided that the title deed of a house to which the regulations applied should, when the title was not registered under the Registration of Title Acts, 1891 and 1942, have endorsed thereon a note to the effect that an undertaking had been given under section 19 of the Act of 1948 by the person erecting the house that, subject to the provisions of the regulations he would not sell the house within a period of 15 years from the date of the undertaking. *Although the defendants could not give a good title to the house*, the contract which they made with the plaintiff was not, in my opinion, illegal." [emphasis added]

If a person who had given the limited undertaking required under section 19 of the Act could not, in breach of his undertaking, give a good title to the property it appears to me that a person who had given the much more stringent undertaking required under section 20 of the Act could not give a good title either. The first named defendant in the present case was, at one time, an officer of the Public Utility Society. Even assuming that what took place in the present case was not a device to evade the undertaking, no attempt has been made to show that the first named defendant was a *bona fide* purchaser for value without notice of the undertaking. It would be surprising, therefore, if he could hold the lands on terms more favourable than those on which the Public Utility Society held them.

I accept that the liquidator of the company, once appointed, had no choice but to realise the assets of the company, but it does not follow that he had power to convey the property, freed from the undertaking, to a person not shown to be a *bona fide* purchaser for value without notice of the undertaking.

Under these circumstances it appears to me that the first named defendant cannot hold the property on terms any more favourable than those on which it was held by the Public Utility Society.

Alistair Rutherdale
Barrister

H. Albert De Bary and Co. NV v. T.F. O'Mullane and Others: High Court 1989 No. 15668p (Barron J) 2 June 1992

Company law – Group of companies – Loan facility granted by plaintiff bank to two companies in the group – Security for loan – Money used to finance operations of group – Breach of terms of loan – Whether bank could call in loan – Whether time should have been given to defendants to arrange their affairs – Veil of incorporation – Whether sums could be recovered against all the companies in the group – Whether justice required that companies be treated as one entity – Fraud – Deceit

Facts: The first named defendant was the principal shareholder in the various incorporated defendants. These defendants consisted of a holding company and various subsidiaries which were set up to deal with different aspects of the group's business in the butter trade. The companies' accounts were mainly in Irish currency, but one subsidiary had its account in sterling and another in Dutch Guilders ("the foreign currency companies"). Some of the business of the group involved storage of butter pursuant to a scheme known as "Aid to Private Storage" under which butter would be stored in the summer months and released in the winter months when butter was not so plentiful. The bank financed the cost of acquiring this butter and took such butter as its security. Once the bank received a warrant from the warehouse to the effect that the butter stored by it was held on behalf of the bank it then released the agreed level of financing. When it became time to sell the butter out of store, once the butter was invoiced to the customer the bank received an assignment of the account receivable on foot of the invoice which it took in place of the warehouse warrant which was released.

From 1987 this facility was granted to the foreign currency companies only and from the terms of the facility letter and accompanying documentation it was made clear that the facility was being made available for the purchase and resale of butter by the borrowers in such a way that butter was always available as the underlying security. The method of dealing between the bank and the borrower was that when debts receivable came into existence, they were assigned to the bank by telex. The monies for the payment of butter were paid in accordance with instructions set out in the telex to one of the Irish currency companies in the group. Such monies were then deducted from the account of one of the foreign currency companies as appropriate. The various dealings in butter included numerous inter-company invoices involving a number of companies in the group which purported to show that the butter passed from one company in the group to another. In or around June 1989 the bank became concerned that they did not have sufficient information to monitor the accounts of the companies and in particular that they had no information about the financial position of the Irish companies.

Discussions took place between the banks representative and the first defendant during which it was agreed that the first defendant would sign all telexes and the defendant informed the bank that some of the sales contracts had fallen through. He also informed the bank that there was a debt of some £600,000 owing to Bailieboro Co-op which he was unable to meet. The bank was prepared to meet this liability on foot of an existing guarantee of the liabilities of the Irish companies but not otherwise. It subsequently became clear that in fact the defendants had no existing valid contracts for sale at that time and furthermore that the butter which would have been necessary to service such contracts did not exist either. It further emerged that the defendant had arranged for some purchasers to pay to an account of the Irish companies in a bank in Cork and not to the plaintiff bank. The companies were given the opportunity of coming up with proposals which would reduce their deficit with the bank but these were considered to be totally inadequate. As a result, letters were sent to both foreign currency companies calling in the loan.

The defendants denied that the bank was entitled to call in the loan as it did. It was submitted that there was no breach of the terms of the loan; that, if there was, there was no notice of default given prior to the termination; and that, even if there had been, the defendants were entitled to time to arrange their affairs. The bank contested these submissions. It further submitted that the position of the foreign currency companies was based upon deceit and lack of good faith and that this alone entitled the bank to call in the loan without notice. The bank also contended that, as well as being entitled to recover the amount of the debt from the two foreign currency companies, it was entitled to go behind the veil of incorporation of the several companies and to recover against the assets of any of them. Finally the bank claimed damages for deceit from Mr O'Mullane and the several companies both on the grounds of deceit plain and simple and upon the ground of conspiracy.

Held by Barron J:

(1) The relationship between the bank and the defendants was governed by Dutch law.

(2) Under Dutch law, the bank was not entitled to call in a loan on demand as it would be under Irish law. If there was a breach, time must be given to the debtor not only to ensure that the breach is brought to the attention of the debtor but also ample time had to be given to remedy the breach.

(3) Under the terms of the facility letter, the defendants were under an obligation to have underlying butter as security for loans obtained by the bank; this they had failed repeatedly to comply with. The defendants were accordingly in very serious breach of contract and under those circumstances there was no need for a separate notice of default and the termination of the loan was valid.

(4) The veil of incorporation of the several companies should be lifted as justice required that all the companies in the group should be treated as one entity. All the companies were inextricably intertwined and living off one another; they should all be jointly and severally liable for the debts of the foreign currency companies to the bank.

(5) The defendants knowingly made several representations to the bank which were false with the intention of inducing the bank to advance the money. These representations were made with the authority of the first defendant and the tort of deceit had been established. The first defendant was liable to the bank for the losses which it has sustained.

Cases referred to in judgment

Crowley v. Northern Bank Finance Corporation [1981] IR 353
In re Watson (1890) 25 QBD 27
Yorkshire Railway Wagon Co. v. Maclure (1882) 21 Ch D 309

Counsel's and solicitors' names not available

BARRON J **2 June 1992**

The plaintiff (hereinafter referred to as "the bank") is a bank carrying on business in Holland. From in or about the year 1979 it had been financing business operations on the part of companies with which the first named defendant is associated. The first named defendant ("Mr O'Mullane") had for many years been involved in the butter trade both in this country and in several other European countries. He is or was at all material times the principal shareholder or beneficially interested in the principal shareholdings in the several incorporated defendants. The remaining individual defendants are related to him and have small minority shareholdings in some of these companies. Mr O'Mullane is the second generation in the business and at the time when he came into it, it was being carried on in the name of O'Mullane Brothers Ltd. This company ceased trading on 1 July 1987. In or about that time it changed its name to O'Mullane Brothers (Holdings) Ltd. This company was referred to in the evidence as Company H and I propose to so refer to it in this judgment.

As the business of Company H expanded subsidiary companies were formed to deal with particular aspects of that business. O'Mullane Brothers Sales Ltd ("Sales") was formed in 1972 to deal with sales of butter to manufacturers in the United Kingdom. O'Mullane Brothers (Exports) Ltd ("Exports") was formed later in the same year to deal with sales of tinned butter to the West Indies. Highland Traders Ltd ("Highland Traders") was formed the following year. Its main business was the sale of Irish creamery butter and Irish Whey butter to customers in continental Europe. Firstfarm Ltd ("Firstfarm") was formed in or about the same time as a separate business in the United Kingdom and was involved in the import of cheese from Holland and West Germany. O'Mullane Brothers Ltd commenced trading in place of Company H on 1 July 1987. Its previous name was Avonview Ltd and it changed its name in or about that time to O'Mullane Brothers Ltd. It was referred to in the evidence as Company A and I propose to so refer to it in this Judgment. Cork Warehousing Cold Storage and Pure Ice Co. Ltd ("Warehousing") carried on business as a warehouse until a fire destroyed its premises in or about 1979. Since then the site upon which it previously stood has been used as a car park. Evernia BV. ("Evernia") was incorporated in Holland and was in fact a shelf company which the bank made available to Mr O'Mullane.

Company H, Firstfarm and Evernia were held directly by Mr O'Mullane. Sales, Exports, Company A and Warehousing were all subsidiaries of Company H. Highland Traders may originally have been held directly by Mr O'Mullane. For some time prior to February 1987 it had also been a subsidiary of Company H, but in that month, its shares were transferred to Mr O'Mullane and thenceforth it was held directly by him. References to Mr O'Mullane as a shareholder include such other shareholders as were from time to time interested. Originally 50 per cent of the shareholding in Firstfarm was owned by a Mr Nott, but this was transferred to Mr O'Mullane in 1989. Company accounts were in the main made up to 30 June in each year. References to company accounts for a particular year will where appropriate be references to accounts for the period ending in that year. So, for example, the 1989 accounts in relation to Firstfarm mean the accounts for the year commencing on 18 July 1988 and ending on 30 June 1989.

These several companies were set up over the years on professional advice to deal with specific parts of the group's business. Exports ceased trading in or about the year 1982 and it has no place in the issues raised in these proceedings. Much of this case involves consideration of dealings in foreign exchange carried out by Mr O'Mullane and in the fact that Firstfarm's accounts were made up in sterling and that the accounts of Evernia were made up in Dutch guilders. To distinguish between those companies in which the currency was denominated in Irish pounds in its accounts and those companies in which it was not, I propose to refer to Company H, Company A, Highland Traders and Sales as the Irish companies; Firstfarm and Evernia as the foreign currency companies; and the several companies collectively as the group.

Company H became a customer of the bank in 1979 and Firstfarm became a customer the following year. Some of the business of the group involved storage of butter pursuant to a scheme known as Aid to Private Storage. What happened was that during the summer months when butter was in oversupply it was put into storage so that it could be released during the winter months when butter was not so plentiful. In the course of this type of business butter was in store for between four to seven months. The owners storing their butter received subventions to include the cost of storage and the interest on the money involved. The bank financed the cost of acquiring this butter and took such butter as its security. Once the bank received a warrant from the warehouse to the effect that the butter stored with it was being held on behalf of the bank it then released the agreed level of financing. When it became time to sell the butter out of store, once the butter was invoiced to the customer the bank received an assignment of the account receivable on foot of the invoice which it took in place of the warehouse warrant which was released. In this way the bank security was dependent upon the existence of the butter. Until 1985 the amount financed by the bank was 100 per cent of the cost of the butter. This was however dependent upon a guarantee from Allied Irish banks which effectively reduced the amount being financed to 90 per cent of the cost.

Sometime in or about 1985 the Allied Irish Banks gave notice to Mr O'Mullane that it wished to withdraw its guarantee. At the same time Mr O'Mullane had been having difficulties with the Central Bank in relation to foreign exchange dealings. He indicated his problems to the bank and it was suggested that he should set up a company in Holland, and as a result Evernia became one of the group. At the same time, terms of the facility being granted by the bank had to be renegotiated having regard to the withdrawal by Allied Irish banks of its guarantee. These continued until 1987 and were crystallised in a facility letter dated 1 July 1987 in accordance with which facilities were thenceforth granted only to the foreign currency companies.

During this period between 1985 and 1 July 1987 when the altered arrangement with the bank came into operation, a number of events occurred which were of considerable importance and have been the subject of conflicting evidence. These were:

(1) Both Sales and Highland Traders in respect of which there had been longstanding applications for certification as export sales relief companies received such approval from the Revenue in 1986.
(2) Company H declared dividends between 30 June 1986 and 30 September 1986 to an aggregate of £950,000.
(3) Two devaluations of the Irish Pound took place, one in September 1986 and one in January 1987. These devaluations caused considerable loss to Company H said to amount to some £1.7 million.
(4) Two accounts, referred to as the split accounts, were prepared for Company H for 1987; the first for the period 1 July 1986 to 30 September 1986, and the second from 1 October 1986 to 30 June 1987.
(5) The shares in Highland Traders were transferred in early 1987 to Mr

O'Mullane.

(6) Both Company H and Company A applied for change of name on 26 June 1987. Company A took over the assets and liabilities of Company H and as from 1 July 1987 commenced trading in its place.

In the period prior to the approval of Sales and Highland Traders as export sales relief company Mr O'Mullane had been paying himself tax-free dividends of approximately £50,000 a year in anticipation of such approval. These payments were taken by way of loan and as a result Mr O'Mullane built up a director's loan account with Company H which at the date of the 1986 accounts amounted to £539,000. Once the approval was obtained, this enabled monies to be paid out to Mr O'Mullane by way of tax free dividends, part of which he was then in a position to use to pay off his director's loan.

The relevant paragraphs of the facility letter dated 1 July 1987 were as follows:

> "Dear Sirs,
> We take pleasure in confirming that under simultaneous retraction of the facility granted to O'Mullane Brothers Ltd we are prepared to grant you under your mutual liability both collectively and individually until further notice and within the scope of our bank's general terms and conditions a credit facility in current account to the amount of 8 million Dutch guilders or the counter value in convertible currencies. . . .
>
> As security for this facility will serve:
> —Assignment of your debts receivable, to which a disbursement rate of 90 per cent will apply;
> Fiduciary transfer of ownership of stocks on hand and trading stock to which a disbursement rate of 90 per cent of the value as determined by the lower of the EEC intervention price or market price will apply,
>
> Deeds to which together with the Deed covering your joint liability please find enclosed.
>
> in this context it is understood that
> —the transactions involved have been concluded;
> —the exchange risks are covered;
> — the account receivables involve only first class debtors.
>
> It is further understood that your total equity will be raised by 900,000 Dutch Florins before 31 December 1988 which will be financed by your combined retained earnings over said period.
>
> The availability of the facility is subject to the additional condition that
> —O'Mullane Brothers Ltd grant you a subordinated loan of IR£250,000 (partial) redemption of the subordinated loan is permitted on the condition

that the aggregate of equity and subordinated loan remains minimally 3,000,000 Dutch Florins;
—you refrain from accepting credit facilities from and/or granting security to third parties.

In consistence with normal banking practice we expect to be kept informed regularly as to the state of affairs and business prospects of your companies, in which context we trust to receive your annual auditor's reports and interim financial statements.

We trust that the credit facility as outlined above will meet your requirements and kindly request you to return the attached copy of this letter together with the enclosed deeds regarding our security duly signed by the parties concerned as a token of your approval with its contents to us.

Yours faithfully."

The documents which came into existence following the acceptance of the terms of this letter were:

1. An all in one agreement;
2. A deed of subordination;
3. A fiduciary transfer of ownership of stock on hand and trading stock and
4. A deed of assignment.

The all in one agreement was merely an agreement accepting that the liability of the foreign currency companies was joint and several. The deed of subordination related to a sum of 750,000 Dutch guilders and provided that Company H subordinated its claims against Evernia to that amount in favour of claims by the bank. The fiduciary transfer of ownership of stock on hand and trading stock was an agreement whereby the ownership in stock on hand was transferred to the bank. The deed of assignment was a document necessitated by Dutch law since there could not be assignments of future debts and it provided for the assignment of debts as they became owing to the foreign currency companies. In addition the relationship between the parties was governed by general terms and conditions applicable to all bank lending in Holland.

Nothing turns upon the terms of the first three documents. Articles 1, 2 and 3 of the deed of assignment were as follows:

"Article 1
For additional security both for the credit granted and to be granted to him/her by De Bary and for all other debts which are or will become due to De Bary by assignor on whatever account assignor binds him/herself to assign to De Bary all debts which are or will become due to him/her by his/her clients.

Article 2
The assignment of debts receivable shall take place by sending to De Bary periodical Statements of Assignment completed and signed by the assignor accompanied by the invoices relating to the respective items. The acceptance of each assignment by De Bary will appear either from an acknowledgment in writing or from the mere fact that De Bary takes possession of and retains the statement delivered by assignor.

Article 3
The assignor is obliged immediately to hand over to De Bary each payment he/she him/herself receives from a client or from a third party on behalf of the former."

The terms of this letter and the documentation brought into existence show that the facility was being made available for the purchase and resale of butter by the borrowers in such a way that butter was always available as the underlying security.

The relevant clauses in the general conditions of the banks were as follows:

"2. *Duty of care of the bank*
When executing orders of the customer and when performing other agreements with the customer the bank shall exercise due care and in doing so the bank shall take into account the customer's interests to the best of its ability. In all other transactions with the customer the bank shall exercise due care as well. The bank shall be liable if any shortcoming in the execution of the aforesaid orders or in the performance of any other agreements referred to above or any shortcoming in the fulfilment of any other obligation towards the customer is imputable to the bank. None of the following articles may be construed as affecting this principle.

21. *Immediately due for payment*
If the customer after having been given notice of the default fails to perform any of its obligations towards the bank the bank shall be entitled to make the customer's debts to the bank immediately due and payable by giving notice. Such notice shall be in writing and shall specify the reason for the giving thereof.

30. *Notice to terminate the relationship*
Both the customer and the bank may terminate the relationship between the customer and the bank. If the relationship is terminated by the bank, it shall, upon request, inform the customer of the reason for such termination.

After notice of termination has been given, the existing individual agreements between the customer and the bank shall be settled as soon as possible but subject to the applicable time periods. During such settlement, these general conditions shall remain in full force."

In October 1988 the terms of the facility were changed and the amount was increased from 8,000,000 Dutch guilders to 23,000,000 Dutch guilders. The terms are set out in a facility letter dated 14 October 1988 which so far as is material is as follows:

> "Dear Sirs,
> We refer to our several telephone conversations and confirm that we are prepared to increase, under your mutual liability and within the framework of our bank's general terms and conditions your credit facility up to a total amount of 23 million Dutch guilders or the counter value in other convertible currencies.
>
> The facility can be divided as follows:
> Eight million Dutch guilders. Basic facility valid until further notice. This facility is applicable in current account and all covenants and conditions as agreed with our letter dated 1 July 1987 remain unchanged.
> Fifteen million Dutch guilders. Transaction financing facility, valid until further notice but not later than March 1st 1989. This facility replaces our additional facility of 7 million Dutch guilders as agreed with our credit letter 17 June 1988 and will be available to finance your sales of butter and milk powder on a so called transaction basis.
>
> Transaction financing is to be understood as financing merchandise bought from a reliable source and at the moment of financing sold to a third party on conditions as customary in the trade; each transaction has to be approved by us on beforehand. A condition is that all parties concerned and the methods of payment are acceptable to us and that we can follow the flow of the goods in detail.
>
> Within the total facility we shall finance unsold goods to a maximum of 4.5 million Dutch guilders. The unsold milk powder stock will not exceed 3.5 million Dutch guilders.
>
> Inventory as collateral will be advanced by us as follows:
> 90 per cent of the lower of purchase price or market value if presold to first class addresses;
> 85 per cent of the lower or purchase price or market value if unsold and stored up to six months.
>
> All other covenants and conditions as mentioned in our credit letter dated 1 July 1987 remain unchanged.
>
> We trust that the credit facility as outlined above will meet your requirements and kindly request you to return the attached copy of this letter duly signed by the parties concerned as a token of your approval

with its contents to us.

Yours faithfully."

During the period when the foreign currency companies were operating the loan facility provided to them by these letters the method of dealing between the bank and the borrower did not alter from the course of dealing which had existed previously. After 1 July 1987 the system continued as before. When debts receivable came into existence they were assigned to the bank by telex. The wording of the telex was as follows:

> "The following invoices are now assigned by us to you."

Details would then be set out of the seller, invoice number, purchaser and amount involved. The telex would then continue:

> "With reference to the deed of assignment of our debts receivable as listed above which are herewith assigned by us to you and transferred in full ownership."

The monies for the payment of the butter were paid in accordance with instructions set out in the telex to one of the Irish companies in the group. Such monies were then deducted from the account of Firstfarm or Evernia as appropriate. The amount of finance at any one time outstanding was dependent upon the amount of cover available to the bank by reason of both the warehouse warrants and the assignments of the debts receivable.

The various dealings in butter included numerous inter-company invoices involving a number of companies in the group. From what date this occurred was not the subject of evidence. It is reasonable to hold that it occurred at least as early as 1 July 1987. Documentation adduced in evidence relates in the main to 1989, but it can be accepted that it reflects what was happening earlier. At this period also considerable change was taking place in the business of the group. While previously various dairy commodities had been bought and sold, the group seems to have become almost totally reliant upon butter. Before July 1988, Irish sources of butter had been less than 25 per cent of total turnover. From that date when an agreement was entered into with Bailieboro Co-op to take its entire output, 75 per cent of the group's purchases were from this source. Another major source was Imokilly Co-op. It is probably reasonable to suppose that from July 1988 these two co-ops were virtually the sole source of the group's product.

The cheese business of Firstfarm ceased about 1985. At the period from 1 July 1987 and certainly by July 1988, the offices of Firstfarm in England appeared to have obtained the status of a store. Its staff which at one time had comprised five employees was reduced to one. Certainly at this period, the group had no storage facilities in this country; its main storage facilities being on the Continent. The staff employed in the business in Ireland apart from Mr O'Mullane, his wife and two sons, comprised three girls who carried out office duties, Mr Harrington, the internal auditor, and Mr Riordan, the operational manager. Only Mr O'Mullane was involved in the buying and selling of butter.

What occurred was as follows: Mr O'Mullane sold to customers in Holland, Belgium and West Germany. This sale was conducted on the telephone and would normally be confirmed in writing, though the sale was binding by reason of the telephone call alone. Purchases were made on a similar basis, though in relation to Bailieboro Co-op there was presumably some means by which Mr O'Mullane became aware of the quantities which he was purchasing. When the time for delivery took place, an invoice was made out to the purchaser. This invoice was made out in the name of one of the foreign currency companies and in the currency of the purchaser. At the same time, other invoices were made out which purported to show that the butter passed from one company in the group to another. An example will show what was done. The purchase order was made out from Bailieboro Co-op to Company A. Invoices which were then made out might have been Company A to Highland Traders; Highland Traders to Firstfarm; Firstfarm to Evernia; Evernia to a customer in Belgium or West Germany; or the chain of invoices might have included sales, but if so Highland Traders would have been excluded. The chain might also have ended with Firstfarm invoicing the ultimate purchaser. No purchase orders existed in relation to the intermediate invoices all of which by coming into existence on the same date as the invoice to the ultimate purchaser would have postdated the date of that purchaser's order.

In April 1989 Peter Farkas was appointed manager of the commodity department of the bank. By June 1989 he had familiarised himself with a number of accounts including that of the foreign currency companies. It was apparent to him that the bank did not have sufficient information from the defendants to monitor the account properly. In particular he was dissatisfied with the fact that no invoices were being provided, that the accounts from the foreign currency companies were made up to different dates and that he had no information as to the financial position of the Irish companies. He set about seeking this information from the defendants. It had become even more important since an increase in the facility to 30 million guilders was sought about this time. He wrote to Mr O'Mullane on 26 June 1989 as follows:

> "Ref: Credit facility granted to Firstfarm Ltd/Evernia BV
>
> Dear Mr O'Mullane,
> During the discussion at your last visit at our bank together with Mr J. Harrington on 13 June 1989 you asked us to consider to temporarily increase your credit line to NLG 30 million until 30 September 1989. In order to enable us to consider proposing this temporary increase to our shareholder we would like to receive your reaction as to the possibility of restructuring the *modus operandi* as follows:

1. We would like to start monitoring the use of the facility on transaction basis as it was originally envisaged, namely:

> (a) To receive all relevant information of the transaction (seller, quantity, price, potential buyer/receiving warehouse (of stock), sale price, conditions) at the same time as we receive your payment order.
> (b) To receive always copies of your invoices together with your duly signed assignment to us of your accounts receivable.

2. The wording of the respective warehouse will have to be changed. You will soon receive an example from us.
3. We would like to receive continuously copies of your monthly management reports.
4. Since Evernia's present accounting year ends at 30 April, we would like to receive your internal (not audited) statements of all companies of your group as per 30 April 1989 in order to enable us to have a complete financial view of your group as a total entity at a certain moment (*i.e.*, 30 April).
5. As mentioned during the meeting the total equity should be not less than 15 per cent of your credit facility (Firstfarm and Evernia combined). We would accept a subordinated loan in order to arrive at the said 15 per cent.

Hoping that you will find enough operational flexibility for accommodating of our proposal.
We remain,
Yours sincerely."

To this letter Mr O'Mullane replied by telex as follows dated 28 June 1989:

"We acknowledge receipt of your Fax letter ref PF/MEP 3009J received 26 June 1989 at 16.54 hours. Your request in this letter represent a change of policy of our banking arrangements. We will have to put these requests to our directors for deliberation and discussion.

This may take 10-14 days whereby we should be able to respond to you with agreement and/or positive counter suggestions.

Furthermore our financial accountant, Mr Harrington, is on his annual leave and his presence is important in this matter.

Regards."

A further reply to Mr Farkas' letter was dated 7 July 1989 in which the request for a temporary increase in facilities to 30 million Dutch florins was withdrawn. In the same letter the defendants indicated that they hoped to be able to reduce their level of borrowing to between 15 and 18 million guilders. By letter dated

17 August 1989 they replied to the specific points raised by Mr Farkas as follows:

> "1. (a) We send assignment for sales where receivables are paid within eight weeks of sale date.
> (b) We send you a copy of our sales' invoices once per week.
> 2. We await your revised wording.
> 3. We agree to send you our monthly management reports. These are usually one month in arrears.
> 4. Following consultation with our external auditor we can send you financial accounts for Firstfarm Ltd and management accounts for Evernia BV for 31 December 1989. Please note that you receive management accounts for both companies twice per year at the moment.
> 5. Total equity is not less than 15 per cent of total credit facility (Firstfarm Ltd and Evernia BV combined). We will take this into account if and when we are making application for increased facilities."

In an effort to advance matters Mr Farkas and one of his officials Mr Ingenhousz, being the bank's official in charge of the account, went to Cork where they met Mr O'Mullane, Mr Harrington and Mr Riordan on 8 September.

This meeting was not very successful so far as the representatives of the bank were concerned. They were unable to get clear answers to their questions. However they appear to have obtained agreement on the part of the defendants to furnish invoices and to sign telexes and this was done from mid-September to the beginning of November. They also asked for a statement of the affairs of the various companies as of one date and it appears that it was agreed that this would be provided for them.

By mid-October two events occurred which caused increasing concern to the bank. First of all the value of sterling started to fall and secondly the prevailing price of butter also started to fall. Because of the fall in the value of sterling the bank was becoming increasingly concerned about potential deficits on forward exchange contracts under which the defendants had purchased sterling. A further meeting took place in Amsterdam on 8 December 1989. At this meeting Mr O'Mullane produced the accounts of the Irish companies which he had promised. They purported to be a statement of the group's financial position as at 30 June 1989 of the Irish companies. They comprised an accountant's report, a group balance sheet, and notes. The accountant's report which was signed by the auditors to the group was as follows:

> "We have prepared the attached group accounts without carrying out an audit from the books and records of the individual companies.
>
> Since the formal group structure does not exist, normal consolidation principles were not appropriate. The accounting policies utilised are outlined in the notes on page 4."

That accountant's report is dated 6 December 1989. A group balance sheet as at 30 June 1989 was set out as follows:

"Employment of capital	IR£000
Fixed assets	209
Net current assets	470
	679
Represented by	
Shareholders' funds:	679
	679

The notes were as follows:

1. Companies included.

The assets and liabilities of the following companies have been included in the group balance sheet:
O'Mullane Brothers Ltd
O'Mullane Brothers Sales Ltd
O'Mullane Brothers Exports Ltd
Highland Traders Ltd
Cork Warehousing Cold Storage and Pure Ice Co. Ltd

2. Accounting Policies

1. The group balance sheet represents the assets and liabilities of the individual companies amalgamated to reflect the overall financial position of the Irish companies.
2. Fixed assets are stated at an original cost less accumulated depreciation."

It can be seen that Company H was omitted from the list of companies even though the evidence indicates that its financial position was included in the figures furnished.

Two matters of importance emerged from that meeting. First, Mr O'Mullane told the bank that some of his sales contracts had fallen through. Secondly he told the bank that there was debt of some £600,000 owing to Bailieboro Co-op which he was unable to meet. A discussion took place concerning the contracts which had fallen through and Mr Farkas did not show any particular concern since he was covered to 90 per cent of the invoice price and so far as he was aware there was no reason why the sales could not be renegotiated. It never occurred to him at that stage as was later conveyed to him that the underlying butter to meet those contracts was non-existent. At that stage Mr O'Mullane had been signing the telexes sent to the bank assigning the accounts receivable. At that meeting Mr Farkas had five such telexes which had not been signed and he produced these to Mr O'Mullane for his signature which Mr O'Mullane provided. As regards the debt to Bailieboro Co-op Mr O'Mullane was anxious that the bank should pay this on his behalf. The bank already had a contingent liability to meet this debt on foot of an existing guarantee of the liabilities of the Irish companies to a maximum of £600,000. So as to avoid any possibility of creating a double liability Mr Farkas was prepared to meet the liability on foot of this guarantee and not otherwise.

Subsequent to this meeting there were a number of telephone conversations passing between the bank and either Mr Riordan or Mr Harrington on behalf of the defendants. The matter of the payment of the £600,000 to Bailieboro Co-op was pursued. I am satisfied that Mr Farkas did not at any stage agree to pay this debt other than in pursuance of his obligation under the guarantee. In the course of these conversations it became apparent that not only had some of the contracts fallen through but they had all fallen through and at that date the defendants had no existing valid contracts for sale. Although Mr O'Mullane did not give the bank this information until this meeting he had been aware of it since the latter part of October. At a food fair in Cologne at that time he had met his various customers of whom he had between 10 and 12 and had discovered that save for three of them none was interested in making further commitments nor prepared to honour commitments already made.

A further meeting was held in Cork on 17 and 18 December. It was on this occasion that the defendants made it clear to the bank that not only had their contracts for sale fallen through but that the butter which would have been necessary to service such contracts did not exist either. These contracts were those for which invoices were set out in the five telexes signed by Mr O'Mullane on 8 December and on another eight telexes. They informed the bank that serious losses had occurred in the foreign companies amounting to some 12 million Dutch guilders. The bank could not understand how so much could have been lost. They calculated that the drop in sterling would have caused the loss of some three million Dutch guilders; that the drop in value of butter would have caused a further loss of 1 million Dutch guilders; and that overheads for the previous six months, if in fact no trading had been carried out, would have amounted to some half million Dutch guilders. The drop in sterling was a matter of concern on two heads. First, the group had a deposit on £6 million sterling which was used to offset in part the liability of the foreign currency companies which was in Dutch guilders. This deposit was kept in sterling because the interest receivable on sterling was considerably higher than on guilders and presumably there was a benefit in so doing. However, save for a reference to the existence of this deposit, neither party adduced any evidence to suggest that its existence materially affected any of the issues in the case. Secondly, the vast bulk of forward currency transactions entered into by the foreign currency companies involved the purchase forward of sterling.

It was in the course of this meeting that Mr O'Mullane informed the bank representatives that he had arranged for some purchasers to pay not to the bank but to an account of the Irish companies in a bank in Cork. In the course of the trial six invoices were produced each for approximately the sum of £60,000 in accordance with the terms of which the ultimate purchasers of the butter were asked to pay not the bank but National Irish Bank Ltd at a branch in Cork. It was said on behalf of the defendants that these invoices came into being because of the refusal by the bank to pay Bailieboro. The dates on the invoices seem to contradict this. Three of them are dated 28 November 1989 and three are dated 8 December 1989. It is said that the first three were duplicates of earlier invoices which had been sent with goods to the purchasers named therein. I will refer again to these invoices but at this stage it is perhaps significant to note that the invoices to the ultimate purchasers were made out not by one of the foreign currency companies but by Company A. Mr Farkas was very disturbed by this news and told Mr O'Mullane that he was in serious breach of his contract with the bank. Arrangements were made for the defendants to make proposals as to how the matter of their very considerable deficiency could be resolved.

By letter dated 20 December 1989 Mr, Harrington on behalf of the defendants wrote to Mr Farkas as follows:

> "Dear Sir,
>
> Further to your visit to Cork I now enclose for your attention summaries of stocks, debtors, creditor and bank balances. The figures are up to 15 December 1989.
>
> Notes.
>
> 1. The O'Mullane Group does not constitute a legal group as defined by the Irish Companies Acts and the informal consolidation given is a matter of courtesy only to help explain the present position.
> 2. The external debtors of Firstfarm Ltd are made up of insurance claims.
> 3. The figures do not provide for the payment of Bailieboro Foods Ltd under guarantee.
> 4. No provision is made for bank interest payable or receivable.
> 5. The figures are denominated in the home currency of the company concerned and no allowance is made for rate of exchange transactions.
> 6. These figures are compiled at short notice and although normal care has been taken in preparation, they are given without prejudice and without responsibility on the part of the directors and staff of O'Mullane Brothers Ltd.
>
> Yours sincerely."

The figures provided were as follows:

O'Mullane Bros. Group	IR£(000)
Fixed Assets	209
Stocks Net	1,020
Assets — (Liabilities)	(392)
Funding provided by shareholders	837

Firstfarm Ltd		Stg£(000)
Stock		Nil
Debtors — external (insurance)		170
Inter co.		— 170
Creditors — external	208	
Inter co.	7,913	
		(8,121)
Bank balances		6,617
		(1,334)
Evernia BV		D. fl.(000)
Stocks		Nil
Debtors — inter co.		31,270
Creditors — taxation		(65)
Bank balance		(30,382)
		823

With this letter was also a letter signed by Mr O'Mullane headed Re: Restructuring. It was as follows:

> "It is evident that the present situation will leave the existing companies with a debt which normal market conditions will not allow to service. Our proposal is that this debt be divided into two elements.
> 1. An element which will be serviced in the normal way.
> 2. A non-serviced element which will be represented by redeemable preference shares which will participate in future profits and can be redeemed at a premium at some future date.
>
> Details of the above will have to be discussed and may involve the establishment of a new company. We anticipate the involvement Irish interest in the form of share capital. H. Albert De Bary will provide finance on a transaction basis.
>
> The above is an outline of our proposal. We will be pleased to discuss the detail at a mutually convenient time in the near future.
>
> Yours sincerely"

While this letter refers to O'Mullane Bros Ltd as did the accounts furnished on 8 December, the bank was unaware that the name O'Mullane Bros Ltd at that time applied to Company A and not to Company H. It was not until after the proceedings had issued that the bank became aware of the existence of both companies. In fact Company A was not joined as a defendant in the proceedings until October 1990.

Mr Farkas regarded this letter and its enclosures as totally inadequate and showing an extreme naivety on the part of the defendants. He had similarly regarded the statement of group financial position furnished on 8 December. He realised that no serious effort was being made nor would be made to deal with the very serious situation which had arisen and immediately determined to bring the relationship between the parties to an end and to call in the loan which was then very significant. Letters dated 21 December 1989 were sent to both of the foreign currency companies as follows:

> "Re: Your credit arrangement
>
> Dear Sirs,
>
> Hereby we terminate with immediate effect the credit-facility which has been granted to you by the facility-letter dated 14 October 1988 (subject to the convenants and conditions set out in the letter of 1 July 1987) and terminable at notice.
>
> We have decided on this termination since our confidence in you has been shaken by, amongst others, your established violations on the covenants and conditions under the credit-agreement and your refusal to provide us with information in relation to the credit-agreement in spite of our repeated requests for that purpose.
>
> In specific:
> 1. The combined debit-balance, calculated at the foreign exchange-rate as per 20 December 1989 (NLG 11,400,514.29) has become to a large extent uncollateralised due to, as has been asserted by Mr O'Mullane, the non-existence of accounts-receivable (and their underlying contracts), assigned to us on our payment to your suppliers (amounting to NLG 8,446,873) as well as to the absence, according to the statement of Mr O'Mullane, of stock matching our payments. We regard this as a clear violation of the credit-agreement, the more so as in various conversations you appeared to have been unwilling or unable to give us an acceptable explanation of this shortfall of the collateral.
> 2. There is a potential loss of approximately NLG 8 million forthcoming from your foreign exchange forward contract positions, which were highly speculative. You maintained that these contracts would be completely matched by physical transactions. In spite of the fact that we insisted that you would give us proof of these underlying commercial contracts, you were unwilling or unable to do so. In spite of the fact that we repeatedly asked you so, you neither provided additional security for this potential loss.
>
> In connection with the above, we request, and if necessary, someone new to pay your debt to our bank (NLG 11,400,514.29), to be increased with interest and costs (estimated at about NLG 350,000) before, but at the

> utmost at, 29 December 1989. Also we request you, and if necessary someone new, to place into a deposit with our bank latest by 29 December 1989 NLG 8 million as security for the repayment of the potential loss on the aforementioned foreign exchange forward contracts.
>
> If both conditions are not met we shall have to deal with your foreign exchange exposure as we in our condition consider suitable.
>
> We reserve to ourselves the right to take any measure in order to safeguard our interests.
>
> Yours sincerely."

Following upon the delivery of these letters the present proceedings were instituted and the plaintiffs subsequently obtained varying interim and interlocutory reliefs.

The defendants deny that the bank was entitled to call in its loan when it did. It is submitted that there was no breach of the terms of the loan; that, if there was, there was no notice of default given prior to the termination; and that, even if there had been, the defendants were entitled to time to arrange their affairs. The bank contest these submissions. It submits that there was a serious default; that notice of default was given and that the circumstances were such that the bank was entitled to act as it did. It further submitted that the position of the foreign currency companies was based upon deceit and lack of good faith and that this alone allowed the bank to call in the loan without notice.

The first question which must be determined is the true nature of the legal relationship between the bank and the defendants. It was agreed by the parties that this relationship was subject to Dutch law. Accordingly, each party called a Dutch lawyer specialising in banking law who gave evidence as to the appropriate Dutch law. The first question in that issue is whether or not the defendants were in breach of the terms of the facility letter by failing to have underlying butter to fulfil the transactions notified to the bank. The defendants submitted that part of the facility was intended to be used as an ordinary overdraft. There are a number of reasons why it seems to me that this could not have been so. It means that in relation to eight million Dutch guilders no security was required. This is clearly contrary to the terms of the facility letters which indicate the form of security, being either butter or the account receivable upon the sale of that butter. If the situation was as the defendants submit then there was no need in the 1988 facility letter for the limits being placed upon the amount of product which could be held unsold at any one time nor for the reference to following the flow of goods in detail. Again the need for the foreign currency companies to have a particular net worth could only have been understood in the context that that net worth was security against a fall in the value of the butter held as security. If, as the defendants now submit, they were entitled to have an unsecured overdraft of some three times the amount of this net worth without corresponding assets, there would have been no sense to the term. We are dealing here with whether or not drawing down other than to purchase butter was a breach of contract. The argument seems to me to have another flaw. Even if it would have been permissible for either of the foreign currency defendants to draw down without giving a reason, the direction for the monies to be paid to one of the Irish companies must have been a representation that the monies were required to purchase product. Another result of this submission that the money could have been used for ordinary expenses leads inescapably to the conclusion that the defendants were aware that the money was in fact a loan for the use of the group as a whole since it was the Irish companies which were paying the bulk of the ordinary expenses.

As a matter of law, Mr Hammerstein, the expert witness called on behalf of the defendants accepted that the terms of the facility letter required the defendants to have security whether in the form of warehouse warrants or in the form of assignments of accounts receivable in respect of the monies advanced. Notwithstanding the case made on behalf of the defendants I am satisfied that Mr O'Mullane and those dealing with the bank were fully aware of their obligation to have underlying butter as security for the loans obtained from the bank. Payment instructions were included on the telexes which purported to transfer the accounts receivable. These in the context in which they were given were clearly intended to enable the defendants to purchase butter. The telex put in evidence by the defendants to show that the bank knew that they did not have to have butter to match the level of the borrowings does not support their case. This was a telex dated 30 June 1987 from the bank to O'Mullane Bros Ltd Cork for the attention of Mr Riordan. It commenced as follows:

> "Assignments still open with us per 26.6.1987. Your tlx ref Invoice NR."

The telex then set out lists of invoices relating to both Firstfarm and Evernia, giving the number, customer and price for each invoice and also setting out the total of invoice prices for each company. The telex then ended:

"Stock (Not warranted):
Colso 3 X 21M/T butter
Goole 1 X 21M/T butter

Assignments at	90	7.870.130,90
Stock at	90	563.220,00
Total cover		8.433.350,90

Regards"

This telex shows clearly by its reference to total cover and its reference to 90 which must be a reference to 90 per cent of the total value that it is a reference to the amount of security being held at that time by the bank.

Nor was it permissible to create an account receivable based solely upon a contract of supply. Accounts receivable were either created by sales of products subject to warehouse warrants in which case one security — the warrant — was being substituted for another — the account receivable; or as a result of a sale of product which the defendants had agreed to buy — in which case the telex gave payment instructions which enabled the product to be bought and the security for such payment was the account receivable.

That was the system which the bank believed was being operated. Clearly, it was not the system which the defendants were operating. If it had been, then the butter necessary to perform the contracts which fell through would have been bought and would have been available to the bank as security or at least as an asset which would have been available to it. The absence of the butter can probably only be explained by the following scenario. The defendants telexed an assignment of accounts receivable together with payment instructions. The money is sent; no product is purchased. The contract is a genuine one. It must be fulfilled, but the money to purchase the underlying butter has been spent. Unsold butter could be taken out of store, but the release of the warehouse warrant would have to be matched by an account receivable which will not be available since it would already have been supplied. Of course other funds might be available, but if so, there would have been no reason not to use the funds supplied to purchase the product for the particular contract. The only way to get funds from the bank would be to assign further accounts receivable with further payment instructions. As a result, the bank unknowingly were financing the purchase of product to fulfil one contract when it thought the money was being used to purchase product to fulfil a different contract.

The defendants say that the bank knew this and have put in evidence a table showing a list of contracts where there was a considerable time delay between the date of the assignment of the account receivable and the relevant invoice. The evidence from Mr Ingenhousz is that payments came in between two and eight weeks after the notice of assignment and that they had no cause to suspect that anything improper was occurring. When recalled to give evidence dealing with this matter he accepted the significance of the delay in the dates when this was drawn to his attention. Although it was clear to him then, it had not been so before. I accept this.

This practice by the defendants gives some weight to the suggestion by the bank that the contracts which fell through were totally fictitious. Such a practice would lead to a temptation to assign fictitious accounts receivable. That the defendants in what was clearly a poor financial position might have yielded to such a temptation is possible. The possibility becomes stronger when it is realised that the defendants were aware through Mr O'Mullane by 24 October 1989 that save for three customers no further sales would be made for some time. The transactions which fell through were referred to in 13 telexes, of these seven post-dated 24 October 1989. The orders purported to be from nine different customers. When one considers that only three customers remained to Mr O'Mullane on his own evidence, that these telexes again on the defendants' case related to contracts and not to invoices and the fact that five of these post 24 October telexes were signed without comment by Mr O'Mullane on 8 December there is certainly a strong case for suggesting that these telexes related to fictitious transactions. Further support for this view is to be found in relation to the six invoices disclosed at the meetings on 17 and 18 December. These six invoices were genuine although made out not by one of the foreign currency companies but by company A, thereby suggesting that the earlier ones were not.

Nevertheless, the bank could have called evidence to support their allegations either in full or in part, but failed to do so, seeking instead to rely upon inadmissible evidence. I am not going to draw any inference in the absence of this evidence which would in effect accept that such evidence was available. Mr O'Mullane referred to the fact of the need to have butter as security. I am quite satisfied that he was fully aware that the facility could not be used to establish an unsecured overdraft and that the manner in which the account was being operated was in breach of his agreement with the bank.

In submitting that the foreign currency companies were entitled to a notice of default and to time to rearrange their affairs the defendants rely upon Clauses 2 and 21 of the general terms and conditions of banking transactions which form part of the relationship between the parties. In substance the submission was that a bank was obliged to act in good faith towards its customer and that it could not simply terminate a loan transaction because it wished to do so. The evidence of Mr Hammerstein in support of these submissions established that the obligation to act in good faith applied equally to the customer and to the bank; that in deciding whether or not the bank or a customer was acting in good faith it was in essence necessary to establish whether or not they were acting reasonably. The obligation of a bank was to consider the whole relationship between it and its customer and that the longer that relationship and *a fortiori* the better that relationship had worked the greater the obligation to ensure that if the loan was called in the customer would have adequate opportunity to find alternative finance.

I am quite satisfied that a bank is not entitled under Dutch law as it would be under Irish law to call in a loan on demand. Time must be given to the debtor, and, if there has been a breach, time must be given to the debtor to ensure that not only is the breach brought to the notice of the debtor but that ample time is given to the debtor to remedy the situation. The bank said that in any event it was entitled to terminate the arrangement under Clause 30. In my view, this clause is relevant only when the bank decides for its own good reasons to call in a loan. In such circumstances, there will be no default and so need for a notice of default. However, since there is an overriding obligation to act in good faith, which in essence means reasonably there would have been an obligation to consider the length of the relationship and how it had operated in practice so as to determine what length of time should have been have been given to a customer.

In a case like the present if the account had been operated in accordance with the terms of the facility letter then even though there was a massive deficit, I think that the bank would have been required to give the borrower time to come up with a reasonable solution to the problem which would then have been existing. That however is not the position which existed in the present case. There would have been no deficit, if there had been no breach. The defendants were not only in breach of contract but in very serious breach of contract.

Secondly although the breach was not strictly capable of remedy they had been given an opportunity to meet the situation in a responsible manner. I accept Mr Farkas' view that the manner in which they sought to meet the situation was naive in the extreme. Certainly in my view Mr Farkas was fully entitled to take the view that no serious effort was being made by the defendants to come up with any reasonable proposal. And that in fact none would ever be forthcoming. Mr Ingenhousz said in evidence that there were three grounds for terminating the facility. First, they did not believe the figures which had been submitted to them; secondly, there were the losses incurred and to be incurred upon the foreign exchange transactions; and, thirdly, there was a lack of collateral. He went on to say also that they were afraid that even more funds would have been diverted. I accept this evidence as being the state of mind of the bank at the time. In those circumstances, there was no need for a separate notice of default. I accept the evidence of Mrs Kellerman that the letter of termination was an adequate notice of default. In any event I also accept the evidence of Mr Farkas to the effect that when he was told about the diversion of funds that he informed Mr O'Mullane that that was a serious breach of contract. I do not think the evidence of Mrs Kellerman was really contested by Mr Hammerstein. His only criticism of the bank was to the effect that their failure to tell Mr O'Mullane that to use the facility for a purpose other than the purchase of butter would be a breach of the terms of that facility. In my view the bank could not be criticised in that regard because I am quite satisfied that Mr O'Mullane and the other officers of the company dealing with the matter were fully aware of the need to purchase butter with any monies advanced on foot of the facility.

Both lawyers accepted that fraud on the part of the defendants would have justified the course taken by the bank. I will return to the question of fraud later but for the present it seems to me that the termination of the loan was valid.

It is now necessary to consider the remedy to which the bank is entitled. Clearly the bank is entitled to recover the amount of the debt from the two foreign currency companies as a breach of contract. The bank however makes two further submissions. First it claims to be able to go behind the veil of incorporation of the several companies and to recover against the assets of any of them. Secondly the bank claims to recover damages for deceit from Mr O'Mullane and the several companies both on the ground of deceit plain and simple and upon the ground of conspiracy.

Whether or not the bank is entitled to either or both of these remedies depends upon the evidence as a whole, but also upon the view which I take as to the credibility of the several witnesses. Mr Fitzpatrick, a chartered accountant, was called by the bank. He had been instructed to examine the accounting records of the defendant companies, to establish their trading relationship, to identify any losses within the defendant companies and to report those findings back to the plaintiffs. He took the view that there was no commercial reason for the manner in which the butter was invoiced through the various companies in the group and that it was improper since it resulted in a loss to a third party. It did not obey the normal rules for armslength transactions. He was of the view that the group was insolvent on 1 July 1987 and should not have continued to trade. In the course of his investigations he also traced various dividends which had been declared and gave evidence of irregularities in relation thereto. It was suggested that some of his conclusions were based upon a mistaken view of some of the documents which he considered and in particular that he mistook the rate of exchange being used by the defendants. In my view he gave his evidence fairly and I accept it. I do not think that any of his conclusions were in any way affected by his failure, if failure there was, to understand fully the documentation which he investigated.

Mr Ingenhousz and Mr Farkas both gave evidence on behalf of the bank. Both were credible witnesses. Mr Ingenhousz in particular was criticised for the fact that the bank was lax in its supervision of the account and that he and the bank ought to have been fully aware of the extensive forward buying of sterling. The bank was undoubtedly lax or Mr Farkas would not have wished to tighten up the procedures. However I do not think that the liability of the defendants can be lessened in any way because of these circumstances.

The witnesses called for the defendants sought to refute Mr Fitzpatrick's conclusions. They supported the inter-company transactions as being the "management of profit". They submitted that this was the commercial reason for such transactions. They also sought to refute the conclusion that the group was insolvent on 1 July 1987. I regret that I found the principal witnesses for the defendants to be unreliable in their evidence. Mr O'Mullane himself on his own evidence withheld the evidence of the loss of his contracts from the bank for over a month. He knew from late October 1989 that these had virtually fallen through *in toto*. It was not until he was forced to disclose this in December that he told Mr Farkas and then only one step at a time, from some to all, and then that there was no underlying butter. The diversion of funds through the six invoices which he disclosed at that time was in similar vein as was his attempted explanation for signing the five invoices which he did sign on 8 December 1989.

Mr Kenny, an independent tax adviser, was responsible for the tax planning of the group. He gave evidence that he was unaware that Company H had been insolvent until January 1989 when the problem had resolved itself. I cannot accept this. On the evidence, the group's financial policy was based upon tax planning. The author of this planning was Mr Kenny and his decisions were implemented in the day-to-day running of the group by Mr Harrington, and interpreted in relation to audit by Mr O'Brien. He must have known of this insolvency at the time and have been responsible for or had a significant input to the decisions made at that time. He was also responsible for the fact that Mr O'Mullane's director's loan account was kept off the balance sheets. In my view he was seeking to distance himself from decisions which he made and which he knew should not have been made.

Mr O'Brien the auditor for Firstfarm and the Irish companies insisted that Company H was not insolvent on 1 July 1987. He also made an obvious mistake in the accounts of Company H for the three month period 1 July 1986 to 30 July 1986. His view of the bank's action in closing the loan was that it was bizarre.

Having regard to his knowledge of events and the evidence which had already been given in the case I found this a very strange comment from a professional accountant. I also found his answers on cross-examination on the meaning of post balance sheet events and his failure to make notations for such events as being in the same vein.

I accept the opinions expressed by Mr Fitzpatrick in preference to those expressed by Mr O'Brien or Mr Kenny or Mr Harrington. I also accept the evidence given by Mr Ingenhousz and Mr Farkas in preference to that given by Mr O'Mullane or Mr Harrington or Mr Riordan. I found the evidence for the plaintiffs more reliable than that of the witnesses for the defence. The evidence of the latter too often sought to contradict the obvious.

The basis upon which counsel for the plaintiff submits that the veil of incorporation of the several companies in the group should be lifted is that justice requires that all the companies in the group should be treated as one entity. It seems to me that there was only one organisation at all times relevant to the proceedings and only one business. There had in the past been several aspects to the business which had been segregated among the several companies. These had ceased and were no longer being carried on. The entirety of the business was that of butter trading. Mr O'Mullane was the sole trader who carried on that trade from his office in Cork.

The business was in reality carried on by Company A although the documentation relating to the trade also involved Highland Traders, Sales, Firstfarm and Evernia. What happened was as I have already indicated. A succession of inter-company invoices came into being when the invoice to the ultimate purchaser was being prepared. There was no commercial reason for all these invoices. They came into being as part of a tax planning exercise. Highland Traders and Sales were both entitled to export sales relief. Transactions were routed through these companies so that the paper profits generated might be free from liability to tax. Sales lost its full exports sales relief on 30 November 1987 and thereafter the majority of the sales were put through Highland Traders. Firstfarm was incorporated in the United Kingdom and was used to take the benefit of the unrestricted foreign exchange regulations in the UK and also lower VAT rates. Evernia was incorporated in the Netherlands and was used solely to take the benefit of unrestricted foreign exchange regulations there.

Although several intermediate invoices were made out, no purchase contracts were made out in relation to the same paper transactions. Some of these invoices contained payment instructions which were incorrect. When this error was raised in the course of cross-examination, it was claimed that old forms were being used. This was a stupid excuse because first, if so, there was still no need to type in the wrong payment instruction or if already printed, no reason why it could not have been crossed out; and, secondly, it was shown conclusively from internal evidence in relation to fax numbers that the forms were contemporaneous. However the invoices purporting to be made out by Company A were in fact made out on old forms applicable to Company H, and could be so identified by the VAT number thereon which belonged to Company H and not to Company A.

In his evidence, Mr Fitzpatrick drew attention to this succession of unnecessary invoices. He took a number of transactions which showed this pattern. These were made the subject of interrogatories and were all admitted substantially by the defendants. From some of his examples, he had assumed the original purchaser to have been Company A but the answers for the interrogatories suggested that it was Highland Traders. This difficulty in pinpointing the actual companies involved was shown in relation to a 1989 purchase from Staple Dairy Products Ltd, the documentation for which has been admitted in evidence. That documentation shows the purchaser from Staple Dairy Products Ltd, as being Company A, but it was Firstfarm which was treated as having been the purchaser. That company then invoiced it to Company A who invoiced it back to Firstfarm who then purported to invoice it on to the ultimate purchaser.

This succession of invoices has been put forward by the defendants as being an exercise in the "management of profit": an expression which to me at any rate indicates all that is alleged to have been wrong with what the defendants were doing. In support of what they were doing, the defendants sought to get Mr Fitzpatrick's agreement to the proposition that it was reasonable to divide the profit being generated equally between the companies sourcing the product and those finding the ultimate purchasers. Mr Fitzpatrick was inclined to agree with some aspects of this proposition, but this limited agreement was subject to his overriding criticism that nothing should be done which would prejudice third parties. However, in the context of this case, the proposition was unreal. It related only to the 1988 results of Highland Traders and Firstfarm respectively. Further, there was only one trader who was both finding the source of and then selling on that product. Finally, the turnover of Highland Traders in 1988 at £4.28m. was approximately one tenth of that of Firstfarm in the same year at Stg£37.74m., the respective gross profit earned being virtually 10 per cent as against marginally over 1 per cent.

There was in the event no need for the exercise carried out by Mr Fitzpatrick. The documentary evidence adduced by the defendants made out his case even more clearly. The sales/packing sheets book shows clearly what was happening. The first document shows a purchase from Imokilly Co-op and a sale on 18 October 1989, to the customer, Hochland in Western Germany. The butter was being shipped from Cork on 20 October for delivery on 26 October. Four invoices are referred to, all being dated 20 October. They were: Company A to Highland Traders; Highland Traders to Firstfarm; Firstfarm to Evernia; and Evernia to Hochland. Another sheet shows the sales contrast of the 2 October 1989 and the customer General Milk Products in Western Germany. Again the butter was being shipped from Ireland. The sailing date was 3 October for delivery on 6 October. Three invoices are referred to: Highland Traders to Firstfarm; Firstfarm to Evernia; Evernia to the customer. In the first case, Company A was the company named was buying from the supplier; whereas in the latter it was Highland Traders. As can be seen the intermediate invoices were all made out on the date of sailing. In effect what was happening was that after the butter had been sold on, the seller was being nominated as a particular company. In fact since the only transaction at the date of the sale to the ultimate purchaser had been the purchases in the name of Company A, and Highland Traders respectively only they would have had title to sell on. This sort of documentation which is only prepared after the event when it is more clear where it is most beneficial to place the profit is a hallmark of irregular, if not illegal transactions. In the field of purported tax planning, which was what was occurring here, it changed what in some circumstances might have been a tax avoidance scheme to simple tax evasion.

This was not the only irregularity. Neither Firstfarm nor Evernia were genuine overseas companies. Both were beneficially owned in this jurisdiction and were being used to circumvent exchange control regulations, and to a much lesser extent to lessen liability to VAT. Indeed Evernia was set up specifically to avoid exchange control regulations.

All of this was occurring in the context of borrowing by the foreign currency companies from the bank where such borrowing was being used to keep the entire group running. I accept the view expressed by Mr Fitzpatrick that all the companies were inextricably intertwined and living off one another. In my view, it is intolerable that a court should even be asked to sanction what was being done, which it would have to do, if it was to hold the assets of the foreign currency companies alone should be available to meet the sums owing to the bank. Those assets are ultimately dependent upon how many invoices Mr O'Mullane had prepared for each transaction and in which names and for what amounts they were completed. I am not prepared to sanction that. It is clearly in the interest of justice that the assets of all the companies should be treated as if those companies were included in the all in one agreement so as to make each company jointly and severally liable on the debt to the bank.

There were very considerable losses on forward currency transactions in the name of the two foreign currency companies. It must be remembered that on the evidence on the defendants, the business was totally dependent upon foreign exchange dealings for its survival. Its margin on butter sales was said to be around one per cent whereas that on its foreign exchange dealings was said to raise this level of profitability to between six and seven per cent. Clearly these transactions in the manner in which they were entered into were made for the benefit of the group as a whole. However, the avowed reason for these forward contracts was to protect the purchase moneys payable in foreign currencies. Whichever way the dealings were looked at, it would be an injustice to the bank to limit recourse in respect to these losses to the assets of the foreign currency companies.

In his evidence Mr Fitzpatrick dealt with dividends which had been declared and paid by the Irish companies since 1 July 1987. In the main, the payment of these dividends involved payments from a bank account of one company through other companies in the group back to the original account. In the course of such travel the monies passed through warehousing and documentation purported to show that its fixed assets became charged in favour of Mr

O'Mullane as a result. These dividends were declared by Highland Traders in December 1988 and by Company A in January 1989. The latter however purported to be paid out of the dormant account of Company H and was later recalled. Finally, in October 1989 a dividend of £2 million was declared and paid by Highland Traders. This was said to have been in anticipation of a 1990 budgetary provision disallowing such relief from then. I am satisfied that these dividends were improperly paid since the group was insolvent at the relevant dates and accordingly it is unnecessary to consider them in detail.

It is now necessary to consider whether any fraud existed. Foreign exchange played a very important part in the trading carried on. It may be said as witnesses for the defendants testified to have been an integral part of the business itself. The evidence on the part of the defendants showed that the actual margin on the resale of butter was increased by skilful manipulation of the currency markets. This is what they may have thought was happening. Unfortunately it is far from the truth. The probability suggests that not only were there no profits from such trading but considerable losses.

Currencies were of importance in two different ways:

(1) In relation to invoicing;

(2) In relation to hedging against foreign currency fluctuations.

In practice, on the advice of management consultants, fixed rates of exchange were used for internal book-keeping purposes. Adjustments were when necessary made in the accounts. While this may have had the merit of simplifying book-keeping transactions, I suspect that it may have operated adversely on the fortunes of the company. Any substantial difference between the fixed rate and the then current rate could have wiped out the believed profit. Mr O'Mullane was buying in Irish currency and selling in either German marks, Dutch guilders or Belgian francs. Obviously by translating the foreign currency into Irish currency, he could immediately see whether he was making a profit on the deal since there were only the two external transactions. This does not seem to have happened because the evidence showed that around the time of the devaluations in 1986 and 1987, owing to the use of an incorrect fixed rate, the assets of the company were some £900,000 less than they were believed to be. Mr O'Mullane believed that he was operating on a combined margin for butter and currency of six to seven per cent although the margin for butter only was one per cent. As a result he believed himself to be in a position to undercut his competitors. It seems to me that, having regard to what happened, this belief led to undercutting resulting in a presumed profit but an actual loss.

The manner in which currency hedging was carried out was equally unsuccessful. The purpose of currency hedging is to ensure that future payment or receipt in a foreign currency will cost or be worth on the date of payment or receipt in terms of the buyers or sellers currency the same as on the invoice date. To ensure this, the relevant currency is either sold or bought forward as of the date of payment. In this way currency fluctuations are eliminated and the cost or value of foreign currency when paid or received would be the same as on the invoice date. The defendants were concerned only with the value of receipts in foreign currencies. They did not operate this system to sell such currencies forward. Instead they sold forward considerably in excess of actual turnover and purchased sterling. This left them in a speculative position as Mr Farkas pointed out to them. If the currency purchased had appreciated, this would have given them a profit. As it depreciated, this caused them loss in the same way as the depreciation in value of any other commodity. This loss was aggravated by the events which occurred between the bank and the defendants. When the loan was called in, the bank was obliged in accordance with Dutch Central bank regulations to close all the defendants' forward currency transactions which resulted in very considerable losses. The defendants were given full details of these losses. Even in the course of the trial, through counsel, submissions were made by the defendants that the bank had failed to furnish information in relation to the closure of these transactions which would, if disclosed, have showed that the losses were not as great as stated. The bank was in effect being accused of fraud. The defendants also submitted that the bank should have left the transactions to run to maturity by which time sterling had virtually recovered and losses would have been relatively light.

These submissions indicated to me that the defendants did not fully understand the nature of forward foreign exchange dealings. When a currency is bought forward that purchase is matched by one in which the same currency is sold forward as of the same date. The bank acts as in effect a broker in both transactions though in reality as principal in each. If, as in this case, the purchaser of the currency fails, then the banker must find another purchaser to replace such purchaser, in this case, the defendant. If the forward value of the currency which has been so purchased has fallen, the cost to the new purchaser would be less than to the defendants. At maturity, the original seller would still be entitled to its price and the bank will have to make good the shortfall between this and the amount being paid by the substitute purchaser. That is the amount for which the defendants become liable. Whereas the original deal involves two transactions, the substitute deal requires only one. The defendants allegation of fraud against the bank is based upon the allegation that the substitute deal also involved two transactions and so a further transaction involving the bank had not been disclosed. There was no such transaction as the defendants should have been fully aware. Some misapprehension might originally have been reasonable because the substitute deals were included in larger transactions taking place at the same time, but this cannot excuse what was an unfounded allegation. One can understand the feeling of frustration felt by the defendants by reason of the fact that the bank did not wait until sterling recovered. Similar suggestions are made when mortgagees do not wait for what the mortgagor says would have been a turn of the market. However that is not relevant unfortunately for the defendants. The bank had to act as it did in accordance with Central Bank regulations. The fact that the defendants must have known this is to be found from the absence of any evidence called on their behalf from any bank or other competent person to suggest that what the bank did in the circumstances was improper.

I have already referred to various matters which occurred in the period 1985 to 1987. These are all interconnected. Once Highland Traders and Sales obtained export sales relief clearance the way was open for the payment of tax free dividends to Mr O'Mullane as the shareholder in Company H. This plan was immediately put into place. The profits available for the payment of dividends in these two companies were paid to Company H by way of dividend: £200,000 from Highland Traders and £1.58 million from Sales. Dividends totalling £950,000 were then declared by Company H. These were paid and Mr O'Mullane was able to close his loan account.

It was after this that the currency losses were incurred by Company H. The devaluations amounted to 11 per cent in total. However, the rates of exchange being used by the group had apparently been misstated in their books and around this time it was found that as a result the assets of the Irish companies were overstated by some £900,000. As the witnesses put it, instead of the devaluations costing 11 per cent, they cost 33 per cent. Why it was put in this way or why there should have been such losses is immaterial. What is significant having regard to the events of 1989 is that the losses sprang from two causes: forward buying of currency and the recording of transactions in foreign currencies at incorrect rates of exchange.

Both the dividends and the losses occurred during what would have been the period of the 1987 accounts. Had they been prepared for the usual period, there would not have been funds from which the dividends would have been paid. They would therefore have had to have been recalled. This would have meant that the export sales relief would have become worthless and that Mr O'Mullane was still indebted on his director's loan. The dividends could not have been rerouted, because both Sales and Highland Traders were subsidiaries of Company H.

A solution to the problem was found. Since the devaluations occurred after 30 September 1986, it was decided to split the accounts for 1987 into two periods, the first for three months to 30 September 1986 and the second for nine months to 30 June 1987. In certain circumstances, I have no doubt that this is a device which is perfectly acceptable. Its justification lay in the assumption that the monies paid tax free to Mr O'Mullane would have been properly payable to him as dividends and not by way of a director's loan account if the export sales relief status had been confirmed at the date of the actual payments. Therefore all that was intended was to give in effect the status of dividends to such drawings.

Mr Fitzpatrick has criticised these accounts and stated that in his belief they do not set out the true financial position of Company H. On the evidence, I must take the same view. The first indication that the accounts were contrived to meet a particular situation is the extent of the revenue reserves on the balance sheet date for the three month accounts. They are a mere £2,767. However there are more serious indicators. The evidence adduced by Mr Fitzpatrick as to the dates upon which this dividend was paid show that as of the balance sheet date some £400,000 had not been paid. The balance sheet however did not show this amount as a liability. Mr O'Brien who prepared the accounts accepted in evidence that this was a mistake. If it was, the mistake was much more far-reaching than even that simple admission suggests. Taken at its face value, the company did not have the money to pay the unpaid balance of the dividend. However, the accounts themselves show in the relevant notes that the entire had been paid. That in my view is more than just carelessness. It shows that the accounts were being prepared to meet a particular situation. The error was probably made good in the nine months accounts, but this is immaterial if the whole purpose of the split accounts was unsustainable.

There was a second question mark hanging over these accounts. We have been told that there had been miscalculations on the rates of exchange used on the group's documentation and that some £900,000 had been overstated in the books on this basis. No evidence was given to identify the period over which this miscalculation had been made. Since it is said to have increased the loss arising from the devaluations from 11 per cent to 33 per cent, it must have been accounted for in the nine month accounts. However the error must have been going on for some time and part of the losses, if not a major part, would have been attributable to the earlier accounts, *i.e.* the three month account and the 1886 accounts.

Mr Fitzpatrick in his evidence said that the group was insolvent at this period and that it should have gone out of business. This is contested by the expert witnesses for the defendants. They maintained that the several companies were able to pay their debts as they became due. If you borrow from Peter to pay Paul, you can always pay Paul provided that Peter is prepared to make the money available. But there is normally a day of reckoning. Our criminal courts as well as our civil courts unfortunately have all too often to deal with persons who obtain money from the public upon the promise of higher than average return on money invested. When such promoters can fulfil their promises only by the flow of money seeking these returns, can it really be suggested that they are solvent merely because such investors are not aware of the situation and are not looking for a return of their money? The answer is obviously, no. There is no substantial difference between this apparently unlikely example and the position of the group on 1 July 1987. Admittedly in the example I have given the day of reckoning must come although perhaps some of these promoters have the hope that they would generate the profits which they have advertised. The position of the group on 1 July 1987 was really no different. They had a hope that they would trade out of their difficulties. The group at that stage existed solely by reason of the bank's lending. The figure involved was £3.3 million. If the bank had known the true position I have no doubt that it would have called in its loans.

In my view the advisers to the group are mistaken as to the meaning of insolvency. Insolvency is essentially a matter of assets and liabilities. If liabilities exceed assets, the position is one of insolvency. But the reverse is not necessarily true. A company is not solvent because its assets exceed its liabilities. It cannot for example take into account assets which it requires to remain in existence save in so far as they may be used as security to raise finance. The test is ultimately, can it pay its debts as they fall due: See *Crowley v. Northern Bank Finance Corporation* [1981] IR 353. I have no doubt that on 1 July 1987 and thereafter, particularly having regard to the events which occurred in 1989, the group was and continued to be insolvent.

There were two further consequences of these events. Highland Traders was transferred into the direct ownership of Mr O'Mullane; and Company A was formed and took over the assets and liabilities of Company H. As a result of the losses sustained by Company H I feel quite sure that the advisers to the group took the view that there might be a danger of fraudulent trading if Company H continued to trade. For this reason Company A was established with that name. Since it took over the assets and liabilities of Company H one would have thought that it was equally liable to be guilty of fraudulent trading. However it carried in its accounts credit from Company H and on this basis its solvency was more real. However there can have been no real justification for carrying forward that credit since Company H having ceased to trade had no real means of support. Admittedly it did have the assets in warehousing and its other subsidiaries which may perhaps as was suggested in the course of the evidence have had asset values in excess of their balance sheet figures.

The existence of Company A was never disclosed to the bank. On the evidence, I am satisfied that this was because of the enquiries which the bank would then have made and the then virtual certainty that it would have called in its loan. I do not accept the reason given nor the evidence as why it was established. It was suggested that this would leave a route free for the payment of dividends direct to Mr O'Mullane, something which would not seem to have been correct since it was a subsidiary of Company H even though Mr Kenny did seem to suggest that turning Company H into a non-trading holding company would be sufficient for his purpose. However, the answer is correct when attributed to the reason to transfer Highland Traders from being a subsidiary of Company H to being directly owned by Mr O'Mullane. In the result what the advisers to the group sought to do was to get over three problems caused by the heavy losses in Company H. These were:

(1) Validating the dividends declared in the period June to September 1986;

(2) Ensuring that the problem would not recur;

(3) Keeping the knowledge from the bank.

This was done by:

(1) Preparing split accounts;

(2) Transferring the ownership in Highland Traders;

(3) Forming a new company with the same name as Company H had had.

I have indicated inferentially that this scheme of events was planned by the group's advisers. Mr O'Mullane said that he was first told of the problems in Company H late in 1986 and later that it was early in 1987. Other witnesses put their knowledge as being acquired later. In particular Mr Kenny said that he did not know until the beginning of 1989. I regret that I cannot accept such evidence. The entire strategy of the group was tax driven. The tax adviser was Mr Kenny. His decisions were implemented on a day to day basis by Mr Harrington and in relation to the audit interpreted by Mr O'Brien. The particular planning started early in 1987. The signing of the split accounts was deliberately delayed until February 1989 because by then those concerned were satisfied that the affairs of the group had recovered. I have no doubt but that Mr Kenny and Mr O'Brien had a reasonably close knowledge of the affairs of the group and that there was no way in which they could have been in any doubt as to the position of the Irish companies in the early months of the year 1987.

This close contemporaneous knowledge of the accounts is equally apparent in relation to the dividend of £2 million declared by Highland Traders in November 1989. The balance sheet of that company for the year ending 30 June 1989 showed a credit to the profit and loss account of some £1.7 million. Yet in November when the earlier accounts had only just been completed, the advisers to the company were in a position to advise the declaration of a dividend of £2 million which turned out to be just possible when the accounts to 1 December 1989 were prepared.

One question which was never fully explained by the evidence is what happened to the monies which were lost by the group. At the meeting in Cork on 17 and 18 December 1989 the unexplained loss varied between 6 and 8 million Dutch guilders. Counsel for the defendants sought to establish in the course of the trial that this loss was explainable by reason of the loss of over £4 million on foreign exchange following the calling in of the loan. There was undoubtedly further loss once the loan was called in. However it is the loss before the loan which was called in which is being considered at the moment. Quite clearly the money had already been lost at that stage. It should in that case have been apparent from the accounts of the Irish companies and the foreign currency companies that that was so. However there is no apparent indication in any of those accounts to support such a suggestion. Counsel for the Irish companies in his closing address submitted that there was always a gap of six million Dutch guilders while counsel for the foreign currency companies submitted that of the missing money eight million Dutch guilders was for payment of goods which had already been sold on and the money received by the bank. Both these submissions were made to show that nothing dishonest had taken place and that no money had been improperly siphoned off from any of the companies in the group. They do however seem to acknowledge that the accounts were incorrect in that they showed this sum as an asset within the group when it had already been lost. It is not necessary for me to speculate as to how this money was lost. It may well be that it was lost because of the manner in which foreign currency transactions were dealt with in the books of the company and that like 1987 when £900,000 was overstated in the accounts that similarly such a sum or even a greater sum was overstated in the accounts in 1988 and 1989. However, the fact that there was an overstatement seems to be something which the defendants must have known about. If they had been operating the account with the bank in the manner intended, that is that there was always underlying butter for the amount of the loan, then the loss or the gap or whatever you wish to call it could not have occurred.

In December 1989, the Irish companies were unable to meet the debt to Bailieboro and they had relatively little butter in stock. Clearly, there was a deficit in their assets at that time and equally clearly it seems that it must have been the result of a gradually worsening position. Unfortunately, the evidence has not been specifically directed to an examination of the accounts over this period. Mr Long called to give evidence that no monies had been improperly withdrawn from the group was not asked to consider this. I regret that his evidence was a total waste because the causes of the problem lay elsewhere. Probably in the pricing masked by the rates of exchange being used in the books of the company. This situation arose before any debts on foot of foreign currency transactions crystallised and it is not in my view credible that these losses can be the cause of the group's problems.

Fraud consists of the making of a representation of present fact which is untrue knowing it to be untrue or being reckless as to whether or not it is untrue for the purpose of inducing particular conduct on the part of the person to whom the representation is made and which does induce that conduct and as a result of which that person is damnified. In the present case it is quite clear that the bank had been damnified. It is equally clear that the bank relied upon what it was told by the defendants. The question to be determined is whether the bank was given false information known to be false or not caring whether it was true or false for the purpose of inducing the bank to continue making advances to the defendants in accordance with the facility agreed.

There were a number of representations made by the defendants to the bank. The first of them which is material relates to the group accounts for the year 1985. These overstated the position of the Irish companies to an amount of approximately £500,000. This is the approximate amount which had been taken out of the company by way of an intended tax free dividend and which were on the balance sheet date in the company and about to be taken out again on the following day. The representation contained in that balance sheet was clearly false. There are circumstances in which there can be two separate and distinct transactions although the purpose of those two transactions is to achieve one particular result. The sale of a chattel to a finance company by a hire purchase agreement whereby that chattel is hired to the original seller by the finance company on hire purchase terms may be accepted as two separate and distinct transactions or it may be treated as one transaction: See *Yorkshire Railway Wagon Co. v. Maclure* (1882) 21 Ch D 309 and *Re Watson* (1890) 25 QBD 27. In the former case the hire purchase agreement is treated as being valid: whereas in the latter case the entire is regarded as creating a charge. Another example where two separate and distinct transactions may be so regarded or may be regarded as one transaction used to occur where schemes existed to save stamp duty on newly erected buildings. Where there was a sale of a plot of land together with a contract to build a house thereon stamp duty was payable on the value of the house unless it could be shown that the two contracts were separate and distinct. A similar situation existed in relation to stamp duty on settlements. If a settlement was set up with a nominal value with the intention of immediately putting considerable funds into the settlement, then the document had to be stamped in accordance with the value of the investments and not in accordance with the nominal amount originally set out in the trust deed. All this is normal commonsense. Similarly, when the director's loan was repaid to the company for the purpose of excluding it on the balance sheet with the intention to repay it to the director the following day, it is clear that there were not two separate and distinct contracts, but only one agreement; and that in effect the balance sheet misstated the position. The next misrepresentation is the failure of the defendants to notify the bank that Company H became insolvent in 1987. It is clear that this was done deliberately.

The next representation which is material was made by Company A granting to the foreign currency companies a subordinated loan pursuant to the facility letter dated 1 July 1987. O'Mullane Bros Ltd on the date of that facility letter was Company A. However, the bank thought it was Company H and had no idea that neither it nor any other of the Irish companies had the ability to give such security. As I have already indicated the whole purpose of what then occurred was done deliberately to keep the bank in ignorance. The establishment of Company A with the same name as Company H and the failure to inform the bank that that had been done can only be regarded as an intention to deceive.

The whole scheme by which the money was advanced by the bank on telex instructions by one or other of the foreign currency companies to pay particular sums to one or other of the Irish companies was dependent upon the representation that that money was being used to buy butter. Once butter was not being bought with such monies then the representation was false. In my view clearly these several misrepresentations were made by the defendants knowing that they were false and with the intention of inducing the bank to advance the money. These representations were made with the authority of Mr O'Mullane and he must bear the responsibility for them. In these circumstances I am satisfied that the tort of deceit has been established and that Mr O'Mullane is liable to the bank for the losses which it has sustained.

I have not dealt with the several cases cited to me because it seems to me that the issues which I had to decide were essentially questions of fact. Lifting the veil of incorporation may be done in a variety of circumstances, but the principle in each case is the same. Where it would be unconscionable not to do so, then it will be done. Wherever one should draw the line, one thing is clear in the present case, it is one where the veil should be lifted.

The claim in deceit is equally one dependent upon the facts. The principles are clear and in my view the allegations are supported by the facts. I have not specifically dealt with the allegation of conspiracy since the relief obtainable on that heading is already available to the bank on my findings.

There is one matter which I have not so far dealt with expressly. The particulars furnished by the bank on 29 May 1991 in reply to a letter for particulars dated 15 March 1991 contain an admission by the bank that Company H had sufficient accumulated profits to entitle it in law to declare the dividend of £950,000. It is now sought to go behind that admission. Even though the bank was then making the case which it made at the trial in relation to fraud and conspiracy, it was apparent both from the amended statement of claim and these answers that the bank was unaware that the dividend had been paid. For this reason, this dividend will also be declared to have been invalid.

Patricia McLaughlin
Barrister

1963 ACT, PART III

Michael P. Fitzpatrick v. Fitzpatricks Footwear Ltd, Thomas P. Fitzpatrick and Others: High Court 1970 No. 148 Sp (Kenny J) 18 November 1970

Company Law – Voting rights – Whether provision in Articles of Association deprived holders of redeemable preference shares of the right to vote at meetings of the company – Whether wording of Article sufficiently unambiguous – Companies Act 1963 (No. 33), section 134(e)

Assignment of office by director – Whether appointment of plaintiff as governing director by a codicil to the will of the deceased governing director was an "assignment of office" – Whether such appointment was required to be sanctioned by a special resolution of the company – Whether it was permissible in deciding the meaning of "assignment of office" to look at the reports of committees on the reform of company law to see what the object of the Act was – Companies Act 1963 (No. 33), section 199

Facts: (1) Prior to 1962 the share capital of the company was £40,000 divided into 20,000 ordinary shares of £1 each and 20,000 5 per cent non-cumulative preference shares. By virtue of article 3A(iii) of the company's Articles of Association, the preference shareholders had no right to vote save at a general meeting where the winding up of the company was proposed. In 1962 a special resolution was passed whereby the capital of the company was increased to £60,000 by the creation of 20,000 redeemable cumulative preference shares of £1 each. Article 3A was amended to reflect the increase in the company's capital. Article 3A(ii) referred to the rights of the non-cumulative preference shareholders in relation to payment of dividends or return of capital in a winding up, but contained no reference to the rights of the redeemable cumulative preference shareholders. Article 3A(iii) contained a similar restriction on voting as before. At a meeting held on 12 May 1970 the holders of the redeemable cumulative preference shares claimed that they had a right to vote conferred by their holding of these shares and with these votes a special resolution was passed by the necessary majority. The plaintiff sought a declaration that such shareholders were not entitled to vote at meetings of the company. The defendants claimed that as article 3A(ii) did not refer to the rights of the redeemable preference shareholders, then the restriction on voting in article 3A(iii) referred only to the holders of the 5 per cent non-cumulative preference shareholders.

(2) Section 199 of the Companies Act 1963 provides as follows:

> "If in the case of any company provision is made by the articles or by any agreement entered into between any person and the company for empowering a director of the company to assign his office as such to another person, any assignment of office made in pursuance of the said provision shall, notwithstanding anything to the contrary contained in the said provision, be of no effect unless and until it is approved by a special resolution of the company."

Article 18 of the company's Articles of Association appointed Thomas Fitzpatrick governing director of the company and bestowed upon him the authority to exercise all powers, authorities and discretions expressed to be vested in the directors generally and that all other directors be under his control. Article 18 further provided that Thomas Fitzpatrick was entitled to appoint any person to be governing director in his place, such appointment to be in writing and executed before his resignation. It also provided that Thomas Fitzpatrick could by will or codicil appoint his successor to the office of governing director. Thomas Fitzpatrick died on 4 October 1969 and by a codicil to his will he appointed the plaintiff as his successor. The parties sought a declaration as to the validity of such an appointment when a special resolution approving it had not been passed.

Held by Kenny J in allowing the two declarations sought by the plaintiff:

(1) The language of any Article in a company's Articles of Association which is relied upon to deprive a holder of any class of share in the capital of a company of the right to vote must be unambiguous; Companies Act 1963 section 134(e) considered.

(2) The restriction on voting in Article 3A(iii) referred to both classes of preference shares mentioned in Article 3A(i) and the holders of the redeemable preference shares had no right to vote at meetings of the company, except where the winding up of the company was contemplated.

(3) Section 199 does not prevent the appointment by a director of an alternative or substitute because an article permitting this is contained in Part II of the First Schedule of the Companies Act 1963 which contains the regulations which apply to a private company limited by shares unless they are excluded (Companies Act 1963, section 13(2)).

(4) When deciding the meaning of "assignment of office" it is permissible to look at the reports on the reform of company law to determine the object which the draftsman of the Act had in view: *Eastman Photographic Materials Company Ltd v. The Comptroller-General of Patents* [1898] AC 571 considered.

(5) The section relates to an assignment of the office of director, an office which a person ceases to hold when he dies. A power to appoint another person by will to be a director after the death of the testator is not an assignment of the office of director as the will only becomes effective when the testator has died.

Assignment refers only to a transaction between living persons: Landlord and Tenant Act (Ireland) 1860 section 11 considered.

(6) The appointment of the plaintiff to the office of governing director by codicil did not require a special resolution of the company to make it effective.

Case referred to in judgment

Eastman Photographic Materials Company Ltd v. The Comptroller-General of Patents [1898] AC 571

Counsel's and solicitors' names not available

KENNY J **18 November 1970**

Fitzpatricks Footwear Ltd ("the company") was incorporated in 1943 with a share capital of £20,000 divided into 20,000 shares of £1 each. The Articles of Association provided that the regulations in Table A in the First Schedule to the Companies (Consolidation) Act 1908 applied to the company except insofar as they were excluded or varied. Regulation 60 of Table A, which read: "On a show of hands every member present in person shall have one vote. On a poll every member shall have one vote for each share of which he is the holder" applied to the company. 14,700 ordinary shares have been issued.

At meetings held in November and December 1948 a special resolution was passed by which the nominal capital of the company was increased to £40,000 by the creation of 20,000 6% cumulative preference shares of £1 each and a new Article 3A, was adopted. It read:

> "3A(i) The share capital of the company is £40.000 divided into 20,000 6% cumulative preference shares of £1 each and 20,000 ordinary shares of £1 each.
>
> (ii) The holders of the preference shares shall be entitled to be paid out of the profits which the directors shall determine to distribute by way of dividend a fixed cumulative preferential dividend at the rate of 6 per cent per annum and to a right on a winding up to be paid all arrears of preferential dividend, whether earned or declared or not, down to the commencement of the winding up and also to be repaid the amount of the capital paid up or credited or paid up on the preferential shares held by them respectively, but shall not be entitled to any other rights in the profits or assets of the company.
>
> (iii) The holders of the preference shares shall not be entitled to receive notice of, or to be present, or to vote either in person or by proxy at any general meeting by virtue of or in respect of such shares save a general meeting at which a resolution is, or is to be, proposed to wind up the company."

At meetings held in January and February 1950 the special resolution passed in 1948 was amended so that the 6 per cent cumulative preference shares became 5 per cent non-cumulative preference shares and a new article 3A(ii) was adopted which read:

> "3A(ii) The holders of preference shares shall be entitled to be paid out of the profits of each year which the directors shall determine to distribute by way of dividend a fixed non-cumulative preferential dividend at the rate of 5% per annum and also to be repaid the amount of capital paid up or credited as paid up on the preferential shares held by them respectively, but shall not be entitled to any other rights in the profits or assets of the company."

At meetings held in June and July 1952 the special resolution passed in 1950 was amended so that the 5 per cent non-cumulative preference shares became 5 per cent cumulative preference shares and a new article 3A was adopted. 3A(iii) remained unchanged.

At a meeting held in December 1962 a special resolution was passed by which the capital of the company was increased to £60,000 by the creation of 20,000 redeemable preference shares of £1 each. The special resolution passed in July 1952 was also amended by the deletion of the word "cumulative" wherever it appeared and the substitution of the word "non-cumulative". A new article 3A (i) was adopted so that the entire article now reads:

> "3A(i) The share capital of the company is £60,000, divided into 20,000 5% non-cumulative preference shares of £1 each, 20,000 7% redeemable cumulative preference shares of £1 each and 20,000 ordinary shares of £1 each.
>
> (ii) The holders of preference shares shall be entitled to be paid out of the profits which the directors shall determine to distribute a fixed non-cumulative preferential dividend at the rate of 5% per annum and to a right on winding up to be paid all arrears of preferential dividend whether earned or declared or not down to the commencement of the winding up and also to be repaid the amount of the capital paid up or credited as paid up on the preferential shares held by them respectively but shall not be entitled to any other rights in the profits or assets of the company.
>
> (iii) The holders of the preference shares shall not be entitled to receive notice of or to be present or to vote either in person or by proxy at any general meeting by virtue of or in respect of such shares save a general meeting at which a resolution is or is to be proposed to wind up the company."

At the meeting held in December 1962, £20,000, part of the balance to the credit of the profit and loss account, was capitalised and used to pay for 20,000 7 per cent redeemable cumulative preference shares which were issued.

At a meeting held on 12 May 1970 the holders of the redeemable preference shares claimed that they had a right to vote conferred by their holding of these shares and a special resolution was passed by the necessary majority which their votes created. If they had not any voting rights conferred by these shares, the resolution would not have had the necessary majority to make it effective. The first question in issue in this action is whether the claim of the holders of the redeemable preference shares that they have a right to vote in all circumstances at meetings of the company is correct.

Section 134 of the Companies Act 1963 reads:

> "The following provisions shall have effect in so far as the articles of the company do not make other provision in that behalf . . . (e) in the case of a company originally having a share capital, every member shall have one vote in respect of each share or each £10 of stock held by him, and in any other case, every member shall have a vote."

The language of the article which is relied on to deprive a holder of any class of share in the capital of the company of the right to vote must, therefore, be unambiguous if it is to have this effect.

Counsel for the holders of the redeemable preference shares (the creation of which was first made permissible by the Companies Act 1959) has said that the phrase "the holders of preference shares" in article 3A(ii) means those who are owners of the non-cumulative shares and that it must be given the meaning in article 3A(iii) which, therefore, would not apply to the redeemable preference shares. But article 3A(ii) deals with the 5 per cent non-cumulative preference shares only and is not relevant to any of the rights of the holders of the redeemable preference shares. And the phrase in 3A(iii) is "the holders of the preference shares".

The 7 per cent redeemable preference shares are preference shares although there is no statement of their preferential rights in relation to payment of dividends or return of capital in a winding up. The preference shares of the company are the two classes of preference share mentioned in Article 3A(i); Article 3A(iii) is so worded that it applies to both these classes.

It follows that, in my opinion, the holders of the redeemable preference shares have got a right to vote at all meetings of the company because of their holdings of these shares.

Article 18 reads:

> "Notwithstanding anything in Table A or in any other article hereinbefore or hereinafter contained, the following provisions shall have effect and shall prevail in case they be inconsistent with any clause of Table A or any other Article contained herein:
>
> > (i) The said Thomas Fitzpatrick shall be the governing director of the company until he resigns or dies or becomes disqualified for any of the reasons mentioned in Article 19, and whilst he retains the said

office he shall have authority to exercise all powers, authorities and discretions by these presents expressed to be vested in the directors generally and all the other directors, if any, for the time being of the company shall be under his control and shall be bound to conform to his directions in regard to the company's business.

(vi) If the said Thomas Fitzpatrick resigns the office of governing director, while still entitled under these articles to remain in such office, he may by writing under his hand executed before his resignation, appoint any person to be governing director in his place and direct and determine what shall be the powers, authorities and discretions of such governing director and what shall be his remuneration and qualifications and how long he shall be entitled to hold office, and in default of such direction and determination such appointee shall have all the powers, authorities and discretions as are by these articles granted to the said Thomas Fitzpatrick while he shall remain governing director.

(vii) If the said Thomas Fitzpatrick dies while he holds the office of governing director, he may by his will or any codicil thereto appoint any person to be governing director in his place and direct and determine what shall be the powers, authorities and discretions of such governing director and what shall be his remuneration and qualifications and how long he shall be entitled to hold office, and in default of such direction and determination such appointee shall have all the powers, authorities and discretions as are by these articles granted to the said Thomas Fitzpatrick while he shall remain governing director."

Thomas Fitzpatrick, the governing director referred to in the articles, died on 4 October 1969. By a codicil to his will he appointed Michael Fitzpatrick, the plaintiff, to be the governing director of the company. Probate of the will and codicils has not yet been granted but the parties wish to have a decision on the validity of the appointment when a special resolution approving it has not been passed.

Section 199 of the Companies Act 1963 reads:

"If in the case of any company provision is made by the articles or by any agreement entered into between any person and the company for empowering a director of the company to assign his office as such to another person, any assignment of office made in pursuance of the said provision shall, notwithstanding anything to the contrary contained in the said provision, be of no effect unless and until it is approved by a special resolution of the company."

Whatever be the meaning of the section, it does not prevent the appointment by a director of an alternate or substitute because an article permitting this is in Part II of the First Schedule of the Companies Act 1963 which contains the regulations which apply to a private company limited by shares unless they are excluded (section 13(2) of the Act of 1963). When deciding the meaning of the expression "assignment of office" it is permissible to look at the reports of committees on the reform of company law to see what was the object which the draftsman of the Act had in view (see the speech of Lord Halsbury in *Eastman Photographic Materials Company Ltd v. The Controller-General of Patents* [1898] AC 571). A section similar to section 199 first appeared in section 83 of the British Companies Act 1928 and was re-enacted in section 151 of the Companies Act 1929 and in section 204 of the Companies Act 1948. The British Act of 1928 was passed to give effect to the recommendations of a committee presided over by Mr Wilfred Greene (as he then was). Their report, which was not referred to during the argument, contained these paragraphs:

> "54. Our attention has been directed to cases where the articles provide that the office of director or manager may be assigned at the will of the holder. It may be questioned whether such a provision is lawful, at any rate in the case of directors, but in any case we consider that the practice is a most undesirable one and that any such assignment should be prohibited unless it is sanctioned by the company. When such a provision is in force the company is deprived of all effective control over its directors and managers and the holder of the office is in a position to force upon the company for his own profit any person, whether suitable or not, who is willing to pay a price.
>
> RECOMMENDATION 55. We recommend that where under provisions contained in the articles or in a contract, directors or managers are empowered to assign these offices, any such assignment should be void unless and until it receives the sanction of a special resolution."

It is, I think, a matter of some significance that articles similar to article 18 (vi) and (vii) have continued to appear after 1929 in the standard text books of company precedents: the authors did not consider that these were affected by the sections I have quoted though their inclusion may have been on the assumption that the appointments would be sanctioned by a special resolution.

The section relates to an assignment of the office of director, an office which a person ceases to hold when he dies. Therefore an assignment can be effective only during the period when the person making it is alive. It follows I think, that a power to appoint another person by will to be a director after the death of the testator is not an assignment of the office of director for the appointment becomes effective only when the testator has died as the will is without effect until then. Assignment means, I think, a transaction between living persons: it is an inappropriate word to describe a person succeeding to an office after the death of the holder. There is an analogy with the law of landlord and tenant under which a tenant may assign his tenancy to a living person but a bequest of it is not an assignment: see section 11 of the Landlord and Tenant (Ireland) Act 1860 which provides "every assignee of the estate or interest or any part thereof of any tenant, by lawful assignment, or by devise, bequest, or act and operation of law, made after the passing of this Act, shall be subject to the observance of all agreements in respect of assignment or sub-letting to the same extent as the original tenant might have been."

In my opinion the appointment of the plaintiff to the office of governing director by the codicil of the late Mr Thomas Fitzpatrick does not require a special resolution of the company to make it effective. I do not propose to express any view on the issue whether an appointment under article 18(vi) requires a special resolution to be valid because that interesting question does not arise in this case.

The two declarations sought by the plaintiff will be made. The company have agreed to pay the costs of all the parties to this litigation.

Patricia McLaughlin
Barrister

Spa Estates Ltd (appellants) v. L. Ó hArgáin (respondents): High Court 1974 No.15 (Kenny J) 20 June 1975

Company – Purchase of land for development – Sale – Shares – Whether profits accrued from a trade within the meaning of Income Tax Act – Whether constituted a business of dealing in developing land – Whether an adventure in the nature of a trade – Objects clause – Income Tax Act 1918 (Ch 40) schedule D – Finance Act 1929 (No. 32), section 12 – Finance Act 1942 (No. 14), section 2

Facts: Moy Construction Company Ltd ("Moy") incorporated in 1955, carried on the business of builders. The company did not purchase lands but contracted with the owners of lands for licences to enter and build and for the grant of a lease to the ultimate purchasers of each house when it was completed. In 1964 the company purchased lands in Lucan by way of sublease. The directors of the company agreed that when the company had completed houses on all sites for which they had agreements, it would cease to trade and a new company would be formed to which the lands at Lucan would be conveyed. On 11 May 1965 the lands at Lucan were demised to Spa Estates Ltd ("Spa") for 900 years at a yearly rent of 5d, in consideration of payment of £30,000. Spa was incorporated in the State on 25 May 1965 and among the objects as set out in the memorandum of association, was one for the development of lands. The directors and shareholders were the same as those of Moy. They sought planning permission to build 127 houses and four shops on the lands but thereafter nothing was done by Spa to develop the lands or build on them. However, when differences arose between the directors, they decided to dispose of the lands at Lucan. They decided to reduce their tax liability by carrying out the sale by means of a transfer of their shares in Spa rather than by selling the lands. A scheme was devised to put this into effect and it was decided that when all arrangements were made, Spa would go into liquidation. Spa duly went into liquidation on 28 January 1967. By an agreement made 4 April 1967 Spa agreed to sell the lands at Lucan and by deed of 2 November 1967 the lands were assigned to the new purchasers for £200,000.

The Revenue treated Spa as having ceased to trade on 28 January 1967 and decided that liability for income tax for the financial year which ended 5 April 1967 had to be based on their profits from 6 April 1966 to 28 January 1967. The Revenue assessed Spa in respect of profits from property dealing rather than from the trade of builders. Spa's appeal to the appeal commissioners was dismissed. On appeal to the Circuit Court, the judge held that the lands at Lucan were the trading stock of Spa and bought by it with a view to sale. The learned Circuit Court judge agreed to state a case to the High Court as to whether his decision to hold that the appellants were liable for income tax and corporation profits tax on profits from property dealing was correct.

Held by Kenny J in answering the case stated in the negative:

(1) The purchase of lands and the application for planning permission were acts preparatory to the carrying on of a trade and not evidence that the trade was being carried on. *Birmingham and District Cattle By-Products Ltd v. The Commissioners of Inland Revenue* (1919) 12 TC 92 followed.

(2) The fact that a company has power under its objects clause to carry on a trade does not involve the conclusion that a company is carrying on the trade which it is empowered to carry on; the existence of the power in the objects clause is undoubtedly relevant to the decision but it is not conclusive of the question. *Balgownie Land Trust Ltd v. The Commissioners of Inland Revenue* [1929] SC 790 and *Wilson Box (Foreign Rights) Ltd v. Brice* [1936] 3 All ER 728, 20 TC 736 followed.

(3) Where no development has been done and no houses have been built, the purchase of land for the purpose of building does not involve the consequence that the taxpayer was dealing in land.

(4) Spa never commenced to carry on a trade of developing lands — the lands were acquired to use them as sites for houses which would be sold by Spa as builders and land developers but not as dealers in property and they never commenced any trade.

(5) The test to be applied when considering whether or not a once off venture is or was "in the nature of a trade" is whether the operations involved in it are of the same kind and carried on in the same way as those which are characteristic

of ordinary trading in the line of business in which the venture is made.

(6) The assessment here was on profits made from property dealing and one transaction, a purchase and a sale, was not evidence of dealing. As a trade was never commenced, the rules in relation to discontinuance in the Act of 1942 did not apply.

(7) The assessments insofar as they related to Schedule A and Schedule B liability were confirmed but insofar as they related to liability for income tax under Schedule D and for corporation profits tax were discharged.

Cases referred to in judgment

Balgownie Land Trust Ltd v. The Commissioners of Inland Revenue [1929] SC 790, 14 TC 684

Birmingham and District Cattle By-Products Ltd v. The Commissioners of Inland Revenue [1919] 12 TC 92

Commissioners of Inland Revenue v. Livingston [1927] SC 251, 11 TC 538

Commissioners of Inland Revenue v. Reinhold [1953] SC 49, 34 TC 389

Edwards v. Bairstow [1956] AC 14, 36 TC 207

Guinness v. The Commissioners of Inland Revenue [1923] 2 IR 186, 1 Irish Tax Cases 1

J. & R. O'Kane v. The Commissioners of Inland Revenue [1922] 12 TC 303

McLellan Rawson & Co. v. Newell [1955] 36 TC 117

Spanish Prospecting Company Ltd [1911] 1 Ch. 92

Taylor v. Good [1974] 1 All ER 1137

Wilson Box (Foreign Rights) Ltd v. Brice [1936] 3 All ER 728, 20 TC 736

Counsel's names not available

Solicitors for the appellants: *McCann Fitzgerald*
Solicitors for the respondents: *A.C.P. Ross*

KENNY J **20 June 1975**

Moy Construction Co. Ltd ("Moy") was incorporated in the State on 19 September 1955 with a share capital of £1,000 to carry on the business of builders. The directors and shareholders were Mr Michael Griffin and Mr James Fleming. The company did not purchase lands but contracted with the owners of lands for licence to enter and build and for the grant of a lease to the ultimate purchaser of each house when it was completed. For about ten years after its incorporation Moy took about 20 sites each year in this way, developed them, built on them and sold the houses.

By a contract made on 12 January 1964 between George Shackleton & Sons Ltd ("Shackleton") and Moy it was agreed that Moy would purchase for £30,000 by way of sublease for 900 years at a nominal rent part of the lands known as Petty Canon at Lucan containing 21 acres 3 roods and 15 perches ("the lands at Lucan") held under a fee farm grant but indemnified against any rent. Moy had never purchased lands before this. After the contract was signed Mr Griffin and Mr Fleming agreed that when Moy had completed the houses on all the sites for which they had agreements, it would cease to trade and a new company would be formed to which the lands at Lucan would be conveyed. The purpose of this was to get the tax advantage which in some cases arises from a cessation of trade.

Shackleton had given the Royal Bank of Ireland a charge on the lands at Lucan and so they had to join in any conveyance of them. By an indenture of 11 May 1965 Shackleton with the consent of the bank demised the lands at Lucan to Spa Estates Ltd ("Spa") for 900 years from 11 May 1965 at a yearly rent of 5p in consideration of the payment of £30,000.

Spa was incorporated in the State on 25 May 1965 with a share capital of £5,000. The memorandum of association contained the usual long list of objects. One of these was:

> "(c) To purchase, take on, lease, or in exchange or otherwise acquire, hold, manage, work, develop the resources of, and turn to account any estates, lands and buildings, tenements and other hereditaments, corporeal or incorporeal, whether freehold, fee farm, leasehold or other tenure, and wheresoever situate, and any life or other interest in any such hereditaments and any rights connected therewith."

Another object was:

> "(y) to develop and turn to account any land acquired by the company or in which the company is interested, and in particular by laying out, and preparing the same for building purposes, constructing, altering, putting down, decorating, maintaining, furnishing, fitting up and improving buildings and by plastering, paving, draining, farming, cultivating, letting on building lease or building licence or agreement and by advancing money to and entering into contracts and arrangements of all kinds with builders, tenants and others."

The directors and shareholders of Spa were Mr Michael Griffin and Mr James Fleming who had been the directors and shareholders in Moy.

Spa had not been incorporated on 11 May 1965 when the lands at Lucan were let to them and so by a deed of 11 July 1965 between Shackleton, the Royal Bank of Ireland and Spa, which was expressed to be supplemental to the deed of 11 May 1965, Shackleton and the bank confirmed the deed of 11 May 1965.

The lands at Lucan were suitable for building and Shackleton had obtained planning permission to built about 100 houses on them when they sold them to Spa. The intention of the directors and shareholders of Spa when they acquired the lands at Lucan was to develop them and build houses on them and they made further applications for planning permission. On 21 May 1965 they sought planning permission to build 123 houses and four shops and later amended this to 127 houses and four shops. Nothing was done by Spa to develop the lands or to build on them.

Towards the end of 1965 relations between Mr Griffin and Mr Fleming became strained. They differed as to how Moy was to be run and it was agreed between them that Moy should complete the houses it was building, that Mr Griffin and Mr Fleming were then to trade on their own and that all business connections between them were to be ended. They decided to dispose of the lands at Lucan as it was not practicable to divide them. They did not intend to sell the lands but proposed to carry out the sale by a transfer of their shares in Spa as they had been advised that if they sold the lands, there was a risk of tax liability on any profits they made and this, they thought, could be avoided by a sale of the shares. Negotiations with MacInerneys Ltd, a well known firm of building contractors, for the sale of the lands at Lucan by a transfer of the shares were opened in 1966 and broke down in September or October 1966. When this happened, negotiations between Mr Fleming, Mr Griffin, Mr Owen and Mr Sean McKone for the purchase of the shares began. Mr Sean McKone was one of three brothers who had formed McKone Ltd and Mr Owens was their financial adviser. Spa owed £28,000 to Mr Griffin and Mr Fleming for a loan which they had made to it and which I infer was made for the purpose of enabling the sale of the lands at Lucan to be completed. Mr Owens and Mr McKone knew of the negotiations with MacInerneys and they offered £83,000 for the lands. This was accepted but in order to avoid the risk of liability to tax, Mr Owens evolved a most ingenious scheme for the transfer of the lands. He decided that the capital of Spa should be reorganised so that Mr Kone Brothers would get non-voting shares while Mr Griffin and Mr Fleming would get A shares which were to have the right to vote, that the lands would be revalued at their current market value of £200,000 and that £167,000, the increase in value would be carried to the credit of a general capital reserve which would be capitalised and used for the payment of new shares to be issued, that the debt of £28,000 due by Spa to Mr Fleming and Mr Griffin was to be assigned to Mr Owens and that when these arrangements had been completed, Spa would go into liquidation and the lands would be transferred to John McKone Ltd for £200,000.

The first step in this scheme was that on 1 December 1966 Mr Griffin and Mr Fleming in consideration of £1,000 gave Mr Owens an option to purchase their entire interests in Spa at a price of £83,000. By the option agreement Mr Griffin and Mr Fleming declared that they were the sole shareholders of Spa and that apart from a loan by them to it, it had no other liabilities.

At an extraordinary general meeting of Spa held on 9 January 1967 a special resolution was passed by which the existing share capital of £5,00 ordinary shares of £1 each was divided into 100 "A" ordinary shares of £1 each and 4,900 "B" ordinary shares of £1 each. The "A" ordinary shares were to have one vote for each share, the "B" ordinary shares were not to confer on the holders thereof any right to receive notice of or to be present at any general meeting of the company and the holders of the existing ordinary shares of the company were to receive one "A" ordinary share and 49 "B" ordinary shares in exchange for every 50 ordinary shares then held. It was also resolved that Article 30(a) of the articles of association be deleted and that this article be substituted:

> "All monies realised from the sale or other realisation of any capital assets

of the company in excess of the price at which such assets stand in the books of the company at the time (hereinafter called "the book value") shall (except in the case of partial realisation of an asset when such monies may be used to write down the book value of the remainder of the asset until it is reduced to nil) be carried to the credit of an account called "General Capital Reserve". There shall also be carried to the credit of such reserve any other sums representing accretions to capital including for this purpose sums resulting from the writing up of the book value of any capital assets. Such reserve shall not be available for dividend but may be used for such capital purposes (including capitalisation pursuant to regulation 30(b) of these regulations) as the directors in their discretion think conducive to the interest of the company. Any loss on the sale of other realisation of capital assets may be carried wholly or partially to the debit of such reserve or charged with other funds of the company as the directors may in their discretion determine."

At a directors' meeting of Spa held on 19 January 1967 at which Mr Griffin, Mr Fleming, Mr Owens and Mr Sean Murray were present, Mr Owens and Mr Murray were co-opted to the board of directors, Mr Griffin and Mr Fleming resigned as directors, and transfers of 100 "A" shares by Mr Griffin and Mr Fleming to Mr Owens, Mr Murray and Mrs Owens and of 4,900 "B" shares to Mr Sean McKone, Mr Edward McKone and Mr Nicholas McKone were approved. At this meeting it was also resolved that the lands at Lucan were to be revalued at their current market value of £200,000 and that in accordance with Article 30(a) the increase in book value of £167,000 be carried to the credit of an account called the General Capital Reserve. The directors noted and accepted the assignment to Mr Owens of a debt of the company of £28,000 formerly due to Mr Griffin and Mr Fleming. At an extraordinary general meeting of Spa held at 12 noon on 20 January a special resolution was passed increasing the share capital of the company to £175,000 by the creation of 3,400 "A" ordinary shares of £1 each and 166,600 "B" ordinary shares of £1 each. At an ordinary general meeting of Spa held on 20 January at 12.15 it was resolved that £166,450 of the sum standing to the credit of the account known as the General Capital Reserve of the company be capitalised and be applied on behalf of the shareholders in paying up in full 3,329 "A" ordinary shares of £1 and 163,121 "B" shares of £1 on the basis of the proportion of each shareholder's holding of shares in the company in the respective classes of shares. At a directors' meeting of Spa held on 20 January at 12.30, 3,392 "A" ordinary shares and 163,121 "B" ordinary shares were allotted fully paid to the two classes of shareholders. At this meeting the directors considered a proposal to wind up the company by a members voluntary winding-up and when they had formed the opinion that the company would be able to pay its debts in full within six months from the commencement of the winding-up, they agreed to make the necessary declaration and lodge it with the registrar of companies. At an extraordinary general meeting of Spa on 28 January 1967 it was resolved that the company be voluntarily wound up and Mr Peter Henry Grant was appointed liquidator.

By an agreement made on 4 April 1967 between Spa and Gerard J. Quinn & Co. in trust, Spa agreed to sell the lands at Lucan held under the lease of 11 May 1965 for £200,000 and by a deed of 2 November 1967 Spa and Mr Grant assigned these lands to John McKone Ltd for £200,000 for the residue of the term of years granted by this lease.

The Revenue decided to treat Spa as having ceased to trade on 28 January 1967, the date when the resolution to wind up was passed and so their liability for income tax for the financial year which ended on 5 April 1967 had to be based on their profits for the period from 6 April 1966 to 28 January 1967. A notice of assessment in respect of ownership under Schedule A and occupation under Schedule B (£33 each) and on "profits from property dealing" for £170,000 was made by the Revenue on Spa who were also assessed to corporation profits tax on the basis that the £170,000 was taxable. It is of considerable importance in this case that Spa were not assessed in respect of profits from the trade of builders but on those from property dealing. They appealed to the Appeal Commissioners who dismissed their appeal and they then appealed to the Circuit Court judge. He held that the lands at Lucan were trading stock of Spa and bought by it with a view to sale because houses cannot be sold without selling the lands on which the houses sit [*sic*] and "Spa which was building houses was necessarily trading in land". He gave his evidence on 22 February 1972 and at the request of counsel for the taxpayer stated this case which is dated 21 January 1974 for the opinion of this court.

Rule 1 of Schedule D in the Income Tax Act 1918 provides that tax under the Schedule is to be charged in respect of the annual profits or gains arising or accruing to any person from any trade. It also provides that the tax is to extend to every trade carried on in the State and is to be computed on the full amount of the balance of the profits or gains of the year immediately preceding the year of assessment for which the accounts of the said trade have been usually made up. Section 12 of the Finance Act 1929 provided that where in any year of assessment a trade is permanently discontinued, then the person charged or chargeable with tax is to be charged for that year on the amount of the profits or gains of the period beginning on 6 April in that year and ending on the date of the discontinuance and also makes provision for the adjustment of tax in respect of the year preceding the year of assessment. Section 2 of the Finance Act 1942 inserted a new rule (rule 19) in the rules for Schedule D to deal with the calculation of profits of a trade which had been discontinued. The relevant part of the rule provided that when a trade has been discontinued, the trading stock belonging to the trade at the date of discontinuance is to be valued at the amount which it would have realised if if had been sold in the open market at the discontinuance of the trade. Trading stock is defined as meaning property of any description which is . . . (a) "property such as is sold in the ordinary course of the trade in relation to which the expression is used or would be so sold if it were mature or if its manufacture, preparation or construction were complete".

The Revenue contentions are that Spa was carrying on the trade of dealing in land and that if they were not, the purchase of the lands at Lucan was an adventure in the nature of trade. The taxpayers contend that they never carried on this trade, that nothing was done to develop the lands or to build houses on them and that the purchase of the lands and the making of applications for planning permission were steps of preparation for carrying on this trade. It is an over-simplification to say that Spa were formed to carry on business as builders. The trade which the directors of Spa intended to carry on was that of developing lands, building houses on them and selling the houses.

The purchase of the lands and the applications for planning permission seem to me to have been acts preparatory to the carrying on of a trade and not to be evidence that a trade was being carried on. This view is supported by the decision in *The Birmingham and District Cattle By-Products Ltd v. Commissioners of Inland Revenue* (1919) 12 TC 92. In that case the taxpayers were incorporated on 20 June 1913 and between that date and 6 October 1913 the directors arranged for the erection of works and the purchase of plant and machinery. They also entered into agreements relating to the purchase of products to be used in the business and to the sale of finished products. On 6 October 1913 the installation of plant and machinery had been completed and the company began to receive raw materials for the purpose of manufacture. For the purpose of Excess Profits Duty the date of commencement of trade was important. The Revenue contended that the taxpayer had begun to trade on 6 October 1913 while the taxpayer argued that it began on 20 June 1913. Rowlatt J held that the taxpayers had commenced to trade on the 6 October 1913. In the course of his judgment he said:

> ". . . The directors at the expense of the company . . . went about and looked at places of business of a similar character in various parts of the country. That was an admirable thing to do preparatory to commencing business but it certainly was not commencing business . . . then they entered into a contract for the erection of works which works were duly erected in July 1913. That again is preparatory. The company were occupying themselves with activities within their powers of course; they were living their life; but they had yet begun to conduct their trade or business. Then they purchased machinery and plant for carrying on the business. That was getting ready. I am bound to say that I think the case is extremely clear and the commissioners having taken the view that they had not commenced business till then, and I do not see the slightest sign of any error in law in the commissioners having taken that view. It seems to me it is the only view both in law and in fact, if I may say so, that they could take."

The fact that a company has power under its objects clause in the memorandum to carry on a trade does not involve the conclusion that the company is carrying on the trade which it is empowered to carry on. The existence of the power in the objects clause is undoubtedly relevant to the decision but is not conclusive to this question. In the *Balgownie Land Trust Ltd v. Commissioners of Inland Revenue* (1929) SC 790; 14 TC 684 the Lord President Clyde said:

> "One is not, however, entitled to infer from the circumstances that a company is professedly formed with trading purposes in view and for trading objects that the transactions in which it engages necessarily constitute a trade or business; because it dies not follow from the fact that it has objects and powers such as I have indicated that it actually uses them for the purpose of conducting the usual business of a company trading in real estate. But the professed objects of the company are not, for that reason, to be left out of account; on the contrary they must be kept in view when considering the transactions in which the company is proved to have been engaged."

A similar view was expressed by Greene LJ in *Wilson Box (Foreign Rights) Ltd v. Brice* (1936) 20 TC 736 at pp. 750-51.

Then it was said that Spa acquired the lands with the intention of selling them to the purchasers of houses and that this necessarily involved the conclusion that they were trading in land from the date of the purchase of the lands at Lucan. This view was adopted by the Circuit Court judge who stated as one of his conclusions:

> "Houses cannot be sold without selling the lands on which the houses sit and Spa which was building houses was necessarily trading in land."

It seems to me that the conclusion drawn by the Circuit Court judge does not necessarily follow from the facts which he stated. It is true that houses cannot be sold without selling the lands on which the houses are situate. But when no development has been done and no houses have been built, the purchase of the land for the purpose of building does not involve the consequence that the taxpayer was dealing in land. In my view the only possible conclusion on the facts in this case was that Spa never commenced to carry on the trade of developing lands, building houses on them and selling the houses nor did they commence the business of dealing in land. The purpose of the acquisition of the lands was to use them as sites for houses which would be sold by Spa as builders and land developers but not as dealers in property and they never commenced any trade (see *McLellan Rawson & Co. v. Newell* [1955] 36 TC 117). There is moreover the cogent argument that what would have been sold to a purchaser would have been primarily a house: it is true that he would have been buying the land on which the house was built but he would not have bought the land only. He would have bought the land developed with a house on it.

The next contention was that the purchase of these lands was an adventure in the way of trade. Trade is defined by section 237 of the Act of 1918 as including every trade, manufacture, adventure or concern in the nature of trade.

The fact that the purchase was the only transaction carried out by Spa does not prevent the transaction being an adventure in the nature of trade because an isolated transaction may be an adventure in the nature of trade. The question whether a transaction is an adventure in the nature of trade is, in my opinion, a question of law on the facts found (*Edwards v. Bairstaw* [1956] AC 14; 36 TC 207).

The test for determining whether an isolated transaction is an adventure in the nature of trade was stated in this way by the Lord President Clyde in *Commissioners of Inland Revenue v. Livingston* (1927) SC 251; 11 TC 538):

> "I think the profits of an isolated venture, such as that in which the respondents engaged, may be taxable under Schedule D provided the venture is "in the nature of trade". I say "may be" because in my view regard must be had to the character and circumstances of the particular venture. If the venture was one consisting simply in an isolated purchase of some article against an expected rise in price and a subsequent sale it might be impossible to say that the venture was "in the nature of trade" because the only trade in the nature of which it could participate would be trade of a dealer in such articles and a single transaction falls as far short of constituting a dealer's trade as the appearance of a single swallow does of making a summer. The trade of a dealer necessarily consists of a course of dealing, either actually engaged in or at any rate contemplated and intended to continue. But this principle is difficult to apply to ventures of a more complex character such as that with which the present case is concerned. I think the test, which must be used to determine whether a venture such as we are now considering is, or is not, "in the nature of trade" is whether the operations involved in it are of the same kind and carried on in the same way as these which are characteristic of ordinary trading in the line of business in which the venture was made. If they are, I do not see why the venture should not be regarded as "in the nature of trade" merely because it was a single venture which took only three months to complete."

The assessment in this case is on profits made from property dealing and one transaction, a purchase and a sale, cannot in my opinion be evidence of dealing. The fact that property is purchased with a view to resale does not of itself establish that the transaction is an adventure in the nature of trade (*Commissioners of Inland Revenue v. Reinhold* (1953) SC 49; 24 TC 389; *Taylor v. Good* [1974] 1 All ER 1137). The purchase and sale of land might be an adventure in the nature of trade for a company which had commenced the business of building or for a building company which bought the land with the intention of selling it at a profit. But an isolated purchase of land by a company which had not commenced any trade or business and which did not but the land with the intention of selling it as underdeveloped land is not evidence from which it can be inferred that the purchase was an adventure in the nature of trade.

In my view the purchase and sale of the lands at Lucan undeveloped was not an adventure in the nature of trade. As a trade was never commenced, the rules in relation to discontinuance in the Finance Act 1942 cannot apply.

It follows in my opinion that the conclusion of the Circuit Court judge was incorrect and that the assessments to income tax under Schedule D and to corporation profits tax should be discharged.

There was, however, another argument put forward by the taxpayer with which I think I can deal. This was that as the sale was made in the course of the liquidation, the profit made on it was a realisation of assets in the winding-up and so was not taxable. If the company was not carrying on a trade at the date when the resolution to wind up was passed, then any profits realised by the liquidator on the sale of the assets cannot be taxable but if the company was carrying on a trade at the date of the winding-up, then profits realised at a sale after the winding-up has commenced may be taxable. Section 254 of the Companies Act 1963 provides that in case of a voluntary winding-up, the company shall, from the commencement of the winding-up, cease to carry on its business, except so far as may be required for the beneficial winding-up thereof, so however that the corporate state and corporate powers of the company shall, notwithstanding anything to the contrary in its articles, continue until it is dissolved. Section 276 of the same Act provides that in every voluntary winding-up the liquidator may with the sanction of a special resolution of the company, exercise any of the powers given by paragraphs (d), (e) and (f) of subsection 1 of section 231 to a liquidator in a winding-up by the court and that he may without sanction exercise any of the other powers by the Act given to a liquidator in a winding-up by the court. One of the powers given to a liquidator in a winding-up by the court (section 231) is:

> "(b) to carry on the business of the company so far as may be necessary for the beneficial winding-up thereof."

These show that the liquidator may carry on a business after the resolution for winding-up has been passed and the argument that the company is not trading after a resolution for winding-up has been passed and that everything realised after that is a realisation of assets and not a profit of trade is inconsistent with the provisions of the Companies Act 1963 and with the decisions in the *Spanish Prospecting Co. Ltd* (1911) 1 Ch 92 and the Irish decision (affirmed by the House of Lords) in *J. & R. O'Kane v. Commissioners of Inland Revenue* (1922) 12 TC 303.

The taxpayers also relied on the decision in *Guinness v. Commissioners of Inland Revenue* [1923] 2 IR 186; 1 Irish Tax Cas 1. In that case the taxpayers, the well-known brewery company, owned large stocks of barley as raw material for the purpose of manufacturing stout but did not normally sell or trade in barley. Orders were made under the Defence of the Realm Regulations by which the stocks were requisitioned at prices subsequently fixed and the taxpayers were directed not to use the barley but to retain it in good condition. Later they were directed from time to time to sell some of the barley to millions at a price equivalent to that at which it had been requisitioned together with an additional amount and 1 per cent for commission. The taxpayers made a substantial profit on the transaction and were assessed to tax on it. The High Court held that they were liable to tax on the profit but a majority of the Court of Appeal held that they were not. It may be that the decision of the majority can be justified on the ground that Guinness were not carrying on at any time the trade of dealing in barley but this was not the basis on which the majority decided the case and I think that the reasons given by the two members of the majority were incorrect. O'Connor MR said that the barley taken over was a capital asset. This is plainly wrong. Ronan LJ said that the effect of the requisition orders was that the taxpayers became warehouse men only and never sold the barley. But if Guinness did not sell the barley to the millers, they sold it to the Commission on Wheat Supplies and the profit on this transaction was taxable. There was, however, no discussion as to the extent to which I am bound by a decision of the former Courts of Appeal in Ireland and so I do not express any opinion on the question whether I should follow the decision in the *Guinness* case.

The answer to the case stated will be that the decision of the Circuit Court judge insofar as he held that the appellants were liable for income tax and corporation profits tax on profits from property dealing was incorrect. I cannot refer the case back to him because he has retired from office. The assessments insofar as they relate to Schedule A and Schedule B liability will be confirmed but insofar as they relate to liability for income tax under Schedule D and for corporation profits tax will be discharged.

Agatha Clancy
Barrister

In the Matter of the Companies Act 1963: Murphy Brothers (Dublin) Ltd v. Stephen Morris, James Malone, and General Woodworking Company Ltd: High Court 1974 No. 362 Sp (Kenny J) 6 October 1975

Company – Debenture – Contract – Whether contract created a trust – Written subcontracts – Whether subcontracts fraudulent – Whether clauses of subcontracts an attempt to create a preference – Whether they constituted an attempt to evade the provisions of the Companies Act 1963 – Whether such clauses were invalid as the debenture prevented the company from creating a mortgage or charge ranking in priority – Whether words used sufficient to create a trust – Nature of a floating charge – No equitable assignment until a receiver is appointed – Whether the bank received monies in good faith – Whether tracing order should be made – Companies Act 1963 (No. 33)

Facts: The company entered into a contract with the ESB ("the employer") for the erection of a large office block. The architects involved in the project were given the power to nominate subcontractors, many of whom, including the third respondent, entered into a standard form subcontract which was stated to be supplemental to the main agreement. The company was paid by the employer on foot of a certificate of payment from the architects which included sums certified as due and owing to nominated subcontractors which sums were to be paid by the company to the subcontractor less any monies retained by the employer pursuant to the main agreement. Clause 11(1)(d) of the subcontract provided that any monies received by the company from the employer in respect of work done or materials used by the subcontractor would be deemed to be held on trust by the company for the subcontractor to be applied in or towards payment of the subcontractor's account. Clause 11(2)(k) stated that insofar as monies retained by the employer pursuant to the main agreement included sums due to the subcontractor, then the company's interest in such sums would be as trustee for the subcontractor. On 25 October 1975 a receiver was appointed to the company pursuant to a debenture issued to Allied Irish Banks on 19 November 1973. This debenture provided that the company would on demand pay to the bank all sums which were due and owing on the balance of the company's account and by it the company charged all its undertaking, property and assets, both present and future. The debenture created a fixed charge over the freehold and leasehold property of the company, the fixed plant and machinery and fixtures thereon and its uncalled capital and goodwill. It further created a floating charge over all other property and assets of the company, both present and future. The debenture prohibited the company from creating any mortgage, debenture or charge over, or permitting any lien to arise on or to affect any of the property charged which ranked in priority to or in *pari passu* with the debenture.

On 14 October 1974 the architect certified that £9,300 was due to the company under the main contract which included a sum of £5,107.17 due to subcontractors, £1,627.25 of which being monies due to the third respondent. On 23 October the employer paid £9,300 to the company and this sum was paid into the company's no. 3 account on 25 October. A further £108.06 had been lodged on the previous day and this balance of £9,408.06 was lodged to the receiver's account on 25 October. On the 17 October 1974 a further certificate was issued showing that the company was due £9,9179.80, £314.50 of which was due to the third respondent.

The company, acting by the receiver, and the general creditors, who did not have a written contract with the company submitted that clause 11 sub-clause 1(d) and 2(k) of the written subcontract did not create a trust in favour of the subcontractors. They argued that these clauses were merely an attempt to secure preference, that they were not effective to create a trust because they were an attempt to evade the Companies Act 1963, that they were unfair to the creditors and that they were not worded in such a way as to create a trust. It was also argued that the trusts created by the sub-clauses were invalid as the debenture in favour of the bank prohibited the company from creating any mortgage or charge ranking in priority to the debenture. It was further submitted that the sums received by the company or certificates from the architect were charged with the sums due on the debentures and that as the debentures were prior in time to the subcontracts, the claim of the debenture holder was first in time and prevailed over the trusts created by the subcontract.

Held by Kenny J that:

(1) The fact that a contract is executed when a company is carrying on business with the intent of securing a preference for one creditor does not render the transaction invalid. The law allows a creditor dealing with a company or individual, who is not contemplating bankruptcy or insolvency to enter into documents which secure preferences subject to sections 286, 287, 288 and 289 of the Companies Act 1963 and section 53 of the Bankruptcy (Ireland) Amendment Act 1872. The subcontracts were not fraudulent.

(2) The clauses undoubtedly worked hardship on the other creditors but this is not a ground on which any court should hold that they are not effective.

(3) The words used in clause 11(1)(b) and (2)(k) were sufficient to create a trust. *Re Kayford Ltd* [1975] 1 All ER 604 and *Re Tont and Finch Ltd* [1954] 1 All ER 12 applied.

(4) The clauses were not ineffective in creating a trust on grounds of public policy.

(5) The trusts were not invalid by reason of the fact that the debenture prohibited the company from creating a mortgage or trust which ranked in priority to the debentures, as a trust, a declaration of trust and an equitable assignment are not mortgages or charges. *Ashby Warner and Co. Ltd v. Simmons* [1936] 2 All ER 697 applied.

(6) The receiver was bound to pay to the subcontractors named in the certificates of 14 October 1974 and 17 October 1974 the amounts certified as due to them which have come into his hands as receiver. These sums were not charged by the debenture as the floating charge did not prevent the company from trading or from assigning its moveable property as there is no equitable assignment of the assets of the company to the debenture holder until a receiver is appointed and the charge crystallises. *Rother Iron Works Ltd v. Canterbury Precision Engines Ltd* [1973] 1 All ER 394 and *Murphy v. the Revenue Commissioners* (unreported Kenny J, 7 February 1974) applied.

(7) However, no valid claim could be made by the subcontractors in respect of any sums certified before 14 October 1974 and not paid as, although such non-payment was a breach of trust, the bank received the cheques payable to the company in good faith and without notice of the trusts which had been created.

(8) No question of a tracing order could arise in connection with sums paid before 14 October because there were no assets of the company which could be identified into which the monies paid had gone and were still in existence. A tracing order could be made only when there are assets available to satisfy the sums misapplied.

(9) The receiver was bound to pay all sums received as retention monies on the subcontracts on receipt of such retention monies from the employer.

Cases referred to in judgment

Ashby Warner and Co. Ltd v. Simmons [1936] 2 All ER 697
Re Kayford Ltd [1975] 1 All ER 604
Murphy v. The Revenue Commissioners, unreported, High Court, Kenny J, 7 February 1974
Rother Iron Works Ltd v. Canterbury Precision Engines Ltd [1973] 1 All ER 394
Re Tont and Finch Ltd [1954] 1 All ER 12

Counsel's and solicitors' names not available

KENNY J **6 October 1975**

Murphy Brothers (Dublin) Ltd ("the company") were a company incorporated in the State which carried out very large building contracts. When a receiver was appointed over their business on 25 October 1974, they were working on about seven large contracts and they had overdrawn their bank account with Allied Irish Banks by £376,010.23. On 18 April 1969 they had given a debenture to the Munster and Leinster Bank (whose assets and liabilities were subsequently transferred to Allied Irish Banks) by which they agreed to pay £75,000 on demand and they charged their assets and specifically charged their goodwill and real and leasehold property with such payment. The debenture was issued subject to and with the benefit of the conditions endorsed thereon which were to be deemed part of it and clause 1 of them read:

> "This debenture is to rank as a first charge on all the assets of the company whatsoever and wheresoever and is to be as regards the real and/or leasehold property now belonging to the company and on its goodwill a specific charge and as regards all other the property and assets of the company present and future a floating security but the company shall not have power to create any mortgage or charge ranking in priority to or *pari passu* with this debenture".

On 13 March 1973 the company entered into a building contract with the Electricity Supply Board (the "employer") for the erection of a large office block at Leopardstown Road, Co. Dublin for the employer. The form of contract used was the 1966 edition of that issued by the Royal Institute of the Architects of Ireland in agreement with the Federation of Builders, Contractors and Allied Employers of Ireland and the Royal Institution of Chartered Surveyors. The terms of this contract are of considerable importance and the relevant ones must be fully set out because cases in relation to building contracts depend largely on the exact words used. The form used was that applicable where quantities form part of the contract. It was recited that the employer wished to build an office block (therein called "the works") at Leopardstown Road, that they had caused drawings and bills of quantities describing the work to be done to be prepared by an architect, that the drawings and bills of quantities had been signed by the parties and that the company had an estimate of the sum which they would require for carrying out the said work shown on a tender dated 14 July 1972. Clause 1 provided:

> "1. For the consideration hereinafter mentioned the contractor (this is a reference to the company) will upon and subject to the conditions annexed hereto execute and complete the works shown upon the said drawings and/or described in the said bills of quantities and conditions all of which together with the agreement are hereinafter referred to as 'the Contract Documents'."

Clause 2 provided:

> "2. The employer will pay the contractor the sum of £349,990 (hereinafter referred to as 'the Contract Sum') or such other sum as shall become payable by virtue of the conditions at the time and in the manner specified in the said conditions".

Clause 14 provided:

> "14. The contractor shall not, without the written consent of the architect, assign this contract or sublet any portion of the works."

Clause 15 provided:

> "15 Where provision is made in the Contract Documents for work to be executed on site and/or materials or goods to be supplied and fixed by a firm to be selected by the architect such firm is hereby declared to be a Nominated Subcontractor employed by the contractor.
> (b) The sums directed by the architect to be paid to Nominated Subcontractors for work, materials or goods comprised in the subcontracts shall be paid by the contractor within 7 days of receipt of payment on the Architects Certificate for the value of such work, materials or goods less only any retention money and cash discount which the contractor may be entitled to deduct.
> (c) Before any certificate is issued to the contractor he shall, if requested by the architect, furnish to him reasonable proof that all Nominated Subcontractors accounts included in previous certificates have been duly discharged, in default whereof the employer may pay such accounts upon a certificate of the architect and deduct the amount so paid from any sums due or to become due to the contractor.
> (d) If the architect desires to secure final payment to any Nominated Subcontractor before final payment is due to the contractor, and if such Nominated Subcontractor has satisfactorily indemnified the contractor against any latent defects, then the architects may in a certificate under

clause 29 of these conditions include an amount to cover the said final payment, and the contractor shall forthwith upon receipt of payment on such certificate pay to such Nominated Subcontractor the full amount so certified less the cash discount and the 'limit of retention fund' named in the appendix hereto shall be reduced in proportion to the amount so certified and the contractor shall be discharged from all liability for the work or materials covered by such certificate except for any latent defects. (e) Neither the existence nor the exercise of the foregoing powers nor anything else contained in these conditions shall render the employer in any way liable to any Nominated Subcontractor.

Clause 16 provided:

"16. Where provision is made in the Contract Documents for materials or goods for the works to be supplied by a firm to be selected by the architects such firm is hereby declared to be a nominated supplier."

Clause 17 provided:

"17. Sums, items or quantities marked provisional included in the bills of quantities shall be at the entire disposal of the architect and shall be expended in whole or part as he may direct. If the architect's instructions under this clause involve the employment of Nominated Subcontractors or Nominated Suppliers, then the amounts expended shall be treated as if they were Prime Costs sums (clause 18). If compliance with the architect's instructions under this clause involve work by the contractor it shall be valued in accordance with clause 12 of these conditions. . . ."

Clause 18 provided:

"18. Sums or rates included in the bills of quantities marked Prime Costs or P.C. shall be the nett amounts to be paid by the contractor to the Nominated Suppliers or Nominated Subcontractor after deducting any commissions, trade or other discount except a discount for prompt payment of 5 per cent on Nominated Suppliers and on Nominated Subcontractors. The sums quoted in the Contract Documents shall be deemed to include these percentages for prompt payment discounts. Such sums shall be used at the sole discretion of the architect and shall be expended in whole or in part as the architect may direct. The contract sum shall be adjusted as necessary to include only the amounts properly so expended by the contractor."

Clause 26 provided:

"26. When in the opinion of the architect, the works are 'practically completed' he shall forthwith issue a certificate to that effect and 'practical completion' of the works shall be deemed for all purposes of this contract to have taken place on the day named in such certificate."

Clause 29 provided:

"29(a) At the period of interim certificates named in the appendix and (it was 4 weeks) the contractor shall (subject to clause 15(c) of these conditions on production of a detailed progress statement be entitled to receive within 14 days a certificate from the architect of the amount due to him from the employer which certificates shall include any amounts allowed in respect of subcontracts, and the architect on request shall specify and show separately the amount (if any) allowed in respect of each Nominated Subcontractor and after issue of such certificate the contractor shall be entitled to payment thereon by the employer upon presentation within the period for honouring certificates named in the appendix (the period for honouring certificates named in the appendix was 14 days).
(b) The amount stated as due in an interim certificate shall be the total value of the work duly executed and of the materials and goods specially prepared for the works delivered upon the site for use therein up to and including a date not more than 7 days prior to the date upon which the contractor shall have applied for the said certificate less an amount to be retained by the employer (as hereinafter provided) and less any instalments previously certified under this clause. Provided that such certificate shall include only the value of the said materials and goods as and from such time as they are, in the opinion of the architect, reasonably properly and not prematurely brought upon the site and then only if adequately stored and/or protected against weather or other casualties. Where in any certificate (of which the contractor has received payment) the architect has included the value of any unfixed materials or goods intended for and placed on or adjacent to the works such materials or goods shall become the property of the employer and they shall not be removed except for use upon the works without the authority of the architect in writing, but the contractor shall remain responsible for loss or damage to them.
(c) The amount to be retained by the employer shall be such percentage of the value of the work and materials aforesaid as is named in the appendix as 'percentage of certified value retained' (the percentage of certified value retained specified in the appendix was 10 per cent.) The total amount to be retained shall not exceed the sum named in the appendix as 'limit of retention fund' (the limit of retention fund specified in the appendix was 10 per cent).

After the total amount retained has reached the sum named in the appendix as limit of retention fund the full value of work and materials as aforesaid shall be certified by the architect.
(d) The amounts retained by virtue of sub-clause (c) of this clause shall

be dealt with in the following manner:

(i) As and when such amounts are so retained they shall be held upon trust by the employer for the contractor subject to the right of the employer to have recourse thereto from time to time where payment of any amount which he is entitled under the provisions of this contract to deduct from any sum due or to become due to the contractor.
(ii) On the issue of the certificate of practical completion the architect shall include in the certificate one moiety of the total amounts then so retained and the contractor shall be entitled to payment within the period for honouring certificates named in the appendix to these conditions.
(iii) The residue of the amounts then so retained shall be included in the final certificate as described in sub-clause (f) of this clause.

(e) (i) Either before or within a reasonable time after practical completion of the works the contractor shall send to the architect all documents necessary for the purpose of the computations required by these conditions including all documents relating to the accounts of Nominated Subcontractors and Nominated Suppliers.

(ii) On compliance by the contractor with sub-clause (e)(i) the measurement and valuation of the works shall be completed within the period of final measurements stated in the appendix to these conditions (the period of final measurement stated in the appendix was 12 months), and the contractor shall be supplied with a copy of the priced bills of valuation not later than the end of the said period and before the issue of the final certificate under sub-clause (f) of this condition. If the contractor fails to comply with sub-clause (e)(i) the architect shall extend the period of final measurement by a reasonable time.

(f) So soon as is practicable but before the expiration of 14 days from the end of the defects liability period stated in the appendix to these conditions (the period was 12 months) or from completion of making good defects under clause 26 of these conditions or from period of final measurement referred to in paragraph (ii) of sub-clause (e) of this clause, whichever is the latest, the architect shall give notice to the contractor of his intention to issue the final certificate and unless the architect receives notice of arbitration within 14 days or such other period as may be stated in the appendix from the employer or contractor he shall issue the final certificate."

On 21 November 1973 the architects wrote to the company in these terms:

"Re: E.S.B. District Office, Dublin South, Leopardstown Road.

Dear Sir,

Will you please accept General Woodworkers Co. Ltd (the third named respondents) tender for the supply and fixing of built-in furniture for the above for the sum of £15,326.32 (including builder's discount of £766.32) plus V.A.T. of £2,988.63. We enclose one set of drawings and details for your information."

Many subcontractors were nominated by the architect for the work at Leopardstown Road. Most of these entered into the form of subcontract issued under the sanction of and approved by the Construction Industry Federation and the Subcontractors and Specialists Association (2nd edition), which was printed in 1971, with the company. This form of subcontract is known in the trade as a pink form subcontract. The company also entered into subcontracts with a number of firms who were not nominated subcontractors and the architect was fully aware that the company had entered into these and did not dissent. The pink form subcontract was used in some but not all of these cases. As the terms of this standard form of subcontract have given rise to the question debated in this summons, it is essential that some of them should be set out. I propose to take as an example the subcontract which was made on 12 March 1974 between the company and the third named respondents. The subcontract is stated to be supplemental to the agreement of 31 January 1973 (this is an error and should read "13 March 1973") between the employer and the company (called "the contractor" in the subcontract) and this agreement of 13 March 1973 is referred to as "the main contract", an expression I propose to use throughout the rest of this judgment. There is a recital that the subcontractor (the third named respondents) are entitled to assume that the agreement and schedule of conditions of building contract into which the contractor has entered is the latest edition of that document issued under the sanction of the Royal Institute of the Architects of Ireland in agreement with the Federation of Builders, Contractors and Allied Employers of Ireland.

Clause 1 of the subcontract provides:

"1. The subcontractor shall be deemed to have notice of all the provisions of the main contract except the detailed prices of the contractor included in schedules and bills of quantities."

Clause 11 of the subcontract provides:

"11(1)(a) The contractor shall, subject to and in accordance with the main contract, from time to time and in any event, unless otherwise agreed, not later than 30 days after receipt of the subcontractors detailed progress statements make application (of which prior thereto the contractor shall give to the subcontractor at least 7 days notice unless otherwise agreed between the contractor and the subcontractor) to the architect for certificates of payments and for inclusion therein of the amount which at the date thereof fairly represents the value of the subcontract works and any variation authorised under this subcontract then executed and of the materials and goods delivered upon the site for use in the subcontract works provided that the application shall include only the value of the said materials and goods as and from such time as they are reasonably properly and not prematurely brought upon the site and then only if adequately stored and/or protected against weather and casualties. The contractor shall also embody in or annex to the said application any representations of the subcontractor in regard to such value.

(b) 14 days after the receipt by the contractor of any certificate from the architect/engineer the amounts certified therein to be due in respect of the subcontract works shall be due by the contractor to the subcontractor and the contractor shall within said time notify in writing to the subcontractor the amount certified in the said certificate to be due to him and any authorised variations thereof less retention money which shall mean in this contract the proportion attributable to the subcontract works of the money retained by the employer in accordance with the main contract and less a cash discount of 5 per cent (if payment is made within 7 days after the contractor himself is paid and if provision is made in the main contract for the allowance of such discount to the contractor) provided always that the subcontractor shall not take steps to enforce payment of such sum until the expiration of such period of 7 days after the contractor has received payment of such certificate unless . . .

(d) Payments made to the contractor in respect of work done and materials used by the contractor shall until received by the subcontractor be deemed to be money or moneys worth held in trust by the contractor for the subcontractor to be applied in or towards payment of the subcontractor's account subject always to the right of adjustment by the architect/engineer in the event of his certifying that adjustment is necessary.

(e)(1) If the contractor does not pay to the contractor the amount certified by any certificate issued by the architect/engineer to be due to the contractor within the period mentioned in sub-clause (b) hereof, then the subcontractor (i) may, but without prejudice to any other right or remedy, apply directly to the employer for and the employer may make payment of the amount certified to be due to the subcontractor direct to the subcontractor and the employer may set off the amount of any payment or payments made by him to the subcontractor against any moneys due or to become due to the contractor. Payment by the employer to the subcontractor direct shall be regarded as payment by the contractor to the subcontractor and shall annul the right of suspension under sub paragraph (ii) of this paragraph (1) or . . .

(h) If before the issue of a final certificate to the contractor under the main contract a period of time equal to the retention period of the main contract

has elapsed since practical completion of the subcontract works the subject of this agreement then the subcontractor may request the contractor in writing to make application to the architect/engineer for a certificate certifying the value of the work executed upon the subcontractor works, and the contractor shall make such application. The provisions of this clause shall apply to such certificates as if they were certificates of payment expressly provided for in the main contract.
(k) If and to the extent that the amount retained by the employer in accordance with the main contract includes any retention money the contractor's interest in such money shall be fiduciary as trustee for the subcontractor and if the contractor attempts or purports to mortgage or otherwise charge such interest or his interest in the whole of the amount retained as aforesaid such mortgage or charge shall in so far as it relates to the retention money be void."

Clause 21 (so far as material) provided:

"21 If for any reason the employment of the contractor under the main contract is determined (whether by the contractor or by the employer) and whether by reason of
(c) a receiver being appointed over the business or undertaking of the contractor then the employment of the subcontractor under this subcontract shall automatically determine and the subcontractor shall be entitled to be paid by the employer directly such sums as he would have been entitled to be paid by the contractor under clause 11 sub-clause (f) hereof had his employment under this subcontract been determined under clause (e) hereof."

On 19 November 1973 the company gave a further debenture to Allied Irish Banks Ltd (the bank). There was no limit of amount on this debenture. It provided that the company would on demand pay to the bank all sums which were then or should from time to time thereafter become owing to the bank by the company on the balance of the company's account and the company charged with the payments aforesaid to the intent that the same should be a continuing security all its undertaking and all its property and assets whatsoever, both present and future, including (without prejudice to the generality of the foregoing charge), its uncalled capital and goodwill and the hereditaments and premises described in the schedule. It was provided that the debenture was issued subject to and with the benefit of the conditions endorsed thereon which were to be deemed part of it. Clause 1 of these conditions provided:

"1 This debenture is to rank as a first charge on all the property and assets of the company within mentioned and such shall

(i) as regards the company's existing freehold and leasehold property (including the property described in the schedule hereto) the fixed plant, machinery and fixtures thereon, its uncalled capital and goodwill be fixed or specific, and

(ii) as regards all other property and assets of the company both present and future be a floating charge.

Provided however that the company shall not during the subsistence of this security be at liberty to create any mortgage, debenture or charge-over, or permit any lien to arise on or to affect any of the property herein charged ranking in priority to or *pari passu* with this debenture."

On 25 October 1974 the bank acting under the powers conferred by the debenture of 19 November 1973 and of every other power which enabled it to do so appointed Mr Noel L. Fox to be receiver and manager of the property and assets of the company charged by the debenture of 19 November 1973.

On the 14 October 1974 the architect issued a certificate to the company that £9,300.99 was due to the company under the main contract. This certificate shows that £381,922.39 had already been certified and when the certificate of 14 October 1974 is taken into account, a sum of £391,223.38 had been certified. The certificate of 14 October 1974 also certified the amounts which were included in it for subcontractors. These amounted to £5107.17 and the sum certified as due to General Woodworking Co Ltd (the third named respondents) was £1627.25. On 22 October the solicitor acting for the third named respondents wrote to the architect enclosing a letter of 22 October from the company consenting to direct payment by the employer to the company of £1,627.25 and this was delivered by hand on 22 October to the architects. This was communicated to the employers on 23 October but despite this, the employers paid the company £9,300 on 23 October. It is however possible that the cheque for £9,300 was issued on 22 October before the third named respondents had delivered their letter to the architect. On 17 October a further certificate for £9,179.80 was issued showing that that sum was due to the company. There was also a list of the subcontractors to whom monies were certified to be due and these included the third named respondents to whom £314.50 was shown as due.

The history of the company's bank accounts is of importance in determining the questions which the receiver has now posed for the court. The company had four bank accounts. The No. 1 account was opened on 31 December 1973 and closed on 25 October 1974 when there was an overdraft of £376,010.23. The No. 2 account was opened on the same date and the last transaction on it was on 4 October 1974. On that date it was overdrawn by £3,567.25. The No. 3 account was opened on 24 October 1974 and on 25 October a cheque from the employer for £9,300 was lodged to it. Another sum of £108.06 was lodged on 24 October so that on 25 October the account was £9,408.06 in credit. This sum of £9,408.06 was transferred to the receiver's account. There was also a wages account which was opened on 25 October. The directors of the company had drawn a cheque for £4,900 in payment of wages and this was honoured by the bank with, I assume, the consent of the receiver and was subsequently debited to the receiver's account. The bank could have exercised their right of set off in respect of the credit of £9,408.06 and refused to pay any sum but they paid the £9,408.06 to the receiver who was, under the debenture, the company's agent.

The company acting by the receiver and the general creditors who did not have a written contract with the company have contended that clause 11 sub-clause 1(d) and 2(k) of the written subcontract did not create a trust in favour of the subcontractor. The first argument was these clauses were, to use counsel's words "merely an attempt to secure preference". They were undoubtedly intended to safeguard the position of the subcontractors and to that extent were intended to do this but this does not make them invalid. The fact that a contract is executed when a company is carrying on business with the intent of securing preference for one creditor does not render the transaction invalid. Pressed to its logical conclusion this argument would mean that the debenture given to the bank was invalid for it certainly was an attempt to secure preference in the event of the appointment of a receiver. The subcontracts were executed some time before the receiver was appointed and were not intended to give a fraudulent preference. The law allows a creditor dealing with a company or individual who is not contemplating bankruptcy or insolvency to enter into documents which secure preference subject to subsections 286, 287 288 and 289 of the Companies Act 1963 and section 53 of the Bankruptcy (Ireland) Amendment Act 1872 as amended by the 11th Schedule to the Companies Act 1963. The subcontracts were not fraudulent and, if I might anticipate a subsequent part of this judgment, were not charges. I reject the argument that the clauses 11(1) (d) and 2(k) were not effective to create a trust because they were an attempt to secure a preference. The next argument was that the clauses were not effective to create a trust because they were an attempt to evade the Companies Act. Counsel did not state which sections of the Companies Act 1963 were evaded by the subcontract but relied on the "general policy" of that Act. In my opinion the clauses were not an attempt to evade any provision of the Companies Act. Then it was argued that the sub-clauses were unfair to the other creditors. The courts administer justice according to law and not according to what any judge may think is unfair. The clauses undoubtedly work hardship on the other creditors but this is not a ground on which any court should hold that they are not effective.

The next contention was that the sub-clauses were so worded that they did not create a trust. I cannot think of any words which are more appropriate to create a trust than those in clause 11(1)(d) and (2)(k). In both the word trust is used, in both the subject matter of the trust is clear and the beneficiary is, by reference to the parties to the contract, named. The monies affected by the trust are stated with clarity and the sub-clauses were effective to create a trust. In this connection the decision of Mr Justice Megarry in *Re Kayford Ltd* [1957] 1 All ER 604 is of considerable interest and supports the conclusion I have reached. See also *Re Tont and Finch Ltd* [1954] 1 All ER 12 where it was decided that words similar to those in this case created a trust.

The next contention was that the trusts created by the sub-clauses were invalid because conditions elsewhere in the debentures prohibited the company from creating a mortgage or charge ranking in priority to the debentures. This argument is based on the fallacy that a trust, and a declaration of trust and an assignment are all equivalent to a charge. A trust, a declaration of trust and equitable assignment are not mortgages or charges. The contention that an assignment by a company which has given a debenture creates a charge was advanced to the Court of Appeal in England in *Ashby Warner & Co. Ltd v. Simmons* [1936] 2 All ER 697 and was decisively rejected by that court who did not find it necessary to call on counsel for the clients who were claiming under such an assignment.

The next argument was that sums received by the company and/or certificates from the architect were charged with the sums then due on the debentures and that as the debentures were prior in point of time to the subcontracts, the claim of the debenture holders was first in time and so prevailed over the trusts created by the subcontract. This argument is based on a misconception of the nature of a floating charge created by a debenture. Such a charge floats over the assets of the company but does not prohibit the company from trading or from assigning any of its moveable property until a receiver is appointed. When a receiver is appointed the charge held by the debenture holder crystallises and one of the effects of the appointment is that there is, on the date when the charge crystallises an equitable assignment of all the assets of the company to the debenture holder. There is however no assignment until he was appointed (see the decision of the Court of Appeal in England in *Rother Iron Works Ltd v. Canterbury Precision Engines Ltd* [1973] 1 All ER 394 and that in *Murphy v. the Revenue Commissioners* (unreported) in which I gave judgment on 7 February 1974). Until a receiver is appointed, the charge floats and does not attach to any of the assets. All the relevant subcontracts were entered into before the receiver was appointed and the claims under them which arise in connection with the certificates of 14 and 17 October 1974 and all subsequent certificates prevail over the claim of the bank. No valid claim can however be made by subcontractors in respect of any sums certified to be due to them before 14 October 1974 and not paid. The failure of the company to pay the amounts certified as due to the subcontractors before 14 October 1974 was a breach of trust but the bank received the cheques payable to the company in good faith and without notice of the trusts which had been created. This however does not apply to the amounts certified for retention on the subcontractors' contracts because these have not yet been paid. If any of the retention monies shown as due to the subcontractors were paid before 14 October 1974 to the company, no valid claim in connection with such retention monies arises. No question of a tracing order can arise in connection with sums paid before 14 October because there are no assets of the company which can be identified into which the monies paid before 14 October went and which are still in existence. A tracing order can be made only when there are assets available to satisfy the sums misapplied.

The sum certified by the certificate of 14 October 1974 was lodged to the number 3 account and this was transferred to the receiver who is the company's agent. The receiver cannot have a better claim to these monies than the company had and he is in my opinion bound to pay the amounts shown as due to the subcontractors in the certificate of 14 October and that of 17 October. His obligation is to pay these sums to the subcontractors now in the cases in which the subcontractors whether nominated or not had subcontracts similar to that of 12 March 1974 called pink form subcontracts.

Clause 11(2)(k) created a valid trust in respect of all retention monies certified as being due to the subcontracts by an architect in any certificate given after the subcontracts were entered into and when these sums are received by the receiver, he is bound to pay them to the subcontractors immediately. The subcontractors have no claim against the employers for payment because the power given to the employers to make payments to the subcontractors does not create an obligation on them to do so but merely gives them authority to do so. It uses the word "may" and not the word "shall".

The answers to the questions in the summons will be:

(a) Monies paid to the company by the Electricity Supply Board (the employer) prior to 25 October 1974 under architect's certificates were received by the company in trust to pay so much thereof as was certified to be due to subcontractors to such subcontractors who had entered into the written contract issued under the sanction of and approved by the Construction Industry Federation and the Subcontractors and Specialists Association 2nd edition.

(b) The receiver is not bound to pay to any subcontractor the amounts certified in certificates issued prior to the 14 October 1974. The receiver is bound to pay to the subcontractors named in the certificates of 14 October and 17 October 1974 the amounts certified as due to them out of any assets (other than the property specifically charged by the debenture) which have come into his hands as such receiver since his appointment. This includes the total amount of £9,409.03 which he received.

(c) All sums received by the receiver as retention monies on subcontracts in the form approved by the Construction Industry Federation and the Subcontractors and Specialists Association are held by him in trust for such subcontractors and he will be bound to pay these to such contractors forthwith on receipt of such retention monies from the employers.

There will be an order directing that the first named respondent be appointed to represent the class of creditors of the company who are subcontractors to the said company under the Construction Industry Federation standard form of subcontract but who were not nominated as subcontractors, that the second named respondent be appointed to represent the unsecured creditors of the company other than such subcontractors and that the third named respondent be appointed to represent the class of creditors of the said company who are nominated subcontractors to the company under the Construction Industry Federation standard form of agreement.

Section 316 of the Companies Act 1963 authorises a receiver of the property of a company appointed under a debenture to apply to this court for directions

In this application the company is named as the applicant. This is an error as the company cannot apply under section 316. The title of the proceedings will be amended by substituting Noel Louis Fox as plaintiff instead of the company.

The first, second and third named respondents will be awarded their costs against the receiver and he will have them as part of his costs of the receivership. He will also be entitled to his own costs of the proceedings.

The work of preparing the papers in connection with this complicated case has been done by the solicitors for the receiver in am admirable manner. I am grateful to them because the proper preparation of papers in a difficult case makes my task very much easier.

Patricia McLaughlin
Barrister

Lee & Co. (Dublin) Ltd and Frank Conroy v. Egan (Wholesale) Ltd and John Roe: High Court 1977 No. 2489P (Kenny J) 23 May 1979 (supplemental judgment delivered 27 April 1978)

Pre-emption clause – Agreement to sell all the issued shares in the company – No authority to do so – Agreement made provision in relation to adjustment of stock – Application to have stock adjusted – Directions sought as to the value of the shares to be offered to other shareholders under the pre-emption clause – Whether majority shareholder should be directed to pass a resolution deleting the pre-emption clause from the articles of association of the defendant company – Whether this would amount to oppression

Facts: This matter is supplemental to the judgment of Kenny J delivered on 27 April 1978 in which the only order that he made was for the lodgment of money in the High Court by the plaintiffs. The parties asked for certain matters to be clarified. The agreement reached in March 1977 for the sale of all the issued shares in the company fixed a price for the shares at £23.29 per share. The agreement made provision for adjustments in relation to stock, to be dealt with by accountants. In relation to the pre-emption clause, the parties submitted that as Mr Roe owned more than 75% of the shares, he should be directed to amend the articles to delete this clause. The parties also sought directions as to what should be inserted in the notice to the other shareholders under the pre-emption clause as to what the fair value of the shares should be. Counsel for the plaintiffs asked for liberty to amend his statement of claim to include a claim against the second named defendant for damages for breach of warranty of authority.

Held by Kenny J:

(1) As the parties contemplated a quick sale, the adjustment in the price in relation to stock should be dealt with as of 30 April 1977.

(2) A resolution to delete the pre-emption clause could be set aside by the other shareholders as being oppressive and would be an abuse of a majority position.

(3) The notice should value the shares as of 17 May 1979 to reflect two years of inflation and an increase in the value of the assets of the company.

(4) Liberty to amend their statement of claim given to the plaintiffs.

No cases referred to in judgment

Counsel's and solicitors' names not available

KENNY J **23 May 1979**

I gave judgment in this matter on 27 April 1978. I intended the parties to come back when they had worked out certain calculations and the only order made was for lodgment of money in the High Court by the plaintiffs. Without coming back, there was an appeal lodged to the Supreme Court which quite rightly refused to hear it because the only order made at that time was an order for lodgment of the money. I intended when the parties came back to give an order for specific performance by Mr Roe by which he would be ordered to give notice to the other shareholders of his intention to sell 7,100 shares in the capital of the first-named defendants. I have been asked now by the parties to decide certain issues which have arisen between them.

The agreement which was made on 22 March 1977, was for the sale of all the 8,802 shares in the first-named defendants. This gives a price of £23.29 per share. The agreement for sale which is set out in the letter of 23 March 1977, written by the late Mr Buckley made provision for adjustments in relation to the stock. This was to be dealt with by the accountants, Mr Finlay Mulligan for the defendants and Messrs Grehan Quinn on behalf of the plaintiffs. The parties contemplated a quick sale and so I think that the adjustment in the price in relation to the stock should be dealt with as of 30 April 1977. I accordingly direct that Mr Finlay Mulligan and a representative of Messrs Grehan Quinn should meet, that all the books necessary should be made available to them, that they should agree on the necessary adjustment for stock and that they should then certify the purchase price of each share having regard to the adjustment. There is no reason why this should not be done within the next six weeks. I sincerely hope that they will be able to agree: if they do not, it will have to go to the examiner and that will be very expensive because large amounts of stamp duty will be payable to the Revenue.

The next matter in dispute relates to Article 31, the pre-emption Article. It is remarkable that there seems to have been no case in the courts in this country or in Northern Ireland or in England or Scotland in which the difficulties created by this pre-emption clause are discussed when an action for specific performance or some of the shares is brought.

Counsel for the plaintiffs have said that as Mr Roe has more than 75 per cent of the shares, he should be directed to amend the articles to delete the pre-emption clause. I think that any such resolution could be set aside by the shareholders as being oppressive. It would be an abuse of his majority position.

The next question is what should be inserted in the notice as being the fair value. The contract was made in 1977 and if the fair value is to be calculated as of 23 March 1977, it is certain that the other shareholders will take up the shares. There have been two years of inflation and I am sure that the assets of the company have increased in value at least 20 per cent. The notice should therefore value the shares as of 17 May 1979 and it seems to me that the best solution is that Mr Finlay Mulligan should be asked to certify the fair value of the shares as of that date and that the figure certified by him should be inserted in the notice to be given by Mr Roe to the other shareholders. This notice must be given within six weeks from 17 May 1979.

Mr Barron, counsel for the plaintiffs has asked for liberty to amend his statement of claim to include a claim against Mr Roe for damages for breach of warranty of authority. This arises from the fact that Mr Roe cannot sell the 900 shares belonging to his wife, the 800 shares belonging to Mr Wallace and the 2 shares belonging to Mr Finlay Mulligan. He undoubtedly led Mr Conroy and Mr Buckley to believe that he could. In the circumstances I will give the plaintiffs liberty to amend the statement of claim in such a way as they think fit and the defendants' defence to the amendment of the statement of claim must be filed within three weeks from service of the amended statement of claim on the defendants' solicitors. The amended statement of claim must be delivered within 28 days from the date of perfection of the order to be made consequent on this judgment.

I earnestly appeal to the parties to try to settle their differences. If this law suit drags on, the costs will be large. In addition the stamp duties payable to the Revenue (and not to the lawyers) will be very large and the parties will ultimately have to pay these.

When these figures as to adjustment of the stock-in-trade and of the fair value of the shares have been reached, the case should be entered again before me to give any necessary directions.

Patricia McLaughlin
Barrister

Lee & Co. (Dublin) Ltd and Frank Conroy v. Egan (Wholesale) Ltd and John Roe: High Court 1977 No. 2489P (Kenny J) 18 December 1979 (supplemental to judgments of Kenny J delivered 27 April 1978 and 23 May 1979)

Pre-emption clause – Agreement to sell all the shares of the company to the plaintiffs – Second defendant had no authority to sell all the shares – Calculation of the true value of the shares – Rule in Bain v. Fothergill *– Whether this applied to the sale of shares – Doctrine of frustration – Whether contract frustrated by the articles of association – Whether the parties had knowledge of the articles – Assessment of damages – Whether the Sale of Goods Act 1893, applied – Definition of "goods" in Act – Section 62 – "All chattels personal other than things in action and money" – Whether a share was a "thing in action" – Date when breach of contract occurred – Sale of Goods Act 1893 (56 & 57 Vic.), section 51(3)*

Facts: This judgment is supplemental to the judgments of Kenny J delivered on 27 April 1978 and 23 May 1979. The parties sought directions as to the fair value of the shares in the company which the second named defendant had agreed to sell to the plaintiffs and the plaintiffs sought damages as against the second named defendant for breach of warranty of authority. Mr Mulligan who was the registered owner of two of the shares in the company and was the auditor of the company, fixed £42 as the fair value of a share and the second defendant offered his shares to the other shareholders at this price in accordance with the pre-emption clause in the articles of association of the company. Mr Wallace, who was the registered owner of 800 shares took 3,400 shares and the second defendant sold his remaining 3,400 shares to the first named plaintiff at a price of £26.70 per share. The contract between the parties provided for an adjustment to be made by the auditors and when this was done the value of each share was £21.54. In relation to the issue of damages counsel for the defendants submitted, firstly, that the plaintiffs were entitled only to nominal damages and secondly that the contract for sale had been frustrated by the provisions of the articles of association and by subsequent events. Counsel for the defendants submitted that damages should be assessed on the basis that section 51(3) of the Sale of Goods Act 1893 applied. The second defendant did not know that Mr Wallace was taking up the number of shares that he did until August 1979 and the plaintiffs first became aware of this on 31 August 1979.

Held by Kenny J:

(1) The rule in *Bain v. Fothergill* (1874) LR 7 HL 158 applies only to the sale of land and has no application to the sale of shares. Therefore the plaintiffs were not simply entitled to nominal damages.

(2) The doctrine of frustration had no application to the case as the second defendant had knowledge of the articles of association and could not rely on his

ignorance of them. Furthermore, pleadings, though amended, contained no plea of frustration.

(3) The Sale of Goods Act 1893 did not apply as section 62 defines "goods" as including "all chattels personal other than things in action and money". A share in the capital of a company is a thing or chose in action: *Re VGM Holdings Ltd* [1942] 1 All ER 224 applied.

(4) 31 August 1979, being the date when the plaintiffs first became aware that Mr Wallace was taking up a proportion of the second defendant's shares was the date upon which the breach of contract occurred and damages should be assessed as of that date.

(5) The value of the shares on that date was £55. The contract price was £21.54 and the difference was therefore £33.46. As Mr Wallace took up 3,700 of the second defendants shares, the first item of damages was 3,700 times £33.46 which gave a total of £123,802.

(6) Although the contract price was £21.54, the shares were offered at £26.70 and the plaintiffs, who bought 3,400 shares were entitled to the difference between the price at which the shares were offered to them and the contract price. Their loss under this heading was £17,544.

(7) The second defendant warranted that he was in a position to sell or have transferred all of the issued shares in the company to the plaintiffs. The plaintiffs were entitled to recover £33.46 for each of the 1,702 shares which were not sold to them, giving a figure of £56,949.

(8) Under the original order the plaintiffs were required to lodge a sum of money in court and they are entitled to the loss of interest on that sum which has been calculated at £2,901.

(9) Accordingly, the plaintiffs were to be given judgment against the second named defendant in the sum of £201,296.

Cases referred to in judgment

Bain v. Fothergill (1874) LR 7 HL 158
Re VGM Holdings Ltd [1942] 1 All ER 224

Counsel's and solicitors' names not available

KENNY J **18 December 1979**

I have already given two written judgments, one on 27 April 1978, and the other on 23 May 1979 in this matter. I do not propose to repeat (except in so far as it is necessary) any of the matters stated in them. Before the contract for sale was made between Mr Conroy, one of the plaintiffs, and Mr Roe, one of the defendants, Mr Roe owned 7,100 shares, Mrs Roe owned 900 shares, Mr Wallace owned 800 and Mr Finlay Mulligan owned 2 shares. Mr Finlay Mulligan, who was the auditor for Egan, fixed £42 as the fair value of a share and Mr Roe offered his shares to the other shareholders at this price. Mr Wallace took 3,700 shares at this price and Mr Roe then sold 3,400 shares to Lee at a price of £26.70 per share.

The contract made between the parties provided for an adjustment to be made by the auditors and when this was done the price of the shares was £189,570 which gave each share a price of £21.54.

On the last day of the hearing, 19 November 1979, Mr Mills, counsel for the defendants raised two points which had not been mentioned before. The first was that the plaintiffs were entitled to nominal damages only because the rule in *Bain v. Fothergill* (1874) LR 7 HL 158 applied. The second was that the contract for sale had been frustrated by the provisions in the articles of association and by what had happened. The celebrated and infamous rule in *Bain v. Fothergill* applies to the sale of land only and has no application to the sale of shares. It is a historical anomaly which I hope will either be rejected by the Supreme Court or removed by statute. The doctrine of frustration has no application to this case: the articles of association were not an event which either of the parties thought of. Mr Roe certainly had knowledge of them and cannot possibly rely on his ignorance of them. There is also the insuperable difficulty that although the defence has been amended, there is no plea of frustration.

Counsel for the plaintiffs said that in assessing damages I should assess them on the basis that section 51 sub-section (3) of the Sale of Goods Act 1893 applied. That Act does not apply because section 62 defines "goods" as including "all chattels personal other than things in action and money." A share in the capital of a company is a thing in action. There are many cases dealing with the nature of a share in the capital of a company but it is now established that a share is a thing or chose in action (see the judgment of Lee Greene MR, a great authority on company law and the chairman of one of the company law amendment committees, in *Re VGM Holdings Ltd* [1942] 1 All ER 224 at p. 226.)

Mr Roe did not know until August 1979 that Mr Wallace was taking up the number of shares which he did and the plaintiffs first became aware of this when they got the letter from Messrs A&L Goodbody of 31 August 1979. This was the date upon which the breach of contract occurred and, in my opinion, I should assess the damages to which the plaintiffs are entitled as of that date.

The first matter to decide is the value of the shares on that date. I had the advantage of hearing the evidence of Mr Christopher Dodd and that of Mr Finlay Mulligan. Though their evidence was very different, both of them were truthful witnesses. The calculation of the value of a share in any company which has not got a Stock Exchange quotation has been, is and always will be a matter of extreme difficulty. It is particularly difficult in this case because the company did not declare any dividends and the distribution of the profits which it was decided to pay out was made by way of salaries and directors' fees. There is the perennial debate as to whether the value should be based on the value of the assets or on a multiple of the earnings. There is debate about the multiplier to be applied and about whether goodwill should be included as an asset. The tendency in modern times has been to omit goodwill as an asset from the balance sheet. The problem has been made even more difficult today by the high rate of inflation and the steep increase in the value of all landed property. Mr Finlay

Mulligan estimated that the net assets of the company after payment of the cost of sale would realise £445,000 which would give a value of £50.58 per share while calculated on an earnings basis using a multiplier of 5, the earnings value was £33.33 for each share. He arrived at his figure of £42 as the fair value by taking the median between these two figures. In evidence he said that he would now regard £45 per share as the value which would be arrived at in bargaining between a buyer or a seller. Mr Dodd laid great emphasis on the asset value and Mr Roy Donovan, a most experienced valuer, said that the value of the principal premises in June 1979 was £500,000 and stated very frankly that his firm had valued the same premises at £325,000 in October 1976.

After much anxious consideration I have come to the conclusion that the value of the shares in August 1979 was £55. When trying to calculate the figure, I did not know whether the plaintiffs or their representatives would be made directors of the company, whether dividends would be paid and what Mr Wallace's policy now that he holds a majority shareholding would be towards the minority.

The value of the shares is £55: the contract price was £21.54 and the difference is therefore £33.46. Mr Wallace took up 3,700 shares when Mr Roe offered his shares to the other shareholders and the first item of damages is therefore 3,700 at £33.46 which gives £123,802.

The next head of damages is that though the contract price was £21.54, the shares were offered by the letter of 31 August 1979, at £26.70. None of the counsel who appeared or the accountants gave me any explanation how that figure of £26.70 was reached but the plaintiffs who bought 3,400 shares are entitled to the difference between the price at which the shares were offered to them and the contract price. The difference is £5.16. They took up 3,400 shares and their loss under this heading is £17,544. There was no offer in the letter of 31 August to sell the shares at the contract price and in my view the plaintiffs are entitled to the difference.

I have no doubt whatever that at the meeting at which Mr Roe, Mr Conroy and the late Mr Buckley negotiated the sale and which took place on 22 March 1977, Mr Roe warranted that he was in a position to sell all the issued shares of Egan. The parties were business men and they fixed the price in terms of assets and earning capacity, not in terms of the price of shares. Mr Roe warranted that he was in a position to sell the whole business and thereby impliedly warranted that he could either sell all the issued shares or have them transferred to the plaintiffs at the agreed price. Mrs Roe, Mr Wallace and Mr Finlay Mulligan have not sold their shares to the plaintiffs at the agreed price. It follows that the plaintiffs are entitled to recover £33.46 for each of the 1,702 shares which were not sold to them. This gives a figure of £56,949.

Under an order made by me, the plaintiffs were ordered to lodge £164,720 in court. I was not given the date when it was lodged or the date it was paid out but Mr Finlay Mulligan has calculated the loss of interest at £2,901. Although the court order directed that the money lodged was to be placed on deposit with the Agricultural Credit Corporation, the cost of borrowing the money to the plaintiffs was higher than the rate of interest earned on the money in court.

The total of these four figures, £123,802, £17,544, £56,949 and £2,901 is £201,196.

The plaintiffs will accordingly be given judgment against the second-named defendant Mr Roe for £201,296. They will also be awarded their costs of the proceedings. The hearing of the case made it necessary that it should be on three different days and the costs are to be taxed on the basis that the case lasted three days. There will be a certificate that discovery was reasonably asked for by the plaintiffs (see Order 31 r. 25).

Patricia McLaughlin
Barrister

Securities Trust Ltd v. Associated Properties Ltd and Estates Development Ltd: High Court 1979 No. 538Sp (McWilliam J) 19 November 1980

Company – Purchase of own shares – Special resolution – Extraordinary general meeting – Resolution to lend money to another company to fund purchase of own shares – Application by shareholder to cancel resolution – Whether resolution authorised by section 60 of Companies Act – Whether authorised by articles of association of company – Subsequent E.G.M. – Resolution to amend articles to include necessary powers – Whether capable of retrospectively validating original resolution – Failure to disclose full circumstances in offer document – Whether breach of faith by directors – Duty of directors to shareholders – Companies Act 1963 (No. 33), sections 60(1), (2), (4), (7), (8), 204

Facts: Section 60(1) of the Companies Act 1963, provided that,

> "Subject to subsections (2), (12) and (13), it shall not be lawful for a company to give, whether directly or indirectly, and whether by means of a loan, guarantee, the provision of security or otherwise, any financial assistance for the purpose of or in connection with a purchase or subscription made or to be made by any person of or for any share in the company. . . ."

Subsection (2) allows such financial assistance,

> "under the authority of a special resolution of the company passed not more than 12 months previously".

Subsection (7) says that,

> "unless all members of the company . . . vote in favour of the special resolution, the transaction whereby such assistance is to be given shall not be carried out before the expiry of 30 days after such resolution has been passed or, if an application under subsection (8) is made, until such application has been disposed of by the court."

On 2 April 1979, an offer was made by Allied Irish Investment Bank Ltd ("the bank") on behalf of the second defendant ("Estates") for the purchase of those shares in the first defendant ("Associated"), not already held by Estates. Estates and Associated carried on business in conjunction, and the directors and managers of the two companies were the same.

The accompanying document stated:

> "(a) No agreement, arrangement or understanding exists between Estates or any person acting in concert with it and or any of the directors or recent directors, shareholders or recent shareholders of Associated having any connection with or dependence on the offers; (c) No contracts material to the offers have been entered into by Estates or associated within the last two years; (e) The bank is satisfied that adequate resources are available to Estates to satisfy full acceptance of the offers."

On 4 May 1979 the bank had offered Estates loan facilities of £2.3m for the purchase of shares in Associated. This offer was accepted by the board of Estates by resolution dated 8 May 1979, by which time the necessary number of ordinary shareholders in each category had agreed to sell their holdings. By 15 May, Estates had borrowed £1.9 m for the purchase of shares in Associated, and further sums were borrowed later to complete the purchase.

On 8 August, the Associated board called an extraordinary general meeting to consider a resolution that Associated make an interest free loan of £1.8m to Estates for the purchase by Estates of shares in Associated. This E.G.M. was held on 15 August. A representative of the plaintiff (a shareholder in Associated) objected on the grounds that Article 5 of the articles of association provided that:

> "None of the funds of the company shall be employed in the purchase of, or lent on, shares of the company."

Nevertheless the resolution was carried.

The plaintiff issued proceedings under section 60(8) of the Companies Act 1963 seeking the cancellation of the special resolution. As a result a further E.G.M. of Associated was held on 21 August, where both the articles of association and the objects in the memorandum of association were amended.

On 15 August, Associated lodged £862,494 with the bank in discharge of part of the loan obtained by Estates to purchase the shares in Associated. On 21

August, after the second E.G.M., Estates repaid Associated this sum. Thereupon Associated lent the sum of £1.8 m to Estates to repay the bank the money borrowed by Estates to purchase the shares.

In his summons the plaintiff claimed: (a) that the special resolution of 15 August was unlawful as it was in contravention of section 60(1) of the Companies Act 1963; (b) that it was also in contravention of Article 5 of the articles of association; (c) that there had been a breach of faith in calling the second E.G.M. to amend the articles and memorandum after the loan had been made, and also in concealing in the offer document that the resources available to pay for the shares were the resources of Associated itself.

Held by McWilliam J, although in making no order as the matter had been settled between the parties:

(1) It was difficult to accept the accuracy of statement (a) in the offer document. It was to be assumed, in the absence of compelling evidence to the contrary, that the parties organising the transaction had worked out the method of completing it before embarking on the transaction.

(2) Minority shareholders whose shares might be acquired compulsorily were entitled to be given full particulars of the transaction, its purpose, the method of carrying it out and its consequences. This had not been disclosed. This was particularly so as directors were to some extent in a fiduciary position to the shareholders.

(3) As a result of the procedures adopted, the plaintiff's shares had been compulsorily acquired prior to the meeting of 15 August, thus depriving the plaintiff, pursuant to section 60(7), of the possibility of preventing the loan transaction being carried out in the way in which it was.

(4) The special resolution of 15 August 1979 was one authorised by the provisions of subsection (2), and so avoided the prohibition contained in section 60(1) of the Companies Act 1963. However the resolution was not within the power of the company, as lending money was not one of the company's objects and the use of funds to purchase the shares of the company was specifically prohibited by Article 7 of the articles of association.

(5) The special resolution passed on 21 August to alter the memorandum and articles of association was effective for that purpose but this would not retrospectively validate the resolution of 15 August. Whilst the correct book entries were made after 21 August in relation to the repaying of the earlier loan and making new loans, what was required at that stage was a new resolution authorising the loan.

Per curiam: When a member's shares are being compulsorily acquired under section 204, he is entitled to be given full particulars of the transaction, its purpose, the method of carrying it out and its consequences.

Semble: In circumstances such as the present, directors may be under a direct fiduciary duty to members to inform them of the full particulars of the transaction.

No cases referred to in judgment

Counsel's names not available

Solicitors for the plaintiff: *Anderson & Co.*
Solicitors for the defendants: *McCann Fitzgerald Roche & Dudley*

McWILLIAM J **19 November 1980**

The plaintiff has brought these proceedings for the cancellation under the provisions of section 60 of the Companies Act 1963, of a special resolution passed on 15 August 1979, by the first-named defendant, hereinafter called Associated. At that time, the second-named defendant, hereinafter called Estates, was in process of acquiring all the shares in Associated under the powers conferred by section 204 of the Act.

The special resolution was in the following terms:

> "That the making of an interest-free loan of £1,800,000 by the company to Estates Development Limited which shall be repayable on demand to assist the said Estates Development Limited to purchase ordinary, ordinary A and preference share in the capital of the company be and is hereby approved."

Associated and Estates are two companies which have carried on business in conjunction for a number of years. The directors and managers of the two companies are the same. At the time Estates commenced the operation for the acquisition of the shares in Associated the plaintiff owned shares of each denomination in Associated, and the Bank of Nova Scotia Trust Company Channel Island Ltd, which supports the plaintiff in these proceedings, owned a number of preference shares.

By letter dated 2 April 1979, sent to all shareholders of Associated an offer was made and recommended by Allied Irish Investment Bank Ltd, hereinafter called the bank, on behalf of Estates for the purchase of the shares in Associated not already held by Estates, at the following prices, that is to say: £7.10 for each ordinary share of £1, £6.75 for each ordinary "A" share of £1, and 65p for each cumulative preference share of £1. Appendix IV to the said letter, which was expressed to form part of the offer, furnished the following information. Under the heading "Responsibility for statements":

> "(a) the information contained in this document in relation to Estates has been supplied by the directors of Estates, who have taken all reasonable care to ensure that the facts stated and the opinions expressed herein in relation to Estates are fair and accurate and that no material facts or considerations have been omitted. All the directors of Estates jointly and severally accept responsibility accordingly.
> (b) the information contained in this document in relation to Associated

> had been supplied by the directors of Associated who have taken all reasonable care to ensure that the facts stated and the opinions expressed herein in relation to Associated are fair and accurate and that no material facts or considerations have been omitted. All the directors of Associated jointly and severally accept responsibility accordingly."

These two paragraphs are probably some sort of "common form" which does not take any account of the fact that the directors of both companies were and are identical. Under the heading "General" are the following paragraphs:

> "(a) No agreement, arrangement or understanding exists between Estates or any person acting in concert with it and any directors or recent directors, shareholders or recent shareholders of Associated having any connection with or dependence on the offers.
> (c) No contracts material to the offers have been entered into by Estates or Associated within the last two years.
> (e) Allied Irish Investment Bank Ltd is satisfied that adequate resources are available to Estates to satisfy full acceptances of the offers (which would entail cash payments by Estates totalling £2.294 million)."

In the letter of offer full particulars were given with regard to the position of Associated. No particulars were given with regard to the position of Estates, except that Estates financed the purchase of houses by tenants of Associated and that the directors and managers of both companies were the same. On 4 May 1979, the bank offered loan facilities to Estates in the sum of £2.3 million for the purchase of the shares in Associated on the security of a letter of hypothecation over all the ordinary and preference shares in the capital of Associated. This offer was accepted by the board of Estates by resolution dated 8 May 1979, by which time the necessary number of ordinary shareholders in each category had agreed to sell their holdings. By 15 May 1979, Estates had borrowed £1.9 million for the purchase of shares in Associated. Further sums were borrowed later to complete the purchases. On 8 August 1979, the directors acting in their capacity as the board of Associated resolved to call an extraordinary general meeting of Associated to consider a resolution that Associated should make an interest free loan to Estates of the purchase by Estates of shares in Associated. This extraordinary general meeting was held on 15 August 1979, and a representative of the plaintiff attended and objected to the proposed resolution on the ground that it was not within the power of Associated to make the loan by reason of the provisions of Article 5 of the articles of association of Associated. Notwithstanding the objection, the resolution was passed and this is the resolution which is challenged in these proceedings. As a result of the objection which had been made on behalf of the plaintiff, a further extraordinary general meeting of Associated was called for 21 August 1979, and, at this meeting, Article 5 of the articles of association was amended, and the objects of Associated as set out in the memorandum of association were also amended.

It appears that, on 15 August 1979, Associated had lodged £862,493.89 with the bank in discharge of part of the loan Estates had obtained from the bank for the purchase of shares in Associated and that, on 21 August 1979, after the extraordinary general meeting Estates repaid Associated the sum of £862,493.89 and that, thereupon, Associated lent a sum of £1.8 million to Estates to repay to the bank the money borrowed by Estates to purchase the shares.

In the summons herein the plaintiff claims that the special resolution of 15 August 1979, was unlawful as being in contravention of section 60, subsection (1) of the Act of 1963 and in contravention of Article 5 of the articles of association of Associated. In argument it was also claimed that there had been a breach of faith in calling the general meeting of 21 August 1979, to pass the resolution altering the memorandum and articles after the loan had been made, and also in concealing in the offer document that the resources available to pay for the shares were the resources of Associated itself.

Section 60 of the Companies Act, 1963 contains the following provisions:

> "(1) Subject to subsections (2), (12) and (13), it shall not be lawful for a company to give, whether directly or indirectly, and whether by means of a loan, guarantee, the provision of security or otherwise, any financial assistance for the purpose of or in connection with a purchase or subscription made or to be made by any person of or for any shares in the company, or, where the company is a subsidiary company, in its holding company.
> (2) Subsection (1) shall not apply to the giving of financial assistance by a company if —
>
> > (a) such financial assistance is given under the authority of a special resolution of the company passed not more than 12 months previously; and
> > (b) the company has forwarded with each notice of the meeting at which the special resolution is to be considered a copy of a statutory declaration which complies with subsections (3) and (4) and also delivers, on the same day as such notices are issued, a copy of the declaration to the registrar of companies for registration.
>
> (4) The statutory declaration shall state —
>
> > (a) the form which such assistance is to take;
> > (b) the persons to whom such assistance is to be given;
> > (c) the purpose for which the company intends those persons to use such assistance;
> > (d) that the declarants have made a full inquiry into the affairs of the company and that, having done so, they have formed the opinion that the company, having carried out the transaction whereby such assistance is to be given, will be able to pay its debts as they become due.

> (7) Unless all the members of the company entitled to vote at general meetings of the company vote in favour of the special resolution, the transaction whereby such assistance is to be given shall not be carried out before the expiry of 30 days after such special resolution has been passed or, if an application under subsection (8) is made, until such application has been disposed of the court.
> (8) If application is made to the court in accordance with this section for the cancellation of the special resolution, such special resolution shall not have effect except to the extent to which it is confirmed by the court."

Article 5 of the articles of association of Associated provided as follows:

> "None of the funds of the company shall be employed in the purchase of, or lent on, shares of the company."

On the facts, as they have been put before me, I have difficulty in accepting the accuracy of the statement at paragraph (a) under the heading "General" in appendix IV in the letter of offer. It may be assumed, in the absence of compelling evidence to the contrary, that, in a transaction involving the borrowing of a sum in the nature of two million pounds, the parties organising the transaction had worked out the method of completing it before embarking on the transaction. As the directors of the two companies were the same, nothing in the nature of a written agreement between the two boards was required.

I do not know what is the reason for the provisions of section 204 of the 1963 Act or why it should be thought desirable that minority shareholders may be compulsorily bought out, but I am of opinion that, on a compulsory purchase of this nature, the people whose shares are being compulsorily purchased are entitled to be given full particulars of the transaction, its purpose, the method of carrying it out and its consequences. The purpose of the transaction and its consequences have not yet been disclosed and the method of carrying it out was not disclosed to the persons concerned.

I have not been addressed on the duty of directors towards their own members or their position as agents or otherwise *vis-à-vis* the shareholders on such a transaction but, although a director is not a trustee for the shareholders, directors are to some extent in a fiduciary position and I am of opinion that, on a transaction such as this, the shareholders are entitled to be given reasonably full particulars by their directors about the matters I have just mentioned. Certainly, in the offer documents in this case there was no indications that the money for the purchase of the shares was to be provided by Associated itself.

As a result of the procedures adopted, the plaintiff's ordinary shares had been compulsorily acquired before the meeting of 15 August 1979, at which, if the plaintiff had then held its ordinary shares, it would have been able, under the provisions of section 60(7), to have prevented the transaction being carried out in the way in which it was carried out. In itself this is not a matter of great importance but it may help to explain the procedures adopted by the directors.

However this may be, I am of opinion that the special resolution of 15 August 1979, was one which came within the provisions of section 60(2) of the 1963 Act so as to avoid the prohibition contained in subsection (1) and would have been effective to authorise the loan had such a resolution been within the power of the company under its memorandum and articles of association.

I am also of opinion, however, that Associated had no power under its memorandum and articles of association to advance money by way of loan or otherwise for the purchase of its own shares. Lending money was not one of the objects in the memorandum and Article 7 stated unequivocally that none of the funds of the company could be employed for the purchase of the shares in the company. Section 25 of the 1963 Act provides that the articles and memorandum bind the company and the members. Accordingly, at the time of the resolution of 15 August 1979, Associated had no power to pass the resolution making the interest free loan of £1.8 million to Estates. This circumstance was brought to the attention of the company and its directors at the meeting but the resolution was passed notwithstanding.

The subsequent proceedings by Associated to rectify the position were unsatisfactory, The general meeting of 21 August to alter the memorandum and articles of association was effective for that purpose but, in my opinion, this would not retrospectively validate the resolution of 15 August. There should have been a new resolution after there was authority to pass it. Again, this is not in itself a matter of great importance but it is a matter which I should take into consideration with regard to the attitude of the directors in conducting the transaction.

I am not impressed by the procedures of repaying the earlier loan and making new loans which are alleged to have taken place immediately after the resolutions of 21 August had been passed. I am sure that the necessary book entries were made but what was required at that stage was a new resolution authorising the loan.

One of the matters mentioned in the arguments on behalf of the plaintiff was that the bank had been left in an invidious position by the statements of the directors. This may be so, but the bank issued the letter of offer under its own name and recommended the offer and advanced the money for the purchase of the shares and was completely identified with the transaction, although I accept it acted in accordance with current practice in such matters.

On the matter being adjourned, the case was settled between the parties and no order of the court is necessary.

Alistair Rutherdale
Barrister

[*Reporters Note:* various amendments have been made to section 60 of the Companies Act 1963, by virtue of section 10 of the First Schedule of the Companies Act 1983 (No. 13) and sections 155(2), 224(1) and 260(1) of the Companies Act 1990 (No. 13)]

Donal Kinsella and Others v. Alliance and Dublin Consumers Gas Company and Others: High Court 1982 No. 9527P (Barron J) 5 October 1982

Company Law – Stock Transfer – Extraordinary general meeting – Failure of company to register some stock transfers prior to meeting – Whether holders of such stock entitled to attend and vote as shareholders – Stage at which transferee becomes entitled to exercise voting rights – Whether chairman should have adjourned meeting – Companies Clauses Consolidation Act 1845 (8 & 9 Vict. c.16), sections 3, 8-9, 14-20, 61-62, 64, 75

Facts: The plaintiffs called an extraordinary general meeting of the company to consider resolutions proposing the removal of the existing board and to replace its members with nominees of the plaintiffs. The voting rights of company members were governed by the Company Clauses Consolidation Act 1845. Under that Act each member had one vote for each share held by him up to ten, one additional vote for every five shares beyond the first ten shares and up to a hundred, and an additional vote for every ten shares held beyond the first hundred shares.

It was seen by each side that it was to their advantage to subdivide large stock holdings, in order to increase the voting power attributable to the stock comprising such holding. In addition the parties purchased additional stock on the market.

As a result, a large number of stock transfers were received for registration in the month preceding the meeting and the company secretary employed a firm of accountants to assist in processing both these transfers, and the 4,000 proxies delivered in respect of the meeting. Despite working very long hours the staff were unable to process some 1,100 transfers in time.

Prior to the meeting solicitors for the plaintiffs wrote to the company solicitors seeking clarification of whether or not unregistered stockholders would be allowed to vote. No response was made to this letter.

At the extraordinary general meeting, held on 10 September 1982, voting was permitted only by stockholders whose names had been entered in the register of shareholders and only such shareholders were permitted to attend the meeting. Persons to whom stock had been transferred and in respect of which transfers had been received by the secretary of the company, but whose names had not been entered in the register of shareholders, were not permitted to attend the meeting.

The plaintiffs issued proceedings challenging the validity of the 10 September meeting.

Held by Barron J in refusing the relief sought:

(1) Until a person entitled to stock in such a company is registered in the register of shareholders, they are not entitled to vote. *Powell v. London and Provincial Bank* [1893] 2 Ch 555 followed; *Pender v. Lushington* (1877) 6 Ch D 70 followed; *Nanney v. Morgan* (1887) 37 Ch D 346 distinguished.

(2) The secretary of the company has a reasonable time in which to register transfers received by him.

(3) There was no evidence of any conscious decision by the board of the company or anyone acting on its behalf to leave the transfers unregistered. The reason was the sheer volume of paper involved and the shortness of time.

(4) An answer should have been provided to the letter sent to the company's solicitors, but the failure to reply did not invalidate the meeting.

(5) Whilst it might have been preferable that the chairman of the meeting put the question of adjournment to the meeting, there was no obligation on him to adjourn the meeting, and the failure of him to do so, did not affect the validity of the meeting or of what took place.

(6) The meeting was therefore a valid meeting, and the decision of the meeting was therefore in accordance with its constitution.

Per Curiam: The plaintiffs were, of course, entitled to call a further extraordinary general meeting with a similar order of business to that of the 10 September meeting.

Cases referred to in judgment
Nanney v. Morgan (1887) 37 Ch D 346
Pender v. Lushington (1877) 6 Ch D 70
Powell v. London and Provincial Bank [1893] 2 Ch 555

Counsel's names not available

Solicitors for the plaintiffs: *Orpen Franks & Co.*
Solicitors for the defendants: *McCann Fitzgerald, Roche and Dudley*

BARRON J **5 October 1982**

This action challenges the validity of the proceedings at an extraordinary general meeting of the company held on 10 September 1982. At that meeting, voting was permitted only by stockholders whose names had been entered in the register of shareholders and only such stockholders were permitted to attend the meeting. Persons to whom stock had been transferred and in respect of which transfers had been received by the secretary of the company, but whose names had not been entered in the register of shareholders were not permitted to attend the meeting.

Before dealing with the legal issues raised I feel it necessary to refer to the facts to show how such a situation arose. The extraordinary general meeting was called upon the requisition of the plaintiffs and those who support them. The resolutions for consideration at the meeting were essentially to remove the existing board and to replace its members with nominees of the plaintiffs. In the ordinary way, this trial of strength would have been decided by the representative shareholdings of the members supporting each side. However in the case of the Gas Company the voting rights of its members are governed by the Company Clauses Consolidation Act 1845. Under this Act, which in the main, comprises the constitution of the company, each member has one vote for each share held by him up to ten, one additional vote for every five shares beyond the first ten shares up to hundred, and an additional vote for every ten shares held by him beyond the first hundred shares. The original shares were of a nominal value of £10 each and for many years had been converted into stock. Reference to a vote per share or number of shares is accordingly a reference to multiples of stock of £10 denomination.

It was seen by each side in the coming trial of strength that it was to their advantage to subdivide larger holdings in order to increase the voting power attributable to the stock comprising such holdings. Because of the need to build up voting strength not only by purchasing stock in the market place but also by subdivision of existing holdings, a very large number of transfers were required and these were delivered to the secretary in the days preceding the date fixed for the meeting. While less then ten such transfers a week was the norm, 380 transfers were lodged in the last week of August, 341 transfers on 2 and 3 September, 1,052 transfers on 6 September, 449 transfers on 7 September, 386 transfers on 8 September and 76 transfers on 9 September.

It was the secretary's duty to register these transfers. As might be expected, the facilities available to the secretary to process such a large number of transfers were inadequate and it became necessary for him to call in registration staff from Craig Gardner & Co., the company's auditors, to assist him in this job. The secretary's task was further complicated by the need to process some 4,000 proxies delivered to him in respect of the meeting. Here again he was obliged to reply upon the assistance of the registration staff of Craig Gardner & Co.

I do not propose to deal in detail with the work done by this registration staff. At first two members of the staff of Craig Gardner's were called in. Later they were joined by two more, and ultimately by a further six. They worked long hours — up to 9 p.m. on some nights, to midnight on others, and the night before the meeting to 4 a.m. They were able to process all transfers received by the secretary of the company up to 4.15 p.m. on Monday 6 September, but none received after that time of which there were approximately eleven hundred. In addition, they checked all the proxies and were able to provide for the chairman of the meeting the number of votes attributable to such proxies. It is in relation to these approximately 1,100 stockholders whose transfers were not registered that the dispute in this action arises.

It became obvious to Mr Jackson, one of the solicitors acting for the plaintiffs that the weight of paper being delivered by him to the company both in the form of stock transfers and proxies was such that there was a serious doubt whether or not all the transfers could be registered in time for the meeting. He telephoned Mr Hogan, his colleague acting for the company, on Wednesday 8 September and asked him whether or not unregistered stockholders would be allowed to vote. Mr Hogan said that he would consider the matter. Mr Jackson rang Mr Hogan again that evening and was told by Mr Hogan that he had no answer for him yet but that he was getting counsel's opinion the following morning. On the following day, Thursday 9 September, Mr Jackson wrote to Mr Hogan as follows:

"Dear Mr Hogan,

Further to my telephone conversation of the 8th instant, I wish to confirm my telephone conversation with you on the 8th in connection with the Alliance and Dublin Consumers Gas Company. My client, Donal Kinsella, shall be claiming a right to vote on foot of proxies lodged in respect of transfers which have been duly delivered to the secretary and accepted by him prior to 11 o'clock on Wednesday the 8 September 1982.

I particularly confirm that I referred you to sections 61, 62 and 64, as well as sections 14 to 20 inclusive of the Companies Act 1845. In addition, I referred you to *Halsbury's Statutes of England*, third edition, volume 5, page 49 and thereabouts as well as the case of *Nanney v. Morgan* (1887) 37 Ch D pages 346 and 353 as well as pages 354 and 356.

My clients' supporters through their proxy of my client will be claiming entitlement to vote on foot of those proxies lodged concerning any stocks that may remain unregistered (but having been duly delivered) at the time of the meeting.

I would also point out that there appears to be no regulation whereby the register of transfers can be closed and it would be my clients' contention that registration in any event can be completed by the time of the meeting of those transfers as yet unregistered in view of the number that were registered on Monday, 6 September 1982.

I felt it best to put the basis of our conversation and my clients' contentions in writing at this stage even though I realise that at the time of writing you are urgently considering the contents of my telephone call.

Yours sincerely."

On the same day Mr Hogan's secretary rang Mr Jackson to say that he had as yet no answer for him. He got no answer that day nor was he able to contact Mr Hogan the following morning prior to the meeting. He attended the meeting and learned from the opening remarks of the chairman of the meeting that the attendance of unregistered stockholders was not being permitted.

The plaintiffs complained that the failure to register all the transfers submitted was as a result of a conscious decision to deprive the transferees affected of their rights as stockholders and that the failure of Mr Hogan to answer the question put to him was part of that conscious decision and deprived them of the opportunity to apply to the court for an injunction to restrain the holding of the meeting.

The evidence adduced shows that no more work could have been done by the registration staff prior to the meeting. It was the decision of Mr Mooney, the senior member actually carrying out the work, made on the afternoon of Tuesday 7 September, that he would be unable to register any more transfers than those upon which he and his staff were then engaged. On the following afternoon, the registration staff were instructed by the secretary of the company acting on the advice of Mr Fitzgerald, another member of the firm of solicitors acting for the defendants, that their priority was to have the proxies processed and that if this meant leaving transfers unregistered this would have to result. I have no evidence that there was any conscious decision by the board of the company or any one acting on its behalf to leave these transfers unregistered. The evidence is all to the contrary as I have indicated. Mr Fitzgerald indicated that they would rely upon the expertise of Craig Gardner & Co. It was through no lack of expertise on their part that the total work could not be completed. In my view, they did much more than could have been expected of them and are to be commended for their efforts. They were beaten by the sheer volume of paper and the shortness of the time available to them.

No reasonable explanation was given for the failure by Mr Hogan to reply to the question raised by Mr Jackson. Although it was not known on the Wednesday evening whether the instruction given to the registration staff would result in any transfers being left unregistered, it was reasonable at that stage to expect that this would apply to a large number of transfers. However, what was known, if not on the Wednesday, then on the Thursday, was that stockholders who were not registered in the register of shareholders at the time of the meeting would not be allowed to vote. Mr Fitzgerald in evidence said that the failure to answer Mr Jackson's question was that both he and Mr Hogan had a lot of things to do and that there was no obligation to answer it. This answer and the manner in which it was given was unfortunate since it tended to support an allegation for which there was no evidence. I think that an answer should have been given.

The basic question raised in these proceedings is the stage at which a transferee of shares in the company becomes entitled to exercise his or her voting rights in respect of such shares. The plaintiffs say it is when the transfer of such shares is acknowledged by the secretary of the company to have been received by him. The defendants say it is when the stockholder is actually registered as a stockholder in the register of shareholders.

In support of his submission counsel for the plaintiffs relies on the wording of section 15 of the 1845 Act and on passages in the judgment of Cotton LJ in *Nanney v. Morgan* (1887) Ch D 346. Section 15 of the 1845 Act in so far as it is material is as follows:

> "15. The said deed of transfer (when duly executed) shall be delivered to the secretary, and kept by him; and the secretary shall enter a memorial thereof in a book to be called the "Register of Transfers", and shall endorse such entry on the deed of transfer, and shall, on demand, deliver a new certificate to the purchaser . . . and on the request of the purchaser of any share an endorsement of such transfer shall be made on the certificate of such share, instead of a new certificate being granted; and such endorsement being signed by the secretary, shall be considered in every respect the same as a new certificate, and until such transfer has been so delivered to the secretary as aforesaid the vendor of the share shall continue liable to the company for any calls that may be made upon such share, and the purchaser of the share shall not be entitled to receive any share of the profits of the undertaking, or to vote in respect of such share".

In *Nanney v. Morgan*, Cotton LJ at pages 353-354 cites section 15 from the words "and until such transfer has been so delivered" until the end of the section and continues:

> "That as regards the company provides that the deed shall not have any effect, so as to put the transferee into the position of the transferor until it has been left with the secretary, and it must be not only left, but accepted by him as properly left, because if the secretary finds that it does not comply with the provisions of the Act it is his duty to refuse to receive it."

Further on in the same paragraph the judge says:

> "I do not place any reliance on the transferee being entered on the register, because when a deed of transfer duly executed is left with the secretary, it becomes the duty of the company to register the transferee as entitled to the shares, and the mere neglect of the company to do that, will not in my opinion affect the right of the transferee to be treated as the legal owner of the shares."

This was the view of the majority of the court, although one member, Lopes LJ regarded it as unnecessary to express an opinion on the point.

The defendants reply to this submission is that it is well settled law that only shareholders are entitled to vote and that, for the purpose of ascertaining who are shareholders, the company, whether incorporated under the Companies Acts or a statutory corporation as in the present case, need look only to its register of shareholders. Counsel for the defendants relied so far as companies governed by the 1845 Act are concerned, upon a passage in the judgment of Linley LJ in *Powell v. London and Provincial Bank* [1893] 2 Ch 555. At p. 560 Linley LJ said:

> ". . . in order to acquire the legal title to stock or shares in companies governed by the Companies Clauses Consolidation Act you must have a deed executed by the transferor, and you must have that transfer registered. Until you have got both you have not got the legal title in the transferee."

Counsel for the defendants also referred to several sections in the 1845 Act in support of his argument. He relied particularly upon sections 3, 8, 9 and 75. These sections are as follows:

> "3. The following words and expressions both in this and the special Act shall have the several meanings hereby assigned to them, unless there be something in the subject or the context repugnant to such Constitution: the word "shareholder" shall mean a shareholder, proprietor, or member of the company; and in referring to any such shareholder, expressions properly applicable to a person shall be held to apply to a Corporation.
> 8. Every person who shall have subscribed the prescribed sum or upwards to the capital of the company, or shall otherwise have become entitled to

> a share in the company, and whose name shall have been entered on the register of shareholders hereinafter mentioned, shall be deemed a shareholder of the company.
>
> 9. The company shall keep a book, to be called the "register of shareholders"; and in such book shall be fairly and distinctly entered, from time to time, the names of the several corporations, and the names and additions of the several persons entitled to shares in the company, together with the number of shares to which such shareholders shall be respectively entitled. . . .
>
> 75. At all general meetings of the company every shareholder shall be entitled to vote according to the prescribed scale of voting, and where no scale shall be prescribed every shareholder shall have one vote for every share up to ten, and he shall have an additional vote for every five shares beyond the first ten shares held by him up to one hundred, and an additional vote for every ten shares held by him beyond the first one hundred shares. . . "

Counsel further submitted that similar sections in the Companies Act 1862 and later Acts had been construed as he suggested and relied amongst other decisions upon *Pender v. Lushington* (1877) 6 Ch D 70.

The provisions of the 1845 Act like any other document must be construed as a whole. I am of the view that they are quite clear. Persons entitled to stock must be registered in the register of shareholders. Until they are, they are not entitled to vote. This is a well established principle and I would be wrong not to follow it.

I do not regard either section 15 of the 1845 Act or the decision in *Nanney v. Morgan* as being contrary to this view. *Nanney v. Morgan* was a case in which the issue for the court was whether a settlor of stock in a railway company held such stock under a legal or an equitable title at the date of the settlement. If he held under a legal title, a settlement would have been invalid, whereas if he had held under an equitable title it would have been good. The court took the view that if a valid transfer had been accepted by the secretary at the date of the settlement, the settlor would have had the legal estate, but that the failure of the company to do what it had to do, *i.e.* register the transferee in the register of shareholders, could not have affected the transferee's rights. Presumably, the court was acting on the equitable maxim that it regards as having been done that which ought to have been done and was not prepared to permit failure by a company to determine whether the settlement was effective.

There is nothing either in section 15 which provides that the right to vote acquired by the transferee shall be exercisable before registration of the name of the transferee in the register of shareholders. Having regard to the view expressed in *Nanney v. Morgan* and the express words of section 15 of the Act, it may be that the true interpretation of that section is that the legal interest when completed by registration relates back to the date of receipt of a valid transfer.

It follows from my decision on the question of voting that the meeting was a valid meeting. Only the vote of those entitled to vote were accepted whether in person or by proxy. The decision of the meeting was therefore in accordance with its constitution.

The plaintiffs' next submission is that nevertheless the chairman of the meeting should have adjourned the meeting to enable the transfers which had not been registered to be registered. His basic argument is that the true verdict of the stockholders of the company could not otherwise have been obtained.

This argument is one with which I have considerable sympathy on a practical rather than on a legal basis. The purpose of the meeting was to test voting strength. The agreement of the board to resign, if the first resolution was determined against them, shows this. Accordingly, when it became apparent that the real purpose of the meeting was not going to be achieved, it would have been in keeping with the intention of the parties that the meeting should have been adjourned to enable the transfers to have been registered so that all the transferees could vote at the meeting.

Nevertheless, the chairman of the meeting had no obligation to adjourn the meeting, nor could he have done so if the majority was against it. The meeting was entitled to proceed on the basis of the register of shareholders as it then existed. In my view, while the failure of the board to put the question of adjournment to the meeting is a matter of comment, it does not affect the validity of the meeting or of what took place at it.

As part of his submission that the meeting should have been adjourned, counsel for the plaintiffs relied upon the failure of Mr Morgan to answer the question raised by Mr Jackson. He submitted that if an adverse answer had been received, he could have applied for and obtained an injunction to restrain the holding of the meeting pending the registration of all the transfers. This might have happened, but the failure to reply did not invalidate the meeting. If it had, my jurisdiction would have been to assume that the majority view, claimed by the plaintiffs to have been in their favour at that date, continued and to restrain any action of the board contrary to such majority view: see *Pender v. Lushington* at p. 80. I would not have been entitled to declare the resolutions carried, but merely to direct the holding of a fresh meeting to determine the matter and to restrain the board in the manner I have indicated until the verdict of such later meeting had been obtained. As it did not, I must leave it to the parties to call such further meeting.

The meeting was properly held on the basis of the register of shareholders as it then existed. I accept that the secretary of the company has a reasonable time in which to register transfers received by him. In the present case, all reasonable efforts were made to register transfers, and the failure to so register them is not a ground on which the plaintiffs are entitled to rely.

In this case, the plaintiffs are not entitled to the relief they seek. This does not however mean that they are not entitled to call a further extraordinary general meeting with a similar order of business to that of the meeting of 10 September 1982.

Alistair Rutherdale
Barrister

In the Matter of A.H. Masser Ltd (In Receivership), William Mary McCann v. Michael Joseph Long: High Court 1985 No. 931 Sp (Barron J) 6 October 1986

Company – Book debts – Whether debenture created a fixed or floating charge – Ambiguity created by clauses in deed – Restriction on mortgagor from charging, assigning or otherwise disposing of its book debts – Intention of the parties

Facts: By Indenture dated 30 March 1981 made between several borrowers, of which the company was one, and a consortium of banks, a charge was created over the book debts of the company. Clause 3.02 of the deed provided that the company 'charges by way of first fixed charge all book debts and other debts now and from time to time due or owing to such company but so that such company shall nevertheless be entitled to make a *bona fide* transfer free of such charge of any book debt against payment therefore by an insurer'. Clause 7.02 provided that:

> "*Debts.* During the continuance of this security each company shall pay into an account or accounts of such company with the banks or any of them all monies which it may receive in respect of the book debts and other debts hereby charged and shall not without the prior consent in writing of the trustee purport to charge, assign or otherwise dispose of the same in favour of any other person but so that such company shall nevertheless be entitled to make a *bona fide* transfer free of such charge of any book debt against payment therefor by an insurer."

Clause 3.04 provided that:

> "*Permitted user of property.* Notwithstanding the charges created by the companies and subject as hereinafter provided the trustee shall permit the companies until the security hereby constituted shall become enforceable as hereinafter provided to hold and enjoy the charge property and subject as herein provided to receive and apply all income arising therefrom and to carry on therein and therewith the business authorised by the respective memoranda and articles of association."

Clause 4.01 provided that:

> "*Events of default.* The security hereby constituted shall immediately become enforceable and all rights of the companies to deal for any purpose whatsoever with the charge property or any part thereof shall cease forthwith if the trustee shall demand payment of the whole or any part of any monies for the time being secured by this debenture in accordance with the terms of repayment thereof."

Clause 7.15 obliged the borrowers on demand *inter alia* to give to the mortgagee "a valid and effectual legal or equitable assignment of its book and other debts". The defendants sought to rely upon the provisions of clause 3.04 and clause 4.01 in support of their submission that the charge thereby created was a floating charge.

Held by Barron J:

(1) The essential provision of the present charge was the restriction on the mortgagor which prevented it from purporting to charge, assign or otherwise dispose of its book debts and other debts. This provision acknowledged that the debts were in equity the property of the mortgagee and, therefore, not available to the mortgagor in the ordinary course of its business.

(2) Although clause 7.15 suggested that the execution of the deed did not effect an equitable assignment of the book debts and other debts, the conflict between various clauses must be resolved in favour of clause 7.02 as the fundamental provisions in relation to book debts and other debts were contained therein.

(3) In addition, the parties themselves by clause 3.02(f) indicated their intention to create a fixed charge.

(4) The deed created a fixed charge over the book debts and other debts of the company.

Cases referred to in judgment

Barclays Bank v. Siebe Gorman [1979] 2 Lloyds Rep 142

Keenan Brothers Ltd [1985] ILRM 641

Counsel's and solicitors' names not available

BARRON J **6 October 1986**

The sole question raised in this case is whether or not on the true construction of an indenture dated 30 March 1981 made between several borrowers of which the company was one and a consortium of banks the charge on book debts which it creates is a fixed charge or a floating charge.

The essential distinction between such charges as indicated by McCarthy J in *Keenan Brothers Ltd* [1985] ILRM 641 is that in the former type the charge is immediately effected upon the execution of the instrument of charge, whereas in the latter type the charge may never be effected. Since the purpose of a floating charge is to enable the borrower to use its property unrestricted by the existence of the charge so long as the charge remains floating, a test to ascertain the true nature of the charge is to determine whether the instrument of charge does or does not permit such unrestricted use of the property charged. A fixed charge creates an immediate assignment in equity of the property charged whereas such equitable assignment in the case of a floating charge is not effected until the charge crystallises. A further test to determine the nature of the charge therefore would be to ascertain when such assignment takes place.

Clause 3.02(f) of the deed provides that the company:

> "charges by way of first fixed charge all book debts and other debts now and from time to time due or owing to such company but so that such company shall nevertheless be entitled to make a *bona fide* transfer free of such charge of any book debt against payment by an insurer."

This clause shows that the parties sought to create a fixed charge. Nevertheless, if the provisions of the deed contradict this expression of intention, it is such provisions which must prevail.

The plaintiffs rely on clause 7.02 of the deed. It is as follows:

> "*Debts.* During the continuance of this security each company shall pay into an account or accounts of such company with the banks or any of them all monies which it may receive in respect of the book debts and other debts hereby charged and shall not without the prior consent in writing of the trustee purport to charge, assign or otherwise dispose of the same in favour of any other person but so that such company shall nevertheless be entitled to make a *bona fide* transfer free of such charge of any book debt against payment therefor by an insurer."

The use of the word "trustee" in the clause is a reference to the trustee appointed by the deed to act on behalf of the consortium of lenders. This clause clearly restricts the manner in which the company can deal with the proceeds of its book debts. It also restricts the company from purporting to charge, assign or otherwise dispose of its book debts and other debts. This is a recognition that the company would not be entitled to do so. If so, then it is a recognition that the book debts and other debts are assigned in equity at the date of execution of the deed or at the date of the creation of such debt if this occurs subsequently. The defendants argue that the saver in favour of the insurers alters this construction. I cannot see how it does. The proviso merely enables the company when it has received the amount of a debt from an insurer to assign the right to claim the debt from the debtor.

The defendants rely upon the provisions of clause 3.04 and clause 4.01. Clause 3.04 is as follows:

> "*Permitted user of property.* Notwithstanding the charges created by the companies and subject as herein provided the trustee shall permit the companies until the security hereby constituted shall become enforceable as hereinafter provided to hold and enjoy the charge property and subject as herein provided to receive and apply all income arising therefrom and to carry on therein and therewith the business authorised by the respective memoranda and articles of association."

Clause 4.01 is as follows:

> "*Events of default.* The security hereby constituted shall immediately become enforceable and all rights of the companies to deal for any purpose whatsoever with the charge property or any part thereof shall cease forthwith if the trustee shall demand payment of the whole or any part of any monies for the time being secured by this debenture in accordance with the terms thereof."

The defendants submit that these clauses allow the company unrestricted use of his assets, while the plaintiff submits that such use is subject to such restrictions as may appear elsewhere in the deed. Clearly, this latter submission is correct and these clauses do not assist in resolving the issue.

Reference should also be made to clause 7.15. This clause obliges the borrowers on demand *inter alia* to give to the mortgagee "a valid and effectual legal or equitable assignment of its book and other debts". It would seem unnecessary to include reference to an equitable assignment if such had already been effected by reason of the charge on the book debts and other debts being a specific rather than a floating charge.

In *Barclays Bank v. Siebe Gorman* [1979] 2 Lloyds Rep 142 the charge on book debts and other debts was expressed as here to be a specific charge. The debenture also contained a clause requiring the borrower to pay the proceeds of book debts into its account in terms similar to those of clause 7.02 in the present case. Clause 5(c) of that debenture was as follows:

> "The company during the continuance of the security shall pay into the companies account with the bank all monies which it may receive in respect of the book debts and other debts hereby charged and shall not without the prior consent of the bank in writing purport to charge or assign the same in favour of any other person and shall if called upon to do so by the bank execute assignment of such book debts and other debts to the bank."

It can be seen that the provision also required the borrower on demand to effect a legal assignment of the book debt and other debts to the bank. The absence of reference to an equitable assignment seems a clear acknowledgement that such had already been effected by the execution of the deed. Slade J indicated that he would have held the charge to be floating had the borrower been free to deal with the proceeds so long as the account was in credit. The basis of his decision lay in the restriction imposed on the borrower in relation to its dealing with the monies.

In *Keenan Brothers Ltd* [1985] ILRM 641 the deed contains a clause requiring the borrower to pay all monies received in respect of its book debts and other debts into a special account. The clause was as follows:

> "The company shall pay into an account with the bank designated for the

> purpose all monies which it may receive in respect of the book debts and other debts hereby charged and shall not, without the prior consent of the bank in writing make any withdrawals or direct any payment from the said account. . . . The company shall not, without the prior consent in writing of the bank, purport to charge, waive, assign or otherwise deal with its book debts or other in favour of any other person."

It can be seen that although this clause was similar to clause 7.02 in the present case, it restricted withdrawals from the account unlike the present clause. As Henchy J said at page 645, these particular assets "were unusable in the ordinary course of business save at the discretion of the bank".

The restrictions imposed upon the borrower in *Keenan Brothers Ltd* were clearly more extensive than those imposed here. Nevertheless it seems to me that the essential provision is the restriction on the mortgagor which prevents it from purporting to charge, assign or otherwise dispose of its book debts and other debts. I regard this provision as acknowledging that the debts are in equity the property of the mortgagee and so not available to the mortgagor in the ordinary course of its business. Undoubtedly clause 7.15 suggests that the execution of the deed did not effect an equitable assignment of the book debts and other debts. Since a conflict accordingly exists I take the view that it must be resolved in favour of clause 7.02 since the fundamental provisions in relation to book debts and other debts are contained in that clause. In addition the parties themselves by clause 3.02(f) indicated their intention to create a specific charge. Accordingly I take the view that the deed created a specific charge over the book debts and other debts of the company.

Patricia McLaughlin
Barrister

In the Matter of Clubman Shirts Ltd And in the Matter of the Companies Acts 1963 to 1977 And in the Matter of sections 205 and 371 of the Companies Act 1963: High Court 1981 No 1825P (O'Hanlon J) 8 June 1988

Minority – Section 205 – Previous order of the court that the petitioner's shares should be bought out by the other shareholders – Valuation report ordered – Application for liberty to bring evidence before the court for the purpose of seeking to establish that the valuation was made on an incorrect basis – Whether court should go behind the valuation already made – Companies Act 1963 (No. 33), section 205

Facts: In a previous judgment in this matter, the court ordered under section 205 of the Companies Act 1963 that the majority shareholders in the company buy out the interest of the petitioner at a valuation based on the true value of his shares as of 31 July 1980 and it was ordered that a valuation of the petitioner's shareholding in the company as of that date be carried out by Mr N.V. O'Neill FCA. The said report was furnished to the court and to the parties in or about the month of November 1987. The respondents were dissatisfied with the valuation and applied for liberty to bring evidence before the court and to make submissions to establish that the valuation was made on an incorrect basis and leave was given to have the matter brought before the court for further consideration. In particular, they objected to the valuation of the company's factory premises at the figure of £300,000; they alleged that the correct figure was £135,000. At the resumed hearing, the petitioner contended that the court could not re-open the matter or go behind the valuation already made by Mr O'Neill.

Held by O'Hanlon J:

(1) The report submitted by Mr O'Neill should be regarded as provisional or conditional in character as he qualified his report by stating that he experienced difficulties in obtaining satisfactory evidence as to current assets and liabilities of the company.

(2) It was proper to admit further evidence which the respondents wished to tender in relation to the report *de bene esse*.

(3) Although the petitioner was justified in complaining that the matters raised by the respondents should have been brought to the attention of Mr O'Neill before the matter came back to court, having regard to the qualification in his report, he should have all the relevant information accessible to the parties in order that he might make a correct valuation of the petitioner's shareholding.

(4) The report should be referred back to Mr O'Neill for his consideration.

(5) The valuation of the factory premises of the company should not be re-opened as the respondents had taken the benefit of an arrangement whereby the premises were assigned to a new company which took over the liabilities of the company, for a sum of £300,000. The respondents used this valuation to apply for a grant-in-aid from the Industrial Development Authority; having received the grant they cannot now challenge the basis on which it was made.

No cases referred to in judgment

Counsel's and solicitors' names not available

O'HANLON J **8 June 1988**

Further to the judgment already delivered in this case on 19 November 1982, Mr N.V. O'Neill FCA was appointed to carry out a valuation of the shareholding of the petitioner, Mr Neal Duggan, in Clubman Shirts Ltd as of 31 July 1980.

Mr O'Neill prepared a valuation of the shareholding and it was furnished to the court and to the parties in or about the month of November 1987.

The respondents, Peter Mooney and Leonard Hayes, being dissatisfied with the said valuation, applied for liberty to bring evidence before the court and make submissions for the purpose of seeking to establish that the valuation was made on an incorrect basis, and leave was given to have the matter brought before the court for further consideration. At the resumed hearing the petitioner, Mr Neal Duggan, contended that the court could not re-open the matter or go behind the valuation already made by Mr O'Neill.

Having considered the submissions made by the parties and having considered the further evidence which was tendered I have come to the conclusion that the report already submitted by Mr O'Neill should be regarded as provisional or conditional in character. In paragraph 4 it states as follows:

> "4. *Valuation*
> Subject to the availability of audited financial statements and a valuation of the fixed assets I value the shares of the petitioner Mr Neal Duggan at IR Pounds 1.96 per share or IR Pounds 68,600 in total."

In paragraph 6 he indicates that he experienced difficulty in obtaining satisfactory evidence about current assets and current liabilities and says that he was not in a position to ascertain if queries raised by Ernst and Whinney about the adequacy of debtors and stock provision were taken into account by the company or Arthur Young & Co. in the intervening period.

This refers to unaudited management accounts prepared by Messrs Arthur Young & Co., Auditors and Accountants, at 31 July 1980, and to unaudited group accounts at 31 January 1980 prepared by Messrs Ernst and Whinney.

Notwithstanding the objections raised by Mr Duggan I concluded that it was proper to admit further evidence which the respondents wished to tender in relation to the contents of Mr O'Neill's Report *de bene esse*, and having heard this evidence it confirms my belief that Mr O'Neill had to operate under considerable difficulties in preparing his report and was justified in qualifying his report in the manner already referred to.

In particular, the respondents contend, and adduced evidence in support of these contentions, that the figure of IR£300,000 taken by Mr O'Neill as the value of the factory premises in his valuation of the shares, was unrealistic and that the true value at the relevant time was in the region of IR£135,000; that the stock figures in the unaudited accounts as of 31 July 1980, were grossly overstated by reason of the fact that these accounts were prepared in great haste at a time when affairs of the company had reached a critical stage, and that revised figures were accepted as correct by Messrs Arthur Young & Co., shortly after 31 July 1980, when further information was made available to them; and that the figures given for creditors and accruals were considerably understated in the said unaudited accounts.

I consider that Mr Duggan is justified in his complaint that these matters should have been brought to the notice of Mr O'Neill for his consideration without waiting for the case to come before the court again, but I consider, having regard to the reservations and qualifications contained in his report that even at this late stage he should be put in possession of any relevant information which is accessible to the parties and which has not already been brought to his attention, so that he can make the best possible attempt to arrive at a correct valuation of Mr Duggan's shares as of 31 July 1980.

For this reason I propose to refer back Mr O'Neill's report to him for further consideration, with a direction that he is to be free to consider any further material relevant to his task which any of the parties can make available to him. This direction is accompanied by a particular reference to the figures for stock-in-trade and creditors and accruals as of the relevant date. I propose to direct, however, that it is not appropriate for the respondents to seek to re-open at this stage the question of the value of the factory premises as the evidence established that an assignment of the said premises was effected for a sum of £300,000 as part of the arrangement under which a new company took over responsibility for all liabilities of Clubman Shirts Ltd, and in doing so, application was made for a grant-in-aid from the Industrial Development Authority and a sum (which I believe may have been as much as £160,000) was paid over on foot of this application. It does not appear to me that it should be open to the company or to the respondents, having taken the benefit of that arrangement at the time, to seek to challenge the basis upon which the grant-in-aid was then made. Mr O'Neill also notes in his report (paragraph 5) that Ernst and Whinney had noted in June 1980 that a valuation of the premises of IR£275,000 had been obtained, and while no further evidence was forthcoming on this point, neither was it contradicted by the respondents. In these circumstances I take the view that the valuation of the factory premises at IR£300,000 as referred to in the said paragraph of Mr O'Neill's report must stand.

In view of the long delays that have already taken place in connection with the valuation of the shares only a limited period can now be allowed for the submission of any further material to Mr O'Neill. I propose to direct that the case be listed again on Friday, 8 July 1988, at 10.30 a.m. for further consideration.

Patricia McLaughlin
Barrister

Pernod Ricard and Comrie plc v. F.I.I. (Fyffes) plc: High Court 1988 No. 8388P (Costello J) 21 October 1988

Takeover – Defendant owner of 20 per cent of the shares in Irish Distillers Group plc – Plaintiff interested in acquiring all of the shares in Irish Distillers – General offer only if defendant agreed to sell all of its shares – Mode of acquisition discussed – Defendant expressed a preference for an "irrevocable" means of transfer – Plaintiff wished to proceed by way of "a compulsory purchase agreement" – Defendant concerned as to the capital gains tax implications – Roll-over relief – Tax clearance certificate – Agreement never reduced to writing – Whether concluded oral agreement reached – Whether production of a tax clearance certificate a condition precedent to the agreement – Whether terms of agreement varied by mutual consent providing for acquisition "irrevocable" – Whether condition as to tax clearance certificate part of new agreement – Capital Gains Tax Act 1975 (No. 20) (Schedule 2) – Finance Act 1982 (No. 14), section 63

Facts: The first named plaintiff became interested in the purchase of the shares in Irish Distillers Group plc in or around August 1988. The defendant owned 20% of the shares in Irish Distillers and Irish Life Assurance Company Ltd owned 10%. The first plaintiff decided that it would only make an offer if it had a good chance of success, and it was determined that no general offer would be made unless it had first secured an agreement from the defendant for the sale of its shares, and then from Irish Life. The first plaintiff established a wholly owned subsidiary in Ireland, Comrie plc, the second named plaintiff, for the purpose of acquiring the shares. Negotiations were entered into with the defendant and amongst other matters the mode of acquisition of its shares was discussed. The plaintiffs were anxious to acquire the defendant's shares by way of "a conditional purchase agreement" rather than the defendant's preferred method of what was known as an "irrevocable agreement". In the former case, the defendant would be bound to transfer its shares once a general offer had been made by the plaintiff, notwithstanding the outcome of this offer, whereas in the latter case, such an obligation would only arise if the general offer were accepted. The defendant's main concern in relation to "a conditional purchase agreement" was the capital gains tax implications of such a transaction. In order to benefit from the roll-over relief provided for in Schedule 2 of the Capital Gains Tax Act 1975, the transaction would have to involve an exchange of debentures for shares and also be part of the type of general offer referred to in paragraph 4 of the Schedule. Furthermore, by virtue of the provisions of section 63 of the Finance Act 1982, in order to obtain the benefit of Schedule 2 the exchange of debentures for shares was required to be effected for *bona fide* commercial reasons and the exchange could not form part of an arrangement or scheme of which the main purpose, or one of the main purposes, was the avoidance of tax. The defendant wished the sale to proceed by way of an "irrevocable" because it was satisfied that if it exchanged its shares for debentures in this way, there would be compliance with Schedule 2. When the plaintiffs insisted that it should go ahead by way of "a compulsory purchase agreement" the defendant required that an opinion be obtained from the Revenue Commissioners confirming that the proposed scheme would qualify for relief under Schedule 2 of the 1975 Act and that this would not be negated by section 63 of the 1982 Act. It was the plaintiffs' evidence that an oral agreement was concluded on the morning of Saturday 3 September 1988 by which the plaintiff agreed to purchase the defendant's shares at 450p per share in exchange for debentures in Comrie plc, that the agreement was conditional upon the plaintiff making a general offer in the terms discussed and upon the production before the time fixed for completion of a tax clearance certificate, and that the transfer would be made within three days of the making of the general offer. The defendant argued that there was no concluded agreement on that morning as no formal written contract was executed. The defendant further urged that the production of a tax clearance certificate was a condition precedent to the execution of the agreement and as this was not available at the time, no agreement was finalised. It then transpired that due to the success of the plaintiff's campaign in securing shares, that the conditions which had motivated the plaintiff in insisting upon the transaction being effected by a "conditional purchase agreement" no longer existed and the plaintiff indicated to the defendant that it would not now object to the transaction proceeding by way of an "irrevocable". The plaintiff alleged that the terms of the agreement were amended by mutual consent and that the condition as to the tax clearance certificate no longer applied as the defendant had indicated throughout that this method was preferred precisely because it attracted the roll-over relief in Schedule 2. The defendant subsequently informed the plaintiff that it had received a higher offer from another company. An interim injunction was granted to the plaintiff on the Sunday night temporarily restraining the defendant from selling its shares otherwise than to the plaintiff. Discussions then took place and the defendant indicated to the plaintiff that if the tax clearance certificate was obtained this might settle the case. The plaintiff took the view that this was not a term of the agreement but nevertheless obtained a verbal opinion from the appropriate tax inspector that the relief under Schedule 2 would be available and that on an exchange of shares for debentures, section 63 of the 1982 Act would not apply. A general offer for the entire share capital of Irish Distillers was made on 4 October 1988 in the terms agreed and the plaintiffs sought specific performance of its agreement with the defendant.

Held by Costello J:

(1) A concluded oral agreement was reached between the parties on the morning of Saturday, 3 September 1988, and an obligation had been imposed on the defendant to sell its shares to the plaintiff if certain conditions were fulfilled by it. The preparation and execution of a formal written contract was merely an incident in the performance of the obligations the parties had

undertaken to one another.

(2) The agreement was conditional upon a general offer being made and upon the production of a tax certificate within three days of such general offer being made.

(3) The mode of effecting the transaction was varied by mutual agreement and the defendant agreed to accept the terms of a general offer if made in accordance with the agreement reached previously and there was no longer any condition precedent in the agreement relating to tax clearance.

(4) The plaintiffs were entitled to have the verbal contract specifically enforced and the defendants restrained from selling its shares in Irish Distillers other than to the plaintiffs.

No cases referred to in judgment

Counsel's and solicitors' names not available

COSTELLO J **21 October 1988**

I

The present takeover battle for the shares in Irish Distillers Group plc began at the beginning of September of this year. These proceedings have resulted from an important engagement in that battle. The contestants in the main struggle are an Irish-based company now called G.C. & C. Brands plc on the one hand and a French-based company called Pernod Ricard on the other. The protagonists in the dispute before me are Pernod Ricard (and its Irish subsidiary, Comrie, plc.) as the plaintiffs, and an Irish company called F.I.I. (Fyffes) plc, defendant, Pernod Ricard claiming that an enforceable agreement exists by which the defendant agreed to sell to its subsidiary its twenty per cent share-holding in Irish Distillers. Partly as background information but more importantly to establish the circumstances in which the parties negotiated and to explain their attitudes to the negotiations, I propose to begin this judgment with a brief description of the companies involved in the present controversies and an outline of certain of the developments which had occurred before the negotiations began.

Irish Distillers Group plc is an Irish company whose main business and that of its subsidiaries is the distilling and marketing of Irish whiskey, which it sells under such well-known brand known names as "Jamesons", Power's", "Paddy", "Bushmills", as well as gin and vodka. By Irish standards it and its subsidiaries comprise a substantial group, employing over 1,000 people in Ireland and enjoying in the year just ended an estimated pre-tax profit of IR £18m. On 30 May of this year G.C.&C. Brands Ltd mounted a bid to acquire all the shares in Irish Distillers, making its formal offer on 27 June. This company had been recently established and was jointly owned by two Irish companies, Gilbey's of Ireland Group Ltd and Cantrell and Cochrane Group Ltd, two companies which were themselves subsidiaries of two very large English companies, in the case of Gilbeys the ultimate parent company being Grand Metropolitan plc, and in the case of Cantrell and Cochrane, Allied Lyons plc. It is accepted that in reality G.C.&C. Brands Ltd was used as a vehicle for a bid for Irish Distillers which was being made by a consortium comprising Grand Metropolitan, Allied Lyons and Guinness plc. Its offer was a cash one namely IR£3.15 for each of Irish Distillers' 25p shares. It was strongly opposed by the board of Irish Distillers who argued that it undervalued the group's assets, that its acceptance would result in the sale of some of its brands and real assets (including the Old Bushmills Distillery) and that its acceptance was not in the interests of either the group's shareholders or its employees. In addition to advising its rejection the board complained to the Commission of the EEC that it infringed community law. In a statement of objections the Commission expressed a view that there had been an infringement of the community's competition rules and following negotiations and the granting of certain undertakings to the commission the panel of Take-Overs and Mergers in London gave a formal ruling that the offer of 27 June had lapsed. This cleared the way to a new offer being made by a reorganised G.C.&C. G.C.&C. Brands Ltd became G.C.&C. Brands plc and a wholly owned subsidiary of Gilbeys and on 22 August it (this time on behalf of Grand Metropolitan alone) made a new bid. Entitled "New and Increased and Final Offer for Irish Distillers" the offer document increased its previous offer from IR 315p to IR 400p per share There are two points about the offer document to be noted; firstly, it was no longer solely a cash offer — Irish Distillers' shareholders could now elect to accept cash or what was termed "an alternative investment in the form of Guaranteed Notes"; and secondly it contained an undertaking that:

> "application will be made to the Irish Revenue Commissioners for their agreement that the exchange of Irish Distillers shares for Guaranteed Loan Notes under the Loan Note Alternative will be effected for *bona fide* commercial reasons and would not, within the meaning of section 63 of the Finance Act 1982, form part of the arrangement or scheme of which the main purpose or one of the main purposes is avoidance of liability to tax" (p. 10).

It is relevant to observe the extremely limited contractual obligation undertaken by G.C.&C. in this offer document; it merely undertakes to apply to the Revenue Commissioners for the agreement stated in the paragraph; failure to obtain it would not in any way affect the parties' obligations resulting from acceptance of the offer document.

This alternative method for effecting a transfer of Irish Distillers' shares brings me to an important aspect of this case, namely the possible tax liability which F.I.I. might have to face on a disposal of shares. It had recently purchased them, it was being offered a price which would result in a substantial capital gain, and it was faced with a possible liability to pay capital gains tax at the rate of 60 per cent under the provisions of the Capital Gains Tax Act 1975. But there was a way by which this liability could with perfect propriety be postponed and diminished, namely if it could avail of the relief afforded by paragraph 4 of Schedule 2 of the Act. By virtue of this section immediate liability would not arise when a company seeking to acquire shares in another company issues debentures in exchange for those shares as a result of a general offer made to the members of the company, the offer having been made on a condition which, if it were satisfied, would result in control of the company passing to the offeror. So, if F.I.I. exchanged its shares in Irish Distillers for debentures in G.C.&C. it could claim relief (in the recondite language used in the world of mergers and takeovers called "roll-over" relief) under the second Schedule as the exchange would have been as a result of the sort of general offer referred to in paragraph 4. Thus it could postpone liability to pay tax until it realised the debentures and could reduce its overall liability because it would be taxed at a lower rate, depending on the length it held the loan notes. It had tried to obtain an offer from G.C.&C. earlier in the year on these terms and had failed. F.I.I. was acutely conscious of the benefit to it of disposing of its shares so as to comply with Schedule 2, which meant that to be attractive to it any rival offer would have to:

(a) involve an exchange of debentures for shares, and
(b) be part of the type of general offer referred to in paragraph 4.

There was a second aspect of the capital gains tax code of which F.I.I. was also aware, namely that arising from the provisions of section 63 of the Finance Act 1982 to obtain the benefit of Schedule 2 the exchange of debentures for shares was required to be effected for *bona fide* commercial reasons and further the exchange could not form part of an arrangement or scheme of which the main purpose or one of the main purposes was the avoidance of tax. This was an entirely different point; it had been dealt with in the G.C.&C.'s final offer document in the way I have already indicated, namely by an undertaking to seek the Revenue's agreement that the transaction was a *bona fide* one and one made without the prohibited purpose specified in section 63.

The tax problem had an important bearing on the negotiations in this case for the following reasons. The manner by which one company goes about acquiring shares in another is likely to vary from case to case, but one of the common ways is for the offeror to attempt to acquire by private negotiations sale commitments from as large a percentage of shareholders in the offeree company as possible before making a public and general bid. Such commitments are made in contracts with individual shareholders by which the shareholder agrees in advance to accept a general offer and when it is made on terms which have been approved in principle. These contracts take the form of irrevocable undertakings to accept the contemplated general offer and were familiarly referred to throughout the negotiations and in these proceedings as "irrevocable". In connection with G.C.&C.'s first bid F.I.I. had signed an "irrevocable" before a general offer had been made. When it came to negotiate with Pernod Ricard it was anxious to contract by means of an "irrevocable" because it was satisfied that if it exchanged its shares for debentures pursuant to the terms of an "irrevocable" there would be compliance with the second Schedule of the 1975 Act.

There is one other aspect of the pre-negotiation developments to which I should refer before turning to the plaintiff herein, that is the role of the Take-Over Panel in London in the situation which existed after G.C.&C.'s "final offer" of 22 August. The evidence establishes that both parties entered into the negotiations on the understanding that G.C.&C. could not make a further bid for Irish Distillers without the permission of the Take-Over Panel and that that permission would only be given if and when another general offer to all Irish Distillers' shareholders was made by another rival bidder. This put the plaintiff in a strong negotiating position because the defendant could not hope for an over-bid from G.C.&C. unless and until a general offer had been made and the plaintiff made clear to the defendant that it would not consider making a general offer unless it at least had got a binding agreement for the sale of the defendant's holding.

The first-named plaintiff in these proceedings, the Pernod Ricard Group, was formed following a merger in 1975 of two very substantial French companies, Pernod and Ricard, as a result of which the group has become the world's largest wine and spirits concern by sales volume. Its involvement in its present attempt to acquire Irish Distillers followed an approach made by the board of Irish Distillers, seeking its assistance to ward off the takeover by the Grand Metropolitan, Allied Lyons, Guinness consortium. Various tentative proposals were considered but these were overtaken by events and the final offer of 22 August. The board of Irish Distillers was as opposed to the second bid from G.C.&C. as it had been to the first, believing that it was "inadequate" and "as ill-conceived as the previous one", as it informed its shareholders. On 28 August the board of Pernod Ricard decided that an offer for all Irish Distillers' shares would be made provided:

(1) it had financing guaranteed by its bankers,
(2) that it had the support of Irish Distillers' and
(3) that it had a good chance of success

and it authorised M. Thiery Jacquillat its president and managing director to negotiate on its behalf. No difficulty in relation to (1) and (2) arose. M. Jacquillat decided to carry out the third condition in a manner which he made perfectly clear to F.I.I. F.I.I., owned 20 per cent of the shares in Irish Distillers and Irish Life Assurance Co Ltd 10 per cent and M. Jacquillat from the very commencement of the negotiations stated that unless he first had agreement that F.I.I. would sell its shares to Pernod Ricard and then Irish Life he would make no bid for the company.

The two major issues that arose in the negotiations which followed were (a) price and (b) method of acquisition. Before he left Paris for Dublin M. Jacquillat had had a meeting with one of the plaintiff's bankers, Messrs Shroder Wagg & Co. Ltd, and as a result a decision was taken on the form of agreement he would propose to F.I.I. It was proposed that it should be asked to agree to sell its shares to Pernod Ricard when (and if) a general offer to all shareholders was made. The distinction between that method of acquisition and an irrevocable undertaking should be noted. If F.I.I. was to accept the form of agreement the plaintiff proposed it would enter into a binding obligation to sell in the event of a general offer being made, so that irrespective of the fate of the general offer it was obliged to transfer its shares. On the other hand if it signed an irrevocable undertaking to accept the terms of a general offer when one was made no transfer of its shares would take place if for any reason the general offer lapsed or was declared invalid. This distinction between: "a conditional purchase agreement" (as it came to be called) and an "irrevocable" was one which the parties fully understood and it loomed large in their discussions for F.I.I. apprehended that a conditional purchase might not afford it Schedule 2 relief whereas if the transaction were to proceed by way of an irrevocable undertaking roll-over relief under the Schedule was available.

Pernod Ricard established a wholly owned subsidiary in Ireland, Comrie plc., the second-named plaintiff for the purpose of acquiring shares in Irish Distillers and on 31 August Mr Dermot Desmond, the managing director of National City Brokers Group was instructed to commence buying Irish Distillers' shares on the stock exchange on Pernod Ricard's behalf. By the afternoon of September he had acquired a holding of between 4.5 and 5 per cent. On Thursday 1 September M. Jacquillat came to Dublin. He had a meeting with the board of Irish Distillers on that day whose support was forthcoming and a preliminary meeting with Mr Haslam of Irish Life. A meeting with F.I.I. was fixed for the following day. But before it took place M. Jacquillat and his advisers were aware of certain aspects of the position that F.I.I. might be expected to adopt and in particular with its apprehended tax problem. On 19 August Mr Hooper of the Investment Bank of Ireland, who were acting as financial advisers to Irish Distillers, had 'phoned Mr Flavin, one of the directors of F.I.I., to inquire whether F.I.I. was still bound by its irrevocable undertaking to G.C.&C. and was informed that it was not. He was informed that before F.I.I. entered into an irrevocable commitment with anyone else it would require a "significant cash inducement", that it had a considerable tax problem in relation to the acquisition of its shares, that anyone making a bid would have to make it as part of a general offer, and it would have to be a "paper offer", that is, the consideration should not be cash but loan stock. The availability of F.I.I. to negotiate a sale of its shares was again confirmed on 31 August to Mr Hooper.

M. Jacquillat had throughout the negotiations as his professional advisers Mr Desmond of National City Brokers, Mr Swallen of Shroder Wagg and Co, and his English and Irish solicitors. Mr Desmond, before the negotiations began, was aware that his clients wanted to acquire by means of a conditional purchase agreement and not by means of an irrevocable undertaking and that F.I.I. wanted to be able to defer its tax liability under Schedule 2. On the evening of 1 September he had in consultation with solicitor and counsel worked on the form of an agreement which he believed could achieve both objectives. He 'phoned Mr Carl McCann on Thursday 1 September, ascertained that F.I.I. shares were available and that F.I.I. was interested in long loan stock in exchange for its shares. A meeting was arranged for 10 a.m. the following morning. It was attended by M. Jacquillat on behalf of the plaintiffs and his advisers, Mr Desmond, Mr Swallen of Shroder, and M. Sorrell of Société Général Merchant Bank plc (the second firm of merchant bankers acting for Pernod Ricard). It was attended on the defendant's behalf by Mr Carl McCann (its deputy chairman), Mr Flavin a member of its board, Mr Anthony Canning Jones of Merril Lynch and Mr Bergin, the company's solicitor. Mr Flavin was there in a dual capacity because not only was he a non-executive director of F.I.I. but he was also chief executive of a very large investment company which was acting as financial adviser to F.I.I. He acted as principal spokesman for F.I.I. in all the negotiations which followed, except on one occasion.

Because of counsel's animadversions on the veracity of two of the plaintiff's witnesses there is a general remark which I think I should make before I consider the progress of the negotiations. It is true that this action has been heard within a few weeks after they had taken place. It is equally true that there is considerable conflict of evidence on some crucial aspects of them. But I am satisfied that all the witnesses before me did the best they could to remember what was said and done, and that the infirmity in recollection where it exists is caused by human fallibility and not malign intent. Quite obviously some witnesses had clearer recollections than others, and where I prefer the evidence of one over that of another I do not intend to impugn the honesty of the witness whose testimony I reject.

II

It is unnecessary for me to review here all the testimony by the participants to the negotiations which took place on the morning of Friday 2 September and it will suffice if I give my conclusions in summary form as to the effect of what was said. M. Jacquillat offered to buy F.I.I.'s shares in Irish distillers at 430p per share, he was prepared to give loan stock in Comrie plc in exchange for them instead of cash, he was prepared to have stock guaranteed by Société Général, and that the stock could be for eight or nine years as required by F.I.I. He made it perfectly clear that he would make no general bid for the shares in Irish Distillers unless he had the prior agreement of F.I.I. as well as Irish Life that they would sell their shares. No agreement as to price was reached at this meeting but it was indicated that F.I.I. was looking for a price in the region of 470 to 480p per share. There was very considerable discussion on the method of acquisition. This was in the main dealt with on the plaintiffs' side by Mr Desmond who explained that it was proposed to acquire the F.I.I. shares by means of a share purchase agreement and not by the execution of an irrevocable undertaking, that he was aware of the tax problems involved, that a scheme had been evolved which would get over them and which that very morning was being discussed between a fellow director and counsel and his colleague was arranging to see the chairman of the Revenue Commissioners that day to obtain his confirmation that the transaction would not attract immediate liability to tax. There was strong opposition from the F.I.I. side to the proposed method of acquisition because of its apprehended tax implications, and on at least three occasions it was strongly urged that acquisition should take place by means of an irrevocable undertaking to be given by F.I.I. F.I.I. clearly left the plaintiffs' representatives with the impression that if this method was adopted it would have no concern about the tax situation. The plaintiffs' representatives insisted that the acquisition be carried out in the way they suggested and so F.I.I. insisted that it should get a "tax clearance certificate" or "tax clearance letter" from the Revenue Commissioners. Because the question of tax clearance has featured prominently in the case I should say a word about it. As a matter of practice, but not because of any statutory requirement, an inspector of taxes may be prepared to consider a proposed transaction and to express an opinion that if the transaction is carried out in the contemplated way it would not attract tax or it would come within some of the relieving provisions of the tax code. Such opinions have no legally binding force, but they do give comfort because provided the transaction is carried out as contemplated they are honoured in practice. F.I.I. made it clear that it wanted an opinion (which was described somewhat inaccurately as a tax clearance certificate) that the proposed purchase agreement would qualify for relief under Schedule 2 of the 1975 Act and that this would not be negated by section 63 of the 1982 Act. Mr Desmond expressed considerable confidence that it could be obtained and on behalf of Pernod Ricard it was agreed that one would be obtained. But this was in the context of a conditional purchase agreement and it was implied by what the defendant's representatives said that one would not be required if instead an irrevocable undertaking was given.

Pernod Ricard also agreed to produce a written agreement the next day and counsel's opinion to the effect that the conditional purchase agreement would qualify for Schedule 2 relief. The precise term of the agreement on this part of the negotiation is important. It has been suggested that Mr Flavin stated that F.I.I. would require the production of a written agreement and that F.I.I. would not be bound until it was signed. That is not so. What Mr Flavin said was that their discussions would be meaningless unless F.I.I. had a piece of paper in front of them, by which he meant that there could be no agreement until they had seen the proposed purchase agreement in written form — a perfectly reasonable and sensible requirement. But he did not specify at that meeting that F.I.I. would be under no contractual obligation until it had signed a written agreement. There are three further comments on this meeting which I should make. Firstly, I think it is unlikely that Mr Carl McCann stated with any degree of force that F.I.I. would have to clear in advance any offer which was made with the Commission of the EEC; in any event it was not a point taken up by F.I.I.'s principal negotiator Mr Flavin and if the statement was made it was never conveyed to the plaintiffs' representative that no agreement would be entered into until it had been approved by the Commission. The matter was not referred to again and the point was forgotten. Secondly, I do not think that Mr Canning-Jones stated that any agreement entered into would be subject to a condition that no transfer would occur if a higher offer was made. Any reference Mr Canning-Jones may have made to the possibility of a higher offer being forthcoming did not convey to Pernod Ricard's representative that such a term should be included in any contact for sale that might be negotiated. Thirdly, there was certainly a discussion about the amount of irrevocable undertakings which Pernod Ricard would require prior to a general offer being made so as to be confident of its success, but there was no agreement that the transfer of F.I.I.'s shares was conditional on any stated amount of irrevocable offers having been obtained prior to the general offer, or that the execution by Irish Life of an irrevocable undertaking in respect of its shares was a pre-condition of the defendant's obligation. The meeting ended with an arrangement for a further meeting the next morning and an agreement on the plaintiffs' part to bring to it a draft contract, and counsel's opinion on the draft.

The following morning the parties' representatives and their advisers met again. M. Jacquillat again represented the plaintiffs and he had with him as advisers Mr Desmond, Mr Swallen and Mr Sorrell as on the previous day and in addition his English solicitor, Mr Chaine and his Irish solicitor, Mr Collins. The defendant was represented by Mr Flavin and Mr Carl McCann, as before, who were joined by Mr Niall McCann, the company's chairman, the financial director, Mr McNamee, and the company secretary Mr Guernon. Its' advisers present were Mr Bergin (who had a colleague Mr Meghan with him), and a tax adviser Mr Mooney. The plaintiffs' representatives had three documents with them, namely a draft contract of sale, counsel's opinion on whether the contract would qualify for relief under Schedule 2 of the 1975 Act, and a draft press announcement which incorporated a draft of the principal clauses of the proposed general offer. When these were distributed the general meeting adjourned. The defendant's legal advisers and tax consultant met separately together and then gave the board of F.I.I. their advice; a second general meeting then took place; it adjourned for a second time. M. Jacquillat and Mr Niall McCann met and negotiated. There then followed a meeting of the board, and after it a second small group comprising M. Jacquillat and Mr Desmond, on Pernod Ricard's side and Mr Niall McCann, Mr Carl McCann and Mr Flavin on F.I.I.'s side which negotiated further. This was followed by a general discussion between the advisers, Mr McCann having by this time left for Belfast and M. Jacquillat for his Dublin hotel. It is the plaintiffs' case that from the discussions at the second general meeting (which took place after the perusal and approval of the plaintiffs' documents) and at the two smaller meetings there emerged an oral concluded agreement for the sale of the defendant's shares.

It is relevant to refer briefly to the three documents given to F.I.I. The draft was a very short and quite simple one. It provided that the defendant would sell its shares to the plaintiffs for a consideration left blank provided a general offer for Irish Distillers' shares was made by the plaintiffs; that the plaintiffs would procure that a general offer be made provided they had before 9 a.m. on 12 September received an irrevocable undertaking to accept the offer from shareholders holding 32 million shares or such lesser number as the plaintiffs might decide; that the defendant would transfer its shares within three days of the making of the general offer against loan notes representing the consideration for the shares. Counsel's opinion was a very brief one. It pointed out that under the proposed agreement the obligation created on the part of F.I.I. to sell its shares would arise from the making of a general offer, that until it was made no obligation to sell existed, that when it arose it would be as a result of the general offer and that accordingly the proposed agreement was within the ambit of subparagraph (2) of paragraph 4 of the Second Schedule to the 1975 Act. The third document was a much longer one. It contained the draft of the terms of an announcement of the principal terms of a general offer. But it was in a form with which F.I.I. would have been perfectly familiar. It contained nothing of a controversial nature; and once price had been agreed the blanks left on the form could have been filled in without difficulty. I am not at all surprised that F.I.I.'s professional advisers readily expressed agreement with counsel's opinion that the draft contract was within the terms of Schedule 2 of the 1975 Act. But Mr Mooney, the defendant's tax consultant, was aware of the provisions of section 63 of the 1982 Act and he had with him the offer document issued by G.C.&C. which contained the provision relating to it to which I have referred and it was his view that a tax clearance certificate should cover both the 1975 Act point and the 1982 Act point.

Again, I do not propose to rehearse here all the evidence adduced from both sides on what took place that Saturday morning; I propose to give my conclusions on the effect of what was said and the legal consequences of what was said.

Before the F.I.I. representatives returned to the meeting Mr Flavin had called Mr Desmond out for a private conversation and said to him that the price of 430p was not good enough and that Pernod would have to do much better. He left Mr Desmond with the impression, as he had made no mention of the tax problem, that F.I.I. was accepting the plaintiffs' views on the tax situation. When the full teams met Mr Desmond's assessment of the situation proved correct. Mr Flavin acted as the defendant's spokesman. He indicated that they were satisfied with the documents. He informed the plaintiffs' representatives that his tax advisers thought the opinion of counsel was a good one, that the proposed method of implementing the transaction was satisfactory to the defendant, but that notwithstanding this view the defendant still required a tax clearance certificate. Whilst indicating the defendant's acceptance of a sale transfer by means of the purchase agreement he stated "I can't understand why you are not going the irrevocable route" and implied, as had been done the previous day, that the "irrevocable route" would have obviated the defendant's tax problems. Turning to the question of price he stated that it was the view of the defendant that it was prepared to sell for 470p to 480p. There was not much discussion immediately following this statement. M. Jacquillat inquired whether what he was told about price was a board decision and when he was informed that it was he asked the board's chairman to join him in a private conversation.

Mr Flavin had called on Mr Mooney to speak during the course of his remarks and Mr Mooney had indicated that he thought counsel's opinion was a correct one but that a tax clearance certificate was nonetheless required on both the 1975 Act and 1982 Act points. A question has arisen as to whether he added that a certificate would be required for whatever route was taken. Whilst I think it is unlikely he said this as the defendant had accepted that the sale be completed in the manner proposed by the plaintiff and furthermore none of the defendant's witnesses recalled him saying so, the point was not taken up by Mr Flavin and it was not made clear to the plaintiffs' representatives that the defendant wanted a tax certificate should the agreement be changed and an irrevocable undertaking executed instead.

Negotiations on price then began. M. Jacquillat and the chairman of F.I.I. met together and alone. M. Jacquillat told him that the plaintiff would not offer 470 or 480, but after a short discussion he made a new offer of 440p. Mr McCann then left the room and met his board to consider this new offer. There was then convened a meeting of M. Jacquillat and Mr Desmond on the one side and Mr Flavin and Mr Niall McCann and Mr Carl McCann on the other. Before leaving this meeting for Belfast Mr Niall McCann stated that he was prepared to sell at 450p. M. Jacquillat then made a 'phone call to Paris and returned to the meeting. He announced that the board of Pernod Ricard was prepared to accept the offer of the sale at 450p per share. There was a spontaneous shaking of hands and Mr Flavin said "we are partners now" and he offered on behalf of F.I.I. to give the plaintiffs help in getting additional "irrevocables" before the public bid was made. M. Jacquillat wanted to know when they could sign the agreement and Mr Flavin said there was a difficulty because their legal adviser had to go to a wedding and that they could sign the following day. He said to M. Jacquillat not to worry about it; "we will arrange all that, we are all together now". M. Jacquillat then 'phoned Mr Niall McCann in his car and told him that he had accepted the offer of sale at 450p. Mr McCann expressed satisfaction and congratulated M. Jacquillat. Having made an arrangement to meet the following day M. Jacquillat also left the premises. The evidence satisfies me that the parties had reached a concluded agreement the terms of which I will indicate later. Mr Flavin returned to the room where the parties' advisers had been waiting and he again repeated that they were now "partners" or that they were now "together" and indicated the readiness of the defendant to use its influence with the institutional shareholders in Irish Distillers to obtain support for Pernod Ricard's bid. A point was raised by Mr Flavin about the possibility of the general offer being higher than the figure they had agreed, which was dealt with. There was some discussion between the parties' legal representatives about making contact the following day if required. All left the building on the understanding that there would be another meeting the following afternoon at 5 p.m.

Prominent in its defence to this action is the defendant's plea that it was under no obligation to sell its shares to the plaintiff until a written contract was executed and that as none was executed no obligation has arisen. I have already expressed my opinion that there was no express term to this effect insisted on by the defendant or accepted by the plaintiff. What happened on that Saturday morning was what frequently occurs in all sorts of negotiations — namely, a point was reached when the parties had made a bargain and agreed that a written document should be executed. When a dispute subsequently arises what the court has to decide is whether the preparation of a further document is a condition precedent to the creation of a contract or merely an incident in the performance of an already binding obligation. I have no doubt that the negotiations had in this case ripened into an agreement, that an obligation had been imposed on F.I.I. to sell its shares to Pernod Ricard if certain conditions were fulfilled by it, and that the preparation and execution of a written contract was merely an incident in the performance of the obligations the parties had undertaken to one another. I have reached this conclusion not only because of the view I have taken of the oral testimony in the case, but also because it is strongly supported by the conduct of the parties subsequent to the Saturday meeting to which I will later refer.

There were other grounds advanced by the defendant as to why it claimed that no obligation to sell existed. It was stated in evidence that it had been agreed that there were no less than six pre-conditions which would have to be satisfied before an obligation to sell arise; one, the production of a tax clearance certificate; two, that Irish Life would agree to the plaintiffs' offer; three, that the plaintiff would obtain shares or irrevocable undertakings to sell shares amounting to not less than 40 per cent of Irish Distillers' shares; four, that a written contract would be entered into; five, that no higher bid would be received; six, that EEC clearance would be given in advance. Of these six, only two were pleaded by way of defence, namely, the need for the execution of a written document with which I have already dealt, and the condition relating to tax clearance which I will turn to in a moment. As to the other four, I cannot accept the defendant's evidence as to the existence of these four pre-conditions and none of them had become a term of the agreement reached when the negotiations had terminated on the morning of Saturday, 3 September. It is true that there were discussions as to the amount of shares which it would be necessary for the plaintiff to acquire to achieve success in its bid but the term in the draft contract which was approved in principle related to the number the plaintiff should acquire before an obligation was imposed on it to make a general offer and not one which operated in the defendant's favour.

As to the tax clearance certificate, I think that the plaintiffs had agreed on the previous Friday when they were urging the share-purchase route as the method of completing the transaction that they would provide a tax clearance certificate and they impliedly, if not expressly, reiterated this agreement on the following morning. As to the form the certificate would take I think it was agreed that it would cover two points which had been raised. But I do not think that the parties agreed that it must be in a form approved by the defendant nor do I think that it was agreed that no contractual obligation would arise until the tax clearance certificate was produced; on the basis of the testimony in the case and the parties' conduct I conclude that the production of the tax clearance certificate was made a condition precedent in the contract and that by this contract the defendant had accepted an obligation to transfer its shares provided the certificate was available within three days of a general offer being made. This meant that the defendant was under an obligation to sign a contract on the following Sunday even if the tax certificate was not at that time available. It is relevant to point out that both parties were confident that a certificate could be obtained, a confidence partly arising from Mr Desmond's assurances but also:

(i) from the nature of the proposed contract document,
(ii) the advices both had received that it complied with the relevant 1975 Act provisions, and
(iii) their knowledge that the transaction was a *bona fide* one which complied with the 1982 Act provisions.

The evidence relating to the negotiations established that a concluded agreement had been entered into by which the defendant had agreed to sell its shares at 450p per share and would receive debentures in Comrie plc in exchange, that this agreement was conditional (a) on the plaintiff making a general offer based on terms in the draft press notice and (b) on the production before the time fixed for completion of a tax clearance certificate, and that the transfer would be made within three days of the making of the general offer. The parties' conduct supports the plaintiffs' testimony. M. Jacquillat had made it perfectly clear that he would go back to Paris unless he obtained the defendant's agreement to sell. Experienced negotiator as he was, it is unlikely that he would have moved to the second stage of his strategy (the acquisition of Irish Life's shares) unless he had successfully concluded the first. Nor would he have told Irish Life that he had the defendant's shares unless he had reasonable grounds for his belief that he had negotiated a concluded bargain. He, Mr Desmond and Mr Swallen met Mr Haslam of Irish Life at 2.30 that afternoon. M. Jacquillat began the meeting by stating "Are you aware that we have a deal with F.I.I.?" Mr Haslam indicated that he was so aware (knowledge which he could have acquired from the defendant) and also of the price which had been agreed but he asked M. Jacquillat to confirm the price, which M. Jacquillat did. He was insistent that Mr Haslam would there and then obtain his board's view on the offer and after leaving the meeting for about half an hour Mr Haslam returned and on behalf of Irish Life accepted Pernod's offer of IR 450p per share and shook hands with M. Jacquillat. It was agreed that the transaction between them would be by means of irrevocable undertaking to accept an offer of 450p per share which would be made in a general offer, and no tax problem in relation to the transaction was raised by Mr Haslam. It was further agreed that they would meet the following day to sign the undertaking.

As to the defendant's conduct; after the successful meeting with Irish Life Mr Desmond and his colleagues in National City Brokers Group began a campaign to have as many shareholders as possible execute irrevocable undertakings before the following Monday. He contacted the Norwich Union (whose holding of 3 per cent in the company made them the third largest shareholder) and because of a reluctance which he encountered he decided to take Mr Flavin up on the offer of support he had at the conclusion of the morning meeting and rang him to ask him to contact the Norwich Union on Pernod's behalf. Mr Flavin readily agreed to do so and added that he had been in touch with Standard Life (on his own initiative) and that they would sell. He rang back at about 7 p.m. to report his efforts to secure the support of the Norwich Union and indicated that they were being cautious and that he would contact them the following day. I think that the offer which Mr Flavin had made on the defendant's behalf to help the plaintiff in its efforts to obtain undertakings from other shareholders to sell their shares to the plaintiff, the actual support which later in the day he gave it, are strongly suggestive that the F.I.I. representatives regarded a deal as having been concluded that Saturday morning.

III

The terms agreed on Saturday morning were varied by mutual agreement on Saturday evening. What happened was this. As a result of obtaining the defendant's agreement as to its 20 per cent holding, Irish Life's agreement as to its 10 per cent holding, the irrevocable undertakings obtained from the directors of Irish Distillers, the success of the campaign to have other shareholders execute irrevocable undertakings, M. Jacquillat realised that having regard to the holding acquired by Comrie it looked likely that he would have obtained more than 50 per cent of the shares in Irish Distillers by Monday morning and that he was likely to win the battle with G.C.&C. so, the considerations which prompted insistence on the sale by conditional purchase agreement no longer applied and he decided to authorise Mr Desmond to approach Mr Flavin and to agree to the defendant's reiterated preference that the transaction with it be undertaken by means of an irrevocable undertaking. It has been accepted by the defendant that a variation that evening was agreed on the terms negotiated that morning as to the method of effecting the transaction; controversy arises as to what was then said about tax clearance. On this part of the case a difference exists between Mr Desmond and Mr Swallen on the one part and Mr Flavin on the other. I have found Mr Desmond's and Mr Swallen's recollection to be more accurate and also more consistent with the parties' subsequent conduct and the probabilities of the case and I accept their evidence.

When Mr Flavin rang back at 7 p.m. he expressed confidence that the Norwich Union would sell the following morning and then asked; "What about the tax clearance?" to which Mr Desmond replied; "You don't have to worry about that. We will take the easy option. We will go your suggested route". Mr

Flavin understood exactly what Mr Desmond meant and willingly agreed on behalf of the defendant (and no suggestion has been made that he had no authority to do so) that the sale would be carried out in the way the defendant had all along wanted, namely by means of an irrevocable undertaking to accept in relation to its shares a general offer if made by the plaintiffs. He then went on to ask "What about roll-over relief?". Mr Desmond understood that Mr Flavin wanted confirmation that the loan stock would be available for exchange for Irish Distillers' shares and that accordingly liability for tax could be deferred under the 1975 Act. Mr Desmond said that there would be no problem getting the relief through and that the best person to confirm this was Mr Swallen. Mr Swallen then 'phoned Mr Flavin and a discussion took place about the roll-over relief and the proposed irrevocable undertaking. Mr Swallen said that he was surprised with the query Mr Flavin had raised as the position would be exactly the same as that which pertained in relation to the G.C.&C. offer and that he had been involved in the United Kingdom in many takeover transactions where roll-over relief was given when shares were exchanged for loan notes without difficulty. The following morning Mr Swallen 'phoned Mr Flavin to try to bring forward the five o'clock meeting because the plaintiffs wanted to announce the offer simultaneously in Paris, London and Dublin and translation problems made this difficult if the meeting was held at five. Mr Flavin agreed to try to meet this request and said he would 'phone him back. He did so and it was agreed to hold the proposed meeting at 4 p.m. Mr Flavin raised again the question of roll-over relief and the irrevocable undertaking and Mr Swallen reiterated the points he had made the previous evening. The conversation ended by Mr Flavin saying "Don't worry" and expressing the view that it would only take about half an hour to sign the documents at the afternoon meeting. It had been clearly implied in the course of the negotiations on Friday and Saturday morning that if the "irrevocable route" was taken the defendant would not require tax clearance and there was nothing said when the new term was agreed which altered that situation. I accept Mr Desmond's evidence that he was not told on Saturday evening that the defendant would require a letter of tax clearance in respect of the irrevocable undertaking, and Mr Swallen's that he was not told the following morning that he was not to presume that they had a deal if tax clearance was not available. Had Mr Swallen been told that the whole deal depended on the presentation that afternoon of the tax clearance certificate I think he would immediately have warned M. Jacquillat, but he did not do so. Had Mr Desmond been told on Saturday evening that the defendant was still insisting on the production of a tax clearance certificate he would have busied himself on Sunday morning trying to get one; instead he played golf with M. Jacquillat. The fact that Mr Flavin agreed to talk to Mr Swallen (who was in no way concerned about getting the tax clearance) indicates that Mr Flavin wanted to satisfy himself that the irrevocable undertaking would enable the payment of tax to be deferred under the relief provisions of the 1975 Act and was not discussing the acquisition of a certificate from the Revenue Commissioners. Furthermore, Mr Flavin was aware of the manner in which the problem raised by the possible operation of the 1982 Act was dealt with in G.C.&C.'s offer document and as he was anxious to sell (believing as he did that the price offered was a good one) I think it is unlikely that he would have insisted on imposing a term on the plaintiffs which he did not require in a possible contract with G.C.&C.

I conclude therefore that the parties had entered into an oral agreement by Saturday evening by which the defendants had agreed to accept the terms of a general offer if made in accordance with the agreements reached on Saturday morning and that there was no longer any condition precedent in the agreement relating to tax clearance.

It is true that no written form of irrevocable undertaking had been produced for the defendant's inspection at the time and that it was understood that one would be executed on Sunday afternoon. But the contract which the parties had entered into was not required by law to be in writing and the execution of a written document was not made a condition precedent to the defendant's liability under the agreement; it was merely a means of implementing a concluded bargain.

As arranged, the plaintiffs' representatives went to the meeting at 4 p.m. on Sunday afternoon. There was no-one there to meet them. Mr Flavin came in alone after an appreciable interval and said "you have probably heard that G.C.&C. have made an offer of 525 and that it had received the authorisation of the Take-Over Panel to make it". This came as a considerable shock to the plaintiffs' representatives who had not heard the news and did not think that a counter-offer could in the circumstances be made. M. Jacquillat said "we have an agreement and I want you to sign". Mr Flavin did not deny the existence of an agreement but having reiterated a couple of times that "a new situation had been created" and having stated that "we have a very difficult situation" he left the room. He returned about ten minutes later and asked Mr Desmond "Have you got the tax clearance". Mr Desmond replied stating that the defendant did not need it as "you are going the irrevocable" and that Jim Kelleher (the plaintiffs' tax consultant) was there and would confirm that there was no problem. Again, this statement by Mr Desmond was not challenged. Fifteen minutes later a meeting between M. Jacquillat and Mr Desmond, Mr Flavin, Mr Niall McCann and Mr Carl McCann was held. When Mr Niall McCann started to speak about the previous day's discussions Mr Flavin counselled him "as your financial adviser" not to say anything. Mr Desmond pointed out that there would have been no new offer from G.C.&C. unless the plaintiff and the defendant had reached an agreement the day before and urged the defendant to sign it. At none of these discussions were the claims made on the plaintiffs' behalf that an agreement existed denied, and at no time was it suggested that the defendant was under any obligation to the plaintiffs because of the absence of a tax certificate or because no written document had been executed. The conduct of the parties on that Sunday afternoon lends support to the plaintiffs' version of what had happened in their negotiations.

It is unnecessary to deal at any length with what subsequently transpired. An application to the High Court was made late on Sunday night and an interim injunction temporarily restraining the sale by the defendant of its shares otherwise than to the plaintiffs was obtained. The following evening just as Mr Desmond was leaving to go to London for a hearing of the Take-Over Panel he received a call from Mr Flavin and a request for what was called a "without prejudice" meeting. This took place. What was said and done thereafter was referred to during the course of the trial, the defendant submitting that the discussions were no longer confidential. When they met Mr Flavin suggested that Mr Desmond would now try to get a tax clearance letter indicating that if it could be obtained this might result in a settlement but that he could not guarantee it. Mr Desmond again stated there had been an agreement and that there was not any need for a tax clearance for "an irrevocable" but he agreed after discussion with M. Jacquillat to adopt Mr Flavin's suggestion. The documents were assembled and a request made for an opinion from the appropriate tax inspector that on the basis of the proposed transaction relief under paragraph 4 of Schedule 2 of the 1975 Act would be available and that on the exchange of shares for debentures section 63 of the 1982 Act would not apply. The inspector took the view that he should not give a letter because of the pending litigation, but he expressed the verbal opinion that there was no problem about tax clearance. Mr Desmond telephoned Mr Flavin to inform him of this and of the willingness of the inspector verbally to repeat his view to him or Mr Mooney. This offer was declined and the attempt to settle the case failed. By consent, terms of the interim injunction were continued until the trial of the action.

On 4 October Comrie plc issued a general offer for the entire issued share capital of Irish Distillers. It has not been suggested that this offer fails to conform to the draft submitted to the defendant on 3 September. The defendant in my view cannot legally resile from the verbal contract it entered into and the plaintiffs are entitled to have it specifically enforced. I will order the defendant forthwith to accept the offer of all shares in Irish Distillers registered in its name or under its control, it being of course understood that it is at liberty to do so by electing to accept the debenture alternative contained in the offer document. I will further order that the defendant be restrained from selling its shares in Irish Distillers other than to the plaintiffs but liberty to both parties to apply will be included in the order.

Patricia McLaughlin
Barrister

Private Motorists' Provident Society Ltd (in Official Liquidation) v. Joseph Moore: High Court 1987 No. 10656P (Lynch J) 18 November 1988

Company – Defendant a dominant member of the committee of management of the plaintiff – Also a dominant member of an associated company – Plaintiff decided to maintain a market in the associated company's shares – Sale of shares in the associated company by members of the committee of management of the plaintiff to the plaintiff – Defendant decided to sell a large number of his shares in the associated company to the plaintiff – Transaction entered into between the defendant and the acting chief executive of the plaintiff – Authorised signatories of the plaintiff signed the cheque – Whether transaction ultra vires *the plaintiff – Whether chief executive authorised by the committee of management to enter into the transaction – Whether transaction in ordinary and usual course of the plaintiff's business – Whether defendant could rely upon section 8 – Whether valid contract concluded – Whether offer and acceptance absent – Companies Act 1963 (No. 33), section 8*

Facts: Under section 5(2) of the Industrial and Provident Societies (Amendment) Act 1978 industrial and provident societies, including the plaintiff, were to be prohibited from accepting and taking deposits. The defendant was one of the founder members of the plaintiff and the dominant member of the committee of management thereof. The defendant was also chairman of the P.M.P.A. Insurance Co. Ltd ("the insurer"), an associated company. The insurer's directors included many of the plaintiff's committee of management and the defendant was also the dominant member of that company and owned in or around three million shares.

In or around 1982 the plaintiff decided to make a market for buying and selling the insurer's shares and the plaintiff commenced to buy and hold such shares as well as acting as an intermediary for the buying and selling of shares by members of the public. For some time prior to October 1983, the buying price was fixed at 40p per share. By September 1983 the plaintiff had purchased a total of 2,224,195 shares in the insurer. Between May and September 1983, the average monthly purchase of the insurer's shares by the plaintiff increased, due mainly to the sales of large numbers of shares by members of the Committee of Management of the plaintiff to the plaintiff during that period at 40p per share. On 19 October 1983, the Insurance (No. 2) Bill 1983 was introduced in the Oireachtas as an emergency measure, and the Bill passed all stages and became law on the same date. During the course of that day, there were very strong rumours that the Bill or Act was aimed at the insurer and as a result, a large number of depositers looked for repayment of their deposits from the plaintiff. On the same date, the defendant decided to sell one million of his shares in the insurer to the plaintiff. Mr Mahon, the administration manager and acting chief executive of the plaintiff effected the transfer of the shares, on the instructions of the defendant, and he made out a cheque in favour of the defendant for £400,000, representing the purchase price of one million shares at 40p per share. The cheque was then signed by two authorised signatories of the plaintiff who did so because they were requested to do so by the defendant through the medium of Mr Mahon and neither of them considered as members of the committee of management of the plaintiff the appropriateness of the transaction and in particular the value of the insurer's shares in the circumstances then obtaining. The plaintiff submitted that the transaction was a nullity and *ultra vires* the plaintiff. The plaintiff further submitted that no valid agreement had been executed due to the absence of any real offer and acceptance.

Held by Lynch J:

(1) The transaction was not *ultra vires* as Rule 54 of the plaintiff's rules permitted the committee of management to invest the plaintiff's funds in any company registered under the Companies Act 1963. Although the rules did not give the plaintiff the specific authority to sell shares, the power to buy shares necessarily involves a power to sell shares and therefore the maintenance of a market of the insurer's shares was not *ultra vires* the plaintiff.

(2) Mr Mahon and other employees of the plaintiff were authorised by the committee of management to buy and sell shares on the plaintiff's behalf in the ordinary and usual course of business.

(3) However, the purchase of one million shares from the defendant was not a transaction in the ordinary and usual course of the plaintiff's business of buying and selling shares in the insurer as it was a transaction of such magnitude and in view of the circumstances at the time which would have required the specific consideration and authorisation of the committee of management. The transaction was effected solely at the behest of the defendant and without any free and genuine assent by or on behalf of the plaintiff. Therefore, the transaction was not binding on the plaintiff.

(4) Furthermore, there was no real agreement as there was no real offer and acceptance. There was no standing offer by the plaintiff to buy the insurer's shares at 40p per share, except in the ordinary and usual course of the plaintiff's business in buying and selling such shares.

No cases referred to in judgment

Counsel's and solicitors' names not available

LYNCH J **18 November 1988**

The plaintiff's claim in this action is for a declaration that a purported contract made on 19 October 1983 between the plaintiff and the defendant did not constitute a valid contract between the plaintiff and the defendant for the sale by the defendant to the plaintiff of one million shares in PMPA Insurance Co. Ltd and for other ancillary declarations and orders.

The defence contained, *inter alia*, a plea of estoppel by record based on the judgment of Murphy J, given on 2 October 1987 in proceedings between the same parties bearing Record No. 10966P of 1986. I heard detailed submissions from counsel for both the plaintiff and the defendant on this issue which was heard as a preliminary issue on 4 October 1988 before any evidence was tendered and I reserved my judgment overnight. On 5 October 1988 I delivered my judgment on that issue not as a written judgment but with a stenographer to make a verbatim note of it. I rejected the defendant's plea of estoppel by record and a subsidiary plea of unfairness to the defendant and I then heard the evidence and submissions in the substantive action.

The facts

The plaintiff is an Industrial and Provident Society first registered as such on 26 April 1958. The defendant is one of the founder members of the plaintiff and at all times material to this action the defendant was a member of the committee of management of the plaintiff and was the dominant member thereof. The defendant was also chairman of an associated company, namely, the PMPA Insurance Co. Ltd (hereinafter called the insurer). The insurer's directors included many of the plaintiff's committee of management in addition to the defendant and the defendant who owned about three million shares in the insurer was also the dominant director of the insurer. The plaintiff and the insurer were in effect members of a large and complex group of companies all under the same ultimate management of whom the defendant was the dominant personality.

The plaintiff had accepted deposits of monies from members of the public and had lent out monies to other members of the public including the defendant. As at 19 October 1983 the defendant owed to the plaintiff just short of £335,000 for monies lent by the plaintiff to the defendant and interest thereon. By virtue of the Industrial and Provident Societies (Amendment) Act 1978 the plaintiff was under an obligation to repay the amount of their deposits to all depositors not later than 14 November 1983 and consequently the plaintiff needed to get in monies lent by it to enable it to make such repayments.

The insurer was a public company whose shares were quoted on the Dublin Stock Exchange until in or about the month of September 1982 when stock exchange facilities were withdrawn. Thereafter the plaintiff decided to make a market for buying and selling the the insurer's shares and the plaintiff itself commenced to buy and hold such shares as well as acting as an intermediary for the buying and selling of shares by members of the public. The plaintiff maintained such market by fixing a selling price and a buying price for the insurer's shares from time to time. In December 1982 the plaintiff advertised its buying price at 39p per share and for some months prior to October 1983 the buying price was 40p per share. Between October 1982 and 27 May 1983 the plaintiff had purchased and itself owned 1,246,715 shares in the insurer.

Between 27 May and 23 September 1983 the plaintiff purchased a further 977,480 shares in the insurer bringing its total holding of shares in the insurer to 2,224,195 at the latter date. On these figures the average purchases per month between October 1982 and May 1983 were 178,102 shares and between May and September 1983 were 244,370 shares per month. The increase in the monthly average from May to September 1983 is accounted for by sales of large numbers of such shares by members of the committee of management of the plaintiff to the plaintiff during that period at 40p per share.

On 19 October 1983 the Insurance (No. 2) Bill 1983 was introduced in the Oireachtas and was dealt with as an emergency measure during that day. The bill passed all stages and became law the same day in the form of the Insurance (No. 2) Act 1983.

During the course of that day, 19 October 1983, there were very strong public rumours that the Bill or Act was aimed at the insurer and this in turn caused a run of depositors looking for repayment of their deposits from the plaintiff. At 4 p.m. on 19 October 1983 the defendant telephoned Mr Gordon Gallagher who was financial controller of the group and more particularly of the insurer to say that he wished to sell one million shares in the insurer to the plaintiff. Mr Gallagher summoned Mr Leo Mahon the administration manager and acting chief executive of the plaintiff to inform him of this communication from the defendant. Mr Mahon had been administration manager for some two years and was acting chief executive officer for about six months prior to October 1983 during which time the permanent chief executive officer, Mr Denis O'Brien, was absent due to illness.

Mr Gallagher informed Mr Mahon that he, Mr Gallagher, would have nothing to do with the proposed transaction even though he was an authorised cheque signatory and that Mr Mahon should be careful about his own position and should make sure that he, Mr Mahon, got and acted on specific instructions from the defendant and did not initiate anything himself. Mr Gallagher made it clear that the reason why he would have nothing to do with the transaction was because he thought it an inappropriate transaction given the Bill then before the Oireachtas and the rumours that the insurer would be the company to be the subject of an application to the High Court pursuant to the provisions of the Bill.

Mr Mahon then obtained from his own office a blank share transfer form and a cheque book of the plaintiff and went to the defendant in the latter's office in the insurer's premises. The defendant confirmed to Mr Mahon that he wished to sell one million of the insurer's shares to the plaintiff and Mr Mahon got the blank transfer form typed up by the defendant's secretary inserting a price of 40p per share being the then current buying rate. The transfer was then signed by the defendant and Mr Mahon then made out a cheque from the plaintiff in favour of the defendant for £400,000 being one million shares at 40p per share.

Mr Mahon then got this cheque signed by two authorised signatories who were also members of the committee of management, namely, Mr Seamus O'Mordha (who is a son of the defendant) and Mr Michael Dore. Neither Mr O'Mordha nor Mr Dore gave evidence before me. In the absence of any evidence from either Mr O'Mordha or Mr Dore I infer and find as a fact that both signed merely as authorised signatories and because they were requested to do so by the defendant through the medium of Mr Mahon and neither considered as members of the committee of management the appropriateness of the transaction and in particular the value of the insurer's shares in the circumstances then obtaining. Mr Mahon was not an authorised cheque signatory nor was he a member of the committee of management and it did not occur to him to query the transaction which did not appear to him to be out of the ordinary. He simply did as he was told to do by the defendant. There is no minute in the plaintiff's minute book indicating that the committee of management ever formally authorised Mr Mahon to buy or sell shares in the insurer on behalf of the plaintiff. I am satisfied however from the volume of dealings both in the form of purchases by the plaintiff itself and in the form of purchases and sales to other persons which exceeded nine million shares by 23 September 1983 that the committee of management did in fact authorise the buying and selling of shares in the insurer in the ordinary course of business of the plaintiff and the insurer and that Mr Mahon and presumably other members of the plaintiff's staff were authorised to implement such sales and purchases.

The submissions

The plaintiff claimed that the sale by the defendant and the purchase by the plaintiff of the one million shares in the insurer was a nullity on three grounds.

First, the plaintiff submitted that the plaintiff itself has no power under its rules to acquire shares although the committee of management may do so on its behalf under rule 54 and in particular the plaintiff submitted that it had no power to maintain a market in the insurer's shares. Rule 54 of the plaintiff's rules so far as relevant for the purposes of this case provides as follows:

> "The committee may invest any of the capital of the society in:
> (c) the shares of or on the security of any other registered society or of a Building Society registered under the Building Societies Acts or of any company registered under the Companies Acts or incorporated under any statute or charter provided that no such investment may be made in the shares of or on the security of any society or company other than one with limited liability."

Secondly, the plaintiff submitted that Mr Mahon was not specifically authorised by the committee of management to enter into this particular transaction and ought to have been so specifically authorised if it were to be valid.

Thirdly, the plaintiff submitted that irrespective of the second submission there was no valid contract between the plaintiff and the defendant because what happened was not an offer by the defendant accepted by the plaintiff or *vice versa* but a direction by the defendant obeyed by the plaintiff through its servants and agents who were in a subservient position *vis-à-vis* the defendant.

The defendant submitted first that there was a standing offer by the plaintiff to buy the insurer's shares at 40p per share and that this offer was accepted by the defendant and that this was a normal transaction.

Secondly, the defendant submitted that no question of *ultra vires* could arise in this case because in fact £400,000 had been paid to and received by the defendant as found by Murphy J in his judgment of 2 October 1987 in the 1986 proceedings and this could not have resulted from a transaction which was a nullity.

Thirdly, the defendant submitted regarding the allegation that the contract was not authorised that this contract was a performed contract and that a performed contract cannot be nullified except for fraud which is not alleged by the plaintiff in this case and furthermore that the rules of the plaintiff do not provide that the committee of management cannot do anything without a written minute of their decisions.

Conclusions

Regarding the plaintiff's submissions that the transaction was *ultra vires* the plaintiff in that the plaintiff could not invest in the insurer's shares although the committee of management might do so on its behalf, in my opinion this submission is not valid. Rule 54 authorises the investment of the plaintiff's funds by the committee of management in any company registered under the Companies Acts which the insurer is. This means that the plaintiff could invest in the purchase of the insurer's shares. The rules do not appear to give any express power of selling shares but the power to buy shares necessarily involves a power to sell shares also because otherwise the funds of the plaintiff would be permanently locked into any shares which the plaintiff might buy and that would defeat the main objects of the plaintiff. Therefore it seems to me that even the maintenance of a market in the insurer's shares was not *ultra vires* the plaintiff although it may have stretched its powers of buying and selling shares to the limit. The maintenance of the market in the insurer's shares was primarily for the benefit of the insurer but it could and did also benefit the plaintiff to some extent by generating funds through the difference between the selling and the buying prices of the insurer's shares.

Regarding the plaintiff's submission that Mr Mahon did not have authority to buy shares on behalf of the plaintiff, I am satisfied that he and presumably other employees of the plaintiff also must have been and were authorised by the committee of management even though there is no formal minute to that effect to deal with the purchase and sale of shares in the ordinary and usual course of such business. Shares were regularly purchased by members of the public who insured their motor vehicles with the insurer in order to gain the discount allowed by the insurer on the premiums when the insured owned not less than 1,000 shares. These shares were also regularly sold by such persons if for example they ceased to be insured with the insurer or perhaps if they required to raise some ready capital quickly.

However, the purchase of one million shares from the defendant was not a transaction in the ordinary and usual course of the plaintiff's business of buying and selling shares in the insurer. It was a transaction of a magnitude and in circumstances and at a time such that it would have required the specific consideration and authorisation by the committee of management and no such consideration or authorisation took place. Mr Mahon did not have power or authority to bind the plaintiff to such a purchase and of course the defendant as a member of the committee of management is not entitled to the benefit of the provisions of section 8 of the Companies Act 1963.

Furthermore, I am satisfied that the plaintiff's submissions regarding the absence of any agreement or contract for want of any real offer and acceptance are also valid. There was no standing offer by the plaintiff to buy the insurer's shares at 40p per share except in the ordinary and usual course of the plaintiff's buying and selling such shares. The purchase in question was not as I have said in the ordinary and usual course of such business. What happened was that the defendant using his dominant position directed that the sale and purchase should be effected and effected immediately and so it was without any consideration by anyone on behalf of the plaintiff as to whether it was or was not a wise, prudent and appropriate purchase on behalf of the plaintiff in the circumstances then obtaining on 19 October 1983. The sale by the defendant and the purchase by the plaintiff were effected solely at the behest of the defendant and without any free and genuine assent by or on behalf of the plaintiff to the terms of such sale and the sale and purchase is and was therefore wholly unauthorised by the plaintiff.

Once I am satisfied as to the lack of authority of the plaintiff's servants or agents to purchase the said shares I see no difficulty in giving relief to the plaintiff just because the defendant received the purchase money as he undoubtedly did and the plaintiff received the one million shares.

I therefore declare that the purchase by the plaintiff from the defendant of one million shares in the insurer for £400,000 on 19 October 1983 as implemented by the servants and agents of the plaintiff was unauthorised by the plaintiff and is not binding on the plaintiff.

I further declare that the said sum of £400,000 paid by the plaintiff to the defendant on 19 October 1983 was and is money received by the defendant to the use of the plaintiff and the defendant is obliged to repay the said sum to the plaintiff.

I accordingly order that the defendant repay to the plaintiff £400,000 with interest thereon at 11 per cent per annum from 19 October 1983 to the date of payment.

I further declare that the plaintiff and its official liquidator hold the said one million shares in the insurer purchased by the plaintiff from the defendant as aforesaid on 19 October 1983 on trust for the defendant and I order that on receipt of the said sum of £400,000 with interest thereon as aforesaid the plaintiff and its official liquidator retransfer the said one million shares to the defendant.

Patricia McLaughlin
Barrister

In the Matter of Credit Finance plc: High Court 1989 No. 6158P (Costello J) 19 June 1989

Application to court to approve the reduction of the share capital of the company – Objections made by shareholder – Purpose of procedure under the Act was primarily to protect the interests of creditors – Court has general discretion as to whether or not the reduction should be approved – Whether it was fair and equitable to reduce the capital having regard in particular to the rights of shareholders – Companies Act 1963 (No. 33), section 73(1)

Facts: The company brought an application under section 73(1) of the Companies Act 1963 seeking the approval of the court of a reduction in its capital as it was experiencing financial difficulties. The company held a meeting in accordance with the provisions of the Act and advertisements were placed in newspapers as directed by the court. A shareholder of the company made a number of submissions to the court suggesting that the court should not exercise its discretion under the section to confirm the reduction in capital. These were, *inter alia*, that the chairman of the company was not entitled to call a poll at the meeting of the company at which the resolution to reduce the capital was approved without first taking a vote by way of a show of hands, that there were irregularities in the circular sent out to members and creditors in that certain inadequate and inaccurate information was given, that the directors of the company had engaged in canvassing, that the scheme did not adequately care for creditors and that the scheme was also unfair to the ordinary shareholders of the company. He further submitted that the scheme involved a variation of shareholders rights as there would be a massive increase in the number of ordinary shareholders of the company and that, accordingly, a special meeting of the class of ordinary shareholders should have been held.

Held by Costello J in making the order approving the reduction of the company's capital:

(1) The main purpose of the elaborate procedure provided for by the Act was for the protection of the creditors of the company.

(2) However, the court had a general discretion in the matter and one of the matters it takes into account is whether it is fair and equitable to reduce the share capital, particularly having regard to the rights of shareholders.

(3) The submissions as to the irregularities in the procedure and voting were not well founded.

(4) The directors were not prohibited from canvassing if they believed that a reduction in the capital of the company was in the interests of the company.

(5) The scheme did not involve the variation of shareholders' rights, therefore there was no need to call a special class meeting.

(6) The scheme was fair as between the classes of shareholders involved. Although the preferential shareholders were to be repaid, it had been established

that where there was a class of shareholders entitled to a preferential repayment on winding up, repayment of such shareholders was permitted. *Re MacKenzie & Co.* [1916] 2 Ch 450.

(7) In all the circumstances of the case the court should exercise its discretion in favour of the company and make the order approving the reduction of the company's share capital.

Case referred to in judgment
Re MacKenzie & Co. [1916] 2 Ch 450

Counsel's and solicitors' names not available

COSTELLO J **9 June 1989**

This is an application to the court to approve the reduction of share capital which the company has undertaken because of the difficult financial situation which it experienced in recent times. The company held a meeting as required by statute and advertisements were circulated in the newspapers in accordance with the direction of the court, one of which was a day late through no fault of the company. The matter now comes before the court for its consideration.

Mr Duggan, who is a shareholder of the company, made a number of points which, of course, he is entitled to do and brought to the attention of the court a number of matters so the court could consider whether or not it was proper for the court to exercise its powers under the section. The main reason for this somewhat elaborate procedure is the protection of the creditors of a company when a company proposes to reduce its share capital and, of course, there are other considerations to be taken into account and, as has been pointed out, the court has a general discretion in the matter and one of the matters it takes into account is whether it is fair and equitable to reduce the share capital, particularly having regard to the rights of shareholders.

A number of submissions made in opposition to the petition were, broadly speaking, relating to an allegation that it was unfair and inequitable to make the order because of the facts and procedures that were adopted. I will deal with this first.

The first point that was made was that the resolution at the meeting called by the company was decided on by a poll and not by a show of hands first. It is quite clear from article 58 and from the information given to the shareholders in a circular sent to them which correctly set out the position that the chairman was entitled to call for a poll before he called for a show of hands and the procedures required by statute and the articles of association were carried out correctly.

Criticisms were made of the circular. It was suggested that inadequate information was given by the company of the IFG Securities and referred to in particular in the notes at page 26 in relation to the subsidiary company and IFG Securities. I think it is relevant to note that the document was prepared by a very experienced firm of accountants reporting on the affairs of IFG Securities and there is nothing in the report or any of the other information before the court to show that no inadequate or incorrect information was given to the shareholders at this meeting.

The point was also made that the information was inadequate or incorrect where given at note (g) on page 32 and at note 4 on page 34 of the said circular, in relation to the Hays share conversion/the "A" shares issue that took place to the shareholders of IFG Securities. This has been explained by Mr McGlinn in his affidavit and should not persuade the court against exercising its discretion in favour of granting the petition.

It was agreed that canvassing by the directors had taken place. There can be no objection at all to the directors doing this if they believe that the resolution was for the benefit of the company and that it was necessary to get support for their point of view.

I come then to more general aspects of the case. First of all, the main consideration in an application of this kind is the position of the creditors of the company. It is clear that the ordinary members will be as well looked after as before. No contingent creditors exist or have appeared to date despite the fact that the matter has been adequately advertised and in the circumstances the apprehension advanced by Mr Duggan that the scheme does not take adequate care of the creditors and that in some way in future the rights of all the creditors may be affected is groundless.

As to the claim made in relation to the ordinary shareholders and the fairness or otherwise of the scheme with regard to the ordinary shareholders and the preference shareholders, it is of some significance — considerable significance, indeed — that Mr Duggan is the only ordinary shareholder to have complained in this way. I would have thought if there was a real problem in this regard that other shareholders who are similarly affected, not being part of the major block of shares held indirectly through Allied Irish Banks would have come to court to make this point. The reality is, the scheme is fair between the classes of shareholders involved — the preference shareholders and the ordinary shareholders. It is true that the preference shareholders are to be repaid but this is perfectly permissible, as the *McKenzie, Re MacKenzie & Co.* [1916] 2 Ch 450 case sanctions, namely, that where there is a class of shareholders entitled to a preferential repayment of capital on winding up, repayment of such shareholders is permitted. A scheme which recognises this effect is unfair to other shareholders who have not that right. In the circumstances, there is nothing unfair to ordinary shareholders in the scheme proposed.

The point was taken that the rights of shareholders should be set out in the petition. It seems unnecessary for this to be done. The rights of respective parties are stated in the memorandum and articles of association exhibited in Mr McGlinn's affidavit. All creditors of the company would be aware of the situation as well as the shareholders. I therefore hold that there is, in fact, no unfairness in the proposal to deal with the respective classes of shareholders.

A further point taken, perhaps more a procedural point than anything else, related to the variation of rights. It was submitted that there is a scheme involving the variation of rights and that there should have been a special meeting of this class of ordinary shareholders and none was held. It seems to me the matter is made clear from Articles 5 and 6 of the articles of association, that when there are variations of special rights then a separate meeting must be held and a class meeting directed by the directors to be held but in this case there is no variation of special rights involved and a special class meeting is not required. It was pointed out that the position of the ordinary shareholders would be diluted — a massive increase in the number of ordinary shareholders of the company. To my mind, this is not a situation which would require a meeting of the special class.

In these circumstances I think this point is not one which should end up by my refusing the application now being made.

A criticism was made of the independence of the advisers employed by the company and that the company employed persons to canvas shareholders. I do not think that criticism is justified. It is not a ground for refusing the application.

In all circumstances it is a case in which the court's discretion should be exercised in favour of the company and I will make an order confirming the reduction which was proposed.

I also approved the draft minute for registration. Notice of the registration is to appear in the *Irish Times* and *Irish Independent* newspapers. I dispense with the need to incorporate the words "and reduced" in the name of the company after registration. I will not make any stay on my order nor will I make an order for costs in favour of Mr Duggan.

Patricia McLaughlin
Barrister

Michael Holland, Brendan Gilmore, L.S. Communications Ltd and Paschal Taggart v. Brian McGill, Daniel Ryan, Olema Consultants Ltd and Leonard McGill: High Court 1990 No. 533P (Murphy J) 16 March 1990

Company law – Pre-emption rights – Whether pre-emption agreement existed – Whether plaintiff represented to defendants that no such agreement existed – Whether defendants relied upon such representations – Whether plaintiff estopped from relying upon agreement – Convening of directors meetings – Notice required to be given – Due notice – Whether director should have been provided with an agenda of the meeting

Facts: The first named plaintiff and the first and second named defendants entered into a joint venture in November 1986 for the purchase of the Harcourt Hotel at Nos. 60 and 61 Harcourt Street in which they were to be equal partners. It was agreed subsequently that the venture would be carried out through the medium of a company in which they or their nominees would have equal shareholdings. The issue in this case was whether or not an agreement had been reached between the parties at an early stage on how they would deal with each other in the event of one of them seeking to withdraw from the transaction. The evidence was that discussions on such an agreement had taken place and a draft agreement had been furnished to the parties but that it had never been signed. On 23 October 1989 Mr Ryan, the second named defendant, made it clear that he wished to sell his shares to either Mr McGill or Mr Holland and a written offer to that effect was circulated to both parties. At this stage, the solicitors on behalf of Mr McGill were concerned about the existence of an agreement which restricted dealings in the shares of the company except in accordance with the pre-emption agreed. Mr McGill traced the written but unsigned agreement which had been given to him by Mr Holland. The solicitor for Mr Holland represented to the solicitor for Mr Ryan that such an agreement had never been executed and that there was no impediment to either party purchasing Mr Ryan's shares. Negotiations took place between Mr Ryan and Mr McGill as to the purchase of Mr Ryan's shares, without the knowledge of the plaintiff, and the transfer of the shares was completed at a meeting of directors held on 11 January 1990. The plaintiff was not aware that this matter would be on the agenda at that meeting. The plaintiff submitted that negotiations between the first and second defendants had taken place prior to the representations made by his solicitor and that, therefore, the defendants did not rely on such representations. The plaintiff also attached importance to the fact that the defendants and their advisers kept secret from him the negotiations taking place and he submitted that this was due to the fact that the defendants were not convinced by, and did not act upon, the representations made by his solicitors and that they still suspected the existence of a pre-emption agreement which would impede the transaction. It was common case that the parties were apprehensive that Mr Holland would move for an injunction notwithstanding the statements emanating from his solicitor. It was further contended that the meeting of 11 January was not validly held as the plaintiff was not given sufficient notice of it and was not made aware of the agenda. As such, the plaintiff submitted that the business completed on that day should be set aside.

Held by Murphy J:

(1) That although there was some measure of agreement as to pre-emption rights as far back as 1986, such an agreement was not executed at that time.

(2) Even if such an agreement existed the plaintiffs were estopped from relying upon it as they represented that no such agreement existed and the defendants acted upon that representation.

(3) The meeting of directors was validly held as due notice is all that is required by law and furthermore, there is no requirement to provide an agenda for director's meetings.

No cases referred to in judgment

Peter Shanley SC with Rory Brady BL instructed by *O'Rourke Reid & Co.* **for the plaintiffs**
Brian McCracken SC and Eoin McGonigal SC with Dominic Hussey BL instructed by *Orpen Franks & Co.* **for the first and fourth defendants**
Brian McGovern BL instructed by *Finbarr Cahill & Co.* **for the second defendant**

MURPHY J **16 March 1990**

Complicated though this matter is, it seems to me that there is nothing to be gained by reserving my judgment. The case largely involves questions of fact and the sooner they are disposed of the better in the interests of all the parties concerned.

This matter started in or about the month of November 1986 when three individuals (the first-named plaintiff Mr Michael Holland, the first-named defendant Brian McGill and the second-named defendant Daniel Ryan) came together to discuss a common venture or enterprise. They had a plan to purchase the Harcourt Hotel at Nos. 60 and 61 Harcourt Street. At the time of their initial discussion they were not certain that they could acquire the hotel but they were considering making a bid for it.

The three individuals whom I have named met together. Mr Holland says that the material meeting took place in the Burlington Hotel. Mr McGill and Mr Ryan dispute that venue but there is a large measure of argument between all three parties as to what took place at the early stage of their planning. It was agreed, for example, and all the parties are united on this, that Mr Ryan would manage the hotel if they succeeded in acquiring it. It was agreed that Mr McGill, who is a building contractor, would carry out the required renovations and, indeed, would do so at cost. It was agreed that Mr Holland would arrange the finances required for the enterprise and would provide other services such as arranging insurance and similar commercial matters.

The significant dispute between the parties relates to whether or not an agreement was made at that early stage on how the parties would deal with each other in the event of one of them seeking to withdraw from the transaction. It was agreed that they would be equal partners, that they would have one-third share each. Subsequently it became clear that the transaction would be carried out through the medium of a company in which they or their nominees would have equal shareholdings.

I am satisfied that there was discussion as to what would happen in the event of one party seeking to withdraw from the enterprise. I believe that this matter was at least touched upon and some consideration given to it. It was not, in my view, canvassed in detail, and for that reason it is understandable that there is some failure by some of the parties to recollect what was said. I am quite convinced that it was the intention of all the parties that these details would be ironed out and properly recorded, and recorded, indeed, in pursuance of the advice to be given by a solicitor or solicitors to be engaged by one or more of them. It was obviously a matter that would involve technical detail and presumably require legal advice. However, the general bones agreed were that if one party wished to withdraw, the other two would have an opportunity of acquiring his interest, that the project would be liquidated if they failed and that all parties would receive their share on the sale of the assets. I believe that, in principle, such an arrangement was adumbrated with the approval of the parties. From there the matter proceeded. The hotel was acquired in December 1986. It was purchased by a company called Olema Consultants Ltd, which was a pre-existing company in which the plaintiffs were interested. The parties contributed finance and subscribed for shareholdings. Each of the three shareholders arranged to subscribe £30,000 for an allotment of shares therein. The shares of Mr Holland were taken in the name of L.S. Communications Ltd, but so far as this matter is concerned that is a detail. Until July 1987 the three individuals were equal shareholders or equal partners, which, I think, would be an adequate expression for them in this enterprise.

The hotel operated for a short period after being acquired and then repairs were carried out by Mr McGill, as arranged. The hotel then re-opened in or about St Patrick's Day 1987. As a result of the cost of the repairs, there was some difficulty with regard to finance and further monies were raised from Mr Holland and Mr McGill. As Mr Ryan did not want any further or additional financial involvement he did not contribute at that stage, so that the shareholdings became unequal and Mr Ryan had a lesser or smaller fraction in the partnership after July 1987.

However, after the re-opening of the hotel and before the allotment of the additional shares a document was produced dealing with the management of the hotel and the rights of pre-emption in the event of shares being sold. This document was prepared by the solicitors retained by Mr Holland (O'Rourke Reid & Co.) and it undoubtedly went to two drafts, if not three. There was a first draft, perhaps an intermediate draft as well as a third draft. It is Mr Holland's evidence that he gave at least one of the drafts, the final draft, to Mr McGill and Mr Ryan. In particular, he says that he discussed one of the drafts with Mr McGill and that, as a result of this discussion with Mr McGill, certain changes were made in relation to the provisions in the agreement dealing with the management of the hotel and the position of the general manager. Mr McGill accepts that he received a copy of a draft of the agreement. He says that he took the document home and that there it remained and that he did not pay much attention to it. Mr Ryan has no recollection of ever receiving a copy of the document or having had any discussion with regard to it.

There are, therefore, differences as to what took place between April 1987 and July of the same year with regard to this document. However, it is agreed by all the parties that no document was executed at that stage and the plaintiffs do not suggest that there was. They rely upon the existence of the draft of the unexecuted document as confirming the recollection of Mr Holland as to what took place at the initial meeting which Mr Holland says was held in Burlington Hotel in October or November 1986. As I say, Mr McGill agreed with this to the extent that the document, when produced to him, did not come as a surprise nor did he object to it, and everything indicates that some such document was anticipated, certainly by Mr McGill.

There the matter rested and nothing occurred material to the issues here until October 1989. Nothing of immediate importance happened, but what occurred is that the relationship between Mr Ryan and the others, Mr McGill in particular, deteriorated and there were long periods during which Mr McGill and Mr Ryan were not on speaking terms. Mr Ryan was dissatisfied with his position and wished to withdraw from the enterprise and both the other parties (Mr McGill and Mr Holland) were anxious to facilitate him; and to achieve this they sought from time to time to arrange the acquisition of a public house or other premises which would satisfy Mr Ryan's needs and facilitate his withdrawal from the enterprise.

There was one other matter which occurred in 1989. Mr Holland drew up a draft agreement in connection with a proposed purchase of Mr Ryan's shares. The matter was not implemented but the document is of some significance as indicating the intention of Mr Holland to purchase Mr Ryan's shares, though it is pointed out that in the draft document Mr Holland was expressed to be purchasing in trust. It was Mr Holland's evidence that he intended to acquire the shares for the remaining shareholders that is to say, Mr McGill and himself, although at that stage further shareholders had been produced who represented the same interest as Mr Holland.

In or about October 1989 an opportunity arose to purchase an hotel in O'Connell Street and in this regard differences arose between Mr McGill and Mr Holland. Mr Holland explained that they had been anxious that Mr McGill would join with them in the new acquisition, that he (Mr McGill) was disinclined to do so and that he subsequently changed his mind and wanted to participate in the new acquisition. This gave rise to some disagreement. From that point on the subject matter of these proceedings moved with greater dispatch.

On 23 October Mr Ryan made it clear that he was anxious to sell his shares to either Mr McGill or Mr Holland and a written offer to that effect was circulated to both parties. At this stage the irony is that the solicitors on behalf of Mr McGill were concerned about the existence of an agreement which restricted dealing with the shares in the company except in accordance with the pre-emption agreed. Mr McGill traced the written but unsigned agreement which had been given to him by Mr Holland. This document was forwarded to the other solicitors and, as a result, inquiries were put in train. The solicitor dealing with the matter on behalf of Mr Ryan (Mr Donovan of Orpen Franks & Co.) 'phoned the solicitor on behalf of Mr Holland (Dermot O'Rourke of O'Rourke Reid & Co.) on a date which I think was 26 October 1989 to inquire whether or not there was such an agreement; and, as I understand it, it was Mr O'Rourke's advice to Mr O'Donovan that as far as he (Mr O'Rourke) was concerned there was no such agreement, that he did recollect preparing a document for the purpose of discussion and for what it was worth, and that it had not been signed. That was the evidence which Mr O'Donovan gave of his 'phone conversation with Mr O'Rourke, Mr Holland's solicitor, and that evidence was not contradicted nor was Mr O'Rourke called to give evidence.

Apart from the evidence of that conversation, there were two letters written by O'Rourke Reid & Co. to Finbar Cahill & Co., the solicitors on behalf of Mr Ryan. They were the letters of 10 November and 29 November. The letter dated 10 November to Finbar Cahill & Co. was headed "without prejudice" and the second paragraph of that letter contains the following statement:

> "We note that negotiations . . . your client also feels the same."

Finbar Cahill & Co. replied to that letter on 27 November and said:

> "We refer to your letter on 10th instant . . . and to the Articles of the Company."

In reply there is a letter of 29 November, also marked "without prejudice", the second paragraph of which contains the following statement:

> "In regard to paragraph 2, there is no agreement . . . of shares in the company."

I pause to comment on the fact that the two letters from O'Rourke Reid & Co. are marked "without prejudice". This arose from the fact that, as all of the parties have indicated and was recognised, in the month of October and into early November negotiations took place with a view to resolving the differences that had arisen between them in relation to the litigation which was then pending. The correspondence relating to those negotiations was marked "without prejudice" and was without prejudice. However, the letter of 10 November which was tendered in evidence was admitted by me because it was clear that the negotiations were at an end from that letter. At any rate, in my view the statement on which the party tendering the evidence wished to rely related to future conduct and not to past conduct and, in particular, not to any matter which was part of any prior negotiations. On that basis I admitted the letter of 10 November in evidence, similarly the letter of 29 November, which was still further removed from the negotiations which had taken place with a view to settlement of the then completed proceedings.

The statements made by the solicitors on behalf of the plaintiffs were, it seems to me, clear: that there was no agreement and that there was no impediment to either party purchasing Mr Ryan's shares.

Now, counsel on behalf of the plaintiffs has analysed the conduct of the defendants with a view to establishing that, notwithstanding these unequivocal representations, the defendants did not rely on the statements contained therein or on the statements or advice given by Mr O'Rourke in his 'phone conversation with Mr O'Donovan. In this regard a number of matters have been referred to. First of all, the evidence has been analysed as to when the negotiations which subsequently took place between Mr Ryan and Mr McGill or their representatives with regard to the sale and purchase of Mr Ryan's shareholding actually took place. Before these statements were made, it is said. That may be so, but if some discussions took place they were pursued with considerable vigour in November and December, and if agreement was reached in principle, it seems to me it was reached at the earliest in December.

I am entirely satisfied on the evidence that a final binding agreement was not concluded until January this year. So whilst it may be that some negotiations took place at an earlier date or that some inquiries were made, perhaps by Mr Leonard McGill, brother of Mr Brian McGill, I feel that the meaningful negotiations did not take place until after the representations were made on behalf of the plaintiffs.

Importance is also attached by the plaintiffs to the fact that the defendants, Mr McGill and Mr Ryan, and their advisers kept secret from the plaintiffs the negotiations taking place between them and undoubtedly they did so. No reference was made to the negotiations and up to the last moment their existence was kept from Mr Holland. What counsel on behalf of the plaintiffs urge is that this secrecy was due to the fact that the defendants were not convinced by and did not act on the representations made by the plaintiffs, that they still suspected that there was an agreement in existence which would impede the sale of the shares and that the plaintiffs, if they became aware of the negotiations, would apply for an injunction to restrain the threatened sale of the shares. It is common case, in fact, that the parties were apprehensive that Mr Holland would move for an injunction notwithstanding the statements emanating from his solicitor to the effect that there was no agreement.

I do not believe that the attitude of the defendants is inconsistent with the belief that they had and that they were induced to hold, that is, that there was no enforceable agreement. The defendants were advised, to my mind, unequivocally by their respective solicitors, and by counsel in the case of Mr McGill, that these representations were such that it would entitle them to proceed on the basis that there was no agreement. They may not have been convinced that this was an unassailable case or that the plaintiffs would accept it without challenge; and if they did take that view, their pessimism was justified because these proceedings were brought and Mr Holland and his colleagues did rely on an agreement which they had indicated did not exist.

Now why was it stated that there was no agreement? The statement emanated from the solicitors for Mr Holland and Mr Holland himself explained that it was made as a "negotiating ploy" to bring the parties back to the negotiating table which they had left not long beforehand. Importance is attached to the fact, rightly, in my view, that the actual author of the letter, Mr O'Rourke, was not called to give evidence. It seems unlikely that Mr O'Rourke would have lent his name to a statement which he knew to be untrue, no matter how commendable the purpose. Furthermore, the statement contained in Mr O'Rourke's letter is wholly consistent with what he himself said on the telephone to Mr O'Donovan.

In the circumstances it seems to me that the statement was made. It was one on which the defendants were entitled to rely and on which they did rely. The curious feature is that Mr Ryan was more inclined to negotiate with Mr Holland because of the differences which he (Mr Ryan) had with Mr McGill but altered his view largely on the advice of Mr O'Donovan. It was Mr McGill who had been invoking the existence of the agreement and Mr Ryan therefore felt it was safer to deal with Mr McGill rather than with Mr Holland who was repudiating the existence of any such restriction. I accept that as being the case. It is consistent with what occurred and, of course, there is evidence of Mr O'Donovan.

I think, therefore, that the defendants were entitled to rely on these statements and to a large extent they did so. I do not suggest or believe that it was the only motivation but I believe it was a powerful one and a factor which influenced both Mr Ryan and Mr McGill. They were influenced in different ways and to a different extent, particularly having regard to the fact that Mr Ryan was under the impression that there had never been any agreement of any description, oral or written, in relation to the rights of the shareholders. But whatever Mr Ryan's personal belief had been, his solicitors had explored the matter and were influenced by the representations made to them and the information received by them and on that basis they proceeded with the distribution of the shares.

With hindsight, one sees that negotiations were taking place between two parties without any information being given to the third. I think it is clear that Mr McGill informed Mr Holland that the directors' meeting arranged for 11 January would discuss certain stock losses and other matters, but no indication was given with regard to an intended transfer of a substantial block of shares in the company or of the resignation of one director and the appointment of another. It can be said, of course, that this matter was not finally agreed and the documentation not executed until after the conversations had taken place between Mr McGill and Mr Holland, but the final execution of the sale agreement was not completed until 8 am on the morning of 11 January. I have no doubt, however, that matters were sufficiently far advanced in the earlier days when the meeting was being convened, that the parties anticipated that this matter would come before the meeting of 11 January, and that that was the reason they were anxious to proceed on that date and not agree to the adjournment sought by Mr Holland.

On the other hand, with regard to the requirements of the convening of meetings of directors, it is common case that the law does not stipulate any defined period as being required for notice to be given. Due notice is what is required and this is usually established by practice among the parties. In the present case, Mr Holland was told when the meeting would be held, agreed to the date and, in fact, he stipulated 9.30 in the morning. Subsequently he was dissatisfied and inconvenienced and more particularly sought an agenda which was not provided. But Mr Holland did know that the meeting was on but did not know the topics to be discussed. Again, the law is clear in that regard. There is no requirement to provide an agenda for directors' meetings, though in practice it may be desirable that it be done occasionally if not frequently.

There can be no complaint, I believe, by Mr Holland that he did not get an agenda for the meeting, but I think he has grounds for complaining that he was misled as to what the agenda would be. There was no obligation on Mr McGill to say what would be on the agenda, but I think he owed a duty not to mislead Mr Holland as to what the parties intended to discuss. That having been done, the reality of the matter is that two directors (Mr McGill and Mr Ryan) were in agreement as to what they intended to achieve at the meeting and were going to achieve their purpose whether the meeting was conducted on the 11th or at a later date. If Mr Holland had been told what was planned, all that he could achieve would be to seek an injunction to restrain the implementation of the transaction.

What counsel on Mr Holland's behalf conceded is that the ultimate outcome could not be altered if the position was as I have held it to be; that whatever agreement existed, the parties were estopped from relying on it as a result of the fact that they represented that no such agreement existed and the defendants acted on that representation. In all the circumstances it is understandable that this should be the case because both parties honestly and properly believed that the matter had been discussed. There was a measure of agreement as far back as 1986 about some such arrangement but it had not been processed at that time and the subsequent effort to do so was not completed either. So in the circumstances it was understandable that there would be a belief that there was an agreement and a belief that there was not an agreement and that ultimately Mr Holland and his colleague came down to saying that there was no agreement. Having been unequivocally informed that that was the position, it was understandable that the defendants should act on it, as I believe they did.

In the circumstances it seems to me that the plaintiffs are estopped from relying on any agreement.

With regard to the meeting of the directors, it seems to me that it was validly held and that the business which was completed at that meeting cannot now be set aside.

I think that justice would be done if I gave the defendants their costs but limited to a two-day hearing. I will allow the defendants their costs in both interlocutory applications.

Patricia McLaughlin
Barrister

George Robinson, Maria Gregg and Elizabeth Robinson v. Mary Theresa Corneill, Rayhill Property Company Ltd and Home Affairs Ltd: High Court 1990 No. 15834P (Keane J) 10 April 1992

Shares – Beneficial interest – First named defendant owned all but one of the shares in each of the defendant companies – Business purchased by second defendant company and operated by third defendant company – First named plaintiff employed as general manager of the business – Relations between the parties broke down – First plaintiff summarily dismissed – Whether dismissal unlawful – Whether defendant had discharged onus of proof – Whether first plaintiff guilty of misappropriation of funds – Payments made by second and third plaintiffs – Whether they were intended to be for the benefit of the first named plaintiff only – Whether the second and third plaintiff acquired a beneficial interest in the companies

Facts: In November 1988, the first named defendant, Mrs Corneill, purchased The Clonmannon Village, a retirement complex, out of her own resources. The first named plaintiff, Mr Robinson, had previously owned the business along with two others but the venture was unsuccessful and a receiver was appointed by the bank. The property was vested in the name of Rayhill Property Company Ltd, and Home Affairs Ltd operated the business. All except one of the shares in each company were vested in Mrs Corneill. Mr Robinson and Mrs Corneill, who had met in England, lived together as man and wife and Mrs Corneill helped the plaintiff out of his financial difficulties. Mr Robinson was appointed general manager of the retirement complex. In or around the summer of 1990, relations between the two parties broke down to such an extent that Mrs Corneill demanded that Mr Robinson leave their home and at the same time the company purported to dismiss him. Two main issues arose in these proceedings. The first was a claim by the first named plaintiff that two of his daughters, the second and third named plaintiffs were entitled to a beneficial interest in the two companies. He claimed that both of these plaintiffs sold their respective properties in England and invested the proceeds in the project. He further said that his nephew, John Robinson, gave him a cheque for £15,000 which was ultimately transferred to Mrs Corneill. He alleged that the agreement was that his two daughters should have a 50 per cent interest in the two companies as he himself could not hold shares as they could be seized by his creditors. Mrs Corneill, whilst accepting that such monies were paid, alleged that they were for the benefit of Mr Robinson. The second main issue concerned the dismissal of Mr Robinson. Mrs Corneill alleged that he was drinking to excess, that he was not attending properly to his duties and was also absenting himself from the running of the village. She further alleged that he was converting monies of the companies to his own use. The evidence was that there were discrepancies in the records of the business as to cheques which had been paid by guests at the village but which had been cashed by Mr Robinson. All of these cheques, except one, had been endorsed by Mrs Corneill. Mr Robinson denied all of these allegations.

Held by Keane J:

(1) On the evidence, the second and third named plaintiffs were entitled to a beneficial interest in 50 per cent of the shares in the two companies.

(2) The burden of proof with regard to the allegations supporting the dismissal of the first plaintiff rested on the first named defendant who failed to discharge that burden.

(3) The cheques cashed by Mr Robinson reflected the informal business arrangement that the parties had and did not amount to conduct which would justify the dismissal of the first named plaintiff.

(4) The first named plaintiff was not employed by the companies for a fixed term, and was entitled to at least six months notice of the termination of his contract and was entitled to £12,500 in lieu of such notice for his wrongful summary dismissal, being half of the salary which he was entitled to.

No cases referred to in judgment

Eamon de Valera SC with Mr O'Leary BL instructed by *C.B. Kingston & Co.* **for the plaintiffs**

Peter Shanley SC and Brian McGovern SC instructed by *Gerard J Haughton & Co.* **for the defendants**

KEANE J **10 April 1992**

The four sets of proceedings before me (three of them in the form of chancery actions seeking certain declarations, and one in the form of a summary summons) were consolidated by order of Carney J. And while three of them are in the form of chancery actions, the case bears more resemblance in some of its features to a matrimonial dispute.

First of all, so far as it is not seriously in dispute, it is necessary to set out the history of the matters which have led to this litigation. In particular, that involves an account of the background to the relationship of the two protagonists, so to speak, in the case, Mr George Robinson and Mrs Mary Corneill.

Mr Robinson is a businessman who spent a lot of his life on the north of England where, over quite a number of years, he met and became friendly with Mrs Corneill. But Mr Robinson's business ventures in the north of England did not prosper; in fact, they were extremely unsuccessful. At some stage in the early 1980s Mr Robinson returned to Ireland. I say "returned" since he himself is of Irish origin as indeed is Mrs Corneill. On his return to Ireland Mr Robinson along with two other people bought part of the lands of Clonmannon near Ashford in County Wicklow belonging to Prince Colonna for the purpose of establishing retirement homes there. This form of retirement village is obviously a familiar type of development nowadays. It consisted of a main house in which the more infirm of the elderly persons would be in receipt of nursing care, while those who would be more active would be accommodated in bungalows but could avail of the facilities in the main house for meals and so on. That was the sort of project that was envisaged and it was duly set up through the medium of two companies with two other persons, one of whom was a Mr Rowland. This project proved to be financially disastrous from Mr Robinson's point of view and presumably from the point of view of his two partners, and in due course a receiver was appointed by the bank. At this stage Mr Robinson was living at The Paddocks in Celbridge. Since his mortgage repayments were in arrears the bank, compounding his difficulties, as it were, were threatening to repossess this house and sell it. It was at this time when Mr Robinson was in these acute financial difficulties that Mrs Corneill came to Ireland.

Mrs Corneill had, in turn, been having problems of a health nature. She had had a violent robbery at her house in Cheshire and she came to stay with Mr Robinson in his house in Celbridge. Whilst there, she had some serious illness which necessitated her being in hospital in Dublin. But during this time, whilst she retained her business interests in England, she and Mr Robinson (who had, as I said, been friendly for a number of years) developed a closer relationship and ultimately lived together effectively as man and wife for a period of time until there arose the differences between them which culminated in these proceedings.

I should recall in relation to Mrs Corneill that she, like Mr Robinson, had had a difficult life, not from a financial point of view, at least not in recent times, but because she had been widowed relatively young in tragic circumstances and then had to bring up her family on her own resources. She built up her business and eventually managed to provide herself with a relatively comfortable style of living, which was due to her own efforts in very difficult circumstances. It was at this stage that a closer relationship developed between these two people.

It was also at this time that the receiver of Clonmannon Village was anxious to dispose of the assets of the two companies (Retirement Ireland Ltd and Retirement International Ltd) which effectively consisted of the retirement village. Mrs Corneill became interested in purchasing the retirement village and in November 1988 the receiver accepted a tender in the sum of £71,000 from Mrs Corneill. The purchase money was provided by her from the sale of The Paddocks. I should intervene to say that, following on Mrs Corneill coming to live in Ireland and the closer relationship developing between herself and Mr Robinson, she helped him out of his current financial crisis in relation to his house by buying the house herself from the bank. That gave Mr Robinson a home but Mrs Corneill subsequently sold The Paddocks and bought Ballinapark Lodge, Wicklow, where she continued to live with Mr Robinson.

Now, the purchase money for Clonmannon Village was provided by Mrs Corneill out of her resources and out of the proceeds of sale of The Paddocks and other funds of Mrs Corneill's. The Clonmannon property was vested in the name of Rayhill Property Company Ltd and Home Affairs Ltd was intended to be the company actually operating the business. The shares in those two companies, at all times material to these proceedings, were vested in Mrs Corneill with the exception of one share, the registered owner of which was Mr Brendan Jeffers who was the company secretary. Mr Robinson was appointed general manager of the retirement complex and, again, it is not in dispute that he was responsible, at least in a general sense, for the management of the complex.

The relationship between Mr Robinson and Mrs Corneill seems to have remained harmonious for some time after the venture commenced. As I have said, the receiver sold the property in November 1988 and it was then operated as a retirement home. Matters seem to have been proceeding relatively harmoniously until some time in the summer of 1990, or possibly later. Certainly not earlier than the summer of 1990 relations between Mr Robinson and Mrs Corneill deteriorated to such an extent that Mrs Corneill demanded that Mr Robinson leave the house in which they were living. At the same time the company purported to dismiss him from his post as manager and a solicitor's letter confirming those matters was in due course received. Following correspondence between the solicitors for the parties these proceedings were issued.

A number of issues arise in the proceedings, but there appear to be two main issues. Of these, the first is the one to which most attention was directed during the hearing and the one which most of the evidence revolved around, and that is, as to whether Mrs Corneill is exclusively entitled to the beneficial interest in the shares in the two companies or whether members of Mr Robinson's family are also so entitled. That is really the principal bone of contention between the parties, although there are others. The second main issue is as to whether Mr Robinson's conduct as general manager of the retirement complex was such as to justify the termination of his managership by the companies. A third issue is whether Mr Robinson is entitled to account to the companies for monies which, it is alleged, he wrongfully converted. There is also an issue as to the ownership of motor cars which were, in the main, imported from the UK by Mrs Corneill.

There was also an issue as to whether Mr Robinson is entitled to any beneficial interest in the property known as Ballinapark Lodge but that does not appear to have been pursued in any way and it is not a matter in which any evidence was adduced to suggest that he had any such interest.

As to the first main issue, Mr Robinson said in evidence that he first interested Mrs Corneill in the Clonmannon Village project. He says that the arrangement between them, once they formed an affectionate and close relationship, was that they would be in business together. He says that Mrs Corneill was obviously aware of his financial situation, that she helped him substantially in relation to his own house and was obviously aware that he had no money of his own. He says that he was anxious to have some stake in this retirement complex apart from running it, and he says that the way in which he was to have a stake in the business was really through members of his own family. Two of his daughters had some property of their own in the Manchester area and he says that they were willing to sell their properties and invest the proceeds of sale in the Clonmannon Village project. He said that one of his daughters, Mrs Maria

Gregg (a plaintiff in one set of proceedings) sold her flat in Manchester and transferred £37,375 to him by cheque, that he in turn paid over to Mrs Corneill. He says that another daughter, Elizabeth Robinson, similarly sold her flat and that the proceeds, after paying off all charges, was £7,400 and that that sum was paid to Mrs Corneill. He says that his nephew, John Robinson, who is a businessman in London, gave him a cheque for £15,000 and that that cheque in turn was ultimately transferred to Mrs Corneill. He says that the intention was — indeed, that the agreement between himself and Mrs Corneill was — that his two daughters should have a 50 per cent interest in the two companies. His reason for not taking the shares himself, he says, was because of the fact that he owed money and had judgments registered against him and that any shares or property in his name could be seized by his creditors. In summary, that is Mr Robinson's account of matters.

Mrs Corneill gives a different version. She agrees that these funds were paid to her but she says that they were transferred in part as to £30,000 to an account in a bank in the Channel Islands and as to £15,000 in payment for one of the cars now in dispute in the proceedings, that that represented the monies owing in respect of the car which was meant to become Mr Robinson's car. Mrs Corneill says that a further sum of £7,000 was retained to enable Mr Robinson to have some spending money. She says that the reason this arrangement was entered into, namely, that a substantial part of the monies was paid into an account in the Channel Islands, was that, if they were paid into Mr Robinson's own account in a bank in Dublin or in Manchester, they would be swallowed up by his indebtedness to the bank. She says (and this is not in dispute) that she paid various sums to another of Mr Robinson's daughters, Fiona, who is not in fact one of the daughters who actually transferred funds to Mrs Corneill. Cheques were undoubtedly paid to Fiona Robinson and I will refer to them later in more detail. That is the evidence of the two principal protagonists in this case as to the shares in the two companies.

As to the dismissal of Mr Robinson from his position as manager of the Clonmannon Village complex, it is accepted that he was manager of the complex. Indeed, a notice was issued by the defendants on the notepaper of Rayhill Property Company Ltd on 15 December 1989 to the effect that he was to be manager for a term of at least five years. It is simply a notice headed "To Whom It May Concern". There was no formal agreement as to Mr Robinson's position. There was no agreement in writing and no formal agreement as to his salary, certainly not in writing. Mr Robinson says it was agreed that he would be paid £25,000 per annum and provided with a car. Mrs Corneill says that no sum was agreed as such, but that he was being provided by her with accommodation, clothing and spending money and that this would, in effect, take care of the salary, that any extra money he needed would be provided by her.

Mrs Corneill had three specific complaints to make about Mr Robinson's conduct as manager of the Clonmannon Village project. First of all, she says that he was drinking to excess, not in the early part of his employment but in the later stages, that he was not attending properly to his duties at a later stage and was absenting himself from the running of the village. She also says that he was converting monies of the companies to his own use. Mr Robinson denies all these claims. For his part, Mr Robinson also asserted that monies were being transferred from these two companies by Mrs Corneill to accounts of hers in the Channel Islands.

In relation to the first of these issues, it has to be said that it is simply not possible to reconcile the accounts given by Mr Robinson and by Mrs Corneill as to the ownership of the shares. There is no way of reconciling the two accounts given of the history of what transpired. Now, I have to bear in mind that the two protagonists have had difficult problems. There is no reason to suppose that their relationship was anything but an affectionate and happy one. Because of their experiences (in Mrs Corneill's case, her health problems, and in Mr Robinson's case his financial difficulties) I think this relationship was originally a source of comfort to both parties and that is why I said at the outset that the case bore a resemblance to a matrimonial case in that the previously affectionate relationship turned to one of great bitterness, with mutual recriminations, and blame, ultimately culminating in litigation about money as much as anything else.

Where people are dealing with matters which they feel emotionally concerned with, one always has to approach the evidence with caution, particularly where there is a great feeling of bitterness involved and where one is in danger of not getting an accurate account of what happened. Bearing that in mind in assessing as best I can the demeanour and credibility of these two witnesses as they gave evidence, Mr Robinson struck me as being relatively straightforward in his account of matters. I find Mrs Corneill to be inclined to justify her own position and to make points rather than give a detached reliable account of what had occurred. It is difficult to expect people to give a detached account of events in a context such as this. However, doing the best I can between these two conflicting accounts, on the whole I find that I would be more inclined to rely on Mr Robinson's account. There is, of course, other evidence which has to be taken into account.

In relation to the factual evidence as to the cheques, it is not in dispute that monies were paid over, but Mrs Corneill has given an explanation as to why that was done. It was suggested that monies were paid by Mrs Corneill to Fiona Robinson, and that this was a circuitous means of dealing with Mr Robinson's money at a stage when it was useful to use Mrs Corneill's bank account to pay these monies to his daughter Fiona.

I now turn to the evidence of Mrs Maria Gregg and Miss Elizabeth Robinson, two of Mr Robinson's daughters, and to the evidence of John Robinson, Mr George Robinson's nephew, all of whom gave evidence that the moneys were paid with a view to investment in the Clonmannon project and with the intention that Maria Gregg and Elizabeth Robinson should have a half interest in the companies along with Mrs Corneill.

There was also the evidence of Mr John Keenan, an architect, who said that he was invited to become secretary of both companies; indeed, his name appears in the companies' returns but is struck out with the name of Mr Jeffers substituted. He said that, having considered the proposal, he decided to reject it. At the time when that proposal was being discussed, he says that he met Mr Robinson and Mrs Corneill and was told that it was intended that Mr Robinson's two daughters were to have an interest in the companies.

I would have to say that I find it extremely difficult to believe that all of these people have simply fabricated this evidence in order to assist Mr Robinson. I found them all to be candid and truthful witnesses, doing their best to recall matters. In the case of the two young women, Maria Gregg and Elizabeth Robinson, it is of course true that natural filial affection would make them not disinterested witnesses. Apart from the fact that they struck me as giving truthful accounts of what they recalled about these matters, I would in any case find it unlikely that they would for no particular reason decide to advance these large sums to their father. It is no answer to say that he was in financial difficulties because that was a fairly common state of affairs with Mr Robinson. It is not suggested that these two young women are well off. And why they should elect to make available to Mr Robinson these (to them) important funds is most unclear were it not for the fact that they were involved in the whole project to the extent that they had assets available for investment and that it would at least keep an interest in this property in the family. From Mr Robinson's point of view, of course, it is less than admirable, particularly in the context of his creditors, that he should be placing this investment in his daughter's names so as to put it beyond the reach of any creditors who might have unsatisfied judgments against him. That may not be a particularly admirable form of activity from the point of view of Mr Robinson's creditors, but I am simply concerned to see what the arrangement was between himself and Mrs Corneill. I find that the arrangement was as stated in evidence by Mr Robinson and as confirmed by the other witnesses. It also concurs with the most likely state of affairs. I do not overlook the fact that these cheques amounting to £24,350 were paid by Mrs Corneill to Miss Fiona Robinson, which sum is, of course, short of the total of the cheques paid to Mrs Corneill. And even if one supposes that Mrs Corneill is correct in her statement in relation to the car, it still falls short of the total funds transferred to Mrs Corneill.

In these circumstances I am satisfied that a case has been made out on Mr Robinson's behalf, or, more accurately, on behalf of his two daughters and that they are entitled to a beneficial interest in 50 per cent of the shares in the two companies. As to the proportion to which they are entitled to those shares, I will return to that later.

As to the next matter in controversy, that is, the management arrangement, the various complaints that were made as to Mr Robinson's conduct of his managership of the complex have already been referred to. As to the complaint of excessive drinking, Mr Robinson denied this assertion. He agreed that he was not a teetotaller and drank in a social fashion, almost invariably in the company of Mrs Corneill and outside his working hours. To an extent, his evidence in this regard was borne out by a number of witnesses who met him in business and social contexts. The undoubted burden of proof rests on Mrs Corneill's side in relation to these allegations. Looking at the evidence as a whole — and I do not overlook the evidence of Mr Rasmussen, who thought that Mr Robinson was drinking to excess — I am satisfied that this complaint has not been made out. I am equally satisfied that it has not been established that Mr Robinson was neglecting his duties as manager of the complex.

As to the question of the conversion of monies, this appears to relate to cheques which were paid by people who stayed in the nursing home, not from the people living in the bungalows. At least, I think that is the position. But the point is that these residents, or patients, settled their accounts monthly by cheque. The secretary and book-keeper, Mrs O'Neill, gave evidence that she found discrepancies in her records in the sense that the invoices did not correspond with the cheques as lodged to the bank account of the companies. When the cheques were ultimately accounted for, it appeared that they had been cashed. She also said that, with the exception of one cheque, all the cheques were endorsed by Mrs Corneill. So what happened in this regard seems to have been that these cheques would be left by the residents in settlement of their accounts, that from time to time Mr Robinson would take them and bring them to Mrs Corneill and suggest that they be used for cash, for which purpose her endorsement would be required. All of that seems to have been, if not a particularly businesslike arrangement, nothing that would amount to conversion of funds because, of course, these two people were living together at the time effectively as husband and wife. This would be a result of the informal arrangements they had when living happily together and of a certain informality in their business arrangements. I accept Mr Robinson's evidence in this regard and I am satisfied that he was not in fact guilty of any particular misconduct which would have justified his summary dismissal.

I have already referred to a document of 15 December 1989 which is headed "Mr George Robinson (Employment)" and "To Whom It May Concern". It is on the notepaper of Rayhill Property Company Ltd and says:

> "Mr George Robinson is commencing full time employment with the above company, together with the full time management of our associated Care Company (Home Affairs Ltd). He will commence employment on 1 January 1990 and will be provided with a two bedroom bungalow within the complex for the duration of his contract which shall not be less than five years."

And it is signed "M.T. Corneill, Managing Director".

As I have said, I am satisfied that grounds for the summary dismissal of Mr Robinson from his employment have not been established by the evidence. At the same time I do not think it would in any sense be realistic to measure the damages which he is undoubtedly entitled to for his dismissal by reference to this five-year contract. Even if one supposes that that was a perfectly valid and binding contract to employ him for a five-year period, questions would have to be gone into as to what the position would be in relation to tax and in relation to his obligation to mitigate his damages by seeking other employment and so on. In any event, I am satisfied that this document is not really a satisfactory document as regards laying the grounds for a five-year contract. It purports to be on behalf of Rayhill Property Company Ltd and Home Affairs Ltd but there is no evidence of any resolution being passed by the directors of these companies authorising this transaction, or, indeed, any resolution appointing Mrs Corneill as managing director, although it was in that capacity that she signed this document. The reality is that this document did not reflect the true nature of the contract, which was highly informal but which still involved Mr Robinson in full-time supervisory duties. It was a responsible position and one which would therefore entitle him to reasonable notice if he and the two companies should, for whatever reason, part company. For that reason I would have thought that he would be entitled to at least six months' notice of termination of whatever contract he had with these companies. Accepting as I do, Mr Robinson's evidence that the agreement was that he was entitled to a salary of £25,000 a year, which would have been paid indirectly by Mrs Corneill in various forms in kind as well as in cash, the fact remains that once it came to the parting of the ways between them he was entitled to at least six months' notice. If he did not get the appropriate salary in lieu, that would entitle him to the sum of £12,500 in respect of what I found to be his wrongful summary dismissal.

As to the question of the cars, Mr Robinson was given the use of one of these cars. All of these cars were Mrs Corneill's cars. In the end they seem not to have played any great part in the evidence. However, it appears that the cars are all now in the possession of the two companies or in the possession of Mrs Corneill and it does not appear to be necessary to give any relief in respect of them. There may be some reason for supposing that their importation into the country may have been, in part, an attempt to evade the relevant excise duties and that is not something the court should countenance. So I propose not to make any order in relation to the cars.

As to Ballinapark House, no claim was pressed in relation to that property.

Counsel have very helpfully reduced to writing the issues and I propose to go through them as they were furnished to me.

Question No. 1 is:

> "Do George Robinson, Maria Gregg or Elizabeth Robinson or any of them have any legal or beneficial interest in the following limited liability companies or either of them:
> (i) Rayhill Property Company Ltd
> (ii) Home Affairs Ltd?"

The answer to that question is that both Maria Gregg and Elizabeth Robinson have a beneficial interest in those companies.

Question No. 2 is:

> "If the answer to question 1 is "Yes", assess the extent of their respective interests."

The answer to that question is that I find that they are jointly entitled to a 50 per cent interest in the share in both companies in the proportions as between them of 37 to 7. I have not worked out the percentages in relation to that question. Obviously it will be understood that I am taking into account their respective financial contributions as proved in the evidence.

Question No. 3 is:

> "Do George Robinson, Maria Gregg or Elizabeth Robinson or any of them have any legal or beneficial interest in ALL AND THOSE the premises known as Ballinapark Lodge, Ashford in the County of Wicklow?"

The answer to that question is "no", so question No. 4 does not arise.

Question No. 5 is:

> "Are Mary Theresa Corneill, Rayhill Property Company Ltd or Home Affairs Ltd indebted to George Robinson, Maria Gregg or Elizabeth Robinson or any of them?"

The answer to that question is "no", save the claim for damages for wrongful dismissal against the companies to which I will come in a moment. I should observe parenthetically that while the suggestion was made at one stage that Mrs Corneill was transferring to the Channel Islands funds which properly belonged to the companies, the evidence on that was fleeting and insubstantial and I would not be prepared to find that that happened so question No. 6 does not arise.

Question No. 7 is:

> "Was George Robinson employed by Rayhill Property Company Ltd and Home Affairs Ltd or either of them for a fixed term from 1 January 1990 until 31 December 1994?"

For the reasons already given, I have serious doubts as to whether Mr Robinson was, in fact, employed in a proper sense for a fixed term so I would answer "no" to that question.

Question No. 8 is:

> "Has the employment of George Robinson with Rayhill Property Company Ltd and Home Affairs Ltd, howsoever arising, been lawfully and validly terminated?"

The answer to that question is "no".

Question No. 9 is:

> "Was George Robinson guilty of converting to his own use monies and assets which were the property of Mary Corneill, Rayhill Property Company Ltd and Home Affairs Ltd or any of them?"

The answer to that question is "no".

Question No. 10 is:

> "If the answer to question 9 is "yes", assess damages?".

I have already indicated damages in the sum of £12,500.

Question No. 11 is:

> "Was George Robinson in breach of his contract of employment with Rayhill Property Company Ltd and Home Affairs Ltd or either of them?"

The answer is "no".

Question No. 12 is:

> "If the answer to question 11 is "yes", assess damages for breach of contract?"

As I understand it, it does not arise.

Question No. 13 is:

> "Has George Robinson wrongfully detained property belonging to Mary Corneill, Rayhill Property Company Ltd and Home Affairs Ltd or any of them?"

The answer to that question is "no".

Question No. 14 is:

> "If the answer to question 13 is "yes", assess damages for detinue."

The answer is that that question does not arise.

The second part of question No. 14 is:

> "Alternatively are Mary Corneill or Rayhill Property Company Ltd or Home Affairs Ltd entitled to an injunction directing him to return the said property?"

The answer to that is "no".

There will be an order made accordingly.

Patricia McLaughlin
Barrister

Donal McAuliffe v. Lithographic Group Ltd: Supreme Court No. 224/93 (O'Flaherty, Egan and Blayney JJ) 2 November 1993 (*Nem. Diss.*)

Agreement – Shares – Pre-emption rights – Written agreement – Interpretation – Service by both parties of purchase notices – Whether obligations mutual

Facts: The plaintiff and his wife entered into an agreement to purchase 40% of the ordinary shares in Mac Publishing Ltd. The remaining shares were held by the defendant.

Clause 4.01 of the agreement provided that where "any of the parties hereto" ("the offeror") wished to dispose of his shares he had firstly to exhaust a right of pre-emption. Such a party was obliged to issue a purchase notice offering to sell the shares being disposed of to the holder of the other ordinary shares. The agreement provided for an audit and a mechanism to calculate the offer price, with arbitration in default of agreement. Within 90 days of the purchase notice, or within 30 days of the arbitrator's award the offeree was to complete the purchase of the offeror's shares.

This clause concluded by stating,

> "PROVIDED ALWAYS that if Donal McAuliffe is the Offeror, then Katrice McAuliffe shall automatically be deemed to have offered her shares under the same Purchase Notice unless otherwise agreed in writing by Lithographic AND FURTHER PROVIDED ALWAYS that in the event of the McAuliffes being the Offeror, then Lithographic shall be obliged to purchase the shares on offer at the price and within the time specified in this clause".

Clause 4.05 provided that "If within 90 days after the service of the Purchase Notice the Offeree has failed to pay as certified, the Offeror shall be entitled to sell the shares to any other person".

The defendant company issued a purchase notice on 6 January 1993, to which the plaintiff did not respond, other than that on 29 March the plaintiff and his wife served their purchase notice on the defendant company.

The High Court (Costello J) held that the obligation to purchase was a mutual one, and that the plaintiff and his wife were therefore obliged to purchase the shares held by the defendant company. The plaintiff appealed to the Supreme Court.

Held by the Supreme Court (O'Flaherty J, Egan and Blayney JJ concurring) in allowing the appeal:

(1) A court is obliged to give effect to each word in a written instrument (unless that produces an absurd result) and an express provision excludes the implication of any provision to the same effect.

(2) The final proviso, which made clear that if the plaintiff was the offeror, then the defendant was obliged to purchase the shares on offer, placed an obligation on the defendant company only.

(3) The binding purchase notice was therefore the one served by the plaintiff on 26 March 1993.

No cases referred to in judgment

Counsel's names not available

Solicitors for the plaintiff: *Gaynor & Co.*
Solicitors for the defendant: *L.K. Shields & Partners*

O'FLAHERTY J (Egan and Blayney JJ concurring) 2 November 1993

This is an appeal brought by the plaintiff from the judgment and order of the High Court (Costello J) of 12 July 1993 whereby he construed a clause in a shareholders agreement of 19 December 1988 as requiring the plaintiff and his wife, Katrice McAuliffe, to purchase the shares held by the defendant company in a company known as Mac Publishing Ltd.

The background facts may be thus summarised. By the said agreement made between, *inter alia*, the plaintiff and the defendant company, the plaintiff and his wife purchased 40 per cent of the 100 ordinary shares in Mac Publishing Ltd. The balance of the shares were held by the defendant company.

It is clear that each party was given a right of pre-emption in regard to the purchase of the other party's shares but the question in this case is: was the obligation to purchase the shares mutual or not?

The clause in the article with which the case is concerned is clause (iii) of Article 4.01 but I think it desirable to set forth some additional relevant clauses aside from that one. I reproduce them as follows:

"TRANSFER OF SHARES

4.01 Notwithstanding anything contained in the Articles of Association of the Companies, the parties hereto HEREBY AGREE and covenant with each other that none of them shall transfer or otherwise dispose of shares in the Companies otherwise than in accordance with the provisions thereof:

> (i) For the purposes of this article where any person is unconditionally entitled to be registered as a holder a share he and not the registered holder of such share shall be deemed to be a member of the company in respect of that share.
> (ii) Save as hereinafter provided no share in the capital of the companies shall be transferred unless and until the rights of preemption hereinafter conferred shall have been exhausted.
> (iii) Save as herein provided at Clause 4.02 and Clause 4.04 in the event that at any time any of the parties hereto ("the offeror") wish to dispose of all or part of their shareholding in the companies, then the party shall unless otherwise agreed in writing forthwith offer by notice in writing ("the purchase notice") to sell all or part of the shares held by them ("the shares") to the holder of the other ordinary shares in the relevant company ("the offeree"). The Purchase Notice once served shall not be revocable. The parties hereto shall procure that within 60 days of the service of the Purchase Notice, an audit shall be carried out (if not already available) of the books of the company for the last period ending 31 March. The Auditors shall as soon as the Audit has been complete value the company as a going concern and the value of any share shall be its value as a percentage of the total without any reduction because of any shareholding being a minority interest. The offer price shall be the relevant multiple of the share valuation save only that in the event that the offer price is less than 7 times the pre-tax trading profits (which term excludes any capital gains or losses or Directors' fees or Management Charges from Lithographic or any of its other subsidiaries) of the company for the relevant year on which the audit has been carried out, the offer price shall be the relevant percentage of 7 times the pre-tax trading profits, proportionate to the number of shares on offer PROVIDED ALWAYS that in the event of either party not accepting the Auditor's valuation, that party may at its own expense obtain a separate valuation and in the event of dispute either party may refer the matter to a single Arbitrator to be appointed in default of agreement between the parties by the President for the time being of the Incorporated Law Society of Ireland and the provisions of the Arbitration Act 1954 or any statute for the time being replacing extending or modifying same shall apply. Within 90 days of the service of the Purchase Notice or within 30 days of the Arbitrator's Award (if relevant) whichever is the later the Offeree shall complete the purchase of the Offeror's shares at the offer price or the price

decided by the Arbitrator as the case may be and on completion the offeror shall deliver to the offeree a transfer of the shares executed by them and the certificate or certificates therefor (or in default of such certificate an appropriate indemnity) and the offeree shall pay to the offeror the price for the shares by way of bankdraft PROVIDED ALWAYS that if Donal McAuliffe is the Offeror, then Katrice McAuliffe shall automatically be deemed to have offered her shares under the same Purchase Notice unless otherwise agreed in writing by Lithographic AND FURTHER PROVIDED ALWAYS that in the event of the McAuliffes being the Offeror, then Lithographic shall be obliged to purchase the shares on offer at the price and within the time specified in this clause."

[I can pass over 4.02, 4.03 and 4.04 as not being relevant.]
Article 4.05 provides:

> "If within 90 days after the service of the Purchase Notice, the Offeree has failed to pay as certified, the Offeror shall be entitled to sell the shares to any other person."

The defendant company served a purchase notice on 6 January 1993, to which notice the plaintiff did not respond in the sense that he did not accept the offer and then, on 26 March 1993; the plaintiff and his wife served their purchase notice on the defendant company. If the obligation to purchase was the same for the two parties it is clear that since the defendant company's purchase notice was served first in time it should prevail.

The matter came before the learned High Court judge by way of special summons pursuant to Order 83 of the Rules of the Superior Courts which entitles a party to apply for the determination of any question of construction arising under any written instrument and for a declaration of the rights of the persons interested.

In the course of his judgment, the learned High Court judge said that while it had been argued that there was an ambiguity in Article 4.01(iii) of the agreement that in his view there is only one way in which the court should construe it. He said:

> "*The parties did intend that if a Purchases Notice was served that the other party would be obliged to purchase his shares. That is what was contemplated by the document.* I am satisfied that the defendant's construction of Article 4.01(iii) is the correct one. While this is an unusual form of clause it has been accepted by the parties. It is clear that it were not for the final proviso the obligation is perfectly clear. I have to determine whether the final proviso affects the clear interpretation of the Article.
>
> That proviso reads:

> "that in the event of the McAuliffes being the offeror, then Lithographic shall be obliged to purchase the shares on offer at the price and within the time specified in this clause".

> It is argued on behalf of the plaintiff that because of this proviso the defendant was obliged to purchase the plaintiff's shares. I do not agree that this is a reasonable interpretation of the Article. It is clear from the earlier part of the Article that the intention had been to place an obligation on both parties."

For the plaintiff it has been submitted that if this construction of the relevant article in the document is to be upheld the following consequences would flow:

(i) The description "offer" would have to be construed in a different way to how it is normally construed in contract law.
(ii) Clauses 4.01(ii) would have to be treated as surplusage.
(iii) The final proviso in the sub-paragraph would also have to be treated as surplusage.
(iv) The provisions of Article 4.05 would have to be disregarded also.

It was submitted that, of course, a court is obliged to give effect to each word in a written instrument (unless that produces an absurd result) and that an express provision excludes the implication of any provision to the same effect.

In the course of the debate before us it was accepted, as one member of the court observed, that this clause (iii) was quite a confused provision. Nevertheless, we must come to grips with it, as best we may.

It seems clear that if either party served a purchase notice then the mechanism whereby the price to be paid should be determined came into operation. Mr Stewart, however, said that the fact that the offeree should complete the purchase of the offerors shares within 90 days of the service of the purchase notice or within 30 days of the arbitrators award pointed to the fact that there was an obligation on the party in receipt of the purchase notice to buy the shares in that manner. He also submitted that the provisions of the clause are clear that the obligation to buy is mutual and that nothing in the final proviso is inconsistent with what is contained earlier on in the clause. I do not agree. The concept of "completing" a purchase involves the prior existence of a binding contract: with an offer and an acceptance in place. While the offer made cannot be revoked by the offeror the clause does not provide for the necessity for an acceptance. It does provide, as I have already pointed out, that a certain mechanism for determining the value of the shares should be put in place. That is as far as the plaintiff and his wife were concerned. However, the final proviso makes clear that if the plaintiff makes the offer then the defendant company is obliged to purchase the shares on offer at the price and within the time specified in this clause. This obligation is placed on the defendant company only, not on the plaintiff.

It seems to me that this interpretation is in harmony and gives effect to the other stipulations in the agreement which have been pointed to and, in particular, Articles 4.01 (ii) and 4.05.

In the circumstances, I would hold that the binding purchase notice in the circumstances of this case is the one served by the plaintiff on 26 March 1993 and I would, therefore, reverse the order of the High Court.

Alistair Rutherdale
Barrister

1963 ACT, PART IV

In the Matter of International Retail Ltd v. Allied Dublin Merchants Ltd:
High Court 1974 No. 143 Sp (Kenny J) 26 July 1974

Company Law – Equitable charge – Particulars not registered as required by Companies Act 1963 – Invalid resolution to wind up company – Application to extend time for registration of particulars under Companies Act – Whether failure accidental or due to inadvertence or some other sufficient cause – Whether or not extension of time would prejudice the position of creditors or shareholders of the company – Whether otherwise just and equitable to extend time – Companies Act 1963 (No. 33), sections 100, 106

Facts: On 2 November 1973, the plaintiff company owed a debt to the defendant society and on that date deposited two leases of property with the society as security for its payment. The deposit created an equitable charge, the particulars of which should have been sent to the Registrar of Companies for registration within 21 days, pursuant to section 100 of the Companies Act 1963. The society was not aware that the particulars of the charge had not been registered by the company. On 22 March 1974 a resolution for the voluntary winding up of the company was passed but this was invalid as two of the three subscribers to the memorandum and articles of association received no notice of the meeting. No mortgages or charges were at this stage registered affecting the property of the company. On 30 May 1974 the society issued a special summons seeking an order that the time for registration of particulars of the deposit be extended. Under section 106 of the 1963 Act, the court has power to extend the time for registration of particulars when the failure to register was accidental or due to inadvertence or some other sufficient cause or is not of a nature to prejudice the position of creditors or shareholders of the company or when on other grounds it is just and equitable to do so.

Held by Kenny J:

(1) The court should not extend the time for registration of a charge against a company's property unless there is evidence that a petition for the winding up of the company has not been presented and that the members are not contemplating a resolution for its winding up.

(2) The extension of time for registration of the particulars would clearly prejudice the position of creditors of the company as the effect of the order would be to make the charge valid and, therefore, the amount secured would

rank before sums due to creditors.

(3) The purpose of section 99 of the Companies Act 1963 was to ensure that every creditor who dealt with the company would know that he was giving credit to a company which had given security for some of its debts and so the charge, if not registered, becomes void when the company goes into liquidation.

(4) A winding up of the company was contemplated by the members as evidenced by the ineffective resolution which had been passed.

(5) The practice of the courts upon such applications was to require evidence that no winding up of the company is pending or contemplated and that no judgments have been recovered against it which are unpaid before extending the time for registration: *Re Bootle Cold Storage Co.* [1901] WN 54 and *In re L.H. Charles & Co. Ltd* [1935] WN 15

(6) The application to extend time was refused as there was evidence that a winding up was contemplated and further there was no evidence that no judgments had been recovered against the company which are unpaid.

Cases referred to in judgment
Re Bootle Cold Storage Co. [1901] WN 54
In re L.H. Charles & Co. Ltd [1935] WN 15

Counsel's and solicitors' names not available

KENNY J **26 July 1974**

International Retail Ltd (formerly Meat Wholesalers Ltd) ("the company") is a company incorporated in the State. On 2 November 1973 they owed a debt to Allied Dublin Merchants Ltd, a society registered under the Industrial and Provident Societies Acts ("the society") and on that date they deposited two leases of property in which they were lessees with the society as security for its payment. This deposit created an equitable charge by the company and so under section 100 of the Companies 1963 Act particulars of it should have been sent to the Registrar of Companies for registration within 21 days after it was created. The company did not send these for registration but none of the officials of the society nor its solicitor were aware of this. The society was entitled to send the particulars to the Registrar of Companies for registration but did not do so.

On 22 March 1974 the company passed a resolution that it be wound up voluntarily. The issued capital of the company is 1,000 shares of which 998 are held by Patrick Hogan, one share by Phyllis Donoghue and one by Olive Lucas. Miss Donoghue and Miss Lucas were the subscribers to the memorandum and articles of association. They did not get any notice of the meeting on 22 March and so the resolution was ineffective and the company is not now in liquidation. There are no mortgages or charges registered which affect the property of the company.

On 30 May 1974 the society issued a special summons seeking an order that the time for registration of particulars of the deposit should be extended. The effect of section 106 of the 1963 Act is that the court has power to extend the time for registration of particulars when the failure to register was accidental or due to inadvertence or some other sufficient cause or is not of a nature to prejudice the position of creditors or shareholders of the company or when on other grounds it is just and equitable to do so. The reason given for the failure by the society to register particulars of the charge is inadvertence because they did not know that the company had not sent the particulars for registration. The affidavits do not give the reason why the company failed to register then nor do they state whether the company is solvent or not. There is no evidence disclosing whether any judgments have been recovered against it.

The extension of time for registration of the particulars will clearly prejudice the position of the creditors of the company for the effect of such an order will be to make the charge valid and so the amount secured by it will rank before sums due to creditors.

It seems to me that the court should not extend the time for registration of a charge against a company's property unless there is evidence that a petition for the winding up of the company has not been presented and that the members are not contemplating a resolution for its winding up. The purpose of section 99 of the 1963 Act (first introduced in the Companies Act of 1900) was to ensure that every creditor who dealt with the company would know that he was giving credit to a company which had given security for some of its debts and so the charge, if not registered, becomes void when the company goes into liquidation. A winding up of this company is contemplated by the members: this is shown by the ineffective resolution which has been passed.

This view is supported by what has been the invariable practice of the courts of Ireland and England on applications such as this. This has been to require evidence that no winding up of the company is pending or contemplated and that no judgments have been recovered against it which are unpaid before extending the time for registration (*Re Bootle Cold Storage Co.* (1901) WN 54: *Buckley on the Companies Acts*, 13th ed., p. 236.) Support for this practice also comes from the decision of Mr Justice Clauson in *In re L.H. Charles & Co. Ltd* (1935) WN 16. In that case a voluntary winding up of the company which gave the charge was in contemplation and the judge made an order extending the time for registration of a charge on an undertaking that if a resolution for winding up became effective within a month from the date of the order and the liquidator within three weeks thereafter applied to discharge the order, the company would abide by any order the court might make for rectification of the register by removing the registration of the charge.

The affidavits filed do not deal with the question as to whether there are any unsatisfied judgments in existence against the company. It has been the practice to require proof on applications such as this that there are no unsatisfied judgments in existence against the company. On this ground the application also fails.

Counsel for the liquidator has attended at the hearing and has said that the company is completely insolvent but as this was not verified by affidavit, I have not relied on it as a ground for this decision.

The application for an extension of time to deliver particulars of the charge to the registrar is therefore refused.

Patricia McLaughlin
Barrister

In the Matter of Telford Motors Ltd and In the Matter of the Companies Act 1963 on the Application of Edmond J Doody, Liquidator of Telford Motors Ltd: High Court 1977 No. 485P (Hamilton J) 27 January 1978

Equitable charge – Particulars of charge should have been registered – Order to extend time granted – Condition of order was that if the company should be wound up within 21 days from the date of perfection of the order then the liquidator might apply to the court to discharge the order – Order stated to be without prejudice to the rights of parties acquired before the particulars were actually registered – Company wound up voluntarily – Whether charge void as against the liquidator and other creditors of the company – Date of registration of particulars – Whether when papers required lodged with Registrar of Companies or whether date of actual registration – Companies Act 1963 (No. 33), sections 99, 100, 106

Facts: By deed of charge dated 2 May 1974 and made between the respondent and Telford Motors Ltd ("the company"), the company charged freehold lands with the payment of the sum of £18,000 and the deed of charge was registered as a burden on the lands on 15 May 1975. However, the prescribed particulars of the charge were not delivered to or received by the Registrar of Companies for registration as required by section 100 of the Companies Act 1963. The respondent was only alerted to this fact when he received a notice that the company was convening a meeting with a view to passing a winding up resolution and that a creditors' meeting was being held. He thereupon applied to the court for an extension of time for registration pursuant to section 106 of the 1963 Act. This was granted subject to the undertaking that in case a resolution for the winding up of the company should become effective within 21 days from the date of perfection of the said order and in the event that the company, by its liquidator, should within 21 days after the commencement of such winding up, apply to the court to discharge the said order, then the respondent would submit to the jurisdiction of the court and would abide by any order that the court might make for the rectification of the register of the company by the removal therefrom of any registration effected under the present order. The order was also stated to be without prejudice to the rights (if any) of parties acquired prior to the time when the particulars of such charge were actually registered. The said particulars were lodged with the Registrar of Companies at approximately 10 a.m. on 18 February 1976 and a resolution to wind up the company was passed on the same date. The particulars of the charge were not actually registered until 20 February 1976. The liquidator brought an application seeking an order discharging the order made on 17 February 1976 and an order for the rectification of the register of the company by the removal therefrom of any registration effected under the said order. Hamilton J took the view that no order was required as the resolution for the winding up of the company was passed before the charge was registered. The premises and lands the subject matter of the said deed of charge were sold by the liquidator and the respondent executed a deed of discharge in order that the sale might be completed on the condition that the monies be lodged in the joint names of the liquidator's solicitors and the solicitors for the respondents. The liquidator sought directions as to whether the charge created by the said deed of charge was void as against him and the unsecured creditors of the company.

Held by Hamilton J:

(1) The order made on 17 February 1976 extending time for registration of the particulars of the charge was expressly stated to be without prejudice to the rights (if any) of parties acquired prior to the time when the particulars of the charge were actually registered.

(2) The object of such a provision was to preserve rights acquired against the property of the company intervening between the expiration of the twenty one days provided for in section 99 and the extended time allowed by the order.

(3) The date of registration of the charge is the date of actual registration and not the date when the papers necessary to secure registration of the particulars of the charge are lodged.

(4) The deed of charge, accordingly, was void against the liquidator and the creditors of the company.

Cases referred to in judgment

In re Ehrmann Brothers Ltd [1906] 2 Ch 697
In re Joplin Brewery Company Ltd [1902] 1 Ch 79
In re Spiral Globe Ltd [1902] 1 Ch 396
Watson v. Duff, Morgan and Vermont Ltd [1974] 1 WLR 450

Counsel's and solicitors' names not available

HAMILTON J **27 January 1978**

In this matter the applicant as Liquidator of Telford Motors Ltd seeks directions in relation to the matters following:—

(a) whether the charge created by Deed of Charge, dated 2 May 1974, and made between the above named Telford Motors Ltd of the one part and Mercantile Credit Company Ltd of the other part, over certain property described in Folio 1168 F of the Register County Queens is void as against the applicant and the unsecured creditors of Telford Motors Ltd ("the company").

(b) whether the rights of unsecured creditors of the company rank prior to the charge of Mercantile Credit Company Ltd created by the said deed of charge and in the distribution of the proceeds of sale of the said premises.

(c) whether the said Mercantile Credit Company Ltd is bound to join in a conveyance of transfer of the said premises by the company (acting by the applicant) to Sherrard (Fethard) Ltd.

The facts relevant to the determination of these issues, may be summarised briefly as follows.

Telford Motors Ltd (hereinafter referred to as "the company") was incorporated on 7 September 1953, under the name of Telford and Kenny Ltd, which name was subsequently changed to Telford Motors Ltd.

The main object of the company was the carrying on of the business of motor garage proprietors. By deed of charge dated 2 May 1974 and made between Mercantile Credit Company of Ireland Ltd (hereinafter referred to as "the respondent") of the one part and the company of the other part, the company charged the lands comprised in Folio 10430 of the Register of Freeholders for the County of Laois with the payment to the respondent of the sum of £18,000 and a new Folio was opened in the Land Registry in respect of the lands the subject of the aforesaid deed of charge and the lands are now comprised in Folio 1168 of the Register of Freeholders Queens County and the said deed of charge was registered as a burden on the lands comprised in the said Folio on 15 May 1975.

Though the deed of charge was registered as a burden on the said Folio, the prescribed particulars of the charge were not delivered to or received by the Registrar of Companies for registration as required by the Companies Act 1963.

Prior to 6 February 1976 it was decided that the company was insolvent and could not continue trading and that it should be voluntarily wound up.

In accordance with the provisions of section 266 of the Companies Act 1963 a notice of the meeting of the members at which the resolution for voluntarily winding up of the company was sent to the creditors and dated 6 February 1976.

Such notices included a notice sent to the respondents. It seems then to have been realised by the respondent that the prescribed particulars of the charge had not been delivered to the Registrar of Companies and on 10 February 1976 a special summons was issued in which the plaintiff claimed an order pursuant to section 106 of the Companies Act 1963 extending the time limit by section 99 thereof for the registration in the Companies Office of the deed of charge.

When the matter was heard by me on 17 February 1976 and being satisfied that the omission to register the charge within the time required by section 99 of the Companies Act 1963 was due to inadvertence I ordered, pursuant to section 106 of the Companies Act 1963 that the time for registration of the particulars of the said charge be extended until 9 March 1976, but expressly provided that the said order was without prejudice to the rights (if any) of the parties acquired prior to the time when particulars of such charge shall be actually registered.

As a condition of obtaining the said order, the respondent undertook that, in case a resolution for the winding up of the company should become effective within 21 days from the date of perfection of the said order and in case the company by its liquidator should within twenty one days after the commencement of such winding up apply to the court to discharge the said order, then the respondent would submit to the jurisdiction of the court and would abide by any order that the court might make for the rectification of the register of the company by the removal therefrom of any registration effected under this present order.

The necessary particulars and documents to secure the registration of the particulars of the said charge were lodged by the solicitor for the respondent in the Office of the Registrar of Companies at approximately 10 a.m. on the morning of 18 February 1976.

The resolution of the company that the company be wound up voluntarily was passed on 18 February 1976 at a meeting of the creditors summoned in accordance with the provisions of section 266 of the Companies Act 1963, held immediately following the meeting of the company at which the resolution to voluntarily wind up the company was passed: the applicant herein was appointed liquidator of the company.

The particulars of charge was not registered by the Registrar of Companies until 20 February 1976.

On 2 March 1976 the applicant, as liquidator of the company issued a notice of motion which was served on the respondent seeking an order discharging the order made by me on 17 February 1976 and an order for the rectification of the register of the company by the removal therefrom of any registration effected under the said order of 17 February 1976.

On the hearing of the said motion I made no order as I did not think it necessary in view of the fact that the resolution proposing the voluntary winding up of the company had been passed prior to the date of registration of the particulars of the aforesaid charge made by the Registrar of Companies in pursuance of the order made by me dated 17 February 1976. The premises and lands the subject of the said deed of charge were sold by the liquidator to Messrs Sherrard (Fethard) Ltd for the sum of £38,000 and in order to enable the sale to be completed and strictly without prejudice to their claims and rights, the respondent executed a deed of charge on a condition that the sum of £28,750 be lodged in the joint names of the liquidator's solicitors and the solicitors for the respondent.

On the basis of the foregoing facts the liquidator seeks directions as to whether the charge created by the said deed of charge dated 2 May 1974, over the property comprised in Folio 1168F of the register County Queens is void as against him and the unsecured creditors of the company and whether the rights of the unsecured creditors of the company rank prior to the charge and in the distribution of the proceeds of sale of the said premises. Section 99 of the Companies Act 1963 provides that:—

> "Subject to the provisions of this Part, every charge created after the fixed date by a company, and being a charge to which this section applies, shall, so far as any security on the company's property or undertaking is conferred thereby, be void against the liquidator and any creditor of the company, unless the prescribed particulars of the charge, verified in the prescribed manner, are delivered to or received by the registrar of companies for registration in manner required by this Act within 21 days after the date of its creation, but without prejudice to any contract or obligation for repayment of the money thereby secured, and when a charge becomes void under this section, the money secured thereby shall immediately become payable."

Sub-section 2 of section 99 provides *inter alia* that the section applied to:

> "a charge on land, wherever situate, or any interest therein, but not including a charge for any rent or other periodical sum issuing out of land."

Despite the learned submissions made by Mr Crivon on behalf of the respondent the position seems to be very clear. The order made by me on 17 February 1976 extending the time for registration of the particulars of the charge was expressly stated to be without prejudice to the rights (if any) of parties acquired prior to the time when particulars of the charge shall be actually registered.

The inclusion of such a provision saving rights acquired before actual registration has as stated by Templeman J in *Watson v. Duff, Morgan and Vermont Ltd* [1974] 1 WLR 450 been common form since the decision in *In re Joplin Brewery Company Ltd* [1902] 1 Ch 79. As stated in many cases the object of this provision is to save rights acquired before actual registration and as stated by Cozens-Hardy LJ in *In re Ehrmann Brothers Ltd* [1906] 2 Ch 697 at 709 the rights intended to be preserved are:

> "Rights acquired against the property of the company or affecting the property of the company intervening between the expiration of the twenty one days and the extended time allowed by the order."

It is also quite clear that when a company goes into liquidation, the liquidator acquires the right and duty to distribute all the assets of the company between its creditors.

It was held in *In re Spiral Globe Ltd* [1902] 1 Ch 396, that:

> "the rights and duties of the liquidator to distribute all the assets of the

company between its creditors is a right acquired against the company's property and is protected by the proviso if before registration of the particulars of charge the company has gone into liquidation."

Mr Crivon has submitted that I should regard the date and time of the lodging of the papers necessary to secure the registration of the particulars of the charge as the registration. I regret I am unable to do so as to do so would be to disregard the terms of the order made by me on 17 February 1976, an order made in ease of the respondent, and the proviso therein contained which is no empty formula but specifically designed to protect the rights over the property of the company acquired prior to the date of actual registration and in common usage since 1902.

I am also satisfied that the position is not in any way affected by the fact that the deed of charge was registered as a burden on the relevant folio.

Consequently I am satisfied that the deed of charge is void against the liquidator and the creditors of the company.

Patricia McLaughlin
Barrister

In the Matter of Euro Travel Ltd and in the Matter of the Companies Act 1963; Robert Dempsey v. The Governor and Company of the Bank of Ireland: High Court 1983 No. 353Sp (Murphy J) 28 May 1984

Company – Banking – Travel agents bond – Guarantee by the bank if company failed to pay – Letter of indemnity – Whether charge requiring registration – Letter of set-off – Whether enforceable – Company in liquidation – Right of bank to set-off monies paid under guarantee with monies held by debtor in different account – Companies Act 1963 (No. 33), sections 99, 280

Facts: The company, a travel agency business, sought to avail of the bonding scheme operated by the Irish Travel Agents' Association ("ITAA"). By an agreement dated 31 December 1982 between the company, the trustees of the ITAA and the Bank of Ireland; the company agreed to pay the trustees the sum of £75,000 if, *inter alia*, prior to 31 March 1983 the company became unable to pay its debts or ceased to carry on business. The bank agreed to guarantee the due payment by the company of the said sum in the event of same becoming payable.

By letter dated 26 March 1981, and prior to the bonding agreement transaction, the company executed the bank's standard form of letter of set-off. The letter, *inter alia*, authorised the bank,

"to set-off and apply such monies . . . in or towards the satisfaction of such

> liabilities entirely at your discretion, without further notice to us and we agree that such set-off would be a good and valid discharge of such monies so applied without the necessity of any further endorsement or authorisation from us whatsoever."

Contemporaneously with the bonding agreement, the company entered an agreement dated 31 December 1982 ("the letter of indemnity") with the bank. By this the company agreed to indemnify the bank against all sums incurred on foot of the bonding agreement and authorised the bank to pay any amounts pursuant to that agreement on demand. This letter provided that the bank might debit any account in the company's name with any sums payable.

By March 1983 the company was no longer able to pay its debts and it ceased to carry on business. By letter dated 29 March 1983, solicitors for the ITAA demanded payment of £75,000 from the bank pursuant to the bonding agreement, which sum was paid by the bank on 19 April 1983. On 11 April 1983, a resolution was passed for the winding-up of the company by means of a creditor's voluntary winding-up.

At the time of entering the bonding agreement a lodgment of £75,000 by the company had been discussed. This sum was in fact lodged to the credit of Bank of Ireland Finance Co. Ltd, a related, but separate legal entity. On 22 March 1983, this sum was transferred by the bank to an account of the company with the Bank of Ireland, and on 20 April 1983 was transferred to the bank's head office and set-off against the amount paid pursuant to the bonding agreement.

The bank had duly registered an equitable deposit of the company's title deeds with the companies office, but apart from that registration no other alleged charges by the company in favour of the bank were registered.

The liquidator instituted proceedings challenging the bank's actions and pursuant to section 280 of the Companies Act 1963, sought directions from the court. He alleged that the letter of indemnity dated 31 December 1982 constituted a charge falling within section 99, Companies Act 1963 as it was a charge on book debts of the company or alternatively was a floating charge on the undertaking of the company, and was thus invalid for want of registration. He further submitted that the bank could not properly set-off the monies.

Held by Murphy J in granting a declaration that the bank were not entitled to set-off the sum of £75,000 paid by them to the trustees of the ITAA against monies held by them in the name of the company, and in holding that, as a consequence, the other orders sought did not arise:

(1) Monies due by a banker to its customer, whether or not recorded in books or other documents, are not properly described as book debts. *Watson v. Parapara Coal Co. Ltd* (1915) 17 GLR 791 followed; judgment of Buckley J in *Independent Automatic Sales Ltd v. Knowles and Foster Independent Automatic Sales Ltd* [1962] 1 WLR 974, discussed.

(2) Nor was the letter of indemnity a floating charge on the undertaking or property of the company.

(3) A bank has a right to set-off what is due by the customer against any sum which might be due by the bank to the customer. This is sometimes described as the right to combine accounts or to adjust accounts.

(4) However, in the present case no part of the money was paid until the company had gone into liquidation. It would be wrong in law for the bank to set off its contractual obligation under the bond, before their obligation under the bond had been discharged. *In Re Fenton* [1931] 1 Ch 85 discussed.

Cases referred to in judgment
Bank of Ireland v. Martin [1937] IR 189
Daintrey, In re [1900] 1 QB 546
Fenton, In re [1931] 1 Ch 85
Independent Automatic Sales Ltd v. Knowles and Foster [1962] 1 WLR 974; [1962] 3 All ER 27
Morris, In re: Coneys v. Morris [1922] 1 IR 136
Paul and Frank Ltd v. Discount Bank (Overseas) Ltd & Another [1967] Ch 348; [1966] 3 WLR 490; [1966] 2 All ER 922
Shipley v. Marshall (1863) 14 CBNS 566
Watson v. Parapara Coal Co. Ltd (1915) 17 GLR 791

Counsel's names not available

Solicitors for the plaintiff: *McMahon & Tweedy*
Solicitor for the defendant: *Richard J. Black, Law Agent*

[Section 99 has been amended non-materially by section 122 of the 1990 Act]

MURPHY J **28 May 1984**

On 11 April 1983 a resolution was passed for the winding-up of the above named Euro Travel Ltd (hereinafter called "the company") by means of a creditor's voluntary winding-up. By that resolution the plaintiff Robert Dempsey was appointed liquidator and his appointment as such was confirmed at a meeting of creditors likewise held on 11 April 1983.

The present proceedings constitute an application by the liquidator of the company for the direction of the court pursuant to section 280 of the Companies Act 1963. The circumstances in which the directions of the court are sought are as follows:

As might be inferred from the title of the company it had been engaged in business as travel agents and was in fact a member of the Irish Travel Agents' Association. The company sought to avail itself of a bonding scheme which had been recommended to the members of the Irish Travel Agents' Association. For that purpose an agreement dated 31 December 1982 had been executed between the company of the first part, the trustees of the Irish Travel Agents' Association of the second part and the Governor and Company of the Bank of Ireland (hereinafter called "the bank") of the third part. Under that agreement the company agreed to pay to the trustees the sum of £75,000 if prior to the 31

March 1983 certain events occurred, one of which was that the company became unable to pay its debts or ceased to carry on business as a result of being unable to pay its debts as they fell due with the result that the company should be unable to carry out or fulfil its obligation to its customers. The bank executed the agreement aforesaid for the purpose of guaranteeing the due payment by the company of the said sum of £75,000 in the event of the same becoming payable in accordance with the terms and provisions contained in the said agreement.

At an earlier date and before any question of bonding arose the company had executed in favour of the bank the bank's standard form of letter of set-off. That letter is dated 26 March, 1981 and expressly authorised the bank pending payment any bills, notes, overdrafts, loans, guarantees or other contingencies to hold any monies which then or thereafter might stand to the credit of the company with any of the branches of the bank as security for all such liabilities. The letter of set-off then went on expressly to provide as follows:

> "Furthermore you are authorised to set-off and supply such monies or any part thereof from time to time in or towards the satisfaction of such liabilities entirely at your discretion, without further notice to us and we agree that such set-off would be a good and valid discharge of such monies so applied without the necessity of any further endorsement or authorisation from us whatsoever."

In addition to that letter of set-off and contemporaneously with the bonding agreement the company entered into an agreement on 31 December, 1982 with the bank (sometimes referred to as "the letter of indemnity") which, after reciting the bonding agreement and in consideration of the bank joining therein, went on to provide that the company should indemnify the bank against all liabilities incurred by it on foot of the bonding agreement and authorising the bank to pay any amounts demanded from it by reason of the bonding agreement on demand being made to the bank and without requiring proof or agreement that the amounts so demanded were due or payable and indeed notwithstanding the fact that the company itself might dispute the validity of such demands. The letter went on to provide in paragraph 3 thereof as follows:

> "You may debit any account in our names with any sums payable by us hereunder."

By March of 1983 it was clear that the company was in financial difficulties. A statement of affairs prepared as at the 23rd of that month showed an excess of liabilities over assets of £13,777 but more particularly showed creditors of approximately £130,000 where the cash and bank balances amounted to only some £35,000. It was recognised by the company and confirmed by the liquidator in the affidavit sworn by him that the company was on 22 March 1983 no longer in a position to pay its debts and that it ceased to carry on business. On behalf of the liquidator the point was made — somewhat tentatively — that the inability of the company to pay its debts and to carry on its business had not necessarily resulted in the company being unable to carry out or fulfil its obligations to its customers. Whilst that point may be valid to the extent that no particular customer had been stranded abroad the former managing director, Mr Kelly, in his evidence clearly recognised that the company would be unable to meet its commitments to its customers.

By letter dated 24 March 1983 the then auditors to the company notified the Irish Travel Agents' Association of the financial position of the company and by further letter dated 29 March 1983 Messrs William Fry and Sons Solicitors on behalf of the association formally demanded payment from the bank of the sum of £75,000 in accordance with the obligations of the bank under the bonding agreement. It was on 19 April 1983 that the bank — in pursuance of their obligation under the bonding agreement — forwarded to the association the bank's draft for £75,000.

At the time, or shortly before the bonding agreement was entered into, the company had agreed in principle with the bank to lodge a sum of £75,000. In fact this amount was lodged to the credit of the company with the Bank of Ireland Finance Company Ltd, a separate legal entity from the bank itself but of course associated with it. It was recognised that the reason for selecting the finance company as opposed to the bank itself was merely to procure more favourable terms in relation to interest. The amount so lodged to the credit of the company with the Bank of Ireland Finance Co. Ltd was, together with the interest accumulated thereon, transferred by the bank to the company's account in Clones with the Bank of Ireland on 22 March, 1983 and on 20 April 1983 the sum of £75,000 was — as I was informed by counsel for the bank — transferred to the head office of the bank and set-off against the amount paid as already mentioned to the trustees of the association.

On 18 February 1983 the bank took from the company an equitable mortgage by deposit of the title deeds relating to certain premises of the company. This security was taken in conjunction with negotiations which were then taking place for the further extension of the bonding agreement. That deposit was duly registered in the company's office but apart from that registration no other alleged charges by the company in favour of the bank were at any time registered in pursuance of the provisions of the Companies Act 1963.

It was contended on behalf of the liquidator that the letter of indemnity dated 31 December, 1982 was and constituted a charge falling within section 99 of the Companies Act 1963 and accordingly was invalid for want of registration. If any such charge was created clearly it would be invalid as against the liquidator having regard to the fact that such charge was not registered as prescribed by that section. To establish that the letter of indemnity constituted a charge it would be necessary to be satisfied first that it was a charge to which section 99 applies and secondly a charge created by the company. To bring the particular transaction within section 99 it was contended on behalf of the liquidator that the letter of indemnity constituted either a charge on book debts of the company or alternatively a floating charge on the undertaking of property of the company as designated in paragraphs (e) and (f) of sub-section 2 of section 99 aforesaid. I find it difficult to accept the proposition that the company was purporting to charge monies in the hands of the bank itself with monies due by the company to the bank. This argument might have been more attractive when and as long as the sum of £75,000 was lodged by the company to the credit of the Bank of Ireland Finance Company Ltd, a legal entity separate from the respondents in the present proceedings. However as the monies were transferred from the accounts in that bank to the respondents on 22 March 1983 the problem can only be viewed as between the company on the one hand and its own bankers on the other. It seems to me that the best definition of the term "book debts" as used in this context is to be found in the decision of Buckley J in *Independent Automatic Sales Ltd v. Knowles and Foster Independent Automatic Sales Ltd* [1962] 1 WLR 974 as explained by Pennycuick J in *Paul and Frank Ltd v. Discount Bank (Overseas) Ltd and Another* [1967] Ch 348 at 361. The definition provided by Buckley J as so revised would read as follows:

> "As far as I am aware, no more precise definition of the meaning of the term 'book debts' has ever been attempted judicially, and I shall not attempt one. *Shipley v. Marshall*, I think, establishes that, if it can be said of a debt arising in the course of a business and due or growing due to the proprietor of that business that such a debt would (in practice) in the ordinary course of such a business be entered in well kept books relating to that business, that debt can properly be called a book debt whether it is in fact entered in the books of the business or not."

In principle I doubt that monies due by a banker to its customer and whether or not recorded in books or other documents would properly be described as book debts in that sense. Such judicial authority as does exists appears to support that view. *Gough on Company Charges* (1978 edition) cites the decision of the New Zealand Courts in *Watson v. Parapara Coal Co. Ltd* (1915) 17 GLR as authority for that proposition. The suggestion that the letter of indemnity might constitute a floating charge on the undertaking or property of the company was not urged with the same vigour and indeed I would have difficulty in seeing how the transaction which did take place could be so described.

However, I have noted the arguments made on behalf of the liquidator in respect of the claim that the letter of indemnity constituted a charge which was in the circumstances invalid and have commented thereon in deference to the arguments made before me. It was clear, however, that this was not in fact the real issue between the parties. The bank do not claim that they have a charge or lien of any description on any part of the assets of the company. Counsel on behalf of the bank explained clearly that the bank sought to rely upon and exercise their right of set-off or as it is otherwise described in relation to banking, the right to combine accounts. Mr O'Neill emphasised this was a right which was given by operation of law and not a right conferred by the parties. In that context he drew attention to the decision in the *Bank of Ireland v. Martin* [1937]

IR 189 where the former Supreme Court affirming Meredith J held that the bank was not entitled to apply monies which their clients deposited with them in reduction of that client's liability on foot of a guarantee without first obtaining the consent of the client. Mr O'Neill suggested that it was the decision in that case which gave rise to the practice of obtaining from clients a letter of set-off in the terms of the document executed in the present case on 26 March 1981. The purpose of counsel in canvassing this historical aspect of the banking practice was of course to make it clear that set-off does not in general derive from the acts of the parties but by the application of settled rules of law.

It seems to me that there are two cases crucial to the resolution of the issue arising in relation to set-off. The first of these cases is *In re Morris: Coneys and Morris* [1922] 1 IR 136 and the second *In re Fenton* [1931] 1 Ch D 85.

In the Irish case, the then High Court of Appeal rejected the contention that a bank has a lien respect of a balance to the credit of a client and held that the only right of the bank was to set-off. In his judgment Sir John Ross C at page 137 quoted from *Harte's Law of Banking* (3rd ed.), page 810, as follows:

> "It is often stated that the lien attaches to the money; but inasmuch as, quite apart from any question of lien, a banker is only bound to pay to, or to the order of, his customer the amount of the balance due to the latter after deducting what is due to the banker himself from the customer, the lien will not normally have any effective application to the monies."

The learned Chancellor then went on to comment as follows:

> "The lien suggested in this case is not like any other kind of lien with which we are familiar. In the ordinary case there must be some specific thing to which the lien can attach, but in this case where is the specific entity to which it attached? In this case there are two accounts — a current account and a deposit account. The lien could not be on the current account, because it was not in funds. How can it be on the deposit account? That account consisted of money paid in by the customer on deposit, and which became the monies of the Bank. There are no indicia of ownership in the hands of the bankers which could be applied by them. The indicia of ownership, the deposit receipts, are in the hands of the creditor, the depositor; and that being so, the right of the bankers is a right of set-off, but that right can be exercised only where there are in existence legal enforceable debts. A banker's right is the right of adjustment of credits and debts, and it is involved in this that the debts must be enforceable."

Again in his judgment O'Connor MR at page 138 commented as follows:

> "But a lien requires for its existence some specific thing on which it operates either by possession of the specific property itself, such as plate or jewels, or by possession of the indicia of ownership, such as title deed,

> a policy of assurance or a bond. The existence of the term 'lien' to a right of set-off against a balance in the bank to the credit of the client is not strictly proper, because there is no specific thing which represents the balance. The balance does not earmark any particular asset in the hands of the bank. It merely indicates a debt by the bankers to the client of a certain amount. It only raises the relationship of debtor and creditor which gives the client a right of action. If when the action is brought the bank has a claim against the client it has a right of set-off which is just as effectual as a lien: but it is only in this sense a lien and not a lien properly so called."

In my view that decision fully supports the approach adopted by the bank in the present case, that is to say, the assertion made on behalf of the bank that they are not claiming a lien (or indeed a charge of any form) but merely the ordinary traditional right granted by law (subject to any special contract between the parties and any special factors affecting the accounts) to set-off what is due by the client. This particular right of set-off is sometimes described as the right to combine accounts or as in the Irish case aforesaid, the right to adjust accounts.

It is ironic that in relation to the set-off issue both parties rely on the decision in the *Fenton* case in support of their conflicting arguments.

On the particular, and somewhat complex, facts of that case it was held that a party with a contingent but undischarged liability on foot of a guarantee was not entitled to operate a right of set-off against the estate of bankrupt debtor. Indeed there are *dicta* within the judgments which do give comfort to both parties.

At page 113 Lawrence LJ stated the position as follows:

> "It has also been decided that, although the date for ascertaining the existence of any mutual debts, credits or dealings which may be made the subject matter of set-off under the section is the date of the receiving order, yet it is sufficient if the account prescribed by the section can be taken when the set-off arises: see *In re Daintry* [1900] 1 QB 546 where the Court of Appeal allowed a set-off in respect of a debt whose existence and amount were alike unascertained at the date of the receiving order."

However, the same distinguished judge dealing expressly with the case where the principal debtor was insolvent went on to express his conclusion — and indeed his reasons for it — at page 114 in the following terms:

> "When, however, as in the present case, the principal debtor is bankrupt, the case assumes a different aspect. In such a case the claim of a surety, who has been called upon to pay but has not yet paid anything to the principal creditors, is in effect a claim for damages for the breach by the principal debtor of his obligation to indemnify his surety on the ground that his bankruptcy has rendered it impossible for him to perform his

> obligation and has made it possible to estimate the amount which the surety can properly claim by way of damages. The reason why, in my opinion, such a claim (although it apparently has the requisite attributes for a set-off under the section and although it is one from which the principal debtor would be released by the order of discharge) cannot be set-off is because so long as the estate of the principal debtor remains liable to the principal creditor the surety will not be permitted to prove against the estate of the principal debtor, as such a proof would be a double proof for the same debt, and would therefore be inadmissible as being concrete to the established rule in bankruptcy."

Indeed it is noticeable that Romer LJ gave the same reason for his conclusion at the foot of page 118 of the report.

Having regard to the decision in the *Fenton* case it seems to me that it is fatal to the bank's case that no part of the monies due on foot of the guarantee were paid until after the commencement of the liquidation. I may add that apart from the reasoning given by the judges in the Court of Appeal in the *Fenton* case it does seem to me that it would be wrong both in law and in logic to allow the form of set-off on which the bank rely, that is to say, a combining or adjustment of accounts in such a way as to enable the bank to set-off in contractual obligation under the bond even allowing that it had crystallised to the extent of constituting an enforceable legal obligation against it before that obligation had been discharged in such a way as to result in the actual accounts between the parties showing the mutual debits and credits which the bank now seek to combine.

Subject to any arguments which the parties may wish to make it seems to me that in the light of the foregoing that section 5 in the special summons herein should be answered in the negative. None of the other questions arise.

Alistair Rutherdale
Barrister

[*Reporters Note:* On 6 December 1985, the Supreme Court (Henchy, Hederman and McCarthy JJ) allowed an appeal by the defendant and directed that the order of the High Court would stand discharged. In lieu thereof the court granted a declaration that the bank were entitled to set-off the sum of £75,000 paid by them to the trustees of the ITAA on 19 April 1983 against monies held by them in the name of the company. See page 328]

In the Matter of St Stephen's Green Safe Deposit plc (In Voluntary Liquidation) and In the Matter of section 280 of the Companies Act 1963: Patrick Nunan v. Group 4 Securitas (International) B.V.: High Court 1985 No. 951 Sp (Blayney J) 28 July 1986

Company – Charge – Loan offer – Charge on leasehold interest in property – Additional agreement by different company to purchase premises if default in loan – Whether agreement constituted a charge – Whether charge requiring registration – Companies Act 1963 (No. 33), sections 99, 280

Facts: The Industrial Credit Corporation ("I.C.C.") offered a loan of £250,000 to St Stephen's Green Safe Deposit plc ("the company") subject to certain terms set out in a facility letter. The terms included the giving of a first charge by the company over its lands and premises, including its leasehold interest in premises at 16 St Stephen's Green. A further term was the execution of an agreement by the respondent that they would buy the premises for £250,000 (less any amount paid under a letter of comfort) should I.C.C. request them to do so, following a default from the borrower.

An agreement was entered into between the respondent, the company and I.C.C. on 2 April 1985, which referred back to the offer letter. The terms included an agreement by the respondent to purchase the premises upon request by I.C.C., and this was to occur only in the event of default as set out in the loan agreement. The agreement also included undertakings by the company not to mortgage or charge the premises to any person other than I.C.C. and that if they were in default they would execute a contract for sale of the premises for £250,000.

The liquidator issued a summons seeking the court's directions as to whether the agreement of 2 April 1985 constituted a charge requiring registration under section 99 of the Companies Act 1963. The respondent submitted that the agreement created "a charge on land wherever situate, or any interest therein", within the meaning of section 99(2)(d), and consequently was registrable. The liquidator submitted that the agreement, whilst a security, was not a charge, and was in fact a conditional agreement for sale.

Held by Blayney J in holding that the agreement did not constitute a charge requiring registration under the provisions of section 99 of the Companies Act 1963:

(1) The agreement could not be looked at in isolation. It was part of the loan security, which included a first charge by the company over its leasehold interest in the premises — a charge which would have allowed I.C.C. to obtain a court order for sale should the company make default. The agreement was therefore ancillary to this charge.

(2) The effect was to give I.C.C. twin options in the event of a default — to proceed by order for sale, or to call on the respondent to purchase. However this

additional option did not create a separate charge.

(3) The substance of the agreement was the agreement of the respondent to purchase the premises. The agreement of the company to sell, in certain circumstances, was a very subsidiary part.

(4) There were no express words in the agreement from which an intention to create a charge could be inferred, nor could such an intention be inferred by regarding the provisions of the agreement as a whole. The agreement was an additional security given by the respondent and not by the company.

(5) The only relief to which I.C.C. was entitled under the agreement would have been an order for specific performance against the respondent of its agreement to purchase, or to obtain specific performance against the company, should it refuse to execute a contract to sell. The agreement in itself would not entitle I.C.C. to obtain an order for sale, which was the usual remedy of a chargeant.

Case referred to in judgment

Carreras Rothmans Ltd v. Freeman Mathews Treasure Ltd & another [1985] Ch 207; [1985] 1 All ER 155; [1984] 3 WLR 1016

Hugh Geoghegan SC instructed by *William Fry & Sons* **for the applicant**
Peter Shanley SC instructed by *Hayes & Sons* **for the respondent**

BLAYNEY J **28 July 1986**

This is a special summons brought by the liquidator of St Stephen's Green Safe Deposit plc (in voluntary liquidation) (to which I shall hereinafter refer to as "the company") to have certain questions determined which have arisen in the course of the winding up of the company. Since the special summons was issued, agreement has been reached between the parties on some of the questions so that one single question remains for determination, namely, whether an agreement in writing made on 2 April 1985 between Group 4 Securitas (International) B.V. (to which I shall hereinafter refer as "Group 4"), the company and Industrial Credit Corporation plc constitutes a charge requiring registration under the provisions of section 99 of the Companies Act 1963.

This agreement came to be executed in pursuance of a term in a facility letter issued by the Industrial Credit Corporation to the company in connection with a loan of £250,000 being made by the I.C.C. to the company. That facility letter provided that the loan to be made to the company should be secured as follows:

> "(1) A sole first floating charge over all the assets of the borrower.
> (2) A sole first specific charge over the land and premises of the borrower which include a leasehold interest in premises at 16 St Stephen's Green Dublin 2. I.C.C. to be satisfied with the terms of this lease.
> (3) Group 4 Securitas (International) B.V. to give a letter of comfort and awareness for £100,000 to I.C.C. with respect to the loan to the borrower. This letter to be in a form satisfactory to I.C.C.'s solicitors.

> (4) Group 4 Securitas (International) B.V. to execute an agreement in a form satisfactory to I.C.C.'s solicitors, that they will buy the premises referred to at (2) above for £250,000 (less any amount paid under the letter of comfort) should we request them to do so and I.C.C. would consider making such a request only in the event of default by the borrower".

It was in pursuance of the last provision of the security requirements that the agreement of 2 April 1985 (to which I shall hereinafter refer to as "the agreement") was entered into.

The agreement was made between Group 4 of the first part, the company of the second part and I.C.C. of the third part. It starts with two recitals in the following form:

> "Whereas:
> (a) By letter of loan offer dated the 5 August 1983 (copy of which is attached hereto hereinafter called "the loan agreement") I.C.C. to make available to the borrower a loan not exceeding £250,000 on the terms and conditions set out therein.
> (b) It was agreed that part of the security for the loan would be the agreement by Group 4 upon the terms and conditions hereinafter contained".

The date of the letter of loan offer is wrongly given in the first recital — it should have been 17 January 1985 — both parties accepted that this was so and the intention was to refer to the letter of loan offer of 7 January 1985.

The reference to the letter of loan offer in the first recital is important. It makes it clear that the agreement is being executed in the context of the security requirements set out in the letter. And the terms of that letter had been accepted by the company on 25 January 1985. The principal terms of the agreement were as follows. Group 4 agreed to purchase the premises of the company at 16 St Stephen's Green, Dublin 2 for the sum of £250,000 should I.C.C. request it so to do but it was provided that such request should be made by I.C.C. only on the occurrence of one or more of the events of default as set out in the loan agreement. The company agreed that during the currency of the loan it would not mortgage or charge the premises in question in favour of any person or company other than I.C.C. The company agreed that in the event of its being in default of the terms of the loan agreement it would execute a contract for the sale of the premises for the sum of £250,000. I.C.C. agreed that on receipt of the proceeds of sale of the premises from the company it would release its mortgage on the premises forthwith.

The agreement contained other terms also to which I shall refer when dealing with counsel's submissions, but the basic terms of the agreement were as I have just set them out.

Mr Shanley, acting on behalf of Group 4, submitted that the effect of the agreement was to create "a charge on land, wherever situate, or any interest therein", within subsection (2)(d) of section 99 of the Companies Act 1963 and accordingly it required to be registered under subsection (1) of that section. For a definition of the nature of an equitable charge he referred me to the judgment of Peter Gibson J in the case of *Carreras Rothmans Ltd v. Freeman Mathews Treasure Ltd and Another* [1984] 3 WLR 1016 at page 1030D:

> "The type of charge which it is said was created is an equitable charge. Such a charge is created by an appropriation of specific property to the discharge of some debt or other obligation without there being any change in ownership either at law or in equity, and it confers on the chargee rights to apply to the court for an order for sale or for the appointment of a receiver, but no right to foreclosure (so as to make the property his own) or take possession".

He also referred me to *Fisher and Lightwood on Mortgages* (9th edition) at page 156 where an equitable charge is defined in very similar terms. Mr Shanley submitted that the effect of the agreement was to appropriate the company's leasehold interest in 16 St Stephen's Green to the discharge of the debt due to the I.C.C. and that this brought the agreement within the definition. He said that the essence of an equitable charge is that it is a security whereby property is appropriated for the discharge of a debt and that the agreement contained this essential element. He submitted that no special form is required to create an equitable mortgage; that what is required simply is the intention to create a security. He submitted that in the present case the intention was clear from the second of the two recitals in the agreement. He pointed to the following terms in the agreement as being the appropriation of the premises to the payment of the debt: clause 3, which prohibited the company from mortgaging or charging the premises in favour of any person or company other than I.C.C. during the currency of the loan; clause 10 by which all dealings by the company with the premises (save and except a charge in favour of I.C.C.) were inhibited except with the consent of Group 4 and I.C.C.; clauses 5 and 6 in which the company agreed to execute the contract for sale and to complete it within three weeks from the date of the consent. Mr Shanley argued that this gave I.C.C. a security. When the agreement was read as a whole the lessee's interest in the premises was clearly appropriated for the discharge of I.C.C.'s debt. The effect of the agreement could best be seen by comparing what I.C.C. could get on a realisation under the fixed charge, and what they could get on a realisation under the charge created by the agreement. The actual open market value of the loan interest in the premises is nil, except for the possibility of selling for £90,000 to a special buyer. It can be seen that the effect of the agreement is to enable I.C.C. to realise a price for the premises vastly in excess of what they could be sold for on the open market.

In answer to my question as to whether I.C.C. could, under the agreement. apply to the court for an order for sale, Mr Shanley submitted that they could. He said that the question was not to be looked at from the point of view of considering whether the terms of the agreement gave the right to an order for sale, but whether they created a charge. If they created a charge, as he submitted they did, it followed as a matter of right that I.C.C. would be entitled to a well charging order and to an order for sale. The right to a sale was an ancillary right which was available once it was established that there was a charge.

Mr Geoghegan, acting on behalf of the liquidator, submitted that one had to start by making a distinction between a security and a charge, While every charge was a security, not every security was a charge. For example, the giving of a guarantee, or the delivery of a bill of exchange could amount to the giving of a security, there would be no question of any charge being created. He submitted that the agreement had none of the recognised features of a charge. He said that one of the essential features was that it should be realisable by a court order of sale; this remedy of sale was always available to a chargeant but it would not be available to I.C.C. under the agreement.

The transaction here was something very different. It was an agreement that in certain circumstances X would buy certain premises from Y for Z pounds. The mere fact that the motive was to get better protection for the secured lender did not make the agreement a charge. He submitted that the correct description of the agreement was that it was a conditional agreement for sale. He submitted that you must first and foremost look at the agreement and see what it means. And while there might be in it an element of appropriation, the sum mentioned in the agreement was not realisable by any of the remedies normally available to a chargeant. All that could be done would be to enforce the sale by getting an order for specific performance or alternatively claim damages for breach of the agreement. He accepted Mr Shanley's submission that a charge could be created informally, but he submitted that for a charge to be created the premises must be appropriated in such a way that an order for sale by the court could be sought. In the light of the terms of the agreement in the present case, the court would be puzzled if a sale were sought. The only real remedy was specific performance. He directed my attention to clause 8 of the agreement whereby I.C.C. agreed that, on receipt of the proceeds of sale of the premises from the company, it would release its mortgage on the premises forthwith. He said that this was clear evidence of an intention that there should be a mortgage by the company to the I.C.C. and further evidence of this was to be found in the agreement in the first recital which stated that I.C.C. had agreed to make available a loan not exceeding £250,000 to the company on the terms and conditions set out in the letter of loan offer, and these conditions included the requirement that the company should give a first specific charge over the premises to I.C.C.

Having considered fully the terms of the agreement and the very helpful submissions of counsel the conclusion I have come to is that the agreement did not have the effect of creating a charge and accordingly it did not require to be registered under section 99 of the Companies Act 1963. My reasons are as follows.

The agreement cannot be looked at in isolation. It constituted part of the security for the loan. This is referred to in the second recital in the agreement. This element is of considerable importance in its interpretation as it means that in construing it, and in trying to determine what the intention of the parties was, one must look at the relationship of the agreement to the other parts of the security.

The other part of the security that is clearly relevant is that the company agreed to give "sole first specific charge over the land and premises of the borrower which include a leasehold interest in premises at 16 St Stephen's Green Dublin 2." So from the time that the company on 25 January 1985 accepted the terms of the loan offer, the company was bound, as one of the terms of the loan, to give a first specific charge on the premises to I.C.C. The effect of giving this charge would be that in the event of the company making default in the repayment of the loan, I.C.C. would be entitled to apply to the court for an order for sale with a view to realising the amount due on the charge.

In my opinion the agreement has to be interpreted in the light of the company's obligation to create this specific charge. The agreement was made on 2 April 1985, the day before the charge was executed, but both Mr Shanley and Mr Geoghegan agreed that no particular significance was to be attached to this, and it seems to me that they were perfectly correct in taking this view. Having regard to the fact that under the terms of the letter of loan offer the company was bound to grant the specific charge, it was immaterial whether the charge was executed before or after the agreement was entered into. On the date of the acceptance of the letter of loan offer, there was a binding obligation on the company to execute the charge and enter into the agreement, and there was a binding obligation on Group 4 to enter into the agreement.

When the agreement is looked at in the light of the obligations created by the letter of loan offer, it seems to me that its relation to the specific charge created the following day is clear. It was ancillary to the specific charge. It ensured that in the event of a default being made by the company in the repayment of the loan, I.C.C. would not have to rely solely on the remedy of a sale by the court which might be useless if the premises had no value on the open market but would have an additional remedy in the shape of being entitled to require Group 4 to purchase the premises from the company for £250,000. So the specific charge gave one remedy, and the agreement gave an alternative one. In my opinion this alternative remedy did not have the effect of creating a second charge on the premises.

The whole thrust of the agreement is that it is a security given by Group 4 and not by the company. The company is a necessary party, because it has to agree to sell the premises and Group 4 is obliged to buy. The substance of the agreement is that Group 4 agrees to purchase the premises. It is this obligation undertaken by Group 4 which is the essence of the security. And this is clear not merely from the terms of the agreement itself but from the manner in which the agreement is described in the letter of loan offer. The description does not contain any reference to the company at all. It says that "Group 4 Securitas (International) B.V. to execute an agreement etc." and the second recital in the agreement states that "It was agreed that part of the security for the loan would be the agreement by Group 4 upon the terms and conditions hereinafter contained." There was no reference to the company. The reference is to the agreement being undertaken by Group 4. And in the agreement itself clause 1 sets out the agreement by Group 4 to purchase the premises at £250,000 as requested by I.C.C.

In the light of this it seems to me that it cannot be said that under the agreement the company was appropriating the premises to the repayment of the loan. That in effect had already been done by the company agreeing to give a specific charge on the premises to I.C.C. In the agreement the company was playing a very subsidiary part agreeing to sell in the event of making a default in repayment of the loan, at which stage the company could not have prevented any sale since I.C.C. would have been entitled to get an order for sale from the court under its charge. So the part played by the company in the agreement was a very subsidiary part only. It was really only concurring in the obligation being undertaken by Group 4 and its concurrence was in effect for its benefit since clause 8 of the agreement provided that once the proceeds of sale had been paid over to the I.C.C. the mortgage on the premises would be released.

As there are no express words in the agreement from which the intention to create a charge can be inferred, if there is any such intention, it can be gathered from regarding the provisions of the agreement as a whole, as Mr Shanley has urged me to do, but even adopting that approach it seems to me that there is no clear evidence of any such intention. And it seems to me in the particular circumstances that very clear evidence of such an intention would be required since at the date of the agreement the company was under an obligation to create a specific charge on the property, and did in fact create such a charge on the following day. Any evidence of intention to create a charge would have had to be evidence to create a charge additional to the specific charge which the company was under an obligation to grant. That the company should have had any such intention would have been unusual since it was totally unnecessary to create an additional charge. But as I said earlier the agreement does not contain any evidence of any such intention. The correct construction to put on it is in my opinion that it was an additional security given by Group 4 and not by the company. Any relief which I.C.C. is entitled to under the agreement is in my opinion confined to obtaining specific performance against Group 4 of its agreement to purchase the premises for £250,000. Having regard to the nature of the agreement which is concerned essentially with Group 4's agreement to purchase the premises, I cannot see how I.C.C. could succeed in a claim against the company for an order for sale. It seems to me that the only relief that I.C.C. could get against the company is an order that it execute a contract to sell the premises to Group 4 for £250,000. So the remedy which is available to every chargeant is not in my opinion available to I.C.C. and this is a further reason for coming to the conclusion that the agreement does not create a charge. Mr Shanley submits that this is not the correct approach; that I should look at the agreement itself first and if I came to the conclusion that it created a charge, then I.C.C. would be entitled to an order for sale. I accept that this is probably the correct approach, and my conclusion is of course that the agreement does not create a charge, but at the same time I think it relevant in considering whether it does or does not take into account the fact that the terms of the agreement are not such as would entitle I.C.C. to apply to the court for an order for sale.

The answer to the question set out in the special summons must be that the agreement does not constitute a charge requiring registration under the provisions of section 99 of the Companies Act 1963.

Alistair Rutherdale
Barrister

Lombard and Ulster Banking Ltd v. The Governor and Company of the Bank of Ireland and Brook House School: High Court 1985 No. 840Sp (Costello J) 2 June 1987

Company – Charge – Provision of security for loan to fund purchase of own shares – Whether compliance with provisions of Companies Act – Proof of formalities – Evidence – Whether transaction illegal – Effect of illegality – Transaction voidable if notice of facts constituting breach – Onus of proof – Deed of Postponement – Alteration after execution by one party – Whether void – Competing interests of creditor banks – Priorities – Companies Act 1963 (No. 33), section 60 – Registration of Title Act 1964 (No. 16), sections 31 and 68(3)

Facts: In early 1981 the plaintiff agreed to lend a trust company, Brook House School Trust Ltd, £275,000 to finance the purchase of 70 per cent of the shares of the second defendant, Brook House School (an unlimited family company), which owned a private school. The family company agreed to guarantee repayment of the loan and to charge its interest in the lands by way of security. This arrangement meant that the family company was indirectly giving financial assistance for the purchase of its own shares.

At the date of the deed of charge, Bank of Ireland, the first defendant held an equitable mortgage of the lands by virtue of an equitable deposit of the land certificate, and the company at this time owed £60,000 to the Bank. As part of the transaction the Bank of Ireland agreed to postpone its security and a deed of postponement was executed. Bank staff erroneously referred in this deed to "Brook House School Trust Ltd" rather than to the unlimited company. Subsequent to its execution by the bank, the deed was corrected by JM, the solicitor for both the trust company and the unlimited company who, deleted the words "Trust Ltd".

In 1985 the plaintiff issued proceedings seeking a well charging order, and a declaration that its charge ranked in priority to the equitable mortgage of the

Bank of Ireland. The liquidator of the second defendant resisted the claim on the basis that the transaction, including the granting of the deed of charge was illegal under section 60 of the Companies Act 1963 for failure to comply with the procedural requirements of subsections (2),(3) and (4) of that section, and that the company could therefore avoid the transaction, by virtue of section 60(14). The plaintiff submitted that the requirements of section 60 were satisfied when the shareholders had authorised their solicitor to take all necessary steps and when by informal consent all the shareholders agreed to what actually was done by some of the members.

As a further defence, the first defendant submitted that the deed of postponement was void, as it had been materially altered after the Bank had executed it. It argued that even if the deed of charge was valid, the plaintiff should get no priority over the equitable mortgage because of the invalidity of the deed.

Held by Costello J in holding that the charge was valid and subsisting and that the sum of £787,670.84 was well charged on foot thereof, and in granting a declaration that the plaintiff's charge ranked in priority to that of the first defendant's equitable mortgage:

(1) There was a non-compliance with section 60 of the Companies Act 1963 in that the required statutory declaration was not made at a directors' meeting on 21 May, and any resolution that might have been adopted at a shareholders meeting could not have been a special resolution.

> (a) The production of a purported statutory declaration of solvency to comply with section 60 from the Companies Office file signed by two directors of the second defendant did not, in the absence of other evidence, prove that such a declaration was made.
> (b) Similarly, the production from the Companies Office file of a document purporting to be minutes of a directors' meeting and a shareholders' meeting for the purpose of adopting a resolution to comply with section 60, did not prove the contents of these documents.
> (c) While there was certain circumstantial evidence from correspondence to suggest that the directors' and shareholders' meetings were held on 21 and 22 May, this did not entitle the court to hold that the resolutions contained in the draft minutes were adopted at them.
> (d) Notices convening the shareholders meeting for the 22 May were not sent out until 21 May, and could not have reached two of the shareholders who were in England.

(2) Where the procedures of section 60(2),(3) and (4) were used to obtain exemption for a transaction in breach of subsection (1), then strict compliance with the procedures was necessary.

(3) A transaction in breach of section 60(1) is, by virtue of subsection (14), voidable at the instance of the company against a person who had notice of the facts which constituted the breach. This requires that there be a non-compliance

with subsections (2), (3) and (4), and that the person knew of the facts which resulted in non-compliance.

(4) Where a plaintiff fails to establish that such a transaction is valid, an onus passes to the company under subsection (14) to show that the plaintiff had "notice" of the facts which resulted in non-compliance, otherwise the transaction is enforceable. "Notice" requires actual notice by the plaintiff, its officials or its agent that the required procedures were not adopted or that they knew the facts from which they must have inferred that the company had failed to adopt the required procedure. It was insufficient to show that had proper inquiries been made the non-compliance could have been identified.

(5) In the instant case although the transaction was rendered illegal by section 60(1) the company was not entitled to avoid it as the plaintiff had no notice of what had happened.

(6) A material alteration to a deed after it has been executed by one party renders it void. *Ellesmere Brewery Co. v. Cooper* [1896] 1 QB 75 followed; *Sellin v. Price* (1867) LR 2 Ex 189 followed; *Suffel v. Bank of England* (1882) LR 9 QBD 555 followed.

(7) Consequently the solicitor was not entitled to amend the executed deed of postponement in the way he did and it was therefore void.

(8) In passing the land certificate to the plaintiff, the solicitor for the Trust Company and the unlimited company was not in breach of a solicitors' undertaking given to the Bank of Ireland as it was clear that the bank expressly agreed to the registration by the plaintiff of its deed of charge.

(9) In respect of priority, the claim of the plaintiff must prevail over that of the first defendant, as there was a concluded and enforceable contract to postpone the claim of the first defendant, a sufficient memorandum of which (if required) was to be found in the letters and accompanying documentation. In addition the provisions of the Registration of Title Act 1964 meant that as owners of the registered charge, the plaintiff's title, in the absence of actual fraud, was not affected by notice of the Bank of Ireland's prior equitable estate.

Cases referred to in judgment

Re Bailey Hay & Co. Ltd [1971] 1 WLR 1357; [1973] 3 All ER 693
Bank of Ireland Finance Ltd v. Rockfield Ltd [1979] IR 21
Cane v. Jones [1980] 1 WLR 1451; [1981] 1 All ER 533
Re Duomatic Ltd [1969] 2 Ch 365; [1969] 2 WLR 114; [1969] 1 All ER 161
Ellesmere Brewery Co. v. Cooper [1896] 1 QB 75; [1895] WN 157
Re Gee and Co. (Woolwich) Ltd [1975] Ch 52; [1974] 2 WLR 515; [1974] 1 All ER 1149
Sellin v. Price (1867) LR 2 Ex 189
Suffel v. Bank of England (1882) LR 9 QBD 555

Counsel's names not available

Solicitors for the plaintiff: *Binchy & Partners*
Solicitors for the first defendant: *Eugene F. Collins*
Solicitors for the second defendant: *Arthur Cox*

COSTELLO J **2 June 1987**

Brook House School is a private school situated in the outskirts of Bray, Co Wicklow. It had been established in 1952 by a Mr Peter Ross but by 1981 Mr Ross had retired as headmaster and his son Mark replaced him. The school was carried on in a large house which, with its surrounding lands, was valued in that year at £700,000. The lands and house were registered lands and were owned by an unlimited company called Brook House School. This, a family company, had been incorporated in 1972 and thereafter it had managed the school. Mr and Mrs Peter Ross owned one third of its ordinary shares between them, and their sons Mark and David held one third each. In 1980 a decision was taken to sell the school and a group of parents and friends came together to buy it. A trust company was formed called Brook House School Trust Ltd whose directors were Mr Jonathan Brooks, Mr Brook Johns, Mr Thomas Campbell and Mr Robert Myerscough. Mr Jonathan Brooks is a solicitor and figures prominently in these proceedings. He and his father Mr Philip Brooks were partners in the firm of Messrs Hickey Beauchamp Kirwan and O'Reilly. Mr Jonathan Brooks acted as solicitor for both the family company and the new trust company, and Mr Philip Brooks (a long-time family friend) acted for three members of the Ross family in the takeover of the school by the trust company. Some of the aspects of that takeover are the subject of these proceedings.

In the early part of 1981 Lombard and Ulster Banking Ireland Ltd (the plaintiffs herein) were approached by Mr Jonathan Brooks to help finance the purchase of the school by the trust company. Originally it was thought that this would be effected by a transfer of assets but eventually it was agreed that 70 per cent of the shares in the family company would be transferred to the trust company for £275,000. Lombard and Ulster agreed to lend this sum to the trust company but naturally it wanted some security for its loan and so it was decided that the family company would guarantee its repayment and charge its interest in its lands at Bray by way of security for the guarantee. Lombard and Ulster and Mr Brooks senior and junior were all well aware that this arrangement meant that the family company was indirectly giving financial assistance for the purchase of its own shares and that the entire transaction would be illegal by virtue of section 60 of the Companies Act 1963 unless the procedures provided for in subsections (2) and (3) and (4) of that section were complied with.

The deed of charge which the family company executed in favour of Lombard and Ulster is dated 21 May 1981 and was duly registered on the folio. The bank now seeks a well-charging order but the liquidator of the family company, (the company having gone into liquidation in 1985) now resists this claim on the grounds (a) that there was non-compliance with the procedural requirements of subsections (2) and (3) and (4) of section 60 and that accordingly the transaction, including the granting of the deed of charge is illegal, and (b) that the company can now avoid the transaction, including the deed of charge, by virtue of subsection (14) of that section.

There is a second and different claim in the case. At the date of the deed of charge the Bank of Ireland had an equitable mortgage over the Bray lands of the family company arising from a deposit of the land certificate at its Bray branch to secure the repayment of overdraft facilities granted to the company. In 1981 the company owed the Bank of Ireland about £60,000. Lombard and Ulster knew about this equitable mortgage and would not lend the money to the trust company unless its proposed security was given priority over that of the Bank of Ireland. The Bank of Ireland agreed to postpone its security and a deed of postponement was executed. The Bank of Ireland now claim this deed is void because it was materially altered by Mr Jonathan Brooks (acting on behalf of the Lombard and Ulster, the family company and the trust company) after the bank had executed it. The Bank of Ireland supports the liquidator's submission that the deed of charge is void and further argues that even if it is valid Lombard and Ulster get no priority over the equitable mortgage because of the invalidity of the deed of postponement. It resists the second claim which the Lombard and Ulster makes in these proceedings, namely a declaration that its charge ranks in priority to the equitable mortgage of the Bank of Ireland.

The proceedings were commenced by special summons and affidavits filed by all parties. It was clear that the issues of fact in this case could only be determined on oral evidence. No formal order was made ordering a plenary hearing or the filing of pleadings but the parties accepted that the issues in the case are to be found in the affidavits and agreed that they should be determined on oral evidence.

I will consider firstly the claim against the company arising from the deed of charge.

Part 1

The deed of charge

(i) *The Companies Act 1963 section 60*

Subsection (1) of section 60 declares that "it shall not be lawful" for a company to give whether directly or indirectly any financial assistance in connection with the purchase of any shares in the company. The plaintiffs accept that by guaranteeing the repayment of loan made to the trust company for the purchase of the Ross family shares and by supporting its guarantee by a deed of charge the company was entering into a transaction made illegal by this subsection. But it points out that certain transactions are exempt from the subsection (1) prohibition and that this was one of them. Subsection (2) of the section provides that subsection (1) is not to apply to the giving of financial assistance if:

> "(a) such financial assistance is given under the authority of a special resolution of the company passed not more than 12 months previously; and
> (b) the company has forwarded with each notice of the meeting at which the special resolution is to be considered a copy of a statutory declaration

which complies with subsections (3) and (4) and also delivers, on the same day as such notices are issued, a copy of the declaration to the registrar of companies for registration."

The statutory declaration (in effect, a declaration of solvency) has to be made at a meeting of directors held not more that 24 days before the date of the general meeting and it has to be made by the majority of the directors when the company has more than two directors (subsections (3) and (4)). Every member of the company has the right to receive notice of the general meeting and attend at it, unless all of the members of the company entitled to vote at the general meeting vote in favour of the special resolution the "transaction whereby . . . assistance is to be given shall not be carried out before the expiry of 30 days after the special resolution" (to give time for an application to be made to the court to annul it).

(ii) *Was there compliance with section 60?*
There were three members of the board of directors of the company in May of 1981, Mr and Mrs Peter Ross and their son Mark. This meant that two of these were required to make the statutory declaration referred to in subsection (2). These three held one preference share in the company each and as these were the only shares with voting rights all had to agree to the terms of the special resolution. But David was a holder of one third of the ordinary shares and he was entitled to obtain notice of the general meeting (although not entitled to vote at it). At the end of May, 1981 only Mr Peter Ross and Mr Mark Ross were in Ireland, David and Mrs Ross being at that time in England.

Mr Mark Ross swore an affidavit in these proceedings to the effect that he did not attend any meetings of directors or shareholders in Mr Brook's offices in Dollard House and did not make the statutory declaration required by the section to validate the transaction. This was not evidence at the hearing, but it means that the plaintiffs were required to prove compliance with the section. An official from the Companies Office produced its Brook House School file. It contains a document which is dated 22 May and purports to be a copy of a statutory declaration made by Mr Peter Ross and Mr Mark Ross in the presence of a Mr Muldowney, a Commissioner of Oaths. But the making of the statutory declarations was expressly put in issue in this case and the production of the Companies Office file does not prove that the declaration was made. Mr Muldowney is dead but the declaration could have been proved by someone familiar with his signature or by evidence from Mr Peter Ross (whose non-attendance at the trial was left unexplained). It has not therefore been established that the declaration of solvency was made by directors as required by the subsection. All the plaintiffs were able to prove was the filing of a document which purported to be a copy of a statutory declaration which had been made on 22 May 1981.

As to the meetings of directors and shareholders, the Companies Office file contains a document purporting to be a minute of a meeting of the directors of

Brook House School and a document purporting to be a minute of a general meeting of its shareholders at which resolutions to comply with section 60 were adopted. Each of these were signed by Mr Peter Ross as chairman. But these documents do not prove their contents. Section 145 of the Act requires that every company should keep minutes of general meetings and directors' meetings in books kept for this purpose. Brook House School had minute books but there is nothing recorded in them for 1981 or subsequent years. The plaintiffs cannot therefore rely on section 145(2), which makes a minute entered into a company's minute book signed by the chairman of the meeting admissible as evidence of what occurred at the meeting. The documents on the Companies Office file do not prove that the resolutions required by the section were passed or even that the meetings were held.

There was no witness called who could give evidence of having attended meetings of the directors or of shareholders of the family company held to comply with the section. Mr Jonathan Brooks had prepared draft minutes of meetings which he contemplated would be held in his offices in Dollard House on 21 May and he included in the drafts resolutions which he contemplated would be adopted to comply with the section. He also contemplated that he and his father would attend the meetings on the 21st and recorded this fact in the draft he had prepared. These documents were drafted before Mr Brooks left for a visit to the United States of America. His visit lasted for a week and he returned on 20 May. He was in his office on Thursday, 21 May and on Friday, 22 May but he says that he cannot now recall any meetings of the board of directors of the family company which were attended by any member of the Ross family on either day, or of any meetings of the shareholders of the company on either day. He does, however, remember a meeting of the board of management of the school out at Bray on the evening of the 21st but it was not concerned with section 60 matters. Mr Philip Brooks died in 1984 but it was established that he was in his office on the 21st and that he may have been there for part of the 22nd. His assistant, Mr Cunningham recalls seeing Mr Peter Ross and Mr Mark Ross in Dollard House on either the 21st or the 22nd, but he says he did not attend any meeting with them and he did not see them execute a statutory declaration on either day. Mr Kirwan, another partner in the firm of Messrs Hickey Beauchamp Kirwan and O'Reilly was acting for Lombard and Ulster in the transaction but did not attend any meetings of the family company or its directors. The documents in the company office were purportedly signed by Mr Peter Ross as chairman of the two meetings. But Mr Peter Ross was not called as a witness and no explanation for his absence was vouchsafed by the plaintiffs. Neither was Mr Mark Ross called to give oral testimony.

There was, however, certain circumstantial evidence offered from which certain limited inferences of fact can be drawn. On 21 May Mr Philip Brooks wrote to Mr David Ross in England in the course of which he observed that his father and brother, Mark, were having meetings that day to pass resolutions necessary to complete the transaction. On 22 May Mr Jonathan Ross telephoned Ulster and Lombard to say that all legal formalities had been complied with.

The deed of charge is dated 21 May and the seal of the company was witnessed by Mr Brooks and Mr Myerscough as directors of Brook House School, a designation which was incorrect unless they had been appointed directors in accordance with the proposals recorded in the minute drafted by Mr Brooks for the meeting proposed for 21 May. In addition the Companies Office wrote on 24 June to Messrs Hickey Beauchamp Kirwan and O'Reilly returning the special resolution and pointing out that this was dated 21 May and that the statutory declaration was dated 22 May.

It is obvious that this letter drew attention to a potentially serious situation, namely, that the documents filed clearly pointed to a non-compliance with the section because the statutory declaration post-dated the meeting. If the documents had inaccurately recorded the date of the meeting it is reasonable to assume that the error would have immediately been rectified. But it was not. No reply was sent to this letter for nearly four years and Mr Brooks gave no evidence to explain this omission. It is true that he then wrote on 1 July 1985 pointing out that the date of the meeting had through inadvertence not been changed in the minutes but he accepts that he is merely assuming that the meeting was held on 22 May as he assumed that the section had been complied with and he agrees that he has no recollection of any meetings on either 21 May or 22 May.

The cumulative effect of this evidence is to raise an inference (a) that meetings of shareholders and directors were in fact held and (b) that they were held on 21 May. But the evidence does not entitle me to hold that the resolutions contained in the draft minutes were adopted at them. And there is further relevant evidence which has to be considered. The notices convening the meeting of shareholders (which contained a consent to short service) were not sent to Mrs Ross and David Ross until 21 May and would not have reached them, at the earliest until 22 May. Accordingly, no special resolution could have been validly passed at any general meeting on 21 May as the requisite notice had not been given for it. It follows that there was non-compliance with section 60 in at least two respects (a) the required statutory declaration was not made at a directors' meeting on 21 May, and (b) any resolution that might have been adopted by the shareholders could not have been a special resolution.

It was urged on the plaintiff's behalf that compliance with the requirements of section 60 was satisfied when (a) the shareholders had authorised their solicitor to take all necessary steps and when (b) by informal consent all the shareholders agreed to what actually was done by some of their members. In this connection reliance was placed on *Re Duomatic Ltd* [1969] 2 Ch 365; *Re Bailey Hay & Co. Ltd* [1971] 1 WLR 1357; *Re Gee & Co. (Woolwich) Ltd* [1975] Ch 52; *Cane v. Jones* [1980] 1 WLR 1451. I cannot agree. The section makes illegal the granting of financial assistance (as defined) and if exemption for a transaction in breach of subsection (1) is claimed because of the adoption of the procedures laid down in subsection (2) and (3) and (4) then strict compliance with the procedure is necessary. It is not sufficient to show that all the shareholders had authorised their solicitors to take the necessary steps and that they subsequently ratified what in fact was done. If the procedural requirements were not adopted the transaction is an illegal one, if in fact it involved the granting of financial assistance contrary to subsection (1).

(iii) *The effect of non-compliance with section 60*
It is now necessary to consider the parties' rights in the light of these findings of fact. Subsection (1) of section 60 declared that subject to certain other subsections "it shall not be lawful for a company to give directly or indirectly financial assistance for the purchase of its own shares", and subsection (14) provided that:

> "Any transaction in breach of this section shall be voidable at the instance of the company against any person (whether a party to the transaction or not) who had notice of the facts which constitute such breach."

What this means is (a) that although a transaction in breach of the section is illegal it is only "voidable", not void, and (b) it is only voidable against a person who had notice of the facts which constituted the breach.

There are three issues arising on the "notice" point in this case. Firstly, the liquidator has argued that the phrase "transaction in breach of the section" means the carrying out of a transaction prohibited by subsection (1) and that as Lombard and Ulster knew that the transaction was prohibited by subsection (1) it had sufficient "notice" for the purpose of subsection (14) to enable the company avoid the transaction. I do not think that that can be correct. The subsection does not permit the avoidance of a transaction which is "in breach of subsection (1) of this section" but "any transaction in breach of this section". And so, if a lender knows that an attempt to validate a prohibited transaction and avoid breaching the section by adopting the procedures set out in subsections (2), and (3) and (4) is to be made I do not think that he has notice of any breach within the meaning of the subsection unless it can be shown (a) that there was in fact non-compliance with the subsections and (b) that he knew of the facts which resulted in non-compliance.

Secondly, as to the onus of proof. If, as has happened in this case, a defendant puts in issue the validity of a transaction prohibited by section 60 the onus is on the plaintiff to establish has case. However, if he fails to establish the validity of a transaction it does not follow that his claim on foot of a deed which is part of the transaction and is otherwise valid fails — the transaction is merely a voidable one. And it seems to me that the onus is then on the company which seeks to avoid it to show that the plaintiff had "notice" as required by subsection (14). This means that in this case the liquidator must establish as a matter of probability that Lombard and Ulster had "notice" that there was non-compliance with the provisions of subsections (2), (3) and (4). If he cannot do so the deed of charge is enforceable.

Thirdly, as to the nature of the "notice", it is not sufficient for the liquidator to show that if Lombard and Ulster had made proper inquiries that they would have ascertained that the company had failed to comply with the subsections. It must be shown that Lombard and Ulster had "actual notice" of the facts which constituted the breach, that is (a) that they or their officials actually knew that the required procedures were not adopted or that they knew facts from which they *must* have inferred that the company had failed to adopt the required procedures, or (b) that an agent of theirs actually knew of the failure or knew facts from which he must have inferred that a failure had occurred (see *Bank of Ireland Finance Ltd v. Rockfield Ltd* [1979] IR 21, 37). "Constructive notice" of the failure is not sufficient for subsection (14).

With these considerations in mind I now turn to the evidence in the case. It is perfectly clear that neither Lombard and Ulster nor any of its officials had any idea that the required procedures which they knew were to be adopted, had not in fact been carried out; on the contrary, they were expressly told by Mr Brooks that all legal formalities were complied with and it was only on that representation that they allowed the loan to the trust company to be effected. What remains for consideration therefore is whether any of its agents had "actual" notice of non-compliance with the statutory procedures. And what is crucial on this issue is that Mr Jonathan Brooks was not the "agent" of Lombard and Ulster.

Mr Brooks knew the directors of Lombard and Ulster well and his firm, Messrs Hickey Beauchamp Kirwan and O'Reilly had frequently acted for the bank. Mr Brooks was, however, acting for the borrowers (the trust company) and the proposed mortgagors (the family company) in this case and on 19 May Lombard and Ulster wrote a formal letter to the family company stating, *inter alia*, that "the solicitor for the Bank in this matter will be A.H.D. Kirwan of Dollard House, Wellington Quay". Thus Lombard and Ulster nominated Mr Kirwan a partner in the firm of Messrs Hickey Beauchamp Kirwan and O'Reilly and not Mr Brooks to act on its behalf. Mr Kirwan (their agent) had no actual knowledge that the provisions of section 60 were not complied with and he knew no facts from which he must have concluded that they were not complied with. He wrote to his clients on 22 May informing them that the section had been complied with but he must have done this from information given to him by Mr Jonathan Brooks because he was in no way involved in the meetings of directors or shareholders of the family company.

It follows, therefore, that even though the transaction was in fact one which was rendered illegal by subsection (1) of section 60 the company is not at liberty to avoid it as the plaintiffs had no notice of what had happened. The deed of charge is valid, and the plaintiffs are entitled as against the company to a well-charging order in respect of the sum of £787,670.84 (the amount now due on Lombard and Ulster's loan) and the usual consequential orders. (The question of its invalidity on an entirely different ground is answered in the plaintiff's favour in part II hereof).

PART II

The priority of the plaintiff's deed of charge

(a) *The agreement to postpone*

Lombard and Ulster's deed of charge is dated 21 May 1981. It was registered on 21 September 1983. The Bank of Ireland's unregistered equitable mortgage arose from the deposit of the land certificate on 29 November 1979. Lombard and Ulster had notice of this prior unregistered equitable estate and made it a condition of its loan to the trust company that its proposed security would have priority over that of the Bank of Ireland. There is no doubt that the Bank of Ireland agreed that this should be so. Originally it was thought that a second charge would be executed and registered in it favour, but on 11 June 1981 it wrote agreeing to the execution of a priority agreement whereby it would postpone its mortgage in favour of the charge to be executed in favour of Lombard and Ulster. On 25 June Mr Brooks sent a draft priority agreement to the Bank of Ireland. On 6 July it was returned with minor amendments. These were acceptable and the agreed draft together with engrossments were sent on to the bank on 6 July.

(b) *The deed of postponement*

The draft having been agreed there then occurred the series of events which have given rise to the claim by the Bank of Ireland that the deed which the parties executed is void. The parties in the agreed draft were to be the Bank of Ireland, Lombard and Ulster and "Brook House School", the unlimited company and registered owners of the land and who in the draft was correctly described as the "mortgagor". Notwithstanding its prior approval of the draft the law department of the Bank of Ireland decided to alter the engrossment by providing that the deed should be made between the Bank of Ireland, Lombard and Ulster and "Brook House Trust Ltd". It effected this change by typing-in the words "Trust Ltd" after the words "Brook House School" in three places in the deed. It then had the deed executed by the bank, explaining in a memorandum to the Bray branch that this execution was "strictly subject to the name of the third party . . . being altered to read Brook House School Trust Ltd since that is the name of the company". On 13 August in a letter headed "Brook House School Trust Ltd" the Bray branch sent to Mr Brooks the executed deed of postponement in duplicate adding "We note that you will now have them completed by Lombard and Ulster Banking and also by Brook House School Trust Ltd". The letter did not expressly point to the change effected in the engrossment.

Mr Brooks did not then notice what had been done and does not now recall when he first realised what had happened. He acknowledged the bank's letter on 20 August and wrote on 16 September stating that the deed of postponement had been completed by Lombard and Ulster "and we are awaiting a meeting of directors of Brook House School Trust Ltd to have it completed early next week". He was obviously still not aware that the draft had been altered and was then apparently prepared to have the deed completed by the Trust Company and not by the unlimited company. Thereafter a long delay occurred and notwithstanding a considerable number of reminders the deed was not executed until the month of June 1982.

It would seem that shortly before its execution Mr Brooks discovered that the engrossments he had sent to the Bank of Ireland had been altered so as to alter the name of the mortgagor. He then concluded that this alteration must have been an error and he erased with the aid of a correction fluid from the engrossments the words "Trust Company" which had been inserted in typescript by the Bank, with the result that the third party to the deed became the unlimited company. The deed was executed by "Brook House School" by the affixation of the seal. He did not draw the attention of the Bank to what he had done, and merely wrote a letter on 18 June 1982 which was headed "Brook House School Trust Ltd" which stated "we regret the delay in sending you the deed of postponement but this has now been stamped and we enclose one copy for your records". The official in the Bray bank who received back the deed did not notice the alteration which was not initialled in any way. It was filed and it was some years later that the bank realised that the deed it had executed had subsequently been altered.

It has long been established that a material alteration to a deed after it has been executed by one party renders it void. The principle has been stated thus in *Halsbury's Laws of England* (4th ed.) Vol. 12, paragraph 1378:

> "If an alteration (by erasure, interlineation, or otherwise) is made in a material part of a deed, after its execution by or with the consent of any party to or person entitled under it, but without the consent of the party or parties liable under it, the deed is made void. The avoidance, however, is not *ab initio*, or so as to nullify any conveyancing effect which the deed has already had, but only operates as from the time of the alteration and so as to prevent the person who has made or authorised the alteration and those claiming under him, from putting the deed in suit to enforce against any party bound by it, who did not consent to the alteration, any obligation, covenant, or promise thereby undertaken or made."

This principle can be illustrated by reference to three cases. In *Sellin v. Price* (1867) (LR 2 Ex 189) a deed of composition was prepared and executed by a debtor. It was purported to have been entered into with creditors named in a schedule to the deed. The schedule was added subsequently and it was held that the addition of the schedule was a material alteration which rendered the deed void. *Ellesmere Brewery Co. v. Cooper* [1896] 1 QB 75 was a case where four persons as sureties executed a bond of suretyship. One of the parties, after three had executed it, amended the document so as to limit his liability below that originally stipulated in the bond. It was held that this was a material alteration which rendered void the entire bond. In *Suffel v. Bank of England* (1882) LR 9 QBD 555 the holder of a note issued by the Bank of England who had purchased it for value unsuccessfully sued on foot of it, the court holding that the unauthorised alteration in the numbers on the note made after its issue was a material alteration and vitiated it.

The situation in this case is a curious one. The bank now accepts that the proper party to the deed of postponement was the unlimited company (Brook House School) and not the trust company (Brook House School Trust Ltd) and that it was in error in changing the engrossment as the trust company was not the owner of the land and had not mortgaged it and could do so. But it argues that it had executed the deed with the trust company as the third party to it and that Mr Brooks had made a material alteration in it after it had done so and so rendered the deed void. I think this submission is correct. To change a party to a transaction, to alter a deed after it has been executed by one party by adding a different party to that provided for in the executed deed, amounts to a material alteration in it. Mr Brooks was right in concluding that the bank had been in error in altering the engrossment, and wrong in the steps he took to rectify that error. He was not entitled to amend the executed deed in the way he did and the result is that the deed is void.

This conclusion by no means ends the case and I now have to consider the effects of this finding on the parties rights.

(c) *The validity of the deed of charge*

I have already concluded that the liquidator's attack on the deed of charge based on the non-compliance with section 60 of the Companies Act fails and I now have to consider the attack on its validity mounted by the Bank of Ireland based on what happened to the land certificate. On 2 April 1979 Mr Brooks received the land certificate from the Bank of Ireland (which had been deposited to secure the indebtedness of the family company) to enable the family company sell off portion of the lands. The usual undertaking in writing was given in respect of it. His firm undertook to hold the land certificate:

> "in trust for the said bank and not to do any act which would enable the property dealt with by them or any part of the said property to be mortgaged or assigned or in any way dealt with without the said bank's consent, or their lien thereon to be in any way postponed or prejudiced."

In May 1981, when the transaction in suit was in train, the land certificate had not been returned to the Bank of Ireland (indeed it seems that it was not returned until 1985) and was still retained by Mr Brooks. In order to have the Lombard and Ulster deed of charge registered in the Land Registry it was necessary for him to produce the land certificate. This Mr Brooks did and it was urged that in parting with it and using it for the purpose of having the deed registered he was acting contrary to the undertaking given to the Bank of Ireland and that the registration thus procured was void.

As I do not think that Mr Brooks acted in breach of the undertaking I do not have to consider the effect on the validity of the registration had he be done so. He was obliged not to do anything which would allow the property to be mortgaged "without the consent of the bank", but it is clear that the bank expressly agreed to the registration by Lombard and Ulster of its deed of charge and it seems to me that in using the land certificate to effect what the bank had agreed to did not involve any breach of the commitment given to it. The deed of charge was, in my view, validly registered.

(d) *The priorities*

So, it is established (a) that the Bank of Ireland is the owner of an unregistered valid estate in the lands, (b) that Lombard and Ulster is the owner of a subsequent valid registered charge, and (c) that the deed of postponement by which the Bank of Ireland postponed its interest to that of Lombard and Ulster is void. Which bank, then, has the first claim to the proceeds of the sale of the encumbered lands?

It seems to me that the claim of the Lombard and Ulster must prevail, and this for two reasons. Firstly, the agreement which the parties entered into for the postponement of the claim of the Bank of Ireland was an enforced agreement. The correspondence to which I have referred clearly shows the existence of a concluded contract. If it was contract which was required by the Statute of Frauds to be evidenced in writing (which I doubt) a sufficient memorandum of it is to be found in the letters and related accompanying documents. The deed of postponement may be void because of the alteration effected in it after it had been executed by the Bank of Ireland but that cannot alter the fact that the bank had prior to its execution entered into an enforceable agreement to postpone its claims. That agreement stands and is not vitiated by the court's findings in relation to the deed which it was intended would give effect to the parties' agreement. The deed is void but that does not prohibit the court from giving effect to the parties' contract.

Secondly, Lombard and Ulster get priority from the provisions of the Registration of Title Act 1964. Its title to the rights conferred on it by the Act as owners of the registered charge is not, in the absence of actual fraud, affected by the notice it had of Bank of Ireland's prior equitable estate (section 31). And the unregistered rights of the Bank of Ireland cannot affect the registered owner of a charge created on the land for valuable consideration (section 68 (3)). The Bank of Ireland could, by holding on to the land certificate, have prohibited the registration of the Lombard and Ulster deed of charge and could thus have preserved its priority. But by agreeing to registration it lost it.

I will make a declaration, therefore, not precisely as sought in paragraph (2) of the indorsement of claim but simply to the effect that the plaintiff's charge ranks in priority to that of the Bank of Ireland's equitable mortgage.

Finally, I stated during the hearing that I would later explain a ruling I made at the end of the plaintiff's case in response to an application by the liquidator of the family company to non-suit the plaintiffs. I will do so, briefly, now. Had, by cross-examination or otherwise, it been shown that there had been non-compliance with the section 60 procedures and that Lombard and Ulster or its agent had actual notice of this then I would have acceded to the application. But this was not how matters stood. The evidence then established that the transaction was an illegal but not a voidable one. As the liquidator could adduce no evidence to put the matter further the plaintiffs were then entitled to the relief claimed.

Alistair Rutherdale
Barrister

1963 ACT, PART V

Sean Hopkins v. Shannon Transport Systems Ltd: High Court 1971 No. 1131 P (Pringle J) 10 July 1972

Company – Directors – Promoters – Failure of promoters and directors to make disclosure of interests in contract with company – Whether failure renders contract void or voidable – Whether company approbated contract – Whether director and promoter entitled to recover profits under the contract – No independent board of directors to whom disclosure could have been made – Whether duty of disclosure extends to subscribers for shares to whom shares had not yet been allotted – Whether agreement collateral to an earlier agreement – Statute of Frauds – Whether there was a sufficient memorandum of the agreement – Approval by company necessary for payment by it to a director for loss of office – Companies Act 1963 (No. 33), sections 186, 194

Facts: The plaintiff and one Mr Gorman were promoters and directors of a private company formed in 1967 to provide a ferry service on the river Shannon. They were also the first shareholders of the company and the initial capital was made up of 100 £1 shares. Prior to incorporation, the plaintiff and Mr Gorman formed a partnership, called "The Shannon Ferry", for the purpose of purchasing three vessels from the company who previously operated the Severn ferry service. It was subsequently decided that only two of the vessels would be retained by the partnership and that one of the vessels would be disposed of by the vendors and the purchase money accounted for in respect of the three vessels. Ultimately, £2,925 was applied towards the purchase money of the three vessels. At the same time lands were acquired for use at the Kildysert terminal of the proposed ferry by the plaintiff, his wife and Mr Gorman, in partnership.

Article 8 of the articles of association of the company stated that any director who entered into a contract or arrangement with the company should disclose the extent of his interest at the meeting of the directors at which the contract or arrangement was to be determined. The articles further provided that the quorum for such a meeting should be two, unless otherwise fixed by the directors and that no director should vote in respect of any contract or arrangement in which he was interested.

On 20 March 1968, the company agreed to purchase from the two partnerships, *inter alia*, the vessels, goodwill and lands acquired by them. The company agreed to purchase what was termed as "The Goodwill of the Shannon Ferry" for £9,000, the two vessels for £11,500 and the land for £10,000. In relation to the sale of lands, the partnership stood to make a substantial profit. No meeting of directors, or general meeting, was held to pass a resolution ratifying the contract.

In the period prior to 20 March 1968 a large number of people had subscribed for shares in the company. On 22 March 1968 the company became a public company and in July 1968 shares were allotted to people who had previously subscribed for them. The monies used in the purchase of the vessels and lands were withdrawn from two accounts into which these monies had been deposited.

In order to obtain State grants for the project, which were critical for its development, it became necessary for the plaintiff to resign from all involvement with the company. The plaintiff's resignation was accepted at a meeting of directors on 20 April 1968. The first part of the plaintiff's claim arose out of an alleged agreement of 11 April 1968, which he claimed was collateral to and a modification of the agreement of 20 March 1968, which he said set out the terms upon which the plaintiff would resign from all involvement with the company. He further relied on the revised statement in lieu of prospectus which he said was drafted after he agreed to resign, and which he submitted constituted a sufficient disclosure to the public, including the subscribers, of his interest. He claimed the sum of £6,833 which was made up of (1) £4,500 for his half share of the sum of £9,000 for what was referred to in the agreement of 20 March 1968 as the "Goodwill of the Shannon Ferry"; (2) A further £1,000 which the plaintiff alleged that the company agreed to pay him in respect of the said goodwill and (3) £1,333 which he said represented his own share of the profits of the sale of the lands.

The defendants denied the existence of the agreement of 11 April 1968, but said that if such an agreement had been concluded, the plaintiff had given no consideration in respect of the sums he claimed. They also claimed that the said agreement was void by virtue of the Statute of Frauds as there was no memorandum of the agreement which included the sale of lands and also was not to be performed within one year. They further submitted that the agreement was entered into by the plaintiff in breach of his duties as a director and was fraudulent as against the company and was void.

The plaintiff claimed a further sum of £1,875 which he said was due to him as assignee of a company known as Organisation Analysts ("O.A."), of which himself and his wife were the only directors and shareholders. The company had entered into an agreement with O.A. for the provision of services and this also had to be terminated in order to obtain the assistance of the Department of Finance. The plaintiff alleged that the company had agreed to pay such sums to release it from its obligations under the contract. The plaintiff also claimed the sum of £2,925 representing the purchase money for the resale of the third vessel sold which he claimed was to be his sole property.

Held by Pringle J:

(1) Under Article 8 of the company's articles, where a contract was to be entered into in which one of the directors had an interest, that interest should be disclosed at a meeting of the directors at which the contract was to be determined

and the interested director should not vote.

(2) Furthermore, such disclosure of interest should be made to the directors who are independent and not to other directors equally interested. *Lagunas Nitrate Co. v. Lagunas Syndicate* (1899) 2 Ch 392; *Gluckstein v. Barnes* [1900] AC 24 and *Erlanger v. New Sombrero Phosphate Co.* (1878) 3 App Cas 1218 applied.

(3) There was no possible quorum at the board for the ratification of the agreement as the plaintiff could not vote on any resolution to ratify a contract in which he was interested.

(4) As the plaintiff and Mr Gorman were not only the directors, but the promoters of the company, any contract made between them and the company under which they were to make a profit was voidable by the company unless full disclosure were made to the persons who had subscribed for shares, even though their shares had not yet been allotted to them. *Lydney and Wigpool Iron Ore Co. v. Bird* (1886) 33 Ch D 85; *Re British Seamless Paper Box Co.* (1881) 17 Ch D 467 and *Regal (Hastings) v. Gulliver* [1967] 2 AC 134 applied.

(5) Failure of a promoter or director to make full disclosure of his contracts with the company renders the contract voidable by the company, but not void and where no question of profit arises, if the company has adopted the benefit of the contract and rescission is no longer possible, the contract can be enforced against the company. *Re Cape Breton Co.* (1885) 29 Ch D 795; *Burland v. Earle* [1902] AC 83 and *Hely-Hutchinson v. Brayhead Ltd* [1967] 3 WLR 1408 applied.

(6) The company approbated the agreement of 20 March 1968 as it eventually took over most of the assets agreed to be sold by both partnerships to the company.

(7) Agreement was reached on 11 April 1968 between the plaintiff and Mr Gorman, acting on behalf of the company, as to the terms upon which the plaintiff agreed to resign.

(8) Such agreement was not void under the Statute of Frauds as it was collateral to the agreement of 20 March 1968 of which there was a sufficient memorandum. Furthermore, the agreement was to be performed within one year.

(9) This contract was voidable by the company for the same reasons as the agreement of 20 March 1968.

(10) The revised statement in lieu of prospectus did not constitute sufficient disclosure to the subscribers for shares as it did not refer to the terms of the agreement of 11 April 1968.

(11) This agreement was adopted by the company insofar as it accepted the resignation of the plaintiff and the renunciation of any rights he had to the allotment of shares in the company.

(12) However, a promoter or director must account to the company for any profit which he has made on the contract, therefore the profit which the plaintiff would otherwise have received on the sale of the lands should be deducted from the plaintiff's claim. *Re Olympia (Ltd) (Registered 1893)* [1898] 2 Ch 153 and

Leeds and Hanley Theatres of Varieties [1902] 2 Ch D 809 applied.

(13) O.A. were entitled to the sum of £1,042, £625 of which was paid and therefore the plaintiff, as assignee of O.A. was entitled to the balance of £417. The plaintiff was also entitled to £500, representing the value to the company of the plaintiff's share of what in the agreement of 20 March 1968 was described as "The Goodwill of the Shannon Ferry".

(14) The purchase money for the sale of the vessel was applied for the benefit of the partnership towards the purchase of the other two vessels and was not due to the plaintiff personally.

Cases referred to in judgment

British Seamless Paper Box Co, In re (1881) 17 Ch D 467
Burland v. Earle [1902] AC 83
Cape Breton Co, In re (1885) 29 Ch D 795
Erlanger v. New Sombrero Phosphate Co. (1878) 3 App Cas 1218
Gluckstein v. Barnes [1900] AC 240
Hely-Hutchinson v. Brayhead Ltd [1967] 3 WLR 1408
Inland Revenue Commissioners v. Muller [1901] AC 217
Lagunas Nitrate Co v. Lagunas Syndicate [1899] 2 Ch D 392
Leeds and Hanley Theatres of Varieties [1902] 2 Ch D 809
Lydney and Wigpool Iron Ore Co v. Bird (1886) 33 Ch D 85
North Eastern Insurance Co. [1910] 1 Ch 198
Olympia (Ltd) (Registered 1893), In re [1898] 2 Ch 153
Regal (Hastings) v. Gulliver [1967] 2 AC 134
Robophone Facilities Ltd v. Blank [1966] 3 All ER 128
Society of Practical Knowledge v. Abbot, 2 Beav 559

Counsel's and solicitors' names not available

PRINGLE J **10 July 1972**

The plaintiff in this action appeared in person and argued his case with great tenacity and considerable ability. The original statement of claim was, by leave of the court, amended in a number of respects, in the first place at the opening of the case and again at the close of the plaintiff's case. As finally amended, the plaintiff's main claims fall under three headings. First, he claims that under an agreement made on 11 April 1968 between himself and the defendant company, which he pleads was collateral to and a modification of an earlier agreement dated 20 March 1968 between himself and others and the defendants, he agreed to resign as a director of the defendant company in consideration of the payment of the sum of £6,833, no part of which he says was paid and he claims this sum of £6,833. Secondly, he claims, as assignee of Organisation Analysts Ltd, the sum of £1,875, the balance outstanding on foot of a contract of October 1967 between that company and the defendants and thirdly, he claims the sum of £2,925 which he pleads was money made available to the defendants in respect of the contract for sale and acquisition of vessels for which the defendants received benefit and he claims this sum as monies paid by him to the use of the defendants. The plaintiff also claims in the alternative a declaration that he is and was at all material times a director and member of the defendant company and that a certain contract dated October 1967 between Organisation Analysts Ltd and the defendants is and was at all material times a full and binding agreement. The plaintiff also claims damages, including interest for the breach of the last-mentioned contract. The defendants in their defence in regard to the first-mentioned claim deny that they entered into the agreement relied on by the plaintiff, either on 11 April 1968 or on any date, and they say that, if any such agreement was entered into, (a) there was no consideration for such agreement, (b) it was entered into by the plaintiff in breach of his duties as director of the defendant company and was fraudulent as against the defendants and void and, (c) there was no memorandum thereof sufficient to satisfy the Statute of Frauds. In regard to the agreement of 20 March 1968 referred to in the statement of claim the defendants do not deny the existence of this agreement, but they say that there was no consideration for the said agreement and that same was fraudulent and void and was entered into in breach of the plaintiff's duty as a director of the defendant company. They also plead the Statute of Frauds in relation to this agreement. In regard to the second claim on foot of the agreement of October 1967, the defendants admit that on or about 8 April 1968 they repudiated an agreement entered into between themselves and Organisation Analysts Ltd under which they were liable to pay that company the sum of £2,500 per annum by equal monthly instalments up to and including 1 December 1968, in consideration of certain services to be provided by that company, and that following 8 April 1968 no services were provided and the defendants paid to the said company the sum of £803 or thereabouts after that date, and they say that this sum represents and is a proper and adequate compensation in respect of their breach of the said agreement, and they further rely on a plea that the sum claimed by the plaintiff is a penalty. In regard to the third claim, the defendants deny that the sum of £2,925 or any sum was made available by them to the plaintiff, as alleged, or that any monies were paid by the plaintiff to the defendants as alleged or at all.

I propose to deal in turn with each of these three claims of the plaintiff, but, before doing so, it is necessary for me to set out the main facts as I find them after a full consideration of the great mass of evidence which was produced at the trial by witnesses on both sides.

The plaintiff, who describes himself as an organisation analyst, is an Irish subject and he is said that before he came to Ireland in 1965 he had had five years training in management services organisation and methods in a well-known company in England. On 24 December 1963 he and his wife formed a private limited company called Organisation Analysts Ltd (to which I shall hereafter refer as O.A.). In his evidence the plaintiff said that in May or June 1966 he conceived the idea of inaugurating a passenger and car ferry service across the River Shannon in the vicinity of Foynes and Kildysert. The basis for assessing the value of such a service was, he said, a report called The Lichfield Report which was then in draft form. One of the main problems was the acquisition of suitable vessels, for which the market was extremely limited.

However, by chance, he ascertained that at that time the Severn Ferry was becoming redundant owing to the opening of a new bridge across the river and in August 1966 he got in touch with the company which had operated that Ferry Service and discussed the question of the purchase of three of their vessels, the "Severn King", "Severn Queen" and "Severn Princess". The plaintiff then started looking round for persons interested in the project and, as the result of an advertisement which he inserted in a paper called *Business and Finance*, Mr James Gorman who was then chairman of Irish and Intercontinental Hotels Ltd replied to the advertisement on 29 September 1966 stating his interest, and, as the result of a series of meetings, it was agreed between the plaintiff and Mr Gorman that they would work together in promoting the project, Mr Gorman to use his influences in procuring the necessary capital and the plaintiff to be responsible for the practical and administrative side of the promotion. It was decided to employ a company called The Economist Intelligence Unit of Ireland Ltd of which Mr Garrett Fitzgerald was a director, to investigate and report on the feasibility of the project and in about May 1967 this company produced a very full comprehensive report dealing with all aspects of the matter and this report was sufficiently favourable to encourage the plaintiff and Mr Gorman to proceed with the project. Negotiations were pursued by the plaintiff with the Severn Company and eventually in January 1968, after considerable bargaining it was agreed that the three vessels would be purchased for the sum of £12,000 by the plaintiff and Mr Gorman who had formed a partnership for this purpose called "The Shannon Ferry" which was registered under the Business Names Act on 22 August 1967. The purchase money for the three vessels consisted of £11,000 for the "Severn Princess" and £500 for each of the other vessels. Subsequently it was decided that only two of the vessels would be retained by the partnership, the "Severn Princess" and the "Severn Queen" and that the remaining vessel, the "Severn King" which the partners had agreed to purchase for £500 would be disposed of by the vendors and the purchase money accounted for in respect of the purchase money of the three vessels from them. The "Severn King" was sold by the vendors for £3,250 and, after accounting for 10 per cent commission, the balance of £2,925 was applied towards the purchase money of the three vessels. This sum of £2,925 is the subject-matter of the third of the plaintiff's claims, and I will deal with it in more detail later. At the same time as these negotiations in connection with the vessels were proceeding, the plaintiff and Mr Gorman were engaged in acquiring options on certain lands for use at the Kildysert Terminal of the proposed ferry. It was important that secrecy should be observed in connection with the negotiations for the acquisition of these lands and it was decided that Messrs P.F. Molony & Co, Solicitors, should be instructed to conduct the negotiations on behalf of Mrs Jennifer Hopkins, the plaintiff's wife, and that a partnership should be entered into between the plaintiff, his wife and Mr Gorman for the purpose of acquiring these lands. This partnership was subsequently registered under the Business Names Act on 2 November 1967 under the name of "Kildysert Estates". Before this, Messrs Molony & Co had entered into two agreements, the first of which was dated 30 May 1967 under which they obtained, in trust, an option to purchase from Daniel and Mary Clancy part of the lands comprised in Folio 6672 Co. Clare for the sum of £600 per statute acre, the sum of £40 being paid for the option. On 31 May 1967 a similar agreement was entered into by Messrs Molony, in trust with James O'Connell giving them an option to purchase the licensed premises known as "O'Connells Bar" for the sum of four thousand five hundred pounds, the sum paid for the option being ninety pounds. A third property comprising two acres and referred to as Hehirs land was also proposed to be acquired but no document was put in evidence in regard to these lands. A sum of £100 was paid on 2 June 1967 by the plaintiff to Messrs Molony in respect of the options on Clancy's lands and O'Connells Bar, but on that day the plaintiff received a cheque from Mr Gorman for £150 and I am satisfied that this was to recoup the plaintiff, *inter alia*, for any monies which he may have advanced in respect of the options. At a later stage a formal contract was entered into for the purchase of O'Connells Bar for £4,500 and I am satisfied that the amount of the deposit £1,125 was paid by Mr Gorman to Messrs Molony & Co on 15 January 1968 and on the following day he paid to Messrs Molony the sum of £3,275, representing the balance of the purchase money after giving credit for the deposit, and this money was lodged in the joint names of the solicitors for the vendors and Messrs Molony & Co. Further references will be made later to the source from which these monies paid by Mr Gorman came.

Mr Gorman had in the meantime been in communication with the Department of Finance and by letter dated October 1967 from the department to him it was stated, that the minister would be prepared to provide certain substantial sums out of the Special Regional Development Fund, subject to certain conditions, such as the provision of certain facilities by the Clare and Limerick county councils and the Foynes Harbour Commissioners and, among the conditions, were the following (1) that the defendant company (which had been formed) had sufficient capital available to enable it to operate the proposed regular ferry services which was stated to be not less than the £73,000 specified in Appendix 16 to the Economist Intelligence Unit Report, plus the cost of the company's commitment in respect of the landing facilities at Foynes. It was further provided that, as a condition precedent to the advance of the money by the minister, the company should hold to the credit of its bankers in Ireland the sum of £45,000 in a separate account and that the company should purchase the three vessels with money over and above the said sum of £45,000. The company was also to undertake to provide ferry services at a certain frequency for a minimum period of five years. The two promoters, the plaintiff and Mr Gorman, were to make a personal commitment to the company in the form of cash subscriptions for shares of at least £2,000 and it was stated that the financial assistance referred to was contingent on the company commencing regular ferry services in 1968. In a note attached to this letter, figures were given to show how the figure of £45,000 was arrived at that is to say: total capital £73,000 plus contribution to Foynes landing facilities £10,000 making £83,000, from which was deducted cost of boats £30,000 and goodwill £9,000: Total £39,000. This letter was addressed to Mr Gorman as chairman of the defendant company which had been incorporated on 20 July 1967 as a private company with a capital of £100 divided into shares of £1 each. The articles provided that, with certain exceptions, the regulations contained in Table A Part 1 and Part II of the First Schedule to the Companies Act 1963 should apply. By Article 3 the qualification of a director was the holding of one share. By Article 4 it was provided that the first director of the company should be nominated by the subscribers to the memorandum and that they should be permanent directors of the company.

It was also provided by Article 8 as follows:

> "No director shall be disqualified by his office from contracting with the company either as vendor, purchaser, or otherwise nor shall any such contract or arrangement entered in to by or on behalf of the company in which any director shall be in any way interested be avoided, nor shall any Director so contracting, or being so interested, be liable to account to the company for any profits realised by any such contract or arrangement by reason of such director holding that office or the fiduciary relationship thereby established, but the extent of his interest must be disclosed by him at the meeting of directors at which the contract or arrangement is determined on and no director shall vote in respect of any contract or arrangement in which he is so interested."

By Article 11 it was provided that the directors should have power from time to time to fix a quorum for their meeting and, unless otherwise fixed, two should form a quorum at a meeting of directors. The subscribers to the memorandum nominated the plaintiff and Mr Gorman as the first directors and 50 £1 shares were allotted to each of them, these each apparently consisting of one share transferred to each of them by the subscribers to the memorandum and 49 shares allotted for cash. By resolution of the directors dated 19 November 1967 Mr Sylvester Barrett was appointed a director of the company, but it appears that he did not acquire the necessary share qualification within two months after his appointment and therefore he ceases to be a director on 19 January in accordance with the provisions of Article 7(c) of the articles of the company.

Prior to the actual incorporation of the company a public meeting had been held in Ennis on 9 June 1967 for the purpose of obtaining financial assistance from the public for the project. As a result of this meeting and, I have no doubt, the personal efforts of the plaintiff and Mr Gorman, a considerable number of people subscribed monies for the purchase of shares in the company. Some of the monies subscribed were paid to Mr Molony, solicitor, and originally lodged to his clients account, but on 7 December 1967 a joint deposit account was opened in the Hibernian Bank in the names of Shannon Transport Systems Ltd, P.F. Molony & Co. and Hardman Winder & Stokes (a firm of solicitors in Dublin) and the monies received by Mr Molony were transferred to this account. £5,500 was lodged in this joint account on 7 December 1967, but £3,000 of this was withdrawn on 7 February 1968 at Mr Gorman's request on his signing an indemnity to Messrs Molony and Mr Stokes. A further sum of £1,700 was withdrawn on 20 February 1968 and £500, which had been lodged on 16 January 1968, was withdrawn on 15 March 1968. The monies which were so withdrawn were used by Mr Gorman towards the purchase money of the two vessels and for other purposes connected with the company. It is not clear from the evidence how many potential shareholders were involved, but among the documents put in evidence is a list dated 24 April 1968 of 19 people who are described as "paid-up members", their subscriptions totalling over £12,000, and four persons described as "allotees" totalling £3,750, and in a letter dated 13 March 1968 from Messrs Haughey Boland and Co., the company's auditors, they set out what they described as the anticipated opening balance sheet for the company in which they included, among the liabilities the sum of £30,986 "Advances from promoters and potential members". In fact it was not until 22 March 1968 that the company was turned into a public company and the capital increased to £100,000 in 5/- shares, and it was not until July of the year that shares were allotted to a large number of shareholders amounting to £62,340, together with £200 to Mr Barrett and £10,056 to Mr Gorman. It is clear therefore that a number of persons had subscribed money for shares prior to the agreement of 20 March 1968 referred to in the statement of claim and the alleged agreement of 11 April 1968 on which the plaintiff's claim is based. Some of these monies were put into the joint account referred to and some into Mr Gorman's No. 3 current account in the National Bank, including a sum of £4,750 subscribed by Mr Bertram Foy, to which I shall have to make further reference. It was out of this latter account that Mr Gorman made the payments of £150, £1,125 and £3,275 in respect of the lands to which I have already referred. There is a dispute as to the legal position in regard to the monies subscribed by the potential shareholders. The plaintiff contends that these monies were personal loans to Mr Gorman and that the persons who had put up the money could not be said to be at the time of the two agreements referred to, either shareholders, or even potential shareholders, in the company. Mr Gorman in his evidence said they were not personal loans to him, but were given to him in trust for the purchase of shares in the company, but he did say that the subscribers agreed that they could, in the meantime, be used for the purpose of the project. He also said that, if he had been asked by any of the subscribers to return their money, he would not have been obliged to do so, his obligations being to provide them with shares. Mr Molony produced in evidence a draft of a letter which he sent to persons who paid money to him in which he referred to "your application for shares in the above-named company" and in which he described his firm as being "stakeholders of the money in question for you and the company". Three of these subscribers gave evidence. Miss Bridget Fox said that Mr Gorman asked her to subscribe for shares in the company and she gave two cheques totalling £150 to Mr Gorman in, she thought, September 1967, that she did not get her share certificate until July 1968, but that, some time after she paid the money to Mr Gorman, he asked her if it could be used in the development of the project and she agreed, but she said that she would not have agreed to this if she had known that Mr Gorman was going to make a profit. Professor Thomas Murphy, registrar of UCD, said that in the autumn of 1967 he gave Mr Gorman £250 for the purchase of shares in the company and that Mr Gorman said that this was going to be used for the purposes of the company and he said he had no objection to this. This sum was sent to Mr Stokes by Mr Gorman with a letter (received on 2 September 1967) in which he said:

> "Here is a cheque for £250 from Professor T. Murphy of 11 Crannagh Road, Dublin 14 which represents a share subscription to Shannon Transport Systems Ltd which I hope you will be able to hold on deposit pending the formal allotment of shares. This subscription is for 250 shares of £1 each."

Mr Bertram Foy also gave evidence that, after a discussion with the plaintiff and Mr Gorman, a company in which he was interested paid by cheque a sum of £4,750 to Mr Gorman and Mr Foy was given a copy of a letter dated 5 January 1968 from the plaintiff to Mr Gorman in which he said:

> "Following our meeting with Mr Foy today he confirmed that he proposed to invest, subject to the Agreement of Shannon Transport Systems to the terms of the arrangement set out below and his accountant's final confirmation, a sum of £5,000 in the company immediately."

The letter then went on to detail an agreement that Mr Foy was to accept managerial and executive responsibility for the development of the project previously known as Kildysert Estates and Amenities Division of the company for which he was to be paid a fee of £1,000 for the period from 8 January to 31 May 1968. The letter also contained the following:

> "It would seem that the use of the shareholders' funds, including Mr Foy's for the acquisition of O'Connells property from Messrs Gorman and Hopkins could be done by means of part payment. Thus the vendors of the company would be prepared to accept a sum of £5,000 as part payment, the balance being paid on the date of for formal transfer of the operating company which at the present time is designated at 31 May. As no element of profit accrues to the vendors from this state of the negotiations, no further acquisition of such shares on their part is required at this time."

Mr Foy in his evidence said that the money was to be used for shares in the company and that, while he agreed to this money being used for the purchase of the O'Connell property, he understood at that time that this property was being purchased for the company and that it was only on 18 January 1968, when the contract of sale was being completed from the O'Connells that he discovered that it was being bought by Messrs Molony in trust for Mrs Hopkins and he said that he only became aware in February 1968 that the property was to be resold by the plaintiff and Mr Gorman to the company. He obviously did not observe that in the letter of January 1968, the vendors to the company were stated to be Messrs Gorman and Hopkins. He also said that, even when he became aware that the property was being initially acquired by parties other than the company, he thought they were to be transferred to the company at the price for which they had been purchased from O'Connell. Furthermore, he asked to arrange for a valuation of the property by Mr De Courcy, auctioneer, Limerick, who valued O'Connells property at £1,500 and Clancy's property at £3,750, making a total of £5,250, which in fact was less than the purchase price agreed to be paid to O'Connell and the Clancys. Mr Foy said that it was not until some time later that he became aware that Mr George Brew, an auctioneer and valuer in Kilrush, had valued the property at £10,000. In this valuation, which bears no date, Mr Brew said that he was aware that the original purchase price of the property was £6,760 and he said:

> "assuming that the proposed ferry service will be in operation during the coming tourist season and that this service will generate traffic in the accordance with the Economist Intelligence Unit forecasts, I estimate that a reasonable valuation of the entire property (which he describes as containing 3⅞ acres also the premises and outbuildings known as O'Connells Bar together with licence) would be ten thousand pounds."

This rather carefully worded valuation was relied upon when the agreement of 20 March 1968 between the plaintiff, his wife and Mr Gorman and the company was entered into. It appears from a letter dated 15 March 1968 from a Mr Duffy, whose firm were auditors for the company (Messrs Turbridy Ltd) who had advanced the £4,750 on Mr Foy's behalf, that they were seriously concerned about the situation and were considering demanding their money back. It is clear that, Mr Foy was aware before 20 March 1968 that the properties were to be sold by Messrs Gorman and Hopkins at a valuation of £10,000 and therefore at a substantial profit and that a figure of £9,000 was to be paid for what is described as "the goodwill of the Shannon Ferry" and, although he said in his evidence that he considered they were being sold to the company at a grossly inflated price and that he questioned those figures, he was by 20 March aware of the position, and he is therefore in a different position to the other investors who were not aware that any profit was proposed to be made by the plaintiff and Mr Gorman on the sale. As regards these other investors, I am satisfied that they paid their money for shares in the company and that Mr Gorman was a trustee on their behalf of these monies for this purpose and that they were not, as submitted by the plaintiff, personal loans to Mr Gorman. No doubt, in the cases of Miss Foy and Professor Murphy, they had agreed that, pending the allotment of their shares, their money could be used for the purposes of the company, but there is no evidence that this was so in the case of the other investors and, in any event, I am satisfied that none of these investors (apart from Mr Foy) was aware of the terms of the agreement of 20 April 1968 and

11 April 1968 on which the plaintiff relies and under which substantial profits were to accrue both to the plaintiff and Mr Gorman. I now come to consider the agreement of 20 March 1968 and the alleged agreement of 11 April 1968 which the plaintiff pleads was collateral to and a modification of certain terms of the agreement of 20 March 1968 as they affected him. Two documents were produced in evidence both dated 20 March 1968, but differing in some respects. One appears to be a top copy typed on note paper with the printed heading "Sean Hopkins, Mount Cashel, Kilmurry, Ennis, Co. Clare" and it reads as follows:

> Shannon Transport Systems Ltd
> 14 Molesworth Street
> Dublin 2 20 March 1968
>
> The Shannon Ferry & Kildysert Estates
> We propose to sell to you the under-mentioned assets for the consideration hereinafter named.
>
> 1. The goodwill of the Shannon Ferry £9,000
> 2. The two vessels known as Severn Princess and Severn Queen now lying in Bristol £11,500
> 3. The vehicle LIE 145 and other sundry chattels £350
> 4. The lands and premises together with options on further lands known as O'Connells Bar, Hehir's land and Clancy's Cross — all situate at Cappanavaroge, Kildysert, Co. Clare £10,160
>
> The formal contracts to be judged as of this date and to be completed forthwith.
>
> Signed James Gorman
> Sean Hopkins
> Jennifer Hopkins
>
> We accept the foregoing and will complete the formal contracts
> For and on behalf of Shannon Transport Systems Ltd
>
> James Gorman Director
> .... Director"

The figures £10,160 are in manuscript and the signature of James Gorman is signed over two threepenny stamps.

The other document produced appears to be a photostat copy of this document, but the figures £350 appear to have been altered in manuscript and are initialled "J.G." and, instead of the figures £10,160, the figures £10,000 appear in manuscript and they are also initialled "J.G.", the word "Judged" is struck out and the word "dated" substituted in manuscript and the document is signed at the end by both James Gorman, as before, but also by Sylvester Barrett opposite the signed word "Director" and both these signatures are over a 6d stamp.

The plaintiff gave evidence that the first of these documents, which he produced, was typed by his wife from a draft prepared by Mr Stokes and that the explanation of the change from £10,000 to £10,160 is that the £160 which had been paid for the options on the lands had been omitted, but the fact remains that the document signed by both Mr Gorman and Mr Barrett has the figure £10,000, whereas the document signed by Mr Gorman has what the plaintiff suggests was the correct figure of £10,160. While the plaintiff is not suing on this document, it is important, in considering the alleged agreement of 11 April 1968, on which the plaintiff's first claim is based, to arrive at a conclusion as to its legal effect. At the date upon which it was entered into the only directors of the company were the plaintiff and Mr Gorman, as Mr Barrett, who had been appointed a director on 19 November 1967 had then ceased to be a director owing to not having acquired his qualifying share by 19 January 1968. The plaintiff and Mr Gorman were also at this date the only shareholders in the company and, at the same time, they were quite clearly the promoters of the company. The position therefore was that the promoters and sole directors of the company purported by this agreement to sell to the company certain assets belonging to them (in the case of the lands together with Mrs Hopkins) as partners. Furthermore, in regard to two of the items, the goodwill and the lands, they were being sold at a substantial profit to the promoters and directors.

Under Article 8 of the company's articles where a contract is being entered into in which the directors have an interest, that interest, in order to make the contract valid, must be disclosed at the meeting of the directors at which the contract is determined on and the interested director must not vote (see also section 194(1) of The Companies Act 1963). Furthermore, it has been held that the disclosure must be to directors who are independent, and not to other directors who are equally interested in the contract in question (see *Lagunas Nitrate Co. v. Lagunas Syndicate* [1899] 2 Ch 392, *Gluckstein v. Barnes* [1900] AC 24, *Erlanger v. New Sombrero Phosphate Co.* [1879] 3 App Cas 1218), nor does it avail when two or more directors are interested to split up the resolution and for each director to abstain from voting on the part in which he is interested (see *North-Eastern Insurance Co.* [1919] 1 Ch 198). Here there is no evidence, and there is no minute, as to any meeting of directors having been held in reference to this agreement and in fact no such meeting capable of passing any resolution could have been held, because the quorum of directors was two and when a director is not entitled to vote he cannot be reckoned in estimating a quorum (see the cases referred to above). Nor is there any evidence of any general meeting having been held to approve of the contract and, in any event the only registered shareholders were the plaintiff and Mr Gorman who owned the entire authorised capital of the company and, while their restriction on voting as directors would not apply to their voting as shareholders at a general meeting,

I do not consider that, even if there was no other persons who had subscribed for shares, this contract could have been legally ratified by a general meeting at which the two parties interested would have been the only persons entitled to vote. But I am satisfied that, as the plaintiff and Mr Gorman were not only directors, but also promoters of the company, any contract under which they were to make a profit would be voidable by the company unless full disclosure were made to the persons who at that time had subscribed for shares, even though their shares had not yet been allotted to them. Lindley LJ delivering the judgement of himself and Cotton and Lopes LJJ, in the case of *Lydney and Wigpool Iron Ore Co. v. Bird* [1886] 33 Ch D at page 94 said:

> "It is perfectly well settled that a promoter of a company is accountable to it for all monies secretly obtained by him from it, just as if the relationship of principal and agent or of trustee and *cestui que trust* had really existed between him and the company when the money was so obtained."

and in *Erlanger's* case at page 1231 Lord Cairns said:

> "I do not say that the owner of property may not promote and form a joint stock company and then sell his property to it, but I do say that, if he does, he is bound to take care that he sells it to the company through the medium of a board of directors who can and do exercise an independent and intelligent judgement on the transaction,"

and at page 1255 Lord O'Hagan said, in regard to the position of promoters of a company,

> "But the privilege given to them for promoting such a company involved obligations of a very serious kind. It required in its exercise the utmost good faith, the completest truthfulness, and a careful regard for the future shareholders"

and at page 1256 he said:

> "the promoters, who so far forget their duty to the company they formed as to give it a directorate without independence of position or vigilance and caution in dealing with its interest, must take the consequences and this without the necessary imputation of evil purpose or conscious fraud. The fiduciary obligations may be violated though there be no intention to do injustice."

Again in *Re Seamless Paper Box Co.* [1881] 17 Ch D 467 Jessel MR at page 471, referring to *Erlanger's* case, said:

> "It makes no difference whatever that the persons who, at the time the

> allotment was made, were in fact the promoters or their nominees, knew of the fraud. You can defraud future allottees as well as present."

and at page 476 James LJ said:

> "If they were intending, although then constituting the whole company, that other people should come in afterwards to whom what had been done would be injurious, the court would feel no difficulty in saying, as Lord Langdale did in the *Society of Practical Knowledge v. Abbott*, 2 Beavan 559, that they intended to commit a fraud."

and Lord Justice Cotton said at page 478:

> "The directors stand in fiduciary relations to the whole company, that is not only to the existing shareholders, but to all whom they intend to bring in. A trustee cannot make a profit for himself without the knowledge of all his *cestuis que trustant* and so the directors of a company formed in the ordinary way stand in a fiduciary relationship, not only to those who are members of the company at the time, but to all who may come in afterwards."

See also the case of *Regal (Hastings) Ltd v. Gulliver* [1967] 2 AC 134.

It appears to be clear therefore that if, as here, there was no independent board of directors to whom disclosure could have been made, and as the promoters themselves were the only actual shareholders, in order to prevent the contract being voidable by the company, full disclosure would have had to be made to the subscribers for shares and this, as I have already found, was not done. It follows that, on one or more of the grounds stated, this contract of 20 March 1968 was voidable by the company and could have been rescinded. But in fact the company did not rescind it and eventually took over most of the assets agreed to be sold by the promoters and directors to the company and I shall have to consider later what the legal effect of this was. The sequence of events after this contract was entered into was that two days later the company was made a public company and the capital increased to £100,000. Then a certain situation of crisis arose. It appears that, for some reason, the Department of Finance intimated that, unless the plaintiff was removed from any involvement in the company, the financial assistance they had promised, and on which the whole project depended, would not be forthcoming. This difficulty seems to have first arisen as early as February 1968, as the plaintiff drafted a letter to Mr Gorman which was originally dated 20 February 1968 in which he said:

> "I realise from your so carefully and tactfully worded remarks of last Thursday that my personal position may be of some embarrassment to those attempting to assist you in launching the ferry. Much as I would like

to take action to protect my good name, you know that to do so would irreparably damage our chances of success in reconstructing Irish Labels Industries. In the circumstances I appreciate that the continued circulation of what we both know is scurrilous innuendo may well adversely affect the Ferry project. Accordingly, if you yourself feel it is in the best interests of the project that I resign my position in the venture, I shall do so without hesitation".

The plaintiff says that he showed the draft of this letter to Mr Gorman in February and that Mr Gorman handed it back to him and later called upon him in April to honour his offer to resign and that he then altered the date on the letter to 9 April 1968. He said that in March Mr Boland told him that his, (the plaintiff's), connection with the company was no longer a problem, but then on 8 April Mr Gorman telephoned him to say that the minister required his resignation forthwith, and that otherwise the grants would be withheld. The plaintiff says that he then had a conversation with Mr Barrett who was sympathetic to him, but said it might be best if he resigned and arrangements made to cover his claims. Mr Gorman says that he does not know when the date on this letter was changed, but that he and Mr Barrett, who was obviously looked upon by both the plaintiff and Mr Gorman as a director, had not agreed to the plaintiff's resignation when the agreement of 20 March was entered into and from the minutes of the meetings of the directors it appears that on 12 April it was recorded that the plaintiff wished to resign as from 24 March and at a further meeting on 20 April, the plaintiff's resignation was accepted. This appears to have been as a result of a letter dated 20 April from the plaintiff to Mr Gorman in which he said:

> "You may therefore take this letter as notification of my resignation from your board. I shall of course place at your disposal my original shareholding in the company and my wife and I will not take up the allotments originally envisaged so you may feel free to seek other sources of capital without the need to consult me."

I am satisfied that the date upon which the plaintiff effectively ceased to be a director of the company was 20 April 1968, so that he was still a director on 11 April, the date of the alleged agreement to which I am about to refer and upon which the plaintiff's first claim is based. When it became clear that his resignation as a director and his severance of all connection with the company was required in order that the grant should be forthcoming, the plaintiff prepared a memorandum setting out the conditions upon which he was willing to resign. He says that he had a meeting with Mr Barrett and went through the points in this memorandum with him and that he had telephone conversations with Mr Gorman on the matter and that both Mr Gorman and Mr Barrett agreed that, if he resigned, he would have to be paid, and that the sums which he would have to be paid were to be agreed on before he resigned and his resignation was not to be handed over until the grants were sanctioned by the department. The all-important meeting of 11 April was held in Mr Gorman's offices at Hainault House at which the plaintiff, Mr Gorman and Mr Barrett were present.

There is a considerable and important conflict as to what took place at this meeting. There is no dispute that the purpose of the meeting was to discuss the terms upon which the plaintiff would resign and there is no doubt the memorandum prepared by the plaintiff was discussed and the plaintiff says that each of the three parties had a copy of this memorandum and he gave evidence that agreement was reached on each of the ten paragraphs therein, with certain amendments which were made as a result of the discussion at the meeting, and he says that the fact that agreement was reached is indicated by the presence of the "ticks" which appear opposite each of these paragraphs on each of the copies of the memorandum which were produced. Mr Gorman, on the other hand, swore that, while there were discussions on each of the points, no agreement was in fact reached. He said that the "ticks" on his copy indicated that he understood each of the paragraphs. He also said that, although he and Mr Barrett wanted to negotiate terms with the plaintiff, he understood that the intention was that any agreement would be put into proper legal form and, in reply to the plaintiff on cross-examination, he said that he (the plaintiff) allowed him to leave the meeting under the impression that the document was to be put into writing in the form of a formal contract. Mr Barrett's account of the meeting was that it was held to arrange for the plaintiff's retirement as a director, that it lasted a considerable time and that the plaintiff put forward proposals as to how he should be compensated. He said that his understanding was that any agreement would be subject to the intending shareholders consenting, and that the plaintiff would only be entitled to receive any monies, if and when monies were available. He also said that he did not remember the items being ticked off. In cross-examination he said:

> "We had hammered out this agreement, but it was to be subject to the agreement of the potential shareholders and the plaintiff said that there would be no problem with the shareholder."

He further said that, while it was his understanding that the shareholders would be involved, he may not have expressed this understanding at the meeting. The plaintiff, in support of his contention that agreement had been reached, relied on the fact that after the meeting he made certain alterations in the draft statement in lieu of prospectus which had to be delivered in accordance with section 35 of the Companies Act 1963 and which had already been drafted, and he contended that these alterations embodied the matters which had been agreed on at the meeting on 11 April and the final draft was signed by Mr Gorman and Mr Barrett with these alterations and it is in fact dated 11 April 1968. The fact that the draft statement in lieu of prospectus would have to be altered was referred to at paragraph 1 of the memorandum. The alterations which appear in the draft statement in lieu of prospectus in the plaintiff's handwriting include, at paragraph 5, the deletion of the plaintiff's name as a director and the deletion of his name and that of his wife from the list of subscribers for shares, and the deletion, in paragraph 18, of the plaintiff's name as a director interested in property purchased or acquired by the company within the previous two years. I have already referred to the fact that the plaintiff wrote on 29 April notifying his resignation from the board and it was accepted on that date. I am satisfied that agreement was reached between the plaintiff, Mr Gorman and Mr Barrett at the meeting on 11 April, as to the terms on which the plaintiff was to resign and that these terms are there embodied in the memorandum as amended. The plaintiff relies on this agreement, together with the revised statement in lieu of prospectus as basis for the first of his claims, that is to say the claim for a sum of £6,833 and also, to a certain extent, for the second of his claims that is to say his claim for £1,875 in relation to O.A. He relies, in regard to the first of these claims on the fact that under paragraphs 4,5 and 6 of the memorandum it was provided that all engagements entered into by the two partnerships (Shannon Ferry and Kildysert Estates) up to and including 8 April 1968 should be implemented in accordance with the undertakings already made with the company, that on the basis that the company completes the contract of 20 March, the monies expended to 8 April should be considered part payment for the assets referred to in what is described as "the letter of contract" of 20 March, and that the balance was to be paid to the plaintiff or his assigns or successors in title on or before 6 September 1968. In his statement of claim the plaintiff pleaded that this agreement was collateral to and a modification of the agreement of 20 March. His first claim for £6,533 is made up as follows:

(1) £4,500 for his half-share of the sum of £9,000 for what is referred to in agreement of 20 March as "The goodwill of the Shannon Ferry".

(2) £1,000 which he says was to be paid to him out of the amount payable under the agreement of 20 March to Mr Gorman as his share of the goodwill, as he says that, in accordance with clause 9 of the memorandum, Mr Gorman agreed to accept £3,500 for his share of the goodwill instead of £4,500. In other words, he claims that the effect of the agreement made on 11 April was that the company would pay him the sum of £5,500 for his share of the goodwill and that the amount payable to Mr Gorman was to be £3,500.

(3) £1,333 which he says was his one-third share of the profit on sale of the lands. This sum he said was arrived at by taking one-third of the difference between the amount to be paid by the partnership for the purchase of the lands (that is to say £6,000) and the sum of £10,000, the sum at which the partners agreed to sell to the company.

The defendants, as well as denying the existence of the agreement of 11 April, say that, if any such agreement was entered into, there was no consideration for such agreement. I am satisfied that there was consideration in that the plaintiff agreed to and did resign as a director of the company and placed his shares at the disposal of the company. The removal of the plaintiff from all connection with the company was clearly of vital importance to its future prospects. The defendants also pleaded the absence of a memorandum in writing under the

Statute of Frauds on two grounds, first that the agreement was, in whole or in part, an agreement for the sale of lands and, secondly that it was an agreement not to be performed within a year. In regard to the first of these pleas, I consider that the agreement of 11 April was, insofar as the sale of the lands was concerned, a confirmation of the previous agreement of 30 March in respect of which there was a sufficient memorandum in writing to satisfy the Statute, and in regard to the second plea, the contract was not one which was not to be performed within a year, as the date for performance was 8 September 1968. These defences therefore in my opinion fail.

The defendants, however also pleaded and relied very strongly on the defence that, if such an agreement was entered into, it was entered into by the plaintiff in breach of his duties as a director of the company and was fraudulent against the company and void.

I have already said that I am satisfied that an agreement was entered into on 11 April between the plaintiff and Messrs Gorman and Barrett who clearly purported to act on behalf of the company. But the same situation arose in regard to this agreement as existed in regard to the agreement of 20 March. Mr Barrett was not a director, or even a shareholder of the company, and therefore he had no power or authority to enter into any contract on behalf of the company. The only other director, apart from the plaintiff, was Mr Gorman and no resolution of the directors could have been passed authorising the entering into the contract on behalf of the company on the sole vote of Mr Gorman, as the plaintiff, being an interested party, could not be counted in order to form a quorum. In fact there is no evidence, either in the minutes or otherwise, of any meeting of the directors to consider the entering into of the agreement, or of any resolution purporting to have been passed in reference thereto by the board, nor was any general meeting of the company held which would be necessary in order to make valid a payment to the plaintiff as a consideration for his retirement from office in accordance with section 186 of the Companies Act 1963 upon which, although not specially pleaded, the company is entitled to rely as a matter of law. Furthermore, as there was no independent board of directors to whom the plaintiff could disclose his interest, his duty to the company as a director was to declare his interest to the subscribers who had put up money for shares in the company (see the authorities which I referred to in relation to the agreement of 20 March), and I am satisfied that this was never done. The plaintiff relied upon the final statement in lieu of prospectus, which was registered in the Companies Office on 18 June 1968, as constituting a sufficient disclosure to the public (including the subscribers) of his interest but, while the statement in lieu of prospectus referred to the contract of 20 March, it did not refer to the agreement of 11 April. It did refer to the fact that Kildysert Estates owned by James Gorman, Jennifer Hopkins and Sean Hopkins had disposed of its properties known as O'Connell's Bar and adjoining lands as Cappanavarogue and its options on property known as Clancy's Cross to the company for a sum of £10,160, but no disclosure was made of the *profit* made by the vendors on such sale. It also referred to the fact that by the agreement of 20 March 1968 the

Shannon Ferry proprietors, James Gorman and Sean Hopkins had sold to the company "The Severn Princess" and "The Severn Queen" and other named assets and goodwill (the latter item for the sum of £9,000). Again in regard to these items, it did not disclose the profit to the promoters or directors at which these items were being sold. No reference is made to the additional £1,000 which the plaintiff was to get for his share of the goodwill under the agreement of 11 April, nor is there any reference to the £2,500 which was to be paid to O.A. I am satisfied that the statement in lieu of prospectus was totally ineffective to operate as notice to the subscribers of the nature and effect of the commitments to the plaintiff alleged to have been entered into by the company in consideration of his resigning as a director: (see as to the non-disclosure in a statement in lieu of prospectus of the profit being made by promoters, *Leeds and Hanley Theatre of Varieties* [1902] 2 Ch D 809). My findings in regard to the alleged agreement of 11 April 1968 are that, although agreement was reached between the plaintiff, Mr Gorman and Mr Barrett, this agreement was not binding on the company. But this is not a complete answer to the plaintiff's claim based on this alleged agreement or on the agreement of 20 March, because the company in fact eventually acted on the agreement of 20 March by taking over most of the assets thereby agreed to be sold and on the agreement of 11 April by accepting the plaintiff's resignation as a director and his renunciation of any rights he had to the allotment of shares in the company. So far from these contracts with the plaintiff being reprobated by the company, they were in fact approbated to a substantial extent. It appears to be clear that failure by a promoter or a director to make full disclosure of his contracts with the company renders the contract *voidable* by the company, but not void (see *Re Cape Breton Co.* (1885) 29 Ch D 795, *Burland v. Earle* [1902] AC 83, 99, and *Hely- Hutchinson v. Brayhead Ltd* [1967] 3 WLR 1408), and where, as in the *Hely-Hutchinson* case, there is no question of a profit arising to the promoter or director, if the company has adopted the benefit of the contract and recission is no longer possible, the contract can be enforced against the company, but this does not mean that the ordinary rule does not apply, that the promoter or director must account to the company for any profit which he has made on the contract (see *In Re Olympia Ltd) (Registered 1893)* [1898] 2 Ch 149 and the *Leeds and Hanley Theatres of Varieties* case referred to above). The plaintiff's claim for £6,833 is, as I have said, made up of three items, the first of which is the sum of £4,500, half share of the sum of £9,000 which in the agreement of 20 March 1968 is described as "The goodwill of The Shannon Ferry". The defendants say that the plaintiff and Mr Gorman had not, and could not have had, any goodwill to sell to the company, because goodwill must be attached to some business and cannot exist in connection with some existing business and they say that, at the time the promoters purported to sell to the company, the goodwill of the Shannon Ferry, there was in fact no business in existence (see *Inland Revenue Commissioners v. Muller* [1901] AC 217 *per* Lord MacNaughton at page 224). The plaintiff relied on paragraph II(12) at page 71 of the Report of The Economist Intelligence Unit which read as follows:

> "The item for goodwill at £9,000 represents approximately 25% of the equity. This is the Sponsors' valuation of the options and arrangements they have negotiated, or are in process of negotiating. The valuation assumes, of course, that arrangements still under negotiations are brought to a successful conclusion. The right to priority, use of shore installations none of which are likely to be duplicated, at least while the company gives a service that is reasonably attained to traffic needs; the agreement to purchase ships from the Severn Company which we understand has been entered into on the basis of our verbal interim report, the options which have been taken on key pieces of property, and the Co-operative relationship established with the Clare Co. Development Team and with local authorities and other statutory bodies, all taken together make up a quasi-monopoly situation in relation to what promises to be a very profitable trade in the long run. Having regard to the returns likely to accrue to the ordinary shareholders, the valuation by the sponsors of their contribution does not appear unreasonable."

It will be seen from this extract from the report that the sum of £9,000 was the plaintiff's and Mr Gorman's valuation of the various activities they had undertaken in relation to the Ferry Project and that these are described as "goodwill". The items, it will be seen, included the agreement to purchase the two vessels which the promoters agreed to sell to the company at their cost price, and therefore at no profit to themselves, the options on the lands which they agreed to sell to the company at a profit of £4,000, and the value of the various negotiations they had undertaken with the Department for Finance in relation to grants and with the local authorities. While these items could not strictly be described as "goodwill", they were obviously of some considerable value to the company which took the benefit of them, but if the vessels and the options on the land for which the promoters were also to be paid under the agreement of 20 March, (in the latter case at a substantial profit), are excluded, as in my opinion they must be, it is clear that the figure suggested by the promoters bears little or no relation to the actual value of the benefits which they agreed to make over to the company under the words "The goodwill of the Shannon Ferry". No evidence was produced before me as to the value of these benefits to the company, or of the profit element involved to the plaintiff and Mr Gorman, the plaintiff claiming that he is entitled to the full sum of £4,500, as his half of the £9,000, and the defendants relying on the fact that there was no "goodwill", properly so called, and that therefore the plaintiff is entitled to nothing. I think it is clear that the words "The goodwill of the Shannon Ferry" were not used in the strict sense of goodwill attached to an existing business, but were meant to include (*inter alia*) the benefits which the company was to acquire, and which it did acquire as a result of the negotiations which the plaintiff and Mr Gorman had conducted with the minister and the county councils and the other work which they had done in instigating the project. The company took these benefits and therefore must be taken to have adopted the agreements of 20 March and

11 April in respect of those benefits and, as under the agreement of 11 April it was clearly recognised that the plaintiff and Mr Gorman each had separate claims against the company, the plaintiff is entitled to be paid by the company whatever his share was worth, but not for any profit thereon. As I have said, the purchase of the vessels and the options on the lands must be excluded, and I think it must also be taken into account that, under the agreement with his company, O.A. hereafter referred to, the plaintiff was remunerated for his service to the company as from 1 November 1967 and this continued up to and after 20 March 1968, so that any contracts he made, or any negotiations which were undertaken during this period were, so far as the plaintiff was concerned, carried out by him while he was, through his own company, employed by the defendants. It is very difficult on the scanty evidence before me to fix a value of the benefits acquired by the company from the plaintiff over and above any element of profit to him but, doing the best I can, and taking all matters which I have mentioned into consideration, I fix a figure of £500 as the value to the company of the plaintiff's share of what is described in the agreement as "The goodwill of the Shannon Ferry". The second item in the plaintiff's claim for £6,833, is the sum of £1,000 alleged to have been agreed on 11 April to be paid to the plaintiff by the company as an addition to his share of the goodwill. As the agreement reached by the three partners on 11 April was not binding on the company and was never adopted or ratified by the company (save insofar as it confirmed the agreement of 20 March), this is not, in my opinion, recoverable by the plaintiff from the company, whatever the position between the plaintiff and Mr Gorman may be, with which this action is not concerned. The third item in this claim is the sum of £1,333, the plaintiff's alleged one-third share of the profit on the sale of the lands to the company. The entire of this sum is clearly, and admittedly, profit and, for the reasons stated, it is, in my opinion, irrecoverable by the plaintiff from the company.

The plaintiff's second claim is for the sum of £1,875 alleged to be due to him as assignee of O.A.

This company was incorporated in England on 24 December 1963 and its purpose was, the plaintiff said, to exploit his management, skill and initiative as an organisation analyst. The capital of the company was £100 and the plaintiff was managing director and he and his wife were the sole shareholders. By agreement contained in a letter dated 12 October 1967, signed by Mr Gorman, the company agreed to employ the services of O.A. for the period from 1 November 1967 to 30 April 1968, with a provision that this period should be automatically extended to 31 December 1968, unless either party notified the other in writing to the contrary not less than 28 days in advance of 30 April 1968. No such notice was given by either party. For their services O.A. were to be paid the monthly sum of £208.6.8, and, in addition, the board of the company could at its discretion refund to O.A. any special out-of-pocket expenses, travel and other costs. The services to be rendered by O.A. were described as:

> "the areas of internal administration, the implementation of all board

resolutions, as and when required relating to the preparations of a Ferry Service across the Shannon River."

The plaintiff in his evidence said that O.A. was to be responsible for preparing all financial papers, and all dealings with auditors, local authorities, the Department for of Finance, consulting engineers and all matters to the marine installations. When the crisis arose in March and April 1968 in connection with the necessity, in the interest of the company, for the plaintiff and his wife to sever all connections with the company, this necessarily involved putting an end to the contract with O.A. and the terms upon which this was to be accomplished were discussed at the meeting in Hainault House and are set out in paragraph 10 of the plaintiff's memorandum.

As originally drafted by the plaintiff O.A. were to discharge the company from all its obligations under the contract on payment of the sum of £1,500, but, as a result of the agreement reached between the plaintiff, acting for O.A., Mr Gorman and Mr Barrett at that meeting, this figure was increased to the sum of £2,500, £1,250 of which might be paid at a monthly rate and the balance was expressed to be "treated as a payment under the goodwill provisions". It is the balance of this sum of £2,500 which the plaintiff now claims, after giving credit for the sum of £625 hereinafter referred to. He relies on an assignment dated 23 November 1970 signed on behalf of O.A. by the plaintiff's wife (under the name of Jennifer Birney), and the plaintiff himself as directors, under which O.A., in consideration of being relieved of any obligation to the plaintiff whatsoever in respect of O.A.'s contingent obligations to the plaintiff consequent upon his carrying out the duties specified in the agreement between O.A. and the company, assigned to the plaintiff the debt alleged to be due by the company to O.A. which was stated to be the sum of £1,041.13.4. It appears that the company did in fact pay O.A. the three monthly payments due in advance on 1 April 1968, 1 May 1968 and 1 June 1968, amounting to £625 and the figure of £1,041.13.4 is the sum alleged to be due to O.A. for the remaining five months up to 1 December 1968. The plaintiff claims in his statement of claim the sum of £1,875 as assignee from O.A., but the assignment was clearly confirmed to the sum of £1,041.13.4. In court the plaintiff claimed that the difference between the £1,041.13.4 and the £1,875 which he claimed was due to him personally under the agreement of 11 April. As I have already held that this agreement is not binding on the company (save insofar as it was subsequently adopted by the company), even if it included an agreement that this balance was to be paid to the plaintiff personally by reason of the reference in clause 10 of the memorandum, which I consider very doubtful, (as it seems to me to envisage the £2,500 being payable to O.A.), the plaintiff cannot recover this balance and his claim under this heading must be confined to the sum of £1,041.13.4. The defendants concede that in April 1968 there was a breach by them of their agreement with O.A. and that the question is what damages O.A. were entitled to arising out of this breach. They say that the three payments made after the breach and when O.A. were not rendering any services under the agreement, that is to say the sum of £625, represents adequate damages for their breach of contract, but in the defence it was pleaded that the defendants had paid four instalments amounting to £803 after the breach, and that this sum was sufficient to satisfy the claim of O.A. This was a mistake, as in fact only the three monthly payments referred to above were made. The defendants also pleaded that the sum claimed was a penalty and they relied on the dissenting judgment of Denning LJ in the case of *Robophone Facilities Ltd v. Blank* [1966] 3 All ER 128, but in the present case there was no provision in the agreement providing for a sum to be payable in the event of a breach, and in my opinion no question of a penalty arises. The measure of damages to which O.A. were entitled is the loss which may fairly and reasonably be considered as arising naturally, that is to say according to the usual course of things, from the breach, bearing in mind that O.A. were bound to mitigate the damages. The plaintiff gave evidence that the principal source of income of O.A. after April 1968 would have been the payments from the defendants under their agreement and that after the breach it became impossible for O.A. to pursue other potential clients as it had no money. But the accounts of O.A. which were produced show that for the year ending 31 December 1967 the nett profit was £273, and for the year ending 31 December 1968 the nett profit was £264, and this was after allowing a provision for bad debts of £1,041, but, as against this, the accounts for 1968 show that there was a bank overdraft of £746 which did not appear in the previous year's accounts. I consider that the fair and reasonable damages to which O.A. was entitled when the breach took place was the sum of £1,042, that is to say five months at £208.6.8 per month, and as £625 was paid the balance due is £417 to which the plaintiff is entitled as assignee of O.A.

The third and final item in the plaintiff's claim is the sum of £2,925, monies alleged to have been paid by the plaintiff to the use of the defendants. This claim arises in connection with the vessels known as the "Severn King", one of the vessels which the partnership of The Shannon Ferry agreed to acquire from the Severn Ferry Company. It appears that in January 1968, after considerable negotiations, it was agreed with the vendors that the three vessels the "Severn King", "Severn Queen and "Severn Princess" would be acquired by the partnership for a sum of £12,000, that is to say £11,000 for the "Severn Princess", £500 for the "Severn Queen" and £500 for the "Severn King" (see the letter from the vendor's solicitors dated 15 January 1968), but later, in February, it was agreed that only "the Princess" and "the Queen" would be acquired by the defendants and that "the King" would be disposed of by the vendors for the best price which could be obtained and, after deduction of 10 per cent commission, the balance of the purchase money would be applied towards payment of the balance of the purchase money of the three vessels due to the Severn Company.

The plaintiff swore that the agreement between himself and Mr Gorman was that he personally was to purchase "the King" and that the purchase money on its resale was to be his sole property and his claim is based on this contention. Mr Gorman, on the other hand, swore that this was "sheer fantasy" and that he never agreed that the plaintiff was to have the entire profit. In the events which happened "the King" was sold by the vendors for £3,250 and, after deducting the commission, the sum of £2,925 was credited to the partnership as against the balance of the purchase money of the three vessels (see the letter from the vendor's solicitors to Mr Stokes dated 9 May 1968). I do not accept the plaintiffs evidence that the purchase money of "the King" was to be his sole property. I am satisfied that it was to be applied, and was in fact applied, for the benefit of the partnership and this is borne out by the letter from Mr Stokes on behalf of the partners to the vendor's solicitors dated 29 February 1968 in which Mr Stokes stated,

> "we confirm our telephone conversation with Mr Francis in which it was agreed that your firm should arrange forthwith to dispose of the 'Severn King' to the purchaser thereof for a minimum price of £3,000 obtaining a larger price, say £3,250, if possible, and that out of this purchase you should pay a commission of 10% to Mr Williams for arranging the transaction and appropriate the balance towards the total price of £8,000 due by our clients to your clients in respect of the three vessels."

As regards the sum of £3,000 referred to in this letter, this was apparently the balance then due by the partnership for the purchase of the three vessels; an initial deposit of £1,000 having been paid at an earlier date, and a further sum of £3,000 in January 1968 by Mr Gorman. It is also to be observed that there was no mention in the plaintiff's memorandum discussed at the meeting on 11 April of any sum being due to the plaintiff by the company in respect of the purchase money of "the King". The plaintiff explains this by saying that he was not aware of the amount of the purchase price of "the King" until the month of May, but one would have thought that, if there was any sum alleged to be due to the plaintiff, it would have been referred to even if the figure was not then available.

The position therefore was that the sum of £2,925 was applied by the Severn vendors in reduction of the balance due by the partnership for the three vessels, and that £500 of this was attributable to the purchase price of "The King", and therefore the partnership, consisting of the plaintiff and Mr Gorman, benefited to the extent of £2,425 from the resale of "the King" as the balance payable on "the Queen" and "the Princess" was reduced by this amount. If the partnership had completed the purchase of "the Princess" and "the Queen", and if the defendants had purchased them from the partnership at their cost price of £11,500, as envisaged in the agreement of 20 March, then the position would have been that the partnership would have obtained the benefit of the £2,925 obtained for "the King", but in fact the purchase of the two vessels from the Severn Ferry was never completed by the partnership and the amount which had been paid on account by the partnership was forfeited by the vendors. The plaintiff's claim is based on the fact that the defendants benefited to the extent of the sum of £2,925 but, there is no evidence that the defendants, as distinct from the partnership, ever benefited or received credit for this sum but, even if they did, the only claim which could be made against them would be by the partnership of The Shannon Ferry, by an action instituted by the partners in their own names "trading as the Shannon Ferry", or in the name of The Shannon Ferry under Order 14 of the Rules of the Superior Courts. No claim could be made by a partner personally for his separate share of the partnership assets. The plaintiff's claim in this action is a claim based on the contention that he was personally entitled to the profit on the sale of "the King" and, as I have said, this contention fails. The plaintiff's position in regard to this claim differs, in my opinion, from that for his share of the goodwill, with which I have already dealt, as his claim in respect of the goodwill is based on the agreement made on 11 April which I have held to have been adopted (in part) by the defendants, when they took the benefit of the goodwill, and under which the plaintiff and Mr Gorman were recognised as having separate shares in the goodwill which each of them was entitled to recover from the defendants.

The result of my findings therefore is that the plaintiff is entitled to judgment for the two sums of £500 and £417, making a total sum of £917 on foot of his first and second claims and that his third claim for £2,925 must be dismissed. It also follows that the claim in paragraph 10 of the statement of claim for a declaration must also be dismissed and the claim in paragraph 11 for damages for breach of contract has already been dealt with and no further order will be made in respect of this claim.

Patricia McLaughlin
Barrister

[*Reporter's Note:* Section 194 of the Companies Act 1963 (No. 33) has been amended by section 47 of the Companies Act 1990 (No. 33).]

In the Matter of Hartigans Garages Ltd and In the Matter of the Companies Act 1963: High Court 1971 No. 2085P (Kenny J) 11 December 1972

Company Law – Scheme of arrangement – Petition for confirmation of the scheme – Application by Revenue Commissioners for an order winding up the company – Whether the court had the power to order the company to be wound up upon a petition for confirmation of a scheme of arrangement – Whether the court had power to compel the directors to summon a meeting to pass a resolution to wind up the company if the proposals in the scheme had not been carried out in full – Companies Act 1963 (No. 33), section 201

Facts: In 1971 Hartigans Garages Ltd had liabilities amounting to £494,205 and assets estimated at £378,000. A receiver was appointed over its assets by a debenture holder to whom £125,387 was due. The company were anxious to avoid liquidation and therefore prepared a scheme of arrangement which provided for the payment of 70 pence in the pound to the unsecured ordinary creditors which was accepted by them in full discharge of their debts. The company had a number of preferential debts and the scheme provided for payment of these in full. Clause 3 of the scheme provided that if the proposals were rejected or "otherwise do not become effective", the directors of the company should forthwith pass the necessary resolution for the winding up of the company. The company issued a summons for the convening of a meeting of the creditors to consider the scheme. This was approved by the majority as specified in section 201 of the Companies Act 1963 and the company presented a petition for confirmation of the scheme under that section. On 28 June 1971, the High Court sanctioned the scheme of arrangement and declared that it was binding on all the secured and unsecured creditors of the company. Preferential claims owed to the Revenue Commissioners were paid in full. However, the Revenue Commissioners were also ordinary creditors for £16,943 in respect of income tax, turnover tax and interest upon these. Although the other creditors were paid the amounts due to them, nothing was paid to the Revenue Commissioners in respect of their debt. The Revenue Commissioners applied by way of motion, in the matter in which confirmation of the scheme of arrangement was sought, for an order that the company should be wound up by the court.

Held by Kenny J:

(1) The court had no power to make an order for the winding up of the company upon a petition to obtain confirmation of a scheme of arrangement.

(2) The procedure for obtaining such an order is prescribed by the Rules of Court.

(3) Under the scheme, the company was under a contractual obligation to distribute its assets in accordance with the scheme.

(4) However, the court had no power to compel the directors to summon a meeting to pass a resolution to wind up the company.

(5) A petition to wind up the company must be brought by the Revenue Commissioners and it must be advertised.

No cases referred to in judgment

Counsel's and solicitors' names not available

KENNY J **11 December 1972**

In 1971 Hartigans Garages Ltd ("the company") had liabilities of £494,205 and assets estimated to be worth £378,000. A receiver over its assets had been appointed by a debenture holder to whom £125,387 was due. As the receiver was about to pay the sum secured, the company were anxious to avoid a liquidation. So a scheme of arrangement providing for payment of 70 pence in the pound to the unsecured ordinary creditors was prepared. This was to be accepted by them in full discharge of their debts. The company had a number of preferential debts and the scheme provided for payment of these in full.

Clause 3 of the scheme provided that if the proposals in the scheme were rejected or "otherwise do not become effective" the directors of the company were forthwith to pass the necessary resolution for the winding up of the company.

The company then issued a summons for the convening of a meeting of the creditors to consider the scheme and when this had been approved by the majority specified in section 201 of the Companies Act 1963, the company presented a petition for confirmation of the scheme under that section. On 28 June 1971 this court sanctioned the scheme of arrangement and declared that it was binding on all the secured and unsecured creditors of the company.

There were preferential claims for monies due to the Revenue Commissioners for income tax and corporation profits tax and these were paid in full. The Revenue Commissioners were however ordinary creditors for £16,943 for income tax and turnover tax and interest on these. I have been told by counsel that the other creditors of the company have been paid the amounts due to them but that nothing has been paid to the Revenue Commissioners in respect of their debt.

The Revenue Commissioners have now applied by motion in the matter in which confirmation of the scheme was sought for an order that the company should be wound up by the court. In my opinion I have no power in this matter to make an order for winding up. The procedure for obtaining such an order is prescribed by Rules of Court and I have never heard of an order for winding up being made in a petition to obtain confirmation by the court of a scheme of arrangement.

The proposals in the scheme were not rejected and they became effective. They were not, however, carried out in full. Under the scheme the company were under a contractual obligation to distribute their assets in accordance with the scheme. There was no duty owed to the court to do this. I have no power to compel the directors to summon a meeting to pass a resolution to wind up.

It has been said that the directors fraudulently preferred some creditors but the directors are not parties in their personal capacities to these proceedings and have not been served with this motion.

A petition to wind up the company must be brought by the Revenue Commissioners and advertised.

I do not accordingly propose to make any order on the motion of 29 November 1972.

Patricia McLaughlin
Barrister

In the Matter of Westwinds Holding Company Ltd and In the Matter of the Companies Act 1963: High Court 1973 No. 1776P (Kenny J) 21 May 1974

Company Law – Oppression – Whether company's affairs conducted or powers of directors exercised in a manner oppressive to the petitioner and in disregard of his interests as a member of the company – Whether single act sufficient to constitute oppression under section 205 – Remedies under section 205 – Companies Act 1963 (No. 33), section 205

Facts: Section 205 of the Companies Act 1963 provides as follows:

> "(1) Any member of a company who complains that the affairs of the company are being conducted or that the powers of the directors of the company are being exercised in a manner oppressive to him or any of the members (including himself), or in disregard of his or their interests as members, may apply to the court for an order under this section.
>
> (3) If, on any application under subsection 1 . . . the court is of the opinion that the company's affairs are being conducted or the directors' powers are being exercised as aforesaid, the court may, with a view to bringing to an end the matters complained of, make such order as it thinks fit, whether directing or prohibiting any act or cancelling or varying any transaction or for regulating the conduct of the company's affairs in future or for the purchase of the shares of any members of the company by other members of the company or by the company and in the case of a purchase by the company, for the reduction accordingly of the company's capital, or otherwise."

The petitioner and Martin Hession were the only two directors and shareholders of the company, and the petitioner was also the secretary. The articles of association stated that Martin Hession was to be the governing director of the company and that he would have five votes for each share that he held, the other directors having one vote per share. Before he subscribed to the company, the petitioner met with Martin Hession and a Mr J.F., an auditor, on 21 July 1965 and they had agreed, *inter alia*, that the articles of association of the company would be amended, removing Mr Hession from the position of governing director in consideration of the petitioner subscribing to the company. This was in fact never done. The articles also required that the affixing of the company seal be witnessed by one director and the secretary.

Martin Hession procured a transfer by the company at a substantial undervalue of a piece of property at Knocknacarra to another company Country Developments Ltd, in which he owned almost all the shares. He forged the petitioner's signature on the deed of transfer. In addition he caused the company to guarantee the liabilities of another company controlled by him, Archers

Holdings Ltd. This guarantee was supported by an equitable deposit of the title deeds to a property at Whitestrand Road owned by the company. Martin Hession created fake minutes of a meeting at which a resolution was purportedly passed, approving the guarantee and mortgage. He had also forged the petitioner's signature on the minutes and on the sealed form of registration of the mortgage. Martin Hession subsequently purported to pass a resolution dismissing the petitioner as director and secretary of the company. The petitioner, who had been unaware of the above transactions petitioned for relief under section 205. Counsel for Mr Hession argued, *inter alia*, that section 205 had no application as there was no minority in that the petitioner and Mr Hession held an equal number of shares.

Held by Kenny J in allowing the application of the petitioner:

(1) There was no binding legal contract between the parties arising out of the meeting of 21 July 1965 as it was anticipated by the parties that a detailed contract setting out their rights would be prepared.

(2) Even if there was a binding contract executed on that date, the contract thereby concluded was rescinded by mutual agreement.

(3) The sale of lands at Knocknacarra by the company to Country Developments Ltd was made at a gross undervalue and was a fraud on the other members of the company.

(4) The sale of lands at Knocknacarra was an exercise by the directors of their powers in a manner which was oppressive to the petitioner and was in total disregard of his interest as a member of the company. On this ground alone the conditions for the exercise of the powers of the court under section 205(3) were fulfilled.

(5) The mortgage by deposit of deeds relating to the property at Whitestrand Road to guarantee the amount which Ardos Holding Ltd owed Allied Irish Banks was an exercise of the powers of the directors of the company which was oppressive to the petitioner and in total disregard of his interest as a member and was fraudulent on the company.

(6) The appropriate remedy was an order directing that Martin Hession purchase the shares of the petitioner at a price fixed by the court.

(7) The word "minority" does not appear in any part of the section and the heading is merely a convenient way of describing the majority of cases in which the section will apply. In addition, Martin Hession, as governing director, had five votes for each share of which he was the holder, therefore, although the two shareholders held an equal number of shares, the petitioner was certain to be out-voted and so was a minority.

Case referred to in judgment

Royal British Bank v. Turquand (1855) 5 E & B 248: (1856) 6 E & B 327

Counsel's and solicitors' names not available

KENNY J **21 May 1974**

Martin Hession Ltd (which subsequently changed its name to Westwinds Holding Ltd and which I propose to call "the company") was incorporated on 31 March 1964. Its principal object was to take over and carry on the business of builders and public works constructors carried on by Martin Hession at Galway. Its authorised share capital was £5,000 divided into 5,000 ordinary shares at £1 each. Article 42 of the articles of association provided:

> "42 So long as there shall be a governing director, such governing director shall have five votes on a show of hands or on a poll for each share of which he is the holder, and every other member shall have one vote for every hundred shares held by him."

The relevant parts of Article 43 read:

> "43 (a) Notwithstanding anything elsewhere contained in these articles, Martin Hession of Knocknacarra Salthill Galway shall be the first governing director of the company and shall hold that office for life or until he resigns and whilst he is governing director, the government and control of the company and all powers, authorities and discretions vested in the directors by the Companies Acts, Table A of these Articles (sic) shall be vested in him alone and all other directors (if any) of the company for the time being shall be bound to conform to his directions in regard to the company's business. The remuneration of the said Martin Hession shall from time to time be determined by him.
>
> (b) The said Martin Hession while he holds the office of governing director may from time to time appoint any other persons to be directors of the company and may define, limit and restrict their powers, and may fix and determine their remuneration and duties and may at all times remove any director however appointed and may at any time convene a general meeting of the company. Every such appointment or removal must be in writing under the hand of the said Martin Hession."

Article 56 provided:

> "No director shall as a director vote in respect of any contract or arrangement in which he is so interested as aforesaid and if he does so vote his vote shall not be counted but this prohibition shall not apply to any contract by or on behalf of the company to give to the directors or any of them any security for advances or by way of indemnity or to a settlement or set-off of cross claims and it may at any time or times be suspended or relaxed to any extent by general meeting."

Article 77 provided:

> "The seal of the company may be affixed in the presence of one director and the secretary and that one director and secretary shall sign every instrument to which the seal of the company is so affixed in their presence."

The minutes of the first meeting of the company, held on 3 April 1964, show that one share was issued to Martin Hession and one to May Doran. Although the principal object of the company was to take over the business of Martin Hession in accordance with an agreement which had been prepared, there is no accord that this agreement was ever adopted by the company and its terms were not proved in this action.

In 1965 Martin Hession had discussions with John F. Dooley, an engineer who was then in the employment of the Galway County Council ("the petitioner") in connection with the petitioner taking shares in the company and becoming a director of it. At a meeting of the directors of the company, held on 29 June 1965, Martin Hession stated that he was negotiating with the petitioner who was contemplating taking shares in the company and joining the board of directors and said that "to facilitate these negotiations" it would be necessary to increase the capital of the company to £10,000 and to make certain alterations in the articles of association. Wednesday 21 July 1965 was fixed as the date of the extraordinary general meeting to pass the necessary resolutions. Miss Dolan tendered her resignation as secretary of the company and signed a transfer of her one share to the petitioner who was then declared a director of the company and was appointed its secretary.

The petitioner, Martin Hession and Mr J. Fitzgerald, an auditor, met at the offices of Messrs MacDermot & Allen, solicitors on 21 July 1965. Mr Allen had formed the company and, at this meeting, was acting as solicitor for the petitioner. A discussion took place about the terms on which the petitioner was prepared to join the company and Mr Allen made a written record of what was agreed. This shows 4,998 shares were to be issued to Martin Hession for assets which were to become the property of the company, that 4,999 shares were to be issued to the petitioner for cash, that Martin Hession was to be chairman and the petitioner secretary of the company, that there was to be no governing director, that Martin Hession and the petitioner were to be directors of the company and that the article in relation to the transfer of shares to a purchaser was to be altered. This written record shows that everybody at the meeting contemplated that a formal written agreement embodying these terms would be prepared. A meeting of the company was held immediately after this at the solicitor's office but no minute of this appears in the company's minute book. However, Mr Allen took a note of the business transacted. A resolution was passed (i) that the share capital be increased to £10,000 consisting of 10,000 ordinary shares at £1 each, (ii) that 5,000 of these were to be issued to Martin Hession and 5,000 to the petitioner, (iii) that the article in relation to the appointment of a chairman was to be altered so that the chairman would be elected at each meeting, (iv) that the article in connection with the transfer of the shares was to be changed and (v) that all references to the governing director were to be deleted. At the end of this written record there is a note "Martin Hession to be chairman". No resolution to alter the articles by deleting the references to the governing director or to make a provision for permanent directors was ever passed by the company.

The petitioner sold some of his assets and there were sums due to him by the company for work which he had done. At a directors' meeting held on 7 February 1966 it was resolved that the shares certificate for the one share issued to Miss Dolan be cancelled and that that share should be issued to the petitioner, who as secretary was instructed to issue 2,599 shares to Martin Hession and the same number of shares to himself. The result was that the issued share capital became 5,200 ordinary shares. Unfortunately, the share register of the company was not given in evidence and all the issues of shares have to be gathered from the minutes of the company. At a directors' meeting held on 15 March 1968, 716 shares were issued to the petitioner and the same number to Martin Hession for cash and this brought the shareholding of each of them to 3,316 shares. At an extraordinary general meeting of the company held on the same day, it was resolved to capitalise £3,368 and to apply it in paying up a corresponding number of shares and that 1,684 shares be allotted to each of them. The result was that each of them held 5,000 fully paid shares in the company.

The first building scheme carried out by the company was on the lands of Kingston where fourteen houses were built. In 1968 the company purchased a site of three acres at Knocknacarra for £6,000. Full planning permission for four houses on the main road was obtained and each of these was built on a site of one rood and was sold. The company applied for planning permission for the remaining two acres, but this was refused because there were no sewerage services and the water supply was inadequate. Mr Hession's counsel argued that these lands at Knocknacarra were not purchased by the company but by another company called Hession (Enterprises) Ltd. This contention was based entirely on an entry in the cheques payment book of Martin Hession (Enterprises) Ltd which shows that a cheque was issued on 14 August 1968 for £730. The explanation for the cheque reads: "Martin Hession Ltd — purchase of O'Hara's land Knocknacarra." If the lands were purchased by Hession (Enterprises) Ltd, I do not understand why they were conveyed to the company and no attempt was made by Mr Martin Hession to explain this. The £730 was, I believe, a loan by Hession (Enterprises) Ltd to the company. I have no doubt that the lands at Knocknacarra were the property of the company.

The lands at Knocknacarra formed part of a folio opened under the Registration of Title Act. By a deed of transfer dated 15 November 1968, the two acres were sold for £600 to a company called Country Developments Ltd in which Mr Hession owned almost all the shares. The deed of transfer was sealed with the company's seal and the affixing of the seal was authenticated by Mr Martin Hession and by what appeared to be the signature of the petitioner, but it was admitted that Mr Hession forged the petitioner's signature to this document. Three justifications for this were advanced. The first was a memorandum dated 19 March 1968 signed by Mr Hession as a director and by the petitioner as secretary and director, by which the company authorised "our chairman and managing director Mr Martin Hession to sign and execute all deeds, documents etc. on behalf of the above company" and the memorandum is written on paper which bore the printed name of the company at the top. The articles of association of the company required that the affixing of the seal should be authenticated by the signature of a director and the secretary and the authority given to Mr Martin Hession authorised him to sign deeds and documents on behalf of the company that did not require the seal of the company. It certainly did not authorise him to sign the petitioner's name. The second justification was that the petitioner had authorised Mr Martin Hession to sign his name. I reject this contention and also the evidence given by Mr Martin Hession that he told the petitioner that he (Martin Hession) had signed the petitioner's name to this deed. The subsequent dealing with the lands and the very large profit made on the sale of them show that Mr Martin Hession was anxious to conceal this transaction from the petitioner and to take all the profit on it. It was also argued that the petitioner knew that these lands had been sold by the company because he signed a general profit and loss account of the company for the period 1 August 1966 to 30 April 1969. These contain two entries in relation to lands at Knocknacarra. The first relates to property described as Kingston/Knocknacarra which was apparently purchased for £150 and sold to Country Developments Ltd for £150: the second relates to lands at Knocknacarra and shows payment of a deposit of £150 and a balance of purchase money and fees of £580 making a total of £730 and then shows a sale to Country Developments Ltd at £730, so that the company made no profit on the transaction. I accept the petitioner's evidence that he did not realise that this meant that the lands had been sold to Country Developments Ltd. The lands were subsequently sold by Country Developments Ltd to a company called Ulster Properties Ltd in which Mr Martin Hession was the owner of most of the shares. He subsequently sold all his shares in Ulster Properties Ltd to a Mr McNella for £15,000.

The company had purchased lands at Whitestrand Road and built houses. Thirty-two leases of these lands were granted and the reversionary interest in two of them was sold. The leases reserved an annual rent of £15 but this sum was never paid to the company. Mr Martin Hession was interested in a company called Ardos Holdings Ltd in which all the shares were owned by Galway Investments Ltd, of which Mr Martin Hession holds almost all the shares. Mr Hession decided that the company should guarantee payment to Allied Irish Banks Ltd of the overdraft granted to Ardos Holdings Ltd up to a maximum sum of £50,000. The bank were furnished with a certified copy of minutes of a directors' meeting of the company which is alleged to have been held on 14 April 1972. The minutes of this meeting do not appear in the minute book. Those present at it are said to have been Mr Martin Hession, Mr Patrick Hession and the petitioner. I am satisfied that the petitioner never received notice of it. A resolution was passed that in consideration of Allied Irish Banks Ltd agreeing to grant banking accommodation to Ardos Holdings Ltd, the company guaranteed payment to the said bank of all sums due by Ardos Holdings Ltd to the bank, provided the maximum liability of the company was not to exceed £50,000, that a guarantee in the form submitted to the meeting was to be signed for and on behalf of the company, that the documents of title relating to the properties described in the schedule to the minute were to be deposited with the bank by way of equitable mortgage as collateral and continuing security for the company's general liabilities and that Mr Martin Hession was authorised to deposit these documents verbally with the bank. The property mentioned in the schedule was the lands at Whitestrand Road together with 27 counterpart leases. The minutes of this meeting were represented to the bank as having been signed by Mr Martin Hession and the petitioner.

A comparison of the petitioner's signature to other documents and that on this minute convinces me that that on the minute is a forgery. Mr Hession certified that the copy furnished to the bank was a true copy of the minutes of a directors' meeting of the company held on 1 April 1972. The deposit creating the equitable mortgage to the bank had to be registered with the Registrar of Companies under section 99 of the Companies Act 1963. Registration is effected by lodging a form sealed with the seal of the company and Mr Martin Hession affixed the seal of the company, signed his own name and then forged the petitioner's signature to authenticate the seal. I am convinced that the petitioner would never have agreed to the creation of this charge and that he did not get notice of the meeting because Mr Martin Hession wished to conceal the business being transacted. This was done at a time when the petitioner was a director and the secretary of the company. When giving evidence, Mr Martin Hession claimed that he had purchased the reversion in the property at Whitestrand Road from the company at the full market price after the last accounts had been prepared, but no evidence of the price paid was given nor were the deeds of conveyance produced.

There were a number of meetings of the company and of the directors of which the petitioner received no notice and it is a matter of some significance that the last minutes signed by the petitioner are those of a meeting on 17 November 1969. The minutes of meetings held on 9 July, 17 November 1970 and 17 November 1971 are not signed and all subsequent minutes are signed by Mr Martin Hession. An inspection of the earlier minutes shows that it had been the regular practice that Mr Hession and the petitioner signed all minutes.

At a meeting of the company, held on 14 March 1973, at which Mr Martin Hession and Mrs Ann Hession were present, it was agreed that Mr Martin Hession be appointed secretary of the company and it was also agreed that the petitioner be removed from office as a secretary and director of the company. An extraordinary general meeting of the company was held on 18 March 1973 at which it was resolved that the name of the company be changed to Westwinds Holding Company Ltd.

Section 205 of the Companies Act 1963, insofar as it is relevant to this action, provides:

"205 (1) Any member of a company who complains that the affairs of the company are being conducted or that the powers of the directors of the company are being exercised in a manner oppressive to him or any of the members (including himself), or in disregard of his or their interests as members, may apply to the court for an order under this section.

(3) If, on any application under sub-section 1 . . . the court is of opinion that the company's affairs are being conducted or the directors' powers are being exercised as aforesaid, the court may, with a view to bringing to an end the matters complained of, make such order as it thinks fit, whether directing or prohibiting any act or cancelling or varying any transaction or for regulating the conduct of the company's affairs in future or for the purchase of the shares of any members of the company by other members of the company or by the company and in the case of a purchase by the company, for the reduction accordingly of the company's capital, or otherwise."

In this petition, presented under section 205, the petitioner claims an order deleting articles 42 and 43 from the articles of association of the company. The basis of this claim is the agreement which was made on 21 July 1965 in Mr Allen's office.

I accept all Mr Allen's evidence and I reject the testimony of Mr Martin Hession in so far as it conflicts with that of Mr Allen or of the petitioner. It seems to me however, that what was agreed at the meeting of 21 July 1965 were the heads of an agreement and that it was intended between the parties that a detailed contract setting out their rights would be prepared. Until this was done there was, in my view, no binding legal contract between the parties. It was undoubtedly agreed at the time the petitioner joined the company that the position of governing director was to be abolished but this was part of a more general agreement and until that became effective, the heads of the agreement did not constitute a contract.

If however, terms were agreed on 21 July 1965, I think that the contract thereby created was rescinded by mutual agreement. No step was ever taken to amend the articles of association and the petitioner never asked that this be done. The heads of agreement contemplated the issue of 4,998 shares immediately to Martin Hession and of 4,999 shares to the petitioner, but this was not done until 1968 and then 3,368 ordinary shares were issued by means of capitalising some of the profits. In the document of 21 July it is stated that the petitioner was to take up 4,999 shares for cash. The petitioner signed a number of minutes in which Martin Hession is described as governing director (see the minutes of 19 November 1966, 2 November 1967, 16 October 1968 and 17 November 1969). No steps to create the office of permanent director or to fill such a position was ever taken. The only possible conclusion from these matters is that the agreement of 21 July 1965 (if there ever was a legally binding agreement) was rescinded by mutual consent.

The sale of the lands at Knocknacarra by the company to Country Developments Ltd was made at a gross undervalue and was a fraud on the other members of the company. In 1968 planning permission for the erection of four houses on the front sites had been obtained and it was certain that adequate sewerage and water services would be available for the rest of the lands in a few years time. Full planning permission for the two acres was granted in 1973. If the lands in 1968 had, as the defendant contends, a value as agricultural land only, it is impossible to understand why they were sold to Country Developments Ltd of which Mr Martin Hession owned almost all the shares. The purchase price ultimately realised, £15,000, within four years after the sale in 1968, shows that the price paid (whether it was £600 or £730) was an undervalue. The sale benefited Mr Martin Hession only at the expense of the company and the petitioner.

The sale of the lands at Knocknacarra was an exercise by the directors of their powers in a manner which was fraudulent and oppressive to the petitioner and was in total disregard of his interest as a member of the company. On this ground alone the conditions for the exercise of the powers of the court under section 205(3) have been fulfilled.

The mortgage by deposit of 24 May 1972 of deeds relating to the property at Whitestrand Road to guarantee the amount which Ardos Holdings Ltd owed Allied Irish Banks was not for the benefit of the company or of the petitioner. It was done solely to benefit Ardos Holdings Ltd in which Mr Martin Hession holds almost all the shares. The forgery of the petitioner's signature to the minutes of the meeting at which this transaction was authorised, and of his signature to the particulars of the charge, which were filed with the Registrar of Companies, indicate that Mr Martin Hession was anxious to conceal the transaction. If it be assumed that the deposit was effective to create any security (and I cannot decide that issue without hearing the bank who will doubtless rely on the rule in *Royal British Bank v. Turquand* (1855) 5 E & B 248: (1856) 6E & B 327), it was an exercise of the powers of the directors of the company which was oppressive to the petitioner and in total disregard of his interest as a member. At a late stage in his evidence, Mr Martin Hession said that he had bought the reversion in the lands at Whitestrand Road from the company at the full market price. No evidence to support this was given and while this may be relevant on the remedy to be given for the oppression, it does not alter the position that the transaction, when carried out, was fraudulent and oppressive.

The is the first case in which the question of the appropriate order under section 205 of the Act of 1963, which made a profound change in the remedies available to a shareholder, has been discussed. The petitioner asks that the transfer by the company of the lands at Knocknacarra to Country Developments Ltd and the charge given to Allied Irish Banks Ltd should be cancelled, but neither of these courses can be taken without hearing the parties to whom the transfer and charge were given. That will involve prolonged litigation. The company has ceased trading and a winding-up by the court would be expensive and involve the liquidator in litigation in connection with the transfer of the lands and the charge given to the bank. It seems to me therefore, that the appropriate remedy is an order directing Martin Hession to purchase the shares of the petitioner at a price fixed by the court. This was the remedy which Mr Parke, appearing for the petitioner, asked for in his closing speech. When fixing the price of the shares however, the court should do so on the basis that the lands sold to Country Developments Ltd are still the property of the company. In relation to the lands at Whitestrand Road, if these have not been purchased by Martin Hession from the company at the full market price, the price of the shares should be fixed without regard to the deposit of 24 May 1972 and the amount secured by it. The company is a private company and the Articles contain elaborate restrictions on the power to transfer shares, but this should not affect the price to be fixed when it has been established that the directors of the company have exercised their powers in a fraudulent or oppressive fashion. The price will therefore be fixed on the basis that there are no restrictions on the transfer of the petitioner's shares in the company and that the directors would sanction the transfer.

Counsel for Mr Hession argued that section 205 did not apply because of the heading "minorities" to the section. The word "minority" does not appear in any part of the section and the heading is merely a convenient way of describing the majority of cases in which the section will apply. In addition, Martin Hession was governing director and under Article 42 had five votes on a show of hands or on a poll for each share of which he was the holder, while every other member was to have one vote for every hundred shares held by him. Although the two share holders held an equal number of shares, the petitioner was certain to be out-voted and so was a minority.

The order to be made will be that the court being satisfied that the powers of the directors of the company have been exercised in a manner oppressive to the petitioner and that those powers have been exercised in disregard of the petitioner's interest as a member, Mr Martin Hession is to purchase all the petitioner's shares in the company at a price determined by an inquiry held before a judge. This price will be the fair price of the shares at the date of the order on the basis (a) that the two acres of the lands at Knocknacarra, being part of the lands on folio 49061 of the register County Galway, sold to Country Developments Ltd are still the property of the company, (b) that if the reversion in the lands at Whitestrand Road was not by Martin Hession from the company at the full market price, then disregarding the deposit of 24 May 1972 and the amount secured by it and (c) that there are no restrictions on the transfer of the said shares and that the directors would sanction a transfer of them by the petitioner.

Patricia McLaughlin
Barrister

Allied Irish Banks Ltd v. Ardmore Studios International (1972) Ltd: High Court 1973 No. 206 (Finlay J) 30 May 1973

Company Law – Directors, acting as agents of the company, arranged a loan for the company – Certificate produced to the effect that a resolution of directors was passed ratifying the loan – The memorandum and articles of association furnished to the plaintiff indicated that there was a third director of whom they had not been notified – No meeting ever took place – Whether the bank had notice that no meeting took place – Whether this constituted an irregularity in the internal management of the company – Whether a person acting bona fides *must enquire into irregularities in the internal management of the company*

Facts: In or around January 1972, the plaintiff bank agreed to provide a short term accommodation loan in the sum of £37,500 to the defendant company for the purpose of acquiring the Ardmore Studios at Bray, County Wicklow. The loan was agreed to on the basis that the directors who arranged it were acting as the agents of the company and that when a print of the memorandum and articles of association were available, the company would open an account with the plaintiff bank and that it would formally take over the overdraft in its own name. At the time the bank was informed that there were only two directors and shareholders of the company. On 28 February, 1972 a certified copy of a resolution signed by Mr Nolan as director and Mr O'Reilly as secretary and managing director of Ardmore Studios International Ltd was presented to Mr O'Halloran of the plaintiff bank. This certified that certain resolutions were passed including a resolution ratifying the loan from the plaintiff bank. At the same time a print of the memorandum and articles of association of the defendant company was supplied to Mr O'Halloran which indicated that there was in fact a third director of the company. Mr O'Halloran then issued the cheque of 28 February 1972 thus transferring the loan from the personal account of Mr Nolan and Mr O'Reilly to that of the company.

The plaintiff bank sought summary judgment of the said sum and interest thereon. The defendants sought to avoid judgment on the basis that a receiver appointed over the assets and property of the defendant company, having caused a search to be made of the books and records of the company, found no record of any meeting of directors of 28 February 1972 nor of any resolution being passed by the directors of the defendant company authorising the borrowing of the said sum from the plaintiff bank.

Held by Finlay J:

(1) Mr Nolan and Mr O'Reilly were appointed directors of the company on 28 February 1972 and were entitled to hold a meeting of directors with a quorum of two, without the attendance of the third director.

(2) A perusal of the certificate of 28 February 1972 and the memorandum and articles of association would not raise any suspicion of an invalidity in the meeting.

(3) Even if the directors gave no notice of the holding of the meeting to the third director, and took no record or minutes of the meeting, these frailties or defaults in their activity are classic examples of an irregularity in the internal management of the company. *Duck v. The Tower Galvanising Co. Ltd* [1901] 2 KB 314 applied.

(4) A person dealing *bona fides* with a company need not enquire into irregularities in the internal management of the company.

Case referred to in judgment
Duck v. The Tower Galvanising Co. Ltd [1901] 2 KB 314

Complete names of counsel and solicitors not available

Mr Farrell BL **for the plaintiff**
Brian McCracken BL **for the defendants**

FINLAY J **30 May 1973**

This matter comes before me on an application for summary judgment by the plaintiffs in respect of their claim for £40,027.30. The claim is made up of a single payment of £37,500 made by the plaintiff on foot of a cheque dated 28 February 1972, the balance of the amount claimed being for interest. There is no dispute that this amount was paid by the plaintiffs on foot of the cheque referred to nor is there any dispute as to the calculation of the interest which is in addition due if the principal sum is recoverable from the defendants.

The defendants seek to avoid judgment upon the grounds that Mr Kelly, the receiver of the property and assets of the defendants appointed on 17 November 1972 by Thomas Farmer the holder of the debenture issued by the defendant company on 3 July 1972, having caused a search to be made in the books and records of the defendant company, which are all in his possession, can find no record of any meeting of directors of 28 February 1972 nor of any resolution being passed by the directors of the defendant company authorising the borrowing of the sum of £37,500 from the plaintiff's bank.

The facts preceding and surrounding the issue of this cheque on 28 February 1972 are fully set out in the supplemental affidavit sworn by Mr Michael B. O'Halloran on behalf of the plaintiffs and filed on 4 May 1973. These facts are not put in issue or dispute by the defendants. Shortly speaking they are, that in the month of January 1972, Mr John E. Nolan, who is a customer of the plaintiff bank, requested a loan from the bank for the purpose of acquiring, through the defendant company, the Ardmore Film Studios at Bray in County Wicklow. He informed Mr O'Halloran that the defendant company was incorporated on 21 January 1972, was known as Ardmore Studios International (1972) Ltd and that he and a Mr George O'Reilly were the sole directors and shareholders of the company. He requested on behalf of the company short-term accommodation in the sum of £37,500 so that the company could place a deposit for that amount and sign a contract for the purchase of the property. On behalf of the plaintiffs Mr O'Halloran agreed to issue a cheque for £37,500 in favour of Messrs Arthur

Cox & Co., solicitors, for the deposit on the strict understanding that Mr Nolan and Mr O'Reilly were in fact acting as the company's agents and that when a print of the company's memorandum and articles of association was available the company would open its bank account at the plaintiff bank and take over the overdraft formally in its name. I have no doubt and it is not seriously disputed that Mr O'Halloran believed in these representations and that there were no grounds for his suspecting that they or any of them were untrue.

On the 28 February 1972 a certified copy of a resolution signed by Mr Nolan as director and Mr O'Reilly as secretary and managing director of Ardmore Studios International Ltd was presented to Mr O'Halloran. This certified that a meeting of the directors of the company was held on 28 February 1972 and that certain resolutions were passed including a resolution instructing the plaintiff bank to pay all cheques, drawn on behalf of the company and signed by Mr Nolan and Mr O'Reilly and providing also that the company do borrow from the bank by way of overdraft on foot of their banking account, from time to time to such extent as may be arranged with the bank. At the same time a print of the memorandum of association and articles of association of the defendant company was supplied to Mr O'Halloran. Mr O'Halloran then issued the cheque of 28 February 1972 which is the foundation of this action thus transferring the loan from the personal account of Mr Nolan and O'Reilly to that of the company. Consideration of the memorandum and articles indicates that the representations with regard to the structure and powers of the company made to Mr O'Halloran were true and correct except in one matter, that is to say that Mr Nolan and Mr O'Reilly, although they were the sole subscribers to the company, were not the sole directors, a Mr John Huston being in addition a director. The provisions of part one of table A are incorporated in the articles of association of the company with certain modifications but these do not affect the provision of Regulation 102 and therefore the articles of association of the company provide for the transaction of business by directors on a quorum to be fixed by them and unless so fixed to be two. There is no suggestion that any quorum was fixed by the directors. The power of the company to borrow from the bank under its memorandum and articles is not in dispute.

On this set of facts which are not being disputed Mr Farrell on behalf of the plaintiff company contends that the appropriate principle of law which must be applied is that a person or firm dealing with a limited liability company and doing so *bona fides* is not required to enquire into irregularities in what is described as the internal management of the company and that its transactions are valid notwithstanding the existence of such irregularities if it has acted *bona fide*. Mr Farrell contends that borrowing from the bank, being within the clear power of the defendant company that if there was in fact no meeting of the directors of the defendant company as is certified by the document of 28 February 1972 this comes within the category of an irregularity within the internal management of the company by which his clients are not bound they having manifestly acted *bona fide* throughout.

Mr McCracken on the other hand contends on behalf of the defendants that this is not an irregularity in the internal management of the company but it is a total gap there being an absence of the fact of a meeting and that this is not something which a person even dealing, as I think he would concede, *bona fide* with the company, can ignore. He further contends that a perusal of the memorandum and articles of association which indicated that there was a third director, though not a third subscriber to the company, should have put the bank, through its agent Mr O'Halloran, on notice that the meeting purporting to have been held on 28 February 1972 had not taken place.

I am satisfied that on these affidavits no issue of fact has been raised, the determination of which is necessary to resolve the general issue between the parties. If the contention made on behalf of the plaintiffs is correct then they are entitled to judgment now, notwithstanding the absence of a record of a directors' meeting, the fact raised by Mr Kelly in his affidavit. If on the other hand the contention of Mr McCracken on behalf of the defendants is correct, it appears to me that the plaintiffs must fail in their action as well as in their claim for summary judgment because it has not been contended by Mr Farrell on behalf of the plaintiff that they would wish an opportunity to adduce further evidence with regard to the holding of a directors' meeting.

I am satisfied that Mr Nolan and Mr O'Reilly were on 28 February 1972 duly appointed as directors of this company and that they were entitled to hold a valid meeting of the directors with a quorum of two, that is to say without the attendance of the third director. A perusal of the certificate of 28 February 1972 and the memorandum and articles of association would therefore not raise any suspicion of an invalidity in the meeting. Even if one assumes on the affidavits before me that they gave no notice of the holding of such a meeting to the third director, who would have been entitled to it, and that they made no record or minute of the meeting, it seems to me these frailties or defaults in the activity of the two directors of this company are classical examples of an irregularity in internal management of the company. Mr McCracken has not contended that the principle, which Mr Farrell urges upon me and which is supported by the case of *Duck v. Tower Galvanising Co. Ltd* [1901] 2 KB 314 is an incorrect principle. Rather he has contended that it does not apply to the facts of the case.

The facts of the case of *Duck v. The Tower Galvanising Co. Ltd* were that a debenture had been issued by the defendant company without authority, no directors of the company having been appointed and no resolution to issue debentures having been passed. The holder of the debenture, however, had, on the findings of the court, no notice of any irregularity in the issue of the debenture. It was there held that the debenture was good and prevailed over the rights of an execution creditor. It seems to me that the irregularities found to have existed in the case which I have just quoted were far more fundamental than those which I assumed to exist in this case.

I am satisfied therefore that applying the principle contended for by Mr Farrell that the plaintiffs are entitled to summary judgment.

Patricia McLaughlin
Barrister

Oliver Moylan v. Irish Whiting Manufacturers Ltd, Francis Counihan, Bernard McMahon and Cormack McGuinness: High Court 1975 No 2747P (Hamilton J) 14 April 1980

Company – Directors – Company without validly appointed directors – Resolution that purported directors retire and present themselves for re-election – Whether court should interfere with internal management of company – Whether resolution ultra vires *– Injunction – Whether resolution constituted removal of directors – Whether resolution illegal, oppressive or fraudulent – Special business – Irregularities in internal management – Companies Act 1963 (No. 33), sections 181, 182*

Facts: The plaintiff and the second, third and fourth named defendants were directors of the first named defendant company, and the plaintiff also acted as chairman of the company. It was clear from the minutes of the annual general meetings of the company held between 1965 and 1975 inclusive that the requirements of Table A were never complied with in relation to the retirement and election of directors but notwithstanding, the plaintiff and the second, third and fourth named defendants continued to act as directors of the company with the plaintiff acting as chairman. Following a disagreement between the plaintiff and his fellow directors a resolution was proposed, seconded and approved at the annual general meeting held on 6 February 1975 that all the directors of the company should retire and seek re-election. This resolution was opposed by the plaintiff but was passed. In the subsequent election, the plaintiff though proposed, was not re-elected to the board of directors of the company. The plaintiff sought a declaration that he was a director of the company and entitled to attend all meetings of the board of directors of the company and an injunction restraining the second, third and fourth named defendants from excluding him from such meetings. He claimed that the proceedings at the said annual general meeting and in particular the passing of the said resolution were invalid as the notice convening the said meeting did not include any agenda for the said meeting or give notice of any special business to be transacted at the said meeting; the time and place of the said meeting was not prescribed by the company in general meeting or by the board; the said meeting was not held at the time prescribed by the articles of association of the company and by the Companies Act 1963; the fourth named defendant was not authorised by the board to summon the said meeting; the letter summoning the meeting did not give notice of the general nature of the special business transacted at the meeting; the plaintiff was not permitted to preside as chairman of the said meeting though required by the articles of association to act as chairman and the second named defendant acted as chairman of the said meeting in contravention of the articles of association of the company. The plaintiff, furthermore, contended that the action taken constituted a removal of the directors otherwise than in accordance with the provisions of section 182 of the Companies Act

1963. The plaintiff also claimed to be entitled to remuneration and expenses as director and managing director of the company.

Held by Hamilton J in refusing the plaintiff's claim:

(1) While there may have been certain deficiencies in the notice convening the meeting and irregularities in the manner in which the meeting was conducted, the majority of the shareholders gave their approval to the course adopted at the meeting and the decisions reached therein.

(2) The courts will not interfere with the internal management of companies acting within their powers unless the actions complained of are of a fraudulent character or are beyond the powers of the company.

(3) There was nothing illegal, oppressive or fraudulent in the proceedings of the majority and, accordingly, the plaintiff was not entitled to the relief sought.

(4) The actions of the defendants were not in any way *ultra vires* the company as the plaintiff was not a duly appointed director of the company at the date of the said annual general meeting.

(5) The circumstances were not such as to justify the court in interfering with the internal management of the company.

(6) The plaintiff was entitled to remuneration and expenses in the sum of £750.

Per curiam: Having regard to the provisions of Bunreacht na hÉireann an exception to the rule in *Foss v. Harbottle* must be made where the justice of the case demands it.

Cases referred to in judgment

Burland v. Earle [1902] AC 83
Foss v. Harbottle (1842) 2 Hare 461
Heyting v. Dupont [1964] 2 All ER 273; [1964] 1 WLR 854
Lord v. Copper Miners Company (1848) 2 Ph 740
MacDougall v. Gardiner (1875) 1 Ch D 13
Mozley v. Alston (1847) 1 Ph 790
Russell v. Wakefield Watertanks Ltd (1875) LR 20 Eq 475

Counsel's and solicitors' names not available

HAMILTON J **14 April 1980**

In this case the plaintiff claims, *inter alia*:

1. A declaration that he is a director of Irish Whiting Manufacturers Ltd, the first-named defendant herein and is entitled to attend all meetings of the board of directors of the said company.

2. An injunction restraining the second, third and fourth-named defendants from excluding the plaintiff from meetings of directors of the said company.

Prior to the incidents of which the plaintiff complains and which led to the institution of the proceedings herein, the plaintiff was the chairman of the board of directors of Irish Whiting Manufacturers Ltd, the first named defendant herein and a company incorporated pursuant to the provision of the Companies

Acts 1908 and 1917, having been so appointed in the year 1972, after serving as a director since 1964.

Prior to 6 February 1975, the board of directors of Irish Whiting Manufacturers Ltd (hereinafter called "the company") consisted of the plaintiff and the second, third and fourth-named defendants, all of whom were shareholders in "the company".

At the annual general meeting of "the company" held on that day, a resolution was proposed, seconded and approved that all the directors of "the company" should retire and seek re-election. This resolution was opposed by the plaintiff and though proposed he was not elected to the board of directors of "the company".

It is alleged by the plaintiff in the statement of claim delivered on his behalf that the proceedings at the annual general meeting and, in particular, the passing of the resolution hereinbefore referred to were invalid because:

(a) The notice convening the said meeting did not include any agenda for the said meeting or give notice of any special business to be transacted at the said meeting.

(b) The time and place of the said meeting was not prescribed by the company in general meeting or by the board.

(c) The said meeting was not held at the time prescribed by the articles of association of the company and by the Companies Act 1963.

(d) The fourth-named defendant was not authorised by the board to summon the said meeting.

(e) The letter summoning the meeting did not give notice of the general nature of the special business transacted at the meeting.

(f) The plaintiff was not permitted to preside as chairman of the said meeting though required by the articles of association to act as chairman.

(g) The second-named defendant acted as chairman of the said meeting in contravention of the articles of association of the company.

It is further alleged in the said statement of claim that the said resolution was invalid in that it constituted a removal of the directors otherwise than in accordance with the provisions of section 182 of the Companies Act 1963 and that it also constituted special business of which notice had not been given in the letter purporting to summon the said meeting.

In these circumstances, the plaintiff claims that the defendants herein have wrongfully treated the said resolution as removing him as a director and as chairman of the board.

In addition, the plaintiff claims to be entitled to remuneration as a director of the company and as managing director of the company and to be entitled to expenses incurred by him in connection with his duties as director and managing director respectively.

In the defence delivered on behalf of all the defendants, it is alleged, *inter alia*, that:

(i) the plaintiff is not entitled to any of the relief claimed on the grounds

that he is seeking the intervention of the court in the internal affairs of the company where nothing has been done which is *ultra vires* the powers of the company;
(ii) the plaintiff was paid all fees due to him as a director and all expenses properly payable to him.

In the said defence, it is denied by the defendants that:

(i) The notice convening the annual general meeting to be held on 6 February 1975 was in any material respect defective;

(ii) the proceedings conducted at the said annual general meeting were invalid;

(iii) the plaintiff's removal or exclusion from the board of directors was wrongful;

(iv) the plaintiff was at the date of issue of these proceedings a director or chairman of the board of directors of the company.

The facts relevant to the determination of the issues raised in this case may be briefly stated as follows:

The company was incorporated pursuant to the provisions of the Companies Acts 1908 to 1917 on 21 September 1932. The articles of association of the company provided that the number of directors of the company should be not less than two nor more than five, that the first director of the company should be appointed by the subscribers by an instrument in writing under their hand and that the directors so appointed should be permanent directors of the company and entitled to hold such office as long as they lived unless disqualified for any of the causes specified in article 20 of the said articles.

The said articles further provided that:

> "15. The directors shall have power at any time and from time to time to appoint any other person to be director of the company, either to fill a casual vacancy or as an addition to the board, but so that the total number of directors shall not at any time exceed the maximum number fixed as hereinbefore mentioned. Any director so appointed shall hold office only until the next following ordinary general meeting, when he shall retire, but shall be eligible for re-election."

Articles 78 to 83 and articles 86 of Table A apply to directors so appointed. These articles provide for the retirement and re-election of directors.

The plaintiff herein was appointed to the board of directors of the company in 1964 upon the death of his father, who had been one of the original shareholders in the company.

The second-named defendant was appointed to the board of directors on 15 September 1969, his father, one of the original permanent directors of the company, having resigned.

The third-named defendant was appointed a director in 1965 and was for a time managing director of the company.

The fourth-named defendant was appointed a director on 24 January 1974 and subsequently executive director.

The plaintiff was on 15 March 1972 elected chairman of the company and continued to act in that capacity until 6 February 1975.

Prior to 6 February 1975, the plaintiff and the second, third and fourth-named defendants constituted the board of directors of the company and at all relevant times, there were no permanent directors of the company.

It is quite clear from a consideration of the minutes of the annual general meetings of the company held between 27 September 1965 and 6 February 1975 that the requirements of Table A with regard to the retirement and election of directors were never complied with.

At the annual general meetings held on 27 September 1965, 19 September 1966, 18 September 1967, 9 September 1968, 15 September 1969, respectively resolutions that the directors be re-appointed collectively and that the outgoing directors be re-elected directors of the company were passed.

Two separate resolutions were necessary at each annual general meeting because of the terms of section 181 of the Companies Act 1963 which provides that:

> "181 (1) At a general meeting of a company, a motion for the appointment of two or more persons as directors of the company by a single resolution shall not be made, unless a resolution that it shall be so made has first been agreed to by the meeting without any vote being given against it.
> (2) Subject to subsections (3) and (4), a resolution moved in contravention of this section shall be void, whether or not its being so moved was objected to at the time.
> (3) Subsection (2) shall not be taken as excluding the operation of section 178.
> (4) Where a resolution moved in contravention of this section is passed, no provision for automatic re-appointment of retiring directors in default of another appointment shall apply."

Though, during this period, the directors did not retire in accordance with rota established by Table A, all were treated as having retired and were re-elected, the resolutions necessitated by the provisions of section 181 of the Companies Act 1963 having been passed.

At the annual general meeting of the company held on Monday 9 November 1970, however, it was proposed by Dr H. Counihan and seconded by Mr McMahon that the same directors be appointed for another year.

It does not appear from the minutes that the resolution necessitated by the provisions of section 181 of the Companies Act 1963 was passed at this annual general meeting.

Due to the illness of the secretary of the company, Mrs McCormack, the minutes of the annual general meeting held in 1971 were never completed.

During this year the chairman of the company died and the plaintiff was appointed acting chairman.

At the annual general meeting held on 15 March 1972, the plaintiff was appointed chairman of the company and it was proposed by Dr H. Counihan and seconded by Mr McMahon that the four existing directors be re-appointed.

There is no record in the minutes that this resolution was passed but I presume it was as the existing directors continued to act in that capacity.

The resolution required by the provisions of section 181 of the Companies Act 1963 does not appear to have been passed at this meeting.

At the annual general meeting held on 24 January 1974 under the chairmanship of the plaintiff, the fourth-named defendant was elected a director of the company.

There is no record in the minutes of the election of any other directors or of the retirement of any directors in accordance with the requirements of Table A but the plaintiff and the second, third and fourth-named defendants continued to act as directors of the company with the plaintiff acting as chairman.

That was the last annual general meeting of the company prior to the annual general meeting at which occurred the events that led to the proceedings herein.

It is clear from the evidence that the company was experiencing certain trading difficulties, was involved in litigation, had to contend with local agitation which culminated in a portion of the mine being blown up and that relations between the directors were not exactly harmonious.

In January 1975 proceedings between the company and a man called Clive, with whom the company was in dispute were settled on the second day of the hearing.

Though the second and third named defendants were present with the plaintiff at the hearing and authorised the settlement, the second-named defendant criticised the settlement as not being in the best interests of the company at the meeting of the board of directors held on 31 January 1975. It appears that the third-named defendant then supported the second-named defendant.

After some heated discussion, the second-named defendant proposed and the fourth-named defendant seconded the proposal that the plaintiff retire as chairman of the company.

The plaintiff asked for time to consider the position and there is a conflict of evidence as to what then transpired.

The plaintiff states that the matter ended there: that the resolution was not voted on as he did not put the resolutions to the meeting.

The defendants, other than the company, however allege that they refused to allow the plaintiff time to consider his position, insisted that the resolution be voted on, that it was voted on and passed.

On the balance of probabilities, I accept the defendants evidence on this point though I am satisfied that the plaintiff is convinced that what he alleges is true.

The evidence of the defendants is confirmed by the minutes of this meeting.

The notice convening the annual general meeting was signed by the fourth-named defendants and states:

> "We wish to inform you that the annual general meeting for the year

ending 31 December 1974 of Irish Whiting Manufacturers Ltd, will be held at these offices on 6 February 1975 at 4.30 p.m."

Having regard to the events which transpired at the said annual general meeting this notice is impugned on the grounds that it:

(a) did not contain any agenda for the said meeting,

(b) did not give notice of any special business to be transacted at the said meeting.

At the meeting held on 6 February 1975 the notice concerning the meeting was read by the second-named defendant, who stated that this understanding was that there were no officials or directors of the company in being and that the correct procedure was to elect a chairman.

After a discussion during the course of which objection was taken to this course, a vote was taken and by a majority it was decided to elect a chairman for the annual general meeting.

The second-named defendant defeated the plaintiff in the vote to elect a chairman.

Subsequently, during the course of the meeting the second, third and fourth-named defendants were individually proposed, seconded and elected as directors of the company.

The plaintiff, was proposed and seconded but not elected as a director of the company.

It is submitted on behalf of the plaintiff that this meeting was invalid for the reasons set out in detail in paragraph 6 of the statement of claim.

It is further submitted that a resolution was passed at the said meeting that all the directors be retired and put up for re-election and that that resolution was invalid in that it constituted a removal of the directors otherwise than in accordance with section 182 of the Companies Act 1963 and in that it also constituted special business of which notice had not been given in the letter purported to summon the said meeting.

I am satisfied that no resolution was proposed or passed at this meeting. What transpired was that the second-named defendant stated his belief that there were no directors or officers of the company in existence and that the meeting should elect a chairman. It is true that subsequently the practice previously adopted of electing the directors collectively was abandoned and that the directors were elected individually but there is nothing unlawful or invalid in adopting this course rather does the law require it in the absence of a specific resolution.

While there may have been certain deficiencies in the notice convening the meeting, such as failure to comply with the requirements of clause 49 of Table A and irregularities in the manner in which the meeting was conducted; it is quite clear that the majority of the shareholders gave their approval to the course adopted at the meeting and the decisions reached at the said meeting and the first question I have to consider is whether I have any jurisdiction to interfere with the conduct by the company of its internal affairs.

In the course of his judgment in *MacDougall v. Gardiner* (1875) 1 Ch D 13 at page 21 Jones LJ stated:

> "I think that it is of the utmost importance in all these companies that the rule which is well known to this court as the rule in *Mozley v. Alston and Lord v. Copper Miners Company* and *Foss v. Harbottle* should be always adhered to: that is to say that nothing connected with internal disputes between the shareholders is to be made the subject of a Bill by some one shareholder on behalf of himself and others unless there be something illegal, oppressive or fraudulent — unless there is something *ultra vires* the company *qua* company or on the part of the majority of the company so that they are not fit persons to determine it: but that every litigation must be in the name of the company if the company really desire it."

In the course of his judgment in *Burland v. Earle* [1902] AC 83, Lord Davey stated at page 93 that:

> "It is an elementary principle of the law relating to joint stock companies that the court will not interfere with the internal management of companies acting within their powers and in fact has no jurisdiction to do so. . . . The cases in which the majority can maintain such an active action are, therefore, confined to those in which the actions complained of are of a fraudulent character or beyond the powers of the company."

In *Russell v. Wakefield Watertanks Ltd* (1878) LR 20 Eq 475, Sir George Jessell, Master of the Rolls, stated:

> "But this is not a universal rule, that is, it is a rule subject to exceptions and the exceptions depend very much on the necessity of the case, that is the necessity for the court doing justice . . . the rule is not an inflexible rule and it will be relaxed where necessary in the interests of justice."

In *Heyting v. Dupont* [1964] 1 WLR page 854C of A Lord Justice Harmond stated:

> "There are cases which suggest that the rule is not a right one and that an exception will be made where the justice of the case demands it."

Having regard to the provisions of Bunreacht na hÉireann, I am satisfied that an exception to the rule must be made when the justice of the case demands it.

Does the justice of this case require that I abandon what has been described as "an elementary principle of the law relating to joint stock companies that the court will not interfere with the internal management of companies acting within their powers and in fact has no jurisdiction to do so"?

While the plaintiff may with a certain degree of justification feel that he has been unfairly treated by his former co-directors the second, third and fourth-named defendants, that is not to say that there has been anything illegal oppressive or fraudulent in their actions and I so find.

Was their action and the action of the company *ultra vires* the company?

Their action could, in my opinion, only be *ultra vires* the company if on 6 February 1975 he was duly appointed director of the company and not due to retire on rotation.

It appears to me that all the resolutions appointing directors of the company passed at the annual general meetings of the company held on 9 November 1970, 15 March 1972 and 24 January 1974 whereby directors were elected collectively were void having regard to the provisions of section 181 of the Companies Act 1963.

Consequently I am not satisfied that the plaintiff was at the date of the annual general meeting on 6 February 1975 a duly appointed director of the company not due to retire on rotation.

It follows that I am not satisfied that the actions of the defendants were in any way *ultra vires* the company.

I do not consider that the circumstances of this case and the plaintiff's complaints with regard to the proceedings adopted by the defendants before and at the annual general meeting are such as to justify the court in interfering with matters which relate to the internal management of the company.

Consequently I will refuse to make the order sought and to grant the injunction sought.

The plaintiff further claims monies due to him by the company as director's fees and travelling and other expenses.

Clause 17 of the articles of association provides that:

> "The directors shall be entitled to be paid out the funds of the company by way of remuneration for their services in each year a sum calculated at the rate of £100 for each director, plus an extra £50 for the chairman. Furthermore, they shall be entitled to be paid all their reasonable travelling and other expenses properly and necessarily incurred by them in and about the business of the company."

With regard to the fees I am satisfied that the plaintiff waived the fees due to him as a director and chairman for all years other than the year ended 6 February 1975 and that he is entitled to the sum of £150 in respect of that year.

I am also satisfied that in his capacity as a director and chairman he incurred travelling and other expenses in and about the business of the company and will award him £750 in respect of same.

Consequently there will be judgment against the company for the sum of £900.

Patricia McLaughlin
Barrister

In the Matter of the Companies Act 1963 and In the Matter of Ray-Ger Ltd; Sean O'Flanagan and Elizabeth O'Flanagan v. Ray-Ger Ltd, Frederick Pope and Mary Bourke: High Court 1980 No. 2858p (Costello J) 28 April 1983

Company – Property – Trust – Purchase of property for director and wife – Monies advanced to other director – Property put into name of company – Whether held on trust – Director ill with cancer – Agreement between directors that on death of one partner, his estate would have no claim to the company or its assets – Whether procured by undue influence – Whether unconscionable bargain

Facts: Premises at 139 St Peter's Road, Walkinstown were originally run by James O'Flanagan and his wife, Elizabeth, the second plaintiff as a grocery business, but when both succumbed to ill-health, their leasehold interest in the shop was sold on 14 December 1973 and the proceeds of £19,000 put into a joint account at a local bank.

James O'Flanagan suffered a series of strokes and was diagnosed as suffering from cancer. In late 1973 Mr Pope a friend of James O'Flanagan and former tenant of a newsagency at 129 St Peter's Road suggested a joint venture between the two to purchase and sell property and use the proceeds to finance a pub. Mrs O'Flanagan was against the scheme but eventually agreed after much persuasion.

In 1974 Mr Pope set up a limited company called Ray-Ger Ltd. Following negotiations an agreement was reached between the O'Flanagans and Mr Pope as follows: (a) The O'Flanagans were to purchase the freehold to 139 St Peter's Road themselves, eventually using the proceeds of sale as capital for the pub, (b) Mr Pope would buy the landlord's interest in 129 St Peter's Road and 48 Sundrive Road, Kimmage and he too would sell on these premises to raise capital (c) The partnership business would be carried on by Ray-Ger Ltd, in which Mr O'Flanagan and Mr Pope would have an equal interest and into which both would put equal amounts, (d) The company, in order to raise further capital, would buy out the landlord's interest in 135A St Peter's Road, and for this purpose, Mr and Mrs O'Flanagan would lend the company £7000 to be repaid when Mr Pope sold 129 St Peter's Road. It was intended that until 139 St Peter's Road was sold that it would belong to Mr and Mrs O'Flanagan and that they would enjoy the rents and profits.

Between February and October 1974 Mrs O'Flanagan made payments totalling £13,700 to Mr Pope which she assumed would be used in accordance with the agreement. However, the defendant gave her a document referring to an "investment in the company" and later one referring to her "25 per cent holding in the company and . . . a 50 per cent interest in the liabilities and proceeds arising out of the purchase and eventual sale of 135A and 139 St Peter's Road."

Instead of using the money to purchase the freehold in 139 St Peter's Road for the O'Flanagan's, the defendant purchased the premises for the company. He then borrowed £7,000 for the company, using No. 139 as security. A minute of a company board meeting in 1974, however, indicated that the expenses and outgoings of the purchase of No. 139 would be the responsibility of Mr O'Flanagan personally and that he would be entitled to the income from the sale of those premises and all other benefits of charges on No. 139 would accrue to him personally.

When Mrs O'Flanagan complained and made approaches to the defendant, he wrote a letter dated 15 May 1975 and marked "without prejudice" which indicated that the company had purchased 139 St Peter's Road in trust for the benefit of her and her husband personally.

In 1976 following a second cancer operation James O'Flanagan called a meeting of the board of directors. Prior to the meeting Mr O'Flanagan reluctantly agreed to meet Mr Pope in a public house.

At this meeting Mr O'Flanagan signed a written agreement with Mr Pope dated 15 March 1976. It stated that the only liability of the company to the heirs of a deceased director was for amounts due on foot of director's loan accounts, and that in the event of one director dying the survivor would have the right to acquire all of the unissued share capital and to appoint another director of his choice. This agreement was stated to cancel all previous agreements in connection with the running of the company. He also signed a receipt acknowledging that rents from 139 St Peter's Road belonged to the company, and that he accepted payment of this money in lieu of the indebtedness of the company to him.

James O'Flanagan died in October 1977 and the first named plaintiff was appointed his executor. Mr Pope then appointed the third defendant as a director and they allocated the shares to themselves. They refused to register the first plaintiff as a shareholder in lieu of his late father. Relying on the agreement of 15 March 1976, they alleged that the O'Flanagan estate had no interest in the company and no claim on its assets.

The plaintiffs issued proceedings claiming (a) that the company held the premises at 139 St Peter's Road in trust for the plaintiffs jointly or for the first-named plaintiff alone, (b) that the written agreement should be set aside as procured by undue influence or that it represented an unconscionable bargain.

Held by Costello J, *inter alia*, in granting a declaration that the premises at 139 St Peter's Road was now held by the company upon trust for the second-named plaintiff, and in declaring that the first-named plaintiff was entitled to be registered as owner of the share in the company owned by his late father:

(1) The premises at 139 St Peter's Road were held by the company upon express trust for James and Elizabeth O'Flanagan, each having an equitable interest in the property as joint tenants. The letter of 15 May 1975 was an admission of this and was not a privileged document. The court would direct

that these premises be conveyed to the second plaintiff free from encumbrances.

(2) Upon the death of James O'Flanagan, Elizabeth O'Flanagan as surviving joint tenant became entitled to the entire beneficial interest in the property.

(3) In using the property for the purpose of securing a loan for the company and by creating a charge for this purpose the company acted in breach of trust.

(4) The second named plaintiff was entitled to the rent from 139 St Peter's Road, and the tenant would be directed to pay the rent to her. An account would be taken of rents received to date.

(5) A court may set aside a transaction based on undue influence if (a) It can be expressly proved that undue influence was exerted, (b) the relationship between the donor and donee at or shortly before the execution of a gift was such as to raise a presumption that the donor had influence over the donee, in which case the court will set aside the transaction unless the donee proves that the gift was the result of a free exercise of the donor's will. *Allcard v. Skinner* (1885) 36 Ch D 145 approved.

(6) The defendant must have used undue influence to procure James O'Flanagan's signature to the agreement of 15 March 1976. The defendant knew that Mr O'Flanagan was ill and infirm and the agreement was clearly unfair to Mr O'Flanagan's wife and family and should be set aside.

(7) It was not necessary therefore to decide whether the agreement represented an unconscionable bargain.

(8) The Court would declare that the first-named plaintiff was entitled to be registered as the owner of the share in the company owned by his father, and that the purported allotment of shares made by the defendants on 25 October, 1976 was invalid.

Cases referred to in judgment

Allcard v. Skinner (1885) 36 Ch D 145
In re Brocklehurst's Estate [1978] Ch 14; [1977] 3 WLR 96; [1978] 1 All ER 767
Cavendish v. Strutt (1903) 19 TLR 483
In re Craig [1971] 1 Ch 95
In re Daintry [1893] 2 QB 116
Dent v. Bennett (1839) 4 My & Cr 269; 8 LJ Ch 125
Fry v. Lane (1888) 40 Ch D 312; [1886-90] All ER 1084
Grealish v. Murphy [1946] IR 35; (1946) 80 ILTR 111
Gregg v. Kidd [1956] IR 183
Huguenin v. Basely (1807) 14 Ves. 273; [1803-13] All ER 1
In the goods of Kavanagh (Deceased), unreported, High Court (Costello J) 24 October 1978
O'Rorke v. Bolingbroke (1877) 2 App Cas 814; 26 WR 239
In re Westbourne Galleries Ltd [1973] AC 360; [1972] 2 WLR 1289; [1972] 2 All ER 492

Counsel's names not available

Solicitors for the plaintiff: *Bell Brannigan, O'Donnell & O'Brien*
Solicitors for the defendants: *Nugent & Co.*

COSTELLO J **28 April 1983**

Introduction

The late Mr James O'Flanagan and the defendant, Mr Pope, entered into a business relationship which involved the formation of a company (the first named defendant) in which each held one share, and the acquisition by the company of a member of properties including, in particular, a shop premises (now worth, I am told, about £100,000) at 139 St Peter's Road, Walkinstown, Dublin. The plaintiff Mr Sean O'Flanagan is a son of the deceased Mr O'Flanagan and the executor of his will. The plaintiff Elizabeth O'Flanagan is the deceased's widow. The first claim in these proceedings which I will consider is that the company holds the premises 139 St Peter's Road in trust for the plaintiffs jointly or, alternatively, in trust for the plaintiff Mr Sean O'Flanagan alone. The second claim relates to the company. After Mr O'Flanagan's death Mr Pope appointed the third-named defendant a director of the company and he and his co-director then refused to register Mr Sean O'Flanagan as a shareholder in place of his late father and, relying on a written agreement of 15 March 1976, they claim that Mr O'Flanagan's estate has no interest in the company and no claim on its assets. The plaintiffs' claim, calling in aid certain well established equitable principles, is that the written agreement should be set aside on the ground (a) that it was procured by undue influence or alternatively (b) that the bargain it represented was an unconscionable one. Injunctive, declaratory and other relief are also claimed.

I propose in Part I of this judgment to deal with the early part of the relationship between the deceased and Mr Pope (who I will call the defendant) which relates in particular (but not exclusively) to the claim that the company is a trustee of the premises; in Part II with the claim to set aside the agreement of 15 March 1976; in Part III to other issues that arise. In Part IV I will give my conclusions on the relief claimed by the plaintiffs.

Part I

Mr and Mrs O'Flanagan had lived for a number of years in England before Mrs O'Flanagan's return to this country in the year 1963. She came for the purpose of finding a suitable premises in which she and her husband could carry on business. She succeeded in negotiating a 21 year lease of 139 St Peter's Road, Walkinstown at an annual rent of £916 and she opened up a grocery business in it. The premises (comprising a shop with living accommodation overhead) was one of several newly constructed buildings which formed a small shopping centre. In another of the premises in the same shopping centre, at No. 129 St Peter's Road, Mr Frederick Pope (the second named defendant) opened up a newsagency business. In the year 1965 Mr O'Flanagan joined his wife and together they set about building up their business. They formed a family company (Greenhills Supermarket Ltd) but the arrangements between them were very informal; the lease of the premises was left in the name of Mrs O'Flanagan and the shares in the company were not divided evenly between them. I am satisfied however, that it was intended that they would run the business on a joint basis and that its profits were to be jointly owned.

Unfortunately their plans did not work out as they had hoped as ill health struck Mr O'Flanagan. He sustained his first stroke in the month of June 1967 and it was a bad one. In July of 1969 he suffered a second one and in the year 1971 a third. These so incapacitated him that Mrs O'Flanagan was required to run the business virtually single-handed until she, in her turn, succumbed to high blood pressure. As a result, early in the year 1973, it was decided to sell the goodwill of the business and the leasehold interest in the premises and on 14 December 1973 a contract was entered into with a Mr Edmund Tunney for a consideration of £32,000. After paying various debts the O'Flanagans had a little over £19,000 left from the sale of the premises. This was put into a joint account in a local bank and I am satisfied from Mrs O'Flanagan's evidence that she and her husband owned this money jointly.

As a result of the series of strokes which Mr O'Flanagan suffered he walked with a limp and the movement of his mouth was impaired. But his misfortunes did not end there. In the month of September 1973 it was found that he had a malignant tumour of the large bowel and he underwent major surgery for cancer. From then on Mr O'Flanagan knew that he suffered from cancer; as did all his friends including, notwithstanding his protestations to the contrary, the second named defendant in these proceedings.

Mr Fred Pope is highly intelligent and a very articulate person with obviously a great deal of business acumen. Originally his relationship with Mr O'Flanagan was a social one. He and Mr O'Flanagan went drinking together over many years at least three or four nights every week. Mrs O'Flanagan was far from happy with this relationship and the effect which it had on her husband as he had been advised by his doctors not to drink because of the effect alcohol would have as a result of drugs he was required to take. But he ignored this advice and very frequently came home so drunk that he fell about the house. At the time of the sale of the O'Flanagan premises (and just after Mr O'Flanagan's first operation) the relationship between Mr O'Flanagan and the defendant changed from being a purely social one into a business one. This development came about in this way.

The solicitors for the landlords of the shopping centre wrote to each of the tenants in March of 1972 offering to sell to them the freehold interest in their properties. The O'Flanagans did not want to take the offer up and gave their purchaser, Mr Tunney, an opportunity to do so of he wished. The defendant however was very active amongst his co-tenants in the shopping centre and endeavoured to negotiate a joint agreement between all the tenants and their landlords. These efforts failed; in particular a Mr Stewart, the lessee of 135A St Peter's Road, did not wish to buy out the freehold. Late in the year 1973 and early in the year 1974 the defendant put forward for Mr O'Flanagan's consideration a scheme for a joint venture between them. He suggested that they should go into partnership to buy a licensed premises; that the O'Flanagans would buy out their landlord's interest and having done so raise capital by selling the property subject to the lease. He would do the same in respect of 129 St Peter's Road and also in respect of other premises he owned at 48 Sundrive Road, Kimmage. Each partner would put an equal amount of capital into the business and the profits would be divided equally.

Mrs O'Flanagan was against the idea from the word go. Not only did she dislike the effect which the association with Mr Pope had on her husband's welfare but also because she considered the investment in the freehold to be a bad one. She urgently needed money and in fact had to go out to seek work to maintain herself, her husband (who was unable to work) and her large family of eight children. It speaks volumes for Mr Pope's powers of persuasion that he eventually succeeded in getting her agreement to his proposals. He did this by constantly coming to her house in the company of her husband and extolling the benefits of the venture which he had in mind.

I need not delay in detailing the course of the negotiations. I should however, make clear that although Mr O'Flanagan was a party to the eventual agreement the defendant was the instigator of the whole plan and in the discussions which took place with Mrs O'Flanagan Mr O'Flanagan was a mere onlooker in the efforts his friend was making to persuade his wife to agree to part with their joint savings. When agreement was reached in February 1974 the defendant's proposals had developed and matured. He told Mrs O'Flanagan that he had formed a company (first named defendant herein); that as part of the scheme for raising capital to buy a licensed premises the company should buy out the landlord's interest in 135A St Peter's Road (Mr Stewart's premises); that the company needed a short-term loan of £7,000 from the O'Flanagans which would be repaid when Mr Pope had effected the sale of his two premises. I am satisfied that what was eventually agreed initially between the partners and then between the partners and Mrs O'Flanagan was as follows:

(a) Mr and Mrs O'Flanagan were to buy out the freehold in 139 St Peter's Road; the property would be theirs and they would enjoy the rents and profits until it was sold for the purpose of providing capital to buy a licensed premises.
(b) the defendant Mr Pope would buy out his landlord's interest in 129 St Peter's Road and 48 Sundrive Road, Kimmage and he too would sell these properties and put an equal amount into the partnership business, as Mr O'Flanagan put in.
(c) The partnership business would be carried on by the company, Ray-Ger Ltd, in which Mr Pope and Mr O'Flanagan would have an equal interest.
(d) for the purpose of raising further capital the company would buy out the landlord's interest in 135A St Peter's Road. For this purpose Mr and Mrs O'Flanagan would lend to the company the sum of £7,000 and this would be repaid immediately on the sale by Mr Pope of 129 St Peter's Road.

Mrs O'Flanagan had no part in the running of the enterprise and she took little interest in it beyond releasing the money when requested to do so by Mr Pope. Not surprisingly her memory is not entirely accurate as to when monies were actually paid over. It is possible, however, to get fairly exact dates from the company's records. It appears that the first drawing on the joint account was made about 20 February 1974. It was for the sum of £3,200, Mrs O'Flanagan having been told by the defendant that this was needed for deposits on the properties which were being purchased. A second payment of £1,000 was made on 1 August 1974 and another of £2,000 on 9 August 1974. A final payment of £7,500 was made on 30 October 1974 (in all a sum of £13,700).

Mrs O'Flanagan was informed that the payment of £1,000 was needed in respect of the purchase of the properties and on 9 August the defendant told her that he was in financial difficulties and on his insistence she authorised the withdrawal of a further £2,000. On 30 October she was again visited by the defendant in the company of her husband. Mr Pope then explained to her that the cost of purchasing 139 St Peter's Road would work out at £13,700 and having deducted the sum of £6,200 which she already paid she was asked to authorise the withdrawal of a sum of £7,500 to make up the balance.

Mrs O'Flanagan presumed that the monies would be used in accordance with her agreement with the defendant. On 1 August the defendant handed Mrs O'Flanagan a hand-written document signed by him and the deceased purporting to be a receipt for the sum of £4,200 "for investment in the above named company" (*i.e.* Ray-Ger Ltd). A similar document was handed to her on 9 August. These documents were very misleading as Mrs O'Flanagan had not agreed to give the money as an "investment in the company" but she paid no attention to them. An even more misleading document was prepared by the defendant and given by him to her on 30 October.

Written on company notepaper it states:

> "It is hereby agreed that Mrs Elizabeth O'Flanagan has a 25 per cent holding in the above company and that she has a 50 per cent interest in the liabilities and proceeds arising out of the purchase and eventual sale of 135A and 139 St Peter's Road, Walkinstown, D.12."

The defendant suggested that this letter truly represented Mrs O'Flanagan's interest both in the company and in the properties it owned but he claimed that her interest changed at a later date. I have no difficulty in rejecting this evidence. There was never any question of Mrs O'Flanagan having an interest in the company. By this letter (as well as the two earlier "receipts") the defendant, it seems to me, was preparing his defences against the inevitable onslaught which he anticipated would result when Mrs O'Flanagan learned what he had done with her money.

Instead of using Mr and Mrs O'Flanagans money for purchasing for them the freehold of 139 St Peter's Road he used it to purchase the premises for the company (of which he owned one of the two issued shares).

He then used 139 St Peter's Road as security for a loan which the company obtained from the United Dominions Trust ("the U.D.T.") for £7,000. He arranged that this sum was to be charged on both 135A and 139 St Peter's Road. In further breach of agreement he bought out the freehold interest in 129 St Peter's Road (with a further loan from the U.D.T.) but never sold his interest and never paid any money into the company.

Again, in breach of contract, he did not buy out the landlord's interest in 48 Sundrive Road. In fact during Mr O'Flanagan's lifetime the defendant never put a penny into the venture, beyond incurring incorporation costs of about £160.

In order to consider the plaintiff's claim that the company holds 139 St Peter's Road as a trustee I must examine more closely exactly what occurred. The company was incorporated on 25 February 1974 and the first meeting of the board of directors was held on 19 March. Mr O'Flanagan's solicitor (who became the company's solicitor) and a representative from his accountant's firm (which became the company's auditors) attended the meeting. Mr O'Flanagan and Mr Pope were appointed directors and one share each was issued to them. Mr O'Dowd, the accountant's representative, prepared draft minutes which recorded his understanding of the parties' agreement about the property to be purchased. Before it was circulated, however the defendant sent on a hand-written note of what the minutes were to contain and this was eventually incorporated in them. His note was significantly different from Mr O'Dowd's draft as it provided that the company was to purchase 139 St Peter's Road. It is thus clear that from the very beginning of the venture the defendant had decided that the monies which he would obtain from the O'Flanagans would be used for the purchase of 139 St Peter's Road by the company and not, as he had agreed, by the O'Flanagans themselves.

It is important to note the exact wording of the minute in relation to this property. It reads as follows:

> "It is expressly agreed that expenses and other outgoings of the purchase by the company of 139 St Peter's Road will be the responsibility of Mr O'Flanagan personally and that the total income from the ultimate sale of 139 St Peter's Road and all other benefits of charges on 139 St Peter's Road shall accrue to Mr O'Flanagan."

The phraseology used by the defendant in preparing this minute is somewhat obscure but it is reasonably clear that he is recording the fact that although the property was to be taken in the name of the company that Mr O'Flanagan was to be responsible for outgoings and that he was to be entitled to proceeds of its sale.

It was not until the year following that Mrs O'Flanagan found out what had happened. By May of 1975 she was in serious financial difficulties. For reasons which I will explain later no rent had been received from 139 St Peter's Road and, of course, Mr O'Flanagan was not able to work. Mrs O'Flanagan therefore decided to raise some money on the security of 139 St Peter's Road. When she asked her husband about the title deeds she discovered for the first time that he and Mr Pope had used the money which she jointly owned with her husband to buy the property in the company's name. Not unnaturally she was extremely angry. She believed herself to have been tricked by the defendant and she rang his solicitor to try to find out what was going on. She asked him was he aware that 139 St Peter's Road belonged to her and her husband, but the defendant's solicitor declined to discuss the matter with her and advised her to get separate legal advice.

After Mrs O'Flanagan's telephone call the defendant was contacted by his solicitors and as a result he wrote a letter of the 15 May 1975 to Mrs O'Flanagan. It was an extremely abusive letter. In the course of it he denied that he had conspired with Mr O'Flanagan to use the company to defraud Mrs O'Flanagan and went on:

> "You are of course very well aware that you have not been and will not be cheated in any way whatever. You are also aware that 139 St Peter's Road was purchased in trust by the company for the benefit of yourself and your husband and that the premises are not part of the company's share capital."

Having complained of her "vicious irrational outbursts and profane telephone calls" he threatened legal proceedings if she attempted further to damage his character.

This letter is, of course, of crucial importance in this case; it acknowledges that the company held the property as trustee and is strongly supportive of the plaintiffs' claim in these proceedings.

Strenuous objection to the admissibility of this letter was taken at the trial on the grounds that it was written on a privileged occasion. The defendant had headed the letter "without prejudice" but these words alone possess no major properties and some more substantial grounds had to be found to justify the defendant's objection to the admissibility of this letter. Before reading it I heard evidence from both the plaintiff and the defendant.

The defendant said that after he received a telephone call from his solicitor he discussed the situation with Mr O'Flanagan in a public house, that Mr O'Flanagan said that he was in trouble at home and that Mr Pope would have to get "Mrs O'Flanagan off his back", that Mr O'Flanagan told him that he had been assaulted by his wife and that he was afraid of further assaults, that Mr O'Flanagan had suggested that he, Mr Pope, should say that the company held the property in trust.

I cannot accept this evidence. Mrs O'Flanagan knew that her husband was terminally ill and, in any event, she is not the sort of person who would strike her husband, and I think it is highly improbable that Mr O'Flanagan told the defendant that she had done so. I accept that Mr O'Flanagan would have conveyed to the defendant that his wife was very angry at what had been done and that he must have urged on him the need to put matters right.

But the relationship between the deceased and the defendant was not such that the deceased could have influenced the defendant to write something that was untrue.

Furthermore, I accept Mrs O'Flanagan's account of what she said to the defendant's solicitor on the telephone and I do not believe that she threatened to issue legal proceedings and I cannot accept that Mr O'Flanagan's solicitor would have misrepresented what she had stated in the way suggested by the defendant.

The rule which excludes documents marked "without prejudice" has no application unless some person is in dispute or negotiation with another and terms are offered for the settlement of a dispute or negotiation (see *In re Daintry* [1893] 2 QB 116, 119). Mrs O'Flanagan did not threaten any legal proceedings; her main concern was to ascertain from the defendant's solicitor what the true position was about her property. Having admitted the document in evidence without having read it my view as to its admissibility was confirmed when I did so as it will be seen that the defendant was not offering to settle a dispute but was making a statement as to the rights of the plaintiff and her husband in relation to the property; in addition he was himself threatening legal proceedings against Mrs O'Flanagan. It is clear that the defendant obviously hoped that by heading the letter "without prejudice" he would be able to ensure that the letter could not be used if Mrs O'Flanagan subsequently attempted to rely on it to support her claim that the company held the property as a trustee for her and her husband.

I am satisfied that the letter was a true admission and acknowledgement that the company held the property in trust. This conclusion gets support from a number of aspects of the case. Mr O'Flanagan must have been well aware that by using the money from the joint account to buy 139 St Peter's Road in the name of the company he was involved in a deception on his wife. It is probable that he went along with the deception on the defendant's assurance that the company would hold the property in trust for himself or for himself and his wife jointly. That the partners so agreed gets support from the minute of 19 March 1974 to which I have referred. In addition, at a meeting attended by the company's accountant, Mr O'Flanagan stated to the meeting that the company held the property in trust and this statement was not corrected by the defendant who was also present. Furthermore, Mr O'Flanagan received rent from 139 St Peter's Road (at a time when the property was in the name of the company) in circumstances which showed that he was asserting his right to it as against the company's right.

The defendants have relied on the manner in which the property was treated in the company's accounts and records and Mr O'Flanagan's apparent acquiescence in such treatment to negative the existence of a trust.

But I do not think that this evidence outweighs the clear statement which is to be found in the letter of 15 May 1975 and the inferences to be drawn from the other evidence in the case to which I have referred.

I conclude therefore that the company held 139 St Peter's Road under an express trust for Mr and Mrs O'Flanagan jointly which had been created at the time it was conveyed into the company's name. Mr and Mrs O'Flanagan had been jointly entitled to the money in their joint account and I think that their equitable interest in the property was as joint tenants. It follows from this that on Mr O'Flanagan's death, Mrs O'Flanagan, as surviving joint tenant, became entitled to the entire beneficial interest in the property.

The trust was an express one arising from the agreement of the directors at the time the property was conveyed to the company. The letter of 15 May 1975 was written with the approval of both the directors of the company and binds the company. I should add that if an express trust had not existed I would have been prepared to hold that a constructive trust arose by operation of law when the deceased and the defendant wrongfully used the money entrusted to them for the purpose of buying property to be put into the names of Mr and Mrs O'Flanagan, for the purpose of taking the property in the company's name.

I also find that in using the trust property for the purpose of securing a loan for the company from U.D.T. and by creating a charge for this purpose the company acted in breach of trust.

I will deal later in this judgment with the appropriate relief to which the plaintiffs are entitled arising from the findings I have just made.

Part II

I come now to consider the executor's claim against the company. At the time of Mr O'Flanagan's death the company had issued two shares of its hundred pound share capital, one to Mr O'Flanagan and one to the defendant Mr Pope. Mr Sean O'Flanagan as executor of his father's will claims to be entitled to be registered as owner of his father's share. After Mr O'Flanagan's death a new director was appointed and unissued share capital was allotted to Mr Pope and his nominee. Registration of Mr Sean O'Flanagan has been refused. In support of this refusal the defendant relies on a written agreement of 15 March 1976 signed by both himself and the deceased and sealed with the company seal.

In this part of my judgment I will deal with the plaintiffs' claim that this written agreement should be set aside because (a) it was obtained by undue influence or (b) it represents an unconscionable bargain. The equitable principles which the plaintiffs call in aid are well established. The cases where a plaintiff seeks to set aside a gift or other transaction on the ground that it was procured by undue influence have been divided into two classes; firstly, those in which it can be expressly proved that undue influence was exercised, in which circumstances the court intervenes on the principle that no one should be allowed to retain any benefit arising from his own fraud or wrongful act; secondly, those in which the relations between the donor and the donee have at or shortly before the execution of a gift been such as to raise a presumption that the donor had influence over the donee. Then, the court intervenes, not on the ground that any wrongful act has in fact been committed by the donee but on the ground of public policy and to prevent the relations which existed between the parties and the influence arising therefrom being abused. The court will set aside the gift unless it is proved (and the onus is on the donee in such cases) that in fact the gift was the result of a free exercise of the donor's will (see *Allcard v. Skinner* (1885) 36 Ch D 145 at 171). The courts have not defined the degree of confidence and trust which must exist in a relationship before it can be said that a donee is in a position to exert undue influence. It has been long established that the relationship of parent and child, guardian and ward, doctor and patient, religious adviser and pupil are relationships which give rise to the presumption to which I have referred. But the categories are not closed and in *Gregg v. Kidd* [1956] IR 183, Budd J held that the relationship raised the presumption to which I have referred in a case in which an uncle settled property on his nephew. Recently in England a majority of the Court of Appeal (in *In Re Brocklehurst's Estate* [1978] 1 Ch 14) took the view that the presumption did not arise from the relationship of friendship between an elderly man and a companion from a different class in the social structure, whilst in *In Re Craig* [1971] 1 Ch 95 it was held that the relationship between an elderly man and his secretary gave rise to the presumption. The presumption does not arise in the case of wills (see *In the goods of Kavanagh, deceased* (unreported) 24 October 1978 in which I held that express undue influence was proved).

Just as the courts have declined to define the exact categories of relationship which will give rise to the presumption of undue influence so too they have declined to define exactly what undue influence is. The approach which Courts of Equity should adopt was suggested by Sir Samuel Romilly (a distinguished Chancery Lawyer and former Solicitor General) in one of the early leading cases on the matter (*Huguenin v. Basely* [1807] 14 Ves 273), an approach which subsequently obtained judicial approval from Lord Cottendham in *Dent v. Bennett* (1839) 4 My & Cr 2877 and from Bryne J in *Cavendish v. Strutt* (1903) (19 TLR 483). The passage to which I refer reads as follows:

> "Where a gift is immoderate, bears no proportion to the circumstances of the giver, where no reason appears, or the reason given is falsified, and the giver is a weak man, liable to be imposed upon, this Court will look upon a gift with a very jealous eye, and very strictly examine the conduct of the persons in whose favour it is made; and if it sees that any arts or stratagems, or any undue means have been used — if it sees the least speck of imposition at the bottom, or that the donor is in such a situation with respect to the donee as may naturally give an undue influence over him — if there be least scintilla of fraud, this Court will and ought to interpose. . ." (quoted in White and Tudor *Leading Cases in Equity*, Vol. 1, p. 216)

The plaintiffs do not rely solely on the equitable principles relating to undue influence. They claim in the alternative that the agreement of 15 March 1976 should be set aside on the ground that it is an unconscionable bargain. The principle relied on was stated by Lord Hatherley in a dissenting judgment in *O'Rorke v. Bolingbroke* (1877) 2 App Cas 814, 823, a case dealing with a sale at undervalue by an expectant heir but which enunciated a principle of wider application. The passage reads as follows:

> "It . . . appears that the principle on which equity originally proceeded to set aside such transactions was for the protection of family property; but this principle being once established, the Court extended its aid to all cases in which the parties to a contract have not met upon equal terms. In ordinary cases each party to a bargain must take care of his own interest, and it will not be presumed that undue advantage or contrivance has been resorted to on either side; but in the case of the "expectant heir" or of persons under pressure without adequate protection and in the case of dealings with uneducated ignorant persons, the burden of showing the fairness of the transaction is thrown on the person who seeks to obtain the benefit of the contract".

This passage was quoted with approval by Gavan Duffy J in *Grealish v. Murphy* [1946] IR 35, a case in which the plaintiff was a mentally retarded adult but in which no undue influence was shown to have been exercised. The transaction which he entered into, however, was set aside on the ground that equity comes to the rescue in cases where the parties to a contract have not met on equal terms, the court holding that the deed was an improvident one and that the plaintiffs' weakness of mind coupled with the inadequacy of the advice he obtained justified the intervention of the court in that case (see also *Fry v. Lane* (1888) 40 Ch D 312, at 322).

As the evidence relating to the relationship between the deceased and the defendant and the evidence relating to the allegation of undue influence are inextricably mixed I propose to examine the facts surrounding the making of the agreement of 15 March 1976 and then save my opinion as to whether or not the plaintiff has made out a case for the intervention of the court on the ground that undue influence was exercised by the defendant in relation to it.

I turn, then, to the facts leading up to the execution of agreement. It is quite clear that after the defendant had written his abusive letter to Mrs O'Flanagan that relations between him and the deceased became severely strained. In the summer of 1975 Mr O'Flanagan had to go into hospital for an operation on his elbow and in November of that year he underwent a second major operation for cancer. The deceased had sufficiently recovered from the operation in the early part of 1976 to enable him to deal with the highly unsatisfactory situation which existed between himself and the defendant. To try to rectify the situation he contacted the company's auditor, Mr Fay, and on his instructions Mr Fay wrote to the defendant to convene a meeting of the directors of the company on 17 February. The defendant's reaction was a very significant one. He obviously was aware that both Mr Fay and the company's solicitor would attend the meeting (as they had on previous occasions) and the defendant refused to attend it, demanding instead that a private meeting be held between himself and Mr O'Flanagan before any formal board meeting took place. Mr O'Flanagan's reaction is equally significant. He wrote back agreeing to a private meeting provided that it was held in Mr Fay's office adjacent to the room where the directors' meeting would be held and provided that it would not last longer than half an hour, and provided that the defendant undertook to attend the directors' meeting directly after the private meeting, a directors' meeting at which the company's solicitor and auditor would be present. It seems to me to be quite clear that Mr O'Flanagan was apprehensive of what would happen if he and Mr O'Flanagan had met in one of their old haunts and he sought to protect himself from the danger he anticipated might exist if he was to meet the defendant alone. The defendant, however, did not agree to a private meeting on the lines suggested by Mr O'Flanagan and instead on 5 March wrote direct to him suggesting that they should meet in a public house. This they did (on two occasions according to the defendant) and as a result there emerged the written agreement of 15 March, signed, as I have said, by both parties and typed on the company's notepaper.

The only evidence of what transpired between Mr O'Flanagan and the defendant is the defendant's own testimony. He stated in evidence that relations between himself and the deceased had been bad for the latter part of the previous year and that they hadn't met for several months. He gave no explanation as to why he wanted a private meeting before the board meeting or why he refused to meet in Mr Fay's office with the deceased. He explained that he and the deceased met in the lounge of the Belgard Public House in the morning time and drank coffee. He said that Mr O'Flanagan was looking very well and that he told him of the operation that he had had (but he did not tell him that he was suffering from cancer). The defendant stated that the deceased said that he was in a bad way for money and that he told the deceased that he also needed money. After discussions which went on that day and on a second day in the Belgard lounge it was agreed that he and the deceased would settle their differences in the manner set out in the written agreement. Hand-written drafts of this agreement had been prepared (but these were subsequently torn up) and on the second meeting he and the deceased went to a small office in the defendant's premises at 129 St Peter's Road where the defendant typed up the agreement. He said that they then went back to the Belgard lounge, that Mr O'Flanagan had the company's seal with him and that they then signed and sealed the document in the Belgard lounge.

At the time that he typed up the written agreement the defendant also typed up a receipt for the sum of £1,384 which the deceased signed. The defendant explained that the company had received rent from 139 St Peter's Road and that the figure in the receipt represented this rent. The deceased had borrowed the money from the defendant and had given him I.O.U.'s in respect of these loans. The defendant said that they added these up and then two cheques were drawn on the company's account, one for £766 and one for £618 (both payable to "cash"). Mr O'Flanagan gave the smaller cheque to the defendant to discharge the debts he owed him and kept the larger cheque. The receipt makes no mention that the money was rent from the company's property (property which the previous year the defendant had agreed was held in trust for Mr and Mrs O'Flanagan) and it is stated to be a receipt of £1,384 "being repayments in part of money lent by me to the company".

As the written agreement is of such importance in this case I think I should set it out in full.

It is dated 15 March 1976 and headed "to whom it may concern" and reads:

> "We the undersigned, James O'Flanagan and Fred Pope being the joint managing directors of Ray-Ger Ltd hereby agree to settle our differences in the company in the following ways.
> 1. We agree that payments made by the company to either of us shall be regarded as being payments of our respective loans in the company's accounts, and that neither of us shall charge the company interest on any loans that we have given or may in the future give to the company.
> 2. We agree that in the event of one of the directors dying, the surviving director shall have the right to acquire all of the remaining unissued ordinary shares of the company, and to appoint another director of his choice.
> 3. We agree that the only liability of the company to the heirs or assigns of a deceased director shall be for the balance due to him in the directors' loan accounts.
> 4. We agree that neither of us shall seek to have the company liquidated.
> 5. We agree that the purpose of this mutual agreement is to protect the company and its directors against demands that might be made by a deceased director's heirs or assigns.
> 6. We agree that this agreement cancels all previous agreements that have been made between us in connection with the running of the company.
> 7. We agree that the company seal shall be fixed at the end of this document along with our signatures and that the contents of this document shall be strictly private until one of us dies or we terminate our association in business.
> 8. We agree that we shall each receive a copy of this agreement and that they shall be placed in string envelopes and that the joints of the envelopes shall be embossed with the company seal and signed by both of us".

The effect of this agreement and the receipt signed by the deceased cannot be in doubt. The previous year the defendant with the knowledge of the deceased had unequivocally stated that the company held 139 St Peter's Road in trust for Mr and Mrs O'Flanagan. But contrary to this statement by accepting the rent in the terms of the receipt the deceased was now acknowledging that the rent of the premises belonged to the company and could be used by it to discharge its indebtedness to him.

Secondly, prior to the agreement the deceased and the defendant jointly owned the share capital of the company. By this agreement Mr O'Flanagan agreed that on the death of a partner the partner's estate would have no claim on the company and the surviving partner would be entitled to the entire share capital in the company. Thus by this agreement Mr O'Flanagan was agreeing that if he pre-deceased Mr Pope neither his wife nor any of his eight children would be entitled to any share in the company's assets which consisted not only of 135A St Peter's Road but also as he was then acknowledging 139 St Peter's Road.

I have the following observations to make on the agreement and the defendant's evidence in relation to it:

(a) I found the defendant's evidence unconvincing and must record my view that he was not telling the truth as to how the agreement came to be made. He failed to give any or any acceptable explanation as to why (a) he insisted on a "private meeting" with the deceased or (b) why he and Mr O'Flanagan should agree that the surviving partner should be entitled to the entire of the company's assets. I am also quite satisfied that the defendant, contrary to what he stated in the course of his testimony, knew full well that Mr O'Flanagan had had two major operations for cancer.
(b) I do not accept (as pleaded in paragraph 8 of the defence) that the defendant in March 1976 wished to wind up the company and that he was prevailed upon by the deceased not to do so. I think it is much more probable that the defendant used the threat to wind up the company as a means for procuring the deceased's signature to the agreement and that he used the I.O.U.'s which the deceased had signed for the same purpose.
(c) The written agreement refers to the fact that each of the partners should receive a copy of it. No copy was ever found amongst the deceased's effects after his death and Mrs O'Flanagan knew nothing about the agreement until the reply to the notice for particulars in this action. I think it is reasonable to assume that the defendant did not give Mr O'Flanagan a copy of it.
(d) In March 1976 the deceased was a very sick man. He had undergone a very serious operation the previous November and a letter written by him on 10 March a couple of days before he met the defendant shows that he had been ill in bed and had been unable to attend a business appointment.
(e) The deceased was aware that he was terminally ill with cancer and must have realised that his chances of surviving Mr Pope were slight. He was not well off and notwithstanding this he was apparently agreeing that on his death the defendant and not his wife or any of his eight children would obtain the benefit of two valuable commercial properties. There is nothing to suggest that Mr O'Flanagan had not the normal love and affection which a husband and father has for his wife and children and no explanation has been forthcoming as to why he should fail to give expression to that love and affection and instead give what was virtually a gift of these properties to Mr Pope.
(f) After Mr OFlanagan's death, as we will see, the defendant sought

advice from his accountant as to the right to appoint a new director and issue the balance of the share capital to himself and nominee. In doing so he did not show him the secret agreement of 15 March 1976. His failure to do so demonstrates a lack of confidence in its validity, which could only have arisen if it was tainted by some wrong-doing on his part.

Taking into account all the evidence in the case I think there is only one conclusion to be reached in relation to this agreement namely that the defendant must have used undue influence to procure it. The defendant has a strong and forceful personality and had obviously exercised considerable influence amounting to domination of the deceased on previous occasions. The deceased was infirm and ill when he signed it. The agreement was egregiously unfair to the deceased's wife and family.

The mutual promises it contained were largely illusory in that both parties knew that it was highly probable that the deceased would predecease the defendant. Furthermore, the lack of candour of the defendant raises very serious suspicions about the circumstances in which it came to be executed. It is unnecessary for me to decide whether the relationship which existed raises any presumption as to what happened. The evidence satisfies me that I should set the agreement aside.

Because I have concluded that the plaintiffs have been able to establish that the agreement was procured by undue influence it is unnecessary for me to decide whether, apart from undue influence, the court should by the application of equitable principles to which I have already referred set it aside on the ground that it represented an unconscionable bargain.

Part III

I now consider some of the other facts of this case which are relevant to some of the issues to which the pleadings have given rise.

Firstly I must say a word about 139 St Peter's Road.

Mr Tunney, the purchaser of the leasehold interest from the O'Flanagans left the premises some time in June 1975 and for a considerable time they were vacant. Ejectment proceedings were taken against him and for some time the rent was paid by Mr Tunney's mortgagees, the Lombard and Ulster Bank Ltd. In 1977 it appears that the mortgagees paid a cheque for £1,916 being a year's rent for the premises. On 27 May 1977 the company's solicitors sent this to Mr O'Flanagan but he claimed (having then fallen out again with the defendant) that he and not the company was entitled to the rent and negotiated the cheque and kept the proceeds. It would appear that no claim in respect of this sum has been made by the company or Mr Pope since then.

At some date after Mr O'Flanagan's death the defendant company obtained possession of these premises. The company reconstructed them and relet them. There are now four tenants in the premises and the premises are worth in the region of £100,000. I presume that the lettings were made by the company but there is no evidence as to whether the company or the defendant received the rents.

The tenant, Mr Tunney, successfully sued the O'Flanagans for damages for breach of contract. I found Mrs O'Flanagan to be a truthful witness and I do not consider that my assessment of her is vitiated in any way by the success of Mr Tunney's claim.

As I have already pointed out the company borrowed £7,000 from the U.D.T. in the early part of 1975 and the U.D.T. obtained a charge both on 139 and 135A St Peter's Road. The company defaulted in its repayments and ejectment proceedings were taken against it in the High Court and apparently a decree for possession was obtained on 21 January 1977. It would appear that the decree was not executed but I have no information as to the terms on which this was arranged.

At the time of Mr O'Flanagan's death the company owed the U.D.T. on foot of its loan £18,000 approximately. In October 1982 this had increased to £26,000 and it is now, I am told, in the region of £30,000. An account was produced which showed that Mr Pope was personally indebted to the U.D.T. in the sum of nearly £41,500 in September 1982. Whether the company's assets are in any way pledged to secure this indebtedness has not been established.

As to 135A St Peter's Road, it would appear from the records kept by the company's auditors that the company purchased these premises in February 1975 for the sum of £6,886.25 and that an annual rent of £500 was thereafter payable by the tenant "Stewart Electric". This rent clearly belongs to the company. What rent the company has received or how it disposed of the rent has not been established.

As to 129 St Peter's Road, it will be recalled that these premises were premises in which Mr Pope carried on his newsagency business. The agreement which the partners made between themselves and then with Mrs O'Flanagan was that the defendant would buy out his landlord's interest and then having sold the premises would reinvest the proceeds in the company so that the company could buy a licensed premises. The proceeds of this sale were also to be used to repay Mrs O'Flanagan the sum of £7,000 which she and her husband lent to the company. Mr Pope purchased the freehold in January 1975 with a loan from the U.D.T., but apparently he never sold the premises as was agreed. He never paid any sum to the company as his share of the proposed undertaking.

After the death of the deceased, however, Mr Pope called a meeting on 25 October 1977 and its minutes record that in consideration of the issue of 78 shares in the company which were issued to him and the payment of £2,000 by the company to him that he agreed to assign 129 St Peter's Road to the company. No conveyance ever took place, but Mr Pope has agreed that the premises belonged to the company and his solicitor explained that it was on his advice that no formal conveyance was executed as a sale of the premises had been contemplated. It appears from the auditor's records that the company received substantial rents from these premises.

I am satisfied that these premises are the company's property and that this conclusion is unaffected by the fact that the allocation of shares to the defendant was, as I will show in a moment, an invalid one.

The original agreement between the partners and the partners and Mrs O'Flanagan was that the defendant would buy out the freehold in 48 Sundrive Road, Kimmage and would sell the premises and use the proceeds for investment in the company to assist in the purchase of a licensed premises. Obviously the deceased was very concerned about this part of the bargain because the defendant wrote to him as secretary of the company on 5 April 1974 confirming the fact that the company was to be his agent for the purposes of purchasing the leasehold of 48 Sundrive Road and selling the property "as quickly as possible". I do not accept that the purchase and resale did not take place because the defendant's landlord refused to sell. I think the reality of the situation is that the defendant had in fact no money to purchase these premises and was unable to borrow for this purpose. It would appear that later he unilaterally decided not to do so. In the result these premises form no part of the company's assets.

I come now to consider briefly certain of the events which occurred after the agreement of 15 March 1976, and after Mr O'Flanagan's death on 15 October 1977.

After the March meeting the deceased's and the defendant's relations returned for a while to their earlier basis. The company's auditor prepared accounts for the company for the year ending 28 February 1975 and the year ending 28 February 1976, and he obtained the signature of a loan certificate from the deceased on 22 June 1976 which showed that the company owed him £13,737. It had been Mr Fay's opinion that the company had owed part of this sum to Mrs O'Flanagan but on Mr O'Flanagan's instructions he changed the records so that the total sum was shown as being due to Mr O'Flanagan personally. It is claimed in the defence that the acknowledgement in the loan certificate and the deceased's signature to the annual accounts constitute a bar by way of estoppel to the claim that the company holds the property in trust.

I cannot agree with this contention. Quite clearly the deceased and the defendant had declared that the company was a trustee of the property for the deceased and Mrs O'Flanagan and by signing the documents to which I have referred the deceased could not in my opinion effect the beneficial interest which had been created. The only significance of these documents is, it seems to me, an evidential one but for reasons which I have already given their significance is far outweighed by the other evidence in the case. I should add that obviously Mr Fay had doubts about the loan certificate signed by Mr O'Flanagan as on 22 November 1977 he wrote to the executors' solicitors pointing out that he may have been incorrect in stating the balance due to the deceased on 28 February 1977, because a "portion of this amount may be due to Mrs O'Flanagan."

After Mr O'Flanagan's death on 15 October 1977 the defendant moved quickly. On 18 October he called to his solicitor and to the company's auditor for the purpose of arranging that a meeting of the company be held. Mr Fay advised him that he could call a meeting of the directors and appoint a new director under regulation 103 of Table A. Mr Fay also advised him (wrongly as he now admits because regulation 5 of Table A does not apply to the company) that the directors could issue the balance of the share capital. A meeting of the directors was held on 25 October attended by Mr Pope and one Mary Burke the third named defendant in these proceedings. The minutes record that Miss Burke was appointed a director of the company and that it was resolved that twenty shares would be allotted to her and seventy-eight to Mr Pope. In addition as I have already pointed out, the directors resolved to pay Mr Pope the sum of £2,000 and it was noted that Mr Pope had agreed to assign 129 St Peter's Road to the company.

Under the provisions of the company's regulations the appointment of Miss Burke as a director of the company was a valid one. The meeting of directors had, however, no power to allot shares to her or to Mr Pope. It is as I have already pointed out significant that when seeking advice about the situation arising from the death of his co-director the defendant informed neither his solicitor nor his accountant of the existence of the secret agreement of 15 March 1976. Mr Fay cannot recollect when the envelope containing this secret agreement was deposited with him but it is perfectly clear that he was unaware of its contents for a considerable time after Mr O'Flanagan's death.

The solicitors for the executor of Mr O'Flanagan's will wrote on 12 October 1979 requesting that he be registered in succession to the deceased as holder of one share in the company. By a letter of 8 December they were informed that at a meeting held on 5 December the directors had decided not to approve the transfer. Thereafter these proceedings were issued. No reason was given as to why registration was refused. Under the company's regulations the executor was entitled to be registered and so it would appear that in refusing registration the defendant was relying on the written agreement of 15 March 1976. As this agreement was an invalid one I must hold that the company and the defendant wrongfully refused to register Mr Sean O'Flanagan as a member of the company.

Part IV

I come to the relief to which the plaintiffs are entitled.

(1) I will declare that the premises No. 139 St Peter's Road is now held by the company upon trust for the plaintiff Elizabeth O'Flanagan. I appreciate that this is not in accordance with the plea in the Statement of Claim but the defendants are not in any way prejudiced by this finding.

(2) I will declare that the company was in breach of trust by charging the premises No. 139 St Peter's Road, Walkinstown in favour of the United Dominions Trust, and is liable in damages for this breach.

(3) I will order that the company do convey the premises 139 St Peter's Road, Walkinstown to Mrs O'Flanagan free from incumbrances.

(4) I will declare that Mrs O'Flanagan is and has been entitled to the rent from 139 St Peter's Road and I will direct the defendant to inform the tenants to pay the rent to her.

(5) I will order that an account be taken of:

(a) all rent received by the company from the premises 139 St Peter's Road;
(b) all monies used by the company in repairs and improvements of a permanent and lasting nature and which enhance the value of the property;
(c) all acts which may have caused the value of the property to depreciate and the value of such depreciation;
(d) an account of any mortgages or charges made on the property.

(6) I will declare that the plaintiff Mr Sean O'Flanagan and the plaintiff Mrs Elizabeth O'Flanagan are entitled jointly to the net profits from the premises up to 15 October 1977 after giving the allowances for sums due on the taking of the account taken at paragraph 5(b) and thereafter that the plaintiff Mrs O'Flanagan is entitled to the nett profits from the premises.

(7) I will order payment of the nett profits to the persons entitled thereto after the taking of the accounts as aforesaid, and after giving credit for any rent received by the deceased in respect of the said property during his lifetime.

(8) I will grant an injunction restraining the defendants or any of them from disposing of any interest in 135A and 139 and 129 St Peter's Road, Walkinstown without the plaintiffs' consent.

(9) I will declare that the first named plaintiff is entitled to be registered as the owner of the share in the company owned by the deceased on 15 October 1977 and direct the defendants to effect such registration for them.

(10) I will declare that the purported allotment of shares at the meeting of 25 October 1976 is invalid and direct the defendants to effect the appropriate amendments in the company's books and records arising from such a declaration.

(11) The plaintiffs have claimed an order that the company be wound up under section 213(f) (on the grounds that it would be just and equitable to do so) or under section 213(g) (on the ground that the powers of the directors are being used oppressively) or alternatively under section 205 of the Act. But an application to wind up the company can only be brought by way of a petition (see section 215 of the 1963 Act) and I have no power in these present proceedings to make such an order. But it seems to me that once Mr O'Flanagan has been registered as a member of the company and once he wishes to obtain such an order that it would be just and equitable to wind up the company (see *In re Westbourne Galleries Ltd* [1973] AC 360) but I do not think it would be appropriate for me to make any declaration to that effect in these proceedings. I have not heard any submissions on the executors' rights to share in the profits of the company since the death of Mr O'Flanagan, but I will give liberty to apply in relation to this aspect of the case.

I will make no order at present in relation to any claims for breach of trust against the company or Mr Pope personally but I will give liberty to apply to the plaintiffs after the taking of accounts which I have ordered have been completed.

This is obviously a case in which the accounts should be taken as speedily as possible and to avoid any delay I propose to order that the defendant company and the defendant Mr Pope do discover on oath all documents in their power and procurement relevant to the accounts to taken, the affidavit to be made by the company to be sworn by Mr Pope. The affidavits to be sworn within 4 weeks should contain references to the company's minutes, books of accounts and records, contracts relating to the company's premises, and any documents relevant to the breach of trust which has been established.

Alistair Rutherdale
Barrister

Oliver Byrne v. Shelbourne Football Club Ltd: High Court 1982 No. 4274; **Oliver Byrne v. Shelbourne Football Club Ltd, Anthony Byrne, John Nolan, Frederick Strahan, Joseph Wilson and Reds Ltd:** High Court 1982 No. 9471P (O'Hanlon J) 8 February 1984

Company – Football Club – Financial advances by director – Money Claim – Whether loan to company – Whether properly vouched – Company – Transfer of assets to new company – Football Club – Company owing large debts – Plaintiff creditor of old company – New company to make only limited provision for debts of old company – Whether arrangement designed to defraud creditors – Obligation of company to do best it can for creditors – Whether obligation fulfilled

Facts: During the early 1980s Shelbourne Football Club was in a difficult financial position, with large accumulated losses and debts. The club accepted an offer from the plaintiff to provide finance until the end of the 1980-81 season.

The situation was no better at the start of the 1981-82 season. The directors, aware that the plaintiff did not have a bottomless purse, made approaches to two other businessmen, Mr Anthony Byrne, the second defendant, and Mr Michael Kelly, who it was felt might be interested in taking control of the club. At this stage control of most shares was in the hands of Gerard Doyle and Anthony Rowan, both of whom were also directors. The plaintiff had also been a director for a short period, but was at that stage banned from football for 5 years because of a confrontation with a referee.

However, a vague arrangement was made with the plaintiff whereby it was envisaged that once his suspension was lifted, Anthony Rowan and Gerard Doyle would transfer their shares to him, in return for money which he would put into the club. The suspension was lifted in May 1982 but by then the envisaged share deal had been overtaken by events.

As a result of the approaches made to them, Anthony Byrne and Michael Kelly expressed an interest in financing and taking control of the club and the directors agreed to transfer their shares to Anthony Byrne. They had second thoughts about the deal, but when proceedings were brought in July 1981 eventually agreed to register Anthony Byrne as share owner, in return for certain payments to Gerard Doyle and the plaintiff for monies advanced to the club in the season ending April 1981.

This settlement was not reached until July 1982, and because an injunction was in place maintaining the status quo, the financial crisis had re-emerged. The plaintiff claimed that he had stepped into the breach with further funding in this period. The arrangements in relation to this were very informal and there appeared to be no formal Board decision in relation to the loans. In respect of the 1981/82 season, the plaintiff claimed to have expended £21,929 for the benefit of the club, but was unable to vouch this sum properly.

In the first action the plaintiff claimed this sum of £21,929 as money lent to Shelbourne Football Club Ltd or as monies paid by him at the request of the club.

After obtaining control of the club, Anthony Byrne set about implementing a scheme to repair the fortunes of the club. Following the passing of a number of resolutions at an E.G.M., a board meeting agreed to dispose of the name and goodwill, and all other assets of the club (including league membership and tenancies of stadia) to a new company, Reds Ltd, which was also owned and controlled by Anthony Byrne. An offer of £10,000 from the plaintiff to buy the company was ignored.

Reds Ltd agreed to pay £500 and set aside a quarter of gate receipts of the 1982/83 season to discharge debts of the old company. At the time of the E.G.M. it was impossible to put an exact figure on the liabilities of the club. Substantial claims existed in respect of P.A.Y.E. arrears, directors' loans and audit and accounting expenses. Against this there were no assets other than the name of the football club.

In the second proceedings the plaintiff suing as a creditor of Shelbourne Football Club Ltd claimed that the defendants entered an arrangement to defraud its creditors, and sought an injunction to restrain the disposal of assets to Reds Ltd, and ancillary relief.

Held by O'Hanlon J in granting the plaintiff judgment for £10,000 in the first proceedings, and dismissing his claim in the second proceedings:

(1) The plaintiff did provide substantial help to the club during the 1981/82 season, and the monies thus paid by the plaintiff should be regarded as a loan to the club. The evidence was just sufficient to support his claim to repayment of these monies. Because of the vouching difficulties, a sum of £10,000 would be allowed.

(2) At the time of the E.G.M. the plaintiff was a creditor of the company. He had an expectation that if things improved he would have a claim for repayment.

(3) Before any limited company can dispose of its assets it must do the best it can for creditors and explore all reasonable possibilities of obtaining a better offer before selling out to a particular bidder. It was incumbent on the defendants

to satisfy the court that they had done this.

(4) On the evidence, the company was right to go ahead with the transfer to Reds Ltd. While the plaintiff had put large sums of money into the company he had run out of steam (in the financial sense) and there was some doubt as to whether he could have supported a bid of £10,000. In the circumstances the impugned agreement with Reds Ltd represented the best solution which could be achieved at the time for the club's financial problems.

(5) The reality was that there was no money for creditors or to finance a liquidation. In providing even a limited fund for past debts, the agreement was in the best interests of the club and its creditors.

(6) The agreement therefore was not intended to, and did not have the effect of hindering, delaying or defrauding creditors of Shelbourne Football Club Ltd.

No cases referred to in the judgment

Fergus Flood SC with Ciaran O'Loughlin BL instructed by *Paul F. Diamond & Co.* **for the plaintiff**
Gerard Lardner SC with James Salafia BL instructed by *Kevans* **for the defendant**

O'HANLON J **8 February 1984**

These two actions were heard together, and this judgment deals with both sets of proceedings. In the first action commenced by summary summons, the plaintiff claims a sum of £21,929 as money lent by him to Shelbourne Football Club Ltd between 31 July 1981, and 30 June 1982, or alternatively, as money paid by him for and at the request of the said defendant between the said dates. In the second action, commenced by plenary summons dated 10 September 1982, the plaintiff, suing in his capacity as creditor of Shelbourne Football Club Ltd., claims that the said defendant has entered into an arrangement to defraud its creditors, and he seeks an injunction to restrain the disposal of the assets of the said defendant in favour of Reds Ltd, the last-named defendant, and other ancillary relief.

The plaintiff and his family have been life-long supporters of Shelbourne Football Club, one of the oldest association football clubs in Ireland, or indeed, anywhere in the world, which has now been fielding soccer teams for the best part of a century, and in the process has built up a distinguished record of successes in senior football. For many years past, however, the club has been in the doldrums. They lost possession of a very fine football stadium at Ringsend, which was their traditional home, and have had to play at different pitches in the Dublin city area, with no fixity of tenure at any time. They have been waiting a long time for a successful run in the league or the cup, and, inevitably, their financial situation has waned in line with the decline in their fortune on the field of play. The club might by now have gone out of existence were it not for the dedicated support of the plaintiff and others like him, who rallied round when the going was hard and dipped into their own pockets to keep the team in professional football.

Matters came to a head in the last few years. At the beginning of the 1980-81 season the club was in dire straits. It had accumulated heavy losses over the previous ten years and owed debts to the revenue authorities and to other creditors which it was quite unable to meet. It had no longer a bank account, and hence, no overdraft facilities. It was propping up the league from a position at or near the bottom of the ladder, and when the gate money was insufficient to meet the wages of the players the deficiency had to be met by temporary loans from individual directors, and by other similar expedients.

During the course of that season, the plaintiff came to the rescue. He had a business of his own, and sold some property in the city which brought him a substantial, but undisclosed, figure from the proceeds of sale. He approached the directors, knowing full well the difficulties they had been facing from week to week, and volunteered to finance the club for the remainder of the season. This offer was gratefully accepted, and the crisis was over for the time being, although the club still finished in its accustomed position near the bottom of the league and had to apply for re-election at the end of the season.

With the approach of the new playing season, 1981/82, the perennial crisis loomed up again for the club. The plaintiff had not a bottomless purse, and the directors thought the time had come to look elsewhere for financial support. Approaches were made to two other businessmen who, it was felt, might be interested in taking over control of the club and putting up the necessary funds to keep it in football. One of these was the second-named defendant in the second set of proceedings — Anthony Byrne. The other was Mr Michael Kelly, who has not featured in the proceedings as a party or as a witness, but who played quite a significant part in the conflict which developed between the other contesting parties.

At this time the vast preponderance of the shares in the limited company which ran the football club were in the hands of two men — Gerard Doyle and Tony Rowan — they were also directors and the people who conducted most of the negotiations with the plaintiff and other possible sources of finance for the club. The plaintiff was, at one time, a director of Shelbourne for a short period, but during the period under review he was living under a cloud as far as the governing body of Irish association football was concerned. An excess of enthusiasm for the fortunes of the team had, apparently, led him, as a supporter, into a confrontation with a referee, with whose decisions he disagreed, and the League of Ireland took so serious a view of the incident that he was banned from football for a period of five years. This did not prevent him continuing his support of the club from the sidelines but it did create difficulties in giving him any share in the control of the club in return for the financial help which he was willing and able to provide.

In these circumstances, a rather vague arrangement was made which envisaged that when his suspension by the League of Ireland was lifted, Anthony Rowan and Gerard Doyle would transfer their shares to him, in return for money which he was to put in to the club to keep it financially viable. The suspension was eventually lifted by the disciplinary committee of the League of Ireland, in or about the month of May 1982, but by then the shares deal had been overtaken by other events, and the plaintiff was no longer pressing for the transfer to him of the majority shareholding in the company.

As a result of the approaches made to them, both Anthony Byrne and Michael Kelly had expressed an interest in taking over control of the club and financing it for the future. The first on the scene was Anthony Byrne and negotiations between him and the two controlling shareholders and directors reached the point where they executed transfers of their shares to him and handed over the transfer documents. Later, they had second thoughts about the deal, when they felt that Anthony Byrne was not living up to what they expected from his side of the transaction, and this resulted in court proceedings brought by him to enforce his rights under the agreement. That action was settled at the door of the court, on terms that he was to be duly registered as owner of the shares in question. The settlement also involved payment by him to Gerard Doyle of £3,000 which Mr Doyle had advanced to the club, and he was also required to pay an agreed balance due to the plaintiff in the present proceedings in respect of his (Oliver Byrne's) financial help to the club during the season, 1980/81. This claim was dealt with by a payment being made by Anthony Byrne to Oliver Byrne of £3,500 in settlement of any claim Oliver Byrne might have in respect of payments for the benefit of the club in the season which ended in April 1981.

That settlement was not concluded until the month of July 1982. Anthony Byrne's action to enforce his claim to the shares had commenced a year previously, and in July 1981, an interlocutory application was brought to prevent the shares being transferred to Michael Kelly (or anyone else) pending the hearing of this action. This application was successful. As the status quo had to be maintained for the time being, the club found itself plunged into a new crisis, with Anthony Byrne being excluded from control *pro tem*, the introduction of Michael Kelly being blocked, and no new source of finance being clearly visible. Once again the plaintiff stepped into the breach — or claims to have done so — although his claim in respect of this period is disputed by the defendants.

What happened, as a matter of history, is that the club continued to function during the 1981/82 season, although under considerable difficulties. The playing record of the team improved on the previous season, but there were no major successes. The gates continued to be small and were quite inadequate to meet the players' wages and other liabilities which arose from week to week. Some person or persons made up the deficiency, to the extent necessary for survival. The plaintiff claims to have volunteered to find the money and to have done so. Clearly his own resources were dwindling at this stage, and he says that he was dependant to a considerable extent on borrowings from Michael Kelly, from members of his family, and from friends generally.

No one else appears to have made any claims to have paid the wages and other outgoings during that playing season, although the evidence strongly suggests that the real source of finance was Michael Kelly, whether directly, or indirectly by means of loans made to the plaintiff.

I am prepared to accept that the plaintiff did provide fairly substantial financial help for the club during that playing season of 1981/82, although where the money came from is by no means clear. He admitted quite frankly that he was no longer in a position to draw cheques on his bank account in favour of the club at that time and that there was a substantial unsatisfied judgment against him by one of his business creditors which has never been discharged.

Secondly, I am prepared to regard the monies thus paid over by the plaintiff as a loan to the club, although all these financial transactions on his part were conducted with a degree of informality which was bound to cause major problems if he ever sought repayment. Meetings of the board of directors were few and far between, and appear to have been virtually suspended between the month of July 1981, and July 1982. Thus, one looks in vain for any formal decision of the board to seek for, or to accept, loans of money from the plaintiff to finance the activities of the club. The plaintiff has to rely on an implication of law arising from the general course of conduct adopted by the club, and I think the evidence of this character is just sufficient to support his claim to be entitled to repayment of whatever moneys he put into the club. Individual directors were putting up large sums of money around the same period — notably a payment of £3,000 by Gerard Doyle, and £2,000 by Joseph Wilson. In those cases, the payments were treated as loans, and have, in fact been repaid. From all the evidence, I am of opinion that there was a recognised practice in the club for directors and other loyal supporters to put up sums of money, required from time to time whenever a critical situation arose, and that there was a clear understanding that if the club unexpectedly found itself in funds at a later stage, these payments would rank as debts which it should meet.

It is much more difficult to determine what amount may legitimately be claimed by the plaintiff. In respect of the previous season he claimed to have paid out about £10,000 but when the settlement of that was being negotiated with Anthony Byrne in March 1981, the plaintiff obviously had great difficulty in producing documentary evidence by way of paid cheques or otherwise to back up a claim of this magnitude, and he eventually accepted a compromise figure of £3,500. In spite of his experience on that occasion, he has come forward again with a very badly-documented claim for the sum of £21,929 which he claims to have expended for the benefit of the club during the season 1981/82 and he has to pay the penalty for being unable to vouch his claim properly.

The plaintiff, in giving evidence in the case, produced a certain number of receipts for payments which had been made in the course of that year in discharge of liabilities of the club, but they do not assist his case to any great extent — first, because they do not indicate where the money came from to pay these charges, and secondly, because they represent in total only a fraction of the full amount claimed by him in these proceedings. He also produced a copy of a statement of account prepared by Brian Cranwell, a former director and secretary of the club, from information supplied to him by Gerard Doyle and the plaintiff concerning income and expenditure of the club for the relevant period in 1981/82. This statement of account gives a figure for total expenditure of £33,775.48; total income, £14,960.57; an excess of expenditure over income of £18,814.91. He also gives a figure for income of the club coming to the plaintiff, Oliver Byrne, of £6,184.40; expenditure by him during the same period of £22,125.18; an excess of expenditure over income attributable to him of £15,940.78.

I propose to allow the plaintiff's claim to the extent of £10,000 and there will be judgment in his favour for that amount against Shelbourne Club Ltd. He has been unable to substantiate a claim to any greater amount by the evidence given by him and on his behalf in the present case, and I have come to the conclusion that the figure I have mentioned represents the maximum which he can claim for advances in respect of the season 1981/82.

What happened after the settlement of Anthony Byrne's action to enforce his claim to the majority shareholding in the club may be stated briefly. Having secured effective control of the club, he proceeded to implement a scheme to repair the fortunes of the club which had been devised for him by John Nolan, who was a friend and adviser on company matters. An extraordinary general meeting of Shelbourne Football Club Ltd was convened on 3 September 1982, to consider a number of proposals — one of them being a resolution that the directors be authorised to sell and dispose of the assets of the company for the purpose of achieving a number of objectives. These included the perpetuation of the name of Shelbourne Football Club, and its continued survival as a football team, while also protecting the best interests of all proven creditors and members of the company.

Having secured the necessary support for such of the special resolutions put to the meeting as were acceptable to the majority shareholders, a board meeting was held, there and then, at which the directors agreed to dispose of the name and goodwill, and all other assets of the club to a new company, called Reds Ltd (the last-named defendant in the second set of proceedings), which was also owned and controlled by Anthony Byrne. As this is the agreement which the plaintiff challenges as being in fraud of the creditors of Shelbourne Football Club Ltd, it is desirable to summarise its terms, which are as follows:

(1) Shelbourne Football Club Ltd assigned to Reds Ltd., all its undertaking and assets, including goodwill, and the right to use the name "Shelbourne Football Club"; the right to membership of the Football Association of Ireland and playing membership of the League of Ireland; any licences or tenancy agreements held under Bord na gCon for the use of Harold's Cross stadium, and with Home Farm Football Club Ltd in respect of Tolka Park stadium.

(2) Shelbourne Football Club Ltd further agreed to change its name to "Ollays Investments Ltd" or such other as might be agreed with Reds Ltd, whereupon Reds Ltd, was to change its name to Shelbourne Football Club Ltd. The old company would then effectively go out of business and cease to have any active function in the world of football.

(3) Reds Ltd agreed to pay Shelbourne Football Club Ltd a lump sum of £500; to discharge four debts of the old company totalling £2,772.50

(including substantial arrears of rental due to Bord na gCon for the use of Harold's Cross stadium during the season 1981/82); and to appropriate one quarter of the net gate receipts of the club for the 1982/83 season to a fund for the benefit of Shelbourne Football Club Ltd and which would be available for the benefit of its creditors. That season has now come and gone, and I am informed that the net gate receipts were in the region of £10,000, and 25% of same, representing about £2,500 has been set aside to meet this liability of Reds Ltd, under the said agreement.

(4) Reds Ltd further convenanted (*inter alia*) "to carry on the business of owning, operating, administering and managing a football club under the name 'Shelbourne Football Club' and do its utmost to perpetuate the continual existence and promote the continual wellbeing of Shelbourne Football Club by the provision of sufficient finance, sponsorship and otherwise to achieve this object."

During the course of the extraordinary general meeting, when details of the proposed agreement with Reds Ltd were being given to those present, the plaintiff (who was there as a proxy-holder for Brian Cranwell) intervened to say that he would give £10,000 "for the club". He was ruled out of order and the meeting proceeded without further reference being made to this offer.

As to the extent of the club's liabilities at the time of that extraordinary general meeting, it is impossible to put an exact figure on them. All kinds of figures were tossed around during the course of the negotiations with Anthony Byrne, and with Michael Kelly, and again during the hearing of these proceedings. Over the past ten years no P.A.Y.E. payments have been made to the revenue and there is an unresolved claim for many thousands of pounds under this heading alone. Thousands more are owed under the heading of the "Directors' Loan Account"; to the company's auditors and to other creditors. The effect of the earlier part of the present judgment is to increase the total, whatever it may be, by a further sum of £10,000.

With regard to the assets of the company, it seems clear that these were to all intents and purposes non-existent, save only for one thing — the possibility that some individual with large sums of money to spare might like the excitement of controlling the destinies of a leading soccer club, and might be willing to pay money to buy his way into that situation. Leaving that possibility aside the club was in a disastrous state financially. It had no tangible assets; no pitch in which it had any security of tenure. It had no money in the bank and no means of obtaining further credit. It owed debts it could not pay to its auditors. It was bad news with hotel owners, with coach operators and with the owners of the football pitches it needed to use. The *coup de grace* could have been administered at any time in the previous few years by the Revenue Commissioners, had they forced on their claim for P.A.Y.E. payments.

At the close of the case for the plaintiff, an application was made by counsel for the defendants, asking me to dismiss the plaintiff's claims at that stage on the grounds that the evidence fell far short of establishing (a) that he was a creditor of the company, and (b) that the agreement between the company and Reds Ltd could be regarded as being calculated or intended to hinder, delay or defraud creditors of the company. I refused that application and I can now state the grounds which impelled me to do so. I took the view that there was a *prima facie* case that monies had been advanced by the plaintiff to the club in the 1981/82 season, in continuation of the practice he had adopted the previous season, and that in line with the informal way the club had always conducted its affairs, there was an expectation on his side which was also recognised by the club, that if things improved, and the ship came home, he would sooner or later have a claim for repayment. I still adhere to that view and it is the basis for the judgment already given in relation to the plaintiff's claim for money due.

Secondly, I took the view that before any limited company can dispose of all its assets, it must do the best it can for its creditors, and explore all reasonable possibilities of obtaining a better offer before selling out to a particular bidder. In the present case the only other potential bidders who had appeared over a period of one or two years were the plaintiff and Michael Kelly. Once the plaintiff intervened with an offer of £10,000 at the extraordinary general meeting, it appeared to me that it was incumbent on the defendants to satisfy the court that they had done all that they could reasonably be expected to do to test the market fully before concluding the proposed deal with Reds Ltd. Whether the plaintiff was entitled to be present at that extraordinary general meeting or not appears to me to be quite immaterial. Once it comes to the knowledge of the directors of a company that another and possibly higher bidder is in the background, they cannot ignore that situation, or they do so at their peril if they proceeded to rush through an agreement which they already have in contemplation, and which leaves the creditors unsatisfied at the end of the day.

Now that both sides have been fully heard, however, I have come round to the view that the company was right to go ahead with the proposed transfer to Reds Ltd on the terms which have already been referred to in the course of the present judgment. The possibility of anyone coming forward with the will and the ability to pour more money into the club and keep it in business for the coming seasons was a very remote one in 1980, in 1981, and again in 1982. The plaintiff did his best for the club in 1980/81 and again in 1981/82, but it was quite clear to everyone connected with the club that he was running out of steam (in the financial sense) when the 1981/82 season was about to commence, and he did not attempt to conceal this fact in the course of his evidence in the case. He was prepared to bow out gracefully in the face of possible take-over bids by Anthony Byrne and Michael Kelly and it is only a clash of personalities rather than the will or capacity to make a genuine bid for control of the club which has brought him back into the arena to challenge the actions of Anthony Byrne and John Nolan. There was evidence to suggest that the plaintiff's own mother, who was present at the extraordinary general meeting, expressed disbelief at the idea that he could support a bid of £10,000, and I am of opinon that in doing so she was expressing the firm belief of everyone who was present that the plaintiff was no longer in a position to face the continuing drain on his resources which would be involved in running the club. From the evidence I have heard from the plaintiff himself, as well as from the other witnesses, I think this belief was well-founded, and that the directors would have been acting very unwisely were they to call a halt to their plans for the reorganisation of the club at the start of the playing season and embark on an assessment of any alternative plan the plaintiff might wish to put forward.

Secondly, while Michael Kelly was clearly a potential bidder of more substance than the plaintiff, and a man whose financial and personal credentials were acceptable to what I will call the old guard in Shelbourne, he had disappeared from the picture a year before the extraordinary general meeting and had not at any time thereafter put forward any concrete proposals for acquiring the assets (such as they were) of the club. Having regard to the history of the club over the last ten years, and the extreme difficulty which was always experienced in finding someone to finance its activities, I have come to the conclusion that the impugned agreement with Reds Ltd represented the very best solution which could be achieved at the time for the club's financial problems. No one ever thought of putting the club into liquidation, because there was no money there even to meet the legal costs of liquidation proceedings. There has been nothing there for the creditors for years past and they have simply had to resign themselves to their fate. Nor was there any real prospect of anything materialising for them in the future had the club managed to survive another few seasons without a radical reorganisation. The agreement with Reds Ltd provided a limited, but not insignificant, fund for past debts, and gave an assurance that the club would commence to trade on a sound financial basis for the future.

I am fortified in my belief that the agreement of 3 September 1982, was in the best interests of the club and its creditors, by the reasonable success which has attended the efforts of the new board of directors of Reds Ltd since the agreement was concluded.

The club's tenure of the stadium at Harold's Cross, which can be regarded as its new home, for the time being at any rate, has been placed on a firm footing, and relations with Bord na gCon, who own the stadium seem to be quite amicable. The team has achieved its best results for years and gate receipts, as might be expected, have moved up in line with that success. It appears to me that the defendants, over the period which has intervened since the execution of the agreement of 3 September 1982, have carried into effect what they said they would do and that they should be supported and not hindered in their efforts to revitalise an old and famous football club.

For these reasons I have come to the conclusion that the agreement of 3 September 1982, was not intended to, nor did it have the effect, of hindering, delaying or defrauding creditors of Shelbourne Football Club Ltd, and I must dismiss the plaintiff's action bearing record number 1982 No. 9471P.

Alistair Rutherdale
Barrister

In the Matter of the Companies Acts, 1963-83, and in the Matter of Pye (Ireland) Ltd, on the Application of Thomas P. Hogan, Aidan P. Kelly, Joseph W. Little and Liam Dillon Digby: High Court 1984 No. 692Sp (Costello J) 12 November 1984

Company – Scheme of Arrangement – Meeting sanctioned by court – Scheme defeated by opposition of Collector General – Second scheme proposed offering some concessions to Collector General – Whether court should call further meetings of creditors and shareholders – Discretion – Particular position of Collector General – Companies Act 1963 (No. 33), section 201

Facts: Section 201(1) of the Companies Act, 1963 provides that:

> "Where a compromise or arrangement is proposed between a company and its creditors . . . or between the company and its members . . . , the court may . . . , order a meeting of the creditors or class of creditors, or of the members of the company or class of members, as the case may be, to be summoned in such manner as the court directs."

Section 201(3) provides that where three-fourths of the appropriate group or class vote in favour,

> "the compromise or arrangement shall, if sanctioned by the court, be binding on all the creditors or the class of creditors, or on the members or class of members, as the case may be. . . ."

The company, with the sanction of the High Court, called meetings of creditors and members in relation to a scheme of arrangement. The scheme proposed that the company cease as a radio and television manufacturer, and become a property management company, obtain planning permission for its lands and sell these off. These meetings were held but the scheme was opposed by the Collector General who was owed at least £522,000 in respect of VAT, PAYE, PRSI and customs duties, and, consequently, the necessary statutory majorities were not obtained.

Shortly afterwards the company proposed a second scheme of arrangement, which was substantially similar but included some concessions in favour of the Collector General. Counsel for the Collector General informed the court that he would oppose the second scheme should the court see fit to authorise the calling of the various meetings.

Held by Costello J in exercising his discretion by refusing the application:

(1) A second application under section 201, should not be entertained unless very exceptional circumstances arise, as to do so would be to allow the section to be used as a means of improving a bid, which had failed under the first scheme, in favour of dissenting creditors.

(2) There were no such exceptional circumstances in the instant case.

(3) The Collector General has a duty to decide how the public interest is best served, and he had decided that the public interest would not be served by postponing the State's debt. Where the Collector General had decided that the scheme was not in the public interest, a court should be slow to order meetings, in the face of his opposition.

No cases referred to in judgment

Brian McCracken SC instructed by *Noel Smyth & Partners* **for the applicants**
R.N. Cooke SC instructed by *The Revenue Solicitor* **for the Collector General**

COSTELLO J **12 November 1984**

This is an application pursuant to section 201 of the Companies Act 1963. The court has been requested to call meetings of the various classes of creditors and shareholders to consider a scheme of arrangement now to be presented to the meeting. This application is an unusual application in that it is the second application to the court to exercise its discretion within a short period of time under the section. Mr Cooke indicated that he was appearing on the application on behalf of the Collector General although he was not a notice party to the proceeding and not having been served with the summons. Mr Cooke on behalf of the Collector General, applied to be heard and I gave him liberty so to appear. The special summons in this case should in the particular circumstances have been served on the Collector General. Mr McCracken agreed that Mr Cooke could appear as if the special summons had been served on the Collector General and Mr McCracken had indicated that he was prepared to serve the Collector General with the summons. Mr McCracken indicated that the other creditors should be heard and this is fully appreciated by me but I am prepared to consider this application on the basis of the attitude of the other creditors remaining unchanged.

The court gave its sanction to the calling of meetings of creditors and members in relation to the previous scheme and those meetings were duly held and the scheme was opposed by the Collector General and consequently did not obtain the necessary statutory majority. Very shortly afterwards a second scheme of arrangement was proposed which is substantially the same as the previous scheme, but contains certain concessions in favour of the Collector General. The Collector General has not modified his position and his counsel has informed me that he will oppose this scheme should the court see fit to authorise the calling of the various meetings.

The matter before me is whether I should exercise my discretion under section 201. In my view the section as interpreted in normal circumstances is that a second application should not be entertained unless very exceptional circumstances arise, as to do so would be to allow the section to be used as a means of improving a bid, which had failed under the first scheme, in favour of dissenting creditors, and it would be undesirable if the section was to be so used.

The consequences of a defeat therefore should flow; I would depart from this view only in exceptional cases. I cannot find that exceptional circumstances exist in the present case and therefore I must decline to exercise my discretion in this case.

There is another reason which requires me to decline to exercise my discretion. The Collector-General is the principal objector to this scheme on the basis, as Mr Cooke points out, that what is proposed is that the company ceases to trade as a radio and television manufacturing company and will instead become a property development company managing its very valuable lands at Dundrum and obtaining planning permission for the lands and selling them off; that is the scheme. No doubt this might well turn out to be of considerable benefit to the creditors and the shareholders. However, the Collector-General is opposed to this proposal.

The court should not regard the Collector-General as just another creditor similar to other creditors; he is charged with the collection of monies due to the State. In this case I do not think that the Collector-General should be required to surrender for the benefit of other creditors contingently money owed to the public. The debt due to the State in respect of VAT, PRSI, PAYE. and Customs and Excise is at least £522,000. In those circumstances if the Collector General has decided that this scheme is not in the public interest, I should be very slow indeed to order these meetings given the opposition of the Collector General. I see no reason to order this scheme to proceed. He has the duty of deciding how the public interest is best served and he has considered the public interest and has decided that the public interest would not be served by postponing the State's debt. I must therefore refuse this application and will make no order as to costs.

Alistair Rutherdale
Barrister

[*Reporters Note* — On 22 November 1984 the Supreme Court (Henchy, Griffin and Hederman JJ allowed an appeal by the applicants and discharged the order of the High Court. The applicants undertook to pay the sum of £52,665 to the Collector General. The Supreme Court ordered that within eight weeks the applicants convene meetings of certain classes of members and creditors to consider and approve (with or without modification) the scheme of arrangement and composition. Classes referred to were (a) 5 per cent cumulative preference shareholders, (b) 7 per cent redeemable cumulative preference shareholders, (c) ordinary shareholders, (d) secured creditors, (e) preferential creditors, (f) unsecured trade and sundry creditors.]

In the Matter of the Companies Acts 1963-83 and In the Matter of Pye (Ireland) Ltd and In the Matter of the Petition of Thomas P. Hogan, Aidan P. Kelly, Joseph W. Little and Liam Dillon Digby: High Court 1985 No. 1452p (Costello J) 11 March 1985

Company – Scheme of arrangement and compromise – Meetings of classes of creditors – Persons to constitute each class – Shareholding and non-shareholding creditors – Duty of company to decide which groups should be treated as separate classes – Whether court should sanction scheme – Companies Act 1963 (No. 33), section 201

Facts: By order dated 30 July 1984, it was ordered, pursuant to section 201 of the Companies Act 1963, that Pye (Ireland) Ltd ("the company") should convene meetings of certain classes of creditors and members for the purpose of considering a scheme of arrangement and compromise. At the meetings held on 19 September the opposition of the Collector General (a preferential and unsecured creditor) meant that the statutory majorities required for the approval of the scheme were not obtained.

A second summons proposing meetings to discuss a new scheme of arrangement was then served on the Collector General. The High Court (Costello J) found his objections valid and declined to make the order sought. However the Supreme Court, following an undertaking by the applicants to pay a preferential debt to the Collector General of £52,665, made an order directing meetings of (a) secured, (b) preferential and (c) unsecured trade and sundry creditors.

The payment to the Collector General was made, and the three meetings proceeded, all endorsing the scheme by the statutory majority of 75 per cent. At the unsecured creditors meeting, however, the vote was close. There were 34 votes in favour (representing £1,313,921.40 or 77.73 per cent) and 1 vote against (the Collector General representing £377,435.82 or 22.32 per cent).

The applicants then petitioned the court for an order sanctioning the scheme under section 201(3).

On behalf of the Collector General it was submitted that the court should not sanction the scheme, not only in the exercise of its discretion, but also because of the failure of the company to hold meetings of different classes of unsecured creditors. It was argued that small trade creditors whom it was proposed to pay in full constituted a separate class. The court was also directed towards a proposal to pay in full a firm called Monkstown Consultants of which the chairman of the company was a director. Thirdly, it was argued that the statutory majority was only reached with the votes of Philips Electrical (Ireland) Ltd, an unsecured creditor which was also a substantial shareholder in the company.

On behalf of the applicants it was submitted that the different creditors' groups had been settled by the Supreme Court order.

Held by Costello J in refusing to sanction the scheme of arrangement:

(1) It was for the company to decide which groups should be treated as

separate classes. However, if the correct meetings are not held the court may not sanction the scheme. Unsecured creditors will normally form a single class except where some are to be treated differently and have different interests from the rest. Judgments of Templeman J in *In re Hellenic & General Trust Ltd* [1976] 1 WLR 123 and Bowen LJ in *Sovereign Life Assurance Co. v. Dodd* [1892] 2 QB 573 quoted with approval.

(2) The small trade creditors whom it was proposed to pay in full did form a distinctive class. However, the failure to hold a separate meeting for them was not a sufficient reason to refuse to sanction the scheme.

(3) Monkstown Consultants should have been placed in the class of small trade creditors whom it was proposed to pay in full. However the fact that the company chairman was a director of this company was not sufficient reason for treating it as a further separate class.

(4) A separate meeting should have been held comprising unsecured creditors who were also shareholders in the company, as they had very different interests from the general body of unsecured non-shareholding creditors.

(5) Whilst the Supreme Court order did refer to the meetings to be held, the points raised in this application had not been argued before the Supreme Court when hearing the section 201(1) summons nor adjudicated upon. As nothing in the nature of an estoppel arose, the court was free to consider the validity of the procedures adopted by the company.

Cases referred to in judgment

In re Hellenic & General Trust Ltd [1976] 1 WLR 123; [1975] 3 All ER 382
Sovereign Life Assurance Co. v. Dodd [1892] 2 QB 573
In re United Provident Assurance Co. Ltd [1910] 2 Ch 477; [1910] WN 199

Brian McCracken SC instructed by *Noel Smyth & Partners* **for the applicants**
R.N. Cooke SC instructed by *The Revenue Solicitor* **for the Collector General**

COSTELLO J **11 March 1985**

By order of 30 July 1984 it was ordered that Pye (Ireland) Ltd should convene meetings of certain specified classes of creditors and members for the purpose of considering a scheme of arrangement and compromise. The order was made pursuant to the provisions of section 201 of the Companies Act 1963. The meetings were held on 19 September but due to the opposition of the Collector General of Revenue who was both a preferential and unsecured creditor the statutory majorities required for approval were not obtained. A scheme of arrangement and compromise was devised and a second application was brought to this court under section 201(1) for an order summoning meetings of different classes of creditors and members for the purpose of considering the new scheme. The summons was served on the Collector General. I considered the objections raised on his behalf were valid and I declined to make the order sought. On appeal the Supreme Court on 22 November 1984, having been given an undertaking by the applicants to pay a preferential debt of £52,665 due to the Collector General, made an order that meetings of three different classes of shareholders be held and that meetings of three different classes of creditors be held, namely meetings of secured, preferential and "unsecured trade and sundry creditors" in the manner specified in the order. The preferential debt of the Collector General was paid, the meetings were duly held, and the scheme obtained the necessary majorities at each of the meetings. The meeting of the unsecured creditors was, however, a close run thing. The total valid poll was £1,690,266.20. The amount or value voting in favour was £1,313,920.40, or 77.73 per cent. The amount or value voting against was £377,345.82, or 22.32 per cent. The number of votes in favour (including proxies) was 34, whilst there was only one vote against. But this vote was that of the Collector General and his unsecured debt of £377,435.82 was nearly sufficient to defeat the scheme. The applicants have now petitioned the court under section 201(3) for an order sanctioning it.

Mr Cooke on behalf of the Collector General has submitted that, apart from any view he would urge that the court in the exercise of its discretion should not sanction the scheme, there are legal objections to the making of the order now being sought. These arise, it is urged, from the failure of the company to hold meetings of different classes of unsecured creditors. Both he and Mr McCracken (on behalf of the applicants) accepted as a correct statement of the law applicable on section 201 applications the views expressed in Palmer's *Company Law* (23rd ed., paragraph 79-10). The author points out that:

> "The Court does not itself consider at this point [i.e. when an application to convene meetings is brought] what classes of creditors or members should be made parties to scheme. This is for the company to decide. . . . If there are different groups within a class the interests of which are different from the rest of the class, or which are to be treated differently under the scheme, such groups must be treated as separate classes for the purpose of the scheme;"

and:

> "Great care must be taken in considering what for the purpose of the scheme constitutes a class. If meetings of the proper classes have not been held, the court may not sanction the scheme."

Indeed it would seem that a failure to hold proper class meetings will generally speaking be fatal to a section 201(3) petition. This was illustrated recently in England in *In re Hellenic & General Trust Ltd* [1976] 1 WLR 123, where Templeman J (at p. 125) stated:

> "Although section 206 provides that the court may order meetings, it is the responsibility of the petitioners to see that the class meetings are properly constituted, and if they fail then the necessary agreement is not obtained and the court has no jurisdiction to sanction the arrangement.

> Thus in *In re United Provident Assurance Co. Ltd* [1910] 2 Ch 477 the court held that the holders of partly paid shares formed a different class from the holders of fully paid shares. The objection was taken that there should have been separate meetings of the two classes, and Swinfen Eady J upheld the objection, saying, at p. 481: "... the objection that there has not been proper class meetings is fatal, and I cannot sanction the scheme".
>
> Similarly Eve J issued a practice direction, Practice Note [1934] W.N. 142, in which he reminded the profession, in dealing with the predecessor of section 206, that the responsibility for determining what creditors are to be summoned to any meeting as constituting a class rests with the petitioner, and if the meetings are incorrectly convened or constituted, or an objection is taken to the presence of any particular creditors as having interests competing with the others, the objection must be taken on the hearing of the petition for sanction and the petitioner must take the risk of having the petition dismissed."

Palmer, like other text book writers, quotes Bowen LJ in *Sovereign Life Assurance Co. v. Dodd* [1892] 2 QB 573, at 583:

> "It seems plain that we must give such a meaning to the term 'class' as will prevent the section being so worked as to result in confiscation and injustice, and that it must be confined to those persons whose rights are not so dissimilar as to make it impossible for them to consult together with a view to their common interest."

And as the author points out (paragraph 79-11) all unsecured creditors will normally form a single class:

> "except where some of them are to be treated in a manner different from the rest and have different interests which might conflict. In such a case fresh classes will be carved out".

Three points are made about the classifications made by the applicants herein:

(i) Attention is drawn to the fact that the scheme provides that a number of unsecured creditors are to be paid their claims in full. (see paragraph B (iii)). These are creditors with claims under £25,000 and are mainly small trade creditors. The total of their claim is £132,554.00, and it is urged that these form a distinctive class from the other unsecured creditors. I agree. The paragraph B (iii) creditors are getting very special treatment under the scheme. As they are to be paid in full within one month of its sanction it is impossible to see how they would vote against it and obviously their interests are different to the less favoured body of unsecured creditors amongst whom is the Collector General. If the scheme is successful the Revenue debt is to be partially paid over a three year period and part of it (the interest component) is not provided for in the scheme at all. But I do not think that is a justification for refusal of sanction as I am not satisfied that if a separate class for the favoured creditors had been created that this would have meant that the scheme would have been defeated. The report of the meeting of the unsecured creditors shows that only 36 votes (including proxy votes) were cast at the poll and it seems that the paragraph B (iii) unsecured creditors did not tip the balance (admittedly a fine one) to create the requisite majority.

(ii) Secondly, it is pointed out that the explanatory memorandum circulated with the scheme on the direction of the Supreme Court reveals that the chairman of the company (and one of the present applicants) is a director of a firm called "Monkstown Consultants", an unsecured creditor for £12,600 whose debt is to be paid in full. The report of the meeting of unsecured creditors discloses that this firm voted by proxy in favour of the scheme. For reasons just given at (i) I agree that this firm should have been in a separate class with other favoured creditors but I do not think the fact the company chairman is also a director of this company is an added reason for creating a further class. In my view this company's special relationship to Pye (Ireland) Ltd is not a reason for refusing sanction.

(iii) Thirdly, attention is drawn to a reference in the Explanatory Memorandum to an unsecured creditor, Philips Electrical (Ireland) Ltd, which is also a substantial shareholder in the company. This company owns 229,425 ordinary 25p shares in Pye (Ireland) Ltd, a significant and substantial proportion of the entire issued ordinary capital of the company. It is owed as an unsecured creditor a sum of £379,000 (excluding interest) and it voted at the meeting by proxy in support of the scheme. Without its vote the statutory majority would not have been obtained. There is no doubt that if the scheme is successful that the prospect for the ordinary shareholders is very much better than in a liquidation (which is the alternative if the scheme is not adopted) in which it would appear the ordinary shareholders are likely to do very badly. So it seems to me that the interests of a substantial unsecured creditor who is also a substantial shareholder are very different to those of the general body of unsecured non-shareholding creditors and that there is in reality no common interest between them — the creditor/shareholder is almost certain to support the scheme, whilst the ordinary unsecured shareholder may have (as happened in the case of the Collector General) what is considered as valid reasons for opposing it. I think therefore that there should have been a separate class created comprising unsecured creditors who are also shareholders in the company.

It was pointed out by Mr McCracken on behalf of the applicants that the different meetings were held in this case pursuant to order of the Supreme Court. That is true, but it has not been suggested that the point I am now considering was raised at the hearing of the section 201(1) summons and adjudicated upon. Normally a section 201(1) summons would not be served on anyone and objectors to the scheme would not have any opportunity to raise a point like this until the hearing of a section 201(3) petition. In this case the Collector General was served with the summons and was represented at the hearings. But it is by no means clear that at that time the information which was contained in the explanatory memorandum (and on which the present objection is based) was known to him. And even if it was and the point now taken somehow overlooked, this is not a reason for granting sanction if the objection is a valid one. If the applicants are not in any way misled and if nothing in the nature of an estoppel arises it seems to me that on the present petition the court should carefully consider the validity of the procedures which have been adopted. In this case had the proper classes been constituted the views of a major creditor (the Revenue) would not have been defeated. In all the circumstances, then, I think I should exercise my discretion by refusing sanction under the section. Even had I jurisdiction to do so, the summoning of fresh meetings of the correct classes of unsecured creditors would be an otiose exercise.

Alistair Rutherdale
Barrister

[*Reporters Note:* The petitioners appealed to the Supreme Court. On 17 April 1985 the Supreme Court (Henchy, Griffin and Hederman JJ) allowed the appeal and discharged the order of the High Court. In lieu thereof they ordered that the scheme of arrangement agreed to between the shareholders and the creditors be sanctioned, and declared that it be binding on the shareholders and the creditors.]

Robert Dempsey v. Bank of Ireland: Supreme Court 1983 No. 353 Sp (Henchy, Hederman and McCarthy JJ) 6 December 1985

Travel agents – Requirement to be bonded – Guarantee executed by bank – Bank contractually entitled to debit sums paid on foot of guarantee from accounts of company with the bank – Liquidation – Bank called upon to pay such sums prior to the date of the winding up – Passing of resolution to wind up – Relevant date – Sums not actually paid until after relevant date – Whether bank entitled to debit sums from company's accounts – Assets of company vested in liquidator – Liquidator only acquires such title as the company had – Equity – Pre-liquidation contract made in good faith – Whether liquidator entitled to approbate and reprobate contractual arrangement

Facts: Eurotravel Ltd carried on the business of travel agents and was a member of the Irish Travel Agents Association. Due to the risky nature of the business, the association required its members to have an enforceable guarantee by a financial institution so that in the event of the insolvency of the firm the guarantor would pay a specified sum of money to the trustee of the association who would use the money for the relief of customers of the firm. In pursuance of this, Eurotravel executed two documents with the Bank of Ireland on 31

December 1982. The first was an agreement between Eurotravel, the trustees of the association and the bank to the effect that Eurotravel would pay £75,000 to the trustees of the association during the period of the agreement if *inter alia* it became unable to pay its debts and was thereby unable to fulfil its obligations to its customers. The agreement was expressed to be effective until 31 March 1983 and the bank guaranteed the said sum. Under the second document, in consideration for the said guarantee, Eurotravel agreed to indemnify the bank against its liabilities under the guarantee. The bank was authorised to pay any monies demanded immediately without requiring proof that the amounts demanded were due and Eurotravel agreed that the bank could debit any account in its name with any such sums payable under the guarantee. On 29 March 1983, before the period of the guarantee ran out, the solicitors for the trustees of the Association wrote to the bank claiming payment of £75,000 under the guarantee as Eurotravel was then unable to pay its debts. The sum was not paid until 19 April 1983. However on 11 April, a special resolution was passed pursuant to section 141 of the Companies Act 1963 putting the company into voluntary liquidation and a liquidator was appointed. The liquidator instituted proceedings seeking a declaration from the court as to whether the bank was entitled to debit against Eurotravel's accounts in the bank the sum of £75,000 paid on foot of the guarantee. In the High Court it was held that the bank was not entitled to do so and the bank appealed.

Held by the Supreme Court (Henchy and McCarthy JJ, Hederman J concurring) in allowing the appeal:

(1) The bank was not seeking to prove its debt in a winding-up: it wished to stand apart from the winding up and enforce its contractual right to recover its debt by debiting it against the company's accounts in the bank and as such it was irrelevant that the bank had not actually paid the monies due under the guarantee before the resolution to wind up was passed.

(2) The relevant date was the date of the winding up which commenced when the resolution to wind up was duly passed and at that date the bank had been called upon to pay the monies and was contractually bound to do so: *Re Fenton* [1931] 1 Ch 85 and *Re A Debtor* [1956] 3 All ER 225 distinguished;

(3) When a liquidator is appointed, the assets of the company vest in him, but he acquires only such title to the assets as the company had. Therefore the monies standing to the accounts of the company became vested in him subject to the right over these accounts that had been created in favour of the bank by the documents of 31 December 1982.

(4) Although the right of the bank was originally a contingent one, when the trustees called upon the bank to pay the said sum they became forthwith bound to make such payment and Eurotravel's accounts became actually, rather than contingently, subject to the bank's right to debit.

(5) Equity required that the guarantee, being a pre-liquidation contract made in good faith and partly performed when the liquidation began, should be honoured in full, and the liquidator is not entitled to approbate and reprobate.

Cases referred to in judgment
Re A Debtor [1956] 3 All ER 225
Re Fenton [1931] 1 Ch 85

Counsel's and solicitors' names not available

HENCHY J (Hederman J concurring) **6 December 1985**

Eurotravel Ltd ("Eurotravel") was a company which carried on the business of travel agents. As its name would suggest, it arranged holidays abroad for its customers. It is apparently a risky business, for a number of such companies have collapsed in recent years. When that happens, there is a danger that financial loss and inconvenience will be suffered by customers of the company, through not being able to get the holidays they have paid for, or through finding themselves stranded at a holiday resort abroad. In an effort to alleviate or avoid such misfortunes, the Irish Travel Agents Association ("the association") requires that its member firms shall be bonded, that is to say, have an enforceable guarantee by a financial institution that in the event of the insolvency of the firm the guarantor will pay a specified sum of money to the trustees of the association, who will use the money for the relief of the customers of the firm.

Eurotravel was a member of the association and accordingly had to be bonded. It arranged to get the necessary guarantee from the Bank of Ireland ("the bank"), who were its bankers. The guarantee was effected by means of two documents which were executed on 31 December 1982. The first was an agreement between Eurotravel, the trustees of the association, and the bank, and was expressed to be effective until 31 March 1983. It provided that Eurotravel would pay £75,000 to the trustees if during the period of the agreement it became (amongst other eventualities) unable to pay its debts and thereby unable to fulfil its obligations to its customers. The bank guaranteed the payment of that sum. The agreement provided that the money payable to the trustees under the guarantee would be used by them for the relief of Eurotravel's customers — for example, in repatriating holiday-makers stranded abroad and in repaying money paid by customers for holidays not yet provided.

The second document was one executed by Eurotravel only and it was addressed to the bank. It provided that, in consideration of the bank joining in the first document as guarantor, Eurotravel would indemnify the bank against its liabilities under the guarantee; the bank was authorised to pay immediately any monies demanded under the guarantee, without requiring proof that the amounts demanded were due; and Eurotravel agreed that the bank could debit any account in its name with any sums payable by the bank under the guarantee.

As far as the bank was concerned, the joint effect of the two documents (validity of which has not been seriously questioned) was clear: if within the three-monthly payments due on 31 March 1983 the trustees of the association called on it to pay £75,000 it would be bound to do so, but it could recover the amount paid by debiting Eurotravel's accounts with the amount of the payment.

Before the period of the guarantee ran out, solicitors acting for the association wrote to the bank on 29 March 1983 claiming payment of £75,000 under the guarantee. Eurotravel was by then unable to pay its debts and could not fulfil its obligations to its customers. The bank was therefore liable under the guarantee, so on the 19 April 1983 it paid £75,000 to the trustees.

Meanwhile, Eurotravel's trading activities had gone from bad to worse. By 11 April 1983 it had ceased trading and it was found that its debts far exceeded its assets, so, as a result of a special resolution pursuant to section 141 of the Companies Act 1963, passed on that date, it was put into voluntary liquidation and the plaintiff was appointed liquidator.

The present proceedings have been brought by the plaintiff as liquidator seeking a ruling by the court as to whether the bank is entitled to debit against Eurotravel's accounts in the bank the sum of £75,000 paid on foot of the guarantee. In the High Court it was held that the bank is not entitled to do so. The bank now appeals against that decision.

Counsel on both sides relied on a number of decided cases, but I do not find those cases particularly helpful, as they mainly deal with the right of a creditor to prove his debt, by set-off or otherwise, in a winding up or in a bankruptcy. As I understand the bank's case, however, what is claimed is not a right to prove the £75,000 as a debt in the winding up, but an entitlement to enforce its contractual right to appropriate that sum by way of debit, notwithstanding the winding up.

Counsel for the liquidator relied mainly on two cases: *Re Fenton* [1931] 1 Ch 85 and *Re A Debtor* [1956] 3 All ER 225, but in my view neither case covers the situation in this case.

In *Re Fenton* the question was whether a bankrupt who had guaranteed a company's overdraft, but had not been called on to pay anything on foot of the guarantee, could prove in the winding up of the company the amount of the overdraft by way of set-off against a debt owed by him to the company. It was held that he could not, because at the relevant date there was no debt (only a contingent liability for a debt) owing by the company to the bankrupt which could be set-off against his debt to the company.

The present case is radically different from that. In this case the bank does not seek to prove its debt in the winding up. It wishes to stand apart from the winding up and to recover its debt by debiting it against Eurotravel's accounts in the bank. Apart from a point about double proof of the same debt (which does not arise in the present case), the reason why the claim in *Re Fenton* to exercise a right of set-off was disallowed was because on the relevant date the bankrupt had not paid or been called on to pay any money under the guarantee, so on that date there was no debt owed by the company to him which could be set-off. The present case is different in that by the relevant date the bank had been called on to pay £75,000 under the guarantee, and under the contractual arrangement the bank was then bound to make that payment. I do not think *Re Fenton* is (as seems to have been held in the High Court) authority for the proposition that it is fatal to the bank's case that it had not paid the £75,000 by the relevant date. The question of (actual payment) would be material only if the bank were seeking (to prove) its debt in the winding up. It is not. It is standing on what it says is its contractual right to recover that debt by debting it against Eurotravel's accounts.

Re A Debtor, which was also relied on by counsel for the liquidator, was to the same effect as *Re Fenton*. The question there was whether a guarantor of a bankrupt's debt could prove in the bankruptcy, by way of set-off, what he alleged was a debt under the guarantee, which debt he had not paid on the relevant date, but had paid later. It was held, following *Re Fenton*, that the set-off claimed could not be allowed because, as the guarantor had not paid anything under the guarantee on the relevant date, there was no debt capable of being set-off on that date; and the payment later could not be held to relate back to the relevant date. It will be seen, therefore, that since (as was the case in *Re Fenton*) the claim was to prove a debt by way of set-off, the case was essentially different from the present one, where the claim is not to prove a debt in the winding-up but to recover it by means of a direct debit pursuant to a contractual arrangement.

I understand counsel for the liquidator and counsel for the bank to agree that none of the reported cases covers the situation in this case. It would seem, therefore, that the matter on which the liquidator seeks a ruling falls to be decided by the application of first principles.

In the case of a voluntary winding up of a company (such as this is), the winding up commences when the resolution for the winding up is duly passed (section 253 of the Companies Act 1963). That is the relevant date. The company then ceases to carry on business except so far as is necessary for the winding up. The liquidator then takes over. The assets of the company pass to him. His primary function is to cause the assets to be collected, converted (where necessary) by sale into cash, and applied in discharge of the company's liabilities according to prescribed rules and priorities. For that purpose the creditors of the company must prove their debts. Where, as is the case here, the winding up is that of an insolvent company, the bankruptcy law applies to debts provable (section 284, Companies Act 1963). This means that the liquidator approaches his task in the same way as the official assignee would deal with the administration of the estate of a person bankrupt.

To say that when the liquidator takes over, the assets of the company vest in him is a less than complete statement of the legal position. The general rule is that he acquires only such title to the assets as the company had — no more, or less. He cannot take any better title to any part of the assets that the company had. This means that he takes the assets subject to any pre-existing enforceable right of a third party in or over them. If that were not so, equities, liabilities and contractual rights validly and enforceably created while the assets were in the hands of the company would be unfairly swept aside and an unjust distribution of the assets would result.

The relevant bankruptcy law (which is the law applicable in a winding up such as this) is succinctly stated as follows in Halsbury's *Laws of England*, vol. 3, para. 594:

> "The general rule is that the trustee in bankruptcy takes no better title to property than the bankrupt himself had. The bankrupt's property passes to the trustee in the same plight and condition in which it was in the bankrupt's hands, and is subject to all the equities and liabilities which enforced it in the bankrupt's hands, to all dispositions which have been validly made by the bankrupt, and to all rights which have been validly acquired by third persons at the commencement of the bankruptcy".

When, on the passing of the winding-up resolution in this case on 11 April 1983, the monies standing to the credit of Eurotravel in its current and deposit accounts in the bank on that date became vested in the liquidator, they became so vested subject to the right over those accounts that had been created in favour of the bank by the documents of 31 December 1982. That right was originally a contingent one and it was to the effect that if the bank was called on before 31 March 1983 by the trustees to pay £75,000, while it would be bound to do so, it could reimburse itself by debiting Eurotravel's accounts in that sum. But when the trustees called on the Bank to pay them £75,000 on 29 March 1983 and the bank became forthwith bound to make that payment, Eurotravel's accounts in the bank became actually rather than contingently subject to the bank's right to debit. It was in that state of contractual liability that those accounts passed to the liquidator on 11 April 1983. Immediately before the liquidator took over on that date, the bank was entitled to say that it was bound to pay the £75,000 and entitled to recover it forthwith by debiting it against Eurotravel's accounts. If it had actually done so, I do not think the debit could have been questioned by the liquidator, for it would have been done under the terms of a guarantee which was entered into in good faith and which in no way offended the statutory provisions applicable in the winding-up.

The fact that the bank did not pay the £75,000 or exercise its rights to debit until after the winding-up had commenced seems to me to be irrelevant for present purposes. What matters is that Eurotravel's bank accounts passed to the liquidator subject to the bank's enforceable right to pay the £75,000 and to debit that sum against those accounts. The intervention of the winding up did not override or pre-empt the bank's ability to give effect to that right, any more than it would effect an enforceable lien or charge on those accounts existing on the relevant date. It follows that the bank's accrued right to debit took precedence over the liquidator's title to the accounts.

This conclusion, it seems to me, may be said to be borne out on another ground. The applicable laws of bankruptcy governing the proof of debts in a winding up are designed to ensure a just and equitable distribution of the assets in accordance with the debts duly proved. Such would not be the result if the bank's claim to the right to debit were to be disallowed. By 29 March 1983 Eurotravel owed the trustees of the association £75,000 under a document of guarantee, and under the same document the bank had become liable to pay that debt to the trustees. On 19 April 1983 (which was after the liquidation had commenced on 11 April 1983) the bank paid that sum to the trustees and it was presumably applied in full in discharge of Eurotravel's liability to customers affected by its collapse. If the liquidator were now to be allowed to maintain successfully that the bank could not exercise its contractual right to debit, the result would be plainly unfair, for Eurotravel would have got the benefit of the £75,000 paid by the bank, which was a benefit it was never intended to have except on condition that the bank could exercise its reciprocal right to debit. Because of that condition, the liquidator is not entitled to maintain (as in effect he seems to do) that Eurotravel should have the benefit of the bank's compliance with its duty to pay under the guarantee and at the same time to reject the bank's right to debit, which was the consideration for the grant of guarantee by the bank. He cannot approbate and reprobate in that way. Equity requires that the guarantee, being a pre-liquidation contract made in good faith and partly performed when the liquidation began, should be honoured in full.

I would hold that the bank is entitled to appropriate by way of debit £75,000 out of the monies in Eurotravel's bank accounts. I would allow the appeal accordingly.

McCARTHY J

I have read the judgment of Henchy J and I agree with the order he proposes. Were it not that we are disagreeing with the conclusion following the careful judgment of the learned trial judge, I would be content merely to state my agreement.

At p. 12, the learned trial judge says:

> "In my view that decision [*In re Morris: Coneys and Morris* [1922] 1 IR 136] fully supports the approach adopted by the Bank in the present case, that is to say, the assertion made on behalf of the Bank that they are not claiming a lien (or indeed a charge of any form) but merely the ordinary traditional right granted by law (subject to any special contract between the parties and any special factors affecting the accounts) to set-off what is due by the client to the Bank against any sum which may be due by the Bank to its client. This particular right of set-off is sometimes described as the right to combine accounts or as in the Irish case aforesaid the right to adjust accounts".

Whilst the bank claims a right granted by law to set-off, it appears to me not merely to claim but to have established a special right of set-off contained in the second document of 31 March 1983. As the learned judge pointed out, the principal authority cited — *In re Fenton* [1931] 1 Ch 85 was relied upon by both parties. I share the view of Henchy J that neither *Fenton's* case nor *Re a Debtor* [1956] 3 All ER 225 are directly in point. I note that in *Fenton's* case Lord Hanworth MR (109) said:

> "The words of the section (section 31 of the Bankruptcy Act, 1914) seem clearly to connote an account capable of ascertainment on either side if

> not immediately, yet based upon authority or liability definitely undertaken. I find it difficult to construe those words or adapt that system to dealings in which there was a debt on one side due to the other, and per *contra* there was not a debt or a certain liability, but one in respect of which there was a right of protection, and no more; a liability which could not be turned into a direct *contra* money claim, unless and until the debit had been paid by the surety, who then, and not till then, would become entitled to give a discharge for the sum paid to him. This he had not done at the date of the liquidation when his rights became determined."

In the instant case, there was a liability definitely undertaken; there was a liability to pay once demand was made in the circumstances that had arisen and were contemplated by the guarantee. The fact that the bank delayed payment until 18 April did not alter the situation that the bank was liable to pay as of the date of receipt of notification from the solicitors acting for the trustees of the Irish Travel Agents Association, whose letter was dated 29 March 1983. If damage had flowed from the failure to pay during the interval, such damage would have been to the association and not otherwise. If, having received the demand, the bank had issued proceedings claiming a declaration of entitlement to set-off and succeeded in having such proceedings heard before what is called the critical date, 11 April, would such a declaration be defeated by the company going into voluntary liquidation? I do not think so. In my view, the reliance on *Fenton's* case was misplaced because the bank is not seeking to prove its debt in the liquidation, but asserting its contractual right.

I would allow the appeal and give the following directions as to the matters raised in the special endorsement of claim:

> "5. The Governor and Company of the Bank of Ireland are entitled to set-off the sum of £75,000 paid by them to the trustees of the Irish Travel Agents Association on 19 April 1983 against monies held by them on any account in the name of the Company."

Patricia McLaughlin
Barrister

Irish Microforms Ltd v. Sean Browne and Anne Clune: High Court 1980 No. 10121P (Murphy J) 3 April 1987

Contract – Defendant a director and in de facto *control of the plaintiff company – Also a director and substantial shareholder of a company which competed directly with the plaintiff – Both businesses run from the plaintiff company's premises – Staff employed worked for both companies – Whether plaintiff knew of the defendant's involvement with the second company – Whether defendant guilty of fraudulent misrepresentation in relation to contracts secured for second company – Conflict of interest – Whether defendant in breach of his fiduciary duty as director of the plaintiff company – Whether defendant misappropriated funds from the plaintiff company – Whether benefit and burden of contract which the defendant had negotiated on behalf of the second company was assigned to the plaintiff company*

Facts: The defendant was a director and in *de facto* control of the plaintiff company. He was also a director and substantial shareholder of a company known as Ellerton Ltd, which traded as Academy Press, and which competed directly with the plaintiff. Both businesses were run from the premises of the plaintiff company and shared staff. The defendant in his evidence stated that staff costs were apportioned between the two enterprises by reference to the amount of work done by them for each business. The defendant did not try to conceal his involvement with Academy Press and it apparently appeared on the agenda at a meeting of the board of the plaintiff company. The plaintiff's cheque payments ledger disclosed numerous payments to Academy Press which were explained by the defendant as representing for the greater part repayments by the plaintiff to Academy Press for monies borrowed by the former from the latter when the defendant's co-directors were not available to countersign cheques on the plaintiff's bank account. The plaintiff made a number of allegations against the defendant. Firstly, the plaintiff submitted that it had suffered loss due to a failure by the defendant to provide certain documentation, including accounts, thereby preventing the plaintiff's auditors from carrying out a proper audit, which they said caused the plaintiff company loss and damage. Secondly, the plaintiff submitted that the defendant had charged invoices to the plaintiff company which did not appertain to the trading activities of the plaintiff. Amongst these, the plaintiff claimed that sums in excess of £4,500 were invoiced to the plaintiff which were attributable to "The Digest of Irish Affairs". In June 1987 RTE entered into a contract with Ellerton Ltd, negotiated by the defendant whilst he was in the full-time employment of the plaintiff, under which the latter undertook to microfilm this current affairs index. The defendant submitted that the benefit and burden of this contract had been assigned to the plaintiff company, although the evidence was that such a proposal had never been put to the board of the plaintiff. The plaintiff further submitted that the defendant had engaged in business in competition with it without the knowledge of the board. Finally, the plaintiff claimed that the defendant had fraudulently warranted to an American company known as Clear Water Publishing Company, New York, that he and Academy Press were interested in the plaintiff company, thus seeking to deprive the plaintiff of the business of that company. These allegations arose out of a letter written by the defendant to the American company on the plaintiff's notepaper wherein he represented that "corporate changes" were pending and that the projects discussed between the defendant and the American company would go ahead under a different corporate name *i.e.*, Academy Press.

Held by Murphy J:

(1) A misunderstanding on behalf of the plaintiff clearly arose by the failure to distinguish between loss and damage occasioned by the absence of proper documentation either authorising or recording a transaction and the loss which might be caused by the transaction itself. In the former case there is no justification for calling upon the officer to pay to the company the full amount of the payment which he neglected to record.

(2) As no evidence was tendered of any loss suffered by the company as a result of the delay in producing the accounts, the first part of the plaintiff's claim failed.

(3) It was clear on the evidence that the defendant carried on the business of publishers trading as Academy Press with the knowledge of the plaintiff company. Although this company was in direct competition with the plaintiff company, the assumption that this formed part of a fraudulent conspiracy was rebutted by the fact that no effort was made by the defendant to conceal such involvement.

(4) In relation to the letter from the defendant to the American company, it was clear that even if the defendant were not guilty of a fraudulent misrepresentation, he certainly acted in breach of his fiduciary duty as a director of the plaintiff company. There was no evidence of any other attempts by the defendant to appropriate any other part of the business or goodwill of the plaintiff company.

(5) Ellerton Ltd did not at any time assign the benefit or burden of the contract which they had entered into with RTE to the plaintiff company. The defendant, as a director of the plaintiff company, was in a fiduciary position in relation to it and there was an obvious conflict of interest between the duty that he owed to Ellerton Ltd and that which he owed to the plaintiff company. It would not have been possible for the defendant as *de facto* executive of the plaintiff company to acquire the contract for the benefit of the plaintiff without the board approving the acquisition in the knowledge that the supplier was a company in which the defendant was a substantial shareholder.

(6) The burden and benefit of the contract remained with Ellerton and all costs, expenses and payments made by the plaintiff company at the behest of the defendant in connection with the contract or to persons engaged in editing or promoting the index were incorrectly debited to the plaintiff and must be

borne by the defendant or Ellerton Ltd.

(7) The matter should be referred to the examiner of the High Court to take account of the monies so misapplied unless some agreement can be reached between the parties.

No cases referred to in judgment

Counsel's and solicitors' names not available

MURPHY J **3 April 1987**

In July last this action was heard as against the first named defendant alone. Due to the indisposition of the second named defendant the trial as against her was adjourned. When the matter was re-entered last November the court was informed that all differences between the plaintiffs and the second named defendant had been resolved. Regretfully I must accept responsibility for the delay which has occurred since then.

The association between the plaintiffs and Mr Browne goes back for approximately 12 years. From the incorporation of the plaintiff company on 8 January 1974 and for six years thereafter Mr Browne was involved with the plaintiff company as a director, shareholder and employee. In the next six year period commencing with the institution of these proceedings on 12 November 1980 much of the time of both parties has been taken up in interlocutory applications relating to these proceedings. The background to the commercial relationship between the parties was as follows. For some time prior to 1975 a company known as Irish University Press Ltd was engaged in the publication of a variety of academic material. The procedure was that that company identified valuable historical material and procured the right to publish it. The company employed the appropriate staff to edit the material to the point where it could be reproduced by a variety of means, one of which was a photographic procedure. In connection with photographic reproduction IUP availed of the services of a company known as Memo Ltd. That company was controlled by Mr G.E. Ryan and his two brothers D.J. Ryan and G.J. Ryan and a fourth member Mr J.A. Martin. They were the directors of that company and between them owned the entire issued share-capital thereof. Memo Ltd carried on business from its premises at Sandymount Road, Dublin.

Sometime in 1974 or 1975 IUP got into serious financial difficulties and a receiver was appointed over the assets and undertaking thereof. The precise date of his appointment was a matter of some dispute between the parties but it does not seem to me to be necessary to resolve that dispute. Two of the employees of IUP a Mr McGlinchey and Mr Browne, the first named defendant, negotiated the purchase from the receiver of the goodwill of IUP insofar as it consisted of outstanding orders for the publication of archive material. The directors of Memo Ltd were approached. Agreement was reached between them and the two former employees of IUP to promote a third company, that is to say Irish Microforms Ltd, the plaintiffs herein, to carry on work similar to that previously undertaken by IUP. The arrangement reached between the parties was that the new company should have a share capital of £6,000 subscribed as to £1,000 by each of the interested parties. Whilst the matter does not appear to have been the subject of any specific agreement it appears to have been the intention of the parties that the plaintiffs would avail of the services of Memo Ltd in the same way and for the same purposes as IUP had done previously. For some time after the incorporation of the plaintiff company its premises were situate at Kildare Street, Dublin. Subsequently they moved to Ranelagh in the suburbs of Dublin. Unfortunately the development of the company was hampered by the death in 1976 of Mr McGlinchey whom all of the parties recognised as a person of considerable expertise and authority in the business in which he was engaged.

It is difficult to analyse satisfactorily the progress made by the plaintiff company. Quite apart from any matter in dispute between the parties there is a surprising lack of consistency in the quality of the records and documents maintained on behalf of the company. Some minutes were taken and preserved in considerable detail. Of other meetings there appears to be either no minutes or else a variety of drafts in respect of which no one version was finally accepted. Indeed there is no book of minutes and no file purporting to include all of the minutes taken. That this should happen in relation to the affairs of a small private company is by no means unusual. However the existence of some records and the absence of others; detailed documentation in relation to some matters and none at all with regard to others, has provided scope for wide ranging argument between the parties.

It seems to me that it can be said with confidence, first that Mr Gerry Ryan was the managing director of the company at all material times. Secondly, that Mr Browne was general manager and secretary thereof. Thirdly, that the actual operations of the company were under the *de facto* control of Mr Browne. Fourthly, that by 1980 the remuneration payable by the company to Mr Browne was a sum of £6,500 per annum. It was said, and I accept that there were considerable disputes between Mr Browne on the one hand and Mr Gerry Ryan and indeed other members of the board in relation to the affairs of the plaintiff company and in particular with regard to the amount from time to time due by one company to the other. The plaintiff company (which instituted these proceedings at the instigation of what I may call the Ryan faction) placed great importance on the agreement which was reached in the month of July 1978 which was attached or was expressed to have been attached to the minutes of the meeting of the board of directors of the plaintiffs held at Sandymount Road on 13 July 1978. Several versions of this document each differing slightly from the other were put in evidence but the point on which the plaintiffs rely is that clause 6 of the agreement provided as follows:

> "Future personnel employed by Irish Microforms Ltd temporary or full-time to be approved by the company's board".

It is contended on behalf of the plaintiffs that this effectively placed an embargo on Mr Browne employing any further staff without the approval of the board and that the payment of wages or salary to staff employed without the consent of the board was and amounted to a misappropriation of the monies of the company. Mr Browne's reply to that argument was first that Mr Ryan and his group neglected to perform the other terms of the contract imposed upon them and secondly that agreement was reached simply to overcome a disagreement then current between the parties and that when this was resolved the agreement fell into disuse. The matter then passes to early 1980. A decision was made by the directors of Memo Ltd to move their operations from Sandymount to Ossory Road in the North Strand, Dublin. The Ryan faction in the plaintiff company took the view that it would be desirable for Irish Microforms Ltd to move its operations from Ranelagh to the Memo premises in Sandymount. It is not clear what merits this step would have had or to whom the benefits would accrue. Certainly there was no significant financial gain to the plaintiff company in undertaking the move. The rents of the Sandymount premises and of the Ranelagh premises were almost identical. On the other hand it does not appear that there was any very serious reason to oppose the move. But it was opposed by Mr Browne. The matter was taken a stage further on 2 July 1980 when the board of directors of Irish Microforms Ltd formally resolved to transfer the business of that company from Ranelagh to Sandymount or Ossory Road as from 1 August 1980 despite the opposition of Mr Browne. Shortly afterwards Mr Browne submitted a memorandum to Mr Allan Martin dated 29 July 1980 in relation to the proposed transfer which apparently it had then been decided would be to Sandymount rather than Ossory Road. In that memorandum he accepted that the transfer would take place. However, the transfer was not implemented on the planned date and there is some difference of opinion as to why that was. At about the same time there was another matter requiring the attention of the directors of the plaintiff company. The auditors Messrs. Reynolds Cooper and McCarron completed the annual audit and produced draft accounts for the company's financial year ended 31 March 1980. In fact four different sets of accounts were produced. The first three sets of accounts were expressly marked "draft accounts". The fourth though not so marked, were never finalised by the signature of the directors or that of the auditors. The adjustment of the accounts does confirm however that some debate took place in relation to the amount of the creditors of the company and probably that the auditors were satisfied that the figure had been overstated in the first draft of the accounts. However, the final breach between the Ryan group and Mr Browne came in the middle of September 1980 when Mr Gerry Ryan visited the company's premises in Ranelagh with a view to persuading Mr Browne to implement the proposed transfer to Sandymount. Mr Ryan described his visit to the company's premises at Ranelagh. The stairway was he said covered in boxes, the place was alive with people, typewriters were clattering everywhere. He described how he met a young lady and asked to see Mr Browne. She enquired who he was and he told her that he was the managing director of the company. She asked him to hold on and when she returned she explained that he would have to make an appointment to see Mr Browne. In fact Mr Ryan went straight into Mr Browne's office and he enquired, according to his recollection, from Mr Browne "Sean, what is going on here?".

There is no doubt that this incident made a strong impression on Mr Ryan and that he was deeply hurt by it. From that point onwards events moved quickly. At times too quickly. On 22 September 1980 Mr Ryan wrote to Mr Browne demanding that certain documentation specified therein should be delivered to him at the Memo Ltd premises in Sandymount. On 14 October the solicitors on behalf of the Ryan group demanded possession of the same documents and some others. It does seem that Mr Ryan had overlooked the fact that by letter dated 23 September 1980 Mr Browne had undertaken to deliver certain documents and that indeed some of those were probably delivered at that time. What has given rise to considerable confusion is the fact that there was a parallel request for other documentation from the auditors. Whether arising from Mr Browne's failure to move the business of the company on the incident which occurred in mid September is not clear but certainly Mr Ryan was very disturbed and one of the steps which he took was to direct the auditors to prepare draft accounts for the period from 1 April to 30 September 1980. There is no doubt that this exercise was approached with some preconception or suspicion by the auditors and a more searching enquiry was carried out than had been undertaken in relation to earlier accounts. In relation to the half yearly accounts the auditors sought from Mr Browne a number of financial documents of the company and it is not clear whether those documents were provided or whether there would have been any difficulty in so doing. However, by 6 November 1980 the accountants, Reynolds Cooper and McCarron, indicated that they were unable to finalise the half yearly account unless and until the information set out in their letter of that date was obtained. Enclosed with that letter was a 15 page document specifying the documents and papers which would be required by the accountants for the purposes of the outstanding account. There were, as I say, therefore, two sets of documents being sought. First the managing director was seeking the transfer of all of the books, records, and documents of the company by Mr Browne from Ranelagh to Sandymount and the auditors were seeking either from Mr Ryan or from Mr Browne certain books and records which they needed to enable them to complete the accounts.

The plenary summons herein was issued on 12 November 1980 and the primary relief sought by the plaintiffs was a mandatory injunction requiring the defendant to deliver up to the plaintiffs various files, invoices, correspondence, stock and other chattels. This was followed immediately by a motion on notice seeking interlocutory relief which was heard by this court on 15 December 1980. That motion was compromised on terms which included an undertaking by Mr Browne to deliver up to the plaintiff company all papers and records and all stock and microfilm in his possession which were the property of the plaintiff company and a further undertaking by both parties to co-operate in the carrying out of a joint audit of the plaintiff's business for the period from 1 April 1977 to 30 September 1980.

In the course of the evidence given by him Mr Gerry Ryan accepted that the defendant had indeed returned all of the company's documents to the plaintiffs or their then auditors Reynolds Cooper McCarron. Indeed it appears in the correspondence which passed between Mr Ryan and the then auditors of the company in February 1981 that the documents which Mr Ryan believed were still outstanding had indeed been safely delivered by Mr Browne to the auditors.

As a result of the joint undertakings given by the parties to co-operate in carrying out a joint audit of the plaintiffs business Mr Michael F. Hargaden, A.C.A., was engaged on behalf of the plaintiffs and Mr Noel Flynn of Messrs Fay McMahon & Co., Chartered Accountants, was engaged by the defendant. Mr Hargaden undertook a meticulous investigation of the affairs of the plaintiff company and produced a detailed analysis purporting to show that Mr Browne was indebted to the plaintiffs in a sum in excess of £40,000.00 or alternatively that Mr Browne had failed to produce appropriate documentation authorising or vouching expenditure by the company in that sum. It was Mr Hargaden's evidence that the meeting was held in a cordial atmosphere and that he sought explanations and vouchers from Mr Browne through Mr Flynn but that no such documentation or explanations were ever received by him. Mr Browne in his evidence accepted that no effort was made by him to meet with the demands made by Mr Hargaden as it was his, Mr Browne's, understanding that a hostile attitude had been taken up by Mr Hargaden which precluded the possibility of any meaningful discussions taking place.

There were, therefore, demands or requests made of Mr Browne by different people, at different times for different documentation. This has undoubtedly given rise to considerable confusion as the parties did not at all times bear in mind the distinction between books and records of the company which did undoubtedly exist and which Mr Gerry Ryan wished to have moved from the company's offices in Ranelagh to the alternative premises in Sandymount and the documentation or vouchers which were sought by the auditors, and in particular Mr Hargaden, which, he says would have been appropriate to verify or authorise certain financial transactions carried out by the plaintiff company.

In these circumstances I turn to explore the claims made on behalf of the plaintiffs.

First it is alleged (see paragraph 8 of the statement of claim) that

> "due to the negligent manner in which he ran the plaintiff company or alternatively due to fraud on his part, the company accountants, Messrs Reynolds Cooper & McCarron were not able to produce a final set of accounts for the period April 1979 to March 1980 due to the fact that they were unable to obtain all the information and explanations which they considered necessary for the purpose of the said audit".

It is further alleged in paragraph 10 of the statement of claim that as a consequence of the defendant's failure to deal with the queries raised by the auditors that the plaintiff "suffered much loss and damage and has been greatly injured in its business and reputation".

Secondly, it was contended (in paragraph 11) that the defendant did "knowingly and fraudulently, without the plaintiff's consent, charge to the plaintiff company many invoices which did not appertain to the trading activities of the plaintiff company".

Thirdly, it was alleged that the defendant engaged on his own behalf in the business of publishers trading as Academy Press without the knowledge of the plaintiff company.

Fourthly, it was alleged that on 9 September 1980 the defendant "fraudulently represented and warranted to Clear Publishing Company New York that he the defendant and Academy Press were interested in and connected with the plaintiff company and thus sought to deprive the plaintiff company of the business of the American Company".

In June 1981 the solicitors then acting on behalf of the defendant sought particulars of certain matters alleged in the statement of claim. Details were sought (among other things) of the fraud alleged by the plaintiffs and the loss and damage sustained by them. In their reply dated 25 August 1981 the solicitors on behalf of the plaintiffs maintained that adequate particulars had been given either in the statement of claim or certain affidavits sworn in the matter. As to the loss and damage, the plaintiffs took the unusual course of maintaining that these were matters to be proved in evidence at the trial and accordingly declined to give particulars. With regard to the allegations of fraud it was made clear to the plaintiffs that whilst the court would entertain an application even at a late stage to amend the pleadings if that should be appropriate the court could not deal with an allegation of fraud otherwise than by reference to express allegations within the pleadings themselves. No application was made for an amendment.

In addition to the problems which arose as a result of confusion between the different categories of documentation and vouchers sought from the defendant, misunderstandings clearly existed due to the failure to distinguish between the loss (if any) occasioned by the absence of proper documentation either authorising or recording a transaction and the loss which might be caused by the transaction itself. Where payments are made with the object and effect of benefiting a company and the officer responsible neglects to make an appropriate record thereof no doubt inconvenience, delay and some financial loss occurs as a result but there would be no justification for equating that loss with the payments actually made. Perhaps the appropriate remedy would be to reprimand or even dismiss the officer responsible. There could be no justification, however, for calling upon the officer to pay to the company the full amount of the payment which he neglected to record.

As no evidence was tendered of any loss suffered by the company as a result of the delay in producing the accounts for the year to April 1980 I reject the first of the claims made as aforesaid by the plaintiffs against the defendant.

As the third and fourth claims adumbrated above involve directly the association of the defendant with a firm known as "Academy Press" and that association arises only indirectly in relation to the second claim it may be more helpful to consider next the third and fourth claims.

The plaintiffs assert that the defendant did at all material times carry on the business of publishers trading as Academy Press and further that he did so without the knowledge of the plaintiff company. It is clear on the evidence that the first of these assertions is correct and that the second is not.

Academy Press is the firm name of a business which was established by the defendant with a Mr Seamus Cashman on 6 May 1976 under which the promoters intended to carry on and did carry on the business of general publishers. That a director and full-time executive of one company should at the same time engage in business on his own account in competition with his employer is one of the most extraordinary features of a commercial relationship which was unusual in many respects. However, the conflict of interest to which his involvement in the two businesses gave rise formed only part of the picture. It appears that Mr Browne and Mr Cashman held between them the entire issued share capital in a company known as Ellerton Ltd which also carried on a publishing business and traded under the name "Academy Press". Furthermore it appears that on 7 October 1980 Mr Browne procured the registration of the business name "Academy Microfilms (Dublin)". Not only does it appear that Ellerton Ltd was in direct competition for business with Irish Microforms Ltd but it is Mr Browne's own evidence that the staff or some of the staff which he engaged on behalf of the plaintiff company and who worked at the company's premises in Ranelagh devoted part of their time to the business of Ellerton Ltd. Mr Browne explained that he apportioned the staff costs between the two enterprises by reference to the amount of the work done by them respectively for each of the businesses. It was not only at staffing levels that the affairs of the two competing businesses were interwoven. The plaintiff's cheques payment ledger discloses numerous payments to the Academy Press and those transactions were explained by Mr Browne as representing, for the greater part, repayments by the plaintiff company to Academy Press of monies borrowed by the former from the latter when Mr Browne's co-directors were not available to countersign cheques on the plaintiff company's bank account. Mr Browne's evidence was that Academy Press acted as bankers for the company.

I would have assumed readily that this extraordinary state of affairs formed part of a fraudulent conspiracy but the evidence makes it clear that such an assumption is unwarranted. No effort was made by Mr Browne to conceal his involvement with Academy Press. The documentation relating to the registration of that business name and the incorporation of Ellerton Ltd were of course matters of public record. The business names of Mr Browne's companies were apparently displayed on the Ranelagh premises. The staff engaged on the Academy Press work were employed in the premises in Ranelagh and the fact of their employment and the nature of the work which they were doing was something which could have been ascertained by any of the directors for the time being of the plaintiff company by visiting the plaintiff's premises at any time as Mr Gerry Ryan ultimately did in September of 1980. Attention should also be drawn to the fact that the auditors of the company Messrs Reynolds

Cooper and McCarron were at the same time auditors to Academy Press. There was, therefore, no attempt at concealment. But that is not all. The involvement of Mr Browne with Academy Press was the subject matter of an article in the *Sunday Independent* in October 1978. Finally, the specific question "what percentage of Sean Browne's time is spent on Academy Press Ltd?" was an express item on the agenda for a meeting of the board of directors of the plaintiff company in October 1979. Indeed there was some controversy between the parties as to how that question was answered at the meeting. On one copy of the agenda a figure of 25 per cent was written in from which it might be inferred that a very significant part of the time which Mr Browne might otherwise have devoted to the affairs of the plaintiff company was being taken up with the business of Academy Press whereas Mr Gerard Ryan's recollection was that the percentage of the time involved was only 10 per cent. It was Mr Browne himself who reconciled this apparent conflict. He explained that the figure of 25 per cent was used in relation to his full working day including several hours of each evening. The figure of 10 per cent represented the intrusion on his ordinary working day which would otherwise have been available for the affairs of the plaintiff company.

In those circumstances the contention that the defendant involved himself in the business of Academy Press without the knowledge of the plaintiff company is clearly unsustainable.

The claim fourthly made by the plaintiff company is that a letter dated 9 September 1980 to the Clear Water Publishing Company constituted a fraudulent representation made with the intention of depriving the plaintiff company of the business of the addressee and furthermore that the representation was made in breach of contract and in breach of trust. The first paragraph of that letter which was written by Mr Browne on Irish Microforms Ltd notepaper includes the following sentences:

> "Pending corporate changes here made it very difficult to get back to you on any of the points covered at our meetings. However, you can take it that most of the projects etc. that we discussed will go ahead albeit under a different corporate name".

The second paragraph of the letter refers to an enclosed invoice and goes on to say:

> "As you will see the invoice is from the Academy Press. This reflects some of the company changes presently occurring. I will fill you in in greater detail on these later".

Mr Browne explained the foregoing statements by reference to the disagreements which were taking place at the date of the letter between himself and Mr Gerry Ryan and his belief that changes would indeed take place. He explained that he made a general reference to "Corporate changes" rather than any specific details because he was anxious to avoid damaging the goodwill of the plaintiff company. In relation to the invoice issued under the name "Academy Press" Mr Browne explained that he was anxious to collect this debt himself which was admittedly due to Irish Microforms Ltd so as to ensure that the *Irish Times* would be paid the monies which were due to them and which formed the greater part of that invoice. In fact the plaintiffs accept that the amount due to the plaintiff company out of the transaction was very modest indeed and reliance was placed on the transaction — which only came to light some time after the proceedings had been instituted — as indicating a course of conduct in which the defendant was engaged. Whilst I suspect that Mr Browne did not fully appreciate the consequences of his actions in writing the letter of 9 September 1980 I think that he may have felt that certain connections of the plaintiff company were of value to him, Mr Browne, but not to Memo Ltd. Nevertheless it is clear that even if Mr Browne was not guilty of a fraudulent misrepresentation he certainly acted in breach of his fiduciary duty as a director of the plaintiff company. However, there was no evidence of any other attempts by the defendant to appropriate any other part of the business or goodwill of the plaintiff company.

The remaining allegation relates to the misappropriation or misapplication by the defendant of the funds of the plaintiff company. The plaintiffs sought to substantiate this allegation by adducing evidence through Mr Hargaden of the innumerable disbursements made by the plaintiff company between the years 1977 and the end of 1980 whilst under the *de facto* control of the defendant and which transactions did not appear from any record available to Mr Hargaden or any explanation given to him by Mr Browne to have been duly authorised by the company or expended for its benefit. There is no doubt but that this analysis of Mr Hargaden was made available to Mr Browne as far back as February 1981 but that Mr Browne did not offer any explanation for sums totalling approximately £45,000 which appear to have been misapplied. Mr Browne's explanation for refusing to co-operate has already been referred to. However, in the course of the hearing the parties were afforded an opportunity of engaging in further discussions and this did result in some adjustment of the figures. It was not feasible for the parties to debate each and every one of the disputed disbursements. However, it is fair to say that Mr Browne was in a position to establish that some of the payments were correctly accounted for.

A rough analysis of the disputed disbursements expressed in round figures is as follows:

1. Sums totalling £17,000 paid to the defendant.
2. Sums totalling £9,000 paid to Academy Press.
3. Sums totalling £7,500 paid to employees or contractors whose employment or retention had not been authorised by the board.
4. Sums totalling £1,500 which was the liability of Academy Press and which was discharged by the plaintiff company.
5. Sums in excess of £4,000 in respect of invoices which were attributable to *The Digest of Irish Affairs*.

The *Digest of Irish Affairs* (or the current affairs index as it was more properly called) was a record of news items compiled by Radio Telifís Éireann for the years 1969 and onwards. On 14 June 1978 R.T.E. entered into a written agreement with Ellerton Ltd (expressed to be trading as the Academy Press and having its place of business at 124 Ranelagh Dublin 6) under which Ellerton undertook to microfilm the current affairs index and to publish it in book form. The contract provided that in addition to providing copies of the cassette film of the work and of the first edition of the book that Ellerton would pay to R.T.E. a royalty in the order of 10 per cent of the publisher's net receipts. The fact that Mr Browne could negotiate such a contract on behalf of Ellerton Ltd at a time when he was in the full-time employment of the plaintiff company illustrates the ludicrous position in which he had placed himself. But that was only the beginning of the story. According to Mr Browne he transferred the film rights in the index to the plaintiff company in or about January or February 1979 in consideration of the payment to Ellerton Ltd of a sum of £800. The evidence in this regard appears to be supported by the accounts of the plaintiff company for the year ended 3 March 1979.

The publication of the index required very considerable academic and skilled research. It also involved, as the contract itself recognised, considerable expense. According to the evidence of Mr Cashman and Mr Browne discussions took place between them with regard to the financing of this work. It was their evidence that Mr Browne insisted upon transferring the R.T.E. contract to the plaintiff company despite the objections of Mr Cashman because he, Mr Cashman, was unable to raise sufficient monies to have the publication completed by Ellerton Ltd.

I am satisfied that Ellerton Ltd did not at any time assign the benefit or burden of the contract which they had entered into in 1978 with R.T.E. to the plaintiff company. It is a common case that neither Mr Cashman nor Mr Browne obtained or sought legal advice as to whether that contract was assignable in law. No written document was ever executed or drafted to give effect to the assignment. it does not appear that the alleged assignment was approved in any formal way by the board of Ellerton Ltd and certainly it was not considered by the board of the plaintiff company. Mr Browne did swear that the current affairs index was discussed by him from time to time with his co-directors in the plaintiff company and I do accept that some references were made to it. However, I do not accept that the board of the plaintiff company was ever invited even in an informal manner to accept a transfer of the interests of Ellerton Ltd under that agreement. Furthermore, I would doubt such a transfer would have been effective, quite apart from any other consideration, without the approval of R.T.E. and that approval was never given nor sought.

As counsel suggested in replying to the defendant's case the execution of the R.T.E. contract and its alleged assignment to the plaintiff company lies at the core of these proceedings. That being so it was unfortunate that the matter was not identified in the pleadings as an issue between the parties.

Again, it was regrettable that no submissions were made to the court as to the consequences in law of the purported arrangement between Mr Cashman and Mr Browne concerning the contract. Mr Browne contented himself with saying that he had been given full power to enter into contracts on behalf of the plaintiff company and the plaintiff in reply to that argument stated that having regard to Mr Browne's fiduciary relationship with the plaintiff company it would have been necessary for him to disclose the special nature of the transaction to at least one other director of the plaintiff company.

Whilst I can see that disclosure to a fellow director might go a long way to negativing an allegation of fraud I know of no principle of law which either requires disclosure to at least one director on the one hand or validates a transaction which would otherwise be void provided it is disclosed to a single director. However, it is clear and necessarily accepted by both parties, that Mr Browne as a director of the plaintiff company was in a fiduciary position in relation to it. It is likewise clear that there was an obvious conflict of interest in relation to the duty which he owed to Ellerton Ltd and that which he owed to Irish Microforms Ltd in any negotiations concerning the R.T.E. contract. This conflict was exacerbated by the fact that Ellerton Ltd had already incurred expenditure in exploiting the contract and was under its terms responsible to incur even more. In those circumstances the acquisition of the publishing rights of the index from Ellerton Ltd would be distinguishable from the general run of commitments entered into by Mr Browne on behalf and for the benefit of the plaintiff company. In my opinion it would not have been possible for Mr Browne in his capacity as *de facto* executive of the plaintiff company to acquire the R.T.E. contract for the benefit of the plaintiffs without the board approving the acquisition of the rights in the knowledge that the supplier was a company in which Mr Browne was a substantial shareholder.

The consequence of this decision is twofold. First of all it follows that the burden and the benefit (if any) of the R.T.E. contract remains vested in Ellerton Ltd and secondly that all costs and expenses and all payments made by the plaintiff company at the behest of Mr Browne in connection with the R.T.E. contract or to persons engaged in editing or promoting the current affairs index were incorrectly debited to the plaintiffs and should and must be borne by the defendant or Ellerton Ltd. It would seem, for example, that all of the invoices attributable to the *Digest of Irish Affairs* were sums wrongly withdrawn from the funds of the plaintiff company at the direction of Mr Browne. Similarly monies paid to employees or contractors, whether nominally engaged by the plaintiff company or not, but whose work related to the index or to the extent to which it so related would likewise constitute misapplications of the company's funds. It may be that other questioned payments likewise constituted misapplications of the plaintiff's monies. It does seem to me that *prima facie* all of the payments made to Academy Press should be refunded unless express justification can be found for any particular payment. The other payments would require to be judged on their merits but with the proviso that a particular payment is not a misapplication merely because the records of the company are inadequate. To be recoverable from the defendant it must be shown that the particular payment was expressly or impliedly authorised by Mr Browne for a purpose which was not calculated to benefit his employer.

Whilst I regret the delay and expense which such a procedure would entail I feel that the matter would have to be referred to the examiner of the High Court to take an account of the monies so misapplied unless some agreement can be reached between the parties so as to avoid this additional burden.

With regard to the defendant's counterclaim there was in fact only one real issue, namely, whether the defendant resigned his employment with the plaintiffs or whether he was wrongfully dismissed. I have no doubt but that he resigned in the manner and in the circumstances of which Mr Gerry Ryan gave evidence. Indeed that account was not seriously disputed. Instead the defendant argued in general terms that he was coerced into his resignation but in my view that contention was unsupported by any evidence.

I will hear the parties in regard to the nature of the order which they suggest should be made having regard to the foregoing judgment.

Patricia McLaughlin
Barrister

Balkanbank v. Naser Taher, Kevin McGrath, Via Holdings Ltd (formerly Taher Investments Ltd), Taher Meats (Ireland) Ltd and Balkan International Ltd: High Court 1990 No. 13479P (Blayney J) 12 February 1992

Company Law – Joint venture company established – Loan obtained – Whether loan obtained pursuant to a valid resolution of the board of directors – Whether Bulgarian directors consented to the loan – Derivative action – Relevant exception to the rule in Foss v. Harbottle *– Fraud on the minority – Whether disbursements made irregularly – Whether these could be approved by a properly convened meeting of the Board – Oppression*

Facts: In the course of 1990 a credit facility was arranged for Balkan International Ltd ("BIL") with the American Express Bank in Vienna in the sum of $7,000,000. BIL was a joint venture company controlled by Balkanbank and Taher Investments Ltd (now Via Holdings Ltd), the latter company being controlled by the Taher family, including Naser Taher. BIL drew down on this facility with American Express Bank in circumstances which led to the commencement of proceedings by Balkanbank claiming certain monies as well as damages for fraud against the first, third, fourth and fifth defendant. Balkanbank claimed that Naser Taher and Kevin McGrath, two of the directors of BIL, had improperly and without authority caused BIL to draw down under its facility and divert the bulk of the $7,000,000 to Naser Taher and others, and that the payments made out of the monies constituted a wrongful disposal of assets of BIL. Balkanbank sought injunctive relief, accounts and orders for repayment and damages for breach of duty, breach of trust and fraud. The defendants contended that the resolution on foot of which the loan was obtained was perfectly valid and, furthermore, that the Balkanbank directors knew that the loan was going to be obtained and assented to it. They further claimed that the disbursements made out of the monies borrowed were made in discharge of liabilities of BIL. One such disbursement was made to cover the start-up expenses of BIL which had been borne by Taher Investments Ltd. BIL also counterclaimed for declaratory relief relating to an agreement between it and Balkanbank whereby the latter agreed to transfer to BIL shares in a company called Air Via Ltd. Under Bulgarian law, such an agreement was subject to the unanimous approval of the members of Air Via Ltd.

Held by Blayney J:

(1) The plaintiff's claim for fraud and breach of duty in relation to the obtaining and drawing down of the loan should be dismissed. The $7,000,000 was drawn with the consent of the Bulgarian directors of BIL.

(2) The counterclaim brought on behalf of BIL should be dismissed. Any agreement between Balkanbank and BIL for the transfer of shares in Air Via Ltd by Balkanbank was always conditional, under Bulgarian law, upon BIL being accepted by all the shareholders as a member of the company and this consent was not forthcoming.

(3) The plaintiff's claim should be treated as a derivative action based upon the relevant exception to the rule in *Foss v. Harbottle* brought on behalf of the plaintiff and all the shareholders. Although Balkanbank and Taher Investments Ltd were equal shareholders, Taher Investments had control of the board through the casting vote of Mr Taher as chairman and therefore Balkanbank were in the same position as a minority shareholder. Liberty to amend the statement of claim granted.

(4) The disbursements made, with the exception of $1.6 million which was intended for BIL's participation in Air Via Ltd. were made irregularly as they were not made pursuant to resolutions of the board passed at regularly convened meetings. They could only be validly confirmed by a properly convened meeting of the board if they did not constitute oppression. The first, second and third defendants should account to BIL for the sum of $1,271,494 which constituted the BIL start-up expenses. The $7,000,000 drawn down from the American Express Bank was obtained on security provided by Balkanbank and although that did not give Balkanbank the absolute right to determine how the funds should be used, Balkanbank would be entitled to object to their being used to defray expenses incurred by its partner, Taher Investments. Furthermore, the defendants should account for the balance of the $7,000,000 still under their control.

(5) Balkanbank must account to BIL for the $750,000 retained by it out of the $1.6 million paid to it in connection with Air Via Ltd.

(6) Liberty given to the defendants to serve a notice of motion seeking an enquiry into damages.

(7) In relation to the counterclaim by BIL seeking to enforce a contract with Balkanbank concerning the transfer of a package of shares in Air Via Ltd, specific performance would not be ordered as such an order could not be enforced against Balkanbank.

(8) Nor would a declaration be granted requiring Balkanbank to attempt to use its powers to procure the registration of BIL as owner of the share package in Air Via Ltd, as such a declaration would have no reality. Under Bulgarian law such a transfer could only be registered with the unanimous acceptance of all the shareholders, and it was clear that the general assembly of Air Via would not now accept BIL as a member.

Cases referred to in judgment

Foss v. Harbottle (1843) 2 Hare 461

Royal British Bank v. Turquand (1856) 6 E and B 327 (Exchequer)

Counsel's and solicitors' names not available

BLAYNEY J **12 February 1992**

The enormous changes that are taking place in Eastern Europe are giving rise to many unexpected problems. This case might be said to be one of them.

The plaintiff, Balkanbank, is a semi-state commercial bank incorporated in Bulgaria. 14 per cent of its shares are held by Bulgarian Foreign Trade Bank and the balance by 160 Bulgarian manufacturing companies. In the latter part of 1989 Balkanbank agreed with the third named defendant, Via Holdings Ltd (then known as Taher Investments Ltd and to which I shall refer as Taher Investments or TIL throughout this judgment) to engage in a joint business venture with a view to taking advantage of the opportunities presented by the liberalisation of trade in Bulgaria. For the purpose of this joint venture a company, the fifth named defendant, Balkan International Ltd (to which I shall refer as Balkan International or BIL) was incorporated in Ireland on 19 February 1990 with Balkanbank and Taher Investments as equal shareholders. The board of directors consisted of two nominees from Balkanbank, Ivan Mironov, the President of Balkanbank, and Assen Ochanov, and two nominees from Taher Investments, Naser Taher, who was chairman of the board, and Kevin McGrath, being respectively the first and second named defendants. The share capital of the company was 100,000 dollars which was contributed equally by the shareholders.

Early in the month of June 1990 Balkanbank made a block deposit of seven million dollars in the American Express Bank in Vienna. The purpose of making such deposit was to provide a security against which Balkan International could obtain loans to finance the projects which were being planned. Shortly after the money had been deposited, Mr Taher and Mr McGrath, acting in their capacity as directors of Balkan International, obtained a loan of seven million dollars from the American Express Bank in Vienna and transferred the entire of that sum to the bank account maintained by Balkan International in the Banque Nationale de Paris in Dublin. Various disbursements were made from that sum and a balance of $4,150,000 is now standing on deposit in the name of Messrs Lennon Heather & Co., the solicitors for the defendants.

Balkanbank claims that in obtaining the loan of $7 million Mr Taher and Mr McGrath acted wrongfully, fraudulently and in breach of their duty in Balkan International; that the board resolution on foot of which the loan was obtained was invalid; that Balkanbank had no knowledge of the resolution or of the fact that the loan was being obtained; and that the payments made out of the monies borrowed constituted a wrongful disposal of assets of Balkan International. As against Mr Taher, Mr McGrath and Taher Investments they seek damages for fraud and breach of trust, together with a number of injunctions; as against the fourth named defendant, a company managed by Mr Taher, an account of monies received by it together with a declaration and certain injunctions, and as against Balkan International certain injunctions.

The defendants contend that the resolution on foot of which the loan was obtained was perfectly valid and furthermore that the Balkanbank directors were aware that the loan was going to be obtained and assented to it. And as for the disbursements made out of the monies borrowed, they claim that they were made in discharge of liabilities of Balkan International.

In addition to defending the action, Balkan International have brought a counterclaim. It concerns shares in a Bulgarian private company, Air Via Ltd, which was incorporated in Bulgaria pursuant to a preliminary contract entered into on 30 March 1990 between Balkanbank of the one part and Interbalkan-Balkantourist, the Bulgarian State tourist company, and three individuals, of the other part. Balkanbank was to have 56 per cent of the shares, and Balkan International contends that it was agreed between Balkanbank and Balkan International that Balkanbank would transfer 87 per cent of its shares, being 49 per cent of the total shares in Air Via, to Balkan International; that Balkanbank failed to perform that agreement, and Balkan International claims damages and other relief for breach of contract.

That is a brief summary of the main issues that arise in the case. It is now necessary firstly to find the facts, which is by no means easy as much of the evidence is conflicting, and then to consider the legal position, which is also complex. While many of the facts are common to both the claim and the counterclaim, so that there is considerable overlapping between the two, I propose to deal with each of them separately as the issues arising in each are quite distinct, and I start with Balkanbank's claim.

There is one aspect of the facts which I propose to take out of chronological order as it renders unnecessary a detailed examination of some of the conflicting evidence. It concerns the defendants' contention that the loan of $7 million was obtained on foot of a valid resolution of the board of directors Balkan International. Two such resolutions were put in evidence: one dated 26 May 1990 and one dated 31 May 1990. Both purport to have been passed at board meetings of

Balkan International held on the relevant dates. But it is clear on the evidence that no board meetings were held at all. The resolutions are signed by Mr Taher and Mr McGrath but they did not meet to pass them. The resolution of 26 May was signed by Mr McGrath in Dublin and by Mr Taher in Vienna. That of 31 May was similarly signed by both without there being any meeting. Mr Taher said in evidence that he was not in Dublin on either 26 or 31 May. He said that the resolutions were simply a formality to enable a bank account to be opened for Balkan International with American Express. Insofar as the bank was concerned, the rule in *Royal British Bank v. Turquand* (1856) 6 E and B 327, clearly applied and they could not be prejudiced by the fact that no meeting was held, but as between Balkanbank and Balkan International this irregularity rendered the resolution invalid and so altogether apart from any question of absence of notice to the Bulgarian directors, or whether the quorum for a meeting of the directors was two or three, the resolution cannot be relied on in isolation by the defendants as justifying the obtaining of the loan.

It is immaterial in the circumstances to resolve two issues of fact which were hotly contested: whether the quorum for the meeting of the directors of Balkan International had been fixed at three by a resolution of the directors passed at a meeting held on 1 March 1990, and whether a copy of the minutes of that meeting, in which it was stated that the quorum had been fixed at three, had been signed by Mr Taher and Mr McGrath, but I will nonetheless indicate at a later stage what conclusion I have reached on each of these issues.

The essential issue of fact that it seems to me that I have to decide is whether the Bulgarian directors were aware of the resolutions and gave their assent to them, and also whether they were aware of the taking of the loan and gave their assent to that also. It is for the purpose of making a finding on this issue that I now examine the relevant evidence.

The decision by Balkanbank and Taher Investments to set up a joint venture company was taken at meetings at Dublin held in the offices of the fourth named defendant, Taher Meats (Ireland) Ltd between 25 and 28 October 1989. The participants in these meetings were Mr Taher, Mr Mironov, Mr Ochanov and Mr Michael Jeliaskov, the head of the Foreign Trading Department of Balkanbank. At the conclusion of the meetings minutes were prepared and were signed by Mr Taher and Mr Mironov. These minutes were as follows:

> "Minutes of Meeting held at Russell House, Stokes Place, St. Stephen's Green Dublin 2. Held between 25 and 28 October 1989.
>
> Present Mr Naser Taher, Chairman Taher Investment (Ireland),
>
> Mr Ivan Mironov,
> Mr Michael Jeliaskov,Commercial Bank
> Mr Assen Ochanov, Balkanbank Sofia
>
> Statement of Intent for Financing of Projects in Bulgaria and other Countries.

(1) Taher Investment Ltd and Balkanbank agreed to establish a joint venture company in Dublin on a 50-50 basis i.e. 50 per cent Taher Investments and 50 per cent Balkanbank to secure credit facilities for execution of various projects in Bulgaria and other countries and to invest in the new technologies in these countries in the field of industry and agriculture.
(2) The Company, Balkan Investments Ltd will have its registered office at Russell House, Stokes Place, St. Stephen's Green Dublin 2.
(3) Each project requiring financial aid shall be approved by the Board of Directors of the Company and the value of the credit facilities shall be determined by the Board of Directors.
(4) The Company shall endeavour to procure finance for Bulgarian projects minimum five years amounting to US $250 million maximum. For other countries the credit facilities will be negotiated on an individual basis.
(5) The authorised share capital of the Company shall be US $100,000 distributed in 100 shares each of US $1,000. 50 shares for Taher Investments Ltd and 50 shares for Balkanbank – Sofia.
(6) The company shall establish a representation in Sofia, Bulgaria, with staff approved by the Board of Directors, in order to study and to propose to the shareholders and the Board of Directors the respective projects for approval.
(7) Taher Investment Ltd shall organise the banking syndicates to provide the credit facilities for the Bulgarian projects and Balkanbank shall guarantee the financing and the repayment of the credits.
(8) The parties shall establish the Company by 31 December 1989 in order to commence operation on 1 January 1990.
(9) The authorised capital of the Company would be used to support the representation in Sofia and the salaries of the staff.
(10) Statement of intent for establishment of leasing services in Bulgaria and other countries
(a) The parties agreed to endeavour to organise a joint leasing company in Bulgaria, Soviet Union and other East European Countries.
(b) By 3 December 1989, the parties will finalise and submit a more detailed proposal in connection with the establishment of the above mentioned leasing Company."

The next meeting in connection with the incorporation of Balkan International took place between 18 and 20 January 1990, also in Dublin. Present at the meeting were Messrs Taher and McGrath and Messrs Mironov and Ochanov. The name given at the time to the joint venture company was Balkan Investments Ltd but subsequently it turned out that this name was not available and so it was changed to Balkan International Ltd. At this meeting 14 separate business projects were discussed and all 14 are referred to in the minutes which were prepared and signed at the end of the meeting. Only one of these projects became a reality. It is dealt with in the minutes as follows:

> "FOREX TRADING AND FINANCIAL SERVICE TO THE BANK:
> It has been agreed to set up a dealing room in Dublin for Balkan Investments. A credit of $223 million has been obtained. Mr Jeliaskov and another person will come to Dublin before the end of March to work with a chief dealer who will be appointed by Balkan Investments. The trading policy will be agreed with Mr Jeliaskov and will be faxed to Mr Mironov to approve and for Mr Taher the same. The objective is to obtain a profit on trading of $7 to $15,000 per day. This project shall commence operations within 45 days.
>
> The credit facility will be obtained in accordance with the financial conditions mentioned in these minutes.
>
> Also Balkan Investments will be in constant touch with Balkanbank and will give whatever financial services are required including forex dealing, deposits etc."

The minutes commenced with the following general provisions in regard to the formation and management of Balkan International:

> "Balkan Investments is a joint venture company set up between Balkan and Taher Investments Ltd on a 50-50 basis. It has a representation in Bulgaria and their aim is to seek out projects in Bulgaria and abroad and to prepare feasibility studies on these projects at the expense of the Bulgarian organisations and submit its findings to Balkan Investments for approval.
>
> Balkan Investments will be established and registered by 1 March 1990 in Ireland. The registration documents will be taken to Bulgaria for presentation to the Bulgarian authorities when the name has been changed from Reilton Ltd to Balkan Investments Ltd. The presentation in Sofia shall be set up after the registration of the company to the Bulgarian authorities.
>
> A management committee will be formed with Naser Taher, Kevin McGrath, Mr Mironov and Mr Ochanov. Mr Taher and Mr Mironov shall be co-chairmen of the company. Mr Ochanov shall be appointed as director of the company and the representation in Sofia. Mr Kevin McGrath will be director in Ireland. Mr Ochanov shall be available from 1 February 1990 to enhance the development of the company. Regarding staff requirements for the representation in Sofia, it was agreed to appoint 3 to 5 people for the beginning. Salaries and other expenses shall be in accordance with the budget of the company — Appendix 1 and 2 — which shall be approved by Mr Mironov on behalf of the Balkanbank before 20 February 1990.
>
> The bank account of the company will be opened in Dublin the week of 22 to 29 January 1990. Balkanbank shall be informed of this by telex

in order to transfer the share capital of US $50,000. Balkanbank and Taher Investments shall transfer its share capital ($50,000) not later than 31 January 1990. The bank account of the representation of the company will be opened in a Bulgarian bank also by the end of January into which both shareholders shall transfer 90,000 levas.

The premises of the representation of the company in Bulgaria shall be in Balkanbank. Two cars will be purchased for the representation in Sofia by the end of February.

The shareholders in Balkan Investments, namely Balkanbank and Taher Investments, after approving the projects shall find credit lines for the finance of these projects. When they find the banks who are willing to submit credit lines they will secure and guarantee this credit on behalf of Balkan Investments. Balkan Investments will use the credit for the execution of the above mentioned projects. Balkanbank will keep Balkan Investments informed on a monthly basis on availability of credit lines with various banks and institutions.

Balkan Investments shall submit an application to the Customs House Financial Centre in order to avail of the new Irish legislation which allows 10 per cent corporation profit tax on their activities."

Balkan International was incorporated by Intercompany Comparisons Ltd on 19 February 1990 on the instructions of Mr Taher. A directors' meeting was held on 26 February and while no direct evidence was given as to what took place at that meeting it was common case that Messrs Mironov, Ochanov and Taher and Ms Liz Curtis were appointed directors and the two shares issued initially were transferred to Balkanbank and Taher Investments respectively. It had been intended to appoint Mr McGrath as a director but he was in the United States of America at the date of the meeting and Ms Curtis, who was Mr Taher's secretary, was appointed instead of him as a temporary measure.

The first meeting of the new board was held on 1 March 1990 at the offices of Messrs Matheson Ormbsy and Prentice. Present were Mr Taher in the chair, Mr Ochanov and Ms Curtis. Mr David Prentice was also in attendance representing Matsack Trust Ltd, the secretary of the company. With the exception of the quorum, to which I have referred already, none of the matters discussed at the meeting was controversial. Mr Taher was appointed chairman of the board and Mr Mironov vice-chairman. While it had been stated in the minutes of the meetings held between 18 and 20 January that Mr Taher and Mr Mironov would be co-chairmen, it had been agreed subsequently between them that Mr Taher would be chairman and Mr Mironov vice-chairman so there was no contest at the meeting in regard to this.

49,999 shares of $1 each fully paid at par were allotted to Balkanbank and a similar number to Taher Investments; both the Banque Nationale de Paris and Ulster Bank Ltd were appointed to be the bankers of the company; Ms Curtis' resignation as director was noted and Mr McGrath was appointed a director in her place, and finally it was resolved that with effect from 8 March 1990 Mr

McGrath should be the secretary of the company in place of Matsack Trust Ltd.

As regards the question of the quorum, Article 14 of the Articles of Association provided that:

> "The quorum necessary for the transaction of the business of the Directors may be fixed by the Directors, and unless so fixed shall be two."

The disputed question is whether the quorum was fixed at three by a decision taken at the meeting as otherwise it would remain at two as provided by Article 14.

The evidence was conflicting. Mr Taher was very positive that he did not agree to a quorum of three, and Ms Curtis said that no conclusion was reached on the question. Mr Ochanov, when asked what was agreed about the quorum, replied:

> "We agreed, finally, that a Bulgarian Director should participate but the exact form we did not agree. We did not accept it. We leave it to be done by Mr Prentice following our understanding and our wishes."

And in cross examination he confirmed that it was correct that they left it to Mr Prentice to formulate what he called "Our solution, our decision, our agreement".

Mr Prentice's evidence was that it was definitely agreed at the meeting that the quorum would be three. He said that this placated Mr Ochanov's concern. What he was referring to was that Mr Ochanov had stated that according to the Bulgarian legislation any participation of Bulgarian companies abroad should be defended by a minimum of one Bulgarian director, and this meant that all kinds of documents should pass obligatorily through the Bulgarian directors. This was said by Mr Ochanov in the context of the management of the company because Mr Taher was insisting that he should be in control of the management. What Mr Ochanov clearly did not appreciate was that Mr Taher, by reason of being chairman of the board, had a casting vote, and so could control the board. The Articles adopted Table A and did not exclude Article 101 which gives the chairman a casting vote. And while Mr Taher was clearly aware of this, he was concerned with being able to have board meetings in Ireland whenever necessary and this would not be possible if it was always necessary for one of the Bulgarian directors to attend.

I am satisfied that a definite decision was taken at the meeting to fix the quorum at three. It seems to me that what happened was that it was left to Mr Prentice to produce a formula that would satisfy Mr Ochanov. He did this including in the minutes a provision that the quorum should be three. But when at the end of the meeting Mr Prentice had these minutes typed up, and gave them to Mr Taher to read, I accept Mr Taher's evidence that he said he would not agree with the quorum of three, and I accept Ms Curtis' evidence that when Mr Taher saw that a quorum of three had been included , he got very annoyed. That evidence is clearly inconsistent with a resolution having been passed that the quorum should be fixed at three. I consider that Mr Prentice did not have an accurate recollection of what happened at the meeting, which is perfectly understandable. He did not appear to remember, since he gave no evidence of it, that he had had the minutes of the meeting typed up before the meeting terminated, and had shown them to Mr Taher, and this clearly happened as Ms Curtis took away the copy and had retained it in one of her files. And it was only Mr Prentice who swore positively that the quorum had been fixed at three. Apart from this, the fact that the minutes were not signed when produced at the end of the meeting is significant, since it was the practice of the Bulgarians to have minutes drawn up and signed at the end of every meeting. If the minutes produced by Mr Prentice at the end of the meeting correctly represented what had been resolved in regard to the quorum, one would have expected Mr Ochanov to have asked Mr Taher and then Ms Curtis to sign them. No such request was made but, as shall appear shortly, Mr Ochanov contended that he had obtained the signatures of Mr Taher and Mr McGrath to the minutes about five days later in Sofia.

On 3 March Mr Ochanov returned to Sofia, and Messrs Taher and McGrath, Ms Curtis and Jasmal Ismail, a Jordanian engineer working for Mr Taher's companies, travelled with him. Over the next few days there were numerous meetings and discussions between Messrs Mironov and Ochanov on the one hand, and Messrs Taher and McGrath on the other. In particular there was a formal meeting on 7 March after which two sets of minutes were signed by all four parties. The first of these contained detailed provisions in regard to the Forex project which was to be started within 45 days with Peter Cruddas as the chief dealer. Mr Cruddas was an experienced dealer working for the Taher group in London. Messrs Ochanov, Taher and McGrath had had a meeting with him in Heathrow Airport on their way to Sofia on 3 March, and at Mr Mironov's request he had also come out to see Mr Mironov in Sofia. Unfortunately for the project, while Mr Cruddas initially had been agreeable to come to Dublin, he subsequently changed his mind and decided to stay in London. But at the date of the meeting of 7 March he was to be the person in charge of the dealing room in Dublin.

The second set of minutes signed on 7 March 1990 dealt with a number of the projects being considered by Balkan International. The only one that it is relevant to refer to is what became known as the Air Via project and which was dealt with as follows:

> "(2) On the private Air Company project the following was decided:
> (A) BIL would participate with this project with 39 per cent, Interbalkan would have 10 per cent and the management and pilots would have 51 per cent.
> (B) BIL would arrange the additional finance required to complete the purchase of three Tupolov 154M aircraft, delivery of which will be in June, July and October 1990. In consideration of BIL supplying the finance the aircraft will be mortgaged to BIL.

(C) The formation of the Bulgarian Company will commence immediately by Assen Ochanov and to be finalised within 45 days after which BIL would set up a joint venture company registered in Ireland with the Bulgarian Company as formed above.
(D) The Irish joint venture company would then lease the aircraft in US dollars from the Bulgarian company thus enabling it to use international routes.
(E) Mr Marangosov would revert to Mr Taher within ten days as to whether he would recommend the purchase of a YAK 40 or a L610 from Czechoslovakia. TIL would then lease the aircraft from the Bulgarian company. The purchase contract for this aircraft would take place within 30 days and Mr Marangosov or his representative would go to USSR or Czechoslovakia.
(F) On 7 March BIL shall receive from the air company a letter of intent agreeing to the above."

It is necessary now to refer back to the minutes of the meeting of 1 March. On 5 March, Mr Prentice faxed a copy of the minutes to Helen Gammell, a secretary employed by Mr Taher's group, at the group offices at Russell Place, Dublin. There was no evidence as to who asked for a copy. Miss Gammell did not give evidence and Mr Prentice was simply asked to recognise the fax which emanated from his office. The cover sheet contains a manuscript note signed by Mr Prentice: "Herewith copy minutes. See Item 7". The copy of the minutes received from Mr Prentice was then faxed to the Sheraton Hotel in Sofia but there was no evidence as to the identity of the individual to whom it was sent, nor as to who received it in Sofia. But it was given to Mr Ochanov and he took it home and typed in at the foot of the second page the names of the four directors of Balkan International. Mr Ochanov said that on the following morning there were a lot of people in the offices of Balkanbank to meet Mr Taher and have discussions. He said that he signed the minutes and then gave them to Mr Taher who signed, and after that to Mr McGrath who also signed. He said that he did not ask Mr Mironov to sign but here his evidence conflicts with that of Mr Mironov. The latter said that Mr Ochanov translated the document for him paragraph by paragraph but that he did not sign because he was not present at the meeting. Mr Ochanov, on the other hand, said that he could not remember if he translated the minutes for Mr Mironov, and that he did not give him the document to sign because he had not been to the meeting. In his evidence Mr Ochanov did say that Mr Taher and Mr McGrath had read the minutes before signing. His evidence was simply that he had presented the minutes to each of them and they had signed.

I have gone through this evidence in some detail because Mr Taher and Mr McGrath both said they never signed the minutes, but signatures bearing a close resemblance to their signatures can be seen at the foot of the second page of the minutes, and a handwriting expert called on behalf of Balkanbank said that the only conclusion he could come to was that their signatures were genuine. As I have come to the conclusion that no resolution was passed at the meeting of 1 March 1990 fixing the quorum at three, it is immaterial whether the copy minutes produced in evidence was signed by Messrs Taher and McGrath or not, but the view I have formed is that it is unlikely that it was or, if it was signed by them I think it unlikely that they were aware of what it was they were signing. The fact that there is no evidence that they read the minutes before they signed is in my opinion very significant. If Mr Taher had read the minutes, as he had in Mr Prentice's office on 1 March, he would certainly not have signed and similarly, if Mr McGrath had read them, I think it unlikely that he would have signed since he had not been at the meeting.

The next event of importance was that on 30 March 1990 Balkanbank entered into a written agreement with Interbalkan-Balkantourist, the Bulgarian State tourist company and three individuals, Ivan Marangasov, Angel Hadjiiski and Georgi Kantchev, to form an air transport company, Balkanbank to have 60 per cent of the share participation and the other parties to have 40 per cent. The agreement provided that Balkanbank could not transfer more than 82 per cent of its shares, being 49.2 per cent of the entire shares in the company, to another party without Interbalkan's consent. The initial capital was to be 200,000 leva divided into 200 shares of 1,000 leva each. Balkanbank was to provide credit for the purchase of three TU-154M aircraft amounting to a total of 38,959,861 transferable roubles, and to transfer immediately 4,000,000 transferable roubles to the vendor as an advanced payment. Shortly after this, the company, Air Via Company Ltd, was incorporated. The initial shareholding was slightly different from that stated in the contract of 30 March. Balkanbank had 56 per cent instead of 60 per cent and the balance was divided as follows: Interbalkan 25 per cent, five individuals with 3 per cent each and another two with 2 per cent each. Article 7 of the Articles of Association provided that:

> "Balkanbank may not transfer more than 87.5 per cent of its share, amounting to 49 per cent of the original share capital, to other corporate bodies and physical persons without the consent of Interbalkan."

This provision was to enable effect to be given to the decision of Balkan International set out in the first set of minutes of 7 March 1990, though with slightly different percentages, since the minutes had stated that BIL would participate in the private air company project with 39 per cent. It is clear that the intention of the parties at that time was that Balkanbank would transfer to BIL 87 per cent of its shares which would have amounted to 49 per cent of the shares in Air Via. This is confirmed by the resolution of the general assembly of Air Via which was passed on 11 May 1990 and is entitled Protocol Number 1, the translation of the relevant part of it being:

> "The General Assembly has taken the following resolution:
> (1) Confirm its approval that Balkanbank may transfer 87 per cent from its own shares to any partner at its own discretion."

Apart from the Air Via project, two other projects were being vigorously pursued by Balkan International, the Forex project and the Aquaba project which was concerned with the acquisition of a timber factory in Jordan. But neither of these projects is directly connected with the issues to which the plaintiff's claim gives rise. So, while a great deal of evidence was given to both of them, I do not propose at this stage to deal with them. The only project that is directly relevant to a consideration of the fundamental issue of fact which I referred to earlier is the Air Via project.

As appears from the minutes of the meeting of the directors of BIL of 7 March 1990, it was already planned that BIL would arrange "the additional finance required to complete the purchase of three Tupolov 154M aircraft" and in consideration of supplying the finance, the aircraft would be mortgaged to BIL. In the minutes of the next meeting of 8 April it is noted that TIL rather than BIL:

> "shall secure till 5th May 1990 a payment for US $1.3 million for the private airline project and Balkanbank, after receiving the above amount, shall purchase roubles and pay the value of the first plane through Interbalkan, Sofia."

This change is significant. It relates to an important aspect of the financing of the purchase of the planes, being an aspect in relation to which there is an acute conflict of evidence. It was common case that provided the dollars to be advanced for the purchase of the planes came from a source outside Bulgaria, they could be changed by Balkanbank into roubles at a most advantageous rate — 10 roubles for 1 dollar — instead of the official rate of 1 rouble for 1 dollar. By being able to benefit from this rate of exchange, Air Via could purchase the planes at $1.3 million each, but the planes would in fact be worth £13 million. It was essential, however that the dollars came from an outside source and it was because of this that it was provided in the minutes that they should come from TIL. An advance by BIL would not be an advance from a foreign source since BIL was partly owned by Balkanbank. Where the conflict of evidence arises is whether the dollars were genuinely to come from TIL or whether they were really to come from BIL, but to be made to appear to come from TIL in order to satisfy the Bulgarian authorities. Mr Taher's evidence was that, while it was agreed between himself and Mr Mironov that the monies should be advanced by BIL, he was directed by Mr Mironov to make it appear that the moneys were coming from TIL. This was vehemently denied by Mr Mironov.

Where all four directors of BIL were in agreement was that the aircraft would be mortgaged to BIL and refinanced, and as a result of the refinancing it was anticipated that BIL would be able to raise a sum in the region of $50 million for its own projects. The evidence as to how this would be done was far from clear, as it would have involved BIL becoming the owners of the aircraft, but I am satisfied that all four directors believed it could be done and that it would result in BIL having substantial funds for its various projects.

Further meetings of the board of directors of BIL were held on 8, 26 and 27

April, on 15 May and finally between 16 and 24 May 1990. The minutes of 8 April, in addition to noting that TIL should secure £1.3 million for the Air Via project, to which I have already referred, and dealing with the Forex project, dealt with other funding as follows:

> "(2) In reference to the other funding for Balkan International Ltd it was agreed that Balkanbank will issue an acceptable guarantee US $8 million from a western bank being 25 per cent of the value of the other projective financial requirements in favour of BIL which will be used as a standby guarantee for the various projects BIL is looking at. In consideration of this TIL shall guarantee to procure a minimum of 75 per cent of the projective financial requirements from their side for the same project. The above shall be done not later than 26 April 1990."

At the next meeting on 26/27 April, it was agreed that:

> "Mr Taher shall inform Mr Mironov by 4 May 1990 of the required text of the standby guarantee and Mr Mironov shall arrange to open the guarantee by 11 May 1990."

There was no further decision at the meeting in regard to the finance for the aircraft.

The minutes of the meeting of 15 May, contrary to the parties' usual custom, are unsigned. Mr Mironov said he did not sign them because there was a delay on the part of TIL in transferring the 1.3 million dollars referred to in the minutes of 8 April, and also because there were things in the minutes which concerned Mr Marangasov, the general manager of Air Via, and he had not had time to speak to Mr Marangasov about them. The unsigned minutes contained the following paragraph in regard to the financing of the aircraft:

> "Taher Investments shall arrange for the payment of the four planes amounting to about US$4 million, being the maximum value of the planes and working capital. However, Balkanbank and other parties in Via Company shall pay within a period of 24 months for their share capital. Until the 15th May 1990, Taher Investments did not transfer the amount of US$1.3 million."

There was a total conflict of evidence between Mr Mironov and Mr Taher as to where the £1.3 million was to come from. Mr Mironov insisted that it was to be from Taher Investments' own resources; Mr Taher said that the payment was conditional on the letter of credit referred to in the minutes of 8 April and 26/27 April being opened by Balkanbank, the intention being that the letter of credit would be used to enable the $1.3 million to be borrowed by Balkan International but the actual payment to Air Via would be made through Taher Investments to make it appear that the dollars were coming from a foreign source. He said this had been agreed on 8 April and when asked about a fax he had received from Mr Ochanov on 1 May saying the transfer of the $1.3 million must be delayed, he said that he had told Mr Ochanov that the money could not be paid until the letter of credit had been opened by Balkanbank.

A number of meetings between Mr Taher and Messrs Mironov and Ochanov took place between 16 and 24 May 1990 in Austria, Switzerland and Germany, and the decisions taken at them are recorded in a Protocol dated 24 May 1990 signed by all three and also by Mr Tachev the general manager of the International Department of Balkanbank. The principal decision recorded in the Protocol was that Balkanbank, instead of opening a standby letter of credit, would block a sum of seven million dollars in an account with the American Express Bank Vienna. This decision is recorded as follows in the Protocol:

> "1.1. Balkanbank will not open a standby letter of credit in favour of Balkan International Ltd/BIL/for the amount of US $10.5 million through Banco di Lavoro, New York, as it had been decided at the extraordinary meeting of BIL's Board of Directors stated in the Protocol of 15 May 1990. Instead of the above mentioned letter of credit, Balkanbank will block the amount of US $7 million under its own account with American Express Bank/AEB/Vienna in favour of BIL, at an interest rate agreed upon between the two banks for a period of one year, against which Taher Investments shall provide facilities in favour of BIL to realise the projects agreed between both parties, amounting from a minimum of US$30 million to US$75 million. The amount of US$7 million which Balkanbank will block under its account with AEB, Vienna will be considered a guarantee that Balkanbank will participate with the minimum of 20 to 25 per cent in financing the projects agreed to be executed by BIL Balkanbank shall arrange the above commitment with AEB not later than 31 May 1990.
>
> The projects are as follows:
> (a) Establishment of an air company agreed upon following the Protocol and Agreements signed till 24 May 1990;
> (b) Organising of a 'dealing room' in Dublin and Foreign Exchange activities through Mr Peter Cruddas and Plamen Stoyanov from the Bulgarian party. Balkanbank will participate with US$2.5 million to ensure a dealing line for US $100 million;
> (c) Purchase of the wood processing factory at Aquaba, Jordan;
> (d) Organising of a translation office at the BIL's representation at Sofia, and a total of US $100,000 will be provided for purchasing the necessary machinery and equipment and payment of salaries and fees."

Paragraph 2 of the Protocol then provided as follows:

> "Taher Investments will transfer within 48 hours the amount of US$1.3 million in favour of Balkanbank, Sofia, to finance the necessary opera-

> tions under the project for establishment and purchase the air company and the aircrafts, after settlement of all agreements, as per item 1 above with AEB Vienna. This amount considered the first plane."

Mr Mironov's evidence in regard to the purpose of this paragraph was that it was to show to the shareholders of Air Via that they would have their money within 48 hours. Mr Taher said that the payment by TIL of their 1.3 million dollars was dependant on the blocking of the seven million dollars. He said that he had explained to Messrs Mironov and Ochanov that he was not going to put one penny more until he got the guarantee and credit facility for BIL.

I am satisfied that Mr Ochanov was in general agreement with Mr Taher on this point. He said that the meaning of paragraph 2 of the Protocol was that the credit facility created by the blocking of the seven million dollars would be used for the 1.3 million dollars. It follows that he, as a director of BIL, was agreeable that Mr Taher should withdraw the 1.3 million dollars from the American Express Bank on behalf of BIL and pay this over for the financing of the aircraft as if it were coming from TIL. I am satisfied that Mr Mironov was agreeable to this also. I do not accept his evidence in regard to the reason why paragraph 2 was included in the protocol.

Other parts of the evidence confirm me in this view. On 22 May 1990 Mr Tachev sent Mr Taher a telex in the following form:

> "Please be informed that Balkanbank has arranged the transfer of US$6 million to its account in American Express Bank Ltd, Vienna and is ready to block these funds like a collateral for credit facilities extended to Balkan International Ltd, Dublin. We shall proceed further, instructing American Express Bank Ltd Vienna accordingly, immediately after receiving your approval in accordance with the recent agreements.

This showed that Mr Taher had an immediate interest in the blocking of the six million dollars (which later was increased to seven million dollars) and his interest clearly was to have a security against which the 1.3 million dollars could be borrowed. In addition, Mr Taher agreed in evidence that there was great urgency in creating the deposit. As none of the other projects which BIL had in hand required funds immediately, the only reason there could have been for this urgency was that funds were required at once for the Air Via project.

As to the opening of the account for BIL with the American Express Bank, Vienna, this was discussed by Mr Tachev at the afternoon meeting with the bank on 25 May. In a telex of 23 May to the bank Mr Tachev had previously asked the bank for particulars of their formal procedure for opening a current account in the name of BIL. It is clear accordingly that it was Balkanbank's intention, as well as Mr Taher's, that such an account should be opened. I accept Mr Ochanov's evidence that Mr Mironov had given Mr Taher full authority to act on behalf of BIL in the negotiations with the American Express Bank, part of which was the opening of a current account. Mr Ochanov also said that the opening of the bank account and the loan which would be provided was agreed by everybody, meaning Mr Mironov, himself and Mr Taher. Mr Mironov denied this. He said that Mr Taher was in Vienna simply to help Mr Tachev. Once again I reject his evidence. I accept Mr Taher's evidence that Mr Mironov told him to go to Vienna on behalf of BIL and arrange the credit facilities and start BIL working.

There is further evidence also that Balkanbank must have been aware of the resolutions of 26 and 31 May signed by Mr Taher and Mr McGrath. Mr Lismore, whose evidence I accept, said that he brought the resolution of 31 May to Vienna on 1 June. There he met Mr Fikov, who was from the BIL office in Sofia. He had with him certain documents in a sealed envelope. It contained the pledge agreement and facility letter and also the resolution of 26 May. Mr Lismore substituted the resolution of 31 May for the latter when he handed over all the relevant documents to the American Express Bank on the afternoon of 1 June but he confirmed that Mr Fikov had had it in his possession. Furthermore, he said that in Mr Fikov's presence he took out the papers that he (Mr Lismore) had with him and the papers which Mr Fikov had brought and sorted them in order to make sure he had what was required before going to the bank. And he obtained from the American Express Bank a receipt for the paper, dated 1 June, one of the papers being the resolution of 31 May.

What is clear from Mr Lismore's evidence is that the resolution of 26 May had been brought to Vienna by Mr Fikov with the pledge agreement signed by Balkanbank, and the facility letter, that is to say, with papers emanating from Balkanbank so that Balkanbank clearly had notice of the resolution.

I am satisfied accordingly that the bank account for BIL with the American Express Bank was opened with the full agreement of the Bulgarian directors of BIL and likewise that they agreed to 1.3 million dollars being borrowed on the security of the seven million dollars deposit in order to provide finance for Air Via.

There remains the question of whether the withdrawal actually made of seven million dollars was made with the knowledge and consent of Mr Mironov Balkanbank's claim is that the drawing down of this money was a fraudulent wrongful act on the part of Mr Taher and Mr McGrath but this clearly would not be the case if it was done with Mr Mironov's knowledge and consent.

The issue turns mainly on whether I accept the evidence of Mr Taher and Mr Ismail of a telephone conversation between Mr Taher and Mr Mironov, on Monday, 11 June 1990. Mr Mironov says he has no recollection of any such conversation and denies that he said any of the things which are attributed to him. Both Mr Taher and Mr Ismail gave a detailed account of it. Mr Taher said he explained to Mr Mironov that the money had been drawn down; they were now ready to work and he was effecting immediately the transfer of the 1.3 million dollars. He said that Mr Mironov said: "this baby starts to walk", referring to BIL which he always referred to as "this baby". He said that Mr Mironov then said:

> "Please make sure that the money comes in via TIL so that we can change

> the dollars into roubles and get ourselves a lot of money."

Mr Taher said they also discussed things in general, including the translation project and the Aquaba project, and he also told Mr Mironov he wanted to get some of the money he had spent and Mr Mironov said:

> "No problem, but be sure to be mortgaging those planes and get back the American Express loan."

Mr Ismail's account of the conversation was somewhat fuller. In addition to the matters to which Mr Taher referred, he said that Mr Taher had asked if Air Via was registered and if BIL was a shareholder. Mr Mironov said "no", but it would be happening soon. He said that Mr Mironov asked about Bulgar Tabac; that he wanted a letter of credit for them, and Mr Taher said that "we would do something for them, but we have to make a profit". He said they discussed the Forex project and agreed to start with $1.25 million rather than $2.5 million. When Mr Taher said he wanted to put back some money into TIL, he said that Mr Mironov was not too happy and said:

> "You know Bulgarian regulations, all this from the Irish side, I cannot accept it this way."

And Mr Taher said:

> "You needn't worry about that. This $7 million will very soon be paid back to American Express Bank as we are going to refinance the planes."

And Mr Mironov said:

> "Please make sure you be back to me as quickly as you can. I don't want you to tell anybody, especially the Air Via people, about this refinancing."

Mr Taher said there would be no problem about that.

Balkanbank asked me to find that this conversation was invented. I do not believe it was. I find that such conversation did take place and accordingly that Balkanbank, through Mr Mironov, was aware that the seven million dollars had been drawn down, and assented to it. I consider that at the time both Mr Taher and Mr Mironov believed that what they were planning would work out, that is to say, that the 1.3 million dollars would be converted into transferable roubles at the rate of 10 roubles for a dollar and would be used to pay for the planes for Air Via; that BIL would become a shareholder in Air Via and the planes would be mortgaged to it, and that BIL would then refinance the planes and repay the American Express Bank out of the proceeds. The telephone conversation is entirely consistent with this having been in their minds.

I am satisfied accordingly that there was no fraud or breach of duty on the part of Messrs Taher and McGrath and that this part of Balkanbank's claim fails.

There remains to be considered the question of the disbursements made by Mr Taher and Mr McGrath out of the seven million dollars. As I am satisfied that that sum was drawn down with the knowledge and consent of Mr Mironov, it became part of the assets of Balkan International so the question is whether Mr Taher and Mr McGrath were entitled to use it in the manner in which they did.

While in the statement of claim Balkanbank alleged that it had suffered damage and loss, and claimed damages and other relief, in the course of his submissions Mr Shanley put the case also on the basis that Balkanbank was suing in its capacity as a shareholder in Balkan International in respect of damage suffered by Balkan International through the breach of duty of the Irish directors, Mr Taher and Mr McGrath. It was submitted that the case came within one of the exceptions to the rule in *Foss v. Harbottle*, being the exception which enabled a shareholder to sue where damage to the company was caused by conduct on the part of the majority in control of the company which amounted to a fraud on the minority.

This particular exception is described as follows in Gower's *Principles of Modern Company Law* (4th ed., 1979) at page 648:

> "Not every wrong to the company will justify a derivative action to remedy it. Normally the wrong complained of must be such as to involve a fraud on the minority, which could not be validly waived by the company in general meeting. What constitutes such conduct has been discussed in Chapter 25. Briefly to recapitulate, it appears to cover conduct of the following types:
> (a) Expropriation of the property of the company or, in some circumstances, that of the minority,
> (b) Breach of the Directors' duties of subjective good faith, and
> (c) Voting for company resolutions not *bona fide* in the interests of the company as a whole."

I adopt that passage as a correct statement of the law. On behalf of Balkanbank it is contended that it entitles them to an order directing Mr Taher and Mr McGrath and Taher Investments Ltd to account to Balkan International for the entire of the seven million dollars drawn down from the American Express Bank. They contend that none of the disbursements could be regarded as having been properly made.

The situation in the case is an unusual one. Balkan and Taher Investments are equal shareholders in Balkan International. As neither has a majority, there is no question of any disbursements being approved by a majority of the shareholders. But they could be approved by a properly convened meeting of the board of directors of Balkan International and if so approved would be binding on Balkanbank provided that such approval did not constitute oppression of Balkanbank. Even though Balkanbank is an equal shareholder, since Taher Investments has control of the board, through Mr Taher having a casting vote as chairman, Balkanbank are in my opinion in the same position as a minority shareholder and the situation has to be looked at in that light.

The disbursements made, with the exception of the $1.6 million which were intended for Balkan International's participation in Air Via, were in my opinion made irregularly since they were not made pursuant to resolutions of the board passed at regularly convened meetings of the directors. They were decided upon either by Mr Taher on his own, or jointly by Mr Taher and Mr McGrath. But even though irregular, if they could be validly confirmed by a properly convened meeting of the board of directors of Balkan International the court would not interfere. But they could be validly confirmed only if they did not constitute oppression of Balkanbank. So the question is whether confirmation would constitute such oppression.

In order to answer this it is necessary to distinguish between the different disbursements made. They are set out in the summary account of receipts and disbursements in Appendix 3 to Mr Patrick McSweeney's report and are as follows:

Forex Losses (dealings by Plamen Stoyanov and Rafiq Petker)	£560,888
Paint for Air Via plane	£6,919
Interest payments to AmEx Bank	£167,709
Bank charges on transfer of $7 million	£12,180
BIL start-up expenses, feasibilities and commitment fees	£1,271,494

It seems to me that no objection could be taken by Balkanbank to the first four items. The Forex losses were clearly the liability of Balkan International. The Forex dealing room was a Balkan International project decided upon by the four directors of Balkan International and while it appears that it was not envisaged that there would be losses, since there were losses, they were Balkan International's responsibility. And even if Mr Mironov did not know of the losses, as he claimed, that could not make any difference.

The paint for the Air Via plane was clearly a Balkan International liability also, as were the interest payments to the American Express Bank and the bank charges on the transfer of the seven million dollars, both of which flowed from the decision to draw down that sum.

The Balkan International start-up expenses etc., are in my opinion in a different category. It has to be borne in mind that the seven million dollars drawn down from the American Express Bank was obtained on security provided by Balkanbank. They were funds procured by Balkanbank for Balkan International. While that may not have given Balkanbank an absolute right to determine how the funds should be used, it seems to me that Balkanbank would be entitled to object to their being used to defray expenses incurred by their partner Taher Investments. I am satisfied on the evidence that it was Balkanbank's intention that the $7 million should be used for capital investment in future projects and that Mr Taher and Mr McGrath were aware of this. It would accordingly be in breach of their duty of subjective good faith if they were to apply part of that sum in discharge of Balkan International's start-up and other expenses incurred by Taher Investments. They would be using the funds for their own benefit and for a purpose never intended by Balkanbank. I am not overlooking the fact that in his telephone conversation with Mr Mironov on 11 June Mr Taher said he wanted to be repaid expenses that Taher Investments had incurred, and Mr Mironov gave a grudging acceptance to this, but this did not in my opinion authorise the actual disbursement which was made, nor would it relieve a decision now by the board to confirm the disbursement from being a fraud on Balkanbank.

I am satisfied accordingly that Mr Taher and Mr McGrath, and Taher Investments, must account to Balkan International for the $1,271,494 disbursed for Balkan International's start-up expenses, feasibilities and commitment fees.

It does not follow that these expenses are not a liability of Balkan International. I am not making any decision on that issue. All I am deciding is that it would be a fraud on Balkanbank to direct their payment out of the monies borrowed from the American Express Bank.

Taher Investments and Mr Taher and Mr McGrath must account to Balkan International also for the balance of the $7 million still under their control, being the two sums referred to in Mr McSweeney's summary account as:

Deposit on offices	$260,000
Cash	$4,144,110

Similarly Balkanbank must account to Balkan International for the $750,000 retained by it out of the $1.6 million paid to it in connection with Air Via.

I will hear counsel on the form that the order should take.

In giving Balkanbank relief on the basis of the relevant exception to the rule in *Foss v. Harbottle*, I have gone outside the pleadings in the case. I have treated this as being a derivative action brought on behalf of Balkan International but in any such action it is necessary for the plaintiff to plead that the action is brought on behalf of himself and all the other shareholders of the company. There is no such plea in the statement of claim. However, the issue was fully dealt with in the submissions of counsel on both sides, and without any objection from the defendants, so I have no hesitation in giving liberty to Balkanbank to make the necessary amendment to the statement of claim.

I now turn to Balkan International's counterclaim. The claim is that Balkanbank agreed to transfer to Balkan International 87.5 per cent of its shares in Air Via, being 49 per cent of the capital of that company, and that it failed to carry out that agreement. In the pleading filed various declarations are sought together with an order for specific performance and damages.

When Mr Clarke was closing the case on behalf of the defendants, I asked him what I could do in regard to the issue raised by the counterclaim. The reason for my question was twofold. Firstly, I had been informed by counsel in the course of the hearing that separate proceedings are pending between Balkan

International and Balkanbank in Bulgaria in relation to the shares in Air Via, and secondly, in the event of my finding that there had been an agreement which had been broken, there was no sufficient evidence before me to enable me to assess damages.

Mr Clarke replied that he did not think I would have jurisdiction to deal with the internal affairs of a foreign company, which seems to me to represent correctly the legal position, but nonetheless, when asked what relief he was seeking, he firstly stated that he was seeking specific performance of the agreement though he conceded that it was possible that effect could not be given to such an order, and he went on to say that it might be more appropriate to seek a declaration that as between Balkanbank and Balkan International, Balkanbank should attempt to take on whatever was within its powers to procure the registration of Balkan International as owner of 49 per cent of the shares of Air Via.

Whether such a declaration would be of any practical value to Balkan International is open to doubt. But I think it is clear that the court could not make an order for specific performance since it would have no way of enforcing it. Not only would it be purporting to make an order regulating the internal affairs of a foreign company, but it would also be purporting to bind by its order a company not amenable to its jurisdiction since it is registered in Bulgaria and has no place of business in the State. Such an order could not be enforced against Balkanbank. So the sole question is whether a declaration in the form outlined by Mr Clarke should be made.

In my opinion, on the facts as they stand at present, such a declaration would have no reality. Air Via is a company registered under the Part 3 Chapter 2 of the Bulgarian Decree Number 56 on Economic Activity which came into force in Bulgaria on 30 January 1989. Article 47 sub-article 3(2) of the decree provides, *inter alia*, that for the admission of a new member of a company or the transfer of shares to a new member a unanimous vote of the general assembly of members is required. So any agreement there may have been between Balkanbank and Balkan International for the transfer of shares to Balkan International was always conditional on Balkan International being accepted by all the shareholders as a member of the company. Whatever the position may have been previously, it is clear that the general assembly will not now accept Balkan International as a member. A Protocol passed by the general assembly on 28 February 1990 commenced with the following paragraph:

> "Protocol No. 3 of the general assembly of shareholders finds that the Irish Company Balkan International Ltd has not fulfilled the conditions in item 1 of the Protocol No. 2 of 'Air Via' concerning the decision taken at the Company's meeting dated 15 June 1990, as it has not transferred $1.6 million to the account of the Company to the final agreed term on 29th 06 90 — 5 p.m. and as a result the aforementioned Company is not accepted as a shareholder in Air Via and the decision of the shareholders must be considered null according to the text and conditions in the aforementioned

> Protocol No. 2 from the meeting of the shareholders of Air Via dated 25th 06 90."

Apart from this, the protocol altered the shareholdings in the company so that Balkanbank, which formerly had 56 per cent of the shares, now only has 31 per cent. So Balkanbank could not, since the date of that protocol, transfer to Balkan International the percentage which it is alleged was the subject matter of the agreement, which was 49 per cent. It follows that a declaration in the form suggested by Mr Clarke would be asking the impossible.

Balkan International has a twofold problem in regard to the shares in Air Via. Firstly, it would have to establish a clear agreement with Balkanbank, and secondly, since any agreement was always subject to Balkan International being accepted as a member by a unanimous vote of the general assembly of Air Via, it had to establish that such a vote had been obtained. This latter point was the main obstacle in the way of Balkan International. There was no contractual relationship between Balkan International and Air Via so there was nothing to prevent the members of Air Via altering the conditions on which they were prepared to give their consent. And this is what happened. In Protocol No. 1, 11 May 1990, the general assembly confirmed its approval that Balkanbank might transfer 87 per cent of its own shares to any other partner at its own discretion. There was disagreement between the experts in Bulgarian law who gave evidence as to the effect in law of this provision. Mr Boyonov, who was called by Balkanbank, was of the opinion that it was only a protocol of intention and it would not have been sufficient to entitle Balkan International to be registered as a member if the shares had been transferred to it. On the other hand, Mr Borisov, who was called by the defendants, considered that the Protocol constituted an actual approval of the transfer of 87 per cent of Balkanbank's shares and would have entitled Balkan International to be registered as a member.

Of the two opinions I prefer that of Mr Borisov but as there was no transfer of the shares at the time, and as the protocol in question was superseded by a later Protocol, it is immaterial which of the experts was correct.

Protocol No. 2 was more detailed. Paragraph 1 provided as follows:

> "The general assembly has decided:
> (1) In accordance with Article 7 of the Statute, Balkanbank informed the other shareholders that it will cede 87.5 per cent of its stake in the share capital, representing 49 per cent of this capital, to Balkan International Ltd in which its proper ownership is 50 per cent.
>
> Interbalkan agrees that this transfer of property should be done under the nominal value of TR 32 million, paid in US dollars on the rate of TR 10 for 1 US dollar.
>
> The new shareholders to be represented in the general assembly by the Vice-President of Balkan International Ltd, Mr Ivan Mironov, or by his authorised delegate from the Bulgarian party.

> 50 per cent from the a.m. amount, equal to US $1,600,000 (one million six hundred thousand only) must be transferred to the Company account with Balkanbank until 5 p.m. on 29th June 1990.
>
> If this transfer is delayed this resolution will become null and void."

Of the 1.6 million dollars which was to be paid 1.3 million dollars had been transferred on 11 June. There was a considerable dispute as to whether the balance of 300,000 dollars was transferred in accordance with the requirements of the Protocol before the time specified. There is no doubt that Mr Taher telexed BCCI on 28 June 1990 to transfer 300,000 dollars to the account of Balkanbank at BCCI Leadenhall Street, London, and it appears that that transfer was made with a value date of 29 June 1990. But Air Via did not accept that the Protocol had been complied with and subsequently the sum demanded for the shares increased to 12 million dollars. In the result, the transfer of the shares to Balkan International was never approved by Air Via and so Balkan International could not be and never was registered as a member of Air Via.

The problem for Balkan International was that, irrespective of any agreement which may have existed between it and Balkanbank, the ultimate decision in the matter rested with the shareholders of Air Via. And their requirements became increasingly more exacting. Initially, as can be seen from Protocol 1, they did not attach any conditions to Balkanbank transferring 87.5 per cent of its shares to Balkan International. Shortly afterwards, it seems clear from the evidence, they required BIL to make a loan of 1.3 million dollars to the company, and in Protocol No. 2 this sum has been increased to 1.6 million dollars and, instead of being a loan, it was to be investment capital, and so non-returnable, a change of which Mr Taher complained bitterly in his evidence. Finally, at a meeting of the shareholders on 17 July 1990 the amount demanded of Taher Investments for his participation in the company was 12.5 million dollars.

The reality of the situation was that Balkanbank was never in a position to make an unconditional contract for the transfer of 49 per cent of its shares to Balkan International. Any agreement was subject to Balkan International being accepted by the shareholders of Air Via which meant that the conditions which they imposed had to be complied with.

In support of their case, the defendants relied on a Protocol of Balkanbank of 28 March 1990 the existence of which only came to light after the case had been heard and which was the subject of an application for further and better discovery. The relevant part of this Protocol was as follows:

> "The Board of Directors made the following decision:
>
> (1) To give its consent Trade Bank Balkanbank to become a partner of the Ltd Company 'Via' with place of residence Sofia.
>
> (2) Trade Bank Balkanbank to participate with 56 per cent in the share capital. The share capital will be 200,000 levs, divided in shares of 1,000 levs. From these 56 per cent, 7 per cent of the share capital, to be left for

> Balkanbank within two months after the establishment of the Company. The rest 49 per cent to be transferred to the Bulgarian Irish Company Balkan International Ltd (50 per cent property of Balkanbank) in accordance to the agreement with Interbalkan, Sofia and the others."

This confirms something of which there never was any doubt, namely, that the intention of the parties was that 49 per cent of Balkanbank's shares in Air Via would be transferred to Balkan International, but it also makes it clear that this was to be done "in accordance to the agreement with Interbalkan Sofia and others", being the persons who at that time were intending to form Air Via, and who are the parties to the letter of intent of 14 February 1990 and the preliminary contract of 30 March 1990. The protocol does not in my opinion add anything to the defendants' case. What it states was in effect what would have happened if the first protocol of Air Via of 11 May 1990 had been implemented. But, as already mentioned, it was not implemented and was then superseded by Protocol No. 2.

The defendants also relied on the certificate given by Balkanbank and signed by Mr Mironov, which is not dated, but appears to have been given on some date in the first half of July. This certificate purports to be a transfer by Balkanbank to Balkan International of 87.5 per cent of its shares in Air Via "on the basis of Air Via Ltd shareholders' decision specified in Item 1 of Protocol No. 2 from 25 06 1990", and it provided that it should be null and void if the 1.6 million dollars referred to in the protocol were not transferred to Balkanbank by 29 June 1990. This is the same condition as that on which the validity of Protocol No. 2 itself depended. The shareholders of Air Via clearly took the view that the condition had not been satisfied, with the result that the protocol became null and void, and the shareholders in these circumstances would hardly have accepted that the position in regard to the certificate would have been any different.

Since there was never any written agreement for the transfer of the shares by Balkanbank to Balkan International, the onus was on Balkan International to establish the existence of an oral contract and its terms. Mr Taher complained that the terms kept changing. This was not quite correct. What seems to have been changing was the requirements of the shareholders of Air Via. And this was something which neither party could control. Furthermore, the onus was on Balkan International to establish that their failure to become registered as owners of 49 per cent of the shares of Air Via was due to the breach by Balkanbank of their agreement. It seems to me that this has not been established. In my opinion it was due rather to the refusal by the shareholders of Air Via to accept the transfer of the shares to Balkan International rather than to the breach by Balkanbank of any agreement they had with Balkan International.

In my opinion Balkan International is not entitled to the relief sought in the counterclaim and it must accordingly be dismissed.

Patricia McLaughlin
Barrister

1963 ACT, PART VI

In the Matter of Shannon Travel Ltd and In the Matter of the Companies Act 1963: High Court 1970 No. 3849P (Kenny J) 8 May 1972

Company – Agreement between the company and Aer Lingus Teoranta that the company would act as an agent of Aer Lingus – Liquidator appointed to the company – Whether monies received by the agent for Aer Lingus tickets sold by them to passengers were received in a fiduciary capacity – Monies lodged in bank account – Whether Aer Lingus had a charge on monies held in the liquidator's bank account – Whether monies traceable – Charge only arises when company becomes insolvent – Whether monies satisfactorily accounted for – Whether liquidator has a duty to take steps to trace any monies received by the company and lodged to the bank accounts

Facts: Shannon Travel entered into a standard form agreement with the International Air Transport Association (I.A.T.A.) under which travel agents were supplied with blank tickets for use on airlines. These tickets were filled in by the agent who collected the fee from the intending passenger. The agreement provided for the payment of commission to the agent by the carrier and for the remission of fees collected by the agent to the carrier. The agreement also provided that the monies collected, including commission withheld, was retained by the agent as the property of the carrier until satisfactorily accounted for and, further, that the agent would indemnify the carrier for any losses incurred in connection with tickets whether or not such loss was occasioned, *inter alia*, by the default or insolvency of a bank in which the agent may have deposited such proceeds, notwithstanding that under the terms of the agreement such proceeds were the property of the carrier and were held in trust by the agent.

On the same day, Aer Lingus Teoranta issued a certificate of appointment to Shannon Travel appointing it as one of their agents. Shannon Travel accounted to Aer Lingus twice a month for sales of air tickets and it also submitted a sales report twice monthly showing the tickets which it had sold together with a cheque for the amount due less its commission. The cheques included the amount due for tickets which had been sold to passengers on credit.

Shannon Travel had an account with Bank of Ireland and when bank officials went on strike on 1 May 1970, a considerable number of cheques sent by Shannon Travel to Aer Lingus had not been cleared. An account was opened by the holding company of Shannon Travel with the First National City Bank and all cash received and cheques drawn on banks which were not closed were lodged to that account by the companies in the group. During the strike, Shannon

Travel continued to send Aer Lingus reports on the tickets which it had sold, with cheques drawn on the Bank of Ireland for the sale price less commission.

It became clear in October 1970 that Shannon Travel was insolvent and Aer Lingus then insisted on receiving cheques drawn by third parties in favour of Shannon in payment of some of its liability for tickets. Cheques totalling £47,932 were sent to Aer Lingus, of which £3,935 was not paid when the bank strike ended.

On 19 November 1970 a provisional liquidator was appointed to Shannon Travel and he took possession of all the cheques and cash of the company and lodged these to an account in the National Bank of Ireland, the ultimate credit of this account being £198,490. £32,694 was sent to the Bank of Ireland from Shannon's office in Limerick, which said monies were held in a suspense account at the bank.

Aer Lingus claimed that Shannon sold air tickets supplied by it at fares of £183,659, that these monies were received by Shannon in a fiduciary capacity and that Aer Lingus had a charge on the amounts standing to the credit of the liquidator's bank account in the National Bank of Ireland for the sums which they can establish were received by Shannon and paid into these accounts and not paid to it. It was submitted by the liquidator that the forwarding of the sales reports with a cheque for the amount which it showed as due meant that the sums for the cheques had been drawn had been satisfactorily accounted for to Aer Lingus. Accountants retained by Aer Lingus inspected the books of Shannon Travel and were able to trace cases in which Aer Lingus tickets were sold by Shannon and paid for by cheques which were subsequently lodged by the provisional liquidator to the account at the National Bank.

Held by Kenny J in allowing the claim by Aer Lingus that:

(1) When a person receives money as a trustee or as one occupying a fiduciary relationship to another, the person who transferred the property or paid the money may recover the property and has a charge on the account to which the money or cheques have been lodged or on property on which the monies received have been spent, provided that the property or money can be traced through the accounts of the debtor into the bank account or buildings or other property and provided that there is money to the credit of the account on which the charge can operate. *Re Halletts Estate* (1880) 13 Ch D 696 and *Sinclair v. Brougham* [1914] AC 398 applied.

(2) When the debtor, having received money in a fiduciary capacity, lodges it to his account, he creates between himself and the bank the relationship of debtor and creditor and the charge does not operate as an assignment of the *chose in action* which he has, but directly on the sum standing to the credit of the bank account.

(3) Such a charge, being an equitable remedy can be called in aid only when the property or funds cannot be recovered from the debtor in an action for money had and received.

(4) It follows that the charge arises only when the debtor being an individual

has become insolvent or bankrupt or being a company is unable to pay its debts. *Re Diplock's Estate* [1948] 1 Ch 465 and *Re Shanahan's Stamp Auctions Ltd* [1962] IR 386 applied.

(5) The effect of the agreement was that the monies collected by the company for all tickets were the property of Aer Lingus and were to be retained by Shannon Travel as such property until they had been satisfactorily accounted for. They never became part of the assets of Shannon Travel and were held by them as trustee.

(6) The forwarding of the sales report with a cheque for the amount which was shown as due did not mean that the sums for which the cheques had been drawn had been satisfactorily accounted for to Aer Lingus. Acceptance of a cheque for a debt is not payment as it is clearly conditional upon the cheque being honoured. The monies which had been received by Shannon Travel in respect of Aer Lingus tickets were not accounted for satisfactorily to the carrier when the cheques were not honoured when the banks opened again.

(7) It was possible to trace monies coming from clients of Shannon Travel in respect of air tickets and going into the account which was now in credit. The charge was confined to the monies to the credit of the bank account with the National Bank of Ireland.

(8) A deduction should be made of £43,996 in respect of monies received by Aer Lingus through the third party cheques sent to it by Shannon Travel.

(9) The official liquidator was not required to take any steps to trace any monies received by Shannon Travel and lodged to the bank accounts. The claim must be prepared by Aer Lingus and submitted to the official liquidator to check, and Aer Lingus was entitled to inspect the books and records of Shannon Travel for that purpose.

(10) Their was no duty on the liquidator to enquire from other creditors whether they claimed that the monies received by Shannon Travel in respect of the sale of their tickets was received in a fiduciary capacity.

(11) The remuneration and legal fees and expenses of the provisional and official liquidator ranked before any fiduciary claims.

Cases referred to in judgment

Diplock's Estate, In re [1948] 1 Ch 465
Halletts Estate, In re (1880) 13 Ch D 696
Shanahan's Stamp Auctions Ltd, In re [1962] IR 386
Sinclair v. Brougham [1914] AC 398

Counsel's and solicitors' names not available

KENNY J **8 May 1972**

Shannon Travel ("Shannon") was incorporated in the Republic of Ireland and carried on the business of selling air, sea and road transportation and booking and organisation of hotel accommodation. It had offices in Dublin, Cork and Limerick. An international organisation, the International Air Transport Association (I.A.T.A.), had prepared a standard form of agreement for use by airlines under which travel agents would be supplied with blank tickets for use on airlines and which could be filled up by the travel agent who would collect the fare from the intending passenger. On 24 September 1969, Shannon signed such an agreement. The relevant clauses read:

> "1. Effectiveness. (a) This agreement shall become effective between the agent and each individual I.A.T.A. member only if such I.A.T.A. member (hereinafter called "the carrier") delivers to the agent a certificate of appointment duly executed by or on behalf of the carrier authorising the agent to represent the carrier subject to the terms and conditions of this agreement.
>
> 5. Commissions. (a) Subject to the terms and provisions of this agreement the carrier will pay or allow the agent the rates of commission as set forth in Schedule A attached hereto and made a part hereof. Such commission shall be accepted by the agent as full compensation for its services rendered to the carrier hereunder. No commission shall be paid to the agent for the sale of any air passenger transportation unless the proper fare applicable to such transportation is collected and paid by the agent to the carrier.
>
> 6. Remittance. (a) The agent shall remit to the carrier the monies due (all monies for sale of passenger transportation excluding monies for transportation sold under the I.A.T.A. travel plan or similar I.A.T.A. approved credit plan, but including monies for any sales against which the agent issues a transportation document, as defined in section B of resolution 810a, being deemed to be due when such document is issued) for the sales made hereunder not less than once each month, at such times under such conditions and in such currencies as the carrier may designate from time to time in writing. Unless otherwise instructed by the carrier the agent shall be entitled to deduct from such remittance the applicable commission as specified on Schedule A attached hereto. If no monies are due, the agent, if required to submit a sales report, shall submit "a no sales report" with the same frequency as the sales report.
>
> (b) All monies collected by the agent for transportation sold hereunder including any commission withheld by the agent pursuant to paragraphs 5 and 6 hereunder are the property of the carrier and shall be retained by the agent as the property of the carrier until satisfactorily accounted for to the carrier. The agent shall not use such monies to engage directly or indirectly in any foreign transactions which are intended to obtain for the agent any monetary advantage additional to his commission.
>
> 11. Custody and issuance of tickets. (a) The carrier may, at his option, furnish the agent free of charge with tickets and/or exchange vouchers/orders and other necessary documents for use in connexion with business transacted under this agreement. . . .
>
> 12. Liability. (c) Further, the agent agrees to indemnify and hold harmless the carrier, its officers, agents, employees and servants from any damage,

> expense or loss incurred for any reason whatsoever in connexion with tickets, exchange vouchers/orders or other materials furnished by the carrier to the agent or any documents issued by the agent on the authority of the carrier or the proceeds thereof whether or not such proceeds have been deposited in a bank and whether or not such loss is occasioned by the default or insolvency of either a purchaser of such forms or documents or of a bank in which the agent may have deposited such proceeds, and notwithstanding the fact that, under the terms of this agreement, such proceeds are the property of the carrier and held in trust by the agent."

On the same day Aer Lingus Teoranta ("Aer Lingus") issued a certificate of appointment to Shannon appointing them as one of their agents. Air tickets were given by Aer Lingus to Shannon who issued some of them to their customers on credit, so that some substantial sums were due when Shannon subsequently was ordered to be wound up by the court. Aer Lingus required Shannon Travel to account for sales of air tickets between the 1st and the 15th of each month within eight days after the 15th and for those sold between the 15th and the end of each month, within eight days after the last day of each month and Shannon sent twice in each month to Aer Lingus a sales report showing the tickets which they had sold with a cheque for the amount due for them less their commission. The cheques included the amount due for tickets which had been sold on credit.

Shannon had its bank account with the Bank of Ireland at O'Connell Street, Dublin where they maintained at least two accounts, one for lodgments and the other for payments. In March and April 1970 relations between the associated banks and their staffs were not good and there were considerable delays in the clearance of cheques. Those which were sent by Shannon to Aer Lingus in connection with monies due for air tickets had not been cleared when the bank officials went on strike on 1 May 1970. Shannon was a wholly-owned subsidiary of Hibernian Transport Company Ltd which succeeded in opening an account with the First National City Bank to which all cheques drawn on banks which were not closed and received by the Hibernian Transport Co. Ltd and its subsidiaries and all cash received by that group were lodged. During the bank strike, Shannon continued to send to Aer Lingus reports on their tickets which it had sold with cheques drawn on the Bank of Ireland for the sale price less the commission.

In October 1970 Shannon tried to persuade Aer Lingus to take over its business and when Aer Lingus examined their books, the insolvency of Shannon became clear. Aer Lingus then insisted that they should get cheques drawn by third parties in favour of Shannon from it in payment of some of their liability for tickets. On 2 November Shannon wrote to Aer Lingus:

> "Please receive endorsed cheques and money orders amounting to £15,775 in payment of the Shannon Travel Ltd ticket returns for the period 1st to the 15th October 1970"

while on 4 November the letter read:

> "Please receive endorsed cheques and money orders amounting to £3,693 in payment of your Shannon Travel Account for £3,693,"

and on 6 November they wrote:

> "Please receive endorsed cheques, postal orders and money orders amounting to £28,461 being deposit on Shannon Travel ticket returns for the two periods from the 16th October 1970 to the 15th November 1970."

The cheques and money orders drawn by third parties in favour of Shannon amounted to £47,931 of which £3,935 was not paid when the bank strike ended.

Hibernian Transport Co Ltd and Shannon had been insolvent for some time before November and on the 19th of that month a petition was presented to this court for the winding-up of Shannon. A provisional liquidator (Mr Ivan O'Neill) was appointed on that day and he took possession of all the cheques and cash of Shannon and lodged these amounting to £229,281 to an account in the National Bank of Ireland. £30,791 was not paid and therefore £198,490 went to the ultimate credit of this account. Shannon's account at the Bank of Ireland, O'Connell Street was overdrawn by £1,452 on 1 May 1970 when cheques which had been issued by Shannon but not cleared before then are taken into account. During the bank strike £32,694 was sent from Shannon's Limerick office to the Bank of Ireland in Dublin and this sum now stands to the credit of a suspense account in the Bank of Ireland.

Aer Lingus now claims that Shannon sold air tickets supplied by them at fares of £183,659, that these monies were received by Shannon in a fiduciary capacity and that they have a charge on the amounts standing to the credit of the liquidator's bank account in the National Bank of Ireland and on the company's bank account in the Bank of Ireland for the sums which they can establish were received by Shannon and paid into these accounts and not paid to them. They base this contention on the decision of the Court of Appeal in England in *Re Halletts Estate* (1880) 13 Ch D 696 but this decision is but one facet of the general equitable principle which will be found expounded in divergent terms in the speeches in *Sinclair v. Brougham* [1914] AC 398. The general principle is that when a person receives money as a trustee or as one occupying a fiduciary relationship to another, the person who transferred the property or paid the money may recover the property and has a charge on the account to which the money or cheques have been lodged or on property on which the monies received have been spent provided that the property or money can be traced through the accounts of the debtor into the bank account or buildings or other property and provided that there is money to the credit of the account on which the charge can operate. When however the debtor having received money in a fiduciary capacity lodges it to his account, he creates between himself and the bank the relationship of debtor and creditor and the charge does not operate as an assignment of the *chose in action* which he has but directly on the sum standing to the credit of the bank account. Moreover such a charge, being an equitable remedy, can be called in aid only when the property or funds cannot be recovered from the debtor by an action for money had and received. It follows that the charge arises only when the debtor being an individual has become insolvent or bankrupt or being a company is unable to pay its debts (see the judgment of Lord Greene MR in the Court of Appeal in England in *Re Diplock's Estate* [1948] 1 Ch 465 and that of Mr Justice Budd in *Re Shannon's Stamp Auctions Ltd* [1962] IR 386. Shannon is insolvent and indeed most of the claims against it are by those who will probably claim that they are entitled to a charge on the bank accounts which will have the result that they rank before the ordinary creditors.

The effect of clause 6(b) of the agreement of 24 September 1969 is that the monies collected by Shannon for all tickets were the property of Aer Lingus and were to be retained by Shannon as such property until they had been satisfactorily accounted for. They never became part of the assets of Shannon and were held by them as a trustee. I do not see any difference between the position which Shannon occupied in relation to money collected by them by the sale of tickets which were the property of Aer Lingus and that of a trustee who being the legal owner of property in which others have the equitable interest is able to collect the purchase money because of the legal title which he has. It was however contended that Aer Lingus had accepted the cheques drawn by Shannon in payment of the sums due for air tickets and that this was done under the arrangement which had been made when the agreement was signed. It was then said that the forwarding of the sales report with a cheque for the amount which it showed as due meant that the sums for which the cheques had been drawn had been satisfactorily accounted for to Aer Lingus. Acceptance of a cheque for a debt is not payment for it is clearly conditional upon the cheque being honoured. The monies which had been received by Shannon in respect of Aer Lingus tickets were not accounted for satisfactorily to the carrier when the cheques were not honoured when the banks opened again. It is significant that the monies collected by the agent by the sale of Aer Lingus tickets including any commission to which Shannon was entitled remained the property of Aer Lingus and that it was these monies which were to be retained by the agent until satisfactorily accounted for.

The accountants retained by Aer Lingus have inspected the books of Shannon and have been able to trace cases in which Aer Lingus tickets were sold by Shannon and paid for by cheques which were subsequently lodged by the provisional liquidator to the account at the National Bank. This shows that it is possible to trace monies coming from clients of Shannon in respect of air tickets and going into the account which is now in credit. Although the cheques given by Shannon for tickets sold in March and April were not paid, there cannot, in my opinion, be a valid claim by Aer Lingus in respect of any cheques received by Shannon and cleared before 1 May 1970. The charge will be confined to the monies to the credit of the bank account in the National Bank of Ireland.

It was said that Aer Lingus should not be allowed to make a claim for the period from 1 October to 15 November because they had received cheques drawn by third parties in favour of Shannon. In one of the documents the sum is described as being a deposit on Shannon Travel ticket returns. I think that the three payments were payments on account and that £43,996 must be deducted from the amount in respect of which Aer Lingus establish that they have a charge in order to arrive at the net amount for which the charge exists.

The official liquidator has not to take any steps to trace any monies received by Shannon and lodged to the bank accounts. The claim must be prepared by Aer Lingus and submitted to the official liquidator who should then check it and Aer Lingus must be allowed to investigate the books and records of Shannon. It is not the duty of the liquidator to enquire from other creditors whether they claim that the monies received by Shannon in respect of the sale of their tickets were received in a fiduciary capacity.

The official liquidator seeks an order that Aer Lingus are entitled to prove — as unsecured creditors only but in my view they are entitled to a charge on the monies in the National Bank. It is not possible to decide whether they have a charge on the monies in the suspense account in the Bank of Ireland because no evidence has been given as to how this account was created. The amount for which a charge exists is the sum received by Shannon less the commission to which they were entitled under the agreement and less the £43,996. In any case where Shannon did not receive payment from the customer for tickets issued by Aer Lingus, the amount will rank as an ordinary unsecured debt.

The remuneration and legal fees and expenses of the provisional and official liquidators rank before any of the fiduciary claims. Although the claim by Aer Lingus succeeds on the ground that the monies received by Shannon in respect of tickets do not form part of the assets of Shannon, the claim for the charge is based on equitable grounds and the court should grant it only on the basis that the officer appointed by it to conduct the winding-up is paid in full. The assets which are not subject to the charge will be the primary fund out of which the liquidator's remuneration and expenses will be paid but if they are not sufficient to do this, the balance of the expense will be paid out of the bank accounts on which there is a charge before any claims on the fiduciary basis are discharged.

I have been informed that other creditors will probably claim on a fiduciary basis but as no evidence has been given as to how the claims arose, I do not intend to express any opinion on their validity.

Patricia McLaughlin
Barrister

In the Matter of Irish Tourist Promotions Ltd and In the Matter of the Companies Act 1963: High Court 1973 No. 1759P (Kenny J) 22 April 1974

Company Law – Petition to wind up company – Company insolvent – No reasonable prospect of directors working together again – Majority of creditors against winding up of company – Whether company should be wound up

Facts: The company was incorporated on 23 April 1970. All the issued shares in the company were held by the petitioner, by a Mr Desmond Mullin and by a third party who intended to sell to the petitioner. The main business of the company was in advertising: it arranged to get space for advertising from commercial concerns, racecourses and hotels, and then let them to those who wanted to advertise. The petitioner applied to the court for an order that the company be wound up as the relationship between himself and Mr Mullin had deteriorated to such an extent that they could never work together again. The company was insolvent at the date of the application but Mr Mullin contended that the company had a reasonable prospect of making substantial profits in the future. The majority of the creditors of the company did not want it to be wound up.

Held by Kenny J in granting the petition:

(1) The company was insolvent.

(2) There was no possibility in the circumstances outlined of the company trading profitably.

(3) The company should be wound up.

No cases referred to in judgment

Counsel's and solicitors' names not available

KENNY J **22 April 1974**

Irish Tourist Promotions Ltd ("the company") was incorporated on 23 April 1970 with a nominal capital of £500 the entire of which has been issued and is fully paid. 218 of the shares are held by Mr James P. Doherty ("the petitioner"), 219 by Mr Desmond Mullin and 63 by Mr Brendan Smith who has agreed to sell his shares to the petitioner but the transfer of them has not been completed.

In July 1973 the petitioner brought proceedings to have the company wound up by the court on the grounds that it was insolvent and that the petitioner and Mr Mullin, who are directors, were on such bad terms that a complete deadlock in the management of the company existed. These proceedings were, at the request of the parties, adjourned on many occasions and were finally the subject of an oral hearing in January.

The company was formed by the petitioner and Mr Smith each of whom had fifty per cent of the issued shares. A company called The Swift Marketing Company became interested in the company and acquired a majority shareholding. The petitioner continued to manage the company. The Swift Marketing Company subsequently decided to sell their shares and the petitioner and Mr Mullin, who was introduced into the company by the petitioner, bought them. The company then moved its offices to 54 Brighton Square, Rathgar. The main business of the company has been in advertising: it arranges to get space for advertisements from commercial concerns and from race courses and hotels and then lets the space to those who want to advertise. They have also obtained the agency for an advertising device called the Rota sign which is illuminated and which gives a continuous electrical show of advertisements. The company owns 66 illuminated notice boards and 65 light boxes. The light boxes are at Leopardstown Racecourse. It owns a number of other machines, many of which are installed in hotels, and those who wish to advertise can rent space in these.

The relationship between the petitioner and Mr Mullin began before the company was formed. Mr Mullin owned a garage where he traded under the name of the Trident Motor Company. The petitioner advanced £3,500 to him for use in the garage business which did not prosper. The petitioner says an arrangement was made that he would be repaid the loan by getting some of the second-hand cars which were part of the stock in trade of the Trident Motor Company. When the petitioner took some of the cars, Mr Mullin disputed the existence of such an arrangement and began proceedings for their recovery.

Relations between Mr Mullin and the petitioner became so bad that the business of the company had almost ceased in May 1973. The petitioner had come to the conclusion that the business of the company could not be carried on and a Mr O'Byrne and he formed another advertising company called the Rota Signs International Ltd and represented that the new company were carrying on the business of the company. An injunction to restrain them making these representations was granted by this court. Mr Mullin has also commenced proceedings under section 205 of the Companies Act 1963 alleging oppression by the petitioner. These proceedings have not yet been heard.

At a meeting of the directors of the company, held on 22 August 1973 of which the petitioner was given notice and which was attended by Mr Mullin and by Mr Smith, the petitioner was removed from the office of chairman of the company and of joint managing director but remained a director of the company.

It has not been seriously contested by counsel for Mr Mullin and for the company that it is now insolvent. The liabilities of the company on 15 January 1974 were £19,912 and its assets, if sold, will realise about £3,450. At least 30 per cent of the liabilities are owing to Mr Mullin and in addition he has guaranteed other liabilities amounting to £4,200. The debate has been whether the company should be wound up because Mr Mullin says that though the company is insolvent, it has a reasonable prospect of making substantial profits in the future and he had submitted an estimate of these which shows that the company could have a gross income of £25,730 before payment of salaries and tax during the first twelve months of its trading if all assets were fully utilised and if this petition were dismissed.

The result of the dispute between the petitioner and Mr Mullin about the motor cars was that the parties have not spoken to each other since May 1973 and Mr Mullin has refused to allow the petitioner to take any part in the running of the business which has not been carried on since that date. There has been a removal of some of the books and records of the company from the registered office and having regard to what has happened between the parties it is impossible that they could ever work together again. As the company is insolvent, the petitioner cannot hope to get anything out of a liquidation: indeed he admits that he will not. His motives in bringing the proceedings are that liquidation will make it possible for the new company which he has formed to get the contract for advertising from Leopardstown. There is also in his mind the hope that Mr Mullin will become liable on his guarantee for the company.

The majority of the creditors do not wish the company to be wound up. Rota Signs Ltd, the English company, to whom £2,077 is due, wish the company to continue trading and objected strongly to the petitioner forming a company called Rota Signs International Ltd.

Substantial sums for wages are due to employees. Mr Mullin is now employed whole-time by another company and has made it clear that he intends to retain this position. Nobody is now employed on a whole-time basis by the company.

Mr Smith has said that he thinks that if the company could be brought back to the stage and position it was in before the dispute between the petitioner and Mr Mullin began, it could be successful.

I think that the estimate of what the company could earn, if it were to trade, is based upon hope and not on reasonable anticipation and that it is entirely false. Mr Mullin has made it clear that he does not intend to give up his position with Murphy & Gunn and he is determined that he will not allow the petitioner to run the business. The petitioner is still a director so no business will be transacted at any meeting at which the two of them are present. I find it impossible to believe that a company could have a turnover of £46,000 (the figure in Mr Mullins' estimate) without one full time employee particularly when the directors cannot meet without the risk of unruly scenes.

The company is insolvent: it cannot pay its debts. There is no prospect that it will ever trade profitably in the present circumstances and I think that it should be wound up by the court.

Before reaching this conclusion I have given consideration to the wishes of the creditors. They believe that they have a better chance of being paid if the company is not wound up as the stock-in-trade will realise little if it is sold on the open market. Despite this, I think that the company should be wound up by the court though the prospects of anyone being paid anything are remote.

Patricia McLaughlin
Barrister

In the Matter of the Companies Act 1963 and In the Matter of Murphy Brothers (Cork) Ltd; Provincial Bank of Ireland v. John C. O'Connor:
High Court 1973 No. 125 Sp (Kenny J) 23 July 1974

Winding up – Resolution to wind up passed before the Companies Act 1963 came into operation – Winding up governed by Companies (Consolidation) Act 1908, section 186 – Liquidator in voluntary winding up may exercise all powers which are given by that Act to a liquidator in a winding up by the Court – Powers listed in Companies (Consolidation) Act 1908, section 151 – Loans advanced by liquidator to shareholder out of company's assets – Not within the powers of the liquidator – Loans made partly to enable shareholder to buy out the interest of another member – Companies Act 1959, section 3 – Criminal offence – Shareholder assigned all monies due to him in the liquidation to the plaintiff – Defendant refused to demand repayment of the loans – Whether the plaintiff was entitled to an order directing the liquidator to recall the loans and pay them into the liquidator's account – Nature of shareholder's interest – Whether the plaintiff was entitled to an order directing the defendant to pay to the plaintiff all monies due to the shareholder arising out of the liquidation – Companies Act 1963 (No. 33), section 398

Facts: By special resolution passed on 22 March 1958, confirmed on 9 April 1958 it was resolved that Murphy Brothers (Cork) Ltd ("the company"), although solvent, be wound up voluntarily and the defendant was appointed as liquidator. Between the date of the resolution and 1963, the defendant advanced a total of £100,000 to a shareholder, Patrick J. Murphy, out of the company's assets. The loans were made in part to buy out the interest of another shareholder in the company. On 24 September 1969 Patrick J. Murphy executed a deed by which he assigned to the plaintiff all the monies which were payable to him in any capacity whatsoever or to which he might become entitled in the course of, or arising out of, the winding up of the company. The defendant was notified of such assignment and informed the plaintiff that he wished to resign as liquidator. No agreement as to his resignation was ever reached. On 15 May 1970, the plaintiff asked for a statement of the position in the liquidation and it then became aware of the loans made to Patrick J. Murphy. If the defendant were to collect the loan he would be able to make substantial interim distributions to the shareholders and a large sum would become payable to the plaintiff as assignee of Mr Murphy's interest. On 10 September 1972 the plaintiff solicitor wrote to the defendant requesting him to demand immediate repayment of the loan. The defendant replied that it was for the plaintiff to take whatever steps it considered suitable to recover the monies advanced to Patrick J. Murphy. The plaintiff sought a declaration that the defendant had acted unlawfully and in breach of his duty in advancing the loans and for an order directing the defendant to recall the loans and that this be paid into the liquidator's account. It further sought an order directing the defendant to pay to the plaintiff as assignees of Patrick J. Murphy all monies properly payable by the defendant as liquidator to Patrick J. Murphy.

Held by Kenny J in making that order:

(1) As the resolution to wind up was passed before the date when the Companies Act 1963 came into force, the effect of section 398 of the Act of 1963 was that the liquidation was governed by the Companies (Consolidation) Act 1908. The title of the summons was incorrect as the 1963 Act has no application to this liquidation.

(2) In a voluntary liquidation under the 1908 Act, section 186 enabled the liquidator to exercise all powers which were given by the Act to a liquidator in a winding up by the court. These powers were listed in section 151 and did not include a power to make loans.

(3) The loans were made partly to buy out the shares of another member of the company and were in breach of section 3 of the Companies Act 1959 and a criminal offence.

(4) The shares owned by Mr Murphy gave him the right to a sum of money, which right he had assigned to the plaintiff. The effect of this is that the plaintiff was entitled to be paid all sums of money payable in the liquidation in respect of these shares and therefore it was entitled to require the defendant to recover the loan. *Borland's Trustee v. Steel Bros* [1901] 1 Ch 279 and *Commissioners of Inland Revenue v. Crossman* [1937] AC 26 considered.

(5) The plaintiff was vitally interested in the proper performance by the defendant of the duty imposed on him by section 186 of the 1908 Act.

(6) The defendant is bound to collect the assets of the company and to distribute them among the members.

Cases referred to in judgment

Borland's Trustee v. Steel Bros [1901] 1 Ch 279
Commissioners of Inland Revenue v. Crossman [1937] AC 26

Counsel's and solicitors' names not available

KENNY J **23 July 1974**

Murphy Brothers (Cork) Ltd ("the company") was incorporated in the State on 21 October 1940. The issued share capital of the company is £15,000 consisting of 15,000 shares of £1 each. At the date of the last annual return made to the Company's Registration Office, Patrick J. Murphy owned 6,000 shares, William Joseph Murphy owned 6,000 shares and Jeremiah Murphy owned 3,000 shares. By a special resolution passed on 22 March 1958 and confirmed on 9 April 1958 it was resolved by the company that it was desirable to wind it up and that the company be wound up voluntarily and the defendant was appointed as liquidator. The company is solvent.

This case has been argued on the basis that the winding up was to be conducted under the Companies Act 1963 but this assumption is incorrect. As the resolution to wind up was passed before the date when the Companies Act 1963 came into force, the effect of section 398 of the Act of 1963 is that the liquidation is governed by the Companies (Consolidation) Act 1908. This section was not referred to in argument. The title of the summons is also incorrect because the Act of 1963 has no application to this liquidation.

Between the date when the resolution to wind up was confirmed and 1963 the defendant lent £40,000 out of the company's assets to Patrick J. Murphy and on 14 February 1966 he made a further loan of £10,000 and on 11 November 1966 advanced £50,000 from the same source to him. These loans were a very gross breach of duty by the defendant as a liquidator has no power to make loans to anyone and certainly should not make advances to a director. In a voluntary liquidation under the Act of 1908, section 186(iv) enables the liquidator to exercise all the powers which are given by the Act to a liquidator in a winding up by the court. These powers are listed in section 151 and do not include a power to make loans. In addition it appears from the correspondence that the loans were made in part to buy out the interest of Mr William Joseph Murphy in the company: this was to purchase his shares and was a breach of section 3 of the Companies Act 1959 and so was a criminal offence. The shares in the company have been transferred since the winding up commenced and since 1968 Provincial Bank (Nominees) Ltd have been registered as owners of 14,900 shares, Mr Patrick J. Murphy has been registered as owner of 50 shares as has his wife.

On 24 September 1969 Mr Patrick J. Murphy executed a deed by which he assigned to the plaintiffs all the monies which were payable to him in any capacity whatsoever or to which he might in any way become entitled in the course of or arising out of the winding up of the company and declared that the receipt of the manager for the time being of the bank's South Mall Cork office should be an adequate discharge to the defendant. On 1 October 1969 the defendant was notified of this assignment and acknowledged receipt of the notice on 3 October and informed the plaintiffs that he wished to retire as liquidator. Correspondence then took place in connection with the defendant's resignation but no agreement as to this was reached. On 15 May 1970 the plaintiffs asked for a statement of the position in the liquidation and when this was given to them, they saw that a loan of £100,000 had been made to Mr Patrick J. Murphy. The assets of the company, including this loan, amount to £210,239 and the liabilities are an estimated sum of £65,000 due to the Revenue Commissioners and an estimated £5,250 for legal fees and the liquidator's remuneration. There is thus a surplus of about £135,000. If the defendant collected the loan which was improperly made to Mr Patrick J. Murphy, he would be able to make a substantial interim distribution to the shareholders and a large sum would become payable to Provincial Bank (Nominees) Ltd and to the plaintiffs.

On 10 February 1972 the plaintiffs' solicitor wrote to the defendant that the plaintiffs as assignees of Mr Patrick J. Murphy's interest in the proceeds of the liquidation requested him to demand immediate repayment of £100,000 from Mr Patrick J. Murphy. This request produced the astonishing reply of 27 March

1972 that it was a matter for the plaintiffs to take whatever steps they considered suitable if they sought to recover the money advanced by the defendant to Mr Patrick J. Murphy. The plaintiffs did not accept this contention and issued a summons in June 1973 in which they claimed a declaration that the defendant had acted unlawfully and in breach of his duty in paying £100,000 to Mr Patrick J. Murphy, an order directing the defendant to recall the said loan and directing that this be paid into the liquidation account and an order directing the defendant to pay to the plaintiffs as assignees of Mr Patrick J. Murphy all monies properly payable by the defendant as liquidator to Mr Patrick J. Murphy.

The purpose of the defendant's refusal to take proceedings against Mr Patrick J. Murphy for the recovery of the £100,000 seems to me to be clear and does not enhance my view of his suitability to act as liquidator. If the loan is not repaid and if it is set off against the amount payable by the defendant to Mr Patrick J. Murphy in the winding up and the balance only is paid to the defendant as liquidator, the sum payable to the bank under the assignment will be substantially reduced. This is supported by the fact that the only defence advanced was that the plaintiffs are not a contributory or creditor of the company and so cannot successfully bring these proceedings. If the proceedings had been brought by Provincial Bank of Ireland (Nominees) Ltd there would have been no defence to them even though that company holds the 14,900 shares as nominees for Mr Patrick J. Murphy and his wife.

Mr Patrick J. Murphy is the owner of 50 shares in the capital of the company. The nature of a share in a company is easier to describe than to define but the most widely quoted and accepted definition is that of Farwell J in *Borland's Trustees v. Steel* [1901] 1 Ch 279 in which he said:

> "A share is the interest of a shareholder in the company measured by a sum of money, for the purpose of liability in the first place and of interest in the second, but also consisting of a series of mutual convenants entered into by all the share holders, *inter se*, in accordance with section 16 of the Companies Act 1862. The contract contained in the articles of association is one of the original incidents of the share. A share is not a sum of money . . . but is an interest measured by a sum of money and made up of various rights contained in the contract, including the right to a sum of money of a more or less amount."

This definition was approved by the House of Lords in *Commissioners of Inland Revenue v. Crossman* [1937] AC 26. The plaintiffs are not the owners of any shares in the company but under the assignment they are entitled to any sum payable to Mr Patrick J. Murphy in respect of his share. The shares owned by Mr Murphy gives him the right, in the words of Farwell J, to "a sum of money" and he has assigned that right to the plaintiffs. The effect is that the plaintiffs are entitled to be paid all sums of money payable in the liquidation in respect of the shares owned by Mr Patrick J. Murphy and in my view that entitles them to require the defendant to recover the loan of £100,000. The plaintiffs are vitally interested in the proper performance by the defendant of the duty which the law imposes on him by section 186 of the Act 1908 which provides:

> "The following consequences shall ensue on the voluntary winding up of a company: (i) The property of the company shall be applied in satisfaction of its liabilities *pari passu*, and, subject thereto, shall, unless the articles otherwise provide, be distributed among the members according to their rights and interests in the company."

So the defendant is bound to collect the assets of the company and to distribute them among the members.

There will be accordingly an order that the defendant as liquidator of the company do recall from Mr Patrick J. Murphy, a director of the company, the loan of £100,000 made by the defendant to the said Patrick J. Murphy and that upon receipt of the same it is to be paid into the liquidation account of the company. I do not think it is necessary at the moment to make any order on the relief claimed at paragraphs (a) and (b) in the summons. The plaintiffs are entitled to their costs of the proceedings against the defendant who will have them as part of his costs and expenses of the liquidation.

Patricia McLaughlin
Barrister

In the Matter of Shannon Transport Systems Ltd and In the Matter of the Companies Act 1963: High Court 1970 No. 4084P (Kenny J) 3 February 1975

Company Law – Petition for winding up of the company -- Judgment recovered by petitioner against the company – Amount of award under appeal – Petitioner claimed that he would be awarded substantially greater damages on appeal – Stay on judgment pending appeal – Company refused to pay the amount awarded to the petitioner unless he withdrew his appeal – Whether assets of company should be controlled by a provisional liquidator pending the outcome of the appeal

Facts: The petitioner presented a petition for the winding up of the company on 9 December 1970, which said petition was adjourned as the petitioner wished to bring proceedings for the recovery of a disputed debt. The petitioner was awarded £917.00 by Pringle J on 10 July 1972. The petitioner then appealed that decision. In the meantime, he applied to the solicitors for the company for payment of the debt but they refused to do so unless he withdrew his appeal, on the ground that the appeal operated as a stay. In response, the petitioner applied for the appointment of a provisional liquidator. He submitted that he would recover substantially more damages on appeal and that all the assets of the company should be controlled by a provisional liquidator.

Held by Pringle J in refusing the application:

(1) A provisional liquidator should only be appointed when there is some real urgency in connection with the application.

(2) In most cases he is appointed immediately after the presentation of a petition so that the assets may be preserved from seizure or so that there may not be any dealings adverse to the interest of the petitioner.

(3) The petitioner had not established any reason why a provisional liquidator should be appointed and until he succeeded in having the amount awarded to him increased substantially, there was no case for the winding up of the company and therefore no case for the appointment of a provisional liquidator.

No cases referred to in judgment

Counsel's and solicitors' names not available

KENNY J **3 February 1975**

On 9 December 1970 the petitioner, Sean Hopkins, presented a petition to this court for the winding up of Shannon Transport Systems Ltd ("the company"). At the hearing of the petition on 18 January 1971 it became clear that the petition was in respect of a disputed debt and I adjourned the hearing of the petition generally so that the petitioner could bring proceedings for the recovery of the debt. The case was heard by Pringle J over nine days in February 1972 and he awarded the petitioner £917.00. The petitioner has now appealed against this judgment but the appeal has not yet been heard. I understand that there was no shorthand-writer present at the hearing and that the preparation of the judge's note is obviously a most laborious task. The company has not appealed.

The petitioner then applied to Messrs O'Donnell and Dundon, the solicitors for the company, for payment of the £917.00. They stated that they had the money to pay the £917 but that they would not do so until the appeal to the Supreme Court had been withdrawn on the ground that the appeal operated as a stay. The petitioner is claiming a sum of about £10,000 damages.

The main item of assets owned by the company is a licensed premises at Kildysart, Co. Clare. The petitioner says that although the property is registered on a folio, the defendants have not been registered as owners of it. Applications to renew the licence have been made and granted on a number of occasions.

The petitioner now applies that a provisional liquidator should be appointed over the assets of the company. A provisional liquidator should be appointed only when there is some real urgency in connection with the application. In most cases he is appointed immediately after the presentation of a petition so that the assets may be preserved from seizure or so that there may not be any dealings adverse to the interests of the petitioner. In my opinion the petitioner has not established any reason why a provisional liquidator should be appointed. He has a judgment for £917 and a firm of solicitors have agreed to pay him this when he withdraws his appeal. He was not awarded the costs of the proceedings before Pringle J. His argument is that on appeal he will get considerably more than the £917 and that all dealings with the assets of the company should be controlled by a provisional liquidator. Until he succeeds in having the amount awarded to him increased substantially, there is no case whatever for the winding up of the company and therefore no case for the appointment of a provisional liquidator.

The application will accordingly be dismissed with costs.

Patricia McLaughlin
Barrister

Thomas Joseph Cawley and Maura Cawley v. Metro Investment Trust Ltd:
High Court (McWilliam J) 28 January 1977

Company in liquidation – Claim by plaintiffs to certain goods and chattels – Contents of house owned by company – Some goods purchased prior to the opening of the company bank account – Plaintiff previously swore that goods belonged to the company – Some of the goods purchased with company money – Whether goods and chattels belonged to the company or the plaintiffs

Facts: The plaintiffs claimed that certain goods and chattels which formed the contents of a house owned by the company, now in liquidation, belonged to them personally. They claimed that some of the goods were bought by Mrs Cawley, some by Mr Cawley and that the remainder were gifts from friends who were involved with the company. The plaintiffs moved into the house in early 1971 and the company bank account was not opened until 28 December 1972. Mr Cawley had sworn on oath on a number of occasions that the goods belonged to the company, for the purpose of discharging himself from bankruptcy and in order to oppose the liquidation of the company.

Held by McWilliam J:

(1) Anything purchased before December 1972 could not have been purchased by the company and there would have had to have been a transfer to put the property in such items in the company.

(2) Everything purchased after December 1972 was purchased from the company bank account. If items were purchased with company money and Mr Cawley has sworn that they belonged to the company then the matter should not be investigated further.

No cases referred to in judgment

Counsel's and solicitors' names not available

McWILLIAM J **28 January 1977**

On this part of the case, the plaintiffs are claiming to be entitled to certain goods and chattels, the contents of Arbrugh House, as set out in two schedules. The numbering of these schedules indicates to me that there is another list of the same goods and chattels prepared for another purpose. It is claimed that most of the goods and chattels in Schedule A were purchased by Mrs Cawley out of her own money and were her property and that the remainder were gifts to Mr Cawley or from friends. It is claimed that the goods and the chattels listed in Schedule B were purchased by Mr Cawley with his own money and were never the property of the company.

Mr Cawley was discharged from bankruptcy on 25 February 1974. For the purposes of his discharge and for the purpose of opposing the liquidation of the company, he appears to have sworn on oath on a number of occasions that the contents of the house were assets of the company. It is clear to me, from the occasions on which Mr Cawley has been before me, that he is prepared to say anything he thinks will suit his purpose at the particular time no matter how it may conflict with what he may have said for another purpose at another time. This makes my task very difficult, but it does not absolve me from the responsibility of trying to ascertain the truth if I can. In addition, although the statement of claim was delivered on 18 December 1975, Mr Cawley has not, until this hearing, sorted out the various cheques or invoices which he says support his claims.

He presented the claim by indicating on Schedule A the items which he alleges were purchased before the company had opened a bank account. This appears to have been on 28 December 1972. He and his wife moved into the house early in 1971 and it seems reasonable to suppose that they then furnished it to some extent. He also indicated a number of items which he claimed as gifts, some to himself from his wife, some from Mr Fegan, some from Mr Horan, some from other people and some purchased by himself in Paris or elsewhere. As I understand it, the balance of the goods are claimed mainly as having been purchased by Mrs Cawley out of her own money and a number of cheques were produced, dated between 17 February 1973 and 21 November 1974, which it is alleged were applied towards the purchase of various items.

Mr Cawley states that Mrs Cawley had no money of her own and got whatever money she had before December 1972, from him and any money she got after that date she got from the company, she being the only person authorised to draw cheques on the company account. He states that Mr Fegan and Mr Horan got money with which they bought items on the list from the company.

It appears to me that anything purchased before December 1972 could not have been purchased with money provided by the company. This being so there would have to be some sort of transfer to the company to put the property in such items in the company. They were in a house owned by the company and

Mr Cawley has sworn, for a different purpose, that they belonged to the company but, having regard to the unreliability of his evidence throughout, this is not necessarily conclusive.

I am satisfied that everything purchased after December 1972 was purchased from the company bank account whether purchased by Mr Cawley, Mrs Cawley, Mr Fegan or Mr Horan. If items were purchased with company money and Mr Cawley has sworn that they belonged to the company, I am not prepared to investigate the matter further.

Invoices were produced for a small number of items alleged to have been purchased before December 1972. I am prepared to allow these items, they are as follows: Nos. [12, 13, 20, 36, 78, 79, 80, 84, 87, 88, 89, 95, 98, 183, 224.]

Of the others, in the absence of any form of corroborative evidence, I will allow No. 170, which appears to be a portrait of Mrs Cawley and the following items only, that is to say: [40, 68, 69, 158, 164, 166, 170, 212, 215, 216, 217, 220, 236, 255, 260, 262, 263, 264, 285, 287, 288, 295, 299, 306, 309.]

Patricia McLaughlin
Barrister

Metro Investment Trust Ltd and the Companies Act 1963: High Court 1974 No. 2741P (McWilliam J) 26 May 1977

Company Law – Promissory note – Winding up – Claim for sum in winding up on foot of a promissory note – Joint and several promissory note given by debtor company and company now in winding up – Whether claim can be opposed on the basis that transaction was not in furtherance of the objects of the company and of no benefit to it – Whether transaction void as being ultra vires *the company – Promissory note expressed to be given for value – One of the objects of the company was to draw negotiable instruments of all kinds – Whether company can be estopped from denying that value was received – Whether payment gratuitous – Whether a third party who enters into a transaction with a company that has power to enter into that transaction must investigate the possibility of the transaction not being for the benefit of the company – Whether forbearance exercised by the creditor sufficient to have the debt admitted*

Facts: Societé Soprico Géstion S.A. ("Soprico") obtained judgment against a company known as Invest of Ireland Ltd ("Invest") for the sum of £85,562.51. Invest and Metro Investments Ltd were under the control of a Mr and Mrs Cawley, Mrs Cawley being a director of both companies. Apart from this there was no evidence of any business or other association between the two companies. A stay of execution was granted on the basis that Invest would pay the sum of £36,563.51 forthwith and pay the balance of £50,000 by five consecutive monthly instalments of £10,000. In consideration of this forbearance, Metro and Invest gave a joint and several promissory note promising to pay the £50,000 in the manner stated. The first two instalments only were paid and Soprico claimed the outstanding £30,000 in the winding-up of Metro.

Held by McWilliam J in allowing the claim that:

(1) Money can only be spent by a company for a purpose reasonably incidental to the carrying on of the company's business.

(2) A third party who enters into a transaction involving a company which has power to enter into that transaction need not investigate the possibility of the transaction not being for the benefit of the company.

(3) Insofar as Soprico had exercised forbearance towards Invest in consideration of the guarantee given by Metro, it was not seeking to enforce a gratuitous payment.

(4) Accordingly, the transaction by Metro was not *ultra vires* and Soprico was entitled to have the debt admitted.

Cases referred to in judgment

Charterbridge Corporation v. Lloyds Bank [1969] 3 WLR 122; [1970] Ch 62
Hutton v. West Cork Railway Co. (1883) 23 Ch D 654
Henderson v. Bank of Australasia (1888) 40 Ch D 170
Re Lee, Behrens & Co. Ltd. [1932] 2 Ch 46
Ridge Securities Ltd v. Inland Revenue Commissioners [1964] 1 WLR 479

Counsel's and solicitors' names not available

McWILLIAM J **26 May 1977**

This application brought by Societé Soprico Géstion S.A. hereinafter described as Soprico, to have a claim for £30,000 admitted in the winding-up of Metro Investment Trust Ltd, hereinafter described as Metro.

The claim is made on foot of a promissory note for the sum of £50,000 which was given under the following circumstances. Soprico brought proceedings against a company called Invest of Ireland Ltd, hereinafter described as Invest, for the sum of £85,563.51. Invest and Metro were under the control of a Mr and Mrs Cawley, Mrs Cawley being a director of both companies. Apart from this, no business or other association between those two companies is alleged by Soprico and the liquidator of Metro has put in an affidavit to the effect that he can find no record of dealings between the two companies in the books of Metro. Whatever the reason for the involvement of Metro, the proceedings against Invest were compromised on terms whereby Soprico got judgment against Invest for the full amount with a stay of execution on the basis that Invest would pay the sum of £36,563.51 forthwith and pay the balance of £50,000 by five consecutive monthly instalments of £10,000 each payable on the 12th day of each month, commencing on 12 March 1974. In consideration of this forbearance, Metro and Invest gave a joint and several promissory note promising to pay the £50,000 in the manner stated. The first two instalments of £10,000 were paid, but the remaining three instalments were not, and Soprico claims the sum of £30,000 in the winding-up of Metro.

The liquidator of Metro opposes the claim on the ground that this transaction on the part of Metro was not in any way in furtherance of the objects of the company and that there is no evidence of any benefit to Metro from the transaction and that it was, therefore, *ultra vires* and void.

On behalf of Soprico it is urged that the promissory note is expressed to be given for value, that one of the objects of the company was to make or draw negotiable instruments of all kinds, that there is a presumption of value received and that Metro is estopped from denying that value was received.

I have been referred to a number of authorities.

Hutton v. West Cork Railway Co. (1883) 23 Ch D 654
Henderson v. Bank of Australia (1889) 40 Ch D 170
Re Lee, Behrens & Co. Ltd [1932] Ch 46
Ridge Securities Ltd v. Inland Revenue Commissioners [1964] 1 WLR 479
Charterbridge Corporation v. Lloyds Bank [1969] 3 WLR 122; [1970] Ch 62.

From these cases the principle appears to be clearly established that money can only be spent by a company for a purpose reasonably incidental to the carrying on of the company's business. Most of the cases to which I have been referred deal with claims to gratuitous payments in one shape or form which had been promised to the claimants, and the question arose in each case whether such gratuitous payments furthered the interests of the company in any way. This seems to me to be a different situation from the present in which Soprico exercised forbearance towards Invest in consideration of the guarantee by Metro; that is to say, Soprico is not claiming a gratuitous payment although, on the evidence, the assistance given by Metro to Invest appears to have been gratuitous. To this extent the *Charterbridge* case most resembles the present case. There, one of a group of companies gave a somewhat similar guarantee of the debt of another member of the group. The court found that such a transaction could, under the circumstances, have been of benefit to the company giving it, but the judgment in this case reviews the authorities very fully and it seems to be clearly indicated that a third party who enters into a transaction involving a company which has power to enter into that transaction is not concerned to investigate the possibility of the transaction not being for the benefit of the company. Accordingly, I am of opinion that, however trifling the detriment to Soprico of the forbearance it agreed to exercise, Soprico is for this reason entitled to have this debt admitted. The position would be quite different were the claim being made by Invest and I express no opinion on the rights Metro may still have against Invest.

Patricia McLaughlin
Barrister

Daniel Kelleher v. Continental Irish Meats Ltd (in Receivership): High Court 1977 No. 2243P (Costello J) 9 May 1978

Company Law – Company insolvent – Receiver appointed – Alleged contract between plaintiff and an employee of company for the sale of a consignment of meat – Whether employee had the authority to enter into the contract – Whether contract concluded before receiver appointed – Whether company bound by contract – Whether contract an attempt to secure a fraudulent preference for the plaintiff – Companies Act 1963 (No. 33), section 286

Facts: The plaintiff was a cattle dealer and supplied meats to the defendant company, Continental Irish Meats Ltd . A receiver was appointed over the assets of the defendant company by the Bank of Ireland on 5 May 1977 pursuant to a debenture. The plaintiff claimed that he had entered into a contract with the company, through its agent, a Mr McMorrow, for the purchase of certain consignments of meat held in cold storage. Mr McMorrow was an employee of the company and had previously had the authority to buy and sell on behalf of the company. Prior to the alleged contract it had become clear that the company was in serious financial difficulties and various meetings took place to discuss these difficulties. Prior to the alleged contract, the plaintiff became aware of these difficulties and was concerned that the company would not be able to meet its commitments to him. Mr McMorrow was also appraised of the difficulties that the company faced and it was alleged that he had been told on 3 May 1977 that no more trading was to be carried out on behalf of the company. A meeting was called on 4 May 1977, at which the plaintiff was present, in an attempt to come up with proposals which would satisfy the bank. It was understood by all present that unless such satisfactory proposals were forthcoming, the bank would appoint a receiver on the following morning. The plaintiff approached Mr McMorrow with a view to purchasing the meat and he submitted that a contract was concluded before the receiver was appointed. The receiver was appointed on 5 May 1977 and the plaintiff attempted to take possession of the meat on the following day. When he was prevented by the receiver from doing so, he issued a summons claiming that he was entitled to the meat.

Held by Costello J in refusing the application:

(1) There was a concluded contract between the plaintiff and Mr McMorrow before the receiver was appointed.

(2) However, the company was not bound by this contract as Mr McMorrow's authority to buy and sell on behalf of the company had been revoked on 3 May 1977.

(3) The plaintiff knew that Mr McMorrow had no authority to conclude the contract.

(4) Mr McMorrow knew well that the company had sustained heavy losses and his actions in entering into the transaction amounted to a fraudulent

preference which was invalid by virtue of section 286 of the Companies Act 1963.

No cases referred to in judgment

Counsel's and solicitors' names not available

COSTELLO J **9 May 1978**

The defendant company ("C.I.M.") was incorporated in the year 1976 to export dressed meat. It carried on its operations in Waterford. Clover Meats Ltd ("Clover Meats"), a well known Irish Company, owned 40 per cent of its issued share capital and a company called Possum Ltd (a company owned by the non-Irish investors in C.I.M.) owned 60 per cent of the issued share capital. Possum Ltd appointed three directors to C.I.M.'s board, one of them, Mr Kongmark being its chairman. Clover Meats appointed two, one of whom was a Mr McDermott, Clover Meats' general manager. The managing director of C.I.M. had been Mr Liam Marks, but he resigned on 15 April 1977. From that time on Mr Kongmark although living in Switzerland assumed the role of chief executive, pending the appointment of a new managing director. The company had in its employment a Mr James McMorrow. Mr McMorrow's position in the company has been the subject of some controversy. A letter was written to him on 25 March by Mr Marks purporting to appoint him as general manager. This appointment was not, however, ever approved by the board. It had been raised informally with the directors but was not taken any further. I do not think that the title attributable to Mr McMorrow's position in the company is of any great significance in this case, as it is clear that from 5 April (when the management structure was re-organised after Mr Marks' resignation) he had authority to buy and sell on behalf of the company. One of the important issues to be determined in these proceedings is whether this authority had been revoked before he entered into the transactions with the plaintiff which I will examine shortly.

The plaintiff is a cattle dealer in a very substantial way of business. He commenced supplying cattle to C.I.M. on a regular basis from January of 1977. By the month of May he and Collins' Brothers Ltd, a firm operating in Waterford for many years, were virtually the sole suppliers to C.I.M. The plaintiff had an arrangement with Clover Meats by which his cattle were slaughtered in Clover Meats' premises in Waterford and the carcasses were then delivered to C.I.M.'s premises.

The meat was processed by C.I.M. and boxed by them. Under an arrangement made with the Department of Agriculture C.I.M. had entered into what were known as "APS" contracts by which the boxed meat was required to be held in cold storage for a stated period. The number of one such contract covering 1,629 cartons of boxed meat was "1,500 A 391". The plaintiff claims that the meat the subject matter of that contract was sold to him and is his. Another meat product produced by C.I.M. is called "Trimmings". The plaintiff says that 3,630 cartons of "Trimmings (code 99)" which, along with the meat the subject of the

APS contract, was kept in cold storage in the premises of Waterford Cold Storage Ltd, were also sold to him, and are his.

On the afternoon of 5 May 1977, a receiver was appointed by the Bank of Ireland over C.I.M.'s assets. The receiver resisted the plaintiff's claim on the basis:

(i) that at the time of his appointment no concluded agreement had been made between the company (through its agent, Mr McMorrow) and the plaintiff;
(ii) that if a concluded agreement for sale had been entered into the company is not bound by it as Mr McMorrow (as the plaintiff well knew) had no authority to enter into it.

The company has now gone into liquidation, and the liquidation commenced within six months of 5 May the date of the purported sales agreement. This has given rise to a third issue in these proceedings. The liquidator, Mr Crowley, says that even if Mr McMorrow entered into a transaction prior to the appointment of the receiver which bound the company it is invalid under section 286 of the Companies Act 1963 because it was a fraudulent preference.

There is a considerable conflict of testimony in this case. The determination of the issues in it depends almost entirely on how I resolve these conflicts. It will, I think, be convenient if I do so when reviewing, chronologically, the relevant events.

From early April 1977 representatives of C.I.M.'s auditors, Messrs Oliver Freaney & Co., were in Waterford preparing the company's accounts. On Thursday 28 April they rang Mr Kongmark in Switzerland with bad news. It appeared that the company was in a serious financial situation, that its losses were much greater than the directors had been led to believe and its overdraft very high. Mr Kongmark decided to come to Ireland immediately and bring with him a representative from a well known firm of management consultants and two French accountants. He telephoned Mr McMorrow on Friday to appraise him of the situation and of his forthcoming visit. He arrived in Waterford on Sunday evening and early on Monday morning he went to C.I.M.'s premises.

Monday 2 May. The plaintiff shortly after eight o'clock met Mr Kongmark in C.I.M.'s premises. They had met twice before and had discussed the possibility of a formal contract between the plaintiff and C.I.M. by which the plaintiff would become C.I.M.'s sole supplier. The plaintiff was in Waterford to obtain money for cattle supplied to C.I.M. Mr Kongmark explained that he had not authority to sign cheques but that the plaintiff could obtain Mr McDermott's signature. In the course of conversation Mr Kongmark explained in a general way why he had come over — he said he was there because there was an "alleged hole" or a "suggested hole" (or words to that effect) in the company and that he had come over to find out what was happening. The plaintiff, by obtaining Mr McDermott's countersignature received two C.I.M. cheques that morning. One was dated 2 May for £55,000; the second was post-dated to 5 May and was for £55,306.64. He received a cheque dated 28 April the previous week for £33,700.08. As the events of the week developed the plaintiff became acutely conscious of the consequences for him if the company was not able to meet its commitments on these cheques.

Mr Kongmark met the plaintiff again at about noon on that Monday morning. He told him that he had a board meeting in London on Tuesday but would be back on Wednesday and the possibility of a meeting between the plaintiff and Mr Kongmark was raised, but not finalised.

Mr Kongmark's meetings with the plaintiff were, of course, only a small part of the day's activities as far as he was concerned. With the gentlemen he had brought with him from abroad and with the assistance of the company's auditors he was trying to discover the truth about the financial situation of the company. One of the matters about which he was gravely worried was the fact that he had learned that a consignment of meat which the company had obtained had in fact been smuggled from Northern Ireland. On Monday afternoon he saw, amongst others, the union representative. What he learned from him caused him further concern. He discussed the company's affairs with Mr McMorrow, including the smuggling case. One of the directions he gave Mr McMorrow on that afternoon was to find out the possible prices which could be obtained for the meat which they had in store.

Tuesday 3 May. Mr Kongmark's investigations continued on Tuesday morning and into the afternoon. By then, Mr Kongmark had a good idea of what had happened and a full appreciation of the serious financial situation the company was in. At 3 p.m. there were present in C.I.M. Mr Tonquist (a representative of the management consultant firm), two French accountants, Mr Byrne (a member of the firm of Messrs Oliver Freaney & Co.) and Mr Wallace, the secretary of Clover Meats. Mr McMorrow was called into the room. A discussion took place between Mr Kongmark and Mr McMorrow about the losses and his explanation for them was called for. Mr Kongmark was unhappy about Mr McMorrow's role in the company's affairs and it is very possible that Mr McMorrow felt that he was being made a scapegoat for what had occurred. I do not accept Mr McMorrow's version of this meeting. I am satisfied that Mr Kongmark told Mr McMorrow that there were to be no more purchases or sales, that all activity was to cease, expect for keeping the plant going, and nothing was to happen until he, Mr Kongmark, returned from the board meeting on Wednesday afternoon. Mr Kongmark had full authority to take these decisions; indeed for him not to have taken them might have amounted to a breach of duty. I find that from Tuesday afternoon Mr McMorrow had no authority to sell any of the company's assets and, in particular, he had no authority to enter into any arrangement for the sale of processed meat to the plaintiff. I also find that he was well aware that this was the position.

Later on Tuesday afternoon Mr Kongmark flew to London where a board meeting of C.I.M. was held in the Excelsior Hotel close to London airport. Mr McDermott was present at this meeting as were the directors nominated by

Possum Ltd. A formal decision to stop trading was taken at the London meeting.

Wednesday 4 May. Mr Kongmark and Mr McDonnell travelled back to Dublin and were at a meeting in the Bank of Ireland at 10.30 on Wednesday 4 May. C.I.M.'s indebtedness to the bank was secured by means of a debenture. The overdraft facilities which had been granted had far exceeded what was originally contemplated and, as far as the bank was concerned, the situation had reached crisis proportions. The meeting concluded on the basis that Mr Doyle, the credit control manager of the Bank of Ireland, would indicate later that day the bank's decision in the light of the representations made to it. Between 4.45 and 5 o'clock Mr Doyle telephoned Mr Byrne in the offices of Messrs Oliver Freaney & Co. informing him that in the bank's view there was a high probability that the company was insolvent and that unless proposals were forthcoming by 12 o'clock the following day both as to fresh financial aid and as to further guarantees relating to the company's indebtedness to the bank that the bank would act to protect its security. It was clearly understood from this communication by C.I.M.'s representatives who were appraised of it that unless a rescue operation could be mounted by 12 o'clock the following day that the bank would appoint a receiver.

Before making his call to Mr Byrne, Mr Doyle had received a telephone call from a Mr Moroney. Mr Moroney was known to him in a different context and he was surprised that he wished to talk to him about the affairs of C.I.M. Mr Moroney stated that he was talking on behalf of Collins' Brothers Ltd and the plaintiff herein and said to Mr Doyle that he wanted the bank to know that his principals were very interested in the company, that they were substantial creditors, and that "his people had an interest in what emerged".

To return to the plaintiff: earlier that morning Mr McMorrow had phoned him with the news that must have shocked him. According to the plaintiff Mr McMorrow told him that he was not to send any more meat to the company. The plaintiff said that some short time after this he phoned his accountant Mr Fox. Mr Fox was a member of the firm of Messrs Oliver Freaney & Co. who were, it will be recalled, also C.I.M.'s auditors. I do not accept the plaintiff's evidence that he phoned Mr Fox on other business and that he took the opportunity to mention to him C.I.M.'s affairs. I accept Mr Fox's account and I find that the plaintiff commenced the telephone conversation by saying "what is wrong with C.I.M.?" In fact, Mr Fox had just learned from his colleague Mr Byrne the seriousness of the situation of C.I.M. and was at pains not to divulge any of the information which he had learned. Mr Fox however informed the plaintiff that a meeting was being held later in the offices of Messrs Oliver Freaney & Co., and he suggested that the plaintiff might consider joining it.

The plaintiff's evidence is that after this call and in the early afternoon he telephoned Mr McMorrow back with a view to purchasing meat from C.I.M. This was a most unusual thing for him to do as his business was buying and selling cattle — not purchasing processed meat. His evidence is that Mr McMorrow told him the prices for which the Trimmings could be sold and the different selling prices of the meat the subject of the APS contract. The plaintiff's evidence was that he decided to think the matter over and that he told Mr McMorrow that that he would get in touch with him again about a possible sale. I am quite satisfied that neither the plaintiff nor Mr McMorrow have given me anything like a full account of the discussions they had on that Wednesday or the following day but I am equally satisfied that no concluded sale took place that afternoon. The plaintiff's account of what subsequently occurred was brief. He says that he drove to Dublin from Limerick after talking to Mr McMorrow, that he thought the matter over in the car and decided to buy at the prices quoted, that before going to the meeting in the offices of Oliver Freaney & Co., he telephoned an employee, Mr Hunter, to go to Waterford the next day to collect the necessary papers relating to the deal, and he joined the meeting sometime around 7.30 or 8 o'clock. It is, I think, revealing that throughout the whole of his testimony the plaintiff gave no evidence which would explain Mr Moroney's call to Mr Doyle at 4.30 that afternoon. It is clear that the plaintiff must have been in touch with Collins' Brothers or Mr Moroney and that he did a great deal more to try to retrieve his position than he divulged in his evidence.

The meeting in Messrs Freaneys' office had begun before the plaintiff got there: what was said by Mr Kongmark to the plaintiff in the course of it is crucial to this case. The meeting was a long one and there was much coming and going during the course of it. It was attended not only by the directors of C.I.M. and their auditors but also by Mr Collins and Mr Fortune, two directors of Collins Brothers Ltd (who, like the plaintiff, were owed very substantial sums by the company) and by Mr Moroney (who, it will be recalled, had told Mr Doyle that he was an adviser to both Collins Brothers Ltd and the plaintiff). I need not delay with reviewing all the evidence as to what transpired that evening; basically, a rescue operation was being mounted by Collins Brothers Ltd and the plaintiff who were proposing that their debts would be converted into an equity in the company and that they would obtain control of the company. As to what occurred of particular relevance to these proceedings I make the following findings. The plaintiff was made fully aware of the disastrous situation the company was in; he was told that the company was heavily indebted to the bank and he knew that the bank required proposals to be put before it by the following morning. He must have also fully appreciated that it was virtually certain that the bank would appoint a receiver the following day unless an arrangement suitable to it was arrived at. Mr Kongmark told the plaintiff what the situation was in Waterford; he told him the instructions which he had given to the staff in Waterford, and that trading had been suspended. I conclude that from what he was told that evening the plaintiff was well aware that Mr McMorrow had no authority to sell any of the company's assets, and, in particular that he had no authority to sell to him any of the company's processed meat. I cannot accept the plaintiff's version of the meeting. I also draw attention to the fact that the plaintiff during the course of that evening deemed it prudent not to mention to the company's chairman or any of its directors that he had at that time opened negotiations with an employee of the company to purchase meat from the company in the order of about £120,000.

I must now revert to one other incident that occurred that Wednesday evening. I have already referred to the plaintiff's evidence to the effect that having considered the matter in the drive up to Dublin he telephoned his employee, Mr Hunter, and gave him certain instructions. In fact, he did not. Mr Hunter has no telephone. He lives in Doneraile, County Cork, about thirty miles from Hospital, County Limerick where the plaintiff resides. I accept Mr Hunter's evidence that the plaintiff's wife travelled by car that Wednesday evening from the plaintiff's home and that she (not the plaintiff) gave him the instructions to which he deposed.

Thursday 5 May. The parties who had met the night before foregathered in Messrs Freaneys' office early on Thursday morning. An inconclusive discussion took place and then the C.I.M. representatives went down to the bank's premises. The plaintiff and the representative of Collins Brothers Ltd did not immediately go there. When they did, they were put in a room into which Mr Doyle came at about twelve o'clock. The discussions between C.I.M. and the bank had been fruitless and Mr Doyle was coming to relay the bank's decision. He said he had a communication for the company and was looking for a director of C.I.M. Somebody present (not the plaintiff) said "we think we know what it is". Mr Doyle left as no C.I.M. director was in the room. I am quite satisfied that the plaintiff then or very shortly afterwards knew that the bank had decided to appoint a receiver. In fact, the appointment was effected at half past three that afternoon.

According to the plaintiff he had phoned Mr McMorrow in Waterford at about a quarter past nine that morning from Jury's Hotel and told him that he had made up his mind to do a deal at the prices which had been quoted to him and that Mr Hunter was in Waterford and would collect the documents from him. Mr Hunter had in fact arrived at eight o'clock that Thursday morning at C.I.M.'s premises. Mr McMorrow was not there then. When Mr Hunter returned at nine o'clock he says he met Mr McMorrow and it was clear that Mr McMorrow knew what Mr Hunter was looking for and, at that time, must have already been in touch with the plaintiff. I accept this evidence. The difficulty of reconciling it with the plaintiff's is obvious. Mr Hunter, later in the morning, received an envelope from Mr McMorrow containing certain documents. He had been told by Mrs Kelleher to wait at C.I.M. until a quarter past twelve and at about that time he got a call from the plaintiff. The plaintiff asked him to open the envelope and to read him the figures on the documents. This he did. The plaintiff told Mr Hunter to ask Mr McMorrow to write out a new set of documents; he said that the ones Mr Hunter had were not right. Later that day Mr McMorrow gave Mr Hunter a further document. It was a single sheet of paper. I am satisfied that what Mr McMorrow gave to Mr Hunter and which later that day Mr Hunter gave to the plaintiff was initially invoice no. 164 in respect of the A.P.S. contract (and copies thereof); another invoice in respect of the Trimmings (and copies thereof); and later a letter to Waterford Cold Stores authorising the release of the meat to the plaintiff.

I must now turn to record the quite extraordinary and highly significant actions taken by the plaintiff and Mr McMorrow in relation to the invoices of the goods the subject matter of the purported sale:

(a) Invoice no. 164 was not signed by Mr McMorrow. It was not totalled. The original and all three copies of it were given to the plaintiff and the usual practice by which the green and blue copies were retained and filed in C.I.M.'s offices was departed from. All copies of this invoice were kept by the plaintiff until the Monday prior to the trial of these proceedings. He then tore them up. Later he retrieved them and produced them in court.
(b) The invoice in respect of the Trimmings which the plaintiff received on Thursday 5 May is not available. This was, in all probability, invoice no. 163. The plaintiff said he tore this up at the same time as he tore up invoice no. 164 but that he was unable subsequently to retrieve it.
(c) Mr McMorrow went to the firm who supplied C.I.M.'s typewriters in the late afternoon of Thursday 5 May. He brought his wife with him who was his secretary/typist. He had a supply of C.I.M. blank invoices with him. He wanted his wife to type out new invoices on a typewriter similar to that used by C.I.M. He says that in fact this was not done. I accept the evidence of Mr Charles, the proprietor of the firm of office suppliers, that Mr and Mrs McMorrow were in his premises for about twenty minutes and that during this time Mrs McMorrow was at a typewriter typing to the dictation of Mr McMorrow.
(d) The invoices produced at the hearing were no. 160 (in respect of the APS contract) and no. 161 (in respect of the Trimmings contract). The plaintiff says that they were typed in the offices of Collins Brothers on the morning of Friday 6 May. Some of the prices on invoice no. 160 differ from the prices on no. 164. It is admitted that these prices were typed in at the dictation of the plaintiff. It is also admitted that the invoice was predated to 5 May at the instigation of the plaintiff. These were signed by Mr McMorrow. The original and the pink copy (called a "delivery note") were given to the plaintiff. The other two copies (the green and blue ones) were brought back by Mr McMorrow and placed on files in the offices of C.I.M.
(e) The plaintiff swore an affidavit in these proceedings on 19 May 1977. In paragraph three of that affidavit he swore that at quarter past nine on 5 May 1977 that he and Mr McMorrow "had agreed a price for the said frozen box of beef under two headings, a total of £40,294.91 which is represented and set out on invoice no. 160 from Continental Irish Meats Exports Ltd which invoice is duly signed by the said James McMorrow and which was delivered to my representative Mr John Hunter". This averment was incorrect. Invoice no. 160 was not given to Mr Hunter on the morning of 5 May.
(f) Mr McMorrow admits that invoice no. 159 which was made out in favour of Collins Brothers Ltd as a result of a phone call made on the 5 May was antedated by him to 4 May.

(g) The evidence of Mr Renishaw, the forensic expert establishes that invoice no. 164 was typed in C.I.M.'s offices but that invoices 160, 161 and 162 (the last invoice being an invoice in favour of Collins Brothers Ltd) were not typed on a typewriter owned by C.I.M. but were all typed on the same machine.

In some instances no explanation was given for this conduct. Such explanations that were offered in relation to the plaintiff's invoices I found entirely unconvincing. I am quite satisfied that the truth of the transaction between the plaintiff and Mr McMorrow has been kept from me.

Whether or not invoice nos. 160 and 161 were typed on Thursday afternoon on a typewriter in Mr Charles' office or on Friday morning on a typewriter in Messrs Collins Brothers' office it is not necessary for me to decide. It is clear that the plaintiff and Mr McMorrow were engaged in a subterfuge; that they did not wish to have these invoices typed in C.I.M.'s offices but that they agreed that copies would be placed on C.I.M.'s files so as to leave the impression that they had been brought into existence in the ordinary course of business.

Friday 6 May. On Friday 6 May the plaintiff had in his possession the letter to Waterford Cold Stores Ltd authorising him to collect the meat referred to in it and in addition he had the two invoices 160 and 161 signed by Mr McMorrow. Armed with these documents he set off to take delivery of the meat. The receiver, however had acted speedily and was able to stop the consignment leaving the premises. The plaintiff countered with the summons which he issued the following Monday in which he claimed that the meat was his. As will have been clear from what I have already said the plaintiff was in my judgment wrong in so claiming.

I am prepared to accept for the purposes of this judgment that sometime subsequent to being told by Mr Kongmark on the evening of 4 May of C.I.M.'s financial situation and the directions he had given to the staff in Waterford that a concluded agreement was reached between the plaintiff and Mr McMorrow. It is not necessary for me to find when this exactly occurred, but I am prepared to hold that it was before the receiver was appointed. Mr McMorrow had at that time no authority to enter into any contract with the plaintiff. He knew this; so did the plaintiff as a result of what Mr Kongmark told him on the evening of 4 May. It follows that the company was not bound by whatever agreement Mr McMorrow and the plaintiff entered into. I am also satisfied that the transaction entered into between the plaintiff and Mr McMorrow is invalid by virtue of section 286 of the Companies Act 1963. From the afternoon of Tuesday, 3 May (if not before) Mr McMorrow knew full well the heavy losses which the company had sustained and was fully aware that it owed a great deal of money not only to the plaintiff and Collins Brothers Ltd, but also to the bank. The inference to be drawn from his conduct is irresistible. He demonstrated a quite extraordinary zeal in furthering the plaintiff's interests and went to quite extraordinary lengths in doing so. He wanted to help the plaintiff to retrieve the loss he was facing, and his substantial and dominant intention in entering into the sale of the company's goods to him was to prefer him. The liquidator has discharged the onus which is on him of establishing that the transaction amounted to a fraudulent preference within the meaning of section 286 and is accordingly invalid.

Finally, I should explain that I did not consider it necessary to adjourn the hearing for the production of the minute-book of the meeting of 3 May or the records of the transactions between Clover Meats and C.I.M. relating to the last two or three days trading of the company about which questions were asked in course of cross-examination. No injustice would be done, in my view, by failing to adjourn for the production of the documents and their production was not necessary for the determination of the issues in this case.

Patricia McLaughlin
Barrister

In the Matter of The Redundancy Payments Acts 1967-1971 and The Minimum Notice and Terms of Employment Act 1973 and John Donnelly, Official Liquidator of Brittain Manufacturing Ltd v. John Gleeson, John Mulhall and Michael Willis Murphy: High Court 1978 No. 95Sp (Hamilton J) 11 July 1978

Appointment of a provisional liquidator to company – Given liberty by court to continue trading – Employees told that they would be employed therefrom on a day to day basis – Whether the appointment of a provisional liquidator operated to discharge the contracts of employment – Whether notice given by the provisional liquidator was sufficient notice to terminate the contracts of employment – Minimum Notice and Terms of Employment Act 1973 (No. 4) – Redundancy Payments Acts 1967-1971 – Companies Act 1963 (No. 33), section 220

Facts: The appellant was appointed provisional liquidator of the company on 26 May 1977 and was given liberty by the court, *inter alia*, to carry on the business of the company. An order to wind up the company was made on 20 June 1977. The liquidator called a meeting of employees and informed them of his appointment and further informed them that from then on they would be employed on a day to day basis. However, there was no mention of a dismissal, the employees did not receive their insurance cards or P.45 forms and they continued to work on the same terms and conditions as before. The employees were subsequently dismissed and they brought proceedings before the Employment Appeals Tribunal claiming compensation under the Minimum Notice and Terms of Employment Act 1973. The tribunal found as a matter of law that the appointment of the appellant as provisional liquidator did not automatically determine the contracts of employment and, further, found as a mixed matter of fact and law that the notice as given to them did not effect the termination of their contracts of employment. The appellant appealed the finding of the Tribunal.

Held by Hamilton J in refusing the appeal:

(1) The court is bound by findings of fact made by the tribunal.

(2) A court order for the winding up of a company is in the ordinary case deemed to be a discharge of the company's servants.

(3) A servant can however be kept on in the same terms as his original contract by being specifically requested to do so.

(4) The effect of a winding up order as a notice of discharge can be waived.

(5) The appointment of a provisional liquidator who has been given liberty by the court to carry on the business of the company and who does in fact carry on the business of the company does not operate to determine the contracts of employment of the employees of the company. Such an order is completely different to an order for the winding up of the company.

(6) The question as to whether the notice given by the appellant was effective to determine the contracts of employment is one of fact and there was ample evidence to enable the tribunal to reach the conclusion that it did.

Cases referred to in judgment

Chapman's case, LR 2 Eq R 346
Doyle v. Equitable Insurance Co. Ltd
Ex parte Harding (1867) LR 3 Eq 341
In re Oriental Bank Corporation, MacDowall's case (1886) 32 Ch D 366

Counsel's and solicitors' names not available

HAMILTON J **11 July 1978**

The respondents in this case are constituent members of the Employment Appeals Tribunal (hereinafter referred to as "the tribunal") which sat on 23 November 1977 to hear appeals brought by employees and ex-employees of Brittain Manufacturing Ltd (hereinafter called "the company"), a company in liquidation and of which the appellant was appointed official liquidator by the court on 20 June 1977, against the decision of the appellant to refuse such employees and ex-employees payment pursuant to the provisions of the Redundancy Payments Acts 1967–1971 and the Minimum Notice and Terms of Employment Act 1973.

By order of court dated 26 May 1977 the appellant herein had been appointed provisional liquidator of the company and had been given liberty by the court:

(a) To continue existing negotiations for the sale of certain assets of the company,

(b) to carry on the business of the company so far as might be necessary for the beneficial winding up thereof,

(c) to appoint a solicitor to assist him in the performance of his duties, and

(d) to convene meetings of members and creditors of the company.

The order that "the company" be wound up pursuant to the provisions of the Companies Act 1963 was made on 20 June 1977.

The tribunal found as a matter of law that the appointment of the appellant as provisional liquidator of the company did not automatically determine the contracts of employment with the company of the aforesaid employees and ex-employees and is alleged to have found as a matter of mixed law and fact that the notice as given to these employees by the appellant did not effect the determination of their contracts of employment.

Insofar as a question of fact is concerned I am bound by the decision of the tribunal and cannot interfere with same if there was available to the tribunal evidence which would justify such finding of fact.

It appears from the report of the tribunal that:

> "Evidence from each of the employees was to the effect that the liquidator called a meeting and informed them that he was appointed liquidator. He also told them that from then on they would be employed on a day to day basis. However most of the appellants stated that there was no mention of a dismissal, all of them stated that they did not receive their insurance cards or P.45 forms and that they continued working on the same terms and conditions as before. No mention was made about any change of identity of their employers."

The report of the tribunal then went on to say that:

> "The tribunal takes the view that the reasoning in *Doyle v. Equitable Insurance Co. Ltd* is applicable to this case and that what happened on the 26 May 1977, does not break the continuity of employment of any of the employees."

The tribunal then went on to

> "find that these employees who continued in employment for varying periods after 26 May 1977, and who were subsequently dismissed are entitled to compensation under the Minimum Notice and Terms of Employment Act 1973 based on continuous service from their respective dates of commencement to the date their employment finally terminated at their agreed outgoing wages. They may also be entitled to further payments under the Redundancy Payments Acts in respect of their period in continuous service."

From this decision and award of the tribunal, the appellant appeals to this court and seeks:

(a) An order declaring that the respondents were wrong in law in deciding that the appointment of the appellant as provisional liquidator as aforesaid did not automatically determine the contracts of all employees of the company.

(b) An order declaring that the respondents were wrong in holding as a matter of mixed law and fact that such notice as was given to the employees of the company did not determine the contracts of the employees thereof.

(c) An order declaring that the contracts of employment with the company were determined on 26 May 1977, together with the ancillary relief sought in the special summons.

Having regard to the matters set forth in the special indorsement of claim and the manner in which the case was argued before me it is quite clear that the primary matter for determination by me is whether the appointment by the court of the appellant as provisional liquidator of the company automatically determined the contracts of all employees of the company.

In support of his submission that it did, Mr Barron on behalf of the appellant relied on *Chapman's* case LR 1 Eq R 346 and in *Re Oriental Bank Corporation, MacDowall's case* 32 Ch page 366 and referred to *Ex parte Harding*, LR 3 Eq 341.

Chapman's case is merely authority for the proposition that an order for the winding up of a company is notice of discharge to the employees of the company and that a servant of the company is entitled to prove for his salary on the footing of having had notice of discharge on the day the order was made.

In *Ex parte Harding* the Vice Chancellor said:

> "If the services of a person in the employ of a company be not wanted — if the concern be hopelessly or irretrievably bankrupt, and there be nothing whatever for clerks to do — I can well understand that if the clerks receive notice at, or shortly after, the making of the winding-up order, that their services will no longer be required, their discharge may be held to date from the winding-up order; but if the company be a continuing company (and it is observed that the appointment of an official liquidator does not destroy a company — the official liquidator is, in effect the company) and there be actual business to occupy the services of clerks — they must then, I think, go on under the old contract".

Chitty J in *MacDowall's* case considered both these cases and in conclusion at page 372 of the report stated:

> "It is said in order to come to the conclusion at which I have arrived I must be overruling Lord Hatherley's judgment in *Ex parte Harding*. I consider that not to be so. The case that Lord Hatherly was considering when Vice-Chancellor was the case in which, as I understand the report, the business of the company as such was continued. No doubt if that were the

case, the liquidator having continued the business, there might be grounds for saying, and the Vice-Chancellor found that there were grounds in that case for saying, that either the notice had been waived or there was a new contract on the same terms. I think that the two cases of *Chapman's* case and *Ex-parte Harding* can stand together."

It seems to me from a consideration of these three cases and in this I do not differ from the view of the tribunal in the case of *Doyle v. The Equitable Insurance Co. Ltd* to which they refer in the course of their decision, that their effect is:

(a) A court order for the winding up of a company is in the ordinary case deemed to be a discharge of the company's servants.
(b) A servant can however be kept on in the same terms as his original contract by being specifically requested to do so, and
(c) the effect of a winding up order as a notice of discharge can be waived.

These cases also appear to me to require that there be an actual order for the winding up of the company and that this order is the discharge of the company's servants.

It is true that section 220(2) of the Companies Act 1963 provided that "the winding up of a company by the court shall be deemed to commence at the time of the presentation of the petition for the winding up."

The petition for the winding up of the company was presented on 26 May 1977, and the appellant was on that day given, *inter alia*, liberty to carry on the business of the company so far as may be necessary for the beneficial winding up thereof and to continue existing negotiations for the sale of certain assets of the company.

In my opinion the appointment of a provisional liquidator who has been given liberty by the court to carry on the business of the company whatever the purpose and who does in fact carry on the business of the company cannot and does not operate to determine the contracts of employment of the employees of the company.

It is different from an order for the winding-up of the company. An order for the winding-up of a company is notice of discharge to all persons in the employment of the company.

An order for the appointment of a provisional liquidator who has been given liberty to carry on business cannot amount to notice of discharge to all the persons in the employment of the company.

Such an order and its effect on the contracts of employment of the servants of the company must be and is completely different to an order for the winding up of the company.

Consequently I am satisfied that the appointment of a provisional liquidator who has been given such liberty does not automatically determine the contracts of all employees of the company.

The question whether the employees were given by the appellant on 26 May 1977, notice effective to determine their contracts of employment is consequently a question of fact and as there was ample evidence to enable the tribunal to reach the conclusion that it reached it is not open to me to interfere therewith even if I disagreed with its findings.

Patricia McLaughlin
Barrister

In the Matter of Lakeglen Construction Ltd (In Liquidation) and In the Matter of the Companies Act 1963: High Court 1978 No. 1582P (Costello J) 20 December 1978

Company Law – Debenture – Winding up – Company insolvent at time when debenture was executed – Floating charge invalid if created when company was insolvent – Charge over book debts of the company – Whether this was a fixed or a floating charge – Whether it created a charge over the assets of company both present and future – Whether assets charged would, in the normal course of business, be changing from time to time – Whether it was intended that company should continue to trade in relation to this class of assets until some future event– Companies Act 1963 (No. 33), section 288

Facts: The company executed a debenture on 24 November 1977 and the winding up of the company commenced some four months later on 13 March 1978. The debenture was issued to a group of creditors referred to as "major creditors" in consideration of their forbearance in enforcing immediate payment of debts due to them. The company was insolvent at the time the debenture was executed and therefore insofar as it may have created a floating charge it would be invalid by virtue of the provisions of section 288 of the Companies Act 1963. Some of the charges created by the debenture were clearly fixed charges and were therefore not invalidated by the terms of the section. A dispute arose between the preferential and unsecured creditors on the one part and the debenture holders on the other as to whether a purported charge in relation to the book debts of the company in clause 3(b) of the debenture should be construed as a floating or a fixed charge. It was clear by the terms of the debenture that it was contemplated by the parties that the company would continue to trade, and provision was made whereby the major creditors could inspect the company's books. The debenture also required the company to lodge immediately to the company's bank account all monies received by it.

Held by Costello J in construing the charge as a floating charge:
(1) The essential feature of a floating charge is that the company is permitted

to deal with the property the subject matter of the charge: *Houldsworth v. Yorkshire Woolcombers Association Ltd* [1903] 2 Ch 284; *Illingsworth v. Houldsworth* [1904] AC 355 applied.

(2) In the absence of provisions to the contrary, when permission to trade is given in a debenture, permission to receive book debts is more readily inferred than an arrangement whereby the company is required to hand them over to a debenture holder.

(3) The debenture gave the company permission to continue to receive the book debts.

(4) A charge on "all the company's book debts" means those presently in existence and (as those in existence may be extinguished in the ordinary course of trading) those which as a result of future trading may come into existence.

(5) As the instant charge embraced existing and future book debts then it could be said to be over assets which in the ordinary course of the company's business would be changing from time to time.

(6) It was clear that the parties intended that the company should carry on its business in the ordinary way.

(7) The debenture was invalid by virtue of section 288 of the Companies Act 1963 to the extent to which it purported to charge the book debts of the company in favour of the creditors to whom the debenture was issued.

Cases referred to in judgment

Houldsworth v. Yorkshire Woolcombers Society [1903] 2 Ch 284
Illingsworth v. Houldsworth [1904] AC 355
Siebe Gorman and Co. Ltd v. Barclays Bank Ltd [1979] 2 Lloyd's Rep 142

Counsel's and solicitors' names not available

[*Reporter's Note:* Section 288 has been amended by section 136 of the Companies Act 1990]

COSTELLO J **20 December 1978**

The official liquidator of Lakeglen Construction Ltd ("the company) has sought the assistance of the court on a problem which has arisen in the course of the winding up. It is this. The company executed a debenture on 24 November 1977. The winding up of the company commenced some four months later on 13 March 1978. The debenture was issued to a group of creditors referred to as "major creditors" in consideration of their forbearance in enforcing immediate payment of debts due to them. It is now admitted that the company was seriously insolvent in November 1977 and it would follow, therefore, that in so far as the debenture may have created a "floating charge" it would be invalid by virtue of the provisions of section 288 of the Companies Act 1963. No difficulties arise in respect of some of the charges created by the debenture — clearly they are fixed charges and cannot be invalidated by the section. But a dispute has arisen between the preferential creditors and unsecured creditors on the one part and the debenture holders on the other as to whether a purported charge in relation to the book debts of the company in clause 3(b) of the debenture is to be constructed as a floating charge or a fixed charge and the question which I am required to determine is whether the debenture is invalid to the extent to which it purported to charge the book debts of the company in favour of the "major creditors".

To answer this question it is relevant to outline the circumstances in which the debenture came to be made. The company is a fully owned subsidiary of another company known as Catalyst Ltd ("the holding company"). Prior to executing the debenture the company entered into an agreement in writing with the major creditors. By this agreement the major creditors agreed not to enforce immediate payment of part of the sums due to them (described as "the frozen balances") and in consideration of this agreement the company covenanted to execute a debenture in favour of the major creditors, to procure a guarantee by the holding company in favour of the major creditors in respect of sums due by the company to the major creditors, and to procure the granting of a debenture by the holding company in favour of the major creditors. The company also entered into certain express covenants with the major creditors in relation to certain debts owed to it by companies registered in the United Kingdom, Northern Ireland, France and this country and in respect of such debts it covenanted to enforce them by whatever means the major creditors considered prudent for their recovery. It is clear that it was contemplated by the parties to the written agreement that the company would continue to trade and provision was made by which the major creditors could inspect the company's books and which required the company to lodge immediately to the company's bank account all money received by it.

In pursuance of this agreement both the company and the holding company executed the debenture of 24 November 1977. Having recited the agreement to which I have just referred and the fact that it was in the best interests of the holding company that it should give security over its assets in the manner contained in the debenture, and that by a guarantee of 24 November 1977 the holding company guaranteed the due repayment to each of the major creditors of all monies owing or to become owing by the company to each of the major creditors with interest thereon, the company and the holding company jointly and severally covenanted to pay the "frozen balances" with interest as therein specified in the manner set out in the First Schedule to the debenture. There then followed a clause containing covenants entered into by the company and the holding company in relation to the payment of interest. There then was a clause (Clause 3) which contained the security for the payment of the "frozen balances" and interest. I think I should quote this clause in full:

> "3. As security for the payment of the frozen balances and interest thereon and all other monies hereby agreed to be paid or intended to be hereby secured (including any expenses and charges arising out of or in connection with the acts or matters referred to in clause 6 hereof) and so that the security hereby created shall be a continuing security:

(a) The company and the holding company as beneficial owners hereby assigned unto the major creditors all their respective fixed and movable plant, machinery, equipment, fixtures, implements and utensils TOHOLD the same unto the major creditors absolutely;
(b) The company and the holding company as beneficial owners hereby charge in favour of the major creditors all their respective book debts and all rights and powers of recovery in respect thereof TOHOLD the same unto the major creditors absolutely;
(c) The company and the holding company as beneficial owners hereby charge by way of first fixed charge in favour of the major creditors their respective goodwill and uncalled capital for the time being;
(d) The holding company as beneficial owner hereby charges by way of first fixed charges in favour of the major creditors:

(i) 49,999 shares of £1 each in the capital of the company.
(ii) shares of £1 each in the capital of O'Sullivan Homes Ltd.
(iii) 19,995 'A' shares of £1 each and 4 ordinary shares of £1 each in the capital of Pembroke Homes Ltd, a limited liability company registered in the United Kingdom.
(iv) shares of £1 each in the capital of Catalyst Management Ltd,
(v) and all rights and interests of the holding company therein or which may accrue in respect thereof and the holding company shall forthwith transfer the said shares to and procure them to be registered in the name of a nominee of the major creditor and shall duly deliver to the nominees the certificate for such shares.

(e) The company and the holding company as beneficial owners hereby charge by way of first floating charge in favour of the major creditors all other their respective undertakings and assets whatsoever and wheresoever both present and future PROVIDED ALWAYS that neither the company nor the holding company shall without the consent of all the major creditors be entitled to create any mortgage debenture or charge upon and so that no lien shall in any case or in any manner arise on or affect any part of the property of the company or of the holding company ranking either in priority to or *pari passu* with the charges created by this debenture."

The clause which I have just quoted contains certain features which are worthy of note. It will be observed that a number of different types of securities are created by it. By sub-clause 3(a) the company and the holding company *assigned* all their fixed and moveable plant machinery etc. to the major creditors. By sub-clause 3(b) they created a *charge* in relation to "all their respective book debts and all rights and powers of recovery in respect thereof" but did not specify whether the charge was a floating charge or a fixed charge. By sub-clause 3(c) they charged "by way of first *fixed charge* their respective goodwill and uncalled capital for the time being". The holding company by sub-clause 3(d) created a charge "by way of *fixed charge*" on the shares specified in the clause and agreed to transfer the shares to a nominee of the major creditors. Finally sub-clause 3(e) contained a *floating charge*. By this sub-clause both the company and the holding company charged by way of "first floating charge" all other their respective undertakings and assets whatsoever wheresoever both present and future". Thus there was an assignment, two fixed charges and a floating charge created by clause 3 of the debentures. The controversy in this case arises by reason of the failure of the debenture explicitly to state whether the charge created in sub-clause 3(b) in relation to the book debts was a floating one or a fixed one.

The legislature has not attempted to define the meaning of the term "floating charge" and the courts have preferred to indicate certain tests by which a security can be identified as a floating or a fixed charge rather than to formulate an exhaustive definition of what a "floating" charge is. In the particular circumstances of this case I think I can best commence the elucidation of the problem of construction involved in it by pointing to the important differences which exist between the consequences which flow when a charge on book debts is a floating one and when it is a fixed one. These have been pointed out in the *Yorkshire Woolcombers* case (see *Houldsworth v. Yorkshire Woolcombers Association Ltd* [1903] 2 Ch 284; and *Illingsworth v. Houldsworth* [1904] AC 355) in the judgments in the High Court, the Court of Appeal, and the House of Lords in England. Farwell J pointed out that if the security he was considering (which had been given in respect of book debts) was to be treated as a specific charge then "the company had no business to receive one single book debt after the date of it". On the other hand if it was intended that the charge was to remain dormant until some future date and that the company was permitted to go on receiving the book debts and using them until the security would contain the true element of a floating charge (see [1903] 2 Ch 288). In agreeing with these views Cozens Harding LJ concluded that the security in the case was to be read as containing a licence or permission by the mortgagee to the mortgagor "to deal with the mortgage property for a certain time as though a mortgage had been executed" (*ibid.*, p. 298), and was to be regarded as a floating one. And in the House of Lords the Lord Chancellor, in agreeing with the interpretation put on the documents by the lower courts had this to say:

> "In the first place you have that which in a sense I suppose must be an element in the definition of a floating security, that it is something which is to float, not to be put into immediate operation, but such that the company is to be allowed to carry on its business. It contemplates not only that it should carry with it the book debts which were then existing, but it contemplates also the possibility of those book debts being extinguished by payment to the company, and that other book debts should come in and take the place of those that had disappeared. That, My Lords, seems to me to be an essential characteristic of what is properly called a floating security (see [1904] AC at p 367)."

And so the question arises in this case; when they executed the debenture did the parties intend that in relation to its book debts the company was free to receive them and bring new book debts into existence as if the debenture had not been created until such time as the debenture holder became entitled to intervene in the company's affairs? In answering this question the first point to bear in mind is that the company was a trading company carrying on a building contractor's business. Secondly, the parties expressly agreed that it was to be permitted to carry on the business. Thirdly, in the normal course of affairs it would obviously create difficulties for a trading company if it was required to hand over to its mortgagees its book debts as it received them from time to time. I conclude, therefore, that in the absence of provisions to the contrary when permission to trade is given in a debenture permission to receive book debts is more readily to be inferred than is an arrangement by which the company is required to hand them over to a debenture holder. Is there anything in the agreement between the parties or in the debenture itself which would tend to displace the inference to which I have referred? I do not think so. On the contrary, support in it for the *prima facie* inference exists. The written agreement (the terms of which the company was required by clause 12(g) of the debentures to observe) made specific reference to certain of the company's debtors at the date of the transaction. (see clause 2(c) and (d) of the written agreement). The company was required to demand immediate repayment of these specified debts; to enforce its demand for payment by whatever means the major creditors considered prudent; to lodge immediately to its bank account all monies received by it; to give access to the major creditors to its books and records (see clauses 2(c), (d), (h) and (1)). Nowhere is there a provision or a direction which requires the company to pay over the monies which it receives from these debtors to its major creditors. The absence of such a direction, bearing in mind the provisions to which I have just referred, supports rather than weakens the inference that it was intended that the company was to be permitted to retain the book debts as they were paid and to create new ones from time to time and thus generally deal with this particular asset in the ordinary course of its business until such time as the major creditors became entitled to intervene in the company's affairs. I have come to the conclusion that I should so construe this deed.

This does not, of course, conclude the problem of construction in this case. Counsel for all the parties have made reference to a much quoted passage from the judgment of Romer LJ in the Court of Appeal in the *Yorkshire Woolcombers* case ([1903] 2 Ch at p 295) and I have been invited to apply the tests therein formulated to the facts of this case. The passage is this:

> "I certainly do not intend to attempt to give an exact definition of the term "floating charge" nor am I prepared to say that there will not be a floating charge within the meaning of the Act, which does not contain all the three characteristics that I am about to mention, but I certainly think that if a charge has the three characteristics that I am about to mention it is a

floating charge. (1) If it is a charge on a class of assets of a company present and future; (2) if that class is one which, in the ordinary course of the business of the company, would be changing from time to time; and (3) if you find that by the charge it is contemplated that, until some future step is taken by or on behalf of those interested in the charge, the company may carry on its business in the ordinary way as far as 'concerns the particular class of assets I am dealing with'."

As to the first test, I am satisfied that the charge in clause 3(b) in the debenture in this case is a charge in respect of monies due to the company from both existing and future debtors. When a company charges "all its book debts" and when it is specifically permitted to continue trading I think such a charge (unless there is some other provisions in the debenture or some fact in the surrounding circumstances which would call for a contrary interpretation) should not be construed in a restrictive sense; it means, in my view, what it says — a charge on "all the company's book debts" means those presently in existence and (as those in existence may be extinguished in the ordinary course of trading) those which as a result of future trading may come into existence. In this case the other provisions of the debentures lend support to this construction rather than contradict it. After creating a number of securities clause 3 ends by reference to a floating charge by which the company and the holding company charge "all other their respective undertakings assets whatsoever both present and future". Mr Blayney, on behalf of the debenture holders, suggested that this clause was intended to embrace future book debts and that the scheme of the debenture was that clause 3(b) created a fixed charge in relation to existing book debts and clause 3(e) created a floating charge on future debts. I cannot agree. In my opinion clause 3(e) when charging "other assets" is referring to assets other than those mentioned earlier in the clause. Clause 3(a) had referred to fixed and movable plant and machinery; clause 3(b) to "debts"; clause 3(c) to goodwill and uncalled assets; clause 3(g) to certain specified shares; and the reference in clause 3(e) to "other assets" must be a reference to assets other than the company's book debts. If this is so, it would follow that when the parties agreed to make provision in relation to a charge on "all the company's book debts" they were dealing with existing and future book debts — otherwise no security would have been given in relation to an important asset of the company, namely its future book debts.

As to the second test suggested by Lord Justice Romer, if the charge in clause 3(b) is one which embraces existing and future book debts (as I believe it does) then it is quite clear that this charge passes the second test being, as it is, a charge on a class of assets which in the ordinary course of the company's business would be changing from time to time. The views which I have already expressed indicate my opinion on the third test. As I have said, I am satisfied that the parties intended that the company should carry on its business in the ordinary way; that it was, in fact, licensed for this purpose to receive payment from its debtors from time to time without regard to the charge created by the debenture over the book debts until some future contingency arose which would justify the intervention by the debenture holders.

In reading the conclusions which I have just stated I should point out that I have not ignored the judgment of Mr Justice Slade in the unreported case recently decided in England (see *Siebe Gorman & Co. Ltd v. Barclays Bank Ltd*: 26 May 1978 [1979] 2 Lloyds Rep 142). Subsequently it seems to me, however, that the provisions of the document which Slade J was considering were considerably different to those in the present case and that no great assistance is to be found from the conclusions he reached on the facts before him. Nor have I overlooked the submissions made by Mr Blayney as to the *habendum* clause contained in clause 3(b) or as to the inferences which I can properly draw as to the existence of substantial book debts when the debentures was executed. As to the *habendum*, it seems to me that it is a neutral factor in the case — the clause is equally applicable to a charge in respect of future book debts as it is to a charge in relation to existing book debts. As to the evidence of what book debts existed when the debenture was executed I agree that the evidence does not permit any very definite conclusions as to their extent. It is, however, reasonable to conclude that it is likely that they were fairly substantial. But this fact does not weaken the conclusions which can be reached from an interpretation of the document itself. Again, it seems to me that the existence of substantial book debts would be a neutral factor in construing the party's intention. It is equally consistent with the parties deciding to allow the company to receive them in the ordinary course of trading as it is consistent with an arrangement to assign them (by means of a fixed charge) to the debenture holders.

I propose, therefore, to answer the question raised by holding that the debenture is invalid by virtue of the provisions of section 288 of the Companies Act 1963 to the extent to which it purported to charge the book debts of the company in favour of the creditors to whom the debenture was issued.

Patricia McLaughlin
Barrister

In the Matter of Palgrave Murphy Ltd and in the Matter of the Companies Act 1963: High Court 1970 No. 3846 P (Hamilton J) 24 February 1979

Preferential payments on a winding up – Claim by Minister for Posts and Telegraphs, subsequently adopted by the Minister for Social Welfare, that monies due in respect of social insurance contributions payable by the company were entitled to the priority conferred by section 285 – Social insurance stamps purchased by company at a number of Post Offices – Cheques not honoured – Whether purchase of stamps constituted payment of contributions under the Social Welfare Acts 1952-1961 – Whether contributions only paid when stamps affixed to employees social insurance card – Whether contributions paid to the Department of Social Welfare – Companies Act 1963 (No. 33), section 285

Facts: Between 6 May 1970 and 11 November 1970, the company purchased social insurance stamps at various Post Offices which they paid for by cheques totalling £3,947.68. On 19 November 1970, the company went into liquidation and none of the relevant cheques was paid. It was claimed on behalf of the Minister for Posts and Telegraphs and the Minister for Social Welfare that the claim was in respect of contributions payable by the company during the next twelve months previous to the relevant date (being the date when the company went into liquidation) as the employees were persons under the Social Welfare Act 1952 and as such were entitled to the priority payment conferred by section 285 of the Companies Act 1963. By virtue of the provisions of section 10 of the Social Welfare Act 1952 and the provisions of the Social Welfare (Powers in Relation to Insurance Stamp Order 1952 (No. 382 of 1952), the Minister of Posts and Telegraphs had power (a) to direct the manner in which insurance stamps should be prepared and issued and (b) to provide for the sale of insurance stamps through the Post Office. It was submitted on behalf of the claimants that the Minister for Posts and Telegraphs acted as the agent for the Minister for Social Welfare in relation to the claim for contributions which had not been paid. It was further submitted that the employer makes contributions to the Department of Social Welfare through the Department of Posts and Telegraphs and as evidence of such contributions, he receives stamps which can be stuck upon the employee's insurance card.

Held by Hamilton J in refusing the claim:

(1) In exercising these powers, the Minister for Posts and Telegraphs was exercising statutory powers given to him and was not acting as the agent of any other Minister.

(2) It was clear from the Social Welfare Act 1952 that no contributions were paid or payable to the Department of Social Welfare but, by virtue of section 3(3) of the 1952 Act, were paid into the fund established by section 39(1).

(3) It was not correct to say that a contributor receives a stamp as evidence of the payment of contributions required to be paid under the 1952 Act. It was clear from a consideration of Article 11(1) of the Social Welfare (Collection of Contributions) Regulations 1952 (SI No. 381 of 1952) that the contribution payable under the Act was paid by the affixing of the insurance stamp to the employee's card and, therefore, the purchasing of an insurance stamp did not of itself amount to the payment of the contribution.

(4) The amount claimed was due in respect of the purchase of insurance stamps and could not be regarded as due in respect of contributions payable by the company under the Social Welfare Acts 1952-1961.

(5) The Minister for Posts and Telegraphs was not entitled to the priority afforded by section 285(2) of the Companies Act 1963 and ranked as an ordinary creditor.

No cases referred to in judgment

Counsel's and solicitors' names not available

[*Reporter's Note:* Section 285 of the Companies Act 1963 has been amended by section 10 of the Companies (Amendment) Act 1982 (No. 10) and, most recently, by section 134 of the Companies Act 1990 (No. 33)]

HAMILTON J **24 February 1979**

This matter came before me by virtue of a request made by the Minister for Social Welfare and the Minister for Posts and Telegraphs for a decision that the ruling of the assistant examiner dated 11 February 1976 be reversed.

The examiner had ruled that a claim originally made by the Minister for Posts and Telegraphs and subsequently adopted by the Minister for Social Welfare for £3,947.68 did not qualify for preferential treatment under section 285 of the Companies Act 1963.

It was claimed on behalf of the Minister for Posts and Telegraphs and the Minister for Social Welfare that this claim was in respect of contributions payable by Palgrave Murphy Ltd during the twelve months next before the relevant date (19 November 1970) as the employees were persons under the Social Welfare Act 1952 and as such were entitled to the priority payment afforded by section 285 of the Companies Act 1963.

It is submitted by the liquidator of Palgrave Murphy Ltd that during the period between 6 May 1970 and 11 November 1970 that the company purchased Social Insurance Stamps at a number of Post Offices, paid for them by cheques totalling £3,947.68 and that the said social insurance stamps to that total value were obtained in exchange for the said cheques.

On 19 November 1970 the said company, Palgrave Murphy Ltd, was placed in liquidation and none of the relevant cheques was paid.

It is not necessary for me to set out in detail the facts in this case. They are set out in detail in the request for the decision of court, the annex setting out the history of the case and the memorandum submitted by the assistant examiner.

Paragraph 3 of the request for the decision of court states that:

> "Under section 10 of the Social Welfare Act 1952 authority has been granted to the Minister for Posts and Telegraphs to sell insurance stamps which are to be affixed by employers to employees' social welfare cards as evidence that social welfare contributions have been made. The expressed authority in relation to insurance stamps is stated in Statutory Instrument No. 382 of 1952 and is entitled Social Welfare (Powers in Relation to Insurance Stamps) Order 1952."

Section 10 of the Social Welfare Act 1952 provides that:

> "Subject to subsection 2 of this section, insurance stamps shall be prepared

> and issued in such a manner as the Revenue Commissioners, with the consent of the Minister for Finance, may direct, and the said Revenue Commissioners may, by regulations made by them, provide for applying, with the necessary adaptations, as respect insurance stamps, all or any of the provisions, including penal provisions, of the following enactments, ... and may, with the consent of the Minister for Posts and Telegraphs, provide for the sale of insurance stamps through the Post Office."

Subsection 2 provides that:

> "The Government may by order provide that any powers and duties of the Revenue Commissioners with reference to insurance stamps shall be exercised and performed by the Minister for Post and Telegraphs, either to the exclusion of the Revenue Commissioners or concurrently with the Revenue Commissioners. . . ."

By virtue of the terms of Article 2 of Statutory Instrument No. 382 of 1952:

> "All powers and duties of the Revenue Commissioners with reference to insurance stamps shall be exercised and performed by the Minister for Posts and Telegraphs to the exclusion of the Revenue Commissioners."

I have been informed by counsel for the Minister for Posts and Telegraphs that no regulation has been made providing for the sale of insurance stamps through the Post Office but with some hesitation and for the purpose of this case I am prepared to hold that a specific regulation to this effect is not necessary and that the Minister for Posts and Telegraphs has provided for the sale of insurance stamps through the Post Office.

Consequently by virtue of the provisions of section 10 of the Social Welfare Act and the provisions of Statutory Instrument No. 382 of 1952, the Minister for Posts and Telegraphs has power to (a) direct the manner in which insurance stamps shall be prepared and issued and (b) to provide for the sale of insurance stamps through the post office.

In exercising such powers he is exercising the statutory powers given to him and not as agent for any other minister.

Paragraph 6 of the request states that:

> "In so far as the Minister for Posts and Telegraphs is concerned, it should be clear that this claim is made as agent for the Minister for Social Welfare in relation to contributions which have not been paid. It should not be suggested, nor is it acceptable, that the Minister 'sells' stamps in the commercial sense or that the employer 'buys' stamps from the Minister for Posts and Telegraphs. The employer makes contributions to the Department of Social Welfare through the Department of Posts and Telegraphs and as evidence of such contributions he receives stamps which can be stuck upon the employees' cards."

I cannot agree with this statement. It is clear from the terms of the Social Welfare Act 1952 that no contributions, whether by an employed contributor or by the employer of an employed contributor, are paid or payable to the Department of Social Welfare.

It is quite clear that such contributions, being those provided for in section 5 of the Social Welfare Act 1952, are by virtue of the terms of section 3 sub-section 3 of the Social Welfare Act 1952 "paid into the fund established by section 39 sub-section 1 of the Act".

Section 39(1) of the Social Welfare Act 1952 provides that:

> "There shall be established a fund (to be called the Social Insurance Fund and in this Act referred to as the Fund) comprising a current account and an investment account."

The Minister for Social Welfare manages and controls the current account of the Fund into which sums payable to the fund are paid unless otherwise specifically provided.

These contributions are not paid to the Department of Social Welfare or to the Minister for Social Welfare but are required to be paid into the Social Insurance fund.

Neither is it correct to say that a contributor receives stamps as evidence of the payment of contributions required to be paid under the Social Welfare Act 1952.

Section 8(1) of the Social Welfare Act 1952 provides that:

> "Subject to the provisions of this Act, regulations may provide for any matters incidental to the payment and collection of contributions and in particular for:
> (a) payment of contributions by means of adhesive stamps (in this Act referred to as insurance stamps) affixed to cards (in this Act referred to as insurance cards) or otherwise, and for regulating the manner, times, and conditions in, at, and under which insurance stamps are to be affixed or payments are otherwise to be made."

In exercise of the powers conferred on him by the said Welfare Act 1952 and in particular section 8 of the said Act, the Minister for Social Welfare made the regulations set forth in Statutory Instrument No. 381 of 1952 Social Welfare (Collection of Contributions Regulations) 1952. Article 11(1) of the said Statutory Instrument provides that:

> "Every weekly employment contribution payable under the Act shall, except as otherwise provided in these Regulations, be paid by the affixing of an insurance stamp of the appropriate value to the insurance card of the employed contributor in the space indicated for that purpose upon the card."

It is quite clear from a consideration of this Article that the employment contribution payable under the Act is required to be paid, subject to the exception provided in these regulations, by the affixing of an insurance stamp of the appropriate value to the insurance card of the employed contributor in the space indicated for that purpose upon the card.

As already stated the Minster for Posts and Telegraphs was empowered to (a) direct the manner in which insurance stamps shall be prepared and issued and (b) provide for the sale of insurance stamps through the Post Office.

As the purchase of the insurance stamps through the Post Office did not, however, of itself amount to the payment of the contribution, the payment of the contribution was made by affixing the insurance stamp to the insurance card. The amount claimed here, £3,947.68 is due in respect of the purchase of insurance stamps paid for by cheques which had been dishonoured.

Can this amount be regarded as due in respect of contributions payable by the company under the Social Welfare Acts 1952 to 1961?

Having given this matter very considerable consideration I have come to the conclusion, not without difficulty and with some hesitation, that it cannot be so regarded. As I have already said, the purchase of the stamps is not the payment of the contribution. The payment of the contribution is made by affixing the stamps to the insurance cards. These are separate and distinct acts.

If, after the purchase of the stamps from the Minister for Post and Telegraphs the said stamps were lost or stolen prior to their being affixed to their employees' insurance cards, could the company, Palgrave Murphy Ltd be regarded as having discharged its obligation to make contributions to the Social Insurance Fund? In my opinion, it could not as the regulation provide that the payment shall be made, not by the purchase of the stamps, but by affixing them to the employees' insurance cards in the space allotted for that purpose.

Consequently I am satisfied that the amount claimed and admittedly due is not due as a contribution under the Social Welfare Acts 1952 to 1961 but merely due in respect of the purchase of insurance stamps which could be used for the payment of contributions under the said Acts.

Consequently I am satisfied that the Minister for Posts and Telegraph is not entitled to the priority afforded by section 285 sub-section 2 of the Companies Act 1963 and must rank as an ordinary creditor.

Patricia McLaughlin
Barrister

Gresham Industries Ltd (in Liquidation) v. Matthew Cannon: High Court 1978 No. 4268P (Finlay P) 2 July 1980

Company – Liquidation – Claim against shareholder and director – Claim on foot of monies advanced to the defendant or monies paid by the plaintiff to the use of the defendant – Counterclaim – Monies paid to or to the use of the plaintiff – Calculation of sums – Right of set-off – Whether right of set-off exceeds to sums which a person had not paid at date of liquidation but might become liable to pay in the future

Facts: The plaintiff company traded in radio and electrical goods. The defendant was the principal shareholder and director, owning 22,498 shares out of 30,000. His brother Anthony owned a further 6,250 and Anthony's wife, Lily Cannon, was a director and secretary, but resigned from both posts in 1976. Prior to the company's incorporation, the defendant had traded in electrical goods through other outlets, firstly Tara Electrics Ltd, and shortly before the incorporation of the plaintiff, through Matthew Cannon Ltd.

The plaintiff company owned no property but traded from various premises, most of which were owned by Paulcar Ltd ("Paulcar") (of which the defendant and Anthony Cannon were the effective beneficial shareholders) another being owned by the defendant personally. In 1975 the defendant formed a company called Tivoli Centre Ltd ("Tivoli") to acquire premises for the use of the plaintiff.

The plaintiff went into liquidation on 25 August 1976 and Paulcar and Tivoli also went into liquidation. The plaintiff issued proceedings against the defendant claiming the sum of £159,280, being monies alleged to have been advanced to the defendant as loans and monies paid by the plaintiff to the use of the defendant, allowing for credits in respect of monies paid by the defendant to the plaintiff. The evidence on behalf of the plaintiff was that for the period up to the end of 1974 the books and records of the plaintiff made available to the liquidator were extremely incomplete and in some cases non-existent. This was alleged to have been due to a fire. From 1975-76 the books, which at that stage were kept by Lily Cannon were complete.

In the first part of its statement of claim, the plaintiff claimed the sum of £90,914 allegedly due between the date of incorporation of the plaintiff and 1975, and made up as follows:

(a) £16,000 in relation to a director's loan used to finance the defendant's purchase of shares in the plaintiff. The defendant alleged that he obtained the shares in consideration of handing over the assets of Matthew Cannon Ltd to the plaintiff.

(b) £74,914 made up of £36,000 paid by the plaintiff for the purchase of a residence, £6,000 paid to the defendant for the purchase of shares in Martin Nugent Ltd, with the balance of £32,914 relating to cheques and goods paid to the defendant. The defendant alleged that he had not received these sums and submitted that they were inadequately proved.

In the second part of the statement of claim the plaintiff claimed the further sum of £73,2000 allegedly due between February 1975 and the liquidation of the company, and made up as follows:

(a) £7,000 on foot of seven cheques each for £1,000 lodged to the personal account of the defendant. The defendant alleged that these were for expenses involved in the setting up of Tivoli.

(b) £15,000 in respect of cheque recorded as "M. Cannon, personal" but actually made out to cash and cashed by the defendant's brother.

(c) £3,000 in respect of a cheque for 22 August 1975 to which the defendant offered a straight denial that he had received the money.

(d) Further sums in respect of a cheque dated 25 August 1975, £700 cash (16 January 1976), and £500 in respect of a payment to Chesham Property Overseas Ltd (17 December 1975). These were admitted by the defendant.

(e) Sums of £17,000, £12,000 and three cheques of £5,000 paid to the defendant, which the defendant defended on the basis that these sums were applied to the Tivoli project. The defendant asserted that these were really sums invested by the plaintiff, which only came through him as a channel.

The defendant disputed the claim and counterclaimed for sums he alleged were paid by the defendant to the use of or to the plaintiff, in particular in respect of sums which he alleged were paid or applied to him through Paulcar or for the purposes of that company, and in 1975 for the project involving Tivoli.

Held by Finlay P in granting the plaintiff judgment in the sum of £101,880.

(1) The defendant was liable for the sum of £84,914 in respect of the first part of the statement of claim.

(a) A sum of £16,000 was due by the defendant in respect of a director's loan used to finance the purchase of his shares in the plaintiff.

(b) The sum of £32,914 relating to cheques and goods advanced to the defendant was sufficiently proved by the surviving working papers and the evidence of the then secretary. This sum was, therefore, also due to the defendant.

(c) The defendant was not liable in respect of the sum of £6,000 advance to Martin Nugent Ltd, as he had never received any shares in that company, and there was evidence that this was a sum paid to the then managing director of that company as compensation for loss of office.

(d) The sum of £36,000 was due by the defendant in respect of the purchase of a residence.

(2) The defendant was also liable for the whole of the sum of £73,200 claimed in the second part of the statement of claim.

(a) The sum of £7,000 was due in respect of the seven cheques paid to the defendant's personal account. The evidence did show that they were sums advanced for the Tivoli project, but even if they were, these sums were not, as a matter of law, sums for which the defendant could avoid liability.

(b) The defendant was liable for the cheque for £15,000, as the evidence of the secretary was that the entries in the book were made after careful and responsible enquiry as to the purpose for which the money was required.

(c) The defendant was liable in the sum of £3,000 for the cheque dated 22 August 1975.

(d) The defendant was liable for the various payments totalling £44,000 in respect of Tivoli, as even had he invested these sums in the Tivoli project, that did not entitle him to deny liability to the plaintiff company.

(3) Taking into account a credit of £4,834 conceded by the plaintiff, the defendant therefore was liable to the plaintiff in the sum of £154,280.

(4) The plaintiff was however entitled to credit of £52,400 (which he could set-off against the sum due to the plaintiff) made up as follows:

(a) The defendant was entitled to credit for the sums of £3,400 paid to the plaintiff, £25,000 in respect of sum paid by the defendant for goods supplied to the company and £24,000, the proceeds of sale of his property, paid to the company in 1972 and 1973.

(b) Even if the defendant was the 100 per cent beneficial owner of all the shares in Paulcar Ltd, he could not for the purpose of settling an account between him and another company be identified with the company. Therefore the defendant could not claim credit for the proceeds of sale of properties owned by Paulcar Ltd, the proceeds of which were paid to the plaintiff or for sums allegedly due by the plaintiff Paulcar Ltd in respect of rent.

(c) The defendant had failed to prove a claim for £19,512 in respect of alleged cash payments made by him for second-hand electrical goods for the company. A further claim for £33,741, in respect of stock which the defendant alleged he purchased when the company was initially promoted, would also be disallowed.

(d) A further claim in respect of a payment to Allied Irish Banks in respect of a debt owing by Martin Nugent Ltd would also be disallowed, as this was not a payment to the plaintiff, and so could not be set-off.

(e) Further payments by the defendant on foot of guarantees for the debs of the plaintiff and Paulcar Ltd, were not paid prior to the presentation of the petition. Pursuant to the bankruptcy rules, where a person owes money to a company at the date of liquidation, sums which that person may become liable to pay in the future are not properly allowable as a set-off against the debt due to the company even though they may have been paid prior to the date upon which an account between the debtor and the company is stated and settled. *Re Fenton* [1931] 1 Ch 85 followed; *Re a Debtor, ex parte The Debtor v. Waite's Trustee* [1956] 1 WLR 1226 followed.

(f) An agreement by the defendant to transfer certain apartments to the two shareholder of Loughrey Sales Ltd, in payment for goods valued at £32,000 supplied by that company to the plaintiff, had never been completed. It was therefore not necessary to decide whether had the agreement been completed it would have amounted to a fraudulent preference, or was a sum which was capable as a matter of law of being set-off.

Cases referred to in judgment

Re a Debtor, ex parte The Debtor v Waite's Trustee [1956] 1 WLR 480; [1956] 2 All ER 94 (Ch D); [1956] 1 WLR 1226; [1956] 3 All ER 225 (CA)

Re Fenton [1931] 1 Ch 85

Counsel's names not available

Solicitors for the plaintiff: *William Fry*
Solicitors for the defendant: *David Walsh & Co.*

FINLAY P **2 July 1980**

This is a claim brought by the plaintiff company by its official liquidator pursuant to sanction of the court against the principal shareholder and director of the plaintiff company for a total sum of £155,280 consisting in effect of advances made to the defendant by way of loan and of monies paid by the plaintiff company on behalf of or to the use of the defendant allowing for credits in respect of monies paid by the defendant into the plaintiff company or on its behalf. The defendant in his defence not only disputed the entire of the plaintiff's claim but in addition claimed that substantial sums of money paid by the defendant to the use of or to the plaintiff company had not been credited and in effect claimed by way of counterclaim or set off in respect of those sums. The matter came for hearing before me on 22 April 1980 and continued at hearing on the two succeeding days. It then became clear that, notwithstanding certain replies to notice for particulars which had been furnished by the defendant a short time previously after a series of applications by the plaintiff, the defendant's case in respect of the state of account between him and the plaintiff company had not been particularised and I adjourned the matter giving specific directions to the defendant with regard to the further particulars and certain documents to vouch them which must be delivered to the plaintiff company before the resumption of the hearing. The defendant was at that time represented by solicitor and counsel. The matter came back before me by way of resumed hearing on 10 June 1980 and was at hearing on that day and for three further days. On 10 June 1980 the solicitor on behalf of the defendant applied to be discharged from the record of the case and I made an order accordingly and the defendant then represented himself.

The general facts and background in connection with these proceedings which are not in conflict between the parties, I find to be as follows.

The plaintiff company was incorporated on 22 October 1971 with a nominal share capital of £50,000 divided into 50,000 shares of £1 each. The amount of capital paid up or credited as paid up is £30,000. Shortly described, it was a trading company formed for the purpose of trading in radio and electrical goods and the shareholders were the defendant who was credited with having been issued with £22,498 paid up shares, his brother Anthony Cannon who was credited as having been issued £6,250 paid up shares, one Cornelius O'Sullivan to whom was credited as having been issued £1,250 paid up shares and two persons holding one share each.

The directors of the company were at all material times the defendant, his brother Anthony Cannon, Mrs Lily Cannon wife of Anthony Cannon who up to a short time before the presentation of the petition for liquidation acted as secretary as well director but resigned from both posts in 1976 and Cornelius O'Sullivan

Prior to the incorporation of this company, the defendant had for many years traded in electrical goods by way of, what might be described as multiple retail outlets. Firstly, in a company entitled Tara Electric Ltd which he sold and for a short period prior to the incorporation of the plaintiff company in a company named Matthew Cannon Ltd.

The plaintiff company did not own any of the premises from which it traded and most of these were registered in the name of a company entitled Paulcar Ltd of which the defendant and his brother Anthony Cannon were the effective beneficial shareholders. One of the premises from which it traded remained the property of the defendant personally. Paulcar Ltd is a company also now in liquidation. In the year 1975 the defendant became involved in a venture to acquire certain premises in which on the evidence before me it was intended that the plaintiff company might use as a warehouse in part and part of which it was intended might be developed as a leisure and shopping centre type of development. For this purpose a company was incorporated named Tivoli Centre Ltd and that company is also now in liquidation.

The plaintiff's claim as set out in the statement of claim was broadly divided into two sums, the first being sums alleged to be due between the date of the incorporation of the plaintiff company and the commencement of the year 1975 in a nett sum of £90,914, the second sum being £73,200 was in respect of sums alleged to be due between the month of February 1975 and the liquidation of the company.

A petition for the liquidation of the company was presented by a creditor on 28 July 1976 and an order for the liquidation of the company was made on 25 August 1976. The present proceedings were instituted by plenary summons issued on 18 July 1978 pursuant to an order giving the liquidator liberty to institute such proceedings made on 6 February 1978. Service of this summons was not affected until 11 November 1978 and an appearance having been entered on 16 November 1978, the statement of claim was delivered on 22 November 1978. A series of notices for particulars were furnished by the defendant to the plaintiffs after that date and were replied to. By notice of motion of 11 June 1979 the plaintiffs applied for judgment in default of defence and by order of the High Court dated 18 June 1979 the defendant was given extended time for the delivery of defence. A defence was eventually delivered on 24 July 1979 and notice of trial was delivered on 12 November 1979. From that time until the initial hearing before me the plaintiff company sought to obtain from the defendant particulars of matters set out in his defence and in particular more specific information with regard to a generalised claim that inadequate credits have been allowed to the defendant. These particulars were eventually furnished by two letters written on behalf of the defendant on 14 April 1980 and 18 April

1980. After the hearing before me in April of 1980 the defendant complied with the directions through his solicitor who was still then acting for him, given by me as to the particulars of his claim necessary to be furnished to the plaintiffs by a letter of 5 May 1980.

The issues which really arose and were tried out before me, largely being issues of fact, were in effect separated into various categories and dealt with *seriatim* by reference to the two letters from the solicitor for the defendant of 14 and 18 April 1980 respectively and the further letter from the solicitors for the defendant of 5 May 1980.

In general the evidence on behalf of the plaintiff fell into two categories. For the period up to the end of 1974 the books and records of the plaintiff company made available to the liquidator were extremely incomplete and in some cases non-existent . This was explained by the defendant as being the result of a fire which occurred in the offices of the plaintiff company before the end of 1974.

From the commencement of 1975 on, except for the period immediately preceding the liquidation of the company, the company's ordinary accounting books were still intact and were kept by Mrs Lily Cannon who was during the relevant period director and secretary of the company and who gave evidence before me. Details with regard to the amounts claimed by the plaintiffs therefore in the latter period were much more precise and more satisfactorily displayed from the books of the company than were those in the earlier period.

A number of the credits claimed by the defendant consisted of monies which he alleged were paid or applied by him either through the agency of the company Paulcar Ltd, or for the purposes of that company and to a large extent in the period from 1975 on in relation to the project which consisted of the Tivoli Centre Ltd. A broad issue therefore as to the right of the defendant to counterclaim or set off against any amounts which may be due by him to this company in liquidation in respect of monies expended or invested by him in these other two companies arose.

I will deal with the various issues in the order firstly, in which the claim of the plaintiff company is set out in the statement of claim and secondly, in the order in which credits and counterclaims are asserted by the defendant in the letters of April and May 1980 to which I have referred.

The first item in the claim of £90,914 contained in the plaintiff's statement of claim is a sum of £16,000 alleged to be due by the defendant in respect of shares issued in the company. It is not disputed that the defendant is credited in the company as the owner of £18,249 £1 shares fully paid up. Neither is it disputed that in respect of those he paid in actual money to the company a sum of £2,249 only, leaving an outstanding balance of £16,000. The then auditor of the company created an account consisting *inter alia* of a statement of affairs of the company as at 18 November 1971 in effect representing the financial situation in the company at the time it took over the business, stock, assets and liabilities of Matthew Cannon Ltd. From that account it is clear that in order to provide the shares issued to the defendant as being fully paid up it was necessary to create a directors' loan to him of the sum of £16,000. That figure contained in the directors loan account is continued and carried on unpaid by the defendant throughout the time when accounts of the company were prepared by their auditor.

The defendant's defence to this portion of the claim was that the arrangement existing at the time of the setting up of the company and the taking over of the assets and liabilities of Matthew Cannon Ltd was that he got these shares in effect as a credit in consideration of handing over the assets of Matthew Cannon Ltd to the company. In support of that he provided evidence of the bank balance of Matthew Cannon but not at the material date.

I am quite satisfied that no such arrangement as is asserted by the defendant was made at the time of the formation of this company and I am confirmed in that view by the total absence of any documentary proof establishing such an arrangement which one would have expected. I am therefore satisfied that this sum of £16,000 is due and owing by the defendant to the plaintiff company. With the exception of three items consisting of two figures of £9,000 and £27,000 being the amount paid by the company for the purchase by the defendant of a residence known as Mountainview House and a sum of £6,000 alleged to have been paid by the company for the purchase by the defendant of shares in Martin Nugent Ltd, the remainder of the sum of £90,914 firstly claimed by the plaintiff company consists of cheques and goods supplied and emanates from the working papers of the auditor of the company which have survived notwithstanding the fire and the loss of the books of the company during the period concerned. In effect the defendant's attitude to these sums in evidence was that they were inadequately proved having regard to the absence of the books and a general denial that he ever received these sums. I have had the evidence of Mrs Lily Cannon who is the person who kept the books during the greater part of this period and of the system which she operated in keeping them. I am satisfied on her evidence that when cheques were payable either to the defendant by name or to cash and when they were in effect drawings by or advances to the defendant that she entered them in the books as a personal account of the defendant and that she did so upon information reliably supplied to her either by the defendant himself or by one of his fellow directors. I am therefore satisfied that these amounts are due and are sufficiently proved by the working papers which have survived and which were proved in evidence before me.

With regard to the purchase of shares in Martin Nugent Ltd in respect of which a claim for £6,000 is made, different considerations in my view apply. This item was originally entered in the working papers to which I have referred as an investment by the company in Martin Nugent Ltd. The defendant gave me concrete evidence that this sum was not for the purchase of shares by him or in his name but it was rather a sum paid to the managing director of Martin Nugent Ltd by way of compensation for getting him out of that company. The books of the company satisfy me as a matter of probability that the takeover in broad terms of Martin Nugent Ltd which never reached any particular legal form was done by the plaintiff company and not by the defendant personally and I am satisfied that no shares in Martin Nugent Ltd issued at any time to the defendant. In these circumstances, I am not satisfied that this sum of £6,000 is due by the defendant to the plaintiffs.

With regard to the sums totalling £36,000 and paid in respect of Mountain-view House in the letter of 5 May 1980 the solicitor then acting on behalf of the defendant agreed those sums. The defendant in evidence sought to dispute them but I am satisfied that they are due.

I therefore conclude that on the first portion of the plaintiff's claim there is due and owing by the defendant to the plaintiff company a total sum of £84,914.

With regard to the second claim of £73,200 made by the plaintiff company, the first seven items are cheques each for £1,000 lodged to the personal account of the defendant at Allied Irish Bank, Santry, on successive dates in the months of April and May 1975. The defendant did not dispute the payment of these amounts into his bank account nor indeed could having regard to the production of his bank account. He did seek to assert however that they were in repayment of sums expended by him in the setting up of the project consisting of the Tivoli Centre. I am not satisfied on the evidence that this is so and in my view they were clearly sums advanced to the defendant from the plaintiff company probably in my view to reduce an overdraft which had gone beyond its permitted limit in his personal account in Allied Irish Bank, Santry at that particular time. Even if they were in repayment for monies invested by the defendant in the project known as the Tivoli Centre for the reasons which I will elaborate at a later stage in this judgment, they would not, in my view, as a matter of law be sums which the defendant could avoid liability for.

The next item is described in the particulars contained in the statement of claim as a cheque dated 13 August 1975 made payable to cash and recorded as "M. Cannon, personal", in the cheque journal by Mrs Lily Cannon. The cheque was in the sum of £15,000. The primary defence of the defendant with regard to this item was that upon inspection of the cheque it was made payable to cash but endorsed and apparently cashed by Edward Cannon, a brother of the defendant. On this evidence the defendant denied that the money was received by him or paid to him. I had the evidence of Mrs Lily Cannon who kept the cheque journal during the entire of this relevant period and who made the entry concerning this sum of £15,000. I am satisfied that she was a careful, accurate and truthful witness and I am therefore satisfied that in regard to this particular transaction as I was satisfied in regard to the other entries in the books of the company that she made these entries after careful and responsible enquiry as to the purpose for which the money was required. The defendant sought in evidence to suggest that this sum was probably cashed by Mr Edward Cannon and the proceeds of the cash applied by the company towards the purchase of wholesale goods for cash. On the evidence I am satisfied that this explanation could not be true because whilst in the year 1976 and shortly prior to the liquidation of the company, the company was buying large quantities of goods for cash because its credit had run out with suppliers, there is no evidence that this has really the situation in August 1975. Furthermore I am equally satisfied that in relation to the purchase of goods for cash these entries were carefully and precisely made by Mrs Cannon in the books of the company and examples of them are to be found there. There would be no reason other than it was its true description therefore why Mrs Cannon should enter this particular sum of £15,000 as personal to the defendant. I am therefore satisfied that this account is payable. The next amount is an amount by cheque dated 22 August 1975 for £3,000 payable to cash and recorded again as M. Cannon, personal. This cheque was not available showing any different or other endorsement on it and the defendant's defence to it was a simple denial that he received the money but he was unable to offer any explanation for the form of the entry in the journal or for what other use or person the money would have been given to. I am satisfied this money is also due. The next amount is for a cheque dated 25 August 1975 made payable to M. Cannon and recorded in the cheque journal as personal in the way that the other cheques were, and is an amount which the defendant has agreed and the reason he has agreed is that it was a cheque made payable to him and traceable to his bank account. Two other items in this portion of the claim, one being a sum of £700 paid on 16 January 1976 to J. Cannon and recorded in the cheques journal as personal to the defendant was admitted by the defendant as being paid in respect of decorative work to his house. The other amount payable on 17 December 1975 payable to Chesham Property Overseas Ltd and recorded in the cheques journal as advertising in the sum of £500 was also admitted by the defendant.

Apart from these items, an item of £17,030, of £12,000 and three separate cheques of £5,000 each were all recorded as paid or payable to the defendant but were demanded by the defendant upon the basis that they were all sums except possibly for a balance of £2,500 out of the cheque £12,000 which were applied by him towards the project known as the Tivoli Centre. This project consisted of the purchase in the late summer or autumn of 1975 of a large warehouse premises which I am satisfied on the evidence the defendant intended should be used in part as a warehouse for the purposes of this company and as to the rest, as a leisure centre to be developed in accordance with certain ideas which he had seen and approved of in Spanish leisure centres and partly for a shopping arcade or shopping centre in association with the leisure centre. In effect the defendant's assertion was that all the monies taken by him out of the plaintiff company and applied towards this venture travelled through him merely as a channel or conduit pipe and really constituted an investment by the plaintiff company in the Tivoli Centre which subsequently was formed as a company known as Tivoli Centre Ltd. With regard to this contention it is of considerable importance that in addition to these sums marked as payable to the defendant personally there are other substantial sums entered in the books of the plaintiff company as being loans or advances made by the plaintiff company to the Tivoli Centre Ltd. Furthermore there is no sign of any documentary evidence or proof that the plaintiff company was entitled to any share either held by the defendant or by anyone else in trust for them or issued directly to them or that they had any form of debenture or mortgage over the property of

Tivoli Centre Ltd in respect of the sums with which I am concerned in this claim. Tivoli Centre Ltd was unfortunately also put into liquidation after the liquidation of the plaintiff company and though the defendant bitterly complains of the price at which the premises were sold by the liquidator of that company it is clear that it is substantially insolvent. Had the position been otherwise and had Tivoli Centre Ltd been an affluent or solvent company there is nothing in the documents and books or correspondence available to the liquidator of the plaintiff company in this case which would have entitled him to make any claim against Tivoli Centre Ltd in respect of the sums with which I am now dealing though, of course, in respect of the sums recorded as advances, the plaintiff company would have been a creditor.

I can to some extent understand the contention made by the defendant in this regard which is associated with and similar to the contention which he has made in regard to the company Paulcar Ltd with which I am later dealing in this judgment. He probably did believe or certainly acted upon a belief during the time when all these companies were trading and in apparently good financial position that he was the owner of an entire group of companies. It seems to me however a fundamental principle of the law that if a person decides to obtain and use the benefit of trading through limited liability companies and if for any purposes whether the limitation of his liability, tax purposes or otherwise he transfers assets from one company to another or makes drawings from one company and invests them in his own name in another company that he cannot subsequently be heard to ignore the existence of the legal entities consisting of the different companies and to look upon the entire transaction as a personal one. I am therefore satisfied that apart from a dispute which existed on the evidence before me as to whether these sums were truly invested by the defendant in the Tivoli Centre Ltd and I am disposed to believe that they were, that that fact does not entitle the defendant to deny liability for them to the plaintiff company now in liquidation. In effect therefore I am satisfied that the entire of the sum of £73,200 claimed in the second portion of the plaintiff's particulars of claim in the statement of claim is due and owing by the defendant to the plaintiff company. This means that allowing for the credit of £4,834 given by the plaintiffs in their statement of claim that my decision is that the total amount due by the defendant to the plaintiff before consideration of his counterclaim or claim for additional credits is the sum of £154,280.

The defendant's counterclaim which is in effect a claim for additional credits is itemised as I have indicated in the letters written on his behalf on 14 April and 18 April 1980.

Of the sums claimed I am satisfied that the following amounts, the issues of which were simply issues of fact, were paid by the defendant to or for the benefit of the plaintiff's company and are credits properly allowable to him.

(1) £3,400 made up of three cheques for £300, £2,000 and £1,100 respectively dated 9 July 1976, 12 July 1976 and 23 July 1976 paid to the plaintiff company for the purpose of paying in part wages, stamps and other immediate outgoings of the company immediately prior to its liquidation.

(2) A sum of £15,000 paid to a firm known as Manchester and Midlands Ltd of Belfast for the purchase of 108 second-hand television sets.

(3) £10,000 paid to Thor Appliances Ltd for electrical goods supplied to the company.

(4) £24,000 the proceeds of the sale of Mountainview House paid to the company in the years 1972 and 1973.

I disallow all the claims made by the defendant in respect of either properties registered in the name of Paulcar Ltd which were sold and the proceeds of which he alleges were made available to the plaintiff company and also the amounts claimed by him as having been discharged on foot of guarantee for the debt of Paulcar Ltd. I also disallow the amount claimed in respect of rent due by the plaintiff company to Paulcar Ltd together with the amount of an insurance claim paid by the insurers to Paulcar Ltd and the plaintiff company in respect of 65 Dorset Street.

All these claims were put forward by the defendant upon the basis that he was the effective beneficial owner of Paulcar Ltd which he asserted was a solvent company and that therefore he must be identified with the rights and liabilities of Paulcar Ltd as if they were his own rights and liabilities and that therefore he was entitled to these as a set-off or credit against the amounts due by him to the plaintiff company in liquidation. For the reasons already set out in this judgment I am satisfied that as a matter of law even a 100 per cent beneficial shareholder in a company cannot for the purposes of the settling of an account between him and another individual or company be identified with the company. In these circumstances apart from any issues of fact with regard to these amounts I am satisfied that they are irrecoverable amounts.

With regard to a claim made by the plaintiff for £19,512 alleged to have been paid in August 1975 for the purchase of miscellaneous electrical goods second-hand I am not satisfied that this claim has been proved before me. The defendant altered the claim in the course of the evidence so as to reduce it by £5,000 and also stated that in the original notice of particulars the date had been misstated. He made this claim upon the basis that he had purchased for cash, in the last days of the trading of the company before its liquidation, considerable amount of goods for the company out of his own personal monies. He sought to support this contention by producing a number of dockets showing the receipt issued by suppliers for cash purchase of goods over that period. I am satisfied that his approach to this in evidence was irresponsible and that he merely found these dockets during the course of investigations after the liquidation of the company and then made a claim of personal payment for the entire of them. The books of the company were at that time in disarray, Mrs Lily Cannon having left the employment of the company, but I am satisfied that it is at least possible to ascertain a significant number of cash transactions at that time out of the company's own assets which probably coincide with the dockets which were produced. If the defendant were to discharge the onus of proof which was on him before me of establishing this claim, it would have been necessary for him to prove it in a much more particular and precise fashion and I do not consider that this evidence on this matter is credible and I disallow this claim. For substantially the same reason namely a question of the credibility of the evidence I also disallow a claim made by the defendant for a sum of £33,741 in respect of stock which he alleges he purchased for the company when it was initially promoted. I also disallow a claim for a sum of £13,303.76 which he asserts is due to him being a balance which he alleges was carried over from Matthew Cannon Ltd in a bank account to the plaintiff company. I do not believe that this transaction took place or that there was any agreement that this sum should be returned to the defendant.

I disallow a sum of £9,500 claimed by the defendant as having been discharged by him to Allied Irish Bank, Santry in respect of a debt owing by Martin Nugent Ltd as this was not a payment to the plaintiff company and in my view is not established to my satisfaction as a set-off.

The defendant in addition made a number of claims in respect of sums which he was obliged to pay by way of personal guarantee either in respect in one instance of a debt directly due by the plaintiff company and another instance of debts due by Paulcar Ltd which he alleged were monies advanced to Paulcar Ltd and provided by that company for the use of the plaintiff company.

None of these amounts were paid prior to the presentation of the petition for liquidation in this case. On the authority of *In re Fenton* [1931] 1 Ch 81 and *Re A Debtor, ex parte The Debtor v. Waite's Trustee* [1956] 1 WLR 480 I am satisfied that applying as I must pursuant to the provisions of the Companies Act the rules of bankruptcy to this liquidation that as a matter of law sums for which a person owing money to the company at the date of the liquidation may in the future become liable to pay are not properly allowable as set-off against the debt due to the company even though they may have been paid prior to the date upon which the account between the debtor and the company is stated and settled.

There remains therefore one further major issue that arose in the course of the case. In the winter of 1975 the plaintiff company commenced substantial purchases of electrical goods from a firm known as Loughrey Sales Ltd. These were purchased on the basis of sight drafts which were dishonoured by the company. The defendant alleges that after considerable discussion with Mr Denis Loughrey of Loughrey Sales Ltd he entered into an arrangement in April of 1976 whereby he handed over certain apartments in Spain to Mr Loughrey and to the other shareholder in Loughrey Sales Ltd in discharge of a sum of £32,000 off the amount due by the plaintiff company to Loughrey Sales Ltd.

The facts proved to my satisfaction with regard to this transaction were as follows. I am satisfied that an arrangement was entered into between Mr Loughrey and the defendant in April of 1976 whereby Mr Loughrey and his co-shareholder in Loughrey Sales Ltd would accept apartments to the value of £32,000 in discharge of £32,000 worth of goods already supplied by Loughrey Sales Ltd to the plaintiff company. I am satisfied that that contract which was a verbal one only and not reduced to writing was a contract in which the amount would be considered by Loughrey Sales Ltd as being discharged off the liability of the plaintiff company to them if, and only if, the apartments with full title were effectively transferred according to Spanish law to Mr Loughrey and his fellow shareholder.

I am satisfied on the facts that what occurred was that a contract was entered into by Erinvest Ltd, a company in which the defendant had a shareholding, to transfer these apartments to the two intended purchasers. I am also satisfied that the intended purchasers were put into possession of the apartments but I am not satisfied that at any stage since then has the title to these apartments been transferred to the two intended purchasers. Although the matter was imprecisely dealt with in the evidence adduced on behalf of the defendant I think it probable, on the evidence which was tendered before me, that the true position now is that Erinvest Ltd was the owner of these and other apartments under a lease or purchase by instalment arrangement from the original developers of a block of apartments and that since the contract entered into between Erinvest Ltd at the request of the defendant and Mr Loughrey and his fellow shareholder that the interest of Erinvest Ltd in the property had been forfeited. It was submitted by the defendant that the evidence adduced before me, should be interpreted by me, as indicating that Mr Loughrey and presumably by implication his fellow shareholder could easily have the title to the apartments made good by proceedings in Spanish courts but that they were unwilling for tax purposes to have the title completed. I am not satisfied that this is the true position nor am I satisfied that it has been established in a manner which is necessary having regard to the onus of proof on the defendant that Mr Loughrey and his fellow shareholder can now achieve a perfection of their title by any proceedings in the Spanish courts.

Whilst therefore counsel on behalf of the liquidator of the plaintiff company made submissions to me of law with regard to the question as to whether if this transaction was completed it was not a fraudulent preference of a creditor of the company and secondly, as to whether if it were now capable of being easily and immediately completed whether as a matter of law that would constitute a set-off bearing in mind that it certainly had not been completed at the date of the presentation of the petition for liquidation, it is unnecessary for me to decide either of these two issues since I am satisfied that it has not been completed at all and that therefore it cannot constitute a set-off by the defendant against the plaintiff company.

The result of these decisions which I have reached with regard to the amounts claimed by the defendant by way of additional credits or set-off is that the total amount which in my judgment is due to him over and above the credits already allowed by the plaintiffs in their statement of claim is a sum of £52,400. Setting this off against the amount which I am satisfied is due to the plaintiff company on its claim of £154,280 I give judgment for the plaintiff against the defendant in the sum of £101,880.

Alistair Rutherdale
Barrister

In the Matter of Pageboy Couriers Ltd and In the Matter of the Companies Acts 1963-1982: High Court 1983 No. 1565P (O'Hanlon J) 27 April 1983

Company Law – Winding up – Petition – Money claim – Failure by company to pay sum because it was disputed – Whether unable to pay its debts – Whether winding up petition appropriate action – Companies Act 1963 (No. 33) section 213(e)

Facts: In June 1982, proceedings were issued against Pageboy Couriers Ltd ("the company") by a Mr Stephen Rabbette ("the petitioner"), in which he claimed the sum of £5,000 allegedly due to him for director's fees, pursuant to an oral agreement with the managing director of Contactaphone Ltd, which held the controlling interest in the company. The company disputed the claim contending that there was no agreement to pay fees, and that even on the petitioner's own case, fees were only due if the company made substantial profits, a situation which had not arisen.

The petitioner allowed these proceedings to lie dormant, and instead issued a petition seeking an order for the compulsory winding up of the company, on the ground that despite demand the company had failed to pay the sum of £5,000, and was thus unable to pay its debts.

The company argued that proceedings to wind up a company were not appropriate where the petitioning creditor was well aware that the company had a substantial and reasonable defence to the money claim on which it proposed to rely to defeat the claim brought against it. The company also strongly disputed the contention that it was unable to pay its debts.

Held by O'Hanlon J in dismissing the petition:

(1) A winding up petition is not a legitimate means of seeking to enforce payment of a debt which is *bona fide* disputed. If a company in good faith and on substantial grounds disputes any liability in respect of the alleged debt, a petition should be dismissed. *Stonegate Securities Ltd v. Gregory* [1980] Ch 576 followed.

(2) Such a petitioner is not a creditor of the company, and the question whether he is or is not a creditor is not appropriate for adjudication in winding up proceedings. *Stonegate* followed.

(3) On the facts before the court the petitioner's money claim appeared to be disputed in good faith and on substantial grounds.

(4) Nor was there any convincing evidence before the court to show that the company was insolvent and unable to pay its debts.

Cases referred to in judgment

In Re Gold Hill Mines (1882) 23 Ch D 210

Mann v. Goldstein [1968] 1 WLR 1091; [1968] 2 All ER 769

Stonegate Securities Ltd v. Gregory [1980] Ch 576; [1980] 3 WLR 168; [1980] 1 All ER 241

Peter Kelly BL instructed *by Matthews & Co.* **for the petitioner**
John D. Cooke SC instructed by *Dockrell, Sheilds and Farrell* **for the company**

O'HANLON J **27 April 1983**

Stephen Rabbette, as petitioning creditor, seeks an order in these proceedings for the compulsory winding up of Pageboy Couriers Ltd. He claims that the company is indebted to him in the sum of £5,000 for director's fees which it has failed to pay after demand duly made, and that it is unable to pay its debts.

The application is hotly contested by the company, which disputes the entitlement of the petitioner to the amount claimed by him or to any amount in respect of director's fees, and further denies the allegation that it is unable to pay its debts.

Proceedings were commenced by Mr Rabbette by summary summons in the month of June 1982, claiming payment of the amount he alleged was due to him by the company, and an appearance was entered to the proceedings at the beginning of July 1982. A letter seeking particulars of the claim was sent on 20 July 1982, in which the plaintiff was asked to state when and by whom it was agreed that he should receive director's fees at the rate of £2,500 per annum. A reply was not received to that request for particulars until the present month, when, by letter dated 8 April 1983, the petitioner's solicitors stated that their client's claim arose on foot of an oral agreement "made between our client and the managing director of Contactaphone Ltd, Donough O'Connor, in or about June 1980. This was later confirmed by the said Mr O'Connor, our client, and Mr Timothy Childs in or about January 1981." (The company, Contactaphone Ltd, to which reference was made is a company holding a controlling interest in Pageboy Couriers Ltd).

The company say that no agreement to pay such fees, or any director's fees to the petitioner was made at any general meeting of the company or by any person having authority to bind the company in this respect. It further contends that on the petitioner's own statement of the terms of agreement he was only to receive such fees if and when the company was making substantial profits, and that this situation has not arisen.

The petitioner allowed the civil proceedings instituted by him in June 1982 to lie dormant after receiving the said notice for particulars of his claim and has not prosecuted them at any time since. Instead, he has brought the present petition to wind up the company in reliance upon the same claim which has at all times been disputed by the company on the grounds already mentioned.

Mr Cooke, for the company, argued that proceedings to wind up a company should not be brought where the person claiming as petitioning creditor is well aware that the company has a substantial and reasonable defence to the claim which it wishes to plead, and on which it proposes to rely to defeat the entire claim brought against it. He relied, *inter alia*, on the decision of the English

Court of Appeal in *Stonegate Securities Ltd v. Gregory* [1980] 1 All ER 241 where Buckley LJ said (at p. 243 of the report):

> ". . . if the company in good faith and on substantial grounds disputes any liability in respect of the alleged debt, the petition will be dismissed or, if the matter is brought before a court before the petition is issued, its presentation will in normal circumstances be restrained. That is because a winding-up petition is not a legitimate means of seeking to enforce payment of a debt which is *bona fide* disputed. Ungoed–Thomas J put the matter thus in *Mann v. Goldstein* [1968] 2 All ER 769 at 775:
>
> > 'For my part, I would prefer to rest the jurisdiction directly on the comparatively simple propositions that a creditor's petition can only be presented by a creditor, that the winding up jurisdiction is not for the purpose of deciding a disputed debt (that is, disputed on substantial and not insubstantial grounds) since, until a creditor is established as a creditor he is not entitled to present the petition and has no *locus standi* in the companies' court and that, therefore, to invoke the winding-up jurisdiction when the debt is disputed (that is, on substantial grounds) or after it has become clear that it is so disputed is an abuse of the process of the court'."

Having adopted that passage in its entirety, Buckley LJ concluded:

> "In my opinion a petition founded upon a debt which is disputed in good faith and on substantial grounds is demurrable for the reason that the petitioner is not a creditor of the company within the meaning of section 224(1) at all, and the question whether he is or is not a creditor of the company is not appropriate for adjudication in winding up proceedings."

I accept the principles there enunciated as being applicable also when considering the propriety of proceedings by way of petition for the winding up of a company under the provisions of our own Companies Acts and when these principles are applied to the facts of the present case I am of opinion that Mr Cooke's submission against the petition is well-founded. The petitioner's claim for director's fees has at all times been disputed by the company since he first started proceedings for recovery of same almost a year ago, and without in any was attempting to prejudge the outcome of those proceedings it can be fairly stated that the claim appears to have been disputed in good faith and on substantial grounds.

Neither was I convinced by the evidence placed before the court at the hearing of the petition that the company has been shown to be insolvent and unable to pay its debts. It is not without significance that the Revenue Commissioners, whose claim against the company far exceeds that of any other claimant, have decided to adopt a neutral stance in relation to the petition. If the evidence clearly indicated a condition of insolvency one would have expected them to lend their wholehearted support to the petition.

In these circumstances I propose to dismiss the present petition for the winding up of the company.

Alistair Rutherdale
Barrister

Re Welding Plant Ltd (In Liquidation) (No. 1) Hugh Cooney v. John Dargan, Patrick Dargan and Allied Irish Banks Ltd: High Court 1983 No 423 Sp (McWilliam J) 27 June 1984

Fraudulent preference – Directors – Personal guarantees – Company in financial difficulties – Transaction – Money lent by bank personally to directors – Used to discharge part of company's indebtedness to the bank – Intention of directors to purchase premises from company – Agreement never executed – Whether transaction amounted to fraudulent preference either to the bank or to the directors – Intention of parties – Companies Act 1963 (No. 33), section 286

Facts: The first and second named defendants were directors of the company, Welding Plant Ltd, which carried on business at premises at Green Lane, Carlow. In September 1981, the company was indebted to Allied Irish Banks Ltd in the sum of £23,000. As security for this money, the bank held an instrument of guarantee limited to the sum of £30,000 executed by the first and second named defendants and undertakings by two letters from the solicitors for the company to lodge the documents of title to the premises at Green Lane, when the registration of the title to the premises was completed. These undertakings were not registered as a charge or charges in the Companies Office and no documents of title were lodged with the bank. At the time the company was in financial difficulties, which was known to the directors. In November 1981 the bank entered into an arrangement with the first and second defendants whereby £10,500 was advanced to each of them personally to enable them to purchase the premises at Green Lane from the company. The total sum of £21,000 was then lodged by the bank to the credit of the company's account in discharge of part of its indebtedness to the bank. The company subsequently went into liquidation and on 31 March 1981 a liquidator was appointed. The liquidator issued proceedings claiming that the payment of £21,000 was a fraudulent preference either to the first and second named defendants or to the bank contrary to section 286 of the Companies Act 1963 and that such monies should be repaid to the liquidator. It was accepted on behalf of the liquidator that the onus was on him to show that the payment to the bank was made in order to prefer either the first and second named defendants or the bank but it was submitted that this had been established by the evidence. On behalf of all defendants it was contended that the liquidator must establish a dominant intention to prefer and that this onus had not been discharged.

Held by McWilliam J:

(1) Whatever agreement was reached, the only steps which were taken were that the bank lent the monies to the first and second defendants which was appropriated to the discharge of the greater part of the debt due by the company to the bank. Although a draft agreement for the sale of the premises by the company to them was drawn up, it was never executed. As a result, the premises at Green Lane were still owned by the company.

(2) Had the property been conveyed to the first and second defendants and a mortgage of it given by them to the bank there would have been grounds for setting it aside.

(3) The transaction did not appear to have accomplished any preference to the Bank or the first and second defendants over the creditors, fraudulent or otherwise, whatever the intentions of the defendants may have been.

Cases referred to in judgment

Corran Construction Co. Ltd v. Bank of Ireland Finance Ltd [1976-77] ILRM 175
Re FLE Holdings Ltd [1967] 3 All ER 553
Re F.P. & C.H. Matthews Ltd [1982] 1 All ER 338
Peat v. Gresham Trust Ltd [1934] AC 252
Re T.W. Cutts (a bankrupt) [1956] 2 All ER 537

Counsel's and solicitors' names not available

McWILLIAM J **27 June 1984**

Welding Plant Ltd (hereinafter called the company) was incorporated on 8 April 1976, and carried on business at premises at Green Lane, Carlow, until September 1981, when it ceased to trade. John and Patrick Dargan and Seamus Dooley were the directors but Seamus Dooley seems to have taken no part in the running of the company and is not concerned with these proceedings. In September 1981, the company was indebted to Allied Irish Banks Ltd (hereinafter called the bank) in the sum of £23,000.

As security for the money due by the company, the bank held an instrument of guarantee limited to the sum of £30,000 executed by John and Patrick Dargan on 22 September 1980, and undertakings by two letters from a solicitor for the company dated 14 July 1977, and 21 November 1977 to lodge the documents of title to the premises at Green Lane when the registration of the title to the premises should have been completed. These undertakings were not registered as a charge or charges in the Companies Office and no documents of title have been lodged with the bank. The first letter related to a leasehold interest in the property and the second related to the fee simple.

In September 1980, the company had an overdraft of £30,000 and it may be assumed that this was the reason why the guarantee by the Dargans was given for that sum. At the same time the permitted overdraft of the company was reduced to £10,000 and the balance of £20,000 was altered to a term loan for five years. It appears that the company's auditor was pressing the directors for accounts from August 1979, until August 1981, but that these accounts were not presented although, in or about August 1981, the directors asked for a statement of affairs to be prepared by the auditor. The auditor commenced to prepare such a statement and soon realised that the situation of the company was very serious, but he was unable to prepare more than a preliminary draft owing to the failure of the directors to provide the necessary information. The last audited accounts had been presented in August 1979, and these showed that the company was then financially sound but that problems were arising, such as a high number of debtors and considerable liabilities, including arrears of Value Added Tax.

The bank was, at this time, writing regularly for audited accounts and for the documents of title to the Green Lane premises. Although the manager of the Carlow branch of the bank stated that he had no reason to believe, at the end of November 1981, that the company was going down, the sequence of events suggests that he must have been getting worried at this stage, particularly having regard to the absence of any title deeds. Whatever about the appreciation of the situation by the bank, there can be no doubt but that the cessation of trading, the requests for information from the auditor and the draft statement of affairs could have left the Dargans under no illusion as to the insolvency of the company. Subsequently the company went into liquidation and on 31 March 1982, Hugh Cooney (hereinafter called the liquidator) was appointed liquidator.

The transaction which is challenged in these proceedings was entered into on or about 30 November 1981 at a meeting between the Dargans and the Carlow manager of the bank. This consisted of an arrangement whereby the bank advanced sums of £10,500 to each of the Dargans personally to enable the Dargans to purchase the Green Lane premises from the company. The total sum of £21,000 was then lodged by the bank to the credit of the company's account in discharge of part of the indebtedness of the company to the bank. I am satisfied that the Dargans assumed that this transaction enabled them to take the Green Lane property free from the undertaking to lodge the title deeds which the manager considered created a lien over the premises in favour of the Bank.

The issues which have been set down for this hearing are:

(a) Whether the payment of £21,000 was a fraudulent preference in favour of either the Dargans or the bank, and
(b) If so, whether they are liable to pay the sum of £21,000 to the liquidator.

Section 286 of the Companies Act 1963, provides, at subsection (1) that:

"any conveyance, mortgage, delivery of goods, payment, execution or other act relating to property made or done by or against a company within six months before the commencement of its winding up which, had it been made or done by or against an individual within six months before the presentation of a bankruptcy petition on which he is adjudicated a bankrupt, would be deemed in his bankruptcy a fraudulent preference, shall in the event of the company being wound up be deemed a fraudulent preference of its creditors and be invalid accordingly."

Section 53 of the Bankruptcy (Ireland) Amendment Act 1872, as substituted by section 399 and the 11th Schedule of the Companies Act 1963, provides as follows:

> "Every conveyance or transfer of property or charge thereon made, every payment made, every obligation incurred and every judicial proceeding taken or suffered by any person unable to pay his debts as they become due from his own moneys in favour of any creditor or of any person in trust for any creditor, with a view to giving such creditor, or any surety or guarantor for the debt due to such creditor, a preference over the other creditors, shall, if the person making, taking, paying or suffering the same is adjudged a bankrupt on a bankruptcy petition or a petition for arrangement, presented within six months after the date of making, taking, paying or suffering the same be deemed fraudulent and void against the assignees or trustees of such bankrupt; but this section shall not affect the rights of any person making title in good faith and for valuable consideration through or under a creditor of the bankrupt."

On behalf of the liquidator it is accepted that the onus is on him to show that the payment to the bank was made in order to prefer either the Dargans or the bank but it is submitted that this has been established by the evidence and that the proper order for the court to make is to direct the bank to repay the sum of £21,000 to the liquidator with interest from the date of the liquidation. I was referred to *Buckley on Companies*, ed. 14, p. 746; *Re T.W. Cutts (a bankrupt)* [1956] 2 All ER 537; *Re F.P. & C.H. Matthews Ltd* [1982] All ER 338.

On behalf of both the bank and the Dargans it was argued that the liquidator must establish a dominant intention to prefer and that this had not been done. I was referred to *Peat v. Gresham Trust Ltd* [1934] AC 252; *Re FLE Holdings Ltd* [1967] 3 All ER 553; and to my own unreported decision in *Corran Construction Co. Ltd v. Bank of Ireland Finance Ltd* [1976-77] ILRM 175.

No arguments were presented as to the effect of this unusual transaction but, to arrive at any conclusion on the issues before me, it seems to me to be necessary to consider what was accomplished by it. What the statutes provide is that every payment made by any person unable to pay his debts as they become due from his own monies with a view to giving any creditor or any surety or guarantor for the debt due to such creditor a preference over the other creditors, etc., shall be invalid.

I am satisfied that the bank was aware that the company was getting into difficulties. Patrick Dargan, who did not give evidence before me, stated at paragraph 7 of his affidavit that the bank offered to lend £21,000 on condition that he and his brother purchased the property from the company and executed a mortgage over it for this sum in favour of the bank and that the £21,000 would be credited against the company's indebtedness to the bank. While John Dargan agreed with this statement in an affidavit sworn by him, in evidence before me he stated variously that he understood that the bank owned the premises, the bank held the deeds and could sell and that the premises were being bought from the bank. Paragraph 7 of Patrick Dargan's affidavit corresponds in the main with the evidence of the Carlow manager of the bank, although the manager stated that the meeting was held at the instigation of the Dargans.

Whatever was said at the meeting, I have come to the conclusion that an agreement was reached whereby the Dargans would take loans in their own names from the bank and with the money lent pay off the major part of the debt owed by the company to the bank, the Dargans would buy the premises at Green Lane from the company for the amount of the loan given to them by the bank and would then mortgage these premises to the bank as security for their loans. I am satisfied that the Dargans believed that the letters of undertaking on behalf of the company would then be released by the bank so that they would hold the property free from any liabilities by the company to the bank although subject to the mortgage by them to secure the loans made to them by the bank.

Whatever agreement was reached, the only steps taken on foot of it were that the bank lent the Dargans £21,000 which was appropriated to the discharge of the greater part of the debt due by the company to the bank and the Dargans got their solicitor to draft an agreement for the sale of the premises by the company to them. This draft agreement is dated 2 December 1981, with the closing date given as the same day and the purchase price expressed to be £21,000. John Dargan stated in evidence that this agreement was not executed and the photocopy exhibited in the affidavit of the liquidator is of an unexecuted agreement. I conclude that it was not executed either by the company or by the Dargans and that the Dargans have no agreement in writing to purchase the property from the company. The bank retained the letters of undertaking given by the solicitor for the company in 1977 and, by letter of 6 May 1982, to the liquidator, stated that the bank would hold the letters of undertaking until similar undertaking was given by the solicitor for the Dargans although the solicitor for the company had, by letter dated 16 April 1982, informed the solicitors for the liquidator that "On 2 December 1981, the company disposed of its interest in the property to John and Patrick Dargan for £21,000 and my undertaking was discharged".

The results seems to be that the company still owns the premises at Green Lane although the Dargans have been using them for their own businesses and may be liable for an occupation rent. The Dargans as guarantors have paid the company's debt to the bank to the extent of £21,000, having been advanced money by the bank for that purpose. It has not been suggested that the Dargans, as guarantors, were not liable to pay the amount due to the bank by the company. Nor has it been suggested that the liquidator and the creditors of the company, other than the bank, could have any claim against the Dargans as guarantors of the debt due to the bank. The question of any possible right of the liquidator to require the bank to rely on the guarantee given by the Dargans before claiming in the liquidation does not arise on this proceeding.

In my opinion, this transaction was entered into by the Dargans at a time the company was insolvent and, as John Dargan stated in evidence, they had been thinking of putting the company into liquidation, and it was entered into by them with a view to obtaining the property at Green Lane to the prejudice of the creditors of the company. Had a conveyance of the property to them been executed and a mortgage of it given by them to the bank there would have been grounds for seeking to have the transactions set aside. That is not the position. The company still owns the property and has paid nothing to the bank or anybody else. The bank still claims some sort of a lien over the property for any money due to the bank. The bank has reduced the amount of the debt due to it by the company by means of a loan to the Dargans who now owe £21,000 to the bank and it is a matter between the Dargans and the bank as to the validity of the loan to them for the discharge of the company's debt.

Under these circumstances, the transaction does not appear to have accomplished any preference of the bank or the Dargans over the creditors, either fraudulent or otherwise, whatever the intention of the Dargans may have been.

As it is unsatisfactory to decide an issue on grounds which have not been argued the matter will be re-entered for argument on the matters which I have raised.

Patricia McLaughlin
Barrister

[*Reporter's Note:* Section 286 of the Companies Act, 1963 (No. 33) has been substantially modified by section 135 of the Companies Act 1990 (No. 33)]

In the Matter of Kelly's Carpetdrome Ltd (In Liquidation) and in the Matter of the Companies Act 1963; Kelly's Carpetdrome Ltd (In Liquidation) and Monck Properties Ltd v. Fergal Gaynor and Patrick Tuffy: High Court 1981 No. 7508p (O'Hanlon J) 13 July 1984.

Company – Liquidation – Fraudulent trading – Accountants – Irregular books – Transfer of assets to new company at discount – Whether accountants party to carrying on of business with intent to defraud – Standard of proof – Companies Act 1963 (No. 33), section 297.

Facts: The liquidator of the Kelly's Carpetdrome Ltd ("Carpetdrome") sought an order pursuant to section 297 of the Companies Act 1963, imposing personal liability on the respondents, members of a firm of accountants, in respect of the debts or other liabilities of the company, on the ground that they were knowingly parties to the carying on of the business of Carpetdrome with intent to defraud the creditors of the company or creditors of some other person or for some fraudulent purpose. In previous proceedings the High Court (Costello J.) had determined that the company's business was carried on with intent to defraud creditors and imposed personal liability on two directors.

Carpetdrome, incorporated in October 1976, had taken over the carpet retailing business formerly carried on by Kelly's Carpet Supermarket Ltd ("Supermarket"), a company to which Mr Gaynor had acted as liquidator. It was alleged that this winding up was a device to enable the business to continue, while defrauding the Revenue Commissioners of outstanding VAT claims, but the evidence was inconclusive on this point.

It was alleged that a huge proportion of the cash transactions of Carpetdrome never found their way into the ordinary books, but were recorded secretly in different books. It was further alleged that the respondents later devised, advised upon and assisted in implementing a scheme whereby Carpetdrome was placed in liquidation, its trade creditors paid off, but where a substantial indebtedness to the Revenue Commissioners would be left deliberately undischarged.

The plan devised transferred the business of the company to Kelly's Carpet Drive-In Ltd ("Drive-In"), with the price of stock tranferred between the two companies being at less than cost. However there was no evidence that the respondents were implicated in this.

A decision was made to wind up Carpetdrome following a VAT demand for £230,000. The creditors meeting was poorly advertised and only two creditors turned up, who left when they were told their claims would be met. A liquidator, Mr Harding, was appointed who was proposed by the respondents. The statement of affairs as presented did not reflect the true picture of the company.

Held by O'Hanlon J in refusing to make the order sought:

(1) The involvement of the first repondent in the winding up of Supermarket did not establish complicity on his part or that of his firm in a scheme of fraud.

(2) Neither respondent had been shown to be fixed with knowledge of the fraud which was taking place in the week-to-week running of the business of Carpetdrome, and the company accountant had not revealed the true picture to them. Indeed the accounts as prepared by the respondents made no attempt to cover up any irregularities in the company's affairs.

(3) The first respondents response to the transfers between Carpetdrome and Drive-In was neutral in tone, and stopped far short of advising the client to carry through any scheme of arrangement in a fraudulent or improper manner. The scheme was initiated from within the company itself and without consulting the

respondents, and had largely been put in effect by the time the respondents were made aware of it.

(4) The respondents must accept responsibility for the preparation of the statement of affairs and its presentation to the meeting in compliance with the statutory obligation imposed on the directors by the Companies Act 1963.

(5) The onus of proof on the liquidator to establish liability under section 297 was a heavy one.

Per curiam: There was some authority for the proposition that as the liability imposed by section 297 involved an allegation of crime in civil proceedings the criminal standard of proof should apply. However there was also authority that where a case involved alternative claims founded on contract or fraudulent misrepresentation, then the same standard should apply to all *i.e.* the civil standard. *Hornal v. Neuberger Products Ltd* [1956] 1 QB 247 considered.

(6) In any case it was not necessary to decide the question of standard of proof, as applying the civil standard, the respondents must still be exonerated from the charges brought against them.

Cases referred to in judgment

Bater v. Bater [1950] 2 All ER 458; [1950] WN 367
Chalmers v. Shackell (1834) 6 C & P 475
Hornal v. Neuberger Products Ltd [1956] 1 QB 247; [1956] 3 WLR 1034; [1956] 3 All ER 970
Statham v. Statham [1929] P 131
Thurtell v. Beaumont (1823) 1 Bing 339
Willmett v. Harmer (1839) 8 C & P 695

R.N. Cooke SC, John D. Cooke SC with Peter Kelly BL instructed by *William Fry* **for the applicants**
Colm Condon SC, Brian McCracken SC and James Salafia BL instructed by *Gerald Byrne, Hardman & Stokes* **for the respondents**

O'HANLON J **13 July 1984**

In these proceedings the liquidator of Kelly's Carpetdrome Ltd invokes the provisions of section 297 of the Companies Act 1963, for the purpose of asking the court to make an order which would have the effect of imposing personal liability on the members of a firm of accountants — Messrs Gaynor, Tuffy & Co. — in respect of the debts or other liabilities of the company. This claim in turn is based on the contention that the two partners in the firm — Fergal Gaynor and Patrick Tuffy — were knowingly parties to the carrying on of the business of Kelly's Carpetdrome Ltd with intent to defraud creditors of the company or creditors of some other person or for some fraudulent purpose.

There are, accordingly, two essential features involved in the claim. In the first place it must be established to the satisfaction of the court that the business of the company was, in fact, carried on in such a manner and with such intent as to achieve one or more of the fraudulent purposes referred to in section 297, and secondly it must also be established to the satisfaction of the court that the respondents were knowingly parties to the carrying on of the business in the manner aforesaid.

The liquidator has succeeded in bringing home the charge of fraud against the company in these proceedings, just as he had already done in earlier proceedings before Costello J, in the course of which an order has already been made under the provisions of section 297 of the Act imposing personal liability on two other persons — Matthew Kelly and Eamon Kelly. The most salient features of fraudulent practices as established against the company in these proceedings will appear in the course of the present judgment.

A company named Kelly's Carpet Supermarket Ltd was incorporated on 6 December 1973, and continued to trade until the year 1976. On 28 October 1976, Kelly's Carpetdrome Ltd was incorporated and effectively took over the carpet retailing business formerly carried on by Kelly's Carpet Supermarket Ltd. On 27 May 1977, a resolution was passed at a general meeting of the members of Kelly's Carpet Supermarket Ltd that the company, by reason of its liabilities could not continue in business and that it should be wound up voluntarily, and that Mr Fergal Gaynor of Gaynor, Tuffy & Co. be appointed as liquidator of the company.

The evidence given in the course of the present proceedings suggested that the claim of all creditors of Kelly's Carpet Supermarket Ltd had been met in full, with the exception of large outstanding claimed for VAT presented by the Revenue Commissioners, and it was contended that the winding-up of the company and the formation of another on that occasion was merely a device to enable the old business to continue under a new name while at the same time defrauding the Revenue Commissioners of the amounts claimed for VAT against the original company. It was further suggested that this was a course of conduct which, with the passage of time, was repeated when Kelly's Carpetdrome Ltd was put into liquidation and the phoenix rose from the ashes again, on this occasion in the shape or guise of Kelly's Carpet Drive-In Ltd. However, the evidence to support the allegation that the winding-up of Kelly's Carpet Supermarket Ltd was part of a fraudulent scheme to which the first-named respondent lent himself in his capacity as liquidator of that company, is inconclusive. The Revenue Commissioners are the only creditor of the company who are still unsatisfied. The winding-up of the company has lain dormant for several years, and the VAT claimed by the Revenue Commissioners, which was disputed in its entirety by the liquidator, has never been finally determined, although the Revenue Commissioners had at all times the means in their powers to press their claim to a conclusion had they elected to do so.

For these reasons, although there is, indeed, a marked similarity between the procedure adopted for securing the transfer of the business and assets of Kelly's Carpets (Supermarket) Ltd to Kelly's Carpetdrome Ltd in the 1976/77 period, and that adopted later when Kelly's Carpetdrome Ltd was put into liquidation and its mantle was assumed by Kelly's Carpets Drive-In Ltd, I think the evidence regarding the earlier transaction remains neutral in character and cannot be relied on to implicate the respondents in any charges of fraud brought against the various companies. For what it is worth, the evidence does show that the services of Messrs Gaynor, Tuffy & Co, as accountants, were being availed of by Mr Matthew Kelly and his associates as far back as the mid-seventies.

Kelly's Carpetdrome Ltd continued to trade in premises in Phibsboro on the northside of Dublin, for about five years from the date of its incorporation and built up a huge turnover as carpet retailers and in allied lines of business. Messrs Gaynor, Tuffy & Co. acted for the company in registering it with the revenue authorities for VAT and PAYE, and were asked by Matthew Kelly to advise on the accounting procedures of the company. Their intervention in this field, however, met with a hostile reception from the accountants' employed by the company and as they were unable to take over the full responsibility of acting as accountants for the company they withdrew from the scene and were thereafter consulted only in relation to specific problems which arose from time to time. I am satisfied that they did not hold themselves out as auditors of the company, or carry out an audit of its accounts at any time, and from what the court was told of the book-keeping practices observed by the company the completion of an audit at any time would have presented any firm of accountants with enormous difficulties.

The evidence of Mr Brendan McGoldrick, who acted as accountant for the company during the last year or two of its existence, conveyed that a huge proportion of the cash transactions conducted by Kelly's Carpetdrome Ltd with its customers never found their way into the ordinary books of account of the company, but were recorded secretly in a different set of books. By this means the accounting system of the company was so conducted as to conceal from the Revenue Commissioners and anyone else charged with investigating the affairs of the company, sales transactions of up to £30,000 per week or £1.5m. per annum. If correct, and no one came forward to challenge or refute this part of his evidence — then it discloses the existence of fraudulent practice on a monumental scale. One consequence of such a finding is that it makes it impossible to take at their face value any of the many accounting documents which have been produced concerning the Kelly group of companies — statements of affairs, balance sheets, and so forth, compiled at different times and for different purposes. If those who controlled the destinies of the company had embarked on a scheme of fraud of the magnitude described in Mr McGoldrick's evidence, then no document emanating from the same source and purporting to throw some light on the financial status of the company at any particular time can be regarded as reliable or trustworthy.

With regard to this first, major allegation of fraud in the conduct of the business of the company, the evidence did not implicate the respondents in the present proceedings in any way. They were not the company's accountants, save to the extent that they were employed in a consultative capacity from time to time. Their involvement with the affairs of the company eventually led them to prepare a four-year set of draft accounts for the company, extending back to the time when it first set up in business and forward to 31 October 1980. The primary object of this exercise was stated to be the resolution of the tax problems of Mr Matthew Kelly, but it seems clear to me that this very onerous task was also undertaken for the benefit of the company itself and substantial payments were made in favour of the respondents out of the company's accounts from time to time in respect of work and services rendered.

Be that as it may, the evidence of Mr McGoldrick and of the staff members employed by the respondents to prepare the four-year set of accounts indicated quite clearly that the existence of a double-accounting system was never disclosed to the respondents or to their representatives and that they were allowed to proceed with the preparation of the draft accounts in blissful ignorance of the fact that much of the base material needed for the project was being deliberately withheld from them.

It may also be said, in the respondent's defence, that when eventually the four-year set of draft accounts were prepared and made available to the Revenue Commissioners in the year 1981, these accounts, when read in conjunction with the working papers which were also made available to the Revenue Commissioners, could not fail to disclose to anyone with an elementary knowledge of accounting procedures that the affairs of the company were being conducted in a highly irregular manner. Very large sums were included in suspense accounts on the basis that they could not be accounted for in any way, and a clear inference could be drawn that creditors had been paid on a large scale out of the proceeds of sales which had been left unrecorded in the accounts of the company. The draft accounts also gave rise to the inference that there were large sums owing by the company for VAT which had not been previously disclosed to the Revenue and which gave rise to a claim which later precipitated the winding-up of the company. From these points of view it might be said that insofar as the respondents were representing the interests of the company as well as those of Mr Matthew Kelly, they did their clients a disservice by the preparation of the draft accounts, since the inevitable consequence was to set in train a much more vigorous investigation by the Revenue of the affairs of the company.

Similarly when Mr Thomas Tiúit of the investigation branch of the Revenue Commissioners came to give evidence concerning his personal contacts with Mr Fergal Gaynor, it showed that Mr Gaynor had been more than candid in disclosing the total unreliability of the books of accounts and accounting systems of the company and of Matthew Kelly himself. At different times Mr Gaynor said to him, (1) that in his opinion, Matthew Kelly had made substantial cash withdrawals from the business, and that he would seek to make full disclosure; (2) that the company showed losses for six years, but that there were no proper accounts, and that he would not certify them; (3) that, in relation to Matthew Kelly's personal tax liabilities, he was at the mercy of Matthew Kelly as to what went into statements of income, because of lack of records; (4) that he could not give an opinion on the accounts of the company as the back-up information was not there; (5) that the accounting systems left a lot to be desired and that he could not be sure that all transactions were recorded in the books of account.

Accordingly, having commenced by finding that the involvement of Mr Fergal Gaynor in the winding-up of Kelly's Carpet Supermarket Ltd does not establish complicity on his own part or that of his firm in a scheme of fraud, I can follow that up by making the further finding that neither he nor his partner has been shown to have been fixed with knowledge of the fraud which was taking place in the week-to-week running of the business of Kelly's Carpetdrome Ltd, and which involved the deliberate exclusion from the ordinary books of accounts of the company of all information concerning cash sales totalling over £1 million in the course of a single year.

The closest the evidence came to implicating the respondents in these fraudulent practices of the company came when Mr McGoldrick testified that when Gaynor, Tuffy & Co. were brought in to prepare the four-year set of draft accounts, he informed Mr Gaynor that "there was a bit of a fiddle going on". His account of this conversation, which he said took place at the company's premises in the first week of June 1980, was as follows:

> "I showed Mr Gaynor a statement document showing liabilities of £650,000 and told him I had grave doubts about the solvency of the company. He pushed the document aside. . . . Later, on the sales floor, I told him that if he was doing the accounts of Carpetdrome, he would have to take into account the accounts of Roundwood Carpets Ltd because of the relationship between Matthew Kelly and Roundwood. There was 0.75m. due by Carpetdrome not shown in the books — £750,000 invoiced to Carpetdrome, but only £500,000 shown in the Carpetdrome books.
>
> Mr Gaynor said he did not want to know anything about Roundwood. I said: 'There is a bit of a fiddle going on'. He said: 'Never discuss the affairs of Carpetdrome with anybody'. I told Fergal Gaynor there was a firm in England called Roundwood, connected with Matthew Kelly and Carpetdrome and if doing accounts for Carpetdrome he could not do so without access to the accounts of Roundwood. There was money in the accounts of Roundwood which belonged to Matthew Kelly and the directors had given an undertaking to bring it into the Carpetdrome accounts. I told Fergal Gaynor he should go to Leeds and have a discussion with Dobby. He said he did not want to know about Roundwood and would not be concerning himself with Roundwood in his work. The discussion ended there."

The respondent, Fergal Gaynor, when he came to give evidence, denied that any such conversation had ever taken place between himself and Brendan McGoldrick and there is a sharp conflict of evidence between the two parties in this respect. Were I to accept in full what was said in evidence by Brendan McGoldrick, and reject what was said in refutation by Fergal Gaynor, it would lead to a finding that Fergal Gaynor was put on notice that there were serious irregularities in the accounts of the company and that he chose to ignore this information when the draft four-year accounts were being prepared in order to meet the claims of the Revenue Commissioners. It is, therefore, necessary to assess the weight which should be attached to the evidence of Brendan McGoldrick on this and on certain other issues and to consider his reliability as a witness.

Mr McGoldrick was employed by the company from mid-August 1979 as an accountant at a rather low salary having regard to the size of the business and the complexity of the accounts he was to be called upon to regulate. No final accounts had been made up for previous years and there were no books of record available which could form the basis for such accounts. No balance sheet had been made up; no profit and loss accounts and no trading accounts. He had to commence by trying to write up the accounts from the time the company started up on business on 1 November 1976.

I believe that he made a conscientious effort to restore some order out of the chaos in which he found the company's accounts and would probably have succeeded had he been given more co-operation by the directors and had time not run out on him before his task was completed. He said, and I am prepared to accept, that he was not made aware of the fraudulent system of double accounting already referred to, for some time after he took over as company accountant, and when it did come to his knowledge he was faced with a choice of giving up his employment or going along with the fraud which was being perpetrated.

He chose the latter course and by this means he was drawn into a network of fraud and must be regarded as having actively participated in it from that time forward. When he gives evidence tending to implicate others in the fraud with him, such evidence had to be treated with the reservations which must always exist when one person claims that others were fellow-conspirators or fellow-accomplices with him in some criminal enterprise. Secondly, while Mr McGoldrick impressed me as a person who was doing his best to assist the court and to give a full account at this late stage of the dubious practices of the company, his recollection of dates and events was shown to be faulty in some respects, and this must tend to undermine one's confidence in the accuracy of his account in other parts of his evidence.

I am not prepared to hold that the alleged conversation between himself and Fergal Gaynor never took place, but I am left in considerable doubt as to the nature and extent of the disclosures made by Mr McGoldrick. If his purpose was to put Mr Gaynor on notice that no reliance whatever could be placed on the books and records of the company in seeking to prepare draft accounts for the Revenue Commissioners, all that was necessary for him to do was to let Mr Gaynor in on the secret of the dual accounting system and the fact that sales of up to £30,000 per week were being effected without being put through the normal books of account of the company. He concedes, however, that he never mentioned this all-important fact to Mr Gaynor but claims that instead of doing so he embarked on an account of a complicated inter-company transaction involving the manipulation by Matthew Kelly of the affairs and finances of a company in England. I think that what probably happened is that Mr McGoldrick hinted at irregularities in the accounting system of the company without being bold enough to reveal the true picture which was well known to him at the time, and that Mr Gaynor, in common with anyone with any inside knowledge of the workings of the company, was already well aware of the fact that the accounting systems of the company were highly irregular and were not calculated to withstand close inspection.

Fergal Gaynor's *bona fides* in relation to this episode can best be tested by reference to what happened afterwards. Members of the staff spent several months endeavouring to compile the four-year set of draft accounts and even with the wisdom of hindsight it has at no stage been suggested that these accounts, or the working papers which formed the basis for them, were designed to cover up any irregularities in the company's affairs or were calculated to do so. Instead, as already indicated in an earlier part of the present judgment, they were calculated to put the trained observer on notice that there were serious irregularities in the conduct of its affairs of the company. The compilation of the draft accounts and the working papers in this form does not seem to be consistent with the suggestion that at the same time the principal of the firm of accountants was bent on ignoring or suppressing other important information about irregularities in the company's accounts.

For these reasons I have come to the conclusion that the evidence has failed to establish any involvement of the respondents or either of them in the fraudulent practices of the company up to the time when the decision was made to wind up the business of Carpetdrome and to start again under the auspices of yet another company — this time, Kelly's Carpet Drive-In Ltd.

The real gravamen of this part of the liquidator's claim against the present respondents is based upon the contention that the respondents "devised, advised upon and assisted in implementing a scheme whereby the first named claimant" (Kelly's Carpetdrome Ltd) "was to be placed in liquidation and its trade creditors paid off but where the substantial indebtedness of the Revenue Commissioners would be left deliberately undischarged". It is also claimed that a similar scheme had previously been implemented in respect of Kelly's Carpet Superdrome Ltd, but I have already indicated that I regard the evidence given in relation to the winding-up of that company as neutral in character.

The developments which led to the winding-up of Kelly's Carpetdrome Ltd appear to be as follows. The four-year set of draft accounts to 31 October 1980, prepared by the respondents with the primary purpose of negotiating a settlement of Matthew Kelly's tax liabilities with the Revenue Commissioners, put the Revenue on notice that the company appeared to have an outstanding VAT liability of £327,612, and the Revenue proceeded to press by payment of the outstanding sum, which had been reduced by payments on account to about

£230,000 in the early months of 1981.

The Revenue claim came as a shock to the directors of the company and to their accountant, Brendan McGoldrick, who appear to have had little if any knowledge of the contents of the draft accounts up to that time, and it produced some kind of crisis in the affairs of the company. Even before this claim came in, however, Brendan McGoldrick claims to have prepared a balance sheet of Carpetdrome as of 28 February 1981, showing the company to be insolvent. When this was presented to one of the directors, Paul Jackson, he (according to Mr McGoldrick) consulted with Eamonn Kelly and Matthew Kelly, and told Mr McGoldrick to go ahead with a plan which had already been devised to transfer the business of the company to Kelly's Carpet Drive-In Ltd.

At this time, Fergal Gaynor was away in the United States for about one month and the first steps to secure the transfer of the business were taken in his absence, and without his knowledge or advice. The bank account of Carpetdrome was closed on 3 March 1981, by means of a transfer of funds from Drive-In Ltd. The new company, which had been incorporated on 17 February 1977, but had been allowed to lie dormant in the meantime, started up in business immediately, making use of the stocks of Carpetdrome and continuing to trade under the same style or title as the former company.

Mr McGoldrick said that his intention was that the new company should take over the assets and liabilities of the old company, so that no one should be the loser as a result of the changeover. Carpetdrome had had a number of judgments registered against it and although these had been satisfied, its creditworthiness had been damaged, particularly on the English market and the English Export Guarantee Board was no longer willing to underwrite the company's indebtedness to its English suppliers. This made its trading position very difficult and Mr McGoldrick felt that if a new company were to take over the business, without being encumbered with large directors' loans and with a better looking balance sheet, the situation could be retrieved. This is the scheme which he claims to have set in motion in the absence of Mr Gaynor and which he says was designed to leave all creditors of the old company in at least as good a position as they were previously.

When Mr Gaynor returned from the United States a meeting took place in his office in the month of 1981, with Mr McGoldrick and Matthew Kelly, Eamonn Kelly and Paul Jackson. Both Mr Gaynor and Mr Tuffy were present. There is a conflict as to the date of the meeting, which I do not regard as important. Mr McGoldrick said there were two meeting with the accountants in March; Mr Gaynor said only one meeting took place, and that on 24 March. It is common case that Messrs Gaynor and Tuffy were informed that the Carpetdrome bank account had been closed on 3 March 1981, and that Drive-In had taken over the business as and from 1 March 1981. Mr McGoldrick says that he informed the accountants that Drive-In had taken over Carpetdrome because of the insolvency of Carpetdrome, that he produced a balance sheet he had prepared for Drive-In as of 1 March 1981. Mr Gaynor says that Mr McGoldrick told them that Carpetdrome was solvent. "I thought everything was alright. Mr McGoldrick said the business was solvent and four of them were putting money in".

As to the advice given by the accountants at that stage, there is not a great deal of conflict between the parties. Mr McGoldrick's account is as follows:

> "Mr Gaynor said I should not have closed the bank account — it would cause problems. He asked had any stocktaking taken place. I said, No. He told me to prepare an analysis of the sales of Drive-In from 1 March 1981 and identify between the sales of Carpetdrome stock and its own stock; to ignore the Drive-In sales, take VAT out of the Carpetdrome sales, identify the cost price to Carpetdrome and names of customers and date of sales as long as sales of Carpetdrome stock continued."

He said he undertook the task, which he described as "very heavy":

> "I was bringing the books of Drive-In over continually and Mr Gaynor was monitoring the work I was doing. In early May Mr Gaynor arrived around 1.30 p.m. at North Circular Road. We were closing down at the time. He said the Revenue were on the warpath. They had got wind of the transfer between Drive-In and Carpetdrome and it had better be completed fast. A final stock-taking took place in mid-May and the remainder of the stock was transferred around 17 May 1981, after the value of the stocks had been gerrymandered."

Mr Gaynor, on the other hand, said that he had never been told about Mr McGoldrick's plan to transfer the business to Drive-In on the basis that the new company would take over the assets and liabilities of the old company and simply stand in its shoes in relation to the creditors of Carpetdrome. He said he told them to make sure the stock was transferred at not less than cost, and to attach the suppliers' invoices — that the Revenue would investigate the affairs of Carpetdrome sooner or later.

Mr McGoldrick says that the value of the stock transferred from Carpetdrome to Drive-In was "gerrymandered" and if this is so, and the new company did not assume any liability for the debts and liabilities of Carpetdrome then a further fraud on creditors was perpetrated. However, Mr McGoldrick did not suggest in the course of his evidence that the respondents were, or either of them was, at any stage made aware of the fact that the figures shown in relation to these transactions were spurious and there was no other evidence tendered which would implicate them in this manner. Mr Gaynor denied that the meeting with Mr McGoldrick at the Carpetdrome premises in early May 1981, ever took place, and in particular denied that he had ever used expressions to suggest that the Revenue Commissioners "were on the warpath", and that the transfer should be completed without further delay. I do not find it necessary to resolve this conflict of evidence as between Mr McGoldrick and Mr Gaynor, as even were I to accept unreservedly what was said by Mr McGoldrick and reject the account given by Mr Gaynor, the content of the conversation would appear to me to be neutral in its tone, insofar as it could be relied on to show participation in fraud. I have no doubt that the Revenue Commissioners were, in a sense, "on the warpath", whenever they first had an inkling of the departure from the scene of Carpetdrome, and not without justification, and even if the transfer of the business from one company to the other were carried through in a completely *bona fide* manner they would have been bound to investigate it very closely. In this kind of situation I feel an accountant would be perfectly justified in advising his client that there was a full Revenue investigation on the way and the sooner the transaction was finalised the better for all concerned. This appears to me to stop far short of advising the client to carry through any scheme of arrangement in a fraudulent or improper manner.

The next development was brought about by the Revenue demand for VAT arrears as against Carpetdrome. It is not clear from the evidence when and why Mr McGoldrick's plan for a takeover by Drive-In of the assets and liabilities of Carpetdrome was finally abandoned. He says in effect that he was brow-beaten at the meeting in April 1981, both by his own employers and by the accountants, and was not given an opportunity to explain what was involved in his own proposals or to press for their adoption. Mr Gaynor, on the other hand, says that on his return from the United States he was presented with a *fait accompli*, with the Carpetdrome bank account closed and its business already taken over by Drive-In and that all he could do was to endeavour to ensure that the transfer of assets from one company to the other would stand up to scrutiny when the inevitable investigation took place. There may have been some breakdown in communication between the two sides at that stages, brought about in part by the diffidence of Mr McGoldrick in fighting his own corner, and the overbearing attitude adopted towards him by Matthew Kelly.

What does emerge from the evidence is that the changeover from Carpetdrome to Drive-In was initiated from within the company itself and without consulting the respondents, and had been largely put into effect by the time the respondents were first made aware of what was proposed, or consulted about the steps which should be taken. Up to the time when Carpetdrome was put into liquidation the extent of the participation of the respondents in the transfer seems to have been confined to advising that full records should be kept of transfers of stock, and monitoring the implementation of that advice. There is no suggestion that Matthew Kelly or his associates went to the respondents and asked them to devise a scheme which would enable Carpetdrome to dispose of all its assets while remaining in good standing with its trade creditors and leaving nothing available to meet any claims of the Revenue Commissioners, nor was there any evidence to suggest that the respondents had produced such a scheme on their own initiative.

The respondents, however, became more directly involved in the affairs of Carpetdrome when a decision was taken in May 1981 to wind up the company. Mr McGoldrick said the VAT demand for £230,000 came as a complete surprise to the company as he considered they were only four months in arrears at the time and only claims for credits had been contested by the Revenue authorities. He continued:

> "On 23 May 1981 I went to see Mr Tuffy with Paul Jackson. Mr Tuffy said Carpetdrome was going into liquidation — did I know what a statement of affairs was. I was asked to furnish him with the information for one, together with £700 for fees. The statement of affairs was prepared in front of me by Mr Tuffy when I brought over the materials. The figure for stock was suggested by Mr Gaynor before he handed over the liquidation to Mr Tuffy. He said he put in £3,000 for stock so that money could be generated to pay the liquidator's fees. Mr Tuffy asked did I know about the debtors. I made a guess — he put in half. . . . He went down the list of creditors and eliminated disputed claims and other claims such as Monck Properties — people who were not expected to prove or appear."

The witness went on to say that when the meeting of creditors was being convened for 3 June 1981, Mr Tuffy said he would put the advertisement in the *Evening Press* for the last Friday in May — that he would bury it in the sports pages on a Bank Holiday weekend, where the least number would notice it, and this was what happened in point of fact.

He described the meeting of creditors which took place in the Sunnybank Hotel, Botanic Road, at 10 a.m. on 3 June 1981 and which was attended by only two creditors' representatives apart from himself, representing Drive-In. Before the meeting commenced Paul Jackson succeeded in satisfying the other two creditors that their claims would be met and they left. The "creditors' meeting" then went through with the appointment of Mr Harding as liquidator — his name having been put forward by the respondents as a suitable person — and with no one else present save Mr Tuffy, Mr Harding, Mr Paul Jackson (a director of Carpetdrome and of Drive-In), and one other person who hoped to be appointed as liquidator.

This was indeed an extraordinary performance in relation to a trading company whose annual turnover was reckoned in millions rather than thousands; which was clearly insolvent, and which a short time previously had a very large number of creditors with claims against it totalling hundreds of thousands of pounds. It was suggested in the course of the present proceedings that it was no more than a charade. The statement of affairs presented to the meeting was an attenuated document giving stocks at £3,000, total assets as £6,000, and liabilities of almost £500,000 — most of it due to the Revenue Commissioners.

For the respondents, Mr Gaynor denies that he ever told Mr McGoldrick to put in a figure of £3,000 for stock "to generate fees for the liquidator" and Mr Tuffy denies that he dealt in the cavalier manner described by Mr McGoldrick with the list of creditors and debtors. The respondents must, however, accept responsibility for the preparation of this statement of affairs and for its presentation to the meeting in compliance with the statutory obligation imposed on the directors by the provision of the Companies Act 1963.

I have a strong impression that this statement of affairs was prepared in great haste and without any great regard to its accuracy by anyone who was involved in the work of compiling it. A balance sheet of sorts had been prepared for the company by the respondent as part of their work in preparing the four-year set of draft accounts, which purported to show the position of the company as of 31 October 1980, and the reconciliation of that document with the statement of affairs as of 29 May 1981, would be a task of considerable magnitude, if, indeed, it could be attempted at all. While no more credence can be attached to the balance sheet than to any other statement of the company's position based on the inaccurate and incomplete information the directors were making available to their accountants, I think the discrepancies between the two documents were of such an order that the respondents should not have concurred in the production of the statement of affairs of 29 May 1981, without first making the most searching inquiries about the material to be included therein.

I have come to the following conclusion regarding the part played by the respondents in the winding-up of Carpetdrome when the decision was finally made to put the company into liquidation. I believe the initial decision to transfer its business to Drive-In was taken without consulting the respondents, and I also believe that the decision which followed a few month later to put Carpetdrome into liquidation was also made by the directors without the direct involvement of the respondents. Once the decision had been taken, the respondents were brought into the picture — as happened previously during the history of Matthew Kelly's companies when some point of particular difficulty or crisis was reached. On this occasion, however, it must have been apparent to the respondents that a very tricky situation was arising both for themselves and for the company. They had a client who had paid very substantial sums in fees to the firm over a period of years and whom they would not wish to ditch in an unceremonious fashion, but they were now being asked to become involved in the winding-up of a company whose affairs, to their knowledge, had been conducted in a highly irregular manner from the time it first commenced in business and which was in the process of divesting itself of all its assets at a time when it was faced with enormous, unsatisfied claims by the Revenue Commissioners.

My impression is that the main concern of the respondents at that stage was to extricate themselves as quickly and as gracefully as they could from all further involvement in the affairs of Carpetdrome. When the winding-up of Carpetdrome was mooted, Mr Gaynor later told Mr Tiúit of the investigation branch that he had put Matthew Kelly in touch with his partner, Mr Tuffy, as the expert in liquidation matters, while at the same time warning Mr Tuffy to have nothing to do with it. The respondents, in evidence, said they felt it would be inappropriate to be involved in the liquidation as they had acted for Matthew Kelly and some of his companies, but this did not deter Mr Gaynor from acting previously as liquidator of Kelly's Carpet Supermarket Ltd. I think Mr Harding was brought in to get the partners "off the hook" while not giving offence to their clients, and I also think that in their anxiety to dissociate themselves from further involvement in the affairs of Carpetdrome the partners did, in fact, lend themselves to the preparation of a completely inadequate statement of affairs, and the holding of a creditors' meeting which could fairly be described as a charade.

Their attitude at that stage was that it was now over to the liquidator, Mr Harding, to sort out the mess in which the affairs of Carpetdrome were to be found, and I think they regarded the preparation of the statement of affairs and the convening of the creditors' meeting as merely a formal compliance with the requirements of the statute, which in no way fettered the liquidator or the creditors in the examination of all claims which thereafter could be made against the company.

I have no reason to believe that Mr Harding, although his experience in the field of company liquidation was of a somewhat limited nature, would have shirked his responsibilities of his office in any way, or would not have carried out his duties in a competent manner, and I do not accept the suggestion that his name was put forward by the respondents as a person who would not be sufficiently equipped to investigate the affairs of the company in a thorough and effective manner.

This concludes the summary I have made from the evidence in the case of the involvement of the respondents with the affairs of Kelly's Carpetdrome Ltd and while I am satisfied that they were employed in an important consultative capacity from time to time not only by Matthew Kelly but also by the company, and while they have laid themselves open to a good deal of criticism for their failure to adopt a much tougher line with clients who gave many indications of sailing windward of the law, I have come to the conclusion that the evidence in the case stops well short of satisfying me that they were, or either of them was, knowingly party to the carrying out of the business of Carpetdrome with intent to defraud the creditors of that company or creditors of any other person or for any fraudulent purpose.

The onus of proof assumed by the liquidator in pressing such a claim must be a very heavy one. Conduct of the type described in section 297 of the Companies Act 1963, as well as giving rise to a possible civil liability on the part of the wrongdoer, is also made a criminal offence by the provisions of subsection (3) of the section. Consequently, what is involved when civil liability is sought to be imposed under the provisions of section 297 is an allegation of crime in civil proceedings, and there is some authority for the proposition that in this kind of situation the same standard of proof is demanded as would apply in a criminal prosecution, that is to say, proof beyond reasonable doubt, and not merely proof of the balance of probabilities, such as would apply in the ordinary run of civil actions. See *Thurtell v. Beaumont* (1823) 1 Bing 339; *Chalmers v. Shackell* (1834) 6 C & P 475; *Willmett v. Harmer* (1839), 8 C & P 695; *Statham v. Statham* (1929) P 131.

The final word may not have been said as yet on this subject, but in *Hornal v. Neuberger Products Ltd* [1956] 1 QB 247, the Court of Appeal in England held that in a case where an action was based in the alternative on breach of contract or fraudulent misrepresentation, the same standard of proof should be applied in each case, and the standard of proof applicable was the civil standard of a preponderence of probability. The court went on to say however, that this was not an absolute standard, since within it the degree of probability required to establish proof might vary according to the gravity of the allegation to be proved. The court further approved the observation of Denning LJ in *Bater v. Bater* [1950] 2 All ER 458, in the course of which he remarked as follows:

> "Many great judges have said that, in proportion as the crime is enormous, so ought the proof to be clear. So also in civil cases. The case may be proved by a preponderance of probability, but there may be degrees of probability within that standard. The degree depends on the subject-matter. A civil court, when considering a charge of fraud, will naturally require a higher degree of probability than that which it would require if considering whether negligence were established. It does not adopt so high a degree as a criminal court, even when it is considering a charge of criminal nature, but still it does require a degree of probability which is commensurate with the occasion."

In the present case I can resolve this legal difficulty by stating that even applying the somewhat lower standard of proof required in civil proceedings I would still feel bound to exonerate the respondents from the charges brought against them of knowing participation in fraudulent transactions of the company.

I must therefore refuse the liquidator the relief sought by him in the present proceedings under section 297 of the Companies Act 1963.

Alistair Rutherdale
Barrister

In the Matter of The Sunday Tribune Ltd (in Liquidation) and In the Matter of the Companies Acts 1963-1983: High Court 1982 No. 10390p (Carroll J) 26 September 1984

Company Law – Winding-up – Creditors – Priority – Newspaper journalists and sub-editor – Whether preferential creditors – Whether employees – Test – Companies Act 1963 (No. 33) section 285

Labour Law – Contract of employment – Newspaper journalists and sub-editor – Whether employees or independent contractors – Whether engaged under contract of service – Test to be applied – Whether under control of employer – Whether work integral to business

Facts: The liquidator of the company applied to court to determine whether certain persons, who did work for a newspaper produced by the company, were employees of the company and thus entitled to be entered in the class of preferential creditors in the winding-up. Three cases were submitted as representative of their respective class.

PW was a part-time worker, working under the same conditions, control and supervision as full-time employees, and was paid by the shift under a contract based on the house agreement applicable to all employees. He worked as a sub-editor, who did initially one, and later two shifts per week. Additional work, done beyond the end of the shift, was paid at overtime rate.

MH was a regular columnist. Her contract agreed a fixed fee of £250 per week for her column, her attendance and participation in editorial conferences and some small news items. Payment was made for two weeks per year when no copy was supplied, and for two further weeks where advance copy was supplied. The salary was separately negotiated and was not a minimum fixed by a trade union agreement.

RL was a regular contributor who was paid for commissioned work, not necessarily appearing weekly, on a rate per word basis. No reference was made to editorial control or attendance at the office.

All three claimants were registered with the Revenue Commissioners under Schedule D and accordingly paid tax on their respective aggregate annual income from journalism.

Held by Carroll J in holding that PW and MH were employees of the company for the purpose of section 285 of the Companies Act 1963, while RL was not.

(1) The determining factor was whether the work was done on foot of a contract of service which created the relationship of employer and employee. In deciding this the court must look to the realities of the situation, regardless of how the parties describe themselves.

(2) The deduction of income tax on a P.A.Y.E. basis was not solely determinative.

(3) Nor was the question of whether the employer possessed the right to control both what work was done, and how it was to be done, determinative. Control is just one of many factors whose influence varies according to circumstances. *Beloff v. Pressdram Ltd* [1973] 1 All ER 241 considered; *Simmons v. Heath Laundry Co.* [1910] 1 KB 543 considered.

(4) A further test is whether on the one hand the employee is employed as part of the business and his work is an integral part of the business, or whether his work is not integrated into the business but is only accessory to it. *Beloff v. Pressdram Ltd* [1973] 1 All ER 241 considered; *Stevenson, Jordan and Harrison Ltd v. McDonald and Evans* [1952] TLR 101 considered.

(5) PW satisfied the simple test of control by the employer. He worked at specified times under the direction of the chief sub-editor. The fact that his work was part-time did not change this position. He was therefore employed under a contract of service.

(6) MH's employment was an integral part of the business of the newspaper. Her column was regular, she took part in editorial conferences and there was a provision for the equivalent of holiday pay. She was therefore employed under a contract of service.

(7) The employment of RL was not an integral part of the business. Her work was as a freelance contributor, and there was no obligation to contribute on a regular basis. If she did not turn up to negotiate a commissioned article, the editor could get articles from other sources. She was, therefore, an independent contractor in respect of the articles she provided.

Cases referred to in judgment

Beloff v. Pressdram Ltd [1973] 1 All ER 241
Ferguson v. Dawson and Partners [1976] 1 WLR 1213; [1976] 3 All ER 817; [1976] 2 Lloyd's Rep 669
Jones v. Scullard [1898] 2 QB 565
Market Investigations Ltd v. Minister of Social Security [1969] 2 QB 173; [1969] 2 WLR 1; [1968] 3 All ER 732
Simmons v. Heath Laundry Co. [1910] 1 KB 543
Stevenson, Jordan and Harrison Ltd v. McDonald and Evans [1952] TLR 101

Counsel's names not available

Solicitors for the official liquidator: *Eugene F. Collins & Son*
Solicitor for the notice party: *Patrick J. Maher, Revenue Solicitor*

[Reporters Note: Section 285 of the Companies Act 1963 (No.33) has been amended by section 10 of the Companies (Amendment) Act 1982 (No. 10) and by section 134 of the Companies Act 1990 (No. 33).]

CARROLL J **26 September 1984**

The liquidator of the Sunday Tribune Ltd has applied to the court to determine if certain people who did work for the paper were employees of the company and therefore entitled as preferential creditors in the winding-up. The liquidator was not prepared to enter them in the class of preferential creditors on the grounds that their remuneration had not had P.A.Y.E. deducted therefrom.

The examiner's memorandum identifies the first claimant as "P.W. of a class for convenience described as "shift workers" whose claim is as a part-time worker working under the same conditions, control and supervision as full-time employees, paid by the shift under a contract based on the house agreement applicable to all employees. This claimant worked two shifts per week."

In a separate affidavit P.W. said that he was employed on a shift basis and in the beginning did one shift per week as sub-editor. He was required to attend at a specified time and then worked under the guidance of the chief sub-editor and to his instructions until the shift was over. The period of the shift was fixed in advance. If any work had to be done beyond the end of the shift, overtime was to be paid. From March 1983 he worked two shifts per week. He worked under the same general terms and conditions of a house agreement between the *Sunday Tribune* and the N.U.J., as full-time employees.

The next claimant is described in the examiner's memorandum as:

> "M.H. of a small class described as 'regular columnist'. Her contract agrees a fixed fee of £250 per week as a journalist in relation to her weekly column, her attendance and participation in editorial conferences and whatever additional small news items came her way. For two weeks of the year payment was to be honoured without having to supply copy. For two additional weeks advance copy was to be accepted by the newspaper. The salary was separately negotiated and was not a minimum fixed by a trade union agreement."

In her affidavit M.H. says she was paid £250 per week to include a regular weekly column. attendance and participation in editorial conferences with such further news items or items of interest which she was able to contribute. Six times a year the column was to be a major piece. For two weeks of the year she was paid without having to supply copy and for two additional weeks advance copy was to be accepted.

The next claimant is identified in the examiner's memorandum as:

> "R.L. of a class described as 'regular contributors' who were paid for commissioned work not necessarily appearing weekly on a rate per word basis. No reference was made to editorial control or attendance at the office."

In her affidavit R.L. said she was a regular contributor. She visited the office of the *Sunday Tribune* approximately once a week and would either suggest a topic for an article or be asked to contribute an article of a certain length on a specific topic. She was then commissioned and paid on the basis of the house agreement between the *Sunday Tribune* and the N.U.J. She said in no case was the work embarked on without a firm commission from the editor.

All three claimants filed affidavits to say they were each registered with the Revenue Commissioners under Schedule D and each accordingly paid tax on their respective aggregate annual income from journalism.

I am satisfied that the fact that P.A.Y.E. was not deducted is not the determining factor in this case. The profession of journalism is such that a journalist may have an income from more than one source under a contract of service or contract for services or both. It appears to have been a matter of convenience at the time permitted by the Revenue to allow payments to be made without deduction of P.A.Y.E. notwithstanding the status of the worker.

M.H. at the time she was working for the *Sunday Tribune* was also working part-time for London Weekend T.V. and also for the *New Statesman*. P.W. who worked part-time on shift for the *Sunday Tribune* also worked for the *Irish Times*, the *Irish Press* Group and the *Irish Independent* Group. He said there was no difference in practice between the way in which those with certificates of exclusion (i.e. those from whom P.A.Y.E. was not deducted) and those without worked.

The determining factor is whether the work which was done by each claimant was done on foot of a contract of service which created the relationship of employer and employee or whether it was done on foot of a contract for services which did not create the relationship.

The court must look at the realities of the situation in order to determine whether the relationship of employer and employee in fact exists, regardless of how the parties describe themselves (see *Ferguson v. Dawson and Partners* [1976] 1 WLR 1213). The simple test is whether the employer possessed the right not only to control what work the employee was to do but also the manner in which the work was to be done. However the test is no longer of universal application. In the present day when senior staff with professional qualifications are employed, the nature of their employment cannot be determined in a simplistic way.

The question is dealt with extensively in the case of *Beloff v. Pressdram Ltd* [1973] 1 All ER 241. One of the issues to be determined in that case was whether copyright in a memorandum belonged to the journalist who wrote it or the newspaper which published it. If the work was written in the course of the author's employment by the newspaper under a contract of service, the newspaper was entitled to copyright in the work under section 4(4) of the Copyright Act 1956. It was not in issue that the memorandum was made in the course of employment but the court had to decide whether the employment was under a contract of service or a contract for services. Ungoed-Thomas J reviewed the earlier law in the course of which he quotes from the judgment of Fletcher Moulton LJ in *Simmons v. Heath Laundry Co.* [1910] 1 KB 543 at 549-550, a portion of which I now quote:—

> "The greater the amount of direct control exercised over the person rendering the services by the person contracting for them the stronger the grounds for holding it to be a contract of service, and similarly the greater the degree of independence of such control the greater the probability that the services rendered are of the nature of professional services and that the contract is not one of service. The place where the services are rendered, i.e. whether at the residence of the person rendering the services or not, will also be an element in deciding the case, but is not in my opinion decisive. . . ."

Ungoed-Thomas J goes on to say (at page 248) that nowadays professional and similarly skilled persons are widely engaged under what are recognised as contracts of service and he reviews recent authorities in relation to particular cases which have been held to be or not to be contracts of service.

The test that Denning LJ applied in *Stevenson, Jordan and Harrison Ltd v. McDonald and Evans* ([1952] TLR 101 at 111) is quoted as follows:—

> "One feature which seems to run through the instances is that, under a contract of service, a man is employed as part of the business, and his work is done as an integral part of the business; whereas, under a contract for services, his work, although done for the business, is not integrated into it but is only accessory to it."

Denning LJ also said in the course of that case (at 110):—

> "It is often easy to recognise a contract of service when you see it, but difficult to say wherein the difference lies. A ship's master, a chauffeur, and a reporter on the staff of a newspaper are all employed under a contract of service; but a ship's pilot, a taximan, and a newspaper contributor are employed under a contract for services."

Ungoed-Thomas J, having reviewed other cases as well, says at page 250:—

> "It thus appears, and rightly in my respectful view, that the greater the skill required for an employee's work, the less significant is control in determining whether the employee is under a contract of service. Control is just one of many factors whose influence varies according to circumstances. In such highly skilled work as that of the plaintiff it seems of no substantial significance. The test which emerges from the authorities seems to me, as Denning LJ said, whether on the one hand the employee is employed as part of the business and his work is an integral part of the business, or whether his work is not integrated into the business but is only accessory to it, or, as Cook J expressed it, the work is done by him in business on his own account."

The court went on to hold that the plaintiff who was political and lobby correspondent of the *Observer* was employed under a contract of service. The job of political and lobby correspondent was essential for and woven into its political coverage. The court held that the plaintiff's job was an integral part of the business of the *Observer*.

In the case of P.W., his employment satisfies the simple test of control by the employer. He worked at specified times under the guidance of the chief sub-editor and to his instructions. The fact that he was part-time does not change the nature of his employment.

A person may be an employee even though employed part-time (see *Market Investigation Ltd v. Minister of Social Security* [1969] 2 QB 173). Also a person may be an employee to different employers. (See *Jones v. Scullard* [1898] 2 QBD 565 at 569).

Therefore I am satisfied that Mr W. was employed by the *Sunday Tribune* under a contract of service.

In the case of M.H. I am of opinion that her employment was an integral part of the business of the newspaper. The column was to run for 50 out of 52 weeks of the year. She took part in editorial conferences. There was provision for the equivalent of holiday pay. Her case is not dissimilar to that of the plaintiff in *Beloff v. Pressdram Ltd.* Therefore I am satisfied that she was employed under a contract of service.

In the case of R.L. I am of opinion that her employment was not an integral part of the business of the newspaper. She was in my opinion a freelance contributor who secured commissions in advance. She was under no obligation to contribute on a regular basis. Presumably if she did not turn up to negotiate a commissioned article, the editor would get articles from some other source. Therefore I am satisfied that she was employed under a contract of service but was an independent contractor in respect of the articles she did provide.

Accordingly, P.W. and M.H. are employees of the company for the purposes of section 285 of the Companies Act 1963 while R.L. is not.

Alistair Rutherdale
Barrister

In the Matter of the Trustee Act 1893; John Kavanagh and Barbara Cantwell (applicants): High Court 1984 No. 672 Sp (Costello J) 23 November 1984

Trust – Mortgage – Company – Company in liquidation – Company entitled to fee simple of mortgaged property – Agreement to transfer property to new company – Transfer never completed – Property held in trust by company for new company – Company dissolved without divesting itself of estate in property – Subsequent contract for sale – No claim by state to fee simple as bona vacantia *– Whether purchasers entitled to order vesting property in them – Trustee Act 1893 (56 & 57 Vict Ch. 53) sections 25, 26 – Companies Act 1963 (No. 33) section 263*

Facts: Section 25(1) of the Trustee Act 1893 provides:

> "The High Court may, whenever it is expedient to appoint a new trustee or new trustees, and it is found inexpedient, difficult, or impracticable so to do without the assistance of the court, make an order for the appointment of a new trustee or new trustees. . . ."

Section 26(ii)(c) provides that:

> "Where a trustee entitled to or possessed of any land . . . cannot be found . . . the High Court may make an order vesting the land in any such manner and for any such estate as the court may direct."

Mr and Mrs Silk mortgaged their fee simple interest in a dwellinghouse at

Glenageary to Moore Paragon Ireland Ltd as security for a loan. On 2 March 1983 that company went into liquidation. The liquidator agreed to transfer the mortgaged property and the right to sue for the mortgage debt to another company, Moore Business Forms Ltd, in consideration for the sum of £42,875. Although this sum was paid on 2 June 1983, only the mortgage debt, but not the mortgaged property, was transferred to the purchasing company.

Its liquidation complete, Moore Paragon Ireland Ltd was dissolved on 28 October 1983, without having divested itself of its fee simple interest.

By contract dated 6 July 1984 Mr and Mrs Silk agreed to sell the property to the applicants. On 20 July the applicants paid the purchase price, and by conveyance of the same date, Mr and Mrs Silk purported to convey the fee simple interest in the premises. By indenture dated 20 September 1984, and in consideration of the payment by Mr and Mrs Silk of the loan monies, Moore Business Forms Ltd purported to release and convey to Mr and Mrs Silk the legal estate in the fee simple in the premises.

The applicants applied to appoint new trustees under section 25 of the Trustee Act 1893 and to make a consequential vesting order under section 26 or, alternatively, for an order vesting directly in the applicants the property referred to in these proceedings.

On 19 November 1984 the Attorney General indicated that the State did not claim that the legal estate vested in the State as *bona vacantia*.

Held by Costello J in ordering that the fee simple or other interest which vested in Moore Paragon Ireland Ltd at the date of its dissolution, would vest in the applicants:

(1) In a case where a company holds property as trustee and is dissolved before it has executed a transfer of property to a purchaser, this is a case where a trustee "cannot be found", and is a proper case for the court to vest the property directly in the purchasers. *In re Richard Mills and Co. (Brierly Hill) Ltd* [1905] WN 36 approved, *In re General Accident Assurance Corporation Ltd* [1904] 1 Ch 147 approved, *In re Taylors Agreement Trusts* [1904] 2 Ch 737 not followed.

(2) The court would declare that immediately prior to its dissolution, Moore Paragon Ireland Ltd was possessed of an estate in fee simple in the premises as trustees for Moore Business Forms Ltd upon a trust within the meaning of the Trustee Act 1893 and the applicants were now entitled to the beneficial interest under the said trust.

(3) The applicants were entitled to an order pursuant to section 26 of the Trustee Act of 1893, that the fee simple or other estate or interest vested in Moore Paragon Ireland Ltd at the date of its dissolution was to vest in the applicants.

Cases referred to in judgment

In re General Accident Assurance Corporation Ltd [1904] 1 Ch 147
In re No. 9 Bomore Road [1906] 1 Ch 359
In re Richard Mills and Co. (Brierly Hill) Ltd [1905] WN 36
In re Taylors Agreement Trusts [1904] 2 Ch 737; [1904] WN 120

Complete names of counsel and solicitors not available

Solicitors for the applicants: *L.B. McMahon & Co.*

COSTELLO J **23 November 1984**

This is an application to appoint new trustees under section 25 of the Trustee Act 1893 and to make a consequential vesting order under section 26, or alternatively, for an order vesting directly in the applicants the property referred to in these proceedings. Clearly, the applicants are entitled to relief under the Act; the only question is the form of order which should be made. I can outline briefly the unfortunate set of circumstances which has given rise to these proceedings (and no doubt caused the applicants some not inconsiderable financial loss). They are as follows.

Mr and Mrs George Silk mortgaged their fee simple interest in a dwelling-house at 24, Sharavogue, Glenageary, County Dublin, to a company called Moore Paragon Ireland Ltd as security for a loan of £45,000. On 2 March 1983 the company went into voluntary liquidation. Its liquidator agreed to transfer the mortgage property and the right to sue for the mortgage debt to another company called Moore Business Forms Ltd in consideration of the sum of £42,875. This sum was duly paid on or about 2 June 1983 but by an extraordinary piece of inadvertence the mortgage debt only, but not the mortgaged property, was transferred to the purchasing company. It is quite clear that certainly from that date Moore Paragon Ireland Ltd held the legal estate in the fee simple of the property in trust for Moore Business Forms Ltd. Its liquidation having been completed Moore Paragon Ireland Ltd was dissolved pursuant to section 263 of the Companies Act 1963 on 28 October 1983 without having divested itself of its fee simple interest.

The error that had occurred did not come to light until recently after Mr and Mrs Silk had agreed to sell their dwellinghouse to the applicants by a contract of 6 July 1984. Paragraph (G) of the Special Conditions of this contract provided that:

> "The purchaser shall not be entitled to delay the closing of the sale herein by reason of the fact that the mortgage by the vendors in favour of Moore Paragan [*sic*] Ireland Ltd on security of the premises in sale has been discharged [*sic*] but shall accept on [*sic*] undertaking from the vendors' solicitors (a) to discharge the amount necessary to redeem the mortgage and (b) to hand over a duly executed Release of the Mortgage as soon as same comes to hand."

On or about 20 July 1984 the applicants paid £56,000 to Mr and Mrs Silk who by a conveyance of that date purported to convey to them the fee simple interest in the premises. Mr and Mrs Silk, of course, did not have the fee simple interest at that time; their estate was an equitable one. By an indenture of 20 September 1984 and in consideration of the payment by Mr and Mrs Silk of all the monies due under the mortgage Moore Business Forms Ltd purported to release and convey to Mr and Mrs Silk the legal estate in the fee simple in the premises which, unfortunately, they did not possess. I have no doubt that the result of these developments is that firstly the Silks and then the applicants became entitled to the beneficial interest (previously enjoyed by Moore Business Forms Ltd) in the trust to which I have referred.

Obviously, the dissolution of Moore Paragon Ireland Ltd raised the question whether the outstanding legal estate vested in the State as *bona vacantia*, but the Attorney General has written on 19 November 1984 stating that the State does not claim it. On this basis I can then proceed to consider sections 25 and 26 of the Trustee Act 1893.

This court, whenever it is expedient to appoint a new trustee, and if it is found impracticable to do so without its assistance, may make an order for the appointment of a new trustee under section 25 of the Trustee Act 1893. *In re No. 9 Bomore Road* [1906] 1 Ch 359 was a case in which a company entitled to a leasehold interest in premises went into liquidation. Its liquidator agreed to transfer all its assets to a new company which duly went into possession. Inadvertently the leasehold interest was never assigned to the new company prior to the dissolution of the old company. The court appointed trustees under section 25 and made a consequential vesting order holding that the property was vested in the new company in equity with the legal estate outstanding and that it was impossible to get the estate vested where it ought to be — namely in the purchaser — except by exercising its section 25 powers.

But the court has additional powers under section 26 of the Act. Where a trustee entitled to any land "cannot be found" (subsection (ii)(c)) the court may make a vesting order vesting the land in "any such person in any such manner and for any estate as the court may direct". In a case very similar to the present one (*In re General Accident Assurance Corporation Ltd* [1904] 1 Ch 147) a company went into voluntary liquidation and sold its property to a new company. The liquidator received the purchase price for the company's assets but by inadvertence no deed transferring a mortgage of 13 April 1899 was executed prior to the company's dissolution. The purchasing company applied to the Crown inquiring whether the Crown would execute an assignment of the outstanding legal estate as *bona vacantia* but were informed that the Crown was not able to admit that that legal estate was vested in the Crown. The purchasing company then petitioned the court under the subsection of section 26 to which I have referred and the court made an order vesting in the company not only the right to sue for and recover the mortgage debt but also the leasehold premises comprised in the mortgage of 13 April 1899 for such estate and interest as vested in the corporation at the date of its dissolution on the basis that this was a case in which the trustee could not be found.

But judicial opinion in England is not unanimous on the interpretation of section 26. In *In re Taylors Agreement Trusts* [1904] 2 Ch 737 Buckley J declined to follow the decision of Farwell J but Farwell J (*In re Richard Mills and Co. (Brierly Hill) Ltd* [1905] WN 36) in another case in which a trustee company was dissolved without having transferred a legal estate again made a vesting order under section 26 pointing out:

> "With great respect to Buckley J, I do not think the difficulty exists that he raises, on the section. If you know where a trustee is, you can locate him. If you do not know where he is then whether it is an individual or a company that has been dissolved, it is the case of a trustee "who cannot be found". There will be an order vesting in the purchaser the freeholds. . . ." (p. 37)

I find myself in agreement with this interpretation of the section. It seems to me that in the circumstances which I am considering it can properly be said that this is a case in which the trustees cannot be found within the meaning of the section so that the court can vest the property directly in the purchasers, the present applicants, and I propose to do so.

I think, then, that I should declare that Moore Paragon Ireland Ltd was at and immediately before the date of its dissolution possessed of an estate in fee simple in the premises the subject matter of these proceedings as trustees for Moore Business Forms Ltd upon a trust within the meaning of the Trustee Act 1893; that in the events that have happened the applicants are now entitled to the beneficial interest under the said trust; that the Attorney General having stated that no claim to the said premises is being made by the State, the trustees of the said trust cannot now be found. I will then order, pursuant to section 26 of the Act, that the fee simple or other the estate or interest vested in Moore Paragon Ireland Ltd at the date of its dissolution do vest in the applicants.

Alistair Rutherdale
Barrister

[*Reporter's Note:* Section 263 of the Companies Act 1963 has been amended by Schedule 1 of the Companies (Amendment) Act 1982.]

In the Matter of Castlemahon Poultry Products Ltd (in liquidation) and In the Matter of the Companies Acts 1963 to 1983 (No. 1): High Court 1984 No. 6784P (Barrington J) 3 May 1985

Company in financial difficulty – Schemes devised – Turkeys held in cold storage sold to first respondent – Whether this amounted to a fraudulent preference – Agreement with second respondent to keep turkeys owned by second respondent in cold storage – Trust – Breach – Liquidation – Dispute as to ownership of monies received on the sale of the turkeys – Whether monies belonged to first respondent – Whether turkeys owned by second respondent had been sold by company – Whether second respondent entitled to such monies as represented the poundage of turkeys owned by them – Right to trace

Facts: Castlemahon Poultry Products Ltd ("Castlemahon") was in the business of rearing, fattening, storing, selling and distributing turkeys and chickens. It had been in financial difficulties for some years and schemes were adopted to keep the company afloat. Golden Vale Co-operative Ltd ("Golden Vale"), the first respondent in the application, was a shareholder in Castlemahon and had close links with it at managerial level. A provisional liquidator was appointed to Castlemahon on 5 September 1984 and an official liquidator was appointed on 8 September 1984. The liquidator sought a declaration from the court as to the ownership of certain monies representing a stock of frozen turkeys which were in cold storage on the premises of Castlemahon at the date of the appointment of the provisional liquidator. Golden Vale claimed that it owned all turkeys in cold storage on the company's premises at the said date whereas the second respondent, International Turkey Ltd (ITL) claimed that it owned a portion of the said turkeys. On behalf of Golden Vale it was contended that as much of Castlemahon's capital was tied up from the late summer to the run up to Christmas due to the build up of storage of frozen birds at that time, the parties devised a scheme whereby Castlemahon would sell its stock of frozen turkeys to Golden Vale. This was first done in 1982 and was evidenced in writing and a similar agreement was entered into in 1983 although this was not evidenced in writing. It was submitted on behalf of the first respondent that in August 1984 it was agreed that Golden Vale would purchase all of the turkeys in cold storage from Castlemahon and that a storage charge would be paid to Castlemahon by Golden Vale.

ITL approached Castlemahon around Christmas 1983 and entered into an agreement under which Castlemahon was to slaughter turkeys for ITL and keep them in cold storage until such time as ITL was in a position to dispose of them. These were placed in Castlemahon bags but were labelled "ITL/Rigney". On 14 March 1984 ITL withdrew 2,295 of its turkeys, leaving a balance of some 3,165 turkeys in Castlemahon. Castlemahon offered to buy a number of the turkeys still in storage, which offer was refused by ITL. However, Castlemahon had in fact appropriated and sold 1,570 turkeys for which ITL was never paid.

On 5 September 1984 employees of Golden Vale entered the store and labelled all the turkeys "property of Golden Vale Co-op" as a result of which it was impossible for the provisional liquidator to identify which were the property of ITL.

Held by Barrington J:

(1) The sale to Golden Vale was not a fraudulent preference but was a *bona fide* transaction.

(2) The transaction entered into on 1 August 1984 between Castlemahon and Golden Vale was for the sale of all turkeys in Castlemahon bags in cold storage and as such the subject matter of the sale was sufficiently identified.

(3) Although no actual delivery of the goods took place as the turkeys were not removed from the premises, no actual delivery was in the circumstances necessary. The title of Golden Vale did not depend upon the execution of any particular document and therefore no question of a bill of sale arose: *Ramsey v. Margrett* [1894] 2 QB 18 considered.

(4) The proceeds of the sale of these turkeys, subject to the claim of ITL, were held in trust by the liquidator for Golden Vale.

(5) The transaction between Castlemahon and ITL was totally genuine and the turkeys held in cold storage remained the property of ITL.

(6) Castlemahon's action in selling these turkeys was clearly a breach of trust and ITL would be entitled to trace the proceeds of the said sale if they could be traced.

(7) Between 1 August and 5 September 1984 Castlemahon sold to Golden Vale turkeys which were the property of ITL.

(8) ITL were entitled as against Golden Vale and the liquidator to such portion of the fund then in the hands of the liquidator as represented a poundage in turkey meat the equivalent of their turkeys sold by Castlemahon.

Case referred to in judgment

Ramsay v. Margrett [1894] 2 QB 18

Full names of counsel and solicitors not available

John Cooke SC **for the liquidator**

BARRINGTON J **3 May 1985**

This is an application in which the liquidator of Castlemahon Poultry Ltd raises questions as to the ownership of certain monies representing a stock of frozen turkeys which were in cold storage on the premises of Castlemahon Poultry Products Ltd on the date on which a provisional liquidator was appointed to the company on 5 September 1984.

Mr Laurence Crowley was appointed provisional liquidator on that date and was subsequently appointed official liquidator on 8 October 1984.

The respondents on the motion are the Golden Vale Co-operative Creameries

Ltd who claim that they owned all turkeys in cold storage on the company's premises on the date on which the provisional liquidator was appointed over the company and International Turkeys Ltd who claim that they owned portion of the turkeys in the cold store. Golden Vale claim to have purchased all the turkeys in the cold store in accordance with the provisions of an unwritten agreement entered into between officials of Golden Vale and officials of Castlemahon on 1 August 1984. As this alleged agreement took place some five weeks before the appointment of the provisional liquidator, and as there was no delivery of the turkeys to Golden Vale, who were not themselves engaged in the business of the sale or distribution of turkeys, the liquidator was justified in having reservations about the genuineness of this transaction. Moreover, Golden Vale were shareholders in Castlemahon Poultry Ltd and had close links with them at managerial level so that the liquidator was concerned that the alleged transaction of 1 August 1984 might amount to a fraudulent preference.

International Turkeys claimed that a portion of the turkeys were turkeys which International Turkeys had, some months previously, delivered to Castlemahon Poultry Ltd for slaughter and storage to be kept at the order of International Turkeys Ltd.

All the turkeys were in Castlemahon bags. Shortly after the appointment of the provisional liquidator, representatives of International Turkeys Ltd called to the Castlemahon premises and after consultation with officials now in the employ of the provisional liquidator claimed title to specific turkeys in the store. It is clear from an examination of the records of the company that the turkeys claimed could not have been the property of International Turkey Ltd because they were not of the correct weight.

The liquidator was therefore entitled to have reservations about the claims of both respondents.

The Golden Vale claim

I shall deal first with the claim made by Golden Vale.

To understand this claim it is necessary to say something about the way in which Castlemahon Poultry Products Ltd conducted its business. It was in the business of rearing, fattening, slaughtering, storing, selling and distributing turkeys and chickens. For some years prior to going into liquidation it had been in financial difficulties and schemes had been invented to keep the company afloat. A rescue packet was, in fact, being negotiated in August and September 1984, and I am satisfied that, up to the early part of September, the company was confident that it would be able to resolve its problems. Because of its known financial difficulties the company had to settle with most of its creditors for cash or within days after delivery of goods to it. In fact I am satisfied that because of the links between the two companies, Castlemahon got better trading terms from Golden Vale than from other suppliers. I may say that, having heard the evidence of all parties, I am quite satisfied that the alleged sale hereinafter discussed, was not a fraudulent preference of Golden Vale, but a *bona fide* transaction, whether valid or not.

The scheme arose in the following fashion. The major sales of turkeys by the company took place at Christmas and, to a considerably lesser extent, at Easter. For that reason the stock of frozen birds in the company's store built up in the late summer and in the months running up to Christmas. As a result a lot of the company's capital was, during these months, tied up in stocks of frozen turkeys. At the same time the company had to feed its stock of live birds and would be faced with disaster if the supply of food for the birds was cut off, even for a short while. Golden Vale was one of the principal suppliers, if not the principal supplier, of foodstuffs for the live birds. At the same time Golden Vale was alarmed at the size of the company's account. For this reason the parties thought of the device of the company selling its stock of frozen turkeys to Golden Vale. This was first done in the year 1982 and was evidenced by a letter from Golden Vale to Castlemahon Products Ltd. The letter was in the following terms:

> "Dear Sirs,
>
> This is to confirm the arrangement agreed between us for settlement of your account and for future supplies by us. In settlement of the sum of £119,180 owed by you to us for the feedstuffs supplied by us to you up to and including 29 September 1982, we will purchase from you 175,266 pounds of frozen turkey at a price of 68p per pound, which represents your current price to distributors, making a total of £119,180.
>
> We will supply further feedstuffs to you against either payment of cash or sale to us of further turkeys and/or chickens at your then current distributors price.
>
> We enclose a copy of this letter which please sign and return to us to confirm your agreement."

The letter was signed by the financial controller on behalf of Golden Vale. Mr O'Dwyer, general manager of Castlemahon, signed a copy of the letter on behalf of Castlemahon Poultry Products Ltd.

This agreement was honoured by both sides and apparently a somewhat similar agreement was entered into in 1983 but was not evidenced in writing.

This forms the background to the alleged agreement of 1 August 1984.

Mr Curley, the secretary of Golden Vale, says that he visited the premises of Castlemahon Poultry Products Ltd on that date. At that stage the scheme to rescue the company appeared to be proceeding very favourably and he was optimistic about Castlemahon's prospects. At the same time he was alarmed at the size of Castlemahon's account. He had a discussion with Mr O'Dwyer, and said that Castlemahon's account was too high. The pair of them went to the cold store and reviewed the stocks of frozen turkeys which Castlemahon had in store. They discussed the number of turkeys and the categories into which they were divided. Mr Curley said that he agreed to purchase all the turkeys in Castlemahon bags. Mr O'Dwyer confirms Mr Curley's evidence. Mr Curley says that as he left the store the turkeys were his. He says "I was paid in turkeys". It was also agreed that Golden Vale would pay to Castlemahon a storage charge which would vary depending on how long the turkeys had to be kept in store before being ultimately disposed of to third parties.

Mr Curley and Mr O'Dwyer, having concluded the agreement, left the details of stock control and accountancy to be worked out by their subordinates. Castlemahon, in a statement from Golden Vale as of 31 July 1984, received credit in the sum of £170,067.20. Later on 25 August 1984, Castlemahon raised an invoice against Golden Vale in the sum of £2,076.24 in respect of storage. On or about 14 August 1984, Castlemahon repurchased three hundred turkeys from Golden Vale at a price of £2,287.50. But Castlemahon also appears to have disposed of other turkeys to a total value of some £19,506.00 without written notice to Golden Vale.

I accept the evidence of Mr Curley and Mr O'Dwyer that the sale was intended to be and was, in fact, a genuine sale of all the turkeys in Castlemahon bags in Castlemahon's cold store on 1 August 1984, and that the sale was complete when Mr Curley left the premises. I am satisfied that the sale was of all the turkeys in Castlemahon bags and that the subject-matter of the sale was therefore sufficiently identified. The turkeys were not removed from the premises and, in that sense, no actual delivery of the turkeys took place but no actual delivery was, in the circumstances, necessary. It was clearly good sense to leave the turkeys in the cold store where they were being kept by persons skilled in operating a cold store. I am satisfied that the sale was complete in itself prior to any document being drawn up in respect of it. The title of Golden Vale did not depend upon the execution of any particular document by Castlemahon and therefore no question of a bill of sale arises. (See *Ramsay v. Margrett* [1894] 2 QB page 18). As there was no bill of sale, no problem arises about the property remaining in the apparent possession of the person who executed the bill of sale. (See *Ramsay* and in particular the judgment of Lord Esher MR at page 24). Any bill of sale in the present case would of course have been void.

In all the circumstances it appears to me that there was a genuine sale of turkeys to Golden Vale on 1 August 1984. A small portion of these turkeys were subsequently bought back by Castlemahon from Golden Vale. But the balance of the turkeys remained the property of Golden Vale and the proceeds of the sale of these turkeys therefore, it appears to me, are, as between the liquidator and Golden Vale, and subject to what is said below, held in trust by the liquidator for Golden Vale.

The claim of International Turkeys Ltd

International Turkeys Ltd operates a hatchery for turkeys and specialises in the breeding and hatching of turkeys. Shortly before Christmas 1983, there was an outbreak of turkey disease in Monaghan. This led to widespread alarm among people engaged in the business of rearing turkeys. As a result there was a dramatic decline in the demand for young turkeys and International Turkeys Ltd found itself with surplus breeding stock on its hands. International Turkeys Ltd does not have facilities for slaughtering turkeys or for keeping dead turkeys in cold store. It accordingly approached Castlemahon and entered into an agreement under which Castlemahon was to slaughter turkeys for International Turkeys Ltd and keep them in cold storage until International Ltd was in a position to dispose of them. As a result, International Turkeys Ltd delivered 5,460 turkeys to Castlemahon Ltd. Castlemahon slaughtered these turkeys and the supply yielded 5,400 turkeys fit for keeping in cold storage. I am satisfied beyond any doubt that this was a totally genuine transaction and that the 5,400 turkeys remained the property of International Turkeys Ltd. International Turkeys Ltd had not got its own turkey bags so that the turkeys, when slaughtered, were placed in Castlemahon turkey bags. But according to Mr Rigney the principal person in International Turkeys Ltd, the pallets on which the turkeys were stored in Castlemahon's cold store carried labels marked "ITL/Rigney".

On 14 March 1984 International Turkeys Ltd withdrew 2,295 of its turkeys, leaving a balance in Castlemahon of some 3,165 turkeys.

On 13 April 1984, Mr O'Dwyer, the general manager of Castlemahon, wrote to Mr Rigney offering to buy 1,570 of the turkeys still held in store.

On 20 April 1984, Mr Rigney wrote to Mr O'Dwyer refusing this offer. But meanwhile it would appear that Mr O'Dwyer, in anticipation of Mr Rigney's consent, had in fact appropriated and sold the 1,570 turkeys. International Turkeys Ltd were never paid for these 1,570 turkeys. Castlemahon's action in selling the turkeys was clearly a breach of trust on its part and International Turkeys Ltd would be entitled to trace the proceeds if they can be traced. The only evidence on this point is that of Mr O'Carroll who, under cross-examination by Mr Butler on behalf of International Turkeys Ltd, said that the proceeds of the sale of these 1,570 turkeys went into the general funds of Castlemahon Ltd and were "used to buy more turkeys".

After this sale Castlemahon should have been holding 1,535 turkeys for International Turkeys Ltd. On 29 May 1984, Mr Rigney visited Castlemahon's premises and saw turkeys stored on pallets and marked "ITL/Rigney". On 5 September 1984, employees of Golden Vale entered the store and labelled all the turkeys "property of Golden Vale Co-op".

As a result it is no longer possible to identify which of the turkeys in the store belong to International Turkeys Ltd as, when the provisional liquidator took possession of them, all the turkeys were in Castlemahon bags and labelled "property of Golden Vale Co-op".

Meanwhile, International Turkeys Ltd had apparently told their bank that they owned a substantial stock of turkeys which they had in cold storage with Castlemahon.

On 3 July 1984, they obtained from Mr G.A. Lewis, the financial controller of Castlemahon, a telex in the following form:

> "We hereby confirm that we are holding on behalf of International Turkeys as at 2 July 1984, 3,058 oven ready turkeys weight 42,135 pounds and we note that Ulster Bank has an interest in this stock."

This was confirmed by a further telex on 1 August 1984 in the following terms:

> "We hereby confirm we are holding on behalf of International Turkeys as at 1 August 1984, 3,058 turkeys weight 42,135 pounds and we note that Ulster Bank has interest in this stock."

It is difficult to make out where the figure of 3,058 turkeys comes from. If one excludes the 1,570 turkeys which Castlemahon wrongly sold the figure should be 1,535. If one includes them the figure should be 3,015. It is possible, however, that the figure of 3,058 turkeys includes the 1,535 turkeys, the property of International Turkeys Ltd, which still remained in the store and that the balance consisted of replacement turkeys bought in to replace the 1,570 turkeys which Castlemahon had wrongly sold.

The matter is further complicated by the fact that Mr Rigney visited the store, after the appointment of the provisional liquidator, and laid claim to a specific stock of turkeys which numbered 3,564 birds.

Mr John Cooke, on behalf of the liquidator, has submitted that the parties were not interested in specific birds but were merely concerned with poundages of turkey meat. There may have been some truth in this so far as stock control was concerned. I am also sure that Mr Rigney would not have been unduly worried if he got back a poundage of turkey meat equivalent to the poundage which he had originally deposited. Nevertheless, the size of the individual birds was of some significance as birds suited to one market might not be suited to another. Also, I am quite satisfied that the arrangement Mr Rigney had was that his company's birds were to be kept separate and labelled separately.

The inevitable conclusion is that on 1 August 1984, Castlemahon sold to Golden Vale turkeys which were the property of International Turkeys Ltd. Turkeys sold included 1,535 turkeys which could have been identified on 1 August 1984. Castlemahon had no title to sell these turkeys and they remained the property of International Turkeys Ltd. The fact that they can no longer be identified results from the wrongful act of Castlemahon in purporting to sell the turkeys and of Golden Vale in re-labelling the stock.

So far as the proceeds of the 1,570 turkeys wrongfully sold by Castlemahon is concerned, the position is more difficult. The only evidence we have of what became of the proceeds of this sale is that they were used to buy further turkeys. Moreover, right up until 1 August 1984, Castlemahon was representing to Mr Rigney and his bank that they held on his behalf a number of turkeys approximating to the 3,105 turkeys which they ought to have been holding on his behalf. Therefore it appears to me to be proper to assume, as against Castlemahon, that on 1 August 1984, they held in trust for International Turkeys Ltd a poundage of turkey meat equivalent to the poundage of these 3,105 turkeys, and that they had no title to sell this meat to Golden Vale. For the same reason it appears to me reasonable to assume that the turkeys sold by Golden Vale and Castlemahon between 1 August 1984 and 5 September 1984, being the date on which the provisional liquidator was appointed, came from stocks that they were entitled to sell, not from stocks which were the property of International Turkeys Ltd. It follows that International Turkeys Ltd are entitled, as against Golden Vale, and the liquidator to such portion of the fund now in the hands of the liquidator as represents a poundage in turkey meat equivalent to these 3,105 turkeys.

My answers to the questions of the liquidator in his letter dated 22 January 1985 would therefore be as follows:

1. Was International Turkeys Ltd entitled to ownership of any (and if so how many) turkeys located in the cold store of the company on 5 September 1984?

Answer: International Turkeys Ltd was entitled to a quantity of turkeys equivalent in weight to the 3,105 turkeys above referred to.

2. Were any (and if so, how many) turkeys owned by International Turkeys Ltd capable of identification as such on the premises of the company on 5 September 1984?

Answer: No specific turkeys were capable of identification as being the turkeys of International Turkeys Ltd.

3. Is International Turkeys Ltd an unsecured creditor of the company in the amount of the value of those turkeys which were owned by it and in the possession of the company prior to 5 September 1984 and which had not been delivered by the company to International Turkeys Ltd?

Answer: No. International Turkeys Ltd are entitled to a portion of the proceeds of the sale of the turkeys which were in the store on 5 September 1984, equivalent to the quantity of turkeys or turkey meat being held in trust for them on that date.

4. Was a purported sale by the company on 1 August 1984 of its stock of turkeys to the value of £170,067.20 a valid and effective transaction?

Answer: The transaction was a valid one but, as regards a proportion of the turkeys was subject to a trust in favour of International Turkeys Ltd.

5. Was the said sale on 1 August 1984 effective to transfer ownership of the said stock to Golden Vale Ltd?

Answer: Yes, subject as in 4 above.

6. Were those turkeys labelled by representatives of Golden Vale Ltd on the premises of the company on 5 September 1984, the property of Golden Vale?

Answer: Yes, subject to the answer to question 4 above.

7. Is Golden Vale an unsecured creditor of the company in the amount of the value of those turkeys labelled by its representatives on the premises of the company on 5 September 1984?

Answer: Golden Vale is entitled to the proceeds representing the said turkeys subject to the prior claim of International Turkeys Ltd.

Patricia McLaughlin
Barrister

In the Matter of Merchant Banking Ltd (In Liquidation) and In the Matter of the Companies Acts 1963-1983: High Court 1982 No. 5555p (Costello J) 29 April 1985

Company Law – Official Liquidator – Remuneration – Inquiry – Whether amount claimed for written report into alleged breaches of criminal law by directors properly allowable – Whether already covered by amount claimed in respect of "miscellaneous work" – Whether amounts claimed for collection of rents and sale of freehold excessive – Companies Act 1963 (No. 33), sections 228, 299 – Rules of the Superior Courts 1962 (SI No. 72) Order 74 r.47

Facts: Merchant Banking Ltd ("the company") was ordered to be wound up on 24 May 1982 and an official liquidator was appointed. Having made five interim applications for fees, the liquidator made application to court to determine finally the remuneration properly payable from the date of his appointment to 12 October 1984, pursuant to section 228 of the Companies Act 1963 and Order 74 r. 47 of the Rules of the Superior Courts. On 3 December 1984, Costello J made an order under r. 47 that the examiner inquire into the claim and report to the court. The Revenue, as principal preferential creditors, attended at the inquiry.

The total sum allowed by the court to date was £331,362.25. This included a sum of £46,460 (plus VAT) in respect of preparing a report submitted to the court under section 299(1) of the Companies Act 1963, relating to a possible reference by the court to the D.P.P. in respect of allegations of criminal wrongdoing by directors and officials. There was also a claim for £53,035.50 in respect of "miscellaneous work", which the inquiry established involved considering transactions between the company and other companies in the group, consideration of fictitious deposits and the examination of possible claims against the company's auditors.

In addition 36.3% of the total claim related to work in relation to the collection of rents (which produced £104,035) and work relating to the sale of freehold (which produced £102,851). The sum of £41,255 was claimed in respect of the collection of amounts due for loans by the company which only realised £41,169.

Held by Costello J in deducting from the fee payment approved to date (£331,362.25) the sum of £46,460 plus VAT and in adding the sum of £500 plus VAT:

(1) Section 299 of the Companies Act 1963 does not require an official liquidator to prepare a "report" for the court. Subsection (2) requires a liquidator in a voluntary liquidation to report a possible criminal offence by a director or officer to the D.P.P. Subsection (1) requires the court in a compulsory liquidation to refer a possible breach of the criminal law to the D.P.P. However, an official liquidator does have a duty to draw the court's attention to relevant matters.

(2) The facts which were contained in the "report" appeared to have been largely obtained during the currency of the "miscellaneous work".

(3) The duty to report possible breaches of the criminal law to the court did not require the elaborate document produced in this case. A simple statement of the facts with copies of supporting documents would have sufficed.

(4) The court would therefore allow the full fee of £53,035.50 in respect of miscellaneous work. The court would disallow the sum of £46,460 plus VAT claimed in respect of the "report" but would allow in its place a fee of £500 plus VAT being an estimated cost of preparing a statement of facts.

(5) Although noting that some parts of the claim appeared excessive if measured against the value of assets realised, the court would allow the various fees claimed in respect of the collection of rents, sale of freehold and collection of loans by the company.

(6) Claims for higher level of fees than that allowed at the interim application, had previously been disallowed and there was nothing to show that such disallowance had been improper.

(7) The Revenue were entitled to their costs of the motion and their attendance at the inquiry out of the assets of the liquidation. The liquidator was not entitled to his legal costs arising from the inquiry out of the assets, as these were incurred in his own interests and not those of the liquidation.

Per Curiam: Given the special circumstances of the case, it should not be taken as a precedent either for the level of rates to be charged or for the means of ascertaining the appropriate amount of remuneration payable. There was a need to establish a more satisfactory way of fixing the remuneration of official liquidators.

No cases referred to in judgment

Counsel's names not available

Solicitors for the official liquidator: *McCann Fitzgerald Sutton Dudley*
Solicitors for the notice party: *The Revenue Solicitor*

COSTELLO J **29 April 1985**

The winding-up order in this matter was made on 24 May 1982 (nearly three years ago) and an official liquidator was appointed. He has applied on five separate occasions for payment on account of his remuneration, and an application has now been made to determine finally the remuneration properly payable from the date of his appointment to 12 October 1984, under section 228 of the 1963 Act and Order 74 r. 47 of the Rules. On 3 December 1984 I made an order under r. 47 that the examiner inquire into the claim and report to the court.

The inquiry was held by the assistant examiner and his helpful report (clarified by a later amendment) is dated 20 February 1985. The Revenue are the principal preferential creditors and they were asked by the court to attend at the inquiry and they did so.

The total amount allowed on account by the court to date in respect of remuneration was £266,782.94 which together with £6,297.58 expenses and £58,281.83 for Value-Added Tax makes a total allowance to date of £331,362.25. The basis of the claim for remuneration and its composition was the subject of the inquiry, and the results obtained have helped me in the exercise of my duties under the section.

In directing the appropriate amount for remuneration the first matter which calls for comment is that the inquiry has disclosed that included in the claims made by the official liquidator is a sum of £46,460 (plus VAT) which is said he should be paid for preparing what is termed a "report" for the court. The official liquidator has called this a "Report submitted to the court under section 299(1) of the Companies Act 1963". It related to a possible reference by the court to the Director of Public Prosecutions of allegations of criminal wrongdoing by directors and officials. It is said that this "Report" was commenced in October 1982 and was completed in late March 1984, and that the general responsibility for its compilation was given to a Mr Sheil. The report (which I have read) deals with a number of formal breaches of the Companies Act which were found to have occurred, but in the main relates to the behaviour of directors and officials in the conduct of the company's business. A liquidator is entitled to remuneration for work done from which facts suggestioning delinquency are ascertained but I note that in addition to the claim for £46,460 there is a further claim for £53,035.50 for what is termed "miscellaneous work" which the liquidator and his staff carried out. The inquiry has established that this work involved considering transactions between the company and other companies in the Gallagher Group, consideration of what are said to be fictitious deposits and the examination of possible claims against the company's auditors. The examiner's report states that 40 per cent of this item of fees is attributable to charges in respect of Mr Sheil's work and that he had responsibility for the management of the liquidation on a day-to-day basis.

It may well be that the claim for £46,460 for preparing this "Report" may have been based on a misunderstanding of section 299 of the Act. The section does not call upon the liquidator to prepare a "report" for the court. Subsection (2) requires a liquidator in a *voluntary liquidation* to "report the matter" to the Director of Public Prosecutions when it appears that a director or officer may have been guilty of a criminal offence. But subsection (1) requires the court in a compulsory liquidation in circumstances which it outlines to direct that the matter of a possible breach of the criminal law be referred to the director. The official liquidator has of course a duty to draw the attention of the court to any matters which may come to his attention relevant to the exercise by the court of its section 299 powers.

The liquidator should be remunerated for all the work he was called on to perform to unravel the inter-company transactions which occurred in this case, and the other matters referred to in the "miscellaneous work" section of his claim, and I am prepared to allow him a sum of £53,036.50 as claimed for his work. But I do not think that he is entitled in addition to a further sum of £46,460 for the preparation of a "Report" whose preparation is said to have spread over a period of seventeen months. It seems to me that the facts which are contained in the "Report" must have been largely if not wholly obtained during the currency of the "miscellaneous work". Furthermore, if the facts disclosed the possibility of breaches of the criminal law the duty to the court to which I have referred did not require the extraordinarily elaborate document which was produced in this case; a simple statement of the facts (with copies of supporting documents, if necessary) would have sufficed, any work over and above this being supererogatory. Bearing in mind the overall figure which I propose to allow I consider then that the liquidator would be reasonably remunerated for the fulfilment of his duty to the court by the sum for "miscellaneous work" I have mentioned, plus £500 for the preparation of a statement of facts plus VAT. I will allow this sum in lieu of the claim for £46,460 (plus VAT). There should therefore be deducted from the figure of payments approved to date (£331,362.25) the sum of £46,460 plus the appropriate VAT and there should be added to the balance thus arrived at the sum of £500 plus appropriate VAT. The resulting balance I will call the "revised balance".

In England liquidators' fees have been fixed by reference to a percentage of the value of assets recovered and realised. By using this method as a counter-check other aspects of the present claim would appear at first sight to be excessive.

The report of the assistant examiner has drawn attention to the fact that 36.3% of the total claim for fees related (a) to work in the collection of rents which produced £104,035 and (b) work relating to the sale of freehold which produced £102,851.

But for reasons given by the examiner I propose to allow this part of the claim. I note also that remuneration amounting to £41,255 was claimed in respect of the collection of amounts due for "loans" by the company which produced £41,169 for the liquidation. But again for reasons suggested by the assistant examiner I think the fees charged should be allowed. The figure for the "revised balance" to which I have just referred is based on payments of fees provisionally approved by the court in the five interim applications, and not on the basis of the claims made by the liquidator on those applications. A claim for fees charged at a rate higher than ordinary rates has been previously disallowed and it has not been shown on this present application that such disallowance was improper.

In view of the attitude adopted by the Revenue at the inquiry and taking into account what has been ascertained during the inquiry I will allow as remuneration to the liquidator from 24 May 1982 to 12 October 1984 the "revised balance". This should be certified by the examiner. He should further certify that the liquidator has refunded the appropriate balance of fees paid on account, and when this certificate is given the liquidator will be discharged from the undertakings given by him on the interim applications.

The Revenue was represented at the inquiry at the direction of the court and their costs and expenses of doing so should be allowed out of the assets as well as the costs on this motion. But I do not think it would be reasonable to allow out of the assets legal charges incurred by the liquidator in relation to the inquiry as these were incurred in his own interests and not those of the liquidation.

For similar reasons I do not think that he is entitled to remuneration for attending on his claim for remuneration. In the ordinary way he is entitled to the costs of the motion I am considering.

I am not aware whether the liquidator's statement as required by section 306 and Rule 131 (required where a liquidation has not concluded within two years) has been filed. I will direct that a statement be filed every six months and that a copy of it should accompany any future application for interim payments.

This case illustrates the need to establish more satisfactory ways of fixing the remuneration of official liquidators. As there are special circumstances in this case it is not to be taken as a precedent either for the level of rates to be charged or for the means of ascertaining the appropriate amount of remuneration payable.

Alistair Rutherdale
Barrister

[*Reporters Note:* Section 299 of the Companies Act 1963 has since been amended by section 143 of the Companies Act 1990 (No. 33)]

In the Matter of Irish Commercial Society Ltd (in Liquidation), Irish Commercial Society Group Ltd (in Liquidation), Irish Savings Building Society Ltd (in Liquidation) and Irish Commercial Finance Ltd (in Liquidation) and in the Matter of the Industrial and Provident Societies Acts 1893-78 and in the Matter of the Building Societies Acts 1976-83 and in the Matter of the Companies Acts 1963-83 (No. 1): High Court 1984 Nos. 1149p 1085p 1148p and 1086p (O'Hanlon J) 10 September 1986

Company Law – Liquidation – Action against other companies seeking aggregation of assets and liabilities – Settlement proposal – Application for approval – Objection – Whether assets of defendants correctly calculated – Whether costs of further litigation would dissipate assets – Whether proper that proposal would prevent possibility of action against one defendant in personal capacity

Facts: The liquidator of the four companies commenced High Court proceedings, with the leave of the court, in March 1984 against Peter Plunkett and five limited liability companies. In the action he sought an order aggregating the assets and liabilities of the second to sixth defendants, with those of the plaintiffs. As against the first defendant, an order was sought restraining him from dealing with certain properties, or any other property held in trust for the plaintiffs, and an order declaring him personally liable for any excess of loans and deposits received by the fourth plaintiff, in breach of the provisions of the Building Societies Act 1976 as amended.

Written terms of settlement were agreed, subject to the approval of the High Court. Under the agreement, the defendants were to pay £320,000 to the liquidator of the plaintiffs, together with a further sum amounting to 75 per cent of the net assets of the defendants as exceeded £600,000, together with a further sum of £5,000 costs in respect of a Supreme Court appeal. The agreement specified that the term "net assets" did not include assets owned by the first defendant personally and not held by him in trust for the defendants. The proposed settlement was stated to be in full and final settlement of all claims of whatever nature which the plaintiffs might have against the defendants. The liquidator calculated the additional payment as £7,182 based on net assets of £609,576.

The liquidator sought the court's approval of the scheme. It was submitted on his behalf that if the action were allowed to proceed, the greater proportion of the monies available would be swallowed up in costs.

The Registrar of Friendly Societies objected to the proposed settlement on behalf of the depositors in the first company (an industrial and provident society) and the third company (a building society). He submitted (a) that the net assets of the defendants should yield a substantially higher figure, (b) that he did not accept that the costs of litigation would dissipate the assets to the extent alleged, c) that he was opposed to the clause in the agreement which effectively prevented proceedings against the first defendant in his personal capacity.

Held by O'Hanlon J in refusing to approve the settlement proposed:

(1) Having regard to the detailed examination carried out by the liquidator, it seemed unlikely that the net assets of the defendant companies would ultimately produce a much higher figure.

(2) The liquidator's estimate of the likely costs involved in litigation seemed the more realistic and might even be conservative.

(3) The report of the inspector appointed by the Registrar suggested substantial grounds existed for bringing separate proceedings against the first defendant in his personal capacity, in respect of the manner in which the funds and other assets of the plaintiffs were dealt with prior to liquidation. As there were *prima facie* grounds for such a claim, the clause releasing the first defendant from further liability, meant the court should not approve the settlement.

No cases referred to in judgment

Counsel's names not available

Solicitors for the Liquidator: *Gerrard, Scallan & O'Brien*
Solicitors for the Registrar of Friendly Societies: *Liam Lysaght & Co.*

O'HANLON J **10 September 1986**

The official liquidator of the above-named companies and societies has applied to the court to approve the terms of a settlement entered into him with certain of the defendants in High Court proceedings which were commenced by the official liquidator with the leave of the court, for the benefit of the above-named liquidations. He further seeks an order permitting him to take all necessary streps to carry into effect the terms of the said agreement.

The High Court proceedings in question were brought in the name of the four above-named companies and societies against six defendants, the first-named defendant being Mr Peter Plunkett, and the remaining five defendants being companies with limited liability. The action was commenced by plenary summons on 15 March 1984, (Record No. 1984 No. 2277P), and an order was sought for the aggregation of the assets and liabilities of the defendants, other than the first-named defendant, with those of the plaintiffs. The relief sought against the first-named defendant was,

> (1) an injunction restraining him from dealing in any way with certain properties set forth in a schedule to the general indorsement of claim, and any other properties held by him in trust for the plaintiffs or the other defendants in the proceedings, and
> (2) an order declaring him personally liable for any excess of loans and deposits received by the fourth-named plaintiff in breach of the provisions of the Building Societies Act 1976, as amended.

The proposed terms of settlement of the action are to be found in a written agreement dated 30 October 1985, under which a sum of £320,000 was to be paid by the defendants to the official liquidator, together with a further sum amounting to 75 per cent of the value of such of the net assets of the defendants as should exceed £600,000. The defendants also agreed to pay a sum of £5,000 for costs of an appeal to the Supreme Court which were ordered to be paid by the defendants. The agreement specified the manner in which the value of the net assets of the defendants was to be ascertained, and provided that the term "net assets" was not to be taken as including assets owned by the first-named defendant personally and not held by him in trust for the other defendants. The settlement was made subject to the approval of the High Court and the official liquidator agreed to recommend approval of the terms of the agreement to the court.

An important provision is contained in Clause Q of the agreement which reads as follows:

> "Q In consideration of the payment of the settlement money and the agreed costs (as defined and referred to at paragraph T below) to the plaintiffs by the defendants, the plaintiffs confirm that the settlement money is hereby accepted in full and final settlement of all claims of any nature whatsoever (including claims of any nature whatsoever not specifically referred to in the proceedings) which the plaintiffs may have against the defendants and each of them PROVIDED ALWAYS that any matters which lie outside the discretion of the official liquidator the plaintiffs and the defendants and each of them are not included in the terms of this agreement."

The liquidator in the affidavit sworn by him for the purpose of the present application on 16 April 1986, gives the further information that the net assets of the defendant companies, calculated in the manner prescribed by the agreement come to a sum of approximately £609,576, so that the sum of £7,182 would be added to the minimum settlement figure of £320,000 referred to in the agreement. He is apprehensive that if the action were allowed proceed to a hearing, the greater part of the monies available would be swallowed up in costs and expenses, and that even total success would amount to no more than a pyrrhic victory yielding a much smaller that the amount now offered by way settlement.

The Registrar of Friendly Societies and Registrar of Building Societies asks the court not to approve the settlement and in doing so his particular concern is on behalf of the depositors in Irish Commercial Society Ltd, an industrial and provident society, and Irish Savings Building Society, a building society, in respect of which societies he has certain supervisory responsibilities under the Industrial and Provident Societies Acts and the Building Societies Acts. In two affidavits sworn by him for the purpose of resisting the liquidator's application he makes it clear that:

(a) he is not satisfied that the net assets of the defendant companies should only yield the amount referred to by the liquidator and he contends that they should yield a substantially higher figure;
(b) he does accept that the costs of litigating the claim to the full against the defendants would dissipate the assets to the extent envisaged by the liquidator, and
(c) he is very much opposed to the clause in the agreement which would effectively put paid to proceedings against the first-named defendant in his personal capacity.

I am indebted to both the liquidator and the registrar for the meticulous care with which the relevant documentary evidence has been put before the court to enable it to consider whether the settlement should be approved or not. I should also pay a particular tribute to the work of Mr Breffni J Byrne, FCA, of Messrs Arthur Andersen and Co., chartered accountants, who was appointed as inspector in the year 1984 by the then Registrar of Friendly Societies to investigate and report to him on the affairs of Irish Commercial Society Ltd. His very comprehensive and clear report in which he examined in considerable depth the workings of the various companies has been of considerable assistance to me in ascertaining the background to the present proceedings.

Having regard to the detailed examination carried out by the liquidator of the present status of the defendant companies it seems unlikely to me that their net assets would ultimately produce a very much higher figure than that referred to in the liquidator's affidavit. With regard to the costs of the proceedings if the action were allowed to proceed to a conclusion, I think the liquidator's estimate of the possible length of the court hearing is more realistic than that of the registrar and my experience would lead me to believe that even the liquidator's estimate may be too conservative. With regard, however, to the question of the release contained in the agreement, of the first-named defendant from further liability, I share the view taken by the registrar that the benefits of the agreement are being purchased at too dear a price. The report of the inspector appointed by the registrar suggests to me that substantial grounds exist for bringing separate proceedings against the first-named defendant in his personal capacity in respect of the manner in which the funds and other assets of the plaintiffs were dealt with prior to liquidation. It is not possible to forecast the outcome of such litigation, nor would it be proper for me to do so. Suffice to say that, in my opinion, the material before me discloses *prima facie* grounds for a claim of such a substantial nature that I am unwilling to approve the settlement which has been entered into by the liquidator.

Alistair Rutherdale
Barrister

In the Matter of Lynch, Monahan and O'Brien Ltd (In Liquidation): High Court 1984 No. 2938p (Costello J) 14 October 1986

Company – Charge – Registered land – Land held in name of solicitor in trust for shareholder of company – Shareholder indicates to bank that property owned by company – Debenture – Debenture not registered – Whether valid against liquidator – Transfer of part of lands to company – Whether captured by debenture – Charge on lands – Charge not registered as burden on folio – Whether valid as against liquidator – Companies Act 1963 (No. 33), sections 99 and 218 – Registration of Title Act 1964 (No. 16), sections 62, 90

Facts: In 1973 Paul Ryan assigned the residue of a lease of property known as Eastham House to Edward Rogers, a solicitor. By a declaration of trust executed on the same day it was recited that Mr Fintan O'Brien had provided the purchase money and that the property was held in trust for Mr O'Brien. Mr O'Brien was the principal shareholder in Lynch, Monahan and O'Brien Ltd ("the company").

On 26 June 1975, the company executed a debenture in favour of the bank charging all estate or interest legal or equitable in all freehold or leasehold property which during the continuance of the security might become the property of the company. This was registered as a charge pursuant to section 99 of the Companies Act 1963 on 16 July.

The Eastham House lands were registered in Mr Rogers' name as full owner of folio 2434L on 28 July 1981, and on the same day an inhibition in favour of Mr O'Brien was entered on the folio. The bank's interest was never registered as a burden on the folio.

Part of the lands in folio 2434L were sold prior to 3 November 1981 and the proceeds lodged with the bank in reduction of the company's indebtedness. A further portion was transferred to Mr O'Brien. On 3 November 1981 Mr Rogers as beneficial owner and for the consideration of £1 executed a transfer of a third part of the lands (4.396 hectares) to the company. This transfer was not registered prior to the liquidation. A dispute arose over the level of stamp duty payable, and Mr Rogers remained as the registered owner.

The bank became concerned about the adequacy of security. On 21 January 1982 a deed was executed granting a legal charge over the lands being transferred by Mr Rogers to the company. This incorrectly suggested that the company was the registered owner. This charge was registered as a charge pursuant to section 99 of the Companies Act 1963 on 11 February 1982, but was never registered as a burden on the folio as the dispute over stamp duty had not been resolved.

By notice of motion the bank sought the court's directions as to (i) Whether the portion of folio 2434L, Co. Meath, the subject of the transfer from Rogers to the company on 3 November 1981, was subject to the debenture made on 26 June 1975, (ii) Whether the debenture of 26 June 1975 was valid against the liquidator, even though not registered until after the winding up, (iii) Whether the deed of 21 January 1982 between the company and the Bank of Ireland was valid as against the liquidator even though not registered in the Land Registry until after the date of the winding up.

The bank submitted that the agreement by Mr Rogers as registered owner to sell the land to the company and the payment of the £1 consideration, created an equitable estate in the lands in the bank which was captured by the debenture, and that this equitable estate was unaffected by the order to wind up the company. They also argued that the 1981 agreement to grant a charge created an equitable interest, which was also captured by the debenture, or in the alternative, that on payment of the correct stamp duty, the company could be registered as owner, and the bank's charge could then be registered as a burden, notwithstanding the order to wind up.

Held by Costello J in answering the questions raised in the affirmative:

(1) As in the case of unregistered land, where there is a contract for sale of registered land and purchase money paid, the ownership of the estate is in equity transferred by that contract. *In re Strong* [1940] IR 382 followed.

(2) Consequently when in 1981 Mr Rogers contracted to sell the lands in folio 2434L to the company and the £1 was paid, an equitable interest was created in the lands in favour of the company, which became subject to a charge in favour of the bank pursuant to the debenture of 26 June 1975.

(3) Even thought it had gone into liquidation, the company continued to enjoy an equitable interest in the land, which was subject to the bank's charge. The liquidator, if he registered the company as owner and sold the lands, would be under a duty to obtain the best price for the lands and to hold the proceeds in trust to discharge the bank's liability under the debenture.

(4) In relation to the registration of the bank's charge as a burden on the folio, it did not appear that this would be a "disposition of the property of the company" after the commencement of a winding up within section 218 of the Companies Act 1963. In any case the court had a discretion to permit such a disposition. Here the liquidator only had an encumbered interest to sell, and the other creditors had no rights which would be infringed by the registration of the debenture. *In re Wiltshire Iron Company* (1868) 3 Ch App 443, discussed.

(5) In relation to the charge of 21 January 1982, section 90 of the Act of 1964 permitted an owner of land, who desired to charge the land before he was registered as owner, to do so in the same manner as if he were registered owner at the time of the execution of the charge.

(6) The 1981 agreement and the 1982 charge did not confer any estate in the lands to the bank which could be made subject to the charge in the debenture of 26 June 1975. However the bank obtained an equity in the lands which would have entitled the court to make an order for specific performance in its favour. In addition because the company had executed a deed of charge, it had a statutory right to have that charge registered. The court therefore should permit the bank to register its charge, as this did not deprive the creditors of any rights under the Companies Acts, because the assets which they were entitled to have sold were so encumbered.

Cases referred to in judgment

Allied Irish Banks Ltd v. Glynn [1973] IR 188
Northern Ireland Banking Co. v. Devlin [1924] 1 IR 90; (1924) 58 ILTR 118
In re Strong [1940] IR 382; (1940) 74 ILTR 177
In re Wiltshire Iron Company (1863) 3 Ch App 443

Counsel's names not available

Solicitors for the liquidator: *McCann Fitzgerald, Sutton and Dudley*
Solicitors for Bank of Ireland: *Mary Gleeson*

COSTELLO J **14 October 1986**

The facts

By an assignment of 31 July 1973 Paul Ryan assigned to one Edward Rogers the residue of a term 999 years created by a lease of 25 April 1956. Mr Rogers was a solicitor in the firm of Rogers and Byron practising in the town of Navan and the property assigned was known as Eastham House and contained about 22 acres. By a declaration of trust executed on the same day it was recited that a Mr Fintan O'Brien had provided the purchase money for the property and Mr Rogers declared that he held the property in trust for Mr O'Brien. Mr O'Brien was the principal shareholder in Lynch, Monahan and O'Brien Ltd, the company which is now in liquidation.

In a letter of 4 July 1975, Mr Rogers wrote to the Bank of Ireland (to which the company was then indebted) stating that he had received instructions from

Lynch Monahan and O'Brien Ltd to lodge with the bank the title deeds of "their property at Eastham House, consisting of two portions of land, one of which contains 7.889 acres and the other 1.289 acres". The letter stated that these properties together with the house and surrounding land had been "bought some time ago and are presently held in trust by our Mr Rogers". It was pointed out that the lands had not yet been registered but that when the land certificate was obtained it would be lodged with the bank. In an affidavit filed in these proceedings on behalf of the bank it is accepted that the company had in fact, at that time, no interest in the land, the legal interest being vested in Mr Rogers and the equitable in Mr O'Brien, and not his company. This seems to be so and no evidence to suggest otherwise has been filed. The bank therefore makes no claim in these proceedings arising from Mr Rogers' undertaking.

Previously, on 26 June 1975 the company's directors had met and resolved to execute a debenture in favour of the bank. This was in fact executed by the company on the same day (but not, apparently, by the bank) and registered as a charge pursuant to section 99 of the Companies Act 1963 on 16 July 1975. The debenture was in the usual form and under its terms the company charged as a specific charge all estate or interest legal or equitable in all freehold or leasehold property which during the continuance of the security might become the property of the company.

Registration of the lands at Eastham House had not been effected when the debenture was executed and indeed first registration did not take place until 28 July 1981 when Mr Rogers was registered as full owner in Folio 2434L of the Register of Leasehold Interests for the County of Meath. On the same day an inhibition in favour of Mr O'Brien was entered on the folio. The bank's debenture was not then nor at any time prior to the liquidation of the company (which occurred on 7 May 1984) registered as a burden on the Folio, nor was a caution entered in respect of its interest in the lands.

Part of the lands comprised in Folio 2434L was sold prior to 3 November 1981 and the proceeds lodged with the bank in reduction of the company's indebtedness. On 17 November 1981, another part of the lands was transferred to Mr O'Brien and a new Folio (Folio No. 2595L) opened in respect of them.

On 3 November 1981, Mr Rogers as beneficial owner and for the consideration of £1 executed a transfer of a third part of the lands (comprising 4.396 hectares) to Lynch Monahan and O'Brien Ltd. This transfer was not registered prior to the liquidation of the company and this has given rise to the problems leading to these proceedings. It was lodged with the Revenue Commissioners by Messrs Rogers and Byron on behalf of the company for assessment and adjudication for stamp duty and they submitted that the transfer should be stamped on a nominal basis only because, it was claimed, the lands had prior to the transfer been held in trust by Mr O'Brien for the company. A dispute on this point arose (the stamp duty office claiming that it should be stamped at market value). This dispute remained unresolved ever since, and Mr Rogers remains to this day the registered owner of the land.

In 1981 the bank, its evidence discloses, had become concerned about the adequacy of the security it held for the money owed to it by the company and it had been instrumental in having the transfer of 3 November executed by Mr Rogers in favour of the company. In addition it sought to obtain as an extra security, a legal charge over the lands which were being transferred by Mr Rogers to the company. This charge was executed by the company on 31 January 1982. This deed recited (incorrectly, for the company was not yet registered) that the chargeant (i.e., the company) was the registered owner of the lands described in the schedule, and "being the registered owner" the company charged the lands in the schedule with payment of monies due by it to the bank and assented to the registration of the charge as a burden on the lands. The lands were described in the schedule as:

> "All that the subject matter of Land Registry Transfer dated 3 November 1981, wherein Edward Rogers transferred that part of the property described in Folio 2434L of the Register, County Meath, specified in the schedule thereto to Lynch, Monahan and O'Brien Ltd."

This charge was registered under section 99 of the Companies Act 1963 on 11 February 1982. But it was never registered as a burden on the folio, as the dispute on the stamping of the transfer of 3 November 1981 had not been resolved when the company went into liquidation.

From these facts two different points arise for consideration. The first relates to the debenture of 26 June 1975. It is urged on behalf of the bank that the agreement by the registered owner of the land, Mr Rogers, to sell the land to the company and the payment of the consideration for the transfer (albeit, a nominal one of £1) created an equitable estate in the lands in the bank which is captured by the debenture and this equitable estate is unaffected by the order to wind-up the company. Secondly, it is urged that the 1981 agreement to grant a charge created an equitable interest which is captured by the debenture. Alternatively, it is claimed that on payment of the correct amount of stamp duty, the company can now be registered as owner of the lands and the bank's charge of 21 January 1982 over them can then be registered by it as a burden, notwithstanding the order that the company be wound up.

The Debenture of 26 June 1975

The principle on which the bank relies is well established as regards non-registered lands. When the owner of an estate contracts with a purchaser for the immediate sale of it the ownership of the estate is in equity transferred by that contract. When the purchaser has paid his purchase money though he has got no conveyance the vendor becomes a trustee for him of the legal estate and he is in equity considered the owner of the estate. The question now for decision is the application of this principle in the case of registered land; a question considered and authoritatively decided by the Supreme Court in *In re Strong* [1940] IR 382. The facts of that case were straightforward. The registered owner of lands in County Meath had sold them by auction. On 8 October 1939 at 11.30

a.m., the purchase money having been paid, the registered owner executed a transfer of the lands in fee simple.

Later that day the purchaser was registered as owner. But on the same day and before her title was registered a judgment mortgage was entered on the register. The purchaser applied to the Registrar of Titles to cancel the judgment mortgage. The Registrar did so. The judgment mortgagee appealed to the High Court. The High Court found in his favour. The purchaser appealed to the Supreme Court. By a three-to-two majority the Supreme Court reversed the High Court decision and held that the purchaser was entitled to have the judgment mortgage cancelled.

The judgment of the majority was delivered by O'Byrne J. His conclusions depended in the main on a construction of section 44 of the 1891 Act (now section 68 of the 1964 Act). This section, having enacted that the registered owner alone was entitled to transfer or charge registered land, went on to provide that nothing in the Act was to prevent a person from creating any right in or over registered land, but such rights would not affect a registered transfer of the land for value unless the right was registered as a burden or was one of the burdens to which though not registered all registered land was subject. The judgment pointed out that this section recognises that "rights" including estates, interests, equities and powers can be created in registered land which do not appear on the register, and that the interest of a person who has entered into a contract for the purchase of registered land and has paid the purchase price is a "right" within the meaning of the section. It concluded that the judgment mortgagee could not be regarded as a transferee for the value of the land and so could not obtain the protection which the section conferred on such transferees. It considered the effect of section 35(2) of the 1891 Act (now section 53(2) of the 1964 Act) which provided that until a transferee is registered as owner of the land the instrument of transfer confers no estate in the lands on the transferee and rejected an argument based on this subsection by pointing out that subsection 44 (2) had provided that unregistered rights could be created in registered land and that the purchaser in the case was relying not on the transfer which had been executed (but not registered before the registration of the judgment mortgage) but on the equitable interest created by the contract of purchase coupled with the payment of the purchase price. Rule 117 of the Rules then in force allowed a judgment mortgage to be removed from the register if it could be shown that "the judgment debtor had no estate or interest capable of being affected by the registration of the Affidavit". The effect of the majority judgment was to decide that the vendor in that case had no estate or interest capable of being affected by the judgment mortgage after the contract for sale had been entered into and the purchase price paid, and to reject the contrary view, advanced in the minority judgment delivered by Murnaghan J, that section 44(2) afforded no protection for whatever right the purchaser had obtained under the contract.

Applying the law as established in *In re Strong* it seems to me to be perfectly clear that when in 1981 the registered owner of the lands, Mr Rogers, contracted with the company to sell to it for £1 the lands in Folio 2434L and was paid the agreed purchase price an equitable estate was created in the lands in favour of the company, and that this is a right which is recognised and protected by section 68(2) of the 1964 Act. This equitable estate immediately became subject to the charge in favour of the bank contained in the debenture of 26 June 1975. The company it seems to me still enjoys an equitable estate in the lands, which is still subject to the bank's charge. And these equitable rights are unaffected by the fact that the company is now in liquidation. Mr Rogers holds the lands in trust for the company, and the company's equitable estate is subject to the charge in favour of the bank. If the liquidator now registers the company as owner (but the bank's debenture is not registered) a purchaser for value without notice of the bank's charge would not be bound by it. But the liquidator would be under a duty to the bank to obtain the best price for the lands and to hold the proceeds in trust to discharge the company's liability under the debenture.

A question also arises as to whether the bank's charge can now be registered as a burden on the folio. Mr Collins on behalf of the liquidator referred to section 218 of the Companies Act 1963 which provides:

> "In the winding-up by the court, any disposition of the property of the company . . . made after the commencement of the winding-up, shall, unless the court otherwise orders, be void."

and suggested that this section would, after the company had been registered as owner, render void the registration by the bank of its debenture as this would amount to a "disposition" within the meaning of the section and the court should not exercise its discretion in the bank's favour and permit such a "disposition" to occur. But I am very doubtful as to whether section 218 applies to the facts of this case. The modern English text books commenting on the corresponding section in 1948 English Companies Act, quote with approval an early authority (*In re Wiltshire Iron Company* (1863) 3 Ch App 443) which decided that a similar section in the 1862 Companies Act only applied to completed transactions and no discretion under the section was given to allow the disposition of a company's property where the transaction had not been completed when the winding-up order was made.

A winding-up order has of course a retrospective effect, and the object of this section is to give the court a discretion to validate transactions *bona fide* entered into in the ordinary course of trade after the presentation of the petition and completed before the date of the winding-up order.

I therefore do not think that the section applies to transfers or dispositions of the company's lands which remain uncompleted at the date of court's order. This does not mean that the transferee is automatically entitled to have the transaction completed; it means that however the court may be seised with the problem (be it in the course of a specific performance action in respect of which liberty to proceed has been given, or pursuant to an appeal from an order of the Registrar of Titles, or, as in the present case, pursuant to an application for directions relating to the parties' rights) and will be required to consider whether the completion of the transaction will infringe the rights which the Act confers on the company's other creditors. If it does, then the transferee will be left to his right to claim damages for breach of contract; if it does not, the transaction can be completed.

Creditors in a winding-up are entitled to have the company's lands sold and the proceeds distributed in accordance with the provisions of the Act. But if the lands have been encumbered by the company prior to the date of winding-up (as has happened in this case) the liquidator has only an encumbered interest to sell. So by permitting the registration as a burden on the folio the charge created by the debenture of 26 June 1975, the court in this case is merely enabling the bank to protect the equitable interest which it already enjoys and subject to which the liquidator holds the lands. In my judgment therefore the creditors have no rights in this winding-up which would be infringed by the registration of the debenture. I propose therefore to answer the first two questions in the notice of motion in the affirmative.

The Charge of 21 January 1982

The evidence establishes that in 1981 Mr Rogers and the company agreed with the bank that the company would be registered as owner of the lands and that it would execute a charge in favour of the bank charging the lands with sums due by it to the bank. Although not so stated, I presume that the consideration for this agreement was the continuance of the bank's overdraft facilities to the company. In pursuance of this agreement a deed of transfer was executed between Mr Rogers and the company and the company executed a charge in favour of the bank on 21 January 1982.

Section 62 of the 1964 Act deals with the creation and effect of registered charges. Subsection (1) provides that the "registered owner of land" may charge the land with the payment of money and that the owner of the charge "shall be registered as such": an instrument of charge in the prescribed form is to be executed, "but until the owner of the charge is registered as such, the instrument shall not confer on the owner of the charge any interest in the land" (subsection 2); on registration the instrument of charge operates as a mortgage by deed within the meaning of the Conveyancing Acts and for the purpose of enforcing the charge the registered owner "shall have all the rights and powers of a mortgagee under a mortgage by deed, including the power to sell the estate or interest which is subject to the charge" (subsection 6).

It will be recalled that when the deed of charge of 21 January 1982 was executed by the company it had not yet been registered as owner of the lands. But section 90 of the Act deals with such a situation. It provides that where a person on whom the right to be registered as owner of registered land has developed by reason of an instrument of transfer made in accordance with the provisions of the Act (as was the position of the company in this case after the execution of the deed of transfer of 3 November 1981) desires to charge the lands before he himself is registered as owner of the land (as the company desires in this case), he may do so "in the like manner and with the same effect as if he were the registered owner at the time of execution of the charge" (subject to certain qualifications which are not relevant for the purposes of this case).

The instruments which the parties executed in this case were therefore executed in accordance with the provisions of the 1964 Act, but until registration they have conferred no estate in the lands on the bank. It becomes necessary, therefore, firstly to consider whether, apart from these instruments the bank obtained from the transactions an equitable interest in the lands and the application of the principles established in *In re Strong* to these transactions. As pointed out in *McAllister* "Registration of Title" (at p. 186) a contract for a charge creates an unregistered right over the land pending registration. But it is necessary to look a little closer at the nature of the right which the bank now enjoys. Counsel has drawn attention to the distinction between an "equity" and "equitable estate". As Kenny J (in *Allied Irish Banks Ltd v. Glynn* [1973] IR 188 at 192) pointed out, "an equity" does not create any estate in the land; it is a right against persons that is enforceable against those who were parties to the transaction which created it. And it has been urged that the 1981 agreement and 1982 unregistered deed of charge has at most given an "equity" to the bank, but conferred on it no estate in the lands. I agree that the bank obtained no estate in the lands. It is well established that the registered owner of a charge created by deed on registered land has no estate in the land (see *Northern Ireland Banking Co. v. Devlin* [1924] 1 IR 90) and I do not think that an agreement to create a charge can create any estate or interest in the lands in the person to whom it is to be granted. This means that this transaction created no equitable estate in the lands in the bank's favour and so the bank obtained no estate which could be made subject to the charge in the debenture of 26 June 1975.

If then the bank has no equitable interest in the lands following these transactions, and if the unregistered deed of charge confers no estate until it is registered, it is necessary to consider whether the bank can now apply to be registered as owner of the charge, notwithstanding the order winding-up the company.

For reasons which I have already given, I do not think that I should consider this problem by reference to the provisions of section 218 of the Companies Act 1963; rather, I should, as in the case of the registration of the charge contained in the debenture, consider whether to do so would be to infringe the rights conferred on the company's other creditors by the 1963 Act.

Let me look at the company's interest in the lands at the date of winding-up; to what rights in the bank's favour were they subject by virtue of the transactions I am considering? Although they created no equitable estate in the lands at the date of winding-up the bank had an equity arising from the agreement to grant the charge which would have entitled the court to make an order for specific performance in its favour. But it had more than this equity; it had, because the company had in fact executed a deed of charge in its favour, a statutory right to have the charge registered.

At the date of winding-up therefore the lands were subject to rights conferred on the bank by statute and what the liquidator has in his hands is an estate in the lands which is encumbered by the bank's statutory rights. If the court permits the bank to register its charge it will not be making an order pursuant to its equitable jurisdiction against the company for the specific performance of a contract to grant a charge; it will be making an order permitting the bank to exercise rights conferred on it prior to the liquidation by the 1964 Act. And it will not be depriving the company's creditors of any rights under the Companies Act because the assets which they are entitled to have sold are encumbered in the way I have described.

I propose, therefore, to answer question 3 in the notice of motion in the affirmative. I will discuss with counsel whether in the light of the conclusions I have reached any further specific questions require to be answered.

Alistair Rutherdale
Barrister

In the Matter of S.H., a Bankrupt: High Court 1987 No. 1964 (Hamilton P) 23 September 1987

Bankruptcy – Petitioning creditor presented petition to have the bankrupt so declared – Bankruptcy proceeded in normal way – Application to have bankruptcy annulled on the grounds that the seal of the petitioning creditor was not properly affixed to the petition – Articles of Association of the petitioning creditor – Whether rules give company powers which it does not have pursuant to its Articles of Association – Whether seal properly affixed – Whether bankrupt estopped from making objections at this stage in the proceedings – Whether proper time to make objections was upon the motion to show cause – Order 76 rule 30(2) Rules of the Superior Courts

Facts: The petitioner was adjudicated a bankrupt on 13 September 1987 as a result of a petition submitted by the petitioning creditor, Clondalkin Concrete Ltd. The seal of the petitioning creditor was affixed to the petition. Order 76 Rule 30(2) of the Rules of the Superior Courts provides that:

> "A creditor's petition by a limited company or body corporate shall be sealed with the seal of the company or body corporate and signed by two directors or by one director and the secretary. Such seal and signature shall in all cases be attested."

Article 37 of the Articles of Association of the petitioning creditor provided that:

> "the seal of the company shall only be affixed . . . in the presence of at

> least two directors and the secretary or acting secretary for the time being, and in pursuance of a resolution of the Board."

The petition was sealed in the presence of two directors but one of the directors was also the company secretary. The bankrupt did not raise this point on the motion to show cause, and he allowed the bankruptcy to proceed in the normal way. He then applied to the court to have the bankruptcy vacated on the grounds that the seal of the petitioning creditor was not properly affixed to the petition.

Held by Hamilton P in refusing the application:

(1) Order 76 Rule 30(2) of the Rules of the Superior Courts does not give a company powers which it does not have pursuant to its own Articles of Association.

(2) The seal was not affixed in accordance with the company's articles as the secretary of the company merely signed the petition in his capacity as secretary and did not presume to act as a director.

(3) Furthermore, from the affidavits, it did not appear that the seal was affixed to the petition in pursuance of a resolution of the board of the petitioning creditor.

(4) However, the bankrupt allowed the bankruptcy to proceed in the normal way and was thereby estopped from raising this point at this stage.

(5) The proper time for making objections as to the adjudication of bankruptcy is on motion to show cause.

No cases referred to in judgment

Counsel's and solicitors' names not available

HAMILTON P **23 September 1987**

The bankrupt in the title hereof was adjudicated a bankrupt on 13 September 1985 as a result of a petition submitted by the petitioning creditor, Clondalkin Concrete Ltd, (hereinafter referred to as the petitioning creditor) on 9 September 1985.

The bankrupt has now applied to this court for an order setting aside the said adjudication on the basis that:—

> (1) It was improper and resulted in documentation containing inaccurate and misleading averments being furnished by the petitioning creditor and/or their lawful agents and;
>
> (2) It was in breach of the Articles of Association of the petitioning creditor as the seal of the company was not affixed to the aforesaid petition in the presence of two directors and the secretary of the petitioning creditor.

This application is grounded on the affidavit of the bankrupt sworn on 15 May 1987, the documents exhibited therein and the affidavit of the bankrupt's solicitor, sworn on 27 May 1987.

Before dealing with the application made on behalf of the bankrupt, it is necessary to outline very briefly the steps which have been taken in the bankruptcy proceedings to date.

The debtors summons herein was issued on 1 May 1985 and was served personally on the bankrupt on Monday, 13 May 1985.

The petition seeking the adjudication of the bankrupt as a bankrupt was presented on 9 September 1985 and accompanied by affidavits for proof of debt and of non-compounding sworn by one N.A., secretary of the petitioning creditor, on 9 September 1985.

The seal of the petitioning creditor was affixed to the said petition.

On 13 September 1985, the bankrupt in the title hereof was adjudged bankrupt.

On 16 September 1985, a duplicate order of adjudication was served on the bankrupt by the court messenger by leaving same with the bankrupt's wife at ..., in the County of ... . A notice of intention to show cause against the adjudication was served by the bankrupt and 25 September 1985 was appointed as the date for the hearing before the court of the cause against adjudication.

This notice was issued on 17 September 1985 by Messrs Nugent & Co., solicitors for the bankrupt.

On 25 September 1985, it was ordered that the matter be referred to the examiner to report the proceedings with a view to the annulment of the bankruptcy.

On 25 November 1985, it was ordered that the motion to show cause against adjudication be dismissed and that the bankruptcy do proceed.

The solicitors for the bankrupt were present at the hearing.

The public sittings were held on 17 February and 3 March 1986.

On 14 February 1986 a notice of change of solicitors was served on the bankrupt, who was then represented by Messrs Gerrard Scallan & O'Brien.

On the application of the bankrupt, an order was made on 18 March 1986 giving the bankrupt liberty to continue in his own name proceedings which had been instituted by him against Kieran Doherty, Ireland and the Attorney General and the court approved the settlement reached in the said proceedings on the basis that the defendants named therein would pay the sum of £25,000 to the bankrupt together with the costs of the said proceedings.

The amount of the settlement and the costs were lodged with the official assignee in bankruptcy to the credit of the bankrupt's estate.

On 29 May 1986, a public sitting in this matter was held before the examiner for the proof and admission of debts and for the vouching of the official assignee's account.

Various affidavits were sworn by the bankrupt and his wife in connection with these matters.

On 13 October 1986, the official assignee was granted liberty to pay to the solicitors who had acted for the bankrupt in the above-mentioned proceedings the sum of £7,506.85 being the cost thereof.

By order made on 1 December 1986, it was ordered, *inter alia*, that a first dividend of 42p in the pound be declared on the sum of £37,221.11 being the amount of the debts due to the creditors proved and admitted. The official assignee was directed to pay the same to the said creditors accordingly after payment of which dividend amounting to £15,632.87 there remained a balance of £2,840.74 to be carried to the next account.

On 6 February 1987, a notice was issued on behalf of the applicant seeking an order in the following terms:—

> "(1) Placing a stay on further seizures or realisation of the bankrupt's assets pending the presentation to the creditors of a composition after bankruptcy or until further order."

This application was adjourned until 23 February 1987, and was grounded on the affidavit of the bankrupt sworn on 9 February 1987.

In his affidavit, he states *inter alia* that:—

> "I say and believe that there is a sum of approximately £5,500 presently to the credit of my estate and that it is my intention to propose a composition after bankruptcy to my creditors of 50p in the pound."

He further avers that:—

> "Whilst I appreciate that there are formalities to be adhered to in any composition, I say and believe that from informal enquiries made by me a number of other creditors would be prepared to accept a compromise of 50p in the pound. My family have instructed Messrs. Eugene F. Collins & Sons, Solicitors of 61 Fitzwilliam Square, Dublin 2 to carry out the necessary procedure."

He further averred that:—

> "I have recently been notified by Messrs. James H. North & Co Ltd., auctioneers of 55 Dame Street, Dublin 2 who are the agents appointed by the official assignee that they will be attending at my home on Monday, 9 February 1987, at 2.30 p.m. for the purpose of removing, storing and ultimately disposing of certain items listed on the court messenger's inventory. . . . I say and believe that in view of the impending composition it would be most unreasonable if further seizure and realisation were to take place and would also be most disruptive to my wife and family who also reside in the home."

On 23 February 1987, an order was made providing that the realisation of the bankrupt's assets be stayed for a period of two weeks from the date of the order and the bankrupt was given liberty to trade for this period and liberty to continue to negotiate with his creditors with a view to making a formal offer of composition.

It is against the foregoing background and the other steps taken in the course of the bankrupt's proceedings which I have not outlined herein that the application now made by the bankrupt must be considered.

An affidavit was sworn by the solicitor for the petitioning creditor on 18 June 1987, in the course of which she deals with certain matters deposed to by the bankrupt in his affidavit sworn on 15 May 1987.

Order 76 Rule 30 (2) of the Rules of the Superior Courts provide that:—

> "A creditor's petition by a limited company or body corporate shall be sealed with the seal of the company or body corporate and signed by two directors or by one director and the secretary. Such seal and signature shall in all cases be attested."

This rule, however, does not give a company powers which it does not have pursuant to its own Articles of Association.

Article 37 of the Articles of Association of the petitioning creditor provides that:—

> "The seal of the company shall only be affixed for any instrument in the presence of at least two directors and the secretary for the time being, and in pursuance of a resolution of the board."

It is submitted on behalf of the bankrupt that the seal of the company was not affixed to the petition upon which the adjudication of bankruptcy was made in accordance with the provisions of the Articles of Association of the petitioning creditor. And consequently, that all proceedings on foot thereof are void.

In her affidavit the petitioning creditor's solicitor states that:—

> "The petition was sealed by Clondalkin Concrete Ltd in the presence of two directors and a secretary, N.A. being both a director and secretary of the said company."

In my view, the seal of the company was not affixed to the petition dated 9 September 1985 in accordance with the requirements of Article 37 of the Articles of Association of the petitioning creditor.

Though Mr Atkinson may be a director of the company he did not presume to so act on the occasion of the fixing of the petition because he merely signed the petition in his capacity as secretary and not as a director.

Neither does it appear from the affidavits before me that the seal of the petitioning creditor was affixed to the petition in pursuance of a resolution of the board of the petitioning creditor.

Neither does it appear that the seal and signatures on the petition were properly attested in accordance with the requirement of Rule 30(2) of Order 76.

However, I am satisfied that it is not open to the bankrupt to rely on this point at this stage to have the adjudication of bankruptcy annulled.

He did not raise this point on the motion to show cause, allowed the bankruptcy to proceed, allowed the realisation of the assets to proceed, allowed the proof of debt sittings to proceed, allowed the interim dividend herein before referred to be paid, negotiated with his creditors for the purpose of making an offer of composition after bankruptcy and generally allowed the bankruptcy to proceed in the ordinary way, and allowed the official assignee to continue to fulfil his statutory functions in this regard from the date of adjudication.

I am satisfied that he is thereby estopped from raising this or any other point with regard to his original adjudication at this stage.

The time for making objections as to the adjudication of bankruptcy is on the motion to show cause and not at this stage of the proceedings.

Consequently, I have no alternative but to dismiss his application.

Patricia McLaughlin
Barrister

In the Matter of G.W.I. Ltd and In the Matter of the Companies Act 1963-1983: High Court 1986 No. 699P (Murphy J) 16 November 1987

Liquidation – Provisional liquidator appointed – Interest of leasehold premises vested in company – Part of demised premises sublet to another company – Petition presented for winding up of company and provisional liquidator appointed – Provisional liquidator vacated part of premises that company had actual occupation of – Order made for winding up of company and official liquidator appointed – Liquidator offered to surrender interest of company under headlease -- Offer not accepted – Liquidator disclaimed company's interest pursuant to an order of the court – Rents due under sublease were paid into company's account under a pre-existing standing order arrangement – Whether rent due under headlease between the date of presentation of petition to wind up and date of disclaimer should be treated as an expense of the liquidation – Whether liquidator had retained possession of any part of demised premises for benefit of the liquidation – Whether receipt of rent under sublease meant that liquidator was maintaining a claim to the entire of the premises for the benefit of the liquidation – Whether headlessor should be compensated under principles of common sense and ordinary justice – Whether liquidator should retain monies received under sublease – Order 74 r.106 Rules of the Superior Courts

Facts: By indenture of lease dated 12 August 1974 Erris Investments Ltd ("Erris") demised certain office accommodation and warehouse space to a company known as Freedox Ltd. In December 1974 the interest in the said premises was assigned to and became vested in G.W.I. Ltd ("G.W.I."). In 1980 G.W.I. sublet that portion of the premises which consisted of office accommodation to Litho Studios Ltd ("Litho Studios") and retained the ownership and occupation of the warehouse space. On 28 January 1986 a petition was presented for the winding up by the court of G.W.I. and a provisional liquidator was appointed. On 10 February 1986 an order was made for the winding up of G.W.I. and the provisional liquidator was appointed official liquidator. The rent payable under the headlease had been paid up to 31 August 1985 and a sum of £22,000 had accrued from that date to the date of the appointment of the official liquidator. On 31 January 1986, the provisional liquidator (as he then was) vacated that part of the demised premises of which the company had actual occupation. On 22 April 1986, the solicitors on behalf of the official liquidator offered to surrender the interest of the company under the headlease but this offer was not accepted. On 23 July 1986 the liquidator, pursuant to an order of the court, disclaimed the interest of the company under the headlease. Litho Studios retained possession and occupation of that part of the premises held by them under the sub-lease. A sum of £3,999.96 was, by standing order, remitted to the credit of the G.W.I. company's account in respect of the rent payable under the sublease from the commencement of the liquidation until the date of disclaimer of the superior interest. Erris applied to have the rent payable by G.W.I. accruing from 28 January 1986 to 23 July 1986, amounting in total to £15,013.00, treated as an expense of the liquidation. It was submitted on behalf of Erris that having regard to the receipt of the rent payable under the sublease the official liquidator had the use and benefit not merely of the premises comprised in the sublease but all of the premises demised by the headlease. The liquidator contended that he did not at any time retain any part of the premises demised by the headlease for the benefit of the liquidation.

Held by Murphy J in refusing the application:

(1) Where a liquidator takes possession or remains in possession of leasehold property for the purpose of the winding-up, the rent of the premises ought to be regarded as a debt contracted for the purpose of winding up the company and ought therefore to be paid in full like any other debt or expense properly incurred by the liquidator for the same purpose.

(2) The courts operate a principle based upon common sense and ordinary justice under which the lessor may be compensated for being kept out of his premises during the period whilst they are being retained by the liquidator for some benefit which he anticipates will accrue to the liquidation as a result of the retention thereof.

(3) The liquidator vacated the premises within some weeks of his appointment as provisional liquidator. He made no positive efforts to collect the rent payable on the sublease and he did not at any time anticipate that he could dispose of the company's leasehold interest with the benefit of the sublease on terms which would be advantageous to the creditors of the company.

(4) There was nothing in the actions or inactions of the liquidator which

would justify an order permitting the liquidator to make any payments in respect of the rent which had accrued on foot of the headlease subsequent to the liquidation.

(5) However, the retention by the liquidator of the rent received by him from the sublessee would amount to an injustice and accordingly the court should order that he pay those sums received by him from the commencement of the liquidation to the date on which the headlease was disclaimed to the headlessor.

Cases referred to in judgment

ABC Coupler and Engineering Company Ltd (No. 3) [1970] 1 All ER 650
Downer Enterprises Ltd, In re [1974] 1 WLR 1460
H.H. Realisations Ltd, In re (1975) 31 P & CR 249
Lundy Granite Company, In re (1871) 6 Ch App 462
M. Power and Sons Ltd, Grant v Aston, In re 103 ILTR 39
Oak Pits Colliery Company (1882) 21 Ch D 322
Tempany v Royal Liver Trustees Ltd [1984] ILRM 273

Counsel's and solicitors' names not available

MURPHY J **16 November 1987**

This is an application by Erris Investment Ltd ("Erris") to have the rent payable by G.W.I. Ltd ("G.W.I.") under an indenture of lease dated 12 August 1974 accruing during the period from 28 January 1986 to 23 July 1986 and amounting in total to £15,013 treated as an expense of the liquidation.

By the said indenture of lease dated 12 August 1974 Erris demised part of the Kylemore Industrial Estate at Ballyfermot, Dublin, to Freedex Ltd for the term of 35 years subject to the rent of £16,711.80 or such greater rent as might be fixed in pursuance of the rent review provisions contained therein. The demised premises consisted as to 2,835 square feet of office accommodation and as to the remaining 14,658 square feet of warehouse space.

It appears that by an indenture of assignment made in the month of December 1974 the interest of Freedex Ltd in all of the premises demised by the said lease were assigned to and became vested in G.W.I.

By an indenture of underlease dated 6 February 1980 made between G.W.I. of the one part and Litho Studios of the other part that portion of the premises demised by the said lease consisting of 2,835 square feet of office accommodation was subleased by G.W.I. to Litho Studios for the residue of the term granted by the headlease subject to the yearly rent of £5,670.00 or such greater amount as might be determined in accordance with the rent review provisions contained therein. The ownership of the warehouse space and the occupation thereof was retained by G.W.I.

On 28 January 1986 a petition was presented for the winding up by the court of G.W.I. and Mr Tom Grace was appointed provisional liquidator thereof. On 10 February 1986 an order was made for the winding up of G.W.I. and Mr Grace was appointed official liquidator.

As at the date of the commencement of the liquidation the rent payable under the headlease was £33,000 per annum and that had been paid up to 31 August 1985. A further £22,000 had accrued due from that to date of the appointment of the official liquidator.

The undisputed facts are that on 31 January 1986 Mr Grace vacated that part of the demised premises of which the company had the actual occupation. On 22 April 1986 the solicitors on behalf of the official liquidator offered to surrender the interest of the company under the headlease and that offer was not accepted. On 23 July 1986 the liquidator, pursuant to the order of this court, disclaimed the interest of the company under the headlease. The amount of the rent which would have accrued due under the headlease from the commencement of the liquidation to the date of the disclaimer was £15,013.03 together with interest payable in accordance with the provisions of the lease amounting to £1,708.10 making a total of £16,721.10. Litho Studios retained possession and occupation of that part of the premises held by them under the sublease dated 6 February 1980. A sum of £3,999.96 was remitted to the credit of the G.W.I.'s account under a standing order in existence prior to the commencement of the liquidation in respect of the rent payable under the sublease from the commencement of the liquidation until the date of the disclaimer of the superior interest.

In these circumstances the official liquidator contends that he did not at any time retain any part of the premises demised by the headlease for the benefit of the liquidation and on behalf of Erris it is contended that having regard to the receipt of the rent payable under the sublease the official liquidator has had the use and benefit not merely of the premises comprised in the underlease but all of the premises demised by the headlease.

In a line of authorities stretching from the decision of the Court of Appeal in England in *Oak Pits Colliery Company* (1882) 21 Ch D 322 to the decision of Keane J in *Tempany and Royal Liver Trustees Ltd* [1984] ILRM 273 it has been established that where a liquidator takes possession or remains in possession of leasehold property for the purposes of the winding up the rent of the premises ought to be regarded as a debt contracted for the purpose of winding-up the company and ought therefore to be paid in full like any other debt or expense properly incurred by the liquidator for the same purpose. This principle was discussed at some length by Plowman J in *ABC Coupler and Engineering Company Ltd (No. 3)* [1970] 1 All ER 650 and VC Pennycuick in *In re Downer Enterprises Ltd* [1974] 1 WLR 1460. The principle was clearly applied though without reference to any decided cases, in *In The Matter of M. Power and Sons Ltd, Grant v Aston*, 103 ILTR 39 where the late Kenny J made an order directing a liquidator to pay rent from the commencement of a liquidation to the date in which the property was disclaimed by him. Indeed this principle is reflected in the Rules of the Superior Courts (SI No. 15 of 1986) Order 74, r.106 (replacing rule 107 of Order 74 introducing SI No. 28 of 1966) which provides as follows:

> "When any rent or other payment falls due at stated times and the order or resolution to wind up is made at any time other than at one of those

> times, the persons entitled to the rent or payment may prove for a proportionate part thereof up to the date of the winding up order or resolution as if the rent or payment accrued due from day to day. Provided that where the Official Liquidator remains in occupation of premises demised to a company which is being wound up, nothing herein contained shall prejudice or affect the right of the landlord of such premises to claim payment of rent during the period of the company's or the Official Liquidator's occupation."

Both Plowman J and Pennycuick VC cited with approval a passage from James LJ in *In re Lundy Granite Company* [1871] 6 Ch App 462 at 466 in the following terms:

> "But in some cases between the landlord and the company, if the company for its own purposes, and with a view to the realisation of the property to better advantage, remains in possession of the estate, which the lessor is therefore not able to obtain possession of, common sense and ordinary justice require the Court to see that the landlord receives the full value of the property."

Apart from the application of principles of common sense and ordinary justice it is easy to see that commercial realities will frequently necessitate the continued payment of rent after the commencement of a liquidation. If the premises are held at something less than a rack-rent it is probable that they will have some realisable value. Clearly if a liquidator is to complete a sale he must discharge all of the arrears of rent. Even if the leasehold premises have no saleable value but the liquidator is coerced into retaining occupation thereof for the purpose of carrying on a trade or otherwise for the advantageous winding up of the company he would be faced with an application by a competently advised lessor with the threat of proceedings either for ejectment for non-payment of rent or perhaps distraint. It is difficult to see how a court could refuse liberty to the lessor to exercise such rights if leasehold premises were being withheld by the official liquidator without paying any rent or fee for the occupation thereof. Indeed it appears that the duty to pay rent or a fee equivalent to the accruing rent was originally seen as the necessary corollary of a prohibition on the right of distress. On the other hand it was clearly held in the *Oak Pits Colliery* case that the right of the landlord to recover was not limited to the amount which could have been realised by a distress but should indeed extend to the full amount of the rent which accrued during the period over which the premises were retained by the liquidator for the purposes of the winding up of the company.

On the other hand it is equally clear that the official liquidator as such is not liable to pay rent. He could not be sued on foot on any covenant or agreement in that behalf. The liability to pay rent remains that of the corporate body and what the courts have done is to operate, as has already been pointed out, a principle based upon common sense and ordinary justice under which the lessor may be compensated for being kept out of his premises during the period whilst they are retained by the liquidator for some benefit which he anticipated will accrue to the liquidation as a result of the retention thereof.

What the applicants contend in the present case is that the liquidator in fact retained possession of the premises the subject matter of the underlease in the only way in which he could enjoy possession thereof, that is to say, by the receipt of the rent payable by the underlessee. The argument then goes on to claim that the receipt of the rent could only be justified or explained by a claim to the interest of the lessee under the headlease so that it followed that the official liquidator, Mr Grace, was, notwithstanding his statement to the contrary, maintaining a claim to the entire of the premises for the benefit of the liquidation. The effect of this argument would be to compel the official liquidator to pay in full a sum in excess of £17,000 for the reason and only for the reason that he had received a sum just under £4,000. Such a consequence would not accord with the principles of common sense and ordinary justice invoked by James LJ.

I am satisfied that Mr Grace vacated, as he said he did, all the demised premises which had physically been in the occupation of the company within some weeks of his appointment as provisional liquidator. I accept that he made no positive efforts to collect the rent payable on foot of the underlease and I believe that he did not at any time anticipate that he could dispose of the leasehold interest with the benefit of the underlease on terms which would be advantageous to the creditors of the company. If Erris had applied to the court for liberty to institute proceedings for recovery of the premises for non-payment of rent or otherwise I anticipate that it would have been granted by the court with the acquiescence of the liquidator. I can see nothing in the actions or inactions of the official liquidator which would justify me in permitting him to make any payment to Erris in respect of the rent which accrued due on foot of the headlease subsequent to the commencement of the liquidation. On the other hand I do accept that the retention by the official liquidator of the rent of nearly £4,000 received by him from the underlessee would represent an injustice and that I should properly order the payment of that sum by the official liquidator to Erris.

The decision of the court falls to be determined not by the particular provisions of any legislation but in accordance with the dictates of justice and common sense as James LJ pointed out or what Templeman J (as he then was) describes as what was "fair and reasonable" or what was "equitable" as between the lessor and the creditors whom the liquidator represents (see *H.H. Realisations Ltd, In re* (1975) 31 P & CR 249).

Applying these principles it seems to me that the appropriate order is to direct the official liquidator to pay to the applicants all of the rent payable under the sublease which was received by him from the date of the commencement of the liquidation to the date on which the headlease was disclaimed.

Patricia McLaughlin
Barrister

In the Matter of Dubned Exports Ltd And in the Matter of the Companies Acts 1963-83: High Court 1986 No. 139P (Costello J) 9 May 1986

Company – Winding Up – Whether company unable to pay debts – Petition – Dispute over debt – Whether petition an abuse of process – Whether dispute a bona fide *one – Whether appropriate to refer dispute to plenary hearing*

Facts: Mr Liam Marks controlled and was the principal owner of, the petitioner, Benburb Ltd ("Benburb"), a company registered in Northern Ireland, and also Dubned Exports Ltd ("Dubned"), registered in the Republic of Ireland. Money was freely transferred between the two companies under Mr Marks' directions.

Benburb subsequently went into liquidation and the liquidator instituted proceedings to wind up Dubned, on the basis that Dubned owed Stg£364,883 to Benburb.

Dubned disputed the debt and alleged that in fact the sum of £65,527 was owing by Benburb to Dubned. It was further submitted that the dispute over the monies should be settled by plenary hearing, and that the winding-up petition was an abuse of process of the court.

A statement of affairs of Benburb prepared by Price Waterhouse, who were also auditors to Dubned, showed that Dubned was indebted to Benburb in the sum of Stg£364,883 at 10 October 1985, and that Mr Marks had offered to make £180,000 available, "which it is proposed will be used to repay part of the balance". In affidavits, however, Mr Marks while accepting that a figure of £203,437 was due by Dubned to Benburb at 31 January 1985, said that a credit note of £160,000 should be debited against this sum. He also referred to a sum to be offset of £247,945 in respect of cash paid by Mr Marks to Benburb. Mr Marks stated in his affidavit that Benburb was 'fully solvent', but adduced no accountancy evidence to support this.

In relation to the credit note, there was evidence that a credit note for £140,000 had been dealt with by Price Waterhouse in the draft Benburb accounts for year ending 31 January 1985 and the notes suggested these accounts were approved by the directors. In relation to the advance from Mr Marks, the statement of affairs referred to this, but suggested that, in discussions with the auditors, Mr Marks accepted that this money was not advanced in reduction of Dubned's debts to Benburb, but was money owed personally to Mr Marks, a debt which he agreed to waive in certain circumstances.

In separate proceedings Mr Marks had sworn affidavits referring to his offer to invest Stg£180,000 in Benburb, and also to waive a sum in excess of £200,000 due to him personally by Benburb. However, he later swore an affidavit stating that this was an error and, in fact, the £220,000 paid by him, was paid on behalf of Dubned to discharge liabilities owed to Benburb.

Held by Costello J in granting the relief sought by the petitioner and holding that the dispute concerning the debt was not a *bona fide* one and that Dubned was now insolvent:

(1) The significant and persuasive evidence tending to establish that the debt claimed was due had not been referred to in the replying affidavits or denied.

(2) The controlling director of the two companies had sworn directly contradictory versions of the financial transactions involved, and no reasonable explanation for these contradictions had been forthcoming.

(3) There was a clear failure to disclose evidence about the financial situation of the company and the inter-company transactions.

No cases referred to in judgment

Counsel's names not available

Solicitors for the petitioner: *Matheson Ormsby Prentice*
Solicitors for the official liquidator: *Whitney, Moore & Keller*
Solicitors for the directors: *Johnston, Lavery & McGahon*

COSTELLO J **9 May 1986**

The petitioner ("Benburb") is a company registered in Northern Ireland which until it went into liquidation was controlled and largely owned by Mr Liam Marks, who lives in Blackrock, Co. Louth. Mr Marks also controls and owns (as principal shareholder) the company ("Dubned") the subject matter of the petition I am now considering. The two companies were closely inter-related; Benburb purchased cattle and slaughtered them, whilst Dubned, carried on business as the manufacturers of meat products in the Republic of Ireland and money was freely transferred between the two companies under Mr Marks directions.

Benburb is now in liquidation and these proceedings are being maintained by its liquidator who claims that Dubned owed Benburb £364,883 sterling on 10 October 1985 and has since failed to pay it and that it is insolvent. This debt is disputed by Dubned who alleges that in fact Benburb is indebted to it in the sum £65,527 and claims that these proceedings are an abuse of the court's process as the dispute between the companies should be settled in the ordinary way by plenary proceedings and not on a petition to wind up the company. The company also denies that it is insolvent. Normally, a denial of liability of a petitioning creditor's debt together with an averment that the company is solvent would at the very least result in the court staying the proceedings on foot of the petition until the dispute had been determined in substantive proceedings. But this is far from a normal case. Lengthy adjournments have been granted so that evidence on affidavit could be filed. On the evidence now before the court it appears (a) that significant and persuasive evidence which tends to establish that the debt claimed is due has not been referred to in any replying affidavits or denied; (b) that the controlling director of the two companies has sworn directly contradictory versions of the financial transactions involving the two companies and no reasonable explanation for these contradictions has been forthcoming; (c) that there has been an obvious failure to disclose evidence about the financial situations of the company and the inter-company transactions. In these circumstances I have come to the conclusion (i) that the dispute which has been raised concerning the debt claimed by Benburb is not a *bona fide* one and (ii) that Dubned is now insolvent. It would be wrong, in these circumstances, not to grant the petitioner the relief in these proceedings to which it is entitled.

I can briefly summarise the considerations which brought me to these conclusions as follows.

Benburb got into serious financial difficulties in the latter part of 1985. A meeting of its creditors was called at which a scheme of arrangement was proposed and a statement of affairs prepared based on a report of Messrs Price Waterhouse, the well-known firm of accountants. Price Waterhouse were auditors of both Benburb and Dubned and in the statement of affairs they prepared they stated that their conclusions were based on information included in the books and records of both companies "together with such other additional information as we were able to obtain". At the same time, very explicit qualifications were included in a covering letter sent to the creditors. In paragraph 7 of the statement of affairs Dubned is known as owing Benburb £364,883 sterling as of 10 October 1985. Price Waterhouse stated that they had access to the records of Dubned for the purpose of preparing the statement and expressed the view that Dubned "had a deficiency of net assets as at 10 October and is illiquid". From this statement it is reasonable to infer that in the opinion of the Dubned's own auditors the company was insolvent as of that date. The same paragraph went on to state that Mr Marks had agreed to make available to Dubned £180,000 sterling "which it is proposed will be used to repay part of the balance". Quite clearly, therefore, Price Waterhouse were informing the creditors of Benburb that Dubned owed Benburb £364,883, that Mr Marks (the principal shareholder in both companies) had discussed this debt with the auditors and that far from controverting it he was prepared to give Dubned financial assistance to enable it to be paid. Nowhere in the many affidavits that Mr Marks has filed in these and other proceedings (to which I will refer in a moment) has he denied that he had this conversation with Price Waterhouse.

In an affidavit sworn on behalf of Dubned by Mr Marks of 25 February, 1986 a completely different position is taken up in relation to its financial dealings with Benburb. It is there stated that Benburb owed Dubned £65,527. The "Summary" showing how this figure is arrived at accepts that there was a balance due to Benburb as of 31 January 1985 of £203,437 but claims that there should be debited against this a sum of £160,000 in respect of a Credit Note for the period of 31st January, which was "not approved or issued". In respect of other dealings recorded in the "Summary" it is claimed that there should be what is termed an "offset" for "cash paid by Liam Marks to Benburb on behalf of Dubned of £247,945." Mr Marks gives no explanation as to why in the Price Waterhouse statement of affairs of which he must of course have been aware (and which in any event was exhibited in the affidavit grounding this petition) he is recorded as having agreed that Dubned owed Benburb £364,883 sterling and volunteered his own personal resources to Dubned to enable it to be paid.

As a result of investigations carried out by Mr Ross, Benburb's liquidator, further information was obtained and made available to the court relating to the two large sums which according to the "Summary", resulted in Dubned being a creditor, not a debtor, of Benburb. The working papers of Price Waterhouse show that a credit note for £140,000 sterling (which it is accepted refers to the credit note for £160,000 in the "Summary") appears in the journal entries made by them. But more importantly, in the draft accounts which they as auditors of Benburb had prepared for the year ended 31 January 1985, some time before the collapse of Benburb this credit in favour of Benburb is reflected. These draft accounts, although not formally adopted, were seen by Benburb's directors and page 6 of the accounts states that they had been approved by the directors on 30 September 1985. In view of Mr Marks' position in the two companies the strong presumption is raised that Mr Marks saw these accounts in September 1985 and approved them, and that he thereby accepted as correct that there was a credit in favour of Benburb of £140,000 sterling properly allowed for in them. He has given no evidence to rebut this inference or to explain why in the year 1985 the company's records indicate that this sum is due by Dubned to Benburb and why the situation should now be reversed. Mr Ross also expressed his professional opinion that if this credit of £140,000 sterling had not been allowed in the Benburb accounts then Benburb would have been insolvent. Again, this opinion has not been challenged, even though subsequently evidence by a professional accountant was filed on behalf of Dubned.

As to the sum of £247,945 claimed as an "offset" because, as claimed in the "Summary", it was paid by Dubned through Mr Marks into Benburb, it is clear that this figure is reflected in the statement of affairs prepared by Price Waterhouse. It is however, treated by the auditors in a very different way. Paragraph 14 gives particulars of a balance due by the company to Mr Marks of £220,174 sterling and contains the statement that "we understand that Mr Marks has agreed to waive the balance due to him in the event that the Scheme of Arrangement is approved. Mr Marks has not yet formally agreed that the balance is correct". Paragraph 14 thus raises the strong inference (a) that Benburb's records showed there was a debt due to Mr Marks by the company in respect of monies advanced to the company by Mr Marks personally; (b) that the company's indebtedness had been discussed with Mr Marks; (c) that he did not suggest that he had advanced the money to the company in reduction of Dubned's debt; and that on the contrary (d) he agreed that he was personally owed substantial sums by the company and that he was prepared to waive his claim in certain circumstances. This conduct is inconsistent with the claim now made but, again, it is to be noted that no attempt has been made to deal with this evidence in any replying affidavit, or to explain why, if it was correct, these statements were made to the auditors if, in fact, they were not true.

Further doubt is cast on the *bona fides* of the dispute now raised by Dubned by reason of contradictions between the evidence filed on the company's behalf and sworn testimony given by Mr Marks in these proceedings. In an affidavit sworn by Mr Marks on 13 December 1985, in proceedings instituted by a Mr Carl O'Neill (a supplier of cattle to Benburb) for damages for fraudulent misrepresentation Mr Marks referred (in paragraph 18) to the creditors meetings at which the scheme of arrangement was proposed and gave this description of what he said to the meeting:

> "At the said creditors' meetings I said I would raise, and pay through Dubned Exports Ltd, the sum of £100,000 sterling within two weeks and a further sum of £80,000 sterling over a 10 week period. I had also certain proposals whereby I would sell my said premises at Blackrock Co. Louth and would cause the net proceeds of sale to be paid through Dubned Exports Ltd into the Scheme, and furthermore that I would waive a sum in excess of £200,000 which was due to me personally by the company, Benburb Meats Ltd."

Mr Marks is stating in this affidavit that he informed the meeting of creditors that Benburb was indebted to him personally for a sum in excess of £200,000 and that he was prepared to waive the debt. He was thus confirming as accurate the statement of affairs and making a statement to the creditors which is wholly at variance with the case now being made, namely that the monies were paid by him in reduction of Dubned's debt and did not create a debt in his favour. A further affidavit in those proceedings was sworn on 14 April (but never filed or delivered to Mr O'Neill's solicitors and was subsequently re-sworn), in which he stated that for reasons set out in it he was under stress and strain at the time he swore his earlier affidavit on 13 December and that in fact the sum of £220,000 was paid to him on behalf of Dubned and that he paid it to Benburb to discharge the debts and liabilities of Dubned. It is to be assumed from this affidavit that Mr Marks is averring that he did not make the statement at the meeting of creditors deposed to earlier. But the earlier affidavit was a long and detailed one and it is difficult to accept that his recollection as to what he said at the meeting was affected by strain and stress particularly as what he recalls he said is consistent with what he had earlier said to Price Waterhouse. And it is to be noted that he does not deny that he had the discussions with Price Waterhouse about this sum and does not claim that they are wrong in stating that he had accepted that the sum shown in the accounts was due to him personally and that he had agreed to waive its payment in certain circumstances.

There are other aspects of the evidence which has been filed which cast further doubts both on the *bona fides* of the dispute now raised by Dubned and on its solvency.

In the affidavit sworn by Mr Marks in these proceedings on 25 February 1986 it is averred that "the company is fully solvent". In support of this averment he stated:

> "By Order of the High Court dated the 25th November, 1985 in an action entitled Carl O'Neill, Plaintiff and Liam Marks, Defendant Record No.

> 1985 No. 9872P assets of the company to the value of £100,000 sterling was and remains frozen in a branch of the Bank of Ireland, Balbriggan, County Dublin,"

and he referred to the said order.

There are two points to be made on this averment. Firstly, it is to be inferred that the case is being made that if this sum was unfrozen that the company would be solvent. It is noteworthy that nowhere in any of the affidavits filed on the company's behalf is the court informed of what the company's assets and liabilities are and no draft statement of affairs has been prepared (even though the services of an accountant were obtained for another purpose in relation to the case) and no evidence of any sort to support the assertion of solvency has been adduced. Nor has it been suggested that Price Waterhouse were incorrect in stating that as of 10 October 1985, there was a net deficiency of assets in Dubned and that the company was illiquid, and no suggestion has been forthcoming to show how, if that view was correct, the company's situation is now any different. Indeed, counsel on behalf of the company whilst suggesting that the petition should be dismissed on the grounds that there was a *bona fide* dispute urged in the alternative that it should be adjourned to see if other directors might be prepared to advance money to the company, a submission that supports the view that it is indeed insolvent.

Secondly, Mr Marks quite categorically states that the £100,000 sterling lodged in the Balbriggan branch of the Bank of Ireland is an asset of Dubned. But this claim is inconsistent with evidence which he gave in the affidavit sworn in the other proceedings to which I have already referred. In paragraph 18 of that affidavit Mr Marks stated that he had informed the creditors at the meeting held on 10 October 1985 that he would raise the sun of £100,000 within two weeks. He went on:

> "As a gesture of good faith and at the specific request of Carl O'Neill made through his solicitor Mr C.B. Turkington the said sum of £100,000 was in fact lodged in Balbriggan in a deposit account in the name of Robert Sinclair, Conn O'Donnell and Noel Gilroy within the said period of two weeks."

And in paragraph 21 of the same affidavit he referred to the fact that horses which he owned were sold in order to inject money into the company and he went on:

> "I had a 75% interest in the Iliad, but early in October, 1985 I sold 50% interest in the Iliad in order to partly finance the sum of £100,000 hereinbefore referred to."

There is no suggestion in this affidavit that the £180,000 sterling lodged in the Bank of Ireland was obtained from Dubned. On the contrary, it is suggested that part of it has been obtained from the sale of a share in a horse which was Mr Marks' own property. No attempt has been made to explain the inconsistency between the two affidavits, and although it is claimed that the money in the bank is owned by Dubned, no explanation has been given as to the source from which it was derived, or who paid it in.

In reaching the conclusion that the dispute which has been raised is not a *bona fide* one and that the company is insolvent and should be wound up I have not ignored the other affidavits sworn on the company's behalf. But these add nothing to the case advanced on the company's behalf, and do not affect the validity of the conclusions to be drawn from the evidence to which I have just referred.

Alistair Rutherdale
Barrister

In the Matter of the Companies Acts 1963-83 and in the Matter of Mont Clare Hotels Ltd (in Liquidation); Ray Jackson v. Pauline Mortell, Brian Mortell and Anthony Hussey: High Court 1986 No. 20 Sp (Costello J) 2 December 1986

Company – Misfeasance – Limitation of actions – Liquidation – Loan to other company – Overlap in directors – Loan not repaid – Assurance by director to board that loan secured – Failure by board to institute proceedings to recover loan – Whether misfeasance or breach of trust by directors – Test – Whether claim statute barred – Companies Act 1963 (No. 33), section 298 – Statute of Limitations 1957 (No. 6), section 44

Facts: Section 298(1) of the Companies Act 1963 provides that:

> "If in the course of the winding up of a company it appears that [*inter alia*] any . . . director . . . of the company, has misapplied or retained or become liable or accountable for any money or property of the company, or been guilty of any misfeasance or breach of trust in relation to the company, the court may, on the application of the liquidator . . . examine the conduct of the . . . director . . . and compel him to repay or restore the money or property or any part thereof respectively with interest . . . , or to contribute such sums to the assets of the company . .. as the court thinks just."

In 1973 Mont Clare Hotels Ltd ("Mont Clare") made a loan of £20,000 to Cluney Construction Ltd ("Cluney"). The loan was made by Brian Mortell who, with his mother, effectively ran Mont Clare. Minutes of the company directors dated 17 April 1973 made reference to the loan, but it, in fact, appeared to have been made earlier. There was no written agreement or security for the loan, but there was an agreement to pay interest at 10 per cent.

Cluney was established by Brian Mortell, who could sign cheques of that company along with its other director, Mr Power. The company was mainly run by Mr Power who had some limited experience in the construction industry. The company began some projects but failed to prosper and was unable to repay its loan to Mont Clare.

On 13 September 1977 Mr Mortell told the Mont Clare directors that £6,000 would be paid off the loan. This was not done. On 29 February 1979 he again informed the directors that the loan was secured. On 14 February 1980 he wrote to Mont Clare's bankers stating that the loan was good and was due to be repaid in four instalments. As a result no proceedings were taken against Cluney to recover the loan.

Mont Clare went into liquidation in 1982, and proceedings were brought by the liquidator pursuant to section 298 of the Companies Act 1963. It was alleged that misfeasance arose through the 1973 loan, and also in the failure of the directors to institute proceedings against Cluney in the period 1977-1980 when it failed to repay the loan. The defendants submitted that the claim, in so far as it related to wrongful acts in the year 1973, was statute barred.

Held by Costello J in dismissing the liquidator's application:

(1) As more than six years had passed since the alleged act of misfeasance in 1973 occurred, it was not open to the liquidator to claim under section 298 of the Companies Act, in respect thereof. The money paid was not "trust property . . . still retained by the trustee . . ." within the meaning of section 44 of the Statute of Limitations 1957, as the money was paid to Cluney and was not retained by the defendants. *In re Lands Allotment Company* [1894] 1 Ch 616 followed.

(2) Not every error of judgment or act of negligence amounts to misfeasance in law. Misfeasance requires an act amounting to gross negligence in failing to carry out a duty owed by a director to his company.

(3) There was no evidence of misfeasance against the first and third defendants, who had no reason to doubt what they were told by the second defendant.

(4) In relation to the second defendant, while he may have been guilty of errors of judgment or undue optimism in giving the assurances to the board and the bank in 1977, 1979 and 1980, there was no evidence that he was guilty of fraud, nor that his statements amounted to misfeasance. It was therefore not possible to establish misfeasance against him as a matter of law.

Case referred to in judgment

In re Lands Allotment Company [1894] 1 Ch 616

Complete names of counsel not available

Vincent Landy SC instructed by *Giles J. Kennedy & Co.* **for the third defendant**

Solicitors for the applicant: *William Fry & Sons*
Solicitors for the first and second respondents: *O'Brien, Sheridan & Co.*
Solicitors for the third respondent: *Giles J. Kennedy & Co.*

COSTELLO J **2 December 1986**

These proceedings have been brought by the liquidator of Mont Clare Hotels Ltd under section 298 of the Companies Act. Mont Clare Hotels Ltd went into liquidation on 26 May 1982 and it was known at the time, knowledge that was confirmed later, that in 1973 Mont Clare Hotels Ltd had made a loan of £20,000 to a company called Cluney Construction Ltd.

It was in relation to the loan to Cluney Construction Ltd that the section 298 proceedings were instituted, and the liquidator has raised for determination by the court whether or not the directors named as the respondents in these proceedings were guilty of misfeasance arising out of, firstly, the making of the loan and, secondly, its non-enforcement at later dates.

The loan was made in the year 1973 by Brian Mortell who was, with his mother, effectively running Mont Clare Hotels Ltd. Although the loan was referred to in a minute of the directors of the company of 17 April 1973 as having been made as of that date, I am satisfied from the evidence that the loan had been made to Cluney Construction Ltd prior to this at Mr Mortell's instigation. The relevance of that is in relation to the claim made against Mr Hussey, who was and is a solicitor and was acting as solicitor to the company, and who was a director of the company and held shares in the company but was not beneficially entitled to them.

The position is that prior to the meeting of 17 April 1973 this loan had been made to Cluney Construction Ltd. It was made in a very informal way. There was no security or nothing in writing for it but there was agreement to pay at the rate of 10 per cent, or that is what was minuted on 17 April 1973, and it is not denied that there was a liability on Cluney Construction Ltd to pay interest at that rate.

The first point in this case arose under Statute of Limitations. It was urged by Mr Landy on behalf of Mr Hussey, and the submission was adopted by Mr Foley on behalf of Mr Mortell and his mother, that the claim, insofar as it related to wrongful acts in the year 1973, is statute barred. The position seems to be clearly established by the *In re Lands Allotment Company* [1894] 1 Ch 616, to which Mr Landy referred, that the Statute of Limitations applied in relation to allegations of misfeasance and breach of trust made against a director. Notwithstanding the facts that these proceedings could not be instituted until after the liquidation, which was more than six years after the wrongful act occurred, the authorities indicates that it is not open to a liquidator to claim that an act of misfeasance can now result in a claim under section 298 after six years. In these circumstances I am satisfied that the reliance on the Statute was permissible in that connection.

I should say that I was referred to section 44 of the Statute of 1957 which provides that no period of limitation fixed by the Act is to apply to an action against a trustee where "(b) the claim is to recover trust property or the proceeds thereof still retained by the trustee or previously received by the trustee and converted to his own use". I do not think that this avails the liquidator because the money paid to the account of Cluney Construction Ltd has not been "retained" by any of the defendants.

That brings me to say a few words about Cluney Construction Ltd. This company was established and run by Mr Mortell, one of the directors of Mont Clare Hotels Ltd, in association with a Mr Power. Mr Mortell had the power of signing cheques for the company but the company was mainly run by Mr Power who had some expertise in the construction industry, but not a great deal of expertise, Mr Mortell having none.

Cluney Construction Ltd started developing in Newbridge and later in Bray but the company did not prosper. The company met very great difficulties in respect of its activities in Newbridge and its bankers insisted on obtaining the funds generated on the sale of its houses. The result of this was that the company was unable to repay the loan given to it by Mont Clare Hotels Ltd, and it is in that connection that the second claim of misfeasance arises, a claim which may not be subject to the Statute.

The evidence establishes that on 13 September 1977 Mr Mortell informed his co-directors that £6,000 would be paid back off the loan. This was not done. I am satisfied there was no fraud in connection with that statement. I am satisfied that Mr Mortell may well have been guilty of errors of judgment in relation to this whole transaction but that he was guilty of any fraud in relation to it, and it has not been shown that he did not believe that what he said would come to pass. Unfortunately it did not come to pass.

On 27 February 1979 the minutes again record that Mr Mortell expressed the view that the loan was secured. Again, I am of the view that it has not been shown that this was said recklessly or fraudulently. It may well have been that Mr Mortell was being over-optimistic and it may well be an error of judgment on his part, but I do not think his statement in itself amounted to misfeasance.

On 14 February 1980 Mr Mortell expressed in writing to the bank, who were then lending money to Mont Clare Hotels Ltd, that the loan was good and that it would be repaid in four instalments, as stated in the letter. Again, in my view it is not been shown that Mr Mortell acted fraudulently in signing this letter. Again, it may well be a case of misplaced optimism on his part.

The relevance of the evidence is this: it is said that there was misfeasance on the part of the directors of Mont Clare Hotels Ltd in failing to enforce the obligation of Cluney Construction Ltd to repay the loan.

In relation to Mr Hussey, I am quite satisfied that during this period Mont Clare Hotels Ltd was apparently financially all right. There was no reason to doubt what he was being told by Mr Mortell and there was no reason to insist that proceedings be instituted against Cluney Construction Ltd. I can exculpate him of any misfeasance for failing to urge, as a director of Mont Clare Hotels Ltd, that proceedings be instituted against Cluney Construction Ltd.

The same considerations apply to Mrs Mortell. There is no evidence to suggest other than that she was merely acquiescing in what her son was informing her and accepting his assurances on their face value. In these circumstances there is no case of misfeasance on her part.

The question arises, however, as to whether or not Mr Brian Mortell was guilty of misfeasance in the way he dealt with this outstanding loan. This is not an easy question to decide but I have come to the conclusion on the authorities quoted by Mr Foley and Mr Fennelly that a case of misfeasance has not been made against him. It is not every error of judgment that amounts to misfeasance in law and it is not every act of negligence that amounts to misfeasance in law. It seems to me that something more than mere carelessness is required, some act that, perhaps, may amount to gross negligence in failing to carry out a duty owed by a director to his company. During this period I think Mr Mortell was genuinely hopeful that the difficulties of the construction company would be overcome.

Mr Mortell was not at this period — in 1977, 1979 and 1980 — in a position where his other company, Mont Clare Hotels Ltd, was in serious financial difficulty. These difficulties arose later at a time when Cluney Construction Ltd was unable to repay the money and when, in fact, he had to mortgage his own dwellinghouse in order to infuse some finance into Mont Clare Hotels Ltd.

So it does not seem to me it has been possible to establish that as a matter of law Mr Brian Mortell was guilty of misfeasance, as alleged, during the time that Cluney Construction Ltd owed the money to Mont Clare Hotels Ltd and no proceedings to recover the money were instituted or authorised by the directors.

It seems to me that it was proper for the liquidator to institute these proceedings and he is entitled to his costs out of the assets. Mr Hussey is also entitled to his costs out of the assets and I will so order.

A question arises as to whether the first and second-named respondents are entitled to their costs. The view I take of Mr Foley's application is this: it seems to me that Mr Mortell has himself to blame to a considerable extent for the fact that these proceedings were instituted. The various actions which he took and the statements which he made, particularly as late as the statement made to the creditors, indicated to the liquidator that there was a situation which justified him bringing these proceedings. It is only now, when the matter has been considered on the oral evidence given by Mr Mortell, that it has been possible to determine that he was not guilty of misfeasance. In those circumstances he contributed, in my view, to the fact that these proceedings were instituted. I think it would be fair not to require him to pay the costs as he has succeeded technically so I will refuse the application that his costs be paid out of the assets. Nor will I allow costs in relation to Mrs Mortell.

Alistair Rutherdale
Barrister

[*Reporters Note:* Section 298 of the Companies Act 1963, has since been amended by section 142 of the Companies Act 1990]

In the Matter of M.F.N. Construction Company Ltd (In Liquidation): On the Application of Patrick Tuffy, Liquidator: Supreme Court 1986 No. 11 (Finlay CJ, Henchy, Griffin, Hederman and McCarthy JJ) 12 May 1988 (*Nem. Diss.*)

Company – Insolvency – Scheme of arrangement devised – Approved by required majority of unsecured creditors and by the High Court – Scheme provided that monies due and owing to the collector general would be frozen and paid as a preferential claim in the winding up of the company – Subsequently wound up – Whether scheme enforceable – Whether section 285 of the Companies Act 1963 should determine priority – Whether parties could agree to waive priority of payment provided for in section 285 – Whether the unsecured creditors could approbate and reprobate the arrangement – Whether liquidator bound by the arrangement – Companies Act 1963 (No. 33), section 201(3)

Facts: In June 1981 the company was insolvent but it had two major contracts with Dublin Corporation which had not been completed. A scheme of arrangement was proposed by the directors with the creditors, including the Bank of Ireland, which was a secured creditor and the Collector General who was only the preferential creditor. The scheme was approved by the required majority of unsecured creditors and was approved by order of the High Court dated 17 June, 1981. The scheme provided, *inter alia*, that £210,250 and interest would be payable to the Collector General as preferential creditor. The scheme also provided for the payment of 40 pence in the pound to the unsecured creditors. The company was wound up voluntarily on 6 July 1982 and a liquidator was appointed. In the explanatory statement of the scheme, issued in compliance with section 202 of the Companies Act 1963, it was stated that a sum of £210,250 was owed by the company to the Collector General for arrears of PAYE and PRSI and that the entire of that sum would rank as a preferential payment in a winding up of the company pursuant to section 285 of the 1963 Act. The explanatory note also stated that the monies to be received up to 31 March 1982 would be sufficient to enable a dividend of at least 40 pence in the pound to be paid to the unsecured creditors after payment of the secured creditor and the preferential creditor. The Collector General sought to enforce the scheme which would give him priority over the unsecured debts. On behalf of the unsecured creditors, it was submitted that the court should disregard the scheme and adhere to section 285 of the 1963 Act as the statutory direction to the liquidator on priority of payments. Reliance was placed upon section 201(3) of the Act as support for the view that the liquidator was bound by such a scheme of arrangement.

Held by McCarthy J (Finlay CJ, Henchy, Griffin, Hederman JJ concurring):

(1) The liquidator was not bound by the arrangement as section 201(3)

applies only to an arrangement made by a company in the course of being wound up.

(2) However, the unsecured creditors could not be permitted to approbate and reprobate: they secured the advantage of the company continuing to trade in the completion of the contracts and they could not now be permitted to deny another part of the same agreement.

(3) The parties unquestionably intended that the preferential claim of the Collector General should stand in the event of a winding up.

(4) As long as all interested parties were involved, those immediately concerned might make a valid and enforceable agreement to waive or amend the order of priority of payment. If other parties not involved in the scheme were to be concerned in the winding up, different considerations would apply.

(5) To order that the parties adhere to the agreement is "in accordance with law".

No cases referred to in judgment

Counsel's and solicitors' names not available

McCARTHY J **12 May 1988**

By special resolution of 6 July 1982, it was resolved that the company be wound up and, on the same day, the applicant was appointed liquidator. Section 285 of the Companies Act 1963 prescribes what are preferential payments in winding up including (subsection 2(a)(iii)):

> "any amount due at the relevant date (here 6 July 1982) in respect of sums in which an employer is liable under the Finance (No. 2) Act 1959, and any regulations thereunder to deduct from emoluments to which Part II of the Act applies paid by him during the period of 12 months by any amount which he was under that Act, and any regulation thereunder liable to repay during the said period, with the addition of interest payable under section 8 of that Act."

As of the relevant date, there was some £34,000 due as the balance of such sums during the period of 12 months next before the relevant date. The liquidator has paid approximately £14,000 and intends to pay the balance of approximately £20,000 as a preferential payment in priority in accordance with section 285. The remaining assets in the liquidation would then be available for distribution amongst the ordinary creditors. The Collector General, however, claims the much larger sum of £210,250 together with interest up to 31 March 1982, being arrears of such statutory sums unpaid between October 1980 and 10 June 1981.

The arrangement

In June 1981, the company was insolvent but it had two major contracts with Dublin Corporation which had not been completed; the directors Michael

McNamara, Patrick Neylon and John Neylon proposed a scheme of arrangement with the creditors including the Bank of Ireland as secured creditor, and the Collector General who would, in the event of a winding up, be a preferential creditor. The scheme was accepted by the required majority of unsecured creditors and was approved by order of the High Court dated 17 June 1981. The major proposals in the scheme were:

(a) to pay the entire of the amount due to the Bank of Ireland as secured creditor;

(b) to pay the sum of £210,250 and interest to the Collector General as preferential creditor;

(c) to pay 40 pence in the pound to unsecured creditors;

(d) to release the directors of the company from joint and several guarantees to the Bank of Ireland and on foot of an insurance bond furnished by the Insurance Corporation of Ireland to Dublin Corporation;

(e) a provision whereby the directors of the company personally guaranteed the dividend of 40 pence in the pound to the unsecured creditors.

Subsequent to the resolution for voluntary winding up the majority of the unsecured creditors were paid at a rate of 40 pence in the pound in respect of their several debts the total sum being £254,548. The sums were paid by John McNamara, Shelley McNamara and Bernard McNamara, Barbara Ceillier, none of whom were directors and Michael McNamara and Company Ltd. They are, accordingly, entitled to prove in the liquidation as unsecured creditors by virtue of subrogation agreements executed in their favour. The latter parties derived their rights from, and only from, the subrogation agreements and, consequently, are identified with the unsecured creditors who sanctioned the scheme of arrangement.

The Collector General, by letter, accepted the scheme which also made provision for the payment of current outgoings, including the statutory sums, of which £146,205 was paid between 5 July 1981 and 5 February 1982 in respect of persons employed in the completion of the Dublin Corporation contracts.

The issue

The Collector, in effect, seeks to enforce the scheme which was approved by order of the High Court and contains, *inter alia*, the following provisions:

> 3. "The sum due to the Collector General as the sole preferential creditor as appears in the Statement of Affairs shall be frozen as of the date hereof but shall continue to carry the rate of interest applicable thereto in accordance with law. Future payments of PAYE and PRSI shall be discharged as and when the same fall due and no part of such future payments shall be appropriated in discharge of the said frozen balances due as of the date hereof.
>
> 10. Subject to the works comprised in the said Building Contracts having been completed by Company and all sums properly payable by Dublin Corporation to the Company having been received, the company shall be

> wound up as of the 31st day March, 1982 and its assets realised and applied in satisfaction of its debts in accordance with law."

The explanatory statement issued in compliance with section 202 of the Companies Act 1963 contains the following statements:

> Page 3: "A sum of £210,250 is owned by the Company to the Collector General for arrears of PAYE and PRSI and the entire of that sum would rank as a preferential payment in a winding up of the Company pursuant to section 285 of the Companies Act 1963."

> Page 5: "The Company is satisfied that monies receivable during the period up to the 31st March, 1982 will be sufficient to finance the works required to complete each contract and that by the 31st March, 1982 the substantial value of the works in progress will have realised sufficient to enable a dividend of at least 40 pence in the pound to be paid to the unsecured creditors after payment of the secured creditor and the preferential creditor. . . ."

The factual issue is whether or not the frozen claim with interest of the Collector General is to be paid in priority to the subrogated debts, thereby at the expense of those to whom subrogation was made; if not, the latter will recoup the 40 pence in the pound that they paid.

Those in the shoes of the unsecured creditors say that the court must disregard the scheme and adhere to section 285 as the statutory direction to the liquidator on priority of payments. They say that the Collector General benefited from the scheme in that he continued to collect the statutory sums where, otherwise, these might have not been received. Whether or not that is a benefit to the Collector General and subsequently to the Revenue, if the work was going to be carried out to complete the contracts, as, no doubt, it must have been, then those statutory sums would have been paid to the Revenue in any event by somebody. It is also said that a winding up at the time, in June 1981, would have left the Collector General short of payment; be it so, but the present argument would also leave him short of payment, in respect of the debt then, in June 1981, due. The effect of yielding to the Collector General's claim, it is argued, would mean overriding the statute.

The Collector General relies upon the enforceability of the scheme of arrangement which involved the Collector General in staying his hand until at least 31 March 1982 and that this scheme is binding on the company, and consequently, on the liquidator. Reliance was placed upon section 201(3) of the Act as support for the view that the liquidator is statutorily bound by such an arrangement; in my view there is no statutory support for such a proposition, since subsection 3, in that regard , is related to an arrangement etc. made by a company in the course of being wound up, whereby the liquidator would be bound. In my view, a more fundamental equitable principle is involved. The unsecured creditors cannot be permitted to approbate and reprobate; they secured the advantage of the company continuing to trade in the completion of the contracts, thereby greatly increasing the amount available for distribution. But they now seek to deny another part of the self same agreement; they cannot be permitted to do so. As long as all interested parties are protected, I see no reason why those immediately concerned may not make a valid and enforceable agreement to waive or amend the order of priority of payment. If other parties not involved in the scheme were to be concerned in the winding up, different considerations would apply. Here, however, the court has before it effectively the two parties to the scheme who have vital interests in the winding up; the liquidator provides the machinery. It is beyond question that the parties intended that the preferential claim of the Collector General should stand in the event of a winding up as of 31 March 1982 (which date was unilaterally extended until 6 July 1982). To order that the parties adhere to the terms of that scheme of arrangement and to give the Collector General the priority claimed seems to me to be "in accordance with law".

I would accordingly answer the questions set out in the Special Indorsement of Claim as follows:

(a) Yes including interest
(b) Does not arise
(c) Does not arise
(d) Does not arise
(e) Does not arise

Patricia McLaughlin
Barrister

[**Reporter's Note:** Section 285 of the Companies Act 1963 has been amended by section 10 of the Companies (Amendment) Act 1982 (No. 10) and more recently by section 134 of the Companies Act 1990 (No. 33).]

In the Matter of J. & L.F. Goodbody (Exports) Ltd (in Liquidation) and In the Matter of the Companies Acts 1963 to 1986: High Court 1984 No. 8813P (Murphy J) 22 March 1991

Modernisation plans of company – New machinery imported– Company advised that if the machinery were imported by a company which sold only by way of export, then the purchase would not be liable to value added tax – Importation of raw materials to be used in the manufacturing process would also be exempt – Name of wholly owned subsidiary changed – Invoices in name of subsidiary – Subsidiary occupied no premises and had no staff – Did not have any permanent significant capital or loan capital available – Did import materials and paid for them – Debits from subsidiary's account accompanied by corresponding credit provided from resources of parent company – Receiver appointed to parent company – Subsidiary wound up and official liquidator appointed – Outstanding invoices – Issue as to whether the parent company or subsidiary was entitled to resulting proceeds

Facts: J. & L.F. Goodbody Ltd ("Goodbody") underwent a process of modernisation in 1983 which involved the purchase of expensive machinery including machinery known as the Barmag Line. The company was advised that if this machinery were purchased and imported by a company which sold only by way of export then Value Added Tax would not be payable on the importation of the machinery or raw materials imported subsequently in connection with the business. As a result, Goodbody changed the name of a wholly owned subsidiary, Shamrock Plastics Ltd, to J. & L.F. Goodbody (Exports) Ltd ("the export company"), and the Barmag Line was purchased and imported in the name of that company. However, it was installed at the premises of Goodbody and it was operated by Goodbody staff. It was clear that the export company did import some materials which were processed on the Barmag Line and which were subsequently exported. All of the goods exported subsequent to the purported reorganisation of the affairs of the two companies were invoiced out on documents which bore the name "J. & L.F. Goodbody (Exports) Ltd". The export company did not at any time own or occupy any premises and did not employ any staff. It did not have any significant permanent capital nor did it have any loan capital available to it from any financial institution. The goods bought and paid for by the export company were funded through the Ulster Bank and debits to the account of the export company were corresponded by credits provided from the resources of the parent company.

On 17 September 1984 a receiver was appointed over Goodbody and on 14 November 1984 the export company was ordered to be wound up and an official liquidator was appointed. As of the date when the receiver was appointed to Goodbody invoices amounting to £567,726.78 in respect of goods invoiced under the name of the export company were outstanding and a question arose as to who was entitled to these.

Held by Murphy J:

On the balance of the evidence available, the export company, having become the owners of the raw materials remained the owners of so much of those raw materials as were incorporated in the finished products ultimately exported.

No cases referred to in judgment

Counsel's and solicitors' names not available

MURPHY J **22 March 1991**

J. & L.F. Goodbody Ltd (Goodbody) carried on business as manufacturers of sacks and related products, originally of jute and subsequently of synthetic materials for many years at Clara, County Offaly. In 1983 Goodbody had under consideration a modernisation programme. This involved the purchase of expensive machinery including what was known as the Barmag Line. It appears that Goodbody were advised by a company which sold by way of export that value added tax would not be payable on the importation of the machinery or indeed on raw materials subsequently to be imported in connection with the business of the company. This advice was taken and implemented by changing the name of a wholly owned subsidiary of Goodbody's known as Shamrock Plastics Ltd to J. & L.F. Goodbody (Exports) Ltd, the company named in the title hereof, and the Barmag Line was imported in the name of that company. The decision to import the Barmag Line in the name of J.& L.F. Goodbody (Exports) Ltd — to which I will refer as "Exports" — was made known to and accepted by the manufactures of the Barmag Line and by An Foir Teoranta and the I.D.A. who co-operated in financing the transaction. The application to import materials free of VAT was made to the Revenue Commissioners in the name of Shamrock Plastics Ltd on 28 November 1983 and the authorisation was granted on 9 January 1984. When the name of Shamrock Plastics Ltd was changed to Exports an amended application was made and a fresh authorisation was granted by the commissioners on 28 June 1984. A curious feature of the application was that it expressly stated that the goods which it was proposed to import and re-export would be manufactured by the parent company of Exports although it does not appear that this fact would justify the grant of an exemption from VAT.

The suppliers of the Barmag Line installed the same in the premises of Goodbody at Clara, County Offaly. It is a substantial machine, or more correctly series of machines, which were bolted to the factory floor. The machine was operated by persons employed by Goodbody. It is clear that Exports did import some materials which were processed or used for the purpose of manufacture on the Barmag Line and subsequently exported. All of the goods exported subsequent to the purported reorganisation of the affairs of the two companies were invoiced out on documents which bore the name "J. & L.F. Goodbody (Exports) Ltd". In addition there was a reference to the word "Goodbody" and to the name J. & L.F. Goodbody Ltd in part of the logo of the company. It is clear, however, that a change did occur in the form of the invoices subsequent to the reorganisation. Certainly there was not and could not have been any reference to the name J. & L.F. Goodbody (*Exports*) Ltd before the reorganisation.

On 17 September 1984 Mr Michael McNulty was appointed receiver over Goodbody and on 14 November 1984 it was ordered that Exports be wound up by the court and that Bernard E. Somers be appointed official liquidator thereof. It appears that as at 17 September 1984, that is to say, the date of the appointment of the receiver over Goodbody, there was due a sum of £567,726.98 in respect of goods exported under invoices which incorporated the name "J. & L.F. Goodbody (Exports) Ltd". The issue in the present proceedings is whether the receiver of Goodbody or the liquidator of Exports is entitled to that sum.

As far back as 7 April 1983 the board of Goodbody had resolved at a meeting held on that date that:

> The whole of the business of J. & L.F. Goodbody Ltd is transferred into a wholly owned subsidiary. This transfer includes:
>
> > The Goodbody name and style.
> > All of the Goodbody employees including their respective contracts of employment. Such employees have a continuation of employment in terms of years of service, rights etc. All of the Goodbody assets, rights and benefits and all of its liabilities including contingent liabilities guarantees and other commitments. The Goodbody goodwill."

The resolution having dealt with certain other matters then went on to record the following observations and directions:

> "While it was noted that the transfer of the business of J. & L.F. Goodbody Ltd would require the permission of interested parties and certain legal formalities would need to be put in place, it is the intention that such transfer should take immediate effect.
>
> The secretary was instructed to arrange the legal formalities in such manner as to minimise the incurrence of taxation and stamp duties."

Whether the change of name of Shamrock Plastics Ltd to Exports and the acquisition of the Barmag Line formed part of the restructuring by that board resolution is not clear. All that can be said with certainty is that Exports did not at any material time own or occupy any premises or employ or pay any staff. It follows that Exports did not itself handle (less still manufacture) any goods. Again it seems clear that Exports did not have any significant permanent capital monies nor did it have loan capital available to it from any financial institution. Such goods as were bought and paid for by Exports were funded through the

Ulster Bank Ltd (Tullamore branch) by means of monies provided by Goodbody. In the period from 14 June 1984 to 31 August 1984 seven items totalling £111,513 were debited to an account of Exports with that branch of the Ulster Bank but as each item was debited there was a corresponding credit provided from the resources of the parent company. One of the seven items was a sum of £52,159 which related to the purchase of the Barmag Line but the remaining six items amounting to £59,352 appear to have related to the raw materials. In addition to that expenditure Exports appears to be indebted to creditors in respect of the supply of raw materials in a sum of £181,218.

There is, therefore, evidence that it was the intention of both Goodbody and Exports that the latter company should purchase raw materials and that Exports should export the raw materials when processed. Furthermore the financial records support the inference that this intention was implemented to the extent that goods were indeed imported in the name of Exports and paid for by it (albeit with monies provided by the parent company) and that the name of Exports was shown on the invoices supplied in respect of the finished goods sold abroad. Unfortunately there is a hiatus in the evidence between the importation and the exportation. As already pointed out it is clear that the goods could not have been processed by Exports as they had neither staff nor premises but what is not known is whether the goods were processed by Goodbody on their own account with perhaps the intention of reselling them to Exports or whether the raw materials were processed by Goodbody on some form of commission basis for Exports. It was the evidence of Mr Lionel Booth who was the chairman of Goodbody from 1979 to 1984 that the raw materials became and remained the property of Exports. However, he fairly recognised that he did not have a clear recollection of all the details of the matter. Indeed it seems to me that the reality is that either the details of the arrangement were not fully thought out or alternatively were not implemented before the ultimate financial collapse of both companies. There is simply no evidence as to the nature of the arrangement implemented to regulate the right and interests of Exports and Goodbody in relation to the ownership of the raw materials and the profit or remuneration for carrying out the industrial process. There were a variety of means by which this could have been carried out but there is no evidence before me as to which of them was intended or adopted. Apparently Goodbody invoiced customers with the sale price of goods sold on the domestic market even though the raw materials had been purchased by Exports. This would suggest that it was intended that the ownership in some of the goods would pass to Goodbody. On the other hand in relation to the goods which were exported there is no evidence at all to suggest that it was intended that goods would be sold by Exports to Goodbody and then repurchased by Exporters prior to resale. Of course it is equally true, in this negative area, that there was no evidence of any agreement providing for the commission or remuneration to be paid by Exports to Goodbody's for the work carried out by them on behalf of Exports if that is what the parties intended.

There is no satisfactory solution to the question raised by the notice of motion herein. It seems to me, however that the better of the two unsatisfactory solutions is the inference that Exports having become the owners of the raw materials remained the owners of so much of those raw materials as were incorporated in finished products ultimately exported. Given the paucity of evidence it seems to me safer to base my conclusion on the known facts relating to the purchase of the raw materials by Exports; the invoices incorporating the name of the export company and the established intention of both companies that the export business should be carried on by Exports rather than to speculate or attempt to draw other inferences as to the transfer of ownership from Exports to Goodbody and perhaps back again. On balance it seems to me probable that what the parties intended and achieved was that the ownership in the raw materials (at least to the extent to which they were subsequently incorporated in goods exported abroad) vested and remained in Exports until ultimately sold by that company. I would assume that Exports incurred a liability to Goodbody on a *quantum meruit* basis if not otherwise in respect of the work done by the parent company on the goods provided by the subsidiary. Again it may be that this liability was discharged or reduced by a set-off of the cost price of the goods imported by Exports and ultimately resold by Goodbody for its own benefit on the domestic market. These factors may require further argument and may indeed involve troublesome computations. Whether it is necessary to pursue that aspect of the matter will depend upon the financial circumstances of the two companies. In any event the issue is not before the court at the present time.

Subject to any submission that counsel may see fit to make in this regard it seems to me that the question raised in the notice of motion, namely:

> "Whether or not the monies received by J. & L.F. Goodbody Ltd in respect of goods sold to non-customers and so issued in the name of J.& L.F. Goodbody (Exports) Ltd (in liquidation) is the property of Exports"

should be answered in the affirmative.

Patricia McLaughlin
Barrister

HKN Invest Oy and Wicabo Finland Oy (PVT) v. Incotrade PVT Ltd, Gunter Knieper, Alfred Eiger and Jurgan Heisler, and Patrick McSwiney, William Lynch, Leonard Lynch, James Patrick Fitgerald and Paul Gilsenan (notice parties): High Court 1991 No 13862P (Costello J) 2 October 1992

Company – Promoter – Pre-incorporation contracts – Whether contracts ratified – Whether ratification inferred from acceptance of sums by principle shareholder – Liquidation – Judgment – Garnishee – Beneficial ownership – Whether contracts could be ratified by liquidator – Equity – Constructive trust – Fiduciary relationship – Whether fiduciary relationship existed prior to incorporation – Whether monies received by promoter as trustee – Whether creditor entitled to order of garnishee – Companies Act 1963 (No. 33), sections 37, 231

Facts: The defendant company was promoted by the three individual defendants and was set up as a bogus loan brokerage business. The plaintiffs were Finnish companies who secured loan facilities for their clients in foreign currencies in international markets. The plaintiffs agreed with the defendants that the latter would provide loans for some of the plaintiffs' clients and that commission would be paid to the defendants in advance of these loans.

Several contracts were entered into both prior to and after incorporation and substantial amounts of commission was paid to the defendants, although the plaintiff believed at all times that the said contracts were with the first defendant. These monies were paid into the personal bank accounts of the second and third named defendants which contained commission paid prior to the incorporation of the company under pre-incorporation contracts, commission paid after incorporation under pre-incorporation contracts and commission paid after incorporation paid under contracts entered into after the date of incorporation.

The defendant failed to secure any loans for the plaintiffs' clients, the individual defendants left the jurisdiction and a liquidator was subsequently appointed to the company which had a large number of creditors at that time. The plaintiff's obtained judgment against the defendant company and conditional orders of garnishee over the monies lodged in the personal bank accounts of the second and third defendants. They sought to have these conditional orders made absolute. The liquidator submitted that the monies were beneficially owned by the company and such could not be subject to attachment under an order of garnishee. It was further submitted that the liquidator had the power to ratify any contracts made prior to incorporation by the individual defendants.

Held by Costello J in refusing to make absolute the conditional orders of garnishee and declaring that the company was beneficially entitled to the monies in the accounts of the second and third defendants:

(1) Pre-incorporation contracts may be ratified by the company by virtue of section 37 of the Companies Act 1963 and it is not necessary to show that a

formal meeting took place to ratify such contracts. However, there was no evidence in this case which would permit the court to infer a post-incorporation ratification of any of the pre-incorporation contracts and such ratification cannot be inferred from the mere acceptance by the principle shareholder of sums paid by commission.

(2) The powers conferred by section 231(2)(i) include an implied power of the liquidator to ratify pre-incorporation contracts as by this means assets could be obtained for distribution to the company's creditors which otherwise would not be available.

(3) The pre-ratification breach of a term of the contract which can be brought into existence under the section does not mean that the contract cannot be ratified. Ratification will mean that as a matter of law the pre-incorporation contracts will have existed from their date of execution and it will not affect the rights of either party arising from the manner in which the contracts have or have not been performed since then.

(4) No fiduciary relationship existed between the second and third defendant and the company with regard to monies received by way of commission on pre-incorporation contracts. *Lydney and Wigpool Iron Ore Co. v. Bird* 33 Ch D 85 considered.

(5) The promoter of a company who received payment on behalf of a company which he is incorporating and pursuant to a pre-incorporation contract which the company is empowered to ratify holds the commission as a constructive trustee for the company and the company is beneficially entitled to the benefit of such contracts.

(6) The same principle applies even if the company did not formally ratify the contracts because as a matter of law the payments made in such circumstances would have been received by the promoter as a trustee for the company he was proposing to establish. The fraud of the promoter does not affect this position as what they did was to act in breach of the trust, not disestablish the trust by their fraud.

(7) Monies paid after incorporation on foot of pre-incorporation or post-incorporation contracts were received by the defendants as fiduciaries for the company, whether as directors or agents of the company.

(8) It follows therefore that as all the monies in these accounts are trust monies to which the company is beneficially entitled, they cannot be the subject of execution by any of the creditors of the second and third named defendants, including execution by means of garnishee proceedings.

Cases referred to in judgment

Hussey v. Palmer [1972] 3 All ER 744
Lydney and Wigpool Iron Ore Co. v. Bird (1886) 33 Ch D 85
Newborne v. Sensolid (Great Britain) Ltd [1954] 1 QB 45

Paul Sreenan SC and Bruce Antoniotti BL instructed by *Ernest J Cantillon & Co.* **for the plaintiffs**

Richard Law Nesbitt BL instructed by *Matheson Ormsby Prentice* **for the first notice party**
Cormac Clancy BL instructed by *Eamon Murray & Co.* **for the second, third and fourth notice parties**
Frank Callanan BL instructed by *Daly Derham & Co.* **for the fifth notice party**

COSTELLO J **2 October 1992**

Gunter Knieper, Alfred Eiger and Jurgan Heilser were three German nationals who came to Ireland in the first half of 1991 and started up in Cork a bogus loan brokerage business by means of which they defrauded a number of Irish and foreign nationals of substantial sums of money. In September 1991 they departed this country hurriedly only a few steps ahead of the Irish and German police. They left behind them a number of angry creditors and a cluster of legal problems as to who is now entitled to the benefit of certain assets which they had failed to take with them. They had formed a company called Incotrade Pvt Ltd incorporated on 13 August 1991. It is now in liquidation and the liquidator claims that certain assets including credits standing in a bank account in the name of Mr Knieper and another in an account in the name of Mr Eiger, and four large expensive motor cars and two large expensive motor cycles, are the company's property and should be available for the company's creditors, whilst the plaintiffs in these proceedings, who have obtained judgment both against the company and the three individuals I have named, maintain that these assets belong to the individuals and that they should be allowed to complete execution against them by way of the garnishee proceedings they have instituted.

What happened to the plaintiffs is probably fairly typical of the unfortunate experiences of other creditors.

The plaintiffs are Finnish companies who provide services for their clients by arranging loan facilities for them in foreign currencies on international markets. In July 1991 two of their representatives travelled to Cork having learnt that a firm call Incotrade Pvt Ltd was offering services as a loan broker. Following discussions with the three defendants it was agreed that loans would be procured for some of the plaintiffs' clients at a rate of 5.5 per cent, that the plaintiffs would pay commission at the rate of 1 per cent on the amount of the loans, that the commission would be paid in advance of any draw down of the loan, that the commission would be repaid if the loan was not advanced in thirty days. The plaintiff paid commission amounting to 670,400 DMs in the months of July and August 1991. When no loan was forthcoming, their representatives travelled to Ireland on 20 September 1991 only to find that the company's offices were deserted and that the three defendants had disappeared. They sued Incotrade and the three defendants individually obtaining judgment in default of appearance on 3 February 1992 for 670,400 DMs (being IR£51,276.86). They ascertained that there was a sum standing of £84,727.35 to the credit of Gunter Knieper in an account No. 20915189 at the Bishopstown Branch of Allied Irish Bank and a sum of £16,181.31 standing to the credit of Alfred Eiger in the same branch. They obtained a conditional order of garnishee over the bank's indebtedness on 2 March 1992. Their motion to have this order made absolute was served on Incotrade's liquidator. As they claimed relief in relation to the vehicles also, another motion dated 26 February was served on three Irish creditors who claimed to have obtained proprietary interests in the vehicles. For the moment I will defer consideration of the issues on that motion and concentrate on the issues relating to the bank accounts, and the garnishee proceedings.

The salient facts as appearing from the affidavits filed and the inferences I draw from them are as follows:

(1) Incotrade was incorporated on 13 August 1991 but for some time before its incorporation the three personal defendants had been carrying on business. They had stationery printed, all of which was headed 'Incotrade Pvt Ltd". Most of the documents emanating from the defendants in relation to loans and the payment of commission were signed by two of the personal defendants purporting to do so on behalf of "Incotrade Pvt Ltd".

(2) Persons carrying on business with the defendants believed that in the negotiations which took place the personal defendants were acting on behalf of Incotrade. When they entered into contracts in respect of loans to be obtained and commission to be paid they understood that the contracts were entered into with Incotrade and that commission was payable to Incotrade. In most, if not all, cases the sums paid by way of commission were made payable to Incotrade and not to the personal defendants. Where contracts, were entered into and payments of commission made before 13 August 1991 none of the persons so contracting and so paying were aware that the company had not been incorporated at the time.

(3) Whilst I have not, of course, have had the benefit of evidence from any of the personal defendants, I think that it is reasonable to infer that they caused the company to be established (or purchased a "shelf" company for this purpose) to avoid any personal liability on any of the contracts that were entered into and that they intended that the business they were purporting to carry on would be carried on by the company when it was incorporated.

(4) A number of contracts purporting to be made by Incotrade were made before the company was incorporated, A number of payments were made to "Incotrade Pvt Ltd" before it was incorporated. Commission was paid after the date of incorporation in respect of contracts made both before and after incorporation.

(5) Gunter Knieper opened a personal account in his own name in the Bishopstown Branch of AIB on 16 July 1991. This is account No.

20915189. He caused to be paid into this account the commission which was payable to "Incotrade Pvt Ltd" both before the company was incorporated and after the company was incorporated. It is accepted that no funds were transferred into the account from the company after it was incorporated, and no sums were lodged from Mr Knieper's own resources into this account.

(6) After the company was incorporated it opened an account in its name in the branch of AIB at 26 Patrick Street Cork on 21 August 1991. This is account No. 10422-010. At the date of liquidation this account was in credit in the sum of £30,250.54. The company opened a second account in this branch on 17 September 1991 (account No. 10422-366) and there was a sum of £81,327.93 standing to the company's credit in this account on the date of liquidation. It appears that even though the company had after incorporation its own account sums payable by way of commission on contracts entered into with the company after incorporation were paid by Mr Knieper into his private account at the Bishopstown branch of AIB.

(7) Not all the commission payments paid into Mr Knieper's Bishopstown account were retained in it, but none was paid over to the company after its incorporation. Substantial sums were paid out of this account on and after 16 August and used to purchase two Mercedes cars and a Porsche car which were registered in the names of the personal defendants.

(8) Mr Knieper had another personal account (with, which this case is not concerned) in the Bank of Ireland, 37 South Mall Cork (No. 07009940). It appears that commission payments were lodged by Mr Knieper into this account before the company was incorporated and that substantial sums were paid out of it on 12 July 1991 for the purchase of another expensive car which was not registered in the company's name.

(9) The issue now for determination is whether the balance now in Bishopstown account No. 20915189 is owned beneficially by Mr Knieper or is owned beneficially by the company. Although I have not got a detailed analysis of this account it is clear that the balance must be made up of (a) commission payments made before the company's incorporation on 13 August 1991 on contracts entered into before that date, and for (b) commission payments made after 13 August 1991 on contracts entered into before that date, and (c) commission payments made after 13 August 1991 on contracts entered into after 13 August 1991.

(10) The sum to credit in an account in the name of Alfred Eiger maintained in the Bishopstown branch of AIB is £16,181.31. This account is No. 18526048 and was opened on 26 July 1991 (*i.e.* before the incorporation of the company). It appears that no funds were transferred

into this account from the company and no funds transferred out of it to the company. It further appears that no sums were lodged into it from Mr Eiger's own resources. Again, this balance is made up of (a) commission payments made before the company's incorporation on contracts entered into before that date, and for (b) commission payments made after the date of incorporation on contracts entered into before that date, and for (c) commission payments made after the date of incorporation on contracts entered into after the date of incorporation.

The law

(a) *Pre-incorporation contracts*
I propose now to consider the law in relation to pre-incorporation contracts. In so doing, however, it is to be borne in mind that this case concerns the beneficial ownership of monies paid under pre-incorporation contracts and not, the enforceability of such contracts.

(i) *At common law*
It is well established that because a company before incorporation has no capacity to contract it follows that nobody can contract on behalf of an unincorporated company. This means that a pre-incorporation contract could not, at common law, be ratified by the company after incorporation (but it could, of course, enter into a new contract after incorporation to put into effect the terms of the pre-incorporation contract). A pre-incorporation contract which is purported to be made on behalf of a company which does not exist is in fact a nullity (see, Palmer, *Company Law* (1987 ed.), para. 20.02 and *Newborne v. Sensolid (Great Britain) Ltd* [1954] 1 QB 45).

(ii) *Statute*
The rigours of, and possible injustices flowing from, the strict common law rules were modified by statute, section 37 of the Companies Act 1963 provides:

> "Any contract or other transaction purporting to be entered into by a company prior to its formation or by any person on behalf of the company prior to its formation may be ratified by the company after its formation and thereupon the company shall become bound by it and entitled to the benefit thereof as if it had been in existence at the date of such contract or other transaction and had been a party thereto."

In this case a question of fact arises as to whether or not the company ratified any of the pre-incorporation contracts which were made prior to its incorporation.

I do not think that any formal meeting to ratify must be shown to have taken place before this section can be applied. Each case must depend on its own facts, but it seems to me that ratification can in certain circumstances occur informally, for example, in a one-man company where after incorporation the controlling shareholder, implements the contract without the benefit of a formal board meeting. However, in this case no evidence of any sort has been produced to permit the court to infer a post-incorporation ratification of any of pre-incorporation contracts and I do not think that I can infer such ratification from the mere acceptance by the principal shareholder of sums paid by commission.

It has been urged on the behalf of the liquidator of Incotrade that he can now ratify the pre-incorporation contracts under section 37. In principle, I can see no reason why this could not be done — the company remains in existence after an order has been made to wind it up (or, in the case of voluntary liquidations when the resolutions required by the Act have been passed) and what has to be ascertained is whether the liquidator has any statutory powers to ratify conferred by the 1963 Act. Certainly, no express powers are to be found but section 231(2)(i) empowers liquidators "to do all such other things as may be necessary for winding-up the affairs of the company and for distributing its assets". As section 37 confers a statutory right on a company to obtain the benefits of pre-incorporation contracts and as this statutory right may properly be regarded as an asset conferred on companies by the section, it seems to me that the powers conferred by section 231(2)(i) includes a power to ratify pre-incorporation contracts as by this means assets could be obtained for distribution to the company's creditors which otherwise would not be available.

But can the liquidator properly ratify these particular contracts? They contained provisions that (a) the company would render certain services and (b) that if they did not do so within 30 days the commission would be repayable. This means that the act of ratification would be in respect of a contract under which the other party is entitled to a return of the money paid under it at the date of ratification, and in respect of which the company had undertaken obligations which it had failed to fulfil and which the liquidator could not fulfil after ratification. But I do not think that the pre-ratification breach of a term of a contract which can be brought into existence under the section means that the contract cannot be ratified. Ratification brings into existence an agreement which would otherwise be a nullity, and it creates contractual rights and obligations on the basis that it had always had a legal existence. Ratification in this case will mean that as a matter of law the pre-incorporation contracts will have existed from their date of execution — it will not affect the rights of either party arising from the manner in which the contract has or has not been performed since then. I will therefore declare that the liquidator is entitled to ratify the pre-incorporation contracts entered into on behalf of the company prior to its incorporation.

Ratification, however, will not determine the issue that arises on this motion — namely the beneficial ownership of the monies in the accounts to which I have referred. To determine that issue it is necessary to refer to and apply the principles of equity which, it seems to me, will apply whether the contracts are ratified or not.

(iii) *Equity*

It is to be borne in mind (a) that our first concerns are with pre-incorporation contracts by which the company purportedly agreed to supply services in consideration for the payment of commission and to refund the commission if the agreed services were not provided and (b) that payments of commission were made pursuant to these purported contracts. The issue in the case is not the enforceability of the pre-incorporation contracts but the beneficial ownership of money paid under them. Secondly, the beneficial ownership of monies paid after incorporation also falls for consideration. If it can be shown that the monies were received by Mr Knieper and Mr Eiger as constructive trustees of the company then it would follow (a) that the company has a proprietary remedy against them for the return of the monies and (b) their creditors cannot levy execution against these sums (by garnishee proceedings or otherwise) to satisfy debt that they may personally owe. Alternatively, if it can be shown that a fiduciary relationship existed between them and the company then they would hold the monies as constructive trustees for the company.

I will consider firstly the position concerning monies received before incorporation by way of commission on pre-incorporation contracts. It seems to me that it would be straining past breaking point the concept of a fiduciary relationship to hold that such a relationship existed at a time prior to the incorporation of the company. This was the view of Lindley LJ in *Lydney and Wigpool Iron Ore Co. v. Bird* (1886) 33 Ch D 85. Dealing with a case in which the promoter of a company received a secret profit prior to incorporation he pointed out (at p. 93):

> "It is not correct to say that James Bird was the agent of the company when it did not exist, nor is it much less objectionable to talk of his being in a fiduciary relation to the company before the company had any existence,"

but he went on to point out (at p. 94):

> "it is perfectly well settled that a promoter of a company is accountable to it for all moneys secretly obtained by him from it just as if the relationship of principal and agent or trustee and *cetuis que trust* had really existed between them and the company when the money was so obtained."

Although, Mr Knieper and Mr Eiger may not have been fiduciaries at the time they received the pre-incorporation commission I think they received it as constructive trustees. A constructive trust will arise when the circumstances render it inequitable for the legal owner of property to deny the title of another to it. It is a trust which comes into existence irrespective of the will of the parties and arises by operation of law. The principle is that where a person who holds property in circumstances in which in equity and good conscience should be held or enjoyed by another he will be compelled to hold the property in trust for another (*Hanbury Modern Equity*, p. 218. *Hussey v. Palmer* [1972] 3 All ER 744, at 747).

It will help the analysis in this case, I think, if I first examine a situation in which no fraud is involved. Let me assume that a promoter who is to be controlling shareholder in a company shortly to be incorporated purports to contract in the name of a company and received advance commission for services which the company is to render. In such circumstances he has received the commission for the benefit of the company which is to be incorporated and not for his own benefit. If before the company is incorporated and before it has either formally or informally had an opportunity to ratify the contract he is adjudicated a bankrupt and ratification then takes place a question would arise as to whether the creditors in the bankruptcy of the promoter are entitled to the commission or whether it can be claimed by the company. It seems to me that as a matter of equity and good conscience the court should uphold the company's claim. The commission was never beneficially owned by the promoter — he held it in trust for the company which he was forming and which was to perform the services he had agreed would be performed. If this was not the case (a) considerable injustice could be suffered by the company, its shareholders or creditors who were deprived of the commission whilst (b) the creditors in the bankruptcy would obtain a greater interest in the property than the bankrupt himself enjoyed. It seems to me therefore that the court should hold that the promoter of a company who received payment on behalf of a company which he is incorporating and pursuant to a pre-incorporation contract which the company is empowered to ratify holds the commission as a constructive trustee for the company.

I think the same principle would apply even if the company did not formally ratify the contract matter of law the payments made in the circumstances I have outlined would have been received by the promoter as a trustee for the company he was proposing to establish and did in fact establish. And I do not think that the fraud of the promoters can affect this position. The fact that the promoters did not pay the commission to Incotrade and that they had no intention of supplying the promised services when they received it and that they misapplied the funds they received does not, in my view, affect the trust which arose when they received the monies — what they did was to act in breach of trust, not disestablish the trust by their fraud.

It follows therefore that insofar as the monies in the two accounts I am considering represent the balance of commission received prior to incorporation on 13 August 1991 this balance is held in trust for the company and cannot be the subject of a garnishee order.

The monies in the accounts may represent in whole or in part commission paid after incorporation in respect of pre-incorporation contracts or post-incorporation contracts and which should have been paid over to the company but instead was retained by Mr Knieper and Mr Eiger for their own use. The position in such cases is clear. If they had been appointed directors of the company (the evidence does not disclose whether formal appointments were ever made) they would have a fiduciary relationship with the company. Even if they had not been formally appointed they would have received the commission as agents for the company and a fiduciary relationship would also exist. As fiduciaries they would hold the commission on a constructive trust for the company. It follows therefore that as all the monies in these accounts are trust monies to which the company is beneficially entitled they cannot be the subject of execution by any of the creditors of Mr Knieper or Mr Eiger, including execution by means of garnishee proceedings. I will therefore refuse to make absolute the order of garnishee and discharge the conditional order. I think it would be, appropriate also to make a declaratory order that the liquidator is entitled to the monies in these accounts as assets of the company.

The motion of 26 February 1992
This motion raised questions as to the ownership of the proceeds of sale of four motor cars and two motor cycles. It has been agreed that these issues can more appropriately be dealt with by an application by the liquidator in the Incotrade winding-up and so no order is now required on this motion.

Patricia McLaughlin
Barrister

In the Matter of Eccles Hall Ltd (In Liquidation) and In the Matter of the Companies Acts 1963-1990: Francis N.A. Kelly v. Linda Scales Practising Under the Style and Title of Scales and Company: High Court 1993 No. 16651P (Barron J) 22 November 1993

Whether retrospective – Presumption – Liquidation – Solicitor claimed lien over documentation – Whether liquidator entitled to such documentation – Whether the right to the lien arises only when it is asserted – Companies Act 1963 (No. 33), section 244A as inserted by Companies Act 1990 (No. 33), section 125

Facts: The respondent was a solicitor and had acted for Eccles Hall Ltd which was in liquidation. The applicant as official liquidator applied to the court for possession of all documentation relating to a hotel which was the main asset of Eccles Hall Ltd which the respondent had in her possession. The respondent claimed that she had a lien over the documentation in respect of costs owed to her by the company. The applicant applied for an order pursuant to section 244A of the Companies Act 1963 as inserted by section 125 of the Companies Act 1990 that the respondent deliver up to him such documentation notwithstanding the lien claimed. The respondent submitted that the lien arose prior to the passing of the 1990 Act and that to grant the relief sought would give section 244A of the 1963 Act retrospective effect.

Held by Barron J in dismissing the applicant's claim:

(1) The lien arose when the work was done by the applicant and there was no need to assert the lien for the right to arise.

(2) In the absence of a clear intention to the contrary, no statute should be given retrospective effect; *In re Raison* (1891) 63 LT 709 approved; *Hamilton v. Hamilton* [1982] IR 466 considered.

(3) The respondent is entitled to the lien claimed.

Cases referred to in judgment

Hamilton v. Hamilton [1982] IR 466

In re Raison (1891) 63 LT 709

Michael Collins BL instructed by *O'Brien & Binchy* **for the applicant**

Frank Clarke SC with Brian O'Moore BL instructed by *Scales & Co.* **for the respondent**

BARRON J **22 November 1993**

This case raises two net issues. First, whether section 244A of the Companies Act 1963 is retrospective; and, secondly, if it is whether it applies where a secured creditor is seeking to raise its security whether or not there will be a balance available to the liquidator.

The liquidator makes two submissions:

(1) that the right to the lien arises only when it is asserted; and

(2) that since the proviso to the section could have included liens, there is an implication that the Act was intended to be retrospective in relation to liens.

In relation to the retrospective operation of statutes, two types of situation exist. The first is the enforcement of the terms of the statute to circumstances in existence of the date of the statute. To do so is to give the Act retrospective effect. The second is the enforcement of its terms in relation to circumstances existing subsequent to its passing but having regard to events which occurred before its passing. To do so does not give the Act retrospective effect since the right being enforced is one given by the Act.

I can see no merit in suggesting that to deny the validity of the lien, the court is not giving the statute a retrospective effect but is merely taking into account past events. That can only occur when a statute creates a right and the past events are permitted to establish the right which before the Act would not have been possible. That is not the case here; the past events had already created the right.

The circumstances giving rise to the lien claimed arose as soon as the work was done. There was no need to assert the lien to establish the right. Accordingly, if the Act is to take away this right, it must be given retrospective effect. I cannot therefore accept the applicant's first submission.

The court leans against retrospective effect. In my view the rule is best expressed by the following passage from the judgment of Cave J in *In Re Raison* (1891) 63 LT 709 as following:

> "There is an old and well known saying with regard to new laws that you

> are not by a new law to affect for the worst the position in which a man already finds himself at the time when the law is actually passed".

Nevertheless, where there is a clear intention in the statute itself that it should have retrospective effect, such effect will be given to it. However, in the absence of such clear intention no such effect will be construed: see *Hamilton v. Hamilton* [1982] IR 466. The applicant has submitted that since the proviso to the section could have included liens there is an implication that the Act was intended to be retrospective in relation to such charges. I cannot accept this submission. In my view there is no clear intention in the Act itself to be derived from this omission, if in fact it is such.

In my view the respondent is entitled to the lien which she asserts. There is accordingly no need to consider the position of a receiver co-operating with a liquidator in the sale of secured assets.

Patricia McLaughlin
Barrister

1963 ACT, PART VII

Constantine A. Angelis v. Algemene Bank Nederland (Ireland) Ltd, Alexander K. Burns, Owen Mulholland, Robert John Armstrong, James Malone, Vincent Nolan and Commercial Ferries Ltd: High Court 1974 No. 2130P (Kenny J) 4 July 1974

Company – Receiver – Debenture – Agreement of debenture holder not to utilise powers provided certain sums paid – Judgment obtained against company by different creditor – Appointment of receiver – Validity of appointment – Fear that assets in danger – Meetings – Member – Request to call meeting of directors – Whether person requesting meeting was in fact a director – Whether appropriate to treat as application by member to call meeting of company – Requirement for notice – Whether directors bound to act on request – Power of court to convene meeting – When exercisable – Companies Act 1963 (No. 33), sections 132, 135

Facts: Commercial Ferries Ltd ("the company") was incorporated on 13 October 1972. The plaintiff and the second, third, fourth and fifth named defendants were shareholders of the company. On 13 May 1974 the company granted a debenture to Algemene Bank Nederland (Ireland) Ltd ("the bank") to secure all monies due by the company to the bank and charged all of its assets and undertakings with payment of the sum due. Some £250,000 was due by the company to the bank. The bank agreed that they would not exercise some of their powers under the debenture if the company paid £7,000 per month off the amount due.

Shortly after the grant of the debenture, Texaco (Ireland) Ltd obtained a judgment against the company and the bank, fearing that the assets were in danger, appointed the second defendant as receiver over all of the assets and undertakings of the company. The company was also indebted to Ulster Bank Ltd in the sum of £49,000 which sum was secured by a guarantee given by the plaintiff.

By letter dated 14 June 1974 the plaintiff purported to convene a directors' meeting for 17 June. On 24 June he commenced proceedings claiming a declaration that the appointment of the receiver was invalid, an order restraining him from interfering with the assets of the company and an order under section 135 of the Companies Act 1963 directing the third defendant to hold a meeting of the company. By notice of motion dated 21 June 1974 he sought an order declaring the appointment of the receiver invalid and an order directing the third, fourth and fifth defendants to assist the plaintiff in holding a meeting of the company or directing the same to be held.

The plaintiff claimed to be the owner of 100,000 of the 150,000 shares in the company. However the other directors disputed this on the grounds that 99,000 of the shares were purchased from sums paid to the plaintiff by the company, some of which related to a deposit which the plaintiff claimed to have paid to a Norwegian firm for the construction of a ship, but which the directors ascertained had not been paid.

Held by Kenny J in refusing to grant any of the relief sought:

(1) The receiver was validly appointed because the assets of the company were in danger of being seized under the judgment.

(2) It seemed probable that the plaintiff had resigned as a director when he purported to call a directors' meeting. Even if the letter of 14 June was taken as a request to call a meeting of the company then, under section 132 of the Companies Act 1963, the directors would have had 21 days in which to convene a meeting after a request by the holder of 10 per cent of the shares. The letter dated 14 June was therefore clearly invalid. In addition the plaintiff had issued his plenary summons on 24 June and that was less than 21 days from 14 June. The directors were therefore not bound to act on his request.

(3) Section 135 of the Companies Act 1963 permits the court to call a meeting where it is impracticable to do so. Here it was not impracticable to call a meeting and the directors could without difficulty call one. The court would not order that a meeting be convened, and as a receiver was in possession of the assets it was difficult to see what purpose would be served by the holding of a meeting.

No cases referred to in judgment

Counsel's names not available

Solicitors for the plaintiff: *Michael B. O'Cleirigh & Co.*
Solicitors for the first and second named defendants: *Gerrard Scallan & O'Brien*
Solicitors for the third, fourth, fifth, sixth and seventh named defendants: *Brendan Walsh & Co.*

KENNY J **4 July 1974**

Algemene Bank Nederland (Ireland) Ltd ("the bank"), the first named defendants, are a banking company incorporated in the State. The second named defendant is a well known accountant who has been appointed receiver by the bank over the assets and property of the defendants, Commercial Ferries Ltd ("the company"). The third, fourth, fifth and sixth named defendants are shareholders in the company. The company was incorporated in the State on 13 October 1972 and the plaintiff, the third named defendant, the fourth named defendant, the fifth named defendant and the sixth named defendant were directors of it.

On 13 May 1974 the company gave a debenture to the bank to secure monies due by the company to the bank and charged all assets and undertakings with payment of the sum due from the company. There is a sum of at least £250,000 due by the company to the bank and this is secured by the debenture. The debenture was subject to certain conditions as to payment and the bank agreed that they would not exercise some of their powers under the debenture if £7,000 per month was paid off the amount due on the debenture. After the debenture had been given Texaco (Ireland) Ltd recovered judgment against the company. It is not necessary to cite authority for the proposition that when the assets charged by a debenture are in danger of seizure, a debenture holder may immediately appoint a receiver. The bank appointed the second named defendant to be the receiver and manager of all the assets and undertakings of the company. The company is also indebted to the Ulster Bank Ltd for £49,800 and this is secured by guarantees given by plaintiff.

The plaintiff began these proceedings on 24 June 1974 in which he claimed a declaration that the appointment of the second named defendant as receiver was invalid and an order restraining him from interfering with the assets of the company. He also claimed an order under section 135 of the Companies Act 1963 ("the Act of 1963") directing the third named defendant to hold a meeting of the company and by motion of 21 June he applied for an order that the appointment of the receiver was invalid and that the third, fourth and fifth named defendants be ordered to assist the plaintiff in holding a meeting of the company or directing the same to be held.

The nominal paid up share capital of the company is £150,000 and the plaintiff appears in the share register as the owner of 100,000 shares. The circumstances surrounding the issue of 99,000 shares to the plaintiff are highly suspicious. The company was shown in its books as being indebted to the plaintiff for a large sum. Part of this sum was alleged to consist of a deposit paid by the plaintiff to a Norwegian firm called Ulstein for the construction of a ship for the company called "the Athenian Trader". The directors subsequently ascertained that no deposit had been paid and that the plaintiff's statement that he paid such a deposit was untrue. The company issued a cheque to the plaintiff for £99,000 in part repayment of the loan and the plaintiff then gave the company a cheque for £99,000 for shares. If the deposit was not paid for the construction of "the Athenian Trader", then the sum was not due. It seems to me to be reasonably clear that the cheque which the plaintiff got from the company was obtained by false statements and that the question whether the shares which he holds were fully paid or whether they were properly issued is very much in contention.

I am satisfied that the appointment by the bank of the receiver was valid because the assets of the company were in danger of being seized under the judgment. I accordingly decline to make any order on paragraphs (a) or (b) of the motion.

It seems to me to be probable that the plaintiff agreed to resign as a director of the company and therefore he cannot convene a meeting of directors. By letter dated 14 June 1974 he purported to convene a directors' meeting for 17 June 1974. If this be read as a requisition to call a meeting of the company, then it was clearly invalid because under section 132 of the Act of 1963 the directors have a period of twenty-one days within which to convene a meeting. Moreover a plenary summons was issued on 24 June 1974 and that is less than twenty-one days from the letter of 14 June. Section 135 of the Act of 1963 gives the court power to call a meeting of a company if it is impracticable to do so. I am not satisfied that it is impracticable to call a meeting of the company. I think that the directors could without difficulty convene a meeting of the company. The requisition served on them to convene a meeting was invalid and they were not bound to act on it. Circumstances have not arisen in which the court should order a meeting of the company to be convened. As a receiver is in possession of the assets of the company I do not see what purpose would be served by holding a meeting of the company. The directors are of course free to convene a meeting at any time they think fit and will have to hold a meeting if members of the company holding not less than one-tenth of the paid up share capital of the company serve a valid requisition on them to hold such a meeting.

As the plaintiff has been charged with certain criminal offences in connection with assets of the company I do not wish to say more than is strictly necessary for the purpose of deciding whether I should grant the relief claimed in the notice of motion of 21 June 1974. For the reasons given I am not prepared to grant any of the relief sought and this application must be dismissed.

Alistair Rutherdale
Barrister

In re Industrial Development Authority: High Court (Butler J) 1 May 1978

Company seal – Receiver – Power of attorney – Transfer of property – Articles permitted granting of power of attorney – Whether receiver had power of attorney to execute deeds within the State on behalf of the company – Whether receiver could affix the seal of the company – Whether power of sale given to receiver included a power to execute a deed to effect such sale – Companies Act 1963 (No. 33), sections 40, 41

Facts: The articles of association of the Cork Shoe Company permitted the directors to borrow and issue securities and article 128 provided for the use of the company seal in the same terms as are prescribed by article 115 of Table A of the first Schedule to the Companies Act 1963. Article 129 which was in the common form provided for an official company seal to be used abroad as provided for in the Companies Act 1963. Article 100 gave the company the power to appoint an attorney. In 1965 the company issued a debenture to the Bank of Ireland which included as a specific charge the lands comprised in Folio 43689 in Co. Cork. The debenture gave the bank power, *inter alia,* to appoint a receiver with power to take possession of, collect and get in the property charged by the debenture and, further, to carry any such sale of the property into effect by deed in the name and on behalf of the company or otherwise to convey the same to the purchaser. The debenture further appointed any such receiver as the attorney of the company in order that he might execute, seal and deliver and otherwise perfect any deed, assurance, agreement, instrument or act which may be required or may be deemed proper. On 12 May 1975 the bank appointed a receiver under the debenture. On 25 July 1976, the receiver contracted to sell to the Industrial Development Authority part of the lands in the folio which was subject to the charge and purported to carry this sale into effect by transfer dated 8 October 1976. The document was expressed to be sealed by the company by the direction of the receiver. The registrar was not satisfied that the receiver had power to affix the seal of the company in the execution of the deed and he referred the matter to the court for directions.

Held by Butler J in upholding the registrar's objections:

(1) The seal is the only tangible existence that a company has and its use must be regulated by the articles of association. In a matter so important and fundamental, strict adherence to the articles is essential and cannot be waived or altered by the directors or the company itself otherwise than by altering the articles.

(2) The use and control of the seal by the receiver which was not authorised by the articles is not in accordance with any valid power. The affixing of the seal by the receiver is not a valid or effective sealing by the company to witness the transfer as its deed.

(3) The importance which the legislature attaches to the company's seal is clearly to be inferred from the Companies Act 1963 itself. The Act provides two ways in which a company can transact outside the State: section 40 enables a company to appoint an attorney to execute deeds on its behalf outside the State and section 41 provides that the company may have an official seal for use abroad. The fact that these specific and detailed provisions were made in the Act indicates that specific statutory authority is required to authorise the use of the seal and the method of affixing it in a manner different from that normally authorised.

(4) The legislature enacted a specific power enabling a company to appoint an attorney indicating that, but for the section, a company would have no such power. Therefore the power is limited to circumstances covered by the provision, namely to execute deeds on its behalf in any place outside the State.

(5) Insofar as the power purported to confer a power to execute deeds on behalf of the company within the State, it is *ultra vires* and void. The deed must be executed by the company itself and have the same effect as if it were under its common seal.

(6) Section 46 of the Conveyancing Act 1881 cannot operate to validate the transaction as the company had no power to appoint an attorney to act on its behalf in the execution of a deed within the State.

Cases referred to in judgment
Blackpool Corporation v. Starr Estate Company [1922] AC 27
Moss v. Whinney [1912] AC 254

Counsel's and solicitors' names not available

Decision of Butler J reversed by Supreme Court. Reported as *Industrial Development Authority v. Moran* [1978] IR 159

BUTLER J **1 May 1978**

1. Cork Shoe Company is a limited liability company incorporated on 1 May 1947. It is regulated by articles adopted by special resolution passed on the 24 July 1973. By the articles the provisions of Table A are not to apply to the company. Article 101 gives the directors all the powers of the company to borrow and issue securities in identical terms with the first four lines of Article 79 of Table A without the limitations contained in the latter part of the Article: Article 128 providing for the use of the seal is in the exact terms of Article 115 of Table A: and, Article 129 is in the common form providing for an official company seal for use abroad under the provisions of the Companies Act 1963. Article 100 is in the following terms:

> "100. The directors may from time to time and at anytime by power of attorney under the seal appoint any company, firm or person or any fluctuating body of persons whether nominated directly by the directors to be the attorneys of the company for such purposes and with such powers, authorities and discretions (not exceeding those vested in or exercisable by the directors under these Articles) and for such period and subject to such conditions as they may think fit, and any such power of attorney may contain such provisions for the protection and convenience of persons dealing with any attorney as the directors may think fit, and may also authorise any such attorney to sub-delegate all or any of the powers authorities and discretions vested in him."

2. The company is the registered owner of the lands comprised in Folio 43689 of the county of Cork subject to certain leases, charges and rights, including the charge next referred to in this judgment.

3. On 23 October 1965 the company issued a debenture to the Bank of Ireland to secure present and future advances. The company charged with the payments secured by the debenture all its property and assets and as a specific charge the lands comprised in the said folio. The conditions of the debenture confer on the bank the fullest and most stringent powers in relation to the security. Clause 10 gives the bank power to appoint a receiver with power to take possession of collect and get in the property charged by the debenture. Paragraph 3 of the paragraphs setting out the powers of the receiver is in the following terms:

> "3. To sell or concur in the selling, let or concur in the letting any of the

property charged by this debenture and to carry any such sale into effect by deed in the name and on behalf of the company or otherwise to convey the same to the purchaser."

The clause further provides that the receiver shall be the agent of the company and the company shall be solely responsible for his acts or defaults.

Clause 14 provides as follows:

14. "The company hereby irrevocably appoints any receiver or receivers appointed as foresaid the attorney or attorneys of the company for the company and in its name and on its behalf and as its act and deed to execute seal and deliver and otherwise perfect any deed, assurance, agreement, instrument or act which may be required or may be deemed proper for any of the purposes aforesaid."

4. On 12 May 1975 the bank appointed Mr Michael Gribben as receiver under the debenture. The instrument of appointment in specifying his powers set out the powers conferred by clause 10 of the conditions including the power to sell and convey property which I have quoted.

5. On 25 July 1976 Mr Gribben contracted to sell to the Industrial Development Authority part of the lands comprised on the folio for £130,000 and purported to carry this sale into effect by transfer dated 8 October 1976. The transfer is by indenture made between the company of the first part the receiver of the second part and the I.D.A. of the third part. It recites the debenture setting out the charge and the relevant conditions in detail; it recites the due appointment of the receiver, and it recites the agreement for the sale by the receiver pursuant to the powers vested in him by the debenture. The property is conveyed in the following terms:

". . . the company, the registered owner (acting by the receiver) doth hereby convey and transfer and the receiver in exercise of the powers given to him by the conditions endorsed on the said debenture dated the 23 October 1965 doth hereby transfer and confirm unto the purchaser. …"

The deed is witnessed as follows:

"In witness whereof the common seal of the company has been hereunto affixed by direction of the receiver as such receiver, pursuant to the powers vested in him as aforesaid and the receiver has signed his name and affixed his seal and the common seal of the purchaser has hereunto affixed the day and the year first herein written."

The document was expressed to be sealed by the company by the direction of the receiver accordingly. It is with this transfer and this sealing by the company that we are concerned. The registrar was not satisfied that the receiver had power to affix the seal of the company in the execution of the deed and has referred the matter to this court. The I.D.A. appeared to support their application for registration and are themselves supported by the receiver. Both were represented by counsel at the hearing. As the company did not appear I was anxious to have the consideration that led the registrar to have doubts presented to me by way of contribution and I am grateful to the Attorney General for his ready co-operation in enabling the registrar to be represented by counsel. I am deeply appreciative of the helpful submissions of counsel for all three interests.

6. The question, though the point is simple and net, is not easy to answer. I am aware that there are conflicting views among conveyancing practitioners. The practice in England, even before the modern legislation, appears to have been less stringent than in Ireland as is evidenced by the provision of forms for the purpose of having a sale carried out in this way by a receiver in standard sets of precedents. Furthermore, it has been decided that on the appointment of a receiver in circumstances such as this, a company cannot itself deal with property (see for example *Moss v. Whinney* [1912] AC 254) and the insertion of a power by the receiver to convey in the name and on behalf of a company is almost commonplace in debentures. Again it was submitted by counsel for the bank that there is no case in the books in which a deed in this form has ever been attacked. Lastly, as Mr Barron submitted if the debenture gives, and validly gives a power of sale to the receiver it is inherent to the effective exercise of that power that he has the means of carrying the sale into effect.

If all these considerations are insufficient to enable me to hold that the transfer was a valid and effective exercise of the power of sale of the receiver I was strongly pressed to hold that the transfer is a valid exercise of the power of attorney conferred on the receiver by the debenture and that the transfer is made valid and effective by virtue of section 46 of the Conveyancing Act 1881. This section provides that the donee of a power of attorney may execute or do any instrument or thing in and with his own name and signature and his own seal where sealing is required and that every assurance, instrument or thing so executed and done shall be as effectual in law to all intents as if it had been executed or done by the donee of the power in the name and with the signature and seal of the donor.

7. Both in principle and by statute the use of a company's seal is obviously a matter of the greatest consequence. The seal is the only tangible existence that a company has and must be used as evidence of the act of the company in any matter of importance. Its use is regulated by the articles which constitute the regulations adopted by the company for the management of its affairs and define the limits within which the shareholders agree that the corporate acts of the company are to be performed. In a matter so important and fundamental strict adherence to the articles would appear to be essential and cannot be waived or altered by the directors or indeed by the company itself otherwise than by altering the articles. If this be correct then the use and control of the seal by the receiver which in this case is not authorised by the articles is not in accordance with any valid power. The affixing of the seal by the receiver is not a valid or

effective sealing by the company to witness the transfer as its deed.

8. The importance which the legislature attaches to the company's seal is clearly to be inferred from the Companies Act itself. Section 18 which sets out the effect of registration of a company provides in subsection (2) that from the date of incorporation the members of the company shall be a body corporate "capable forthwith of exercising all the functions of an incorporated company, and having perpetual succession and a common seal". Where important matters require to be transacted outside the State, the Act deals with the matter in two ways. First, in section 40 by enabling the company to appoint an attorney to execute deeds on its behalf outside the State. I shall return to this provision later, and secondly, by providing that the company may have an official seal for use abroad. A consideration of the conditions attached to this latter power illustrates the importance that the legislature attaches to the company seal and the degree to which its use is to be governed by the articles. First it is given only to companies whose objects require or comprise the transaction of business outside the State; secondly, the possession of such a seal must be authorised by articles; thirdly, the company must in writing under its common seal nominate the person who is to use the seal and the territory in which it is to be used and must authorise that person to affix the seal to any deed or document to which the company is a party in that territory; lastly it was apparently thought necessary to spell out the effect of an instrument so executed. Subsection (2) provides that a deed or other document to which an official seal is duly affixed shall bind the company as if it had been sealed with the common seal of the company. Sections 40 and 41 are re-enactments of previous legislation: section 40 re-enacts section 78 of the 1908 Act which had itself re-enacted section 55 of the 1862 Act; and section 41 re-enacts section 79 of the 1908 Act.

The fact that it was found necessary to make these special and very detailed provisions would seem to indicate that specific statutory authority is required to authorise the use of the seal and the method of affixing it in a manner different from that normally authorised.

9. Because of the submission that the present transfer is a valid exercise of the power of attorney expressed to be given to the receiver by the debenture I have to return to the provisions of section 40 and consider them more in detail. The section is a short one and may be quoted in full.

> "Section 40(1) A company may, by writing under its common seal, empower any person, either generally or in respect of any specified matters, as its attorney, to execute deeds on its behalf in any place outside the State.
>
> (2) A deed signed by such attorney on behalf of the company and under his seal shall bind the company and have the same effect as it were under its common seal".

Natural persons may appoint attorneys freely to do any act which the principal himself may do. That the legislature found it necessary to re-enact this specific provision to enable a company to do so would appear to be a clear indication that but for the section a company has no such power. If this be so the power is limited to the circumstances covered by the provision, namely to execute deeds on its behalf in any place outside the State. It follows in my view that a company has no power to act by attorney to execute deeds within the State. The attorney must be appointed in writing under the common seal of the company. That was done by clause 14 of the conditions of this debenture. However if my view is correct the appointment insofar as it purports to confer a power to execute deeds on behalf of the company within the State is *ultra vires* and void. Again in relation to the power conferred by subsection (1) of section 40 it was apparently thought necessary to provide as is also done in section 41 that the effect of the execution of a deed in the special case is to bind the company and have the same effect as if it were under its common seal.

All these considerations lead me to the view that in the case of a domestic transaction a deed must be executed by the company itself and the seal affixed in accordance with the regulations of the company and not otherwise.

10. There remains the question as to whether the transaction can be validated by section 46 of the Conveyancing Act 1881. The section applies to deeds executed by the donee of a power of attorney. If I am correct in the view that a company cannot appoint an attorney to act on its behalf in the execution of a deed within the state then the section can have no application to the present case. However, there are other grounds which suggest that the section does not apply in the case of companies. As I have noted the provision enabling a company to execute deeds abroad through an attorney has already conferred by section 55 of the Companies Act 1862. If it were intended that section 46 of the 1881 Act should broaden that power to make it general it would have been necessary for the Act to say so explicitly either in the section itself or by separate provision. Had that been done or if as was submitted to me, the section achieves the result without such express references it would have been unnecessary to re-enact section 55 of the 1862 Act by section 78 of the 1908 Act and again by section 40 of the 1963 Act. The general principle of statutory interpretation is *generalia specialbus non derogant.* The application of the principle was explained by Viscount Cave in the classic quotation from his judgement in *Blackpool Corporation v. Starr Estate Company* [1922] AC 27 at page 38:

> "the presumption is that a subsequent and general enactment is not intended to interfere with the special provision unless the intention so to do is clearly manifested."

Accordingly in my opinion the present transfer has not been validly executed, it was ineffective to transfer the legal estate in the property and the registrar's doubts when in withholding registration of the purchasers as full owners were justified.

11. Although this is sufficient to dispose of the matter before me the position of the bank as equitable mortgagees of the property was adverted to in the course

of argument and it may be helpful if I indicate my views on the matter. The bank are the owners of a registered charge on registered land. In the case of unregistered land it would appear that section 21 subsection (1) of the Conveyancing Act 1881 does not empower a mortgage having only an equitable mortgage by deed to convey the legal estate. In the case of registered lands however, section 62 of the Registration of Title Act 1964 provides a code of its own in relation to the creation and effect of a charge on such lands.

Subsection (1) provides that the registered owner of lands may charge the lands with the payment of money either with or without interest and the owner of the charge shall be registered as such. Subsection (6) provides that on registration the instrument of charge shall operate as a mortgage by deed within the meaning of the Conveyancing Acts and the registered owner shall for the purpose of enforcing his charge have all the rights and powers of a mortgagee under a mortgage by deed including the power to sell the estate or interest which is subject to the charge.

The effect of a sale made under this power is clearly set out in subsection (9) which provides that if the registered owner of a charge sells the land under the powers referred to in subsection (6) his transferee shall be registered as owner of the land and thereupon the registration shall have the same effect as registration on a transfer for valuable consideration by a registered owner.

The position would therefore, appear to be clear. The bank as registered owners of the charge can sell and convey the full legal estate of the registered owner in the lands.

I appreciate and regret the effect of this judgment on the present transaction. However, for the reasons stated I can see no alternative to holding as I do and although certain inconvenience will result, the matter can be remedied in a number of ways which it is unnecessary for me to discuss.

Patricia McLaughlin
Barrister

Rex Pet Foods Ltd (In Receivership) and Charles Russell Murphy v. Lamb Brothers (Dublin) Ltd, Lamb Brothers (Marketing) Ltd, Lamb Foods Ltd, W.H. Lamb and Co. Ltd and Lambs (Ireland) Ltd (No. 1): High Court 1982 No. 8937P (Finlay P) 26 August 1982

Company – Receivership – Company wholly owned subsidiary of other companies – Goods produced by company held by defendants – Whether part of assets – Interlocutory injunction to restrain sale of goods – Whether serious question to be tried – Balance of convenience – Injunction – Test – Respective sides finely balanced – Court entitled to take into account relative strength of cases shown on affidavit by the parties

Facts: The receiver of the plaintiff company commenced proceedings seeking declarations that the assets of the defendant companies formed part of the assets of the first named plaintiff and should be aggregated therewith, and, further, that the plaintiff and defendant companies carried on business as a single entity.

The plaintiffs sought an interlocutory injunction pending the trial restraining the defendants from disposing of certain goods, produced by the plaintiff company and then in the possession of the defendants, or, alternatively, to restrain the disposal of such goods pending the hearing, unless the proceeds of sale were preserved in a suspense or trustee account to await the outcome of the action. The plaintiffs claimed that these goods were part of the assets to which the receiver was entitled to have access for the purposes of his receivership.

The plaintiffs said that the relevant defendant companies were 100 per cent owners of the plaintiff company, and that the plaintiff was bound by a distribution agreement to sell its product to the defendants, with the defendants fixing the price of resale. There was also a management agreement with the defendants providing the management of the plaintiff company.

The plaintiffs submitted that the books did not record regular payments in respect of goods supplied, but for significant periods these sums were entered as loans. Payments did not relate to specific goods but rather the need of the plaintiff company to make disbursements to creditors.

The plaintiffs averred that the defendants were about to go into liquidation, and without an injunction the proceeds for sale would go into the general fund. The defendants said they were not imminently insolvent unless they were prevented from disposing of the disputed goods.

Held by Finlay P in granting an interlocutory injunction.

(1) On an application for an interlocutory injunction the first enquiry to be made by the court is whether the claim of the plaintiffs in their affidavit raises a fair or serious question to be tried. If it does not then no question of an injunction arises.

(2) If it does, then the court must consider whether the balance of convenience is in favour of the granting of an injunction. The onus of proof is on the plaintiff. In this regard the court looks at the disadvantage or damage which would be suffered by the respective parties — being damage or disadvantage which is irreparable by an award of money damages. *American Cyanamid Co. v. Ethicon Ltd* [1975] AC 396; [1975] 2 WLR 316; [1975] 1 All ER 503 followed; *Educational Company of Ireland v. Fitzpatrick (No. 1)* [1961] IR 323; (1961) 96 ILTR 161 followed.

(3) When the balance of convenience appears to be relatively finely met, it may not be improper to tip the balance by examining the relative strength of the cases shown on affidavit by the plaintiff and defendant.

Dicta of Diplock LJ in *American Cyanamid Co. v. Ethicon Ltd* [1975] AC 396; [1975] 2 WLR 316; [1975] 1 All ER 503 approved.

(4) The evidence as set out in the affidavits did raise a serious question to be

tried as to whether the three companies involved carried on business as a single entity.

(5) In relation to the balance of convenience, the allegation about the imminent liquidation of the defendants, while baldly stated, was not without support on the facts and exhibits. There was thus a risk that the sale proceeds of the goods would be lost to the liquidator. In these circumstances an onus passed to the defendants to show they had resources if the plaintiffs were ultimately successful in their action.

(6) In these circumstances the court was entitled to consider the fact that in the affidavits the extent of dispute as to the facts was limited, and that the case made by the plaintiff in asserting that the companies were a single entity was stronger than the case made by the defendants that the two companies traded at arms length.

Cases referred to in judgment

American Cyanamid Company v. Ethicon Ltd [1975] AC 396; [1975] 2 WLR 316; [1975] 1 All ER 503

Educational Co. of Ireland v. Fitzpatrick (No. 1) [1961] IR 323; (1961) 96 ILTR 161

Peter Kelly BL instructed by *D.F. Jones & Co.* **for the plaintiffs**

Brian McCracken SC with Patrick Keane BL instructed by *A & L Goodbody* **for the defendants**

FINLAY P **26 August 1982**

This is an application by the first-named plaintiff, Rex Pet Foods Ltd, who are in receivership, and the receiver, Mr Murphy, against Lamb Brothers (Dublin) Ltd, Lamb Brothers (Marketing Ltd, Lamb Foods Ltd, W.H. Lamb & Co. Ltd and Lambs (Ireland) Ltd. It is a claim for an interlocutory injunction by the plaintiffs restraining the defendants from disposing of certain scheduled goods produced by the first-named plaintiffs and presently in the possession of one or other of the defendants, or in the alternative for an order by way of interlocutory injunction that such goods should not be disposed of pending the hearing of the action, otherwise than on terms that the proceeds of the sale of the goods should be held in a suspense or trustee account preserved to await the outcome of the action.

It is clear that on the facts stated in the affidavits the action is in truth maintainable only against two of the named limited companies who are defendants and that the other limited companies do not appear to be involved in the dispute.

On an application for an interlocutory injunction the principles upon which I must decide it are, in my view, clear and well settled. They are to be found set out by the Supreme Court in the *Educational Company of Ireland v. Fitzpatrick* [1961] IR 323 and most recently in the House of Lords in the *American Cyanamid Co. v. Ethicon Ltd* [1975] AC 396.

The statement of principles contained in these two decisions do not differ but to some extent each complements the other in certain aspects of the questions raised. The principles upon which I am obliged to decide this application are therefore in my view as follows.

The first enquiry must be as to whether the claim in aid of which the plaintiffs seek this injunction on the affidavits raises a fair or serious question to be tried. If it does not, or to put the matter in the negative form which it is contained in the decision of Diplock LJ in *American Cyanamid Co. v. Ethicon Ltd*, if it is vexatious or frivolous or an implausible claim then no question of an injunction arises.

If, however, it does raise a fair or serious question to be tried in the action then I must necessarily enquire, the onus of proof being on the plaintiff, as to whether the balance of convenience is in favour of the granting of an injunction.

That enquiry involves, *inter alia*, a consideration on the facts before me of the damage or disadvantage arising to the plaintiffs if the injunction were not granted and if they were successful in the final hearing of the action. It also involves the disadvantages arising to the defendants if the injunction were granted and they were successful in establishing at the hearing of the action that the claim against them was unsustainable. The disadvantage or damage to be considered in balancing the convenience, as it is stated in the authorities, is necessarily damage or disadvantage which is irreparable by giving money damages, in the one case the damages to which the plaintiffs would be entitled if they succeeded and in the other case the damages which would be payable by the plaintiff to the defendants on the undertaking as to damages which is necessarily a pre-condition to the granting of an injunction.

The only other principle which has affected my mind and which I have taken into consideration as a legal principle to apply the law to the facts of this difficult case is that I would follow with approval the remarks made in the judgment of Diplock LJ in *American Cyanamid Co. v. Ethicon Ltd*, that it may not be improper where the balance of convenience appears to be relatively finely met to tip the balance by the relative strength of the cases shown on affidavit by the plaintiff and the defendant.

Applying these principles of law which I believe to be correct principles to the facts of this case the position is as follows:

The claim made by the plaintiffs and significantly and substantially speaking the cause of action in aid of which they seek this interlocutory injunctions is, firstly, for a declaration that the assets of the defendant companies form part of the assets of the first-named plaintiff and should be aggregated therewith and, secondly, for a declaration that at all material times the first-named plaintiff and the defendants were trading and carrying on business as one single entity. The plaintiffs claim that if they are successful in obtaining these two declarations then the finished products presently in the possession of the defendants, which were manufactured or produced by the first-named plaintiff company and have not yet been sold or converted into monies by the defendants are part of the assets which the receiver is entitled to have access to for the purpose of his receivership and that it is necessary in order to preserve that situation until the hearing of the action that either of the two forms of injunction which I have outlined should be granted to the plaintiff.

In relation to the onus of proof which lies on the plaintiffs that this is a serious question to be tried in the action, they rely on a number of factors some of which it is necessary to identify. Firstly, they rely on the fact that the relevant defendant companies are at present and were at the time of the receivership 100 per cent owners of the plaintiff company. Secondly, they rely on two distribution and management agreements, one of which is distribution and the other of which is a management agreement, very shortly and broadly the effect of which is to bind the plaintiff company exclusively to sell all its products to the defendant company and which permitted the defendant company to fix the price at which those products would be resold to retail outlets; which provided for the total management of the plaintiff company by servants or employees or by persons with a consultancy duty acquired by the defendant companies and in particular permitted the financial, book-keeping and other organisational and administrative tasks of the plaintiff company to be under that control. They also rely upon the consequential book-keeping entries and financial transactions between the companies since these agreements came into operation in March of 1981 up to the time of the receivership.

Broadly speaking, they rely upon the fact that there does not appear to have been entered into the books of the plaintiff company regular payments relating in either times or amount to specific invoices for goods delivered and sold but rather that over a significant period in 1981 at least in two months in June and July the payments that are now claimed by the defendants to have been payments for goods sold by the plaintiff to the defendants appeared as loans.

Secondly, in a very great number of instances payments made by the defendant companies to the plaintiff company have not been related either in time or amount to goods produced and delivered as between the two companies but rather had been related to what were clearly urgent and essential disbursements by the plaintiff company in order to deal with those creditors in relation to raw materials and other necessary services for the manufacture of these goods.

They place particular reliance also on the fact that the control of the prices at which these goods would ultimately be sold which determined entirely the prices which would be received by the plaintiff company for them was in the apparent decision of the defendant company. In my view, these and other facts which it is unnecessary for me to enumerate in the affidavits before me and the exhibits referred to in them clearly raise a serious question to be tried as to whether the three companies involved did not trade and carry on business as a single entity and whether as a consequence the assets of the defendant companies concerned do not form part of the assets of the first-named plaintiff.

It then becomes necessary to consider the question of the balance of convenience. The plaintiff's case on this aspect is short and to an extent somewhat baldly stated in the affidavit. The second-named plaintiff says in his affidavit that it has been indicated to him that the defendant companies are imminently going to go into liquidation and if they do, no amount will be recovered in the event of a successful conclusion by the plaintiff of this claim in this action or that some extremely diminished amount is all that will be available if the goods are sold by the defendant company when the proceeds go into their ordinary funds.

The defendants on the other hand in their affidavit state that the defendant companies are not imminently insolvent provided that they can dispose of and apply the monies constituted in these products or arising from the sale of these products but that if they were forced to freeze or hold in suspense these monies or the products that they would be put into a condition of insolvency.

The statement by the plaintiff with regard to his information and belief concerning the state and condition of the defendant companies and the chance of recovering in the event of a successful conclusion of the action is baldly stated in the affidavit but is not without support on the individual facts which arise from the exhibits and certain matters which are uncontested in the affidavits filed on behalf of the defendants.

It seems that the relevant defendants ceased to deal in jams and allied foods in 1981 and I infer from the affidavits quite clearly that since that time their sole trading and commercial occupation has been associated with the first-named plaintiff company. It is clear on the facts and figures available that the first-named plaintiff company is markedly insolvent looking at its assets isolated to the assets in its own books and this fact lends support in my view to the statement of belief and information made by the receiver that if the defendant companies are permitted to sell and absorb the proceeds of the sale of these goods that there would not be available for the satisfaction of a judgment the amounts appropriate were the plaintiffs to succeed in the action. In that situation and with that additional strength behind the expression of belief by the receiver, I feel that the onus of proof to an extent has shifted to the defendants and it is only those who are involved in the defendant companies who are persons peculiarly with the knowledge and information at their disposal to make any detailed or even quasi-detailed assertion of the capacity of the defendant companies to pay the amount of these claims if the plaintiffs were successful in their action. The defendant companies on the other hand assert that they would be forced from a situation of solvency into a situation of insolvency were the goods or the proceeds of the sale of the goods to be frozen or not available to them. I must have regard to the fact that that general statement or assertion is not in any way supported by even the most localised view or account of the state of the assets and liabilities of the defendant companies or of their future trading projections.

Having regard to the appointment of a receiver too and the clear insolvency of the trading company if it were necessary to do so I would be inclined to take in aid the fact that in the affidavits the amount of dispute as to facts as distinct from the inference to be drawn from facts and documents is very limited.

Indeed, I would take the view that the plaintiffs in asserting a single trading entity and an enterprise in which the assets effectively had become aggregated have a relatively stronger case than the case made by the defendants that these were two companies trading at arms length.

Bearing these considerations in mind, I have come to the conclusion that I am forced to grant the interlocutory injunction in this case. I will grant it either in the form of a total restraint on the sale of these products but would prefer to grant it in the form of some effective and simple and heavily supervised method of sale and the suspense and preservation of the proceeds pending the outcome of the action. I would hear counsel on both sides in relation to those provisions.

Alistair Rutherdale
Barrister

Lambert Jones Estates Ltd, Charles Street Ltd and Others v. John Donnelly: High Court 1982 No. 10479P (O'Hanlon J) 5 November 1982

Injunction – Practice and procedure – Interlocutory application – Test – Whether fair or serious question to be tried – Whether balance of convenience is in favour of grant of injunction – Receiver – Property company – Sale of property as single unit – Whether better price obtainable by sale in smaller units with individual planning permission – Claim of breach of duty by receiver – Duty owed by receiver – Whether plaintiffs entitled to injunction restraining sale until the trial of the action

Facts: The first-named plaintiff owned a valuable development site at St Stephen's Green West. On 11 May 1982 the board resolved that to protect the interests of the creditors, they would request the company's bankers, Northern Bank Finance Corporation Ltd to appoint a receiver over the assets of the company mortgaged to that bank. The defendant, John Donnelly, was appointed receiver and manager over the assets of the first-named plaintiff ("the company") and its subsidiary company the second-named plaintiff.

The indebtedness of the company to the bank was £6,461,613, and interest was accruing at £3,206 per day. The defendant worked to improve the property, securing a clear site and getting rid of burdensome claims against the property. He then put the property on the market for sale as a single unit, by public tender, with a closing date for tenders of 5 November 1982.

The plaintiffs (among whom numbered the company, certain of its members, its directors, alleged chargeholders over some of its shares and certain unsecured creditors) claimed that the receiver was acting in breach of his duty as receiver and manager and claimed damages for negligence and breach of duty. They sought to restrain the sale by the receiver in the manner proposed. It was contended that it would be more profitable to divide up the property, seek planning permission for the development of smaller units and then to sell off the parcels in a series of individual transactions.

The receiver was acting on the advice of estate agents and valuers. He did not dispute that a greater price might ultimately be obtained by selling on in smaller units, but felt that the delays and time expended would result in no greater gain as interest was accumulating at £1 million per annum.

The plaintiffs sought an interlocutory injunction to restrain the liquidator and maintain the *status quo*. They were not prepared to have the hearing of the motion treated as the hearing of the action, a course that the receiver indicated would be acceptable to him.

Held by O'Hanlon J in refusing to grant an interlocutory injunction:

(1) In deciding whether to grant an injunction the court should look firstly to whether the plaintiff has shown that there is a fair or serious question to be tried. If he does not do so then an injunction cannot be issued. If he does then the court will go on to consider whether the balance of convenience lies in favour of granting the injunction. *Educational Company of Ireland Ltd v. Fitzpatrick (No. 1)* [1961] IR 323 considered; *Campus Oil Ltd v. Minister for Industry and Energy* [1983] ILRM 258 followed; *Rex Pet Foods Ltd v. Lamb Brothers (Dublin) Ltd & Others*, High Court 1982 No. 8937P (Finlay P) 26 August 1982 followed; *American Cyanamid Co. v. Ethicon Ltd* [1975] AC 396 considered.

(2) It is not appropriate for the court to express a view as to the probable outcome of the proceedings when they go to plenary hearing, or to base its decision on whether to grant interlocutory relief on a forecast of such probable outcome.

(3) A receiver owes a duty of care to the owner of property and possibly also to the creditors of the owner, when he seeks to realise property, for the primary purpose of discharging the secured creditor who appointed him. That duty renders it incumbent on him to take all reasonable steps to obtain the best possible price for the property.

(4) The plaintiff's claim was an implausible one, and the material available to the court failed to disclose any real prospect of succeeding in the claim for a permanent injunction at the trial.

(5) In addition the plaintiffs had failed to establish that damages did not afford them an adequate remedy.

(6) The injunction should therefore be refused and it was not necessary to consider the balance of convenience.

Cases referred to in judgment

American Cyanamid Co. v. Ethicon Ltd [1975] AC 396; [1975] 2 WLR 316; [1975] 1 All ER 504

Campus Oil Ltd v. Minister for Industry and Energy [1983] ILRM 258; [1984] 1 CMLR 465

Educational Company of Ireland Ltd v. Fitzpatrick (No. 1) [1961] IR 323

Latchford v. Beirne [1981] 3 All ER 705

Rex Pet Foods Ltd v. Lamb Brothers (Dublin) Ltd & Others, Irish Company Law Reports (1963-1993) 549

Standard Chartered Bank Ltd v. Walker [1982] 1 WLR 1410; [1982] 3 All ER 938

Eoghan Fitzsimons SC with Peter Kelly BL instructed by *A & L Goodbody* **for the plaintiffs**

T.K. Liston SC, Peter Shanley SC with Kevin Feeney BL instructed by *Matheson, Ormsby & Prentice* **for the defendant**

O'HANLON J **5 November 1982**

In this case the plaintiff seeks an interlocutory injunction to restrain the defendant, in his capacity as receiver, from proceeding with a sale by tender of an extensive and valuable development site abutting onto St Stephen's Green and South King Street in the City of Dublin.

The plaintiffs in the case are very numerous. They include the limited company which owns the property; a minority shareholder in the company; a number of parties who claim to be the owners of a charge over the majority shareholding in the company; a number of unsecured creditors of the company and the directors of the company.

The defendant, John Donnelly, is the receiver and manager of the assets and undertakings of the first and second-named plaintiffs (the first-named plaintiff being the owner of the development site in question which extends over some 3.5 acres at St. Stephen's Green West). At a board meeting of the first-named plaintiff held on 11 May 1982, the directors took the unusual course of resolving:

> "that to protect the interests of the creditors that they should request the company's bankers, Northern Bank Finance Corporation Ltd, to appoint a receiver and manager over the assets of the company mortgaged and/or charged to such bankers without the necessity of any formal notice or demand which are hereby waived and that such request be made immediately".

It was pursuant to this resolution that the defendant was appointed as receiver on 11 May 1982, of the first-named plaintiff and of its subsidiary, the second-named plaintiff in these proceedings.

The defendant in the course of carrying out his duties as such receiver has set about negotiating a sale of what is described as the major asset of the first-named plaintiff, being the parcel of land already referred to, situate at St Stephen's Green West in the city of Dublin. The indebtedness of the first-named plaintiff to their bankers as of 15 October 1982, was in the region of £6,461,613.00 and further interest is accruing thereon at the rate of £3,206 per day, — close on £100,000 per month, and more than £1m. per annum.

The defendant claims that since his appointment as receiver he has been engaged in negotiations and transactions which will make the property more attractive to a potential purchaser — securing a clear site and getting rid of burdensome claims against the property which existed in favour of Green Group Ltd under the terms of an agreement of 28 November 1973, and made between that company of the one part and the first-named plaintiff of the other part. He now says that the property is ripe for sale and has proceeded to put it on the market for sale as a single unit, the sale being by public tender, and the closing date and time for receipt of tenders being Friday 5 November 1982, at 3 p.m.

The plaintiffs bring these proceedings for the purpose of preventing the defendant from carrying through his avowed purpose of selling the entire site as a single unit by public tender in the manner adopted by him. They claim that they have expert advice to the effect that it would be much more profitable to divide up the property into smaller units; to apply for and obtain planning permission for schemes of development of such smaller units, and then proceed to sell off such parcels — individually in a series of transactions. In support of this contention they have put before the court an affidavit by James Kelly, himself a plaintiff and a director of the first-named plaintiff, and a further affidavit by Patrick Joseph Bannon, a partner in the firm of Harrington Bannon, Chartered Valuation Surveyors of 40 Fitzwilliam Place in the city of Dublin. They claim that the receiver is only concerned with getting in sufficient funds to discharge the claims of the bank creditors, and is unconcerned about the fate of the company which owns the property, or of its shareholders, directors or unsecured creditors. Their present application is for the purpose of obtaining interlocutory relief so that the *status quo* may be preserved pending the hearing of the action and they have indicated that they do not wish to have the hearing of the motion treated as the hearing of the action, although this course would have been acceptable to the defendant. It appears to me that when such an application is made the court should look closely at the cause of action upon which the plaintiff relies, and subject to the conclusion it reaches after conducting such examination it may then be necessary to examine the question of the balance of convenience as between granting and refusing the relief sought.

What the object of the exercise should be in looking closely at the plaintiff's cause of action is not very easy to determine by reference to the decided cases on the topic. One of the leading authorities on the principles applicable in granting or refusing relief by way of interlocutory injunction in this jurisdiction is the case of *Educational Company of Ireland Ltd v. Fitzpatrick and Others* [1961] IR 323.

Lavery J cited with apparent approval a number of passage from what he described as "the authoritative text-book, *Kerr on Injunctions*" (6th ed. 1927), some of the relevant extracts being as follows:

> "In interfering by interlocutory injunction, the court does not in general profess to anticipate the determination of the right, but merely gives it as its opinion that there is a substantial question to be tried and that till the question is ripe for trial, a case has been made out for the preservation of the property in the meantime *in statu quo*. A man who comes to the court for an interlocutory injunction is not required to make out a case which will entitle him at all events to relief at the hearing. It is enough if he can show that he has a fair question to raise as to the existence of the right which he alleges, and can satisfy the court that the property should be preserved in its present actual condition, until such question can be disposed of.
>
> The office of the court to interfere being founded on the existence of the legal right, a man who seeks the aid of the court must be able to show a fair *prima facie* case in support of the title which he asserts. He is not

> required to make out a clear legal title, but he must satisfy the court that he has a fair question to raise as to the existence of the legal right which he sets up, and that there are substantial grounds for doubting the existence of the alleged legal right, the exercise of which he seeks to prevent." (p.336).

Lavery J summarised these passages (at p. 337) by saying:

> "The plaintiffs have to establish that there is a fair question raised to be decided at the trial."

Earlier English decisions which suggested that there was an onus on a plaintiff seeking an interlocutory injunction to establish a "probability" of ultimate success, or "a *prima facie* case", or "a strong *prima facie* case", were discarded by the House of Lords in *American Cyanamid Co. v. Ethicon Ltd* [1975] AC 396, where Lord Diplock re-stated the principle applicable in the following terms at pp. 407-8:

> "The court no doubt must be satisfied that the claim is not frivolous or vexatious; in other words, that there is a serious question to be tried. . . . Unless the material available to the court at the hearing of the application for an interlocutory injunction fails to disclose that the plaintiff has any real prospect of succeeding in his claim for a permanent injunction at the trial, the court should go on to consider whether the balance of convenience lies in favour of granting or refusing the interlocutory relief that is sought."

It appears to me that Lord Diplock, while professing to discard the old test of the "*prima facie*" case, went very close to reinstating it in the last sentence of this citation.

These two decisions were referred to by Finlay P in a judgment delivered on 26 August 1982, *Rex Pet Foods Ltd v. Lamb Brothers (Dublin) Ltd & Others*. The learned President concluded that the two decisions were not inconsistent, but complemented each other. He continued at pp. 2-3 of his judgment:

> "The first enquiry must be as to whether the claim in aid of which the plaintiffs seek this injunction on the affidavits raises a fair or serious question to be tried. If it does not, or to put the matter in the negative form in which it is contained in the decision of Lord Diplock in the *Cyanamid* case, if it is vexatious or frivolous or an implausible claim then no question of an injunction arises. If, however, it does raise a fair or serious question to be tried in the action then I must necessarily enquire, the onus of proof being on the plaintiff, as to whether the balance of convenience is in favour of the granting of an injunction."

The recent decisions are again summarised in a useful manner in the judgment of Murphy J in the case of *Campus Oil Ltd & Others v. Minister for Industry and Energy & Others* [1983] ILRM 258.

In many of the cases where the courts have had to consider the principles applicable in granting or refusing relief by way of interlocutory injunction a good deal of stress has been laid on the difficulties facing the court when the facts are in dispute between the parties and it is not possible to resolve such conflict by a perusal of the affidavits. In such circumstances it is clearly inadvisable for the court to express a view as to the probable outcome of the proceedings when they go to plenary hearing, or to base a decision as to interlocutory relief on a forecast of such probable outcome.

The affidavits which have been filed on both sides in the present case disclose some areas of disagreement on the facts but the disputed facts are few in number and appear to me to be relatively unimportant. I believe the essential facts which I have to consider in dealing with the present claim for an interlocutory injunction are not in dispute and can, I think, be summarised as follows:

(1) The defendant was appointed as receiver over the property of the first-named plaintiff, including the St Stephen's Green site, on the initiative of the board of directors of the first-named plaintiff, in or about the month of May 1982, at a time when the indebtedness of the company to its bankers was in the region of £6 million. That figure had risen to close on £6.5 million by 15 October 1982, with further interest accruing thereafter at a rate not far short of £100,000 per month.

(2) For the purpose of discharging this indebtedness the defendant is proceeding to sell off the major asset of the company, consisting of the 3.5 acre site at St. Stephen's Green. This he proposes to do by offering the property for sale by public tender as a single unit, and with the benefit of such planning permissions as have already been obtained in respect of the site and which are still in force.

(3) The defendant is a chartered accountant, and sought and obtained the advice of a prominent firm of estate agents, surveyors and valuers, Messrs Jones Lang Wootton of 10/11 Molesworth Street, Dublin. He claims to have acted on their advice at all stages, and that he is still acting on their advice with regard to the proposed method of sale of the property.

(4) The plaintiffs have consulted other experts in the property field and have been advised that a considerably enhanced purchase price could, in all probability, be obtained for the site if it were sold off in several smaller lots over a period, with planning permission having first been obtained for the development of such smaller units.

(5) The defendant does not set out to dispute the claim that by adopting the method suggested by the plaintiffs a higher sale price might ultimately be obtained for the property taken as a whole. He says, however, that he is advised that the apparent gain to the vendors would in all probability be illusory. They would be likely to be involved in long delays while new development schemes were prepared for the different units and planning permission was sought for

same. In the meantime interest at over £1m per annum would continue to accumulate against the company as long as there was no return from the property. The costs involved in the plaintiffs' alternative plan of campaign would be very heavy and there are no funds available to meet such costs. Indeed, the banks have already had to contribute some £200,000 to enable the defendant to clear the site and the title for the purpose of the sale now proposed. Taking all these circumstances into account, he says he has been advised to proceed to sell in the manner which has been adopted by him, and at the present time.

(6) There is another divergence of views between the experts in relation to one of the grants of planning permission which exists in relation to the property and which is the subject of an appeal to An Bord Pleanála. The defendant says he has been advised to let that appeal lie dormant for the time being until the sale goes through, for reasons which are explained in the affidavits. The plaintiffs say, with the support of their experts, that the sale should be deferred until An Bord Pleanála has given its decision.

(7) The appointment of the defendant as receiver was made by Northern Bank Finance Corporation Ltd and The First National Bank of Chicago in exercise of powers conferred on them by a number of mortgages and debentures which had been entered into by the first-named plaintiffs and their bankers. The debentures in each case are in the conventional form and provide that in the event of a receiver being appointed he shall have power, (*inter alia*):

> "to sell or concur in selling, let or concur in letting and to terminate or to accept surrenders of leases or tenancies of any of the property hereby charged in such manner and generally on such terms and conditions as he shall think fit and to carry any such transactions into effect in the name of and on behalf of the company".

That concludes my summary of what I consider to be the central and undisputed facts of the case.

It is important to bear in mind what is the cause of action upon which the plaintiffs rely in these proceedings. The action is not brought for the purpose of determining which of the two methods of disposal of the property would, in the long run, be more favourable to all the parties who have a material interest in the outcome of the sale. It is brought to restrain the defendant from acting in breach of his duties as a receiver and manager, and seeking damages against him for negligence and breach of duty and other ancillary relief.

I am prepared to accept that a receiver owes a duty of care to the owner of property, and possibly also to the creditors of the owner, when he proceeds to realise property for the purpose of discharging the claims of a secured creditor by whom he has been appointed. That duty of care would render it incumbent upon him to take all reasonable steps to obtain the best possible price for the property. (See *Latchford v. Beirne* [1981] 3 All ER 705 and *Standard Chartered Bank Ltd v. Johnny Walker & Another* [1982] 1 WLR 1410)

Accordingly, in applying the principles governing the grant or refusal of an interlocutory injunction, it appears to me that the first question which must be asked in the present case is the following:

On the material available to the court on the hearing of this application for an interlocutory injunction, have the plaintiffs any real prospect of succeeding in their claim for a permanent injunction at the trial? If the answer to that question is "no", then the plaintiffs have failed to satisfy the test suggested by Lord Diplock in *American Cyanamid Co v. Ethicon Ltd* and would, in my opinion, fall at the first hurdle in their application for an interlocutory injunction.

I can see very clearly on the affidavits that the plaintiffs have radically different ideas from the defendant as to the best way of realising the assets of the company, and that they have the support of a prominent firm of chartered valuation surveyors for the opinion they have formed. It is equally clear, however, that the defendant has also taken expert advice and has acted upon it in deciding how he should proceed with the sale of the property. He is anxious to sell, if at all possible, at an early date, to minimise the enormous burden of interest on the bank debt which is accumulating against the company with each day and month that passes. He does not want to take a course which will involve him in new and costly and protracted planning applications for multiple units of property. He says he has no funds available to finance such transactions and the plaintiffs have not suggested that any source of finance is available to him. Finally, he has stated through his counsel in the course of the hearing, that if and when he is allowed to proceed with sale by tender it is his intention to seek the approval of the court before accepting the highest or any tender.

I fail to see, on the evidence now before the court, how the defendant could conceivably be said to be guilty of negligence or breach of duty as receiver, and in my opinion, any such finding on such evidence as is now available would be perverse. I hesitate to describe the plaintiffs' claim as "frivolous" or "vexatious" since I can appreciate their anxiety to take any step which they feel will guarantee them the best return for the property, but to borrow the expression used by Finlay P, I regard it as an implausible claim, and to borrow the words of Lord Diplock, I consider that the material available to the court at the hearing of this application for an interlocutory injunction fails to disclose that the plaintiffs have any real prospect of succeeding in their claim for a permanent injunction at the trial.

For this reason I propose to refuse the application.

As the matter may go further, it may be of assistance if I express briefly the views I have formed on some other aspects of the case.

It also appears to me that the claim for an interlocutory injunction may not lie in the present case by reason of the plaintiffs' inability to establish that, if their cause of action is well-founded, damages would not afford them an adequate remedy. If the plaintiffs are correct in their argument, and the receiver is proceeding to sell in a manner involving negligence and breach of duty on his part, then the only damage that can thereby be caused to the plaintiffs is financial loss — the difference between what will be realised on a sale by this method and what could be realised by some other method. The plaintiffs contend that such loss is not quantifiable — that it would be too difficult to determine how much had been lost in the process. Where a claim for damages arises, however, the court is not deterred from assessing damages by the difficulty of the task. It is noteworthy that the plaintiffs offer the usual undertaking as to damages in the event of their claim for an interlocutory injunction succeeding and presumably regard the loss which could be incurred by the receiver as being quantifiable, although the difficulty of assessment would appear to be as great in one case as in the other.

By reason of the conclusion already reached as to the unsustainable nature of the cause of action if considered in the light of the evidence now before the court, it is unnecessary for me to consider the balance of convenience as between the parties in granting or refusing the application for an interlocutory injunction. It appears to me, however, that the scales may be tilted in favour of the plaintiffs on this aspect of the case by reason of the rather curious circumstances that if the plaintiffs wrongfully impede the receiver in realising the assets, and money is lost in the process, the main losers will be the plaintiffs themselves. The less the property in St Stephen's Green realises, the more will have to be paid out of whatever other resources are available to the company. The bank, as a secured creditor, could also be put in jeopardy, but as between the parties to the action it would not seem to be a matter of great moment to the receiver if the method favoured by him for the realisation of the property is obstructed, and he is compelled to resort instead to some less profitable means of disposing of the asset. However, this is a matter which I do not have to determine positively, by reason of the conclusions already reached in relation to the first branch of the case, and which form the basis upon which the present application is refused.

Alistair Rutherdale
Barrister

[*Reporter's Note:* By order dated 6 February 1984 the High Court (Keane J) granted the defendant liberty to proceed with the sale of the property to Arch Properties Ltd.

By further order dated 9 April 1984 the High Court (Keane J) dismissed the plaintiffs action for want of prosecution, with costs to the defendant.

The duty of a receiver in relation to the sale of charged assets set out in section 316A of the Companies Act 1963 as inserted by section 172 of the Companies Act 1990. Section 316A(1) requires the receiver "to exercise all reasonable care to obtain the best price reasonably obtainable for the property *as at the time of sale*" (emphasis added).]

The Irish Oil and Cake Mills Ltd and Irish Oil and Cake Mills (Manufacturing) Ltd v. John Donnelly: High Court 1984 No. 2086P (Costello J) 27 May 1983

Company Law – Receiver and manager – Whether duty to account to company – Whether such duty arises from contract – Whether such duty arises from the duty of care owed by the receiver to the company – Whether equitable duty to account

Mandatory injunction – Application to force receiver to account to company – Discretionary relief – Failure of directors of applicant company to file statutory statements of affairs – Companies Act 1963 (No. 33), sections 319, 320

Facts: On 28 October 1983 the Northern Bank Ltd appointed the defendant as receiver and manager over assets which the plaintiff companies had charged under two separate indentures of floating charge.

On 25 January 1984 the defendant agreed to sell one of the assets of the second named plaintiff, an interest in a subsidiary company, Crest Foods Ltd. The second named plaintiff claimed the proposed sale was at an undervalue and instituted proceedings seeking, *inter alia*, interlocutory injunctive relief, an application which was adjourned to the trial of the action.

On 29 February 1984 the plaintiffs' solicitor wrote to the defendant requesting detailed accounts and information relating to the receivership. The plaintiffs then issued further proceedings seeking a mandatory injunction directing the defendant to furnish the information requested in the letter of 29 February.

The plaintiffs contended that (a) under the terms of the floating charge the defendant as receiver and manager was agent for the plaintiffs and so a contractual duty arose as agent to supply the information; (b) alternatively and independent of contract there was a duty of care owed by the defendant to the plaintiffs which obliged him to furnish the information sought; (c) in the further alternative there was an equitable duty to account.

Held by Costello J in refusing the relief sought:

(1) The contract between the companies and the bank, whilst establishing that the receiver be treated as the agent of the mortgagor, was silent as to the nature of his duties. There was no basis for implying a term into the contract in this case which would oblige the receiver to furnish the information sought. *McGowan v. Gannon* [1983] ILRM 516 distinguished.

(2) The receiver did owe a duty of care to the company to take reasonable steps to get the best possible price for the companies' assets. *Standard Chartered Bank v. Walker* [1982] 1 WLR 1410; [1982] 3 All ER 938 followed; *Lambert v. Donnelly*, unreported, High Court 1982 No. 10479P (O'Hanlon J) 5 November 1982 applied.

(3) However, the receiver was not in breach of that duty. There was no

evidence to show that, with the information sought, the company could prepare a scheme of reconstruction or arrangement which would mean that the price for the assets would be greater than that recoverable on a sale on the open market.

(4) Nor was there evidence to support an assertion that the information would have assisted two of the company directors to formulate a bid for the company which would be higher than would otherwise be obtained.

(5) The receiver's duty to take reasonable steps to secure the best possible price for the companies' assets does not include a duty "to keep the company appraised of how the business of the company is going".

(6) There may in some circumstances be an equitable obligation on a receiver to account, but there is no general legal obligation to do so. The extent and nature of the duty and the extent and nature of the accounts to be furnished must depend on the facts of each individual case. *Smiths Ltd v. Middleton* [1979] 3 All ER 842 explained.

(7) A claim for the information sought in the letter of 29 February was wholly exceptional, and there was nothing in the evidence to justify the grant of the interlocutory relief sought.

Per Curiam: The failure of the directors of the companies to furnish a statutory statement of affairs pursuant to sections 319 and 320 of the Companies Act 1963 would in any event disentitle the companies through their directors to the discretionary relief sought.

Cases referred to in judgment

Campus Oil Ltd v. Minister for Industry and Energy [1983] IR 88; [1984] ILRM 45
Lambert v. Donnelly, Irish Company Law Reports (1963-1993) 55
McGowan v. Gannon [1983] ILRM 516
Shepherd Homes Ltd v. Sandham [1971] 1 Ch 340
Smiths Ltd v. Middleton [1979] 3 All ER 842
Standard Chartered Bank v. Walker [1982] 1 WLR 1410; [1982] 3 All ER 938

Complete names of counsel not available
Eoin Fitzsimons SC instructed by *Vincent & Beatty* **for the plaintiff**

Solicitors for the plaintiffs: *Vincent & Beatty*
Solicitors for the defendant: *A & L Goodbody*

[Section 319 has been amended by Schedule 1 of the 1982 Act. Section 320 has been amended (again non-materially by section 173 of the 1990 Act.]

COSTELLO J **27 May 1983**

INTRODUCTION

The plaintiff companies owed the Northern Bank Ltd a sum in excess of £1.9m and on 28 October 1983 the defendant was appointed by the bank receiver and manager over the assets the plaintiffs had charged under two separate indentures of floating charge. The defendant decided to carry on the business of the second named plaintiff (that of manufacturing and distributing vegetable and other oils) with a view to selling it as a going concern and began the task of realising the assets by advertising them for sale on 11 November 1983. One of the company's assets was its interest in a subsidiary company, Crest Foods Ltd. On 25 January 1984 the defendant agreed to sell this asset, but the second named plaintiff herein claimed that the sale was at an undervalue and instituted proceedings against him. An application for interlocutory injunctive relief was adjourned by consent to the trial of the action. After this had happened the plaintiffs' solicitor wrote to the defendant on 29 February 1984 requesting detailed accounts and information of the receivership. Before his solicitors could reply otherwise than by means of a formal acknowledgement an article appeared in a Dublin daily paper stating that an offer had been made for the plaintiffs' business. The plaintiffs' directors met on 8 March and authorised the institution of these present proceedings. They then applied to the court for interlocutory relief. Their first claim is for a mandatory injunction directing the defendant to furnish the information requested in the letter of 29 February but in addition they asked for an order that such information as they might request in the future in relation to the affairs of or the disposal by the defendant of the assets of the plaintiffs be given to them. Mr Fitzsimons on their behalf has however indicated that the claim is now limited to a request for a mandatory order directing the furnishing of the information in the February letter only. They also claimed an order restraining the defendant from selling the plaintiffs' assets at an under value:

> "or until such time as the information sought by the plaintiffs . . . is furnished by the defendant in relation to such sale or proposed sale."

There has, however, been no evidence filed to suggest that the defendant is proposing to sell any asset at an undervalue and the relief claimed in paragraph 3 of the plaintiffs' notice of motion has not been pressed at the hearing. In effect what I have to decide is whether the plaintiffs are entitled to an order directing the defendant to furnish them with the information sought in the letter of 29 February.

A great deal of evidence was filed on behalf of the plaintiffs and replied to by the defendant concerning the conduct of the receivership by the defendant and the financial strength of the plaintiff companies. Mr Fitzsimons says that it is unnecessary for me on this motion to decide the many issues of fact that arise on the affidavits or otherwise to reach conclusions on them, and he admits that his case is in essence a simple one — as a matter of principle the defendant he says is under a duty to furnish the information sought and the court should order him to fulfil his duty. The duty he says arises because under the terms of the floating charges the defendant as receiver and manager is agent for the plaintiffs and so a contractual duty as such agent exists to supply the information. Alternatively and independent of contract there is a duty of care owed by the defendant to the plaintiffs which obliges him to furnish the information sought.

In the further alternative there is an equitable duty to account which on the authority of a recent case in England (*Smiths Ltd v. Middleton* [1979] 3 All ER 842) obliges him to account as requested.

Before examining these submissions I should refer in greater detail to the information which the plaintiffs say the defendant is obliged to give them. The letter of 29 February 1984 requests the following information:

> "1. Financial management account for all periods from 1 October 1983 to date.
> 2. Latest balance sheet analysed as to:
>
> > (a) All debtors and stocks.
> > (b) All creditors — showing separately pre and post receivership preferential creditors.
>
> 3. Details of all tonnages and costs of raw materials purchased since 29 October 1983.
> 4. Details of refinery programmes since 29 October 1983.
> 5. Details of sales made, by tonnage price and commodity since 29 October 1983.
> 6. The present manufacturing/sales programme.
> 7. Staff levels by job description to include management, administration and refinery indicating present and proposed (if different) and salary/wages levels.
> 8. Receiver's estimate of break-even point and how calculated.
> 9. Details of all sales and purchase contracts.
> 10. Present status of amounts due to and by foreign traders arising out of 10CM raw material purchase and sale contracts prior to 29 October 1983."

The net question which now arises is this:

Is this information which, as a matter of law, a receiver and manager is, after four months of his receivership, obliged to give the company?

The plaintiffs' first submission is that the receiver is under a contractual duty to provide the requested information.

The receiver derives his appointment and his authority from the contract entered into between the parties. In this case, as is usual, the parties agreed that he is to be treated as the agent of the mortgagors, the plaintiffs herein. The provision protects the debenture holders from liability as mortgagees in possession and establishes the relationship between the receiver and the company. But the contract is silent as to the nature of his duties and the plaintiffs here submit that there is to be implied an obligation to account as claimed in the February letter. The agency here is of course very different from the ordinary agency arising every day in commercial transactions. Here the receiver has been appointed by the owner in equity of the companies' assets with the object of realising their security and for this purpose to carry on the companies' business.

The exceptional nature of his status is to be seen from the fact that notwithstanding his appointment as agent he is to be personally liable under contracts entered into by him (with a right of indemnity out of the assets) unless the contract otherwise provides (section 316 (2) Companies Act 1963).

I can find no basis for implying a term into the contract in this case which would oblige the receiver to furnish the information now sought.

I think that the company has a right to an account from a receiver, as I will point out later, but I think it is an equitable right and that the plaintiffs herein have not a right arising from an implied term in the debenture for the information claimed in their February letter.

McGowan v. Gannon [1983] ILRM 516 does not help their case on this point. That was a case dealing with the proposed sale by a receiver of a company's premises. The receiver had given information about the sale to the company's directors, but not to a guarantor of the company's debts who was challenging the sale. Whilst in that case the receiver had vouchsafed information about a sale to the directors there is nothing to suggest that he gave them details of his trading accounts and the court was in no way concerned with the point raised in this case, namely, the existence of a receiver's duty to account to the board of directors whilst managing the company's business.

The second basis on which the claim is put forward is that the defendant threatens to breach a duty of care which he owes to the plaintiffs. The argument proceeds as follows. It is said (a) that a duty of care lies on the receiver to take reasonable steps to get the best possible price for the company's assets and that this is a duty which he owes to the company (see *Standard Chartered Bank Ltd v. Walker* [1982] 3 All ER 938 and *Lambert v. Donnelly*, High Court 1982 No. 10479P O'Hanlon J, 5 November 1982, (b) in failing to give the information sought the receiver is in breach of this duty in that (i) with its assistance the company could prepare a scheme of reconstruction or arrangement which would mean that the price for the assets would be greater than that recoverable on a sale in the open market and (ii) alternatively two of the directors of the company, Mr Rabbitte and Mr Senexio, are interested in purchasing the companies' assets and that if the company gets the information sought it will be available to these directors and enable them to formulate a bid for the company which would be higher than otherwise be obtained.

The receiver does not deny that he owes a duty to the company as alleged, but he urges that he has not been nor is he in breach of it. As to the sale which has already taken place of part of the company's assets Mr Fitzsimons accepts that the issues of fact surrounding it will be determined in other proceedings and I am not required to express any view on them on this motion. As to the receiver's present intentions, Mr Fitzsimons agreed that I do not have to decide now whether as is stated in the affidavits grounding this motion the receiver is acting *mala fide*. The plaintiffs' claim to the information is based on the general legal principles which they claim are applicable and not on any allegation of wrongdoing on the receiver's behalf.

As to (i), (the argument based on the possibility of a scheme of re-construction) it is not, in my judgment, sufficient on a motion of this sort for a company merely to assert the possibility that such a scheme would be forthcoming with the assistance of the information sought and that a receiver is under a duty to await the formulation of such a scheme before selling the assets. The uncontradicted evidence in this case is that before the receiver was appointed the directors had approached the debenture holders, informed them of the company's financial difficulties following speculation on the commodity market (which had resulted in debts of nearly £4m.) and the directors had negotiated with creditors of the company and Foir Teoranta to see if a rescue plan could be implemented. Foir Teoranta stated that it was not prepared to support a plan because it believed that funding necessary to finance it was not forthcoming. The uncontradicted evidence also establishes that on 2 December Mr Rabbitte, the managing director of the plaintiff companies wrote stating that "he had proposals to pay off the Northern Bank in full together with the receiver's fees" and that Mr Hooper of the Investment Bank of Ireland would contact the receiver about them. But no proposals were forthcoming, either at that time or since. Nearly five months have elapsed since the receiver was appointed and in the absence of a satisfactory explanation for (a) the failure to put forward a realistic scheme, and (b) as to how the information sought could assist in ensuring that the financial backing necessary would be available, and (c) in the absence of satisfactory evidence to show that purchase of the assets under the proposed scheme could avoid a sale of the assets or produce a better price than their sale in the ordinary way, the plaintiffs have not satisfied me that the receiver is acting in any way in breach of his duty to the company on the ground I am now considering.

The second ground is a different one. It is said that if the company got this information two of its directors would been be in a position to make a bid for the company's assets. But the companies' assets have been advertised for sale since 11 November 1983 and whilst an offer was made for part of the assets of the group none has ever been made for the companies' principal assets.

Again to justify the court making the entirely novel and wholly exceptional order, which is now claimed, it is not sufficient for the company to assert that the information sought would produce the result suggested. To justify the court in holding that the receiver is in breach of a duty of care to the company it should be shown that evidence in support of the assertion is available. This has not been done to my satisfaction in this case. The receiver is of course prepared to give to the directors the same information which is available to other prospective purchasers. He is entitled to make a commercial judgment in the matter and decide that it would not be conducive to procuring an enhanced price to give these directors any more information. The evidence falls short in showing that by so concluding he is in breach of duty.

The plaintiffs advanced a second argument to support the contention that the receiver is in breach of the duty of care he owes to the company. It is said that apart from the special facts of this case the general duty on a receiver and manager to take reasonable steps to secure the best possible price for the companies' assets includes a duty "to keep the company appraised of how the business of the company is going". This is a very far-reaching proposition, unsupported by any authority and I must reject it. There may well be special circumstances in which, to ensure that the best price possible is obtained for the assets, trading information since the appointment of a receiver should be given to the company's directors. But in the absence of special circumstances which might favourably affect the price, a receiver/manager is not under any duty of care which involves him in reporting as suggested to the directors on his management of the business.

It cannot be said that a receiver/manager is under *no* duty to account to the company whose affairs he is managing nor did the defendant so urge in this case. The extent and nature of the duty and the extent and nature of the accounts he must furnish will depend on the facts of each individual case. *Smiths Ltd v. Middleton* [1979] 3 All ER 842 illustrates this point. That was a case in which an account was ordered after a receivership had come to an end, the court holding that as agent an equitable obligation to account existed which had not been obviated by statute. But the plaintiffs (having perhaps been misled by the headnote to the report) are not correct in finding in that case a general legal proposition to support their contentions in this case. I am not required now to lay down any general principles, and I gladly refrain from doing so. I am merely adjudicating on the claim to the detailed information sought in the letter of 29 February. As I have said a claim to such information is wholly exceptional, and I can find nothing in the evidence to justify me acceding to it on this motion. As pointed out by the Chief Justice in *Campus Oil Ltd v. Minister for Industry & Energy* [1983] IR 88 mandatory injunctions at the interlocutory stage are only granted in exceptional cases and I agree with McGarry J in *Shepherd Homes Ltd v. Sandham* [1971] 1 Ch 340 that on such applications the court must feel a high degree of assurance that at the trial it will appear that the injunction was rightly granted. I feel no such assurance in this case and so must refuse the relief claimed.

There is one final observation to be made. The directors of these companies are under a statutory duty under sections 319 and 320 of the Companies Act 1963 to furnish a statement of affairs to the receiver. This requirement has not been complied with and certainly cannot be regarded in this case as a mere formality whose breach the court should readily excuse. A statutory statement of affairs verified by affidavit is specially required here for a number of reasons; including the fact that the companies' managing director is associated with companies who owe the plaintiff companies sums in excess of £9m. and may be associated with other companies indebted to the plaintiffs, and because of the need to explain adequately the status of the debts amounting to £4m. incurred on speculating on the commodity market to which no reference is made in a recent statement of affairs prepared by the directors. The information was not sought in the February letter for the purpose of preparing the statutory statement of affairs and as it relates almost exclusively to the receivership the failure to respond to the letter does not excuse breach of statutory duty by the directors.

As the relief claimed now is a discretionary one the failure of the companies through their directors to comply with this important statutory requirement would in my judgment in any event have disentitled them to relief.

Alistair Rutherdale
Barrister

[*Reporter's Note:* The plaintiffs appealed the order of Costello J to the Supreme Court. On 4 July 1986, the appeal was ordered to be struck out with costs to the defendant.]

W. and L. Crowe Ltd and Laurence Crowley v. Electricity Supply Board: High Court 1982 No. 7544P; **Ionos Ltd and Laurence Crowley v. Electricity Supply Board:** High Court 1982 No. 7545P (Costello J) 9 May 1984

Receiver – Contract – Supply of Electricity – Company – Refusal by Board to enter new contract with receiver while existing debts of companies remained unpaid – Obligation to supply – Extent of Board's obligations – Discretionary powers – Whether abuse of discretionary powers – Gasworks Clauses Act 1871 (34 & 35 Vict c.41), section 11 – Electric Lighting Act 1882 (45 & 46 Vict c.56), section 19 – Electric Lighting (Clauses) Act 1899 (62 & 63 Vict c.19), Schedule section 27 – South Wales Electrical Power Distribution Company Act 1900 (63 & 64 Vict c.282), section 40 – Electric Lighting Act 1909 (9 Edw. 7 c. 34)– Shannon Electricity Act 1925 (No. 26) – Electricity (Supply) Act 1927 (No. 27), sections 19, 34, 93 – Companies Act 1963 (No. 33), section 316(2)

Facts: Section 93 of the Electricity (Supply) Act 1927 provides:

> "Where a supply of electricity is provided in any part of an area for private purposes, then except insofar as is otherwise provided by the terms of the order or special Act authorising such supply, every person within that part of the area shall, on application, be entitled to a supply on the same terms on which any other person in such part of the area is entitled under similar circumstances to a corresponding supply."

The second plaintiff was appointed receiver of W. and L. Crowe Ltd ("Crowe"). Crowe owed arrears of £9,459.37 to the defendant in respect of their contract with the defendant for the supply of electric current. Clause 16 of the contract dated 21 January 1972 permitted the defendant to disconnect supply without notice if the customer failed on demand to make a payment due.

The second plaintiff wrote to the defendant seeking a new account in his name as receiver. He undertook to be responsible for all services used from the date of his appointment. The defendant replied, pointing to arrears of £29,958.38 owed by the Gallagher group (of which Crowe was a part), and sought immediate payment of that sum and an undertaking by the second plaintiff to be responsible for all future bills during the continuance of the receivership. If he did not agree, supply would be terminated. The second plaintiff refused to discharge the debts incurred prior to appointment. As a result supply was disconnected.

The second plaintiff was also appointed receiver over Ionos Ltd ("Ionos"), the principal asset of which was a property known as Straffan House, Kildare, the private dwelling house of Mr Gallagher. Arrears for electricity totalled £5,959.10 and again the receiver refused to pay the existing arrears, and supply was discontinued.

The second plaintiff commenced proceedings seeking the court's determination as to whether there was a statutory duty on the defendant to enter a new contract for the supply of electricity with a receiver of a company who failed to pay arrears due to the board under an existing contract.

On behalf of the second plaintiff it was accepted that the board could terminate the existing contracts, but it was submitted that the receiver was entitled to a new contract. It was submitted that section 93 of the Electricity (Supply) Act 1927 gave an entitlement to members of the public to have (a) a right to a supply and (b) a right to a supply on the same terms as others in similar circumstances in the same area. It was also argued that a right to a supply arose from the fact that the Act gave the board a monopoly for the supply of electricity in the State.

Held by Costello J in dismissing the actions:

(1) There was no obligation on the board to provide a supply to every "owner or occupier" as that obligation imposed by section 27 of the Schedule to the Electric Lighting (Clauses) Act 1899, had been repealed and was not re-enacted by the Electricity (Supply) Act 1927. In any case it would appear that a receiver and manager was not to be treated as an "owner or occupier". *Paterson v. Gas Light and Coke Co.* [1896] 2 Ch 476 considered.

(2) Whilst the board could make regulations in addition to its statutory obligations, its regulations contained no obligations similar to those contained in section 27 of the Schedule to the Act of 1899.

(3) An obligation imposed by section 19(c) of the Act of 1927 to "distribute, utilise and sell" the electricity it generated, imposed no specific obligation to supply electricity to any person who might apply for a supply.

(4) Section 93 of the Act of 1927 contained a prohibition on the board against discrimination but it did not contain any obligation on it to supply. *Husey v. London Electric Supply Corporation* [1902] 1 Ch 411 considered.

(5) The provisions of the Act, therefore, did not impose a duty on the board to supply a person with current. However they certainly empowered the board to enter into supply contracts. The board thus had a discretionary power which it could not abuse.

(6) Whilst the board could not refuse supply because a previous owner left arrears, here there was no change of ownership, as the plaintiff companies remained in occupation of the premises through their agent and caretaker, the receiver. In this situation, therefore, by refusing to enter into a new supply contract with the receiver so long as arrears remained unpaid, the board had not abused its discretionary powers.

Semble: The result might well be different if a liquidator were appointed or if a mortgagee took possession.

Cases referred to in judgment

Granger v. South Wales Electrical Power Distribution Co. [1931] 1 Ch 551
Husey v. London Electric Supply Corporation [1902] 1 Ch 411; [1902] WN 31
Marriage, Neave and C., In re [1896] 1 Ch 663
Paterson v. Gas Light and Coke Co. [1896] 2 Ch 476

John Blayney SC instructed by *Gerrard Scallan & O'Brien* **for the plaintiff**
T.K. Liston SC instructed by *Arthur Cox & Co.* **for the defendant**

COSTELLO J **9 May 1984**

I tried these two actions together as they involved the determination of the same issue, namely, whether there is a statutory duty on the Electricity Supply Board to enter into a new contract for the supply of electricity with the receiver of a company which, at the date of his appointment, had failed to pay arrears due to the board under an existing contract. The facts of each case are not identical, but the differences do not affect the point of law which falls to be considered.

The plaintiff companies in the two actions were companies in the Gallagher group of companies, a group engaged in different aspects of the construction industry whose spectacular collapse attracted a good deal of public attention a couple of years ago.

W. and L. Crowe Ltd (hereinafter "Crowe") carried on business manufacturing trusses and machining timber at premises at Kilshane Cross, Finglas. The company had entered into a contract with the board for the supply of electric current to these premises but owed on 30 April 1982, the day on which Mr Laurence Crowley (the second-named plaintiff) was appointed receiver, and receiver and manager, arrears of charges amounting to £9,459.37. After his appointment Mr Crowley continued the company's business for a number of months, eventually disposing of it and the company's assets to a purchaser. The company's contract with the board was dated 21 January 1972. The contract incorporated the board's current terms and conditions. Clause 16 of those conditions gave the board the right to disconnect supply without notice if a consumer failed on demand to make any payment due. The board's right to determine this contract is not in question.

On 3 May Mr Crowley notified the board of his appointment and added:

> "Please arrange to open a new account in my name as receiver. I shall be responsible for all services used by me from the date of my appointment".

The board's solicitors replied on 7 May referring to the fact that Mr Crowley had been appointed receiver of all the companies in the group, that at that time the companies (including Crowe) owed the board £29,958.38 and stating that as a condition for the continuance of electricity supplies to the companies at the addresses specified the board required the immediate payment of that sum and an undertaking from Mr Crowley to pay all future bills during the continuance of the receivership. Mr Crowley was informed that if he did not agree to these requirements by 14 May supplies would be discontinued without further notice.

Mr Crowley believed that the board was not entitled to insist on the requirements in the letter of 7 May and refused to agree to discharge the debts incurred prior to his appointment, although he was fully prepared to undertake to discharge personally any of the board's charges arising during the receivership. On 26 May supply to Crowe's premises was discontinued. On 28 May these proceedings were instituted and an application for an interlocutory injunction was brought. On 2 June 1982, the board undertook to continue supply until the determination of the proceedings and Mr Crowley undertook to set aside out of the company's assets a sum sufficient to meet the amount of arrears owing to the board at the date of his appointment and to discharge the costs of electricity incurred from the date of his appointment until further order.

In the case in which Ionos Ltd are plaintiffs Mr Crowley was appointed receiver over the company's assets pursuant to a charge in a deed of mortgage of 26 February 1980. The principal asset, a property known as Straffan House, Co. Kildare, was the private dwelling house of Mr Gallagher (the ultimate beneficial owner of the companies' shares) and the contract for the supply of electricity to it was entered into by a company known as Gallagher Group Properties Ltd. There was due to the board on foot of this contract the sum £5,959.10. The board's attitude to the receiver's refusal to pay off these arrears was as I have just described, and proceedings were instituted by Ionos Ltd and Mr Crowley which took the same course as that taken in the proceedings instituted by Crowe. Mr Crowley as receiver allowed Mr Gallagher to remain on in Straffan House until the premises were eventually sold.

The plaintiffs do not now seek any relief by way of injunction and they do not deny the right of the board to terminate the existing contracts. Their claim is that Mr Crowley is, as both receiver and as receiver and manager, entitled to obtain a new contract from the board. This right is not a contractual one but arises, it is said, from the board's obligations under the Electricity (Supply) Act 1927.

To assist in an understanding of the provisions of the 1927 Act and an appreciation of the authorities to which I have been referred a brief reference should be made to the earlier legislation which the 1927 Act repealed. The Electric Lighting Act 1882 made provision by which the Board of Trade could by provisional order authorise any authority, company or person to supply electricity for any public or private purpose within a specified area, the provisional order remaining in force until confirmed by Act of Parliament. The Act contained detailed provisions relating to the powers of local authorities and undertakers empowered to supply electricity under the Act, including a section, section 19, which reads as follows:

> "Where a supply of electricity is provided in any part of an area for private purposes, then except in so far as is otherwise provided by the terms of the licence, order or special Act authorising such supply, every company or person within that part of the area shall, on application, be entitled to a supply on the same terms on which any other company or person in such part of the area is entitled under similar circumstances."

The whole of the 1882 Act was repealed by the 1927 Act, but section 19 was re-enacted with minor amendments as section 93. I will refer to this section in greater detail later in this judgment.

The next Act to which I should refer is the Electric Lighting (Clauses) Act 1899. This was an Act:

> "to incorporate in one Act certain provisions usually contained in Provisional Orders"

made under the 1882 Act by the Board of Trade. It provided that the provisions contained in the schedule would form part of every provisional order unless expressly excepted by the order, also, that they should be contained in any special act confirming a provisional order unless expressly excepted. Section 27 of the schedule placed a very explicit and clear statutory duty on undertakers in the following terms:

> "The undertakers shall, upon being required to do so by the *owner or occupier* of any premises situate within fifty yards from any distributing main of the undertakers, give and continue to give a supply of energy for those premises. . . ."

This obligation was subject to a number of conditions of which one was that the owner or occupier who required a supply should serve a notice on the undertaker specifying, *inter alia*, the premises to which supply was required and enter into a written contract (if asked by them to do so) with the undertakers in relation to payment for the proposed supply.

A number of points about this section are to be noted. Firstly, this specific obligation imposed on undertakers by it had not been contained in the 1882 Act. Secondly, the obligation to supply electric current (*i.e.*, an obligation to supply the "*owner or occupier*" of premises) was expressed in identical terms to the obligation on undertakers who were authorised to supply gas under section 11 of the Gasworks Clauses Act 1871 (to which I will refer in a moment). Thirdly, the 1899 Act was repealed by the 1927 Act and the obligation contained in section 27 of the schedule was not re-enacted nor any comparable obligation imposed on the board.

I referred to two English authorities on the point that falls for consideration in these actions. Section 11 of the Gasworks Clauses Act 1871 was considered in *Paterson v. Gas Light and Coke Co.* [1896] 2 Ch 576. That was a case in which receivers were appointed over a company which at the time of their appointment owed a gas undertaker £90 for gas supplied. The gas company threatened to cut off the supply unless the debt was paid. The receivers then instituted proceedings to restrain it from so doing, claiming that they were entitled by virtue of section 11 of the 1871 Act to a supply of gas. They succeeded in the High Court, Kekewich J holding that the receivers and managers were in the position of new tenants or new occupiers and so entitled to a new supply. He was reversed in the Court of Appeal, the court holding that the receivers and managers were not "owners and occupiers" of the premises within the meaning of section 11 and so the gas company owed them no obligation under the section.

A receiver had a more successful outcome in *Granger v. South Wales Electrical Power Distribution Co.* [1931] 1 Ch 551. That was a case in which a colliery company owed a sum of money to an electrical distribution company at the time a receiver was appointed. The distribution company threatened to cut off supplies unless payment of the arrears was guaranteed. The receiver obtained an injunction from the High Court restraining them from doing so. The judgment of Bennett J makes clear why the receiver in *Granger* was successful whilst the receiver in *Paterson* failed: namely, the obligation to supply electricity imposed on the electrical distribution company by the private Act under which it operated was different to the obligation to supply gas under section 11 of the 1871 Act. The private Act in question was the South Wales Electrical Power Distribution Company Act 1900. It did not incorporate section 27 of the Electric Lighting (Clauses) Act 1899 which I have just quoted but instead provided by section 40 that the company "shall give a supply of energy to *any person* who requires a supply . . . upon that person entering into a binding agreement. . . ." as provided in the section. The court held that the receiver was a "person who requires a supply" within the meaning of the private Act, and as the words "being an owner or occupier" of the premises were not contained in the section and should not be read into it the case was different to the *Paterson* case considered earlier by the Court of Appeal.

It is obvious that neither of these cases helps the receiver in the instant cases. The receiver/plaintiff in *Paterson* failed to get a supply of gas even though there was a statutory duty to supply an "owner or occupier" who was prepared to enter into a contract; the court held that the receiver could not be regarded as either an "owner" or an "occupier". The receiver/plaintiff in *Granger* succeeded because there was a specific statutory duty in the private Act to supply a person who requires a supply — a provision strikingly absent from the 1927 Act.

As I have already pointed out the 1927 Act repealed the 1899 Act and did not re-enact section 27 of the Schedule and no comparable obligation was imposed on the board to supply "an owner or occupier" of the premises prepared to enter into a supply contract with it. In this connection it should be noted that under section 34 of the 1927 Act the board is empowered to make regulations in lieu of or additional to the provisions of the 1899 Act and the Electric Lighting Act 1909 and all regulations so made "shall be incorporated into and form part of every special order made by the board constituting the board to be an authorised undertaker", save insofar as they may be specifically excepted by the special order. It is common case that the board has constituted itself an authorised undertaker but its regulations contain no obligations similar to those contained in section 27 of the Schedule to the 1899 Act.

The 1927 Act which established the board made provision for the handing over to it of the works carried on at Shannon for the production and generation of electricity under the provisions of the Shannon Electricity Act 1925. Section 19 of the 1927 Act sets out the duties of the board. By subsection (a) it was required to produce and generate electricity in the Shannon works and transmit electricity through the transmission system of the Shannon works and extensions thereof. It was required by subsection (b) to maintain the Shannon works in good repair. Subsection (c) (the subsection on which the plaintiffs rely as justifying the receiver's claim for a new contract) placed the following duty on the board; namely a duty:

> "to distribute, utilise, and sell the electricity generated by the board in the Shannon works and to promote and encourage the purchase and use of such electricity."

I cannot see however how this subsection helps the plaintiffs' case. The subsection places a general duty on the board to "distribute, utilise and sell" the electricity it generates, but it imposes no specific obligation on it to supply electricity to any person who may apply for a supply. The Oireachtas, it seems to me, imposed a general public duty on the board by this subsection, but has not conferred any collateral rights on individual members of the public by it.

The plaintiffs then rely (and I think I am correct in saying that this is their principal argument) on the provisions of section 93 which as already pointed out virtually re-enacts section 19 of the 1882 Act. Because it is so central to the plaintiffs' case I should quote it in full. It reads as follows:

> "Where a supply of electricity is provided in any part of an area for private purposes, then, except insofar as is otherwise provided by the terms of the order or special Act authorising such supply, every person within that part of the area shall, on application, be entitled to a supply on the same terms on which any other person in such part of the area is entitled under similar circumstances to a corresponding supply."

The plaintiffs submit that this gives a double entitlement to members of the public who want a supply for private purposes; (a) a right to a supply and (b) a right to a supply on the same terms on which others in similar circumstances in the area are entitled to a corresponding supply. Again, I find myself in disagreement with the plaintiffs' construction of the statute. It seems to me that the section certainly contains a prohibition on the board against discrimination but it does not contain any obligation on it to supply. It begins by postulating that a supply of electricity exists in a part of an area of supply and then confers an entitlement on every person in that area:

> "to a supply on the same terms on which any other person in such part of the area is entitled under similar circumstances to a corresponding supply."

If it was intended to confer a right to a supply to every person who saw fit to apply for one the section, it seems to me, could have easily so provided by putting a full stop after "shall, on application, be entitled to a supply". And if it was intended to give a double entitlement then it would have been simple to add a new sentence to the effect that when a supply is provided it shall be on the same terms as others obtain it.

This view of the section is strengthened by the fact that although a similar section was contained in section 19 of the 1882 Act it was considered necessary to make specific provision in the 1899 Act imposing an obligation on undertakers to grant a supply of electricity to owners and occupiers who were prepared to enter into supply contracts — surely a piece of supererogation if the obligation existed already in the 1882 Act. It also gets support from the decision of the Court of Appeal in *Husey v. London Electric Supply Corporation* [1902] 1 Ch 411. That was a case in which the private Act confirming an earlier provisional order contained a clause which required the undertakers upon being required to do so by the owner or occupier of the premises to give and continue to give a supply of energy, subject to the obligation on the owner or occupier to enter into a supply contract with it. A receiver had been appointed over the assets of a company which was indebted to the undertakers, but it was held that the undertakers were entitled to discontinue the supply until the receiver had entered into a new contract with them. The court, however, was not asked to and did not hold that section 19 of the 1882 Act gave any right to a supply contract. As Cozens Hardy LJ pointed out (p. 424) this section contemplates that a contract has been entered into between the undertaker and the occupier and it gives an entitlement by arrangements entered into between the parties to a supply on the same terms on which others have been supplied in the same area. The section assumes (as Vaughan Williams LJ pointed out at p. 420) that there will be a contract — but it confers no right to such a contract.

An additional argument was advanced in support of the plaintiffs' claim based not on any specific section of the Act but on the existing situation arising from the fact that the board now have a monopoly for the supply of electricity throughout the State from which fact it is said a duty to supply the receiver arises under the Act. This submission involves firstly a consideration of the present factual situation. On this there is in fact no controversy — no member of the public, subject to some insignificant exceptions, can obtain a supply of electricity unless the board is prepared to supply it. Secondly, it involves a consideration of the status of a receiver and that of a receiver and manager of a company's assets and business appointed by a debenture holder or mortgagee. (Parenthetically, it can here be mentioned that counsel's submissions have not sought to make any distinction between the duty of the board *vis-à-vis* a receiver appointed by the court and a receiver appointed without the aid of the court).

The receiver derives his appointment and authority from the contract entered into between the parties. In each of these cases the parties have agreed that the receiver is to be treated as the agent of the plaintiff company, a position which, of course, protects the debenture holder and the mortgagee from liability as mortgagees in possession. After his appointment a receiver can, of course, enter into contracts and if he does so he is personally liable on foot of them (with a right to be indemnified out of the company's assets, unless the contract otherwise provides (section 316(2) of the Companies Act 1963)). But it is important to note that when a receiver and manager is appointed over a company's business the company is still legally in occupation of the premises in which the business is carried on; the receiver is a caretaker of them. This was pointed out in *Paterson*; "The relation between the mill company" (that is, the mortgagors) "and the plaintiffs" (that is, the receivers) "is not the relation of outgoing and incoming tenant, nor of vendor and purchaser, but that of owner and caretaker" (see [1896] 2 Ch at p. 483, and see also *In re Marriage, Neave, and Co.* [1896] 1 Ch 663).

Therefore on the appointment of the receiver in these cases the legal position was that the plaintiff companies remained in occupation of the premises through their agent and caretaker, the receiver, and no change of occupation occurred after his appointment. The business which he managed in the *Crowe* case was the company's business, notwithstanding the fact that the receiver may have been personally liable on the contracts he entered into and that the profits may have belonged to the debenture holder as equitable owner. The property over which he was appointed receiver in the *Ionos* case had been in the physical occupation of Mr Gallagher with the company's permission prior to the receiver's appointment and so remained with his permission until Straffan House was sold.

The provisions of the Act do not, as I have already pointed out, impose any specific duty to enter contracts with every person who applies for a supply of current. But it certainly empowers the board to enter into supply contracts. What has to be considered, therefore, in these cases is the exercise of a discretionary power and the issue is whether the board has abused its powers by refusing to enter into contracts with the receiver. It is accepted by Mr Liston on the board's behalf that the discretion is not an absolute one and that it must be exercised in accordance with principles established by the common law and in particular that it must be exercised in a reasonable manner.

Mr Blayney on the plaintiff's behalf says that the board has acted wholly unreasonably and urges that just as it would be unreasonable for the board to refuse to enter into a contract with the purchaser of a dwelling house until he discharged the arrears due to the board by the vendor so too it is unreasonable for the board to refuse to contract with the receiver in the new situation arising from his appointment by the debenture holders. But the analogy is not an exact one. I would have little difficulty in holding that the board would abuse its powers if it refused to enter into a contract with a purchaser of premises until a previous occupant's arrears were paid, but here the receiver is the agent for the companies and is a caretaker of premises of which legally they remain occupiers: no change of occupation has occurred by his appointment. The board, it seems to me, is entitled to have regard to the position in law which pertains. If a company appointed a new board of directors to manage its affairs each of whose members were prepared personally to enter into or guarantee a new supply contract in respect of the premises occupied by the company the board would, I believe, be entitled to refuse to contract with them until arrears due under the existing contracts with the company had been discharged. If a receiver takes control of a company's assets as a result of a contract which the company had entered into the board can properly and reasonably adopt the same attitudes — in each case the defaulting company remains in occupation of the premises to which the supply is given.

Obviously different considerations might arise if the company goes into liquidation or if a mortgagee instead of appointing a receiver goes into possession of mortgaged property. Whilst not deciding either point now I draw attention to them to contrast the different and special position which results from the appointment of a receiver from that resulting from the appointment of a liquidator or from that arising when a mortgagee enters into possession of the company's property. I conclude, therefore, that by exercising its contractual right to terminate the supply contract because of the company's default, and by refusing to enter into a new supply contract with the receiver as long as the arrears remain unpaid, the board has not abused its discretionary powers. It was pointed out that by acting in this way the board is effectively obtaining a preferential payment of its debt ahead of the secured creditors. This is true enough. But this follows from the factual situation which the parties to the debenture and mortgage have themselves created by the appointment of a receiver and there is certainly nothing unlawful and to my mind nothing unreasonable in the board taking what advantage it can from this situation.

As no breach of statutory duty has been established the plaintiffs' claims in these two actions fail.

Alistair Rutherdale
Barrister

John Moore v. John Donnelly: High Court 1985 No. 2707P (Carroll J) 17 June 1985

Receivership – Landlord and tenant – Company – Arrears of rent – Judgment against guarantor – Charge over assets of company – Receiver appointed over assets including the premises and adjacent premises – Whether receiver in occupation – Whether beneficial use – Whether obliged to pay arrears of rent in priority to discharging the mortgage debt

Facts: By lease dated 9 September 1982, Anne Sheridan leased premises at 5 Clyde Lane, Dublin to Gilbert Ashe Construction Ltd ("the company"). The plaintiff was one of the guarantors for the rent. The freehold of 6 Clyde Lane, was owned by Moore Construction Ltd. Both companies granted charges over their assets, including the premises, to the Industrial Credit Corporation ("I.C.C.").

On 24 May 1983, the defendant was appointed receiver by I.C.C. over the assets of both companies. A petition for their winding up had been presented on 28 April, and on 3 June 1983, Vincent O'Neill was appointed liquidator.

The landlord sued the company in liquidation, the receiver and the liquidator in the Circuit Court for arrears of rent. In a separate action she sued the guarantors. Judgment was granted against the company (but not the receiver) and Mr Moore as guarantor.

Under clause 12 of the debenture granted to I.C.C. the payment of outgoings affecting or payable in respect of the mortgaged property, ranked above the discharge of the mortgage debt.

The plaintiff claimed that the defendant had entered into possession of No. 5 Clyde Lane, and made use of it as receiver, and removed papers. There was evidence that the two premises were interconnected, that there were toilet facilities only in No. 5, that the defendant changed all the locks of the two premises, that he held the keys to both premises, and that a partition was erected between the two premises.

There was also evidence that the leasehold of No. 5 was put on the market by the receiver, and only withdrawn when it was discovered that it was of no value.

Held by Carroll J in holding that the receiver was in beneficial occupation and possession of premises, but in adjourning the matter to allow the debenture holder to be heard:

(1) It being conceded that if the receiver enjoyed use of the property he should discharge the rent in priority to the mortgage debt, the issue was a factual one as to whether the receiver made use of the property to the exclusion of the liquidator, or whether he "walked away".

(2) A receiver has no power to disclaim onerous leaseholds.

(3) On the evidence it appeared that the receiver had sole control of the keys

and his staff did make beneficial use of the premises at No. 5. The receiver never walked away by handing the keys to the landlord.

(4) The receiver was in beneficial occupation and possession of the premises from the date of his appointment. Accordingly he was bound to discharge the outgoings on the property in priority to the mortgage debt.

(5) As the declarations sought affected I.C.C. the matter would be adjourned to give them an opportunity to be heard.

No cases referred to in judgment

Counsel's names not available

The plaintiff appeared in person
Solicitors for the defendant: *A & L Goodbody*

CARROLL J **17 June 1985**

This case came before the court on a plenary summons on the basis that there was only one net point to be decided.

The plaintiff went guarantor for the rent reserved by a lease dated 9 September 1982 made between Anne Valerie Sheridan of the first part, Gilbert Construction Ltd of the second part, John Moore (the plaintiff) and Joseph Buddock of the third part comprising premises situate at No. 5 Clyde Lane, Ballsbridge, Dublin at the yearly rent of £12,250 payable by quarterly instalments.

No. 5 adjoins No. 6 Clyde Lane which are freehold premises and which were owned by an associated company, Moore Construction Co. Ltd. Gilbert Ashe Construction Ltd granted a fixed and floating charge over its assets including a fixed charge over the premises at No. 5 Clyde Lane to the Industrial Credit Co. Ltd by debenture dated 22 September 1982. Moore Construction Co. Ltd also granted a debenture over its assets including the premises No. 6 Clyde Lane to the Industrial Credit Co. Ltd on 22 September 1982.

By appointment dated 24 May 1983 the defendant John Donnelly was appointed receiver of the assets of Gilbert Ashe Construction Ltd and on the same date he was also appointed receiver of Moore Construction Co. Ltd. A petition for the winding up of both companies was presented on 28 April 1983 and Vincent O'Neill was appointed liquidator on 3 June 1983. The rent was not paid, nor was the rent for the quarter August to October 1983 or the quarter November to January 1984. The landlord sued the liquidator, the company in liquidation and the defendant as receiver for the rent. In a separate action she also sued the guarantors. Judgment was given in the Circuit Court against the company but not against the receiver, Mr Donnelly. Judgment was also given against Mr Moore as guarantor.

Clause 12 of the debenture provides as follows:

> "All monies received by a receiver appointed hereunder shall be applied as follows:

(a) In payment of all sums necessary or proper in or for the purpose of the exercise of the powers and duties of such receiver hereunder.
(b) In discharge of all outgoings affecting or payable in respect of the mortgage property.
(c) In payment of his remuneration.
(d) In payment of premiums on fire and other insurances and the cost of executing necessary or proper repairs to the mortgage property.
(e) In payment of the interest on the mortgage debt and other monies (if any) other than the mortgage debt due or payable under this deed and in such order as the lender may direct.
(f) In or towards the discharge of the mortgage debt.
(g) In payment to the company of the residue of the monies received by the receiver."

The plaintiff claims that the defendant entered into possession of the property at No. 5 Clyde Lane and made use of it as receiver which was denied by the defendant.

The evidence was as follows:

On his appointment Mr Donnelly changed all the locks on Nos. 5 and 6. No. 6 provided the main entrance to the two properties, there being however a rear entrance to No. 5. The premises were interconnected in that a substantial portion of the dividing wall had been removed sometime in the past. All the lavatory accommodation was in the premises No. 5. Furniture belonging to Gilbert Ashe Construction Ltd was in No. 5 as also were the books of the company.

Mr Moore was employed by Mr Donnelly to assist him as receiver in recovering monies due to the company. He worked in both No. 5 and No. 6 going through files and papers. He was there approximately five to six weeks when by his choice he worked at home. Early in 1984 he visited No. 5 and No. 6. No. 6 was then separated by a partition with plaster-work on both sides. He entered No. 5 by a rear door and said that papers, documents and furniture were still in the building. The premises No. 6 were sold in May 1984 and prior to that all documents and furniture were taken out.

The business of the company ceased at the time of the liquidation and was not carried on afterwards. The receiver had staff in No. 5 and No. 6 and they used the toilets in No. 5 as there were none in No. 6.

Mr Donnelly's evidence was that he was appointed receiver in May 1983 of Gilbert Ashe Construction Ltd and also of Moore Construction Co. Ltd. He changed the locks on all the premises. There was no business to carry on so that it was a case of realising the assets for the receivership. He engaged Mr Moore to negotiate with people who owed monies to the company for work in progress. Concerning the use of Nos. 5 and 6 he said that his attitude was the staff should use No. 6 for the receivership as they had clear title to the property. The only use they made of No. 5 was for the toilet facilities. He took advice as to value from Messrs Jones Lang and Wootton. They advised there could be value in the leasehold of No. 5. He instructed them to advertise both for sale (this was done in August). When it was discovered there was no value in No. 5, they advertised No. 6 only. When they sold No. 6 they were told they must divide the two premises so they got a contractor. The key to No. 5 was given to Mrs Sheridan, the landlord, before they did the separation of the premises.

When asked if the receiver derived any benefit, Mr Donnelly said he did not realise anything for it. He said he did not make use of the premises and he said it was no use to him. There were papers stored in No. 5 and there was furniture there. The papers were subsequently removed to a store and the furniture disposed of. He said the liquidator came to see him on his appointment to ask what his plans were. He said he wanted to realise the assets and they arranged that he would look over the premises at Nos. 5 and No. 6. He went through papers with the directors. Mr Donnelly held the keys of the changed locks all the time. The two premises appeared from the inside to be one unit. A substantial portion of the wall had been removed. The liquidator never got his hands on anything.

The issue is not whether the receiver was liable to the landlord to pay rent accruing due while he was in possession. It is clear that a *vis-à-vis* the landlord he is not liable. Indeed this is the issue which was determined in the Circuit Court. At first it seemed the issue was whether the receiver is obliged to discharge rent accruing due while he was in beneficial occupation and possession of the property in priority to the mortgage debt. But then it was conceded that if the receiver did enjoy the use of the property he should also discharge the rent in priority to the mortgage debt. Therefore the issue comes down to an issue of fact namely whether the receiver took possession of the property and made use of it to the exclusion of the liquidator or whether he "walked away".

A receiver has no power to disclaim onerous leaseholds. Only a liquidator has this power if given leave by the court. This was not done in this case. However the receiver returned the keys to the landlord in February 1984 and he accepted them and only claimed rent due to January 1984.

I am satisfied on the evidence:

(1) That the staff employed by the receiver (and therefore the receiver) did make beneficial use of the premises at No. 5. Indeed it would have been impossible to confine the receivership to No. 6 because of the lack of toilet facilities.

(2) That the premises were under the sole control of the receiver, as he alone had the keys. The visit the liquidator made was by arrangement.

(3) That the receiver did not at any stage "walk away" from the leasehold. The building of the partition wall between Nos. 5 and 6 commissioned by the receiver post-dated the handing over of the keys to the landlord.

Therefore the receiver was in beneficial occupation and possession of the premises from the date of his appointment. The receiver was bound under Clause 12 of the debenture to apply the monies received in discharge of the outgoings on the property in priority to the mortgage debt.

The issue has been put as an issue between the plaintiff as surety for the rent and the defendant as receiver. However, the declarations sought affect the

Industrial Credit Corporation as debenture holder. Before making any declarations they should be given an opportunity to be heard. The matter will be adjourned pending communication with them.

Alistair Rutherdale
Barrister

[*Reporters Note:* The matter was adjourned for mention until 1 July 1985. On that date Miss Justice Carroll read a letter from solicitors for the I.C.C. to the effect that they did not wish to pursue the matter further. She therefore ordered that the rent, the subject matter of the Circuit Court judgment, was an expense of the receivership, and that the receiver had to pay same in priority to sums due and owing to the debenture holder. Secondly she ordered that the defendant indemnify the plaintiff for all loss, damage and expense suffered pursuant to the Circuit Court judgment.]

Rex Pet Foods Ltd (in Receivership) and Charles Russell Murphy v. Lamb Bros (Dublin) Ltd, Lamb Brothers (Marketing) Ltd, Lamb Brothers Ltd, W.H. Lamb and Co. Ltd and Lambs (Ireland) Ltd (No. 2): High Court 1982 No. 8937p (Costello J) 5 December 1985

Company – Debenture – Formerly independent company – Becomes wholly owned subsidiary of defendant company – Deterioration in financial situation – Receivership – Separate legal personality – Whether company should be treated as branch of defendant company – Defendant company distributor of plaintiff's goods – Whether receiver entitled to goods manufactured by plaintiff in possession of defendants – Counterclaim – Excess payments by defendants to plaintiff – Companies Act 1963 (No. 33), section 286

Facts: The plaintiff company existed independently of the defendant companies until March 1981. In that month the first defendant purchased 52 per cent of the shares in the plaintiff company and appointed some directors to the board of the plaintiff company. Management of the plaintiff company remained as before.

The plaintiff company and the first defendant entered into two agreements, under which the defendant group became the sole distributors of the plaintiff company's goods and supplied management services to the plaintiff company.

Later that year the plaintiff company started to get into financial difficulty. During this period the plaintiff company's board met, and it operated as a separate legal entity, with separate books of account.

In March 1982 the situation changed, and because of the deteriorating financial position, the first defendant company took up the balance of the shares in the plaintiff company, so that it became a wholly owned subsidiary of the first defendant. A manager was appointed from the defendant group.

In July 1982 a receiver was appointed to the plaintiff company by the Agricultural Credit Corporation, a debenture holder. He issued proceedings and sought to have the assets of the defendants and the plaintiff company aggregated, and a declaration that the business of the plaintiff company and the defendants was one.

On behalf of the receiver it was submitted that the plaintiff company should be regarded merely as a branch of the defendant group because (a) the defendants discharged the creditors of the plaintiff company from time to time, (b) invoices from suppliers were sent directly to the defendant, (c) there was an overlap in management, (d) there were no meetings of the plaintiff company's board, particularly after March 1982, (e) the defendant group was the sole distributor of the plaintiff company's goods.

In addition the receiver claimed in respect of certain goods manufactured by the plaintiff which were in the possession of the defendants at one of their warehouses at the time the receiver was appointed. This stock was sold on by the defendants, with an invoice being raised at the end of each month. A separate account was kept for these goods entitled the "LIL account with Rex Pet Foods Ltd". The records showed that in actual fact the defendants had paid in excess of the costs of goods supplied, and that the plaintiff company owed a sum in excess of £131,000 for goods not yet supplied. The defendants counterclaimed, asserting title to the goods in question and to their proceeds.

Held by Costello J in dismissing the claim and allowing the defendants' counterclaim.

(1) There was no evidence that would justify the court making a declaration that the plaintiff company be regarded as a branch of the defendant group. Any changes which occurred after March 1982 did not affect the fact that the plaintiff company was a separate legal entity. The fact that members of the defendants sat on the plaintiff board, was normal where a group of companies was controlled by a parent. Taken together the five factors argued by the receiver did not raise the inference sought to be raised.

(2) Even if there was evidence which would suggest that the companies were one, the court would not be justified in making an order for aggregation, as there was no evidence to suggest that funds had been siphoned off by the defendants.

(3) In relation to the claim for the goods supplied, the "LIL account" was an accurate record of the dealings, and during the relevant period the defendants paid the plaintiff for goods supplied.

(4) Title to the goods in the warehouse at the end of June 1982 and goods delivered in early July, was effectively passed by the raising of invoices on 2, 8 and 14 July.

(5) There was no fraud involved in any of the transactions, and in the absence of any proceedings under section 286 of the Companies Act, no question of a fraudulent preference arose. The plaintiff company therefore had no title to the goods.

No cases referred to in judgment

T.C. Smyth SC with Peter Kelly BL instructed by *D.F. Jones & Co.* **for the plaintiffs**
John Cooke SC, Daniel O'Keeffe SC with Mary Finlay BL instructed by *William Fry & Sons* **for the defendants**

COSTELLO J **5 December 1985**

This case arises because of a claim made by the receiver and manager of the plaintiff company who was appointed on 15 July 1982. The receiver submits that the assets of the defendant companies and the plaintiff company should be aggregated and seeks a declaration that the businesses of the plaintiff company and defendant companies are one. A separate claim exists in these proceedings arising from certain goods which were in possession of the defendant companies at the time the receiver was appointed.

The facts of this case, which I find from the evidence adduced by the plaintiff company, are as follows:

The plaintiff company had an existence independent of the defendant companies up to the month of March 1981. In the month of March 1981 the first-named defendant company, Lamb Bros (Dublin) Ltd, was seeking a means of entering into a new line of business and purchased 52 per cent of the shares in the plaintiff company. There no doubt that the plaintiff company remained a separate legal entity at that time. Some members of the board of directors of the defendant group of companies went on to the board of directors of the plaintiff company but the minority shareholding in the plaintiff company existed and was represented on the board of directors of the plaintiff company. What is of equal significance is that the management of the plaintiff company remained as it had been.

The plaintiff company manufactured pet food in a factory premises near Athy. At the time the shares in the plaintiff company were purchased two agreements were entered into between the plaintiff company and the first-named defendant company, one being a distributorship agreement and the other a management agreement. The effect of these agreements was that the defendant group of companies became the sole distributors for the plaintiff's goods and supplied management services to the plaintiff company, arrangements which are by no means unique and which do not in any way affect the separate corporate entities of the companies concerned.

It is clear that the plaintiff company started to get into financial difficulties some time later that year and that these difficulties became aggravated. During this period there were meetings of the board of directors of the plaintiff company and the minutes were produced to show that it operated as a separate legal entity from the defendant group of companies.

What is of equal importance is that separate books of account were maintained and I have had the benefit of the evidence of Mr Robert Gentleman, who later became the secretary of the plaintiff company and who was the accountant of the group of companies formed by the defendant companies. His evidence made it clear that at all times separate books of account were kept for the plaintiff company and their separate legal entities were at all times recognised by the defendant companies.

That situation existed up to March 1982, and the trading arrangement between the parties was governed by the two agreements to which I have referred. The distributorship agreement, it is true, was not carried out to the letter of the agreement in that prices were not fixed in writing but mutual agreement prices were fixed otherwise than in writing.

In March 1982 the situation changed. Because of the deteriorating financial position of the plaintiff company, the defendant group of companies or, to be more precise, the first-named defendant company, took up the balance of the shares in the plaintiff company as a result of which the plaintiff company became a wholly owned subsidiary of Lamb Bros (Dublin) Ltd. The reason for this change in the shareholding of the plaintiff company was the hope that the plaintiff company could become financially sound by a change in the management structure in Athy. A change in management was brought about and the existing members were dispensed with. Mr Middlesborough, who was a manager of the defendant group, became manager of the plaintiff company; Mr Lyons became managing director of the plaintiff company and Mr Gentleman became secretary of the plaintiff company.

In these circumstances it seems to be clear that the change of management that occurred in March 1982 was one which was a perfectly normal commercial decision and did not affect the separate corporate entity of the plaintiff company although, of course, the relationship between the two became, as I have indicated, one in which the plaintiff company was now 100 per cent owned by Lamb Bros (Dublin) Ltd.

The case that is made on the plaintiff's behalf depends on a number of aspects of the trading of the defendant group of companies and of the plaintiff company to which I will now refer.

It is alleged that the plaintiff company should be regarded merely as a branch of the defendant group, as its manufacturing arm because, firstly, the defendants discharged the creditors of the plaintiff company from time to time. The evidence establishes that this in fact occurred, particularly from the month of April 1982 onwards, but this to my mind did not in any way affect the separate legal entity of the plaintiff company and was a normal enough arrangement for companies trading in a group such as these companies were trading. Secondly, it is suggested that the claim is supported by the fact that invoices from suppliers of the plaintiff company were sent direct to the defendant company. Factually that is so. From time to time creditors of the plaintiff company, in particular suppliers of goods and raw materials to the plaintiff company, sent invoices to one or other of the defendant companies but this does not raise any claim or sustain any claim that the two companies should be treated as one legal entity. It does, perhaps, reflect some confusion but not to the extent which would justify the claim now being made on the plaintiff's behalf. Thirdly, it is suggested that the management of the plaintiff company was such that the claim being made is justified. The management changed in the way I have indicated. The explanation for the change is a reasonable one and in my view does not of itself justify the claim that has been made. Fourthly, it was suggested that there were no regular meetings of the board of directors of the plaintiff company. There were meetings of the board of directors and meetings were held up to March 1982. Thereafter it seems that no inference such as is now being sought to be drawn arises from the fact that the board of directors comprised members of the parent company for this is a situation which is normal and is to be found where a group of companies is controlled by a parent company.

Finally, the point was raised that the defendant company was sole distributor for the plaintiff company, but this was a situation which was in no way unique or which raises the inference which the plaintiffs seek to raise.

The question arises whether all these factors taken together raise the inference sought to be raised but I cannot agree that this is so. There have been some cases which counsel have referred me to where the courts have treated companies as being one legal entity but these have been cases in which the facts are very different to those which the evidence establishes in the circumstances of this case.

So in my view the plaintiffs have failed to make out a case which would justify me in making the declaration which is sought. I should add that even if the situation were different and there were circumstances in which the court should regard these companies as being one for some reason or other, this would not justify the court making another order which, is a separate order in relation to the aggregation of assets because it seems to me there has been no evidence to suggest that any funds of the plaintiff company were siphoned off into any of the defendant companies in such circumstances as would raise an equitable claim to assets of any of the defendant companies.

I now turn to the second part of the plaintiff's case. In turning to this I should point out that this part of the case was also relied on as evidence of the close relationship between the two companies which would justify the order sought and I think that reliance on this second part of the case does not assist the plaintiffs on the first part of the case and that the goods in the warehouse which I now come to deal with were treated in circumstances which do not permit the plaintiff company validly to claim on either part of the case.

What happened in relation to the goods in the warehouse of the defendant group of companies on the Naas Road was this: Under the distributorship agreement goods manufactured by the plaintiff company were consigned to a warehouse on the Naas Road and then sold on by the defendant group to purchasers in this country and elsewhere. The practice developed that at the end of each month an invoice was raised arising from the goods consigned in the previous month and the invoice was based upon the prices which the goods had reached less agreed charges, *e.g.*, a four per cent discount and freight and other charges, permitted under the terms of the contract. During the period Lamb (Dublin) Ltd kept a separate account which has been proved in evidence and which is headed "LIL Account with Rex Pet Foods Ltd", and I accept this account as an accurate record of the dealing. This account is supported by other records produced by Mr Gentleman.

I am satisfied from these records and in particular from the document "LIL Account with Rex Pet Foods Ltd" that in the relevant period the defendant group were paying the plaintiff company for the goods which the plaintiff company supplied, partly by cheques and partly by means of payments made to creditors of the plaintiff company. This was a perfectly permissible way of paying its indebtedness for the goods which the plaintiff company supplied to them.

In the course of dealings between the companies the records show that the defendant group paid sums in excess of their indebtedness to the plaintiff company so that at the end of June the plaintiff company owed for goods not yet supplied a considerable sum of money, a sum in excess of £131,000.

I think it is clear from the evidence that at the end of June the directors of the plaintiff company, who were the same persons as the directors of the defendant group, were aware that the plaintiff company was insolvent. Goods were supplied and were in the warehouse at the end of June 1982 and at that time the stock was taken and an invoice was raised in respect of those goods on 2 July 1982, and it was the intention of the parties that the title of the goods then in the warehouse would be transferred to Lamb Bros (Ireland) Ltd. In my view this was effectively done by the raising of this invoice and the goods then in stock became the property of Lamb Bros (Ireland) Ltd. Thereafter further goods were supplied by the plaintiff company and consigned to the warehouse. These consignments occurred on 5, 6 and 8 July. The value of these goods was ascertained and an invoice was raised in respect of these goods on 8 July for the sum of £19,336.69. In my view the raising of this invoice transferred the property in these goods to Lamb Bros (Ireland) Ltd.

There were further deliveries on 9, 12, 13, and 14 July and in respect of these goods an invoice was raised on 14 July for £32,910.20. In my view this invoice effectively transferred title of the goods to Lamb Bros (Ireland) Ltd.

The situation, therefore, was that when the debenture which the Agricultural Credit Corporation owned crystallised on 15 July by the appointment of the receiver, these goods were no longer the property of the plaintiff company but the property of Lamb Bros (Ireland) Ltd. Had proceedings been instituted as a result of the liquidation of the company under section 286 of the Companies Act, the question might have arisen as to whether or not there was any fraudulent preference within the meaning of that section involved in the transactions to which I referred, but this did not occur.

The question now arises as to whether or not any claims can be made in respect of these goods in the circumstances which I have outlined. It is perfectly clear there was money owed by the plaintiff company to the defendant company at the time these goods were supplied and that the figures set out in the document "LIL Account with Rex Pet Foods Ltd" are correct. In these circumstances it seems to me that there was no fraud involved in any way by the actions carried on at the times as indicated in the evidence of Mr Gentleman.

It seems to me that the plaintiff company has been unable to establish that any tort was involved in what was done. No question of fraudulent preference arises because the provisions of section 286 do not arise; so I must hold that the title to the goods having been passed and there being no validity in relation to that which has been established, the plaintiff company have no entitlement to the goods and no entitlement to the proceeds of the goods which, I understand, are now on deposit.

In these circumstances the defendants are entitled to a direction and I will dismiss the claim.

First of all, I will make an order dismissing the claim and an order on the counterclaim under the terms of paragraph A. I can see no reason why the ordinary rule should not apply, the plaintiffs having failed in this claim, so I will order that the defendants' costs of defending this claim be paid by the plaintiffs, such costs to include the costs of any order such as the order for discovery and the order on the injunction. I give liberty to apply to the defendants on the undertaking as to damages.

Alistair Rutherdale
Barrister

[*Reporters Note:* By order made *ex parte* of same date it was ordered that (a) the proceedings be struck out as against the second, third and fourth named defendants, (b) That Patrick Campbell replace the late Charles Russell Murphy as plaintiff.]

In the Matter of Bamfords Ireland Ltd (in Receivership and in Liquidation) Robert Stewart v. Patrick Campbell: High Court 1985 No. 323 Sp (Carroll J) 13 June 1986

Receiver – Duty of receiver to render proper accounts of his receipts and payments if required to do so by liquidator – Whether "receiver" referred to in section 322 includes references to his predecessor – Whether default of duty referred to in section 322(1)(b) referred to the duty of a receiver under section 319(2) to prepare an abstract every six months to be filed with the Registrar of Companies – Receiver appointed after the death of a previous receiver – Whether receivership should be regarded as continuous – Costs – Whether liquidator reasonable in bringing petition – Whether receiver should be obliged to provide a report without charge – Companies Act 1963 (No. 33), section 322 (1)(b)

Facts: The plaintiff as liquidator of the company brought an action against the defendant as receiver for an order under section 322(1)(b) of the Companies Act 1963. The subsection provides:

"(1) If any receiver of the property of a company —

> (b) having been appointed under the powers contained in any instrument, has, after being required at any time by the liquidator of the company to do so, failed to render proper accounts of his receipts and payments and to vouch the same and to pay over to the liquidator the amount properly payable to him;

the court may, on an application made for the purpose, make an order directing the receiver to make good the default within such time as may be specified in the order."

The receiver was appointed on 25 April 1984 as successor to the previous receiver who had died on 12 April 1984. His solicitor sent a letter dated 30 November 1984 to the liquidator's solicitor enclosing, *inter alia*, what purported to be the receiver's receipts and payments account. The receipts and payments account referred to was an abstract of receipts and payments with no detail. The liquidator further requested a full accounting report of the receivership, without charge, to include full details of all receipts and payments during the period of the defendant's receivership to date, details of the present position regarding any preferential claims and an analysis of the receiver's fees charged to date. In his reply the receiver referred to the documents already provided and informed the plaintiff that he had not as yet drawn any fees. The liquidator found the reply unsatisfactory and requested, *inter alia*, full details of all receipts and payments during the period of the receivership to date, during his period and during his predecessor's period and also full details of fees charged by the previous receiver.

The liquidator submitted that if a receiver is appointed without undue delay on the death or removal of a previous receiver, the receivership may be regarded as continuous. The receiver, in his affidavit, submitted that the duty imposed under section 322(1)(b) refers to the duty of a receiver under section 319(2) to prepare an abstract every six months to be filed with the Registrar of Companies, and that all such abstracts had been filed by both the previous receiver and himself. It was further submitted in court that the requirements of section 322(1)(b) had been complied with when the receiver's solicitor furnished various documents to the liquidator's solicitor on 30 November 1984.

Held by Carroll J:

(1) References to a "receiver" in section 322 do not include the receiver's predecessors in title as it is not specifically provided for: sections 319(4), 320 and 322 compared.

(2) The case did not concern the concept of a continuous receivership as the issue in this case was whether the present receiver had failed to comply with the statutory duty imposed upon him by section 322(1)(b).

(3) However, both parties believed that an account of the entire period was

necessary, therefore the liquidator acted reasonably in requiring more than an abstract of receipts and payments which would not have required much additional work for the receiver.

(4) It was unreasonable for the liquidator to require the receiver to produce a full accounting report without charge. Accordingly, the receiver would be entitled to reasonable charges for necessary work done.

(5) In the circumstances, both parties should bear their own costs.

Case referred to in judgment
Re White's Mortgage [1943] Ch 166

Counsel's and solicitors' names not available

CARROLL J **13 June 1986**

The plaintiff as liquidator of Bamfords Ireland Ltd has brought this action against the defendant as receiver appointed by the Bank of Ireland on foot of a debenture dated 5 May 1978 for an order under section 322(1)(b) of the Companies Act 1963.

Section 322 (1)(b) provides:

> "(1) If any receiver of the property of a company—
>
> > (*b*) having been appointed under the powers contained in any instrument, has, after being required at any time by the liquidator of the company to do so, failed to render proper accounts of his receipts and payments and to vouch the same and to pay over to the liquidator the amount properly payable to him; the court may, on an application made for the purpose, make an order directing the receiver to make good the default within such time as may be specified in the order."

The receiver was appointed on 25 April 1984 as successor to the previous receiver who had been appointed on 9 June 1980 and died on 12 April 1984.

Both parties filed lengthy affidavits. In addition the liquidator's assistant, Mr Riordan, and the receiver himself gave oral evidence. In his affidavit the liquidator complained that he had only received summaries of receipts and payments accounts which were insufficient to identify when, from whom and for what the monies were received, the movement of monies within the receivership, and when, to whom and for what monies were paid out. He also sought a breakdown and analysis of fees charged in respect of the receivership.

The receiver in his affidavit claimed that default of duty under section 322(1)(b) refers to the duty of a receiver under section 319(2) to prepare an abstract every six months to be filed with the Registrar of Companies, and that all these abstracts had been filed by both the previous receiver and the receiver.

The case made in court differed from this in that counsel for the receiver submitted that compliance with the requirements of section 322(1)(b) had been made once the enclosures sent with the letter dated 30 November 1984 from the receiver's solicitors to the liquidator's solicitors were sent. These were:

1. Receiver's receipts and payments account (to the nearest £1,000).
2. Copy receiver's last abstract.
3. Estimated projection in respect of funds remaining on hand (to the nearest £1,000).

The receipts and payments account referred to is an abstract of receipts and payments with no detail.

Following that letter, agreement was reached that the liquidator could go through the receiver's books. Mr Riordan attended the receiver's offices on 25 January 1985, and a conflict of evidence arises over what happened at that meeting. The liquidator was not satisfied with the outcome and among other things required by letter dated 29 January 1985:

> "A full accounting report of your receivership without charge to include:
>
> (a) full details of all receipts and payments during the period of your receivership to date;
> (b) details of the present position regarding any preferential claims;
> (c) analysis of receiver's fees charged to date."

A detailed reply to that request was made by letter dated 7 March 1985. The receiver referred to the documents sent on 13 November 1984, and said:

> "Your solicitor has acknowledged receipt of this information and has acknowledged that we have requested you to let us have details of any further information, if any, which you require. To date we have not received particulars from you in this regard."

He also said:

> "I do not understand your reference to a report without charge and perhaps you might be kind enough to clarify. As to your request for an analysis of receiver's fees charged to date I can confirm that as receiver I have not as yet drawn any fees in this case since the date of my appointment in April last."

The liquidator found the detailed response unsatisfactory. The summons was issued in May 1985. In a letter dated 21 May 1985 the liquidator required, *inter alia*, full details of all receipts and payments during the period of the receivership to date, i.e., during his period and during his predecessor's period and he required full details of fees charged on 28 August 1981 by the previous receiver.

A further meeting took place on 24 May 1985 and a conflict of evidence also arises over this. The meeting did not solve the matter.

It was submitted by counsel for the liquidator that if a receiver is appointed without undue delay on the death or removal of a previous liquidator, the receivership may be regarded as continuous. The authority cited is *Re White's Mortgage* [1943] Ch 166. That case deals with a special statutory situation under the Courts Emergency Powers Act 1939 where the question to be determined was whether leave of the court was required on replacement of a receiver, where the remedy had already been exercised as distinct from a first appointment. The court took the view that leave was not required if the appointment was made to maintain continuity but if a long interval passed, a new receivership was created and leave of court was required.

Kerr on Receivers at page 357 (15th Edition) takes the view based on *Re White's Mortgage*, which he acknowledges relates to a special statutory situation, that if a fresh receiver is appointed without undue delay the receivership may be regarded as continuous. He says this is important as regards undischarged statutory duties such as the duty to discharge preferential debts.

But whether there can be a concept of a continuous receivership with resulting legal effect on undischarged statutory duties, it does not really go to the issue I have to decide, which does not concern an undischarged statutory duty by the previous receiver. The issue here is whether the present receiver has failed to comply with the statutory duty imposed on him by section 322 (1)(b), *viz.* to render proper accounts of his receipts and payments after being required to do so.

Under section 319(4) where the obligation to furnish a statement of affairs to a receiver has not been complied with before that receiver dies or ceases to act, reference to the receiver includes references "to his successor and to any continuing receiver". Under section 320 reference is made to the statement of affairs to be made "to the receiver (or his successor)". This is obviously a reference back to section 319(4).

It therefore appears to me that since it is not specifically provided for, the "receiver" in section 322 does not include references to his predecessor. The statutory duty to render proper accounts is referable to receipts and payments received or made by him personally and does not include a duty to render proper account of receipts and payments made by his predecessor. If that duty exists (and I am not saying it does not exist if the concept of a continuous receivership exists) it does not lie in section 322.

However, both parties believed the duty under section 322 referred to the accounts of the receivership from the beginning. Since the initiation of proceedings, in particular since March 1986, all outstanding matters which the receiver was in a position to deal with, have been cleared up and this action is really about who is to pay the costs.

Even though the receiver never furnished accounts referable only to his receipts and payments, I cannot award costs against him on that basis, as neither the liquidator nor the receiver adverted to that point until very late in the day. So I have looked at the matter from the point of view of reasonableness on both sides. Given that both parties believed an account of the entire period was necessary, it seems to me that the liquidator was reasonable in requiring more than an abstract of receipts and payments and it would not have required massive additional work for the receiver. To give one example, in this case the receiver's cash receipts book consists of 18 double pages. It seems to me it would have been simple to furnish copies of that.

As against that the liquidator told the receiver that he required a full accounting report without charge. This was unreasonable as the receiver would be entitled to reasonable charges for necessary work done. There has been a certain amount of misunderstanding and there are faults on both sides. In my opinion the fairest thing to do is to let both sides bear their own costs.

With regard to the conflict of evidence, I think both Mr Riordan and the receiver gave their evidence to the best of their recollection. While it is not possible to reconcile their evidence, no purpose is served at this late stage by expressing a view on the facts based merely on the balance of probabilities.

Patricia McLaughlin
Barrister

In the Matter of Irish Commercial Society Group Ltd (in Receivership and in Liquidation); Irish Commercial Finance Ltd (in Liquidation); Irish Commercial Society Ltd (in Liquidation) and Irish Savings Building Society (in Liquidation) and in the Matter of the Companies Acts 1963 to 1986 (No. 2): High Court 1984 No. 1085P (Lynch J) 12 February 1987

Statutory prohibition on investment trust companies accepting deposits – Group company issued bonds – Trust deed entered into with the issue of bonds – Floating charge created over assets of the group company – Power to appoint a receiver – Whether this transaction was tainted with illegality – Whether the group company was an investment trust company at the date when the bonds were issued – Whether the issues of bonds were null and void as a sham attempt to circumvent the statutory prohibition of the 1978 Act – Definition of an investment trust company – Whether certain mortgages, loans and leased assets were the property of the group company and captured in the receivership – Whether property properly assigned – Whether consideration paid by the group company – Mortgages on houses and lands – Whether agreement evidenced in writing – Part performance – Central Bank Act 1971 (No. 24), section 2 – Industrial and Provident Societies (Amendment) Act 1978 (No. 23), section 36 – Statute of Frauds

Facts: A receiver was appointed to Irish Commercial Society Group Ltd ("the group company") by virtue of a power contained in a trust deed which was entered into by the group company on the issue of bonds to the public and by which a floating charge was created over its assets. The receiver claimed that certain mortgages, loans and leased assets were the property of the group company and thereby caught in the receivership and that they were not the property of the company's subsidiaries or former subsidiaries as claimed by the liquidator. Upon the hearing of the motion the liquidator submitted that the transaction pursuant to which the receiver was appointed was tainted with illegality in that it was claimed that at all material times the company was an investment trust company and that the issue of bonds was merely a sham attempt to circumvent the prohibition in section 36 of the Industrial and Provident Societies (Amendment) Act 1978 on an investment trust company accepting deposits. The liquidator relied upon the company's memorandum of association, the description of the company's activities in the prospectuses accompanying the issue of the bonds and the accounts of the company from 1978 to 1982. He further stated that the terms and interest rates of the bonds were identical to those of the deposits previously accepted by the subsidiary company. The receiver conceded that on the date of the first issue of bonds, the group company was an investment trust company but denied that it was on the second and third issues as he contended that its main business at those times was not investment of its funds in securities. He relied on an item of £694,000 invested in properties shown in the accounts at the date of the second issue and submitted that as of the date of the third issue, there was really no investment in securities of any substance in the 1982 accounts despite the figure therein of £360,107. The balance sheet also showed investments which represented the mortgages, loans and leased assets the subject matter of the motion, therefore the question as to whether the group company was or was not an investment company at the date of the third issue depended upon whether these were in fact the property of the group company. This involved a consideration as to whether purported assignments of these interests were effective. Category 1 related to the majority of mortgages and loans and category 5 dealt with all the leased assets. Five agreements were entered into in relation to these two categories, each of which contained an identical clause to the effect that the completion date of each transaction should be not later than 30 June 1983. In fact, no formal assignments were ever executed. However, full consideration was paid by the group company in respect of them all. Category 2 comprised of two mortgages alleged to have been transferred from one subsidiary to the group company on 20 December 1983 and category 3 comprised a number of loans and mortgages alleged to have been transferred by another subsidiary between 1 January and 31 December 1983. Although there were entries in the account books of the group company showing that full consideration had been paid and in a minority of cases there was correspondence by the group company with third parties, there were no formal documents whatsoever showing any written agreement, assignment or form of transfer by these subsidiary companies in favour of the Group company. Some of the properties the subject matter of categories 2 and 3 consisted of mortgages of houses or lands. Category 4 comprised a number of transactions entered into by a third subsidiary with third parties the benefit of which the receiver alleged were transferred to the group company. In addition to paying consideration for these, the group company paid a seven and a half per cent premium to one of the subsidiaries, Irish Commercial Finance Ltd.

Held by Lynch J:

(1) The group company was an investment trust company at the date of the issue of the first and second bonds.

(2) The group company was not an investment trust company at the date of the third issue of bonds.

(3) The bonds issued when the company was an investment trust company were not illegal and were not simply deposits in another name. Therefore they were not contrary to section 36 of the Industrial Provident Societies (Amendment) Act 1978.

(4) Although the clause in all the agreements contained in categories 1 and 5 as to the completion date was initially of the essence of the agreement, the respective parties waived the same by the payment and acceptance of the consideration and the equitable interest in the property the subject matter of the agreements passed to the group company.

(5) The receiver failed to establish to the satisfaction of the court that the mortgages in categories 2 and 3 were assigned or transferred to the group company as while the entries in the account books and bank accounts of the various companies show as a matter of probability that consideration was paid, they do not show the precise nature or purpose of such payments. Insofar as the properties consisted of mortgages of houses and lands, the entries in the accounts of the various companies do not constitute sufficient part performance to overcome the provisions of the Statute of Frauds because they are completely ambiguous.

(6) Although the same criticisms could be levelled in relation to the category 4 transactions, the important difference is that in these cases, the group company paid a premium which is consistent only with an arrangement whereby the group company was to become owners of these mortgages and loans and is sufficient part performance to come within the rulings in *Steadman v. Steadman* [1976] AC 536.

Cases referred to in judgment

Dempsey v. Bank of Ireland Irish Company Law Reports (1963-1993) 328
Murphy v. The Revenue Commissioners [1976] IR 15
Steadman v. Steadman [1976] AC 536
Tempany v. Hynes [1976] IR 101

Counsel's and solicitors' names not available

LYNCH J **12 February 1987**

This is a motion brought by the receiver Mr John Donnelly against the liquidator Mr David Hughes of Irish Commercial Society Group Ltd (hereinafter called the group company) to determine whether certain mortgages, loans and leased assets are the property of the group company and captured in the receivership by virtue of the documents under which the receiver was appointed to be receiver or whether they are the property of one or other of the group company's subsidiaries or former subsidiaries and therefore not so captured, namely Irish Commercial Finance Ltd (hereinafter called the finance company), Irish Commercial Society Ltd (hereinafter called the commercial society) and Irish Savings Building Society (hereinafter called the building society).

The notice of motion is dated 2 July 1985 but as a result of the complexity of the matters which appeared to be in issue between the receiver and the liquidator the court directed the delivery of pleadings between them. Pleadings were accordingly delivered comprising a claim on behalf of the receiver dated 30 June 1986, a defence on behalf of the liquidator dated 12 November 1986, a notice for particulars on behalf of the liquidator dated the same date, a reply thereto dated 21 November 1986, a letter on behalf of the liquidator giving further particulars dated 18 December 1986, a letter for particulars on behalf of the receiver dated 17 December 1986 (these letters crossing in the post), a reply on behalf of the liquidator dated 14 January 1987, a letter on behalf of the receiver dated 12 January 1987 and a reply thereto on behalf of the liquidator dated 14 January 1987.

These pleadings and documents delivered between the receiver and the liquidator raise quite a number of issues which broadly speaking resolve into two main issues. The first is whether the transactions pursuant to which the receiver was purported to be appointed receiver were tainted with illegality so that such transactions and appointment are null and void. That issue of illegality in itself involves two separate questions: (1) whether the group company was at the time when certain bonds were issued by it an investment trust company and (2) if it was an investment trust company whether the issues of the bonds were null and void as a sham attempt to circumvent the prohibition in section 36 of the Industrial and Provident Societies (Amendment) Act 1978 on accepting or holding deposits by an investment trust company. If the issue of illegality should be determined in favour of the receiver then the second main question arises which is as to whether in fact such mortgages, loans and leased assets were effectively assigned to the group company.

I propose to deal with the issues in the order in which they have been set out above but as the two questions involved in the issue of illegality are to some extent inextricably bound together they must be dealt with to some extent together.

The facts relevant to the issue of illegality are as follows.

The commercial society is an industrial and provident society. Prior to 1978 the commercial society held £4,4902,217 deposited with it for periods of three months, six months, eleven months and five years. By virtue of section 5 of the Industrial and Provident Societies (Amendment) Act 1978 the commercial society was required to repay all such deposits and to cease accepting deposits by 15 November 1983.

The monies which the commercial society held on deposit in 1978 formed a large proportion of the finance available to the group company and its subsidiaries at that time. The activities of the group company and its subsidiaries are accurately described in a prospectus dated 5 October 1979 as follows:

> "Irish Commercial Society Group Ltd through its resources primarily in providing loans to prime borrowers on the security of real and leasehold property and leasing facilities to industry and commerce. It also trades in industrial and commercial property".

In order to replace the finance which the commercial society was required to shed it was decided that the group company should issue five year bonds to the public in amounts of not less than £500. The group company was originally incorporated under the name Seapoint Holdings Ltd on 3 October 1973 as a private company and it changed its name to Irish Commercial Society Group Ltd on 14 April 1978. By a special resolution passed on 27 September 1979 by the group company the articles of association were amended so as to convert it into a public company, thus entitling it to seek subscriptions from the public.

Following that the prospectus dated 5 October 1979 was prepared and issued and the provisions of the Companies Act 1963 were complied with regarding invitation to the public to subscribe to the bonds offered by the prospectus. This issue of bonds raised less than £200,000 and was inadequate to replace the capital which would have to be lost by the Commercial Society. Hence it was decided by the group company to make a further issue of bonds, this time of eleven months' duration.

A prospectus was accordingly prepared and issued dated 21 June 1982. Again the provisions of the Companies Act 1963 were complied with regarding seeking subscriptions from the public. This issue of bonds raised £2,100,000 of which £900,000 was new money, that is to say subscribed by members of the public not already depositors with the group company or any of its then subsidiaries. £1,200,000 of this issue was old money, that is to say, money which in effect changed from being deposited with the Commercial Society to bonds with the group company.

In order to retain the use of the monies so raised the group company decided to make further issues of bonds in the hope that persons who had subscribed for the eleven month bonds in 1982 would on these bonds expiring and being repaid reinvest the moneys in the new bonds. Hence a prospectus was issued dated 21 April 1983. The activities are described in this prospectus as:

> "Irish Commercial Society Group Ltd through its subsidiaries employ [*sic*] its resources primarily in providing loans to prime borrowers on the security of real and leasehold property and leasing facilities to industry and commerce."

In fact the group company had prior to this prospectus disposed of all its subsidiaries except the building society and Irish Commercial Trust Ltd which had an issued share capital of only £2. The prospectus of 21 April 1983 offered for sale to the public three month bonds, six month bonds, eleven month bonds and eleven month monthly income bonds all of which were fixed interest rate bonds, the minimum subscription to be at least £100.00. This issue of bonds raised £2,400,000 of which £1,000,000 was new money and £1,400,000 was old money. This £1,400,000 came from within the group company and its former subsidiaries and a large proportion of it was subscribed by way of reinvestment of monies repaid from the 1982 issue of eleven month bonds of which only £33,000 now remain outstanding. In effect therefore a large proportion of the 1982 eleven month bonds were "rolled over" by way of reinvestment in 1983 eleven month bonds. The amounts outstanding on the three issues of bonds are:– 1979 bonds £99,000: 1982 bonds £33,000: and 1983 bonds £2,400,000, making an overall total of £2,532,000.

With each issue of bonds a trust deed was entered into by the group company with Chambers Trust Corporation Ltd (hereinafter called Chambers Trust) creating a floating charge on all its assets as security for the bonds with powers to Chambers Trust to appoint a receiver. It is pursuant to such powers that the receiver was appointed to be receiver of the company on 1 February 1984. The liquidator was appointed to be provisional liquidator of the company, the finance company, the commercial society and the building society on 2 and 3 February 1984 and an order winding up the same companies was made on 27 February 1984 and the liquidator was appointed to be liquidator of the same companies.

The objects clause in the group company's memorandum of association commences by stating that:

> "The objects for which the company is established are:
> (1) to carry on the business of a Trust and Investment Company and to invest the funds of the company in or upon or otherwise acquire hold and dispose of property real or personal of every kind which without limiting the generality of such description shall be deemed to include (a) shares stocks rights to new issues debentures debenture stocks bonds mortgages and securities of every kind and description issued or guaranteed by any company constituted or carrying on business in Ireland or elsewhere and etc."

The description of the group company's activities in the first prospectus of 5 October 1979 has already been quoted and an identical description appeared in the second prospectus of 21 June 1982 and the description of its activities in the third prospectus of 21 April 1983 has also already been quoted.

It was agreed by counsel for the respective parties that the onus of proof of the issue of illegality rested on the liquidator. It was submitted by counsel for the liquidator that the group company was an investment trust company at all material times. An investment trust company is defined in section 2 of the Central Bank Act 1971 as meaning "a company whose main business consists of the investment of its funds in securities".

Securities are defined as meaning (a) shares in the share capital of any body corporate, (b) securities of the Government, and (c) rights in respect of monies lent to or deposited with Industrial and Provident Societies and Building Societies *inter alia.*

Counsel for the liquidator relied on the terms of the memorandum of association and the prospectuses and the accounts of the group company and in particular the balance sheets for the years 1978 to 1982 inclusive as indicating that the group company was at all material times an investment trust company.

The receiver in evidence conceded under cross-examination that as at the date of the first prospectus on 5 October 1979 the group company was an investment trust company and I so find. The receiver further almost conceded that the group company as at the date of the prospectus of 21 June 1982 might be an investment trust company but he contended strongly that it was not an investment trust company as at the date of the third prospectus of 21 April 1983.

Counsel for the receiver submitted that the group company was not an investment trust company either at the date of the second prospectus 21 June 1982 or the third prospectus 21 April 1983 and further contended that the evidence indicated that its main business was not investment of its funds in securities as at either of those dates. He relied strongly on the item of £694,000 investment in properties in the 1981 accounts and on the fact that there were really no investments in securities of any substance whatever in the 1982 accounts despite the figure therein of £360,107.

As regards the prospectus of 21 June 1982, at that time the group company held properties in Hanover Quay and Weatherwell Industrial Estate in Dublin which it had acquired in late 1981. It did nothing with these properties and sold them in December 1982 to the finance company and sometime later repurchased them in 1983 and then again resold them in July 1983. It seems to me that this sort of dealing with these properties cannot alter the fact that the main business of the group company as described in the accounts of 31 December 1981 was then:

> "The company acts as holding company co-ordinating the activities of its various wholly owned subsidiaries, the activities are divided into principal divisions lending and property as listed below."

I find that the group company was an investment trust company at the date of issue of the prospectus of 21 June 1982.

It is in respect of the issue of the bonds on foot of the prospectus of 21 April that the greatest conflict arises on the question as to whether the group company was or was not an investment trust company. The objects in its memorandum of association remained unchanged. The group activities as described in the prospectus have already been quoted above. These activities are described in the accounts of the group company for the year ending 31 December 1982 as:

> "The company acts as holding company co-ordinating the activities of its

wholly owned subsidiaries. The company is also involved in lending and leasing. The activities of its subsidiary companies are listed below. Irish Savings Building Society – Building Society – Irish Commercial Society Trust Ltd – Trustees."

The balance sheet for the year ending 31 December 1982 shows an item of £360,107 as investment in subsidiaries. This is an unrealistic figure because the subsidiaries in question had already been sold off and nevertheless it was claimed in the balance sheet that the goodwill of the subsidiaries remained with the group company. The truth is that as at the date of the balance sheet the group company's investment in subsidiaries was only £1,337 – as shown by notes 9 and 10 to the accounts for the year ending 31 December 1982.

The balance sheet also shows investments referred to as "Secured Loans, Unsecured Loans and Leased Assets" totalling £1,470,000. Whether the group company in fact owned these investments depends on my decision to be given later in this judgment as to whether or not the mortgages, loans and leased assets were effectively assigned to the group company. If it is assumed for the purposes of deciding the issue of illegality that the mortgages, loans and leased assets or the greater part thereof were effectively assigned to the group company then at the date of the third issue of bonds on 21 April 1983 the group company's funds were not invested in securities and such investment was not its main business and therefore the group company would not have been an investment trust company on that date. If on the other hand the mortgages, loans and leased assets or the greater part thereof were not effectively assigned to the group company then there was no real change in the nature and activities of the group company and it thus remained an investment trust company as defined in section 2 of Central Bank Act 1971.

As the group company was an investment trust company at the dates and on the occasions of the issues of bonds on 5 October 1979 and 21 June 1982 and may have been such on 21 April 1983 I next have to decide whether the bonds were in truth no more than deposits in another name and therefore contrary to section 36 of the Industrial and Provident Societies (Amendment) Act 1978.

The group company had never held deposits before 4 October 1978 and was therefore not entitled to hold or accept deposits after the passing of the 1978 Act on 15 November 1978 by virtue of section 36 of that Act. Counsel for the liquidator submitted that the issue of the bonds was really a sham and that they were no more than deposits by another name intended to replace the deposits of similar duration, namely five years, eleven months, six months and three months which had been obtained prior to 1978 by the commercial society and which had to be repaid by that society not later than 15 November 1983 by virtue of section 5 of the 1978 Act. The terms and interest rates of the bonds are identical with the terms and interest rates of the deposits and counsel for the liquidator submitted that this was an obvious attempt to evade the statutory prohibition.

Counsel for the receiver submitted that the bonds were debentures and perfectly lawful. He conceded that they were issued in the hope of replacing capital lost to the commercial society by having to divest itself of its deposits but he submitted that there was nothing wrong in seeking to replace such lost capital by other means of finance and that the method adopted was lawful and was within the rights and powers given to companies and their directors by the Companies Acts 1963 to 1986. He pointed out that on each of the three occasions the prospectus complied with Part III of the 1963 Act and was a public issue and therefore the group company was entitled to use the money so raised for any purpose of the group company which the directors might decide.

Counsel for the receiver further submitted that to the extent that the bonds were secured they tended to achieve the purpose of the 1978 Act in giving some added protection to members of the public who would subscribe for them over and above the protection and remedies of a mere depositor: that while the bonds bear many of the characteristics of the former deposits taken by the commercial society nevertheless they are not in fact deposits: they are a form of secured debenture bonds: there is no definition in Irish law of what is or is not a deposit but a distinction seems to be drawn between bonds which are referred to in the definition of securities in the Central Bank Act 1971 at paragraph (a) of that definition and deposits which are referred to at paragraph (c) of that definition: and he referred also to the definition of debentures in section 2 of the 1963 Act.

Counsel for the receiver also pointed out that so far as subscribers to the bonds are concerned the only point made by the liquidator against them was that such subscribers would not appreciate the difference between deposits and bonds but counsel pointed out that there was no way of knowing whether they would or would not appreciate the difference. So far as the bonds on their face value appeared they were lawful and subscribers were innocent contributors in the absence of any notice of illegality. They made their contributions on the terms of the trust deed and a floating charge secured thereby and the bonds and charge and the powers of the trust deed must be valid in their favour.

I have come to the conclusion that the submissions of counsel for the receiver on this aspect of the case are correct. Accordingly, I find that the bonds were not illegal and the transactions constituting the same resulting in the appointment of the receiver to be receiver of the group company are lawful and valid transactions and appointment respectively.

It follows from the foregoing conclusions that the other major issue falls for decision that is to say the effectiveness of the purported assignments of the mortgages, loans and leased assets to the group company.

At the hearing before me five booklets were produced and admitted in evidence relating to five different categories of transaction which it is not disputed comprise all the purported assignments of mortgages, loans and leased assets to the group company. Category 1 deals with the majority of the mortgages and loans and Category 5 deals with all the leased assets and the facts relevant to these two categories are as follows.

By an agreement in writing dated 31 December 1982 the commercial society agreed to transfer 16 loans to the group company for £293,502.85 and the finance company agreed to transfer eight loans to the group company for £8,694.78.

By a second agreement in writing dated 31 December 1982 the commercial society agreed to transfer 44 mortgages to the group company for £163,802.99.

By a third agreement in writing dated 31 December 1982 the finance company agreed to transfer 37 mortgages to the group company for £64,676.28.

By a fourth agreement in writing dated 31 December 1982 the commercial society agreed to transfer the lessors interest in 43 leasing agreements to the group company for £47,982.29.

Finally, by a fifth agreement in writing dated 31 December 1982 the finance company agreed to transfer the lessors interest in 582 leasing agreements to the group company for £218,563.29.

Each of these five agreements contained an identical clause as follows:

> "It is hereby agreed between the parties hereto that completion and performance of this agreement shall take place on a date to be agreed between the parties as soon as all legal formalities in respect thereof have been arranged provided that the completion shall take place not later than 30 June 1983.
>
> Completion shall take place at the offices of Messrs Hickey Beauchamp Kirwan & O'Reilly, Dollard House, Wellington Quay, Dublin 2."

No such formal assignments were ever executed as envisaged by the five agreements. However, the inter-company accounts and the bank accounts of the respective companies established that full consideration was paid by the group company to the finance company and the commercial society respectively. Very few of the third party borrowers or lessees were notified of the transfers or assignments or intended transfers or assignments.

Counsel for the liquidator submitted that the clause as to completion by 30 June 1983 was included in the five agreements in order that if the issue of bonds provided for by the prospectus of 21 April 1983 should fail to attract sufficient finance the group company could escape liability to complete the transactions and thus liability to pay the monies required for their completion. Counsel further submitted that the reason for and the wording of the clause was such as to make completion by 30 June 1983 of the essence of each of the agreements and on the failure so to do the group company and the receiver had no right to completion and therefore no equitable right to the property agreed to be transferred by these five agreements.

Counsel for the receiver submitted that the books of account of the various companies as between themselves and their respective bank accounts showed that the transactions were in fact completed and accordingly that the mere failure to execute the formal assignments or transfers of the legal interest or estate could not affect the equitable interest or estate. Counsel submitted that the equitable interest or estate in the property the subject of these five agreements had passed pursuant to the agreements and the payments made thereunder by the group company to the finance company and the commercial society respectively.

I have come to the conclusion that the clause in question was inserted for the reasons submitted by counsel for the liquidator but I also conclude that the group company in fact paid the finance company and the commercial society the full amount of the consideration for the transfer of the property the subject matter of the five agreements. In these circumstances I conclude that even if the clause was initially of the essence of the agreements the respective parties waived the same by the payment and acceptance of the consideration and the equitable interest in the property the subject matter of the agreements passed to the group company. Some of the mortgages, loans and leased assets had been discharged by the third parties prior to 31 December 1982, and therefore those mortgages, loans and leased assets had ceased to exist as at 31 December 1982 – for example of the 105 mortgages and loans in Category 1 (45 negotiated by the finance company and 60 by the commercial society) only 65 or 66 were still subsisting as at 31 December 1982.

Therefore, in relation to the Category 1 mortgages and loans still subsisting at 31 December 1982, and in relation to the Category 5 leased assets still so subsisting, I make the declaration sought by the receiver in paragraph 1 of his notice of motion of 2 July 1985, and I further make the orders sought in paragraph 2 and paragraph 3 of the said motion in relation to the said properties. I do not think it necessary to make the order sought in paragraph 4 of the motion because no doubt the liquidator and the receiver will go into the accounts as between themselves and resolve this matter but I give liberty to apply in relation thereto in case that any difficulty arises.

There now remains for decision the question of the effectiveness of the alleged or purported assignments of the mortgages and loans the subject matter of Categories 2, 3 and 4.

I shall deal first with Categories 2 and 3 which I find I can deal with together.

Category 2 comprises two mortgages for a total of £94,020 alleged to have been transferred by the building society to the group company on 20 December 1983. Category 3 comprises a number of mortgages and loans for a total of £44,848 alleged to have been transferred by the Commercial Society to the group company between 1 January and 30 April 1983.

It should be noted that a booklet of the accounts of the group company for the years ending 31 December 1978, 1979, 1980, 1981 was produced on behalf of the liquidator and admitted in evidence. The accounts for the year ending 31 December 1982 state under the heading "report of the directors" that on 31 December 1982 the group company disposed of a number of its subsidiaries including the finance company and the commercial society but not including the building society. The group company and its subsidiaries when they were subsidiaries had common directors and were under the same control and management and notwithstanding the fact that the finance company and the commercial society may have ceased to be subsidiaries of the group company on 31 December 1982 it is apparent from the course of dealing between these companies and I so find as a matter of probability that the finance company and the commercial society still remained subject to the control and management of the directors who were common directors with the group company.

The receiver relies on entries in the account books of the group company, the commercial society and the building society, respectively as establishing that the Category 2 and Category 3 mortgages and loans were transferred to the group company. These entries are found in inter-company journals and account books. There are also some entries in bank accounts of the respective companies tending to show the payment of the consideration set out above by the group company to the commercial society and the building society respectively. In a minority of cases there is correspondence by the group company with some of the third parties. There are however no formal documents whatever. There is no trace of any written agreement, memorandum, assignment or form of transfer by the building society or the commercial society in favour of the group company. I find that the inter-company journals, account books and bank accounts established as a matter of probability that the group company paid to the building society £94,020 in respect of the Category 2 mortgages and to the commercial society £44,848 in respect of the Category 3 mortgages and loans. Such books of account do not however in any way show the precise nature or purpose of such payments by the group company to the building society and commercial society respectively. Such payments could have been as payment for the outright transfer of the mortgages and loans to the group company: alternatively the payments are consistent with a transfer by the commercial society and the building society respectively to the group company by way of security for advances by the group company to the commercial society and the building society. Alternatively, the payments are consistent with simple loans by the group company to the building society and the commercial society respectively to help finance their respective businesses.

It is not open to companies simply because they are associated with each other in some way or other even if they have ceased to be subsidiaries one of the other to by-pass all the rules of property and law in regard to transferring assets from one to the other by such ambiguous and informal entries in account books. Insofar as the properties the subject matter of categories 2 and 3 consist of mortgages of houses and lands there is no sign anywhere of a memorandum much less a formal agreement of transfer signed by or on behalf of the building society or the commercial society. The entries in the accounts of the various companies are not sufficient part performance of the alleged agreements because they are completely ambiguous and it is in my view open to the liquidator to make this case and rely on the Statute of Frauds because part performance was specifically pleaded by the receiver and specifically denied by the liquidator.

Furthermore insofar as these transactions might be transfers by way of security for monies advanced by the group company on loan to the building society and the commercial society there is no evidence that such securities were ever registered in the respective company's register of charges or with the Registrar of Companies.

Counsel for the liquidator submits that entries such as are given in evidence relating to Category 2 and Category 3 are mere book entries which could be cancelled at any time by making counter-entries. The fact that no such counter-entries have been found in the case of the particular transactions does not alter the ability of the companies to do so and that ability to cancel the transactions at any time if they so wished indicates that no final transfers or assignments or intention to transfer or assign can be inferred in relation to Category 2 and Category 3 transactions.

Counsel for the receiver relied on the Supreme Court decision on 6 December 1985 in *Dempsey v. Bank of Ireland* (unreported) Supreme Court, 6 December 1985 and in *Tempany v. Hynes* [1976] IR 101 and on the High Court decision in *Murphy v. The Revenue Commissioners* [1976] IR 15. It seems to me however that the facts in those cases are completely different from the situation in the present case. In each of the three cases *Dempsey, Tempany* and *Murphy* there was a clear and definite transaction of a specific nature and the only issue was as to what was the effect of this clear and definite transaction in the circumstances of the case. In the present case what is in issue before me is whether any such transaction as alleged in fact took place and if any such transactions took place then as to what was the nature of the transactions rather than the effect of clearly existing transactions of a clearly defined nature.

As to Category 2 mortgages and Category 3 mortgages and loans (if any) without mortgages the receiver has not established to my satisfaction that any of these were assigned or transferred to the group company. Accordingly I decline to make the orders sought in the notice of motion of 2 July 1985 so far as these categories 2 and 3 are concerned.

Finally, there remains for decision the question as to whether the category 4 as mortgages and loans were effectively assigned by the finance company to the group company. Category 4 comprises a number of transactions entered into by the finance company with third parties the benefit of which the receiver alleges was transferred on the same day to the group company. The Booklet 4 comprising documentation relating to the Category 4 mortgages and loans which was tendered in evidence on behalf of the receiver comprises fourteen mortgages to a total value of £95,000 and two personal loans to a value of £3,800. In addition to making payments in the foregoing sums totalling between them £98,800 the group company also paid a seven and a half per cent premium to the finance company which totalled £7,410.

Much the same criticisms can be levied and were levied by the liquidator in relation to the category 4 transactions as in relation to the category 2 and 3 transactions. It seems to me however that there is one very important distinguishing feature of the category 4 transactions. The finance company granted loans to third parties as to fourteen of them on the security of houses and lands and as to the other two on personal security only. The finance company was reimbursed the amount that it advanced to the third parties by the group company and in addition the group company as already stated paid a premium or commission to the finance company of seven and a half per cent of each of these advances.

It seems to me that the payment of this premium or commission is inconsistent with the payments of the principal by the group company to the finance company being a mere loan of monies by the group company to help the finance company to fund its business. It also seems to me to be inconsistent with a payment by the group company to the finance company by way of loan only to be secured by the transfer to the group company by the finance company of the mortgages and loans as security for the advances made to it by the group company. It seems to me that the payment of the principal monies by the group company to the finance company in respect of the day's mortgages and loans negotiated by the finance company with third parties together with the payment of a premium or commission of seven and a half per cent is consistent only with a purchase by the group company of the 14 mortgages and two personal loans from the finance company. The payment of the seven and a half per cent premium or commission establishes to my satisfaction that the finance company really entered into these sixteen transactions with third parties as agent or trustee for the group company. Having entered into the transactions as such agent or trustee it seems to me that no question arises of the Statute of Frauds applying even though 14 of the transactions relate to mortgages by third parties of their interest in houses and lands to the finance company but even if the Statute of Frauds could arise it seems to me that the payment of the commission or premium is such that it points only to an arrangement whereby the group company was to become owner of these mortgages and loans and is a sufficient part performance to come within the rulings in the House of Lords case of *Steadman v. Steadman* [1976] AC 536.

For the foregoing reasons I make the declaration sought by the receiver in paragraph 1 of the notice of motion of 2 July 1985 so far as the Category 4 mortgages and loans are concerned and I also make the orders sought in paragraphs 2 and 3 of the said notice of motion and whilst not making the order sought in paragraph 4 I give the receiver liberty to apply in case that any difficulty should arise.

In addition I give liberty to both parties to apply generally. It also follows from the foregoing conclusions that the group company was not an investment trust company on the occasion of the third issue of bonds pursuant to the prospectus dated 21 April 1983.

Patricia McLaughlin
Barrister

Michael J. Wymes and Others v. Laurence Crowley and Others: High Court 1986 No. 6624P (Murphy J) 27 February 1987

Practice – Procedure – Order for Inspection – Ore Body – Trespass – Bore holes – Principles – Addition of further plaintiffs – Whether abuse of process – Whether attempt to stultify or frustrate activities of receiver – Rules of the Superior Courts 1986 (SI No. 15) Order 50 r. 4

Facts: Bula Ltd ("Bula") owned certain lands in Co. Meath under which lay a valuable ore body. Bula was owned 49 per cent by the State, 40.8 per cent by Bula Holdings (controlled by the family interests of Thomas C. Roche, Thomas J. Roche, Richard Wood and Michael Wymes) and 10.2 per cent by members of the Wright family.

In October 1985 the first defendant was appointed receiver of Bula. In 1986 the plaintiffs issued proceedings alleging negligence on the part of the receiver in failing to detect the alleged systematic larceny of the Bula orebody by the owners of an adjoining mine Tara Mines Ltd.

The plaintiffs obtained an interim injunction restraining the receiver from selling the assets of Bula on or prior to 18 July 1986. The injunction was disposed of at the interlocutory stage by the receiver's undertaking to seek High Court approval for any offer for the purchase of the assets. No objection was made, however, as to the validity of the debenture or the receiver's appointment.

In January 1987 the existing plaintiffs issued a motion seeking (a) to add Bula Ltd, Thomas C. Roche, Thomas J. Roche and Richard Wood as plaintiffs — the defendants did not object to the addition of the three individuals, but objected to the addition of Bula Ltd; (b) to amend the plenary summons; (c) an order directing the first defendant to permit the plaintiffs to inspect certain lands and the minerals thereunder.

The defendants contended that the intended proceedings were an abuse of the process of the court, in that the plaintiff was seeking to "stultify or frustrate the receiver's activities" contrary to the terms of the debentures, even though no challenge had been made to his appointment. They argued that the extended claim presaged further injunction applications designed to delay the realisation of the assets of Bula.

In relation to the inspection claim the plaintiffs objected to inspection conducted through Tara Mines using Tara's plans, as their own advice was that the alleged mine trespass might not be shown on the plans, and it would still be necessary to drill for positive proof. The receiver was concerned that drilling might damage the orebody, while he might be put at risk of liability for damage as a result of works carried out.

Held by Murphy J in granting the relief sought:

(1) Insofar as the proceedings sought to prevent the realisation on improper terms of the company's assets, this could not be contrary to the legitimate interests of the debenture holders. Therefore Bula could properly be added as a

plaintiff. *Newhart Developments Ltd v. Co-operative Commercial Bank Ltd* [1978] QB 814 discussed.

(2) The defendants' concerns in relation to further applications should the court accede to the amendment of the claim were unwarranted. In any case the plaintiffs would have been free to discontinue the proceedings and start afresh. Therefore, the amendment to the claim should be allowed.

(3) The general principles of inspection were that where there was an allegation of injury to land, based on *prima facie* evidence, and the only way of ascertaining that fact was by inspection, then the court should allow it. *Bennitt v. Whitehouse* (1860) 28 Beav 119, quoted with approval.

(4) Bula here was making a claim as to alleged larceny of the Bula orebody, by the owners of the adjoining orebody, Tara Mines Ltd. In addition, Bula was in fact seeking to inspect its own property or at any rate property in which subject to a charge in favour of the banks, it held the equity of redemption. In that sense, Bula was, in fact, asking for liberty to inspect its own property, or, at least, property in which it had a very substantial interest.

(5) It was not possible to resolve the conflict between the geologists as to the potential for damage to the orebody by drilling. The plaintiffs should however be facilitated, while protecting the defendants from liability. The receiver should therefore put the named experts in possession of the lands, to the exclusion of the receiver, during a specified period, for the purpose of drilling not more than eighteen boreholes of a stipulated diameter, subject to certain obligations being set out in a contractual document.

Cases referred to in judgment

Bennitt v. Whitehouse (1860) 28 Beav 119

Cooper v. Incehall Company [1876] WN 24; (1876) 2 LT 45

Newhart Developments Ltd v. Co-operative Commercial Bank Ltd [1978] QB 814; [1978] 2 WLR 636; [1978] 2 All ER 896

Counsel's names not available

Solicitors for the plaintiffs: *Dockrell, Shields & Farrell*
Solicitors for the first defendant: *William Fry & Sons*
Solicitors for the second, third and fourth defendants: *Whitney, Moore & Keller*

MURPHY J **27 February 1987**

By motion dated 7 January 1987 three orders were sought by the plaintiffs. First, that a company and certain individuals should be joined as plaintiffs, secondly that the plenary summons should be amended and thirdly that the first named defendant should be directed to permit the plaintiffs to conduct an inspection of certain lands and the minerals thereunder. Having regard to the urgency of the matter I made the first and second of the orders sought but postponed giving my reasons for so doing until the conclusion of the hearing of the remainder of the motion.

In so far as the first of the motions sought to have the named individuals

Thomas C. Roche, Thomas J. Roche and Richard Wood joined as plaintiffs no difficulty arose and no serious objection was made by any of the defendants. However, all of the defendants disputed the right of the plaintiffs to join as an additional plaintiff Bula Ltd. Bula Ltd is the owner of certain lands at Nevinstown, Co. Meath and it appears to be clearly established that there is a valuable orebody under those lands. The shareholding in Bula Ltd is owned as to 49 per cent by the State, 40.8 per cent by Bula Holdings and 10.2 per cent by members of the Wright family. Bula Holdings in turn is effectively owned and controlled by the family interests of Thomas C. Roche, Thomas J. Roche, Richard F. Wood and Michael J. Wymes.

The second, third and fourthly named defendants (the defendant banks) have loaned sums of money in the order of £16,000,000 for principal and interest to Bula Ltd. The repayment of those monies was secured, *inter alia*, by means of debentures granted by Bula Ltd to the defendant bankers on foot of which the first named defendant, Laurence J. Crowley, was appointed receiver on 8 October 1985.

In these proceedings an interim injunction was granted on 2 July 1986 restraining the receiver from selling the assets of Bula Ltd on or prior to 8 July 1986. On the latter date the interlocutory application came on for hearing and was struck out on consent on the undertaking of the receiver to apply to the High Court for approval for any offer for the purchase of the assets of Bula Ltd and his undertaking to notify the plaintiffs of such application. It was not contended then or at any time that the appointment of the receiver was invalid or that there was any defect in the debenture under which he was so appointed. No challenge has been made as to the right or power of the receiver to dispose of the assets of Bula Ltd charged by the debentures. The concern of the plaintiffs has related to the terms on which they are sold and more particularly the price to be obtained for them. No doubt the undertaking of the receiver not to dispose of the assets charged without the sanction of the court obtained on notice to the plaintiffs is a procedure which fully protects the interest of both the plaintiffs and the receiver.

On 14 February 1986 a petition was presented by the defendant banks for the winding up of Bula Ltd. That petition was contested by Bula Holdings and others and was adjourned from time to time until 18 July when an order was made by Justice Costello winding up the company and appointing Mr William McCann as official liquidator thereof. An appeal was lodged against that order which is, I understand, listed for hearing on 10 March 1987. In the meantime a stay has been placed on the winding up order.

The defendants properly recognise that the appointment of a receiver in pursuance of the powers in that behalf contained in a mortgage debenture does not terminate the powers vested by law in the directors of the company. The combined effect of the mortgage debenture and the appointment of a receiver is to appoint the receiver as the attorney of the company to deal with and dispose of the assets charged in accordance with the terms of the contractual documents and subject to certain statutory provisions which are applicable in those circumstances. References have been made to "the residual powers of the directors" notwithstanding the appointment of a receiver. This expression may be appropriate as in practice the security granted by a company would ordinarily extend to all of its assets present and future and impose thereon a fixed or floating charge as might be appropriate to the nature of the assets and include in addition — as is done in the present case — a power to carry on the business of the company. In such cases and with that range of powers irrevocable delegated to the receiver, the areas in which directors may lawfully and effectively exercise powers in no doubt limited but, as I say, that is the practical consequence of granting an extensive charge over the assets of the company. If the parties were to confine themselves to a specific or limited area of charge or at any rate to exempt some of the properties of the company from the mortgage debenture it would be appreciated more clearly in principle that the powers of the receiver are those conferred upon him for the purpose of realising the security over which he is appointed and that all of the other powers to manage the affairs of the company remain vested in the board of directors thereof.

I have no doubt but that the directors of Bula Ltd retain their power to institute proceedings in an appropriate case. The limitation on their powers is that they must not deprive the debentureholders of the security granted to them and the very practical difficulty that the extensive nature of the charge deprives the company of the means of financing litigation. That the directors of Bula Ltd would be entitled to institute proceedings in the name of that company to sue for negligence a receiver appointed over the assets of that company could not be questioned as a matter of law.

What was urged on behalf of the first named defendant was that the intended proceedings were an abuse of the process of the court in as much as the company was seeking to restrain the receiver disposing of the assets charged in favour of the defendant banks notwithstanding the fact that no challenge had been raised to the validity of the debentures or the appointment of the receiver. It was contended that the proceedings were seeking to "stultify or frustrate the receiver's activities" contrary to the terms of the debentures as had been held by Chapman J in *Newhart Developments Ltd v. Co-operative Commercial Bank Ltd.* That decision was reversed on appeal [1978] QB 814. At page 821 of the Report Shaw LJ explained the position in the following terms:

> "I see no principle of law or expediency which precludes the directors of a company, as a duly constituted board (and it is not suggested here that they were not a duly constituted board when they took the step of instituting this action) from seeking to enforce the claim, however ill founded it may be, provided only, of course, that nothing in the course of the proceedings which they institute is going in any way to threaten the interests of the debenture holders."

If and insofar as it is suggested that the purpose of these proceedings is to prevent the realisation *on improper terms* of any part of the assets of the company that could not be contrary to the interest of the debentureholders and I cannot see that the allegations made in the interlocutory proceedings or the relief sought in the plenary summons, if supported by appropriate evidence, could be seen as a threat to the legitimate interests of the debentureholders.

In the circumstance I directed that Bula Ltd should be joined as a co-plaintiff.

The second order sought on the notice of motion was the amendment of the plenary summons herein. This order was opposed by the defendant banks largely on the grounds that the amended claim seeking extended injunctive relief presaged further applications for interlocutory injunctions designed to delay the realisation of the assets of Bula Ltd. In my view that suspicion is unwarranted. As I have already pointed out the existing arrangement in relation to the interlocutory position with regard to the realisation of the assets appears to protect the interest of all parties and it is difficult to see how or why there would be any further relief sought in that regard. In relation to this aspect of the matter there is too the reality that the plaintiffs would be free to discontinue the existing proceedings and start afresh. In my view there is nothing to be gained by putting them to that expense and perhaps causing the defendant unnecessary delay. Accordingly I granted the relief sought.

The third order sought was the most contentious. The plaintiffs are seeking the right to inspect — by suitable technical procedures — the orebody beneath the Nevinstown lands of Bula Ltd (the Bula orebody). The right of inspection is sought under Order 50 r.4 of the Rules of the Superior Courts (1986) which provides as follows:

> "4. The Court, upon the application of any party . . . for the purpose of obtaining full information or evidence."

The principles on which that rule may be invoked were explained many years ago — coincidentally in a mining case — in *Cooper v. Incehall Company* [1876] WN 24. The material part of the judgment of Lindley J was as follows:

> "An order for inspection of this kind is so common in Chancery that I should have thought this was a matter of course. My impression is that the plaintiffs are entitled almost as a matter of course to inspect the defendants' mines about the alleged boundaries."

In an earlier case — *Bennitt v. Whitehouse* (1860) 28 Beav 119 the Master of the Rolls had pointed out the necessity for establishing a *prima facie* case when he explained the right to inspection in the following terms:

> "Wherever it appears that a person has power to make use of his land to the injury of another, and there is *prima facie* evidence of his doing so, though it is contradicted, still, as the only way of ascertaining the fact is by an inspection, the court always allows it, if it can be done without injury to the defendant."

In the absence of a statement of claim it is difficult to speak with precision of the nature of the plaintiffs' claim as against the defendants or any of them but a reading of the numerous affidavits and documents exhibited therein indicates that the gist of the plaintiffs' claim as against the receiver is the alleged failure of the latter to detect at any time since his appointment (in October 1985) the continuing and apparently systematic larceny of the Bula orebody by the owners of the adjoining orebody, namely, Tara Mines Ltd. Whilst the allegation against the receiver is no doubt serious the allegation against Tara is vastly more so. Not merely is it alleged that they have misappropriated the Bula orebody but apparently the allegation made in this and in other proceedings is that this expropriation has continued for upwards of ten years.

Whilst the defendants is the present case emphatically deny the claims made by the plaintiff there is a significant difference between the present proceedings (the Bula action) and certain proceedings by the same plaintiffs against Tara Mines Ltd and others (the Tara action). The parties to the Bula action have a common interest in maximising the value of the Bula orebody and any other assets of Bula Ltd. The greater the price realised the better the prospect of the defendant banks being paid in full and an even more successful outcome would result, presumably, in a surplus for the individual plaintiffs. At any rate the better the price obtained the lesser their liabilities on foot of the various guarantees. There is also the fact that now, as a result of an order already made by me herein, the owner of the Bula orebody is a plaintiff in these proceedings. This ownership is of course subject to the charge in favour of the defendant bankers but the equity of redemption — and it has suggested that this could be of enormous value — remains in Bula Ltd. In this sense, therefore, Bula Ltd is in fact asking for liberty to inspect its own property or at any rate property in which it does have a very substantial interest. Indeed one of the objections raised by the defendants is the failure of Bula Ltd to undertake the proposed inspection during the period from 1976 to 1985 when that company had apparently untrammelled occupation of the lands in question.

It is in these circumstances that the receiver entered into negotiations with the plaintiffs, and in particular Mr Wymes, with a view to facilitating the enquiries which the plaintiffs were pursuing. The receiver, on the basis of the advice given to him by appropriate experts, suggested that the allegations of trespass (and larceny) could best be pursued by conducting an inspection and survey through the Tara mines with the assistance of the plans or drawings prepared by Tara for the purposes of their mining operations.

This proposal was rejected by the plaintiffs as a result of a report received by them dated 21 January 1987 from A.B. Malkin, consulting geologist. It was his advice as provided in that report that:

> "The procedures of plan examination followed by physical examination and surveys is constrained by (1) uncertainty as to the interpretation of the data obtained and (2) the time to carry out the operations. At the conclusion of this work it could still be necessary to resort to drilling for

positive proof.

In the past instances of deliberate mine trespass it was common to find that the trespass workings were not shown on the working plan of the mine. Plan examination in these circumstances was thus of no value for ascertaining the existence of the trespass. Because of this situation there will be no way of knowing whether any plans produced for inspection will be complete or not."

Mr Malkin summarised his conclusions in the penultimate paragraph of his report in the following terms:

> "There are thus clear advantages in time and costs in short-circuiting the above procedures and moving directly to the drilling of the exploratory boreholes which could, in any event, still be required even if the procedures are followed. Such boreholes would penetrate the maximum distance through the orebody and be spaced sufficiently close together to ensure that they intersected any workings that may be present. Back-fill, collapsed ground or mined out voids should be clearly indicated by the drilling and would identify with certainty the presence of any trespass."

Mr Crowley's objections to the works proposed by Mr Malkin were twofold. First he was concerned that damage might be caused to the Bula orebody and secondly he was concerned that he might expose himself (or others) to liability for damage to persons or property as a result of works carried out on or under property in his possession or under his control. Mr Crowley's concern was based partly on general legal principles but also on the express advice given to him by his geological experts Messrs MacKay and Schnellmann. Lengthy correspondence has passed between the solicitors on behalf of the parties with a view to resolving their differences and protecting their respective interests. However, it was not surprising to find that the lawyers could not resolve the problem seeing that it was based on a fundamental difference of opinion between experts in a different discipline, namely, the geologists engaged.

Mr Malkin is fully confident that the works which he proposes will not give rise to any of the possible adverse consequences of which Messrs MacKay and Schnellmann are apprehensive. In his report dated 26 January 1987 Mr Malkin deals with the possibility of damage to the orebody in the following terms:

> "2.1 In paragraph (f) it appears the receiver is concerned that the proposed drilling operation could cause damage to the orebody and place it at risk. No information is provided to define the nature of such damage or the risks to which the orebody might be exposed.
> 2.2 I understand that no circumstances are known which could have given rise to damage during the previous explorations and I know of no cause of damage or potential hazards which could arise from such boreholes drilled into a sulphide orebody set in bedded limestone strata and overlain

by only a nominal thickness of cohesive overburden.
2.3 Approximately eighteen boreholes are planned and these will be similar to the previous two hundred or so boreholes already drilled into the orebody. So far as I am aware no damage has been caused or potential hazards created by this previous work. In any event, adequate insurance will be carried by the contractor to deal with damage as yet undefined, caused by his drilling operations.
2.4 In these circumstances I believe that acceptance of the receiver's proposals would lead to unwarranted restrictions on the conduct of the drilling operations."

There is no way in which I can resolve the conflict, such as it is, between Mr Malkin and Messrs MacKay and Schnellmann with regard to the potential for damage to the orebody whether by penetrating aquifers or otherwise. At best this difference could be resolved only after an oral hearing.

However it seems to me that (notwithstanding the paucity of evidence in support of the plaintiffs' claim) inspection along the lines sought should be facilitated if that can be achieved whilst at the same time protecting the interests of the defendants. I believe that this can be achieved by deferring to the confident and optimistic opinions expressed by the experts engaged by the plaintiffs. I see no prospect of balancing the actions of one party and the supervision by the other. It seems to me that this would lead to disagreements and perhaps expose both parties to liability at the suit of others. What I propose to do is to require the receiver to put the named experts in possession of the appropriate part of the lands of Nevinstown (defined by reference to a suitable map) to the exclusion of the receiver during a specified period of time for the purpose of drilling not more than eighteen boreholes of a stipulated diameter. I envisage the obligations of the experts being set in a contractual document to which the receiver will be a party solely for the purpose of receiving the benefits of certain specific contractual obligations including the following:

(1) That no damage whatsoever will be caused to the site or to Bula orebody (or to any other property or person) other than damage consisting of first the drilling of the stipulated boreholes and the removal of the cores therefrom and secondly the despoiling of the surface of the lands as a result of the introduction of vehicles or other heavy equipment on the site for the purposes of the drilling operations.

(2) Covenants will provide that the plaintiffs' experts will be bound to restore and make good the damage aforesaid by back-filling the boreholes to the full depth thereof (save that in the case of boreholes encountering a void it will be necessary only to back-fill the borehole to the point where it intersects with the void). Secondly the experts will restore the site to the reasonable satisfaction of some appropriate expert by reseeding the grass and repairing any fences or similar works.

(3) The experts will provide a bond for the due completion of the restoration works in a sum of £20,000.

(4) The experts will be fully liable to the defendants and in particular the receiver for any other damage howsoever caused as a result of any works carried on by the experts or under their control or as a result of or during the course of their occupation of the site. Any possible liability of the experts under these headings to be secured by an insurance bond in the sum of £1,000,000.

(5) The agreement would expressly provide of course that the experts should be entitled to procure counter indemnities and securities from any contractors, miners or other operatives engaged by them.

(6) The contract will provide that the experts will ensure the maintenance and preservation of detailed records of all drilling carried out and of the results and interpretation of those drillings and their agreement to provide all such information to the receiver free of charge.

I do not propose to impose any term requiring the plaintiffs to make any payment (at this stage) in respect of any experts which the defendants or any of them may think fit to engage in relation to the inspection or otherwise.

I would be hopeful that the parties could agree upon the terms of the necessary legal documentation to give effect to such an agreement but in the event of a dispute due to a difference in drafting I will arrange to have it resolved by counsel appointed by the court (if necessary) and any other insoluble problem can be referred back to the court for decision.

A matter of the greatest concern, however, are the anticipated time limits. It has been suggested that a period of eight weeks would be required to bore four of the intended eighteen boreholes. If the correct inference from this is that it would take more than six months to complete the inspection it might be necessary for me to review the position and to hear the parties further on the matter. Clearly a commercial case of this importance and involving the allegations to which I have already referred must be heard without any unnecessary delay. Indeed I would expect the parties to be in a position to go trial not later than the month of July of this year.

Alistair Rutherdale
Barrister

Hurstridge Finance Ltd v. Lismore Homes Ltd (In Receivership): High Court 1989 No. 15292P (Costello J) 15 February 1991

Discovery – Legal professional privilege claimed – Principles to be applied – Whether communications between solicitor and client were for the purpose of drafting legal documents or whether they were for the purpose of obtaining legal advice – Whether privilege covers notes of telephone conversations between solicitor and client – Whether privilege extends to notes of meetings which were prepared as an aide memoire *at which the client was not present – Whether privilege covered notes made by solicitor for purpose of preparing a draft letter – Whether they were documents which came into existence for the purpose of advising the client company of the correct legal steps to take*

Facts: The third party in the motion entered into a number of transactions in January 1986 with the defendant relating to building land in County Dublin under which £1,115,000 became payable by the defendant to the third party. The plaintiff claimed that by an assignment of 22 September 1989 the third party's rights and remedies against the defendant were assigned to it. In early 1989 the Bank of Ireland agreed to make financial facilities available to the defendant. A condition of the provision of such services was that the third party's claim against the defendant be postponed and the defendant and third party entered into two agreements giving effect to this on 28 February and 30 March 1989. The bank later appointed a receiver who conducted the proceedings on behalf of the defendant. The defendant pleaded that the plaintiff, as assignee of the third party, was bound by the agreements to postpone the rights of the third party. An order of discovery was made on 28 May 1990 with which the plaintiff complied. In the affidavit of discovery the plaintiff disclosed the existence of relevant documents which were in the possession or procurement of the plaintiff but which were the property of the third party. Legal professional privilege was claimed in respect of these. On the hearing of the motion, Costello J directed that the defendants should apply for third party discovery as, if privilege existed, it would vest in the third party and not the plaintiff. This was done and on the hearing of the application legal professional privilege was claimed in relation to certain documents.

Held by Costello J:

(1) The first category of documents were communications between the person who apparently controlled the third party and the company's solicitor prior to the two 1989 contracts and such communications took place not merely for the purpose of drafting legal documents but also for the purpose of obtaining advice. Such documents were privileged: *Smurfit Paribas v. AAB Export Finance Ltd* [1990] ILRM 588 applied.

(2) The privilege in relation to these transactions covers written communications and notes of telephone conversations made by the solicitor.

(3) The privilege does not extend to notes of meetings which are kept as an *aide memoire* which the solicitor attended but which the client did not. Such notes are not communications between a solicitor and client.

(4) Notes made by the solicitor for preparing a draft letter are privileged as they came into existence for the purpose of advising the client as to the correct legal steps to take.

Case referred to in judgment
Smurfit Paribas v. AAB Export Finance Ltd [1990] ILRM 588

Counsel's and solicitors' names not available

COSTELLO J **15 February 1991**

The dispute on this motion (brought by the defendant) is whether a third party's claim of legal professional privilege in respect of certain documents in its possession relating to the issues between the plaintiff and the defendant is well founded.

It arises in the following way.

A company called Finance Indemnity Company (Ireland) Ltd which has been referred to throughout as "Ficoil" and which is the third party in the motion I am considering, entered into a number of transactions with the defendant herein, Lismore Homes Ltd, relating to building land in County Dublin. Under three agreements made on 28 January 1986 it is said that the sum of £1,115,000 became payable by Lismore Homes to Ficoil. The plaintiff claims that by an assignment of 22 September 1989 Ficoil's claims rights and remedies against Lismore Homes were assigned to it. These proceedings follow the assignment. As assignee the plaintiff now claims to be entitled to a lien over the lands to which the three agreements related.

In the early part of 1989, Bank of Ireland Finance Ltd entered the scene and agreed to make financial facilities available to Lismore Homes. But it required that Ficoil's claims against Lismore Homes be postponed in favour of the claims which might arise by the bank under the facilities it was proposing to grant. As a result Ficoil and Lismore Homes entered into two agreements on 28 February 1989 and on 30 March 1989 by which, *inter alia*, Ficoil's claims under the 28 January 1986 agreements were postponed. Later the bank appointed a receiver of Lismore Homes and it is the receiver who is conducting these proceedings on its behalf. Lismore Homes has pleaded the two 1989 agreements in its defence and claims that the plaintiff, as assignee of Ficoil, is bound by them and that they bar its present claim. But the plaintiff has countered in its reply by pleading that there were breaches of these agreements and of pre-contractual representations which mean that they no longer bind either Ficoil or the plaintiff. Thus the two 1989 agreements and the facts surrounding their execution have become an important issue in this case.

An order of discovery was made on 28 May 1990. The plaintiff complied with it by an affidavit of 29 June 1990. In this the plaintiff disclosed the existence of relevant documents which were the property of Ficoil but which were apparently in the possession or procurement of the plaintiff. It was claimed that legal professional privilege in respect of them existed and inspection was refused. On the hearing of a motion which contested this view I directed that the defendant should apply for a third party order against Ficoil because it seemed to me that if privilege existed it was Ficoil's and not the plaintiff's. This was done. On the hearing of this application it was urged on Ficoil's behalf that in reference to the following documents referred to in the affidavit of 29 June 1990 legal professional privilege existed, namely; document numbers 171, 174 to 180, 182, 184, 187, 188, 194, 195, 199 and 211.

I have examined these documents in the light of the principles enunciated by the Chief Justice relating to legal professional privilege in *Smurfit Paribas v. AAB Export Finance Ltd* [1990] ILRM 588. Having referred to the distinction to be made between (a) communications between a solicitor and his client where litigation was in existence or in contemplation, (b) such communications seeking legal advice when no litigation was in contemplation, and (c) such communications seeking legal *assistance* (as distinct from advice) the Chief Justice pointed out in relation to (b) and (c) at p. 594 as follows:

> "Where a person seeks or obtains legal advice there are good reasons to believe that he necessarily enters the area of potential litigation. The necessity to obtain legal advice would in broad terms appear to ensivage the possibility of a legal challenge or query as to the correctness or effectiveness of some step which a person is contemplating. Whether such query or challenge develops or not, it is clear that a person is then entering the area of possible litigation.
>
> Having regard to those considerations I expect that where it is established that a communication was made between a person and his lawyer acting for him as a lawyer for the purpose of obtaining from such lawyer legal advice, whether at the initiation of the client or the lawyer, that communication made on such an occasion should in general be privileged or exempt from disclosure, except with the consent of the client."

The Chief Justice then added that similar considerations did not apply to communications made to a lawyer for the purpose of obtaining his legal *assistance*, other than advice, and such communications would not be privileged.

Applying these principles to the facts of this case and to the documents which I have examined I have reached the following conclusions.

(1) Most of the disputed documents are communications between a Mr Taylor and a solicitor in the firm of Messrs Binchy and Partners who acted as solicitors for Ficoil. Mr Taylor's position in Ficoil has not been clarified but I assume that he controlled the company. The two 1989 contracts were entered into only after Mr Taylor had consulted his solicitors and I think it is a reasonable inference from the surrounding circumstances and the documents themselves

that he consulted the company's solicitors not merely for the purpose of drafting legal documents but for the purpose of obtaining advice as to the best course that Ficoil should adopt in the critical financial situation which had developed in its relationship with Lismore Homes. It was reasonable for him to obtain the advice of a lawyer on the situation which then existed and I think the assistance requested and given went well beyond the mere drafting of documents.

(2) The privilege claimed covers written communications between Messrs Binchy and Partners and Mr Taylor relating to these transactions. In respect of these communications it is correctly claimed. In addition I think the privilege covers notes made by Mr Taylor's solicitor of verbal telephone conversations between him and them. This means that the following are privileged; Items 175, 178, 179,180, 182, 184, 187, 194, 195, 199, 211.

(3) The privilege does not extend to notes of meetings which are kept as an *aide memoire* which Ficoil's solicitors attended which their client did not. Such notes are not communications passing between a solicitor and a client. Had they been made by the client himself they would be privileged. This means that item 171 can be inspected. So can items 176 and 177. These latter two items are notes of meetings held on 20 February 1989. These meetings were, apparently, held on a "without prejudice" basis but privilege on this ground has not been claimed for the record of what transpired at the meetings.

(4) Item 177 consists of notes made by Ficoil's solicitor for preparing a draft letter. They are documents which came into existence for the purpose of advising Ficoil as to the correct legal step to take and I think are covered by legal professional privilege.

There is one final matter, not raised on this motion, to which I feel I must refer. Paragraph 41 of the affidavit of the receiver sworn on 15 May 1990 refers to the fact that he had caused a search to be carried out in the Companies Office in relation to the plaintiff company. He ascertained that no annual returns had been filed by it since July 1967 and that it has an issued share capital of £10. The non-compliance with the provisions of the Companies Acts may well have some significance in this case. It seems to me that the court should take steps to ensure compliance with the law in appropriate cases and that I should refer the fact of this apparent non-compliance of the plaintiff with its statutory obligations to the officer charged with its statutory responsibility in this area. I therefore propose to direct the registrar of the court to forward to the Registrar of Companies the affidavit of the receiver of 15 May 1990 and a copy of this judgment so that he can take such steps as he may consider appropriate.

Patricia McLaughlin
Barrister

1990 ACTS

In re Goodman International and Related Companies: The Companies as Hereinafter Defined v. The Creditors and Members of the Companies: High Court 1990 No. 12132P (Hamilton P) 28 January 1991

Examiner – Appointed to related companies – Examiner obliged to conduct an examination of the companies – Report to the court – Contents of report – Purpose of Act – Proposals formulated for a compromise or scheme of arrangement – Meeting of members and creditors – Consideration of report by court – Parties entitled to be present – Modifications – Whether court obliged to convene a further meeting of members and creditors to consider the proposals as modified – Objections – Whether scheme "unfairly prejudicial" to creditor – Whether undertaking of companies capable of survival as a going concern – Whether proposed scheme would facilitate such survival – Whether this would be more advantageous to the members as a whole and the creditors as a whole than a winding up of the companies — Companies (Amendment) Act 1990 (No. 27), sections 2, 4, 5, 15, 16, 17, 18, 19, 22, 24, 25

Facts: An examiner was appointed to Goodman International and a number of related companies, divided into what were termed "the companies" and the Cork companies". On 30 October 1990, the examiner presented his report to the court in which he expressed the opinion that the whole of the undertaking, with the exception of certain non-essential subsidiaries, was capable of survival as a going concern, that the formulation, acceptance and confirmation of proposals for a compromise scheme, work-out or other arrangement would facilitate such survival and that the attempt to continue the whole of the undertaking would be likely to be more advantageous to the members as a whole and the creditors as a whole than a winding up. He expressed the view that the assets of the Cork companies should be disposed of in an orderly manner and that this did not require the formulation of proposals for a scheme of arrangement and that there was no need for such a scheme in relation to Goodman International. In accordance with the provisions of section 18 of the act, he formulated proposals for a scheme of arrangement in respect of the companies, which were considered at meetings of members and creditors. The members voted unanimously in favour of the scheme, with the exception of three companies. The required majority of banking creditors was obtained save in respect of five companies, three of which were non-trading and the other two which were insolvent and no order was required in respect of these. Certain modifications were suggested by a number of creditors and these were accepted by the examiner as not being contrary to the spirit and terms of his proposals. Two of the banking creditors claimed that if the proposals were implemented, their respective claim or interest would be impaired. Banco Bilbao submitted that clause 3.18.1 was contrary to public policy, that it would be unfairly prejudiced if the scheme were confirmed, that there should have been separate proposals in respect of each company and that the court had no jurisdiction to confirm the proposals with modifications without referring such modifications back to the members of the company and their creditors. Banco Bilbao was further opposed on the ground that it had issued a petition in Northern Ireland for the winding up of a company in Northern Ireland which had transferred its assets to a company within this jurisdiction which was under the protection of the court. Midland Bank also objected on the ground that the proposed scheme was unfairly prejudicial to it as it was the only creditor whose exposure would be increased if the scheme were implemented. A modification proposed by Midland Bank was not accepted by the examiner as it violated the underlying principle of the scheme that all the banking creditors would be treated equally.

Held by Hamilton P in approving the scheme:

(1) It was not necessary to convene a further meeting of the members and creditors to consider the proposals as modified as section 24(3) of the Act gives the court an absolute discretion to confirm, confirm subject to modifications or to refuse to confirm the scheme.

(2) The overall policy of the Act is to protect the rights of the members of the company as a whole and the creditors as a whole. This would be nullified if the examiner were not entitled to take into account the position with regard to each and every one of the related companies and to formulate a scheme of arrangement which would deal with the overall picture.

(3) The fact that Banco Bilbao had issued proceedings for the winding up of the company in Northern Ireland is irrelevant as that company was not under the protection of the court.

(4) The proposals were not unfairly prejudicial to Banco Bilbao and clause 3.18.1 was not contrary to public policy.

(5) Although the proposed scheme was prejudicial to Midland Bank, it was not unfairly prejudicial and the modifications suggested should not be accepted.

(6) The undertaking was capable of survival as a going concern, the proposed scheme with modifications would facilitate such survival and an attempt to continue the undertakings of the companies concerned was likely to be more advantageous to the members as a whole and the creditors as a whole than a winding up of the companies, therefore the proposals with modifications should be confirmed.

No cases referred to in judgment

Counsel's and solicitors' names not available

HAMILTON P **28 January 1991**

It is quite clear from a consideration of the terms of the Companies (Amendment) Act 1990 (herewith called "the Act") that its purpose is not to give the continued protection of the court, as set forth in section 5(2) of the Act, to all insolvent companies and to deprive the creditors of their legitimate rights against such companies.

In accordance with the provisions of section 2 of the Act an examiner to the company may be appointed by the court upon presentation of a petition, for the purpose of examining the state of a company's affairs and where such an examiner is appointed, the court may at the same or any time thereafter make an order appointing the examiner to be the examiner for the purpose of the Act to a related company, (section 4) as defined by the Act.

Section 5(1) of the Act provides that:

> "During the period beginning with the presentation of a petition for the appointment of an examiner to a company and (subject to *section 18(3) or (4)* ending on the expiry of three months from that date or on the withdrawal or refusal of the petition, whichever first happens, the company shall be deemed to be under the protection of the court and the provisions of 5(2) to have effect."

The examiner is obliged to conduct an examination of the affairs of the company to which he is appointed and report to the court within 21 days of his appointment or such longer period as the court may allow the result of his examination in accordance with section 16.

Such report must include, *inter alia*,

> "(e) a statement of opinion by the examiner as to whether the company, and the whole or any part of its undertaking, would be capable of survival as a going concern and a statement of the conditions which he feels are essential to ensure such survival, whether as regards the internal management and controls of the company or otherwise,
> (f) his opinion as to whether the formulation, acceptance and confirmation of proposals for a compromise or scheme of arrangement would facilitate such survival,
> (g) whether, in his opinion, an attempt to continue the whole or any part of the undertaking of the company would be more likely to be more advantageous to the members as a whole and the creditors, as a whole, than a winding up of the company".

Section 17 of the Act provides that:

> "Where, in a report made under *section 15*, the examiner expresses the opinion that:
> (a) the whole or any part of the undertaking of the company to which he

has been appointed would not be capable of survival as a going concern, or
(b) the formulation, acceptance or confirmation of proposals for a compromise or scheme of arrangement would not facilitate such survival, or
(c) an attempt to continue the whole or part of the undertaking of the company would not be likely to be more advantageous to the members as a whole or the creditors as a whole, than a winding up of the company, or
(d) there is evidence of a substantial disappearance of property that is not adequately accounted for, or of other serious irregularities to the company's affairs,
the court shall, as soon as may be after receipt of the examiner's report, hold a hearing to consider matters arising out of the report."

Following such hearing the court may make any order it deems fit including, *inter alia*, the discharge from the protection of the court of the whole or any part of the assets of the company and the winding up of the company.

I have referred to these sections of the Act for the purpose of illustrating that the Act does not give continued protection to an insolvent company where the examiner expresses an opinion that the whole or any part of the undertaking of the company would not be likely to be more advantageous to the members as a whole or the creditors as a whole than a winding up of the company.

Where, however, in the opinion of the examiner —

(a) the whole or any part of the undertaking of the company would be capable of survival as a going concern, and

(b) an attempt to continue the whole or any part of the undertaking of the company would be likely to be more advantageous to the members as a whole, and to the creditors as a whole, than a winding up of the company, and

(c) the formulation, acceptance and confirmation of proposals for a compromise or scheme of arrangement would facilitate such survival,
the examiner is obliged by virtue of the terms of section 18 of the Act to formulate proposals for the compromise or scheme of arrangement and is obliged to convene and preside at such meetings of members and creditors as he thinks proper to consider such proposals and report thereon within 42 days of his appointment or such longer period as the court may allow.

Section 19 of the Act sets forth the matters which must be included in the report and section 22 sets forth the matters to be dealt with in the proposals for a compromise or scheme of arrangement.

The examiner's report under section 18 must be set down for consideration by the court as soon as may be after receipt of the court and the following persons are entitled to be heard at the hearing:

(a) the company,

(b) the examiner,

(c) any creditor or member whose claim or interest would be impaired if the proposals were implemented.

At the hearing the court may, as it thinks proper, subject to the provisions of sections 24 and 25 of the Act confirm, confirm subject to modifications or refuse to confirm the proposals.

Section 24(4) of the Act provides that:

> "the court shall not confirm any proposals —
> (a) unless at least one class of members and one class of creditors whose interests or claims would be impaired by implementation of the proposals have accepted the proposals, or
> (b) if the sole or primary purpose of the proposals is the avoidance of payment of tax due, or
> (c) unless the court is satisfied that —
>
> > (i) the proposals are fair and equitable in relation to any class of members or creditors that has not accepted the proposals and whose interests or claims would be impaired by implementation, and
> > (ii) the proposals are not unfairly prejudicial to the interests of any interested party".

Section 25 of the Act provides that:

> "(1) At a hearing under *section 24* in relation to proposals a member or creditor whose interest or claim would be impaired by the proposals may object in particular to their confirmation by the court on any of the following grounds —
> (a) that there was some material irregularity at or in relation to a meeting to which section 23 applies,
> (b) that acceptance of the proposals by the meeting was obtained by improper means,
> (c) that the proposals were put forward for an improper purpose,
> (d) that the proposals unfairly prejudice the interests of the objector.
>
> (2) Any person who voted to accept the proposals may not object to their confirmation by the court on the grounds —
> (a) that such acceptance was obtained by improper means, or
> (b) that after voting to accept the proposals he became aware that the proposals were put forward for an improper purpose.
>
> (3) Where the court upholds an objection under this section, the court may make such order as it deems fit, including an order that the decision of any meeting be set aside and an order that any meeting be reconvened."

Section 24(5) provides that:

> "Where the court confirms proposals (with or without modification), the proposals shall be binding on all the members or class or classes of

> members, as the case may be, affected by the proposals and also on the company."

Sub-section 6 provides that:

> "Where the court confirms proposals (with or without modification) the proposals shall, notwithstanding any other enactment, be binding on all the creditors or the class or classes of creditors, as the case may be, affected by the proposals in respect of any claims against the company and any person other than the company who, under any statute, enactment, rule of law or otherwise, is liable for all or any of the debts of the company".

The confirmation by the court, with or without modification, of the proposals, undoubtedly affects the rights of members and creditors of the company but only arises in exceptional circumstances, *viz.*

(1) when the company is insolvent,

(2) when it is capable of survival as a going concern,

(3) when an attempt to continue the whole or any part of the undertaking would be likely to be more advantageous to the members as a whole, and to the creditors as a whole than a winding up of the company,

(4) when the scheme of arrangement would facilitate such survival,

(5) when at least one class of members and one class of creditors, whose interest or claims would be impaired by implementation of the proposals have accepted the proposals,

(6) when the court is satisfied that —

> (i) the proposals are fair and equitable in relation to any class of members or creditors that has not accepted the proposals and whose interests or claims would be impaired by implementation, and
> (ii) the proposals are not unfairly prejudicial to the interests of any interested party, and

(7) that there are none of the grounds set forth in section 25.

Consequently, the Act is designed not only to protect the rights of the members of the company as a whole but also the creditors of the company as a whole and the policy of the Act is such.

On 29 August 1990 Peter J. Fitzpatrick was appointed as examiner to Goodman International in accordance with the provision of section 2 of the Act.

On 31 August, he was appointed as examiner to the companies listed at Appendix 1 to the judgment, the said companies being related companies of Goodman International and hereinafter referred to as "the companies".

On 28 September 1990, he was appointed examiner to a further 30 related companies to Goodman International, which are set forth in Appendix 2 to this judgment and are hereinafter referred to as "the Cork companies".

On 30 October 1990, the examiner delivered to the court his report in respect of the companies, the Cork companies and Goodman Holdings in accordance with the provisions of section 15 of the Act, the time for delivery thereof having been extended by the court.

A report was delivered in respect of each individual company.

In his report he expressed the opinion that the whole of the undertaking with the exception of certain non-essential subsidiaries was capable of survival as a going concern, the formulation, acceptance and confirmation of proposals for a compromise scheme, work-out or other arrangement would facilitate such survival and an attempt to continue the whole of the undertaking is likely to be more advantageous to the members as a whole and the creditors as a whole than a winding up.

In the case of the Cork companies he expressed the opinion that their assets should be disposed of in an orderly manner and that this did not require the formulation of proposals for a scheme of arrangement.

In the case of Goodman Holdings which is a holding company for the companies and the Cork companies he expressed the opinion that there would be no need for a scheme of arrangement.

In accordance with the provisions of section 18 of the Act, he formulated proposals for a scheme of arrangement in respect of the companies.

The proposals were considered at meetings of members of the companies and creditors of the companies convened by and presided over by the examiner on 10 December 1990 as set forth in his report.

With regard to the members of the companies all voted unanimously in favour of the proposals with the exception of three companies AIBF Nenagh Exports, Nenagh Chilled Meats Ltd and AIBF Southern where a minority representing 25 per cent voted against.

With regard to the creditors, the requisite majority of banking creditors was obtained save in respect of five companies *viz*. Irish Agricultural Development Company, AIBP Carlow Exports, Anglo Irish Meats, Ven Air and Munster Proteins. The first three of these companies are non-trading and the other two are solvent and no order is required in respect of same.

Certain modifications to the examiner's proposals were made and accepted by the examiner as appear in his affidavit.

The report of the examiner pursuant to the provisions of section 18 of the Act was presented to the court on 11 December the time for presentation thereof having been extended by the court and was set down for consideration by the court on 19 December 1990.

The persons entitled to appear and be heard at such hearing were the company, the examiner and any creditor or member whose claim or interest would be impaired if the proposals were implemented.

All such parties were notified of the date fixed for consideration by the court of the proposals.

At the hearing the following parties appeared: The examiner; Goodman International; Lloyds Bank; Banco Bilbao; Credit Agricole; Banque National de Paris; West Deutsche Landesbank; Monaghan Nominees Ltd; Midland Bank; Barclays Bank.

The matter was heard by me on 19, 20, 21 and 28 December 1990.

It is not necessary for me to set forth in detail what transpired during the course of these hearings as a transcript of the proceedings is available.

Certain modifications to the proposals were suggested by counsel on behalf of Banque National de Paris, West Deutsche Landesbank, Goodman International, Lloyds Bank and Barclays Bank and were accepted by the examiner as not being contrary to the spirit and terms of his proposals.

I also am prepared to accept the said modifications. The only serious question which arose in connection with these modifications was whether it was necessary to convene a further meeting of the members and creditors of the companies to consider and approve of the proposals as modified.

Section 24(3) of the Act provides that:

> "at a hearing under *sub-section (1)*, the court may, as it thinks proper, subject to the provisions of this section and *section 25*, confirm, confirm subject to modifications, or refuse to confirm the proposals."

This section appears to me to give absolute discretion to the court in this regard. It is of course a discretion that must be exercised judicially and if the modifications suggested were to fundamentally alter the proposals which had been considered by the members and creditors of the companies, then a court would be slow to modify the scheme in a fundamental manner without having the modifications considered by members and creditors. I am however satisfied that the modifications to the scheme do not fundamentally alter the proposals.

Miss Finlay on behalf of Monaghan Nominees Ltd being the minority shareholder in the three companies hereinbefore referred to originally objected to the implementation of the proposals on the grounds that they were unfairly prejudicial to her clients but she subsequently withdrew her objection. That left Banco Bilbao and the Midland Bank.

Mr Fitzsimons on behalf of Banco Bilbao opposed the confirmation on the following grounds:

(1) That the insertion of Clause 3.18.1 in the proposals was contrary to public policy.

(2) That his client had issued a petition in Northern Ireland for the winding up of ABP Holdings Ltd, a company registered in Northern Ireland, which had transferred its assets to Shoreditch Ltd, a company registered within this jurisdiction and which is under the protection of the court.

(3) That his client would be unfairly prejudiced if this scheme were confirmed.

(4) The proposals as made by the examiner and sought to be confirmed relate to a group of companies and that there should be separate proposals in respect of each company, and

(5) That the court had no jurisdiction to confirm the proposals with modifi-

cations without referring them to the members of the company and their creditors.

With regard to this latter point, I have already ruled that the court has jurisdiction so to do.

The examiner has prepared and submitted to the court a report in respect of each of the companies to which he has been appointed examiner.

Each of the companies is "a related company" to Goodman International and by virtue of the terms of section 4 of the Act the court is empowered at the same or any time after the appointment of an examiner to a company to appoint him to be an examiner for the purpose of the Act to a related company.

I have already set forth in the course of this judgment what I consider to be the purpose of the Act which I consider would be nullified if the examiner were entitled to take into account the position with regard to each and every one of the related companies and to formulate a scheme of arrangement which would deal with the overall picture and I am satisfied that this ground of objection must fail.

With regard to the fact that Mr Fitzsimons' client has issued proceedings for the winding up of ABP Holdings Ltd in Northern Ireland, in my view this fact is irrelevant to the issues which I have to deal with.

ABP Holdings Ltd is a company registered in Northern Ireland, is not under the protection of this court and there is nothing in the scheme before me which would inhibit Mr Fitzsimons' client from proceeding with his petition in Northern Ireland if it so wishes.

The majority of the creditors in this case are satisfied that the proposals submitted for consideration by the court are likely to be more advantageous to the members of the company as a whole and the creditors as a whole than the winding up of the companies. I am satisfied that the proposals are not unfairly prejudicial to the interests of Banco Bilbao.

Neither am I satisfied in any way that the insertion of Clause 3.18.1 is in any way contrary to public policy or that the scheme is fundamentally flawed by its insertion.

Being so satisfied I disallow the objection to the confirmation of the scheme by Banco Bilbao.

That leaves Midland Bank. Mr McDonald on its behalf is not seeking an order for the winding-up of the companies.

He has submitted that the proposed scheme is unfairly prejudicial to his client and has suggested a modification to the scheme that would protect his client's interest.

He appears for the only creditor bank whose exposures would be increased if the scheme were implemented, from £250,000 to £2.5 million.

The modification proposed by Mr McDonald has not been accepted by the examiner because the acceptance thereof would violate the principle underlying the scheme that all the banking creditors would be treated equally.

I am satisfied that the proposed scheme is prejudicial to Mr McDonald's client, the Midland Bank, but having considered the entire of the matter am not satisfied that the proposals are unfairly prejudicial to the interests of the Midland Bank and will not accept the modification to the scheme as suggested by him.

Having considered the report of the examiner presented on 11 December 1990 and his earlier reports I am satisfied that the undertaking of the companies would be capable of survival as a going concern, that the proposed scheme with the modifications agreed at the meeting of creditors held on 10 December 1990 and the modifications accepted by the examiner during the course of the hearing would facilitate such survival and that the attempt to continue the undertakings of the companies referred to in the said reports is likely to be more advantageous to the members as a whole and the creditors as a whole than a winding-up of the companies.

Consequently, I will make an order confirming subject to the modifications to which I referred the proposals for the scheme of arrangement presented by the examiner and I direct that the proposals shall come into effect on 18 February 1991 which is 21 days from this date and that the companies other than Irish Agricultural Development, AIBP Carlow Exports, Anglo Irish Meats, Ven Air and Munster Proteins, the Cork companies and Goodman International remain under the protection of the court until that date.

Patricia McLaughlin
Barrister

APPENDIX 1

AIBP Cahir Exports
AIBP Carlow Exports
AIBP Central
AIBP Northern
Coolock Trading Company
Irish Agricultural Development Company
Malones Meats
Munster Proteins
Munster Proteins Exports
Silvercrest Foods Exports
Ven Air
AIBP Exports
AIBP Nenagh Exports
AIBP Southern
Anglo Irish Beef Processors International
Anglo Irish Beef Processors Nenagh
Nenagh Chilled Meats Ltd
Anglo Irish Beef Processors
Shannon Meat
Shannon Meat International Ltd
DJS Meats Ltd
DJS Meats Ireland Ltd
James Doherty (Carrigans) Ltd
Ardee International Projects Consultants Ltd
Anglo Irish Meats
Shoreditch Ltd
Idlewild Ltd
Celandine Ltd
Garamboree Ltd

APPENDIX 2

Rumil
Ingamell
Ardrossan Company
Rubicille
Renoir Investment Company
Bamburgh Company
Larkit Investments
Penaross
Carrigart Investments
Ison Developments
Provost Company
Tiobrand Ltd
Veracruz
McGinnity Holdings Ltd
McGinnity Stevedores
Fretter Ltd
Pescatina Ltd
International Hide and Skin Company
Sleelver Ltd
Portlaw Leathers International Ltd
Central Hide and Skin Ltd
Irish Hide and Skin Markets Company Ltd
T.P. Waste Disposal
Seven Kings
Silver Sky Ltd
Reynolds Electronics
Reynolds Electronics Manufacturing
Channel 2
Reynolds Electronics (International)

In the Matter of Selukwe Ltd and In the Matter of the Companies (Amendment) Act 1990: High Court 1991 No. 1157P (Costello J) 20 December 1991

Appointment of an examiner – Presentation of report to court – Objections by creditors – Whether scheme should be approved – Whether company capable of survival as a going concern – Whether modifications should be made to proposals – Companies (Amendment) Act 1990 (No. 27)

Facts: An examiner was appointed to the company and he prepared proposals for a scheme of arrangement under section 18 of the Companies (Amendment) Act 1990. Meetings were held of different classes of creditors and the matter was set down for consideration by the court under section 4 of the Act. Two creditors objected to the scheme proposed and asked the court not to confirm it. Under the scheme, Allied Irish Banks, who were due £50,262.86 plus interest, would obtain 10 per cent of its total indebtedness over a five month period. As security for this debt the bank had obtained joint and several guarantees executed by two of the company directors but under the scheme, the bank was required to revoke these personal guarantees and the security obtained on foot of them would be nullified. The bank's principal objection to the scheme was that there was no justification in releasing the personal guarantees of the two directors. The bank also submitted that the proposals were invalid as they operated retrospectively to affect contracts entered into prior to the coming into operation of the Act. Furthermore, it submitted that conversations took place between the new investors and the directors of the company before the presentation of the petition which amounted to a ground for refusing the petition. The Revenue Commissioners also objected to the scheme and suggested that the company be wound up. The principal objections related to the manner in which the directors had carried on the business of the company, the fact that no proper records or books were kept, that there had been a total disregard of their obligations to the Revenue Commissioners, that the company had conceded its total indebtedness prior to the presentation of the petition, that it had failed to pay current taxes after the presentation of the petition and that the directors had failed to inform the Revenue Commissioners of a meeting of creditors held earlier in the year.

Held by Costello J:

(1) There was no justification for releasing the personal guarantees of the two directors and any proposal containing such a provision was not fair and equitable to the bank.

(2) However, it was not necessary to refuse the proposals, which could be modified by the deletion of the paragraph releasing the directors from their personal guarantees. This paragraph should further provide that the directors would not be entitled to be subrogated to any rights of the bank against the company unless they paid more than 90 per cent of the debts of the company to the bank.

(3) The scheme of the Act was to allow contracts which were entered into before the Act came into operation to be affected insofar as they are necessary for the preparation of proposals to make the company viable and this was not a ground for refusing to sanction the scheme.

(4) In certain circumstances, there may be collusion which might justify the court in refusing to exercise its power to confirm proposals, but it had not been established in this case.

(5) The objections of the Revenue Commissioners, although well founded, do not constitute a ground for non-confirmation either under section 24(4) or section 25 of the Act. However, they do constitute grounds for modification under section 24(3) and the proposals should be modified to include a provision that the two directors against whom the complaints were made should cease to act as directors of the company.

Per curiam: The court should not turn down proposals notwithstanding any doubts that it may entertain, if there is any prospect of saving 30 jobs.

No cases referred to in judgment

Counsel's and solicitors' names not available

COSTELLO J **20 December 1991**

On 29 July 1991 the petition was presented by the company under section 2 of the Companies (Amendment) Act 1990. The petition was verified by an affidavit of Mr Stack, a director of the company. On 7 August 1991 the court appointed Mr Jenkins examiner. On 4 September 1991 the examiner's section 15 report was presented and subsequently the examiner prepared proposals for a scheme of arrangement under section 18 of the Act. This scheme of arrangement is dated 2 November 1991.

Meetings were held of different classes of creditors and a report of these meetings under section 18 was prepared and it has now been set down under section 4 for consideration by the court. The company and the examiner and two creditors were represented at the hearing. The two creditors represented are the Revenue Commissioners and Allied Irish Bank. These two creditors objected to the proposals and asked me not to confirm them.

I will deal firstly with the objections taken by Allied Irish Bank. The bank's debt is £50,262.86 plus £7,338.90 interest to date. This debt is due by the company on an overdraft facility which was granted by the bank to the company. As security for this debt the bank obtained joint and several guarantees executed by two of the directors of the company, Mr Byrne and Mr Stack, on 24 June 1990. Under the proposals in the scheme of arrangement the bank will obtain 10 per cent of its total indebtedness over a five-month period. The bank is required to revoke its personal guarantees so that the directors will be freed from any liability on foot of them and the security obtained from the two directors will be nullified.

In addition the sum of £10,000 which was placed to the credit of Mr Stack was placed in circumstances the validity of which is, to say the least, very doubtful, is to be returned and it is then to be paid to the class of creditor of which Allied Irish Bank is the principal creditor. As a result, Allied Irish Bank will obtain most of this £10,000.

The principal but not the sole objection taken by the bank is its claim that there is no justification for releasing the personal guarantees of the directors. I agree with the submissions made on the bank's behalf in this connection. I can find no reason for depriving the bank of this security.

The reason advanced for this proposal, namely, that the new investors did not wish the directors to face the problem of perhaps having to face bankruptcy proceedings does not justify the examiner's proposal. As long as the proposals contain this provision I think that they are not fair and equitable in so far as the bank is concerned. So I would have to refuse confirmation of the proposals unless I am prepared to modify them.

I think I need not refuse the proposals because I think I can modify them and I propose to do so. I propose to delete sub-paragraph A of paragraph 3 of the proposals on page 6 and I will provide for a new paragraph which will read:

> "Nothing herein will affect the liability of the directors on foot of the personal guarantees to Allied Irish Bank".

The paragraph should further provide that the directors will not be entitled to be subrogated to any rights of the bank against the company unless they pay more than 90 per cent of the debts to the bank, in which event their subrogation rights will be limited to the sums paid in excess of 90 per cent of the debt. The reason for this is to make clear that they are not entitled to claim against the company for all sums they may pay on foot of their guarantees. The situation should be that the company's liability to the bank in relation to this transaction should be limited to 10 per cent as provided in the scheme. If such a provision was not contained in the proposals it might well upset the whole balance of the proposals and defeat their object.

The other points which have been raised on behalf of the bank can be dealt with briefly. I do not think that the proposals are invalid because they operate retrospectively to affect contracts entered into prior to the coming into operation of the Act. I think that the scheme of the Act is to allow such contracts to be affected in so far as they are necessary for the preparation of proposals to make the company viable. I do not think that the fact that these contracts were entered into before the Act came into operation is a reason for refusing confirmation. Furthermore, I do not think that the evidence that conversations took place between the new investors and the directors of the company before the presentation of the petition is a ground for refusing confirmation. In certain circumstances there may be collusion which might justify the court in refusing to exercise its power to confirm proposals but I do not think that such collusion has been established in the circumstances of this case.

I turn now to the position of the Revenue Commissioners. The Revenue are now owed a sum of approximately £326,770.26. On 7 August 1991 when liberty to proceed on foot of the petition was given the debt was £298,196.22. Of this sum £143,987.68 would rank as a preferential debt in a winding up.

The proposals will result in the payment of £37,219 to the Revenue as a preferential creditor. In addition, the Revenue will be entitled to a further payment but will only receive 10 per cent of the balance of their debt in two parts — on 31 December 1991 and on 30 April 1992. The total amount which the Revenue will receive under the proposals is £99,820.

The Revenue Commissioners have objected to confirmation of the proposals and suggest that the company should be wound up. The principal objections of the Revenue Commissioners are as follows:

(a) It is pointed out that the manner in which the directors carried on the company's business was very unsatisfactory and that no proper books and records were maintained by the company.

(b) There was a total disregard by the directors of their obligations to the Revenue Commissioners.

(c) The directors conceded the true position of the company's indebtedness to the Revenue in their discussions with representatives of the Revenue Commissioners prior to the presentation of the petition. Indeed, the directors failed to pay the proper amount of tax due by other companies with which they were associated.

(d) The directors failed to pay current taxes due after the presentation of the petition until ordered by this court to do so.

(e) The holding by the directors of the creditors' meeting in April of this year without informing the representatives of the Revenue that they were doing so.

I must hold that these objections are well founded. But I do not think that they constitute a ground for non-confirmation either under section 24(4) or under section 25 of the Act. They do, in my view, constitute grounds for modification of the proposals which I propose to do under section 24(3) of the Act. The modifications which I propose to make are as follows:

I propose that Mr Stack and Mr Byrne will cease to act as directors of the company. This means that paragraph 9 on page 11 of the proposals should be amended by providing that Mr Stack and Mr Byrne should resign as members of the board and should cease to act as directors of the company as soon as new directors have been appointed.

I should explain why I think that these modifications are proper:

(1) The criticism of the directors' conduct of the affairs of this company which was made in the affidavit of Ms Crotty of 20 November 1991 is fully justified. The conduct of the directors in relation to their obligations to the Revenue is such as to disentitle them to continue to act as directors of the company.

(2) The examiner informed the meeting of creditors on 4 November 1991 that the reconstituted board would not include either of the two existing directors of the company. It now transpires that the present proposals, if confirmed, would contain no such condition. The information which was given at the creditors' meeting might have had a significant effect on their attitude to the proposals so I think it is not proper to allow the proposals to be implemented otherwise than in accordance with what I have already proposed.

(3) There has been a lack of candour about the position of the directors in the presentation of these proposals. The creditors were told at the meeting that the directors would not continue to act, but in a recent submission made to the IDA they (the IDA) were informed that Mr Stack would continue to be managing director of the company. The report is silent about this aspect of the matter and I think this lack of candour is a further reason for modifying the proposals.

Finally, I should explain why I have decided to exercise my discretion under the section to confirm the proposals subject to the modifications which I have already outlined. I have had serious reservations about these proposals. I am not by any means certain that the company is viable.

I point to the fact that in his first report the examiner stated that £250,000 was needed by way of an injection of new capital. It now transpires in his second report that the amount of new capital available will be considerably less than this sum, namely, £120,000. In addition, in his first report the examiner pointed out that the IDA grant was necessary. Even though that grant is now going to be made available, the sum which was originally considered necessary is not going to be reached. Furthermore, the proposals were made on the basis that valuable machinery would be made available to the company. It is clear that this is not going to be the position. Furthermore, there was a lack of *uberrima fides* in the original application. This is a new Act and has not been in operation for very long. I think it should be made clear that the utmost good faith is required when an *ex parte* application is made for the appointment of an examiner. The directors of a company, if they are responsible for presenting a petition, are required to act with the utmost good faith. It is a *uberrima fides* application. In my experience this is the second petition in which there has been a considerable lack of good faith in the presentation of the petition. In this case the petition, which was verified by the sworn affidavit of one of the directors, stated that the debt due to the Revenue was £75,000. In fact, the debt was over two-and-a-half times that amount to the knowledge of the directors.

The third factor which caused me considerable concern in this case was the lack of candour to which I have already referred. I do not know where the responsibility for this lack of candour lies but the court should not be put in the position of putting itself into an inquiry into matters which should have been obvious at the time the report was presented. But the position in this case is such that these considerations to which I have referred are outweighed by what I consider to be the main consideration in this case, namely, the fact that there are 30 jobs at stake. I do not think the court should turn down the proposals if there is any prospect of saving those jobs. So notwithstanding the doubts which I have expressed I have decided to confirm the proposals subject to the modifications to which I have referred.

Patricia McLaughlin
Barrister

In the Matter of Section 8 of the Companies Act 1990 and In the Matter of the Minister for Industry and Commerce v. Siúcre Éireann CPT, and In the Matter of section 13(1)(a) of the Companies Act 1990 and In the Matter of Order 75(b), rule 3(d) of the Rules of the Superior Courts: The Minister for Justice v. Siúcre Éireann CPT, Greencore plc, Sugar Distributors (Holdings) Ltd, Gladebrook Co. Ltd, Sugar Distributors (Exports) Ltd, I.S.M. Investments Ltd, Trilby Commodity Trading Ltd, Trilby Trading Ltd, Talmino Ltd (under investigation): High Court 1991 No. 738 Sp Ct 6 (Lynch J) 1 May 1992

Company Law – Company – Investigation – Costs and expenses of investigation – Repayment – Application by Minister for Justice to recover costs – Investigation of company formerly owned by State in respect of irregularities occurring during period of State ownership – Whether appropriate to order recovery of costs against company – Whether possible injustice to present shareholdres – Application also against company not under investigation, but referred to in report – Whether body corporate "dealt with in report" Whether company "carrying on business in the State" – Companies Act 1990 (No. 33), sections 8, 9, 13, 17

Facts: Section 8(1) of the Companies Act 1990 provides, *inter alia*,

> "the court may on the application of the Minister appoint one or more competent inspectors to investigate the affairs of a company and to report thereon . . . if the court is satisfied that there are circumstances suggesting—
>
> > (a) that its affairs are being or have been conducted with intent to defraud its creditors or the creditors of any other person or otherwise for a fraudulent or unlawful purpose or in an unlawful manner or in a manner which is unfairly prejudicial to some part of its members . . ., or
> > (b) that persons connected with its formation or the management of its affairs have in connection therewith been guilty of fraud, misfeasance or other misconduct towards it or towards it members, or
> > (c) that its members have not been given all the information relating to its affairs which they might reasonably expect."

Section 9 of the Act, allowed the inspector, with the approval of the court to investigate also, "the affairs of any other body corporate which is related to such company. . . ."

By virtue of section 17 of the Act, sections 8-9 applied to "all bodies incorporated outside the State which are carrying on business in the State or have at any time carried on business therein as if they were companies registered under the Principal Act. ..."

Section 13(1) of the Act provided that the cost of such investigations, "shall be defrayed in the first instance by the Minister for Justice but the court may direct that any person being—

> (a) a body corporate dealt with in the report, or
> (b) the applicant or applicants for the investigation,

shall be liable ..., provided that no such liability on the part of the applicant or applicants shall exceed in the aggregate £100,000."

Subsection (2) allowed the court to direct that "any person who is—

> (a) convicted on indictment of an offence on a prosecution instituted as a result of an investigation,
> (b) ordered to pay damages or restore any property in proceedings brought as a result of an investigation, or
> (c) awarded damages or to whom property is restored in proceedings brought as a result of an investigation,

may, in the same proceedings, be ordered to repay all or part of the expenses. …"

On 16 September 1991, the High Court, on the application of the Minister for Industry and Commerce, made an order pursuant to section 8 of the 1990 Act appointing two inspectors to investigate the affairs of the first named respondent. On 18 September 1991, the court, on the application of the inspectors, made an order pursuant to section 9 of the 1990 Act, authorising the inspectors to investigate the other respondents, but not including Talmino Ltd.

The application of 16 September 1991, was grounded on affidavits sworn by officials from the Departments of Industry and Commerce and Justice, which proved the possibility of serious irregularities in the formerly State-owned Siúcre Éireann CPT between 1998 and its privatisation in 1991. The inspector's report identified various irregularities and other possible irregularities which occurred or which may have occurred between 1988 and the privatisation of the enterprise in 1991.

The minister brought an application pursuant to section 13(1)(a) of the 1990 Act, for the reimbursement to him by the respondents of expenses totalling £1,150,000 incurred by him of and incidental to the investigation of the respondents (excluding Talmino Ltd). That company was, however, referred to in the report.

On behalf of the Minister for Justice it was submitted that liability for the expenses of the investigation was placed on the minister in the first instance, and it was then intended by section 13 that the minister should be reimbursed by the companies dealt with in the report. Companies made liable might have a right to contribution or indemnity. While Talmino Ltd was not formally investigated, it was submitted that it should be liable to reimburse the minister, jointly and severally with the other respondents.

On behalf of Siúcre Éireann and the related companies, it as submitted that the matters under investigation occurred while the enterprise was owned by the State, and that the State should therefore bear the costs, rather than pass them on to shareholders, the vast majority of whom had nothing to do with the company during the period investigated. Talmino submitted that it was not "dealt with" in the report, that adverse comment about it did not fix liability under section 13(1), but under section 13(2) only, and in any case Talmino Ltd never carried on business in the State, so by virtue of section 17, section 13 did not apply to it at all.

Held by the High Court (Lynch J) in refusing the application:

(1) The costs of attendance by the inspectors in court, including the initial application on behalf of the Minister for Industry and Commerce were part of the costs and expenses actually incurred in the investigation.

(2) A a general rule and subject to the facts of each individual case, the minister should be reimbursed the expenses of such an investigation, and it would be wrong that the State should have to pay such expenses.

(3) *Prima facie*, companies dealt with in a report, even though not adversely dealt with therein, should reimburse the State pursuant to section 13(1) and then in appropriate circumstance seek reimbursement themselves under section 13(2).

(4) The present case, however, had special factors; in particular, the fact that the State owned the enterprise at the time of the period investigated, and that 70 per cent of the current members were not involved at that time.

(5) The realities of the case allowed the court to look beyond the legal personality of Siúcre Éireann, Greencore and the companies forming the enterprise, and to see who was the beneficial shareholder at the time of the wrongdoing. *Foss v. Harbottle* (1843) 2 Hare 461, considered.

(6) The effect of an order against the company for the recovery of the costs, would be to penalise the majority of innocent present shareholders to the benefit of the State. In addition the enterprise had itself incurred substantial costs in meeting the inspectors requirements and carrying out an internal inquiry. In the circumstances it was not appropriate to make an order against any of the first nine respondents.

(7) Taking the ordinary meaning of the words "dealt with", Talmino Ltd was a body corporate "dealt with" in the inspector's report. However, the intention of the legislature and the meaning of the words "a body corporate dealt with in the report" as used in section 13(1) was to limit the power of the court to order repayment of expenses by such bodies corporate only as were under investigation and dealt with in the report.

(8) However, in any case Talmino Ltd had never "carr[ied] on business in the State" within the meaning of section 17 of the Act, and therefore the court had no power to order it to repay expenses of the investigation, pursuant to section 13. *Cripps Warburg Ltd v. Cologne Investment Co. Ltd and others* [1980] IR 321, considered.

Cases referred to in judgment

Cripps Warburg Ltd v. Cologne Investment Co. Ltd and others [1980] IR 321
Foss v. Harbottle (1843) 2 Hare 461
Re Gibson's Settlement Trusts [1981] Ch 179; [1981] 2 WLR 1; [1981] 1 All ER 233

Brian McCracken SC and Esmond Smyth BL instructed by *The Chief State Solicitor* ***for the Minister for Justice and the Minister for Industry and Commerce***
Dan O'Keeffe SC and Rory Brady BL instructed by *Arthur Cox & Co.* **for the first to ninth named respondents**
Nial Fennelly SC and Jerry Healy BL instructed by *Michael Hourihan & Co.* **for the tenth named respondent**
Dan Herbert BL instructed by *Cawley, Sheerin, Wynne* **for the Inspectors**

LYNCH J **1 May 1992**

This is an application brought by the Minister for Justice pursuant to section 13(1)(a) of the Companies Act 1990 for the reimbursement to him of expenses incurred by him of and incidental to an investigation of, *inter alia*, the respondent companies but not including the last named respondent (Talmino) which is a foreign company registered in Jersey in March 1989 and insofar as the title to the proceedings as brought by the Minister for Justice suggests that that company was under investigation the title is erroneous.

The investigation was ordered by the High Court on 16 September 1991 on the application of the Minister for Industry and Commerce under section 8 of the 1990 Act for the appointment of two inspectors to investigate the affairs of the first named respondent (Siúcre Éireann). On 18 September 1991 on the application of the inspectors an order was made pursuant to section 9 of the 1990 Act authorising the inspectors to investigate, *inter alia*, the other respondents being companies related to Siúcre Éireann but not including Talmino.

The investigation carried out by the inspectors was a very thorough and detailed investigation and to quote from the written submissions of the applicant the Minister for Justice filed in court in advance of the application "their findings, and indeed the attention to detail in the report, fully justifies the amount of time and effort expended by the inspectors".

Pursuant to section 11 of the 1990 Act the inspectors issued two interim reports on 7 October and 11 November 1991 respectively a copy of the first of which was transmitted to the Minister for Industry and Commerce only and a copy of the second to that minister and to the second respondent (Greencore) pursuant to section 11(3) of the 1990 Act. The inspectors' final report was presented to the High Court on 25 February 1992 and it together with the two interim reports were pursuant to section 11(3)(c) ordered to be printed and published by order of the High Court made on 3 March 1992.

The affidavit of Mr Crowley of the Department of Justice sworn on 27 February 1992 grounding this application by the Minister for Justice for reimbursement proves that the expenses of and incidental to the investigation amount to approximately £1,150,000 inclusive of VAT and exclusive of VAT (which goes back to the State any how) to approximately £960,000.

The facts

The inspectors' final report sets out in detail the matters investigated and the facts found and opinions formed by the inspectors. It is sufficient for me to state in this judgment just a few facts which seem to me to be particularly relevant to the issues to be decided by me on this application by the Minister for Justice.

Siúcre Éireann was established in 1933 pursuant to the Sugar Manufacture Act 1933. Thereafter the Minister for Finance on behalf of the State held all the share capital of Siúcre Éireann and exercised a dominant position in relation to the board of directors of Siúcre Éireann. The powers of the Minister for Finance were extended to subsidiary companies by the Sugar Manufacture (Amendment) Act 1962 but have not otherwise materially altered. The Minister for Finance's powers were again extended by the Sugar Manufacture (Amendment) Act 1973 and section 4 of that Act provided as follows:

"4. The schedule to the Principal Act is hereby amended by the substitution of the following for paragraph 3:

> 3. The Articles of Association of the company shall provide:
> (a) that the directors of the company shall be of such number not exceeding ten as the minister may from time to time determine;
> (b) that a majority of the directors (being the smallest majority in any particular case) shall be nominated by the minister;
> (d) that a person shall not be capable of being appointed auditor of the company unless the approval of the minister to the nomination of that person to the office of auditor of the company has been given."

The Minister for Finance on behalf of the State continued to own the entire share capital of Siúcre Éireann until 1991. In or about June 1990 it was decided that the Minister for Finance should dispose of approximately 55 per cent of the State's holding in Siúcre Éireann by means of privatisation. Towards this end a holding company Greencore was formed under the Companies Acts 1963-1990 on 14 February 1991. Under powers accorded to him under the Sugar Act 1991 the minister exchanged the ordinary shares owned by him in Siúcre Éireann for shares in Greencore amounting at that time to 100 per cent of the equity of Greencore. This exchange took place on 20 March 1991.

On 18 April 1991 the Minister for Finance sold 27,400,000 of his shares in Greencore and Greencore issued 12,056,544 new shares to members of the public all at the price of 230p per share except for 6,500,426 shares which were offered for sale at 184p each to certain employees and beet growers. The Minister for Finance thus reduced the State's holding in what I will call the enterprise (meaning thereby Greencore and all its various subsidiary companies) from 100 per cent to 45 per cent. The said minister in or about February 1992 disposed of a further 15 per cent of his shareholding so that the State's interest in the enterprise is now only 30 per cent and the 70 per cent balance is owned by approximately 8,800 private shareholders and by several different institutions including I infer pension funds in which ordinary working men and women who never owned a company share in their own right in their lives would have an interest as the source and guarantee of their pensions.

The order of the High Court of 16 September 1991 was made on foot of an affidavit by Mr Sean Dorgan, Secretary of the Department of Industry and Commerce and an affidavit of Mr Denis G. Hickey of the Department of Finance both sworn on 16 September 1991. Those affidavits proved the possibility of serious irregularities in Siúcre Éireann between 1988 and its privatisation in 1991 such as to justify an investigation pursuant to section 8 of the 1990 Act and the order of the High Court of 16 September 1991 was accordingly made.

The inspectors' final report finds various irregularities and possible and probable irregularities in the conduct of the enterprise. These irregularities all occurred between 1988 and the privatisation of the enterprise in 1991. The only criticism in the report of the board of directors of Greencore since privatisation is that they ought to have dismissed Mr Comerford forthwith on 3 September 1991 instead of agreeing to his resignation on terms. That is not a matter that gave rise to the investigation of the enterprise.

The law

The applicant's claim for reimbursement of the expenses of and incidental to the investigation must be considered separately as against the first nine respondents being part of the enterprise on the one hand and as against Talmino which is not part of the enterprise on the other hand. It is desirable to summarise in part and to quote in full where necessary the relevant provisions of the Companies Act 1990 especially as this is the first time that the issues raised on this application have come before the courts for consideration.

The investigation was ordered and carried out and the application for reimbursement of the expenses of and incidental to the investigation is now made under the provisions of Part II of the 1990 Act. By virtue of section 1(3) that Act and the Companies Acts 1963–1986 are to be construed together as one Act.

By virtue of section 2(1) of the Companies Act 1963 "company" means a company formed and registered under the 1963 Act or an existing company at the date of that Act. And by section 2(3) of the 1963 Act it is provided:

> "2(3) References in this Act to a body corporate or to a corporation shall be construed as not including a corporation sole, but as including a company incorporated outside the State."

By virtue of section 3(1) of the 1990 Act "related company" has the meaning assigned to it by section 140 of that Act which it is sufficient for the purpose of this case to say means that a company is related to another company if that other company is its holding company or subsidiary company.

It is important to bear in mind that Talmino is not related to any of the companies in the enterprise nor does it form part of the enterprise.

Section 17 of the 1990 Act provides as follows:

> "17. Sections 8 to 11, 13, 18 and 22 shall apply to all bodies corporate incorporated outside the State which are carrying on business in the State or have at any time carried on business therein as if they were companies registered under the Principal Act, subject to any necessary modifications."

The effect of section 17 of the 1990 Act is to restrict for the purposes of Part II of that Act the meaning of "body corporate" as defined in section 2(3) of the 1963 Act in the case of companies incorporated outside the State to such companies only as also carry on business in the State and to apply the specified sections of Part II of the 1990 Act to such foreign companies only.

Section 7 of the 1990 Act entitles a company (which means an Irish company only) or a director thereof or shareholders having not less than a specified interest in the company to apply to the High Court for the appointment of an inspector to investigate the affairs of the company. In relation to the second respondent, Greencore, the Minister for Finance, was such a shareholder but he did not apply under section 7.

Section 8 entitled the Minister for Industry and Commerce to apply to the High Court for the appointment of an inspector to investigate the affairs of a company (including a foreign company carrying on business in the State) and as this is the section under which the inspectors were appointed I quote in full subsection (1):

> "8.(1) Without prejudice to its powers under section 7, the court may on the application of the minister appoint one or more competent inspectors to investigate the affairs of a company and to report thereon in such manner as the court shall direct, if the court is satisfied that there are circumstances suggesting:
>
> > (a) that its affairs are being or have been conducted with intent to defraud its creditors or the creditors of any other person or otherwise for a fraudulent or unlawful purpose or in an unlawful manner or in a manner which is unfairly prejudicial to some part of its members, or that any actual or proposed act or omission of the company (including an act or omission on its behalf) is or would be so prejudicial, or that it was formed for any fraudulent or unlawful purpose; or
> > (b) that persons connected with its formation or the management of its affairs have in connection therewith been guilty of fraud, misfeasance or other misconduct towards it or towards its members; or
> > (c) that its members have not been given all the information relating to its affairs which they might reasonably expect."

The order of the High Court of 18 September 1991 giving the inspectors power to investigate certain subsidiary companies of Greencore was made pursuant to section 9 of the 1990 Act which is as follows:

> "9. If an inspector appointed under section 7 or 8 to investigate the affairs of a company thinks it the purposes of his investigation to investigate also the affairs of any other body corporate which is related to such company, he shall, with the approval of the court, have power so to do, and shall report on the affairs of the other body corporate so far as he thinks the results of his investigation thereof are relevant to the investigation of the affairs of the first mentioned company."

As has been seen from what I have said above by virtue of section 17 a body corporate referred in section 9 includes such a body registered outside the State which carries on business within the State provided of course that it is also a related company.

Section 13 of the 1990 Act is the section under which this application is brought by the Minister for Justice and I therefore quote it in full:

> "13(1) The expenses of and incidental to an investigation by an inspector appointed by the court under the foregoing provisions of this Act shall be defrayed in the first instance by the Minister for Justice but the court may direct that any person being:
>
> (a) a body corporate dealt with in the report, or
> (b) the applicant or applicants for the investigation,
>
> shall be liable, to such extent as the court may direct, to repay the Minister for Justice, provided that no such liability on the part of the applicant or applicants shall exceed in the aggregate £100,000.
>
> (2) Without prejudice to subsection (1), any person who is:
>
> (a) convicted on indictment of an offence on a prosecution instituted as a result of an investigation,
> (b) ordered to pay damages or restore any property in proceedings brought as a result of an investigation, or
> (c) awarded damages or to whom property is restored in proceedings brought as a result of an investigation,
>
> may, in the same proceedings, be ordered to repay all or part of the expenses referred to in subsection (1) to the Minister for Justice or to any person on whom liability has been imposed by the court under that subsection, provided that in the case of a person to whom paragraph (c) relates, the court shall not order payment in excess of one-tenth of the amount of the damages awarded or of the value of the property restored, as the case may be, and any such order shall not be executed until the person concerned has received his damages or the property has been restored, as the case may be.
>
> (3) The report of an inspector may, if he thinks fit, and shall, if the court so directs, include a recommendation as to the directions (if any) which he thinks appropriate, in the light of his investigation, to be given under subsection (1)."

The inspectors did not include in their report any recommendation pursuant to subsection (3) above nor did I direct them to do so.

The submissions

I adjourned consideration of the Minister for Justice's application for the expenses of and incidental to the investigation from 3 to 31 March 1992 and I gave all parties liberty to file affidavits and written submissions in advance of the latter date if they so wished and the three contending parties the Minister for Justice, the first nine respondents and Talmino availed of this liberty. The written submissions were argued and expanded upon in open court on 31 March and 1 and 2 April 1992 and are briefly summarised below.

Counsel for the Minister for Justice submitted that the scheme of Part II of the 1990 Act imposes the liability for the expenses of and incidental to the investigation whether under section 7 or section 8 on the Minister for Justice in the first instance and it is then intended by section 13(1) that the minister should be reimbursed by the company or one of the companies dealt with in the report as soon as possible. Such companies so made liable might then have a right to contribution or indemnity pursuant to section 13(2) if the circumstances mentioned in subsection (2) should arise. Talmino, counsel for the minister submitted, although not a related company and therefore not formally investigated is dealt with extensively in the report, is at the root of much of the controversy: and is therefore liable to reimburse the Minister for Justice jointly and severally with the other respondents.

Counsel for Siúcre Éireann and the other respondents forming part of the enterprise submitted that the matters giving rise to the investigation all occurred during the time when the enterprise was owned and controlled by the State and it was right that the State should therefore bear the costs of the investigation rather than pass them on to the enterprise at the time when the State has transferred 70 per cent of its shareholding ownership to new owners the vast majority of whom had nothing to do with the enterprise when the alleged irregularities occurred.

Counsel for Talmino submitted that Talmino was not "dealt with" in the report: that adverse comment in the report was not a proper criterion for fixing liability on a body corporate under section 13(1) and was only appropriate in the context of subsection (2): furthermore Talmino never carried on business in the State to satisfy the requirements of section 17 and therefore section 13 does not apply to Talmino at all.

Counsel for the inspectors submitted that the costs and expenses of all the various attendances by the inspectors in court and also the first attendance on behalf of the Minister for Industry and Commerce and all the orders obtained on such attendances were part of the costs and expenses of and incidental to the investigation in addition to such expenses actually incurred in the investigation itself. I can deal with that submission at once by ruling that that is so as regards the costs and expenses of the inspectors, the Minister for Industry and Commerce and the Minister for Justice.

Conclusions as regards Siúcre Éireann and the enterprise

In the course of his oral submissions counsel for the Minister for Justice submitted that *prima facie* the minister should be reimbursed his expenses of such an investigation and that it would be wrong that the State should have to pay such expenses.

As a general rule and subject to the facts of each individual case I completely agree with this submission. Companies are creatures of the law and are controlled by the law and it falls to the executive power of the State to supervise them. Hence the scheme of the Act provides for in effect guaranteeing by the State of the costs and expenses of an investigation including the fees of the inspector because of necessity an inspector must be a highly qualified professional person whether an accountant or a lawyer. Hence although the State may have no interest in a company which might even be a private company circumstances of such irregularity may arise as to require an investigation either under section 7 or section 8. If under section 7 the court may require security for the costs (not exceeding £100,000) from the applicant for the investigation but if under section 8 it is a matter of such public concern even though the State has no direct interest in the company that no security for the costs is required. In such circumstances it is *prima facie* only right and proper that the company or companies dealt in the report even though not adversely dealt with therein should reimburse the State the costs and expenses pursuant to section 13(1) and then in appropriate circumstances such companies can seek reimbursement themselves under subsection (2). It will be noted that under subsection (1) it is only a body corporate that can be ordered to reimburse the Minister for Justice whereas under subsection (2) individual persons can be ordered to reimburse either the minister or a company which may already have done so under subsection (1).

The facts of each case have to be taken into account however and in this case there are very special facts.

The alleged wrongdoing in the enterprise giving rise to the investigation all took place when the enterprise was wholly owned by the State and under the control of the State through a board the majority of whom were appointed by the Minister for Finance on behalf of the State. Since then and without any knowledge of the irregularities the State sold 55 per cent of its shareholding ownership to citizens and institutions who bought such shareholding without any such knowledge. Later still the State sold another 15 per cent of its shareholding ownership with knowledge of the likelihood of serious irregularities in the enterprise apparent from the inspectors' first two interim reports and the reports of an inspector appointed by the Minister for Industry and Commerce under section 14 of the 1990 Act and who issued an interim report on 2 October 1991 and a final report on 4 December 1991. Those who bought such 15 per cent shareholding of the State did so with knowledge of the then ongoing investigation and the likelihood of serious irregularities appearing from the said reports of October and December 1991 of the inspector appointed under section 14 of the 1990 Act.

Thus the State has before the application by the Minister for Justice divested itself of 70 per cent of its shareholdlng ownership and nonetheless seeks to impose liability on the enterprise even though now 70 per cent owned by institutions and persons the vast majority of whom had nothing whatever to do with the enterprise when the irregularities giving rise to the investigation occurred.

As an example of the foregoing matters one of the irregularities appearing from the inspectors' report (pages 163 to 178) is a claim by Sugar Distributors Ltd to be entitled to pay corporation tax at the manufacturing rate of 10 per cent instead of the usual corporation profits rate of 43 per cent and the actual payment of such tax at 10 per cent in the year preceding privatisation. The irregularity relates to the issue of 900,000 convertible redeemable preference shares in Sugar Distributors Ltd to Siúcre Éireann so as to confer manufacturing status on Sugar Distributors Ltd through Siúcre Éireann and thus qualify for the 10 per cent rate. The issue of those shares appears to be invalid and void and accordingly tax should have been paid by Sugar Distributors Ltd at the 43 per cent rate and the inspectors' report suggests that the difference will exceed £400,000 for the year ending September 1990 and of course continuing thereafter. At the time of privatisation neither the State nor the general public was aware of these matters but in fact the State had the benefit of the extra monies retained as part of the assets of the enterprise when selling it to the public in April 1991.

If the State now recovers through the Revenue Commissioners these monies the State will benefit on the double at the expense of the innocent public subscribers on privatisation and perhaps indeed benefit treblely if substantial penalties are imposed. On the other hand if notwithstanding the inspectors' strongly expressed views to the contrary at page 177 and 178 of their report where they refer to fraud and forgery the enterprise succeeds in avoiding these tax payments as they say they are going to attempt to do by retrospectively ratifying the invalid issue of the 900,000 shares and the other steps taken invalidly to qualify for the manufacturing tax rate the State still does not lose anything because it privatised the enterprise on the basis that no such liabilities arose and accordingly the State had the benefit of those retained monies in the enterprise in the sale price of the shares in Greencore.

It was submitted on behalf of the State that the rule in *Foss v. Harbottle* (1843) 2 Hare 461 precludes me from looking behind Siúcre Éireann, Greencore and the companies forming the enterprise to the shareholder owners thereof but having carefully considered that case I do not think that it so precludes me. And I am of opinion that the realities of the case require me to bear in mind who was the beneficial shareholder owner at the time of the wrongdoing and who is now the beneficial shareholder owner at the time when the expenses of and incidental to the investigation are sought to be imposed upon the enterprise.

Apart altogether from the fact that innocent shareholder owners of the enterprise would now be damnified by an order in favour of the State there is the factor of who was in ultimate control of the enterprise at the material time. As between the body having ultimate control of the enterprise at the time of the alleged wrongdoing and successors to that ultimate control especially insofar as they are without any notice of the wrongdoing it seems to me that it is more equitable that those in ultimate control at the time of the wrongdoing (even though unaware of it at that time) should bear the costs of the investigation rather than their successors especially to the extent that such successors were wholly unaware of any such wrongdoing. On this basis it might be suggested that the enterprise should pay 45 per cent or 30 per cent of the expenses seeing that the State retained ownership of those percentages as above but I do not think that that follows because the wholly innocent present shareholder owners will still be penalised to the benefit of the State.

Moreover the enterprise has incurred very substantial costs and expenses itself in meeting the inspectors' requirements and also the requirements of the section 14 inspector as well as an internal inquiry by independent accountants and inquiries by the Revenue Commissioners. In all the very special circumstances of this case I do not think that it would be just or equitable to direct that any of the first nine respondents being part of the enterprise should be liable to repay to the applicant the Minister for Justice any of the expenses of and incidental to the investigation by the inspectors and I accordingly refuse the minister's application as against those respondents.

Conclusions as regards Talmino

As already stated Talmino is not part of the enterprise nor is it related to any of the companies in the enterprise.

It was incorporated and registered in Jersey in March 1989 for the purpose of acquiring shares in the respondents Gladebrook Co. Ltd which had just purchased the 49 per cent shareholding in Sugar Distributors Ltd not owned by Siúcre Éireann. It duly acquired those shares and about one year later sold and transferred them to Siúcre Éireann and received the consideration therefor in the form of a loan note for £2,104,900.

The first matter which I consider on the claim by the Minister for Justice as against Talmino is whether Talmino is a body corporate dealt with in the report within the meaning of section 13(1)(a) of the Companies Act 1990.

In the first paragraph of p. 39 of the report the inspectors say:

> "Some of the key issues in our investigations into the affairs of Siúcre Éireann CPT and related companies are in respect of Talmino Ltd, the Siúcre Éireann loan note which it holds and the actual ownership of the company. We have set out below details of our investigations in relation to these matters and a number of related matters."

In the last paragraph of p. 39 the inspectors say:

> "During the course of our investigations, we did not examine financial statements of either Talmino or Serrat Finserco on the grounds that their only relevance to this investigation is in the context of their ownership and the location of their financial assets, namely the Siúcre Éireann loan note."

There follows a discussion of these matters which takes up some 30 pages to the top of p. 69 of the report.

The discussion is indeed limited to the ownership of Talmino and consequently the beneficial ownership of the loan note and does not examine the financial status of that company. Nevertheless the discussion is so wide ranging and detailed on these matters that I have come to the conclusion that giving the words "dealt with" their ordinary meaning in the absence of any special definition in the Companies Acts 1963-1990 Talmino is dealt with in the report.

I must next consider whether the legislature in enacting paragraph (a) of section 13(1) of the 1990 Act intended to widen the range of companies which might be ordered to repay the Minister for Justice the expenses of and incidental to the investigation, to include companies dealt with in the report even though not actually under investigation, or intended to narrow the range to exclude companies ordered to be investigated but not at the end of the day dealt with in the report.

In the present case the primary investigation was into the affairs of Siúcre Éireann but by the High Court order of 18 September 1991 the inspectors were authorised to investigate 33 related companies and these are set out at Appendix I of the report. As appears from Appendix II of the report the inspectors had suspended their investigation into seven of these related companies by 7 October 1991 and by 11 November 1991 they had suspended their investigation into a further 13 of such companies and it was not necessary to investigate further any of those 20 companies and none of them are dealt with in the report. Clearly the court would have no power to order that any of those 20 companies should repay the Minister for Justice any of the expenses of and incidental to the investigation and the minister makes no such application as against those 20 companies.

If the court has power to order a company dealt with in the report but not actually under investigation to pay these expenses it could lead to strange results in that the company might never have had a proper opportunity of itself putting its case to the inspectors who might nevertheless have power under section 13(3) to recommend that such company should bear such expenses.

I have come to the conclusion that the intention of the legislature and the meaning of the words "a body corporate dealt with in the report" is to limit the power of the court to order repayment of the expenses by such bodies corporate only as were under investigation and are dealt with in the report and not to extend the power to bodies corporate which are dealt with in the report but were not under investigation.

The foregoing conclusion is sufficient to decide this application by the Minister for Justice as against Talmino but I think that I should also deal with the question as to whether or not Talmino carried on business in the State within the meaning of that phrase as used in section 17 of the 1990 Act as this point was fully argued before me. If Talmino did not carry on business in the State then section 13 does not apply to Talmino at all and the court would have no power to order it incidental to the investigation.

The expression "to carry on business" is not defined in the Companies Acts 1963 to 1990 and must therefore be given its ordinary meaning. In my opinion its ordinary meaning presupposes some sort of continuum of activity as contrasted with one or two isolated transactions.

The meaning of the phrase was considered in the context of section 6 of the Moneylenders Act 1900 by D'Arcy J in the case of *Cripps Warburg Ltd v. Cologne Investment Co. Ltd and Others* [1980] IR 321. Section 6 of the Moneylenders Act 1990 provides as follows:

> "6. The expression "moneylender" in this Act shall include every person whose business is that of moneylending, or who advertises or announces himself or holds himself out in any way as carrying on that business."

At p. 339 of the report D'Arcy J says:

> "Apart from the loan which is the subject matter of this claim and matters flowing from or ancillary to that claim, such as the taking of the guarantee and the mortgage, at material times the plaintiffs were only involved in two transactions connected with Ireland. Neither of these involved the making of a loan. They involved the providing of banking expertise, knowledge and advice. In two of these transactions one of the parties was Irish.
>
> I find that at all material times the plaintiffs were not carrying on the business of moneylenders in this jurisdiction. The one isolated loan which is the subject matter of these proceedings did not constitute them moneylenders for the purpose of the Act of 1900, as amended. I hold that the making of the loan and the taking of the guarantee and securities were not void or illegal by reason of the fact that the plaintiffs had not a moneylender's licence under the relevant Act. They did not require it. In this jurisdiction they were not carrying on the business of moneylending. In England they had a certificate of exemption under the appropriate legislation there."

In the title "Companies" in Halsbury's Fourth Edition Reissue Volume 7(1) at paragraph 22 dealing with associations of persons exceeding 20 in number which need not be registered as a company it is stated:

> "Business is carried on only where there is a joint relation of persons for the common purpose of performing jointly a succession of acts, and not where the relation exists for a purpose which is to be completed by the performance of one act. If therefore more than twenty persons between whom no contractual relation exists subscribe to a fund to be invested in the shares of companies by trustees for the subscribers, the subscribers do not carry on a business, and probably the trustees, even if more than twenty, do not do so either even though the shares are acquired with the object of pooling them and promoting an amalgamation with another company."

The only activity of Talmino in this State was to acquire 2,425 shares in Gladebrook Co. Ltd in 1989 and to sell and transfer those shares to Siúcre Éireann in 1990. The consideration for such sale and transfer was £2,104,900 which was received and held by Talmino in the form of a loan note in that amount issued to it by Siúcre Éireann.

In my opinion the foregoing transactions do not constitute carrying on business in the State by Talmino and therefore section 17 of the 1990 Act does not operate to apply section 13 to Talmino and the court has no power to order any part of the expenses of and incidental to the investigation to be repaid by Talmino to the Minister for Justice.

The application of the Minister for Justice for repayment of such expenses by Talmino must therefore be refused far the foregoing two reasons namely that Talmino was not under investigation by the inspectors and that it is a foreign company not carrying on business in the State.

Alistair Rutherdale
Barrister

In the Matter of Wogan's (Drogheda) Ltd (under the protection of the court) and in the Matter of the Companies (Amendment) Act 1990 (No. 1): High Court 1991 No. 15465P (Costello J) 7 May 1992

Company – Scheme of arrangement – Application to confirm scheme – Order placing company under protection of court – Petition – Undervaluing of liabilities – Whether abuse of process – Scheme conditional on orders extinguishing tax liabilities – Whether court should make such orders – Defects in scheme – Whether remediable – Position of employees – Wage cuts – Purpose of legislation – Whether scheme fulfilled purposes of legislation – Duties of examiner – Companies (Amendment) Act 1990 (No. 27) sections 2, 15, 18

Facts: On 13 January 1992 the High Court made a protection order in respect of the company, pursuant to section 2 of the Companies (Amendment) Act 1990, and an examiner was appointed. The examiner's report under section 15 into the affairs of the company was presented on 10 February 1992, and he prepared a scheme of arrangement and presented it to members and creditors at meetings on 31 March 1992. He then presented his report under section 18 on the scheme of arrangement to the court.

The scheme proposed an investment in the company by Dublin Providers Ltd ("DPV Ltd"). It affected the two major creditors in the following ways: (a) a debt of £462,300 owed to Hill Samuel (Ireland) Ltd ("the bank") was to be written down to £235,000 and restructured as a seven year term loan; (b) of a debt of £293,402 owing to the Revenue Commissioners, the scheme allowed only for payment of £73,467 (later raised to £92,317 after the Revenue proposed to utilise section 15 of the Finance Act 1986 to recover book debts in priority to the bank). Both the bank and the Revenue Commissioners voted against the scheme and objected to its confirmation by the court.

Held by Costello J in refusing to confirm the scheme:

(1) There was an abuse of the process of the court at the time of the original application for protection on 13 January 1992. The petition understated liabilities and overstated assets and, in particular, understated the debt due to the Revenue Commissioners. At least two of the directors had chosen not to seek to wind up the company, but to seek a protection order so as to obtain personal advantage.

(2) An application to be placed under the protection of the court pursuant to the Companies (Amendment) Act 1990, requires the utmost good faith and an applicant has a duty not to deliberately mislead the court by false evidence.

Per Curiam: It is desirable that when making a protection order, a court should make it subject to any further order that might be made, terminating an examiner's appointment, on foot of an application to re-enter a matter by the examiner. The order should impose a duty on an examiner to consider whether any evidence adduced at the hearing was misleading in any material aspect, and to re-enter the matter where this is so.

(3) The abuse of the process of the court was such as to require the court to refuse to sanction the scheme of arrangement proposed, as it was prepared consequent to an improperly obtained order of the court.

(4) The court would also refuse to confirm the scheme as it was conditional on the making of certain orders on taxation matters which the court would not make. The court would refuse to make orders that PAYE/PRSI, VAT and corporation tax liabilities be extinguished for transactions up to the date of implementation of the scheme.

(5) There were a number of defects in the scheme which the examiner had negotiated with the new investor of such a nature as to preclude its confirmation.

(a) The scheme failed to deal with a money claim against the company by the mother-in-law of a director, or with the question of any subrogation rights the directors might claim against the company should they be found liable on foot of personal guarantees to the bank.

(b) The agreement was conditional, and purported to allow the investor to withdraw or amend the agreement at a later stage.

(6) The agreement obliged the examiner to impose new wage rates on the employees, and to terminate their employment in default of agreement. As the interest of employees was one of the objectives of the protection legislation, the scheme failed to achieve this objective. The scheme was in essence designed to establish a new commercial enterprise.

(7) In addition the scheme failed to deal with the cost of any claims for wrongful dismissal, should the examiner have dismissed any of the employees.

No cases referred to in judgment

Counsel's names not available

Solicitors for the Examiner: *Paul W. Keogh & Co.*
Solicitors for the Revenue Commissioners: *Frances D. Cooke, Revenue Solicitor*
Solicitors for Hill Samuel (Ireland) Ltd: *Gerrard Scallan & O'Brien*

COSTELLO J **7 May 1992**

The facts
Wogans (Drogheda) Ltd was established in 1981 and thereafter carried on business in Drogheda as traders in hardware products and suppliers to the building trade. Initially the company traded successfully achieving a turnover of £1.8m by 1985 and employing more than 20 employees. However, from 1 April 1989 to 31 December 1990 it sustained a substantial loss of £454,000 and continued trading at a further substantial loss in 1991. It became insolvent, but instead of applying to wind up the company a petition was presented by the company on 19 December 1991 under section 2 of the Companies (Amendment) Act 1990. It is a family company run by two of its three directors. The petition under section 2 of the 1990 Act was heard on 13 January 1992 and a protection order was made and an examiner appointed. The examiner's section 15 report was presented on 10 February 1992 (the time for doing so having been extended). He prepared a scheme of arrangement and presented it to the members and creditors at meetings on 31 March 1992. He then presented his report under section 18 to the court and I heard the application to confirm the scheme on 29 and 30 April 1992.

The company has continued to trade at what the examiner described as a small loss.

The scheme involves the investment in the company of a Dublin firm (Dublin Providers Ltd) which has successfully traded in the hardware trade in different parts of Ireland. The scheme will involve the purchase by the new investors of the issued share capital and the appointment of new directors (although one former director will be retained as an employee). The scheme will materially affect the interests of the company's two major creditors, one of which is Hill Samuel (Ireland) Ltd, which is owed approximately £462,300 which is secured by a mortgage and a fixed and floating charge. The scheme proposed will result in the debt being written down to £235,000 and the revised amount being restructured as a seven year term loan with a moratorium on repayment of principal for one year, thereafter payments to be made by equal quarterly amounts with interests as specified on the reducing balance. The other major creditor is the Revenue Commissioners. The total due to the Revenue Commissioners on 13 January 1992 was £293,402.71, of which only a portion was a preferential debt. Under the proposed scheme the preferential amount was to be £82,598. The scheme involved a total payment to the Revenue Commissioners (over a period of years) of £73,467, that is about 25 per cent of the total taxes due. Both the bank and the Revenue Commissioners voted against the scheme and objected to its confirmation. The total debt due to the unsecured creditors is £857,800 approximately. Most of these creditors are small creditors and they are to be paid 10 per cent of the sums due to them. A majority in number and value of the unsecured creditors voted to accept the scheme.

An issue in the course of the protection period relating to the fixed charge over the company's book debts to which the bank claims to be entitled. The High Court decided that the fixed charge did not capture the book debts. On appeal the Supreme Court held that it did. But section 145 of the 1986 Finance Act enables the Revenue Commissioners to recover those book debts in priority to the bank. As they propose to operate the section, this means that the Revenue Commissioners will become entitled to a payment of £92,317 or about 31 per cent of the total tax due on 13 January 1992. Notwithstanding this improvement, the Revenue Commissioners maintain their objections.

Having carefully considered the scheme (and the suggested amendments to it proposed during the hearing) and the submissions made, I have come to the conclusion that I should not confirm it (a) because the evidence discloses that there was an abuse of the processes of the court at the time of the original application for protection on 13 January 1992; (b) because confirmation is conditional on orders being made relating to certain taxation issues which I do not think I should make; (c) because there are defects in the scheme which the examiner negotiated with the new investor of such a nature which preclude its confirmation.

The abuse of the processes of the Court

The petition was presented in the Central Office on 19 December 1991 by the company itself. The petition set out in summary form the company's balance sheet. This showed that the company's principal creditors were (a) the bank at £430,000, (b) the Revenue Commissioners at £124,000 and (c) the directors at £100,000. Its total assets were shown as £1,026,000, its total liabilities at £1,364,000, leaving a deficiency of £338,000. The truth of the statements in this petition were verified by the affidavit of Mr Brian Waldron sworn on 18 December 1991.

Section 14 of the Act requires the directors after an appointment of an examiner to swear an affidavit giving particulars, *inter alia* of the company's assets, debts and liabilities. The examiner was appointed on 13 January 1992. Complying with section 14, the directors swore an affidavit shortly afterwards which disclosed a situation considerably and materially different to that shown in the petition and which had been verified by an affidavit of one of the directors of the company. The new balance sheet showed a deficit of £776,578. The examiner's view was that the discrepancy between the two balance sheets arose because the assets had been overstated by £151,000 and the liabilities understated by £287,000 in the December petition. Of most significance, however, was that the section 14 affidavit disclosed that the debt due to the Revenue Commissioners had been undervalued in the petition by £180,000 approximately. This undervalue was not due to any bookkeeping or accounting error. The undisclosed debt to the Revenue Commissioners was made up of approximately £111,000 for PAYE and PRSI due on wages paid by the company to its employees and not disclosed to the Revenue, and interest on arrears of tax (mainly in respect of PAYE and PRSI liabilities) and £10,000 in respect of other liabilities. Furthermore, in his section 15 report the examiner concluded that the deficit shown in the section 14 affidavit was itself understated. According to him, the true deficiency was £973,294 (not £776,578) on 13 January 1992.

I am satisfied:

(1) that the failure of the company to pay the sums due to the Revenue Commissioners in respect of PAYE and PRSI was a deliberate and conscious decision known to at least two of its directors.

(2) that at least two of the directors must have known that the petition filed by the company contained information that was incorrect and that the verifying affidavit contained a deliberate untruth relating to the debt due to the Revenue Commissioners.

(3) that had the court been informed of the company's true position, namely, that the company's deficit was £973,294 (or even that it was £776,578) and that the directors had for some time been consistently defrauding the Revenue Commissioners, the court would not have made the protection order on 13 January last and the company would now be in liquidation.

When an application is made by a company for a protection order under the 1990 Act, it seems to me that the directors and all those associated with the application (including their professional advisers) are obliged to exercise the utmost good faith and that such a duty exists not just on an *ex parte* application to appoint an interim examiner but also on the application itself. This is because (a) of necessity, the court must depend to a considerable extent on the truth of what it is told by the company and (b) because of the potential injustice involved in the making of a protecting order when the proper course is to wind up the company. This duty involves an obligation to disclose all relevant facts material to the exercise by the court of its discretion. *A fortiori*, it involves a duty not to deliberately mislead the court by false evidence.

Not every breach of duty to exercise good faith will amount to an abuse of the court's processes. But where an application for a protection order is made on evidence which is known to be false this amounts to an abuse of process. And when an application is made for an improper purpose, this also amounts to an abuse of the processes of the court.

In this case I must conclude that the evidence used to obtain the order must have been known to be false by at least two of the directors. Apart from any other aspect of the statement of affair the directors knew that the debt due to the Revenue Commissioners was grossly understated and that the true deficit was much greater than that shown in the petition. Furthermore, I think it a reasonable inference that two of the directors decided not to wind up the company but instead decided to seek a protection order in order to obtain personal advantage and that in doing so they then abused the court's processes. Two of the directors had personal guarantees to the bank of £100,000 each. Counsel tells me that the directors believed that the scheme of arrangement would discharge them from liability on foot of those personal guarantees. I think it is reasonable to conclude that it is probable that the directors decided to apply under the 1990 Act and not to disclose the true state of affairs to obtain such a result. There may, of course, have been other reasons why the directors did not want the company's affairs investigated by a liquidator, but I express no view on this now.

It was urged by counsel on behalf of the examiner that I should not take into account the circumstances which I have just outlined in considering the scheme of arrangement.

Creditors whose interests are impaired by a scheme of arrangement may object to it on the grounds set out in section 25. But the court's discretion under section 24(3) to confirm, or to confirm subject to modifications, or to refuse to confirm the scheme proposed is not limited by the grounds set out in section 25. If an abuse of the court's processes has been established, I do not think that the court should ignore it and consider on its merits a scheme which had subsequently been prepared. To do so would be to condone the abusive behaviour and encourages similar conduct in the future.

In my view the abuse of the processes of the court in this case is such as to require the court to refuse to make an order sanctioning the scheme of arrangement prepared consequent on an order of the court improperly obtained.

There is a second way in which the court was misled at the hearing of the petition. Four reasons were given to explain the company's present financial position: (1) the recession in the building trade; (2) poor management; (3) theft of the company money and other property to the amount of £80,000; (4) the failure of related companies in Balbriggan and Dunleer. But the examiner's section 15 report establishes that the losses due to theft occurred in 1986 (see p.16) and that the main trading loss occurred since 1988. This is additional evidence as to the breach of the duty which was owed to the court when the petition was presented.

This is the third case under the 1990 Act which has come before me in which it was shown that the original protection order was based on misleading evidence. When an examiner is appointed his duty is to examine the affairs of the company and deliver a report as required by section 15. If he considers that the company is capable of surviving as a going concern, the court is presented with the report and has no function until the section 18 report is drawn up. In the light of what has happened in this and other cases, it seems to me to be desirable that, when making a protection order under section 2, the order should state that it is subject to any further order the court may make terminating the appointment of the examiner pursuant to an application to re-enter by the examiner, and that the order should impose a duty on the examiner under section

15(2) to consider whether any evidence adduced at the hearing was misleading in any material respect and to re-enter the matter for further consideration should this be so before preparing a report under section 15.

The court orders required by the investor

The examiner has informed the court that the investor requires the court to make three different relating to certain taxation matters and that the investor will withdraw from the scheme if these orders are not made.

(a) The first order relates to pre-13 January 1992 taxes. Paragraph 13 of the Heads of Agreement provides:

> "The Examiner to obtain a tax clearance certificate from the Revenue Commissioners indicating that at the date of the approval by the court that the Wogans' taxes are up to date.
>
> This certificate and approval of the scheme of arrangement will indicate to DPV Ltd that the taxation affairs are in order and that the liabilities are limited to those arising from the scheme of arrangement."

To give effect to this paragraph the examiner's "Proposals for a Scheme of Arrangement" contained the following paragraph:

> "The Revenue Commissioners to provide a certificate indicating that at the date of the approval by the Court of the scheme that all tax, PRSI and levies due by the company are up to date and in order providing the scheme is approved and implemented." Paragraph 13(f).

The object of this provision was to indicate to the investor that the taxation affairs are in order as on implementation of the scheme of arrangement. The Revenue Commissioners refused to give the certificate required in the scheme in his section 18 report to the court the examiner recommended in paragraph 12:

> "(g) . . .in addition to approving the proposals for a scheme of arrangement that the court approves the following which are the main conditional aspects of the Dublin Providers Ltd agreement:
>
> (1) That on ratification of the scheme the Court indicates that all PAYE/PRSI, employment/health levies and VAT liabilities of the company as at 13 January 1992 will be extinguished by the implementation of the scheme."

As the Revenue Commissioners have refused to give a tax clearance certificate, the investor requires the court to order that all liabilities which may exist in respect of the taxes referred to be extinguished.

I think that the attitude of the Revenue Commissioners was a reasonable one and I do not think that the court should make the order sought. In view of the fact that the directors had been defrauding the Revenue Commissioners over a considerable period of time and that one of the directors had sworn an affidavit which to his knowledge was untrue, I do not think that the Revenue Commissioners should be required to certify in the manner provided. Furthermore, in his section 15 report the examiner pointed out that the company did not have a stock control system and expressed concern that stocks had been reduced by about £60,000 between 5 October 1991 and 13 January 1992, pointing out that without a stock control system it was not possible to examine this aspect of the company's trading. On the information before me, the request made by the investor is not a reasonable one and I must refuse it.

(b) Two orders are required relating to taxation issues arising from the scheme of arrangement.

The examiner in his section 18 report has raised two further taxation issues which were not included in the scheme of arrangement which was presented to the creditors and in respect of which the investor requires orders, one relating to Corporation Profits Tax and one relating to VAT.

1. *Corporation Profits Tax*

In paragraph II(i) of the section 18 report the examiner stated that there are "some further taxation issues of principle that need to be clarified before the intending investor will acquire the company". In his recommendations (at paragraph 12(g)(iii)) the examiner asked the court to order that, on approval of the scheme, corporation tax liabilities be deemed to be extinguished for all transactions up to that date including those arising under the scheme of arrangement, and that any rights which the company may have to taxation losses shall also be deemed to be extinguished.

The reason for the order sought is that under section 14(1) of the Finance Act 1970 debts foregone are assessable on the beneficiary. As the beneficiary (that is, the company) would have already received a deduction for the full invoiced cost of purchases for corporation tax purposes, if the full purchase price is no longer payable under the scheme of arrangement then an adjustment for tax purposes would have to be made. The Revenue Commissioners have refused to forego the "clawback" to which they are entitled (while accepting that losses forward by the company would be available against profits clawed back under the section). I think that this attitude is a reasonable one. I agree with the view expressed by the Revenue Commissioners that this requirement should have been included in the scheme of arrangement. But apart from this criticism, I do not think that I should impose a further detriment on the Revenue Commissioners in addition to that suffered by them by the scheme of arrangement. The ordinary taxation rule should apply if the company is permitted to continue to trade.

2. *VAT*

In paragraph 12(g)(ii) a request is made for a further order, one restricting the rights of the Revenue Commissioners in relation to VAT refunds arising from the scheme of arrangement.

When there is a downward adjustment of the purchase price of goods (as would happen under the scheme of arrangement) then the vendor who has paid VAT on the full sale price will seek a refund of VAT from the Revenue Commissioners. The purchaser (in this case the company) will have been given a credit for the full VAT charged. Consequently there will be an undercharge to VAT against the purchaser arising from the revised and reduced VAT payable by the vendor. The amount of the VAT repayable to the vendor would be the same as the new VAT liability of the company. What the investor requires is an order that the VAT implications of the scheme of arrangement be treated as bad debt relief in a liquidation and the creditors would not provide VAT inclusive credit notes to the company and that a future VAT liability to the company be avoided. The Revenue Commissioners have refused to agree that such an order be made.

It has not been made clear to me the exact form which the order sought should take. If I am required to make an order whose effect would be to disentitle the company's suppliers from making a claim for a refund of VAT, I do not think I should do so in the absence of their agreement. If I am required to make an order which will result in the suppliers obtaining a VAT refund (or equivalent VAT credit) but which will prohibit the Revenue Commissioners from a corresponding liability on the company, this would impose an additional burden on the Revenue which I do not think it reasonable to ask it to bear. Again, I think there should be no interference with the operation of the law arising from the implementation of the scheme should trading continue, and a case has not been made out for the order which the investor seeks.

As the investor's willingness to implement the scheme depends on the court making the three orders to which I have referred, it follows that the scheme cannot be confirmed. Even though the conclusions which I have given determine the application before me, the parties may wish to have my views on the principal issues that arose on the terms of the scheme itself and I should briefly give them.

Defects in the scheme of arrangement

The scheme of arrangement negotiated between the examiner and the investor is unsatisfactory in a number of respects, containing as it does a number of defects only some of which are capable of remedy.

(1) The arrangement negotiated with the investor was described in a document as "Heads of Agreement", paragraph 16 of which provides that the parties "agreed to convert the heads of an agreement into a legally binding contract". This has not been done and it is very doubtful that the "Heads of Agreement" document itself constitutes a concluded legally binding agreement. I have, however been informed that the investor regards the heads of agreement (as amended by an addendum) as binding and I can so provide should the scheme be confirmed.

(2) The "Heads of Agreement" were not made part of the scheme of arrangement and were not produced to the principal creditors until late in these

proceedings. In my opinion, any concluded agreement with a potential investor should form part of the scheme and must be disclosed to interested parties and to the court. I can so provide should the scheme be confirmed.

(3) The financial obligations of the investor under the "Heads of Agreement" were ambiguous and imprecise, as were these obligations in the scheme prepared by the examiner. I interpret them as requiring the investor to make a payment of £264,000 into a trust account (paragraph 13) out of which be paid the examiner's fees, costs and expenses, the balance being used for "working and development capital". There is no further obligation to make any further payment to or on behalf of the company by the investor. However, I was informed at the hearing that the investor is now prepared, should the scheme be confirmed, to make the following payments forthwith: (a) £245,292; (b) £235,000 to be paid in discharge of the debt due to the bank; (c) £78,703 to be paid over three years or two years to discharge the Revenue debt. I can so provide should the scheme be approved.

(4) There is a serious omission from the scheme which cannot be remedied. The scheme ignores the existence of two contracts of guarantee entered into between the directors and the bank.

On 28 March 1991 two of the directors, Mr Brian Wogan and Mr Gerard Wogan, entered into separate contracts of guarantee with the bank by which each personally guaranteed up to a limit of £100,000 the repayment of the company's indebtedness to the bank. The scheme of arrangement makes no reference to these guarantees and the examiner did not refer to them in his section 18 report. When the matter was raised at the hearing I was informed by counsel that the question of the guarantees was discussed by the examiner with the directors and that they had indicated that in their view the effect of the scheme was to discharge their liability under the guarantees. The examiner gave evidence to the effect that he took the view that the question of the personal guarantees was a matter with which he was not concerned and did not consider that they should form part of the scheme of arrangement. I think he was in error in this regard.

Firstly, if a creditor has a security for the repayment of a debt on the company's property, his objection to a scheme of arrangement which limits his rights to realise his security may carry less weight if it is shown that he has another security in the form of a personal guarantee to which he can turn for payment of the debt. The existence of a valid personal guarantee and the effect of the scheme on it are therefore relevant matters for the court to take into consideration.

Secondly, the effect of the scheme on personal guarantees is relevant for another reason. If the personal guarantees are not discharged by confirmation of the scheme by the court, then a contingent liability exists against the company — if payment is made on foot of the guarantee the guarantor has subrogation rights against the company. Unless the scheme of arrangement limits those subrogation rights the company may face a claim by the guarantor which would jeopardise the whole of the scheme of arrangement. So the court cannot conclude that the scheme which it is considering will facilitate the company's survival.

It is not necessary for me to express any concluded view on the effect of the scheme of arrangement on the two guarantees in this case. It suffices if I say that there are arguments of considerable force to support the view that the guarantees are not discharged by the present scheme and that the directors may well be personally liable on foot of the guarantees. This means that this scheme of arrangement is defective.

Firstly, the directors of the company were allowed to vote on the scheme on a misunderstanding of the legal position to which, it may be claimed, the examiner contributed. Secondly, the real risk of a claim arising from subrogation rights has not been removed or limited by a suitable provision in the scheme.

(5) If the scheme is approved and if the heads of agreement form part of the scheme, then the investor may nonetheless withdraw from or amend the scheme under one of its provisions (paragraph 6) and the scheme will collapse. Paragraph 6 provides that the examiner is to prepare a revised statement of affairs after 29 February 1992, that the investor is to be given full access to the company's records, that after it has examined them it is "to confirm the acceptability or otherwise of the aggregate current assets". The paragraph goes on:

> "At this time if the current assets have been depleted compared with the statement of affairs in the examiner's section 15 report DPV (that is, the investors) will have the right to withdraw from or amend this agreement."

Should the investor withdraw then the deposit it has paid is to be refunded. Objection was taken at the hearing to the conditional nature of the investor's agreement and to the fact that no indication had been given as to whether or not the investor has given the confirmation required by this paragraph. I think that this is a valid objection. Firstly, unnecessary costs might be incurred (to be borne ultimately by the company's secured or preferential creditors) should, after a confirmation hearing, the investor decide not to implement the scheme. Secondly, the court cannot confirm a scheme which the investor may subsequently amend because the court cannot conclude that the scheme as amended is likely to facilitate the survival of the company.

(6) The scheme does not satisfactorily deal with the claim by Mrs McGueron to be paid £49,200 and accumulated interest. Mrs McGueron is the mother-in-law of one of the directors. This claim appeared in a statement of affairs verified by affidavit under section 14 by one of the directors. She has maintained her claim through her solicitor. The examiner, however, has come to the conclusion that the money was lent to the company not by Mrs McGueron but by two of the directors and he informed me that he considered that it had been repaid to them by means of a contra account in the company's records. In these circumstances there seems to me to be a risk of some substance that this creditor may claim that she is not bound by the court's approval of the scheme as she has not

been treated as a creditor. Should her claim be a valid one, she could successfully sue the company and cause its collapse. Secondly, no adequate explanation has been given as to why, if there has been a reduction of the company's liabilities by £49,200 as shown in the directors' statement of affairs, this reduction has not been reflected in the assets side of the statement of affairs as originally prepared. Thirdly, I think the creditors are entitled to a fuller explanation than that which has been forthcoming about the loan which the directors swore had been given by Mrs McGueron, wrongly in the examiner's view. The creditors are entitled to have this transaction investigated by a liquidator, which would not be possible should the scheme be approved.

I think I should add that examiners are not liquidators and are not required to adjudicate on disputed claims or on disputes between creditors. They can admit persons claiming to be creditors to meetings on a "without prejudice" basis and in their report indicate how creditors whose claims are disputed have voted. The court can give whatever weight it considers appropriate to the views of creditors whose debts are in dispute.

(7) Finally, I come to a serious defect in the scheme which might more appropriately have been mentioned at the beginning of this judgment. The heads of agreement provide (paragraph 9) that the investor is to supply to the examiner a list of wage rates they wish "to have in place before the date of acquisition" and that the examiner is to secure the written agreement of the affected staff to those rates, that if no agreement is obtained, then the employment of individual employees is to be terminated in advance of the acquisition by the investor.

The Oireachtas did not enact the 1990 Act to create investment opportunities in ailing companies. It enacted it so that orders could be made to help the survival of companies in suitable cases in the interests, amongst others, of their employees. So any scheme of arrangement submitted for confirmation under the Act must be carefully scrutinised to see how it affects the future employment of a company's employees. I am required in this case to confirm a scheme which may require the examiner, at the request of the investor, to dismiss some or all of the company's employees. No information has been disclosed as to the investor's intentions or as to how the investor proposes to operate this provision of the scheme. As the scheme fails to achieve one of the main objectives which the statute is designed to achieve, and as it is in essence a vehicle to establish what is in reality (if not in name) a new commercial enterprise (there being new directors, new shareholders and new employees) to the probable detriment of the preferential and secured creditors of the old enterprise, I do not think that it should be confirmed by the court.

A further defect arises from this paragraph. If the examiner is required to terminate even some of the contracts of employment, it is reasonably probable that substantial claims for damages for wrongful dismissal will follow which, it would appear, are likely to be successful and destroy the scheme. These would not be barred by the confirmation of the scheme by the court. Because of this, therefore, I cannot be satisfied that this scheme is likely to facilitate the survival of the company as a going concern.

I must therefore refuse to confirm the scheme of arrangement. I will hear submissions on the application made on behalf of the Revenue Commissioners that the company be wound up.

Alistair Rutherdale
Barrister

In the Matter of Hefferon Kearns Ltd (Under the Protection of the Court) and In the Matter of Section 33 of the Companies (Amendment) Act 1990; On the Application of Dublin Heating Company Ltd; Dublin Heating Company Ltd v. Thomas Hefferon, Michael Kearns, Cosmo Mellon and Finbar O'Neill: High Court 1990 No 14426P (Lynch J) 14 January 1993

Application by creditors of company for a declaration that the directors and officers of the company should be held personally liable for the debts or other liabilities of the company – Whether directors, while officers of the company, were knowingly parties to the carrying on of the business of the company in a reckless manner – Examiner appointed to company – Report – Scheme of arrangement – Scheme should not come into operation if section 33 application brought – Liquidation – Fraud – Section not retrospective – Whether acts or omissions prior to commencement date relevant – Collective or individual liability – "Reckless trading" – Power of court to relieve officer of personal liability despite finding of reckless trading – Proof of loss or damage condition precedent to relief – Whether loss or damage trivial – Companies (Amendment) Act 1990 (No. 27), section 33

Facts: The plaintiffs were creditors of Hefferon Kearns Ltd ("the company") and brought an application pursuant to section 33 of the Companies (Amendment) Act 1990 seeking a declaration that the defendants as directors and officers of the company be personally liable without limitation for the debts and liabilities of the company on the grounds that they were, while officers of the company, knowingly parties to the carrying on of the business of the company in a reckless manner. The first named defendant was the *de facto* managing director of the company. At the material time, the company was engaged in three main contracts for the development of luxury apartments. The company was not the owner/developer of the lands involved in either of the projects. A company known as Senna Ltd owned the lands involved in the first project and the first and second named defendants held 57% of the shareholding in that company equally. Darwood Builders Ltd owned the lands being developed in the second contract and the first and second defendants owned all the issued shares in that company. There was no formal building contract with regard to either of these developments. An independent company, IDN Ltd, was the owner/developer of the lands involved in the third transaction and a formal building contract was entered into with regard to same. The plaintiff was engaged as a sub-contractor on these contracts and had assumed that the company owned and developed all of these lands. The company was also involved in a number of other minor contracts, including work on the defendants' own homes performed at little over cost price.

The company began trading in January 1989 and management accounts prepared for the half year ending 30 June 1989 showed a net loss of £73,101. However, although the figures indicated insolvency, the defendants were confident that the losses could be reversed and the audited accounts for the year ending 31 December 1989 showed a net loss of only £8,113. Henceforth, the company obtained bi-monthly accounts which showed losses on the next three successive occasions giving a net loss for the half year ending 30 June 1990 of £134,394 giving in total a balance sheet deficit at 30 June 1990 of £142,507.

In May 1990 the first and second defendants borrowed £45,000 from merchant bankers which said sums were applied to the company's account in the form of various payments on behalf of related companies which were indebted to the company. Although the company's cash flow was improved thereby, this did not alter its balance sheet position since the same amount of debts due by related companies were discharged.

In or around the same time an independent surveyor engaged by Senna had rejected the company's claim to an interim payment of £50,000 on the grounds that the company had already been overpaid by £17,000.

After reviewing the half year accounts on 27 August 1990 the defendants concluded that the losses could be reversed as the completion of the three contracts would either yield a profit or would at least release monies retained. In particular it was thought that the third contract, under which the company was already owed £200,000, would be completed by November 1990.

All the debts due by the company on 31 August 1990 were met.

However by mid-September it was clear that the company would not be able to meet its debts at the end of that month and the defendants resolved to continue only with the third project from which they believed a net profit of £150,000 would be realised and which IDN Ltd had agreed to finance on a weekly basis so that the company would not incur further debts.

At a meeting of creditors held on 11 October 1990 a majority resolved to apply for the appointment of an examiner and an interim examiner was appointed on the following day. The examiner's report found an excess of liabilities over assets of £432,379. In his second report he proposed a scheme of arrangement for the survival of the company but stated that this could only operate if an application under section 33 was not proceeded with. Ultimately the company went into liquidation.

Held by Lynch J in dismissing the plaintiff's claim:

(1) Section 33 did not require the plaintiffs to prove fraud.

(2) Although the provisions of section 33 were not retrospective in their

effect, the court could have regard to acts done or omitted before the date when the section came into operation in deciding whether such acts between such date and 11 October 1990 (when it was resolved that an application to appoint an examiner should be made), constituted reckless trading.

(3) The plaintiff was not sufficiently aware of the company's financial state to be prohibited by section 33(4) from obtaining the relief sought.

(4) Section 33 of the Companies (Amendment) Act 1990 did not impose a collective responsibility on a board of directors in respect of the manner in which a company has been run. Section 33 operates individually and personally against the officers (which includes the directors) of a company and the onus rests on the plaintiff to prove in relation to each of the defendants that his conduct falls within the ambit of conduct prohibited or liable to be penalised by section 33.

(5) The inclusion of the word "knowingly" in section 33(1)(a) of the 1990 Act requires that the director be party to carrying on the business in a manner which the director knows very well involves an obvious and serious risk of loss or damage to others and yet ignores that risk because he does not really care whether such others suffer loss or damage or because his selfish desire to keep his own company alive overrides any concern which he ought to have for others.

(6) The first defendant was not a party to the carrying on of any business of the company in a reckless manner within the meaning of section 33(1)(a) of the 1990 Act: he and the second defendant had borrowed money personally in order to improve the company's cash flow; the decision to continue trading had been taken in the belief that to do so would improve the position of the creditors and this was supported in the examiner's report; the decision had been taken on the basis that the company would not incur further debts and the first defendant, in common with the other defendants had co-operated fully with the examiner.

(7) Section 33(2) of the Act does not affect or extend the meaning of subsection (1)(a) but it extends the application of subsection (1)(a) to the cases mentioned in paragraph (a) and (b) of subsection (2) even though the director was not guilty of reckless trading within the meaning of subsection (1)(a) itself.

(8) Subsection (2) deems a director to be guilty of reckless trading in the circumstances set out in paragraphs (a) and (b) and that presupposes that otherwise he would not be so guilty.

(9) By virtue of subsection (2)(a) a director is deemed to have been knowingly guilty of reckless trading if he ought to have known that his actions or those of the company would cause loss to creditors of the company or any of them: it was not sufficient that there might be some worry or uncertainty as to the ability to pay all creditors.

(10) The first defendant did not fall within the ambit of section 33(2)(a) for the period between 29 August and 27 September 1990.

(11) The first defendant was neither within the ambit of section 33(2)(b) during that period as the plaintiff had not established that he had not honestly believed on reasonable grounds that the company would be able to pay its debts when they fell due, taking into account the contingent and prospective liabilities.

(12) However, after that period the company continued to incur debts when

all the defendants knew that it was insolvent and therefore the first defendant came within section 33(2)(b) for that period.

(13) In all the circumstances the first defendant should be relieved of personal liability under section 33(6) as he had acted honestly and reasonably. The court can relieve an officer from personal liability even if the evidence did not show that he had taken every step to minimise loss that he ought to have taken.

(14) These findings applied to all defendants.

(15) It was a condition precedent under section 33(3)(b) to the granting of such a declaration under section 33(1) that the plaintiff prove that it had suffered loss and damage and the loss and damage suffered during the time that the defendants were held to have been guilty of reckless trading was so trivial as not to be within the meaning of loss or damage contemplated by section 33(3)(b).

Cases referred to in judgment

Albert E. Reid & Co. Ltd v. London and Rochester Trading Co. Ltd [1954] 2 Lloyds Rep 463
Andrews v. DPP [1937] AC 576
Angus v. Clifford (1891) 2 Ch 449
Battle v. Irish Art Promotion Centre [1968] IR 252
Breslin v. Brennan [1937] IR 350
Donovan v. Landys Ltd [1963] IR 441
Excelsior Wire Rope Co. Ltd v. Callan [1930] AC 404
Gardner v. Lucas (1878) 3 App Cas 582
Hamilton v. Hamilton [1982] IR 466
In re Hefferon Kearns Ltd (No. 1) [1993] 3 IR 177
In re Hunting Lodges Ltd (in liquidation) [1985] ILRM 75
O'H. v. O'H. [1990] 2 IR 558
R v. Bates and Russel [1953] 1 WLR 77
R v. Grunwald [1960] 3 All ER 380
R v. MacKinnon [1959] 3 All ER 657
Re Produce Marketing Consortium Ltd (No. 2) [1989] BCLC 520
Re West Mercia Safety Wear [1988] BCLC 250
Salomon v. Salomon & Co. Ltd [1897] AC 22
Shawinigan v. Vokins & Co. [1961] 1 WLR 1206

Frank Clarke SC and Bill Shipsey BL instructed by *Matheson Ormsby Prentice* **for the plaintiff**
John Cooke SC and Brian O'Moore BL instructed by *Beauchamps* **for the defendants**

LYNCH J **14 January 1993**

This is an application pursuant to section 33 of the Companies (Amendment) Act 1990 (the Act) brought in the course of proceedings under the Act relating to a company known as Hefferon Kearns Ltd ("the company") for a declaration that the defendants and each of them as directors and officers of the company at all material times be personally responsible, without any limitation of liability, for the debts or other liabilities of the company on the grounds alleged that they were, while officers of the company, knowingly parties to the carrying on of the business of the company in a reckless manner. The plaintiffs are creditors of the company and bring this application as such creditors.

The Facts

The plaintiffs are heating and plumbing contractors and have been in that business for many years in the Dublin area. The principal shareholders of the plaintiffs are Mr Patrick Mahon and Mr Maurice Mortell, both of whom manage and control the plaintiffs and work full time in its business. Mr Mahon's wife has a minority shareholding. Mr Mahon personally supervises the heating and plumbing work on site and Mr Mortell looks after the office and accounts of the plaintiffs. The plaintiffs are engaged in the domestic rather than the industrial market and they work mainly as heating and plumbing sub-contractors to a main contractor who would be building a scheme of houses.

The company was incorporated in May 1988 and commenced trading in January 1989. It has an issued paid up share capital of only £202 and the shares are held as to 27.5% by the first defendant: as to 27.5% by the second defendant: as to 15% by the third defendant: as to 15% by the fourth defendant: and as to 15% by a person no longer a party to these proceedings because he ceased to take any part in the running of the company before the matters giving rise to these proceedings arose.

The first and second defendants became partners in the building industry many years ago and had connections with Sligo as well as Dublin. They formed a building company called H.K. Contractors Ltd of which they were the sole equal shareholders and which did building work in Sligo and Dublin. The first defendant was mainly engaged in negotiating and pricing contracts as well as supervising: the second defendant was mainly engaged in site supervision and getting the work done. H.K. Contractors Ltd prospered and the first and second defendants found themselves over stretched between jobs in Sligo and increasing business in Dublin. Accordingly they took on the third defendant as office manager and financial controller and the fourth defendant as quantity surveyor to assist in pricing and supervising jobs and generally advising as to costs. Originally it was envisaged that the third and fourth defendants would join H.K. Contractors Ltd and take a shareholding in that company but on advice of that company's auditors, who also became auditors to the company, it was decided to incorporate a new company namely the company in which the third and fourth defendants would and did take a shareholding as already set out. The main reason for this was to protect the third and fourth defendants against possible unforeseen liabilities in H.K. Contractors Ltd if they were to become shareholders and employees of that company.

The company took over the business but not the liabilities of H.K. Contractors Ltd as from 1 January 1989. H.K. Contractors Ltd continued to exist and discharged all its liabilities and carried on business in a minor way especially as it was a member of the National Builders Guarantee Scheme of which the company was not. For this reason on sales of houses built by the company H.K.

Construction Ltd were named as the builders in order to give the benefit of the National Builders Guarantee Scheme to the buyer and the company, although the real builder, was treated as sub-contractor to H.K. Contractors Ltd.

At all material times the company had three main contracts which require to be considered. Firstly there was a development of top of the market type houses at Simmonscourt Road, Ballsbridge, Dublin 4. This development was planned to be carried out in three phases, the first comprising seven houses, the second comprising seven or eight houses and the third comprising four or five houses. The owner/developer of the lands being so developed at Simmonscourt was a company called Senna Enterprises Ltd (Senna). The issued shares in Senna were held as to 57% between the first and second defendants equally, as to 33% by a Mr Barra Flynn, Solicitor of Athlone and as to 10% by Mrs Kilfeather, wife of the auditor of the company and of H.K. Contractors Ltd. The first phase of this development at Simmonscourt was intended to be commenced by the company in 1989 but was in fact not commenced until January 1990. No formal contract was ever entered into between Senna and the company and the work was undertaken on the basis of a quotation furnished by the company to Senna in 1989 which was itself based on a bill of quantities prepared for Senna by Mr Donelan of Messrs George C. Kavanagh & Co, Quantity Surveyors.

The second main contract on which the company was engaged at the material times was a development of high class houses not quite as luxurious as the Simmonscourt houses, at Grove Road, Malahide, County Dublin. The owner/developer of these lands at Malahide was a company called Darwood Builders Ltd (Darwood). The issued shares in Darwood were all held equally between the first and second defendants. Again no formal contract was ever entered into between Darwood and the company and the work was undertaken on the basis of a quotation by the company to Darwood based either on estimates prepared by the fourth defendant or there may have been an independent quantity surveyor for this scheme also but this was left unclear by the evidence.

The third main contract on which the company was engaged at the material times was a development of mixed type dwellings at Rathgar Road, Dublin 6. The owner/developer of these lands at Rathgar Road was a company called Irish Daily News Ltd (I.D.N.). None of the defendants had any shareholding or interest in I.D.N. and the work was undertaken by the company pursuant to a formal building contract executed by I.D.N. and the company. This development at Rathgar was the only work being done by the company at the material times for a completely independent and unrelated person or company. The company at the material times was also doing some other less extensive contract work for other related companies and minor work for some of the defendants personally on their dwelling houses.

As already stated the company commenced trading in January 1989. Management accounts prepared for the half year ending 30 June 1989 by the company's auditors showed a net loss of £73,101 which might well be regarded as indicating insolvency at that time. However the summer had arrived: the company had good contracts on hand: and the defendants as directors, having considered the position, were confident that the losses could be reversed and were proved right in that the audited accounts for the year ending 31 December 1989 showed a net loss of only £8,113.

As a result of the loss for the year 1989 the defendants on the advice of their auditor decided to obtain bi-monthly management accounts in an effort to keep the trading position of the company under closer scrutiny and control. Bi-monthly accounts accordingly became available for the two months ending 28 February 1990 on 9 April 1990: for the two months ending 30 April 1990 on 18 June 1990: and for the two months ending 30 June 1990 by telephone on a very brief basis to the first defendant on 31 July 1990 and shortly thereafter in writing but arriving during the time of the building trade's annual holidays and not coming to the attention of the defendants until on or shortly after 22 August 1990. These three sets of bi-monthly accounts showed net losses respectively of £23,965, £38,747 and £71,682 giving a total net loss for the half year ending 30 June 1990 of £134,394. Adding the loss of £8,313 in the year ending 31 December 1989 and crediting paid up issued share capital of £202 left the balance sheet deficit at 30 June 1990 at £142,507. If a deficit of approximately £73,000 at 30 June 1989 indicated a possible insolvency at that time obviously a deficit of over £142,000 at 30 June 1990 indicated a very serious crisis as to the viability of the company at that time.

In May 1990 the first and second defendants had borrowed £45,000 from Merchant Bankers and had paid the same directly into the company's bank account with Allied Irish Banks Plc in Crumlin. As this was not exactly what was intended, that sum was repaid to the first and second defendants on 10 July 1990 but on the same day was again paid in to the company's account in the form of various payments on behalf of related companies which were indebted to the company. The effect of this transaction was that the company's cash flow was improved by £45,000 but this did not alter its balance sheet position since the same amount of debts due by related companies were discharged. Nevertheless it did involve the first and second defendants in incurring personal liability to the merchant bank in order to improve the company's cash flow. That transaction was initiated following the receipt of the accounts for the two months ending 28 February 1990 showing a loss of £23,965 and was adjusted on 10 July 1990 following receipt of the accounts for the two months ending 30 April 1990 showing a loss of £38,747. Those latter accounts were considered at a meeting of the company's directors on 24 June 1990. The company had ample work on its books: the summer was at hand, and the defendants' directors were of the opinion that they should be able to reverse these losses in the second half of the year 1990 just as they had done in the case of the losses incurred in the first half of 1989.

In April 1990 the fourth defendant was very busy with other work and accordingly the company engaged an independent quantity surveyor Mr Brian Hollingsworth to value the work done by the company on the Simmonscourt site with a view to making claims for further interim payments and ascertaining the likely outcome of that contract for the company. Mr Hollingsworth prepared a claim for an interim payment, number 6, which was certified by the architects and duly paid in the sum of £174,269 less retention. Mr Hollingsworth thereafter prepared a claim for the seventh interim payment in the sum of approximately £68,000 but also in or about May 1990 Mr Barra Flynn who had no interest in the company but had a 33% interest in Senna was anxious to ascertain the likely total cost and outcome of phase 1 of the Simmonscourt Development. Accordingly on behalf of Senna he engaged Mr Donelan, the quantity surveyor who had prepared the bill of quantities to carry out a comprehensive valuation of the work done by the company in Simmonscourt. Mr Donelan contended that up to and including the sixth interim payment the company had been overpaid by £85,000 and that accordingly not only was the seventh interim payment not due but that giving credit for the work done since the sixth interim payment the company was still overpaid by some £17,000. This was strenuously contested by the company who were confident that at least £50,000 was due by way of a seventh payment but this dispute was never resolved before the company was taken under the protection of the court pursuant to the Act.

The building trade holidays ended on Tuesday, 21 August and building work resumed on Wednesday, 22 August 1990. In the days immediately following 22 August the accounts to 30 June 1990 were considered by the defendants individually. The defendants normally met for informal directors' meetings on Mondays and on Monday, 22 August 1990 they met and considered the position of the company in the light of the accounts to the half year ending 30 June 1990.

At their meeting on 27 August 1990 it was agreed that an urgent review of the company's trading was required and different directors were assigned to examine the prospects of the jobs on hand. The first defendant valued the Simmonscourt development and came to the conclusion that the cost of completion of the first phase of that development would equal the balance price and the only benefit to the company would be the release of the retention monies of approximately £30,000. The first defendant also valued the Malahide development and concluded that it would be profitable but not until about the latter end of November to mid-December 1990. The fourth defendant valued the Rathgar contract and concluded that the completion of that contract would yield substantial monies because that contract provided for the retention of very large sums pending completion and there was at the end of August 1990 over £200,000 of work already done and not paid for. The timescale for Rathgar was also better in that it might be completed by the middle of November 1990. The defendants were most anxious to complete the Rathgar contract so as to get in these monies for the benefit of the company and its creditors and were fearful that if they were unable to complete it they might lose the substantial retention monies which had already been earned. In addition the defendants were confident that there was at least £50,000 due on the Simmonscourt contract for work done before 30 June 1990 despite Mr Donelan's claims and these monies were not included in the June accounts and if included would reduce the loss to the end of June 1990 to about £80,000 to £90,000, not all that much different from the position at 30 June 1989. Moreover the third defendant and through him the other defendants were reasonably confident that the company would get in enough monies from debtors at the end of August and beginning of September 1990 to enable the company to discharge all debts falling due to creditors on 31 August 1990. The defendants therefore decided at their meeting on 27 August 1990 to continue trading: to give priority to the Rathgar contract whilst trying to complete the other contracts also: and to try to control and reduce costs as far as possible. In addition the defendants required the company's auditors to prepare accounts for the two months and the eight months ending 31 August 1990 and to do so on a doomsday basis, that is to say charging and assuming everything possible against the company, in order to assist the defendants in deciding whether the company was viable and what should be done about the company and its affairs.

The company did succeed in getting in at the end of August and beginning of September sufficient monies to enable it to discharge all debts falling due to its creditors on 31 August 1990 but by mid-September 1990 the third defendant and through him the other defendants knew that the company would have great difficulty in paying the accounts which would fall due for payment on 30 September 1990. On Monday, 17 September a meeting of the defendants as directors was arranged to consider the position further, the meeting to be in the third defendant's house.

The first defendant arrived at the third defendant's house before the second and fourth defendants and almost at once collapsed and had to be removed to St Vincent's Hospital where he was detained as an in-patient until 27 September 1990. Notwithstanding that the first defendant had been advised by his doctors to rest for a week following his discharge from hospital, within hours of his discharge on 27 September a meeting of the defendants as directors took place in his house. At that meeting on Thursday, 27 September which was continued into Friday, 28 September 1990, the first defendant made rough manuscript minutes which I am satisfied accurately record the proceedings and decisions taken at that meeting. I quote these minutes translating abbreviations into full words as follows:

> "Hefferon Kearns Ltd Board meeting
> 27, 28 September 1990
> Present all defendants
>
> Reviewing the situation since the August 27 meeting.
>
> There is considerable doubt as to whether we can finish Simmonscourt for the amounts in the balance.
>
> Therefore the £35,000 approximately of retention is not available. Therefore we should abandon Simmonscourt contract.
>
> It is generally agreed that there are profits of £20,000 to £30,000 to be earned in Malahide but it is felt too far to stretch management. We should rescind this contract.
>
> Rathgar has £300,000 to come in plus extras and claims with £150,000 to go out and this represents our best chance to get money for creditors.

How do we do it?

Cullen has agreed to pay cash as needed to finish Rathgar job. Therefore we take no further credit from any supplier. Therefore third defendant ensure this is done.

The first and third defendants to approach all creditors to get their agreement starting with Chadwicks on Monday.

We will require a moratorium from all creditors and will have to be seen to be fair to each of them as per resolution proposed. Such an arrangement will be fairer to all suppliers and sub-contractors than liquidation.

Action

Cease with Hefferon Kearns (or perhaps it is Michael Kearns) and sort out Darwood — for second defendant.

Work in progress valuation for Hefferon Kearns in Malahide 30/9/90 — for first defendant.

Inform Flynn/Kilfeather re: Senna — for first defendant.

Move out of office. Set up in Rathgar — for third defendant and first defendant.

Rathgar value at 30/9/90 — for fourth defendant.

Arrange new set of communications — for third defendant.

Meet Monday morning to draw up list of key creditors — for first defendant and third defendant.

Advise Dave Cullen and Brendan Bushell — for first defendant and third defendant".

The reference to a Mr Cullen is to the person representing I.D.N. regarding the Rathgar contract. He and I.D.N. agreed with the first defendant to assist the company in carrying out the Rathgar contract without incurring further debts by financing the company on a weekly as needed basis.

The accounts for the two months and the eight months ending 31 August 1990 were prepared on or about 25 September 1990 but were not available for the meeting of the defendants on 27 and 28 September 1990 and did not become available until the first week of October 1990. These accounts showed a balance sheet deficit of £411,679. However even on a doomsday basis these accounts seem to be erroneous in that the balance sheet shows debtors and prepayments to be only £18,647 whereas the balance due as at 31 August 1990 on the Rathgar contract was £207,696 but then, as appears later in this judgment, the examiner appointed by the court arrived at a similar deficit figure in his reports.

The first and third defendants began calling to see the company's creditors on Monday 1 October 1990. They had hoped to inform each creditor personally and get his co-operation in half an hour or so, but this proved impossible and discussions with individual creditors would go on for hours. This was a very difficult exercise for the first and third defendants and in addition people called to their houses and in general I accept the third defendant's description at this stage of the matter as involving extreme pressure and a nightmare. Eventually the first and third defendants decided that it was impossible to see all creditors individually and instead the defendants decided to call a meeting of creditors for 11 October 1990 at which the creditors by a majority decided to apply for the appointment of an examiner under the provisions of the Act. The examiner was provisionally appointed on 12 October 1990 and confirmed on 22 October 1990.

In his first report dated 12 November 1990 the examiner found an excess of liabilities over assets of £432,379. In his second report dated 7 December 1990 the examiner proposed a scheme of arrangement for the survival of the company. This scheme included provision, with the consent of the first and second defendants, for making available for the benefit of the creditors of the company, of the first and second defendants' shareholding in Senna and Darwood. The scheme was accepted by the Revenue Commissioners and was also accepted by a majority of the creditors. However the examiner also reported that if proceedings under section 33 of the Act for alleged reckless trading were brought, the proposed scheme ought not to be implemented and this is in fact what has happened and the company is now in liquidation. It is not disputed that the plaintiffs are creditors of the company and therefore entitled to bring this application under section 33 of the Act but the amount of their debt is disputed. The plaintiffs' claim that the company owes them £41,694. The defendants claim that the amount of the debt is £31,500. I am satisfied that the plaintiffs are correct and that the company is indebted to them in the sum of £41,694. The plaintiffs as already stated are in the domestic housing market and while profitable they are not in a very big way of business. Through Messrs Mahon and Mortell the plaintiffs have always run their business in a careful and prudent manner such that they can pay their creditors promptly and fully provide a good living for their directors and owners.

A bad debt of £41,694 or indeed even £31,500 is a very severe blow to the plaintiffs and Messrs Mahon and Mortell justifiably felt very let down by what happened to the company. They were both under the impression that the company was the owner of the valuable sites at Simmonscourt and Malahide where the plaintiffs were working for the company. With this belief the plaintiffs were not unduly worried when a cheque for £10,000 was dishonoured in July 1990 but immediately honoured on re-presentation and when there was considerable slowness in getting in the balance outstanding at the end of August 1990. However, neither the company nor any of the defendants had ever stated to the plaintiffs that the company was the owner of either of those sites and the plaintiffs simply assumed that that was so. It was a great shock to the plaintiffs in the persons of Messrs Mahon and Mortell when they learned for the first time at the meeting of creditors on 11 October 1990 that the company did not own those sites and that they were instead owned by Senna and Darwood respectively. What up to then had seemed to the plaintiffs to be a debt which would be overdue for sometime but would ultimately be paid suddenly began to look like a bad debt of a devastating amount for the plaintiffs.

The plaintiffs in the persons of Messrs Mahon and Mortell were furious and extremely suspicious of the motivation behind the ownership of the sites by separate development companies rather than by the company. They were convinced that a fraud had been perpetrated on the plaintiffs and the other creditors of the company and they remained so convinced right up to the trial before me and quite possibly still remain so convinced. They emphasised the attempt by Senna to write down the value of the work done on the Simmonscourt site by £85,000. Mr Mahon stated in evidence that the company had built a house for the third defendant which must have cost about £160,000 to build as it exceeded two thousand square feet in area and only £50,000 was paid for it. Mr Mortell stated in evidence that there were large undercharges by the company to Senna and Darwood and the first and second defendants were the beneficiaries of the losses in the company. It was apparent to me that the plaintiffs' real claim was against the first and second defendants and not really the third and fourth defendants and was motivated by the belief that the first and second defendants were either the sole owners or substantial owners of various related companies including Senna and Darwood for which the company was doing building work and that all such building work was being done at wholly uneconomic prices to the benefit of the first and second defendants through their related companies and to the detriment of the company and its creditors. The third and fourth defendants were joined as defendants really for conformity only on the basis that they were directors of the company but without any real wish to fix them with liability despite Mr Mahon's evidence about the third defendant's house. That allegation that the third defendant had a house built for himself by the company for one third of its cost was not even put to the third defendant in cross-examination.

The foregoing perception of the first and second defendants by Messrs Mahon and Mortell is very genuinely and indeed vehemently held but I am satisfied is unwarranted. The prices quoted by the company on the contracts, including the wholly third party contract with I.D.N. for the Rathgar site, were keen but when account was taken of the widespread use of country labour instead of Dublin labour by the company the prices could have realised a modest profit and the contracts were entered into at arm's length. With keen prices however, it was essential to exercise very close supervision of jobs so as to avoid any cost over-runs whether through waste labour or waste material. Because in the year 1990 especially the company had too many jobs on hand spread over too wide an area in Dublin, stretching from Dalkey to Malahide, it was not possible to exercise that close supervision which was required and this, rather than the keen prices, was the real cause of the losses sustained by the company and its failure.

So far as work done on their dwelling houses for the defendants personally is concerned I am satisfied that this was charged at cost plus 5% nominal profit, plus 10% VAT. This price was agreed by the defendants as directors at the outset of the company's trading and was designed and intended to ensure that any work done by the company for any of the defendants/directors would not cost the company anything and would generate enough gross profit to cover overheads and perhaps leave a nominal profit.

As regards the first and second defendants benefiting through Senna and Darwood from the losses in the company, this is wholly misconceived by Messrs Mahon and Mortell. The first and second defendants made their shareholding in Senna and Darwood available for the benefit of the creditors of the company in the scheme of arrangement proposed by the examiner. This is not to say that such shareholding would have been of much if any value. The company and Senna and Darwood were unlucky to be caught by a serious downturn in the property market which happened quite suddenly in the summer of 1990. As a result the houses in Simmonscourt which had been expected to make on average over £250,000 each had to be sold for less than £200,000 average. Senna collapsed owing over half a million pounds and with it went a valuable property in Fosters Avenue which had been given as security to the bank to help finance the purchase of the Simmonscourt site. The whole Simmonscourt project ended up as a disaster and as the first defendant put it in common parlance in evidence before me "all our money went down the tubes". This would not have happened if the Simmonscourt show-house had been ready in January 1990 as had originally been planned with contracts for the sale of houses following shortly thereafter but the work did not in fact start until January 1990 and because of various unusual and sophisticated features of the houses, proceeded much more slowly than was anticipated and the showhouses did not unfortunately open for viewing until June of 1990.

As regards the suggested write down of £85,000 in the value of the work done by the company at Simmonscourt for Senna, this matter has already been shortly referred to. It arose when Mr Flynn, who had a 33% interest in Senna but no interest in the company, became concerned at the costs arising in the Senna development from claimed extras and variations as well as at the quality of some of the work done. He engaged Mr Donelan to value the work done and advise as to the likely total cost of the job to Senna. The company for its part engaged Mr Hollingsworth on a like exercise on its behalf and both these gentlemen were independent qualified quantity surveyors. The claimed write down of £85,000 was never accepted by the company and the dispute was never resolved but it is quite clear to me that there was nothing sinister or collusive in this matter. As regards the existence of separate development companies the third defendant stated in evidence that he believed that the plaintiffs through Messrs Mahon and Mortell were aware that there were separate development companies and the third defendant gave two instances from which he said such knowledge followed. He said that Mr Mahon passed a remark in February 1990, when upset about chopping and changing of the work done at Simmonscourt, that they never knew whether they were working for the developer or the builder. The third defendant also said that he showed Mr Mortell around the showhouse in Simmonscourt in June 1990 and that Mr Mortell said that the plaintiffs do the day-to-day things and the developer profits. Despite the third defendant's opinion it is clear to me that it does not follow from these two remarks that the plaintiffs through Messrs Mahon and Mortell knew that the company was not the owner of the sites at Simmonscourt and Malahide. I am in fact satisfied that they did not know this and that they took the references by some of the defendants to slowness in getting contracts signed for the sale of houses in Simmonscourt and Malahide as meaning that the company owned those sites. Messrs Mahon and Mortell were indeed shocked to learn for the first time at the creditors' meeting on 11 October 1990 that the company did not in fact own those sites. Nevertheless the existence of a development company as owner of a development site and separate from the building company which will actually do the work on the site is the norm rather than the exception and is so for good commercial reasons. The unchallenged evidence was that banks will readily lend to a separate development company as owner of the lands but will be reluctant to lend to a building company who owns the lands in view of the uncertainties in the building trade. I am satisfied that it was for these and other sound commercial reasons that the Simmonscourt and the Malahide sites and other sites on which the company was working were owned by development companies and not by the company. In any event in the case of Simmonscourt I accept the evidence that the bank required the security of another valuable property in Fosters Avenue which was owned as to half by Mr Flynn, one sixth by Mr Kilfeather and one third equally between the first and second defendants and the bank was not satisfied with the security of the Simmonscourt lands alone. I am satisfied that there was nothing underhand or sharp or wrong in that the various building sites were owned by development companies and not by the company.

Finally regarding the belief of the plaintiffs that the first and second defendants profited from the failure of the company, the unchallenged evidence before me was that on 9 October 1990 the first and second defendants signed personal guarantees in respect of the company's indebtedness to Allied Irish Banks Plc in Crumlin. As I have already said the whole venture with the company ended up as a financial disaster for everybody.

The law and submissions

Introduction

Although the plaintiffs' motivation for these proceedings is a belief that a fraud was perpetrated on them by the defendants and especially the first and second defendants, these proceedings are not based on an allegation of fraudulent trading under section 297 of the Companies Act 1963, which in any case only applies in a winding-up, but are based on an allegation of reckless trading under section 33 of the Act which only applies in the course of examinership proceedings under the Act. It is necessary for me therefore to consider the facts in the light of section 33 and to put aside the motivation of the plaintiffs insofar as it is irrelevant to section 33. If the plaintiffs are entitled to relief under section 33 then they must be granted such relief and the fact that they erroneously believe themselves to be more wronged than is necessary for them to prove under section 33 is irrelevant.

Section 33 of the Act provides as follows:

> "33.–(1) If in the course of proceedings under this Act it appears that:
> (a) Any person was, while an officer of the company, knowingly a party to the carrying on of any business of the company in a reckless manner: or
> (b) Any person was knowingly a party to the carrying on of any business of the company with intent to defraud creditors of the company, or creditors of any other person or for any fraudulent purpose:
> The court, on the application of the examiner, or any creditor or contributory of the company, may, if it thinks it proper to do so, declare that such person shall be personally responsible, without any limitation of liability, for all or any part of the debts or other liabilities of the company as the court may direct.
> (2) Without prejudice to the generality of subsection (1)(a), an officer of a company shall be deemed to have been knowingly a party to the carrying on of any business of the company in a reckless manner if —
> (a) He was a party to the carrying on of such business and, having regard to the general knowledge, skill and experience that may reasonably be expected of a person in his position, he ought to have known that his actions or those of the company would cause loss to the creditors of the company, or any of them, or
> (b) He was a party to the contracting of a debt by the company and did not honestly believe on reasonable grounds that the company would be able to pay the debt when it fell due for payment as well as all its other debts (taking into account the contingent and prospective liabilities).
> (3) Notwithstanding anything contained in subsection (1) the court may grant a declaration on the grounds set out in paragraph (a) of that subsection only if —
> (a) paragraph (a), (b) or (c) of section 214 of the principal Act applies to the company concerned, and
> (b) an applicant for such a declaration, being a creditor or contributory of the company, or any person on whose behalf such application is made, suffered loss or damage as a consequence of any behaviour mentioned in subsection (1).
> (4) In deciding whether it is proper to make an order on the grounds set out in subsection (2)(b), the court shall have regard to whether the creditor in question was, at the time the debt was incurred, aware of the company's financial state of affairs and, notwithstanding such awareness, nevertheless assented to the incurring of the debt.
> (5) On the hearing of an application under this section, the applicant may himself give evidence or call witnesses.
> (6) Where it appears to the court that any person in respect of whom a declaration has been sought under subsection (1)(a) has acted honestly and responsibly in relation to the conduct of the affairs of the company or

any matter or matters on the ground of which such declaration is sought to be made, the court may, having regard to all the circumstances of the case, relieve him either wholly or in part, from personal liability on such terms as it may think fit.

(7) Where the court makes any such declaration, it may —

(a) give such further directions as it thinks proper for the purpose of giving effect to the declaration and in particular make provision for making the liability of any such person under the declaration a charge on any debt or obligation due from the company to him, or on any mortgage or charge or any interest in any mortgage or charge on any assets of the company held by or vested in him or any company or person on his behalf, or any person claiming as assignee from or through the person liable or any company or any person acting on his behalf, and may from time to time make such further Orders as may be necessary for the purpose of enforcing any charge under this subsection.

(b) Provide that sums recovered under this section shall be paid to such person or classes of persons, for such purposes, in such amounts or proportions at such time or times and in such respective priorities among themselves as such declaration may specify.

(8) This section shall have effect notwithstanding that —

(a) the person in respect of whom the declaration has been sought under subsection (1) may be criminally liable in respect of the matters on the ground of which such declaration is to be made: or

(b) any matter or matters on the grounds of which the declaration under subsection (1) is to be made have occurred outside the State.

(9) Subsection (1)(a) shall not apply during a period when the company is under the protection of the Court.

(10) For the purposes of this section —

assignee includes any person to whom or in whose favour, by the directions of the person liable, the debt, obligation, mortgage or charge was created, issued or transferred or the interest created, but does not include an assignee for valuable consideration (not including consideration by way of marriage) given in good faith and without notice of any of the matter on the grounds of which the declaration is made:

Company includes any body which may be wound up under the Companies Acts: and

Officer includes any auditor, liquidator, receiver, or any person in accordance with whose directions or instructions the directors of the company are accustomed to act".

There are some matters arising out of the foregoing provisions which I should deal with first before turning to the submissions made on behalf of the parties.

First, the Act was passed and became operative on 29 August 1990. A preliminary issue in this case has already been before the High Court and was decided in a reserved judgment delivered by Murphy J on 5 July 1991. That judgment declared that section 33(1) of the Act is not retrospective in its effect and that the plaintiffs were not precluded from bringing proceedings under section 33 by section 5 of the Act. It follows from Murphy J's decision that the only period in respect of which the defendants could incur liability for reckless trading is the period from 29 August to 11 October 1990 inclusive, the company having come under the protection of the court on 12 October 1990. This does not mean that I cannot have regard to acts done or omitted or knowledge acquired by the defendants before 29 August 1990 in deciding whether or not acts done or omitted between 29 August and 11 October 1990 constituted reckless trading. To quote from Murphy J's judgment at page 8:

> "Another example of legislation referring to earlier events but not itself operating retrospectively is to be found in the decision of Mr Justice Barron in *O'H. v. O'H.* in a judgment delivered on 22 June 1990. As Mr Justice Barron pointed out (at page 6 of the transcript) a distinction must be drawn between applying the new law to past events and taking past events into account in applying the new law. He quoted with approval a further passage from *Craie* on Statute Law as follows:
>
>> But a statute is not properly called a retrospective statute because a part of the requisites for its action is drawn from a time antecedent to its passing".

As regards the debts or other liabilities of the company for which the defendants might be made personally responsible if found guilty of reckless trading between 29 August and 11 October 1990, counsel for the plaintiffs submitted that they might be made liable for all such debts or liabilities whether incurred before or after the 29 August 1990. I disagree and I quote again from the judgment of Murphy J at page 9 and 10 of the transcript:

> "That legislation should operate in this way is not readily inferred. Again the Common Law principles in this regard are summarised in the decision of the Chief Justice in *Hamilton v. Hamilton* [1982] IR 466 (at page 474) by reference to the decision in *Gardner v. Lucas* (1878) 3 App Cas 582, 601 as follows:
>
>> "Unless there is some declared intention of the legislature — clear and unequivocal — or unless there are some circumstances rendering it inevitable that we should take the other view, we are to presume that an Act is prospective and is not retrospective'."
>
> The Common Law construction was based on the presumption that parliament did not intend to create the injustice which would normally flow from retrospective legislation. In this country one can deduce with

greater certainty the intention of the legislature because of the particular obligations imposed upon it by the Constitution. In the case of *Hamilton v. Hamilton* a retrospective construction of section 3 of the Family Home Protection Act 1976 would have prejudiced the rights of the purchaser of premises which, subsequent to the date of the purchase, became a family home by virtue of that Act. It followed that such a construction not merely conflicted with the presumed intention of the legislature under Common Law but would have involved a conflict with the constitutional rights of the citizen and the constitutional obligations of the Oireachtas. As O'Higgins CJ said (at page 477):

> "However when one considers that this is an Act of the Oireachtas, the proposition that it was intended to affect and frustrate pre-existing contractual rights becomes unstateable. Were this legislation to have the effect contended for, it would constitute an unjust attack upon and a failure by the State to vindicate the property rights of (the purchaser) and of others similarly situated, and would constitute a clear infringement of the provisions of Article 40, Section 3, subsection 2 of the Constitution."

If a defendant in this case were made liable for a debt of the company incurred before 29 August 1990 on the basis of reckless trading after that date, that would involve making that defendant liable for an act done or omitted by him before 29 August which at the time of its commission or omission created no liability in the defendant personally and was no infringement of the law by him at that time. Consequently a personal liability cannot be imputed to a defendant for such a debt contracted before 29 August 1990 having regard to the decision of Murphy J and also to Article 15, section 5 of the Constitution. If the plaintiffs succeed in this claim therefore the maximum liability which could be imposed on the defendants would be a personal liability for all the debts or other liabilities of the company incurred between 29 August and 11 October 1990.

Secondly, it is not in dispute that the company is unable to pay its debts and that section 214 of the Companies Act 1963 therefore applies to the company so as to fulfil the condition contained in section 33(3)(a) of the Act.

Thirdly, it is not seriously disputed and I find as a fact that the company's indebtedness to the plaintiffs increased by approximately £4,500 between 29 August and 11 October 1990. Consequently if reckless trading is established and if it is also established that such trading caused or contributed to that extra indebtedness, the plaintiffs would have satisfied the condition contained in section 33(3)(b) of the Act.

Fourthly I find as a fact that the plaintiffs were not sufficiently aware of the company's financial state of affairs to be affected by section 33(4) of the Act.

Submissions on behalf of the plaintiffs

Section 33 of the Act is an extension of directors' obligations towards the shareholders and creditors of the company, both of whom as well as the examiner can apply under the section. The Oireachtas took the view that the balance in the case of limited liability companies had gone too far in favour of those who managed such companies.

Section 33(2) gives an indication of the type of activities condemned and also contemplates that a director who does not know but ought to know that continued trading will cause loss to creditors may be held to be reckless. It follows that the test as to both paragraphs (a) and (b) of subsection (2) is an objective and not a subjective test and, moreover, a defendant can be made responsible not only for his own acts but also for the acts of the company. The objective nature of the test of recklessness is emphasised by subsection (6) which presupposes that a director may be reckless although he acted honestly and responsibly. The plaintiffs must show that the defendants took an unjustified risk but that is to be assessed on the basis of what they ought to have known and not merely on what they in fact knew. Merely continuing with the business when that fact involved an unjustifiable risk and caused loss to creditors is enough. One would not blame directors if some disastrous event like a fire or the unexpected insolvency of a big debtor caused collapse of their company but one can and should blame them where they continued trading on a serious and increasing loss making basis. While directors are entitled to some time to consider what to do about a loss making position, the time allowed by section 33 is short and they must act promptly because otherwise they are gambling with the creditors' money. If they apply for the appointment of an examiner under the Act the creditors get a hearing: if they do not and just carry on, on their own initiative, the creditors get no hearing although their money is being gambled.

In this case the defendants were aware before 29 August 1990 that three consecutive bi-monthly management accounts showed rapidly increasing losses and that a doubt existed about the monies to be expected from the Simmonscourt development in view of Senna's contention that the work already done had been overvalued and overpaid as at the sixth interim payment by about £85,000. The defendants should have known in August 1990 that there was no reasonable prospect of trading out of the critical position in which the company found itself and they were reckless in resuming work on all sites after the holidays on 22 August 1990 and continuing on all sites until 28 September 1990, a period of some five weeks. During that period the defendants invited the plaintiffs back to do work for the company and so increased the company's indebtedness to the plaintiffs which the company had no reasonable prospect of discharging. There was no prospect of any windfall from Senna or Darwood because lucrative sales of Simmonscourt houses were falling through and being replaced by sales at unprofitable prices and much the same situation applied in Malahide.

In this case a number of creditors are significantly worse off by the continued trading through September and into October and it is not an answer for the defendants to say that on a bulk basis the creditors are not much worse off in view of the reference in subsection (2)(a) to creditors of the company or any of them and in paragraph (b) to the contracting of a debt by the company. In relation to any monies which the court may order any of the defendants personally to pay, priority should be given to the plaintiffs' debt pursuant to subsection (7)(b) because the plaintiffs undertook the risks of the litigation.

Counsel for the plaintiffs, in the course of his submissions, referred to the following authorities: *In The Matter of Hunting Lodges Ltd (In Liquidation)* [1985] ILRM 75; *Re Produce Marketing Consortium Ltd (No. 2)* [1985] BCLC 520 and *Re West Mercia Safety Wear* [1988] BCLC 250.

Submissions on behalf of the defendants

Section 33 involves a radical departure from previous company law and is exceptional and draconian in nature. A court should therefore require strong clear evidence before applying the section and there is no such evidence in this case.

An application under section 33 is part of the court's protection exercise under the Act. Such an application may be made by the examiner and he is required by section 16(i) to include in his report to the court his opinion as to whether an application under section 33 is warranted or not. The examiner, unlike the plaintiffs, had full access to all the books and records of the company and, as he confirmed in his evidence, he had full co-operation and assistance from the defendants. In his second report dated 7 December 1990 the examiner did not recommend that proceedings under section 33 should be undertaken although he did advert to the then threat of such proceedings by the plaintiffs. While the court must make up its own mind, it should give particular weight to the views of the examiner which were not resiled from in any way in his evidence in the course of which he expressed his firm opinion that the defendants were not reckless.

It would be appropriate for an individual creditor like the plaintiffs to bring an application if he was the victim of a particular transaction and so based his case and sought an order to compensate him for the loss occasioned by such transaction. That is not the plaintiffs' case here. They make a case which would be more appropriately made by the examiner. They make a generalised allegation that, because the defendants continued to trade with knowledge of the company's financial problems, they were reckless. That is not so. The plaintiffs must prove some identifiable reckless conduct after 29 August 1990 by some one or more identified defendants and that such behaviour caused identifiable loss to the plaintiffs — subsection (3)(b). Section 33(1)(a) imposes individual personal responsibility and not a collective responsibility on the board of directors as such.

Subsection (1)(a) requires proof that a defendant was not merely reckless but was knowingly reckless. The word reckless is not defined. It is more carelessness. It requires a wilful disregard of a clear risk to creditors from a particular transaction or transactions. A defendant must be shown to have participated knowingly in the business or transaction not inadvertently or mistakenly and he must have had a clear understanding of the risk involved for creditors and gone ahead taking that risk not really caring about the creditors.

As regards subsection (2)(a) the plaintiffs must prove that one or more of the defendants ought to have known that his actions would cause loss to creditors. Thus proof of actual or imputed knowledge is essential: proof of a worry or doubt or uncertainty that loss might be caused to creditors is not enough: it must be knowledge that loss would be caused to a creditor or creditors.

As regards subsection (2)(b) the plaintiffs must prove that one or more of the directors contracted debts after 29 August 1990 with no honest belief that they could be paid and no such evidence has been adduced.

None of the allegations or particulars in the points of claim delivered by the plaintiffs on 7 January 1991 have been established. Section 33 is not intended to give an opportunity to other persons to second guess the commercial judgment of the directors with the benefit of hindsight. The defendants were long established, well respected, hard working members of the building trade and kept average books and records. If there were fraud or reckless trading one would expect at best scanty books and records. Just because a company incurs losses does not mean that it must immediately stop trading. This is especially so where, as in this case, the company has long-term contracts where profits or losses are unlikely to be ascertained with any accuracy until the completion of the contracts. Moreover there may be good reasons to continue trading in order to mitigate losses to creditors rather than liquidate the company. A liquidation causes immediate losses through the write down of debtors and assets and such can be avoided by continuing to trade. In this case the company, by continuing to trade into September, collected over £100,000 from the Rathgar development and also got the support of I.D.N. towards completing that development. These were prudent and reasonable steps negativing reckless conduct.

Regarding subsection (6) this is clearly intended to be a qualification of subsection (2)(a) and (b). It could not apply to subsection (1)(a) because directors could not be both knowingly reckless and honest and responsible at the same time. Sub-section (2)(a) and (b) are not examples of subsection (1)(a). They are extensions of the application of subsection (1)(a) which of itself applies only to a director who was knowingly guilty of reckless trading.

The examiner concluded that the defendants acted responsibly and honestly. If contrary to these submissions the court should find that any of the defendants breached subsection (2)(a) or (b), the court should also find in agreement with the examiner that such defendant acted honestly and responsibly and should therefore apply subsection (6) so as to relieve such defendant wholly from personal liability.

Counsel for the defendants, in the course of his submissions, referred to the following authorities: *Salomon v. Salomon and Company Ltd* [1897] App Cas 22; *Battle v. Irish Art Promotion Centre Ltd* [1968] IR 252; *Donovan v. Landys Ltd* [1963] IR 441; *Angus v. Clifford* (1891) 2 Ch 449 and section 214 of the English Insolvency Act 1986

Conclusions

At the outset I should say that I am satisfied that section 33 of the Act does not impose a collective responsibility on a board of directors as such in respect of the manner in which a company has been run. Section 33 operates individually and personally against the officers (which includes the directors) of a company and the onus rests on the plaintiffs to prove in relation to each of the defendants in this case that his conduct falls within the ambit of conduct prohibited or liable to be penalised by section 33. For example, it was conceded on behalf of the plaintiffs that, as between the defendants, they had adduced the least evidence against the fourth defendant but it was nevertheless contended that the court should infer that the fourth defendant had full knowledge of the company's parlous financial state and assented to the continuance of the business notwithstanding such knowledge and was therefore liable to an order under section 33.

The plaintiffs' case was most strongly made against the first defendant and linked with him was the second defendant. The first defendant appears to have been the most authoritative of the directors and to have been regarded as the *de facto* managing director of the company although it does not appear from the evidence that any such office formally existed in the company. I intend to consider the case in the first instance therefore mainly as against the first defendant and thereafter to deal with the case as against the other three defendants.

I must first consider the meaning of section 33(1)(a) of the Act. The meaning of the expression "reckless" has been considered under different branches of the law including the criminal law and law of tort. In *Halsbury*, 4th Edition re issue volume II(1) at paragraph 14 it is stated:

> "Recklessness on the part of the accused is sufficient *mens rea* for certain statutory offences and the common law crime of manslaughter: and for these purposes a person is reckless if he has done an act which in fact involves an obvious risk of causing injury or damage and either (1) he fails to give any thought to the possibility of there being any such risk: or (2) having recognised that there is some risk involved he nonetheless goes on to take it."

In the law of torts the meaning of "reckless' was considered by the Supreme Court in the case of *Donovan v. Landys Ltd* [1963] IR 441 in which at pages 460 to 462 Kingsmill Moore J said:

> "The varying opinions of judges can be illustrated from recent cases. In *R v. Bates and Russell*, Donovan J had to consider the meaning of the reckless making of any statement in section 12, subsection (1) of the Prevention of Fraud Investments Act. He held that recklessness connoted no more than a high degree of negligence. In *R v. MacKinnon*, Salmon J construing the same words held that reckless making of a statement meant a statement not caring whether it was true or false and imported an element of dishonesty or fraud. In *R v. Grunwald*, Paul J rejected both those interpretations and held that the statement must be a rash statement made

by a person who had no real basis of fact on which he could support it. Lord Atkin in *Andrews v. Director of Public Prosecutions* at page 583 suggests that, even in popular speech, recklessness connotes an indifference to risk involving an appreciation of the risk and a willingness to take it. Devlin J in *Albert E. Reid & Co. Ltd v. London and Rochester Trading Company Ltd* construing the meeting of recklessly supplying an unseaworthy barge in the London Lighterage Clause, said that recklessly means something more than mere negligence or inadvertence. I think it means a deliberately running an unjustifiable risk. Finally we come to the judgement of Megaw J in *Shawinigan v. Vokins*. He had to consider the same words in the London Lighterage Clause as had been considered by Devlin J and he rejects the test propounded by Devlin J insofar as it is a subjective test depending upon the mentality of the doer. Instead he proposes an objective test. I quote his words at page 1214 at some length because they seem to me to go to the root of the matter and to constitute the best and most realistic test of recklessness which has yet been propounded in cases of tort:

> "In my view reckless means grossly careless. Recklessness is gross carelessness — the doing of something which in fact involves a risk whether the doer realises it or not: and the risk being such having regard to all the circumstances that the taking of that risk would be described in ordinary parlance as reckless. The likelihood or otherwise that damage will follow is one element to be considered not whether the doer of the act actually realised the likelihood. The extent of the damage which is likely to follow is another element not the extent which the doer of the act in his wisdom or folly happens to foresee. If the risk is slight and the damage which will follow if things go wrong is small it may not be reckless however unjustified the doing of the act may be. If the risk is great and the probable damage great recklessness may readily be a fair description however much the doer may regard the action as justified and reasonable. Each case has to be viewed on its own particular facts and not by reference to any formula The only test in my view is an objective one. Would a reasonable man knowing all the facts and circumstances which the doer of the act knew or ought to have known describe the act as reckless in the ordinary meaning of that word in ordinary speech? As I have said my understanding of the ordinary meaning of that word is a high degree of carelessness."

I think Megaw J is correct in holding that the test to be applied must be objective and that the necessity of an objective test is clearly involved in the decisions in the *Excelsior Wire Rope* case and *Breslin v. Brennan*. If I ask the question. ought the doer of the act to have known that trespassers were present within the ambit of possible danger or were very likely to be

> so present? I am propounding an objective test, the test of the observant and intelligent man. If I ask the further question, having regard to the knowledge which in the circumstances must be applied to the doer of the act that it was very likely that trespassers were present, was his action grossly careless? Again I am propounding an objective test. The two questions are interconnected. The greater the probability of trespassers present in the zone of danger the more careful I must be."

The inclusion of the word "knowingly" in subsection (1)(a) of section 33 must have been intended by the Oireachtas to have some affect on the nature of the reckless conduct required to come within the subsection. I think that its inclusion requires that the director is party to carrying on the business in a manner which the director knows very well involves an obvious and serious risk of loss or damage to others and yet ignores that risk because he does not really care whether such others suffer loss or damage or because his selfish desire to keep his own company alive overrides any concern which he ought to have for others.

As appears from the facts already set out in this judgment the first defendant jointly with the second defendant borrowed £45,000 in May 1990 with a view to improving the company's cash flow. When matters became critical he was concerned about the effects of a forced liquidation on creditors and traded on in the hope and belief that creditors would do better by the company so trading for a time rather than by immediate liquidation. That this belief was not unreasonable is confirmed by part 6 of the examiner's first report showing that on a winding up creditors would probably be £88,000 worse off than under a scheme of arrangement. The first defendant was diligent in trying to achieve profitable trading with minimum risk to creditors by getting the co-operation of I.D.N. in financing the company in regard to completing the Rathgar development on a weekly as needed basis. The first defendant jointly with the second defendant guaranteed the company's debt with Allied Irish Banks Plc in Crumlin and was willing to surrender his shareholding in Senna and Darwood for the benefit of the company. In addition the first defendant, together with the other defendants, fully assisted and co-operated with the examiner.

As is stated in most of the cases cited to me all these cases must ultimately be decided on their own facts. Taking account of all the facts in this case, I am not satisfied that the first defendant was a party to the carrying on of any business of the company in a reckless manner within the meaning of subsection (1)(a) of section 33 of the Act.

I now turn to subsection 2 of section 33. Subsection (2) does not affect or extend the meaning of subsection (1)(a) but it extends the application of subsection (1)(a) to the cases mentioned in paragraphs (a) and (b) of subsection (2) even though the director was not guilty of reckless trading within the meaning of subsection (1)(a) itself as interpreted by me above. Subsection (2) deems a director to be guilty of reckless trading in the circumstances set out in paragraphs (a) and (b) and that presupposes that otherwise he would not be so guilty.

By virtue of subsection (2)(a) a director is deemed to have been knowingly guilty of reckless trading if he ought to have known that his actions or those of the company would cause loss to creditors of the company or any of them. I consider the position first as at 29 August 1990 when the Act became law. In the month of September 1990 the company paid £38,961 to its creditors but it incurred further debts of £78,114 resulting in an increase in the amount due to creditors of £39,153. Probably some invoices that were received in September related to earlier months thus the deficit for September may have been lower but even if so the total indebtedness of the company would be the same.

At the directors' meeting of 27 August 1990 the first defendant had good reason to believe that the company would be able to pay all its creditors falling due for payment on 1 September 1990 and so it transpired. In addition the three main contracts at Simmonscourt, Malahide and Rathgar were nearing completion and the first defendant reasonably expected extra monies as these contracts would be completed and sums held by way of retention would at least be partly released as well as the balance due on the contracts being paid. The first defendant reasonably expected that no further losses would be incurred on those contracts but rather because for example the difficulties in Simmonscourt created by the special features of stone work, of old fashioned windows and of three storey houses were by then overcome and the workforce thenceforth was well able to carry out such specialised work within a reasonable time scale. What paragraph (a) of subsection (2) requires is knowledge or imputed knowledge that the first defendant's actions or those of the company would cause loss to creditors: it is not sufficient that there might be some worry or uncertainty as to the ability to pay all creditors. The requirement is that the first defendant knew or ought to have known that his actions or those of the company would cause loss to creditors. I am not satisfied that as at 29 August 1990 and the weeks immediately following the first defendant fell within the ambit of section 33 (2)(a).

By virtue of subsection (2), paragraph (b) of section 33 a director is deemed to have been knowingly guilty of reckless trading if he was a party to the contracting of a debt by the company and did not honestly believe on reasonable grounds that the company would be able to pay the debt when it fell for payment as well as all its other debts (taking into account the contingent and prospective liabilities). For the same reasons as set out in relation to paragraph (a) except for the different wordings of the two paragraphs, I am not satisfied that as at 29 August 1990 and the weeks immediately thereafter the first defendant did not honestly believe on reasonable grounds that the company would be able to pay the debt when it fell due for payment as well as its other debts (taking into account the contingent and prospective liabilities).

I am of the opinion that the position of the first defendant in relation to subsection (2) of section 33 as just found by me continued until 27 September 1990 especially having regard to the first defendant's hospitalisation from 17 September to that date.

At the meeting of the directors on 27 and 28 September 1990 decisions were taken as set out in the minutes already quoted by me and these decisions were implemented with reasonable expedition although I do not overlook the evidence of Messrs Mahon and Mortell that the defendants were thereafter still trying to complete the Malahide scheme. In any event the company was, to the knowledge of the defendants, insolvent at that time and up to the 11 October 1990 the company paid creditors £12,721 but incurred further debts in a total of £24,481, thus increasing the indebtedness of the company by £11,760. This continued trading after 28 September was done honestly by the first defendant mainly in the interests of the creditors because the first defendant believed that an immediate winding-up would be far more detrimental to creditors than continuing to trade in an effort to complete at least the Rathgar contract. Nevertheless the first defendant, whilst acting honestly and *bona fide* in what he considered to be the best interests of the creditors, was in fact party to the contracting of debts by the company at a time when he knew that those debts, together with all the other debts of the company, including contingent and prospective liabilities, could not be paid by the company as they fell due for payment. In these circumstances in respect of the period from 28 September to 11 October 1990 the first defendant falls within the ambit of paragraph (b) of subsection (2) though not necessarily also within the ambit of paragraph (a) because he believed that the loss (if any) to be caused to creditors or any of them would be less than an immediate liquidation.

Paragraph (b) of subsection (2) appears to be a very wide-ranging and indeed draconian measure and could apply in the case of virtually every company which becomes insolvent and has to cease trading for that reason. If, for example, a company became insolvent because of the domino effect of the insolvency of a large debtor, it would be reasonable for the directors to continue trading for a time thereafter to assess the situation and almost inevitably they would incur some debts which would fall within paragraph (b) before finally closing down. It would not be in the interests of the community that whenever there might appear to be any significant danger that a company was going to become insolvent, the directors should immediately cease trading and close down the business. Many businesses which might well have survived by continuing to trade coupled with remedial measures could be lost to the community.

I think that it is because subsection (2) and especially paragraph (b) is so wide-ranging that subsection (6) was included in section 33 of the Act. The English Insolvency Act 1986 at section 214(3) is not quite as widely drafted as subsection (6) of section 33 of the Act and accordingly in the *Produce Marketing Consortium* case it was held that, while the court could take account of the absence of any fraudulent intent so as to lesson the amount ordered to be paid by the directors, unless the evidence showed that the directors had taken every step to minimise loss to creditors that they ought to have taken, an order should be made against them. It seems to me that the expression "acted honestly and responsibly in relation to the conduct of the affairs of the company" is wider than the corresponding provisions in subsection (3) of section 214 of the English

Act and the court in this jurisdiction is given specific power to relieve such a director from any personal liability whatsoever.

I am satisfied that the first defendant acted honestly and responsibly in relation to the conduct of the affairs of the company to such an extent that having regard to all the circumstances of the case I relieve him wholly from any personal liability without imposing any terms.

What I have said and decided in relation to the first defendant applies equally if not *a fortiori* to the other three defendants and insofar as the fourth defendant is concerned the evidence is so skimpy that I do not think that the case is made out against him at all.

In view of my findings as to the limited time within which reckless trading must be deemed by subsection (2)(b) to have taken place, there arises a further basic problem so far as the plaintiffs are concerned. Mr Mahon stated in his direct evidence that the last work which the plaintiffs did for the company was on 21 September 1990 and that they decided to and did stop work on that day. That being so the plaintiffs have not proved to my satisfaction that they suffered loss or damage as a consequence of any behaviour mentioned in subsection (1) by any of the defendants. That behaviour is deemed by subsection (2) to be knowingly carrying on the business of the company in a reckless manner between 28 September and 11 October 1990. Subsection (3)(b) makes the proof of such loss or damage where the plaintiff is a creditor a condition precedent to the right to obtain a declaration under subsection (1). In the absence of such proof the court has no power to grant a declaration at the suit of a creditor.

I do not overlook the fact that it might be argued that the increase of £11,760 in the debts of the company between 28 September and 11 October 1990 could possibly diminish the dividends which creditors might get on their debts in the liquidation. If that be so the diminution would be about 2 per cent which applied to the plaintiffs £4,500 would result in a diminution of £90. In my opinion that is such a trivial amount as not to be within the meaning of loss or damage as contemplated by subsection (3)(b) of section 33 and neither was the case argued on that basis on behalf of the plaintiffs.

It follows from all the foregoing that the plaintiffs' claim must be and is hereby dismissed.

Patricia McLaughlin
Barrister

In the Matter of Wogans (Drogheda) Ltd and In the Matter of the Companies (Amendment) Act 1990 (No. 2): High Court 1991 No. 15465P (Costello J) 9 February 1993

Examiner – Proposals for scheme of arrangement not approved by the court – Directors abused processes of court – Court misled as to true position of company's indebtedness – Defects in scheme – Company ordered to be wound up and official liquidator appointed – Application by examiner under section 29 of the Act for payment of his remuneration, costs and expenses – Whether examiner had been in breach of his duty to the court – Whether court should refuse to sanction his remuneration, costs and expenses – Whether defects in scheme were such as would justify the court in refusing to sanction payment under section 29 – Whether costs of creditors should be paid by the directors and/or the company and/or the examiner – Companies (Amendment) Act 1990 (No. 27) sections 18, 29

Facts: The applicant applied to the court under section 29 of the Companies (Amendment) Act 1990 for payment of his remuneration, costs and expenses arising out of his appointment as examiner to the company. Section 29 requires that the examiner's remuneration, costs and expenses be paid in the way specified in subsection (2) "unless the court otherwise orders". After his appointment as examiner, the applicant had prepared a report under section 15 of the Act and a further report under section 18 of the Act. Costello J refused to confirm the proposals for a scheme of arrangement contained in this report on the basis, *inter alia*, that there had been an abuse of the processes of the court by the company's directors in that they must have known that the petition contained false information about the state of the company's indebtedness to the Revenue and that the grounding affidavit contained a deliberate untruth. Furthermore, Costello J concluded that there were seven defects in the scheme as proposed and as only some of these could be remedied, this constituted further reason for non-sanction. Two creditors of the company, the Revenue Commissioners and Hill Samuel, submitted that the examiner's application for payment of his remuneration, costs and expenses should be refused on the grounds that he failed in his duty to the court and that he conducted the examinership in a manner which disentitled him to the remuneration and costs. It was clear that prior to the presentation of the *ex parte* application for the appointment of the applicant as interim examiner (which was refused), the applicant had been made aware that the company had made "under the counter payments" to staff and that he had failed to inform the company's legal representatives of this fact. Furthermore, he failed to inform the court that from the date of that application he had provided services to the company and had acted in the capacity of what was termed as an "informal examiner" to the company until his formal appointment. It was further submitted that the manner in which the examiner carried out his duties and, in particular, the preparation of a defective scheme of arrangement disentitled him to an order for remuneration and costs. The main defects complained of were that the examiner had failed to report adequately to the court on the legal problems raised by personal guarantees entered into by two of the directors to Hill Samuel, that he had failed to inform the creditors of the company of arrangements which he had entered into with proposed investors and the requirements of such investors, the inclusion of a provision permitting the investors to withdraw at their discretion, the manner in which he treated the claim of a Mrs Gueron, the mother-in-law of one of the directors who was a creditor of the company, the failure of the examiner to disclose the fact that proposed investors intended to retain the employment of nine out of a staff of sixteen of the company's employees, and the defect in the scheme relating to the way payment of the examiner's fees was to be effected.

A further issue arose due to criticisms made by the examiner of the receiver in relation to the sale of the company's premises, the purchase price of which he alleged was distorted by the receiver to prevent or make it more difficult for him to be repaid his remuneration, costs and expenses from the proceeds of the company's assets. Finally the two creditors, the Revenue Commissioners and Hill Samuel, claimed that they were entitled to their costs as against the directors and/or the company and/or the examiner.

Held by Costello J:

(1) The applicant acted in breach of his duty to the court at the date of the presentation of the interim application in that he did not take reasonable steps to ensure that the court was not misled. He did not inform the court or the company's legal advisers of the information given to him by the director of the company.

(2) The applicant also failed in his duty on the date of the petition to take steps to ascertain what the true position of the company's indebtedness was and by failing to bring to the court's attention, through the company's legal advisers, that the statement of affairs in the petition was incorrect.

(3) He also failed in his duty to the court by failing to inform it that he had been employed by the company prior to the presentation of the petition. If he had fulfilled his duty he would not have been appointed as examiner and it was, therefore, unfair to expect the creditors to pay his costs.

(4) The defects in the scheme which justified the court in refusing to sanction the examiner's remuneration and costs were his failure to make provision in the scheme relating to the directors' guarantees and his failure in his statutory duty to report fully and frankly to the court in relation to this aspect of the company's affairs; the manner in which he dealt with Mrs Gueron's claim; the inclusion in the scheme of a provision permitting the withdrawal by the investors at their discretion and the provision in the scheme relating to the company's employees. Taken together, these defects constitute an additional ground for refusal of the claim for remuneration.

(5) The charge made against the receiver was made without foundation. The receiver did not distort the price he obtained for the property and he never

intended to prevent or make it difficult for the examiner to get paid his remuneration, costs and expenses.

(6) The court had no power under the 1990 Act to order that the costs of the creditors be paid by the directors of the company. The costs incurred are not "debts or other liabilities of the company" under section 297A of the Companies Act 1963 (inserted by section 138 of the Companies (Amendment) Act 1990). The creditors cannot rely upon the general power to award costs given by Order 99 of the Rules of the Superior Court as the directors were not parties to any of the proceedings under the 1990 Act.

(7) There is no power under section 29 of the 1990 Act to make an order for costs in favour of the creditors as against the company.

(8) There is no power under section 29 of the 1990 to make an order that the examiner should pay the costs of any party to proceedings under the Act. Order 99 r.1 Rules of the Superior Courts, which provides that the costs incidental to every proceeding in the Superior Courts shall be in the discretion of the court, confers power to make orders relating to the costs incurred by parties including creditors who appeared in proceedings under the 1990 Act. However, the circumstances in this case were not such to justify an order made against the examiner under Order 99.

Cases referred to in judgment

Selukwe Ltd, In re, Irish Company Law Reports (1963-1993) 633

Wogans (Drogheda) Ltd, In re, Irish Company Law Reports (1963-1993) 653

Counsel's and solicitors' names not available

COSTELLO J **9 February 1993**

Wogan (Drogheda) Ltd, a company carrying on a retail hardware business in Drogheda, petitioned the court for protection under the provisions of the Companies (Amendment) Act 1990. It presented the petition on 19 December 1991. On an *ex parte* application for directions on that day Murphy J refused an application that Mr Brian Jenkins be appointed examiner of the company on an interim basis. On 13 January the petition was heard and an order made, notwithstanding the objection of some of the creditors, that Mr Jenkins be appointed examiner. His section 15 report was presented on 10 February, and his section 18 report was considered on 29 and 30 April. Having reserved judgment to 7 May 1992 I refused to confirm the proposals for a scheme of arrangement contained in his report and I made an order winding-up the company and appointing Mr Liam Dowdall as official liquidator. The present application is by Mr Jenkins under section 29 of the Act for payment of his remuneration, costs and expenses amounting in all to a sum of £92,558.50 plus VAT amounting to £19,257.54. It is strongly resisted both by Revenue Commissioners who hold were owed £293,402.71 by the company and by Hill Samuel Ltd who were owed £462,300 approximately and hold were fixed and floating charges over the company's assets. They both say not only that a section 29 order should be refused but that their costs be paid by the examiner and/or that the directors should pay them and/or the company.

To understand the issues that arise I should briefly refer to some of the conclusions I reached in my judgment of 7 May. I held (1) that there had been an abuse of the process of the court by two of the company's directors in that they must have known that the petition contained false information about the state of the company's indebtedness to the Revenue, that the grounding affidavit contained a deliberate untruth, that the abuse of process was such as to require the court to refuse its sanction to the scheme of arrangement; (2) that the investor required the court to make three different orders relating to taxation matters, (a) an order that because of the refusal of the Revenue Commissioners to give a tax clearance certificate the court should order that all PAYE/PRSI employment/health levies and VAT liabilities of the company as at 13 January 1992 be extinguished, (b) that all corporation profit tax liabilities be deemed to be extinguished, including those arising under the scheme, and (c) an order restricting the rights of the Revenue in relation to VAT arising from the scheme. I did not think that such orders should be made and accordingly I could not sanction the scheme; (3) I concluded that there were seven defects in the scheme as proposed and as only some of them could be remedied these constituted further reasons for non-sanction.

The statutory provisions relevant to this application are to be found in section 29 of the Companies (Amendment) Act 1990 which provides as follows:

> "(1) The court may from time to time make such orders as it thinks proper for payment of the remuneration and costs of, and reasonable expenses properly incurred by, an examiner.
> (2) Unless the court otherwise orders, the remuneration, costs and expenses of an examiner shall be paid and the examiner shall be entitled to be indemnified in respect thereof out of the revenue of the business of the company to which he has been appointed, or the proceeds of realisation of the assets (including investments).
> (3) The remuneration, costs and expenses of an examiner which have been sanctioned by order of the court shall be paid in full and shall be paid before any other claim, secured or unsecured, under any compromise or scheme of arrangement or in any receivership or winding-up of the company to which he has been appointed.
> (4) The functions of an examiner may be performed by him with the assistance of persons appointed or employed by him for that purpose provided that an examiner shall, insofar as is reasonably possible, make use of the services of the staff and facilities to assist him in the performance of his functions.
> (5) In considering any matter relating to the costs, expenses and remuneration of an examiner the court shall have particular regard to the proviso to subsection (4)."

It will be noted that the statute requires that the examiner's remuneration, costs and expenses be paid in the way specified in subsection (2) "unless the court otherwise orders". The Revenue and Hill Samuel ask me to order otherwise and to refuse the claim made under the section.

Extensive affidavit evidence was filed and I heard oral evidence and submission over four days. I propose to examine the issues now to be considered in the following order:

(1) The examiner's duty to the court and the claim that as he failed in that duty he is disentitled to remuneration and payment of the costs he incurred.

(2) Whether the manner in which the examinership was conducted disentitles him to remuneration and costs.

(3) The examiner's criticism of the receiver appointed by the bank in relation to the sale of the company's premises.

(4) The claim by the two creditors for costs against the examiner, and/or the directors and/or the company.

(1) *The Examiner's duty to the court*

(a) *In relation to the abuse of the court's processes*

The petition under the 1990 Act was presented in the Central Office on 19 December 1991. It set out in summary form the company's balance sheet. This showed that the company's principal creditors were (a) the bank and (b) the Revenue Commissioners at £124,000 and (c) the directors at £100,000. Its total assets were shown at £1,026,000 and its total liabilities at £1,364,000 leaving a deficiency of £338,000. The truth of the statements in the petition were verified by affidavit. It transpired, when the directors later prepared a sworn statement of affairs under section 14, that the financial affairs of the company were considerably and materially different to that shown in the petition. The new balance sheet showed a deficit of £776,578. The discrepancy arose for several reasons, the principal being that the debt due to the Revenue Commissioners had been undervalued in the petition by £180,000 approximately. This undervalue arose because of an undisclosed debt to the Revenue of approximately £111,000 for PAYE and PRSI due on wages paid by the company to its employees and not disclosed to the Revenue and interest on arrears of tax (the so-called "under-the-counter" payments). In considering this aspect of the case on the confirmation application I stated:

> "When an application is made by a company for a protection order under the 1990 Act it seems to me that the directors and all those associated with the application (including their professional advisers) are obliged to exercise the utmost good faith and that the statutory duty exists not just on an *ex parte* application to appoint an interim examiner but also on the application itself. This is because (a) of necessity the court must depend to a considerable extent on the truth of what it is told by the company and (b) because of the potential injustice involved in the making of a protection

order when the proper course is to wind-up the company. This duty involves an obligation to disclose all relevant facts material to the exercise by the court of its discretion. *A fortiori*, it involves a duty not to deliberately mislead the court by false evidence. Not every breach of duty to exercise good faith will amount to an abuse of the court's processes. But where an application for a protection order is made on evidence which is known to be false this amounts to an abuse of the process. When an application is made for an improper reason, this also amounts to an abuse of the processes of the court.

In this case I must conclude that the evidence used to obtain the order must have been known to be false by at least two of the directors. Apart from any other aspect of the statement of affairs, the directors knew that the debt due to the Revenue Commissioners was grossly understated and that the true deficit was much greater than that shown in the petition."

I concluded that the abuse of the processes of the court disclosed in the evidence before me required me to refuse confirmation of a scheme of arrangement prepared following an order of the court which had improperly been obtained.

I turn now to consider the evidence in relation to the examiner's knowledge of the director's conduct.

Mr Bouchier-Hayes a partner in Messrs Butler & Co. had acted as auditor for the company until he resigned in January 1991. Later in that year he met Mr Brian Wogan one of the company's directors. Mr Wogan informed him of the company's very serious financial difficulties and of the steps which had been taken to remedy them and explained that there was a need for outside investment. Although Mr Bouchier-Hayes warned him against this way of handling the difficulties, Mr Wogan insisted that an attempt be made to rescue the company in the way he suggested. This occurred in the month of October or November 1991 and Mr Bouchier-Hayes invited Mr Wogan to the offices of Dublin Providers Ltd for the purpose of putting a proposal to that company for its investment in Wogan (Drogheda) Ltd. These negotiations were unsuccessful and a decision then was taken to operate the provisions of the 1990 Act. Mr Bouchier-Hayes explained that it would be inappropriate for him to act as examiner and recommended Mr Jenkins' name to the directors. The figures which were given in the petition were prepared by Mr Bouchier-Hayes who forwarded them to the company's solicitor. They were based by him on management accounts and discussions with Mr Brian Wogan but Mr Bouchier-Hayes did not carry out any examination of the company's books or records and he was unaware of the fraudulent figures contained in the accounts. On 19 December 1991, meetings took place in the offices of Mr Bouchier-Hayes just prior to the presentation of the petition and the *ex parte* application for directions and the application to appoint Mr Jenkins interim examiner. Mr Bouchier-Hayes had discussions with Mr Brian Wogan and Mr Gerard Wogan had discussions with Mr Jenkins. This was the first time that Mr Jenkins had met Mr Gerard

Wogan. Both were aware that an application to appoint Mr Jenkins as an interim examiner was to be made later that morning. A conflict of evidence as to what was said at this meeting existed but I am satisfied, both on my view of the witness and the probabilities of the case, that Mr Wogan's version of the discussion is the correct one. I am satisfied that Mr Wogan told Mr Jenkins that what have been called "under-the-counter payments" had been made to the staff, that he promised that he and his brother would open all the company books to Mr Jenkins and would hide nothing from him when he was appointed. Mr Wogan did not tell Mr Jenkins the extent of the "under-the-counter payments" nor did Mr Jenkins ask. Whilst Mr Jenkins thinks that he did not have at that stage a copy of the petition, I am satisfied that he had a copy of a statement of affairs on which the figures given in the petition were based. I am further satisfied that, as an experienced accountant, he would have been aware of the significance of what he had been told, namely, that it followed from the existence of under-the-counter payments the amount due to the Revenue in the statement of affairs must have been understated.

Mr Jenkins did not inform the company's solicitors of the information divulged to him by Mr Wogan. He attended the court later that morning and was present when an *ex parte* application was made for directions including an application that he be appointed interim examiner. This application was refused. Notwithstanding this refusal and for reasons to be explained later, Mr Jenkins proceeded to act in a capacity referred to in the present application as an "informal examiner" until his formal appointment on 13 January following was heard. Both the application for a protection order and his appointment were strenuously opposed by the Revenue and by Hill Samuel but notwithstanding this opposition the court made a protection order and appointed Mr Jenkins examiner. The court was not informed on 13 January that the statement of affairs disclosed in the petition was incorrect, nor had Mr Jenkins informed the legal advisers to the company of what Mr Wogan had informed him, and that figures presented on the petition must be incorrect.

On 14 January a meeting was held in the Drogheda offices of the company. This was attended by Mr Bouchier-Hayes who was asked to assist the directors in the preparation of a statement of affairs required by section 15 of the Act. On 15 January Mr Bouchier-Hayes decided to terminate his involvement with the matter, for reasons which have not been explained. As I pointed out in my judgment of 7 May 1992 not only the directors but all those associated with an application for a protection order under the 1990 Act, including the company's professional advisers, are obliged to exercise the utmost good faith in applications under the Act. Did that apply to Mr Jenkins? On 19 December Mr Jenkins was not employed in any professional capacity by the company nor was he so employed on 13 January at the time of the application. But he was associated with the application in that (a) he allowed his name to go forward for the position of examiner on 19 December and again on 13 January and (b) had carried out professional services for the company between 19 December and 13 January. It seems to that on 19 December he owed a duty to exercise good faith to the court, and that in the circumstances of this case that duty involved him in taking reasonable steps to ensure that the court was not misled. It seems to me further that he failed to fulfil the duty he owed to the court when he kept the information given to him by Mr Wogan to himself and in neglecting to inform the solicitors for the company of what he had been told. Had he done so I think the petition would not then have been presented by the company's legal advisers. Whether or not it would be presented later is highly problematical.

A further breach of duty to the court occurred on 13 January. Mr Jenkins made no enquiries about the extent of the under-the-counter payments and made no effort to ascertain the consequent extent of the understatement of the company's liabilities to the Revenue, although his engagement by the company would have enabled him to do so. I think he was in breach of his duty to the court (a) in failing to take steps so to ascertain the true position, and (b) in failing to bring to the notice of the court, through the company's legal advisers, that the statement of affairs in the petition was incorrect. After his appointment he gave his assistant specific instructions to inquire into the full position.

(b) *Pre-appointment of the examiner and payment of fees*

When the court later refused to sanction the scheme of arrangement the Revenue applied to wind up the company and a winding-up order was made and Mr Liam Dowdall was appointed official liquidator. An affidavit sworn in this present application established that Mr Jenkins had invoiced the company in respect of professional services rendered to the company between the date of the presentation of the petition and the protection order and that he had been paid on foot of this invoice £3,700 plus VAT shortly after 8 January 1992. A further ground of objection to the present application is based on the examiner's failure to disclose his appointment and this payment on 13 January 1992.

The facts relating to this issue are as follows:

(1) At the hearing relating to the appointment of an examiner on 13 January 1992, a creditor called Woodfab Ltd and a creditor called John C. Doherty Timber Ltd objected to Mr Jenkins' appointment and proposed instead the appointment of Mr Rory O'Farrell. Objections to his appointment was supported by Hill Samuel and they supported the nomination of Mr O'Farrell. In his judgment Mr Justice Blayney stated that the nominee of the company seeking protection should be appointed examiner unless there were good reasons to the contrary. As none had been disclosed he appointed the company's nominee, Mr Jenkins.

(2) None of the creditors were then aware that Mr Jenkins had given professional assistance to the company between the date of protection and 13 January and that he had been paid £3,700 plus VAT in respect of the services he had rendered.

(3) Mr Jenkins did not disclose to the court that he had assisted the company between 20 December 1991 and 8 January 1992.

(4) The official liquidator found in the company's files an invoice dated 8 January from Mr Jenkins addressed to the company's general manager. It was

for the sum of £3,700 plus £777 VAT for:

> "Professional services for the period from 20 December 1991 until the 8 January 1992 as agreed with Mr B Wogan on the 20 December 1991."

The official liquidator sought an explanation as to the payment of this invoice and received a letter of 21 May 1992 from Mr Jenkins in which he was informed that on 19 December at the hearing of the application for protection his counsel had sought an order that he be appointed as an interim examiner,

> "that Mr Justice Murphy made no appointment of an Interim Examiner but did make a reference to having no objection to the company engaging in professional assistance",

that on 20 December he travelled to Drogheda and met Mr Brian Wogan and the company's general manager. His letter went on:

> "At that meeting it was agreed that both myself and Mr Byrne (his assistant) would provide assistance and support for the company during this interim period and to do some basic groundwork that would be useful at the commencement of the examination. It was by no means certain that I would be appointed Examiner and I made it clear to Brian Wogan, at that meeting. that I would expect to be paid before 13 January 1992. This was agreed."

The evidence as to what professional services were given by Mr Jenkins to the company has not been very specific but his counsel referred to him as acting as an "informal" interim examiner during this period, and it is clear that one of the tasks he undertook was to make contact with the company's principal creditor, Hill Samuel with a view to discussing an outline of a possible scheme of arrangement.

I am quite satisfied that the fact that the examiner proposed by the company had been employed by it was a material fact which should have been divulged to the court. An examiner appointed by the court must be impartial between the company's shareholders and its creditors and the court is very slow to appoint as examiner an accountant previously associated with the company. Furthermore, it was a material fact of which the court should have been informed that (a) an application to appoint Mr Jenkins as interim examiner had been made and refused and (b) notwithstanding this refusal he had acted as an informal interim examiner and had been paid fees for doing so. I think it is highly probable that had Mr Jenkins fulfilled the duty he owed to the court on 13 January he would not have been appointed examiner of the company.

I will consider later the consequences of these conclusions.

(c) *Service contracts entered into by the examiner*

At the hearing of this application it was established that the examiner employed no professional staff himself, that he requested a firm of accountants Messrs O'Hare Barry and Associates to supply him with an assistant from their staff, that at that time Messrs O'Hare Barry acted as accountants to Dublin Providers Ltd (the firm with whom he later negotiated the scheme of arrangement and with whom the company had previously negotiated), that the examiner also entered into a contract with a firm called Byrne and Associates who carry on business in Waterford to assist him. It was urged on behalf of Hill Samuel that (a) the examiner ought to have disclosed to the court at the time of his appointment that if appointed he would have to recruit staff, because of the likely extra costs which would result and (b) the details given by him later in a document exhibited in his affidavit of 20 May 1992 to justify the fees charged make no mention of the recruitment of outside staff. No point is taken that he acquired a professional assistant from the firm who acted for the proposed investor.

There has been no evidence that on the application to appoint an examiner a question as to the comparative costs between rival applicants was raised. If it had been then Mr Jenkins would have clearly been under a duty to inform the court of how he would conduct the examinership. I do not think the non-disclosure of the arrangements he made would justify me refusing an order for his remuneration — those arrangements of course would clearly be relevant on an issue as to the quantum of costs payable.

(2) *Conduct of the Examinership*

I come now to the second heading under which a challenge to the examiner's application is made.

It was urged by the Revenue and Hill Samuel that the manner in which the examiner carried out his duties and in particular the preparation of a defective scheme of arrangement disentitled him to an order for remuneration and costs. In my 7 May judgment I referred to a number of defects in the scheme of arrangement some of which were remediable and some of which were not. What now falls for consideration is whether the defects which justified the non-confirmation of the scheme also justify a refusal of the present application.

I propose to consider the evidence (affidavit and oral) in so far as it is relevant to that issue and give my conclusions now on controversial issues of fact in so far as it is necessary for me to do so. In the light of these conclusions I will later consider their relevance to the exercise of my discretion under section 29.

(a) *The contracts of guarantee*

On 28 March 1991 two of the directors entered into separate contracts of guarantee with Hill Samuel by which each personally guaranteed up to a limit of £100,000 the repayment of the company's indebtedness to the bank. The scheme of arrangement ignored the existence of these guarantees. I pointed out in my previous judgment that as the personal guarantees would not be discharged by the confirmation of the scheme a contingent liability might exist from the subrogation rights that would arise should the directors be required to make payments to the bank on foot of them. At the hearing of this application evidence was given by Mr Gerard Wogan, which I accept, that a meeting took place between the examiner and the directors in the Boyne Valley Hotel in Drogheda on 11 March 1992; that the examiner was accompanied by his solicitor and counsel, Mr Forde; that both the examiner and Mr Forde expressed the opinion that the legal effect of the confirmation of the scheme of arrangement was this would discharge the directors' liability on their guarantees, but that the directors should if they wished obtain independent legal advice on the point. Mr Wogan understood that he was being advised that the scheme of arrangement, if approved, would mean that his guarantees would be "dropped", that he acted on this advice, and that it materially effected his decision as a member of the company to approve the examiner's proposals and that he was not in a position to get other legal advice of his own. Whether or not the examiner's advice was correct is not now relevant; the defect in the scheme was in failing to make provision in it for the very real risk of the existence of a contingent liability arising from the guarantees. The objecting creditors urge that the non-disclosure of this meeting and the advice given to the director is a ground for refusal of costs, in addition to the defect in the scheme itself. In his oral evidence to the court on the hearing of the confirmation proceedings the examiner made no mention of the meeting and stated that his attitude to the guarantees was that they were matters with which he was not concerned and that he did not consider that they should form part of the scheme of arrangement.

But this evidence was not a full account of what had occurred. The examiner omitted to tell the court that he was well aware of a judgment I had given in *Selukwe Ltd* on 20 December 1991 (he had been the examiner in the case) which had a direct bearing on the treatment of directors' guarantees in schemes of arrangement under the Act; that he had sent a copy of the judgment to the Wogan brothers; that he had formed an opinion as to the legal consequences of the confirmation of his proposals on the Wogans' guarantees (*i.e.*, that they would be discharged by it); that he had brought counsel to a meeting with the directors to convey this opinion to them; and that the purpose of so doing had been to influence a decision on their part favourable to acceptance of the proposals he was formulating.

The examiner has functions and duties imposed by statute. He is required by the 1990 Act to examine the affairs of the company and report thereon to the court as directed by the Act. I think that his reports must be full, frank and comprehensive ones and I must conclude that he failed in the duty imposed on him by the statute in failing to report adequately to the court on the legal problems raised by guarantees and the manner in which he dealt with them.

(b) *Non-disclosure of the Heads of Agreement with the investors and the addendum thereto*

I indicated in my judgment on 7 May last that the "Heads of Agreement" entered into between the examiner and the investor were not produced to the principal creditors until late in the proceedings and I expressed the view that any concluded agreement should be produced to interested parties and should form part of the scheme of arrangement which the court is asked to confirm. This aspect of the case has become relevant to the present application because of information which arose after the hearing. What happened was this.

The creditors' meeting to consider the examiner's proposals was held on 31 March 1992. These proposals referred to tax matters in a very general way. The Revenue was dissatisfied with the proposals and on 16 April wrote requesting a copy of the "Heads of Agreement". A long reply was sent to this letter by the examiner's solicitor on 23 April. It dealt with the request for a copy of the heads of agreement by simply ignoring it. At a casual meeting in the Four Courts the request was repeated and as a result a document was handed over entitled "Heads of Agreement" containing nine pages with one page added headed "Addendum". At the hearing of the application on 29 April I requested a copy of the Heads of Agreement and I and the other parties were given the nine page "Heads of Agreement" with a one-page "Addendum" attached to it.

Shortly after the hearing at a meeting with the representatives of Hill Samuel one of the Wogan directors produced a three page document headed "Addendum" which was signed on 30 March 1992 by the investors and later by the examiner. It was clearly an agreement between the examiner and the investors modifying and amending the "Heads of Agreement". The first page of this document was the page attached to the Heads of Agreement given to the Revenue before the hearing, and to the court on 29 April. The last two pages of the addendum had not been included. If the examiner had deliberately misled the court and the creditors by suppressing part of a document this would disentitle him to order sought. On the evidence before me, it appears that an error was made which amounted to a most serious act of negligence on the part of whoever was involved but I am satisfied that it was not done with intent to deceive.

It now transpires from a perusal of the complete "Addendum" that the original agreement was considerably amended and that in fact a new term was incorporated at the insistence of the investors contained in a letter of 27 March from their tax adviser, Mr Twohig. The last paragraph of the "Addendum' states "Also subject to the letter from Liam Twohig dated 27 March 1992". This clearly means that the whole agreement was subject to compliance with Mr Twohig's requirements. That letter was never produced to any of the parties or to the court. In fact it contained the requirement which the examiner later incorporated in his report relating the demand by the investor that (a) a tax clearance certificate be obtained or given, (b) that corporation profit taxes be deemed to be extinguished either by agreement or court order and (c) a restriction of the rights of the Revenue to certain VAT payments be obtained or made the subject of a court order. Significantly, the last page of the addendum contains comments on Mr Twohig's letter by the examiner which read "I am not convinced that all the aspects of this letter can be complied with".

As I have previously stated, it is my view that an examiner should incorporate into a scheme of arrangement to be placed before the members of the company and its creditors any agreement which he has entered into with a proposed investor because (a) the investor should be legally bound by the agreement and (b) the creditors should know what the proposals are for the future of the company so as to make a fully informed judgment on the proposals, particularly when part of their debt is being deferred. In this case it was particularly important that the examiner should have informed the Revenue of the investor's requirements relating to tax matters. In the event, the Revenue voted against the proposals without knowing the extra terms which it was proposed the court would be asked to impose on them but this might not have been the case. In my opinion the examiner acted improperly in failing to inform the Revenue of the investor's requirements. Furthermore, in view of their serious extensive implications and the acknowledged likelihood that they would not be approved the examiner should have applied to the court for advice under section 7(6) of the Act, thus limiting to some extent at least the costs of the examinership.

(c) *Mrs Gueron's debt*
The evidence on this application confirmed the view expressed in my judgment that there was a risk of some considerable substance that Mrs Gueron (a mother-in-law of one of the directors who had claimed that she was a creditor of the company) might be able to claim successfully that she was a creditor of the company.

(d) *The company's employees*
A further defect noted in my judgment in the scheme related to the terms negotiated with the investor concerning the continued employment of the company's workforce. Under the agreement the investor was permitted to require the examiner to dismiss some or all of the company's employees. No information was forthcoming at the hearing either from the examiner or the investor (represented at it by senior counsel) of the investor's intention in relation to the company's staff and I concluded that as the scheme failed to achieve one of the main objectives which the statute was enacted to achieve, namely the adoption of schemes or arrangements to enable companies to survive in the interests of, *inter alia*, their employees, that it should not therefore be confirmed. In affidavit evidence filed on this application the examiner has stated that in April 1992 before the hearing on the 29th the investors had in fact agreed to employ nine employees but were to make six redundant. No explanation has been given as to why this information was not forthcoming at the hearing. It was highly relevant as it would have enabled the court to consider whether the employment of nine out of a staff of sixteen would outweigh the injury to the creditors which they claimed the scheme would cause then.

(e) *The provision for the examiner's costs in the scheme of arrangement*
I should also refer to an aspect of the scheme not adverted to in my judgment.

In his section 16 report the examiner informed the court that Dublin Providers Ltd agreed to acquire the company and to undertake a "total capital commitment figure" of £559,000, made up of (a) secured bank facility with Hill Samuel Ltd, (b) deferred payment arrangements for the preferential creditors and (c) "cash injection into the company by way of additional equity" [paragraph 2(g) and (h)]. It stated further that Dublin Providers had given a conditional indication that "they will inject £264,000 by way of additional share capital into the company and that they are prepared to inherit liabilities amounting to circa £295,000" [paragraph 5(a)]. It appears however from the "Heads of Agreement" (to which reference was later made in the section 18 report) that the "cash injection for new equity" was to cover the costs of what was termed "the reconstruction budget" and that the reconstruction budget covered (i) cash payments to the company's creditors (ii) "the examiner's remuneration and costs" and (iii) any payment to be made for the existing share capital. The original agreement was that the examiner's remuneration and costs would not exceed £65,000, but it was agreed in the addendum that the figure for costs and remuneration would be increased to £75,000 if the examiner lost the appeal to the Supreme Court relating to the construction of Hill Samuel's debenture. It was agreed that a payment by Dublin Providers would be made into an examiner's trust bank account and the payment out of it would be made by the examiner for (a) the liabilities arising from the scheme of arrangement and (b) "the agreed examiner's remuneration and costs". This means that out of the so-called "estimated cash injection" of £264,000 there would be paid to the examiner (and not to the company) a sum which might amount to £75,000 should he lose the appeal.

This provision of the scheme of arrangement which the court was asked to approve could not legally be made without an express order of the court permitting it. Section 29 of the 1990 Act provides that the examiner's remuneration and costs:

> "shall be paid . . . out of the revenue of the business of the company ... or the proceeds of realisation of the assets"

unless otherwise ordered. The examiner did not request the court to make such an order and advanced no reason why such an order should be made.

Conclusions

I come now to the conclusions I have reached on the examiner's entitlement to fees under section 29 of the Act.

(1) *As to examiner's duty to court*

(a) I think the breach by the examiner of his duty to the court arising from his knowledge of the abuse of the court's processes by the directors was a most serious one and disentitles him to be remunerated for the work he performed or to be reimbursed for the costs and expenses he incurred. I must so hold (a) because the court must ensure the fulfilment of duties owed to it by professional persons in the interests of justice, and should not condone what happened by the order the examiner now seeks and (b) because in this case it is highly probable that had the court been informed of the fraud which had taken place and which was compounded in the petition an order for protection would not have made. In such circumstances it would be unjust to require the company's creditors to remunerate the examiner or indemnify him for services which, had this duty been fulfilled, would not have been performed.

(b) I must conclude also that the breach by the examiner of his duty to the court in failing to inform it that he had acted for the company prior to his appointment and that he had acted as an informal interim examiner disentitles him to the order he seeks. Had he fulfilled this duty I think it is highly probable that he would not have been appointed to the office of examiner. It would therefore not be just to ask the creditors to make the payments sought to a person who should not have been appointed to the position had this duty been fulfilled.

(2) *As to other aspects of the conduct of the examinership*

(c) The court refused confirmation because, *inter alia*, the requirements in the scheme relating to orders relating to a tax clearance certificate and other orders limiting the investor's tax liabilities. This defect in the scheme could be relevant to the date up to which costs should be paid but not on issue of entitlement to costs.

(d) The non-disclosure of the heads of agreement to the creditors, the failure to incorporate them in the scheme of arrangement, and the negligence in relation to furnishing part of the addendum are matters which might be relevant on issues relating to the date up to which costs should be paid but are not in my judgment factors which would in themselves justify an order refusing the order sought.

(e) The defect in the scheme relating to the way payment of the examiner's fees was to be effected could have been remedied at the confirmation hearing had the scheme of arrangement been approved, either by the court making a special order for the payment of costs in the way proposed or by requiring that the costs be paid in the manner provided in section 29. I do not think it is such as to justify a refusal of the order sought on this application.

(f) The other defects in the scheme and the conduct of the examiner in relation to one of them together oblige the court, in my judgment, to refuse sanction for examiner's remuneration and costs. (a) The failure to make any provision in the scheme relating to the directors' personal guarantees was, for the reasons already given, a most serious defect in it. Furthermore, the examiner failed in his statutory duty to report fully and frankly to the court in relation to this aspect of the company's affairs or the way he dealt with it. (b) The manner in which he treated Mrs Gueron's claim was also a serious defect in the scheme, as was (c) the inclusion in it of a provision permitting the withdrawal by the investors at their discretion. (d) The term in the scheme relating to the employment of the company's staff by the investor was for the reasons given in my judgment of 7 May 1992 a serious defect in it, and the information given since to the effect that some of the staff were to be employed by the investor only remedied the defect in part. Perhaps if the scheme had not contained all these defects it might have been possible to overlook those that had in fact occurred. But taken together they have resulted in a situation in which I think it would be unjust to ask the creditors to remunerate the examiner for the work he has done and to indemnify him for the costs and expenses he incurred in doing it. They constitute a ground of refusal additional to those at (1)(a) and (b) above.

The result is that I will make an order under section 29 of the Act refusing the application for payment to the examiner of remuneration costs and expenses.

(3) *The examiner's criticism of the receiver*

Mr Patrick McSwiney was appointed receiver of the company on foot of Hill Samuel's mortgage debenture on 7 May 1992, the day on which the confirmation of the examiner's scheme was refused and an order made winding up of the company. Thereafter the receiver realised some of the stock in trade of the company and sold some of it to Dublin Providers Ltd. On 18 May he sold the property to Dublin Providers for £411,000. In paragraph 18 of an affidavit filed on 5 October 1992 the examiner referred to the circumstances of this sale, and to previous valuations of the property he had obtained and then stated:

> "It is my firm belief that the figure of £411,000 attributed by the receiver to the mortgage property is distorted to prevent or make it far more difficult for me to get paid my approved remuneration, costs and expenses from the proceeds of the company's assets."

Mr McSwiney was served with the examiner's present motion and swore an affidavit on 29 May 1992 indicating that he was not concerned on the issue, but in the light of what was said in the examiner's affidavit of 5 October he swore a further affidavit and was represented by counsel at the hearing of the examiner's motion and strongly contested the attack made on him by the examiner.

I am quite satisfied that the charge made was without foundation and that the receiver did not distort the price he obtained for the property and that he never had any intention to prevent or make it difficult for the examiner to get paid his remuneration, costs and expenses. I can find no reason why this allegation was made. It is true that in the balance sheet in the company's petition the premises were valued at £439,000, that in his section 15 report the examiner had written down the value of the premises to £250,000 and that the directors had objected to his doing so, but neither the bank nor the Revenue had suggested that his doing so was a reason for refusing his application under section 29.

(4) *The creditors claim against the directors and the examiner and the company for costs*

Both the Revenue Commissioners and Hill Samuel appeared on the initial application for protection and again on the confirmation application and have incurred liability for legal fees in doing so. They both asked the court to order that their costs should be paid by (a) the directors, and/or (b) the company, and/or (c) the examiner.

As to (a), it is urged that the directors should bear their costs because they had abused the processes of the court in authorising the application for protection thereby vitiating all the proceedings under the Act. I do not think that I have any power to make such an order. Section 29 of the 1990 Act gives power to make orders only in relation to the examiner's costs. Section 297A of the Companies Act 1963 (inserted by section 138 of the Companies Act 1990) only gives power to make an order in proceedings under the Companies (Amendment) Act 1990 when declarations are made that directors are personally responsible for the "debts or other liabilities of the company". But the costs incurred by the applicant creditors in these proceedings are not "debts or other liabilities of the company", for reasons to be explained in a moment and so they cannot rely on this section. I do not think that they can rely in the general power to award costs given by Order 99 of the Rules of the Superior Courts because the directors were not parties to any of the proceedings under the 1990 Act.

As to (b), there is no power under section 29 of the 1990 Act to make an order in favour of the creditors against the company, I do not think that I should make an order under Order 99 as the liability of the company for the directors' wrongdoing is far from clear and such an order would be unfair to the company's unsecured creditors. The creditors costs are not therefore "debts or other liabilities of the company" within the meaning of section 297A of the 1963 Act.

As to (c), there is no power under section 29 of the 1990 Act to make an order that the examiner should pay the costs of any party to proceedings under the Act. Order 99 r. (I)(1) of the Rules of the Superior Courts provides that the costs of and incidental to every proceeding in the Superior Court shall be in the discretion of those courts respectively. I think that this confers power to make orders relating to the costs incurred by parties including creditors who appeared in proceedings under the Act may be made. Having given the matter careful consideration I do not think the interests of justice require me to make an order that the examiner should pay the creditors' costs. I think that such an order might be made in very exceptional circumstances but whilst the circumstances in this case were such as to justify the refusal of an order in the examiner's favour under section 29 I do not think they would justify an order against him under Order 99. I must therefore refuse this application.

Final comments

Finally, I cannot conclude this judgment without this further brief comment. Firstly, in relation to the proceedings taken by the examiner against Hill Samuel claiming that debenture did not charge the book debts. When this claim was denied he instituted proceedings in the High Court and lost the point on appeal to the Supreme Court. He estimated that the extra costs involved in these proceedings were £20,000. His case now is that his remuneration and costs (including these costs) should be paid out of the proceeds of sale of the company's property obtained by Hill Samuel under their debenture. If he is right then Hill Samuel would be required to pay (a) their own costs of the proceedings and (b) the examiner's costs, even though they won the case. This illustrates a view I wish to express about the 1990 Act; I do not think that examiners save in exceptional circumstances of urgency should institute proceedings without leave of the court obtained under section 7(6) of the 1990 Act. Secondly, because the examiner is not a receiver or a liquidator I do not think he should adjudicate on claims as was done in this case in relation to Mrs Gueron's claim. If there are real grounds for dispute such claims can be put in a separate class, written down in the same way as others in the scheme of arrangement and provision made for later adjudication on them. Should the claims be valid the confirmation order will limit them in the same way as other creditors claims are limited.

Patricia McLaughlin
Barrister

In the Matter of Don Bluth Entertainment Ltd and In the Matter of the Companies Acts 1963-1990: High Court 1992 No. 5218(A)P (Murphy J) 24 May 1993

Examiner – Application for remuneration, costs and expenses – Certificates issued under section 10 of the 1990 Act – Expenses incurred in presentation of petition – Whether recoverable – Whether petition brought in name of company – Whether court could interfere with decision of examiner – Examiner purported to certify liabilities already incurred by the company – Claim in foreign currency – Date of conversion in punts – Companies (Amendment) Act 1990 (No. 27), sections 10 & 29

Facts: The applicant was appointed interim examiner to Don Bluth Entertainment Ltd and its three subsidiaries on 7 August 1992 which said appointment was confirmed on 27 August. The examiner reported to the court on 8 October 1992 that in his opinion the company was not capable of survival as a going concern as the necessary finance was not forthcoming from Dutch financiers MKB Ltd and an order was made terminating the protection period under section 26(1)(h) of the 1990 Act. The same order reserved the costs of the examiner and made no order in relation to any of the other parties who appeared in the examinership matter and a liquidator was subsequently appointed to the company. The examiner sought the sanction of the court under section 29(3) of the 1990 Act with regard to:

(1) Remuneration of the examiner (including outlay and VAT) from 7 August 1992 to 8 October 1992 amounting to £104,230.90.

(2) The examiner's legal costs (including outlay and VAT) amounting to £40,817.75.

(3) Liabilities of the company which the examiner purported to certify amounting to IR£350,901 and $1,427,238.

On behalf of the official liquidator and the Dutch financiers, it was contended that the certificates given by the examiner under section 10 of the Act were bad in form and in substance to the extent that they purported to certify liabilities not incurred by the company but by some of the directors (in whose names the petition to appoint an examiner had been presented); that the liabilities certified had already been incurred or were to be incurred in the future; and that certain of the liabilities had no relevance to the survival of the company as a going concern during the protection period.

MKB advanced US$1,050,000 subsequent to the order of the court appointing the examiner, although this was not recorded in any document passing between the bankers and the company. The payment of interest was not expressly agreed in the negotiations which took place between the examiner and the financier and the examiner was emphatic that his certificate did not, and was not intended to, extend to interest. It was argued on behalf of MKB that the advance made was intended to be on the same terms as the previous substantial advances as to the payment of interest. A further issue arose as to the date on which those liabilities should be translated into Irish currency. MKB argued that section 29(3) provides that the remuneration, costs and expenses of the examiner which have been sanctioned by the court should be "paid in full".

Held by Murphy J:

(1) As the combined operation of sections 10 and 29 of the 1990 Act will frequently result in some creditors of the company being paid in full at the expense of creditors who hold securities over the assets of the company or creditors who would have enjoyed a statutory preference under section 285 of the Companies Act 1963 Act if the insolvency had resulted in a liquidation rather than an examinership, it is important that an examiner should exercise great care and professional expertise in issuing certificates under section 10 aforesaid.

(2) Notwithstanding the fact that the petition to appoint an examiner was presented in the names of three of the five directors of the company, they were acting on behalf of the company and the services rendered by the solicitors were rendered at the request and for the benefit of the company itself.

(3) The examiner was entitled to the remuneration claimed.

(4) Legal costs reasonably and properly incurred by the examiner for the purpose of the performance of the duties imposed upon him by the Companies (Amendment) Act 1990 and the order of the court made thereunder were recoverable by the examiner.

(5) Insofar as the examiner purported to certify liabilities already incurred, the certificate had no statutory effect and the court could not sanction as expenses of the examiner for the purpose of section 29 of the Act, any liabilities incurred by the company to its solicitors insofar as these related to proceedings

to obtain the protection of the court or the appointment of an examiner under the 1990 Act.

(6) Notwithstanding the absence of any documentation with regard to the transaction between the Dutch financiers and the company, it was implicit in the transaction that the advance to the company would carry interest on the same terms as previous advances and that this was the liability which was certified by the examiner and, accordingly, that the court should sanction repayment of the loan with interest thereon.

(7) The claim by MKB should be converted into Irish pounds as of the date of the presentation of the petition. The fact that the currency is converted at a given date does not of itself mean that something less than the debt is paid. It merely means that both parties accept the risk that they may lose or gain as a result of currency swings between the conversion date and the date of payment: *In re Lines Brothers* [1983] Ch D 1 and *In re Lines Brothers (No. 2)* [1984] Ch D 438 applied.

Cases referred to in judgment
In re Clare Textiles Ltd [1993] 2 IR 213
In re Lines Brothers [1983] Ch D 1
In re Lines Brothers (No. 2) [1984] Ch D 438
Smyth v. Tunny, High Court (Murphy J) 8 August 1991, unreported

Counsel's and solicitors' names not available

MURPHY J **24 May 1993**

This is an application by Patrick McSwiney, formerly the examiner of Don Entertainment Ltd and its three subsidiary companies for an order under section 29 of the Companies (Amendment) Act 1990. Section 29 aforesaid (so far as material) provides as follows:

> "29(1) The court may from time to time make such orders as it thinks proper for payment of the remuneration and costs of, and reasonable expenses properly incurred by, an examiner.
> (2) Unless the court otherwise orders, the remuneration, costs and expenses of an examiner shall be paid and the examiner shall be entitled to be indemnified in respect thereof out of the revenue of the business of the company to which he has been appointed, or the proceeds of realisation of the assets (including investments).
> (3) The remuneration, costs and expenses of an examiner which have been sanctioned by order of the court shall be paid in full and should be paid before any other claims, secured or unsecured, under any compromise or scheme of arrangement or in any receivership or winding up of the company to which he has been appointed."

In addition to expenses actually incurred by an examiner, section 10 of the 1990 Act provides that certain liabilities incurred by the company over which the examiner is appointed should be deemed to be expenses incurred by the examiner. Section 10 aforesaid (as enacted) provided as follows:

> "10(1) Where an order is made under the Act for the winding up of the company or a receiver is appointed, any liabilities incurred by the company during the protection period which are referred to in subsection (2) shall be treated as expenses properly incurred, for the purpose of section 29 by the examiner.
> (2) The liabilities referred to in subsection (1) are those certified by the examiner at the time they are incurred to have been incurred in circumstances where, in the opinion of the examiner, the survival of the company as a going concern during the protection period would otherwise be seriously prejudiced.
> (3) In this section "protection period" means the period, beginning with the appointment of an examiner, during which the company is under the protection of the court."

The company, Don Bluth Entertainment Ltd and its subsidiaries were (and are) engaged in the production and distribution of animated cartoon films. It was a very substantial company and retained some 480 employees. As I pointed out in a judgment delivered in this matter on 27 August 1992, the nature of the business in which the company was engaged created special financial problems. The production of a film and its distribution is both costly and lengthy. Substantial investment is required and a long delay, some 24 months, may elapse before there is any return on the investment. About last August the company had three films in production. Two were close to completion but the third would require several months before it was ready for distribution. Substantial sums of money were required to complete the films and to keep the company in production until a profit would be realised even on those films which were ready for distribution. The company experienced great difficulty in obtaining the requisite finance.

The share capital in the parent company was owned as to 93% by a Dutch company known as Bestvest N.V. A further 4% of the share capital of the company was owned or held between Don Bluth, Gary Goldman and John Pomeroy and the remaining 3% of the issued shares in the capital of the company were held by the Industrial Development Authority. There were five directors, namely, Andrew Fitzpatrick, Don Bluth and Gary Goldman who resided in Ireland and Jan-Dirk Paarlberg and Michael Vredegoor who were resident in Holland. The Dutch directors were nominees of or associated with the principal shareholder Bestvest. By August 1992 Dutch Financiers, M.K.B. Investment, either directly or through Bestvest N.V. had made available a sum in the order of 50,000,000 dollars to the company.

It was against that background that a petition was presented on 7 August 1992 by the said Andrew Fitzpatrick, Don Bluth and Gary Goldman seeking the appointment of Mr Patrick McSwiney as examiner of Don Bluth Entertainment Ltd and its subsidiary companies. On the same day Morris J made an order appointing Mr McSwiney as interim examiner until Wednesday 19 August 1992 for the purpose of examining the state of the company's affairs and performing such other duties in relation to the company as are set out in the provisions of the 1990 Act.

Notwithstanding the opposition of the Dutch directors and the Dutch financiers, an order was made on 27 August 1992 confirming the appointment of Mr McSwiney as examiner of the company and its subsidiaries. One ground of opposition by the Dutch interests was that the petition was presented in the names of three of the directors and it was contended that the Act required a petition, where presented in the name of directors, to be presented in the names of all of them. Whilst I rejected that submission, the judgment emphasises the obvious fact that the petition was indeed presented in the names of directors and not of the company and the lawyers who appeared on behalf of the petitioners purported to appear on behalf of directors rather than on behalf of the company.

A further special feature of the order made by me on 27 August 1992 in the examinership matter was expressed in the following terms:

> "The Court doth hereby refuse (pursuant to Section 29 of the Companies (Amendment) Act 1990) to sanction any expenses incurred after the making of this Order which are or would be deemed to be expenses by virtue of section 10 (1) of the said Act save to the extent that the liabilities of the company certified by the Examiner after the making of this Order to M.K.B. (or such other bankers, financiers or investors as may be approved by the Court) in respect of borrowings by the company not exceeding in total 1,000,000 Irish pounds".

That particular order arose from the concern expressed by the opponents of the petition on the grounds that the alleged purpose of the petitioners in presenting the petition was to achieve a position in which the examiner appointed by the court would issue certificates under section 10 of the 1990 Act in respect of liabilities incurred to creditors other than M.K.B.

It appears that the difficulty of the company, as the examiner saw it, was the need to raise finance in the order of $45,000,000 and this he was satisfied could not be done without the willingness of M.K.B. to compromise their claim against the company. As the co-operation of M.K.B. was not forthcoming, the examiner reported to the court on 8 October 1992 that, in his opinion, the company was not capable of survival as a going concern. On that date an order was made under section 26(1)(h) of the 1990 Act terminating the protection granted to the company and its subsidiaries. The same order reserved the costs of the examiner and made no order in relation to any of the other parties who appeared in the examinership matter. It is also significant to note that the order of 8 October 1992 contains a recital in the following terms:

> "and this application having been adjourned to this day and coming on in

the presence of the said respective counsel (counsel for the petitioners now having instructions also on behalf of the company)".

On 9 October 1992 Mr John McStay, chartered accountant, was appointed provisional liquidator in the present proceedings and on 2 November 1992 an order was made for the winding up of that company by the court and Mr McStay was appointed official liquidator for that purpose.

The notice of motion in the present case was originally returned for 7 November 1992. It was adjourned from time to time, partly to facilitate the court and partly to enable interested parties to be served with that notice. In particular the former examiner was directed to serve Messrs A&L Goodbody, solicitors, who were interested parties in as much as the examiner had certified certain costs payable to them by the company.

The items in respect of which the sanction of the court is sought under section 29(3) of the 1990 Act are as follows:

(1) Remuneration of the examiner (including outlay and V.A.T.) from 7 August 1992 to 8 October 1992 amounting to £104,230.90.
(2) The examiner's legal costs (including outlay and V.A.T.) amounting to £40,817.75.
(3) Liabilities of the company which the examiner purported to certify amounting to IR£350,901 and US$1,427,238.

(1) Of the examiner's fees it must be said that he charges in respect of his own time at a rate of £145 per hour and at £130 an hour for his partner. I think it can be said that the figure of £145 per hour is probably the highest hourly charge proposed by any accountant for services of this nature. On the other hand, it is recognised that it is an important case involving enormous sums of money; an exceptional business with a large and highly qualified labour force. The most important consideration, however, weighing with me is that the parties who will ultimately bear these costs, or will bear them to the greatest extent, are the Dutch financiers and they are not opposing the remuneration claimed. Accordingly, I will sanction the payment thereof. However, I think I should make it clear that in so doing I am not accepting in general that a fee of £145 per hour would be appropriate in other cases.

(2) With regard to the legal fees incurred by the examiner, I propose to refer these to the Taxing Master for taxation. I will direct the Taxing Master to tax the legal costs reasonably and properly incurred by the examiner for the purpose of the performance of the duties imposed upon him by the Companies (Amendment) 1990 and the order of the court made thereunder.

(3) Liabilities which the examiner purported to certify under section 10 of the 1990 Act:

Argument was directed to a number of items comprised under this heading and the consideration of further issues was delayed until additional evidence could be obtained. A number of the arguments were common to all or most of the items included under this heading.

First, it was contended on behalf of the examiner that section 10 conferred upon the examiner a discretion which could not be reviewed by the court. Alternatively, it was contended that, if the decision of the examiner could be reviewed at all, it would only be by analogy to the principles applicable where a judicial review is made of an administrative decision and that, accordingly, the decision of the examiner should not be set aside unless it was made:

(a) In bad faith,
(b) for an improper purpose, or
(c) on a basis that was manifestly unreasonable.

It was then emphasised that if the court declined to sanction (under section 29 of the Act) the expenses certified by the examiner under section 10, this would in fact render null and void a decision properly made by the examiner and defeat the reasonable expectations of creditors who had dealt with the company in reliance on the statutory power which the examiner purported to exercise.

On behalf of the official liquidator of the company and the Dutch financiers, it was contended that the certificates given by the examiner were bad in form and in substance to the extent, first, that they purported to certify liabilities not incurred by the company but by some of its directors, secondly, that the liabilities certified had already been incurred or were to be incurred in the future and thirdly, that certain of the liabilities had no relevance to the survival of the company as a going concern during the protection period. Furthermore, it was emphasised that the word "may" in subsection 1 of section 29 clearly conferred upon the court a discretion in relation to the payment of remuneration costs and expenses. Again attention was drawn to the word "reasonable" with regard to expenses as indicating that the court had a function to exercise in determining whether expenses incurred were reasonable or otherwise. In fact Costello J has held in *Clare Textiles Ltd* [1993] 2 IR 213, that the court does have a discretion in the matter.

As the combined operation of sections 10 and 29 of the 1990 Act will frequently result in some creditors of the company being paid in full at the expense of creditors who hold securities over the assets of the company or creditors who would have enjoyed a statutory preference under section 285 of the 1963 Act if the insolvency had resulted in a liquidation rather than an examinership, it is important that an examiner should exercise great care and professional expertise in issuing certificates under section 10 aforesaid. I would anticipate that an examiner from whom a certificate is sought would require the directors managing the business of the company to submit to him their proposals in relation to any particular liabilities which they proposed to incur and to satisfy him as to how the services or goods to be obtained would benefit the company and in particular how they would contribute to the survival of the company "during the protection period".

The certified liabilities which were challenged in whole or in part were as follows:

(a) Legal costs claimed by Messrs A&L Goodbody, solicitors to Don Bluth Entertainment Ltd. The total amount of their bill is £50,811.

In appendix two to a report to the High Court exhibited in his grounding affidavit, the examiner comments on that item as follows:

> "A&L Goodbody Solicitors were the company's solicitors and represented them to the court from the presentation of the petition right through the hearing of the petition and at each adjournment up until my removal as examiner. They also advise the company in relation to agreements, the conduct of various board meetings and dealings with the company's bankers. As this was essential work to the continuation of the company I certified these costs insofar as they are certifiable by me".

As already noted the petition was in fact presented in the names of three of the directors of the company and not by the company itself so that *prima facie* it would appear that the costs incurred in the presentation and hearing of the petition were liabilities of these directors and not liabilities of the company capable of certification under section 10. It was for that reason I directed the examiner to give notice of the motion to Messrs A&L Goodbody. On behalf of the solicitors it was contended that they in fact acted on behalf of the company. This is undoubtedly so. They had been solicitors for the company and the correspondence and bills and documentation generally would indicate that they purported to act on behalf of the company. Although they and counsel instructed by them presented a petition in the name of directors and informed the court that they appeared on behalf of the petitioners, counsel contended that this was essentially a device (or perhaps even an error) and that the directors by whom the petition was presented, having made their decision to present the petition at a meeting of the board of directors properly convened, were acting on behalf of the company, even though the petition was presented in the names of a majority of the directors. I believe my view of this argument is valid. I accept that, notwithstanding the names in which the petition was presented, the services rendered by the solicitors were rendered at the request and for the benefit of the company itself.

The actual certificate given by the examiner is undated but was issued on 11 August 1992 and was expressed in the following terms:

> "I am of the opinion that the costs of services rendered by you from 7 August 1992 to the date on which my appointment as interim examiner or examiner is terminated are payable under section 10 of the Companies (Amendment) Act 1990 subject to approval by the company. I am accordingly issuing this certificate in respect of the services rendered and consequently the amount would become a priority expense under the provisions of the said Act in the event of

> the company subsequently being wound up or placed in receivership subject to there being assets of the company available to discharge it.
>
> Please note that this certificate is issued in respect of the services rendered by you to the company and imposes personal liability on me as examiner."

From the narrative bill furnished by Messrs A&L Goodbody on 19 November 1992 and counsel's fee note, it would seem that a substantial part of the costs were attributable to the presentation and hearing of the petition for the appointment of the examiner.

It is contended on behalf of the Dutch financiers and the official liquidator that the certificate of the examiner in relation to this item is defective. It does not identify the particular services to be rendered by the firm of solicitors involved. It does not indicate the extent of the liabilities entailed. It is comparable to a blank cheque in as much as there is nothing to indicate that the liabilities in respect of which the certificate was issued is confined to services rendered or to be rendered which would directly affect the survival of the company. The point is made specifically that the certificate is not confined, as the section requires, to liabilities certified at the time they are incurred but both by reference to date and subject matter includes items which had been incurred before the date of the certificate and other liabilities which might be incurred thereafter.

What is said on behalf of the solicitors is that the purpose and effect of the certificate was to ensure that an examiner would be appointed and, it was pointed out, that this was held in my earlier judgment to have been essential for the survival of the company.

The 1990 Act does not confer any priority on the costs of persons petitioning for the appointment of an examiner and indeed on 18 October 1992 no order was made for the costs of the petitioners. Furthermore, the general scheme of the Act could not have envisaged the petitioner procuring a priority for his costs by means of certification under section 10 as ordinarily the examiner would not be appointed until after the expense of the petition had been incurred. It would seem to me to be inappropriate to alter the scheme of the Act by the fortuitous event that a provisional or interim examiner might be appointed and that his certificate would give to the petitioner a priority which the legislation had withheld. Insofar the examiner purported to certify liabilities already incurred, it is clear that the certificate has no statutory effect. Insofar as the liabilities related or may have intended to relate to contemporaneous liabilities in respect of proceedings for the appointment of an examiner, it seems to me that the certificate is likewise invalid for the reason offered by counsel on behalf of the official liquidator, namely, that the protection period during which the survival of the company falls to be considered is a period which commences with and postulates the existence of an examiner so that the appointment of an examiner or proceedings for that purpose can have no bearing on the survival of the company during the relevant period.

Insofar as the company required the services of their solicitors to advise them in relation to the execution of documentation with regard to the various substantial borrowings required to meet the weekly wages bill and for other current purposes, it is easy to see how an examiner could regard the failure to incur such liabilities as prejudicial to the survival of the company as a going concern during the protection period.

In the circumstances, it seems to me, that the court can not sanction as expenses of the examiner for the purposes of section 29 of the 1990 Act any liabilities incurred by the company on foot of the bill furnished by Messrs A&L Goodbody insofar as the same relates to proceedings to obtain the protection of the court or the appointment of an examiner under the 1990 Act.

Having regard to the amount of the bill and the attitude adopted by the Revenue Commissioners, it seems to me to be appropriate to direct taxation of the bill as all or part of it will be a debt provable in the liquidation. Certain brief fees and the refreshers referred to in the bill would not appear to be in line with the figures of which evidence was given and accepted by me in the appeal from taxation which I heard in *Smyth v. Tunney* and in which I gave judgment on 8 August 1991. However, it would be a matter for the Taxing Master to express his judgment on the quantum of the fees but I will expressly direct that he should segregate the costs and issue a certificate as to those relating to the proceedings for the appointment of the examiner and a certificate in relation to the balance of the work done.

(b) It is common case that the Dutch financiers M.K.B. advanced US $1,050,000 subsequent to the order of the court dated 27 August 1992. It does not appear that this substantial advance was recorded in any document passing between the bankers and the company. It would appear from the affidavit sworn by Erik Lagendijk, a lawyer in the employment of the parent company of M.K.B., that the loan was negotiated at a meeting attended by the examiner, his legal adviser and representatives of M.K.B. Mr Lagendijk states that:

> "Messrs McSwiney & O'Neill explained that the borrowing of the money by the examiner from the bank was similar to normal lending by a bank to a company".

The only documents exhibited in relation to the substantial loan are two certificates of the examiner dated 3 September 1992 and 11 September 1992, each in the sum of $600,000. Whilst these certificates refer to advances being made by M.K.B. Investments they do not refer to the company as the borrower or the fact which was the subject of dispute between the parties, the payment of interest on the loan.

It would seem clear that the payment of interest was not expressly agreed in the negotiations which took place between the examiner and the lender. Indeed Mr McSwiney is emphatic that his certificate does not extend, nor was it intended to extend, to the payment of interest.

What Mr Lagendijk argues is that the advance made by his company was intended to be on the same terms as the previous substantial advances as to the payment of interest, that is to say, "at the rate of interest of libor (3 months) plus one per cent" and furthermore that it was a matter of Dutch banking practice that loans to companies would imply that such lending would be subject to the commercial rate of interest from time to time attaching to such commercial loans.

I did not mention in my judgment of August last that one of the surprising features of the case was the fact that large sums were made available to the company without the use of documents recording precisely the terms on which the transactions were negotiated. I can only repeat my amazement that highly experienced commercial and professional men could leave to implication the rights and duties of parties in relation to such a substantial transaction.

Notwithstanding the absence of express agreement and indeed the absence of any reference to interest in the certificate of the examiner, I believe that it was implicit in the transaction that the advance to the company would carry interest on the same terms as previous advances and that this was the liability certified by the examiner and accordingly that the court should sanction repayment of the loan with interest thereon.

(c) Undoubtedly this advance and the liability to the company's American lawyer, Mr Labowitz, were incurred in US dollars. The sum due to the American lawyer being a sum of US dollars, $18,398. The outstanding issue is the date on which those liabilities should be translated into Irish currency.

Whilst the creditors concerned direct attention to the provisions of section 29(3) which require that the remuneration, costs and expenses of an examiner which have been sanctioned by the court should be "paid in full", this statutory obligation must be read in the context of the procedure by which the assets of the debtor are realised so as to enable these claims to be discharged. The debtor company is in liquidation and it is the action of the liquidator acting under the direction of the court which will enable these certified creditors to be paid in accordance with the procedure prescribed by the statute. Accordingly, it seems to me that the rules established for the conversion of foreign currencies into national legal tender in a liquidation as established by the decision of *In re Lines Brothers* [1983] Ch D 1 should be applied. It follows that the claims by M.K.B. and Mr Labowitz should be converted into punts as of 8 October 1992, the date of the presentation of the petition herein. The fact that the

> currency is converted at a given date does not of itself mean that something less than the debt is paid. It merely means that both parties must accept the risk that they may lose or gain as a result of currency swings between the conversion date and the date of payment.
>
> Interest payable after the date of commencement of the liquidation will be payable on the debt as converted into Irish currency in accordance with the decision of *In re Lines Brothers (No. 2)* [1984] Ch D 438.

The remaining issue between the parties concerned the liability of the company in respect of certain employees whose services were provided by what was described as an American Payroll Tax Company.

It would seem that the examiner purported to certify the liability of the company/employer to the US Payroll Companies, whilst the individuals actually providing the service contend that it is they who should have received the certificates. As the factual position in relation to the dispute had not been adequately explored the matter was adjourned for further consideration.

In the meantime I will direct the official liquidator to make forthwith the following payments:

(1) The sum of £104,230.90 to the examiner to cover all of his fees and outlay including Value Added Tax.

(2) The punt equivalent as of 8 October 1992 of the sum of US $1,050,000 (together with interest from the date or dates on which that sum or its constituent parts were advanced to the company up to the date of conversion, together with further interest on the Irish equivalent of the amount advanced from that date until the date of payment) to M.K.B. Investments B.V.

(3) The amount of the examiner's legal costs as and when taxed and ascertained.

(4) The expenses certified by the examiner in respect of which no dispute arises (including the debt due to Mr Labowitz, converted as aforesaid).

I will then direct the taxation of the cost incurred by the company to its solicitors A&L Goodbody and direct the payment by the official liquidator of so much of those costs as relate to services rendered to the company subsequent to 7 August 1992 and not relating to the proceedings seeking the protection of the court or the appointment of an examiner. I will further direct the official liquidator to admit Messrs A&L Goodbody as a creditor in the winding-up matter for the remainder of the taxed costs of the solicitors.

Patricia McLaughlin
Barrister

In the Matter of Edenpark Construction Ltd and in the Matter of the Companies Acts 1963-90: High Court 1992 No. 957P
In the Matter of Edenpark Homes Ltd and in the Matter of the Companies Acts 1963-90: High Court 1992 No. 1530P (Murphy J) 17 December 1993

Company law – Examiner – Fees and Expenses – Application for approval of payment – Extent of fee – Whether examinership should have been terminated at earlier date – Certification of liabilities being incurred by company – Whether written certification required – Whether certification required to be at time expenditure being incurred – Whether examiner entitled to claim for costs of company's solicitors incurred prior to his appointment – Companies (Amendment) Act 1990 (No. 27), sections 5, 10, 16, 29

Facts: Patrick McSweeney was appointed interim examiner of Edenpark Construction Ltd. ("Construction") on 11 February 1992, and appointed examiner on 2 March 1992, pursuant to the provisions of the Companies (Amendment) Act 1990. On 9 March he was appointed examiner of Edenpark Homes Ltd ("Homes"). On 25 May 1992 both examinerships were terminated by the High Court on the application of the examiner, having lasted 105 and 77 days respectively. Both companies were ordered to be wound up and A.I.B. plc appointed a receiver over the assets of both companies.

By notice of motion dated 15 July 1992 the examiner sought payment of his fees and expenses. He claimed a total sum of £241,727 including £127,618 as his professional fee in respect of Construction, £17,279 in respect of fees for the examiner's solicitors and £33,321 for a firm of solicitors who acted for the company.

The notice parties (A.I.B. plc, Anglo Irish Bank plc and the Revenue Commissioners) made a number of submissions:

(a) They were concerned at the enormous expenses, particularly for a company with a known deficiency of £500,000.

(b) That the examiner should have alerted the court at an earlier stage to irregularities (including the conduct of directors), which might have led the court to end the examinership earlier.

(c) That the presentation by the examiner of a petition to appoint an examiner to Homes, made it clear that from that date he accepted Construction was not capable of survival as a going concern.

(d) That because of the company's severe financial problems the examiner had effectively acted as a receiver or liquidator, and should not be remunerated as an examiner.

(e) That certain claimed expenses for Construction arose before the examinership period.

(f) That certain other expenses were not properly certified by the examiner "at the time they were incurred, to have been incurred in circumstances where, in the opinion of the examiner, the survival of the company as a going concern during the protection period would otherwise be seriously prejudiced", as required by section 10 of the Companies (Amendment) Act 1990.

In relation to the latter point the examiner had approved certain expenditure by a verbal certificate, with a later written certificate. Some of the certificates referred to sums already payable or services already supplied, while others failed to state that without the expenditure the survival of the companies would be "seriously prejudiced during the protection period". A valuation report from Lisney's while billed to Construction appeared to have been requested by the examiner, rather than the company.

Held by Murphy J in reducing the fee claimed by 20 per cent and in disallowing certain other expenses claimed:

(1) The examiner erred in the manner in which he purported to certify the liabilities of the company.

(a) Section 10 required certification at the time a liability was incurred, and the "serious prejudice" referred to must relate to the period between the appointment of the examiner and the cessation of the protection period.

(b) While the section did not specify certification in writing, this would appear to be an obvious and inescapable administrative necessity.

(c) An examiner is appointed to examine the affairs of the company and to prepare a report thereon. He does not have an executive role, akin to that of a receiver or liquidator, which usurps the functions of the board. His role in relation to expenditure is to review, at the request of the directors, liabilities intended to be incurred during the protection period, and assess whether the company's survival would be seriously prejudiced if such liabilities were not in fact incurred.

(2) The examinership should have terminated some weeks before it did. It was difficult to assess the precise date when this should have occurred and the effect this would have on the fees proposed. However, it was appropriate for the court to reduce the fee by 20 per cent to £84,376 plus VAT.

(3) The claim in respect of the examiner's own professional advisers and his own solicitors should be allowed in full.

(4) In relation to Construction's solicitors, any liabilities incurred by the company, prior to the date of appointment of the examiner, and in particular costs in relation to the presentation of the petition, should be disallowed.

(5) Costs of the presentation of the petition to appoint an examiner to Homes should not be allowed, as the examiner could not have formed the view that failure to do so would have seriously prejudiced Construction as a going concern during the protection period, as during the protection period its position was safeguarded by section 5 of the 1990 Act.

(6) Emoluments paid to certain former directors of Construction during the protection period were proper expenses of the examiner.

(7) In respect of the Homes examinership, costs of the examiner's solicitors would be allowed, but those of the company's solicitors would be disallowed, unless these were incurred subsequent to the appointment of the examiner to Homes. The examiner's fee would also be reduced by 20 per cent to take account

of the fact that the examinership should have ended previously.

(8) In relation to the apportionment of fees between Construction and Homes, there were no grounds for going behind the apportionment made by the examiner himself.

(9) The Revenue Commissioners would not be prejudiced by the payment of the expenses as, insofar as they included elements of tax, these must be paid by the recipients to the Revenue authorities.

Cases referred to in judgment
In re Atlantic Magnetics Ltd [1993] 2 IR 561
In re Clare Textiles Ltd [1993] 2 IR 213

Counsel's names not available

Solicitors for the Examiner: *Eugene F. Collins*
Solicitors for the Liquidator: *Whitney, Moore & Keller*
Solicitor for the Revenue Commissioners: *Frances Cooke, Revenue Solicitor*
Solicitor for Allied Irish Banks plc: *James McGillion*
Solicitors for Anglo Irish Bank: *Hanby Wallace*

MURPHY J **17 December 1993**

On 11 February 1992 the directors of Edenpark Construction Ltd (Construction) presented a petition for the appointment of an examiner pursuant to the provisions of the Companies (Amendment) Act 1990. On the same date Mr Patrick McSweeney F.C.A. was appointed interim examiner. He was appointed examiner on 2 March 1992.

On 9 March 1992 a petition was presented by the same directors for the appointment of an examiner in respect of Edenpark Homes Ltd (Homes), a company which was related to Construction to the extent that Construction owned 25 per cent of the shareholding in Homes and two directors were common to both companies. Mr McSweeney was appointed examiner of Homes on 9 March 1992. On 25 May 1992 both examinerships were terminated by the court on the application of the examiner. In the case of Construction, the examinership had endured for a period of 105 days and in the case of Homes it had lasted 77 days. On 11 May 1992 it was ordered that Construction and Homes be wound up by the court and that Mr Sean Sheehan be appointed official liquidator of both companies. On 26 May 1992 Allied Irish Banks Plc appointed Mr Tom Grace receiver over each of those companies.

The present motions are for orders approving "the Examiner's fees and expenses" and are dated 15 July 1992. The matter came before the court on 21 April 1993 grounded upon the affidavits of Mr McSweeney sworn on 15 July 1992 and 8 December 1992 and affidavits sworn by Messrs Morris Buckley and Tom Grace on behalf of A.I.B. and Mr Thomas J Browne on behalf of Anglo Irish Bank Corporation as well as affidavits sworn on behalf of the Revenue Commissioners, who were also given notice of the application. Subsequent to the hearing on 21 April last, Mr McSweeney was given liberty to file and did file an affidavit exhibiting certificates which he had purported to issue pursuant to section 10 of the Companies Act 1990 during the course of the examinership. The matter was re-entered on 6 December 1993 to afford the parties an opportunity of commenting on the certificates aforesaid which had not been before the court at the date of the original hearing.

The amounts claimed by Mr McSweeney in relation to Construction were set out in a schedule or exhibit to the affidavit sworn by him on 15 July 1992. That document shows the total amounts (including VAT) at a sum of £241,727.00. Of that sum £127,618.00 (inc. VAT) is the amount claimed by Mr McSweeney as his professional fee for the services rendered by him as examiner of Construction. The sum of £17,279.00 (including VAT) is the fee claimed by Messrs Eugene F. Collins & Son who clearly acted as solicitors to Mr McSweeney in his capacity as examiner and it must be inferred that those fees are claimed as an expense of the examinership. Of the remaining sums claimed the largest is a sum of £33,321.00 due to Messrs A&L Goodbody who acted as solicitors to Construction. It is less clear whether the other indebtedness (particularly that in favour of certain auctioneers, valuers etc. amounting to £14,245.00) was an expense of the examinership or a liability of Construction. The matter was dealt with in Mr McSweeney's affidavit of 8 December 1992 in the following terms:

> "19. In the course of the examination, it was necessary to certify certain expenses which are detailed in a schedule exhibited to my Affidavit. Each of those liabilities were certified by me at the time they were incurred because I considered that they were necessary to ensure the survival of the companies. I now beg to refer to a schedule setting out the reasons for incurring such expenses and I now beg to refer to the same upon which marked with PMS 3 I have signed my name before the swearing hereof".

The exhibit (PMS 3) is not very informative as to the identity of the person by whom the indebtedness was created though I would infer that under the heading of wages, salaries, fees and expenses the services obtained from Messrs Michael McDonald, Pat Cooney and Mark Irwin, the directors and secretary of the company, were obtained for the benefit of the examiner because it is stated in the exhibit that "without the assistance of these individuals it would have been impossible for the examiner to gain a proper understanding of the company's affairs".

Before considering further the claims made by Mr McSweeney and the challenge presented to them by the respondents, it is necessary to review to some extent the business and assets of both Construction and Homes.

Construction was incorporated on 10 March 1988. Apparently it carried on business as builders and developers. It had a paid up capital of £100. The majority (if not all) of the directors together with the secretary and the auditors were resident in England. The statement of affairs prepared by the directors on which the petition for the appointment of the examiner was based a deficit of

£587,000.00. The liabilities were shown at £2.8 million approx. and the assets at £2.3 million. The liabilities included bank lending in excess of £1.2 million which was secured and the Revenue were creditors for at least £400,000 some of which they would have been preferential in event of a liquidation. The nature and value of the assets are more difficult to identify. The largest single item is "work in progress (Palmerstown)" at £913,000. Apart from any difficulty the examiner might have had in verifying the amount or value of the work in progress, it does seem that the lands in question were the property of Homes and that Construction held a mere licence (no doubt coupled with some other contractual rights) to develop the same. None of the parties before the court was in a position to explain the precise relationship between Homes and Construction in this regard or to express any view as to whether the proprietorial or contractual interest of Construction in the sites subsisted. In addition to the sites in Palmerstown, Construction had a variety of other, but less valuable, interests. However, it was clear that on any reckoning and even on the most beneficial realisation and disregarding all costs of same that there would be still a massive shortfall for the ordinary trade creditors. It seems difficult to see how Construction could have traded their way out of their disastrous financial position. Nor is it obvious why the secured or potentially preferential creditors would acquiesce in such a course. It could hardly have been for the benefit of the employees as there were a maximum of nine employees (including the directors and secretary). Indeed it is difficult to see what entity or business could have been preserved.

Counsel on behalf of the respondents made it clear that they did not challenge in any way the integrity of the former examiner. They did, however, express in general terms concern at what they considered to be the enormous expenses or liabilities in respect of which the examiner sought payment, namely, the sum of £241,727. It is understandable that concern should be expressed where a company with a known deficiency of at least £500,000 incurs further expenses or liabilities in the order of £250,000 which must be borne by parties who had no prospect of benefiting from the expensive exercise. But the respondents make other and more particular points, namely,

1. That the date on which the examiner delivered his section 15 report, namely, 2 March 1992 he could and should have alerted the court to irregularities in the manner in which the affairs of the company had been conducted. Certainly the examiner must have been aware even at that early stage that no accounts of the company had been audited since the date of its incorporation and that no management accounts had been prepared since 31 December 1990. If such irregularities had been identified then the court might have convened a hearing for the consideration of that report with the probable result that the examinership would have terminated.

2. Again it is said that the fact that a petition was presented at the instigation of Mr McSweeney for the appointment of an examiner over Edenpark Homes Ltd on 2 March 1992 makes it clear that Mr McSweeney had accepted by that date that Construction was not capable of survival as a going concern except on

the basis that some arrangement would be made with this unrelated company.

3. That the nature of the company's assets and the extent of its financial problems were such that the activities of the examiner were essentially those of a receiver or liquidator disposing of or organising the disposal of the assets thereof and accordingly that he should not be remunerated as examiner. This was an argument which had been invoked successfully in resisting part of the claim of an examiner to fees or remuneration in Clare Textiles Ltd decided by Mr Justice Costello on 2 October 1992.

4. That the information contained in Mr McSweeney's report of 25 May 1992 as to the questionable conduct of the directors and the management of Construction must have emerged some considerable time before the date of that report and accordingly should have been brought before the court at a much earlier date.

5. That certain liabilities of Construction should not be paid in the priority claimed by the former examiner because:

(a) the indebtedness was incurred before the appointment of the examiner, or

(b) that the indebtedness was not correctly certified in accordance with the requirements of section 10 of the 1990 Act.

The Companies (Amendment) Act 1990, section 29 gives to the remuneration costs and expenses (including liabilities of the company which are deemed to be expenses) of an examiner an extraordinary priority. If sanctioned by the court such remuneration costs and expenses are payable not merely in priority to other claims against the company concerned but in priority to those creditors who are the legal owners by way of security of the assets to which recourse may be had for the payment of such indebtedness. Perhaps this provision might not have seemed so far-reaching were it not for section 10 of the same Act which deemed certain liabilities of the company itself to be expenses of the examiner and accordingly to enjoy the same priority. Section 10 aforesaid (as originally enacted) provided as follows:

> "10(1) Where an order is made under this Act for the winding up of the company or a Receiver is appointed, any liabilities incurred by the company during the protection period which are referred to in subsection (2) shall be treated as expenses properly incurred, for the purpose of section 29, by the examiner.
> (2) The liabilities referred to in subsection (1) are those certified by the examiner at the time they are incurred, to have been incurred in circumstances where, in the opinion of the examiner, the survival of the company as a going concern during the protection period would otherwise be seriously prejudiced.
> (3) In this section "protection period" means the period, beginning with the appointment of an examiner, during which the company is under the protection of the court."

It follows, therefore, to elevate liabilities of the company to the status of expenses of the examiner the following must occur:

(1) The liabilities must be certified by the examiner to have been incurred in circumstances where the survival of the company as a going concern would otherwise be seriously prejudiced.

(2) That the prejudice must be foreseen as occurring in the period which commenced with the appointment of an examiner and terminating with the cessation of the protection.

(3) That the certification by the examiner must take place at the time when the liabilities are incurred.

Thus it can be said at once that a liability incurred by a company in procuring the appointment of an examiner could not be a "certifiable" liability as the relevant period would not have commenced when the liability was incurred. Again it is obvious that an expense incurred by the examiner is not a liability of the company and does not require certification. The section does not expressly provide that the examiner should certify *in writing* and accordingly it was argued by counsel on behalf of the former examiner that verbal or parol certification sufficed. Whilst no authority was opened in support (or in rebuttal) of that proposition, I would accept that ordinarily the word "certify" does not necessarily connote a document in writing. Where such is required a draftsman would be expected to include the words "in writing". However even accepting that a certificate in writing is not a legislative requirement, one would have thought that it was an obvious and inescapable administrative necessity. Even where written documentation exists in the present case, it is by no means clear that the examiner directed his mind to the essential ingredients of a certificate for the purposes of section 10 aforesaid. In the absence of such documentation it is difficult to ask those creditors whose rights are postponed to accept that the parol certification was correct in its terms and in its content.

In the paragraph which I quoted from the second affidavit of Mr McSweeney, he stated that "it was necessary to certify certain expenses". Whilst I would have assumed that the word "expenses" was an error and should have read "liabilities", undoubtedly the schedule referred to includes both expenses and liabilities. But it is also significant that in the same paragraph the examiner states that the liabilities were certified by him "at the time they were incurred" and goes on to say that he considered they were necessary to ensure the survival of the companies but he does not say that it was his opinion that the survival of the companies would be seriously prejudiced "during the protection period". It seems to me there is a vast difference between these two situations. As the Supreme Court noted in *Atlantic Magnetics Ltd* [1993] 2 IR 561, the 1990 Act provides time limits which are strictly limited. Indeed it is envisaged that the entire process would be completed in 51 days. Of course these limits may be extended but they represent the time scale envisaged by the Oireachtas and afford guidance as to how the actions of the parties concerned should be judged. Clearly there is a difference between forming an opinion that the survival of a company might be seriously prejudiced during a period limited to six or seven weeks and a period which is wholly indefinite. Furthermore, it is significant that the paragraph from Mr McSweeney's affidavit makes no reference to a parol certification.

In the supplemental affidavit sworn on 6 May 1993, Mr McSweeney exhibits two booklets which he says contains the certificates by him under section 10 of the Companies (Amendment) Act 1990 to various entitles with whom Construction and Homes dealt during the course of the period of court protection. In two specific cases (those mentioned at paragraph 4(b) and (f)) he identifies items in respect of which he states that he gave a "verbal certificate". I had inferred that the other documents exhibited were documents purporting to be certificates under section 10 aforesaid. I gather that that is not in fact the case. It has been explained that even where written documentation exists, the actual certification in some cases consisted of a verbal statement and that the written documentation was merely confirmatory. For example, it is clear that the document purporting to be a certificate for the purpose of section 10 aforesaid and issued to Messrs A&L Goodbody on 20 May 1992 was in respect of services rendered — and presumably liabilities incurred — between 1 May 1992 and 25 May of that year.

Again the certificate issued to Messrs Lisneys on 24 April 1992 by the then examiner is somewhat surprising. It is expressed in the following terms:

> "I certify that a sum of between £2,000 and £2,500 (excluding V.A.T. and dispersements) is payable to you under section 10 of the Companies (Amendment) Act 1990 in order to pay for the valuation report supplied by your firm to the above company. This amount will be paid by Edenpark Construction Ltd (under the protection of the court)."

It would be noted that the liability appears to be current in as much as it is "payable" and the indebtedness appears to be in respect of a past event in as much as the report described it as "supplied by your firm" and not a report "to be supplied". Finally in relation to this brief certificate it is noticeable that the fee is to be paid by Edenpark Construction Ltd thus suggesting that it is a liability of the company rather than an expense of the then examiner. In fact the report from Lisneys is dated 27 February 1992. Both it and the subsequent invoice dated 6 May 1992 were addressed to the examiner by name; at his professional address and not the registered office of Construction. Indeed it would appear to be significant that the report is introduced with the following paragraph:

> "I refer to your meetings and your instructions to provide you with a preliminary estimate of the current realisable values of the property set out hereunder and confirm that we have inspected the various properties and make the following comments."

Certainly it would appear that Lisneys understood and appeared to have had reason for understanding that their instructions came from the examiner and not the directors or other management of Construction.

It has been pointed out in many cases that an examiner appointed under the Companies (Amendment) Act 1990 does not as such have an executive role. He does not have functions akin to those of a receiver or liquidator. In the absence of some particular order of the High Court, he may not usurp the functions of the board of directors of the company over which he is appointed and it is the board or its officials who will continue to manage the business of the company during the period of protection and the continuance of the examinership. The important function which the examiner must perform during the strictly limited period of the statutory moratorium provided by the 1990 Act is to examine the affairs of the company and to prepare and deliver a report containing the information specified in section 16 of that Act. In particular the examiner must state his opinion as to whether the whole or any part of the undertaking would be capable of survival as a going concern and indicate whether the formulation and confirmation of any proposals for a compromise or a scheme which would facilitate such survival. Nobody doubts the importance or difficulty of that task nor would one question the professional expertise which may be involved in performing it.

An executive role, if it may be so described, which is likely to fall to most examiners would be the duty to review at the request of the directors (or perhaps a potential creditor) liabilities intended to be incurred by the company during the protection period with a view to forming an opinion as to whether the survival of the company as a going concern during the protection period would be seriously prejudiced if such liabilities were not in fact incurred. Clearly the examiner would be conscious of the fact that the certification of his opinion in that behalf would give to such liabilities a very special priority and cause an unexpected deferment or postponement of other creditors. Good housekeeping would suggest that the circumstances in which the liability was intended to be incurred and the nature thereof would be recorded in writing for submission to the examiner and that the examiner in turn would certify, again in writing, his opinion as to the effect which the failure to incur such liabilities would have on the survival on the company during the protection period. Certainly one would expect the examiner to maintain a clear distinction between expenses which he incurred and the liabilities incurred by the corporate entity whether or not those liabilities were certified by him under section 10 aforesaid.

Whilst allowance must be made for everybody dealing with the novel provisions of the Companies (Amendment) Act 1990, I feel I must conclude, first, that the examinership should have terminated at least some weeks before it did and secondly that the examiner erred in the manner in which he purported to certify the liabilities of the company under section 10 aforesaid. It would be impossible to identify the precise date upon which the examinership should have been terminated and it would be difficult to assess what effect the earlier completion would have on the fees proposed by the examiner. But doing the best I can, I feel that the fees proposed by the examiner should be allowed at the rate proposed by him but reduced as to the time expended by an overall figure of 20 per cent. Accordingly, I would allow his fee at £84,376 plus V.A.T.

Whilst I think it may have been imprudent of the examiner to retain the services of what are described as "the professional advisers" having regard to the nature of his role as examiner, I cannot say that it was wrong of him to do so and accordingly I feel that the total of the sum of £11,818 should be allowed as claimed under that heading as an expense of the examiner rather than as a liability of the company. It was of course necessary for the examiner to retain the services of Messrs Eugene F. Collins, solicitors and I would be prepared to allow the costs claimed by them amounting to £14,685 unless any of the parties concerned insist upon taxation of the bill. The items included under the heading "site costs" amounting to £7,790 were liabilities incurred during the protection period to improve or preserve the assets of the company during that period and accordingly, in my view, that claim should be allowed in full notwithstanding any infirmities in the certificates issued in respect thereof.

As to the item entitled "Overheads", it seems to me that the costs claimed by A&L Goodbody amounting to £28,280 must be adjusted so as to exclude any liabilities incurred by the company prior to the date of the appointment of Mr McSweeney as examiner and in particular any costs in relation to the presentation of the petition herein. Subject to any submissions which Messrs A&L Goodbody may wish to make in that regard, I would be prepared to consider measuring their costs on a bill so adjusted if the respondents to the present motion agree to that course.

The item of £5,000 payable to Mr P. McGee under the heading of "Overheads" relates to the cost of presenting the petition for protection in Homes and in the appointment of Mr McSweeney as examiner of that company. In my view there was no basis on which Mr McSweeney could properly have reached the opinion that the failure to appoint an examiner over Homes (or the failure to incur liabilities for expenses in that regard) would prejudice Construction as a going concern *during the protection period*. Whatever advantages might accrue from the appointment of an examiner over Homes, these could only accrue at the conclusion of that protection period. During the period itself Construction was safeguarded by the provisions of section 5 of the 1990 Act.

Whilst I understand the concern expressed on behalf of the respondents at the emoluments paid to the former directors of the company having regard first, to the failure of the company, secondly the irregularities which the examiner appears to have uncovered and, thirdly, the failure of the directors to provide all of the information required by the examiner himself, I think that these costs too must be treated as expenses incurred by the examiner and allowed accordingly. Accordingly I would allow the amounts claimed under the heading "Overheads" and the balance of the sum due to A.I.B. subject to the adjustment of the A&L Goodbody fee and the disallowance of the sum payable to Mr McGee.

In relation to Homes only three items are claimed. Of those I would be prepared to allow the examiner's solicitors costs of £3,085 (plus VAT) as an expense of the examiner unless any of the parties require the sum to be taxed. With regard to the figure of £3,370 claimed by Messrs A&L Goodbody, that would appear to relate largely, if not exclusively, to the appointment of Mr McSweeney as examiner and accordingly for the reasons already given cannot, in my view, be allowed. To the extent that any of these costs were in fact subsequent to the appointment of the examiner of Homes, they are of course payable. Finally with regard to the examiner's fees it seems to me that in this case too and for the reasons already mentioned there should be an abatement of a similar percentage so that the figure which I would allow in respect to the examiner's fees would be £6,224 plus VAT.

Two further matters were canvassed in argument. First it was argued on behalf of Anglo Irish Bank Corporation that a larger part of the fees and expenses should have been apportioned to Homes. Whilst I can see the merits of that proposal, I do not feel that I can go behind the evidence of Mr McSweeney as to how and by whom and for whose benefit these costs and expenses were incurred. Secondly, counsel on behalf of the Revenue Commissioners expressed concern as to the manner in which certain claims of his client had been dealt with. However, in relation to the present claim and the order to be made herein, I cannot see that the Revenue are prejudiced in any way. Insofar as monies are to be paid pursuant to the order made herein, such sums insofar as they consists of or comprise an element of tax, whether it be VAT or PAYE, must be paid by the payer (in this case presumably the receiver) to the appropriate Revenue authority. I do not understand that the former examiner or any of the other parties dispute that this is the case. However, if further clarification should be required the matter can be re-entered for that purpose.

I will hear the parties, if necessary, as to the funds out of which the payments should be made and, if necessary, I would entertain applications with regard to the correction of any of the figures hereinbefore referred to as it must be accepted that over the period when this matter has been under consideration by the court errors may have arisen.

Alistair Rutherdale
Barrister

TABLE OF CASES

Cases in bold are reported in this volume

TABLE OF LEGISLATION

IRELAND

UNITED KINGDOM

Statutes

INDEX